E-Business
Legal
Handbook

E-Business Legal Handbook

Michael L. Rustad
Cyrus Daftary

ASPEN LAW & BUSINESS
A Division of Aspen Publishers, Inc.
Gaithersburg   New York

This publication is designed to provide accurate and authoritative information in regard to the subject matter covered. It is sold with the understanding that the publisher is not engaged in rendering legal, accounting, or other professional services. If legal advice or other professional assistance is required, the services of a competent professional person should be sought.

—From a *Declaration of Principles* jointly adopted by
a Committee of the American Bar Association and
a Committee of Publishers and Associations.

Printed in the United States of America

2 3 4 5 6 7 8 9 0

Library of Congress Cataloging-in-Publication Data

Rustad, Michael.
    E-business legal handbook / Michael L. Rustad, Cyrus Daftary.
      p.   cm.
    Includes bibliographical references and index.
    ISBN 0-7355-1726-6
    1. Electronic commerce—Law and legislation—United States. I. Daftary, Cyrus, 1969–
II. Title.

    KF889.3.R87   2000
343.7309'944—dc21   00-053127

About Aspen Law & Business

Aspen Law & Business—comprising the former Harcourt Professional Publishing, Prentice Hall Law & Business, Little, Brown and Company's Professional Division, and Wiley Law Publications—is a leading publisher of authoritative treatises, practice manuals, services, and journals for accountants, auditors, attorneys, financial and tax advisors, corporate and bank directors, and other business professionals. Our mission is to provide practical solution-based how-to information keyed to the latest legislative, judicial, and regulatory developments.

We offer publications in the areas of accounting and auditing; banking and finance; bankruptcy; business and commercial law; construction law; corporate law; pensions, benefits, and labor; insurance law; securities; taxation; intellectual property; government and administrative law; real estate law; matrimonial and family law; environmental and health law; international law; legal practice and litigation; and criminal law.

Other Aspen products treating intellectual property and technology law issues include

The Commercial Law of Intellectual Property
Corporate Partnering
Drafting License Agreements
Federal Telecommunications Law
Guide to Registering Trademarks
Intellectual Property for the Internet
Internet and Technology Law Desk Reference
Law and the Information Superhighway
The Law of Electronic Commerce
Law of the Internet
Multimedia Legal Handbook
Scott on Computer Law
Scott on Multimedia Law
Software Patents
Technology Transfer Guide

ASPEN LAW & BUSINESS
A Division of Aspen Publishers, Inc.
A Wolters Kluwer Company
www.aspenpublishers.com

For Chryss, James, and Erica

M.L.R.

To my wife, Faranak, and my parents Jaleh and Ali Daftary
for their guidance and support.

C.D.

SUMMARY OF CONTENTS

CONTENTS

Chapter Two
ESTABLISHING AND MAINTAINING
AN IDENTITY ON THE INTERNET **43**

CONTENTS

Chapter Five
TORT LIABILITY IN CYBERSPACE **335**

Chapter Six
THE LAW OF E-COMMERCE TRANSACTIONS 423

CONTENTS

Chapter Seven
EXPOSURE TO LAWSUITS
IN DISTANT FORUMS: JURISDICTION 569

Chapter Eight
CONDUCTING A LEGAL AUDIT AND MANAGING RISK 617

Chapter Nine
E-MAIL AND INTERNET USAGE POLICIES 723

ABOUT THE AUTHORS

Michael L. Rustad, Ph.D., J.D., LL.M, holds the Thomas F. Lambert, Jr. endowed chair and is a Professor of Law and the Director of the High Technology Law Program at Suffolk University Law School in Boston, Massachusetts, where he teaches Internet Law, Torts, Computer Law, and Commercial Law. Professor Rustad was a former associate of the Boston law firm Foley, Hoag and Eliot. During the summer of 2000, he taught Global Internet Law in Suffolk's summer program at the University of Lund in Sweden. He is a member of the Massachusetts, U.S. District Court of Massachusetts, First Circuit U.S. Court of Appeals, and U.S. Supreme Court bars.

He is also a member of the American Law Institute's Member Consultative Group revising Articles 2 and 2A of the Uniform Commercial Code. He was a task force leader of the American Bar Association's Subcommittee on Information Licensing. He is the author of *The Concepts and Methods of Sales, Leases and Licenses* (Carolina Academic Press, 1999) and numerous law review articles.

Cyrus Daftary, J.D., LL.M., is Director of Tax Technology at PricewaterhouseCoopers and an adjunct professor in Suffolk University Law School's High Technology Law Program and in Suffolk University's Frank Sawyer School of Management. He received his J.D. from the University of Dayton School of Law and his LL.M. Corporate Tax from Temple University. Mr. Daftary has served as a corporate counsel and consults with law firms and companies throughout the country on the use of technology in law practice. He was founder of Suffolk University Law School's first course in Cyberspace Law.

He teaches law students and lawyers throughout the country on the use of electronic research methods and Cyberlaw-related issues as well as teaches e-Commerce to business students. He is a member of the Indiana, U.S. District Court, U.S. Court of Appeals, and U.S. Supreme Court Bars.

ACKNOWLEDGMENTS

Many people contributed their time and talent to this manuscript, and we appreciate their help. The authors would like to thank Adele Barnaby of Suffolk University Law School and Jenny Lee of PricewaterhouseCoopers, who provided us with excellent administrative support. Our students in our Computer and High Technology Law, Internet Law, and Cyberspace Law seminars have been a great resource to drawn upon. There have been many persons who have contributed to the ideas in this book. The Suffolk University Law Schools High Technology Law Program has been a great resource. Many of our evening students work in the software industry and for dot.com companies in the Boston area. Professor Stephen McJohn made useful suggestions for the book proposal.

During the early drafts of our book, our research assistants at Suffolk University Law School were especially helpful: Mindi Bellis, Catherine Connelly, Barry Gaiman, Tricia Gray, Brian Henneghan, Corey Lee Hutchinson, Dan Maranci, Joseph McCarthy, Ted Pirrera, Thomas Reith, Anita Sharma, Brian Sullivan, Kate Toomey, Jen Whalen, and Joe White. Bob Johnson, Executive Director of the New York Electronic Commerce Association, provided valuable materials and suggestions during the Spring of 1999. Our research assistants in 1999-2000 were: Ellie Chronas, Tim Hadley, Tricia Gray, Shennan Kavanaugh, Thomas Holloway, Allison K. Jones, Jonathan Nielsen, Alanna Prills, Denise Ross, and Tracy Savy. Allison K. Jones also provided useful editorial suggestions in the summer of 2000. Susan Sweetgall, Betsey McKenzie, and Brian Flaherty of the Suffolk University Law Library provided useful reference materials.

Lori Eisenschmidt, Esq. and Harold Leach, Esq. of Computer Solutions provided useful materials on Information Security. Sanjeev Doss, Esq., Eric Doyle, Esq., and Fred Sroka, Esq., of PricewaterhouseCoopers provided valuable help and editorial suggestions to the tax, framing, and linking sections. Chris Mitchell of PricewaterhouseCoopers provided valuable technology and strategic counsel as to the workings of the Internet. Mary Jean Capodanno, Esq., also provided useful suggestions. Mark Maier, Bobby Hazelton, Lucy Elandjian, and Kim Vagos authored preventive law pointers. Peter Stecher, Suffolk University Law School Class of 2004, provided editorial suggestions for each chapter as well as research on statutory and case law development. Attorney Iris Geick, a trademark specialist, provided editorial suggestions for the trademark discussion. Julie Ross, Esq., now an attorney with the cybercrime unit of the Massachusetts Attorney General's office, provided insights into civil liability issues. Mark Silvern, Esq., of Verisign, Inc., provided cutting edge information on digital signatures.

We would like to thank Dawn McGuire, Esq., of PricewaterhouseCoopers for her written, editorial, and strategic contributions to Chapters 1, 2, 6, and 8. Similarly, we should like to thank Todd Kreiger, Esq., of the Bose Corporation for his written, editorial, and strategic contributions to Chapters 1, 2, 4, 7, and 8. Both were instrumental in focusing our vision and challenging us as to the overall structure of each chapter.

A book of this magnitude would not be possible without the assistance of many people at Aspen Law & Business. We would like to recognize Frank Quinn and Larry Wexler for their editorial support.

Finally, Professor Rustad would like to thank his wife, Chryss Knowles, for her editorial work on this project.

October 2000

Michael Rustad and Cyrus Daftary
Boston, MA

OVERVIEW:
THE RISE OF THE INTERNET

[The] Internet's pace of adoption eclipses all other previous technologies. Radio was in existence thirty-eight years before fifty million people tuned in; television took thirteen years to reach that benchmark. Fifty million people were using desktop computers only sixteen years after the first personal computer (PC) kit came out. Once opened to the general public, the Internet surpassed that fifty million mark in just four years.[1]

Although the World Wide Web did not begin to become an integral part of the popular culture until 1995, within a few years, it will be difficult to imagine a world without bandwidth, browsers, and bytes. About 100 million people are now online, and experts are predicting that by 2005, one billion will have access to the Internet.[2]

The rise of the Internet has dramatically changed the ways in which business is conducted. Cyberspace is increasingly the place where millions of people pay bills, do their banking, consult professionals, shop for gifts, communicate electronically, and make connections with family and friends. More than 70 million Americans now use the Internet, and over 44 million have shopped on it.[3] America Online, one of the many Internet Service Providers, currently has 17 million subscribers who spend an average of 55 minutes online each day, compared to ten minutes in 1998.[4]

The online selling of goods and services is the success story of the late 1990s. Online consumer sales increased 100% from 1997 to 1998, and Visa International projects that consumer e-commerce will grow by as much as 67% annually during the next five years.[5] Visa's revenues from online purchases will

---

[1] U.S. Dep't of Commerce, The Emerging Digital Economy 12 (Apr.1998).

[2] John L. Hawkins, E-business Opportunities: Year 2000 and Euro, E-Business Advisor, June 1, 1998.

[3] John Chambers, CEO of CISCO, "Internet is Reshaping Economy," Quarks and Bits, Dec, 2, 1998 (visited Feb. 13, 1999) <http:www.lahaaland.com/it-Internet/opinions/opinions2.html>.

[4] America Online Membership Hits 17 Million, Wall St. J., Apr. 15, 1999 at B7.

[5] Bob Woods, Consumer E-Commerce to Grow by 67% Yearly Report, CNN FN The Financial Network, Sept. 24, 1998.

increase from $1.4 billion in 1998 to almost $3 billion in 2002, and consumer online purchases are projected to increase from $15.3 billion in 1998 to $100.5 billion by 2002.[6] Total online sales, including both business-to-consumer and business-to-business, should exceed one trillion dollars per year by the year 2001.

Consumers are shopping on the Internet for a broad range of goods and services, and companies have been eager to take advantage of this new sales channel. Purchases of gifts and flowers online, for instance, brings in $413 million.[7] Amazon.com already has the world's largest online bookstore with nearly a million volumes in stock and will soon have an online music store of comparable size. The number of web sites that accept credit card payments has tripled in the last year.[8] In financial services, 15 million Americans researched mortgages online in 1998,[9] and almost as many have conducted at least one online banking transaction.[10] By 2000, one out of every two banks in the U.S. will offer online banking services.[11]

With a sales volume five times that of consumer transactions, business-to-business transactions receive less attention from the media but play a much larger part in e-commerce. Dell Computers now processes orders worth five million dollars every day from its web site, while Cisco Systems sells nine million dollars a day of computer hardware on the Internet. Forrester Research projects that "business-to-business Internet commerce will skyrocket to $1.3 trillion by 2003.[12]

Some analysts predict that the Internet will be the most important technological development since the Industrial Revolution.[13] The spectacular adoption of the Internet has spawned instantaneous communication and commerce and resulted in a radical paradigm shift to a truly interconnected global marketplace never before seen in the world economy. This paradigm shift can be attributed to several separate but distinct changes:

1) **Technology.** Phenomenal technological advances have been achieved in the last 30 years. On one level, we have moved from a noncomputer to a mainframe computer environment, and leaped to a PC-network-based society. Accelerating this movement is the fact that the cost of change

---

[6] *Id.*

[7] Martha Mendoza, Internet Romance Thrives —and so do Related Sales, San Francisco Chronicle, Feb. 12, 1999 at 1 (visited Feb. 16, 1999) <http://www.sfgate.com/cgi-in/article.cgi.national 0112EST0445.DT&type=tech_article>.

[8] Ecommerce Reports, Surveys & Trends (visited Apr. 1, 1999) <http://www.allEC.com/allec/News/rs.htm>.

[9] America Online Membership Hits 17 Million, Wall St. J., Apr. 15, 1999 at B7.

[10] Gerry Gottlieb, Financial Services Online? You Can Bank On It, Net Commerce, Mar. 1999, at 6.

[11] *Id.*

[12] Ecommerce Reports, Surveys & Trends (visited Apr. 1, 1999) <http://www.allEC.com/allec/News/rs.htm>.

[13] Harvard Conference on the Internet and Society, 67 (O'Neill & Associates 1996).

has become relatively low. State-of-the-art PCs are now available for as little as $500.

2) **Community.** There has been a radical change in the way society perceives itself. We have moved from a national to a global focus; our sense of community has been extended to cover larger territory than our own backyards. Some individuals find more similarities within a world-wide Internet community than with their next-door neighbor. There are many examples of this, ranging from the introduction of this global focus, from the introduction of the EURO to NAFTA.

3) **Economy.** Finally, the economics of our world has changed. The world has moved from an industrial-based economy to an information-based economy. As barriers to global trade fall, goods and services are exchanged in a global economic system.[14]

These recent trends stemming from the rapid development and adoption of technology and the Internet have revolutionized the way society interacts and does business.

1. New Legal Challenges

The rise of the information society is displacing the traditional legal paradigm that matured as a response to an economy based on the national distribution of durable goods. As the Internet continues to become an integral part of our lives, business professionals and their legal advisers must address many new challenges. The following is an example of a dialogue that you might face in your practice or company:

> **Mike:** Cyrus, I need some legal advice. One of my customers claims that I sold a substandard computer. He now threatens to take legal action to refund the purchase price and pay damages for the harm that it allegedly caused to his internal systems.
> **Cyrus:** I didn't realize that you had a computer store, where is it located?
> **Mike:** Suffolk Personal Computers (SPC) is a virtual storefront on the Internet . . . You know, one of those "dot com" businesses.
> **Cyrus:** Where do you keep your inventory?
> **Mike:** I don't maintain any inventory. Everything is drop shipped directly from the manufacturer. Orders are automatically e-mailed to the distribution point—I never even see the product. We have already expanded into 50-plus markets worldwide.
> **Cyrus:** Have you spoken with the customer to find out the nature of the problem?

---

[14] David Johnston et al., "Cyberlaw: What you need to know about doing business online." 11 (1997).

Mike: We have only communicated via e-mail. He is in France and wants to sue under some European law. They claim to have jurisdiction since my web site can be accessed from anywhere in the world. What can I do to avoid being sued in a European court?

This dialogue illustrates how technology and the Internet have drastically changed the way businesses and customers interact. For many businesses, a web site or an e-mail address has become more important than a telephone number. Although several years ago this kind of legal dilemma would have been foreign to most people, the increasing popularity and power of the Internet, coupled with the affordability and dependability of personal computers, have made problems like this one presented all too routine. This book will help you answer some of the more common questions that you will face in practice as a result of the Internet.

What makes the Internet different as a legal landscape? Much of the commercial law governing Internet transactions was conceived 50 to 100 years ago, decades before the rise of the information age. The Uniform Commercial Code (UCC) is based upon a legal paradigm conceived 50 years ago, long before the rise of the software industry, and in its day was a new paradigm that displaced nineteenth century "horse law and haystack law."[15] But legal principles that made sense when people signed contracts on paper cannot be applied easily to online contracts that parties do not sign but expect to be enforceable.

Traditional commercial law principles are being overhauled to accommodate the global Internet. State legislatures in the vast majority of states are enacting or considering digital signatures to facilitate electronic commerce. The entire UCC is being revised to adapt to cyberspace law, software licensing, and information access contracts. The state legislatures in 40 states have enacted or are contemplating legislation to validate electronic forms signing or digital signatures. In addition, other areas of law—protecting intellectual property rights, data privacy, data security, consumer protection, and regulations affecting public network operators—are also evolving at an exponential pace as a result of the Internet.

Doing business on the Internet raises a host of challenging issues relating to how to deal with electronic cash, online banking, commercial transactions in digital information, and digital signatures. Privacy regulation and jurisdiction questions, too, have been especially pressing. For example, Intel's release of the Pentium III inspired a firestorm of controversy from privacy advocates.[16] Intel's plan was to "hardwire a unique Processor Serial Number into each PIII chip to

---

[15] Grant Gilmore, Note, On the Difficulties of Codifying Commercial Law, 57 Yale L. J. 1341 (1948).

[16] Top of the News, Intel Adds ID Number to PIII—Should You Worry About Big Brother Inside?, PC World, Apr. 1999, at 56.

enhance security for e-commerce."[17] Privacy advocates characterized the tracking device as "supercookie" that permits users to be monitored by webmasters.[18]

The global nature of the Internet raises difficult problems of sovereignty and jurisdiction, both because the Internet is not governed by any single entity[19] and because many online activities cut across multiple jurisdictions and could potentially be regulated by hundreds of jurisdictions.[20] These challenges are compounded by the fact that every country has its own unique and complex legal system. None of these legal systems anticipated the development of the Internet, and a number of them are rethinking how their existing laws apply to the Internet. Consumer protection rules, global privacy standards, and of course taxes are just a few of the issues being debated and decided by many jurisdictions.

Traditional concepts of jurisdiction must be adapted to the global nature of the World Wide Web. The federal government is increasing its regulatory scrutiny of online commerce. The Federal Trade Commission (FTC) has begun to investigate the use and abuse of personal data of consumers using the Internet and is proposing greater consumer protection in international online transactions. Businesses will have to be aware of any new FTC regulations. A number of other agencies are also considering increased regulation of Internet commercial transactions.

The European Union's approach to privacy illustrates how privacy and sovereignty concerns can intersect. The United States has traditionally had a free market approach to information privacy, which conflicts with Data Protection Directive adopted by the European Union (EU). The European Commission has sought "formal authority to negotiate with the United States to establish a code of conduct for American companies that would create a 'safe harbor' of compliance."[21] The U.S. Commerce Department has proposed principles for enforcing EU data protection principles.[22] Such conflicts are likely to rise up in other countries too: the Global Internet Liberty Campaign surveyed 50 industrialized countries and concluded that most had either enacted or were considering new protection for the privacy of individual data.[23]

---

[17] *Id.*

[18] *Id.*

[19] James West Marcovitz, Note, Ronald@McDonalds.com "Owning a Bitchin' Corporate Trademark as an Internet Address-Infringement?, 17 Cardozo L.Rev. 85, 89-90 (1995) (noting the Internet is primarily run by a voluntary organization (ISOC) rather than by a governmental body or corporation).

[20] *See generally* Dennis Campbell, Law of International On-Line Business: A Global Perspective 1-1 (1998).

[21] Microsoft Law & Corp. Affairs, Summary of Global Internet Legal Developments for the Period Oct.1998, at 61 (Jan. 1999).

[22] *Id.*

[23] Global Internet Liberty Campaign (GILC), Privacy and Human Rights: An International Survey of Privacy Laws and Practice (1998) at <http://www.gilc.org/privacy/survey/> (last visited Mar. 5, 1999).

Increasingly, the law of the Internet is found in industry standards such as those formulated by the International Standards Organization (ISO). To the business community, self-control is the most effective form of social control. The Internet Law and Policy Forum (ILPF) argues that Internet industry standards will create a predictable legal environment for e-commerce and are a desirable alternative to "thick" government regulation.[24] The ILPF urges that Internet law be market- and industry-standard driven as opposed to strong public regulation.[25] The recent ILPF report on authentication acknowledges a traditional role for government in consumer protection and fraud prevention,[26] but industry "accreditation is preferred to licensing . . . which should be consistent with or rely on private sector practices."[27]

2. Organization of the Book; The SPC Hypothetical Example

E-Business Legal Handbook provides a guidebook to the rapidly evolving laws and industry standards governing online transactions. E-business transforms more than business; it is imperative to understand and embrace how the online environment is changing the law. This book is designed for corporate counsel, general practitioners, business professionals, and corporate executives who want to harness the power of the Internet and need a basic understanding of the various legal issues that may be encountered in this new medium. In providing a detailed review of specific legal and business issues, each chapter peels back the layers of traditional law as well as global Internet legal developments to help firms avoid liability and protect their rights in cyberspace.

To better illustrate the legal issues and challenges confronting us, the following chapters will use this hypothetical example for demonstrative purposes.

> In 1996, cofounders Mike Rustad and Cyrus Daftary, along with four employees, launched Suffolk Personal Computers (SPC), a C Corporation, with its headquarters at One Temple Street, Boston, MA. Within two years, SPC had achieved phenomenal growth, with revenues in excess of $4 billion in 1998. SPC owned 65% of the Northeast PC market and had employed 4,000 professionals. SPC sold and distributed custom-built PCs through its own retail stores, catalogs, and third-party retail stores like Circuit City and CompUSA. In order to expand SPC's existing client base and compete against the likes of Dell and Gateway Computers on a national level, Mike and Cyrus decided that it was time for SPC to engage in electronic commerce.

---

[24] Internet Law & Policy Forum, "Legislative Principles for Electronic Authentication and Electronic Commerce," Oct. 24, 1997, (visited on Mar. 20, 1999) <http://www.ilpf.org/digsig/principles.htm>.

[25] *Id.*

[26] *Id.*

[27] *Id.*

Chapter One provides an overview of the Internet, its related terminology, and the accelerating pace of related legal developments. Each succeeding chapter seeks to guide the reader through difficult legal and business issues that arise during each stage of conducting business online. We examine the broad range of Internet activity and discuss how individuals, companies, and firms access and use the Internet. Finally, we preview the power of the Internet as a commercial tool. In addition, each chapter analyzes the law related to doing business online and nearly all chapters offer practical checklists as well as practice pointers (called "Preventive Law Pointers," which are highlighted by an arrow call-out symbol in the chapter synopses and the text), to help in resolving legal dilemmas that frequently arise out of Internet-powered business activity.

A word about preventive law: The business community is ill served when legal liability on the Web is portrayed as casino-style random lightning strikes. In our view, legal liability stems from a firm's failure to anticipate legal problems before they arise, and lack of planning is the hallmark of liability. Much of our country's common law is based upon common sense: balancing the risk of harm against the cost of prevention. Like preventive medicine, the logic of preventive law is that it is cheaper to prevent the conditions leading to liability or the loss of rights in cyberspace. The lesson of our common law is that liability is avoidable and preventable even in the uncertain legal landscape of cyberspace

Our thesis is that the rational corporate response to the risks posed by doing business on the Internet is to carry out a high-level legal audit. The type of risk analysis will vary depending on the type of online activity and the type of products or services offered on the Internet,[28] but a thorough legal audit serves the interests of the company in a number of ways. The recordkeeping necessary to measure and avoid Internet liability may help the firm not simply to prevent liability but also to uncover management and other problems. Without centralized safety audits, a firm may not spot a pattern of developing dangers until it is in a protracted legal war fighting for its life, not just its market share.

Preventive law is cheaper than financing defense costs. The goal of preventive law is to anticipate and resolve problems before they become full-blown punitive damage cases. Companies that do not conduct legal audits before conducting business in cyberspace do so at their peril.

---

[28] The Law Firm of Clifford Chance, The Internet: Identifying and Managing Legal Risk 1 (1999).

E-Business
Legal
Handbook

INTRODUCTION

§ 1.01   OVERVIEW

Companies are looking for ways to integrate the Internet into their future business strategies and objectives. The term *e-business* refers to a company's organizational changes to conduct business transactions on the Internet. Computer-to-computer business transactions are referred to as *e-commerce*. As of early 1998, more than one-fourth of U.S. businesses with more than ten employees had established an Internet presence.[1] Companies that fail to harness the potential of the Internet may lose current customers and market share, while companies that use the Internet may reach new markets and raise their market share. E-commerce is evolving rapidly as a business tool as companies try to reach the rapidly increasing number of Internet users.[2]

While many companies have successfully established a presence on the Internet, relatively few have completed a legal audit of the risks and liabilities stemming from e-commerce. This book covers the full range of Internet-related issues, including the following:

1. *Creating and establishing a corporate identity*: Balancing the current corporate name and identity with the selection of an appropriate domain name;[3] protecting and establishing trademark and other related intellectual property issues.

2. *Going online*: Developing an Internet site and accessing the Internet via an Internet Service Provider.

3. *Entering into and enforcing contracts*: Identifying the parties, determining the location of parties, selecting the applicable law, and enforcing agreements (such as webwrap, web linking, and web development agreements); limiting liability for damages and warranties; using digital signature technology as necessary to permit the electronic "signing" of documents.

4. *Collecting revenue*: Establishing payment systems, digital cash; encryption; establishing merchant account; setting up a virtual storefront.[4]

---

[1] PricewaterhouseCoopers, Technology Forecast: 1999, at 182 (1999).

[2] From 1998 to 1999, the number of Internet users increased by 55 percent. Electronic Commerce: Worldwide Growth of the Digital Economy, Congressional Digest, Feb. 2000, at 37. During the same period, new Web address registrations increased by 137 percent. Id. By May 1999, 171 million people had access to the Internet, with more than 50 percent of the users in North America. *Id.*

[3] A domain name is the last part of an Internet address, such as *suffolk.edu*. The top level domain name (i.e., the last part: *.edu*) indicates what kind of organization runs the site. Some examples include *.edu*, for education, *.org*, for nonprofit groups, and *.gov*, for government. The top level *.com* signifies commercial entities.

[4] *See generally,* Rebecca Quick, AOL Members Spend $80 Each Web Shopping, Wall St. J., Jan. 5, 1999, at A1.

5. *Establishing a marketing presence*: Creating links to and from a corporate web page; drafting a disclaimer of endorsement of and liability for linked sites.

6. *Distributing products*: Expanding corporate presence by distributing software products; developing and distributing corporate software: licensing, clickwrap, complying with UCC and other laws limiting warranties, excluding consequential damages, and limiting remedies; complying with the Uniform Information Transfer Act and the Uniform Computer Information Act (UCITA) and the Uniform Electronic Transactions Act (UETA); drafting clickwrap or webwrap agreements that comply with UCITA; webwrap agreements that condition access to site to agreement with terms of service.

7. *Planning for taxation*: Contemplating tax planning opportunities; value added tax (VAT), products versus services, sales and use, nexus, and the Federal Internet Tax Freedom Act.[5]

8. *Anticipating jurisdiction*: Planning for strategic use of jurisdiction, venue, conflict of interest, and choice of law, and selecting choice of law, forum, and venue provisions.

9. *Expanding into foreign markets*: Extraterritorial legislation and legal issues surrounding international sales; complying with European Union data protection and privacy directives, consumer protection, and distance selling rules applicable to the Internet.

10. *Protecting intellectual property*: Protecting domain names, use of metatags and hyperlinks, and the copyrightability of a web site; disclaimers of liability for infringement claims for materials posted by third parties.

11. *Drafting and implementing privacy policies*: Disclosures of privacy practices of web sites; the Federal Trade Commission as the chief federal agency policing the collection of consumer information over the Internet;[6] compliance with best industry practices for privacy.

12. *Employee training*: Devising an Internet usage and e-mail policy; training employees on the proper use of facilities; enforcement of usage policies.

---

[5] *See* Federal Internet Tax Freedom Act, Pub. L. No. 105-277, 112 Stat. 2681-719 (1998) (codified at 47 U.S.C. §151 (2000)) (placing a three-year moratorium on taxes on Internet access and "multiple or discriminatory taxes on electronic commerce").

[6] Privacy Limits on Collecting Personal Information Via the Internet, 15 Computer Law 17 (June 1998).

§ 1.02 THE DEVELOPMENT OF INTERNET LAW

[A] The Development of the Internet

Many people are credited for making the Internet what it is today. The next few pages provide a brief, general summary of the evolution of the Internet from a legal perspective.[7] To paraphrase Oliver Wendell Holmes, we must study history in order to understand the path of the law.[8]

The precursor to the Internet was established when the United States Defense Department wanted to link its network, ARPANET, to various radio and satellite networks.[9] The goal of the network was to ensure that the United States could withstand a nuclear strike. This vision of a robust network and the investment that went into its creation enabled the Internet to grow, unrestricted by boundaries, regulations, or preconceived notions of what it should look like.[10] Today, the Internet is comprised of sophisticated protocols such as XML, improved programming languages and utilities such as Java and Java Beans/Script, and interactive databases such as Oracle, Sybase, and SQL.

The cooperative effort and vision of many creative minds in the United States government and at corporations such as BBN, IBM, MCI, AT&T, Microsoft, Oracle, and Intel has influenced and shaped the evolution of the Internet. Internet law is rapidly evolving as industry groups, governments, and international organizations formulate new standards, regulatory initiatives, statutes, and court decisions.

[B] Global Legal Developments: Selected Case and Statutory Development Timeline

1990

5/16/90: First case in which a court mentioned the Internet: United States v. Morris[11] for the famous Internet worm that caused hundreds of educational

---

[7] *See also,* Stephan Segaller, Nerds 2.0.1: A Brief History of the Internet (1998) (for a comprehensive overview of the history of the Internet).

[8] Oliver Wendell Holmes, Jr., The Path of the Law, in Collected Legal Papers, ed. Harold J. Laski (N.Y. 1920).

[9] Rita Than, CRS Report for Congress: Welcome to Cyberia: An Internet Overview, 2-3 (Mar. 12, 1996).

[10] O'Neill and Associates, Harvard Conference on the Internet and Society, at 67 (1996).

[11] 928 F.2d 504 (2d Cir. 1991) (upholding conviction under 18 U.S.C. §1030).

and military computers to crash. The defendant was convicted under the Computer Fraud and Abuse Act of 1986.

1990: One of the first convictions of a computer hacker under the Computer Fraud and Abuse Act of 1986. In that case, hackers were able to gain unauthorized access to Bell South's 911 computer files and published the proprietary information in a hackers' newsletter.[12]

1990: The National Science Foundation assumed control of the system of interconnected computers that evolved into the Internet.[13]

1991

10/29/91: The first case where an online service provider was held not liable for a content owner's publication of defamatory statements.[14] The court found that the provider was not a publisher, but more like a conduit, because it had no control over content.

1991: The first case to hold that post-sale terms in a mass-market license agreement were unenforceable under Article 2 of the Uniform Commercial Code governing the sale of goods.[15]

1991: Tim Berners-Lee at CERN created the World Wide Web.[16]

1991: The United States Supreme Court enforced a forum selection clause in a consumer contract that required aggrieved consumers to litigate all claims in Florida. The Court enforced the clause because the consumer had notice of the forum and because there were valid reasons for trying all claims in Florida, the company's corporate residence.[17]

---

[12] United States v. Riggs, 743 F. Supp. 556 (N.D. Ill. 1990) (upholding wire fraud indictment).

[13] Antony J. McShane and Orrin S. Shifrin, Special Technology Issue: Protecting Trademarks and Copyrights in the New Millennium, 14 CBA Record 32 (April 2000).

[14] Cubby, Inc. v. CompuServe Inc., 776 F. Supp. 135 (S.D.N.Y. 1991) (ruling that ISP's role was similar to that of a newsstand or bookstore).

[15] Step-Saver Data Systems, Inc. v. Wyse Technology, 939 F.2d 91 (3d Cir. 1991) (holding that shrinkwrap license was unenforceable under § 2-207, the battle of the forms provision of Article 2).

[16] Ben Segal, A Short History of Internet Protocols at CERN (April 1995) http://wwwinfo .cern.ch/pdp/ns/ben/TCPHIST.html (visited Sept. 14, 2000).

[17] Carnival Cruise Lines, Inc. v. Shute, 499 U.S. 585 (1991) (forum selection clause in seven-day cruise ticket).

1992

12/31/92: The National Science Foundation entered into a contract with Network Solutions Inc. (NSI) to develop a domain name registration system.[18]

1993

12/9/93: The first case to find a computer bulletin board liable for copyright and trademark infringement for distributing and displaying copyrighted photographs on its computer bulletin board.[19] Subscribers to the bulletin board could download copyrighted materials belonging to Playboy. The court rejected the operator's fair use defense argument and ruled that the operator also violated Section 43(a) of the Lanham Act for unfair competition by making materials available for downloads by paid subscribers.

1993: The court upheld the Secret Service's seizure of a bulletin board operator's computer system, rejecting the operator's claims that the government violated the federal wiretap statute and the Privacy Protection Act.[20]

1993: A court ruled that a software program was copied for purposes of the federal Copyright Act each time a diagnostic engineer booted up the computer and copied the program into the computer's random access memory (RAM).[21]

1994

4/12/94: The first case to hold that merely obtaining access to a database in another state over the Internet did not subject the defendant to personal jurisdiction: Pres-Kap v. Prestige Travel.[22] The court dismissed the case, holding that an out of state travel agency whose only contact with the forum was logging into a computerized reservations database did not satisfy the minimum contacts test.

10/28/94: The first case considering conflicting rights between a domain name registrant and a trademark owner: MTV Networks v. Curry.[23] While a

---

[18] McShane and Shifrin, *supra* note 13.
[19] Playboy Enters., Inc. v. Frena, 839 F. 1552 (M.D. Fla. 1993).
[20] Steve Jackson Games v. United States Secret Service, 816 F. Supp. 432 (W.D. Tex. 1993).
[21] MAI Systems Corp. v. Peak Computer, Inc., 991 F.2d 518 (9th Cir. 1993).
[22] 636 So. 2d 1351 (Fla. Dist. Ct. App. 3d Dist. 1994).
[23] 867 F. Supp. 202 (S.D.N.Y. 1994).

video disk jockey at MTV, Adam Curry registered the domain name *www.mtv.com* and developed a web site. He refused to relinquish the domain name when he left the network, and MTV sued. The domain name was transferred to MTV as part of a pre-trial settlement.

12/28/94: The first Internet copyright case, United States v. LaMacchia,[24] for pirating software over the Internet. The case against LaMacchia was dismissed because the court found that the criminal penalties of the wire fraud statute were inappropriate for the illegal-copying of software.

1994: The first Internet copyright infringement case in which an electronic bulletin board was found to be liable for contributory infringement under the Copyright Act for operating a bulletin board where subscribers uploaded without permission files containing copyrighted materials.[25] Sega obtained an injunction against the operator of an electronic bulletin board who encouraged subscribers to copy Sega's games.

1995

2/28/95: Utah enacts the United States' first digital signature legislation.

6/21/95: The first case to quash an indictment for transmitting threats of kidnapping over the Internet. Dismissal of a federal criminal indictment of a former University of Michigan student who sent sadomasochistic stories to one of his classmates. The Court ruled that the indictment must be dismissed, as the defendant could not be prosecuted for interstate transmission of threats in the absence of proof that these were "true threats."[26]

11/21/95: The first case to absolve an Internet Service Provider (ISP) of secondary liability for permitting infringing material to be posted on its web site. Religious Technology Center v. Netcom On-line Communication Service, Inc.[27]

1995: A state court held that Prodigy was a publisher of defamatory statements made on electronic bulletin boards because it advertised itself as a family-oriented provider that monitors content.[28]

---

[24] 871 F. Supp. 535 (D. Mass. 1994).

[25] Sega Enterprises Ltd. v. MAPHIA, 857 F. Supp. 679 (N.D. Cal. 1994).

[26] United States v. Baker, 890 F. Supp. 1375 (E. Mich. 1995).

[27] 907 F. Supp. 1361 (N.D. Cal. 1995).

[28] Stratton Oakmont, Inc. v. Prodigy Services Co., 23 Media L. Rep. (BNA) 1794 (Sup. Ct. N.Y. 1995).

1995: The Clinton Administration proposed the so-called Clipper Chip, which contains a single-key algorithm preventing private parties from using encrypted cellular-based communications for drug deals, spying, and other illegal activities. The Clipper Chip was opposed by academics who argued that the government's role as escrow agent for the decryption keys created the potential for illegal domestic surveillance.[29]

1995: President Clinton signed the Federal Trademark Dilution Act of 1995, which protects famous trademarks from blurring or tarnishment by cybersquatters.[30]

1996

6/12/96: The first major case successfully attacking the Communications Decency Act (CDA) of 1996: ACLU v. Reno.[31] The CDA criminalized the transmission of obscenity via the Internet. Section 230 of the CDA was not affected by the Supreme Court's decision.

6/20/96: The first case in which a shrinkwrap software license was enforced even though the terms were not disclosed prior to purchase: ProCD, Inc. v. Zeidenberg.[32] The court held that the licensee was bound to the terms of a license agreement for a software package called SelectPhone because the licensee had an opportunity to review the license prior to being bound. The licensee violated the licensor's copyright exceeding the scope of the license, which was for a single user, when the licensee disseminated the software on the Internet.

1996: In United States v. Thomas,[33] the court found jurisdiction to be proper in Tennessee for electronically transmitting computer files containing obscene images from California. The Sixth Circuit held that it was not unconstitutional to subject Internet distributors of obscenity to varying community standards.

10/28/96: The first case to restrain an e-mail spammer from using false return addresses on unsolicited messages to subscribers of an online service.

---

[29] *See generally* A. Michael Froomkin, The Metaphor Is the Key: Cryptography: The Clipper Chip, and the Constitution, 143 U. Pa. L. Rev. 715-16 (1995).

[30] 15 U.S.C. § 1125(c) (2000).

[31] 929 F. Supp. 824 (E.D. Pa. 1996), *aff'd,* 117 S.Ct. 2329 (1997).

[32] 86 F.3d 1447 (7th Cir. Wis. 1996).

[33] 74 F.3d 701 (6th Cir. 1996).

CompuServe prevailed on the basis of common law trespass for the spammer's unauthorized use of the provider's computer system.[34]

11/1/96: The first case to challenge the domain resolution dispute process and the first case to treat cybersquatting as a significant contact for personal jurisdiction: Panavision Int'l, L.P. v. Toeppen.[35] Court found that a cyber-pirate made "commercial use" of Panavision's trademark in his scheme of registering famous marks for profit.

11/29/96: The first case where a domain registrar transferred the resolution of a domain name dispute to a federal court: Network Solutions v. Clue Computing, Inc.[36] The court dismissed Network Solutions' interpleader and returned the case for resolution in the state court.

12/20/96: WIPO Copyright Treaty concluded at Geneva, Switzerland. The WIPO Treaty grants copyright protection to databases and remedies for circumvention of technical measures protecting copyrighted works.[37]

1996: The first case to rule that defendant's use of a trademark similar to plaintiff's presents a danger of tarnishment because of unfavorable associations with the mark. The use of a domain-name combination for a sexually explicit web site diluted the plaintiff's trademark, "Candyland," for a children's game.[38]

1996: Congress enacted the Communications Decency Act of 1996 (CDA), which provided a safe harbor for Internet Service Providers for liability for information provided by third parties. Section 230 of the CDA was designed to overrule the Prodigy case.

1996: The first court to rule that an e-mail spammer did not have a First Amendment right to send massive amounts of unsolicited, commercial e-mail to Internet subscribers.[39]

---

[34] CompuServe Inc. v. Cyber Promotions, Inc., 962 F. Supp. 1015 (S.D. Ohio 1997).

[35] 945 F. Supp. 1296 (C.D. Cal. 1996), *aff'd,* 141 F.3 1316 (9th Cir. 1998).

[36] 946 F. Supp. 858 (D. Colo. 1997).

[37] The European Community "has adopted a directive creating a *sui generis* right of extraction of substantial noncopyrightable facts or elements from a database." Jesse M. Feder, Copyright Office, Congress and International Issues, Advanced Seminar on Copyright Law 1998, Practicing Law Institute (No. G4-4035, May 1998).

[38] Hasbro, Inc. v. Internet Entertainment Group, Ltd., 1996 U.S. Dist. LEXIS 11626 (W.D. Wash. 1996). *See also* Hasbro, Inc. v. Clue Co., 66 F. Supp. 2d 117 (D. Mass. 1999) (holding that registration of the domain name *clue.com* did not automatically dilute the Clue trademark).

[39] Cyber Promotions, Inc. v. America Online, Inc. 948 F. Supp. 436 (E.D. Pa. 1996).

1997

1/16/97: The first case to develop a sliding scale to determine whether web site activity was sufficient to find that a nonresident "purposefully availed" itself of the forum: Zippo Mfg. Co. v. Zippo Dot Com.[40] The court found that in addition to the web site, the fact that defendant entered into service contracts with members of the forum state availed them of the protection of Pennsylvania law.

1/28/97: The first case validating the right of a public university to restrict Internet access to objectionable sites: Loving v. Boren.[41] The court found that the plaintiff had no standing to challenge the statute because he had not been injured by the university's blocking access to obscene Internet newsgroups.

2/20/97: The first framing case: Washington Post Co. v. Total News, Inc.[42] Total News' web page framed pages from various news sources but included its own advertising, logos, and name, eliminating that of the original sources. The parties reached an out-of-court settlement permitting Total News to link to but not frame the sites.

2/26/97: The first case denying personal jurisdiction for a nonresident whose contacts with the forum were access to a web site and use of an e-mail address: Hearst Corp. v. Goldberger.[43] The court held that these two factors were insufficient contacts for personal jurisdiction.

4/28/97: The first unfair competition case predicated upon deep linking: Ticketmaster Corp. v. Microsoft Corp.[44] Microsoft created a deep link to the Ticketmaster site that went directly to the ticket purchase page, bypassing Ticketmaster's introductory advertising pages. The parties settled before the court could determine whether an unauthorized deep link could constitute trademark dilution or unfair competition.

5/28/97: A Massachusetts court held that a state police report transmitted electronically to the Registry of Motor Vehicles satisfied the state's requirement for a signed writing.[45]

---

[40] 952 F. Supp. 1119 (W.D. Pa. 1997).

[41] 133 F.3d 771 (10th Cir. Okla. 1998).

[42] No. Cv. 97-1190 (S.D.N.Y Feb. 20, 1997).

[43] 1997 U.S. Dist. LEXIS 2065 (S.D.N.Y. Feb. 26, 1997).

[44] No. Cv. 97-3055 (C.D. Cal. April 28, 1997).

[45] Doherty v. Registry of Motor Vehicles, 97CV0050 (Mass. Dist. Ct., Suffolk Cty., May 28, 1997), reported in Perkins Coie LLP: Internet Case Digest (June 5, 1999), http://www.perkinscoie.com/resource/ecomm/netcase/Cases-05.htm.

8/29/97: The first case mentioning metatags (machine-readable code for search engines): Playboy v. Calvin Designer Label.[46] The defendant was enjoined from infringing upon Playboy's trademark in metatags, domain names, or web content.

12/16/97: President Clinton signed the No Electronic Theft Act of 1997 (NET). NET broadens criminal liability for copyright infringement even where no financial gain or profit is involved. NET closed the loophole in United States v. LaMacchia,[47] where the criminal indictment for wire fraud was dismissed because there was no proof that the defendant had received financial gain or profit from the infringing acts of illegal copying.[48]

11/17/97: The first case to hold the NSI domain name registrar not liable for direct infringement or dilution because it had not made use of the mark in its role as registrar.[49]

1997: The first appellate case extending the safe harbor provisions of Section 230 of the CDA to immunize a provider from liability for defamatory statements posted anonymously by one of its subscribers. Section 230 was held to preempt state law claims for negligence in permitting the distribution of defamatory material.[50]

1997: The first state attorney general to restrain a fraudulent online business that solicited orders and payment but failed to deliver goods to Internet customers.[51]

1997: In a trademark infringement case involving a web site, a court ruled that it could not exercise jurisdiction over a small Missouri cabaret using the name "The Blue Note," which was the trademark of a famous New York jazz club: Bensusan Resturant Corp. v. King.[52] The court observed that applying trademark law in the fast-developing world of the Internet is somewhat like

---

[46] 985 F. Supp. 1218 (N.D. Cal. 1997).

[47] 871 F. Supp. 535 (D. Mass. 1994).

[48] 18 U.S.C. § 2319 (1997) (punishing Internet copyright piracy).

[49] Lockheed Martin Corp. v. Network Solutions, Inc., 985 F. Supp. 949 (C.D. Cal., Nov. 17, 1997), *aff'd,* 1999 U.S. App. LEXIS 26771 (9th Cir. 1999) (holding domain name registrar not liable for failing to prevent registration of names that infringed third party's trademarks).

[50] Zeran v. America Online, Inc. 129 F.3d 327 (4th Cir. 1997).

[51] People v. Lipsitz, 663 N.Y.S.2d 468 (Sup. Ct. N.Y. 1997).

[52] 126 F.3d 25 (2d Cir. 1997).

boarding a moving bus.[53] The court refused to extend jurisdiction to the Missouri club, whose business operations were local.

1997: The Federal Trade Commission held the first public workshop on the collection of personal information from web site visitors.[54]

1997: The first spamming case to bar defendant from using false headers or any false references to plaintiff in spam e-mails.[55]

1998

2/29/98: The District of Columbia appeals court rejects Microsoft's argument that its depositions be conducted in private to protect trade secrets. Court rules that the Sherman Act requires depositions to be conducted in open court.[56]

3/25/98: The first Internet gambling payout case: Thompson v. Handa-Lopez Inc.[57] Thompson had won thousands of dollars on the defendant's Internet gambling site and sued to recover his winnings.

5/13/98: The European Parliament adopts the report on electronic commerce of the Committee on Economic and Monetary Affairs and Industrial Systems.[58]

5/18/98: The United States Department of Justice and several state attorneys general file a civil antitrust case in the United States District Court for the District of Columbia charging Microsoft with various antitrust violations. The principal claim was predicated upon Microsoft's market share for its Internet Explorer product.[59]

---

[53] *Id.* at 26.

[54] Online Privacy Overview: Current Laws and Controversies, Congressional Digest, Feb. 2000, at 39.

[55] CompuServe, Inc. v. CyberPromotions, Inc., 962 F. Supp. 1015 (S.D. Ohio, 1997).

[56] United States v. Microsoft, 165 F.3d 952 (D.C. Cir. 1999).

[57] 998 F. Supp. 738 (W.D. Tex. 1998).

[58] Electronic Commerce and the European Union (visited Aug. 8, 1999), http://www.ispo.cec.

[59] United States v. Microsoft Corp., 1998 U.S. Dist. LEXIS 14231 (D.D.C. 1998) (describing Microsoft antitrust litigation); *see* United States v. Microsoft Corp., 2000 U.S. Dist LEXIS 7582 (D.D.C., June 7, 2000) (finding that Microsoft violated the Sherman Act and illegally tied its web browser to its operating system).

5/28/98: A Bavarian judge convicts a former head of CompuServe of Germany of distributing child pornography simply for failing to block a third party's transmission of pornography using the provider's services.[60]

6/4/98: The Federal Trade Commission released a report concluding that the vast majority of 14,000 commercial web sites collected personal information and only 14% of the sites gave visitors notice as to their information practices.[61]

7/23/98: The first case to hold that private litigants had no standing to challenge the sale of alcohol on the Internet under state licensing statute.[62]

9/14/98: The filing date for United States v. Microsoft Corp.[63] The case dates back to an original antitrust action filed by the government on July 15, 1994.

9/22/98: The first court to rule that a defendant linking to a third party's web site could not be liable for infringing material on the linked site.[64]

9/30/98: The first case denying liability for a host web site that was linked to a web site containing copyright infringing materials: Bernstein v. J.C. Penney.[65] The court found that linking to an infringing web site does not constitute infringement because the link does not copy the web site.

10/24/98: The European Directive on Privacy Protection goes into effect, requiring Member Countries to impose minimum standards in the processing of personally identifiable information collected and disclosed to third parties.

10/24/98: Sweden enacted the Swedish Data Protection Act, including regulations about web site personal information.[66]

---

[60] Germany v. CompuServe Deutschland, et al. (Bayern, May 28, 1998) reported in Perkins Coie LLP: Internet Case Digest (June 5, 1999), http://www.perkinscoie.com/resource/ecomm/netcase/Cases-05.htm.

[61] Federal Trade Commission, Privacy Online: A Report to Congress (June 1998), http://www.ftc.gov (visited Sept. 9, 2000).

[62] Wine and Spirits Wholesalers of Mass, Inc. v. Net Contents, Inc., 10 F. Supp. 2d 84 (D. Mass. 1998) (dismissing plaintiff's claim that Virtual Vineyards Inc. was violating Massachusetts alcohol licensing laws).

[63] 65 F. Supp. 2d 1 (D.D.C. 1999).

[64] Bernstein v. J.C. Penney, Inc., 1998 U.S. Dist. LEXIS 19048 (C.D. Cal. 1998) (dismissing complaint against J.C. Penney for merely linking to Swedish web site containing infringing materials, including copyrighted photographs of actress Elizabeth Taylor).

[65] 26 Media L. Rep 2471 (C.D. Cal. 1998).

[66] Microsoft Law & Corporate Affairs, Summary of Global Internet Legal Developments 78 (for the period Oct.-Dec. 1998).

10/28/98: Hessen became the first German *Land* (state) to adopt a data protection law "in line with the EU Data Protection Directive."[67]

10/28/98: Congress passed the Digital Millennium Copyright Act (DMCA), which creates a safe harbor from copyright infringement claims when providers act as a mere conduit distributing content posted by others. Title I of the DMCA implements WIPO's Copyright Treaty of 1996. The DMCA amends the Copyright Act to provide new provisions for Internet Service Providers and rules for anticircumvention technologies.

11/18/98: The European Commission adopted an Electronic Commerce Directive addressing issues such as caching, electronic contracts, digital signatures, and online dispute resolution.

12/15/98: The first Circuit U.S. Court of Appeals affirms district court's denial of Microsoft's motion to compel production of research materials compiled by two academic investigators for its defense in its antitrust case. The material requested by Microsoft was research for the book *Competing on Internet Time: Lessons from Netscape and its Battle with Microsoft*.[68]

1998: The District of Columbia federal circuit court dismissed America Online from defamation lawsuit filed by White House employee Sidney Blumenthal for statements made by political columnist Matt Drudge posted on the AOL system. Drudge had an exclusive contract to electronically publish his gossip column on AOL, but the provider was immunized by Section 230 of the CDA.[69]

1998: Expiration of the cooperative agreement between National Science Foundation and Network Solutions Inc. (NSI) for domain name registration services.[70]

1998: The Children's Online Privacy Protection Act of 1998 (COPPA) enacted. COPPA requires web sites to "obtain parental consent before collecting personal information from children, and a measure criminaliz[es] identity theft using such personal information such as credit card and Social

---

[67] *Id.*

[68] In re Cusmano v. Microsoft Corp., 162 F.3d 708 (1st Cir. 1998).

[69] Blumenthal v. Drudge, 992 F. Supp. 44 (D.D.C. 1998).

[70] McShane and Shifrin, *supra* note 13.

Security numbers."[71] COPPA requires parental consent before collecting information from children under thirteen.

1998: The United States Department of Commerce entered into agreement with the Internet Corporation for Assigned Names and Numbers (ICANN) to replace NSI in administering the domain name registration system.[72]

1998: The Federal Trade Commission proposed fair information practices for the Internet. The FTC requires "fair information practices, which include 'consumer awareness, choice, appropriate levels of security, data integrity and consumer access to their personally identifiable data.'"[73]

1998: The Seventh Circuit U.S. Court of Appeals enforces an arbitration clause in a software license agreement mailed *inside* a software box sent to customers. The court found the consumer accepted the terms by silence by retaining the computer system beyond the 30-day period specified in the agreement. This was the first case to find acceptance of mass-market agreement by silence or the failure to reject and return computer software.[74]

1998: President Clinton signed the Sonny Bono Copyright Term Extension Act of 1998 (CTEA), which increases the copyright term an additional 20 years.[75]

1999

1/1/99: The Euro became the official currency of the Member States of the European Union on January 1, 1999.

1/6/99: The first *in rem* jurisdiction lawsuit against a domain name. Porsche Cars North America filed the *in rem* case against 130 domain names allegedly infringing or diluting the Porsche trademark.[76] The Fourth Circuit

---

[71] Foreword, Internet Privacy: Protecting Personal Information Online, Congressional Digest, Feb. 2000, at 33.

[72] McShane and Shifrin, *supra* note 13.

[73] Notice Requesting Industry Guidelines and Principles Regarding Online Information Practices, 63 FR10916 (March 5, 1998).

[74] Hill v. Gateway 2000, 105 F.3d 1147 (7th Cir. 1998) (finding license agreement was enforceable even though software license agreement could not be reviewed prior to payment).

[75] Copyright Act, 17 U.S.C. § 304 (2000) (amended by the Sonny Bono Copyright Term Extension Act of 1998).

[76] Porsche Cars North America, Inc. v. Porsch.com, 51 F. Supp. 2d 707 (E.D. Va. 1999).

later held that the Anticybersquatting Consumer Protection Act enacted during Porsche's appeal permitted an *in rem* remedy and applied retroactively.[77]

3/10/99: The first case to rule that use of a competitor's trademark in metatags and domain names violated the Lanham Act because it caused "initial interest" confusion: Communications, Inc. v. West Coast Entertainment Corp.[78] The court held that consumer confusion may still ensue despite the different products and services offered.

5/99: The Ninth Circuit held that the government's ban on the export of encryption products violated the First Amendment free expression rights of an Illinois mathematics and computer science professor who developed an encryption method and reported it in academic journals.[79]

5/3/99: Release of World Intellectual Property (WIPO) Internet Domain Name Process by Francis Gurry, Assistant Director General.[80]

6/24/99: The first case denying an action for trademark infringement against Internet search engines for arranging combinations of advertising to appear on the results screen when the user selected the words "playboy" or "playmate" as search terms. Playboy, Inc., was held to have failed to show provider's commercial use of trademarks in interstate commerce.[81] The court ruled that search words were protected by the First Amendment and in any event protected by the Lanham Act's fair use doctrine.

6/15/99: The Ninth Circuit denied an injunction that would have prohibited the marketing of the RIO PMP 300, a handheld digital recording device.[82]

7/7/99: A major Fourth Amendment case on admissibility of records seized from an Internet Service Provider: United States v. Hambrick.[83] The court

---

[77] Porsche Cars North America, Inc. v. Allporsche, 2000 U.S. App. LEXIS 12843 (4th Cir., June 9, 2000).

[78] 174 F.3d 1036 (9th Cir. Cal. 1999).

[79] Bernstein v. U.S. Department of Justice, 199 WL 274111 (9th Cir., May 6, 1999) (holding that the federal government's export administration regulations operated as an impermissible prepublication prior restraint offending the First Amendment).

[80] World Intellectual Property, WIPO Internet Domain Name Process: Final Report, May 3, 1999 (visited May 24, 2000), http://ecommerce.wipo.int/domains/process/eng/wipo1.html.

[81] Playboy Enterprises, Inc. v. Netscape Comm. Corp., 55 F. Supp. 2d 1070 (C.D. Cal. 1999).

[82] Recording Industry Assoc. of America v. Diamond Multimedia Systems, Inc., 1999 U.S. App. LEXIS 13131 (9th Cir. June 15, 1999) (ruling that RIO was not classifiable as a "digital recording device" under the Audio Home Recording Act of 1992).

[83] 55 F. Supp. 2d 504 (W.D. Va. 1999).

held that a user may have no reasonable expectation of privacy for information submitted to an ISP in registering a screen name identity. The court still held open the option of civil damages if the ISP provided the information without being presented a valid warrant.

7/29/99: The National Conference of Commissioners on Uniform State Laws (NCCUSL) approved the Uniform Electronic Transactions Act (UETA) for enactment in the states.[84] UETA validates electronic documents, signatures, and filings as the legal equivalent of "paper and pencil" records in diverse legal fields.

7/29/99: NCCUSL approved the Uniform Computer Information Transactions Act (UCITA) for enactment in states.[85] UCITA governs computer information transactions including access agreements, software licenses, and countless other Internet-related contracts. UCITA validates mass-market license agreements such as "terms and conditions" or webwrap agreements.

8/18/99: The first case to recognize local toll calls to an ISP subject to reciprocal agreements for telecommunications reciprocity: Bellsouth Telcoms. Inc. v. Itc Deltacom Communs., Inc.[86] The court held that calls that terminate at a local ISP point of presence are local and not interstate.

8/23/99: Defendant's registration of *avery.com* and *dennison.com* for use as e-mail addresses for persons with those surnames did not violate the Federal Trademark Dilution Act of 1995 because the Avery/Dennison mark was distinctive, but not famous.[87]

10/20/99: The first case in which the Securities and Exchange Commission filed against individuals offering securities on an online auction site.[88]

---

[84] The Uniform Electronics Transaction Act is available at http://www.law.upenn.edu/bll/ulc/fnact99/1990s/ueta99.htm.

[85] The Computer Information Transaction Act is available at http://www.law.upenn.edu/library/ulc/ulc.htm.

[86] Bellsouth Telcoms, Inc. v. ITC Delta Communs., Inc., 62 F. Supp. 2d 1302 (M.D. Ala. 1999); *see also* BellSouth Telcoms, Inc. v. ITC Deltacom Communs., Inc., 180 F.R.D. 693 (M.D. Ala. 1999) (permitting posting of supersedeas bond to stay execution of reciprocal compensation judgment).

[87] Avery Dennison Corp. v. Sumpton, 189 F.3d 868 (9th Cir. 1999)

[88] Securities and Exchange Commission, SEC Internet Enforcement Program (visited June 8, 2000), http://www.sec.gov/enforce/intrela.htm (settling case by issuance of cease and desist order against selling securities on Internet auction site).

10/20/99: Organization of Economic Cooperation and Development (OECD) proposed a tax treaty through which a company is not liable for income tax on business profits merely because it has a web server in another country.[89]

11/2/99: The court refused to enforce a statute criminalizing dissemination by computer of material harmful to minors because enforcement of the statute violated the First Amendment and Commerce Clause.[90]

11/29/99: The Anticybersquatting Consumer Protection Act of 1999 (ACPA) became law designed "to protect consumers and American businesses . . . promote the growth of online commerce, and . . . provide clarity in the law for trademark owners by prohibiting the bad-faith and abusive registration of distinctive marks as Internet domain names with the intent to profit from the goodwill associated with such marks."[91]

12/9/99: President Clinton signed the Digital Theft Deterrence and Copyright Damages Improvement Act to increase statutory damages for copyright infringement targeting software piracy.[92]

12/12/99: President Clinton signed the Deceptive Mail Prevention and Enforcement Act to "provide for the non-mailability of certain deceptive matter relating to sweepstakes, skill contests, and facsimile checks."[93]

1999: Court grants summary judgment for employer, holding that a racially charged e-mail message did not constitute sufficient evidence that the employer embraced a pattern of racial discrimination.[94]

1999: President Clinton signed the Economic Espionage Act, which makes it a crime to transmit, receive, or possess stolen trade secrets.[95]

1999: The court found domain name *moviebuff.com* was confusingly similar to a senior trademark owner's mark and restrained the use of "moviebuff" in

---

[89] Ecommercetax.com, International Taxation of E-Commerce, Oct. 20, 1999 (visited May 8, 2000), http://www.ecommercetax.com/InternationalTax.htm.

[90] ACLU v. Johnson, 194 F.3d 1149 (10th Cir. 1999).

[91] 15 U.S.C. § 1125 et al. (2000).

[92] Digital Theft Deterrence and Copyright Damages Improvement Act, amending 17 U.S.C. §5504 and 28 U.S.C. §9841 (2000).

[93] Deceptive Mail Prevention and Enforcement Act, 39 U.S.C. §3017 (2000).

[94] Evans v. Toys R Us-Ohio, Inc., 32 F. Supp. 2d 974 (N.D. Ohio 1999), *aff'd*, 2000 U.S. App. LEXIS 14076 (6th Cir. June 2, 2000).

[95] 18 U.S.C. § 1832 (2000).

domain names and metatags because of "initial interest" rather than source confusion.[96]

2000

1/00: WIPO's first international domain name dispute was initiated when the World Wrestling Federation (WWF) submitted a dispute over the domain name *www.worldwrestlingfederation.com* to WIPO in Geneva. The WIPO arbitrator ruled that the registrant acted in bad faith by offering to sell the domain name for a significant profit. The arbitrator found that the domain name was confusingly similar to WWF's trademarks and service marks.[97]

1/10/00: The first case filed to to enjoin web sites distributing software that made unauthorized copies of copyrighted movies. The federal court enjoined the defendants from posting DeCSS and enjoined the use of electronic links to other sites posting DeCSS.[98] DeCSS is computer code to defeat the encryption algorithm used for DVDs, that is, for digital versatile disks or digital video disks.

1/18/00: The first case to rule that a domain name registrar did not violate the Sherman Act.[99]

2/7/00: The first case filed on rebroadcast of television programs on the Internet without permission of the copyright holders. Canadian and U.S. television broadcasters and film companies filed intellectual property infringement lawsuits against iCraveTV, a Toronto webcaster who distributes television programs on the Internet.[100]

2/00: Amazon.com filed a complaint against Barnesandnoble.com alleging that its "Express Lane" method infringed Amazon.com's "1-Click" e-commerce patent for ordering goods from web sites.[101] The court ordered Barnes and Noble to stop using Amazon.com's business method.

---

[96] Brookfield Communications v. West Coast Entertainment Corp., 174 F.3d 1036 (9th Cir. 1999).

[97] WIPO Press Release, First Cybersquatting Case Under WIPO Process Just Concluded, PR/2000/204 (visited Jan. 14, 2000), http://www.wipo.org/eng/pressrel/2000/p204.htm.

[98] Universal City Studio v. Reimerdes, 2000 U.S. Dist. LEXIS 11696 (S.D.N.Y., Aug. 17, 2000).

[99] Thomas v. Network Solutions, 176 F.3d 500 (D.C. Cir. 2000).

[100] Christine McGeever, Webcasting Suit Might Affect Online Copyrights: Coalition Members Complain iCraveTV Is Ignoring Their Broadcast Primacy, Computerworld, Feb. 7, 2000, at 42.

[101] Brian Logest, Brian Logest's Software Patent News: Patent Software Inventions, Oct/Nov. 1999 (visited Feb. 25, 2000, www.softwarepatentnews.com.

2/28/00: The European Council adopts European Community Directive on Electronic Commerce treating issues such as validation of digital signatures, spam, electronic money, digital copyright protection, electronic contracting, online dispute resolution, and other issues.[102] The European Parliament approved single market rules for electronic commerce applying to 15 European Union countries.

2/28/00: The court held that a criminal defendant who violated employer's Internet usage policy as well as criminal law had no reasonable expectation of privacy in his government office or computer.[103]

3/1/00: The American Law Institute released the revised draft of Article 2 on Sales of the UCC. Revised Article 2 validates electronic contracting and provides for electronic authentication and digital signatures.[104]

3/14/00: The Securities and Exchange Commission brought charges against 19 individuals for an $8 million trading scheme in which the Internet was used to pass inside information.[105]

3/21/00: The Advisory Commission on Electronic Commerce, which was formed to study among other things the Internet Tax Freedom Act and other Internet tax policies held its final meeting and submitted its findings in a report to Congress on April 12, 2000 (See *http:/www.ecommercecommission.org/report.htm*).

3/22/00: The first preliminary injunction was granted under the Anticybersquatting Consumer Protection Act in federal court.[106]

3/27/00: A federal court rejected the claim that deep linking practices violated the federal copyright act. In that case, Ticket.com extracted factual data from Ticketmaster and placed it in its own form. The federal court ruled that the federal law of copyright couldn't protect purely factual data or compilations.[107]

---

[102] Directive on Electronic Commerce, 2000/C I28/02 (adopted by the Council on Feb. 28, 2000).

[103] United States v. Simons, 206 F.3d 392 (4th Cir. 2000).

[104] The American Law Institute, Uniform Commercial Code [NEW] Revised Article 2 Sales (March 1, 2000), ALI Members Consultative Group Draft.

[105] Securities and Exchange Commission, SEC Internet Enforcement Program (visited June 8, 2000), http://www.sec.gov/enforce/intrela.htm.

[106] Shields v. Zuccarini, 89 F. Supp. 2d 634 (E.D. Pa. 2000) (granting preliminary injunction for misuse of Joe Cartoon's animations on political protest page).

[107] Ticketmaster Corp. v. Tickets.com, Inc., 2000 U.S. Dist. LEXIS 4553 (C.D. Calif., March 27, 2000).

4/00: The Recording Industry Association filed suit against Napster and other MP3 programs that permit copyrighted music to be freely downloaded from the Internet.[108]

4/3/00: The first case to rule that web site postings on an electronic bulletin board were excluded as hearsay for evidentiary purposes.[109]

4/3/00: U.S. District Judge Thomas Penfield Jackson ruled that Microsoft violated the Sherman Antitrust Act and used anticompetitive means and tying arrangements to maintain its monopoly position over the Windows operating system.[110]

4/4/00: The first case to rule that encryption code was protected by the First Amendment, although the protection is not absolute and may be overruled by national security interests.[111]

4/21/00: The Federal Trade Commission's regulations for children's online privacy implementing the Children's Online Privacy Protection Act (COPPA) went into effect.[112]

5/4/00: The first court to uphold limits on consequential damages found in a mass-market license agreement.[113]

5/5/00: The European Commission proposes its Directive on Electronic Commerce, validating electronic signatures and electronic records and providing safe harbors for Internet Service Providers.[114]

5/16/00: The first court to validate choice of venue clauses in a mass-market license agreement to avoid litigating in a distant forum.[115]

---

[108] Tom Spring, Swap MP3s, Go to Jail? CNN.com, April 14, 2000, at 1.

[109] United States v. Jackson, 208 F.3d 633 (7th Cir. 2000) (upholding fraud conviction because defendant did not disclose the substance of testimony sought from excluded postings, and Internet postings were excluded as hearsay evidence).

[110] United States v. Microsoft Corp., 875 F. Supp. 2d 30 (D.D.C. 2000).

[111] Junger v. Daley, 209 F.3d 481 (6th Cir. 2000) (holding the computer encryption product was protected by First Amendment).

[112] Federal Trade Commission, New Rule to Protect Parent's Online Privacy Takes Effect April 21, 2000 (visited May 5, 2000), http://www.ftc.gov/opa/2000/04/coppa1.htm.

[113] M.M. Mortenson Co. v. Timberline Software Corp., 2000 Wash. LEXIS 287 (Wash. App. Ct., May 4, 2000).

[114] The European Commission, Electronic Commerce: Commission Proposes Electronic Signature Directive (visited May 5, 2000), http://europa.eu.int/comm/internal_market/en/media/sign.htm.

[115] American Eyewear v. Peeper's Sunglasses, 2000 U.S. Dist. LEXIS 6875 (N.D. Tex., May 16, 2000).

6/7/00: Judge Thomas Penfield Jackson orders bifurcation of Microsoft into companies that separate the operating system and applications system as a remedy in the antitrust lawsuit. Judge Jackson observes that Microsoft's lack of repentance was a factor leading to the remedy of divestiture.[116]

6/30/2000: President Clinton signed the Electronic Signatures in Global and National Commerce Act, which validates digital signatures and records.[117]

2000: UETA was adopted in Arizona, California, Delaware, Florida, Hawaii, Idaho, Indiana, Kansas, Kentucky, Maine, Maryland, Minnesota, Nebraska, North Carolina, Ohio, Oklahoma, Pennsylvania, Rhode Island, South Dakota, and Virginia.

2000: Court ruled that MP3.com violated copyrights of a large number of music companies and awarded damages of $25,000 per CD.[118]

2000: First appellate case considering the applicability of the Anticybersquatting Consumer Protection Act to a domain name dispute. The Second Circuit affirmed the federal district court's order to transfer "sporty's.com" domain name to Sportsman's Market. The court found "sporty's" to be a distinctive trademark but declined to make a determination whether it was a famous mark triggering protection of the federal antidilution act.[119]

July 2000: Napster, the popular MP3 swapping service, was shut down by a preliminary injunction issued by Judge Marilyn Patel, a federal district judge. The preliminary injunction ordered that all copyrighted materials be removed from Napster's network. Judge Patel ruled that the Recording Industry Association of America had a strong likelihood of prevailing on its claim that Napster was liable for direct copyright infringement.[120]

Figure 1-1 on page 24 shows the number of cases mentioning the Internet for a five-year-plus period since 1995, pointing to an overall spurt in "mentions" since 1996.

---

[116] State of New York v. Microsoft Corp., No. 98-1233 (D.C. Dist. Ct., June 7, 2000).

[117] Mary Mosquera, President Makes Digital Signatures Legal, TechWeb News, June 30, 2000, at 1.

[118] Larry Neumeister, MP3 Loses Ninth Circuit Copyright Suit, Awarded in Millions; Music Site Ordered to Pay Record Firms, Chi. Tribune, Sept. 7, 2000, at 1; *see also* RIAA v. MP3.COM, 2000 U.S. Dist. LEXIS 5761 (S.D.N.Y. 2000).

[119] Sporty's Farm LLC v. Sportsman's Market Inc., 202 F.3d 489 (2d Cir. 2000).

[120] RIAA v. Napster, 2000 U.S. Dist. LEXIS 6243 (N.D. Cal. 2000) (granting RIAA's request for a preliminary injunction stayed shortly after by Ninth Circuit).

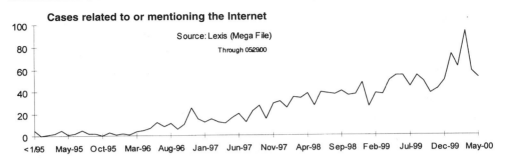

FIGURE 1-1

§ 1.03   WHAT IS THE INTERNET?

The answer to the question "What is the Internet?" varies depending upon whom you ask. Technically speaking, the Internet is a worldwide interconnected collection of computers. Computers are interconnected with each other so long as they share "information."[121] This, of course, is an oversimplified explanation. To really answer this question, consider the following scenario. Suppose Suffolk Personal Computers, or SPC, the hypothetical company used in this book, wants to connect two computers to exchange information. This can be accomplished by connecting the two computers using a set of cables. Linking the computers in this way creates a personal network that makes it possible to exchange files.

Then SPC expands its staff from 2 to 100 employees, all in the same building. To allow the exchange of files among all 100 employees, SPC would connect all 100 computers, via cables, into a Local Area Network, or LAN.[122] If SPC expands into 14 cities on the East Coast, a Wide Area Network, or WAN[123] would be used to exchange information among the various offices.

Now take the WAN concept and multiply it by infinity. That is the Internet. Numerous privately run networks allow businesses to connect their LANs and WANs. These privately run networks span the world, creating both redundancy and stability. Copper connects each network; fiber optic landlines, wireless links, and intelligent devices called "routers" conjoin to route data over the many networks. This infrastructure enables every computer to send and receive data from anywhere in the world. Information is exchanged in the form of "packets," which

---

[121] George B. Delta and Jeffrey H. Matsuura, Law of the Internet, 1-5 (1998).

[122] A LAN consists of computers that are geographically close together (that is, in the same building). It is normally a computer-to-computer cabling system that daisy chains computers together into a linear or circular network so that they can share data storage devices and printers.

[123] WANs differ from LANs in that the computers are farther apart and are connected by telephone lines or radio waves rather than cables.

do not take predesignated routes to their destinations. The packet switching system is simply a means of using routing options for efficient traffic control.[124] Consequently, physical boundaries are erased as data containing text, graphics, audio, video, and much more is transmitted and received by interconnected computers.

§ 1.04 WHAT ARE PEOPLE DOING ON THE INTERNET?

The Internet is a multifunctional tool that offers the world a powerful means of communication, a method of doing research in a virtual library, a way to exchange data, and a system for buying and selling goods and services.[125] These activities can be categorized into (1) e-mail, (2) online services, (3) private networks, (4) publishing, and (5) e-commerce.

[A] E-mail and Online Service Providers

It is estimated that electronic mail (e-mail) messages outnumber regular mail by ten to one.[126] E-mail is a form of communication. E-mail allows people to send and receive messages from almost anywhere in the world. Generally speaking, if a user has access to a telephone line and an e-mail account with an Internet Service Provider ("ISP"),[127] e-mail messages can be accessed at any time and from any place.[128] E-mail has become more widely used than are fax machines because it is relatively inexpensive (not requiring an additional, dedicated piece of machinery, the fax machine), and it is an efficient medium that can be employed throughout an organization. E-mail messages also have the advantage of enabling an individual to send text messages instantly and simultaneously to multiple recipients.

E-mail systems range from those that carry only simple text messages to other, more complex systems that allow users to incorporate typed memos, spreadsheets, photographs, and video clips in their messages. Senders can also "carbon

---

[124] *Supra* note 40, at 1-5.

[125] *See* Reno v. ACLU, 117 S.Ct. 2329, 2335 (1997) (explaining the Internet and its value to users).

[126] 1998 Cisco Systems Shareholder Report (visited Mar. 5, 1999), http://www.cisco.com/shareholder/1998.

[127] ISPs are companies, such as AOL, CompuServe, or Prodigy, that provide access to the Internet. For a monthly fee, the service provider gives its subscribers a software package, username, password, and access phone number. Equipped with a modem, the user can then log on to the Internet and browse the World Wide Web and USENET (discussion groups, which are similar to public bulletin boards), and send and receive e-mail. In addition to serving individuals, ISPs also serve large companies, providing a direct connection from the company's networks to the Internet. ISPs themselves are connected to one another through Network Access Points (NAPs). ISPs are also sometimes called Internet Access Providers (IAPs).

[128] Those craving constant access to e-mail may achieve it today without even using a computer. Cellular phones, pagers, and other wireless devices enable people to access their e-mail messages without being tied to a computer or telephone line.

copy" or "blind carbon copy" multiple recipients. This flexible functionality provides users with an audit trail that can be followed, should the need arise. E-mail messages create electronic records that can be traced to assist the sender or to provide a smoking gun in lawsuits.[129] E-mail smoking guns were star witnesses in the government's antitrust case against Microsoft, and they are frequently invaluable in bolstering a client's position in a lawsuit.[130]

E-mail messages are delivered using an address scheme specific to computer networks. Sending an e-mail to Cyrus Daftary at Suffolk University, for example, would require the sender to type *cdaftary@acad.suffolk.edu* in the address line. This e-mail address can be broken down into its components, much as the address on the envelope of a letter indicates both local and regional points. *Cdaftary* identifies a specific user, Cyrus Daftary. The @ symbol, connecting the specific e-mail recipient with the latter part of the address, represents the computer network on which Cyrus Daftary is a member. The *acad.suffolk.edu* indicates that Cyrus is affiliated with Suffolk University; the *.edu* suffix identifies the organization as being an academic institution.

Likewise, the e-mail address for Michael Rustad, *ProfRustad@aol.com*, can be broken down as follows: *ProfRustad* is the naming convention used to indicate Professor Rustad; *aol.com* indicates that Michael Rustad is a member of AOL; *.com* shows that AOL is a commercial institution. The primary endings of e-mail addresses in the United States include *.com*, *.edu*, *.net*, *.org,* and *.gov.*

After an e-mail message is sent, it is broken into packets of data and routed through a network of computers until it arrives at its final destination, where all the packets come together and are reassembled. Despite the many wonderful things that can be said about e-mail, it is vulnerable at two points. Messages are sometimes lost, and hackers may compromise the message or network security.

For lawyers exchanging confidential or sensitive information with clients, the risk of interception raises particular concern. One way companies and lawyers can protect against having their e-mail intercepted is by using encryption[131] software, or a system of codes. Encryption and encoding scrambles the contents of a message so that the message can be deciphered only by a recipient that has the keys needed to unscramble the message.[132] Many governments, including the

---

[129] Please *see* Chapter Seven for a detailed discussion of e-mail messages and smoking guns.

[130] *See* America Online, Inc. v. IMS, 1998 U.S. Dist. LEXIS 20645 (1998).

[131] *Encryption* is the translation of data into a secret code and the most effective way to achieve data security. To read an encrypted file, one must have access to a secret key or password that enables decryption. Unencrypted data is called plain text; encrypted data is referred to as cipher text.

[132] One of the more popular encryption packages is called Pretty Good Privacy (PGP). PGP Security, Inc., helps companies worldwide easily secure their e-business operations through firewall, encryption, intrusion detection, risk assessment, and VPN (virtual private network) technologies. *See* http://www.pgp.com (visited May 15, 2000).

United States, place limits on the use of encryption, particularly restricting the import and use of cryptographic products.[133]

Many people have access to e-mail either through their employers or through affiliations with organizations that provide members with free e-mail accounts. Many employers, however, restrict how e-mail may be used by their employees. Consequently, for personal use, most Americans look to third-party online service providers (OSPs) to obtain online services, such as e-mail. OSPs provide an infrastructure in which subscribers can communicate with each other, either by e-mail messages or by participating in online conferences, forums, or chat rooms (online, real time "conversations" conducted by typing messages by turns). In addition, most OSPs offer proprietary content, developed either in-house or through licensing arrangements, and can connect users with an unlimited number of outside information and service providers through the Internet.

Subscribers can receive up-to-date stock quotes, news stories, articles from magazines and journals, and any other information available in electronic format. Accessing all this data carries a price, of course, but it is a price that many subscribers pay happily. Collectively, the three largest online services, America Online (AOL), CompuServe, and Microsoft Network (MSN), provide approximately 25,000,000 people with access to the Internet.[134]

The landscape of commercial online services changes almost daily, so comparison-shopping is important. Companies are constantly merging or buying each other out. America Online recently purchased CompuServe, one of its main competitors, and in early 2000, in a move of historic proportions, "little" America Online purchased the publishing powerhouse Time Warner.

[B]   Electronic Bulletin Boards

Computer bulletin boards (BBS)[135] and Internet newsgroups provide sites on which anyone may post text, photographs, software, and videos to share with the larger Internet community. Most bulletin boards are a part of a system called USENET,[136] a global system that hosts more than thirty thousand newsgroups.

---

[133] Edward J. Radlo, Protecting E-Mail: Navigating the Legal Limits on Encryption, 4 Intell. Prop. Strategies 1 (July 1998).

[134] AOL and CompuServe have respectively 21 million and 2.5 million members. *See* http://corp.aol.com/whoweare.html? (last visited Mar. 5, 1999). While no specific numbers are available on MSN membership, at the end of 1998 the network's reach spanned 31 countries. *See* http://microsoft-online-sales.com/audience.asp (last visited Mar. 5, 1999).

[135] BBS is shorthand for a dial-in computer service that is used for exchanging e-mail, reading notices, and other services.

[136] USENET is a worldwide bulletin board system that can be accessed through the Internet or through many online services. USENET contains more than 14,000 forums, called newsgroups, covering every imaginable interest. USENETs are accessed daily by millions of people around the world.

Bulletin boards function similarly to e-mail. An e-mail message, however, is private, intended for a specific individual or group of individuals, whereas a bulletin board posting is intended to reach a larger, nonspecific audience. Newsgroups broadcast and publish messages and related responses for any and all members of the newsgroup to read.

Many observers of the Internet have said that the collective knowledge of mankind is posted and transmitted each day on USENET. On a daily basis, as many as 70,000 messages may be posted.[137] Newsgroups vary in the subjects they treat, which can range from world hunger to e-commerce to a popular culture phenomenon. Anyone can create a newsgroup or participate in a newsgroup. In today's rapidly changing world, newsgroups on the hot topic of the day can quickly flower, flourish, and then die as people gain and lose interest and no more messages are posted.

[C] Mailing Lists

Mailing lists are another communication tool that function similarly to newsgroups, but they require membership. In essence, a mailing list is an automated e-mail notification service that brings together, via e-mail, groups of people who share a common interest.[138] Lists require individuals to send an e-mail note to the list manager asking to "subscribe."[139] Once a user has successfully subscribed, the subscriber, like other members of the list, will automatically receive whatever e-mail messages are posted to the list. The recipients of these e-mails may, in turn, respond with a message to the entire group or by private e-mail to the original sender.

To avoid disruptive or unrelated messages, some lists may have moderators that filter out inappropriate messages. Those lists that do not have moderators will have no way to filter out unwanted messages. Consequently, a member of the list may post inappropriate commercial solicitations or spam[140] messages. If this occurs frequently, subscribers who find this unacceptable may withdraw from the

---

[137] ACLU v. Reno, 929 F. Supp. 824, 834 (E.D. Pa. 1996).

[138] Mailing lists are sometimes referred to as "listservs," but LISTSERV is a registered trademark of L-Soft International, Inc., which distributes software for managing mailing lists. See http://www.lsoft.com/manuals/1.8d/user/user.html. See also Law News Network for information on its various lists: http://www.lawnewsnet.com/forum/aca-1/dispatch.cgi (visited Mar. 5, 1999).

[139] To subscribe to the CYBERIA-L listserv on the law and policy of computer networks, for example, interested parties must subscribe by sending an e-mail to listserve@eagle.birds.wm.edu.

[140] Spam is an unsolicited posting, usually off the topic, sent to many newsgroups or lists simultaneously. Spam e-mail ranges from online advertisements proclaiming ways users can get rich fast to political messages or commentaries to pleas for help in finding missing children. One court has defined spam as "unauthorized bulk e-mail advertisements." America Online, Inc. v. IMS, 24 F. Supp. 2d 548, 549 (E.D. Va. 1998).

list; members have the option of suspending (for vacations and so on) or canceling their subscriptions at any point.

[D] Private Systems

A server or file server is a "computer in a network that stores application programs and data files accessed by the other computers in the network."[141] Private systems consist of local or wide area networks, client server applications, UNIX[142] machines, and intranets.[143] Each of these systems is a series of personal computers connected to each other through a common server[144] linked by fiber optic cable or connected by the Internet.

Private networks can be used to create what is called an intranet, not to be confused with the Internet. An intranet consists of all HTTP nodes on a private network, such as a Local Area Network,[145] which may or may not be connected to the Internet. An intranet connects clients using standard protocols such as TCP/IP[146] or HTTP.[147] The purpose of an intranet is to increase communication in a business or corporate environment, to coordinate projects and tasks, and to coordinate schedules—all using the same interface or "look." An intranet can deliver such services as an institutional directory, e-mail, filing, printing, and network management to those connected to it. Intranet software also includes application and development tools and utilities, databases, e-commerce, and distribution capabilities, messaging, and groupware software. Using any or all of these tools raises

---

[141] American Eyewear v. Peeper's Sunglasses, 2000 U.S. Dist. LEXIS 6875 (N.D. Tex., May 16, 2000) (quoting Microsoft's Encarta World English Dictionary).

[142] UNIX is an operating system developed by Bell Telephone Laboratories. UNIX was developed originally as a portable program development environment that could be ported to many different computers so that Bell engineers designing telephone switching systems could move easily among machines made by IBM, Digital, Hewlett Packard, or any other manufacturer without needing retraining.

[143] *Intranet* has no widely accepted definition. This book uses the term in its most common sense, as a network of computers accessible only by individuals within a particular enterprise via a Local Area Network (LAN).

[144] A server is a computer, attached to the Internet, capable of offering one or more Internet services.

[145] *See* Intranet Design Magazine, Intranet FAQ: Intranet Basics (visited May 30, 2000), http://idm.internet.com/faqs/whatis/2.html.

[146] TCP/IP is an abbreviation for Transmission Control Protocol/Internet Protocol that permits computers to communicate on a network. "TCP/IP was developed by the Department of Defense for the Defense Data Network and has since been widely adopted as a networking standard." Indiana University Knowledge Base, What Does TCP/IP Mean? (visited May 30, 2000), http://kb.indiana.edu/data/abkr.html?cust=12632.

[147] HTTP stands for Hypertext Transfer Protocol. When the abbreviation appears as part of an Internet address or URL, that is the Internet protocol being used. Hypertext is a "standard web formatting language." Shea v. Reno, 930 F. Supp. 916, 929 (S.D.N.Y. 1996).

security concerns, just as with e-mail. Institutions utilizing an intranet generally invest in a separate software application to provide the requisite security.[148] Standard protocols make it possible to bridge the gaps between browsers with different configurations.

Extended intranets or extranets[149] function in the same manner as intranets, but they allow access through the Internet to people outside the enterprise, such as customers or suppliers.[150] An extranet is essentially a "web-based analog of LAN [Local Area Network] and WAN [Wide Area Network]."[151] Industry-specific extranets have been designed for the automobile industry, healthcare, financial services, telecommunications, and other industries.[152] A corporate web connecting trading partners is known as a business-to-business web or extranet.[153] Due to relatively low maintenance costs, it is not unusual to find corporations that maintain intranets, extranets, and a public Internet web site.

Traditionally, company computer networks at different locations have been connected by dedicated lines or switched dial-up lines. A dedicated line, sometimes called a leased line,[154] is a "telecommunications path between two points available 24 hours a day for use by a designated user." A dedicated line is a non-switched line, as opposed to a switched dial-up line, used by many users.[155] A company may lease lines from a carrier or use public switched lines with secure message protocols.

A virtual private network (VPN) is an innovation that allows secure exchange of information among multiple locations via the Internet, rather than through more costly dedicated lines or switched dial-up lines. VPNs are usually

---

[148] One of the leading intranet security application companies is Secure Solutions Expert, which is a Siemens Company. See http://www.sse.ie/ tool (last visited May 15, 2000). Other leading intranet software companies include Applix, Inc.; INTERSHOP; Netegrity; Netscape Communications Corp.; Open Text; and Wallop.

[149] Extranets are based on TCP/IP network and on Internet standard protocols and services.

[150] *See* Commerce One at http://www.commerceone.com (last visited May 15, 2000). Commerce One works with many companies to set up extranets. General Motors and Commerce One are working on a proposed product, to be proprietary to GM and intended as a marketplace for GM suppliers to which those wanting to enter must enroll as members.

[151] Intranet Design Magazine, Intranet FAQ: What Is an Extranet? (visited May 30, 2000), http://idm.internet.com/faqs/whatis/10.html.

[152] *Id.*

[153] Intranet Design Magazine, Intranet FAQ (visited May 30, 2000), http://idm.internet.com/faqs/whatis/2.html.

[154] "A leased line is a telephone line that has been leased for private use. . . . Typically, large companies rent leased lines from the telephone message carriers (such as AT&T) to interconnect different geographic locations in their companies. The alternative is to buy and maintain their own private lines. Whatis.com, What Is . . . A Leased Line (A Definition) (visited May 30, 2000), http://www.whatis.com/leasedli.htm.

[155] *Id.*

supported and maintained by ISPs to enable secure Internet-based access to computer networks. VPNs permit organizations to use the Internet as a "private enterprise backbone infrastructure to provide secure access to telecommuting employees, business partners and customers."[156] At a minimum, a VPN must have the following features: authentication, data encryption, user access control, and event logging.[157] Data may be transmitted from a telecommuting employee's PC to a firewall, where the data is encrypted and transmitted through the company's access line to the company's ISP. The information is then "tunneled"[158] through the Internet to arrive at the receiver's firewall, where it is decrypted. A remote receiver can then dial into the VPN and gain access to the decrypted data via a remote server. VPNs are a cost-effective and secure way of delivering business information using the Internet.

[E] Computer Networks/Protocols

[1] Telnet

Telnet provides a means to access and obtain data from another computer. Telnet makes it possible for users to log into a remote computer and use programs and data made available by the remote owner. Telnet is a "user command and an underlying TCP/IP protocol"[159] permitting the user to log into mainframes,[160] midrange systems, or UNIX servers.

Telnets come in a wide range of applications, but the two basic types are "rlogin" and "TCP3270." Functionally, these protocols operate identically. Both allow a user to connect to a remote computer via the Internet and to use programs and data as if they were installed locally on the user's own computer. Telnet, while still used by many educational institutions and universities, is no longer widely used by corporations.

Many library catalogs are available only by Telnet, although libraries are gradually converting to web-based catalogs. Through Telnet, researchers at another university can connect to the Suffolk University e-mail server (Pine) or to

---

[156] Tim Armstrong, How Virtual Private Networks (VPNs) Save Money and Improve Security, Dec. 1998, White Paper, Electronic Security University (visited May 30, 2000), http://www.v-one.com/whitepapers/vpn_v_ras.htm.

[157] *Id.*

[158] *Tunnel* is a term describing the encapsulating and encrypting of information through Internet Protocol packets.

[159] Whatis.com, What Is . . . Telnet (A Definition) (visited May 30, 2000), http://www.whatis.com/telnet.htm (noting that technical details are available at Telnet Protocol at http://www.metrowerks.com/tcpip/spec/telnet.stm).

[160] Mainframes are very large computers that can perform a huge number of instructions per second, servicing a large user group so quickly that all appear to be receiving service simultaneously.

the Suffolk University Law School Library Online Catalog for example. An example of a Telnet command request is *telnet the.libraryat.Suffolk.edu.* These Telnet sites permit a remote user to request data from anywhere in the world, assuming the user has a password or user ID. From a Serial Line Internet Protocol (SLIP), Point to Point Protocol (PPP), or ethernet[161] connected account, a user can type a Telnet URL[162] into the location window of the browser.

[2] TCP3270

TCP3270 is a special type of Telnet sometimes needed to connect to IBM mainframe sites. Although regular Telnet may work, the key presses and commands are not user friendly. A TCP3270 client is a useful tool for communicating between machines. TCP3270 is highly recommended for libraries because of add-on functionality, which permits record and session capturing.[163] Session capturing permits all activities on a screen to be captured on a file, "a function useful for viewing the information later and compiling bibliographies."[164] Record capturing permits individual records from a Telnet application to be saved or captured.[165] TCP3270 runs under Microsoft Windows and is downloadable, along with good documentation.[166] Netscape also has a TCP3270 web site.[167]

[3] FTP

Transferring files and sharing data is the heart and soul of the Internet. The types of files that can be transferred include documentation, graphics, software,

---

[161] Bob Metcalfe, the founder of 3Com, invented ethernets. An ethernet is one of several local area networks that can be used to connect multiple PCs so that they can share files, programs, and printers. Ethernets generally can handle seventy to eighty computers for printer and file sharing, as long as the network traffic is not too heavy.

[162] A URL, or a Uniform Resource Locator, is a "generic set of all names/address that are short strings that refer to resources," but the term also includes "explicit instruction on how to access the resource on the Internet." Web Naming and Addressing Overview (visited May 30, 2000), http://www.w3.org/Addressing. A URL is "a networked extension of the standard filename concept: not only can you point to a file in a directory, but that file and that directory can exist on any machine on the network [and] can be served via any of several different methods." NCSA, A Beginner's Guide to URLs (visited May 5, 2000), http://www.ncsa.uicuc.edu/demoweb/url-primer.html.

[163] National Library of Australia, Information Facilities Branch, TCP3270 for Windows—Supplementary Documentation for ABN Users (visited May 27, 2000), http://www.abn.nla.gov.au/tcp3270.

[164] *Id.*

[165] *Id.*

[166] *Id.*

[167] *Id.*

sound, and video. These files can contain megabytes[168] worth of information. One method of receiving such files is to use a program called File Transfer Protocol (FTP).

FTP is an Internet protocol that permits users to transfer files between two systems.[169] FTP provides a medium through which two computers can retrieve copies of files and place new files online as needed. When using FTP software to log into a specific site, users are prompted for and must enter a username and a password to gain access. Some sites will allow the users to identify themselves as "anonymous."

[F]   Publishing and Research

The ease of creating a web site has allowed a large number of people to publish information cheaply and easily. An Internet web page can be built using free applications, such as Hotdog, Notepad, or Wordpad, or by using a sophisticated web-publishing tool, such as Microsoft's Front Page. These publishing tools convert information into Hypertext Markup Language (HTML), the universal language understood by computers connected to the Internet. HTML tells an application running on a computer connected to the Internet how to display the text of the document, as well as any movies, audio, video, or links within the document.

The mere ability to publish information is no guarantee of the ability to do it well. Before a company sets up a web site, it must establish goals for the site and minimize its risks of liability. In the corporate world, the various corporate stakeholders, including marketing, sales, management information systems (MIS), and the finance, tax, and legal departments need to determine and agree on the goals for the site.

The content of a web page or pages can be designed either in-house or off-site. In either case, it has been observed that there is an abundance of poor quality web page design on the Internet, and finding good quality designers is not always easy. To build an effective corporate web site, a design team familiar with corporate goals, coupled with a sophisticated webmaster or designer, will be crucial. The Internet itself constitutes a valuable source of ideas for content design and provider resources. The Sun web site,[170] for example, provides many relevant guides and links.

---

[168] A megabyte is 1,048,576 bytes of data, the rough equivalent of 1,000,000 characters, or the text on 33,000 typewritten pages. Data transfer rates are often described in megabytes per second, or MBps.

[169] A File Transfer Protocol (FTP) is a "set of standard codes for transferring files over the Internet. FTP is usually used for retrieving large files or files that cannot be displayed through a browser." Glossary, Terms Used in E-Commerce, Congressional Digest, Feb. 2000, at 36.

[170] *See* http://www.Sun.com (visited Mar. 5, 1999).

The cost of setting up a web site depends on the level of complexity desired for the site. A novice using an off-the-shelf HTML design software package such as NetFusion or Microsoft Front Page can design a "passive" page that simply provides information. A sophisticated linked set of pages that includes online-shopping, security functions, and interactive multimedia, such as streaming video, will require an experienced web site designer.

Though complex graphics and multimedia files work well on some sites, they can detract from the chief goal of most business web sites: disseminating the company's message quickly to site visitors. Many users will not wait for memory-heavy graphics to load, especially if they are accessing the Internet at low-speeds over telephone lines; they will simply leave the site in frustration.

Like other forms of publishing, information publishing on the web can create liability. Before publication, an attorney knowledgeable about Internet business should review the costs and benefits of content. An intellectual property attorney can examine the proposed web site and give advice on whether linking, framing, metatags, or references to a competitor's trademarks is advisable. The attorney can offer guidance on a variety of other issues, including the most beneficial corporate structure of the web business, its tax implications, and any corporate liabilities that may stem from ineffective or absent postings on privacy policies, disclaimers, and other web-related agreements.

[G] Electronic Commerce

The Internet offers today's businesses a global marketplace that operates 24 hours a day, 365 days a year. An organization can now modify every aspect of its business operations to harness the potential of the Internet. Companies can now, for example, (1) enable their customers to price, submit orders, and monitor the distribution and processing of their orders online; (2) respond to customer inquiries; (3) increase professional staff efficiency; (4) recruit new professionals online; (5) reduce operating costs; (6) expand sales opportunities and clientele; and (7) connect various business operations together in real time meetings.[171] By

---

[171] Cisco Systems reported third quarter sales of $4.92 billion, as compared to $3 billion for 1999. Cisco Systems, May 9, 2000, Press Release: Cisco Systems Reports Third Quarter Earnings (visited May 30, 2000), http://www.cisco.com/warp/public/146/presroom/2000/may--/corp_050900.htm.

Cisco projected that 80 percent of its revenues for 1999 would result from orders received via the Internet. Cisco handles 70 percent of its customer inquiries via the web, and it receives more than 70 percent of all resumes via the Internet, which has led to an $8,000,000 reduction in recruiting fees. The company has quadrupled in size since 1994 without increasing its operating expenses, which has resulted in savings of approximately $500,000,000. 1998 Cisco Systems Shareholder Report (last visited Mar. 5, 1999), http://www.cisco.com/business solutions/1998. Cisco has gained even more momentum because traditional business models are being transformed into Internet-based models. May 9, 2000, press release, *id.*

utilizing the full potential of the Internet, customers, suppliers, employees, and business partners can collaborate in ways that allow them to be more productive, to adapt rapidly to change, and to make more effective business decisions.[172] With these capabilities, the Internet has penetrated all parts of the globe, making it possible to reach customers and achieve efficiencies that were unimaginable just a few years ago.

Coined by Lawrence Livermore in 1989, the phrase "electronic commerce," or e-commerce as it has come to be called, refers to the electronic network of commercial transactions that bring the entire supply chain (suppliers, customers, and vendors) online through an electronic infrastructure. More specifically, e-commerce is the use of computer networks—the Internet, intranets, extranets, and private networks—to engage in business transactions.[173]

Great opportunities abound for both small and large businesses that are able to gain worldwide access to millions of consumers by effective use of the Internet. E-commerce is attractive to companies because of its relatively low operational costs, its convenience, its potential for customization, and the astounding access it provides to a global marketplace never before realizable on this scale. Moreover, e-commerce now enables a corporation to advertise, sell products, and even exchange goods with a larger client base while maintaining lower operational costs than is possible using traditional methods. For consumers, e-commerce enables them to shop for a variety of products and services from their own homes and offices using their credit cards.

E-commerce transactions can be broken down into business-to-consumer e-commerce (B2C) and Business-to-Business e-commerce (B2B). Business-to-consumer refers to using the Internet to sell products or services to consumers just as in a retail store, direct sales, or catalog or phone ordering. One of the primary goals of B2B is to provide a more efficient distribution model. The most successful e-commerce businesses include Cisco Systems, Dell Computers, and Amazon.com, which respectively report *daily* sales in the millions of dollars.

Cisco Systems reported net sales of $4.92 billion for the third quarter of fiscal 2000 and net sales of $13.18 billion, an increase of 53 percent over the third quarter for 1999.[174] Cisco has a multifaceted business model and is expanding into the service provider marketplace as well as the optical market, the enterprise market, and small and medium-sized business markets.[175] Cisco's Internet products are for data, voice, and videocommunications. Cisco's horizontal business model is built upon "internal development, acquisitions and partnerships."[176]

---

[172] 1998 Cisco Systems Shareholder Report (visited Mar. 5, 1999), http://www.cisco.com/interneteconomy/1998.

[173] *Supra* note 1, PricewaterhouseCoopers, at 192.

[174] Cisco Systems, *see supra* note 171.

[175] *Id.*

[176] *Id.*

Dell Computer Corporation has become the "world's largest direct computer systems company with revenues of $25.3 billion for the fiscal year ending January 28, 2000."[177] Dell's direct business model delivers custom-built computer systems, eliminating the network of wholesalers, retailers, and distributors interposed elsewhere between the computer customer and seller.[178] Dell expanded its Internet business with the launch of *www.gigabuys.com,* creating an online store for 30,000 competitively priced products.[179] The company use of direct customer service is coupled with "customer paperless purchase orders, approved product configurations, global price, real-time order tracking, purchasing history, and account team information."[180]

Amazon.com opened its web site in July 1995 and has since sold products to 17 million online shoppers in more than 160 countries.[181] Sales grew from $610 million in 1998 to $1.64 billion in 1999, a phenomenal 169 percent increase.[182] From 1998 to 1999, Amazon.com added 10.7 million new customers. Amazon.com had $2 billion in annualized sales, requiring just $220 million in fixed assets, and $318 million in fixed assets in the fourth quarter of 1999.[183]

These three companies all have in common one highly successful sales strategy, a strategy that allowed them to vault to the top of the Fortune 500 rankings within a very short time period: In ordinary parlance, they "cut out the middleman." Each of these companies has expanded products and services in the global marketplace. By doing so, these companies have achieved several objectives:

- Create an immediate connection with the customer.

- Offer every visitor a relatively unlimited selection of products, without being constrained by floor space, store hours, or advertising costs.

- Create targeted marketing efforts that entice visitors to buy products and services that they may not have been looking for.

- Implement a detailed transaction record allowing increased ease in post-sale dialog with the customer.

- Reduce inventory.

---

[177] Dell Computer Corporation, Form 10-K, Annual Report for the Fiscal Year Ended Jan. 28, 2000 (visited May 30, 2000), http://www.dell.com/downloads/us/corporate/sec/10k-00.htm.

[178] Alsop on Infotech; Helping the Governor Figure Out E-Commerce, Fortune, June 8, 1998, at 269.

[179] Dell Computer Corp., Form 10-K, *id.*

[180] *Id.*

[181] Amazon.com, Amazon.com Annual Report for 1999 (visited May 30, 2000), http://www.amazon.com/exec/obidos/subst/misc/investor-relations/199.../104-8139596-215993.

[182] *Id.*

[183] *Id.*

Although Amazon.com, Dell, and Cisco are regarded as some of the most successful e-commerce businesses, many other corporations have experienced phenomenal revenue growth through effective use of business-to-consumer e-commerce. The Disney Store, for example, currently sells as much merchandise online as it sells in eight of its traditional stores combined.[184]

Buy.com does not sell any merchandise and does not have a brick and mortar storefront anywhere. Instead, Buy.com collects qualified leads and resells goods, to be delivered by other vendors, thus relying heavily on distributors. At times, Buy.com may sell goods at a loss, but it hopes to capture enough visitors with its super-low prices that it can make up the difference with advertising revenue for ads sold on its web site.[185]

Business-to-business e-commerce integrates the use of private networks and the Internet to automate business transactions between companies. B2B can be subdivided into several categories: electronic data interchange (EDI);[186] "buy side" procurement;[187] and "sell-side" catalog-based sites.[188] Companies that opt to engage in business-to-business e-commerce agree to enter into a contractual relationship to do business either by extending a line of credit or by implementing a purchase order process.[189] In the spring of 2000, the Big Three automakers decided to band together and create a business-to-business relationship that would enable them to share and sell parts among themselves, rather than allowing a new entrant into the marketplace. The Automotive Network, eXchange, is the resulting extranet now connecting the Big Three automobile manufacturers.[190]

---

[184] *Supra* note 1, PricewaterhouseCoopers, at 192.

[185] Mall of America 2010, Wired, March 1999, at 120.

[186] EDI is the electronic transmission of documents from one company to another using a set of standard forms, messages, and data elements. The following is a partial list of EDI service providers: GEIS, IBM Global Services, Sterling Commerce, Harbinger, TranSettlements, AT&T, MCI, Railnc, EC Company, Sprint. *Supra* note 1, PricewaterhouseCoopers, at 193.

[187] Buy-side procurement involves linking all the individuals or organizations involved in the procurement process. Each entity plays a distinct role, for example, requesting or approving the expenditure, negotiating the purchase, processing the payment, or keeping financial records. Buy-side procurement companies include Ariba, Commerce One, Fisher, and Harbinger. *Supra* note 1, PricewaterhouseCoopers, at 197.

[188] Sell-side sites accomplish the steps needed to track and record the various elements of a transaction's life-cycle. These elements include product description and pricing, tracking inventory, processing and filling orders, and financial reporting. *Supra* note 1, PricewaterhouseCoopers, at 197.

[189] *Supra* note 1, PricewaterhouseCoopers, at 193. (The entire business transaction is linked to the purchase order, including origination and processing of the order, delivery, receipt, invoicing, payment, and related financial recording).

[190] Intranet Design Magazine, How Are Internet Standards Evolving to Facilitate Business Internetworking? (visited May 30, 2000), http://idm.internet.com/faqs/whatis/12.html.

Inherent in these business activities is the need to provide a secure and reliable mechanism so that buyers and sellers can confidently undertake these transactions and safely transfer funds. Requirements include a secure payment gateway for processing the transaction and transferring funds, a back office system for tracking core business components, and a storefront system.

The success of business-to-consumer e-commerce and of business-to-business e-commerce has had a profound effect on the American workforce. Recent reports indicate that 7,000,000 people in the United States work at home, and this figure may grow to 15,000,000 people over the next decade.[191]

§ 1.05   ACCESSING AND USING THE INTERNET

Individuals and corporations can access the Internet in a number of ways. To determine the best option for accessing the Internet in a particular situation, one must consider such things as the purpose for being on the Internet, the potential number of users, the types of sites to be visited and transactions to be made, and the required response time needed. Access to the Internet requires access to a computer with a web browser, a modem, or some similar connection and a subscription with an ISP.

[A]   Internet Service Providers (ISPs)

ISPs offer Internet access to businesses and consumers. Small office and residential consumers typically connect to the Internet via a 56 Kbps modem, which carries data over analog (telephone) lines or Integrated Services Digital Network (ISDN) lines. In the event that users or small businesses need higher speed access to the Internet, Asymmetric Digital Subscriber Lines (ADSL) or cable modems serve as faster options and can provide an uninterrupted Internet connection. Large enterprises link to ISPs through dedicated connections on larger pipelines.

Regardless of which access option an enterprise or consumer chooses, ISPs generally assess a monthly fee. This fee varies depending on the size of the connection needed, for example, whether the user is a corporation purchasing access for conducting its private enterprise or an individual using the service for personal home access. Fees for personal use (by individual(s) for nonwork-related purposes) usually fall between $9.99 and $19.99. Fees for analog service (accessing/connecting to the Internet with a standard telephone line connection) can be as much as $32 per month, with fees for cable lines and DSL approaching $50 monthly. For very limited use of DSL lines, however, fees may be as low as $5. In general, costs depend on the service, access, and technical support desired. Some plans do not allow unlimited Internet access, imposing a time limit on use per pay

---

[191] John L. Hawkins, E-Business Opportunities: Year 2000 and Euro, E-Business Advisor, June 1, 1998, at 1.

period. Notwithstanding the hardware costs, the perception that the Internet is essentially free is a misperception. The minimum cost is the monthly ISP access fee.

[B] Internet Connections

[1] Modem Access

The least expensive method of connecting a user to the Internet is via modem, a connection between a computer and an ISP via an analog telephone line. Over the past several years, modem speeds have improved, enabling users to transfer data at a faster rate. Today, most computers connect to the Internet with either a 28.8 Kbps or a 56 Kbps modem. Modems capable of 56 Kbps transmission range in cost from $99 to $250. Once a user has a computer and a modem, no additional hardware is necessary to connect to the Internet. In recent years, computers have been designed with built-in modems.

[2] Cable Modems and ADSL Lines

Cable modems offer a faster alternative for Internet access. Media giants, such as Media One, can use their cable systems to link clients to the Internet. These fiber optic cables carry data faster than can modems, without requiring users to invest in dedicated lines such as T1s or ISDNs. Although cable modems are faster than traditional modems, they do have speed limitations. Cable connections are limited by the available bandwith,[192] which must be shared by all of its users. The number of cable modems in use in the United States is expected to grow to seven million as prices fall to the $50 to $100 range.[193] The cost of cable is already down to about $50 for installation and $50 per month, and even cheaper in some areas, making cable an attractive option for the average Internet consumer.

ADSL is a dedicated line between the subscriber and the ISP. Purchasing certain guaranteed bandwidths of ADSL service may be possible in certain areas, but in practice, the telecommunications companies have had difficulties keeping up with the demand for this service. Verizon has been an important player, developing solutions for the problems the industry has encountered in trying to meet consumer demand.

[3] ISDN

Integrated Services Digital Network (ISDN) is a technology that delivers high-speed data and voice over a single telephone line. Although not as fast as T1

---

[192] Bandwidth is a term used to describe the fastest speed attainable by a particular data transmission protocol.

[193] *Supra* note 1, PricewaterhouseCoopers, at 75.

lines, ISDN lines are considerably faster than modem connections. An ISDN connection differs from a modem connection in that it can transfer data in its original digital format end-to-end, whereas a modem connection requires converting data from a digital to an analog signal for transmission over telephone lines. Because ISDN requires no such conversion, data can be transmitted and received four times faster than using a modem. ISDN connections are more popular in Europe and, consequently, more ISDN lines have been installed in Europe than in the United States. ISDN prices are predicted to drop to approximately $30 per month by 2001, however, leading International Data Corporation (IDC) to project a growth in ISDN line installations in the United States of 40 percent per year.[194]

[4] T1 and T3 Lines and Beyond

A T1 or T3 connection is a dedicated point-to-point connection that runs from an enterprise or user site directly to the ISP's communication center. The data transmitted on a T1 or T3 line travels on fiber optic wires, enabling data to travel 100 times faster than through a modem connection. Establishing a T1 or T3 connection requires installing a dedicated physical line, at a cost in excess of $1000. Recently, however, these costs have decreased greatly in some areas. In addition, the monthly access charge may run in excess of $1000 per month, depending on the location of the enterprise and the distance to the ISP's communication center.

[C] Web Browser

A web browser enables a user to browse HTML pages and Internet newsgroups and to communicate with standard e-mail services that conform to POP3 or IMAP standards. Today two companies dominate the web browser market: Microsoft and American Online (AOL). Microsoft's product is called Microsoft's Internet Explorer (IE); AOL's product is called Netscape Navigator. Both products have essentially equal market share and process web pages similarly, since web sites are published in a fairly standard format.

[D] Navigating the Web

Depending on the type of access, users have the ability to transmit or receive data in various mediums. The most common network on the Internet is the World Wide Web (WWW).[195] The two primary ways to navigate the WWW are first, to

---

[194] *Supra* note 1, at 75.

[195] The World Wide Web is a network of computers on the Internet that maintains documents that users can read and transfer with a variety of programs. These documents may include graphics, full-

type in the IP address[196] or URL[197] of the desired destination, and second, to use a search engine.[198]

Search engines are often characterized as spiders, worms, or crawlers, by analogy to the way some creatures move in the real world, and as indexes, sub-grouped according to how they index web pages. Not all search engines index words in the same way. Some index each visible word on every web page, while

---

motion video, and sound, as well as text. Users access the web through a computer program known as a browser, which creates the graphical interface necessary to view images as well as text.

[196] An IP address has four groups of three digit numbers. An address might be, for example, 10.2.24.167. Each group of three digit numbers may range from zero to 255. Rather than require web surfers to memorize series of numbers, access to a specific destination can be achieved by entering a domain name. *See* Chapter Two for a more detailed explanation of IP addresses.

[197] A URL is an address through which to gain access to World Wide Web pages. It generally consists of a protocol or program (such as http, gopher, or telnet), followed by a colon or a colon and two slashes, followed by the address of the site. Suffolk University Law School's home page, for example, is http://www.law.suffolk.edu/. A home page is the gateway to the site; it often serves as a main menu, listing documents or graphics (such as product data or legal treatises) that a company, association, or individual maintains in a computer as part of its World Wide Web site.

[198] Searches on the Internet can be conducted to sites in various ways. The following is a partial list of search engines and their web addresses:

AOL	http://netfind.aol.com
AltaVista	http://altavista.com
Ask Jeeves! Smart Answers Fast	http://askjeeves.com
CNN Webspace Search Engine	http://cnn.com/SEARCH/index.html
Direct Hit	http://www.directhit.com
Dog Pile	http://www.dogpile.com
Excite	http://www.excite.com
Fast	http://www.alltheweb.com
Google	http://www.google.com
HomeWiz	http://www.800go.com/homewiz/homewiz.html
HotBot	http://www.hotbot.com
Infoseek	http://www.infoseek.com
Jump City	http://www.jumpcity.com/NEWHOME.html
LawCrawler	http://www.lawcrawler.com
LookSmart	http://www.looksmart.com
Lycos	http://www.lycos.com
Magellan	http://www.mckinley.magellan.excite.com
MetaCrawler	http://www.metacrawler.com
News Index	http://www.newsindex.com
Northern Light	http://www.northernlight.com
OpenText	http://www.opentext.com
Snap	http://home.snap.com
Starting Point	http://stpt.com
Yahoo!	http://www.yahoo.com

Other search tools include Wide Areas Information Server, Gopher, Archie, Jughead, and Veronica.

others also index by *metatags*, words that are *not* visible.[199] Irrespective of the indexing technique, once a search request has been entered, the search engine will traverse the Internet in search of the information or sites requested.

Two of the more popular search engines are Yahoo! and Alta Vista. Yahoo! functions like an Internet Yellow Pages; it is organized using a tree-like structure that lets users search for web sites conceptually, as well as by text. Numerous web sites are listed under each category. Web sites related to the Supreme Court, for example, can be found under the category Government: U.S. Government: Judicial Branch: Supreme Court. Users can input several key terms and search categories, or, if they are uncertain about the correct category, all listed sites.

In contrast, Alta Vista searches millions of web pages by specified search terms. A simple search can be conducted by typing in key words, while a more advanced search can utilize Boolean search logic. Boolean search logic on the web resembles that used by the legal databases LEXIS® and Westlaw.

---

[199] A metatag is a special HTML tag that provides information about a web page. Unlike normal HTML tags, metatags do not affect how the page is displayed. Rather, they provide information about who created the page, how often it is updated, what it is about, and the keywords that best represent the page's content. Many search engines use this information when building their indices. *See* Chapter Two for a detailed discussion of metatags.

CHAPTER TWO

ESTABLISHING AND MAINTAINING AN IDENTITY ON THE INTERNET

§ 2.05   Advertising Your Products and Drawing Traffic to Your
         Web Site
  [A]   Introduction
         [1]   Banner Ads
         [2]   Interstitial Advertising
         [3]   Web Page Sponsorship
         [4]   Other Advertising Strategies
         [5]   Editorial and Search Engine Priority
  [B]   Internet Advertising Law
         [1]   Federal Trade Commission
                [a]   Claim Substantiation
                [b]   Deception and Unfairness
         [2]   Misrepresentation and False Advertising
         [3]   National Advertising Division of the Council of the
                Better Business Bureau
         [4]   Other Considerations
         [5]   Advertising to Children
  [C]   Linking
         [1]   Introduction
         [2]   Legal Implications of Linking
                [a]   Direct Linking
                [b]   Third-Party Links
         [3]   Linking Precautions—Look Before You Link
  [D]   Framing
         [1]   Advantages of Framing
         [2]   Legal Issues in Framing
         [3]   Resolving Framing Controversies
                [a]   Protecting Your Web Site
                [b]   Framing Other Web Sites
  [E]   Marketing Through E-Mail
         [1]   Advantages of E-Mail
         [2]   Opt-In versus Opt-Out E-Mailing
         [3]   Legal Challenges to E-Mail Marketing
         [4]   Solutions for E-Mail Marketing
  [F]   Metatags
         [1]   What to Include in Metatags
         [2]   Tips on Using Metatags Effectively
         [3]   Legal Issues and Limitations
  [G]   Attorney Advertising on the Internet
         [1]   Advantages of Legal Advertising on the Internet

[2]   **Ethical Issues in Attorney Advertising on the Internet**
  [a]   **Language Restrictions**
  [b]   **Multistate Compliance**
  [c]   **Disclaimers**
  [d]   **E-Mail Solicitation**
  [e]   **Chat Rooms**

§ 2.01   INTRODUCTION: DOING BUSINESS IN CYBERSPACE

It seems as if everyone is talking about e-business. On any given day, newspaper and magazine headlines tout the value of and opportunities possible with e-business. See Figure 2-1.

If you don't have your major Internet initiatives already running you're already behind

Peter Slovik, CIO, Cisco Systems

"If the projections are even half right, in 1998, this market will be measured in billions of dollars. We are enormously bullish."

Lawrence Calcano, Vice President, Goldman Sachs

"CEO's in Asia plan a major push toward electronic business as a competitive necessity, and with expectations that doing so will lead to major revenues within the next five years."

James Schiro, CEO, PwC

"In today's competitive world, time-to-market is everything."

Jim Kessler, Director, AMP eMerce Internet Solutions, AMP

"We plan on enhancing our work flow systems so that, ideally, a lot of what people do will be done right on the Intranet."

Barry Marshall, Manager, Interactive Communications, Domino's Pizza

"We believe the Internet is the future of Schwab"

Karen Askey, Vice President, Electronic Brokerage Marketing, Charles Schwab

"We'll do what it takes to keep our people connected to the information that helps them do their jobs

Steve Reimer, Manager, Emerging Technologies, K-B Toys

"The potential of electronic commerce rides on one fundamental thing, and that is not technology it's policy."

Dr. Nicholas Negroponte, Director, MIT Media Laboratory

"With the application on our intranet anyone in the country who talks to a customer can access instant information to manage the whole customer relationship."

John Ashton, Leader, Aerospace Equipment System excellence programs, Allied Signal

FIGURE 2-1

These headlines capture the attention of management in all organizations. Consequently, management teams become convinced that to increase revenues and enter new markets, their organizations must establish a presence on the Internet. On the World Wide Web, any company can market its products in a virtual shopping center 24 hours a day, 7 days a week, to a global market.[1] The opportunities seem endless, and failing to establish a presence on the Internet could be detrimental to your company's existence. But before engaging in e-commerce, an organization should address a number of issues: Proper strategic planning can help ensure a successful e-business site.[2]

This chapter explores the business issues and legal challenges of going online, including the importance of management support; the benefits of being online; the purpose of the web site; and the organization, development, and maintenance of the site. Later, we examine the complex legal and business issues

---

[1] Businesses learn quickly: "If superstores don't get you, cyberstores will." *See* Iven Patterson, A Bookseller Gives Up in Battle with Internet, N.Y. Times, June 27, 1999, at 24.

[2] *See* http://www.ibm.com/e-business/features/firststeps01.html (visited May 15, 2000).

involved in domain names, online advertising, linking, framing, and legal advertising.

[A]   Preparing to Go Online

Traditional bricks and mortar companies need a presence on the Internet to survive.[3] The question is no longer *if* a business should have a web site, but *how* and *what kind*. Businesses must ask how they can establish a web site while avoiding liabilities and protecting their legal rights. Becoming a successful online business is a challenging task requiring a careful balance between costs and benefits. The benefits may seem endless, but so too may be the issues to be resolved, such as content, scalability, advertising, security, bandwidth, and keeping everything manageable and up to date. To meet all of these challenges requires that senior management support the online initiative and that important executives play an integral part in formulating the corporate vision as it will be represented in the online business.

For most businesses, going online represents a significant paradigm shift; thus, unless corporate goals and expectations are manageable, the online venture is likely to fail. Accomplishing every objective or fulfilling everyone's needs is impossible. A well thought-out vision, coupled with a comprehensive strategic business and tactical plan, can help ensure success.

[B]   Management Support

Strong support from senior management is vital to the long-term viability of a commercial web site. Management must fulfill three core functions. First, the initiative must receive adequate funding, including both start-up costs and the ongoing costs associated with updating and maintaining the web site as the business continues to grow. Second, management must decide on the type of content it wishes to make available. As Herbert Simon noted: "A wealth of information creates a poverty of attention."[4] Information is a powerful tool, and the type and quality of information published on a commercial web site can make or break a business. Finally, management must constantly update its vision, strategies, and tasks. Having an online presence requires that organizations keep in touch with customers, potential customers, vendors, and market demands on a daily basis. Consequently, organizations must more than ever be responsive and flexible in meeting changing market demands. The following table identifies some of the organizational strategy issues that management must review.

---

[3] Number of Massachusetts Software and Interactive Firms Continues to Climb, Mass High Tech (Sept. 20-26, 1999), at 23 (reporting boom in "dot com" companies).

[4] Carl Shapiro and Hal R. Varian, Information Rules: A Strategic Guide to the Network Economy, 6 (1999) (quoting Nobel laureate Herbert Simon).

TABLE 3.1
Potential Management and
Organizational Issues to Address in Going Online

Challenges	Considerations
Who will manage the web site? • Is there a need for a central team? • Should the group include sales, marketing, corporate communications, legal, and information technology? • What is the scope of each unit's responsibility? • What is the purpose of the site?	Why a web site? What would be the goal of this web site? • Management needs to decide the potential value of the web site. • Most companies know they need to go online, but they must prioritize activities.
What are the costs of building the web site? • Software, people, hardware, graphics, security, databases, web server, vendors, ISPs, experienced graphics designers. • Deciding whether to hire a web site designer.	What are the benefits of being online? • May need to move in stages. • Cost-effective means of contacting markets. • Cost-effective customer service. • Inexpensive means of promoting the company's products. • Easy communication and coordination of orders with suppliers. • Web sites can attract and help retain customers. (Cisco Systems has proven that savings can be achieved through an Internet customer-service strategy). • Customers can order goods and services from their homes, offices, or in remote locations around the globe. • Greater than 50% of all Internet users are outside the United States, so the Internet offers a global market. • An online company can improve communications with and among its employees, subsidiaries, consultants, and trading partners. • Governments have not restricted e-commerce in most countries. • An Internet presence can improve core business process by streamlining marketing, procurement, and chain management.

continued

TABLE 3.1
Potential Management and
Organizational Issues to Address in Going Online (Continued)

Challenges	*Considerations*
	• New, easier to use web-programming languages, such as Extensible Markup Language (XML), and the decreasing costs and increasing availability of Internet devices.
What are the hardware and software requirements?	What hardware or software is essential and what amounts to overkill?
• Is an HTML editor needed?	• What are the choices?
• Are any other web design tools required?	• Must a company always use the latest technologies?
• Is a graphics editor needed?	• Are graphics needed? How much?
• Is a database tool needed?	• How much data will be stored and managed?
• Is an internal web server needed?	
• What would be required for effective IT systems management?	• What are the costs and what internal resources are available?
How should the web site be organized?	What is the business purpose of the web site?
• What are the logical categories?	• What goals does the web site serve?
• Who is the target audience being sought?	• Does its audience include both customers and vendors?
• What are the design considerations?	• How will viewers access the site?
• What are the content considerations?	• Will viewers get the answers they need within a few mouse clicks?
• How will the site keep pace with e-business developments?	• Are speed and ease of use a high priority?
• How can navigation and consistent "look and feel" issues be managed?	• Will the site be a virtual marketplace for products, raw materials, parts, and services?
• Will music, video, or virtual tours be included? Will it be easy for visitors to turn off music, video, or other multimedia?	• Will it aim to reduce customer service costs?
• Is the web site accessible to text-only browsers? Is the text readable? Are the colors of the photographs or videos accurate and clear?	• Will it offer improvements in handling marketing, procurement, and other business processes?
• Is Java included on the site?	
• Will the site have a contact person, feedback form, or real-time customer service contact person?	

50

TABLE 3.1
Potential Management and
Organizational Issues to Address in Going Online (Continued)

Challenges	*Considerations*
• Does the overall "look and feel" of the site attract visitors? Has the "look and feel" of the site been assessed by the web site development team?	
• Is the web site accessible using a large variety of browsers? Has the site been tested using a wide variety of browsers?	
What are the sales and marketing goals?	How do these goals differ from the traditional sales and marketing initiatives?
• Should the site offer product information?	• Would product brochures, rather than a web site, suffice?
• How will information be updated?	
• What information will be required from customers?	• Will the site provide lead tracking for new products?
• What information will the site contain about competitors?	• Will the site help or hurt sales?
• Should the site advertise future products?	• Can the web be another channel through which to launch product offerings?
What are the security and quality issues?	What are our goals for Network Security?
• Are the correct data and prices being published?	• Local area networks.
	• Storage area networks.
• Is the information up to date and accurate?	• Operating systems, personal computers in the networked environment, telecommuters.
• Can the site be compromised by competitors, hackers, or other intruders?	• Audit of online security risks for the business.
• What security tools are available? Consider firewalls, passwords, biometrics systems, encryption, virtual private networks, security audit products, and physical security calibrated to the risks specific to online companies.	• Attractiveness to hackers, corporate espionage, computer crimes, denial of service, viruses, protection against imposters, natural disasters, social engineering.
	• Emergency response to intrusions, viruses, and other data disasters.
	• Assessing potential liabilities due to Internet intrusion or viruses.
What are the potential uses, misuses and abuses of online advertising?	Is online advertising better than print or other traditional forms of advertising?
• What value do links offer?	• How deep should a link be?

continued

TABLE 3.1
Potential Management and
Organizational Issues to Address in Going Online (Continued)

Challenges	Considerations
• How can potential visitors be reached?	• Can too many links annoy viewers?
• Are metatags useful?	• Will the site be registered by search engines?
• Is advertising used as a source of revenue? Does revenue depend upon clickstreams or actual purchases?	• Can the inclusion of metatags create liability because they include trademarks of competitors?
• What are the legal limitations?	• Can this site give the appearance of false advertising or misrepresentation?
• Can advertising minimize the annoyance factor? Are visitors mousetrapped to secure advertising revenue?	
• What personal data is collected on visitors? Are cookies used to track visitors? Do advertising practices comply with privacy regulations and best industry practices?	
How will sales be processed online?	What are the qualities of the new sales model?
• Will all sales be conducted online?	• Sales may still be made by phone or visits by sales representatives.
• Who will manage credit card transactions? Will "backroom" functions, such as accounting, invoicing, reconciliation, and payment, be outsourced?	• Support for a new global market.
• Must customer service be available 24 hours a day, 7 days a week?	
What third party vendors are needed?	What resources are in-house?
• Webmaster.	• Maintain webmaster in-house or outsource?
• Web Hosting.	• Maintain web hosting in-house or outsource?
• ISP.	• Who has the best services/price?
• Web site design firm or consultants.	
What is involved with updating a web site?	How often should a site be updated?
• Who should remove outdated content?	• Can the same person both add and delete content?
• Who posts and manages changes?	• Who within the organization should have ultimate responsibility for site content, and what reviews are needed?
• How are the changes made?	
• Who monitors or responds to customer concerns?	• Is an FTP tool needed?

continued

TABLE 3.1
Potential Management and
Organizational Issues to Address in Going Online (Continued)

Challenges	*Considerations*
• Who periodically tests graphics, JPG images, GIF images, and other features? • Who periodically assesses web site design? • Who monitors legal developments, such as new advertising regulations, children's privacy regulations, or intellectual property developments?	• Does a committee need to review all activity on the web site?
How will a web site enhance customer service? • Can the site provide sales support? • Can it provide product information and support? • How can order tracking be managed? • Are site-related news releases valuable? • Do customers care about other current clients?	How is the organization currently servicing clients? • How are clients served? • Is traffic monitored? • Is content updated?
What legal issues should be considered? • Copyright notices on the web site. • Trademark notices for the site and any links provided. • Patent pending notices for e-commerce patents. • Notice of intellectual property and usage guidelines. • Policy on direct or indirect reproduction. • Disclaimer of warranties, express, implied, or statutory, including implied warranty of merchantability or fitness for a particular purpose and warranties as to accuracy, completeness, or adequacy of information. • Privacy policy posted. • Posting of designated agent for making complaints about copyright infringement to satisfy Digital Millennium Copyright Act.	Information is power in this economy, and the value in many e-businesses is its in-depth customer knowledge. What information will we get, and what legal rights must be protected? • What data will be collected on visitors to the site? Customer list? Spending patterns? (Information is today's goldmine: Amazon's huge value is largely pinned to its 16,000,000-strong customer list and its knowledge of its customer spending patterns.) • Is there an opt-out provision for visitors who do not wish to provide personal information? • Is the online company's privacy policy posted conspicuously? • Does the company comply with the Federal Trade Commission's rules on advertising to children under 13 years old? Does the company require verified parental consent before collecting personal data?

continued

TABLE 3.1
Potential Management and
Organizational Issues to Address in Going Online (Continued)

Challenges	*Considerations*
• Disclaimers of warranties and limitations of consequential damages. • Web site user contract in which user accepts terms and conditions by using the site; warranty; choice of law; choice of forum; choice of venue. Disclaimer of soliciting customers where sales or services are forbidden. • Compliance with European Union Directives and international intellectual property protection. • Tax issues.	• If the online company is a bank, insurance company, securities firm, or medical institution, is there effective and legally enforceable privacy protection? • Does the webwrap agreement or terms or condition agreement give visitors the opportunity to review the terms before manifesting assent?

When examining some of the management and organizational issues listed in the table, companies must also recognize that the Internet will bring many new challenges. These include new marketplace; new technologies; new distribution channels; new product offerings; enhanced business processes; new client and revenue expectations; new organizational priorities; new partners; and new insights. Without proper planning and a well thought out strategy, these challenges can cause chaos in companies, disrupting their current business operations.

[C] Benefits of Being Online

Addressing the organizational strategies may seem like a daunting task. As each issue is considered, however, numerous benefits of being an online company will immediately become apparent. If done right, web commerce can help companies increase revenue, reach new markets, and improve customer service. The benefits will vary by company, but \will ultimately enhance shareholder value. The table on pages 55-56 outlines some common value drivers.

To identify some key organizational issues, assume we've been hired by SPC, our business model, to handle all legal matters and provide business advice for its web site launch. As you recall (Overview, page xli), SPC's product line consists of personal computers built to customer specifications.

In an effort to assist SPC with its desire to develop an online presence, we have prepared a preliminary business plan.[5] At a minimum, the business plan requires that SPC address the following:

---

[5] For an example of a comprehensive model business plan, *see* Appendix A – SPC Business Plan.

54

TABLE 3.2
Value of Being Online

Business Value	Tangible Benefits
Increased competitiveness: Demonstrates that your company is up to date, aware of the potential of e-business, and able to harness technology to improve its business processes while reducing operational costs.	• Effective way to promote products and their value to client base. • Online catalog and pricing is always current. • Pricing can be changed at any time.
Expanded sales opportunities: Encourages potential customers to learn more about company products and services. Reaching new markets and clients enables businesses to achieve higher market share.	• Products and services can be sold 24 hours a day, 7 days a week. • Access to a global marketplace without the need for offices in numerous locations. • Shorter sales cycles and faster delivery of goods. • Ability to electronically profile customers' needs and purchasing habits.
Improved access to customer information and dissemination of company information: Gathering customer information leads to more pointed contact with customers. Newsletters and product explanations help educate consumers.	• Ability to publish whatever is deemed necessary. • Quality information can be made readily available. • Information can be distributed independent of user platform. • Information can be shared instantaneously. • Information can be shared with business partners. • Supplemental or updated product information can be made available.
Reduction in costs: Costs decline while mechanisms to distribute information and provide better customer service and sales support improve.*	• Online catalogs only need updating when changes occur relative to particular items. • Reduced cost of paper, publications, mailing, and distribution. • Consistent "look and feel" can be achieved for all communications. • Core information can be accessed faster.

continued

TABLE 3.2
Value of Being Online (Continued)

Business Value	*Tangible Benefits*
Enhanced customer service: Service, customer loyalty and trust, and improved name and brand recognition grow simultaneously.	• Better service for less money than can be provided by a customer service staff required to be available 24 hours a day. • Time is never a factor: Service is always available. • Answers to frequently asked questions can be posted. • Sites can provide access to internal resources or experts.

*Gail L. Grant, *Business Models for Internet and New Media*, 505 PLI/Pat 49 January 1998.

1. Decide on the business purpose for the web site and what peripheral information should be published on it. Who should be the contact person? Will real-time customer service be available 24 hours a day, 7 days a week?

2. Determine whether or not a third-party consultant should be hired to develop and maintain the commercial web site.

3. Choose and register a domain name encompassing the company's valuable trademark and not infringing on similar marks owned by others.

4. Determine what products to advertise and what sales or services to offer.

5. Plan for sales of products via a secure web server.[6]

6. Develop an Internet model that satisfies the firm's needs.

§ 2.02   PURPOSE OF THE WEB SITE

The Internet has rapidly expanded with the promise of changing business processes and increasing business opportunities. The question of what to include on a web site is a very difficult one to answer. Most users who surf the Internet casually spend, on average, anywhere from thirty seconds to two minutes at a given web site. This short time does not allow the web-site owner, or host, to distribute much information. Companies must meet the challenge of finding creative ways to translate surfing into online orders and to engender brand loyalty. The

---

[6] Please *see* Chapter Three for an in-depth discussion of product sales via a secure web server.

accomplishments will require making difficult decisions about what and how much information to include on the site.

[A] Introduction

Most companies concentrate on what they want to say or show but spend little time considering who might be viewing their pages and how these viewers will access the site. Every organization must first know who its target audience is and then design and advertise the web site accordingly. Some of the key questions that arise when organizing a site include the following:

Customer-Related Issues

- What customers are you trying to attract?

- Are your target customers currently using the web?

- How can the web be used to keep current customers?

- Does your web site provide the information your customers need?

- Who else might be in your target audience?

- How will your site maintain information on customers' profiles and preferences?

Connection-Related Issues

- How will users access or enter your site? Will the site have multiple access points?

- What kind of network connection will users have?

Product- or Service-Related Issues

- What information or products will users be looking for?

- How will you organize your site to build brand loyalty?

- Will your site allow for commercial sales? For advertising?

- Could your site be used to communicate with third parties, such as banks, business partners, or suppliers?

[B] Organizing Your Web Site

After answering these questions, companies must decide how to organize their sites. Generally speaking, a company should organize its site into logical sections. A commercial web site may be broken down into sections such as Welcome,

About the Company, Services and Products, Order/Response Form, and FAQs. Depending on the company, a variety of other categories may make sense, such as pricing, service guarantees, performance, professional staff profiles, markets, locations, competition, ancillary products or services, and so on.

Each section should note disclaimers and disclosures, the company contact person, acceptable use policies, and indemnity statements. Irrespective of how a web site is organized, the site must reflect the image the company wants to project, as illustrated in Figure 2-2. A well-constructed web site will provide visitors with various levels of information, ranging from brief overviews to thorough specifications or other details.

[C]   Web Site Content

The two most important pieces of information on a site are what products the sponsor sells and how its customers can reach it. The web site should interest viewers enough that they browse through the site, buy goods, and return as a repeat

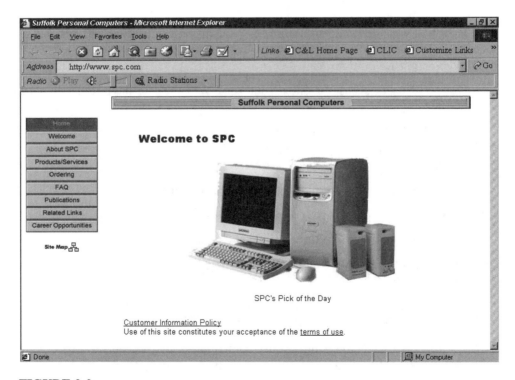

FIGURE 2-2

customer.[7] Web sites use images, illustrations, designs, icons, graphics, and streaming audio and video to convey a corporate image and to enhance good will. In addition to selling to customers, web sites offer an unprecedented opportunity for companies to seek feedback, criticism, suggestions, and ideas *from* customers. Virtual focus groups can provide invaluable feedback. Beyond that, the company might want to include on the site information promoting the company and its products and services, testimonials of successes, and competitive analyses. The options are endless if brand loyalty can be maintained. Consider the following approaches:

- Start each page with a short paragraph summarizing the content displayed on that page. On every page, the most useful information should appear at the top.

- Incorporate corporate logos, branding, or other intellectual property notices into the site.

- Provide detailed product, service, and pricing information.

- Include hypertext links to other pages within your site or to other ancillary sites.

- Provide current information, such as new product releases, press releases, or information about job openings.

- Include persuasive sales literature promoting products and specials, including online catalogs, ordering information, and order systems.

- Maintain and manage consumer registration and profile information.

- Provide a statement on the site relating to company policy, annual reports, and quarterly reports or include a corporate mission statement.

- Minimize the number of mouse clicks needed to get to useful information.

- Make navigation easy and information useful, so that viewers will have a reason to return.

- State when the web site was last updated and provide contact information.

- Insert metatags so that search engines will be drawn to your site.[8]

§ 2.03   DEVELOPING AND MAINTAINING A COMMERCIAL WEB SITE

The procedures for establishing a commercial presence on the Internet have evolved rapidly since 1991, when the ban on commercial use of the Internet was

---

[7] For an example, *see* the Gap's website at http://www.gap.com/onlinestore/gap (visited May 15, 2000).

[8] *See* § 2.05[F] for a more in-depth discussion of metatags.

lifted. But creating a web site that attracts and maintains potential customers is not easy. Companies should visit many other web sites to see how others are doing it. By analyzing various sites and business models, you can determine what works and what to avoid. Companies have spent as little as $500 and as much as $1,000,000 or more to establish and maintain their sites. Companies that have successfully branded themselves on the web have done so by creating web sites that provide potential visitors with a reason to come, to stay, and ultimately to buy a particular product or service.

[A] Internal versus External Development and Maintenance

After deciding to create a web site, the next critical decision a company must make is whether to outsource the web site development or to develop the site internally. Firms have several options. First, they may have the personnel and resources in-house to construct an effective web site. An Internet-based company may have better design capabilities than the average site developer. This viable option is considerably less expensive as long as the internal resources are capable of handling the fundamentals of going and staying online. Second, a company may decide to hire a third-party consultant to build and maintain the web site. The danger with this option is that a consultant may use a cookie cutter approach, resulting in a web site that looks and feels like all the others developed by that consultant. For some companies, however, this may be appealing, since outside vendors specializing in such services can build efficient, creative web sites and maintain them for reasonable fees. Third, a company may elect to use a combination of internal resources and outside consultants. Depending on deadlines, resources available, and costs, this option may be best.

Keep in mind that if your organization chooses an option involving outside vendors, management should negotiate contracts that allow for the appropriate transition and ownership rights. One of the key negotiating points is ownership of the copyright and virtual trade dress of the web site. If content is provided by consultants, indemnification agreements with bullet-proof hold harmless clauses are also vital. The contract with the web site developer must, at a minimum, cover payment, pricing, warranties, and remedies and dispute resolution, as well as "address company growth, changes in company direction, even downturns."[9]

[1] An Example of Building a Web Site Internally

For purposes of our hypothetical case, assume that since SPC is a computer company, senior management has decided to build the web site in-house.[10] The

---

[9] Daniel Tully, Hammering Out a Contract? Hit These Points for a Good Deal!, Mass High Tech (Sept. 20-26, 1999), at 27.

[10] A firm setting up a web site needs IT professionals who can plan, design, build, test, launch, and maintain the site. A firm should not attempt to create a web site internally unless it has the required knowledgeable, experienced personnel within the organization.

executives at SPC, having established the corporate vision for the web site, met with their programmers to talk specifically about building SPC's web site. Senior management requests that the programmers inform them of what tools they need to build a web site. Accordingly, the programmers present the following list.

1. *Either a MAC or a PC.* The faster the machine and the more memory it has, the better. A solid Apple/Macintosh should have at least a PowerPC G3, 350 MHz, 120 MB RAM, 12GB hard drive and a MAC OS 8.5.1. An IBM clone should have at least a Pentium III, 500 MHz, 128 MB RAM, 13.6GB hard drive, and a Windows 98 operating system.

2. *A web design tool.* A successful web site design appeals to sensory, conceptual, and reactive needs. In general, three types of web design tools are useful: a word processor; a web authoring tool; and a web site management tool. Word processors like Microsoft Word or WordPerfect may be used to create a simple web site using Hypertext Markup Language (HTML), a nonproprietary language that enables users to create web pages using simple commands. Web authoring tools differ from word processors, in that they allow design of web pages without an understanding of HTML code.[11] The site management tools used by sophisticated designers can create much faster web sites that are easier to maintain. Two of the more popular site management tools are Cold Fusion and NetObjects Fusion.

3. *A web browser.* Anyone developing a web site should design it to work with at least Microsoft Internet Explorer 4.0+ and Netscape Navigator 4.0+. Not all code renders the same output with a given browser.

4. *A graphics editor.* The developer must be able to manipulate the graphic images featured in most commercial web sites. Popular graphic editor programs include Adobe PhotoShop and Paint Shop Pro.

5. *A database tool.* A database tool is necessary to sell products or services or to manage customer data. A company may elect to build such a database in Oracle or Sybase or to tie into an existing database offered by a third-party vendor.

6. *A web server or host server.* In order to make the contents of the web site accessible to the world, a web server is required. The web server manages all of the HTML pages, databases, and credit card transactions needed to manage a commercial web site. If a company chooses to hire a web hosting company to host their site, they should consider the following: the hosting company's available technical support, services, and bandwidth; the speed of its connections and peering; the quality of its

---

[11] Some of the more popular web authoring tools include AOLPress; Microsoft's Front Page; Netscape's Navigator Gold; Adobe PageMill; and Sausage Software's Hot Dog.

site administration, security, and customer service; and the price it charges.[12]

In short, building a commercial web site internally involves a number of costs as well as benefits that should be carefully analyzed before beginning. A number of effective tools[13] may be used, but regardless of which software packages, graphics design tools, web server hardware and hosting, network connections, and ISP are utilized, each will have its associated expenses—and these can become very high. Failure to manage these expenses may affect the core business decisions that a company subsequently makes about its site.

[B]   Updating Your Web Site

Web sites, like the products they sell, have a short shelf life. Firms need to stay at the leading edge and to create dynamic content, products, and services that can be marketed creatively on the Internet. It makes absolutely no sense to build a commercial web site and then never update it. Is a customer likely to return to, let alone buy a product from, a company web site still advertising Spring 1999 prices?

Maintaining a web site can become a full-time job, considering the range of tasks involved. These include removing outdated content; continually posting changes and updates; responding to customer demands; developing new content on a weekly basis; and redesigning enhancements to the site for things like personalized web pages or messages. The corporate webmaster must be familiar with the latest web site tools, web technologies, and security vulnerabilities.

In continuing to develop its web site, the programmers at SPC came up with a few questions for the management team:

* What does management want to use as a domain name? Should the domain name incorporate an existing registered trademark? Other companies have already registered *www.SPC.com*, *www.suffolk.com*, and a few other obvious selections. Some child in Batesville, Indiana, has already registered *www.suffolkpcs.com*, but is willing to part with it for $50,000. Should SPC license or share the domain name?

* SPC is spending a lot of money to be on the Internet. How will it get people to visit the site?

---

[12] For a detailed discussion of host qualifications, *see* http://www.exeat.com/host.html (visited May 15, 2000).

[13] Tools include Adobe Acrobat, browsers, databases, diagnostic tools, editors, filters, firewalls, forms, gateways, graphics libraries, Java applets/scripts, Real Audio, search tools, security, Shockwave, tracking tools, viewers, and VRML, to name a few.

- Should SPC provide links to their software vendors, even though some of them have links directly to its competitors?

- Should SPC create new pages for the technical specifications of its products or can it just frame the web sites of its suppliers? What about other web sites that will frame SPC's site just to do price comparisons?

- Is SPC willing to pay money to protect its proprietary data, intellectual property, and consumer data? What are the risks if SPC fails to do this?

The remaining sections within this chapter address the various issues raised by the above questions and provide some guidance in resolving them.

§ 2.04 STAKING A CLAIM IN CYBERSPACE: HOW TO CHOOSE A CORPORATE IDENTITY FOR THE INTERNET

With the explosive growth of e-commerce and the projected number of new companies slated to establish a presence on the Internet, many existing and new companies are uncertain about how best to inaugurate their presence on the Internet.[14] Before jumping online and engaging in business transactions, the first thing a company needs is an address on the Internet, that is, an IP address or domain name. Unlike a traditional street address, the Internet address generally reflects the corporate name or identity.[15]

The best domain names are easy to remember and help brand a company's products or services. Where possible, in an effort to maintain their corporate identity, companies register a domain name in the form of "corporate-name.com." Companies must take great care to register the appropriate domain name. Failure to procure the proper identity may result in a loss of potential customers, business partners, or other opportunities, which can translate into lower earnings.

Domain names arise from the Internet Protocol that makes the Internet possible. Every computer connected to the Internet has a unique Internet Protocol (IP) number, which allows information to be sent to that computer.[16] Because the IP

---

[14] Network Solutions, Inc. registered more than 8,000,000 domain names between 1994 and 1999. Beth Fitzgerald, "Loans.com" Is the Latest Domain Name to Draw Big Bucks, Star Ledger, Jan. 28, 2000, available in LEXIS, News Library, Curnws file. Individuals and companies creating an online presence are registering domain names at a rate of 15,000 per day; by 2003, the total number of registered names is expected to reach 100,000,000. *Id.*

[15] *See* Gayle Weiswasser, Domain Names, The Internet, and Trademarks: Infringement in Cyberspace, 13 Santa Clara Computer & High Tech L.J. 137, 163 (1997) (noting domain name may include trademark).

[16] 63 Fed. Reg. 8826. *See also* Josh Goldfoot, Note, Antitrust Implications of Internet Administration, 84 Va. L. Rev. 909, 913 (1998).

number is a difficult to remember string of digits, the Domain Name Service provides a means for associating the number with a more easily remembered alphanumeric address. Corporations and individuals may register unique domain names for their web sites.[17] Domain names thus generally have two addresses. The first is a series of numbers, separated by a period or a dot, such as "123.456.543.21,"[18] and the second an alphanumeric address, such as *microsoft.com.*[19] Numerical addresses are assigned by the Internet Assigned Number Authority (IANA), which allocates blocks of numerical addresses to regional registries. Entering the alphanumeric address *microsoft.com* in a web browser triggers a data transmission that obtains the IP number (such as 206.111.111.11) associated with that domain name. This transmission ultimately engages Microsoft's host server, which renders Microsoft's home page for display on the inquiring user's computer screen. The alphanumeric names are assigned for ease of use, but they are not necessary to access a specific site.

Domain names are hierarchical and consist of two levels, the top level domain (TLD) and the second level domain (SLD).[20] In *microsoft.com*, for example, the top level domain, *.com*, indicates that the domain name owner is a commercial entity. The second level domain, *microsoft*, is the name of the commercial entity. Together, the TLD and SLD create the specified domain name *microsoft.com*.[21] The most common TLDs in the United States include *.com* (commercial organizations), *.net* (network service providers), *.gov* (government entities), *.mil* (military organizations), and *.edu* (schools, colleges, and universities).[22]

---

[17] *See* Dale Dallabrida, Companies Vying for Internet Domain Names, Gannett News Service, Sept. 15, 1997, at S12 (defining domain name).

[18] The first number signifies the computer's geographic region; the second number, a specific ISP; the third number, a specific group of computers; and the fourth number, a specific computer within that group. G. Peter Albert, Jr., Eminent Domain Names: The Struggle to Gain Control of the Internet Domain Name System, 16 J. Marshall J. Computers & Info. L. 781, 784 (1998).

[19] Hearst Corp. v. Goldberger, 96 Civ. 3620 (PKL) (AJP), 1997 U.S. Dist. LEXIS 2065, at *7 (S.D.N.Y. Feb. 26, 1997).

[20] Department of Commerce, Management of Internet Names and Addresses, 63 FR 111 (June 10, 1998).

[21] Guy T. Donatiello, Internet Domain Names: What's All the Confusion?, Legal Intelligencer Intell. Prop. Supp., Mar. 24, 1997, at 3.

[22] Additional TLDs have been proposed, including the following:

Proposed TLD	Intended Use
.firm	Businesses or firms
.store	Businesses offering goods for purchase
.web	Entities emphasizing activities relating to WWW
.arts	Entities emphasizing cultural and entertainment activities
.rec	Entities emphasizing recreation and entertainment activities
.info	Entities providing information services

Domain names administered in other countries may have different TLDs;[23] in fact, currently over two million TLDs exist worldwide. In foreign countries, TLDs are often two characters representing the country or origin of the domain name, such as *.uk* for the United Kingdom or *.fr* for France.

Companies try to register domain names that reflect their corporate trademark[24] since it symbolizes their corporate identity and good will. The purpose of trademarks is to prevent consumer confusion as to the source of goods and services, and trademark rights relate to the mark as used with particular goods or services. As a result, different companies can have different trademarks that share the same name. The search engine Alta Vista, for example, has a separate and distinct trademark from that of Alta Vista Sports.[25] In their respective markets, consumers are not confused between the two companies.

While multiple trademarks may exist contemporaneously in different countries and in different product classes in the United States, Internet domain names are unique worldwide.[26] Consequently, alphanumeric domain names that incorporate trademarks have descended into a litigation explosion pitting trademark owners against domain name registrants.[27]

---

[23] *See* Internet Domains List (visited May 15, 2000), http://www.tw2.com/webresources/domains.html (listing country domain codes). The address www.tw2.co.uk, for example, would represent a site address in the United Kingdom. *See id.* Alternative top level domain names, such as *.web* and *.per*, are administered by approximately two hundred other registrars. *See* Internet Stumbles Towards Domain Name Consensus, Network Briefing, Aug. 15, 1997, available in LEXIS, News Library, Curnws File. Some efforts to create new alternative domain names, which may have jeopardized trademark rights in the United States, may be short lived. *See* U.S. Seeks More Internet Names, Buffalo News, Jan. 31, 1998, at 9b.

[24] Trademarks are defined as words, symbols, or devices used to denote one's products or services as a way to distinguish them from all others.

[25] *See* http://www.cuattheraces.com (visited May 15, 2000).

[26] *See* Legal Update, Brand Strategy, Sept. 19, 1997, at 21 (identifying Internet domain name trademark conflicts). Multiple owners of identical trademarks are also a source of domain name conflicts in the United States. *See* Bob Woods, Spree.com Sues Sprint in Preemptive Move Over Domain Name, Newsbytes, Sept. 18, 1997, available in LEXIS, News Library, Curnws File (outlining conflict between Internet retailer Spree.com and Sprint's Spree telephone cards). Internet addresses are unique, allowing only one "spree.com" site address. *See id.*

[27] *See* Electronic Intellectual Property Protection: Hearings on H.R. 3163 Before the Subcomm. on Courts and Intellectual Property of the House Comm. on the Judiciary, 105th Cong. (1998) (testimony of Theodore H. Davis, Jr., Chairman, Federal Trademark Legislation Committee of the Section of Intellectual Property Law of the American Bar Association) (noting tension between business community's trademark interests and needs of overall Internet community); *see also* Sharon Schmickle, Slumberland's Legal Battle Over Internet Site Name Is Indicative of Larger Unrest, Minneapolis Star Trib., Apr. 19, 1998, at 1A (questioning whether commercial entities can register premium domains while individuals must settle for second rate names).

[A] Registering Names

Commercial use of the Internet has led to a domain name gold rush with a colorful cast of cybersquatters, pirates, and scoundrels. Traditionally, domain names have been assigned on a first-come, first-served basis, which allows a registrant to register any desired name as long as it is available at the time. Consequently, nothing guarantees that a trademark owner will be able to register the desired domain name.[28] When Hess Oil Corp., for example, wanted to register *hessoil.com*, they found the soil-testing company HES Soil had already registered the domain.[29] Similarly, *delta.com* is owned by a small technology firm, not by Delta Air Lines, which uses *delta-air.com*.[30] Because the Internet does not have a comprehensive directory and users may have difficulty finding a company's web site, companies usually want a memorable Internet address like *www.fedex.com* rather than the more unwieldy *www.suffolk.edu/law/hightech/classes/spring99*.[31]

---

[28] *See* Dallabrida, *supra* note 17 (listing multiple trademark owners who would want same Internet address). Network Solutions Inc., which distributes domain names, operates on a first-come, first-served basis. *See* David Noack, Newspapers Sue Over Net Domain Names, Editor and Publisher, Nov. 22, 1997, at 28. NSI does not determine which domain names infringe trademarks; it relies on the trademark owner to enforce his or her rights. *See id.* Trademark holders who find an infringing Internet site that was registered by NSI may request that NSI put the domain name on hold until the domain name owner and the trademark holder resolve the dispute. *See* InterNIC Moves to Establish Mechanism for Trademark Owners to Retrieve Cheeky Domain Names, Computergram, Aug. 25, 1995, available in LEXIS, News Library, Curnws File.

Other countries also favor the first registrant of a domain name in their domain name systems. *See* Rob Hosking, New Zealand: Internet Name Case Favours Earlybirds, Nat. Bus. Rev., June 6, 1997, available in LEXIS, News Library, Curnws File (noting New Zealand's first-come, first-served Internet domain name registration policy); British Court Says First Domain Name Registrant Gets to Keep It, Computer & Online Industry Litig. Rep., July 15, 1997, at 24431 available in LEXIS, News Library, Curnws File (detailing results of dispute between two trademark holders in United Kingdom); Heiner Buenting, The New German Multimedia Law—A Model for the United States?, Computer Lawyer, Sept. 1997, at 17 (illustrating trademark conflicts under Germany's first-come, first-served domain name registration system); Chu Moy, Trademark Strategies and Offensives in E-Commerce, E-Business Advisor, Nov. 1998, at 12 (noting Belgian court's adoption of first-come, first-served domain name policy for companies).

[29] *See* Ron Fluery, et al., Inadmissible, N.J.L.J., Nov. 24, 1997, at 3 (noting Hess Oil's domain name lawsuit).

[30] *See* Eryn Brown, The Net Name Game, Fortune, Feb. 16, 1998, at 124 (highlighting concern about Internet governance); *see also* Morning Business Report: ABC World News This Morning (ABC television broadcast, transcript # 98021604-j03, Feb. 16, 1998) (commenting on Nabisco's challenge to individual's registration of www.oreos.com).

[31] *See, e.g.,* Leora Herrmann & Andrew T. Tarshis, Domain Names and the Courts, Conn. L. Trib., Oct. 6, 1997, available in LEXIS, News Library, Arcnws file (explaining value of easy to find web address); *see also* Arun Natarajan, The Utility of a Bouncing Web Address, Bus. Line, Oct. 8, 1997, at 7, available in LEXIS, News Library, Arcnws File (recognizing brand benefits and ease of memorizing exclusive domain name).

Another advantage to registering a distinctive domain name is that consumers tend to guess when trying to find a particular company's web site.[32] Several cases have recognized that people surfing the Internet guess at a company's domain name by entering the company name between *www* and *.com*.[33] Having the right domain name is, therefore, essential to an effective marketing strategy that reaches the desired customer base; it is also likely to prove to be a valuable organizational asset.[34]

When guessing at a domain name, consumers do not know what company they have reached until the vendor's web site is opened, showing who actually owns the domain name.[35] A few years ago, for example, users who entered *AltaVista.com* were surprised to learn that they had not reached the Alta Vista search engine but had stumbled on another company that had registered Alta Vista as its domain name. The search engine company Alta Vista ultimately bought the domain name for over $3,000,000.[36] Shopping on the Internet can at times be analogous to walking into what one thought was a grocery store, only to find automobile parts on the shelves.[37]

[B] Selecting and Registering a Domain Name and Resolving Domain Name Disputes

Internet sites clearly represent valuable commercial commodities for companies because they offer 24-hour-a-day exposure to potential customers.[38] By

---

[32] *See* Trademark Confusion Is Tangling Up the Web, Companies Decry Net Address Chaos, Online Buyers Are Left Guessing, St. Louis Post-Dispatch, Feb. 18, 1998, at A5 (comparing process of looking for company on Internet to "shopper's roulette").

[33] *See generally,* Cardservicec Int'l, Inc. v. McGee, 950 F. Supp. 737, 741 (E.D. Va. 1997).

[34] Panavision Int'l v. Toeppen, 1998 U.S. App. LEXIS 7557, at *32 (9th Cir. April 17, 1998). The court held that "a domain name mirroring a corporate name may be a valuable corporate asset, as it facilitates communication with a customer base." *Id.*

[35] *See* Paul Carlyle, Why Squatters Aren't Budging from the Domain, Scotsman, Dec. 17, 1997, at 7 (explaining that companies may resort to litigation to resolve domain name confusion issues). Although consumers may not be confused between a sporting goods company and a software manufacturer, they may not know which company they are accessing until they are already in the Internet site. *See id.*

[36] Briefs: Microsoft Files Suit Over Cybersquatting/Online Organizing for Living and Work, Ventura County Star, Jan. 4, 1999, at E01.

[37] *See supra* note 32 (comparing Internet shopping to finding computer software for sale at fast food restaurant).

[38] *See* Haelan Products Inc. v. Beso Biological, No 97-0571, 1997 U.S. Dist. LEXIS 10565, at *10 (C.D. La. July 14, 1997) (comparing temporary nature of magazine and television advertisements to Internet); SF Hotel Co. v. Energy Inv. Inc., 985 F. Supp. 1032, 1034 (D. Kan. 1997) (recognizing Internet facilitates worldwide commerce from desktop computer).

using domain names identical to their corporate names, companies facilitate communication with potential customers.[39] In addition to reaching domestic customers, a domain name can be a corporation's "passport across the border into cyberspace."[40]

Popular domain names have increased in value, with some selling for many times the $100 registration price.[41] *Business.com*, for example, sold for $7.5 million in 1999,[42] which may have been a reasonable price, since many Internet users in the United States represent a desirable demographic profile. An easy to find and remember domain name can facilitate corporate access to those users.[43] Popular trademarks such as McDonald's or Marlboro are valued in the billions of dollars, so it should come as no surprise that related domain names are also becoming valuable assets.[44]

Corporations must also consider in which domain their name will reside.[45] The most popular Internet domains, such as *.com* or *.net*, are in high demand, while domestic alternatives, such as *.us*, are not commonly used.[46]

---

[39] *See* MTV Networks v. Adam Curry, 867 F. Supp. 202, 204 n.2 (S.D.N.Y. 1994) (identifying domain name as potentially valuable corporate asset); Gary W. Hamilton, Trademarks on the Internet: Confusion, Collusion or Dilution?, 4 Tex. Intell. Prop. L.J. 1, 5 (noting that many may argue that domain names function as trademarks).

[40] David Post, Breaking Up the Domain Name Monopoly, Recorder, Sept. 25, 1997, Business and Technology, at 4 (warning that without a domain name, one becomes invisible on Internet).

[41] Memorable domain names are now selling for millions of dollars. Dot-Com Squatters Lose Cyberwars, Toronto Star, Jan. 23, 2000, available in LEXIS, News Library, Curnws File. One observer noted that a name on the Internet may be worth the $100 it cost to register it as a domain name, but in court it is worth "damages in an amount to be determined at trial." Gina Fann, Country Stars' 'Net Suit Eyed; First Amendment Rights an Issue, Tennessean, Apr. 11, 1998, at 1E.

[42] *See* Prices Skyrocket for Choice Internet Sites, Deseret News, Jan. 23, 2000, at M5 (noting competition for popular domain names). The domain name *business.com* originally set a price record in 1997 when it sold for $150,000. USA: Record Price Paid for Internet Name, Computergram, June 6, 1997, available in LEXIS, News Library, Arcnws File.

[43] *See* Luxury Items Attract Upscale Web Shoppers; Consumers Graduate from Buying Books and Baubles Online, San Jose Mercury News, Dec. 20, 1999, at 2 (noting Internet users tend to be better educated and wealthier than the average population). As more individuals obtain access to the Internet, however, the demographics migrate more towards the general population. Shannon Oberndorf, Know Thy Buyer, Customer Profiles Differ by Medium, Catalog Age, Oct. 1999, available in LEXIS, News Library, Curnws File.

[44] *See* GreatDomains.com, which offers to assist clients in buying and selling domain names: http://www.greatdomains.com (visited May 15, 2000).

[45] *See* Andrew Craig, U.S. Domain Extension May Ease Shortage, TechWeb News, Feb. 21, 1998, available in LEXIS, News Library, Curnws File (explaining popularity of some top level domains and lack of interest in others).

[46] *See id.* (noting business risk of using *.us* instead of *.com*).

[1] Trademarks

Businesses must protect their valuable trademarks in cyberspace.[47] Trademark owners in the United States can protect their marks by registering with the Patent and Trademark Office.[48] Not every trademark, however, can be registered.[49] Examples of some restrictions include the refusal of the Patent and Trademark Office to register a descriptive trademark, a trademark similar to another registered mark,[50] or an immoral or scandalous mark.[51] Domain names already in use, such as *yahoo.com*, can be registered as trademarks,[52] but domain names that do not have a corresponding Internet site may not be registered as trademarks.[53]

A visible brand name, by fostering consumer recognition and differentiating its products from others in the marketplace, can be a competitive advantage for a company.[54] By registering a trademark, the trademark holder helps to protect its valuable brand name.[55] Popular trademarks may be worth billions of dollars in sales because of the value of brand recognition.[56]

---

[47] A trademark is a distinctive "word, name, symbol, device," or combination that identifies goods or services and distinguishes them from other goods and services. Restatement (Third) of Unfair Competition § 9 (1995).

[48] *See* Lanham Act § 1, 15 U.S.C. § 1051 (1996) (delineating trademark registration procedures in the United States).

[49] *See* Lanham Act § 2, 15 U.S.C. § 1052 (1996) (listing grounds for refusing trademark registration).

[50] *But see* Park 'N Fly, Inc. v. Dollar Park & Fly, Inc., 469 U.S. 189, 191 (1985) (defining incontestable, descriptive trademark that has acquired secondary meaning). A registered trademark can become incontestable after five continuous years of use.

[51] *Id.*

[52] *See* Sabra Chartrand, Patents; The Process of Filing an Application Is Slowly Catching Up with the Technology Available, N.Y. Times, Jan. 26, 1998, at D2 (explaining applicants registering domain names as trademarks must show that Internet site exists for name). One observer noted a large increase in the number of applications to register domain names as trademarks. *See* Molly Buck Richard, It's Easier to Protect Some Intellectual Property, Texas Lawyer, Nov. 30, 1998, at 34 (noting Patent and Trademark Office's recognition that domain names may function to identify source of goods or services).

[53] *Id.* (outlining restrictions on registering domain names as trademarks). To qualify for registration, the domain name must identify and distinguish the goods or services and indicate their origin. *See id.* Domain names that are only "directional references," such as addresses or telephone numbers, may not be registered as trademarks. *See id.*

[54] *See* James Saunders, How Best to Keep Rivals' Hands Off Your Brands, Scotsman, Oct. 22, 1997, at 7 (citing additional benefits of having Internet presence). Trademark protection on the Internet protects both trademark holders and Internet users by ensuring credibility. *See* IPR Protection on Net to be Discussed, Businessworld, Apr. 2, 1998, available in LEXIS, News Library, Curnws File (quoting World Intellectual Property Organization).

[55] *See* Saunders, *supra* note 54 (advocating brand owners to protect their trademarks).

[56] *See* Category Charts, Superbrands, Ad Week Supplement, Oct. 20, 1997, at 110 (listing sales revenue and total advertising by brand).

In our earlier example, SPC could register a domain name that reflects its trademark, provided that the domain name were available. *SPC.com*, a natural choice, has already been taken, so SPC would need to consider other possible names. SPC might use a name with broad reach, such as *www.personalcomputers.com*, as its domain name, but this would not be a protectable trademark, and SPC would not be able to register it as such.

[2] Registration Process: Domestic and Foreign Registrations

Once a company has chosen a domain name, or collection of domain names, it must register it. In the early 1990s, Network Solutions, Inc. (NSI) had an exclusive government contract to build a database and registry system for the *.com*, *.org.*, *.net*, *.gov*, and *.edu* domain names.[57] NSI was awarded this authority under a contract from the National Science Foundation (NSF).[58] NSI established InterNIC to carry out this process. Under the NSI system, in order to register a domain name, applicants had only to pay a $70 registration fee for the domain name they sought to be assigned to them for the two-year period then allowed.[59]

This process and the associated fees have changed, now that the U.S. government has deregulated the sales of domain names. Registrants can now choose among a number of domain name registrars, many of which offer different options for pricing and web site hosting.

To start the registration process, an applicant must select a registrar.[60] Once a registrar has been selected, registration requires three further steps. The first step requires a search to determine whether the desired domain name is available. To assist with this issue, InterNIC and other registrars maintain a "Whois" database recording all registered domain names.[61] The search will reveal whether a domain

---

[57] *See* Kelly Flaherty, NSI Focus of Internet Talks in Congress, Recorder, Oct. 2, 1997, at 1 (detailing NSI's Internet address domain).

[58] *Id.*

[59] Applicants can visit InterNIC's web site at http://rs.internic.net (visited May 15, 2000). *See also,* Domains 'R' Us, Communications Today, Apr. 22, 1999.

[60] For a list of accredited registrars, visit http://www.internet.net/origin.html (visited Sept. 16, 1999). Registrars pay a $10,000 licensing fee for use of the NSI software as well as an $18 fee to license a domain name on behalf of each customer for two years. As of October, 1999, 76 domain name registrars were accredited, although not all of them were active. David Lake, Web Spotlight: The Rush for Domain Gold, The Standard (visited May 15, 2000), http://www.thestandard.com/metrics/display/0,2149,1023,00.html. *See* Laura Lorek, Don't Overpay for Domain Name, Sun-Sentinel (Fort Lauderdale), July 28, 1996, at 1E (explaining information about foreign domain name registries also available at the InterNIC web site).

[61] *See* John Hill, Stake Your Claim with a Domain Name, Columbian (Vancouver, Washington), Feb. 11, 1998, at C1 (explaining "who is" Internet query to see if someone has registered domain name). The Whois database can be found at http://rs.internic.net/cgi-bin/whois (visited Sept. 16, 1999).

name is available and how to obtain information on holders of already registered names. For the second step, the applicant fills out a registration application, usually completed online at a registrar's web site. Finally, the registrant submits the completed application to the registrar. Applicants may receive written or e-mail confirmation, depending on the particular requirements of the individual registrar.

Once approved, the applicant must pay the registration fee or the domain name may be revoked. Additionally, accredited registrars will transfer domain names to other owners if requested to do so by the registered owner, upon an order from a court or tribunal, or based on a decision from an administrative panel.[62] While domain names were once available for only two years, some registrars now allow longer terms.[63]

[3] Registering Multiple Names

In today's competitive marketplace, given the importance of domain names, companies should consider registering multiple domain names. Our hypothetical company, SPC, for example, might want to consider registering *www.spc.com*, *www.suffolkpc.com*, and *www.suffolkpersonalcomputers.com*. Absent a challenge, any or all of these domain names can be readily assigned, ensuring that several different domain names lead consumers to SPC.[64]

Several other important reasons exist for companies to register multiple domain names. First, they may need to reserve the names for future products or services. Nothing requires that the registered domain name be used immediately or within a specified time period. The lack of such a restriction allows companies as yet unprepared to create an Internet presence to reserve domain names for future use,[65] and many companies reserve or register names for products under development.[66]

Another popular reason to register multiple domain names is to capture users who inadvertently misspell or use variants of a domain name. Domain names registered by other firms that exploit typing or other errors could arguably dilute a

---

[62] The current domain name dispute resolution policy is available at http://www.domainmagistrate.com/disputepolicy (visited Sept. 16, 1999).

[63] Patricia Jacobus, Register.com to Offer 10-Year Net Name Registrations, CNET News.com, Jan. 5, 2000 (visited Jan. 20, 2000), http://www.register.com/domain-news/jan052000.cgi?1 [843279433].

[64] Many companies try to register as many domain names as possible, including domain names that would result from commonly made typographical errors or other mistakes. Lotus, for example, has registered Lotus.com as well as Lotus.net.

[65] See $50 for Domain Name Register & Free Domain Name Research Tool, Business Wire, Sept. 30, 1997, available in LEXIS, News Library, Arcnws File (advertising service reserving domain names pending customer activation on Internet).

[66] See Dallabrida, *supra* note 17 (noting Dupont registers products in development).

company's online value.[67] Fidelity Investment, for example, owns *www.fidelitu.com* and other variations.[68] Large companies with valuable names should register potential name variations and misspellings to assist consumers in finding the site and to prevent others from exploiting these errors.[69]

Finally, a company may want to avoid negative publicity deriving from parody sites or sites that may cause confusion.[70] Not all use of trademarks in domain names is infringing: News commentary and other noncommercial uses of a trademark, for example, are not actionable under the Lanham Act.[71] Individuals have registered Microsoft parody sites, including *www.microsnot.com* and *www.microsos.com*.[72] Bell Atlantic registered *bellatlanticsucks.com* and *bigyel-*

---

[67] *See* Lawrence Magid, Sex Sites Capitalizing on Misleading URLs, L.A. Times, Mar. 2, 1998, at D3 (listing now defunct *www.disnie.com* and *www.nasa.com*, adult web sites). A current list of such so-called stealth sites is available at http://www.webchaperone.com/stealthlist.html (visited Sept. 16, 1999). *See id.* New sites, however, quickly replace those that have been shut down. *See* Jon Swartz, Government Parasites; "Stealth" Web Pages Feed Off Addresses, San Francisco Chron., June 3, 1998, at D1 (noting proliferation of such sites has prompted legislation). While NASA was successful in eliminating "nasa.com," for example, other registrants created *nassa.com*, filling the site with pornographic photos. *See id.*

[68] *See* Todd Wallack, If It's Rude, They Want It—Companies Eat Up Internet Names, Boston Herald, Dec. 30, 1997, at 1 (noting another company registered misspellings of "Fidelity" to try to increase traffic to its web site).

[69] *See id.* (suggesting Fortune 500 companies should register almost anything relating to their trademarks). Domain name registrants trying to exploit misspellings of trademarks may face legal action. Copy-Cat Domain Names Can Spell Trouble, Deutsche Presse-Agentur, Jan 23, 2000, Available in LEXIS, News Library, Curnws File.

[70] *See id.* (illustrating corporate preemptive strike to avoid angry customer's registration of pejorative domain name). In addition to exposure to confusion or criticism, some trademark holders have discovered that hate groups registered their trademarks as domain names and sent visitors to a white supremacist web site. *See* Mary McLachlin, Internet Surfers Hijacked to West Palm Hate Site, Palm Beach Post, Dec. 21, 1998, at 1A (noting hate group registered name variations of fourteen newspapers). Following legal action, the newspapers were able to have the infringing sites transferred or shut down. *See id.*

[71] *See* Lanham Act § 43(c)(4), 15 U.S.C. § 1125(c)(4) (1996). Compare Cliff Notes, Inc. v. Bantam Doubleday Dell Pub. Group, Inc., 886 F.2d 490, 497 (2d Cir. 1989) (finding no infringement in Spy magazine's Cliff Note parody "Spy Notes," which was marked "satire"), and L.L. Bean, Inc. V. Drake Publishers, Inc., 811 F.2d 26, 34 (1st Cir. 1987) (allowing High Society parody of L.L. Bean Catalog, "L.L. Beam's Back to School Sex Catalog"), with Anheuser-Busch, Inc. v. Balducci Publications, 28 F.3d 769, 796-97 (8th Cir. 1994) (concluding Snicker magazine's "Michelob Oily" parody advertisement infringed "Michelob Dry" because trademarks not sufficiently altered), and Mutual of Omaha Ins. Co. v. Novak, 836 F.2d 397, 403 (8th Cir. 1987) (finding likelihood of confusion with antinuclear protester's "Mutant of Omaha" T-shirts and Mutual of Omaha Insurance).

[72] *See* Rebecca Quick, In High Jeer; Home-Page Parodies Proliferate on Free-Wheeling Web, Pittsburgh Post-Gazette, Mar. 23, 1998, at D3 (comparing parody sites and corporate responses); *see also* Hormel Foods Corp. v. Jim Henson Prods., 73 F.3d 497, 507 (2d Cir. 1996) (finding puppet "Spa'am" did not infringe "Spam" because likable character did not cause negative associations).

lowsucks.com, after discovering that an individual had registered *nynexsucks.com*.[73] Unfortunately, when Bell Atlantic let the domain name expire, critics quickly posted a new web site at *bellatlanticsucks.com*.[74] In one similar case,[75] a federal district court held that the defendant's use of "Bally Sucks" neither constituted federal trademark infringement nor diluted the plaintiff's mark, because the defendant's criticism was not a common use of Bally's mark.[76]

In short, every company could potentially face one or all of the aforementioned issues, which would require multiple registrations. Absent economic constraints, registering multiple domain names is a sound business decision.

[4] Resolving Domain Name Disputes

Before companies were fully aware of the value of domain names, entrepreneurs registered many names, including some using valuable trademarks, and then offered to sell them to the trademark holders for a lucrative premium.[77] These registrants are referred to as cybersquatters.

But see Deere & Co. v. MTD Prods., Inc., 41 F.3d 39, 45 (2d Cir. 1994) (finding fearful deer parodying Deere logo in competitive advertisement diluted trademark).

[73] *See* Wallack, *supra* note 68 (discussing Bell Atlantic's alarm at vulgar Internet sites using company name).

[74] *See id.* (claiming company focuses on customer service rather than preventing customers from creating forums for complaints). Unfortunately, derogatory terms are too numerous for companies to hope to register every one. *See id.*

[75] Bally Total Fitness. v. Faber, 23 F. Supp. 2d 1161 (C.D. Cal. 1998).

[76] Microsoft's Law & Corporate Affairs, Summary of Global Internet Legal Developments 63 (April 1999) (reporting decision).

[77] *See* Panavision Int'l. v. Toeppen, 938 F. Supp. 616, 618 (C.D. Cal. 1996) (returning *panavision.com* to Panavision International), aff'd, 141 F.3d 1316 (9th Cir. 1998). Toeppen demanded $13,000 to discontinue using *panavision.com* after Panavision asked to use the domain name. *See id.* at 619. Rather than returning the name, Toeppen registered another Panavision trademark, *panaflex.com*. *See id.* Toeppen had registered other trademarks as domain names, including *lufthansa.com*, *neiman-marcus.com*, and *intermatic.com*. *See id.*; *see also* Intermatic Corp. v. Toeppen, 947 F. Supp. 1227, 1229 (returning *intermatic.com* to Intermatic Corp.); American Standard, Inc. v. Toeppen, No. 96-2147, 1996 U.S. Dist. LEXIS 14451, *2-3 (C.D. Ill. Sept. 3, 1996) (granting American Standard's request for preliminary injunction against use of *americanstandard.com* domain name); Tom Campbell, Reynolds Domain Is Foiled for Now; Trademark Lawsuit Focuses on Web Site, Richmond Times Dispatch, Dec. 30, 1997, at A1 (examining Reynolds Metals discovery that another company had registered *reynoldswrap.com*). The World On Net, Inc. had registered *reynoldswrap.com* in addition to *davematthewsband.com*, *tysonscornercenter.com*, and *dustinhoffman.com*. *See id.* World On Net, Inc. claimed they had registered the names for noncommercial commentary and parody. *See id.* Noncommercial use, news reporting, and news commentary are not actionable under federal false description of origin or dilution claims. *See* Lanham Act § 43 (c)(4), 15 U.S.C. § 1125(c)(4) (1996) (listing federal trademark infringement exceptions).

[a] Legal Remedies

Courts in the United States and other countries have provided relief from individuals who registered infringing domain names for the sole purpose of reselling the domain name to others.[78]

In one landmark case, two British domain name dealers were ordered by the United Kingdom High Court to pay £65,000 (U.S. $110,000) in legal costs and to transfer the infringing domain names to the trademark owners.[79] Cybersquatters in the United States may be liable for $1,000 to $100,000 per infringing domain name.[80] A trademark holder may, therefore, reasonably pursue litigation to obtain the infringing domain name and even, potentially, to recover attorneys' fees and damages.[81]

In the United States, trademark owners may employ a variety of causes of action to pursue cybersquatters. Keep in mind that trademark law is designed to protect consumers and not to provide businesses with a monopoly on the English language. Gateway 2000, for example, was unable to convince a judge that *gateway.com* infringed on their famous trademark, since there was no evidence that Gateway 2000 had used the term "gateway" independently.[82] Domain name registrants have broad rights in fair use of trademarks, including descriptive terms, crit-

---

[78] *See* American Standard, 1996 U.S. Dist. LEXIS 14451 at *1-3 (citing trademark owner's redress against infringing domain name registrant in United States); Judge Bans Internet Name Dealers, Irish Times, Dec. 1, 1997, at 18 (noting U.K. court's ruling against registrants of trademarks as domain names); Germany: Internet Domain Name Dealers Challenged, Handelsblatt, June 10, 1997, available in LEXIS, News Library, Curnws File (discussing German court's support of victims of domain grabbing).

[79] *See* Terence Shaw, Internet Dealers' Name Game Ended, Daily Telegraph, Nov. 29, 1997 at 9 (citing numerous domain names registered by dealers). The domain name dealers had registered many trademarked names through their company, One in a Million, including *buckinghampalace.org*, *marksandspenser.com*, and *burgerking.co.uk. See id.* One in a Million had approached Burger King and offered to sell it the name *burgerking.co.uk* for £25,000 (U.S. $40,000). *See id.* The judge found that "[t]he threat of passing off and trademark infringement, and the likelihood of confusion arising from infringement of the mark, are made out beyond argument." Internet Pair Lose Trade Names Case in Highcourt.co.uk., Herald (Glasgow), Nov. 29, 1997, at 3 (quoting Deputy Judge Jonathan Sumption QC).

[80] *See* United Greeks, Inc. v. Klien, No. 00-CV-0002, 2000 U.S. Dist. LEXIS 5670 (N.D. N.Y., May 2, 2000) (awarding $10,000 damages to trademark owner).

[81] *See* New York State Society of Certified Public Accountants v. Eric Louis Associates, 99 Civ. 3030 (LBS) 1999 U.S. Dist. LEXIS 18543 at *79 (S.D. N.Y., Dec. 2, 1999) (assessing $46,818 in attorneys' fees against domain name registrant exploiting trademark); Britain Puts End to Net Scam Involving Sale of Site Names, Straits Times (Singapore), Dec. 2, 1997, available in LEXIS, News Library, Curnws File (discussing U.K. court's award of legal fees and return of domain names containing trademarks).

[82] Gateway 2000, Inc. v. Gateway.com, Inc., No 5:96-CV-1021-BR (3), 1997 U.S. Dist. LEXIS 2144, at *10 (E.D. N.C., Feb. 6, 1997).

icism, and commentary.[83] Trademark holders should seek competent counsel before contemplating a suit against a domain name holder who may have a legitimate claim to the name. Conversely, domain name owners who registered names in good faith should not cede their names to a business threatening to sue without the advice of legal counsel.[84]

[b]   Legal and Statutory Causes of Action

Trademark holders whose names have been exploited online have a veritable toolbox of legal actions, ranging from a federal trademark dilution suit to the ICANN (Internet Corporation for Assigned Names and Numbers) domain name dispute resolution policy. Some of these causes of action may not apply to domain names registered in other countries not adhering to the ICANN domain name dispute resolution policy. A list of the various remedies and their applications appears on page 76.

Prior to the Anticybersquatting Consumer Protection Act (S. 1948)[85] and the modification of the dispute resolution policy, trademark holders often had little recourse against foreign or unknown registrants of infringing domain names or cybersquatters who did not use the names in commerce. Porsche Cars of North America, for example, was unable to sue registrants of several infringing domain names, since the company could not identify the defendants.[86] The Federal Trademark Dilution Act did not allow individuals to sue domain names directly in *in rem* proceedings. Now trademark holders can obtain recourse through the ICANN Dispute Resolution Policy or the Anticybersquatting Consumer Protection Act.[87] Liability begins at the point of registration, and statutory damages can range from $1,000 to $100,000.[88]

Another possible avenue for relief is through ICANN's Domain Name Dispute policy.[89] Certified domain name registrars require registrants to agree to the ICANN policy. Prior to the new policy, a trademark holder could get an infringing domain name suspended until the resolution of the dispute. While this was effective at getting the attention of the registrant, domain name suspension became a disruptive tool used against legitimate online businesses.[90]

---

[83] David King, Dot.squatters Law Doesn't Hamper All, San Antonio Express-News, Jan. 16, 2000, at 1C.

[84] Henry C. Dinger, When You Hang Your Web Shingle, Don't Be Bullied, Mass High Tech, Oct. 25, 1999, at 24.

[85] S.1948 Intellectual Property and Communications Omnibus Reform Act of 1999.

[86] Porsche Cars North America, Inc. v. Porsh.com, 51 F. Supp. 2d 707 (E.D. Va., 1999).

[87] Henry C. Dinger, New Anti-Cybersquatting Act Still a Bit Fuzzy, Mass High Tech, Jan 3, 2000, at 15.

[88] Sporty's Farm LLC v. Sportsman's Market, Inc., 202 F. 3d 489 (U.S. Ct. App. 2d Cir. Feb. 2, 2000).

[89] Available at http://www.icann.org (visited May 15, 2000).

[90] Juno Online Services v. Juno Lighting, Inc., 979 F. Supp. 684 (N.D. Ill. 1997).

TABLE 3.3
Trademark Holders' Causes of Action/Remedies in Domain Disputes

Cause of Action	Statute	Effective Against	Limitations	Notes
Federal Trademark Dilution Act	15 U.S.C. § 1125 (c)(1)	Dilution of famous trademarks	Only applies to famous mark; infringement must be in commerce	State cause of action may be similar
Federal Trademark Infringement Act	15 U.S.C. § 1114 (1)	Infringement of trademarks	Infringing mark must be likely to cause confusion, in the same product class, and in commerce	State cause of action may be similar
Federal Unfair Competition Act	15 U.S.C. § 1125 (a)	Domain names that cause mistakes in terms of affiliation, connection, or association with another mark—i.e., bait and switch domain names	Domain name must be in commerce	Also effective against web sites that allege endorsement
Anti-Cybersquatting Consumer Protection Act	15 U.S.C. § 1125 (d)(1)	Domain names registered in bad faith that are identical or confusingly similar to a trademark	Damages available only for marks registered after 11/29/99	Provides a broad cause of action and substantial damages
ICANN Dispute Resolution Policy	www.domain-magistrate.com/ disputepolicy	Domain names registered in bad faith that are identical or confusingly similar to a trademark	Must be registered through top level domain that subscribes to the policy	Arbitration mechanism provides an alternative to litigation

The new policy does not allow suspension, but it does permit trademark holders to submit a dispute to an administrative proceeding to determine if the domain name is infringing and registered in bad faith.[91] The World Wrestling Federation, for example, was able to recover *www.worldwrestlingfederation.com* from a cybersquatter by employing the new dispute policy.[92]

[c] Purchasing a Domain Name

Another option for obtaining a desired domain name is to purchase it from the original registrant. Although potentially expensive, purchasing the domain name could prove to be a more cost-effective alternative than filing suit against the cybersquatter.[93] It should be noted, however, that a company will have little legal recourse against a domain name registrant who actually owns the same trademarked name in a different product class.[94]

Despite all of the discussion of cybersquatters, many of them have not profited from their vacant web sites and may be willing to part with them for a reasonable price.[95] Reasonable domain name prices range between $500 and $2,000, which could be less than the potential legal expense and effort of filing a lawsuit.[96] The web site *www.farside.com*, for example, was sold for $225 by a domain name broker.[97] While some companies have paid more than $10,000 to purchase infringing domain names from cybersquatters, companies now are less likely to pay huge sums than to assert their trademark rights in a legal forum.[98]

[d] Registering a Name in Another Domain

After exploring every option, it is possible that a corporation may not be able to register or purchase the domain name it desires. Although this may be disappointing, it does not mean all is lost. Companies encountering this problem still

---

[91] *See* http://www.domainmagistrate.com/dispute-policy.html (visited May 15, 2000).

[92] Ed Hore, Lawyers Weekly (Canada) Jan. 21, 2000, available in LEXIS, News Library, Curnws File.

[93] *See* Stephen McGookin, Name Best Kept To Yourself, Financial Times, June 3, 1998, at 12 (recommending companies purchase domain names instead of resorting to time consuming and costly legal action); James Saunders, How Best to Keep Rivals' Hands Off Your Brands, Scotsman, Oct. 22, 1997, at 7 (indicating legal costs may put smaller companies at disadvantage).

[94] *See* William A. Tanenbaum, Rights and Remedies for Three Common Trademark-Domain Name Disputes, Computer Law., Sept. 1997, at 9 (noting lack of established case law for common trademark domain name dispute).

[95] *See* Damon Darlin, I Got Here First, Forbes, Dec. 16, 1996, at 326 (explaining lawyers are real winners in legal disputes over domain names).

[96] *See id.*

[97] *See id.*

[98] Dot-Com Squatters Lose Cyberwars, *supra* note 41.

have two choices. The first is to obtain their desired domain name through an alternative registry, such as *www.tonic.to*, which registers the domain *.to*, for Tonga.[99] Other countries also sell domain names, although these countries may have lengthy application processes or exorbitant registration fees.[100] Registrants of domain names in the *.tv* domain, for example, must pay at least $2,500 or more per name.[101]

[e] Registering with Search Engines

Another option for companies unable to secure a desirable domain name is to rely on search engines. Recall that consumers can still find a specific business by using a search engine, rather than by typing in the domain name. This choice requires every company to carefully consider the content of its web page.[102] By giving serious thought to each word and to all possible metatags,[103] companies assist in directing customers to their corporate web sites.

Irrespective of how a consumer arrives at a company's web site, the next hurdle to overcome is providing easy access to the desired information. Failure to do so may result in potential customers turning elsewhere for goods or services.[104] More specifically, a web site should serve the target audience and reflect the business strategies of the company.[105] With the right focus, a company that goes online can improve its corporate image and service, find prospective clients, and expand into new markets.[106] Domain names can become a significant strategic asset of a company and an important component in a marketing plan.[107]

---

[99] *See* Elizabeth Corcoran, Tiny Tonga Expands Its Domain; A Web Site Offering Internet Addresses Puts the Islands on the Online Map, Washington Post, July 1, 1997, at C1 (noting Tongan domain registry reserved popular trademarks to avoid trademark controversies occurring in other domains).

[100] *See id.* More than 70 countries permit nonresidents to register domain names. *See* Peter H. Lewis, The Great Domain Name Hunt, N.Y. Times, June 4, 1998, at G1 (explaining that some countries only require some sort of local presence to register domain name).

[101] *See* http://www.tv (visited May 5, 2000).

[102] *See* Neil Winton, Corporate Web Sites Ubiquitous But Feeble—Report (visited Feb. 23, 1998), http://biz.yahoo.com/finance/980222 /computers_1.html (observing corporate web sites are often disappointing).

[103] Metatags enable web site owners to slip key words or phrases onto the web site; these are invisible on the web site itself, but can be found using the indexing mechanism of the various search engines.

[104] *See* Central Corporation Redefines Internet Navigation, Bus. Wire, Mar. 12, 1998, available in LEXIS, News Library, Curnws File (citing study showing 15.9 million Americans canceled their Internet service because of difficulty finding information).

[105] *See id.* (arguing Internet is more than passing fad).

[106] *See* Linda Tsang, Weaving Trade from the Web, Lawyer, Feb. 17, 1998, at 45 (suggesting Internet strategies).

[107] *See* Epoch Internet Becomes Domain Name Registrar Approved by the Internet Council of Registrars, Bus. Wire, Nov. 18, 1997, available in LEXIS, News Library, Curnws File.

§ 2.05   ADVERTISING YOUR PRODUCTS AND DRAWING TRAFFIC TO YOUR WEB SITE

[A]   Introduction

You need to buy a disk drive for your computer at work and decide to gather information from the Internet. After you type a few words into a search engine, an advertisement from a disk drive manufacturer dances across the top of your browser, offering an inexpensive solution. Intrigued, you ignore the search results, click on the ad, and go to the manufacturer's web page.

After exploring this site, you return to the search engine and are surprised to find some unknown manufacturers listed in the results before the national brands. It turns out that the unknown brand paid the owner of the search engine for the privilege of being listed first in an appropriate search.

Later, you find a web site in which a columnist makes recommendations for several manufacturers, accompanied by links to their sites. The editor of the online publication fails to disclose that the recommended web sites paid for their endorsements.

Welcome to the world of Internet advertising. Advertising on the Internet can appear in many different forms and may provide a company with an inexpensive conduit to new customers. In 1998, Internet advertisers spent $2 billion,[108] a 100 percent increase in Internet advertising revenue from 1997.[109] Online advertisements invite customers to visit a web site or to try a product that they might not have found on their own.

The bottom line is, to get people to visit your site, you must advertise. Failure to do so will mean no visitors, no matter how great the web site. Web advertising has also become critically important to site owners as a way to recoup the costs of maintaining their site. Most site owners prefer to fund web site development costs by selling advertising space on a portion of their site, rather than charge visitors a fee.[110] Internet marketers have measured the success of advertising initiatives based on the length of time visitors spend at the site.[111] The following

---

[108] Lee Hall, *Internet Coalition Wants Ad Standards*, Electronic Media, Mar. 8, 1999, at 5.

[109] Frances Katz, Atlanta Tech; IXL's IPO Scheduled to Come Next Week, Atlanta Journal and Constitution, May 12, 1999, at 9D. Procter and Gamble doubled their Internet advertising in 1998, and in the fourth quarter alone, the company spent $3 million for online ads. Kate Maddox, P& G: Interactive Marketer of the Year, Advertising Age, May 3, 1999, at S1.

[110] *But see* the Wall Street Journal Interactive Edition (visited January 28, 1999) http://www.wsj.com.

[111] The average time spent at any given site varies from between three to five minutes. Charles Papas, Don't Just Count Hits—Generate Hits that Count and Turn into Sales, Home Office Computing, January 1999, p. 90. Enticing visitors to stay at your site for a given length of time is called *stickiness*. Stickiness can be defined as "[t]he quality of attracting longer and more frequent repeat visitors to a web site." *Id.*

table identifies several different ways to advertise products or services on the Internet. Regardless of which method you use, online advertising is constantly evolving. Although the table identifies certain methods of advertising, the primary revenue generating forms of Internet advertising include banners, interstitials, and web page sponsorship.

TABLE 3.4
Methods of Advertising on the Internet

Method	How It Works
Search Engines	Search engines are the primary ways in which people find information on the Internet. For each page included in a site, decide on a few key words that, when searched for, will return that page. You may register your web site using either *Submit-It* or *Add Me*. Other popular search engine sites include: • Alta Vista • Excite • Infoseek • Lycos • Yahoo!
E-Mail	E-mail various online magazines with details about your site.
Exchange Links	Look for third party vendors with which you do business and ask if you can post links from their site to yours, and vice versa. Additionally, you may want to find companies that sell services similar to yours and ask if they would help promote your site and services.
Free Web Link Sites	There are sites that will allow you to post your web site free of charge. These sites may provide a surge of temporary visitors. Such sites include: • WebStep Top 100 • Free Links: The Ultimate Web Site Traffic Builder
Internet Link Exchanges	Advertise your site for free using banners that are displayed on other people's sites.
Newsgroups	Feel free to advertise your site in newsgroups related to your business or corporate mission.
Signature Files	At the end of your e-mail or newsgroup messages, advertise your site. The things to include would be: • "Check us out . . ." • Company Name • URL (e.g., *www.suffolk.edu/law*)

[1] Banner Ads

Banner ads appear at the top of many web pages and are currently the most common form of advertising on the Internet. Many companies employ animated banners to grab a web site visitor's attention. The ads provide a link to a company's web site, where the customer can learn more about what was advertised on the banner.

Internet users are growing more sophisticated, however, and are responding to banner ads less frequently than in the past. The novelty of the animated ads has diminished, and in 1999, only 0.5 percent of Internet users who saw a banner ad actually clicked on it to learn more about the offer,[112] a sharp decline from 1998, when 1 percent to 2 percent of Internet users responded to banner ads.[113] Still, banner ads are an inexpensive way to help generate traffic to a web site.

[2] Interstitial Advertising

Interstitial advertisements fill the browser window while another web page downloads. The ad may have a banner at the top and links to other pages. Since they usually consume the entire screen, interstitial ads are hard to ignore and may be more effective than banner ads.[114]

A variation of the interstitial is the pop-up ad, which appears in a new browser window. Pop-up ads usually contain links and are more elaborate than banner ads. Though intrusive, pop-up ads will certainly generate more traffic than will a banner ad. Some Internet users do not like to have pop-up ads interfere with their web surfing. Both interstitial and pop-up ads require programming knowledge and may be beyond the technical capacity of many web site hosts.[115]

[3] Web Page Sponsorship

Web page sponsorship is similar to television advertising. Sponsors pay to have their links and logos on a popular web site. This provides the sponsor with potential exposure and the web site with revenue with which to generate content.

---

[112] Donna Puscaldo, Web Brokerages Dumping Banner Ads for New Marketing Strategies, Financial Net News, Mar. 15, 1999, at 1.

[113] *Id.*

[114] Matthew Reed, Going Beyond the Banner Ad, Marketing, Apr. 29, 1999, at 25.

[115] *Id.*

While it is difficult to directly attribute specific profitability to web page sponsorship, it may be a facet of successful Internet campaigns.[116]

[4] Other Advertising Strategies

Many successful Internet ad campaigns are coordinated with traditional advertising media.[117] Lotus, for example, successfully launched a new product in the United Kingdom by combining traditional newspaper advertising with Internet banner ads.[118] Procter & Gamble created an effective campaign in the United States by coordinating television and Internet ads.[119]

Other Internet advertisers have fully integrated online strategies that include e-mail advertising, banner ads, and site sponsorship. To obtain new customers, for example, First USA paid Microsoft $90,000,000 for the exclusive right to advertise its credit cards across Microsoft's MSN Internet network for five years.[120] The credit card company hoped to reach customers who do not respond to traditional media, such as mail or telemarketing campaigns.[121]

[5] Editorial and Search Engine Priority

While banner ads are popular and overt, advertising pervades many other facets of the Internet. Some advertising is subtly placed within editorial content. Advertisers may also purchase key words within search engines so that their links receive priority in any relevant search. Advertisers may also purchase banner ads that appear on search engines any time the key word is used in a search,[122] allowing more targeted banner advertising.

In one example of subtle sponsorship, publishers paid the online bookstore Amazon.com for prominent placement of favorable book reviews.[123] Visitors to the Amazon.com site who looked at reviews under the heading "What We're Reading" were likely to see book reviews subsidized by the books' publishers. Such hidden

---

[116] Irv DeGraw, Don't Change That Channel, On Wall Street, Sept. 1, 1998, available in LEXIS, News Library, Curnws File.

[117] Adam Woods, A Software Company Saw a Positive Response to the Launch of Its All-In-One Intranet Package Through a Web and Conventional Press Push, Precision Marketing, Apr. 20, 1998, at 10.

[118] *Id.*

[119] Alasdair Reid, P&G Looks Beyond Banner Ads to Boost Its Web Presence,

[120] Largest Internet Ad Deal Signed, Bank Marketing Int'l, Dec. 1998, at 7.

[121] *Id.*

[122] *See supra* note 114.

[123] *See* Saul Hansell and Amy Hoarmon, Subtly Trolling for Online Shoppers, National Post, Feb. 27, 1999, at D11.

sponsorship, if deceptive, may run afoul of the law and will likely be received unfavorably by the public.[124]

[B] Internet Advertising Law

The Internet is no longer like a developing country or the Wild West, with informal frontier justice governing advertising. Because of the many different forms of advertising, many different regulatory agencies become involved, and a wide variety of issues arise.[125] Many jurisdictions are now devoting resources to protecting consumers online, and agencies worldwide are working together to punish offenders and deter advertising scams across jurisdictions.[126] The Federal Trade Commission (FTC) has a special bureau that combs the Internet for deceptive advertising.[127]

[1] Federal Trade Commission

Consumer protection that applies to traditional commercial activities has been extended to cyberspace. The FTC rules, guidelines, and disclosures developed for other media apply to the Internet.[128] Mandatory disclosures must, for example, be clear and conspicuous. The FTC's enforcement of online advertisement focuses on three key issues: claim substantiation, deception, and unfairness.[129]

[a] Claim Substantiation

Advertisers must have a reasonable basis for their advertised claims.[130] Advertisers or web site designers who are unable to substantiate claims may be

---

[124] It is possible that the Federal Trade Commision may file an enforcement action if the "hidden sponsorship" is considered to be an unfair and deceptive trade practice.

[125] Mark Sableman, Business on the Internet, Part II: Liability Issues, 53 J. MO. B. 223, 223 (1997).

[126] See Special Report—Protecting the Consumer: To Boldly Go into Space Chasing Rogues, London Daily Telegraph, Dec. 7, 1998, at 28 (illustrating cooperative pursuit of Japanese company advertising miracle cures).

[127] See supra note 123.

[128] Federal Trade Commission, Dot.Com Disclosures (visited Sept. 14, 2000) http://www.ftc.gov/bcp/conline/pubs/buspubs/dotcom; Federal Trade Commission, Advertising and Marketing on the Internet: The Rules of the Road (visited April 28, 1999), http://www.ftc.gov/bcp/conline/pubs/buspubs/ruleroad.htm (describing how FTC Act's prohibition on "unfair or deceptive acts or practices" applies to Internet advertising, marketing, and sales).

[129] Arent Fox, Advertising Law Internet Site (visited Apr. 28, 1999), http://www.advertisinglaw.com.

[130] FTC Policy Statement Regarding Advertising Substantiation Program (visited Apr. 28, 1999), http://www.webcom.com/~lewrose/adsubpol.html.

subject to fines or other remedies levied by the FTC. If Suffolk Personal Computers advertised on the Internet that they had the fastest computers available, then, they must have proof substantiating the claim, or they may be exposed to a possible enforcement action.

Subjective claims or opinions, such as "At Suffolk Personal Computers, we have the best looking keyboards in the world,"[131] are permitted. Such sales talk or puffery requires substantiation only when it suggests the company has consumer support or agreement, as in phrases such as "More PC users prefer Suffolk PC's keyboards." Companies advertising on the Internet should endeavor to separate seller's talk or puffery from factual claims.

[b] Deception and Unfairness

"Unfair advertising" is a catch-all classification for advertising that offends public policy or injures consumers or competitors.[132] Deceptive acts in Internet advertising can subject a company to FTC or state enforcement against unfair or deceptive advertising. A deceptive act is one that misleads consumers and influences their behavior or decision to purchase the product.[133]

Both failure to disclose material facts and affirmative acts may constitute deception. If Suffolk Personal Computers advertises a new computer for $100, but forgets to mention that the offer is only good with the purchase of a $2,000 monitor, the advertisement is deceptive. Internet advertisers should be clear about what they are offering, and they must avoid any hidden charges or "bait and switch" sales tactics, that is, advertising one item with the intent of selling another. In one case, Virgin Atlantic Airways had to pay a $14,000 fine to the U.S. Department of Transportation for failing to clearly disclose a $38.91 tax applicable to tickets it had advertised on the Internet.[134]

[2] Misrepresentation and False Advertising

FTC regulations are not the only guidelines for advertisers. The Lanham Act imposes liability for advertisers who misrepresent their own or someone else's

---

[131] Roscoe B. Starek, III, Regulatory Enforcement of Your Web Site, Who Will Be Watching? (visited Apr. 28, 1999), http://www.ftc.gov/speeches/starek/onlinweb.htm.

[133] See supra note 128.

[134] Lewis Rose and John P. Feldman, Internet Marketing: Practical Suggestions for International Advertising and Promotions (visited May 25, 1999), www.webcom.com/lewrose/article/intl.html.

products to the consuming public.[135] Any comparisons or representations of competing brands should not be disparaging or false. If Suffolk Personal Computers employed a false banner ad showing defective circuits and phantom bugs in a competitor's computers, they may be liable to that company if it found itself to be damaged by the misleading ads.

[3] National Advertising Division of the Council of the Better Business Bureau

The Better Business Bureau (BBB) has a national advertising division (NAD) with guidelines for voluntary self regulation of advertising. Like the FTC, the NAD is concerned with consumer protection and the corrosive effects of false or misleading advertising.[136] NAD investigates truth in national advertising and may ask noncomplying advertisers to modify or discontinue unsubstantiated claims.[137] Since Internet advertising may be considered national in scope, online advertisers should conform to the NAD's guidelines and recommendations.

[4] Other Considerations

Since Internet advertising regulations are still evolving, many companies are cautious in their approach. IBM, for example, recently announced that it would advertise only on web sites with a clear privacy policy.[138] Advertising techniques popular in the United States may also be contrary to local laws in other countries. While comparative advertising is a popular practice in the United States, for example, other countries impose broad restrictions. Since the Internet is a worldwide medium, advertisers should proceed conservatively with any comparisons. The following are a few of the countries that place restrictions on comparative advertising: Australia, Argentina, China, The Czech Republic, El Salvador, Germany, Greece, Italy, Japan, Malaysia, The Philippines, and Switzerland.[139]

---

[135] Lanham Act § 8, 15 U.S.C. § 1125 (a)(1)(B) (1996).

[136] Better Business Bureau, Promoting Honest Advertising (visited May 28, 1999), http://www.bbb.org/advertising/index.html.

[137] National Advertising Division (visited May 28, 1999), www.caru.bbb.org/advertiserAssist.html.

[138] Jeri Clausing, I.B.M. Vows to Pull Ads From Web Sites that Lack Clear Policies on Protecting Consumer Privacy, N.Y. Times, Apr. 1, 1999, at C4.

[139] Stephen P. Durchslag, Comparative Advertising Doesn't Always Work Overseas, Promo, Jan. 1, 1999, available in LEXIS, News Library, Curnws file.

Companies selling their products and services on the Internet are in a complex legal environment where there is a risk of violating some local advertising regulation. Advertising only in English and stating that any offer is available only in the United States may minimize the risk of liability. Advertisers who venture into other countries should engage local counsel to assess the local advertising regulatory landscape. In Denmark, for example, advertising targeting children is prohibited.[140] In another interesting example, Italian clothing designer Benetton was held liable in both German and French courts for print advertising that was held to exploit emotions.[141]

[5] Advertising to Children

Although children represent a substantial portion of the Internet surfing population, Internet advertising aimed at children is carefully monitored and should be approached with caution.[142] The Better Business Bureau has a children's advertising review unit to help prevent advertisers from taking advantage of children's naiveté.[143] The review unit has published self-regulatory guidelines to provide advertisers with a framework to help avoid exploiting children.[144] The guidelines and principles articulate the NAD's concerns about children's advertising and suggest reasonable solutions for making parents and advertisers comfortable.[145]

The Children's Online Personal Protection Act (COPPA) imposes federal restrictions for collecting personal information on children. COPPA requires any site that targets and collects information on children under the age of 13 to have a conspicuous privacy policy and to obtain parental consent for any personal data collected, among other requirements.[146] COPPA applies only to com-

---

[140] Roscoe B. Starek, III, Unfairness, Internet Advertising and Innovative Remedies, (visited Apr. 28, 1999), http://www.ftc.gov/speeches/starek/aaffub.htm.

[141] *See supra* note 134.

[142] Denise Caruso, A Push to Provide "Safe Playgrounds" in Cyberspace, International Herald Tribune, Feb. 19, 1999, at 10.

[143] *See* Children's Advertising Review Unit (visited May 28, 1999), http://www.bbb.org/advertising/childrensmonitor.html (defining the review unit and its jurisdiction).

[144] Guidelines for Children's Advertising (visited May 28, 1999), http://www.caru.bbb.org/caruguid.html.

[145] *Id.*

[146] 15 U.S.C. §6501 et seq. (2000). The FTC filed its first COPPA enforcement action against an insolvent Internet toy retailer that offered to sell its customer database to pay creditors. Federal Trade Comm'n v. Toysmart.com, 17 Computer & Online Indus. Litig. Rptr. 9 (Aug. 2000) (charging Toysmart.com with collecting personal information from children under age 13 without obtaining parental consent).

mercial web sites or online services directed to children under 13. At minimum, the web site operator must post a clear and conspicuous privacy policy. Verifiable parental consent is required prior to collecting, using, or disclosing personal information from a child. A web site should comply with self regulatory programs that have been granted "safe harbor" status by the Federal Trade Commission.

While other state and federal regulations are emerging slowly, web site operators should be careful in collecting personal information about anyone under 18; they should either obtain parental consent or correlate the data to a screen name rather than a real-world identity.[147] By using screen names, children are guaranteed anonymity within the web site, yet the web site operator can still keep a record of the user's activities. The Children's Advertising Review Unit has developed advertising guidelines geared toward protecting children.[148] These guidelines include the following points:

1. Advertisements should not mislead about the performance of a product.
2. Do not exploit a child's imagination.
3. Products should be shown being used in safe ways and environments.
4. Children should not be urged to ask parents or others to buy products.
5. The name of the sponsoring company should be prominently displayed.
6. Claims should be presented in ways a child can understand.
7. Some act should be required to represent an intentional joining of a club or acceptance of an offer.
8. Parents may not be obligated to fulfill sales contracts entered into by children.
9. Ordering instructions must clearly state that a child must have a parent's permission to order.
10. Mechanisms should be clear for cancelling an order after it has been placed.[149]
11. Privacy measures must be implemented to protect the identities of children.
12. Words that create a sense of urgency should not be used (for example, "Call now!").

---

[147] Richard Raysman and Peter Brown, Privacy and the Internet, N.Y.L.J., May 12, 1998, at 3. The Direct Marketing Association also provides advice to advertisers about online data collection at www.the-dma.org.

[148] *See* Better Business Bureau, The Children's Advertising Review Unit, 1997 Self Regulatory Guidelines for Children's Advertising. *See also* Federal Trade Commission, How to Comply with The Children's Online Privacy Protection Rule, Nov. 1999 (visited Sept. 15, 2000), http://www.ftc.gov/bcp/coline/pubs/buspubs/coppa.htm.

[149] *Id.*

[C] Linking

[1] Introduction

Linking, or hyperlinking, is one of the primary methods of navigating the Internet.[150] By clicking on highlighted text or an image, Internet users can move quickly and directly to the linked web site, file, or segment of the current web page. Many business web sites use links extensively, allowing visitors to move quickly among pages within the site or to connect easily to another company's web site for further resources or information. If linking were not available, companies on the Internet would have to do more to educate the public about their web addresses andweb site content through traditional advertising media; this would raise a cost barrier for smaller companies seeking to do business on the Internet. A web page with useful links serves as a valuable tool for web users while generating traffic for the site's host. Although simple linking is generally unobjectionable, some practices may create legal liabilities.

Linking is useful: An Internet user searching for a new computer monitor, for example, might use a search engine to find computer equipment vendors and reviews. The search results would be composed primarily of a list of links to vendors' web sites. The user can enter the vendor's web site by clicking on the hyperlink in the search results.

The first page of the link is usually the home page or "front door" of the web site. In the case of a vendor, the home page often contains many image and text links to other pages describing products, specials, company policies, and technical support. Each successive link may lead the viewer deeper into the web site. The site might also provide links to software vendors, who in turn might provide links back to the original computer equipment company. These links are symbiotic, increasing the traffic to both sites, which usually results in increased sales.

A link to a web site that bypasses the web site's home page is called a deep link. The link to the software company may be a "deep link" that goes right to a discount page or other targeted page. Deep links cause greater legal hazards than do regular links.

[2] Legal Implications of Linking

For several years, courts were relatively silent in linking disputes, and cases did not yield a clear legal direction. Recent cases, however, illustrate that judges are reluctant to impose liability for links.[151] Despite this reluctance,

---

[150] The other methods of connecting to a web site, by typing in the desired address or URL in the address bar of the Internet browser or returning to a site that the user had "bookmarked" earlier, are effective only if the Internet user already knows the web site's address.

[151] *See* Ticketmaster Corp. v. Tickets.com, Inc, No. CV 99-7654 HLH (BQRx), 2000 U.S. Dist LEXIS 4553 (C.D. CA, Mar. 27, 2000) (finding deep link does not amount to unfair competition);

several linking controversies have illustrated how some links can create legal hazards.

The most controversial question is whether permission is needed to link to another site. A web site linking agreement serves as a good preventive measure. Most Internet companies believe that web site hosts, merely by publishing their sites, are making those sites available for linking—provided the linking site acts in good faith.[152] This widespread belief is largely based on two theories, both of which are independent of whether the owners of the linked pages are aware of the links.[153]

Under the first theory, creating a hyperlink does not entail reproduction of content, only reproduction of the site address or Uniform Resource Locator (URL).[154] The URL itself is not subject to copyright protection because it lacks creative elements.[155] Some legal commentators take the position that providing a hyperlink is no different from providing a phone number or street address.[156] Other commentators make the novel argument that the link may potentially infringe the copyright owner's right to distribute its work by delivering the linked page.[157]

A growing number of academics argue that courts should not hold the owner of the linking site directly liable for infringement absent evidence of copying or distributing the material.[158] The linking site may be liable, however, for contributory infringement for providing the means by which the viewer can copy the work.[159]

The second theory is based on an implied license or estoppel.[160] Subscribers to this theory cite strong public policy reasons to preserve the web's virtually uninhibited navigation system.[161] Commentators argue that parties who voluntarily post copyrighted material on the web do not have a reasonable expectation of being free from unwelcome linking.[162] This does not mean that web site owners have no intellectual property protection for materials or content on the web site.

Kelly v. Arriba Soft Corp., 77 F. Supp. 2d 1116 (C.D. CA S.D. 1999) (finding no evidence of harm from search engine's deep link to plaintiff's web site).

[152] Richard Raysman and Peter Brown, Dangerous Liaisons: The Legal Risks of Linking Web Sites, N.Y. L.J., April 8, 1997, Computer Law, at 3.

[153] Donald Sovie, Downloading from the Net Is Dangerous, Nat'l L. J., December 14, 1998, at B5.

[154] Id., citing Echerou, Linking to Trouble: Legal Liability Emanating from Hyperlinks on the World Wide Web, 10 No. 2 J. Proprietary Rts. 2, 3 (1998) (referring to a Uniform Resource Locator as an Internet address that identifies the type and location of an Internet resource).

[155] Kara Beal, The Potential Liability of Linking on the Internet: An Examination of Possible Legal Solutions, BYU L. Rev. 703, 724 (1998).

[156] Id.

[157] Sovie, *supra* note 153.

[158] Id.

[159] Id. Proof of contributory infringement, however, requires that the owner of the linking site have knowledge of the infringement and actively aid that infringement. Carl S. Kaplan, Can a Web Link Break Copyright Laws?, N.Y. Times, September 25, 1998, at B10.

[160] Sovie, *supra* note 153, at B5 (referring to an estoppel theory where the linked party would be barred from alleging harm because of that party's own act of publishing on the Internet).

[161] Id.

[162] Id.

Rather, site proprietors may disclaim implied licenses by placing an express warning on their home pages denying access by hyperlink.[163] Sites that have expressed warnings or "terms of use" usually incorporate language that binds the visitors to its terms in exchange for viewing its contents.[164]

Linking controversies have largely been decided under copyright law, though a link often highlights a trademarked symbol or company logo.[165] Trademark law, on the other hand, lends itself more easily to the Internet than does copyright law because trademark law does not unreasonably restrict the flow of information any more than it restricts information presented in more traditional media.[166] Linking cases may also be recast as state unfair competition or federal trademark infringement or dilution claims.[167]

Trademark claims come in two forms: infringement[168] and dilution.[169] Links created with a proprietary name, image, or logo may be subject to a trademark infringement claim.[170] Liability turns on whether a perception of "sponsorship" arose.[171] Even the appearance of sponsorship between the two linked sites, whether that link incorporates a logo or text, may be sufficient to bring an action for trademark infringement against the linking company.[172] Without sponsorship, some lawyers argue, unauthorized linking is not a true instance of trademark

---

[163] *Id.*

[164] *Id. (See, e.g.,* http://www.real.com/company/legal.html (visited February 14, 2000).)

[165] Lisa Green and Heather Meeke, Hyperlinking License; It Is Common for Hyperlinking License Provisions to Be Reciprocal, Intell. Prop. Strategist, October 1998, at 2; *see, e.g.,* Intellectual Reserve, Inc. v. Utah Lighthouse Ministry, Inc., 75 F. Supp. 2d 1290 (D. Utah 1999) (linking to site containing infringing materials did not constitute copyright infringement); *cf.* Playboy Enterprises, Inc. v. Universal Tel-A-Talk, Inc., No. Civ. 96-CV-6961 1998 U.S. Dist. LEXIS 8331 (E.D. Pa., June 1, 1998) (holding that defendant's use of a federally registered trademark "Playboy" in a link did not constitute trademark counterfeiting).

[166] Beal, *supra* note 155, at 727.

[167] *Id.*

[168] A party with rights in a particular mark can bring a trademark infringement claim against a third party if the third party's use of the mark creates a "likelihood of confusion." 15 U.S.C. § 1114 (1998). Specifically, the use of a trademark in connection with the sale of goods constitutes infringement if it is likely to cause consumer confusion as to the source of those goods or as to the sponsorship or approval of such goods. For a more detailed discussion, *see* § 4.03[F].

[169] Under federal law, a party with rights in a particular mark can bring a dilution claim to protect "famous" marks. A court will consider the following factors in deciding whether a mark is famous: (1) the degree of inherent or acquired distinctiveness; (2) the duration and extent of use; (3) the amount of advertising and publicity; (4) the geographic extent of the market; (5) the channels of trade; (6) the degree of recognition in trading areas; (7) any use of similar marks by third parties; (8) whether the mark is registered. 15 U.S.C. § 1125(c) (1998). For a more detailed discussion, see § 4.03[G].

[170] Beal, *supra* note 155, at 727.

[171] Green and Meeke, *supra* note 165.

[172] *Id.*

infringement.[173] Nevertheless, a cautious site owner should obtain a trademark license before implementing such a link.[174] Links that incorporate a distinctive mark, such as a trademark logo or icon, are more egregious than those that simply use a text trade name in the URL.[175] Moreover, use of the trade name in a URL may constitute a fair and descriptive use of the mark.[176]

Most trademark claims that concern unwelcome links, however, arise under a dilution theory.[177] The Federal Trademark Dilution Act of 1995[178] makes dilution of "famous" trademarks actionable.[179] Liability arises under the act when site owners use links, images, or framed materials in a way that diminishes the value of the mark.[180] The value of a mark is measured by its capacity to identify and distinguish goods or services.[181]

[a]   Direct Linking

Many web site operators want to control who links to their sites and to which of the site's web pages the link connects.[182] In a high profile case, Ticketmaster sued Microsoft over a deep link from a Microsoft online entertainment guide.[183] The link bypassed Ticketmaster's main web page, which contained Ticketmaster's logo and third-party advertising.[184] Ticketmaster claimed that the link from the Microsoft page exploited Ticketmaster's trademarked name.[185] Ticketmaster also alleged that, through the link, Microsoft was displaying and publicly distributing

---

[173] *Id.*

[174] *Id.*

[175] Beal, *supra* note 155, at 727.

[176] *Id.*

[177] *Id.*

[178] Trademark Dilution Act, 15 U.S.C. § 1125 (1998).

[179] *Id.*

[180] *See supra* note 152. The Direct Marketing Association also provides advertisers with insight into online data collection at www.the-dma.org (visited May 15, 2000).

[181] *Id.* In a dilution claim, plaintiffs argue that the link creates an association between the two organizations that tarnishes the plaintiff's image in the eyes of the consumer. Beal, *supra* note 155, at 727. As many practitioners recognize, the Federal Trademark Dilution Act gives plaintiffs a big stick with which to obtain judicial recourse. Trademark Dilution Act, 15 U.S.C. § 1125 (1998). Steven E. Shapiro, Use of "Mead Data" Test Dilutes the Dilution Act, Nat'l L.J., May 12, 1997, at C02. Courts seem willing to grant summary judgment on trademark dilution while denying a summary judgment on trademark infringement, for example, which further illustrates the Act's power. *Id.*; *see, e.g.,* Intermatic Inc. v. Toeppen, 40 U.S.P.Q.2d 1412 (N.D. Ill. 1996); Panavision International, L.P. v. Toeppen, 938 F. Supp. 616 (C.D. Cal. 1996), *aff'd*, 141 F.3d 1316 (9th Cir. 1998).

[182] Sean M. Mead, The Internet—Legal Resources, Legal Issues (visited May 6, 1999), http://www.blueriver.net/~wyrm/iclef/98Iclef.html.

[183] Ticketmaster Corp. v. Microsoft Corp., No 97-3055 DDP (C.D. Cal. filed 4/29/97).

[184] Beal, *supra* note 155, at 713.

[185] *Id.* at 714.

the content of Ticketmaster's copyrighted web site.[186] Microsoft removed the link when the complaint was filed, and the parties settled before the court could issue an opinion.[187]

A more compelling case against linking was that of Shetland Times Ltd. v. Wills.[188] The Shetland News posted links using headlines from the competing Shetland Times.[189] The headlines linked directly to the Shetland Times articles, bypassing its home page and advertising, leading readers to believe that they were still at the Shetland News page.[190]

Yet another potential pitfall in linking to a web page at another site is the possibility that a company will subject itself to the personal jurisdiction of a remote state.[191] Most courts have held that operating a web site does not in itself subject the operator to the jurisdiction of any state in which the site is viewed when the basis for exercising jurisdiction is the web presence alone.[192] Some plaintiffs have attempted to erode this trend, however, by arguing that the creation and use of a hyperlink constitutes a tort and, accordingly, subjects the operator of the site to jurisdiction on the basis that the tort was committed within the jurisdiction.[193]

[b] Third-Party Links

The Suffolk Personal Computer web site contains links to third-party web sites. SPC's disclosures should state that SPC neither endorses nor has control over the content of linked sites. SPC is only providing these links as a convenience, and does not imply an endorsement of the linked site. Is the use of third-party links valuable to entities on the Internet? A California court dismissed a case against a web site operator for a third party's infringing web site, which was connected by a link.[194] If the plaintiff had been successful, the case would have

---

[186] Nichole M. Bond, Linking and Framing on the Internet: Liability Under Trademark and Copyright Law, 11 DePaul Bus. L.J. 185, 198 (1998).

[187] The Perkins Coie Internet Case Digest (visited May 3, 1999), http://www.perkinscoie.com/resource/ecomm/netcase/Cases-27.htm.

[188] 1997 F.S.R. 604 (Ct. Sess. O.H.) (Ireland Oct. 24, 1996).

[189] Perkins Coie Digest, *supra* note 187.

[190] *Id.*

[191] For a complete discussion of jurisdiction, *see* Chapter Seven.

[192] Minimum Contacts in Cyberspace: A Taxonomy of the Case Law, 35 Hous. L. Rev. 453, 469, 474, 476, 480 (1998).

[193] Bensusan Restaurant Corp. v. King, 126 F.3d 25 (C.A.2, 1997). Although the Court in Bensusan found that there was no personal jurisdiction, the decision was based upon an inferred requirement in New York's Long Arm Statute that a defendant must be physically present in order to commit a tortious act within the state. Many courts do not require physical presence, however. *See, e.g.,* United Conveyor Corp. v. King, 1992 WL 265852 (N.D. Ill.).

[194] Bernstein v. J.C. Penney Inc., No. 98-2958 R (ex) 1998 U.S. Dist. LEXIS 19048, at *2 (C.D. Cal. Sept. 30, 1998).

resulted in potential liability for all web sites containing links, thus reducing the use of links on the Internet.[195] In another case, a United States district court held that the operator of a "visual search engine" did not commit a copyright infringement by displaying a "thumbnail image," lacking copyright management information, as a means of linking to larger versions of the image, located on another web site.[196] The court stated that the "Plaintiff's images are vulnerable to copyright infringement because they are displayed on Web sites."[197]

Congress enacted the Digital Millennium Copyright Act (DMCA)[198] to implement two copyright law treaties promulgated by the World Intellectual Property Organization (WIPO). The DMCA is an attempt to merge technical remedies with legal remedies. Section 512(a) of the DMCA provides a safe harbor for web sites that transmit allegedly infringing material. The DMCA may be used to limit the liability of any party that transmits, routes, or provides connections for infringing materials.[199] While businesses operating on the web should take precautions to ensure that their directly linked pages are noninfringing, they are not expected to monitor third party links that connect to linked pages.

[3] Linking Precautions—Look Before You Link

Linking is a great way to add value to your web site and to generate traffic. Nevertheless, prudent web site operators should obtain permission from other sites before linking.[200] While Microsoft can afford to test the court's opinion regarding linking without permission, most businesses cannot afford the expense of litigation. Even sites that permit unlimited linking to their home page may object to deep links that bypasses their identification or content.

Conversely, if a web site you do not want associated with your business links to your site, you must send it a request to remove the link. If the site refuses, you may be able to thwart the link by slightly modifying the address of the linked page. This is especially helpful in eliminating unwanted deep links. Ticketmaster for instance, modified the web page targeted by Microsoft's unwanted link. Internet

---

[195] CA Judge Dismisses Copyright Claims Based on Linking, Software Law Bulletin, Nov. 1998, at 213.

[196] Kelley v. Arriba Soft Corp., 1999 WL 1210918 (C.D. Cal.).

[197] *Id.*, at 6.

[198] 17 U.S.C. § 1202, et seq.

[199] Alan J. Hartnick, The New Limitations on Online Copyright Liability, N.Y. L.J., Feb. 5, 1999, at 5.

[200] The American Bar Association published a book of model web linking agreements and policies. The book, Web-Linking Agreements: Contracting Strategies and Model Provisions, is available at http://www.abanet.org/buslaw/catalog/5070311.html (visited May 15, 2000). Additionally, some companies may give permission to link to their web sites. *See* http://www.batesville.com/html/link.htm (visited February 14, 2000).

users who clicked on the link would see a message informing them that the link was unauthorized.

Since the courts have not issued opinions regarding linking, legal action should be a last resort. A simple cease-and-desist letter from counsel will probably deter most unwanted links.

Web sites should contain a clear policy regarding linking. Unless your business is unconcerned with who may be linking to your web page, you should post a clear policy requiring written permission for all links. Finally, make sure that all links start at your home page and do not bypass whatever content or advertising you want everyone to see when they enter your site.

[D] Framing

Frames are used to display portions of multiple web pages within a single page. This allows Internet users to navigate through the content of different web pages while still maintaining the original frame and menu of the framing page. Frames may be employed seamlessly, giving visitors the illusion that they never left the original web page, even though they have clicked through numerous web sites.

[1] Advantages of Framing

Frames aid the Internet user by facilitating navigation. Internet pages with frames often contain various navigation buttons, allowing users to search the web site or to explore other pages while still maintaining the frame. Web page operators can maintain a consistent look across the web site and beyond. Framing sites can keep their logo and advertising in front of the viewer longer than would be the case if the user continued through the Internet via other links.[201]

Suffolk PCs, for example, may want to provide technical information about the computers they sell online. Rather than recreating the manufacturer's information, a web page within the Suffolk PC site can frame the latest technical information straight from the manufacturer's web site. SPC may also want to frame many of its own web pages. Through the frame, any changes to the site navigation menu would require only a change to a few web pages rather than every page on the site. This would be advantageous, for example, if Suffolk PCs wanted to have dynamic links to a few special offers on the side of every web page.

[2] Legal Issues in Framing

Since framed pages can be made to look like part of the original page, some web site owners object to framing, and several legal theories support that position.

---

[201] Beal, *supra* note 155, at 717.

Unauthorized framing may violate the framed page's copyright by creating a derivative work,[202] defined in the Copyright Act as "work consisting of editorial revisions, annotations, elaborations, or other modifications."[203] A derivative works claim in a framing case is an especially viable approach for plaintiffs because evidence of copying is not necessary to support such a finding.[204]

A framed link may also invoke liability under trademark infringement and dilution.[205] Under infringement principles, liability would result from the unauthorized use of proprietary marks for commercial purposes, however they appear on the framed page.[206] Dilution principles also apply to framing when the display of the trademarks within the framed page includes the logo and URL of another organization.[207] Framing tends to create great confusion over the owner of the site and can mislead a user into inferring a commercial relationship between the two organizations.[208]

The frame may also infringe upon a web site's trademark by causing confusion and diminishing the value of a protected mark.[209] While courts have not provided decisive precedent regarding framing, web operators should take precautions to avoid the expense of initiating or defending against a lawsuit.

The most notable framing dispute was Washington Post v. TotalNews, Inc.[210] The TotalNews Internet page provided links to the web sites of hundreds of newspapers.[211] Visitors to the web page could view the newspapers' web sites through the TotalNews frame by clicking on links containing their trademarked names and logos.[212] The frame contained TotalNews' advertising and links while providing the content of other web sites.[213]

The TotalNews frame obscured or eliminated the advertising from the target newspapers' framed pages.[214] While some web sites were eager to be linked to the

---

[202] Daniel A. Tysver, Linking and Liability (visited May 6, 1999), http://www.bitlaw.com/internet/linking.html.

[203] 17 U.S.C. § 101 (1998).

[204] Mirage Editions, Inc. v. Albuquerque A.R.T. Co., 856 F.2d 1341 (9th Cir. 1988) (holding that mounting copyrighted artwork onto ceramic tiles is a derivative work for copyright purposes).

[205] Beal, *supra* note 155, at 727.

[206] *Id.*

[207] *Id.*

[208] David Mirchin, Liability for Hypertext Linking: Recent Cases, Internet News: Legal & Bus. Aspects, May 1998, Vol. 3, No. 2, at 5.

[209] *Id.*

[210] 97 Civ. 1190 (PKL) (S.D.N.Y., Feb. 20, 1997).

[211] David L. Hayes, Application of Copyright Rights to Specific Acts on the Internet, Computer Lawyer, Aug. 1998, at 1.

[212] Nichole M. Bond, Linking and Framing on the Internet: Liability Under Trademark and Copyright Law, 11 DePaul Bus. L.J. 185, 196 (Fall/Winter, 1998).

[213] Carol Ebbinghouse, Webmaster Liability, Searcher, Feb. 1998, at 19.

[214] Hayes, *supra* note 211.

TotalNews page, others objected to the use of trademarked logos as links, to the frame obscuring their advertising, and to the commandeering of content.[215] Parties in the controversy settled before the court could issue a ruling. TotalNews agreed to remove the frame and to eliminate links containing stylized logos, leaving only plain text links.[216] As a small web site, TotalNews had little chance of success going against several large newspapers, each of which could afford a lengthy battle.

[3] Resolving Framing Controversies

[a] Protecting Your Web Site

The first step in avoiding costly litigation over framing is to post a clear framing policy. Web sites that violate the policy should respond to a well-crafted cease-and-desist request. Unwanted frames may also be side-stepped through proper programming of the web site.[217]

[b] Framing Other Web Sites

Before you frame another web site, obtain its host's written permission. If you are already framing other sites, and they object, eliminate the links and determine whether the other sites object to unframed links. Frames can be a very effective way of providing content that keeps visitors within your web site for a long time. SPC, for example, may want to give its customers access to Intel's web site whenever it makes reference to its use of the Pentium III chip. Framing Intel's web site within SPC's web site enables SPC to leverage Intel's content without any rewriting. With a few legal precautions, companies can take advantage of Internet framing technology.

[E] Marketing Through E-Mail

E-mail is a marketer's dream. For minimal cost, a company can communicate with thousands of prospective and current customers. E-mail advertising ranges from informative messages directly requested by the recipients to bulk "spam," which can be a convoy of unsolicited messages clogging the information superhighway.

---

[215] Beal, *supra* note 155, at 718.

[216] Online Advertising? Beware of Dangers (visited April 28, 1999), http:www.lgu.com/cy45.htm.

[217] Andrew J. Hollander, Do-It-Yourself Source-Code Firewalls, Internet Newsletter: Legal and Business Aspects, May 1998, at 4. The code to avoid frames is available online at www.netscapeworld.com/netscapeworld/nw-05-1997/nw-05.html (visited May 14, 1999). *Id.*

[1]   Advantages of E-Mail

As the response rates to banner ads and other advertising formats on the Internet diminish, e-mail marketing is becoming an important medium.[218] E-mail can be used to develop traffic to a web site and to distribute information about new products and special promotions.[219] Sending an advertisement via e-mail is similar to mailing traditional solicitations, without the high costs of designing, printing, and postage. Unlike printed advertisements, potential customers may receive e-mails within minutes of their transmission. E-mail ads may contain direct links to the advertised web site or even enclosures of pictures, movies, or other media to intrigue customers.

[2]   Opt-In versus Opt-Out E-Mailing

The most effective method of e-mail advertising is to send messages to people who have registered at the host's Internet site to be on its e-mailing list; this allows the host to target mailings based on the recipients' interests and needs, and it eliminates unwanted messages. In June 1999, half of all e-commerce web sites provided visitors with the option of e-mail registration.[220] Even Internet groups who oppose traditional e-mail solicitations agree that the "opt-in" model is an acceptable form of e-mail advertising.[221]

In one creative example, Calvin Klein Cosmetics incorporated opt-in e-mail advertising into a traditional television, print, and radio campaign.[222] The ads in traditional media contained an e-mail address for the various featured characters.[223] Those who sent e-mails to the advertised addresses received a fictitious correspondence from the characters.[224] This campaign illustrated many of the benefits of e-mail advertising by combining an "opt-in" mailing list culled from traditional advertising media with an intriguing correspondence that subtly advertised products.

---

[218] *See* Ian Oxman, Opt-In E-mail—Who's the Fool?, DM News, Mar. 22, 1999, at 24 (comparing e-mail advertising to other methods of Internet marketing).

[219] *See* Marketing News and Resources, Marketing Department Management Report, Feb. 1999, at 8 (illustrating economics of e-mail advertising).

[220] *Id.*

[221] *See* Roberta Fusaro, Groups Eye Model for E-Mail Ads; Antispam Summit, Computerworld, Dec. 21, 1998, at 47 (reporting agreement between direct marketing group and antispam coalition).

[222] Patrick Allossery, You've Got E-Mail: An Internet Soap Opera from Calvin Klein: New Medium Carries the Storyline for the Campaign, National Post, Dec. 14, 1998, at C4.

[223] *Id.*

[224] *Id.*

Opt-out e-mail advertising, on the other hand, is considered offensive and in bad taste.[225] Opt-out advertising requires the recipient of an unsolicited advertisement to send an e-mail to a specific address to be removed from the mailing list. Since e-mail marketing is so inexpensive, some companies are willing to risk irritating thousands of people in order to get a few respondents.[226]

[3] Legal Challenges to E-Mail Marketing

When the technology for bulk e-mailing was developed, advertisers were quick to recognize its value. Unlike traditional mailed advertisements, however, e-mail solicitations are viewed as intrusive and unwelcome. The first bulk e-mail incident, in 1994, aroused an uproar across the Internet community.[227]

Compared to printed advertisements, unsolicited bulk e-mails may be burdensome to the recipient and costly and time-consuming for Internet Service Providers. Unsolicited e-mail advertising may be likened to selling products via collect telephone calls.[228] Recipients of e-mail still pay the Internet connection charges and phone line rental whether or not they requested the advertisement.[229] According to one estimate, large companies lose $500,000 annually as a result of spam.[230]

Unsolicited e-mail represents 5 percent to 30 percent of America Online's e-mail traffic.[231] Other ISPs face similar spam burdens, which slow down servers, consume disk space, and cost money to filter out. America Online, Compuserve, and other ISPs have successfully sued several intrusive e-mail marketing companies on a variety of legal theories, ranging from the common law tort of trespass to the Computer Fraud and Abuse Act.[232]

Unscrupulous e-mail marketers have also aroused the ire of ISPs by forging return addresses. This practice, known as "spoofing," benefits the e-mail sender by keeping its return address unknown while masking its identity with an address that looks innocuous. Additionally, recipients have no way to reply to the e-mail and

---

[225] Erika Rasmusson, Spam Gets Slammed, Sales & Marketing Management, Dec. 1998, at 56.

[226] Kimberly Patch and Eric Smalley, E-mail Overload; Companies Risk Getting Crushed by All Those Messages If They Don't Devise Strategies for Handling the Burden, Network World, Oct. 26, 1998, at 1.

[227] Margaret Loftus, Great Moments in E-mail History, U.S. News and World Report, Mar. 22, 1999, at 56.

[228] Rasmusson, *supra* note 225.

[229] Four Reasons Why It's Wrong to Spam, Computimes (Malaysia), Apr. 15, 1999, *available in* LEXIS, News Library, Curnws file.

[230] Patch and Smalley, *supra* note 226.

[231] *Id.*

[232] *See* The Perkins Coie Internet Case Digest: Spam (Junk E-Mail) (visited May 3, 1999), http://www.perkinscoie.com/resource/ecomm/netcase/Cases-23.htm (listing e-mail controversies).

little hope of tracing its origins. Spoofing was once a popular method for trying to draw traffic to shady web sites purveying get rich quick schemes or pornography.[233] Recent state and federal laws, however, have prohibited false return e-mail addresses. America Online used trademark law and local computer statutes, among other theories, to win a substantial legal victory against a bulk e-mailer who sent unsolicited e-mails with false return addresses to AOL subscribers.[234]

As spam becomes more burdensome to companies, individuals, and ISPs, plaintiffs are employing state and federal laws to protect themselves.[235] States have been adopting legislation requiring caution on the part of any company planning to use e-mail for advertising. Virginia, for example, imposes statutory damages of $10 per message or up to $25,000 per day for falsifying a return address.[236] A Washington superior court judge ruled that Washington's Unsolicited Electronic Mail Act was unconstitutional because it violated the Commerce Clause.[237] California has several requirements for bulk e-mail, including providing a toll free telephone number or an e-mail address through which to request removal from the e-mailing list.[238] California also requires companies that send out mass e-mailings to begin the subject line with "ADV" for advertisement, and it gives ISPs standing to sue spammers.[239]

[4] Solutions for E-Mail Marketing

Companies using e-mail marketing should limit mailings to individuals who ask to be put on their mailing lists.[240] Sending unsolicited e-mail detracts from a company's image and could result in retaliatory bulk e-mail responses, which can

---

[233] Court Rulings Give AOL Three New Victories in the Battle Against Junk E-Mail, Business Wire, Dec. 21, 1998, available in LEXIS, News Library, Curnws file.

[234] American Online, Inc. V. LCGM, INC., 1998 U.S. Dist. LEXIS 20144 (E.D. Va Nov. 10, 1998). *See also* Court Rulings Give AOL Three New Victories, *supra* note 233 (listing legal victories against bulk e-mailers and return address forgers).

[235] For a comprehensive list of current a proposed legislation, *see* Existing and Emerging Anti-Spam Law (visited May 19, 1999), http://www.tigerden.com/junkmail/laws.html.

[236] Mark Grossman, No Matter How You Slice and Dice It, Spam's a Problem, Broward Daily Bus. Rev. Apr. 30, 1999, at B1.

[237] State v. Heckel, No. 98-2-25480-7DEA (Wash. Super. Ct., King Cty. March 10, 2000), *reported in* 17 Comp. & Online Indus. Litig. Rptr. 14 (April 10, 2000).

[238] California Laws 1999, LA Times, Jan. 1, 1999, at A3.

[239] Rob Turner, Relief From Online "Spam" Attacks?, Money, Dec. 1998, at 104. For an analysis of the California e-mail regulations, *see* California's New Anti-Spam Laws (visited May 19, 1999), http://www.wsgr.com/resource/intprop/pubs/articles/spam.htm.

[240] Consumers can volunteer to have their names put on a mailing list by registering at a given web site. But consumers have found their names on mailing lists for which they had not specifically registered. This happens primarily because many companies sell their customer lists to other marketers.

slow down or cripple a server.[241] Since e-mail advertising is not as well accepted as printed advertising, companies should proceed cautiously in utilizing their e-mailing list. Using e-mail to support traditional mass marketing strategies can backfire and result in a robust e-mailing list of customers who ignore your e-mails.[242] Start slowly and on a small scale to test how consumers respond.

Additionally, all e-mail advertisements should follow the laws of the most restrictive state. Advertisers should use the following checklist as a precaution:

1. Use only opt-in advertising and archive all consumer requests to be part of the e-mailing list. If a recipient claims that the e-mail was unsolicited, you may need to prove that they actively sought to be on the list.
2. Minimize the number of e-mail advertisements sent at one time to avoid burdening the ISPs and recipient's servers.
3. Make sure that your return e-mail address is accurate.
4. Put 'ADV' in the subject line, along with an accurate description of the e-mail's contents.
5. Provide your company's name, address, e-mail address, and telephone number clearly within the body of the e-mail.
6. Provide recipients with an e-mail address or toll free number to contact should they wish to be removed from the e-mailing list.
7. Never sell your e-mailing list or purchase one from others.
8. Check your own ISP's policy regarding distribution of e-mail solicitations. You may have certain restrictions within your contract.
9. Keep the content of e-mail advertising brief. The e-mail should contain a link to your web site for those looking for more information.
10. Define a clear, corporate-wide e-mail advertising policy. This will help prevent recipients from receiving multiple e-mails from different departments of the same company.
11. Make sure that your e-mail policy is compatible with the privacy policy on your web site. The opt-in web page should state exactly why personal information is being collected and the use you intend to make of it.

[F] Metatags

Metatags are hidden HTML codes in the head portion of your various web pages; they are not visible to site visitors, but they contain key words, phrases, or descriptions used by many search engines. Search engines will provide a higher

---

[241] Four Reasons Why It's Wrong to Spam, *supra* note 229.

[242] Erika Rasmusson, What Price Knowledge? Marketers Should Understand Consumer's Wish for Privacy, Sales and Marketing Management, Dec. 1998, at 56.

search result ranking to your site if the metatag used is the proper one for your content. Every page, therefore, should include a metatag.

[1]   What to Include in Metatags

As a general rule, web designers suggest that every metatag on a given web page include a title, a few keywords, and a brief description. Titles are generally created by HTML editing programs. If the tool you use does not create a title for each page, be sure that you otherwise include one. Keywords represent a subjective list of concepts relevant to a site or page. Metatags should also include brief descriptions. Internet searches return the URLs of relevant sites along with a brief description of each. This description, if compelling, helps convince people that the site is worth a click. This is often the only chance site owners have to attract potential customers.

[2]   Tips on Using Metatags Effectively

Metatags are invaluable for generating traffic to a site, and their use can be enhanced in a number of ways.

- Some search engines prefer shorter metatags composed of relevant keywords.

- Metatags should also be provided for on frames.

- Do not cut-and-paste a metatag from one page to another.

[3]   Legal Issues and Limitations

In the past, some web site operators exploited metatags by using other company's trademarks and company names to siphon off visitors looking for another site.[243] Courts have now ruled against such metatag abuse.[244] Metatag users should, therefore, use the following precautions against the appearance of misuse.

1. In creating metatags, do not use anyone else's trademark without permission.
2. Never mention the names or products of competitors in a metatag, even if the names are not trademarked.

---

[243] *See* Playboy Enterprises, Inc. v. Calvin Designer Label, 985 F. Supp. 1220, 1221-22 (N.D. Cal. 1997) (prohibiting use of Playboy trademark in computer code that indexed page on Internet search engines).

[244] Intellectual Property Court Watch Roundup of Recent Developments, Intell. Prop. Strat., Nov. 1997, at 10. The court focused on the defendants' unauthorized use of the registered trademark.

3. If you carry third-party products, get permission before using other brand names or products in metatags.

4. Include your own brand name and product names in metatags.

5. Use descriptive terms for your products or service in metatags. (Suffolk PCs, for example, might use the terms "computer, monitor, CPU, hard drive," among other words, in its metatags.)

A carefully written metatag can be effective in drawing web traffic without inciting a legal dispute. For a complete discussion of the legal issues related to metatags, see § 4.03[M][6].

[G]   Attorney Advertising on the Internet

The Internet is an ideal medium for attorneys seeking to enhance their legal practice through cost-effective information access, advertising, and client communication. Legal web sites range from simple advertisements listing practice areas and biographical information to comprehensive resources with small libraries of information. For a minimal investment, the Internet can enable a solo practitioner to compete with large firms.

[1]   Advantages of Legal Advertising on the Internet

Internet advertising can be an effective way to obtain new clients,[245] and the annual cost of designing and posting a legal web site on the Internet may be less than 20 percent of an advertisement in the Yellow Pages.[246] Many attorneys, ranging from solo practitioners to large firms, have already established Internet presences. According to a recent survey, almost 75 percent of law firms with more than 75 lawyers use the Internet to grow their client base.[247]

While the style of legal web sites varies widely, most fall into one of the following three categories: business card sites; brochure sites; and value-added or free information sites.

Business card web sites resemble small, simple Yellow Page advertisements. The sites are essentially a permanently posted electronic calling card, although they may include some additional information, such as areas of practice and bio-

---

[245] Deborah Marchini and John Defterios, Computer Associates COO Sanjay Kumar: "Prospects Look Good," CNN Business Day Transcript # 98102102V07, Oct. 21, 1998.

[246] *See* Lorelie S. Masters, Professionals Online: Advice for Travels on the Information Super-highway, Computer Lawyer, March, 1999, at 1 (discussing opportunities for attorneys on the Internet).

[247] *See* William E. Hornsby, Jr., Practice Development: In Search of the Ethical Compass for Advertising in an Online World, A.B.A. Law Practice Management, Oct. 1998, at 49 (examining Internet and lawyer advertising).

graphical profiles. Business card sites are inexpensive to develop and maintain and can be updated easily. The business card site can be a valuable resource to lawyers because an Internet user searching for attorneys by practice area, geographic location, profile, or name will find them easily.

Brochure sites provide an in-depth online brochure about an attorney or firm. The site may include articles written by the attorney, case histories, or extensive profiles in addition to the basic information contained in the business card web site. A brochure site can have more impact than a simple business card site, and it can be an effective tool to showcase an attorney or firm.

The value-added site is the most comprehensive of all legal web sites, providing layers of information, articles, or links. The information can be an effective way to generate traffic to a web site and for an attorney or firm to gain exposure and credibility. Unlike a simple business card or brochure web site, a value-added legal page may require extensive programming and content development and maintenance. Value-added sites may generate new clients who use the information on the web site as a resource and then contact the sponsoring attorney or firm when they require more personalized legal assistance.

[2] Ethical Issues in Attorney Advertising on the Internet

Legal advertising in the twentieth century was first permitted in 1977, quite a few years after the Internet's inception.[248] Since legal advertising is relatively new, state bar associations are still exploring the limits of legal advertising in print, radio, and television, as well as online. Consequently, attorneys should approach web site development and Internet advertising with the same restraint dictated by the ethical standards imposed on lawyer advertising in traditional media. Even value-added, informational web sites sponsored by law firms may be construed as advertising by some jurisdictions, so the ethical restrictions cannot be ignored by any attorney with an Internet presence.[249]

Some states have particular restrictions on advertising that have been interpreted to apply to the Internet. In Texas, for example, a federal district court deemed online information services as advertising to the public and thus as subject to the same rules applicable to other lawyer advertisements.[250] Lawyers with

---

[248] *See* Elizabeth D. Whitaker and David S. Coale, Professional Image and Lawyer Advertising, 28 Tex. Tech. L. Rev. 801, 803 (1997) (exploring history of modern legal advertising); ABA Professional Conduct on the Internet, White Paper, July 1998 (visited May 26, 1999), http://www.abanet.org/legalserv/advertising.html.

[249] *See generally* Will Hornsby, Professional Ethics and Lawyer Advertising on the Internet (visited May 25, 1999), www.collegehill.com/ilp-news/hornsby2.html (caution attorneys about the challenges of advertising online).

[250] *See* Texans Against Censorship, Inc., v. State Bar of Texas, 888 F. Supp. 1328, 1370 (E.D. Texas Mar. 31, 1995) (analyzing definition of "public media" for advertising).

web sites practicing in Texas must submit copies of the pages to an advertising review committee for approval,[251] and some other states, as well, require printed copies of Internet advertisements. Clearly, all attorneys operating online should monitor their state's requirements.[252] South Carolina, for example, amended its rules of professional conduct in 1998 without mentioning Internet or e-mail advertising,[253] but has since propounded e-mail and Internet-related ethics opinions.[254]

Lawyers should not rush to establish an online presence in the hope of finding new clients until they assess local and state ethics regulations about such issues as active online solicitation of clients. An attorney in Tennessee, for example, was disbarred for his aggressive e-mail advertising campaign.[255] A legal web site rushed into operation, moreover, may contain errors, exposing the sponsor to liability from site visitors as well as violations of ethics regulations.[256] Finally, attorneys establishing an online presence should check that their insurance covers any Internet or e-mail activities.

[a] *Language Restrictions*

The American Bar Association prohibits misleading language in legal advertising.[257] Comparative terms and phrases that would not be considered misleading in nonlegal advertising can be broadly construed as violating ethics requirements. A firm advertising itself as "full service" or "complete service," for example, must provide an entire range of every type of legal service.[258] While comparative advertising is encouraged as a way to aid consumers, many phrases in legal advertising may violate ethics guidelines unless they are substantiated. In Pennsylvania, for example, attorneys may not advertise themselves as "caring" or "competent," because use of the terms may suggest that other attorneys are not caring or sym-

---

[251] Christopher R. Lavoie, Have You Been Injured In an Accident? The Problem of Lawyer Advertising and Solicitation, 30 Suffolk U.L. Rev. 413, 430-431 (1997). Attorneys advertising in Texas are required to have all print and television advertising approved by the review committee as well. *Id.* at 431.

[252] *See* Ronald D. Rotunda, Professionalism, Legal Advertising, and Free Speech in the Wake of Florida Bar v. Went For It, Inc., 49 Ark. L. Rev. 703, 718 (1997) (warning of Florida's Internet legal advertising requirements).

[253] Wyn Bessent Ellis, The Evolution of Lawyer Advertising: Will It Come Full Circle? 49 S.C. L. Rev. 1237, 1258 (1998).

[254] *See* Ethics Opinions (visited May 25, 1999), http://www.legalethics.com/opins.htm (listing recent ethics opinions relating to attorney advertising on the Internet).

[255] Ashley Craddock, Spamming Lawyer Disbarred, Wired News (visited May 25, 1999), http://www.wired.com/news/politics/story/5060.html.

[256] *See* Elizabeth Davidson, Legal Advice on Net Could Send SIF Claims Spiraling, Lawyer, Nov. 24, 1998, at 6 (cautioning English firms about potential liability for incorrect legal advice online).

[257] *Supra* note 247.

[258] *Id.*

pathetic.[259] More broadly, the terms "expert" or "highly qualified" may also violate local ethics standards.[260] Consequently, adjectives should not be used in any firm or attorney profile on the Internet unless the targeted jurisdiction articulates the threshold for misleading descriptions.

Attorneys must also use caution in selecting domain names that conform to the conduct standards. The name *www.thebestlawyers.com*, for example, would invite trouble, compared with *www.johnsmithesq.com*. Metatags for legal web sites should also fall within the realm of ethics standards and warrant the same degree of restraint as does the content of the web site.

[b] Multistate Compliance

Complying with the ethical rules of multiple states is one of the more challenging aspects of maintaining an attorney's web presence.[261] The web sites of all firms and individual practitioners must comply with the ethics rules of the states in which the attorney(s) are licensed. Larger firms should endeavor to have their web sites conform to the ethical requirements of every state. Pennsylvania, for example, requires a disclosure of geographic location and principal place of business.[262] Common sense, however, would dictate that any legal web site would contain at least as much information as does the firm or attorney's business card, in addition to biographical and licensing information. The local bar association and many other online resources can be helpful in monitoring ethics opinions.[263]

---

[259] *Id.*

[260] *Id.*

[261] *See* Hornsby, *supra* note 249 (listing strategies for contending with online multistate ethical compliance).

[262] *See* Masters, *supra* note 246 (comparing advertising restrictions of different states).

[263] ABA/BNA Lawyers' Manual on Professional Conduct (visited May 15, 2000), http://www.bna.com/prodhome/bus/mopc.html.

   ABA Center for Professional Responsibility (visited May 15, 2000), http://www.abanet.org/cpr/home.html.

   American Legal Ethics Library (visited May 15, 2000), http://www.law.cornell.edu/ethics.

   Law Journal Extra—Professional Responsibility (visited Sept. 16, 1999), http://www.ljxextra.com/practice/professionalresponsibility/index.html.

   LegalEthics.com (visited May 15, 2000), http://www.legalethics.com/states.

   Legal Ethical Opinion Database (visited May 15, 2000), http://www.mwbb.com/leo/leo.htm.

   Massachusetts Ethics Rules (visited May 15, 2000), http://www.massbar.org/rules/contents.html.

   Massachusetts Ethics Opinions (visited May 15, 2000), http://www.state.ma.us/obcbbo.

   NetEthics (visited May 15, 2000), http://www.computerbar.org/netethic/netnav.htm.

   State Legal Advertising Restrictions (visited May 15, 2000), http://www.wld.com/direct/restrict.htm.

[c]   Disclaimers

A lawyer's web site should have a clear disclaimer that lets visitors know that no attorney-client relationship will exist before a specific agreement is signed.[264] An attorney who lacks the resources to ensure compliance with regulations in every state should post a disclaimer stating that the site only complies with the legal advertising regulations of their licensing states.[265] Additionally, the disclaimer may clearly state that the web site is not intended as an advertisement or solicitation in any state other than the state in which the attorney is admitted.[266] Online legal activities to states in which an attorney is not licensed will be construed as the unauthorized practice of law.[267]

[d]   E-Mail Solicitation

E-mail advertising by lawyers is generally viewed with distaste and is not a recommended method of gaining new clients. As the section of this chapter on general e-mail advertising suggested, restrictions are growing against e-mailing anyone who did not request to be on an e-mail list. While the Supreme Court has held that attorneys can use direct mail to advertise to those in need of legal services, attorneys should exercise restraint in using e-mail.[268] A more recent case upheld a thirty-day waiting period before advertising to potential clients in personal injury or wrongful death cases.[269] Attorneys considering e-mailing prospective clients should check the rules of their jurisdiction.

[e]   Chat Rooms

Interactive chat rooms and web sites can help marketers lure customers. An auto company, for example, might host a chat room about certain of its new models. Such web sites and chat rooms open up several issues of concern for the FTC, including wrongful content, false and deceptive advertising, improper employee postings, and labor law issues.[270]

---

[264] Jay G. Foonberg, How to Start and Build a Law Practice, 143 (1999).

[265] *Id.*

[266] Cf. Drew L. Kershen, Professional Legal Organizations on the Internet: Web Sites and Ethics (visited May 25, 1999), http://www.legalethics.com/articles/kershen.html (providing model disclaimers for attorneys advertising on the Internet through a professional legal organization).

[267] Masters, *supra* note 246.

[268] Shapero v. Kentucky Bar Association, 486 U.S. 466 (1988).

[269] The Florida Bar v. Went For It, Inc., 115 S. Ct. 2371 (1995).

[270] Peggy Miller, Creative Marketing and the Future of the Electronic Commerce, 520 PLI/Pat 607-611 (1998).

Chat room communications should be approached very cautiously, if at all, as a way for lawyers to generate new business. Utah already prohibits client development through chat rooms, and other states may adopt the same opinion.[271] Any chat room discussion should contain a disclaimer that no attorney-client relationship exists and that the practice is limited to jurisdictions in which the attorney is licensed. Attorneys should limit their marketing efforts to other Internet channels.

---

[271] *See* ABA Professional Conduct on the Internet, White Paper, July 1998 (visited May 26, 1999), http://www.abanet.org/legalserv/advertising.html (comparing ethics rules for emerging technologies).

INTERNET SECURITY

§ 3.01   OVERVIEW

Information security is critically important to protect the intellectual property and other intangible assets of an e-business.[1] Because the Internet has the potential to compromise mission-critical information, such as databases, customer lists, and other inside information, network security is a critical area for any dot-com company.

This chapter reviews the information security measures that a networked company must adopt to protect its fuel supply of information. The concepts and methods of information security are illustrated by references to Suffolk Personal Computers (SPC), our hypothetical e-business. Because SPC has product divisions in a networked world, its information security is especially difficult to implement. The Internet's interconnected nature offers SPC great potential benefits, but it also poses great dangers. SPC has a duty to provide security capable of protecting its trade secrets, proprietary and confidential information, customer lists, and personal data about its employees and customers. SPC realizes that the Internet and its virtual store require it to make a fundamental change in its business model.

Section 3.02 of this chapter introduces the basic principles underlying internetworking technologies, explores the various components of network security, and assesses information security technologies. Client and server computers, mass-market security products, owner-distributed security products, customized security, and the basics of the Internet security audit are explained. Information security technologies introduced include firewalls, passwords, biometrics security devices, encryption, virtual private networks, and customized security products.

Section 3.03 examines the radius of the risks to information security. Threats can come from hackers, computer criminals, viruses, impostors, or information thieves; each is examined and relevant suggestions made for reducing the radius of that risk. Section 3.04 examines the elements of a comprehensive information security program. The evolving information security law for common law negligence, professional malpractice, product liability, sales warranties, and other legal issues are explored in Section 3.05.

How much security is enough? Network security begins with implementation of commercially reasonable practices and state-of-the art technologies.

---

[1] This chapter updates themes found in Michael Rustad and Lori Eisenschmidt, The Commercial Law of Internet Security, 10 High Tech. L.J. 213 (1995).

§ 3.02   AUDITING INTERNET SECURITY TECHNOLOGIES

[A]   Assessing Internet Security Technologies

[1]   Network Security

Information security differs from home security in two important respects. Home security is primarily designed to prevent the theft of *tangible* personal property, such as jewelry, electronics, computers, and other valuables. In contrast, network security addresses the theft of *intangibles*, such as software, customer lists, and intellectual property. An information heist may occur without leaving a trace, unlike most burglaries of a home or business. Uncovering digital fingerprints will require the efforts of computer forensic experts.

Consumers without adequate security protection for their computers leave their systems vulnerable to attack. If a user leaves a "home computer running Apple's Mac OS or Windows 95 or 98 without the maker's latest security updates or additional security software, it is the closest thing to an unlocked door they are likely to find."[2]

Companies without adequate security are vulnerable to attacks by hackers that can threaten to compromise information owned by third parties. For SPC, inadequate security threatens the integrity of its trade secrets, which, by definition, require reasonable security measures. Failure to implement reasonable security also exposes SPC to the possibility of lawsuits by third parties whose data, confidential information, or personal data is stolen or compromised by hackers.

Even though software may travel on physical disks or CD-ROMs, it is the intangible collection of magnetically fixed electronic impulses and optically stored data that constitutes the value of digital information. Network security must, therefore, protect magnetic data from unwanted intrusion and theft. If this were not the case, security for computers would be limited to prevention of physical harm and theft, much like security for computer hardware. Precautions and safeguards correlate directly with the level of risk. The greater the danger, the greater the burden of precaution.

Just as products, devices, and methods (that is, steel doors, locks, bars, security monitors, and guards) have been developed against unwanted physical intrusion, a growing information security industry has arisen to deter electronic invasions of computer systems. Unlike a home burglar, a cybercriminal does not need physical access to a computer to accomplish an unauthorized entry; electronic access is sufficient. Intrusion-detection systems are emerging as a critical tool for bridging the gap between the Internet and internal networks.[3] Computer crime statutes punish and deter intrusions even if computer files are not altered,

---

[2] Ian Austen, High-Speed Lines Leave Door Ajar for Hackers, N.Y. Times, July 8, 1999.

[3] Security Tools and Technology for Locking Up Agency Networks, Federal Computer Week (visited Dec. 13, 1999), http://www.fcw.com/ref/hottopics/security.htm.

corrupted, or otherwise damaged. Another difference between home security and network security has to do with the interconnectivity of the Internet and of computer networks in general.

Remote computers connect with one another via the Internet by transmitting packets of data over wires, modems and telephone lines, optical fibers, and radio waves. Once computers are connected to the Internet, their precious intangible assets of information and stored data become vulnerable. The first step in preventive law for information security is to survey the basic principles of networking technologies. The probability of an intrusion depends on the type of computer hardware used, the degree of connectivity to external networks, the number and type of security devices in use, and the nature of the users (that is, nonprofit educational institution, governmental entity, or Fortune 500 company).

[a]   Local Area Networks

A network is a broad term referring in the information technology context to computers and communications equipment connected so that users may share data, programs, and peripheral devices. A local area network (LAN) is a specific kind of network that connects computers, software, and communication channels within a limited or local area. As its name suggests, a LAN is a local, delineated network, as opposed to the Internet's global network.

SPC may find it cost-effective to have a LAN, which allows employees to share data, programs, and peripheral devices. A LAN does not pose a risk from external hackers, because it has no connection to the Internet, being a stand-alone internal network. A LAN can be hacked into remotely, however, by or from any other computer connected to or able to connect to the LAN, if it is connected to other networks or to the Internet. This is the essence of the security threat known as remote intrusion. The LAN, without Internet connectivity, simply limits physical access to SPC's server to trusted personnel, thus preventing in-house security threats.

LAN operating systems are "secure" or "insecure," depending on how hardware or software is configured. A company that complies with best industry practices for network security is unlikely to be held liable if a hacker gains entry.

A properly secured LAN network permits work groups to "send memos, letters, and documents in electronic form to other users,"[4] allowing an efficient use of shared software, fax machines, storage devices, and other communications resources.[5] A server refers broadly to any device that offers a service to network users. The LAN client/server architecture employs high-speed, high-capacity workstations, called servers, to manage the activities of the network and to distribute data and programs as requested by client desktop computers.[6]

---

[4] *Id.*

[5] *Id.*

[6] *Id.*, at 561.

An *intranet* is a LAN that connects company computers in an internal network and permits users to share programs, data files, and electronic- or e-mail. The intranet also permits a company to share printers, plotters, imaging devices, hard disks, or other data transfer technologies and storage devices. In effect, a LAN is a miniature version of the Internet, or a mini-Infobahn, with one of its computers designated as the resource manager or server.

Extranets permit trusted outsiders to connect to company computers. The Department of Defense, for example, permits potential bidders, suppliers, and vendors to learn the details of requests for proposal through its extranet.

The way users connect to the LAN depends on physical location. Desktop computers connect to the corporate Intranet using network interface cards and "network police." Access is also dependent on recognition of the hardware address of the network card[7] and the user's log-on account and password, and it is screened by the use of firewalls.[8] A personal computer at home may be connected to an ISP server and other servers on the Internet through a telephone or cable connection. The ISP's computers function as servers, providing news and mail services as well as routing data between the client computer and the rest of the Internet.

Every metropolitan city in the United States has at least one ISP with dial-up services. In the Boston metropolitan area, for example, Internet connectivity services are available from a number of ISPs, including, to name just a few, North Shore Access, of Lynn; Novalink, of Westborough; The Internet Access Company, of Bedford; and the Complete Internet Access Company, of Cambridge. In recent years, America Online, CompuServe, cable companies, and other commercial services have offered Internet access for their customers, some over digital subscriber lines (DSL), which provide users with a fast, constant link to the Internet. DSL

---

[7] Most systems will only log the network address of a client. An attacker may easily spoof the network address by binding a legitimate address to their network card or interface. Computers connected to a LAN or intranet in a corporate environment will use a Network Interface Card (NIC). Each NIC will have a unique Media Access Controller number "stamped" into the firmware. Auditing the MAC address will require attackers wishing to spoof a network administrator to have access to the physical system for the MAC address.

[8] "Although firewalls are usually placed between a network and the outside untrusted network, in large companies or organizations, firewalls are often used to create different subnets of the network, often called an Intranet. Intranet firewalls are intended to isolate a particular subnet from the overall corporate network. . . . The decision to use an Intranet firewall is generally based on the need to make certain information available to some but not all internal users, or to provide a high degree of accountability for the access and use of confidential or sensitive information." National Institute of Standards Technology, Internet Firewall Policy, Internet Security Policy (Washington, D.C.: NIST, 1999): A Technical Guide (Dec. 14, 1999), http://csrc.nist.gov/isptg/html/ISPTG-6.html.

lines are increasingly targets of hackers using probing, scanning, and sniffing techniques.[9]

Popular wisdom has it that a pure client computer or client computer network is "bullet-proof" and invulnerable to hackers. An intermediary—the ISP server computer—shields it. Even if the ISP server is compromised, the client computer is still safe, this reasoning goes, because it lacks the communications protocols necessary to enable the hacker to establish a connection with it. Yet, if the client computer connects to the ISP computer via a Serial Line Internet Protocol (SLIP) or Point to Point Protocol (PPP) connection, it *is* vulnerable—because it is connected to the Internet. This vulnerability, however, does not arise unless the client computer itself runs programs downloaded from the Internet or attempts to act as a server. A client can act like a server by running programs referred to in computer jargon as a daemon.[10] These daemons run in the background without user interaction, waiting to respond to packets of data received over a network.

The greatest threat to the security of client computers is not the Internet hacker, but rather the enemy within, the in-house hacker. Insiders who have otherwise nominal access privileges can invade the computer system by "shoulder surfing,"[11] intercepting the passwords of individuals with higher-level clearance or access to additional network resources. Screen-locking programs are critical for reducing the risk of shoulder surfing.

In this context, PC and Mac-based LANs are more vulnerable to Internet security attacks than are mainframe computers: Mainframe computer systems have traditionally had a department of Management Information Systems (MIS) dedicated to backups and security; no such well-established practices were institutionalized in the LAN environment.[12] Most large corporate network and MIS groups, however, are now concerned with security and with providing backups for a company's servers. In order to reduce maintenance costs, some corporations have been concentrating their server resources into fewer, more powerful computers in a single location, which is reminiscent of the mainframe-computing environment.

---

[9] *Supra* note 2.

[10] Windows NT refers to daemons as services or server processes. The term *server process* may be more familiar to devotees of the Microsoft operating systems. In mythology, a *daemon*, according to Webster's, was "an attendant power or spirit." *Daemons* can be confused with *demons*, which has a different but similar meaning. The New Hacker's Dictionary describes a *daemon* as a program that runs by itself directly under the operating system; a *demon*, however, is part of a larger application program. What Is . . . a Daemon (A Definition) (visited Sept. 19, 1999), http://www.whatis.com/daemon.htm(quoting Eric S. Raymond, The New Hacker Dictionary).

[11] Looking over another person's shoulder, or "shoulder surfing" is a means of gaining credit card numbers as well as passwords.

[12] Network Help Desk, Network World, Nov. 21, 1994, at 2.

[b]   Storage Area Networks

In the late 1990s, network storage evolved as a method of managing large storage requirements on the LAN, versus the traditional host-connected storage systems.[13] This method of data storage evolved into what is generally known as the SAN. The Storage Area Network, or SAN, is a "high-speed channel storage network relying on hubs, switches and gateways."[14] The SAN adds a new dimension to information security as well as to the capacity for a common storage-sized system.[15] The online company cannot afford to be without a backup in the event that the company's computer systems fail because of natural disasters, viruses, or computer crimes.[16] Three decades ago, companies stored data files on magnetic disks and tapes, which were connected to mainframe computers. Mass storage devices evolved in the mid-1980s and were used primarily by companies with large online databases.[17] Computer systems were traditionally backed up by online disk and tape library systems.

An off-line traditional business, let alone a web-based business, cannot afford to be without a backup for data and storage accessibility. The SAN permits a company to recover from a disaster that threatens mission-critical databases. IBM, for example, has a storage hub that supports data speeds as high as 100 MBps. IBM's storage server "starts with 18 [gigabytes] of storage capacity and can handle as much as 1 terabyte using six expandable storage units."[18]

The median cost for a single network outage is "$140,000 in the retail industry and over $450,000 in the securities sector."[19] Backups are thus critical to any information security policy. The traditional means of backing up company data was to add tape drives to traditional servers. One problem with traditional host-attached storage was that when something went wrong with the server, the storage also became inaccessible.[20] Today's storage-area networks are chiefly based upon

---

[13] David Doering, Up the SAN BOX, E-media Professional, July 1999, at 54.

[14] *Id.*

[15] IBM Enterprises Storage Server is an example of a SAN product developed in the late 1990s for high capacity, reliable off-site storage.

[16] "To support recovery after failure or natural disaster, a firewall like any other network host has to have some policy defining system backup. Data files as well as system configuration files need to have some backup plan in case of firewall failure." Firewall Failure, Internet Security Policy (Washington, D.C.: NIST, 1999): A Technical Guide (visited Dec. 14, 1999), http://www.csrc.nist.gov/isptg/html/ISPTG-6.html.

[17] Larry Long, Introduction to Computers and Information Processing 147 (1984).

[18] Nancy Weil, IBM Details Storage Area Network Initiative, InfoWorld Electric (Feb. 17, 1999) (visited Aug. 2, 2000) http://www.infoworld.com/cgi-bin/displayStory.pl?990217.ecibm-san.htm.

[19] SAN Summit '99 (visited Aug. 2, 2000), http://www.creative-expos.com/san.html.

[20] *Id.*, at 52.

"fibre channel."[21] Fibre channel, approved by an American National Standards Institute (ANSI), enables gigabits/sec connectivity.[22]

A SAN is a centrally managed repository or centrally managed networked pool[23] that creates a dedicated storage network, versus a multiple application storage system.[24] Compaq, EMC, IBM, StorageTek, and Sun are a few of the major storage vendors.[25] A company like SPC needs to keep its virtual store open 24 hours a day, 7 days a week. A denial of service attack could result in significant lost revenues. SPC needs to have available a backup of its web-based information should its site be compromised. SPC needs to consider setting up a dedicated network to offload storage traffic.[26] SPC may save money now by replacing departmental backup with a large-scale centralized storage model.[27]

[2]   Routers/Gateways and Bridges

Routers and bridges transmit information from one network area to another. A gateway is the network point that acts as an entrance to another network. A switch is a "network device" that selects how data gets to the next destination. These devices may be used to transmit data from the Internet to LAN destinations and vice versa. When SPC evolves into a full-grown e-business, it may connect many LANs together in a Wide Area Network (WAN). The WAN will utilize routers to transmit data between LANs.

Gateway nodes are traffic cops for a company's computer network and the Internet.[28] A gateway may also be used if the LAN does not recognize Internet protocols such as the Transmission Control Protocol/Internet Protocol (TCP/IP).[29] An IP switch using this protocol is based upon packet switching. Packet switches divide data messages into bytes.

Gateways convert diverse and disparate network protocols to a single protocol compatible with its network system. This can be done using either a router or

---

[21] Brian Robinson, Is Fibre Channel Losing SAN Dominance? Fed. Comp. Wk. (Dec. 6, 1999) (visited Dec. 13, 1999), http://www.fcw.com/pubs/fcw/1999/1206/fcw-specfibre-12-06-99.html.

[22] *Id.*

[23] Thomas Hughes, Special Report: Storage Area Networks: Shifting SANs, Global Tech. Bus.31 (June 1999).

[24] *Id.*

[25] *Id.*

[26] Robinson, *supra* note 21.

[27] *Id.*, at 33.

[28] Whatis.Com, Definitions (visited March 2, 2000), http://whatis.com/gateway.htm.

[29] Most modern Network Operating Systems (NOS) and mainframe hosts now support TCP/IP. Previously, the Network administrator would have to connect mainframe systems that used the System Network Architecture (SNA) and proprietary LAN protocols, such as Novell's IPX/SPX protocols.

a bridge. Additional protocols can be added to allow error detection and connections for bookkeeping functions. Routers are necessary if companies are to directly access the Internet. Routers/gateways filter messages destined for recipients outside the local network and receive messages from remote networks to be delivered locally on the LAN. Just as a group of computers in an office can be linked together to share files and e-mail through a LAN, so can they be networked on a worldwide scale.

SPC, which is headquartered in Massachusetts, may link to computers located in offices around the world through secure Internet connections. Any company using a router or gateway to send and receive messages from the Internet is potentially vulnerable, since the router is a single, obvious access point into the corporate network. If SPC's systems administrator does not take proper security precautions, the router/gateway may become a vulnerable link in a computer network. SPC's security policy should state who has responsibility for managing the company's computer system.[30]

[3] Operating Systems

An operating system (OS) is the systems software designed to operate many of the essential processes of the computer. One of the original PC operating systems was the Disk Operating System, or DOS, an operating system sold by Microsoft (MS-DOS), IBM (PC-DOS), and Digital Research (DR-DOS).[31] IBM's PC-DOS "was developed by Microsoft at IBM's behest."[32] The DOS operating systems were character-based: Users would interact with the system by typing commands to a command interpreter. Most modern operating systems include a graphical user interface (GUI), which permits users to interact with the computer through pictorial metaphors, known as *icons*.

Today's most widely used PC operating system is Microsoft's Windows. Microsoft Windows contains operating system functions, a graphical user interface, and network connectivity capability.

---

[30] The Chief Information Security Officer may also designate persons responsible for managing firewalls. "Each firewall administrator shall provide their home phone number, pager number, cellular phone number and other numbers or codes in which they can be contacted when support is required." NIST, Firewall Administration, Internet Security Policy (Washington, D.C.: NIST, 1999): A Technical Guide (Dec. 14, 1999), http://csrc.nist.gov/isptg/html/ISPTG-6.html.

[31] DOS and its variants were born from a clone of Digital Research's CP/M written by hacker Tim Patterson of Seattle Computer Products. MS-DOS Jargon Dictionary, DOS (visited September 19,1999), http://www.netmeg.net/jargon/terms/m/ms-dos.html. The original name for the product was QDOS for Quick and Dirty Operating System. *Id.* A rather interesting history exists surrounding IBM's choice of DOS over CP/M for their PC line of products. It is well documented in the PBS Special, "Triumph of the Nerds." The full transcript is available at http://www.pbs.org/nerds/transcript.html.

[32] Nat Gertler, Computers Illustrated 204 (1994).

Security on the Internet is inseparable from the security of the computers that access and/or serve the Internet. Operating systems frequently contain security "soft spots," which can be exploited by cybercriminals. At the operating system level, security can be breached on several fronts.

The majority of the computers connecting through the Internet use UNIX-based or compatible standardized operating systems. UNIX-based operating systems were not originally designed with security in mind; they contain scores of well-known security loopholes. Hackers exploit these security soft spots to infiltrate the OS. UNIX-based operating systems do not have a monopoly on hacker interest, however; Windows NT based servers are also a frequent target of hacker attacks. SPC's primary vulnerability lies in its ISP server's OS.

Finding the front door secured, hackers use the back door to break into Internet sites. The back door in the send-mail feature, for example, has been used to break into UNIX operating systems. A hacker may be able to exploit these loopholes to access and copy a list of the server's accounts (that is, the computers and companies that utilize that ISP to access the Internet); browse e-mail stored on the computer for some or all of the accounts; or disclose or damage ISP data files. In cases of severe breach, the hacker can actually disrupt or halt the operation of the server's programs and may be able to extend this destructiveness to other computers by introducing a malicious routine, such as a computer virus or worm.

Since UNIX-based operating systems have numerous inherent security flaws, the industry has filled the gaps with informal trade usages. Some of the widely used industry practices include monitoring for hacker programs, worms, and viruses; blocking repetitive failed access attempts; maintaining adequate log-in and audit trail records; and trolling for suspicious activities or possible trouble. Now that extensive means are available to overcome the original security loopholes, operating system security is a "reasonable" proposition.[33] SPC has a duty to keep informed about ways to take prompt remedial measures once a security hole is found.

The federal government certifies agencies' operating systems as secure if they meet the federal standards for C2 security classification.[34] Certified C2 systems include NetWare 4.x, Windows NT Server, Trusted Network Computing Environment, and Cordant's Assure.[35] Companies that contract or partner with federal agencies may be required to comply with C2 certification as a condition of

---

[33] The other main tenets of network security—survivability and availability—are not addressed in this chapter. *Survivability* refers to the ability to maintain or restore hardware, software, and data integrity in the event of an electronic or natural disaster. *Availability* refers to the consistency and continuity of network functioning.

[34] Cf. Roger Addelson, Making Your Customer's Network Secure, Stacks: The Network Journal, Dec. 1994, at 27.

[35] *Id.*

doing business. At a minimum, SPC will need to enact network security systems that comply with reasonable industry standards. If it intends to register with the Defense Department's online procurement system, for example, it will need to be certified as C2 compliant.

Operating systems, such as Digital Equipment Corporation's Open VMS/VAX 6.0 and Security Enhanced VAX/VMS, have been evaluated by the Department of Defense's National Computer Security Center (NCSC) and have been rated as meeting or exceeding security specifications for C2[36] security classification.[37] These O/S systems, however, comprise only a small part of the backbone of the Internet.

Individual workstation security is also related to LAN security because workstations can be used as unauthorized ports of entry. Disk, screen, and keyboard locking mechanisms can be used to prevent unauthorized access when employees have stepped away from their computers. It is also critical that laptops be equipped with functionally equivalent locking mechanisms to protect the business traveler. In addition, certain programs prevent unauthorized alteration of configuration and startup files.[38] Programs may automatically notify SysAdmins of

---

[36] The D to A1 rating system was designed by the NCSC, a division of the National Security Agency (NSA), based on a collection of 36 color-coded books known as the "Rainbow Series" (including the widely-referenced "Orange Book"). Under the 1987 Computer Security Act, C2 ("Controlled Access Protection") is the minimum rating which federal agencies must achieve to protect sensitive but unclassified information. All hardware and software on the systems, including security features, must periodically be tested to ensure proper functioning. Files can be shared, but file access must be controlled, and only authorized personnel may assign user rights. User identification and authentication is required, data must be protected from unauthorized users, and the computer system must protect itself from outside tampering. Accountability is stressed, requiring a detailed audit trail and logging. *See* Susan Biagi, How the Government Looks at Security, Stacks: Network J., Dec. 1994, at 37. The NSA has responsibility for classified national security issues, while the National Institute of Standards and Technology is responsible for nonclassified information. The guidelines are two of only a few published standards on computer system security, and commercial-sector standards are derived therefrom. *Id.*

[37] Bob Melford, "Six-O" for Security and Things that Take Six Years, Digital News & Rev., Sept. 27, 1993, at 11.

[38] Important configuration files for PC-based systems are CONFIG.SYS and AUTOEXEC.BAT. "Most large programs now come with installation programs (usually called INSTALL.BAT or SETUP.EXE or something similar) that automatically set up their own directories on your hard disks, copy the files, etc. Many of these will alter your AUTOEXEC.BAT and CONFIG.SYS files without you knowing about it." Gertler, *supra* note 56. AUTOEXEC.BAT is "a batch file program that is run by DOS at startup. *Id.*, at 72. Batch files "are programs (easily changed by the user) which are interpreted by the operating system. Generally they're made up mostly of commands just like you would type at the DOS prompt. When you load MS-DOS, it automatically looks for the batch program AUTOEXEC.BAT, and runs that." *Id.*, at 73. Newer operating systems may have a variety of configuration files that could be targeted by virus makers. The Back Orifice Trojan virus, for example, developed by the Cult of the Dead Cow, attached itself to the Windows registry, enabling it to restart each time the computer was rebooted.

any attempts to change program initiation (that is, authorization specification) files. Finally, armoring products prevent either computer booting through the floppy disk drive, where password security could be bypassed, or resetting computer clocks to make former passwords or SuperUser access retroactive.[39] Fischer International Systems Corp. markets a suite of products that perform these and other protective functions.[40] Many companies hire information security consultants who are expert in pricing security products and who may also provide negotiating tips.

Client computers and LANs that have modems are also vulnerable to external intrusion from outside the local network. The modem "acts as an interface between your computer and a phone line."[41] Computers communicate with other computers via telephone lines, with the help of modems or dedicated communication equipment.[42] A common, and effective, method of preventing intrusions employs a "call-back" protocol. An authorized user who wishes to dial in to an office computer first dials up the computer via its modem. The computer, programmed to allow remote use from only certain, preauthorized phone numbers, receives the call-in and immediately terminates the connection; it then checks the number from which the call came against its list of authorized numbers and calls the user's computer back if the number is found to be an authorized one. While effective, this procedure may be problematic for the telecommuting employee who may dial in from a variety of different client sites or hotel telephones.

When the connection is reestablished, the user must log in and successfully complete the rest of the user identification and authentication challenges in order to initiate the remote session with the computer.[43] Security products exist that permit centralized security administration, user management, and access controls to LANs. One company has developed software agents installed on protected application servers "designed to create the authenticated, secure connection from the desktop to the application server."[44] Organizations will frequently hire security consultants that provide turnkey solutions for protecting a LAN as well as extranet and intranet applications. An intranet minimally has four characteristics: (1) e-mail capability; (2) online publishing; (3) online searching; and (4) distributed applications.[45]

---

[39] *See* Horace Labdie, Digital Crime Watch: Developing an Effective Security System, Comp. Shopper, Mar. 1994, at 594.

[40] *Id.*

[41] Gertler, *supra* note 32.

[42] *Id.*, at 227.

[43] This concept *authentication* refers to the identity of a computer user. Authentication, for example, is required before a user can access a company computer.

[44] Security Dynamics and RSA Unveil Enterprise Application Security Strategy, RSA Data Security Conference, San Jose, California, Jan. 18, 1999 (visited on Feb. 5, 1999), http//www.rsa.com/pressbox/html/990118-1.html.

[45] Nabil R. Adams, Electronic Commerce: Technical, Business & Legal Issues 123 (1999).

[4] Firewalls

Firewalls authenticate data and identify users, while "hiding information like system names, network topology, network device types, and internal user ID's from the Internet."[46] The purpose of a firewall is to prevent intruders from accessing computers. Router-based firewalls do not require user identifications or user authentication, whereas host-based firewalls provide for different kinds of authentication such as (1) usernames and passwords, (2) one-time passwords, and (3) digital certificates.[47] Organizations should design the architecture of their firewalls to match their risk profile.[48] SPC will install firewalls as gatekeepers between its computers and the Internet, which will serve to block unwanted traffic, hide vulnerable computer systems, and log traffic to and from the web site. SPC may configure its firewalls using a number of different architectures and various levels of security, choosing among three basic types of firewalls: (1) packet filters; (2) proxy servers; and (3) stateful inspection.[49]

[a] *Packet Filters*

The File Transfer Protocol (FTP) was developed to move information by breaking files into packets "and made sure that each packet arrives with its data intact."[50] Firewalls create a shell of protection between a computer network and possible intruders. Although they are commonly used to restrict information from leaving or entering a company's computer or LAN via a modem, firewalls are increasingly being designed and integrated into routers/gateways in order to regulate the flow of information between a LAN and the Internet. Firewalls are increasingly being designed to perform packet filtering, for example. Firewalls may be conceptualized as part of system-wide computer policy used in conjunction with password protection, data encryption, and workstation security or biometrics security devices.

The firewall, typically housed on the router, functions by filtering all the electronic data packets sent to it from the LAN and the outside connection. Routers attached directly to the Internet employ "packet filters," which are essentially rule-based programs that instruct a router to accept only certain types of

---

[46] NIST Special Publication 800-10, Keeping Your Site Comfortably Secure: An Introduction to Internet Firewalls (visited Dec. 14, 1999), http://www.csrc.nist.gov.

[47] NIST, Internet Firewall Policy Internet Security Policy (Washington, D.C.: NIST, 1999): A Technical Guide (visited Dec. 14, 1999), http://csrc.nist.gov/isptg/html/ISPTG-6.html.

[48] *Id.*, at Firewall Architecture.

[49] Brian Robinson, Special Report on Security: Firewalls: The First Line of Defense, Fed. Comp. Wk., March 29, 1999.

[50] *Id.*, at 182.

traffic from specified network addresses.[51] The firewall permits only verified electronic data packets to be passed on by its packet filter. The firewall must be properly configured to screen electronic data packets; for example, a firewall must be configured to accept and process only e-mail type communications data-packets and to accept mail for only a particular set of addresses. In such a case, an intruder attempting to initiate a file-transfer request would be thwarted, as the firewall would detect the unauthorized communications protocol and reject it. In fact, without the proper server program on the host computer, the computer would have no mechanism for responding to such a request.

Packet filters use Internet Protocol (IP)[52] addresses or other identifiers to control information in the network. Access is granted or denied based on source address, destination address, or port. Packet filters may block designated sites or IP addresses. The security risks inherent in packet filtering include: (1) IP or DNS address spoofing; (2) attacks with direct access to any host after getting past the firewall; (3) lack of strong user authentication; and (4) weak or nonexistent logging capability.[53]

[b] Proxy Server or Application Gateway

The proxy server, or application gateway, runs on the firewall. One advantage of application gateways is that they perform user authentication and logging. Application gateways are strongly recommended for medium to high-risk sites such as the military.[54] The proxy acts as an intermediary point between user programs, application programs, and Internet content. Specific proxies check for security information.[55] The firewall can be configured "as the only host address that is visible to the outside network, requiring all connections to and from the internal network to go through the firewall."[56]

[c] Hybrid Firewalls

Hybrid or complex gateways combine different types of firewalls and implement them in series to enhance security.[57] The National Institute of Standards and Technology (NIST) describes the hybrid gateway as the best solution for a high-risk environment.[58]

---

[51] Ted Doty, The Whole Truth About Network Security, Data Comm., Nov. 1994, at 150.

[52] For more on Internet Protocols, see section 1.04[E].

[53] Internet Firewall Policy, Internet Security Policy (Washington, D.C.: NIST, 1999): A Technical Guide (visited Dec. 14, 1999), http://csrc.nist.gov/isptg/html/ISPTG-6.html.

[54] Id.

[55] Id.

[56] Id.

[57] Id.

[58] Id.

[d]   Special Problems with Firewalls

Firewall architecture is based on variables such as desired level of security, cost of installation, and the number of network interfaces.[59] A multi-home host is defined as a host "that has more than one network interface, with each interface connected to logically and physically separate network segments."[60] A dual-homed host, for example, has two network interface cards (NICs).[61] With a dual-homed host, the firewall "must always act as an intermediary."[62] If the dual-homed firewall allows "traffic coming in from the untrusted network to be directly routed to the trusted network," the firewall is circumvented, and the intruder will gain access to the system.[63] Firewalls may also employ a firewall architecture that uses a "bastion host to which all outside hosts connect, rather than allow direct connection to other, less secure internal hosts."[64] The bastion host is also sometimes called a screened host.

[e]   Firewall Administrators

The firewall is the chief means of information security. Accordingly, it requires well-trained firewall administrators, appointed by the online company's chief information officer. The firewall administrator needs the following qualifications:

1. understanding of network concepts such as TCP IP protocol;
2. understanding of LAN administration;
3. hands-on experience configuring and designing firewalls; and
4. training in network security.[65]

The firewall administrator needs to ensure that "operational procedures for a firewall and its configurable parameters be well documented, updated, and kept in a safe and secure place"[66] and must provide for physical firewall security, handle firewall incident reporting, upgrade the firewall, and revise or update the firewall policy.[67] The administrator of the firewall is also responsible for logging traffic on the firewall's audit trail logs.[68]

---

[59] *Id.*

[60] "Multi-homed Host," *Id.*

[61] *Id.*

[62] *Id.*

[63] *Id.*

[64] *Id.*

[65] These guidelines are drawn from Qualification of the Firewall Administrator, Internet Security Policy (Washington, D.C.: NIST, 1999): A Technical Guide (visited Dec. 14, 1999), http://csrc.nist.gov/isptg/html/ISPTG-6.html.

[66] *Id.*

[67] *Id.*

[68] *Id.*

[5] Passwords

Firewalls are only secure as long as strong authentication systems, such as passwords, are used to control access. Subject-oriented security generally permits users to gain access or permission to access a computer system based on passwords.[69] Remote access over the Internet, for example, requires "strong authentication such as one-time passwords."[70] Passwords were one of the earliest developed security devices, having first evolved in the mainframe-computing environment. Windows 98, for example, requires a network password for Microsoft Networking. Passwords are frequently easy to crack because many people choose passwords easy for hackers to guess, such as their own first names. Windows 98 for Dummies recommends keeping "your password short and sweet: the name of your favorite vegetable, for example, or the brand of your dental floss."[71] It is estimated that more than half of the passwords in use are the first names of spouses or children, dates such as birthdays and anniversaries, or the names of popular culture "super-heroes."[72] Some companies routinely run a program, such as Cracker, to detect easy-to-break passwords. Systems administrators may install electronic agents that force e-mail computer users to change their cracked password.

In general, the shorter the password, the faster it will be cracked. Hacker dictionary programs operate by trying every word in the dictionary (including variant spellings of words and names) until a password match is found. Given the comprehensiveness of these dictionary programs and the high speed of today's computers, most common passwords can be cracked within a few minutes or less. If the vulnerable password is on a router/gateway computer, then the weak password risks the integrity of information assets the equivalent of corporate crown jewels. A company's security system is vulnerable not only from unauthorized company employees, but from outside Internet hackers as well. A successful password system requires employee training and support.

Passwords are frequently subverted by a cavalier corporate attitude about their significance. Trade secrets remain trade secrets only if they are kept secret. The same may be said about passwords. A security expert illustrated poor organizational attitudes toward passwords in a demonstration in which he posed as a computer-room operator. He was able to get a telephone company switchboard operator to give him a critical, top-secret password to the company's computer,

---

[69] David M. Kroenke, Database Processing: Fundamentals, Design, and Implementation 506 (4th ed. 1992).

[70] NIST, Remote Firewall Administration, in Internet Security Policy (Washington, D.C.: NIST, 1999): A Technical Guide (visited Dec. 14, 1999) http://csrc.nist.gov/isptg/html/ISPTG-6.html.

[71] Andy Rathbone, Windows 98 for Dummies 62 (1998).

[72] Eric H Steele, Software Review: Security, 5 Comp. Couns. 39 (Aug. 1993).

thereby gaining access to the names and addresses of all of the company's customers.[73] Such socially engineered dial-in access is the result of failing to train employees in the importance of keeping passwords secret.

Socially engineered lapses of security have no technological remedy. More passwords are lost through employee carelessness than are stolen across the Internet. A successful password system thus requires full employee training and support. One expert suggests emphasizing the following principles to achieve a good password system:

- Good password management will stop most security attacks.

- Common words, such as last or first names, are bad passwords, since they are easily guessed.

- Since passwords are often stored in an encrypted state in a publicly readable file, passwords appearing in a common dictionary may be open to offline dictionary attacks.

- To create strong but still user-friendly passwords, convert an easily remembered personal saying. "Suffolk Law is A number 1," for example, would yield the password of "SLiAn1." This fanciful password is not in any dictionary and thus will be difficult to guess.[74]

The British hacker Paul Bedworth was able to enter numerous government and corporate computers because of their inadequate security. Many of these facilities were protected only by a password established by the installing engineer. A number of computers were accessible merely by typing in the simple default supplied by computer hardware or software licensors. Passwords are sometimes written down or posted in conspicuous places, such as on the computer monitor or a whiteboard above it.

Corporations must institute comprehensive programs to protect passwords. Information security consultants can recommend security programs that detect attempts to "crack" passwords and set off an alarm. Another technique is to install software that requires employees to change their passwords regularly. Increasingly effective password-protection programs are available for a moderate price. Vendors have a variety of technological solutions for password protections.

Some of the more useful solutions, however, are sociological. One expert recommends choosing "hard to guess, but easy to remember passwords [by] concatenat [ing] unrelated words: What1Now or letters of a nonsense phrase:

---

[73] Susan Watts, The BT Hacker Scandal: BT "Flouted Its Own Advice to Government," Consultants Are Fighting a Losing Battle to Persuade Companies to Protect Their Computer Systems, Network World, Feb. 13, 1995, at 37.

[74] Carl-Mitchell Smoot, Internet Security 2.8 (1999).

MhalGwhw (Mary had a little Goat with hairy wool)."[75] The use of uppercase letters and numbers is a simple technique that makes "dictionary attacks more difficult.[76]

Another simple protective measure is to use a *passphrase*, as opposed to a *password*. Another option is to use a two-factor identification, rather than a mere password. The two-factor ID method requires a user to insert a card or token belonging to the user alone and then to give the proper password. "A cryptocard is a physical token or program which: authenticates via a cryptographic exchange; each exchange is unique and cannot be guesses or snooped; eliminates the risk of password interception or eliminates the risk of password guessing."[77]

Companies need security systems to protect computers that are left unattended.[78] The best password programs assign different passwords that permit the user to access different levels of data or information, depending on their need to know. Norton Disklock 3.5 for Windows and DOS provides "password protection against unauthorized system access, selective file locking and encryption." Norton's Disklock also automatically activates a screen-saver to block access when an employee steps away from the computer for a few moments. Such a feature would be useful for the business traveler, helping to defeat snoops or business spies. Disklock also calibrates file protection for different levels of security.[79]

The Department of Defense has long used dynamic synchronized password schemes that change the password in both the host and the user token every few seconds. The DOD's classified computer system, which stores this nation's most sensitive data, is not connected to the Internet.[80] The greatest threat to the DOD is employees within the DOD having access to classified information. The DOD, however, has detected and thwarted internationally coordinated hacker attacks. The Pentagon denies that hackers have penetrated its secret networks.[81]

Another relatively new product is the software-token-based challenge-response system, which uses strong encryption to ensure the security of all transactions.[82] An example of an advanced password product is one combining

---

[75] *Id.*, at 2.12 (1999).

[76] *Id.*

[77] *Id.*, at 2.14.

[78] Symmantec, Norton Disklock 3.5 for Windows and DOS: Easy-to-use Password Security, File Locking, and Encryption (visited Feb. 5, 1999), http://www.symantec.com/region/can/eng/product/disklock/fs_dsklpc.html.

[79] *Id.* (describing how different kinds of encryption offer different levels of security; DES for maximum security and a lesser standard security).

[80] CNN, DOD Confirms Cyberattack "Something New," Mar. 6, 1999 (visited on Aug. 2, 2000), http:www.cnn.com/TECH/computing/9903/06/dod.hacker.update.idg/.

[81] *Id.*

[82] *See generally* Winn Schwartau, New Keys to Network Security, Infoworld, May 15, 1995, at 51 (reviewing a number of password security products).

two-factor identification with dynamic synchronization. The password on the synchronized card changes every 30-to-60 seconds, and thus is good only for the duration of a single log-on session. This smart card is called SecurID and is manufactured by Security Dynamics, Inc., of Cambridge, Massachusetts.

SecurID is a password authentication program, used as a unique personal identification number that restricts network access to authorized users. These programs are available in various forms, including credit card-sized hardware tokens and key fobs, as well as software tokens.[83] Each SecurID form is based upon an "algorithm that generates a one-time, pseudo-random code that changes every 60 seconds."[84] The SecurID is an all purpose network resource restricting user access to those with the "one-time Code with a PIN."[85] "The 6 digit password changes each minute and may be synchronized with a server. A user enters a 4-8 digit PIN followed by the 6 digit number displayed on the card."[86] Another smart card vendor is Enigma Logic, Inc., which produces a competing product called Safeword.[87] But each year a new generation of secure methods for authenticating user identity appears.

Even a computer armed with state-of-the-art security will not remain impregnable for long if the institution does not support training for corporate employees in how to maintain good security. No bulletproof security systems exist, however, even in the most rationally managed organization. High-tech hackers will continually find new means by which to obtain unauthorized access to computer systems. Like automobile antitheft devices, Internet security devices must continue to evolve over time. Steps must be taken so that the technological fixes stay ahead of enemies both inside and outside the organization. A future enhancement to password protection, for example, might be the use of biometrics.

SPC's security administrator will run a dictionary attack periodically, and warn users who have insecure passwords. SPC consumers will be warned to choose a password they will remember but that is not obvious.

[6]   Biometrics Systems

SPC may decide to install biometrics technology for personal authentication by retinal scanning, fingerprint identification, signature recognition, or voice recognition. Biometric security products are so sophisticated that they recognize

---

[83] Security Dynamics Technologies, Inc. Press Release, Security Dynamics Breaks the Barrier for Outsourced Network Security, Dec. 8, 1998 (visited on Feb. 5, 1999), http//www.securitydynamics.com/press/pr/pr 1998-12-15.html.

[84] *Id.*

[85] *Id.*

[86] Smoot, *supra* note 74.

[87] *See generally* Tom McCusker, Take Control of Remote Access, Network Security Measures Datamation, Apr. 1, 1994, at 62.

the unique way a user inputs his or her password or passphrase. Biometric devices are increasingly replacing passwords or ID cards to protect computer networks.[88] Electronic fingerprint-authentication technologies are available to protect networks, laptops, cell phones, and even credit cards.[89] Biometrics devices can recognize the "imprint of a human finger, offering . . . a new way to protect laptops, cell phones, and even credit cards from unauthorized use."[90] Veridicom of Santa Clara, California, for example, has patented software that "checks the imprint against a mathematical representation or template stored in a compact memory bank or computer database."[91]

Face recognition is increasingly being used in retail, financial, security, healthcare, and E-business applications[92] to thwart fraud in check cashing, theft, piracy, and counterfeiting.[93] Hand geometry can also be used to verify a person's identity.[94] Hand geometry reads an individual's hand three dimensionally computing a number of different measurements "including length, width, thickness, and surface area."[95] The scanning of the hand by the reader results in a mathematical representation that can be retrieved and compared to an exemplar.[96] Hand geometry readings may also be transferred to a computer or other media.[97] Biometrics security devices such as hand geometry are used in high security operations such as nuclear power plants.[98]

Since many biometric devices have retail costs under $200 per unit,[99] it may be economically feasible to install fingerprint readers at each desktop. For highly secure systems, SPC may combine biometrics and passphrase authentication for system access.

[7] Encryption

Cryptography is the science of secret writing, "a science that has roots stretching back hundreds, and perhaps thousands of years."[100] Encryption

---

[88] Schwartau, *supra* note 82.

[89] How to Let Your Fingers Do the Walking and Talking, 2 Business Vision for the Entrepreneurial Spirit, Magazine for Key Bank Clients (Time Inc., Mar. 1999).

[90] *Id.*

[91] *Id.*

[92] Michael Kuperstein, Biometrics, SC Magazine, Mar.1999, at 19.

[93] *Id.*, at 20.

[94] *Id.*

[95] *Id.*

[96] *Id.*

[97] *Id.*

[98] *Id.* (noting that more than 90 percent of U.S. nuclear plants do have hand geometry systems on their main entrances).

[99] *See* ACT, SecureTouch Fingerprint Reader (last visited Oct. 31, 1999), http://www.altcomp.com/products/bac/securetouchannounce.htm.

[100] Bernstein v. U.S. Dept. of Justice, 1999 WL 27411 (9th Cir. May 6, 1999).

"involves running a readable message known as 'plaintext' through a computer program that translates the message according to an equation or algorithm into unreadable 'ciphertext.'"[101] Decryption translates ciphertext back to plaintext.[102] The two generic types of encryption are "conventional or symmetric and public-key or asymmetric cryptography."[103] Symmetrical cryptography uses a single key to encrypt and decrypt messages.[104] Public-key cryptography employs a pair of complementary keys: a private key and public key,[105] and is based on algorithms such as RSA and DSA.[106]

Global sales of encryption products will reach $200,000,000,000 by 2002.[107] Encryption products are available from more than 900 companies in 30 countries.[108] Encryption is the principal tool for ensuring the authenticity and integrity of data and messages transmitted on the Internet. Electronic checks, for example, currently being developed in Singapore, will contain a private digital signature code.[109] Encryption in a company's information infrastructure protects its "software databases, network products, telecommunications equipment, computer peripherals, electronic commerce and financial services."[110] Digital signatures employ the technology of encryption and "provide users the ability to certify and authenticate the message and therefore trust that the message is authentic."[111] In addition to ensuring secrecy, data integrity, and authentication, encryption facilitates nonrepudiation, which is the process of linking a specific message to a specific sender.[112] Once the plaintext messages are transformed into coded messages, a key is required to decrypt them.

The federal government has used Data Encryption Standard (DES), a 56-bit single key encryption technology, since the mid-1970s for its sensitive, but not

---

[101] *Id.*, at *1.

[102] *Id.*

[103] Lorijean G. Oei, Primer on Cryptography, Chapter 31 in Thomas J. Smedinghoff, ed., Online Law: The Spa's Legal Guide to Doing Business on the Internet 497 (1996) (describing basic concepts of cryptography).

[104] *Id.*, at 499.

[105] *Id.*, at 500.

[106] Oei notes that RSA is named after Rivest, Shamir, and Adelman; DSA stands for Digital Signature Algorithm (DSA). *Id.*, at 501.

[107] Prepared Testimony of Craig McLaughlin, Chief Technology Officer, Privada, Inc., before the House Judiciary Committee Subcommittee on Courts and Intellectual Property, reprinted in Federal News Service, Mar. 4, 1999.

[108] *Id.*

[109] Microsoft Law & Corporate Affairs, Summary of Global Internet Legal Developments (for the period Jan.-Mar. 1999), Apr. 1999.

[110] *Supra* note 107.

[111] *Id.*

[112] *Id.*, at *2.

classified, information. Encryption works by "converting plaintext into ciphertext, an unreadable string of numbers and letters."[113]

DES was developed by the National Security Agency (NSA) to protect the confidentiality of classified military information that could be transmitted in digital form.[114] The National Bureau of Standards, predecessor to the National Institute of Standards and Technology (NIST), worked with NSA, the Department of Commerce, and IBM to develop DES.[115] NIST is currently developing the Advanced Encryption Standard (AES), scheduled to replace DES later in the century.[116]

Encryption algorithms can be used to secure a corporate computer network that would otherwise be subject to cyberattacks. With the help of encryption, corporate computer networks may be "configured to control access, authenticate users, hide some or all of a corporate network from the public and to protect live corporate data."[117]

Different kinds of encryption may be tailored for different types of business applications. High-speed, but lower strength algorithms may suit some messages. StorageTek's BorderGuard employs four different encryption algorithms: "DES (Data Encryption Standard), 3DES (triple DES), IDEA (International Data Encryption Algorithm) and NSC1 (a proprietary, high-speed algorithm)."[118] StorageTek's software uses different encryption for different purposes: "one type of encryption for suppliers and another for customers."[119] Selective encryption makes it possible to tailor security according to the standard of care required. A firm may decide to use encryption selectively or to use high-speed algorithms, depending upon the business activity.

The Department of Defense policy of overclassifying information had the unanticipated consequence of devaluing the currency of secrecy. A business that uses strong encryption for every data transmission may unwittingly fall into the same trap. On the other hand, a lackadaisical attitude toward security may create unnecessary risks in the cyberworld. If information security software is difficult to use and locks employees out of their workplace, serious problems will result. The information audit must, therefore, include connections to trusted business partners, suppliers, remote sites, and any other party sharing access.

---

[113] Mai-Tram B. Dinh, The U.S. Encryption Export Policy: Taking the Byte Out of the Debate, 7 Minn. J. of Global Trade 375 (1998).

[114] RSA Laboratories, Frequently Asked Questions About Today's Cryptography (visited Feb. 3, 1999), http://www.rsa.com/rsalabs/faq/html/1-6.html.

[115] Id.

[116] Id.

[117] Joanie Wexler, Users Send Out an SOS to Internet Providers, Network World, Feb. 13, 1995, at 37.

[118] StorageTek, BorderGuard: Can You Trust Your Network?, Press Release, Feb. 5, 1999 (visited Feb. 5, 1999), http://www.storagete...Tek/network/NetSentry/BorderGuard/.

[119] Id.

Entities with high security requirements will need to employ bulletproof measures to assure that security. One company has announced that it would incorporate a more complex coding formula, along with a coding string ten times longer than its predecessor—the equivalent of a 50-digit RSA key.[120] A law student may not be concerned with the possibility that a foreign government might attempt to use brute force to crack a 64-digit RSA key; on the other hand, a defense contractor may want to employ a 170-digit RSA key. As with home security, the "haves" will require stronger security programs than the "have-nots."

[8] Public-Key Cryptography

The concept of public-key encryption is a technology built upon trust. Public-key encryption is the Swiss Army Knife of Internet security technology in that it provides an all-purpose solution to the problem of ensuring secure e-business, extranet, and Internet applications. Public key cryptography was first conceptualized in 1975, when Whitfield Diffie published an article describing the dual key system. RSA's public key/private key encryption technology uses a private key, known only to the sender, and a widely published public key. Assuming that the private key is not inadvertently disclosed or stolen, the result is message confidentiality as well as secure transmission of data or information. Assume that Sender A transmits a message using the recipient B's public key; only the proper recipient, B, has the private key necessary to decode it.

Conversely, when sender A transmits a message encoded with her own private key, any recipient with sender A's public key can decode it; the private key acts as a digital signature, authenticating that A is, in fact, the sender and that the message has not been altered. Barring what is known in the security trade as a "man in the middle" security breach, recipient B knows that the message could only have been sent by A. RSA's implementation of a Public Key Infrastructure (PKI) has an additional level of security not available under DES. With DES, each party had to have knowledge simultaneously of the secret key. With an RSA-based PKI, only one person holds the private key.

SPC may choose from a number of software vendors that market public key infrastructure products. Security Dynamics Technologies Inc., for example, developed Keon Desktop, a PKI-ready security software program, for worldwide distribution. The Keon software features a certificate server as well as "PKI system interoperability . . . and PKI-enabled application including e-mail, virtual private

---

[120] John Markoff, Software Security Flaw Put Shoppers on Internet at Risk, N.Y. Times, Sept. 19, 1995, at A1.

networks and Internet-based and e-business applications."[121] Currently, PKI processing is much slower than that of DES: 100 times slower in software and 1,000 times slower in hardware.[122] Vendors, however, are working to find ways to speed it up.

One solution to the slow speed problem is to use RSA primarily to transmit short messages. RSA encryption can be used for longer messages if sent to the recipient with a one-time single key encryption scheme, which can then be used to send longer messages.[123] Since the single key encryption scheme is used only one time, the security of the transmission is not compromised. Digital envelopes that combine DES and RSA can also speed up transmission. A message is first encrypted using a "random DES key and then, before being sent over an insecure communications channel, the DES key is encrypted with RSA. Together, the DES-encrypted message and the RSA-encrypted message are sent."[124]

Any encrypted key can be broken with enough "brute force." To do this, one or more computers are programmed to try every combination of numbers, letters, or symbols conceivable until the key is unlocked. Now that many governments and private entities have the resources to crack a 64-digit RSA key, most RSA keys are made many times longer than that. The longer the key, the greater the security. Entities with great security needs will have longer keys and will combine them with additional security software to gain as much security as possible. The company StorageTek, for example, uses strong encryption in conjunction with filters. Companies now also have the ability to construct 'private sleeves,' which protect data as it goes across the Internet or another network and prevent it from being sent by others. Private sleeves also authenticate that data is from an authorized transmitter or user.[125] StorageTek's BorderGuard, for example, employs filters to segment users by group and to prevent access to hosts on the Internet.[126]

Company employees using encryption should be required to use key-recovery or escrow in the event that the company needs to access information during the absence or after the death of an employee.[127]

---

[121] Security Dynamics Technologies, Security Dynamics and RSA Unveil Enterprise Application Security Strategy, Press Release, Jan. 18, 1999 (visited Feb. 5, 1999), http//www.securitydynamics.com/press/pr/pr1999-1-18_2.html.

[122] Bruce Schneier, Applied Cryptography 285 (1994).

[123] Id.

[124] RSA, RSA's Frequently Asked Questions About Today's Cryptography (visited Mar. 1, 1999), http://www.rsa.com.

[125] StorageTek, BorderGuard: Can You Trust Your Network? Press Release, Feb. 5, 1999.

[126] Id.

[127] Vincent Polley, Electronic Communication Guidelines, Joint Presidential Presentation, ABA Section on Business Law, American Bar Association Annual Meeting, Toronto, Ontario, Aug. 2, 1998.

[9] **Digital Signatures**

The American Bar Association's Science and Technology Committee defines digital signatures as an electronic signature "created and verified by means of cryptography, the branch of applied mathematics that concerns itself with transforming messages into seemingly unintelligible forms and back again."[128] Digital signatures use two different keys. "Public key or asymmetric cryptography uses two keys that are mathematically tied together. If one key is used to encrypt a message, the other must be used to decrypt the same message (and vice-versa). One of the keys is kept secret. The other key made available to the general public, is known as the public key."[129]

A private key can transform a real message or data into a gobbledygook string of characters and/or numbers in a process called *encryption*. The public key can be used to transform the gobbledygook back into a real message. This is called *decryption*.[130] A private key and encryption technology can be used to transform another real message or data into an additional string of gobbledygook characters, thus generating a digital signature. This additional string of characters, the digital signature, can be appended to the primary data or message and will serve to authenticate it as to its source and contents, an authentication confirmable by using the public key. These public key applications permit the safe conduct of e-business transactions. Web browsers, web servers, e-mail, and databases may be protected through public key cryptography.

Digital signatures, designed to insure against falsification or alteration, are well established in the information security industry. Digital signatures have an evidentiary, authenticating, and ceremonial role in electronic commerce.[131] Paper-based signatures may be authenticated by watermarks, semipermanent ink, time stamps, post-marks, and examination for erasures, modifications, or deletions.[132] Functionally equivalent safeguards are necessary for digital messages and signatures. Digital messages "are simply strings of bits—zeros and ones—represented by fractions of a volt. The problem is how to distinguish your volts from my volts."[133] At least 36 states have enacted or are considering enacting legislation legitimating digital signatures. Within five years, the federal government will

---

[128] Information Security Committee, American Bar Association, Committee on Science and Technology, Digital Signature Guidelines With Model Legislation (Chicago: American Bar Association, 1995).

[129] Information Security, All Eyes on PKI (visited Feb. 9, 1999), http://www.infosecuritymag.com/oct/pki.htm.

[130] *See generally, Id.*

[131] Adams, *supra* note 45.

[132] Michael S. Baum, Secure Electronic Commerce, Doing Business and Avoiding Liability in Cyberspace, Suffolk University Law School, May 10, 1996.

[133] *Id.*

require all transactions to be electronic, and it is studying electronic signatures, electronic authentication, and privacy issues to this end.[134]

[10] Certificate Authorities

A certificate authority (CA) is a third-party entity whose business it is to issue and revoke certificates that establish the validity of public keys. This entity is the trusted third party that vouches for the user's identity and issues public-key certificates.[135] Certificate authorities are the equivalent of a passport office for Internet commercial transactions.[136] The CA, a trusted intermediary between two trading partners, issues digital certificates that certify a holder's identity and authority. The CAs "embed an individual's or an organization's public key along with other identifying information into each digital certificate and then crypto-graphically 'sign' it as a tamper-proof seal, verifying the integrity of the data within it and validating its use."[137] VeriSign is the world's largest CA; it has issued more than 100,000 certificates validating the identity of the user and the integrity of the data.[138] VeriSign's method for issuing digital signatures is the "electronic equivalent of a business license."[139] A public key certificate contains: (1) a subject name; (2) a subject public key; (3) an issuer name; (4) notice of the validity period for the information; (5) a serial number; and (6) an issuer's signature.[140]

VeriSign issues what it calls a Server ID, vouching for the users' rights to use a company name and serial number web address. The function of the CA is roughly analogous to what a "Secretary of State does when it issues Articles of Incorporation."[141] The role of the CA is to review an applicant's credentials to ensure that the organization's agents are who they claim to be. When a CA issues a certificate, it is, in effect, "an electronic credential that a business can present to prove its identity or right to access information."[142] In concept and methods, the

---

[134] The lead agency is the U.S. Office of Information and Regulatory Affairs of the Office of Management and Budget (OMB) which "issued draft guidelines detailing how agencies should comply with the Government Paperwork Elimination Act, which requires the federal government to make all transactions electronic within five years." Microsoft Law & Corporate Affairs, Summary of Global Internet Legal Developments (for the period, Jan.-Mar. 1999) 124 (Apr. 1999).

[135] *Id.*

[136] Netscape, Certificate Authority Program (visited May 1, 1999), http://home.netscape.com/ security/caprogram/index.html (comparing certificate authorities to the digital world's equivalent of passport offices).

[137] *Id.*

[138] VeriSign, Inc., White Paper—Securing Your Web Site (visited May 1, 1999), http:// www.verisgn.com/whitepaper/server/secure/secure.html.

[139] *Id.*

[140] *Supra* note 132.

[141] *Id.*

[142] *Id.*

CA's role is that of trusted intermediary, one who can verify the credentials or identity of online trading partners. Trust is essential to an online business and the CA's rigorous authentication practice plays a role as important as the implementation of physical security for databases or networks. Corporate subscribers should carefully examine the certification authority's statement of the practices it uses in issuing certificates.

[11] Export Controls on Encryption

In November 1999, the Clinton Administration released proposed regulations to control the export of encryption products.[143] Prior to this, companies had to obtain a license for key lengths of 56+ bits before exporting them to any country. Encryption has many positive business applications. RSA Data Security, Inc., is a leading vendor of encrypted software and has supplied "more than 330 million copies of RSA encryption and authentication technologies."[144]

"The length of its key, which is measured in bits and the complexity of the algorithm measure the strength of DES. Each bit doubles the number of possible key sequences; thus, as the number of bits increase, the encryption becomes dramatically stronger."[145] The Bureau of Export Administration of the Department of Commerce has a web site describing the latest export rules,[146] regulations, and lists.[147] The Bureau develops export control policies; issues export licenses and prosecutes violators.[148]

In May 1999, the Ninth Circuit U.S. Court of Appeals held that the government's ban on the export of encryption codes violated free expression.[149] Bernstein v. U.S. Dept. of Justice[150] dealt with the situation of an Illinois mathematics and computer science professor who had developed an encryption method based upon a one-way hash function he dubbed "Snuffle."[151] The State Department told Professor Bernstein that he would need a license to export his research paper, source

---

[143] Nancy Weil, United States Grants PGP Encryption Export License, Infoworld.com (Dec. 13, 1999).

[144] Security Dynamics Technologies, Security Dynamics Breaks the Barrier for Outsourced Network Security, Press Release, Dec. 8, 1998 (visited Feb. 5, 1999), http://www.securitydynamics.com/press/pr/pr1998-12-15.html.

[145] Id., at 376.

[146] An export of software includes any release, including an oral exchange of information, to a foreign country or a foreign national within the United States. 15 C.F.$. § 734.2(b)(2) & (3).

[147] Home page, Bureau of Export Administration, Welcome to the Bureau of Export Administration Web Site (visited May 12, 1999), http://www.bxa.doc.gov.

[148] Id.

[149] Bernstein v. U.S. Dept. of Justice, 1999 WL 274111 (9th Cir. May 6 1999) (holding that the government's Export Administration regulations operated as a prepublication prior restraint offending the First Amendment).

[150] Id.

[151] 1999 WL 274111, *1 (9th Cir. Cal.).

code, and instructions on using Snuffle. Bernstein and the government were unable to agree on the scope and application of the export regulations applicable to Snuffle, and Bernstein filed an action challenging the constitutionality of the export regulations. The district court held that the regulations were facially invalid as a prior restraint on speech. The Ninth Circuit affirmed, holding that the challenged regulations violated the First Amendment.

The court was concerned that export regulations allowed the government to restrain speech indefinitely with no clear criteria for review.[152] The court observed that prior restraints on speech are viewed "with suspicion because such restraints run the twin risks of encouraging self-censorship and concealing illegitimate abuses of censorial power."[153] The *Bernstein* court found that the source code used by cryptographers parallels the expression of scientific ideas used by mathematicians and economists.[154] The court concluded that source code is expressive for First Amendment purposes and entitled to the protections of the prior restraint doctrine.[155]

In September 1999, the Clinton administration liberalized export controls further, in a policy decision applauded by the software industry. The new policy permits software products of any key length to be exported without a license, except to countries considered terrorist states.[156]

The software industry has been in a pitched battle with the Clinton administration over U.S. government encryption controls since the early 1990s.[157] The Federal Bureau of Investigation (FBI) seeks "real-time access to all encrypted data without notifying the user or the company that owns the lines for the data."[158] The FBI seeks legislation that would require all companies to hand over private keys to "encrypted data stored on drives."[159]

The NSA designed the so-called Clipper Chip using the single-key based algorithm SKIPJACK to defeat cellular-based security breaches.[160] The Clipper Chip had the single purpose of defeating private parties from using encrypted cellular-based communications for drug deals, spying, and other illegal activities.[161]

---

[152] *Id.*, at *8.

[153] *Id.*, at *4.

[154] *Id.*, at *5.

[155] *Id.*

[156] The Industry Standard's Intelligencer, Encryption Prescription, The Week in the Internet Economy, Sept. 17, 1999.

[157] Jim Kerstetter, Key Uprising: Tighter Crypto Limits Shake IT, PC Week Online, Sept. 29, 1997 (Feb. 9, 1999), http://www.zdnet.com.au/pcweek/news/0929/29crypt.html.

[158] *Id.*

[159] *Id.*

[160] Privacy Issues in the Telecommunications Industry: Testimony Before the Subcommittee on Technology and the Law of the Senate Committee on the Judiciary, 103d Congress, 2d Session (1994) (statement of Stephen T. Walker, President, Trusted Information Systems).

[161] *See* Stephanie Stahl (with Mary E. Thyfault), About Face on Clipper—Privacy Advocates Draw Conflicting Conclusions on Encryption Policy, Info Week, Aug. 8, 1994, at 24.

Inaugurating the Clipper Chip involved a complex balancing of interests. On the one hand, the government would provide the private sector with a strong encryption technology, certified by the NSA as "unbreakable." Recipients, however, would need to allow selected government enforcement agencies to hold the secret keys to this "unbreakable" encryption in escrow.[162]

The Clipper Chip initiative was meant to establish a complex system in which the keys would be divided into two parts and housed with escrow agents at two different government agencies, the Treasury Department's Automated Systems Division and the U.S. Department of Commerce's NIST, both executive branch offices.[163] The government's key escrow recovery system would permit keys to be obtained for law enforcement purposes in the face of valid warrants.[164] The secret keys would then permit law enforcement officials to decode any Clipper-encrypted communications. A functionally equivalent system of key escrow, entitled the Capstone algorithm, was envisioned for database information.[165] The Clipper Chip and Capstone were opposed by civil libertarians, who viewed the government's role as an escrow agent able to break strong cryptography at will as the first step toward Big Brother.[166] Legal academics, too, challenged the Clipper Chip as violative of the right to privacy, freedom of association, free speech, and unreasonable search and seizure.[167]

Government agencies such as the Securities and Exchange Commission, the Food and Drug Administration, and the Atomic Energy Commission, however, argued that they also had a compelling law enforcement interest in the Clipper Chip and Capstone secret keys. Regulatory agencies would like access to encrypted materials in order to have "the capability to eavesdrop on the industries they watch over under hostile circumstances."[168] The federal government has endorsed the public/private key encryption technology, but seeks its own exclusive access to deter and punish terrorists seeking to unleash an "Electronic Pearl Harbor."

[12] Virtual Private Networks

A Virtual Private Network (VPN) uses the Internet as a backbone for connecting company computers, servers, databases, and other key infrastructure.

---

[162] A. Michael Froomkin, The Metaphor Is the Key: Cryptography, The Clipper Chip, and the Constitution, 143 U. Pa. L. Rev. 715-16(1995).

[163] *See* Rochelle Garner, Clipper's Hidden Agenda, Open Computing, Aug. 1994, at 54.

[164] *Id.*, at 54.

[165] Allan McDonald, Federal Bureau of Investigation, Protecting Enterprise Information in the Digital Age: Digital Telephony, Privacy and Security, Presentation at the American Bar Association, Section of Science & Technology, Annual Meeting, Chicago, Illinois (Aug. 7, 1995).

[166] Rochelle Garner, Clipper's Hidden Agenda, Open Computing, Aug. 1994, at 54.

[167] *Supra* note 162, at 810.

[168] *See* Rochele Garner, Clipper's Hidden Agenda, Open Computing, Aug. 1994, at 52 (quoting Donn Parker, program manager of information and security, SRI International, Menlo Park, California).

The VPN gives off-site employees, telecommuters, business partners, and other trusted parties secure access or a tunnel into a company's network.[169] A VPN makes it possible for a company to communicate on the Internet in a secure private environment through the technology of strong user authentication. Businesses with telecommuting employees are on the increase, as are companies with remote sites. A company must know that those entering its systems are authorized employees, not impostors. Businesses must ensure that only authorized users can gain access to the company's information assets. The traditional network, however, by not permitting business partners, customers, or telecommuters to access company computers over the Internet, can sometimes leave them marooned.[170] VPN technology replaces "costly leased communications facilities with encrypted channels across public networks, such as the Internet."[171]

The common hazard of the VPN is the exposure of company assets to hackers and unauthorized users. The Internet Architecture Board issued a 1994 directive that concluded that any Internet-based system required security "from unauthorized monitoring and control of network traffic as well as the need to secure end-to-end traffic using authentication and encryption."[172] A VPN may be vulnerable to cyberattacks such as IP spoofing, in which intruders give packets false IP addresses, eavesdropping, and packet sniffing, which cyberthieves use to read information transmitted over the Internet.[173] IP spoofing would be foiled by a filtering router, which drops "outside" packets with an "inside" source address.[174] Proposed Internet Standards, such as IPSec, are evolving "to secure communications across LANs, private and public WANs and the Internet."[175] The IPSec standard uses encryption to authenticate all traffic and applications including "remote logons, client server, e-mail, file transfer and Web access."[176]

A number of vendors are implementing the IPSec industry standards with an array of new products. One way to achieve a VPN is to use an encrypted point-to-

---

[169] GTE, Virtual Private Networks-VPN (visited April 27, 1999), http://www.bbn.com/groups/vpn/service/.

[170] An extranet allows access to company computers over the Internet.

[171] Edward Skoudis, Fire in the Hole, Information Security: A World of Information for the Security-Conscious (visited on Feb. 9, 1999), http://www.infosecuritymag.com/fire.htm.

[172] William Stallings, A Secure Foundation for VPNS Information Security: A World of Information for the Security-Conscious (visited Feb. 9, 1999), http//www.infosecuritymag.com/vpn.htm.

[173] Id.

[174] Security First Network Bank, Security Issues: A Closer Look at SFNB's Security Architecture (1996).

[175] Id.

[176] Id.

point tunnel to transmit company data and applications.[177] The tunnel model mode provides protection in the following way:

> To achieve this, after the ESP [Encapsulating Security Payload] fields are added to the IP packet, the entire packet along with its security field is treated as the payload of a new outer IP packet with a new outer IP header. The entire original, or inner, packet travels through a "tunnel" from one point of an IP network to another; no routers along the way are able to examine the inner IP header. Because the original packet is encapsulated, the new packet may include different source and destination addresses, adding to the security. Tunnel mode is used when one or both ends are a security gateway, such as a router or firewall that implements IPSec.[178]

Authentication and encryption give "highly secure remote access and extranet uses" in business-to-business commerce.[179]

The risk factor is far less for SPC's private computers accessing the Internet through a dial-up ISP than it is for a corporate network with Internet access provided directly by an Internet backbone company. The larger the company, the more likely it is to be targeted by hackers. Government offices are the second most likely targets for security crimes, followed by educational institutions. At least for now, the private home is the least likely target for a security attack. Technologies such as the VPN, however, make it possible to thwart many security attacks.

[13]   Security Audit Products

SPC must make critical policy choices about how it will implement information security at the operating system level. One possibility is to hire a computer consulting firm or a consultant specializing in information security. SPC should complete a security audit to determine what holes it has in its system and then research ways to patch its particular security soft spots. A number of products have been developed for making security audits. Internet Security Systems, Inc., for example, markets Internet Scanner, which they claim is the most comprehensive "attack simulator" available;[180] it has the capacity to perform audits for more than 100 security vulnerabilities.[181]

---

[177] Security Dynamics Technologies, Inc., Security Dynamics and Aventail Enter Strategic Relationship to Provide Secure Remote Access and Extranet Solutions, OEM Licensing and Distribution Agreement to Enhance Security Dynamics' Enterprise Security Solutions, Press Release, July 7, 1998 (last visited Feb. 5, 1999), http//www.securitydynamics.com/press/pr/pr1998-07-07.html.

[178] *Supra* note 172.

[179] *Id.* (quoting Chuck Stuckey, president, chairman, and CEO of Security Dynamics).

[180] Thomas Noonan Joins Internet Security Systems as President, Business Wire, Aug. 30, 1995.

[181] *Id.*

Internet security consultants, too, can provide multifaceted audits that tell a company where its network is vulnerable, what holes it has, and how to plug them.[182]

The information security industry is one of the fastest growing sectors of the information-based economy. Diagnostics products include the controversial Security Administrator Tool for Analyzing Networks (SATAN) program, COPS, OmniGuard/Enterprise Access Control UNIX, and NetProbe. SATAN is controversial because of its dual nature: It functions by probing its target across the network from another host, and thus can be used to crack systems as well as to defend them.[183] Using SATAN, a hacker can systematically exploit any system weakness it discovers.[184] SATAN and COPS can be downloaded from various servers on the Internet for no charge. The other products, available commercially, run directly on the target host and operate as self-diagnostics.[185] These products enable a Systems Administrator to find and plug O/S security holes before hackers can exploit them.

[14] Physical Security

The online company must also provide for adequate physical security to prevent unauthorized use of its equipment or other information intrusions. The firewall, for example, must be protected by physical controls to preclude unauthorized use. In a high security environment, "the company firewall should be located in a controlled environment, with access limited to the Network Services Manager, the firewall administrator, and the backup firewall administrator."[186] Adequate physical security measures are calibrated on the basis of how critical a company finds it to protect sensitive data and information.[187] Computer systems must be protected adequately from fire, water hazards, electric power supply losses, shifts in humidity, natural disasters, and magnetic surges; finally, good housekeeping procedures

---

[182] Internet Security Systems: Plugging Network Holes: New Network Security Software Uses Simulator to Scan Network for Vulnerabilities, Wall Street & Technology, Jan. 1, 1997, at 28.

[183] Jason Levitt, Techview: Dealing with the Devil, Information Week, Apr. 17, 1995, at 2.

[184] See Winn Schwartau, The Key to Defeating SATAN Is Understanding How it Can Bedevil You, Network World, May 1, 1995, at 32.

[185] Rutrell Yasin, Vendors Fire Up Wares to Vie with SATAN, Communications Week, Apr. 10, 1995, at 4.

[186] Physical Firewall Security, in NIST, Internet Security Policy (Washington, D.C.: NIST, 1999): A Technical Guide (NIST, 1999), (visited Dec. 14, 1999) http://www.csrc.nist.gov/isptg/html/ISPTG-6.html.

[187] Traditionally, mainframe computers were so heavy that the computer room was located in the basement, making the systems prone to flooding. In a PC environment, it may make sense to locate computers on upper floors. The physical security of the computer system should not necessarily be based on traditional methods.

protect against damage from dust and dirt.[188] Additional measures must be tailored to the specific physical, human, or environmental risks.

[B] Mass-Market Security Products

Most information security products consist of sets of instructions for performing designated security functions housed on diskette or CD-ROM. Norton Anti-Virus and MCA Anti-Virus are examples of mass marketed information security products that perform a single primary security function, patrolling for viruses and controlling viruses. Norton's Disklock is a more comprehensive security product that can be used on a single computer or in a network to restrict access to hard drive directories and files to authorized users only. Businesses as well as consumers use mass-market products that are distributed to the desktops and updated automatically.

Mass-marketed firewall software products include FireWall-1, sold by CheckPoint Software Technology, Inc., of Lexington, Massachusetts. FireWall-1 is installed like any other mass-market software, without any customized modifications. Firewalls for UNIX-based software gateways are increasingly being designed to perform packet filtering. (A packet is "[a] group of characters transferred from one computer to another, including control information."[189])

Vendors offer a wide array of firewalls to protect Internet routers/gateways.[190] Network Systems, for example, markets BorderGuard for the protection of remote sites. Another product employs proxies, which are "slimmed-down versions of applications that are open to outside users and serve to protect the 'real' application behind the firewall from bugs."[191] IBM's NetSP Gateway enforces network access rights based on user-determined rules. It also takes action if hacking is suspected, based on an analysis of address pairs and requested services.[192] Harris Corp. makes a computer safeguard called CyberGuard Firewall, which places a computer between a company's LAN and its outside connections.[193] Trusted Information Systems, Inc., developed Gauntlet, a firewall based on Pentium hardware, using a modified version of UNIX.

Custom-designed security products or systems may be necessary where the mass-market product provides insufficient protection. The firewall industry is changing rapidly as companies seek firewalls that serve as Internet gateway filters.

---

[188] These standard environmental safeguards should be implemented for all computer systems.

[189] Gertler, *supra* note 32.

[190] Some users also employ public-domain firewall tools, such as SOCKS.

[191] Joanie Wexler, Users Send Out an SOS to Internet Providers, Network World, Feb. 13, 1995, at 37.

[192] *Id.*

[193] Frank Ruiz, ECI to Build E-Mail Security Chip for U.S., Tampa Tribune, June 8, 1995, at 1.

[C] Owner-Distributed Security Products

A number of network security products are not mass marketed but distributed by the developers or their authorized distributors. Developer-distributed security products include Ace/Server and ACM, from Security Dynamics Technologies, Inc., and properly configured network servers, such as SecureManager from Cylink Corp. The typical owner- or developer-distributed product tends to have more complex functions than do mass-marketed products. Frequently, these products combine hardware and software and have more detailed installation and update procedures. The trend in the information security industry is to license these products with a services component.

[D] Customized Security Products

Network security professionals may also custom-design security products or systems for companies. The network security professional may custom-develop a security product or system in response to a request for a proposal (RFP) or another software contract. The role of the security consultant is to conduct an internal investigation of security solutions for a business. A consultant may determine that the online business faces the potential of intrusions or other information security risks and then custom-designs a solution. As with preventive law, it is best to hire a consultant to forecast a security problem as opposed to being forced to plug a hole after a security breach has occurred. Information security professionals can aid companies in determining the presence of security dangers and can suggest solutions. Because businesses vary significantly in form and function, the information security consultant should be experienced in a given industry. The International Organization for Standardization (ISO) is in the process of proposing a set of minimum standards for assessing the security features of computer products.[194]

➤ [E] Preventive Law Pointer: Continuous Security Improvement

Where to Find Your Hacker "Huggy Bear"

Bobby Hazelton[195]

SPC must make a decision as to which of its company officers will have complete access to confidential data or information. As with any information-

---

[194] NIST, International Organization for Standardization (ISO) (visited July 22, 1999), http://www.csrc.nist.gov/cc/cem/cemlist.htm#CEM2.

[195] Bobby Hazelton, an information technology consultant and certified information systems' auditor, drafted the tips contained in this section.

based company, SPC's confidential data and trade secrets are its crown jewels or lifeblood. Some security choices offer low risk. Implementing a firewall or virus protection product from an established vendor, for example, does not require exposing information to any third party. Vendor selection may be done with the help of outside consultants or through an internal technology selection process.[196]

At some point, companies must establish a trust relationship with an in-house security administrator (SA) or choose a reputable external security auditor to assist in setting up their IT security policy. Turning over the keys to the kingdom may be scary; however, relying on references or certifications can make the choice easier.[197] Unfortunately, this is but the first step in a long process. Technology changes rapidly, and the procedures designed to stop today's intruders will offer little resistance to tomorrow's invaders. Staying protected means keeping the company's Information Security Program current. Staying current requires a channel to information about the latest advances in security breaches and remedies.

Large resources will be earmarked for keeping hackers out, but a small sum should be allotted to letting a few in. Despite the noble attempts of security consulting companies, hackers still remain the best security oversight service in the industry. Their efforts will expose any software security loopholes that could leave a firm's data prone to a variety of malicious attacks. Even though the Back Orifice software from Cult of the Dead Cows has been used for malevolent purposes, it has also helped to expose the security flaws in user access rights and procedures in Windows 95. Attrition.org's errata page provides an excellent resource for determining the true radius of risk, as opposed to media hysteria.[198]

It is natural to want to keep hackers away from information resources. Additionally, the hacker culture may not be compatible with the corporate environment. Their choice of language, graphics, and political messages may be contrary to the desired workplace image. One way to insulate a company from both problems is to view hacker web sites and to communicate with hackers through a low risk meeting place. Maintaining dial-up ISP accounts for security administrators allows contact to be made without compromising or even divulging the location of the corporate network. Maintaining a security test lab on the public side of a firewall will allow security administrators to experiment with new hacks without inadvertently causing harm to actual production resources.

---

[196] ISACA, an independent security assurance corporation, maintains a list of security products having an objective minimum of the necessary specifications. *See* ISACA, Product Certification (last visited September 22, 1999), http://www.icsa.net/services/product_cert/products.shtml.

[197] The Information Audit and Control Association has established a set of universal Control Objectives for Information and Related Technologies (CobiT). The Certified Information Systems Auditor (CISA) must possess comprehensive knowledge of these objectives and adhere to a strict guideline of professional ethics. *See* ISACA (last visited Sept. 22, 1999), http://www.isaca.org.

[198] Attrition.org, Errata (last visited Sept. 22, 1999), http://attrition.org/errata/.

The 1970s TV show "Starsky and Hutch" featured two street wise detectives that knew their way around the criminal underworld. Although capable police officers, they still relied on Huggy Bear, an informant who was even closer to the criminal element. Thankfully, SAs don't need bright orange Ford Torinos to find their hacker Huggy Bears. Hackers are building security related sites everywhere. Choosing the sites and/or persons with which to maintain contact, however, will be an individual decision for each SA.[199]

§ 3.03   THE RADIUS OF RISK

The only way a company can protect prevent potential legal problems is by formulating and implementing a comprehensive information security policy. The policy must emphasize the high standard of care with which employees should treat confidential information. A company should also appoint a systems administrator in charge of information security. The system administrator should construct a Frequently Asked Questions (FAQ) document for employee reference. The company should conduct regular training seminars to make employees aware of the dangers of breaches in information security, as well as the proper use of the technologies available to protect sensitive information. Our hypothetical company, SPC, will need to appoint a rota of contact persons to provide coverage 24 hours a day, 7 days a week, so that SPC will be able to take prompt remedial steps in the face of a computer intrusion, virus, or denial of service attack.

Companies might consider installing e-mail firewalls, which permit administrators to enforce security policies.[200] Employees should be warned of the risk of Internet e-mail attacks, such as address spoofing, in which a cybercriminal uses false headers to obtain proprietary information. Another danger is the potential interception and alteration of an e-mail message. Companies should consider using message encryption, sometimes referred to as Privacy Enhanced Mail or PEM. Message encryption should be used for all sensitive information transmitted by e-mail.

Security policies have little value if the supporting infrastructure does not enable a company to prosecute their plan. SPC must not choose its security products randomly. A viable security solution must not overemphasize functionality at the expense of the sociology of application. Information security depends on educating and socializing employees, consultants, and customers to follow security protocol. Careful attention must be given to how each security component will be

---

[199] A few of these sites can be found at http://attrition.org/, http://www.cultdeadcow.com/, http://astalavista.box.sk/, and http://neworder.box.sk/. Potential visitors should be warned that the content at some of these sites may be explicit.

[200] Mike Elgan, The Dangers of E-Mail, CMP Net: The Technology Network.

implemented. This section describes the various components of a typical network, the associated security issues (as identified by SPC), and some insights into differentiating among competing products. Information security must be tailored for the specific computer systems, including servers, all systems for data storage and applications, and routers, hubs, and networks. The security audit should review each computer component or application.

For SPC, its formal security audit or assessment should be tailored to its Internet-based virtual store. An online company attracts web users to its site in order to increase business and advertising revenue. SPC faces liability risks from materials posted online or generated by its site's users. SPC must also prevent its employees, consultants, and other users from exchanging or distributiing materials deemed harmful to children. In particular, the company needs some mechanism to report violations of federal child pornography laws.[201]

If an online company employs a "reward" program that entitles users to receive points redeemable for merchandise, such as books or music, it must provide security measures to prevent fraud.[202] Further, the online company must protect its payment systems and the privacy of its customers.[203] SPC sells computer software and hardware directly over the Internet. Customers entering SPC's web site need to be assured that its payment system is secure. SPC incorporated a secure ordering system that protects the integrity of the credit card numbers it is given. SPC employs a "1-Click" technology, providing customers with a secure, streamlined ordering process.[204] SPC and all online businesses must address online fraud by professional thieves and amateurs. One method is to monitor ordering logs to detect fraudulent orders. Internet fraud may originate from any where in the world—Pakistan, Russia, Israel, the United Kingdom, Mexico, or a host of other countries.

SPC needs security that will protect its numerous site management, customer interaction, and transaction-processing services. Any online company's process of accepting, authorizing, and charging customer credit cards must be protected. Systems security must be tailored to protect its rapidly evolving virtual businesses. Online businesses need disaster response to "fires, floods, power losses, telecommunications failures, break-ins, earthquakes and new risks" of "electronic break-ins and disruptions and the loss of critical data."[205]

---

[201] Yahoo! 10-K SEC Disclosure (visited July 2, 1999), http://www.sec.gov/Archives/edgar/data/1011006/0001047469-99-025415.txt.

[202] *Id.*

[203] *Id.*

[204] Amazon.com, 10-K SEC Disclosure (visited July 2, 1999), http://www.sec.gov/Archives/edgar/data/1018724/000089102-99-000375.txt. We base our SPC example on Amazon.com's 10-K SEC Disclosure.

[205] *Id.*

[A] Hackers

An empirical study of Internet security found nearly 70 percent of the companies surveyed had experienced at least one episode of information theft,[206] and half reported at least one theft of property worth $10,000 or more.[207] Trusted company employees, consultants or insiders, committed nearly one in five computer crimes.[208] The military, one of the first beneficiaries of Internet technology, has also become a primary target of hackers. The Pentagon has 650,000 terminals and workstations; the military has at least 10,000 local computer networks and 100 long-distance computer networks. The Pentagon experienced an average of two hacker attacks per day in 1995, "more than double the rate of 255 a year in 1994."[209]

Intruders have stolen, altered, and even erased data in Pentagon computers.[210] Robert Ayers, Chief of the Information Warfare Division of the Defense Information Systems Agency (DISA), acknowledges that the Pentagon's electronic infrastructure is "not safe and secure."[211]

To prevent unauthorized access to, and leaking of, classified documents, the U.S. Department of Defense (DOD) had developed firewalls for computers and networks in the mid-1980s.[212] Yet an August 1999 report by the Government Accounting Office (GAO) found extensive security flaws in the Defense Department's computer system.[213] Even such sensitive information as our country's nuclear secrets, kept on computers unplugged from the Internet, are not safe. In January 1999, President Clinton announced a new initiative to combat cyber-intruders seeking to break into critical computer systems.[214]

Many companies hire information security consultants or outside companies to design firewalls to protect their sensitive information. Many law firms seek the assistance of companies such as Computer Solutions Inc., of Boston, Massachusetts, to

---

[206] *Id.*, at 183-84 (reporting survey of COMEEC BBS).

[207] *Id.*, at 184.

[208] *Id.*

[209] John J. Fialka, Pentagon Studies Art of "Information Warfare" To Reduce Its Systems' Vulnerability to Hackers, Wall St. J., July 3, 1995, at A20.

[210] David Bernstein, Insulate Against Internet Intruders, Datamation, Oct. 1, 1994, at 49.

[211] Neil Munro, The Pentagon's New Nightmare: An Electronic Pearl Harbor, The Washington Post, July 16, 1995, at C-3.

[212] Gary H. Anthes, Hackers Stay a Step Ahead, Computerworld, Oct. 17, 1994, at 14.

[213] Extensive Security Gaps Persist in DOD Networks, Fed. Comp. Wk., August 27, 1999 (noting that DOD employees were not following security protocols and that at least 70 employees had the authority to change source code without supervision).

[214] President Bill Clinton, Remarks by the President on Keeping America Secure for the 21st Century, Jan. 22, 1999, National Academy of Sciences (visited on Jan. 26, 1999), http://library.whitehouse.gov.

help tailor their information security technologies. Frequently, information security will consist of both mass-marketed and customized software programs.

SPC's systems administrator needs to probe for unauthorized devices, such as modems connected to user PCs.[215] The Carnegie-Mellon Computer Emergency Response Team (CERT) recommends that systems administrators conduct daily audits for anomalies or unauthorized devices.[216] SPC's systems administrator should conduct a monthly inspection of the computer system to look for any other anomalies.[217]

The term *hack* was first used to describe the antics of Cal Tech students who obtained a blueprint of card codes for football halftime entertainment to be provided by the University of Washington marching band at the 1961 Rose Bowl. The Cal Tech pranksters switched the codes so that the Washington marching band displayed cards that proclaimed "Cal Tech," rather than Washington. The term *dark-side hacker*, in contrast, refers to hackers who commit calculated economic crimes or malicious acts.[218]

The broad term *hacker* refers to persons who obtain "unauthorized access to computer systems and those who simply enjoy using computers and experimenting with their capabilities as 'innocent' hobbyists."[219] Information security breaches could prove to be costly to online companies. The FBI reports that intellectual property losses from foreign and domestic espionage may have exceeded $300,000,000,000 in 1997.[220] Hackers have a distinctive subculture, seeing themselves as electronic Robin Hoods, with their own lingo, ideas, and practices.[221] Hacker culture was originally based on intellectual curiosity and grew out of the challenge of mastering computers and systems security.[222] Among the first hackers were MIT students who broke into computers to satisfy their intellectual curiosity.[223]

A wave of attacks against major web sites and portals occurred in February 2000, knocking a number of businesses off-line. E-businesses such as Yahoo!, MCI WorldCom, E*Trade, Amazon.com, Microsoft's MSN.com, CNN.com, Buy.com, and other companies were inaccessible as a result of denial-of-service

---

[215] Modem banks are a key part of the information infrastructure of many businesses. When unauthorized modems are present, however, wrongdoers may gain access to company computers.

[216] *Anomaly* is the general term used for any suspicious or unusual activity, code, or device in an automated information security system.

[217] *See* Carnegie-Mellon Computer Emergency Response Team (CERT) Advisories at www.cert.org.

[218] Jargon Dictionary, Dark-Side Hacker (visited Sept. 1, 1999), http://www.netmag.neg.

[219] Michael D. Scott, Internet and Technology Law Desk Reference 231 (1999) (citation omitted).

[220] Curtis E. A. Karnow, Computer Network Risks: Security Breaches and Liability Issues, Comp. L. Strat Feb. 1999, at 1.

[221] *Id.*, at 196-238.

[222] *Id.*

[223] Bruce Sterling, The Hacker Crackdown: Law and Disorder on the Electronic Frontier (1992).

attacks.[224] The online auction house, eBay, suffered an outage of five hours, cutting into the company's daily revenue of $10,000,000.[225] The denial-of-service attacks came in at a "rate of one gigabyte per second."[226] The attack on Yahoo! involved a coordinated attack by a large number of servers.[227]

The denial-of-service (DOS) attacks reenforce the notion of an Internet where everyone is vulnerable. Even the most powerful web companies can be shut down by unknown and, perhaps, unknowable forces. No bulletproof solution seems to exist for defeating crackers, snackers, smurfs,[228] sniffers,[229] stalkers, spoofers, phracks,[230] phreaks,[231] cyberpunks,[232]and other creepy web crawlers.[233]

---

[224] Robert Lemos, Hunting Web Attackers "Impossible." ZDNet News , Feb. 10, 2000 (visited Feb. 11, 2000), http://www.news.excite.com/news/zd/000210/hunting-web-attackers.

[225] Jennifer Mack, Attack Victims Count Their Losses, ZDNet News, Feb. 10, 2000 (visited Feb. 11, 2000), http://news.excite.com/news/zd/000210/18/attack-victims-count.

[226] The Industry Standard's Media Grok, Can you, Uh, Yahoo? Feb. 8, 2000.

[227] CNET.COM, Yahoo! Claims Outage a Deliberate Attack (visited Feb. 10, 2000), http://interactive.wsj.com/articles/SB949974774122805106.htm.

[228] Smurfs were those cute little blue characters in mushroom villages that were the rage in the 1970s and 1980s. A "Smurf attack" is a denial-of-service (DOS) attack. Typically, the wrongdoer will forge source addresses, creating packet loss. A Smurf attack may cause loss of packets or the overwhelming of Internet links.

[229] Internet cultural anthropologists distinguish among *crackers*, *snackers*, and other kinds of hackers. A *cracker* is a person who thrives on the challenge of breaking into a supposedly invulnerable corporate computer. In contrast, a *snacker* tries whatever is interesting. A *sniffer* is a special program that seeks out confidential information. A *hacker* is one who breaks into a computer out of the sheer intellectual curiosity and is not driven by desire for financial gain. A *phreak* breaks into telephone systems to make free long distance telephone calls. What Is . . . a Phreak (A Definition) (visited Sept. 19, 1999), http://www.whatis.com/phreak.htm (quoting Eric S. Raymond, The New Hacker Dictionary).

[230] Phrack Magazine, a periodical, subdivides the difference between Internet hackers into phracks, pirates, hackers, and phreakers. *See* http://www.phrack.com.

[231] Sherry Turkle writes:

> One of the most famous [phone freaks] was known as Captain Crunch, who took his name from breakfast cereal. In every box there was a toy whistle, like the prize in Cracker Jacks. The whistle produced a 2600-cycle tone. A young man just entering the Air Force as a radio technician, Crunch was fascinated with electronics, circuitry, and winning. He was a hacker without a computer. He discovered that the Crunch whistle was a lock pick to one of the most complex closed systems ever designed. First you dial a long-distance telephone number. Then you blow the Crunch whistle. This disconnected the dialed conversation but kept the trunk open without further toll charge. From that point on, any number of calls could be dialed free.

Sherry Turkle, The Second Self: Computers and the Human Spirit 226 (1984).

[232] *See generally,* Katie Hafner and John Markoff, Cyberpunk: Outlaws and Hackers on the Computer Frontier (1991).

[233] Maggie Cannon, A Life in the Big City: Internet Concerns, MAC User, May 1995, at 17 (describing the creepy crawlers of the World Wide Web and the Infobahn).

"Cyber-terrorists, political activists, and hackers—and even governments themselves" have attacked government Internet web sites.[234] A 22-year-old cracker, for example, compromised eBay's security, causing the online auction's web site to crash and resulting in the loss of revenue.[235] A 16-year-old high school student hacked into a Massachusetts ISP, gaining access to more than 15,000 customer accounts.[236] Internet threats are difficult to understand, let alone avoid. "There are more laws that apply to your site, from more states and countries, than anyone can track."[237]

➤ [1] Preventive Law Pointers

[a] Computer Emergency Response Team/Coordination Center (CERT/CC)

Kim Vagos

The CERT/CC is a federally funded research and development facility located at Carnegie Mellon University. The main function of CERT/CC is incident response, but it also provides training to incident response professionals, conducts research into the causes of security vulnerabilities, and provides suggestions for improving network and internet security.

SPC's administrators may contact CERT/CC by telephone, fax, or e-mail or through the Internet. To use CERT/CC's services, SPC's administrators will need to conduct an internal investigation to gather the following information: (1) all general contact; (2) the name of SPC's host; (3) the IP address and timezone of the affected machine(s); (4) the IP address and timezone of the source of the attack; (5) information on contacts, if any, between the attack and the victim; and (6) a description of the incident, including (a) the date(s); (b) the methods of intrusion; (c) the intruder tools used; (d) software versions and patch levels in use on the target computer(s); (e) intruder tool output; (f) details of the vulnerabilities exploited; and (g) any other relevant information.

CERT officials will review and research the information provided by SPC, prioritizing the report. CERT officials will then give SPC various patch tools with which to remedy the vulnerability. Patches have been devised to plug most known holes in mass-marketed software programs, such as Windows 95 or 98. If no

---

[234] Jon G. Auerbach and William M. Bulkeley, Web in Modern Age Is Arena for Activism, Terrorism, Even War, Wall St. J., at B1 (Feb. 10, 2000).

[235] CNN Financial News, Hacker Crashes e-Bay's Web site, CNN Fin. News (Mar. 22, 1999).

[236] ISP Hacked By 16 Year Old, Geek News, Mar. 22, 1999.

[237] Lance Rose, Built a Safer Web Site: Webmasters Can Lower Their Legal Risks, Even When the Laws Are Uncertain (visited May 23, 1999), http://www.netlaw.com/safer.htm.

patches exist for a particular software or specific type of intrusion, CERT will notify the commercial vendors of the software of the existence of the vulnerability so they can addres the problem and prevent similar attacks in the future. CERT/CC's website, *http: www.cert.org*, provides the latest information on various types of incident response resources.

CERT distributes reports and studies covering Internet security vulnerabilities, available training and education opportunities, survivability research, technical tips, and various advisories on current security issues. CERT/CC is an important resource that SPC should utilize to help it in maintaining a commercially reasonable information security.

[b] Hacker Insurance

IBM and Sedgwick, a London-based insurance company, have combined to provide Internet security consulting and insurance services. A corporate client that implements their information security tools may also insure for loss of business revenues. Sedgwick offers insurance covering business interruption losses from $5,000,000 to $15,000,000. Coverage may be available for $50,000,000 or more for losses due to information security intrusions.

[B] Information Warfare

A *Wall Street Journal* reporter described the unknown and possibly unknowable dangers of Internet threats as an "eerily quiet day at the beach. [W]e're standing on the shore, wondering what the weather's going to be like, while a 300-foot tidal wave is mounting unseen at sea."[238] The unseen tidal wave represents the possible loss of marketable information products, such as software, but also proprietary information, such as customer lists, product designs, marketing plans, and other material protected by trade secrets. Malicious hackers, white-collar criminals, career criminals, members of organized gangs, and terrorists could thwart the growth of e-business. Many business executives fear that the potential Internet gold rush will suddenly veer into the Infobahn Hell of unknown or unknowable cybercriminals who infiltrate corporate computer networks. Consequently, companies on the Internet must ensure that their sites are secure and that they have a comprehensive information security policy in place. Information security is to e-business as having a parachute is to skydiving. "If at first you don't succeed in e-business, so much for skydiving."[239]

A recent IBM advertisement for Internet security features two 20-something hackers who have infiltrated a computer network containing confidential executive

---

[238] Frederick Rose, ModaCad Aims to Bridge Gaps in Virtual Mall, Wall St. J., May 14, 1998.

[239] I attribute this quotation to Victor O'Reilly, Games of the Hangman (1992).

compensation information.[240] The young woman hacker observes that the other company vice presidents would be surprised to know what one of the other vice presidents made. Her accomplice says: "They know. I just sent an e-mail to everyone in the company." This IBM advertisement uses fear to sell information security software: The fear that a company can lose its trade secrets and valuable proprietary information at the click of the mouse.

[C] Computer Crimes

As mentioned earlier, an empirical study of Internet security found that nearly 70 percent of surveyed companies had experienced at least one episode of information theft,[241] and half of the responding companies reported at least one theft of property of $10,000 or more.[242] Trusted company employees, both consultants and insiders, committed nearly one in five of these crimes.[243] SPC may build technological solutions, such as firewalls, to help keep external threats at bay, but it must not fail to monitor internal threats, such as the violation of SPC company security policies. The enemy within poses the most serious risk management problem for SPC. "Financial losses from unauthorized insider access are 30 times greater than from system penetrations."[244]

Information security is compromised by an epidemic of data leakage, piggybacking, wiretapping, and other information heists. *Data diddling*, generally done by insiders, means making false data entries, to embezzle funds or perpetrate other fraudulent schemes. The rise of e-business as a significant sector of our economy is likely to attract organized criminals, as well, and to keep white-collar criminals interested. Donn Parker describes how one enterprising information security expert absconded with $10.2 million in a funds-transfer fraud from a bank at which he had served as a security system analyst and consultant.[245] Some cybercriminals break into computers for the same reason Willie Sutton robbed banks: "That's where the money is." Carnegie Mellon University researchers found a statistical association between intrusions into Internet hosts and the monthly increase in Internet connections.[246]

---

[240] Hackers generally have a negative reputation. The term "hacker," however, at first designated someone who was a computer virtuoso. At MIT in the 1960s, a hacker was merely someone who could design innovative ways around difficult problems. Wade Rousch, Hackers: Taking a Byte Out of Computer Crime, Technical Review, Apr. 1995, at 32.

[241] *Id.*, at 183-84 (reporting survey of COMEEC BBS).

[242] *Id.*, at 184.

[243] *Id.*

[244] Consul Risk Management, Inc, Your Greatest Security Threat, an advertisement in SC Magazine, March 1999, at 26 (citing 1998 CSI/FBI Computer Crime and Security Survey).

[245] Donn B. Parker, Fighting Computer Crime: A New Framework for Protecting Information 19 (1998).

[246] April Streeter, Don't Get Burned by the Internet, LAN Times, Feb. 13, 1995, at 58.

The escalation of computer crime and its damage to confidence in Internet commerce has not been lost on the U.S. government. In mid-2000, Senator Kay Bailey Hutchison (R-Texas) proposed new legislation that would double the five-year penalty for "fraud or related activity in connection with computers."[247] This new revision to Title 18 of the U.S. criminal code would also double sentences for second offenses to 20 years and establish a "National Commission on Cybersecurity."[248] The executive branch of the U.S. government has also begun efforts to combat cybercrime. Both legislative and executive efforts, however, will likely stop short of full-scale Internet regulation. While the executive branch has called for increased expenditures for protecting the critical infrastructure, Department of Commerce Secretary William Daley quickly pointed out that "this is not about the [U.S.] government regulating this."[249]

[D] Denial of Service

The February 2000 denial-of-service (DOS) attacks heightened awareness of the damage a cybercriminal can impose on the marketplace. DOS attacks were once considered mere pranks, a macho show of computer prowess made by denying others the ability to gain access. Now, however, DOS attacks can threaten a corporation's ability to do business. A spokesperson for Senator Hutchison described the problem in a statement regarding the proposed amendment to Title 18 that would allow businesses to recoup "pain and suffering damages."[250] Although it cost eBay $5,000 to repair the problem one has to answer yes to the question, "Did [eBay] lose [more than] $5,000.00 in lost opportunities, market capitalization, and customer dissatisfaction[?]."[251]

Even though the February 2000 DOS attacks gained headlines because of the large e-commerce companies whose businesses ground to a halt, the real hack victims went largely unnoticed.[252] DOS attacks occur when Internet sites are flooded with so much traffic that legitimate users cannot gain access.[253] To conceal the source of the attack, hackers may break into and launch their attacks from corporate, small business, or educational computers,[254] using Trojan horse programs or

---

[247] Robert MacMillon, Sen. Hutchinson Seeks to Double Hacker Sentences, Newsbytes (visited Feb. 21, 2000), http://www.newsbytes.com/pubNews/00/143996.html.

[248] Id.

[249] Micheal Perine, White House Cybersummit Yields Pledge of Cooperation, The Standard (visited Feb. 21, 2000), http://thestandard.com/article/display/0,1151,10428,00.html.

[250] MacMillon, supra note 247.

[251] Id.

[252] Nancy Weil, Real Denial-of-Service Hack Victims Weren't Web Sites, Computerworld (visited Feb. 21, 2000), http://computerworld.com/home/print.nsf/all/00211E986.

[253] Id.

[254] Id.

distributed denial-of-service (DDOS) agents. Simon Perry, the director of security at Computer Associates International (CA), described the three characteristics of computers most vulnerable for use in cyberattacks: "They are turned on all of the time and connected to the Internet; they have high bandwidth access; and they are located at places like universities, small businesses, and increasingly in homes with Digital Subscriber Lines (DSL) or cable modem services."[255]

The battle against DOS attacks must be fought on two fronts. First, the web site must be protected from facial DOS attacks. Second, the internal computer infrastructure must be protected against being used as a pawn in the hacker's plan. CA's InnoculateIt and eTrust Intrusion detection products can help to detect DDOS programs such as Trinoo, Tribal Flood, and tntf2k.[256] The FBI's National Infrastructure Protection Center (NIPC) has also released a program for scanning for DDOS programs running on Linux or Solaris servers.[257]

➤ **[1] Preventive Law Pointer: Denial-of-Service Protection**

SPC's corporate culture should guard against DOS attacks by implementing procedures designed to thwart DDOS agents. SPC's employees need to be instructed to actively scan for viruses, Trojan horses, and other breaches in PC security. Additionally, employees should be instructed to log-off their systems and to shut down their computers for any periods of prolonged inactivity. Company antibreach software programs should be updated frequently, and systems administrators should constantly monitor NIPC alerts and messages from other security periodicals for possible planned hacking activities. New scanning software should be downloaded and implemented, as it becomes available.

If SPC encounters a facial DOS attack, a response team should implement a response plan and continuity of business plan. The response plan should include steps for identifying the offending IP addresses, notifying the offending party of discovery and, potentially, terminating their service, and reporting the attack to state and local authorities. The continuity of business plan should provide for maintaining essential business functions without the aid of Internet resources, alternative processing facilities, and where applicable, alternative methods for customer service and fulfillment.

---

[255] *Id.*

[256] CA, CA's InoculateIT and eTrust Solutions Protects e-Businesses against Windows Zombie Attacks (visited Feb. 21, 2000), http://www.cai.com/press/2000/02/etrust_zombie.htm.

[257] NIPC, National Infrastructure Protection Center Information; Trinoo/Tribal Flood Net (visited Feb. 21, 2000), http://www.fbi.gov/nipc/trinoo.htm.

[E] Computer Viruses

A 1999 survey of computer viruses concluded that the virus problem is getting worse. Three organizations had 263,784 virus encounters on personal computers during the 26 months between the start of 1997 and the end of February 1999.[258] Damages caused by viruses cost U.S. businesses $7,000,000,000 in the first half of 1999.[259] Of the survey respondents, 43 percent had experienced at least one virus disaster, defined as infection of 25 or more personal computers or of a server.[260] One in four respondents had experienced infections caused by outside diskettes brought into the workplace.[261] Two out of three virus disasters "were caused by macro viruses infecting Microsoft Word and Excel files."[262] A few respondents took up to 1,000 hours to recover following a virus disaster. The median response was that recovery took five person-days.

The U.S. media warned the country about the destructive virus Chernobyl, which was set to strike on April 26, 1999, the anniversary of the Russian nuclear disaster. Chernobyl disabled computers in Hong Kong, and despite the warnings, it also infected computers in the United States. The Computer Emergency Response Team (CERT) tracks viruses such as Chernobyl much like the U.S. Weather Service tracks hurricanes. Many viruses, like hurricanes, have first names, for example, the virus Melissa, which crippled corporate servers around the world on March 26, 1999. Melissa exploited an e-mail program, Microsoft Outlook, and Microsoft Word. "CERT reported that at least 300 organizations and 100,000 machines were affected" by the Melissa virus.[263] "Virus-planting pirates" are continually creating new viruses.[264] A recent corporate survey concluded, "Melissa was more than 38 times more frequent as the cause of virus disasters" and caused greater server down-time than any other virus.[265] Bubble Boy "is the first e-mail virus that could activate by simply being read or previewed in a computer user's Microsoft Outlook or Outlook Express e-mail program."[266]

---

[258] Michael E. Kabay, et al., Fifth Annual ICSA Survey, Anti-Virus Prevalence Survey (1999) (visited Dec. 13, 1999), http://www.icsa.net.

[259] Aidan Turnbulll, Don't Let the Hackers Beat Your Bank Security, Shore to Shore, Winter 1999/2000, at 27 (quoting Michael Vatis, FBI's National Infrastructure Protection Center).

[260] Id.

[261] Id.

[262] Id.

[263] Steven Levy, Biting Back at the Wily Melissa, Newsweek, Apr. 12, 1999, at 62.

[264] Id.

[265] Michael E. Kabay, et. al., Fifth Annual ICSA Survey, Anti-Virus Prevalence Survey (1999) (visited Dec. 13, 1999), http://www.icsa.net.

[266] Carlene Hempel, Anatomy of a Virus (visited Dec. 12, 1999), http://www.techserver.com/noframes.

Many viruses masquerade as useful programs. Trojan horses received their name from the Trojan horse in Homer's *Iliad*, delivered by the Greeks to the gates of the city of Troy.[267] One type of Trojan horse, for example, is "a program that is advertised as something desirable, but is actually something undesirable." The group calling itself Cult of the Dead Cow wrote one of the most infamous Trojan Horse programs, Back Orifice. Back Orifice would invade a system through a benign program, such as an animated greeting card attachment. After the user ran the benign program, Back Orifice would copy itself to the computer's hard driver.[268] Back Orifice would then log computer activity and open a back door for malicious users to usurp control of the system and read confidential information.[269]

Cyberspace criminals have also constructed viruses that permit the introduction of destructive code into computer systems. Electronic mail attachments were used to transmit the virus known as Chernobyl, which struck hard drives on machines running Microsoft Windows 95 and 98.[270] The Melissa virus also struck through e-mail attachments.[271] Many other documented cases demonstrate the misuse of legitimate protocol for destructive purposes.[272]

SPC's systems administrators should perform periodic spot checks for viruses using antivirus software. Further, before a visitor is allowed to download anything from SPC's web site, he or she should be warned (using a pop-up window) about the risks involved and the necessity of running antiviral software on all files downloaded from the site. SPC's antivirus software should be updated often, as new viruses are spread almost daily. Already, experts have found "more than 45,000 known viruses, and many new and altered viruses [are] discovered every day."[273] In the rapidly changing Internet, some risks will continue to be unknown

---

[267] VWA Glossary, Trojan Horse (visited Sept. 22, 1999), http://members.aol.com/mmxbytes/glossary.htm.

[268] NW Internet, The Back Orifice Backdoor Program (visited Sept. 19, 1999), http://www.nwinternet.com/~pchelp/bo/bo.html.

[269] *Id.*

[270] Keith Bowers and Iolande Bloxsom, CIH "Chernobyl" Set to Detonate, ZDTV, Apr. 26, 1999 (visited Sept. 17, 1999), http://web-e6.zdnet.com/zdtv/cybercrime/viruswatch/story/0,3700,2246676,00.html.

[271] *Id.* (noting that the Melissa virus caused an Internet traffic slowdown, whereas the CIH "Chernobyl" destroyed data by disabling flash bios).

[272] The Internet depends on standardized protocol to permit millions of host computers to communicate across diverse cultures and diverse programming languages. Examples of protocols are those rules developed by the International Organization for Standardization (ISO) and the standard ASCII character set for transmitting data. The misuse of protocols can result in widespread destruction not previously possible in the prehistory of the Internet.

[273] "Now there are around 45,000 known viruses. This time last year there were 25,000." Mark Ward, "Cornered: Virus Alert Over New Years Day," The Daily Telegraph (England), Dec. 23, 1999 at 2.

and unknowable. Yet many Internet security risks *are* known and knowable. Only the risk of known viruses can be reduced by state-of-the art antivirus programs, hence the need for continual updating. The risk of property damage from a newly developed virus cannot be eliminated entirely.

➤ [1] Preventive Law Pointer: Antivirus Protection

Antivirus rules need to be instituted as part of SPC's corporate culture. Avoiding viruses is a more effective means than allocating responsibility for the consequences of viruses. Scanning every disk, program, or data file may combat viruses. SPC's employees need to be instructed not to load any application, program, or data file without scanning them first for viruses. Antivirus software programs should be updated frequently.[274] Systems administrators should look for "strange occurrences" to minimize the effects of viruses.[275] Strange or anomalous occurrences include program loading that takes longer than anticipated, unusually large program files, or a sudden reduction in available disk space.[276]

Worms and viruses are programmed to propagate havoc automatically, *ad infinitum*.[277] A *worm* is a program that travels from one computer to another without attaching itself to the operating system of the computer it infects.[278] A *virus*, on the other hand, while also a migrating program, attaches itself to the operating system of any computer it enters and can affect any other computer that uses files from the infected computer.[279] Technicians may also differentiate a virus from a worm according to how the malicious program implements itself on the computer. In this sense, a worm is a type of virus or replicative code that situates itself in a computer system in a place where it can do harm.[280] A virus is a piece of programming code inserted into other programming that causes some unexpected and, for the victim, usually undesirable event.[281]

---

[274] Symantec Corporation, Norton AntiVirus Product Information (visited Oct. 11, 1999), http://www.norton.com/nav/index.html.

[275] *Id.*

[276] *Id.*

[277] A Cornell University student released an Internet worm in 1999. Worms are "self-contained programs containing malicious code that copy versions of themselves across electronically connected nodes." Michael D. Scott, Internet and Technology Law Desk Reference 555 (1999) (quoting U.S. General Accounting Office, Information Superhighway).

[278] United States v. Morris, 928 F.2d 504, 505 n.1 (2d Cir.), cert. denied, 502 U.S. 817 (1991) cert. denied, 502.

[279] *Id.*

[280] Whatis.com, What is a Worm (A Definition) (visited Sept. 19, 1999), http://whatis.com/wormviru.htm.

[281] Whatis.com, What is a Virus (A Definition) (visited Sept. 19, 1999), http://whatis.com/virus.htm.

The United States Department of Energy has developed a database of viruses, a project of the Computer Incident Advisory Capability (CIAC). The National Institute of Standards and Technologies of the Commerce Department also compiles an antivirus database. It is estimated that several hundred new computer viruses come online each month, rendering virus databases quickly outdated. Companies that purchase antivirus programs must have the latest version. Even so, new viral attacks may not yet have been detected by even the latest antiviral programs.

[F]   Integrity of Data

SPC has also made the decision to maintain an internal network, or intranet, not connected to the Internet, to help counter some of the potential problems of insecure data transfers. SPC's intranet is located behind the company's firewall and is dedicated to performing internal transactions. SPC has also established an extranet to handle transactions between vendors and other trusted suppliers. Isolating transactions with intranets and extranets will help prevent external wrongdoers from using network analysis tools to snatch passwords, credit card numbers, and other information.

Originally developed by Network General and now sold by Network Associates,[282] Sniffer was the first network capture and analysis tool. It became so popular that all similar tools became known as "sniffers." SPC's security precautions need to be calibrated to guard against the theft of proprietary and confidential information.

[G]   Protection Against Impostors

Forgers, impostors, and other wrongdoers specialize in altering data. A payment order, for example, may be altered or compromised by adding extra zeros or changing the name or address of the beneficiary. The security administrator needs object and subject-oriented authentication and access controls to protect data integrity. Object authentication will authorize a user to use a specific component of the information system, such as a parcel of data or a specific server; it allows companies to define who can use an object and how that object can be used.[283] Subject authentication authorizes an individual to use an application system or set of resources; it is typically implemented by a username/password combination.

---

[282] Network Associates, Inc., Sniffer Total Network Visibility (visited Oct. 11, 1999), http://www.sniffer.com/asp_set/products/tnv/intro.asp.

[283] Object Level Security (visited Nov. 22, 1999), http://as400.rochester.ibm.com/tstudio/ca400/odbobj.htm.

[H] Natural Disasters

One in ten companies have a comprehensive contingency plan for recovering their computer system in the event of a natural disaster.[284] Most data losses occur due to system malfunction, but they can also result from natural disasters, such as hurricanes or earthquakes.[285] A disaster contingency plan should establish a contact person within the company who will be responsible for coordinating emergency responses to disaster. Well-constructed contingency plans will also include provisions for the off-site backup of data, continuity of business, and computer restart procedures.

SPC needs a comprehensive system of Internet security to communicate securely over the Internet. Information security is only as good as its implementation. Scott Adams' Dilbert describes how a company purchased laptop computers for their employees to use while traveling—then the chief information officer permanently attached the laptops to the employees' desks to prevent theft.[286] SPC's chief information officer must tailor the security policy to the organization's culture. A growing number of companies are finding it more cost effective to outsource the building of an information infrastructure, such as a private network. GTE, for example, offers as a service to design standards-based Virtual Private Networks (VPN). GTE's VPN, for example, works with each company's Information Technology (IT) staff to implement security across all connections.[287]

Many ISPs now offer VPN services to their customers. The World Wide Web Version of *InternetWeek* magazine dedicates a section of its web site to tracking the VPN industry.[288] The site includes information on hardware vendors, service providers, and other news about the VPN industry. Whether Internet security is designed in-house or is outsourced, a company must take an active role in implementing effective security. No magic silver bullet exists for solving Internet security issues.[289] No technological fix can, for example, prevent employees from stealing trade secrets.

A comprehensive security policy supplements a technological infrastructure with employee hiring, training, and education procedures. Before rolling out a

---

[284] Jo Faragher, Special Report Disaster Recovery, Dealing with Disaster, Global Tech. Bus., June 1999, at 37.

[285] *Id.*

[286] Scott Adams, Dilbert Principles 11 (1996).

[287] GTE, Products, VPN Advantage (visited Apr. 27, 1999), http:www.bbn.com/productds/vpn.htm.

[288] InternetWeek Online, VPN Source Page (visited Sept. 19, 1999), http://www.internetwk.com/VPN/default.html.

[289] Evan I. Schwartz, Digital Darwinism: Strategies for Surviving in the Cutthroat Web Economy 5 (1999) (noting the tendency of the business community to seek magic bullet solutions to the problems of e-business).

web site, an online business needs to develop policies and practices to protect the integrity and confidentiality of information assets. As one security expert notes: "You cannot secure what you don't understand."[290] The online company needs to implement, test, fix, and again test its security.[291]

[I] Social Engineering Hazards

Social engineering refers to the use of deception or artifice to gain illicit access to computers. SPC may have the most sophisticated firewalls available, but it will still be infiltrated by a cybercriminal able to convince a low-level SPC employee that he is a computer or telephone repairman. Well-organized criminals have been able to gain unauthorized access to the computer system at the San Diego Supercomputer Center, compromising programs belonging to Tsutomu Shimomura and to the center itself.[292] Increasingly, companies are testing their systems by hiring hacker-gurus to attempt to break down ISP security measures.

Since confidential information is increasingly transmitted on the Internet, business executives must ask the critical question: "Just how secure is the World Wide Web?" An SPC telecommuter, for example, may give his child a company computer password. The SPC employee's child may in turn give the password to his entire online buddy list, which may result in an unknown third party gaining illicit access to SPC's trade secrets and other computer information. Comprehensive technological security solutions will likely fail without proper employee training. The social engineering aspects of firewalls and other information technologies cannot be ignored in the search for comprehensive information security.[293]

[J] Privacy and the Corporate Criminal

In a world of hackers, crackers, careless employees, and corporate espionage agents, it can be difficult to stay on top of computer security. Forgetting about any potential security breach may expose a business to incredible losses both tangible and intangible. Even faced with this degree of risk, many companies remain negligent in providing proper security. Yet even the most diligent company often forgets one very important protection—protection against its own actions.

---

[290] Bruce Schneier, "A Plea For Simplicity: You Can't Secure What You Don't Understand" (visited Dec. 12, 1999), http://www.infosecurity.mag.com.

[291] *Id.*

[292] *Id.*

[293] Firewalls serve as gatekeeper between company computers and the Internet. The purpose of a firewall is to prevent intruders from accessing SPC's computers. A knowledgeable insider may, however, bypass a seemingly bulletproof firewall.

Long before the Internet was opened to commerce and our vocabulary enriched with words such as e-business, deep linking, and cyberspace, businesses knew the value of information. Information was harvested and fed into computer systems to quickly determine new competitive advantages and potential market entry points. The Internet has merely expanded the reach of companies into the homes and lives of billions of potential consumers. With this new channel of information, new problems are born. How much can a company do with the information it gathers? How much information can they require from consumers? What are the ethical limits in the use of information? What are the contractual rights of each party when collecting and disseminating consumer information?

The world of legislation and policy around consumer privacy continues to evolve. The Electronic Privacy Information Center (EPIC) catalogues many of the current initiatives that shape this movement.[294] Recently, the FTC has become more active and has begun to investigate such heralded e-commerce giants as DoubleClick, Ebay, eToys, and Amazon.com.[295] EPIC has filed suit against DoubleClick for "unfair and deceptive industry practices."[296] The complaint against DoubleClick alleges that consumers do not know that their web behavior is being tracked, and in response, DoubleClick has changed its privacy policies over the last two years.[297] Perhaps the largest concern was the merger of DoubleClick's data acquisition mechanisms with the tracking capability of Abacus Direct, one of the nation's largest catalog shopping database firms.[298]

While many industry analysts, such as Michele Slack of Jupiter Communications, doubt that DoubleClick will be held liable,[299] companies must take care to ensure that controls are in place to limit accessibility to consumer data within the corporation. The Direct Marketing Association (DMA), the oldest and largest trade association for users and suppliers in the direct, database and interactive marketing field,[300] has taken steps to help its members regulate policies regarding consumer privacy.[301] In October 1997, the DMA issued a privacy promise assuring that all of its member organizations would comply with a set of rules regarding the collection and use of consumer data.[302] The DMA promise contains four provisions:

---

[294] *See generally* EPIC, EPIC Archive (visited Feb. 21, 2000), http://www.epic.org/security.

[295] Patricia Jacobus, FTC Investigates DoubleClick's Data-Collection Practices, CNET News.com (visited Feb. 21, 2000), http://news.cnet.com/news/0-1005-200-1551521.html.

[296] *Id.*

[297] *Id.*

[298] *Id.*

[299] *Id.*

[300] The DMA, Privacy—Privacy Promise (visited Feb. 22, 2000), http://www.the-dma.org/library/privacy/privacypromise.shtml.

[301] *Id.*

[302] *Id.*

1. Provide customers with notice of their ability to opt out of information exchanges;

2. Honor customer opt-out requests that their contact information not be transferred to others for marketing purposes;

3. Accept and maintain consumer requests to be placed on an in-house suppress file to stop receiving solicitations from the member company; and,

4. Use the DMA Preference Service suppression files, currently available for mail and telephone lists and soon to be available for e-mail lists.[303]

The details of each provision may be seen at the DMA's web site.[304]

Although company security administrators will not want to thwart the decisions of management or counsel, they should make sure that information exchanges among departments conform to corporate guidelines. Furthermore, SAs must evaluate the possible impact to corporate security whenever any new data management resource is introduced into the infrastructure.

 [1]   Preventive Law Pointer: Protecting Consumer Privacy

SPC has resolved to maintain the highest standard of ethics when dealing with consumer information. SPC's data collection and use policies will be clearly posted on their web site, and these rules will not be altered unless a compelling advance in technology, legal, or social policy emerges. Whenever SPC changes its data collection policy, it will provide reasonable and fair notice to all its consumers before implementing the change.

SPC will not sell consumer data, nor will it collect any data on consumer behavior that does not directly relate to its ability to improve its service to its customers. In any instance in which consumer data may be collected, SPC will provide a clear and easy mechanism for the consumer to opt out of the data collection procedure. If SPC must collect data to complete its contractual duty, it will offer consumers an alternative means of providing information with the assurance that no information will be obtained or used beyond the purpose of fulfilling the transaction and maintaining normal business records for accounting, regulatory, or other legal purposes.

SPC will ensure that all personal data dealing with consumer behavior will not be provided to any employee not having a business-related need for the information. SPC will apply all security mechanisms used to forestall external attacks to prevent inadvertent access to information by nonauthorized employees. SPC's security manager will be part of an infrastructure team that will review the implementation of any new hardware or software that provides data management, data

---

[303] *Id.*

[304] *See Id.*

mining, or other data analysis services for possible breaches of its stated privacy policies.

If SPC requires consumer data collected by other parties, it will ensure that the data is processed and filtered by a trusted third party. At no time will the SPC request or accept consumer behavior data that does not assist it with improving its customer service. Information needed for marketing or increasing business development will be gathered from published industry sources or through clearly marked polls on the SPC web site. All polls will state the underlying business rationale for acquiring the data, and SPC will guarantee that the information will be used only for that purpose.

All SPC security management and regulatory counsel will review industry sources, such as EPIC, The DMA, and the Electronic Frontier Foundation, to ensure that its privacy policy addresses consumers' concerns. Should SPC discover that its privacy policy does not meet the high standards of these organizations, it will adjust its policy in favor of consumer protection and provide the proper notification to its customers.

§ 3.04   IMPLEMENTING INFORMATION SECURITY SYSTEMS

The security risks of a business connecting to the Internet are not merely anecdotal horror stories. Real companies' computer networks may have holes in their electronic-mail systems that permit network break-ins.[305] Companies that have implemented off-the-shelf e-mail and other Internet applications without having a security plan may be at greater risk since they do not even consider themselves vulnerable to attack.[306] Many mass-marketed network security products take a "one-size-fits-all" approach to the problems of the Bad Network.[307] They make great claims, as well. One new security product was described as being close to "bullet proof."[308] Other information security products are represented as being "hacker-proof."[309] One marketing director stated that his company had comprehensive solutions "to provide hacker-proof security across any network."[310]

---

[305] Patrick Thibodeau, Security Experts Warn of Christmas Day Hack Attacks, ComputerWorld, Dec. 16, 1996 at 1.

[306] A large number of network security products exist to provide firewalls, antivirus checks, and plug-ins for Internet security. Terrisa Systems, for example, sells plug-ins for Internet security, as do Symantec and Norton, which both specialized in plug-ins for detecting and disinfecting computer systems affected by viruses and other malicious codes.

[307] See Anne Knowles, UUNET Suite Tightens Security: System Offers Firewall, Encryption for Virtual Private Networks, PC Week, May 29, 1995, at 14; Erica Roberts, Network Systems to Secure Hubs, Routers, Comm. Wk., Feb. 20, 1995, at 1.

[308] Network Systems, Network Systems Offers Public, Private Network Data Security, Network Management Systems & Strategies, Nov. 15, 1994, at 1043.

[309] Roberts, *supra* note 307 (statement of Tom Gilbert, marketing director at Network Systems Corp).
[310] *Id.*

SPC's systems administrator needs to probe for unauthorized devices such as modems connected to user PCs.[311] CERT also recommends that systems administrator conduct daily audits for anomalies or unauthorized devices. SPC's systems administrator should conduct a monthly inspection of the computer system to search for any other anomalies.[312] Companies need a contingency plan in the event of a disaster, a hacker attack, or any other security problem. Disaster recovery, emergency preparedness, and backup facilities are critical to retrieving any data lost during a computer outage and are vital for all companies.[313]

[A] Emergency Response to Data Disasters

SPC needs to discover as quickly as possible the name of the ISP through which the hacker attack is made and should keep on hand as many ISP emergency telephone numbers as it can. If a hacker infiltrates SPC's web site using AOL, Prodigy, or CompuServe, for example, the ISP will typically be able to provide records useful in investigating and dealing with the breach. The faster SPC acts after an attack, the greater the probability that the intruder will be detected. Some hackers, however, use anonymous services to conceal their identities, or commit their attacks using another person's identity. Law enforcement agencies profile hackers based upon the methods used to compromise the target site and the type of damage done to the target computer system.

[B] Qualified Webmasters[314]

SPC's webmaster needs to monitor its web site, especially because SPC has a substantial computer network. The webmaster needs to be a dedicated position or the likes of a systems administrator. The webmaster will have root, or superuser, access to the computers that comprise the Internet infrastructure. Each server should generate log files recording the Internet address of each visitor to the site. A special administrative computer may be configured that consolidates the log files from each SPC web server and application computer. This administrative computer may also contain defensive programs that generate statistics from the

---

[311] Modem banks, a key part of the information infrastructure of many businesses, are not the problem. The problem is unauthorized modems that can provide wrongdoers with access to company computers.

[312] *See generally* Carnegie-Mellon Computer Emergency Response Team (CERT) Advisories at www.cert.org.

[313] Two kinds of companies are doing e-business today: companies who *have* experienced computer failure due to viruses, hacking, or natural disasters, and, companies who *will* experience such a computer disaster.

[314] Vincent J. Froio, Jr., a former computer systems administrator who is now a Boston patent lawyer, drafted this section.

log files and monitor specific attacks against the SPC web site. SPC's webmaster must examine log files to determine potential intruders and to promptly uncover security risks.

[C] Allocating Security Risks

The use of indemnification agreements, hold harmless clauses, and other contractual devices may limit the online company's exposure for liability claims arising out of information security incidents. A webwrap "click through" agreement, in which visitors click an "I accept" or "I decline" icon before entering the web site, may be used to limit security claims from web site visitors.

The webwrap agreement is the e-business equivalent of a contract. A vendor or licensor of a product or service will display an information screen containing the terms of the license or agreement. The consumer will be asked to assent to the terms of the agreement before completing the sale, entering into the license agreement, or using the service. This agreement forms the basis of an offer and indicates acceptance of the contract terms. Unfortunately, the matter may not always be resolved so simply. Serious questions may arise over whether the consumer actually understood the terms of the agreement sufficiently well to bind both parties.

As of mid-2000, webwrap agreements had not undergone significant litigation; their predecessors, however, the software shrinkwrap agreements, have progressed through the court with mixed results.[315] Software shrinkwrap agreements generally accompany a program's installation disk, and they are most often found on the media envelope inside a sealed package.[316] Early court decisions were very conservative and reluctant to restrict parties to terms they had not been aware of when forming the initial contract.[317] More recent holdings have liberalized this attitude, holding shrinkwrap agreements to be more binding than had previously been held.[318]

Both webwrap and shrinkwrap agreements are used to limit liability beyond the standard protection offered by copyright law or the UCC. The shrinkwrap agreement differs from the webwrap agreement in that the online consumer usually has an opportunity to read and assent to the terms before completing the contract. If consumers cannot understand the terms, however, either because they are expressed confusingly or because the consumers do not read English well, this difference will evaporate.

---

[315] For a complete discussion of shrinkwrap and webwrap agreements, *see* § 6.03[A][2].

[316] *See* Brian Covotta and Pamela Sergeeff, Intellectual Property: A Copyright: 1. Preemption: (b) Contract Enforceability: ProCD, Inc. v. Zeidenberg, 13 Berkeley Tech. L.J. 35 (1998).

[317] *Id. See also*, Step-Saver Data Systems, Inc. v. Wyse Technology, 939 F.2d 91 (3d Cir. 1991).

[318] *Id.* Discussing a comparison between Step-Saver, 939 F.2d at 104 (shrinkwrap licenses found invalid by Third Circuit), with ProCD II, 86 F.3d at 1447 (shrinkwraps deemed enforceable contracts by Seventh Circuit).

SPC may still need to draft such an agreement. One strategy SPC may use is to place a link to the agreement, translated into various languages, on the webwrap page. SPC may also want to place a large notice on the webwrap page indicating that all questions regarding the terms of the agreement should be forwarded to its customer service department. A hyperlink with the customer service e-mail address could also be provided.

Each of these options will be considered and reviewed by SPC management. When it took its business to the Internet, SPC immediately entered the global marketplace. A small investment in planning could save costly litigation in the future. To prevent large opportunity costs, SPC could incrementally make the other language agreements available based on the demographics of its consumers, information that could be gathered through a simple questionnaire. Additionally, SPC could reduce its customer service costs by publishing a listing of FAQs with corresponding answers on its web site.

➤ **[1]   Preventive Law Pointer: Hold Harmless Clauses**

SPC management will not limit their planning regarding webwrap service agreement to contracts with its consumers. SPC might also want to seek special assurances in its paper-based contracts with suppliers. SPC may also wish to enter into agreements with trading partners about allocating the risks of information security. SPC may seek indemnification from its ISP, for example, if the corporate web site is hacked by unknown parties. (A thorough legal audit of ISP's security protection mechanisms would be a prudent precondition for an agreement.) The following indemnification clause is a simple "hold harmless" adaptable to most information security agreements:

INDEMNIFICATION

> _____, at your own expense, agrees to defend, indemnify and hold harmless Suffolk Personal Computer (SPC), its affiliates and their respective officers, directors, employees and agents, from all actions, claims, liabilities, losses, damages, and expenses, including reasonable attorneys' fees, arising out of or relating to the use of any material supplied by _____ including, without limitation, claims arising out of or relating to the content provided by _____, and the use of the domain name provided by _____ to Suffolk Personal Computers (SPC) for use with the _____ web site.[319]

---

[319] Vincent Froio, Jr., Esquire, drafted this clause.

[D]   Checklist for Internet Security Policy

Why does an online company need a security policy for Internet-related issues? First, the Internet is a networked world "not designed to be very secure."[320] The Internet is based upon open and interoperable standards. It is relatively easy to eavesdrop, spoof, and monitor e-mail, passwords, and file transfers.[321] In a six-month period in 1999, 60 federal World Wide Web sites were hacked and defaced because of a hole in a Microsoft product.[322] SPC needs an overall security policy for maintaining the security of its electronic transactions.

SPC's company employees need to be trained in the following protocol for reducing information security hazards:

1.   SPC employees should not leave computers running unattended. Screen-lock may prevent unauthorized access.[323]

2.   SPC's computer users should be instructed to make frequent backups. SPC's systems administrators need an overall backup and disaster recovery plan.

3.   SPC's antivirus systems must be updated regularly, and their use mandated, to reduce the risk of viruses from downloaded software or data.

4.   SPC needs to complete security audits to determine whether all software is licensed.

5.   Outdated databases or information should be discarded under a formal record retention policy.

SPC's security policy must be tailored to the security risks unique to its organizational culture. SPC's systems administrators will need to implement general security precautions, especially regarding known hazards with web browsers, Java, and web servers.

SPC's Internet security needs and standards should be made part of its training and education programs. The amount and type of training necessary will depend upon the policy instituted. SPC's executives, for example, will need to know about policy-level Internet security principles if they are to make informed

---

[320] National Institute of Standards, Internet Security Policy (Washington D.C.: NIST, 1999): A Technical Guide (visited Dec. 14, 1999), http://csrc.nist.gov/isptg/html/ISPTG-1.htm.

[321] Id.

[322] Win2000 Gives Security Boost, Federal Computer Week, Nov. 15, 1999 (visited Dec. 13, 1999), http://www.fcw/com/ref/hottopics/security/background/fcw-mktwin20000-11-15-99.html.

[323] Screenlock differs from commercial or operating system screen-savers. A screen-blanker is generally part of a comprehensive security package that refuses system access without a password. A screen-saver is a product originally designed to preserve the life of a computer monitor. Rebooting the system may easily defeat whatever security it provides. If no other security measures against unauthorized access are present during a system reboot, a cybercriminal may easily gain access to the data on the computer's hard drive.

decisions about what computer and security programs the company will implement. Internet security has a significant economic impact on any online business. Senior executives must be on board so security policies are given sufficient financial support. Managers, on the other hand, need to understand the chief threats and vulnerabilities of SPC's web site and automated information resources. The chief information officer or equivalent will need to design, execute, and evaluate Internet security procedures and practices. SPC must publish its information security guidelines for all employees.

Each SPC employee should receive a copy of the information security policy and should be asked to acknowledge their responsibility for complying with it. SPC's policy should make it clear that any employee's violation of SPC's network security or information security policy may result in disciplinary action. SPC's policy should also make it clear that security violations may also carry criminal or civil liability, as well as sanctions including dismissal. The information security officer should audit records and transmissions and should try to determine whether users are following the guidelines. In addition, the policy should be posted on SPC's intranet, extranet, and web site. Finally, the policy should be periodically reviewed and updated to prevent it from becoming a dead-letter regulation.

Information Security Guidelines

1. Publish authorization rules. SPC must publish its computer authorization rules in its employee handbook, on its web site, and in its training materials. After determining what security policies it needs to protect its valuable information, SPC must publish them in a publicly conspicuous manner. In addition to posting a hardcopy in a common area such as near the water cooler, SPC should have senior manager e-mail a softcopy to every person in the organization.

2. Provide information about company procedures and policy regarding basic security, authentication, and authorization. SPC's policy should explain its security technology and guidelines for safeguarding the company's information assets. SPC employees should be trained in using any newly acquired technologies as they are instituted. SPC's corporate culture must support information security: A bulletproof firewall will be useless if SPC's employees are lackadaisical about security measures.

3. Involve senior management in formulating security policies. Responsibility for assessing risk levels and determining the resources and support necessary to ensure computer security should fall to senior management.

4. Block any potential interference with or disruption in Internet service. Although denial of service may be less destructive than other security attacks, the downtime resulting from these attacks can be costly for the company. Specific steps should be taken to prevent denial-of-service attacks.

5. Prohibit the downloading of any illegal or obscene content or the excessive use of bandwidth by employees who download unauthorized video or massive amounts of data. Large amounts of data can flood SPC's computer network and result in downtime. If SPC has a low bandwidth network, large downloads should be scheduled during nonpeak hours. SPC employees need to be warned about the negative consequences of occupying bandwidth with non-critical data.

6. Implement automatic antiviral program to detect worms, viruses, Trojan horses, and other destructive code. SPC employees must be trained in how to avoid posting or transmitting files containing destructive code; they must also be instructed not to bypass security procedures. If viruses or other malicious code is detected or suspected, prompt reporting may minimize their consequences.

7. Require employees to use their own names in online communications. SPC employees should know, understand, and use forms of communication considered acceptable to the company. An employee's online conduct affects the image of the employer.

8. Maintain both hardware and software security. A number of information security protections can be built into a company's hardware and software. Users may, for example, be given limited access to files, or may have only specific devices allocated to them. Software may also be engineered to incorporate security features. Operating system software should control user access to authorized resources and capabilities. Both programs and data areas may be restricted.

9. Give notice that the company will cooperate with the investigations of local, state, and federal law enforcement agencies whenever security violations are suspected. Company policy should inform employees that SPC will adhere to industry standards and all laws applying to Internet use and commerce.

10. Hire and supervise personnel with security goals in mind. All online companies need personnel policies and procedures that emphasize the security of trade secrets, business plans, and other confidential information. A printed and circulated copy of company policy should include the names of a contact person who can answer questions about Internet security. Because "insiders" commit ninety percent of e-business security breaches, background investigations of employees and access limited to information and devices employees need to do their jobs are as important to information security as are firewalls and other technological barriers to invasion from outside. Finally, employees must be trained and supervised to ensure proper security.

11. Hold individuals accountable for proper information security. The online company must train its employees in the proper use of its information technology systems. As security technology improves and company security policies and procedures change, employees will require periodic security updates. SPC's web site, too, must be updated so that its security policy statements reflect its current practice. The company should give employees notice that from time to time the company will change its Internet security procedures and that employees will be expected to abide by amended rules.[324] Employees that violate security procedures should lose access privileges and face sanctions, including termination.

12. Report incidents and violations promptly. The online company must implement procedures for minimizing the costs and effects of an intrusion, virus, or security breach. Timely detection and reporting of actual or suspected security breaches can help to mitigate damages.

13. Develop contingency and disaster recovery plans. The online company needs to undertake contingency planning for the following emergency response activities: (a) backup and retention of data and software; (b) selection of alternate operations strategy; (c) emergency response actions; and (d) efficient resumption of normal operations.[325]

Information Security Checklist

• **Has the company designated key personnel for auditing its security policy?** Have systems administrators, network administrators, and security personnel been trained to recognize signs of intrusion?[326]

---

[324] The President's Commission on Critical Infrastructure Protection (PPCIP) studies the radius of the risk of cyberattacks on the government's operating systems. The U.S. government has a Computer Emergency Response Team (CERT) that tracks vulnerabilities and warns systems administrators to fix them. CERT provides technical assistance, security alerts, technical documents, and seminars relating to computer security problems. The CERT Coordination Center evolved out of a computer emergency response team formed by the Defense Advanced Research Projects Agency (DARPA) in 1988 in response to the first reports of Internet worms. The center works with private computer consultants and vendors to develop patches or workarounds for known computer security problems.

By subscribing to CERT's free mailing lists, SPC can have CERT's security advisories sent directly to its e-mail account. SPC's chief information officer must regularly consult CERT's alert list and advisories. (CERT advisories may be accessed at http://www.cert.org.) CERT also publishes vendor-initiated bulletins on their producs' security problems. In addition to subscribing to CERT's advisory mailing lists, SPC's system administrators should attend relevant CERT presentations, workshops, and seminars.

As Internet horror stories multiply, so, too, does the need for comprehensive network security. One malevolent cyberspace netizen, for example, set up a site called INFES-Station BBS, an anonymous file-transfer protocol (or FTP, which permits transfers of files between internetworked computers) with the sole purpose of distributing virus codes. The abuse of this FTPs, which normally ensure the orderly and reliable transfer of data, and the resulting undetected transfer of infected data, caused substantial harm to many company computer networks.

[325] These principles are based on Defense Department policies implemented by DOCT IT Security Managers. *See* Contingency and Disaster Recovery Planning (visited Dec. 14, 1999), http://csrc.ncsl.nist.gov/secplcy/doc-poli.txt.

[326] Carnegie-Mellon's Software Engineering Institute has a center for responding to computer intrusions. *See* the Carnegie-Mellon Computer Emergency Response Team web site, www.cert.org.

- **Has the company completed an audit of its information assets to determine what it needs to protect?** What tools have been implemented for auditing information security?

- **Has the appropriate level of network security been established, calibrated to the importance of the material to be protected?** Are secret documents available only on a "need to know" basis? Has a scale been established indicating levels of confidentiality (for example, confidential, secret, and top secret)?

- **Have access controls for levels of security been implemented and are they being enforced?**

- **What procedures have been instituted to train employees in the organization's policy for e-mail and Internet usage?** Does user education include how to respond to security breaches or other suspicious incidents?

- **Does the company web site follow accepted standards for information security to ensure transactional integrity? Is the web site secure for credit card sales?** Is the web site certified as meeting high-level accepted industry standards?[327]

- **Are procedures in place to protect the company's computer system from malicious code, such as Trojan horses, network worms, or other computer viruses?** Do employees know what to do if they receive a virus?

- **Is there a standard computer incident reporting form?**[328]

- **Have tests been run on the web site to check for security holes?** Has the company used the equivalent of "flight simulators" to check the security of computer networks?[329]

- **Have servers been reconfigured to block third-party e-mail relays by spammers?**[330]

- **Does the company have established procedures for informing employees of the organization's information security policy and of any changes to it?**

- **Does the company have a disaster recovery procedure in the event of an information intrusion?**

---

[327] *See, e.g.,* Verisign's CPA Web Trust Seal program, which certifies web sites that meet Certified Public Accounting (CPA) practices (visited Dec. 12, 1999), http://www.cpawebtust.com.

[328] Companies may use the computer incident form devised by the Computer Security Technical Center at the Lawrence Livermore National Laboratory (visited Dec. 12, 1999), http://ciac.lln/gov/ciac/tools/testemail.html.

[329] *Id.*

[330] CIAC, Securing Mail Servers to Block Third Party Mail Rely (visited Dec. 12, 1999), http://www.ciac.iln/gov/ciac/tools/testmail.html.

➤   **[E]   Preventive Law Pointers**

[1]   Sample Notice to Users

This computer system is the property of Suffolk Personal Computers. It is for authorized use only. Users (authorized or unauthorized)
have no explicit or implicit expectation of privacy. Any or all uses of the
SPC computer system may be disclosed to or intercepted, monitored,
recorded, copied, audited, or inspected by, any authorized site supervisors.

Unauthorized or improper use of the SPC system may result in
administrative disciplinary action and civil and criminal penalties. By
continuing to use this system, you indicate your awareness of and consent to these terms and conditions of use. LOG OFF IMMEDIATELY if you
do not agree to the conditions stated in this notice.

[2]   Responding to a Computer Intrusion

Kim Vagos

SPC has recently been victimized by a computer intrusion and a series of
denial-of-service attacks. SPC is willing to prosecute computer intruders to deter
future hackers who might be tempted to tamper with its computers or digital information in the future. Prosecution is worthwhile for the company because of the
time and resources it must expend to remedy the effects of security intrusions.
Corporate espionage places SPC's future at stake if the loss of business models,
customer lists, trade secrets, or other confidential information impedes its ability
to become a fully developed e-business.

Until recently, companies victimized by computer crime have been reluctant
to report intrusions to law enforcement agencies because of adverse publicity. A
growing number of high profile online companies, however, are now cooperating
with law enforcement officials to prosecute intruders to deter other computer criminals. Successfully combating a computer intrusion or denial-of-service attack
requires prompt remedial measures following the attack. The compromise of a
computer system or network often causes confusion in a company, making it all
the more important to take quick decisive action.

SPC should designate a person in charge of dealing with security intrusions.
This emergency response team head should maintain a chronological log of all
events. Systematic documentation helps prevent key evidence from being dispersed, overlooked, or misplaced. A well-documented log helps law enforcement
officials and prosecutors obtain convictions.

Network security managers should be notified immediately following the
discovery of a computer intrusion. At SPC and other online companies, the net-

work security managers have the best knowledge of company computer systems. The network security manager will be the key person to assist law enforcement in seizing and protecting evidence as well as in understanding the nature of the intrusion.

SPC will need to document the amount of damage that occurred before reporting the security intrusion to law enforcement. Law enforcement is far more likely to be willing to become involved in the case if the damage is great. SPC's network security manager should calculate the costs of the time needed for post-attack recovery. Both law enforcement and prosecuting officials will need these figures to proceed with the investigation. State and federal laws governing computer intrusion incidents observe certain damage thresholds, and only cases reaching these thresholds can be tried in court.

SPC's managers must consult with security officers, legal counsel, or law enforcement on how to proceed once an estimate of the damage from the intrusion has been calculated. The head of SPC's disaster recovery team should then contact the state police and the local Federal Bureau of Investigation (FBI) office. Telephone numbers for the state police and FBI are located on the inside cover of every phonebook, and the offices for both are open 24 hours a day. When contacting the state police, the head of SPC's internal investigation team should ask to speak with an officer on the High Technology or Computer Crime Unit. Most states have specific units devoted to computer crime, and an increasing number of states have units devoted to Internet-related crime.

In many computer intrusions, the FBI will have jurisdiction, due to federal computer crime statutes. The Computer Fraud and Abuse Act is the key federal statute governing intrusions, viruses, or unauthorized access.[331] In addition, the Electronic Communications Privacy Act of 1986 prohibits the interception of electronic messages.[332]

SPC's head of its internal investigation should request to speak with one of the National Infrastructure Protection Center (NPIC) agents, who have specialized knowledge of computer crimes. An agent will likely conduct an interview with SPC's internal investigation chief. The FBI investigates only violations of federal laws. If it is not clear which law enforcement entity has jurisdiction over the situation, the FBI is a good place to start. State officials may prosecute a computer intrusion if the FBI decides against a full-scale investigation.[333]

SPC's administrators must take steps to secure physical evidence, such as copies of intruder-damaged files and system audit logs. Companies often overwrite valuable system logs automatically after a certain period of time, destroying

---

[331] 18 U.S.C. § 1030 (West Supp. 1999).

[332] 18 U.S.C. §§ 2510 et seq. (Law. Co-op LEXIS 1999).

[333] Every state has enacted a computer crime statute. Many of the states model their statutes after the Computer Fraud and Abuse Act.

evidence needed for their case. SPC needs to limit access to evidence of the intrusion in the event that it is a trusted insider acting in concert with an outsider. In any case, all evidence, including backup tapes, needs to be secured, with limited authorized access, until the case is closed.

SPC must be aware of the hazards of transmitting or receiving e-mail from a compromised system. Many companies respond to an intrusion by replacing the computer system. SPC's managers must avoid corresponding via e-mail about the computer intrusion incident. Computer hackers often maintain access to the compromised system for some time following the incident and can intercept these communications. If SPC sends e-mails on a compromised e-mail system, it may unwittingly be providing a hacker with information about its computer system and emergency response and the criminal investigation.

If SPC documents each step and preserves evidence at every stage it will increase the probability of a successful conviction. A successful prosecution of a computer criminal, resulting in a ten-year prison sentence in a federal facility for maliciously unleashing a computer virus, will both deter the individual criminal and signal to others that such destructive behavior will not be tolerated. Deterrence depends upon certain and severe punishment following actions that threaten the social order. Criminal punishment expresses societal disapproval by ratcheting up the price of wrongdoing. The message of deterrence is that computer crime does not pay.

§ 3.05   LEGAL TROUBLES FROM INTERNET INSECURITY

Each episode of the 1940s radio program "The Shadow" commenced with a mysterious-sounding voice asking: "Who knows what evil lurks in the hearts of men? The Shadow knows."[334] A sinister laugh followed this statement of the Shadow's omniscience. That sinister laugh is emblematic of lack of security on the Internet. The anonymity provided by the Internet has led hackers to create web sites the sole purpose of which is to post software for launching attacks.[335]

[A]   Common Law Negligence[336]

A business may be liable for negligence if its conduct falls below the standard established by law for protecting others against an unreasonable risk of harm.

---

[334] John M. Carroll, Confidential Information Sources: Public and Private xi (2d ed. 1991) (comparing the loss of privacy due to the government's assembling of data files with the loss of privacy inherent in the concept of "The Shadow").

[335] The number of cyberattacks increased from 2,000 in 1997 to 8,000 in 1999. News Analysis & Commentary, Bus. Wk., Feb. 28, 2000, at 34.

[336] For a complete discussion of negligence in the Internet context, *see* § 5.08. Mark Maier, Esq., drafted the practice pointers in this section.

Negligence "is a departure from the conduct expected of a reasonably prudent man under like circumstances."[337] Businesses are held to the standard of the reasonable business, while professionals in a given business are held to the "diligence ordinarily possessed by well-informed members of the trade or profession."[338] When attempting to apply these standards to parties in the information economy, however, little authority exists on the standard of care expected from Internet security professionals and consultants. The evolving standard holds businesses liable for the failure to implement effective computer systems.

One starting point for extending the doctrine of negligence into this new type of conduct is that consultants are expressly or impliedly promising to perform security audits in a diligent and reasonably skillful manner. Therefore, the appropriate standard of care must be calibrated to the level of risk. One question is whether a company has a duty to protect the plaintiff from the type of harm that occurred from a given breach of Internet security. Is the risk of harm causing injury to a plaintiff beyond the scope of any duty to provide protection? A prior history of similar security breaches may establish foreseeability. In the absence of a history of similar intrusions and security breaches, foreseeability is based on all facts and circumstances.

This situation could arise from SPC's implementation of a telecommuter program through which its employees work from home via an Internet connection to the SPC internal network. If adequate security measures are not taken, hackers could gain access to the SPC network and harm SPC or any other parties with confidential or valuable information on its network. Third parties may thus have causes of action in the event of an attack, holding that SPC let "their [computer] systems be commandeered."[339]

In general terms, SPC would not have a duty of care arising out of a company telecommuting program. More typical circumstances involve plaintiffs who suffer a physical injury, such as from a slip and fall on the sidewalk of a telecommuter's house. Courts have found that SPC would not be liable where the major use of the telecommuter's house was residential. Only where the property had a predominately commercial use could vicarious liability be extended to SPC.[340]

---

[337] Pence v. Ketchum, 326 So.2d 831, 835 (La. 1976).

[338] Data Processing Servs, Inc. v. L.H. Smith Oil Corp., 492 N.E.2d 314, 319 (Ind. Ct. App. 1986); *see also* Young v. McKelvey, 333 S.E.2d 566 (S.C. 1985) (employee expressly or impliedly promising to perform work in a diligent and reasonably skilled manner).

[339] News Analysis & Commentary, Bus. Wk., Feb. 28, 2000, at 34 (quoting James Dempsey, General Counsel for Democracy and Technology).

[340] *See* Wasserman v. W.R. Grace & Co., 656 A.2d 453 (N.J. Super. Ct. App. Div. 1995), where the plaintiff was injured on the sidewalk in front of the telecommuter's house. Since the home had only a single-room office for telecommuting, and thus the majority of the home's use was residential, the house was not a commercial property of W.R. Grace, and the company had no vicarious liability. *See also* Hungate v. U.S., 626 F.2d 60, 62 (8th Cir. 1980), where the U.S. government, as property owner, was not found liable due to an absence of some special use or conversion of the sidewalk.

The analysis differs, however, where the injury arises out of the telecommuter's Internet connection to the SPC network. In this case, SPC could be found to have additional duties arising out of the use of its network by the Internet telecommuter, beyond those of any employee. These new duties could be based on telecommuting being a hazardous situation in plain view, or the employer itself creating the peril, or from a contractual relationship.[341]

The duty arises from the fact that the Internet connection is a separate, external pipe used predominately by employers such as SPC in telecommuter programs. Since this pipe would be paid for and provided by SPC to access the SPC internal facilities, it is similar to providing a company car to employees or to opening a retail store to the public. As such, employers would be held directly liable for inadequate maintenance, insurance, and control of its equipment.[342] Likewise, SPC could be directly liable for inadequate security and control of the Internet connections that lead to the injury.[343]

Once a duty has been established, SPC's particular standard of care must be calibrated or set. These standards could be found by applying a risk-utility analysis or a professional malpractice standard. The risk-utility analysis is discussed in this section, and the malpractice standard in the following section.

The risk-utility analysis was initiated by Judge Learned Hand in the hallmark case *Carroll Towing*,[344] in which a barge suffered damage because a crew member, known as a "bargee," was not stationed onboard during the night. Had a bargee been onboard, the damage could have been avoided. To answer the question of whether the bargee should have been on board, Judge Hand introduced the economic formula of identifying three factors:[345] one, the liability (L) of the potential damage without precautions; two, the probability (P), that the damage would actually occur; and three, the burden (B), of the cost of reasonable precautions adequate to prevent the damage from occurring. The product of the liability and the probability, known as the risk, is compared to the burden. If the risk is less than the burden, the standard of care does not require the investment in the precautions. If the risk is greater than the burden, however, the standard of care does require the investment in the precautions.

---

[341] Mark J. Maier, The Law and Technology of Internet Telecommuting SMU Computer L. Rev. & Tech. J., 28 (Fall 1999).

[342] For premise liability analysis, *see* Tillman v. Great Lakes Steel Corp., 17 F. Supp.2d 672, 679 (E.D. Mich. 1998), and Gellerman v. Shawan Road Hotel Ltd. Partnership, 5 F. Supp.2d 351, 353 (D. Md. 1998).

[343] *See* Maier, *supra* note 341, at 29-30.

[344] U.S. v. Carroll Towing Co., 159 F.2d 169, 173 (2d Cir. 1947).

[345] "[I]t serves to bring this notion into relief to state it in algebraic terms: if the probability be called P; the injury, L; and the burden, B; liability depends upon whether B is less than L multiplied by P: i.e., whether B less than PL." *Id.*

In the case of SPC telecommuters, the liability (L) of the potential damage would be based on the value of the information to which the telecommuter has access. On one side of the scale, would be placed items of little to no value, such as the tentative schedule of employee mid-morning coffee break, while on the other side of the scale, would be placed important trade secrets and confidential information worth thousands or millions of dollars, such as the secret recipe of a popular soft drink.[346]

The probability (P) that damage will actually occur must be calculated on a case-by-case basis. In the case of a SPC telecommuter, the probability can be determined with the following multiset process. First, most Internet domains[347] experience approximately one attack incident per year, and of these attacks, 57.9 percent[348] are successful. This is expressed as 0.579. The probability that an attack would come via the telecommuter would be 0.0001236.[349] Taking the product of these two numbers (0.579 × 0.0001236) reveals a probability that damage would occur to information stored on SPC's internal network of 0.0000715.[350]

The burden (B) to protect these SPC telecommuters varies with how secure one could make them. For telecommuters without access to valuable information, a proportionately small amount of security would be necessary. To protect information with a modest value, however, basic tunnel protection, which encrypts the information, is readily available from vendors such as AltaVista or Microsoft.[351] The cost to implement this type of protection for 1,000 telecommuters would be approximately $5 per telecommuter.[352] For a higher level of advanced tunnel security, products available from Altiga, 3Com, and Cisco encrypt information as well as prevent access to the telecommuter's computer. The cost for this kind of protection for 1,000 telecommuters would be approximately $55 per telecommuter.[353]

In order to identify the necessary standard of care, risk of harm from a telecommuter attack is first determined by taking the product of the liability and probability (0.0000715). This value is then compared to the burden (B). Starting

---

[346] *See* Maier, *supra* note 341, at 21-22.

[347] An Internet domain is a group of computers within the same organization, such as all the computers in the *suffolk.edu* domain. For information on Internet domains, see John D. Howard, An Analysis of Security Incidents on the Internet: 1989-1995, Carnegie Mellon University (1997), at Chapter 2, http://www.cert.org/research/JHThesis/Chapter2.html.

[348] The 57.9 percent accounted for root break-ins of 31.0 percent and account break-ins of 26.9 percent. The percentage of unsuccessful attacks was 42.1 percent. *Id.*, at Chapter 7, http://www.cert.org/research/JHThesis/Chapter7.html.

[349] *See* Maier, *supra* note 341, at 23.

[350] *Id.*

[351] Microsoft Corp., Virtual Private Networking: An Overview (May 29, 1998), http://msdn.microsoft.com/workshop/server/feature/vpnovw.asp.

[352] *See* Maier, *supra* note 341, at 25.

[353] *Id.*, at 27.

with the case of information of little or no value, the risk would be approximated by multiplying $0 by 0.0000715, which gives a result of $0. Thus, in this case, no protection would be required. For more important information, however, valued at $100,000, for example, multiplying that amount by 0.0000715 would give a result of $7.15. Since this is greater than the cost of basic tunnels ($5), but less than the cost of advanced protection ($55), the standard of care would require only basic tunnel protection. Finally, for highly valuable information, the risk to which could amount to $1,000,000, that amount multiplied by 0.0000715 would give a result of $71.50. Since this is greater than the cost for both basic tunnels ($5) and advanced tunnel ($55) protection, the standard of care would require advanced tunnel protection.

[B] Professional Malpractice

No general professional standard exists, but industries such as hospitals, insurers, banks, and other regulated institutions may have a statutory duty to protect the confidentiality of client records.[354] A plaintiff injured by a disclosure of confidential information may be able to maintain an action against an information security professional for failing to provide adequate security. Such an action would be analogous to Cruz v. Madison Detective Bureau Inc.,[355] in which a movie theater usher assaulted by a patron was permitted to maintain a negligence action against a contract security system for failing to provide adequate security. In that case, the security company was held to be negligent for failing to provide adequate security and for failing to following its own security procedures. It may similarly be sufficient to raise an issue of negligence if an information security company fails to meet industry standards or otherwise fails to provide adequate security.[356] In order to prevail in a negligence action, the plaintiff must prove that the consultant's conduct was a cause-in-fact of the harm to plaintiff caused by the disclosure of private information. Moreover, the defendant must be shown to have owed the plaintiff a duty of care to protect against the risk involved and that the defendant breached the duty, resulting in harm. To find professional malpractice for security professionals, the elements are even more challenging. Plaintiff would have to show the existence of minimum educational requirements,[357] a certification

---

[354] See Holtz v. J.J.B. Hilliard W.L. Lyons, Inc., 185 F.3d 732, 744 (7th Cir. 1999), where the special relationship between the parties created a duty to act in a reasonable manner.

[355] Cruz v. Madison Detective Bureau Inc, 528 N.Y.S.2d 372 (Sup. Ct. of N.Y., App. Div., 1st Dept. 1988).

[356] See Stanford v. Kuwait Airways Corp., 89 F.3d 117, 123 (2d Cir. 1996), where the standard was to have such as "superior attention . . . knowledge, intelligence, and judgment ... . . ," as well as, Heath v. Swift Wings, Inc., 252 S.E.2d 526, 529 (N.C. App. 1979).

[357] Michael Rustad and Lori E. Eisenschmidt, The Commercial Law of Internet Security, 10 High Tech. L. J. 213, 249 (1995).

process, and a prevailing discipline, and that the employer held itself as a professional organization.[358] In regards to the entrance requirement, although a number of technical certification bodies with challenging requirements exist,[359] certification is optional and is not required of any organization prior to its claiming to offer professional security.[360]

---

[358] Steiner Corp. v. Johnson & Higgins of California, 135 F.3d 684, 688 (10th Cir. 1998), where a professional that held himself out as a professional is liable for the negligent performance of duties undertaken. *See also* In re Daisy Systems Corp., 97 F.3d 1171, 1175 (9th Cir. 1996), where a duty of professional care required the plaintiff to show the defendant should have used such skill, prudence, and diligence as other members of his or her profession commonly possessed and exercised. *See also* Hospital Computer Systems, Inc. v. The Staten Island Hospital, 788 F. Supp. 1351, 1361 (D. N.J. 1992).

[359] Certifications exams are provide by Cisco Systems Inc., Cisco Certified Internetwork Expert (CCIE) (visited Apr. 18, 1999), http://www.cisco.com/warp/public/625/ccie/; Microsoft Corp., Microsoft Certified Professional (MCP) (visited Apr. 18, 1999), http://www.microsoft.com/mcp/; and Novell, Inc., Certified Novell Engineer (CNE) (visited Apr. 18, 1999), http://education.novell.com/cne/cnebroch.htm.

[360] *See* Maier, *supra* note 341, at 39.

CHAPTER FOUR

PROTECTING INTELLECTUAL PROPERTY IN CYBERSPACE

§ 4.01 OVERVIEW

This chapter is designed to help a company protect its intellectual property rights (see Table 4.1) while conducting e-commerce. Copyright, trademark, and patent law comprise the three primary branches of intellectual property law, and this chapter will discuss each in turn.

Copyright law is the federal law that protects original works of authorship: literary, dramatic, musical, artistic, software, and other works. Traditional copyright law is being challenged on several fronts by the rise of the Internet, and any company operating online must be aware of these issues.

Trademarks and domain names[1] are also important components of intellectual property on the Internet. If a competitor registers and uses trademarks of another company as a domain name, that company may have an action for trademark infringement and false designation of origin under section 43(a) of the Lanham Act. Similarly, companies must be aware of laws designed to protect trade secrets in cyberspace in the form of business plans, customer lists,[2] and other proprietary information.

Finally, e-commerce patents and the licensing agreements to use these patents are a critical factor for an online company, which must be aware of the latest developments in computer-based business method patents.

Throughout the chapter, references will be made to Suffolk Personal Computers (SPC), our hypothetical dot-com company, which will be used to demonstrate the practical impact of intellectual property issues. SPC maintains a hypothetical web site on the Internet at *http://www.spc.com* (the SPC site) that permits users to search for and access content that it has developed for its site. The reader should assume that SPC's web site consists of digital content including software, photographs, databases, and streaming video, all of which is classifiable as intellectual property. We will demonstrate how the company should protect its copyrighted software, trademarks, domain names, trade secrets, and patents while selling goods and services on its web site and also how SPC has rights not only in the digital information sold on its web site, but also in the web site itself.

---

[1] A domain name means any alphanumeric designation registered with domain name registrars or other authorities.

[2] Courts are sharply divided on whether trade secret protection is available for customer lists. H. Ward Classen, General Counsel, CSC Intelicom Inc., Fundamentals of Software Licensing, Presentation at Fourth Annual High Technology Law Conference: Licensing in a Network Environment, Mar. 10, 2000, Suffolk University Law School.

TABLE 4.1
Summary of Intellectual Property in Cyberspace

Intellectual Property	What Is Protected?	Length of Term/Registration
Copyright rights (federal)	To be copyrightable, digital works must be (1) an "original work of authorship;" and (2) be "fixed in a tangible medium of expression . . ." 17 U.S.C. § 102(a) (1999). The requirement that a work be "fixed in a tangible medium of expression" is satisfied by computer software. Copyright protection extends to source and object code. Copyright works apply to diverse works of authorship on the Internet (i.e., clip-art, video games, thumbnails of copyrighted images, music, DVD movies, and photographs). A copyright owner of a web site has exclusive rights to produce the work, distribute copies, prepare derivative works, rights to public performance, display and make digital performances. 17 U.S.C. § 106 (1999).	Author's life plus 70 years, works made for hire, 120 years from creation for works made for hire; term for joint work: 70 years after death of last surviving author; Registration in the United States Copyright Office. Copyrights may also be registered in foreign countries. The Digital Millennium Copyright Act of 1998 provides new rules for Internet-related copyright activities. The Sonny Bono Copyright Term Extension Act of 1998 increased the copyright term by 20 years.
Trademarks (federal and state) The Lanham Act governs the federal registration of trademarks. Section 43(a) governs unfair competition. Trademark registration is also made in the states, though protection is quite limited.	A trademark is a distinctive symbol used in commerce to identify goods and services. SPC may trademark symbols, designs, and names. Trade dress protection for web site design may also be available under section 43(a) of the Lanham Act. The more distinctive the trademark, the greater the protection. Fanciful or coined marks such as EXXON or KODAK have the highest degree of protection. Generic terms are not protectible. The likeli-	Trademark protection is indefinite, unless abandoned. Federal trademark protection is obtained by registering a trademark application in the U.S. Patent and Trademark Office (USPTO). A trademark applicant may also register trademarks in individual states. Protection may be obtained under the unfair competition provisions of the Lanham Act, federal or state anti-dilution law. Foreign registration may be advisable since registration with the USPTO applies only within the United States. A single registration for European Union

TABLE 4.1
Summary of Intellectual Property in Cyberspace (Continued)

Intellectual Property	What Is Protected?	Length of Term/Registration
	hood of confusion is the touchstone of trademark infringement and means roughly that a customer is confused about the source of goods or services. The use of another's trademark in a domain name may also dilute the trademark through tarnishment or blurring.	countries is made in Alicante, Spain. State trademark protection provides only limited protection.
Trade secrets (state only)	Commercially valuable secret information such as customer lists, business models, formulas, or business methods.	Trade secret protection is indefinite so long as reasonable efforts are made to maintain secrecy and the information does not become generally known. Protection lasts until the information is disclosed and no longer secret. Most states have adopted the Uniform Trade Secrets Act. There is no provision for registering trade secrets.
Patents Patents are registered with the United States Patent & Trademark Office ("USPTO").	Patents protect inventions securing a monopoly for a limited period in return for disclosure of the invention. To qualify for patent protection, inventions must be novel, utilitarian, and non-obvious ("one-click" method) of ordering goods and services online, methods for the real-time processing of loans. Processes, products, and plants may be patentable subject matter. Patent protection is for inventions which are nonobvious, useful, and novel.	Exclusive rights for 20 years from the date of application. Patent protection is obtained by registering a patent claim with the USPTO. The three statutory requirements for obtaining a patent are (1) novelty, (2) utility, and (3) nonobviousness.

continued

TABLE 4.1
Summary of Intellectual Property in Cyberspace(Continued)

Method for obtaining protection	An infringer may be found liable for direct infringement for unauthorized copying. Direct copyright infringement is a strict liability offense, whereas contributory infringement requires proof of a defendant's knowledge. A defendant is liable for vicarious liability even if the defendant did not know of the infringing activity of a third party. To prevail on a contributory or vicarious copyright claim, a plaintiff must show direct infringement by a third party. A court found that visitors to Napster site engaged in direct infringement and that Napster had knowledge of the infringing activity and contributed to infringing conduct of site visitors. The court also found Napster was vicariously liable because it had a direct financial interest in the visitor's infringing activities.[a] A federal court does not have jurisdiction of a copyright infringement claim until the copyright is registered.
Remedies for infringement	Copyright infringement occurs if there is copying done without copyright owner's authorization. Remedies for infringement include (1) injunction; (2) seizure of infringing articles; (3) actual damages plus profits and statutory damages; (4) costs; and (5) criminal penalties. The No Electronic Theft Act of 1997 permits federal prosecution for willful copyright infringement even if the infringer does not act for a commercial purpose or for private financial gain.[b]

[a] Contributory infringement results when a defendant knowingly contributes to infringing conduct of another party. Vicarious copyright infringement occurs if a defendant has a right to supervise the direct infringer and financially benefits from the direct infringer's conduct. SPC is vicariously liable for an online partner's infringing conduct if SPC had a right to supervise and receive profits from the infringing activity. An employer such as SPC could be directly liable for its own infringement and be liable for vicarious or contributory infringement for the acts of its employees, coventurers, or partners.

[b] The No Electronic Theft Act closed the loophole in United States v. Lamacchia, 871 F. Supp. 535 (D. Mass. 1994) (holding that a defendant could not be prosecuted for criminal copyright infringement under the wire fraud statute where no commercial purpose or financial gain was proven).

§ 4.02 COPYRIGHTS IN CYBERSPACE

[A] Overview

The federal law of copyright protects original works of authorship fixed in a tangible form,[3] and a copyright owner has the exclusive right to reproduce copy-

---

[3] See A & M Records, Inc. v. Napster, Inc. 2000 U.S. Dist. LEXIS 11862 (N.D. Ca., Aug. 10, 2000) (enjoining Internet company because of a reasonable likelihood of success on contributory and vicarious copyright infringement claims for assisting site visitors in copying plaintiffs' copyrighted music).

righted work, distribute copies, and display the copyrighted works publicly.[4] Courts have had little difficulty ruling that copyright protection extends to online materials.[5]

The Internet has made it easier to copy artwork, photographs, streaming video, text computer software, and other information, and recent changes in copyright law are accommodating changing technologies. Web sites are a collection of data, video, sounds, and images accessible to hundreds of millions of Internet users. Many of these materials have their own copyrights, and a web site as a whole may also have copyright protection as a work of authorship.[6]

A company operating online must register its copyright to protect the original elements of its own web site. The company will also be subject to direct copyright infringement for using images, music, clip art, video, and other copyrighted materials on its web site without the owner's permission or authorization[7] or even if one of its employees uploads or downloads copyrighted materials without permission.

[B] Constitutional and Statutory Authority

The United States Constitution provides for the protection of intellectual property by granting Congress the power to "promote the Progress of Science and useful Arts, by securing for limited times to Authors and Inventors the exclusive Right to their Writings and Discoveries."[8] The power to determine the duration of copyright terms rests with Congress. Congress extended the length of the copyright term four times in the past century. It is crucial to be aware of the length of the copyright terms because, after expiration, the copyright work descends into the public domain where it may be freely copied.

[C] The Copyright Act of 1976

Copyright is a federal statutory privilege that applies to works "fixed in a tangible medium" that satisfies a minimum threshold of creativity. Copyright protects literary and dramatic works but not facts, ideas, systems, or mechanics of operation. Section 102(a) of the Copyright Act provides:

> Copyright protection subsists . . . in original works of authorship fixed in any tangible medium of expression, now known or later developed, from

---

[4] 17 U.S.C. § 106 (1999).

[5] Playboy Enterprises, Inc. v. Starware Pub. Corp., 900 F. Supp. 433, 437-38 (S.C. Fla. 1995).

[6] Copyright Act, 17 U.S.C. § 401(D) (1999).

[7] *See, e.g.*, Marobie-FL., Inc. v. National Assoc. of Fire Equipment Distributors, 983 F. Supp. 1167 (N.D. Ill. 1997) (finding defendant liable for using copyrighted clip art on web site without permission or authorization).

[8] *See* U.S. Const. art. I, § 8, cl. 8.

which they can be perceived, reproduced or otherwise communicated, either directly or with the aid of a machine or a device.[9]

An online company may protect content on its web site and in the web site itself by registering with the United States Copyright Office (Copyright Office). A prima facie case for infringement is made when a copyright owner shows proof of ownership and copying. Third parties may be liable for vicarious or contributory infringement even if they have not copied or displayed protected material,[10] although copyright infringement that occurs solely outside the territorial boundaries of the United States is outside the scope of federal copyright protection.[11] An online company needs to register individually in the countries where it seeks copyright protection.

[1] Copyright Terms and Extensions

The history of copyright has been a continuous expansion in the copyright term. Copyrighted works created after January 1, 1978, are protected for the life of the author plus 70 years. For joint works, protection is life of the last surviving author plus 70 years. If a work was created (fixed in tangible form for the first time) on or after January 1, 1978, it is automatically protected from the moment

---

[9] 17 U.S.C. § 102 (1999).

[10] To establish a prima facie case of copyright infringement, the plaintiff must prove ownership of copyrighted material and "copying" by the defendant. Infringement occurs when a defendant violates one of the exclusive rights of the copyright holder. These rights include the right to reproduce the copyrighted work, the right to prepare derivative works, the right to distribute copies to the public and the right to publicly display the work. 17 U.S.C. § 106(1) (3) & (5) (1999). There are two general types of infringement: direct and imputed. A copyright owner need not prove knowledge or intent to establish liability for direct copyright infringement. 17 U.S.C. § 504(c). Imputed liability, in turn is divided into contributory infringement or vicarious liability. Contributory infringement is established where the defendant "with knowledge of the infringing activity, induces, causes or materially contributes to the infringing conduct of another." Gershwin Publishing Corp. v. Columbia Artists Management, Inc., 443 F.2d 1159, 1162 (2d Cir. 1971); Sega Enterprises, Ltd. v. MAPHIA, 857 F. Supp. 679 (N.D. Calif. 1994). Liability for contributory infringement evolved out of the common law doctrine that one who knowingly participates or furthers a tortious act is jointly and severally liable with the prime torfeasor. Gershwin, id. at 1162. Actual knowledge material was copyrighted is not required. Rather, all that needs to be proven is that the infringer had reason to know of copying. Cable/Home Communications v. Network Production, Inc., 902 F.2d 829, 833 (11th Cir. 1999). The principal difference between contributory infringement and vicarious liability is the degree of knowledge. A defendant may be liable for vicarious liability even if he had no knowledge of the infringing activity. One may be vicariously liable if he has the right ability to supervise the infringing activity where the defendant has a direct financial interest in the infringing activities. Gershwin, id. at 1162. Vicarious liability extends beyond the employer-employee relationship and a vicarious liability extends to acts of independent contractors. Gershwin, id.

[11] Subafilms, Ltd. v. MGM-PATHE Communications Co., 24 F.3d 1088 (9th Cir. 1994) (holding that extraterritorial copyright infringement did not state a claim for relief under the U.S. Copyright Act).

of its creation and is ordinarily given a term enduring for the author's life plus an additional 70 years after the author's death. For works created, published, or registered before January 1, 1978, the copyright lasts for a first term of 28 years from the date it was secured. During the last (twenty-eighth) year of the first term, the copyright was eligible for renewal.[12]

Table 4.2 describes the copyright term *after* the Sonny Bono Copyright Term Extension Act of 1998 (CTEA), which became law on October 27, 1998.[13] The CTEA extends the copyright duration for individual and corporate entities by an additional 20 years. Individual authors now receive copyright protection for life plus 70 years.[14] Corporate entities receive copyright protection for a "work made for hire" to 95 years from publication or 120 years from creation, whichever is shorter. These rights apply to works created on or after January 1, 1978.

The CTEA also immediately extends copyrights still in their renewal term at the time the Act was passed. The effect of the law is to delay the entrance of copyrighted material into the public domain. In Eldred v. Reno,[15] an Internet publisher sought a declaratory judgment that the CTEA was unconstitutional as a retroactive extension of copyright exceeding Congress' enumerated powers under the copyright clause of the United States Constitution. The federal district court for the District of Columbia granted the defendant's motion on the pleadings holding that the CTEA copyright extension was within Congress' extension.[16] The court rejected the plaintiff's First Amendment claim with a single sentence that "the Court rejects Plaintiffs' First Amendment claim."[17] The court also rejected the plaintiff's argument that the CTEA violated the public trust doctrine.[18]

[2] Copyright Term for Joint Works

Joint works are works created by "two or more authors with the intention that their contributions be merged into inseparable or interdependent parts of a unitary whole."[19] The duration of a joint work not classified as a work for hire is 70 years after the last surviving author's death. The duration of copyright in joint works is generally computed in the same way as for works created on or after January 1, 1978: the life-plus-70 or 95/120-year terms apply to them as well. The Copyright

---

[12] The basic copyright rules described in this section are based upon the publication of the United States Copyright Office, Questions Frequently Asked in the Copyright Office (visited March 1, 2000), http://www.lcweb.loc.gov/copyright/faq.html.

[13] Sonny Bono Copyright Term Extension Act of 1998, Pub. L. No. 105-298, 112 Stat. 2827 (1998).

[14] *Id.*

[15] 74 F. Supp. 2d 1 (D. D.C. 1999).

[16] *Id.* at 3.

[17] *Id.*

[18] *Id.* at 9.

[19] 17 U.S.C. § 10 (1999).

TABLE 4.2
Copyright Terms

Type of Work and Date of Creation	Length of Term
Single author: On or after 1/1/78	Life of author + 70 years after the author's death
Joint authors: On or after 1/1/78	Life of last surviving author + 70 years
Works made for hire: On or after 1/1/78	95 years from first publication or 120 years from creation, whichever is shorter
Work originally created before 1/1/78, but not published or registered by that date	Duration is same as for work created on or after 1/1/78: author's life + 70 or 95/120-year terms apply to them.
Work originally created and published or registered before 1/1/78	Extends renewal term of copyrights still subsisting on that date by an additional 20 years (renewal term of 67 years and a total term of 95 years).*

*If a work is unpublished as of January 1, 1978, protection lasts for the life of the author plus 70 years, but the term expires no earlier than December 31, 2000. If a previously unpublished work is published between January 1, 1978, and December 31, 2002, the term extends until December 31, 2047.

Act provides that in no case will the term of copyright for works in this category expire before December 31, 2002, and for works published on or before December 31, 2002, the term of copyright will not expire before December 31, 2047. The CTEA expanded copyright an additional twenty years.

[3] Copyright Renewal

The Copyright Act states that the parties entitled to the renewal and extension of copyrights are: (1) the author of such work, if the author is still living; (2) the widow, widower, or children of the author, if the author is not living; and (3) the author's executors, if the author, widower, or children are not living; or (4) next of kin.[20] The 1976 Act extended the renewal term from 28 to 47 years for copyrights that were subsisting on January 1, 1978. Pre-1978 copyrights restored under the Uruguay Round Agreements Act (URAA) are eligible for a total term of protection of 75 years.[21] The CTEA further extended the renewal term of copyrights still subsisting on that date by an additional 20 years, providing for a renewal term of 67 years and a total term of protection of 95 years.[22]

---

[20] 17 U.S.C. § 304(a)(1)(c).

[21] *Id.*

[22] *Id.*

The Copyright Act creates copyright protection for the author's life, plus 50 years for individual works, and 75 years for commissioned works or works for hire.[23] When an author dies before the renewal period begins, his or her executor is entitled to the renewal rights unless the author has assigned those rights to another party, such as a publisher. The author may, during the first term of the copyright, assign renewal rights. Section 304(b) of the Copyright Act provides:

> Copyrights in Their Renewal Term or Registered for Renewal before January 1, 1978. The duration of any copyright, the renewal term of which is subsisting at any time between December 31, 1976, and December 31, 1977, inclusive, or for which renewal registration is made between December 31, 1976, and December 31, 1977, inclusive, is extended to endure for a term of seventy-five years from the date the copyright was originally secured.[24]

[4]   Exclusive Rights of Copyright

The Copyright Act grants the copyright owner the right to display "literary, musical, dramatic, and choreographic works, pantomimes, and pictorial, graphic, or sculptural works, including the individual images of a motion picture or other audiovisual work publicly."[25] Copyright ownership refers to the exclusive rights granted by section 106 of the 1976 Copyright Act: (1) to reproduce the copyrighted work in copies or phonorecords; (2) to prepare derivative works based upon the copyrighted works;[26] (3) to distribute copies or phonorecords of the copyrighted work to the public by sale or other transfer of ownership, or by rental, lease or lending; and, (4) in the case of literary, musical, dramatic, and choreographic works, pantomimes, and motion pictures and other audiovisual works, to perform the copyrighted work publicly.[27] A performance or display of a work means to perform or display it at a place open to the public.

[a]   What Is Copyrightable?

Copyright law protects "original works of authorship" that are 'fixed' in a tangible medium of expression."[28] In other words, copyright protects expression but not ideas, facts, nonoriginal databases, and public domain and government materials. Quantum theory is not copyrightable. A book describing how quantum

---

[23] *Id.*

[24] 17 U.S.C. § 304(b) (1999).

[25] *Id.*

[26] A "derivative work" is a work based upon a preexisting work. A motion picture version of *Oliver Twist* is a derivative work.

[27] 17 U.S.C. § 106 (1999) (stating the exclusive rights of owners of copyrights).

[28] 17 U.S.C. § 101 (1999).

theory explains the periodic chart of the elements, however, is copyrightable.[29] Inventions, based upon quantum theory, such as the laser or microchip, are patentable. Einstein's general theory of relativity is an idea not copyrightable, but a book on Albert Einstein's thought experiments in the 1930s is copyrightable. In an online environment, a company must obtain copyright protection for all created works of authorship, including software code, images, clip art, text, software, audio, HTML, and other digital information.

The Copyright Act recognizes eight categories of authorship, all of which may be displayed in an Internet transmission: (1) literary work; (2) musical works, including any accompanying words; (3) dramatic works, including any accompanying music; (4) pantomimes and choreographic works; (5) pictorial, graphic, and sculptural works; (6) motion pictures and other audiovisual works; (7) sound recordings; and (8) architectural works.[30] Section 106 of the 1976 Copyright Act sets forth the six exclusive rights of copyright owners (these also apply to online content):

1. *To reproduce* the work in copies or phonorecords;
2. To prepare *derivative works* based upon the work;
3. *To distribute copies or phonorecords* of the work to the public by sale or other transfer of ownership, or by rental, lease, or lending;
4. *To perform the work publicly,* in the case of literary, musical, dramatic, and choreographic works, pantomimes, and motion pictures and other audiovisual works;
5. *To display the copyrighted work publicly,* in the case of literary, musical, dramatic, and choreographic works, pantomimes, and pictorial, graphic, or sculptural works, including the individual images of a motion picture or other audiovisual work; and
6. In the case of *sound recordings, to perform the work publicly* by means of a *digital audio transmission.*

Several categories of works are generally not eligible for federal copyright protection. Works so fleeting and ephemeral that they are not fixed in a tangible form of expression are not copyrightable. No copyright covers works written in the sands of a Cape Code beach or etched on a frosty windshield. An unrecorded improvisational speech is not copyrightable. Titles of books or periodicals are not copyrightable. Short phrases and slogans such as "Got Milk?" are not copyrightable, but they may be trademarked. Familiar symbols, designs, and variations in typographic lettering or coloring are not copyrightable. Lettering or colorings are not copyrightable. Federal copyright law does not protect:

---

[29] *See, e.g.,* J.P. McEvoy and Oscar Zarate, Introducing Quantum Theory 3 (1997).

[30] 17 U.S.C. § 102 (1999) (defining the subject matter of copyright).

1. Ideas, procedures, methods, systems, processes, concepts, principles, discoveries, or devices, as distinguished from a description, explanation, or illustration.

2. Works consisting *entirely* of information that is common property and that contains no original authorship (for example: standard calendars, height and weight charts, tape measures and rulers, and lists or tables taken from public documents or other common sources).[31]

[b]   Originality

A work needs some minimum degree of originality to quality for copyright protection, and a work is original if it was independently created by the author and possesses some minimal level of creativity. Copyright law protects any content a company places on its web site as well as postings by visitors, although most compilations of data lack the creativity necessary for protection. In Feist Publications, Inc. v. Rural Telephone Service Co., Inc.,[32] the Supreme Court found that a telephone directory consisting of white and yellow pages lacked the minimal originality to receive copyright protection. The Court rejected a "sweat of the brow" theory that the time and effort in compiling and organizing a database satisfied the originality requirement for copyright protection.[33]

Since *Feist*, there has been intense lobbying to create additional database protection.[34] The European Union adopted database protection in a directive that requires individual signatory countries to develop conforming amendments. In fall 1999, the House Judiciary Committee considered a bill, H.R. 354, "that would grant copyright protection to collections of computerized data and make it illegal for competitors to copy, repackage, and sell information obtained over the Internet or from CD-ROMS." The bill would impose civil and criminal liability for the unauthorized extraction of a database, providing that the extraction adversely affected the market for the product or service incorporating the database.[35]

---

[31] 17 U.S.C. 102(b) (1999).

[32] Feist Publications, Inc. v. Rural Telephone Service Co., Inc., 499 U.S. 340 (1991).

[33] Federal Legislation: Collections of Information Antipiracy Act, H.R. 354: Congress Introduces Database Piracy Bill for Third Time, 12 Software Law Bull. 185 (Sept. 1999) (discussing proposed bill granting copyright protection to computer databases). The statutory purpose of the proposed Collection of Information Anti-piracy Act is to revive the "sweat of the brow" doctrine struck down in *Feist*.

[34] The supporters of the Digital Millenium Copyright Act introduced a provision for database protection added to the Conference Report. Jonathan Band, Digital Millennium Copyright Act (visited June 6, 1999), http://www.dfc.org/issues/graphic/2281/JB-Index/JB-Memo/jb-memo.html.

[35] Microsoft Law & Corporate Affairs, Summary of Global Internet Legal Developments (for the period Jan.-Mar. 1999) 56 (Apr. 1999).

[c] Fixation

The second requirement is that the work be fixed in a tangible medium of expression. A work is fixed in a tangible medium of expression when it is sufficiently permanent or stable to permit it to be perceived, reproduced, or otherwise communicated for a period of more than transitory duration.[36] The Copyright Act provides that copyright protection may be obtained "in original works of authorship fixed in any tangible medium of expression, now known or later developed, from which they can be perceived, reproduced, or otherwise communicated, either directly or with the aid of a machine or device."[37] Software inscribed on a diskette or CD-ROM is sufficiently tangible to meet the fixation requirement.[38]

Material on a web site is fixed because it may be perceived, reproduced, downloaded, or transmitted. The Ninth Circuit, in MAI Systems Corp. v. Peak Computer,[39] held that simply loading a computer operating system into RAM constituted the making of a copy for purposes of the Copyright Act.[40] The act of transmitting e-mail or viewing a web page also stores copies in the user's computer operating system and creates copies. The web site visitor makes a temporary copy each time a browser visits a web site.

[5] First Sale Doctrine and Licensing

The "first sale doctrine" of Section 109 of the Copyright Act provides that the *owner* of a copy lawfully acquired may use, dispose of, or display it without risk of infringement.[41] Copyright owners have exclusive distribution and display rights. Copyright is therefore licensed to circumvent the "first sale doctrine" of the Copyright Act. If a copyright owner licenses a copyrighted work, the owner retains rights of distribution and display. A licensee of computer software may, for example, own the physical diskette or CD-ROM but not the copyrighted information inscribed on the diskette.

[6] Derivative Works

A derivative work arises out of a preexisting work and includes translations, arrangements, films, recording, or condensations, and an owner of a copyright has

---

[36] *Id.*

[37] 17 U.S.C. § 101 (1999).

[38] MAI Systems Corp. v. Peak Computer, Inc., 991 F.2d 511 (9th Cir. 1993) (holding that loading a program in a computer's random access memory constituted a copy for purposes of the Copyright Act).

[39] 991 F.2d 511.

[40] *Id.*

[41] 17 U.S.C. § 109 (1999). *See also* Bobbs-Merrill Co. v. Straus, 210 U.S. 339, 349-350 (1908) (holding that owner has no exclusive rights after first sale of a copyrighted work).

the right to prepare derivative works of preexisting works such as "a translation, musical arrangement, dramatization, fictionalization, motion picture version, sound recording, art reproduction, abridgment, condensation, or any other form, recast, transformed, or adapted."[42]

A Spanish translation of a Robert Parker novel is a derivative work, as is a French translation of the American film *Eyes Wide Shut*. New versions of e-commerce software or enhancements to search engines constitute derivative works. If a company has a multimedia web site incorporating film, video, images, photographs, text, and animation, these may be classifiable as derivative works.

[7] Automatic Creation and Notice

Copyright protection is automatically conferred upon a work of authorship when two requirements are fulfilled: (1) the work is fixed in a tangible medium of expression, and (2) it qualifies as an original work of authorship. Copyrights may be secured for all unpublished works, regardless of nationality or domicile. The Copyright Act of 1909 also required the copyright owner to affix a notice of publication on each copy published or offered for sale.[43] Before 1989, authors would lose their copyright by failing to comply with the notice requirement.

Companies should always include a copyright notice—the letter *c* in a circle, ©, or the word "Copyright" and the first year of publication of a work (Copyright 2001)—so that a defendant in a copyright infringement lawsuit cannot use an "innocent infringer" defense to mitigate actual or statutory damages. The proper affixing of copyright notice gives global Internet users around the world notice that its web site and content is protected by copyright.

[8] Works Made for Hire

The Copyright Act treats works prepared for an employee within the scope of employment as a work for hire, which means that the company for whom the work is prepared is considered the author. Works for hire includes work "specially ordered or commissioned for use as a contribution to a collective work in motion pictures or audiovisual works."[44] Section 101 of the Copyright Act defines a "work made for hire" as:

> (1) A work prepared by an employee within the scope of his or her employment; or

---

[42] 17 U.S.C. § 101 (1999) (defining derivative works).

[43] *Id.* at Chapter 1, § 10.

[44] *Id.*

(2) A work specially ordered or commissioned for use as a contribution to a collective work, as a part of a motion picture or other audiovisual work, as a translation, as a supplementary work, as a compilation, as an instructional text, as a test, as answer material for a test, or as an atlas, if the parties expressly agree in a written instrument signed by them that the work shall be considered a work made for hire. . . .[45]

[9]   Collective Work

A web site is a collective work if it includes separate contributions from different content providers. Copyright in collective work vests initially with the author of the contribution and includes the whole work. A co-branded site may include contributions from at least two creators of content, each of which has an ownership interest in the site as a collective work. Each author contributing copyrighted text, photographs, images, or other material to the web site may have a copyright ownership interest to the web site if it is a collective work. If a visitor posts photographs or text in publicly accessible areas of web site, for example, the site owner needs to obtain worldwide, royalty-free, and nonexclusive licenses to reproduce, modify, adapt, and publish such content.

[10]   Music

MP3 permits rapid conversion of CDs into electronic files that can be copied by Internet users. Copyrights may attach to the written music and lyrics as well as the performance. Hundreds of thousands of songs are downloadable at MP3.com, but a federal court has held that MP3.com, which permitted Internet users to copy MP3 files, willfully infringed copyrights in making unauthorized copies of compact discs.[46] In another case, a court held that the RIO digital recording device was not subject to the Audio Home Recording Act of 1992 and refused to grant an injunction.[47] Rights to use video clips may be retained by syndicators, and may only be licensed to a network.[48] Napster is an online application that permits the downloading of MP3 music from the Internet.[49] A court rejected Napster's argument that it was not liable for direct or contributory copyright infringement

---

[45] Copyright Act, 17 U.S.C § 101 (1999).

[46] UMG Records, Inc. v. MP3.Com Inc., 2000 U.S. Dist. LEXIS 13293 (S.D. N.Y., Sept. 6, 2000) (concluding that MP3.com was a willful infringer and imposing statutory damages of $25,000 for each copyrighted compact disc in the defendant's online database).

[47] Recording Industry Assoc. v. Diamond Multimedia Sys., Inc., 1999 U.S. App. LEXIS 13131 (9th Cir. June 15, 1999).

[48] James R. Burdett, et al., A Wake Up Call From Virtual Reality, Mid-Winter Inst., The Law of Computer Related Tech. 131 (1995).

[49] Tom Spring, Swap MP3s, Go to Jail?, CNN.com, Apr. 14, 2000, at 1.

because it was immunized by the Digital Millennium Copyright Act's safe harbor provision.[50] Napster's service of enabling Internet users to copy digitized files of copyrighted music without payment or permission is likely to constitute contributory and vicarious infringement.

[D] Copyright Infringement

To establish a claim of copyright infringement, SPC must demonstrate (1) ownership of a valid copyright; and (2) "copying" of protectable expression by the defendant. The case law recognizes three types of infringement: (1) direct infringement; (2) contributory infringement; and (3) vicarious infringement (see Table 4.3).

[1] Direct Copyright Infringement

If a company posts materials of another without permission, it can be subject to a direct copyright infringement lawsuit. Direct infringement is a strict liability offense that requires no specific intent or particular state of mind, although willfulness is relevant to the awarding of statutory damages.[51] Likewise, someone who posts a copyrighted photograph on a web site is liable for direct infringement.[52] To establish copyright infringement, the copyright owner must prove: (1) ownership of the copyrighted material, and (2) copying by the defendant.

[2] Contributory Infringement

An online company may be liable as a contributory infringer, which applies where there is knowledge and substantial participation in the primary infringer's activities.[53] A company is a contributory infringer to the extent it induces or materially contributes to the infringing conduct of another with knowledge of the infringing activity.[54]

---

[50] A & M Records, Inc., et. al. v. Napster, Inc., 2000 U.S. Dist. LEXIS 11862 (N.D. Ca., Aug. 10, 2000).

[51] 17 U.S.C. § 504(c) (1999). *See, e.g.*, Playboy Enterprises, Inc. v. Frena, 839 F. Supp. 1552 (M.D. Fla. 1993) (holding that knowledge is not an element of infringement and "thus even an innocent infringer is liable").

[52] Sega Enterprises Ltd. v. MAPHIA, 857 F. Supp. 679, 683 (N.D. Cal. 1994) (holding computer bulletin board operator directly liable for copyright infringement where it solicited subscribers to upload files containing copyrighted video games). *See also* Playboy Enterprises, Inc. v. Webbworld, 968 F. Supp. 1171 (N.D. 1997), *aff'd,* 168 F.3d 486 (5th Cir. 1999) (upholding direct and vicarious infringement).

[53] *See* Sony Corp. v. Universal City Studios Inc., 464 U.S. 417 (1984).

[54] *Id.* (citing Gershwin Publishing Corp. v. Columbia Artists Management, Inc., 443 F.2d 1159, 1162 (2d Cir. 1971)).

TABLE 4.3
Types of Copyright Infringement

Type of Copyright Infringement	*Primary Exposure and State of Mind*
Direct Infringement	Company is *strictly liable* for copies infringed by its employees committed within the scope of employment. Intent or knowledge is not an element of infringement.
Contributory Infringement	Company or its employees *knowingly contribute* to an act of infringement by another party.
Vicarious Infringement	Company is liable for a primary infringer's activities based upon the company's right to control and receiving a direct financial benefit derived from the infringing activities.

[3]   Vicarious Infringement

Contributory infringement requires proof that the defendant has knowledge of the infringement. A defendant may be vicariously liable for copyright infringement even if it has *no knowledge* of the primary infringer's action, such as when a company is held liable for the conduct of its employees. It must be shown that the company has the right and ability to supervise an infringing activity and has a direct financial interest in such activity.

[E]   Defenses to Copyright Infringement

[1]   Fair Use

Fair use evolved as a judicial doctrine and was codified in Section 107 of the Copyright Act of 1976. Fair use is an exception to the copyright owners' exclusive right "to reproduce the copyrighted work in copies."[55] The defendant has the burden of proving that its copying constitutes fair use.[56] Four factors are considered in determining whether use of a copyrighted works constitutes fair use:[57] (1) "the purpose and character of the use including whether such use is of a commercial nature or is for nonprofit educational purposes; (2) the nature of the copyrighted work; (3) the amount and substantiality of the portion used in relation to the copy-

---

[55] 17 U.S.C. § 106(1) (1999).

[56] American Geophysical Union v. Texaco Inc., 60 F.3d 913, 918 (2d Cir. 1995).

[57] UMG Recordings, Inc. v. MP3.com, 92 F. Supp. 2d 349 (S.D.N.Y. 2000) (rejecting fair use defense of Internet company for copying recordings and replaying them for subscribers on its computer system).

righted work as a whole; and (4) the effect of the use upon the potential market for or value of the copyrighted work."[58]

If a company's use of the copyrighted work on a web site is to carry out a commercial function, this statutory factor weighs against fair use. If a company's use of copyrighted works benefits science or scholarship, this factor would weigh in favor of a defense of fair use.

The second statutory factor is the nature of the copyrighted work. This factor focuses on whether the copyrighted work is published and informational or creative.[59] In other words, is the nature of the work being copied close to the core of intended copyright protection?[60]

The third "fair use" statutory factor is the amount and substantiality of the copyrighted work copied and displayed. The amount and substantiality element focuses upon whether the portion constitutes the essence of the work.

The fourth factor is the effect of the display of copyrighted materials upon the potential market for the work. Will posting works on the Internet, for example, have a negative effect on the copyright owner's market? If so, this will be a factor against a finding of fair use.

[2] Permitted Copying of Computer Programs

Section 117 of the Copyright Act permits an owner of a copy of software to make a new copy if it is an "essential step" in the utilization of the program.[61] It is not an infringement for the owner of a copy of a computer program to make or authorize the making of another copy or adaptation of that computer program provided: (1) that such a new copy or adaptation is created as an essential step in the utilization of the computer program in conjunction with a machine and that it is used in no other manner, or (2) that such copy or adaptation is for archival purposes only and that all archival copies are destroyed in the event that continued possession of the computer program should cease to be rightful.[62] Section 117 is a narrow exception, which applies only to backup copies of computer programs, but does not extend to copying for commercial purposes.[63]

---

[58] 17 U.S.C. § 107 (1999).

[59] Religious Technology Center v. Netcom On-Line Communic. Services, Inc., 907 F. Supp. 1361 (N.D. Cal. 1995).

[60] Campbell v. Acuff-Rose Music, 510 U.S. 569 586 (1994).

[61] Section 117 was enacted in response to MAI Systems Corp. v. Peak Computer, Inc., 991 F.2d 511, 518 (9th Cir. 1993), in which the Ninth Circuit held that a repair person was not authorized to use a computer owner's licensed operating system and infringed an operating system when he turned on the computer loading the operating system into RAM. The court held that infringement occurred when the operating system was loaded into the computer.

[62] 17 U.S.C. § 117 (1999).

[63] Mark A. Lemley, et. al., Software and Internet Law 201 (2000) (citing ProCD v. Zeidenberg, 908 F. Supp. 640 (W.D. Wis. 1996), rev'd on other grounds, 86 F.3d 1447 (7th Cir. 1996)).

[3]   ISP Limited Liability

Congress enacted the Digital Millennium Copyright Act (DMCA) providing a "safe harbor" for Internet Service Providers (ISPs) for intermediate and temporary storage of digital copies. A service provider is an entity that transmits, routes, or otherwise provides connections for digital online communications.[64]

The DMCA permits online service providers to make cached copies of popular Internet web pages provided that a provider meet several requirements such as including a designated agent.[65] Section 512(c) of the U.S. Copyright Act of 1976 (Copyright Act) implements DMCA's safe harbor for limiting infringement liability. The DMCA overruled case law making service providers liable for copyright infringement.[66]

[a]   *Transitory Digital Network Communications*

The DMCA limits the liability of providers for a wide range of Internet-related activities such as caching or making temporary copies of web sites. A service provider is not liable for transitory digital network communications initiated by third parties.[67] To qualify for this immunity, the transmission or storage of network communications must be an automatic response to the request of another person.[68] The provider is not liable for material online so long as the material is routed without selection of the material, no copy is made, and the content is not modified.[69]

[b]   *Immunity for System Caching*

The DMCA provides immunity for system caching or the temporary storage of copyrighted materials on a computer system.[70] Before the passage of the DMCA, the court in MAI Systems Corp. v. Peak Computer, Inc.,[71] held that a copy is created at the moment information is loaded into the computer's operating system.[72] The *MAI* court held that there would be copyright infringement if a computer repair person who was not authorized to use a computer system turned on

---

[64] 17 U.S.C. 512 (k)(1)(A)(B) (1999).

[65] 17 U.S.C. § 512(c)(2) (1999).

[66] *See, e.g.*, Playboy Enters. Inc. v. Webbworld, Inc., 968 F. Supp. 1171, 1174 (N.D. Tex. 1997), *aff'd,* 168 F.3d 486 (5th Cir. 1999)).

[67] 17 U.S.C. § 512 (1999).

[68] 17 U.S.C. § 512(2)(3) (1999).

[69] 17 U.S.C. § 512(1)(5) (1999).

[70] 17 U.S.C. § 512(b) (1999).

[71] MAI Systems Corp. v. Peak Computer, Inc., 991 F.2d 518 (9th Cir. 1993).

[72] *Id.* at 518.

the computer, thus making a temporary copy in the memory of the computer's hard drive.[73]

The DMCA overruled *MAI* by permitting the temporary storage of copyrighted material on a network provided the material "is made available online by a person other than the service provider."[74] The DMCA permits this copying only if there is no other purpose than maintenance or repair. The DMCA overruled *MAI Systems* to the extent that it would find that cached copies of web sites infringed the copyright law.

[c] Qualifications for ISP "Safe Harbor"

A company must satisfy three conditions for eligibility for a service provider "safe harbor" for Internet-related liability. First, it must have "adopted and reasonably implemented" a policy where it will terminate subscribers who are repeat copyright infringers.[75] Secondly, it must notify its subscribers and account holders of the service provider's system and method of canceling accounts.[76] Third, it must accommodate and not interfere with "standard technical measures."[77]

If a company wishes to obtain a safe harbor for caching, it will need to appoint an agent to receive notification. The webmaster must post information on its web site about the name, address, telephone number, and electronic mail address of the agent and other contact information.[78] A provider is not liable for removing or disabling material "claimed to be infringing based on facts or circumstances from which infringing activity is apparent."[79] In addition, it is advisable to take other steps to publicize its policy by e-mail or pop-up warnings.

While the DMCA is the law of the United States, uncertainty exists about whether caching constitutes infringement in other countries. The Copyright Directive proposed by the European Parliament would make Internet Service Providers liable for caching.[80] The European Internet Service Providers Association

---

[73] Marobie-FL., Inc. v. National Ass'n of Fire Equip. Distrib., 983 F. Supp. 1167, 11179 (N.D. Ill. 1997) notes that liability for copyright infringement for this type of scenario ultimately lies with the person who caused the infringing material to be loaded onto the computer.

[74] 17 U.S.C. § 512(b)(1)(A) (1999).

[75] 17 U.S.C. § 512(I)(1)(A) (1999).

[76] *Id.*

[77] 17 U.S.C. § 512(I)(1)(B) (1999).

[78] 17 U.S.C. § 512(2)(A)(B) (1999).

[79] 17 U.S.C. § 512(g) (1999).

[80] Amended Proposal for a Directive on Copyright and Related Rights in the Information Society (21 May 1999) (visited Sept. 23, 2000) http://europa.eu.int/comm/internal_market/en/intprop/intrprop/docs/index.htm.; *see* Lee Kimber, "European Ruling Could Outlaw Web, TechWeb News 1 (Feb. 16, 1999) (reporting that European Parliament refused to grant a broad exemption for temporary copies from the reproduction right.).

(EuroISPA) argues that the ban on caching would grant greater protection to authors, musicians, and artists but would slow Internet traffic and bring the "Net to its knees."[81]

[F] Works Made for Hire

The "work for hire" doctrine does not automatically apply to consultants or others working on a company's web site who are classified as independent contractors. To make it apply, a company should enter into a "work made for hire" agreement, vesting ownership for content posted on its site with the company (see Table 4.4). The signed agreement, licence, or other agreement should broadly include all media, including web site and print publication, for works prepared for the company, including illustrations, tables, charts, pictures, sounds, pictorials, or graphical works.

[G] Linking Issues

[1] Linking

A hyperlink is a link from one site to another on the Internet. A web site is a specific location on the World Wide Web identified by the Universal Resource Locator (URL). The URL can be a string of letters, such as *http://www.spc.com*, or it may include letters, numbers, or slashes.[82] Links permit Internet users to click on highlighted text and surf from web page to web page without typing in URLs.[83]

A simple link between sites will not normally be problematic, but it may be a violation of netiquette[84] not to request permission to link. In fact, many web sites will welcome linking. An adult entertainment web site that linked to the Papal Visit web site owned by the Archdiocese of St. Louis, however, was found liable for trademark dilution by tarnishment.[85] A company should give a notice that it has

---

[81] Jane Wakefield, EU Directive Poses Anti-Caching Threat (visited June 4, 1999), http://www.zdnet.co.uk/news/1999/5/ins-6942.html.

[82] Web novice.com, Reading Internet Addresses (visited Oct. 8, 1999), http://www.web novice.com/web address.htm (explaining that a Universal Resource Locator or URL is a string of letters, numbers, slashes or others symbols that "point to a specific place on the Internet").

[83] Intermatic Inc. v. Toeppen, 947 F. Supp. 1227 (N.D. Ill. 1996).

[84] *Netiquette* is a term used to describe informal norms that have evolved among Internet users as to what is proper online conduct. When an Arizona law company deluged listservers with spam e-mail about immigration services, it was considered a gross violation of netiquette. Internet users responded by a counter attack of spam mail that shut down the law company's web site. Those who violate important Internet-related norms may face similar self-help measures.

[85] Archdiocese of St. Louis v. Internet Entertainment, Inc., No. 99CV27SNL (E.D. Mo., Feb. 2, 1999) (holding that the use of the domain names "papalvisit1999.com" and "papalvisit.com" by adult entertainment defendant was likely to tarnish the marks' image and that the plaintiffs were likely to prevail on their federal and state law dilution claims).

TABLE 4.4
Methods of Acquiring Copyright

Copyright Ownership Interest	Legal Significance
1. Web site and content created by company's employees	The company owns content even if it was created by employees because "work-made-for-hire" automatically applies to works created in the scope of duties.
2. Commissioned "work-made-for hire" for web site	The company owns the web site and its content only if a "work-made-for-hire" agreement exists.
3. Web site content purchased, assigned, or licensed	An agreement to purchase or assign works from independent contractors or joint authors is superior to a license agreement or assignment. The license agreement must specify that the company has the right to modify content.

no control over linked sites and resources and does not endorse or is not otherwise liable for materials on linked sites.

The practice of simple linking is "unlikely to constitute infringement, because it is probably protected either by an implied license or under the copyright doctrine of fair use."[86] Linking, however, may infringe trademarks by implying an association between the initial site and the linked site. It is unlikely that a company would be liable for copyright infringement if it links to a web site that contains infringing materials.[87]

[2] Deep Linking

When web site visitors click on a deep link, they are transferred to an interior web page, bypassing the home page of the second site. Deep linking occurs when a web site creates a link from its site to a web page deep within the second web site. Deep linking has been the subject of litigation based on copyright infringement or unfair competition. A federal court in Ticketmaster Corp. v. Tickets.com, Inc.[88] dismissed Ticketmaster's claim that Tickets.com's deep

---

[86] *See* Maureen O'Rourke, Fencing Cyberspace: Drawing Borders in a Virtual World, 82 Minn. L. Rev. 609 (1998).

[87] In Bernstein v. J.C. Penney, Inc., 1998 U.S. Dist. LEXIS 19048 (C.D. Cal., Sept. 29, 1998), a federal district court dismissed a claim against a perfume manufacturer for copyright infringement because its product was promoted on a web site that in turn was linked to a third web site with infringing photographs.

[88] 2000 U.S. Dist. LEXIS 4553 (C.D. Calif., Mar. 27, 2000).

linking practices violated the federal copyright act. Ticketmaster has a web site that permits customers to purchase tickets to various events through an Internet connection with its pages.[89] Ticketmaster had exclusive agreements with the events on its web pages so that tickets were not generally available except under the web site.[90] Tickets.com, the defendant, operated a web site performing a different ticketing service. Tickets.com sells tickets at its site, but it also provides visitors with information on how to obtain tickets to events.[91] If Ticketmaster is the exclusive ticket broker, the visitor is transferred to an interior page in Ticketmaster's site, that is, Tickets.com has a "deep link" into Ticketmaster's site.

The federal court granted Tickets.com's motion to dismiss the infringement complaint because copyright cannot protect factual data. In this case, Tickets.com extracted factual data from Ticketmaster and placed it in its own form.[92] The court rejected Ticketmaster's argument that there may be copyright infringement on base facts from publicly available web pages.[93] The court observed that "hyperlinking does not itself involve a violation of the Copyright Act . . . since no copying is involved, the customer is automatically transferred to the particular genuine web page of the original author."[94] The court also noted that it may not have had jurisdiction over the copyright infringement claim since it was unclear whether Ticketmaster's event pages were registered in the Copyright Office.[95]

The Supremacy Clause of the Constitution mandates that the federal copyright law overrides any state contract or tort causes of action with which it conflicts.[96] In *Ticketmaster*, the court found many of the plaintiff's contract and torts claims overridden by the Copyright Act. The court also denied Ticketmaster's breach of contract claim, noting that simply placing terms and conditions on the web site without requiring the visitor to take further action does not create an enforceable contract.[97] The court also rejected the Lanham Act claim and ruled that Ticketmaster's misappropriation and trespass claims were preempted.[98]

---

[89] *Id.*

[90] *Id.* at *5.

[91] *Id.* at *4.

[92] *Id.* at *5.

[93] *Id.*

[94] *Id.* at *6.

[95] A federal court does not have jurisdiction of a copyright infringement claim unless the owner registers its copyright with the U.S. Copyright Office. The web site of Ticketmaster Corp. was registered with the U.S. Copyright Office. However, "the events pages changed from day to day as old events are dropped out, and new ones are added." The court found an ambiguity in the scope of copyright registration: Did the registration cover only the homes page or also each of the event pages? *Id.* at *6.

[96] U.S. Const. Art. VI, cl. 2.

[97] *Id.* at *8.

[98] The court also found the plaintiff's state unfair business practices claim preempted to the extent that it covered Tickets.com's taking and publication of factual data. *Id.* at *9. The court also found

Deep linking was also the issue in the litigation between Ticketmaster and Microsoft. Microsoft deep-linked Ticketmaster's site through its Sidewalk city guides. Ticketmaster sued Microsoft, alleging that the deep linking deprived it of advertising revenues, caused its trademark to be diluted, and hence created an atmosphere of unfair competition.[99] After the settlement of the case, Microsoft stopped deep linking and now links to Ticketmaster's home page.[100] Advertising revenues are raised by attracting users to web sites, measured by the number of "hits." The practice of deep linking diverts attention within the second web site that has received the deep link.

[3] Liability for Remote Links

A federal court enjoined hackers from electronically "linking their site to others that posted a computer program called DeCSS that allowed motion pictures to be copied.[101] A federal court found no liability could be imposed for deep linking to a web site with allegedly infringing materials.[102] The practice of linking to sites containing infringing or illegal content may make a site susceptible to criminal prosecution in a foreign venue. Germany, for example, has criminal laws against the publication of materials on National Socialism. At a minimum, companies should prohibit links to sites containing illegal or objectionable content to avoid the loss of good will.

[4] Framing

The practice of framing causes the plaintiffs' web site to appear in a form other than the one envisioned by the web site developer. Framing permits a party to superimpose its advertising on all the web sites to which links are made.[103] The practice of framing goes well beyond deep linking by creating a frame around the

---

the plaintiff's unjust enrichment claim to be preempted. The court did not, however, rule out the possibility of tortious interference with prospective business advantage. *Id.* at *12.

[99] Ticketmaster Corp. v. Microsoft Corp., No. 97-3055 (C.D. Cal., Complaint filed Apr. 28, 1997, settled Jan. 22, 1999).

[100] Glasser Legal/Works, Update, 11 Cyberspace Law 18 (Feb. 1999).

[101] Universal City Studies v. Reimerdes, 2000 U.S. Dist. LEXIS 11696 (S.D.N.Y., Aug. 17, 2000) (enjoining Defendants from posting DeCSS and linking to other sites where anticircumvention software was posted).

[102] Bernstein v. J.C. Penney, Inc., No. 98-2958-R (C.D. Calif., Sept. 22, 1998) (reporting that federal judge dismissed complaint that J.C. Penney linked to a Swedish web site that allegedly infringed the plaintiff's copyrighted photographs of actress Elizabeth Taylor).

[103] The plaintiff argued: "Although Defendants, too, derive revenue by selling advertisements placed within the totalnews.com web site, defendants provide little or no content of their own. Instead Defendants have designed a parasitic web site that republishes the news and editorial content of others' web sites in order to attract both advertisers and users." *Id.*

web site that hides its advertising and substitutes the defendant's advertising. Framing was "introduced by Netscape in Version 2 of its Navigator product. A framing site, by virtue of certain commands in its HTML code, links to another site, and displays that site within a window or frame."[104] In Washington Post v. TotalNews, Inc.,[105] the newspaper contended that TotalNews infringed its copyrights and trademarks and misappropriated their news material.[106]

The plaintiffs included diversified communications channels, including *Time Magazine, Entertainment Weekly,* and *The Los Angeles Times,* all of which had online versions of their publications.[107] These and other publications were displayed in a *TotalNews* frame. The plaintiff in the *TotalNews* case argued that framing was a parasitic practice that diverted advertising revenues generated by online publications.[108] The plaintiffs also argued that framing was the "Internet equivalent of pirating copyrighted materials from a variety of famous newspapers, magazines, or television news programs."[109] In the *TotalNews* case, the plaintiffs' objection was that the defendant's framing method made its web sites appear in an altered form:

> The totalnews.com web site consists of lists of numerous "name-brand" news sources, including the famous trademarks exclusively associated with Plaintiffs in the public mind. When a user of totalnews.com "clicks" on one of those famous trademarks with the computer mouse, the user accesses a Plaintiff's corresponding web site. . . . Plaintiff's site, however, does not then fill the screen as it would had the user accessed either plaintiff's site directly or by means of a hyperlink from a web site that does not "frame" linked sites. Nor does Plaintiff's URL appear at the top of the screen as it normally would. Instead, part of the site is inserted in a window designed by the defendants to occupy only a part of the screen. Masking part of Plaintiff's site is the totalnews.com "frame," including . . . the "TotalNews" logo, totalnews.com URL, and advertisements that others have purchased from Defendants.[110]

Each of the named plaintiffs in *TotalNews* had registered trademarks and

---

[104] *See supra* note 86.

[105] Washington Post Co. v. TotalNews, Inc., No. 97-1190 (S.D.N.Y. filed Apr. 28, 1997, settled Jan. 22, 1999).

[106] Misappropriation is the acquisition of a "trade secret by 'improper means' or from someone who has acquired it through 'improper means.'" National Conference of Commissioners on Uniform State Laws, The Uniform Trade Secrets Act: A Summary (visited Mar. 19, 2000), http://www.nccU.S.l.org/summary/utsa.html.

[107] *Id.*

[108] *Id.*

[109] Washington Post v. TotalNews, Inc., Complaint ¶ 8 (visited Sept. 18, 1999), http://www.ljx.com/Internet/complain.html (reprinting complaint filed by Debevoise and Plimpton on behalf of the plaintiff).

[110] *Id.* at ¶ 30.

were copyright owners as well.[111] The court ordered *TotalNews* "not to directly or indirectly cause any Plaintiff's web site to appear on a user's computer screen with any material . . . and to permanently cease the practice of 'framing' Plaintiffs' web sites."[112]

A federal appeals court upheld a district court's denial of a preliminary injunction to restrain the defendant from employing a framed link to a plaintiff's web site in Futuredontics Inc. v. Applied Anagramic Inc.[113] The plaintiff's argument was that the framed link falsely implied an association between the parties. The court found no evidence that the defendant has caused the plaintiff to lose business or goodwill due to the framing.

[H]   Digital Millennium Copyright Act

President Clinton signed the Digital Millennium Copyright Act (DMCA) on October 28, 1998. Title I of the DMCA implements copyright treaties of the World Intellectual Property Organization (WIPO), with amendments to the federal copyright act. The DMCA amends the federal copyright law to adapt to Internet-related technologies. The DMCA provides limitations on liability for Internet-related copying, such as caching and routing. ISPs receive an exemption for copyright infringement provided they designate an agent to receive notices of copyright infringement. The DMCA has a number of provisions related to online copying and third-party liability.

[1]   Defense to Caching: Section 512

Companies sometimes mirror their sites so that if one web site is busy, the identical or mirrored site is accessible.[114] During the 1998 Winter Olympics, for example, IBM created "five mirror sites in Japan, the United States and Germany to enable web servers throughout the world to get easy and rapid access to the latest results from the winter games."[115] The Internet Society estimates that up to a third of all content is cached.[116] Caching is the practice of replicating identical web

---

[111] The plaintiffs' lawsuit was based upon misappropriation, Federal trademark dilution, trademark infringement, false designations of origin (false representations and false advertising), dilution under state law, deceptive acts and practices, copyright infringement, and tortious interference. Counts I-X of Plaintiff's Complaint.

[112] Washington Post v. TotalNews, Inc., No. 97 Civ. 1190 (PKL) (S.D. N.Y. 1997) (order granting settlement and dismissal).

[113] Futuredontics Inc. v. Applied Anagramic Inc., 1998 WL 417413 (9th Cir. July 23, 1998) (unpublished opinion reported in Perkins Coie Internet Case Digest (visited May 26, 1999), http://www.perkinscoie.com/resource/ecomm/netcase/Cases-04.htm.

[114] *Id.*

[115] *Id.*

[116] *Id.*

pages to improve the speed of access to web pages. Caching is a technological fix for bottlenecks that reduces "the need to re-transmit information from the source server."[117]

The three types of caching are (1) PC or browser caching; (2) proxy server caching; and (3) mirror caching, or mirroring.[118] All forms of caching make temporary copies of sites just visited to permit faster response time for accessing web pages. With PC caching, images of web pages are stored on the computer user's own computer. Users need only click the back button of their browsers to retrieve an image of the previous site.[119]

A proxy server copies and stores web pages on a separate server. Mirroring or mirror caching sets up identical sites, called mirrors, on different servers.[120] The Global Internet Project predicts that a form of caching, called "replication," will gain momentum. "Replication refers to duplicating data on servers at several points on the network, in anticipation of user demand, rather than caching it in response to user demand."[121] By the end of 1998, "there were 140 million users on the Internet worldwide . . . web pages increased by an estimated 300,000 per week . . . and some ISPs see traffic growth of 1,000% a year."[122]

Section 512 of the DMCA, "Limitations on Liability Relating to Material Online," immunizes from infringement action ISPs that make temporary cache copies of Internet web pages. The immunity from copyright infringement action applies as long as cached pages are not accessible by anyone other than the user. The DMCA requires three conditions to quality for a caching safe harbor. First, the material is available online to a person other than the ISP. Second, the party transmits the information through the ISP to a third party without modification. Third, the storage of the material is carried out through an automatic technical process for making the information available to other users.[123] The DMCA also

---

[117] *Id.*

[118] *Id.*

[119] *Id.*

[120] Jon Knight and Martin Hamilton, Cashing in on Caching (visited June 6, 1999), http:www.ariadne.ac.uk/Issue4/caching/.

[121] Global Internet Project, presented at the Fourth Annual High Technology Law Conference, Suffolk University Law School, Boston (Sept. 1998).

[122] Global Internet Project, Preventing Internet Bottlenecks: The Role of Caching (visited June 4, 1999), http://www.gip.org/caching.htm.

[123] DMCA, § 112 includes the following language:

> (a) TRANSITORY DIGITAL NETWORK COMMUNICATIONS—A service provider shall not be liable for monetary relief, or, except as provided in subsection (j), for injunctive or other equitable relief, for infringement of copyright by reason of the provider's transmitting, routing, or providing connections for, material through a system or network controlled or operated by or for the service provider, or by reason of the intermediate and transient storage of that material in the course of such transmitting, routing, or providing connections, if—

permits computer maintenance workers to make temporary copies during the performance of computer maintenance duties without liability for copyright infringement.[124]

In order to qualify for the "safe harbor" for liability related to Internet materials, the provider must designate an agent for notification of claimed infringement. SPC needs to designate an agent to receive notification of claimed copyright infringement.[125] The Copyright Office does not have a specific printed form for filing an Interim Designation of an Agent but does have a suggested format.[126]

The minimum information that must be submitted about the designated agent includes: (1) the name, address, phone number, and electronic mail address of the agent; (2) legal name and address of the Internet Service Provider (ISP); (3) all names under which the ISP does business; (4) a filing fee of $20; and (5) display of the agent's name and contact information on the web site. The Register of Copyrights may require other contact information when the final regulations are approved.[127] Section 512(c)(2) requires the designated agent provide contact information to the Copyright Office and notice through the provider's publicly accessible web site.

[2] Copyright and Management Systems

Chapter 12 of the DMCA, entitled "Copyright and Management System," proscribes the circumvention of copyright protection systems.[128] The DMCA

---

(1) The transmission of the material was initiated by or at the direction of a person other than the service provider;

(2) The transmission, routing, provision of connections, or storage is carried out through an automatic technical process without selection of the material by the service provider;

(3) The service provider does not select the recipients of the material except as an automatic response to the request of another person;

(4) No copy of the material made by the service provider in the course of such intermediate or transient storage is maintained on the system or network in a manner ordinarily accessible to anyone other than anticipated recipients, and no such copy is maintained on the system or network in a manner ordinarily accessible to such anticipated recipients for a longer period than is reasonably necessary for the transmission, routing, or provision of connections; and

(5) The material is transmitted through the system or network without modification of its content.

[124] The DMCA contains a special interest piece of legislation in providing special *sui generis* protection for boat hulls.

[125] 17 U.S.C. § 512(c) (1999).

[126] U.S. Copyright Office, Designation by Service Provider of Agent for Notification of Claims of Infringement (visited Apr. 12, 2000), http://www.loc.gov/copyright/onlinesp.

[127] 17 U.S.C. § 512(c)(2) (1999).

[128] 17 U.S.C. § 1201(a) (1999) (noting that the circumvention of a technological measures is to "descramble a scrambled work, to decrypt an encrypted work, or otherwise avoid, bypass, remove, deactivate, or impair a technological protection measure").

makes it a crime to create or sell technologies to circumvent copyright protection devices. Section 1201(b) of the DMCA prohibits the manufacture of anticircumvention devices, which bypass technical measures controlling access to copyrighted works.[129] A prohibited device has three attributes: (1) it is primarily designed for circumvention; (2) it has limited uses for legitimate commercial purposes (other than circumvention); and (3) it is marketed for use in circumventing copyright protection. Section 1201(f) permits software developers to reverse engineer circumvention devices to achieve interoperability of independently created computer programs.[130]

Section 1201 of DMCA prohibits technological measures to bypass copyright protection. Such measures are defined as means to descramble a scrambled work, to decrypt an encrypted work, or otherwise to avoid, bypass, remove, deactivate, or impair a technological measure, without the authority of the copyright owner. A technological measure "effectively controls access to a work" if the measure, in the ordinary course of its operation, requires the application of information, or a process or a treatment, with the authority of the copyright owner, to gain access to the work.

Section 1201 (b) prohibits the manufacturing, importing, offering to the problem or other technological protection devices to control access to copyrighted works. Section 1201(b) permits the manufacture of devices to circumvent copyright control technologies. Section 1202(b) of the DMCA prohibits, unless authorized, several forms of knowing removal or alteration of copyright management information.[131] A violation of Section 1201 may result in civil and criminal penalties, provided there is proof that a competitor made copies of copyrighted work separated from a copyright information management measure.

[3] Digital Copies for Libraries

Title IV of the DMCA amends Section 108 of the Copyright Act to permit libraries to digitize analog materials without the permission of the copyright owner for archival purposes. Libraries may make up to three digital copies of copyrighted materials for archival purposes. The DMCA permits libraries to reproduce published works in their last 20 years of protection for the purposes of scholarship, research, and preservation.

---

[129] DMCA, § 1201.

[130] DMCA, § 1201(f).

[131] Section 1202(b) of the DMCA provides that "No person shall without the authority of the copyright owner or the law—(1) intentionally remove or alter any copyright management information . . . (3) distribute . . . copies of works . . . knowing that copyright management information has been removed or altered without authority of the copyright owner or the law, knowing, or, with respect to civil remedies under section 1203, having reasonable grounds to know, that it will induce, enable, facilitate, or conceal an infringement of any right under [federal copyright law]."

[4] DMCA Case Law

In Kelly v. Ariba Software,[132] the owner of copyrighted thumbprint photographs displayed on an Internet web site sued the operator of a visual search engine for copyright infringement. The court held that the defendant's use of copyrighted images constituted fair use under the Copyright Act. In *Ariba*, the defendant operated a "visual search engine." Like other Internet search engines, the user obtained Web content in response to a search query. Unlike other search engines, however, the defendant had retrieved images in addition to text.[133] In addition, the defendant was held not to have violated the DMCA.

[I] Noncopyright-Related Issues

[1] VARA Moral Rights

Companies must also obtain clearance for authors' moral rights associated with digital information displayed on its web site. Visual artists contributing to a web site have moral rights of attribution and integrity, as described in § 106(A) of the 1976 Copyright Act. On an international level, the Berne Convention gives authors moral rights even if they are employees or contractors.[134] A French court, for example, might find that the digitalization of a photograph constitutes an alteration of an author's moral rights.

The term *droit morales* is a French term that "refers not to 'morals' . . . but rather the ability of authors to control the eventual fate of their works."[135] The doctrine of *les droits morales* refers to "the belief that an artist injects his spirit into a work (s)he creates and that the integrity of the work—and therefore the artist's spirit and personality—should be protected and preserved."[136] The right of attribution, integrity, and *droit de suite,* or the right to resale, are well-developed moral rights in the French legal system.[137] The doctrine of moral rights accords the author a continuing interest in the integrity of his or her artistic work after it is sold

---

[132] 53 U.S.P.Q. 1361 (C.D. Calif. 1996).

[133] *Id.* at 1117.

[134] H. Ward Classen, Fundamentals of Software Licensing, Fourth Annual High Technology Law Conference: Licensing in a Network Environment, Mar. 10, 2000. *See generally,* M. Holderness, "Moral Rights and Authors' Rights: The Keys to the Information Age," 1998 (1) The Journal of Information, Law & Technology (visited Aug. 16, 2000), http://elj.warwick.ac.uk/JLT/intosoc/98_/bold/.

[135] Betsey Rosenblatt, Moral Rights Basics (visited Mar. 13, 1998), http://cyber.law.harvard.edu/property/library/moralprimer.html.

[136] Patrick W. Begos, Artists' Moral Rights (1997) (visited June 7, 1999), http://www.molton.com/artlaw/artlaw.html.

[137] *Id.*

or assigned. France recognizes four separate moral rights: (1) The right of disclosure assures that the artist is the sole judge of whether his or her work is a completed creation, and whether it should be submitted to the public;[138] (2) the right of withdrawal; (3) the right of paternity; and (4) the right of integrity.[139]

The right of integrity is "inalienable and perpetual," protecting the artist against "any distortion or alteration of his or her creation once the completed work has been transferred or made the subject of publication or performance."[140] The Berne Convention for the Protection of Literary and Artistic Works protects artists' moral rights.[141] Article 6(b) of the Berne Convention provides that "the means of redress for safeguarding the [right of integrity] shall be governed by the legislation of the country where protection is claimed."[142] Article 6(b) recognizes principles of paternity and integrity as inalienable personal rights of the artist.[143]

The United States is a signatory of the Berne Convention, but it has been slow to recognize the concept of moral rights of authors. If a work is first published in the United States, or simultaneously in the United States and another nation, the "country of origin" under the Berne Convention would be the United States. A work is governed by the Berne Convention if the authors are nationals, domiciles, or habitual residents of the United States.[144]

The United States' implementation of the Berne Convention in 1988 did little to protect artists' moral rights.[145] Our Copyright Act, unlike that of many civil code countries, does not generally protect against destruction or mutilation of works.

The moral rights of artists were fortified when Congress passed the Visual Artists Rights Act of 1990 (VARA). VARA protects the artist's moral rights that a visual work will not be revised, altered, or distorted, even if sold or assigned to another party. "The author of a work of visual art . . . shall have the right . . . to prevent any destruction of a work of recognized stature, any intentional or grossly negligent destruction of that work is a violation of that right."[146] VARA protects only works of visual art, which have attained the status of "recognized stature."[147]

---

[138] Flore Krigsman, Section 43(a) of the Lanham Act As a Defender of Artists' 'Moral Rights,' 73 Trad. Rep. 251 (May-June 1983).

[139] *Id.*

[140] *Id.*

[141] *Id.*

[142] Patrick W. Begos, The Berne Convention (1997), http://www.molton.com/artlaw/berne.html.

[143] Krigsman, *supra* note 138.

[144] 17 U.S.C. § 101(3)(A)(B)(1)(A)-(D)(2)(3) (1999).

[145] *Id.*

[146] 17 U.S.C. § 106A(a)(3)(b) (1999).

[147] The court in Carter v. Helmsley-Spear, Inc., 861 F. Supp. 303 (S.D. N.Y. 1994), *aff'd in part, vacated in part, rev'd in part,* 71 F.3d 77 (2d Cir. 1995) (defining meaning of "recognized stature" under VARA).

Under VARA, a creator may restrain the alteration of the work in a manner that is prejudicial to his or her literary or artistic reputation. Section 106A recognizes "rights of certain authors to attribution and integrity."[148]

The Second Circuit determined in Carter v. Helmsley-Spear, Inc.,[149] that a sculpture made from recycled materials was not of "recognized stature."[150] The sculpture in that case was made from recycled materials affixed to the walls and ceiling.[151] The work "included a giant hand fashioned from an old school bus, a face made of automobile parts, and a number of interactive components."[152] To qualify as a work of "recognized stature" requires:

> that the visual art in question has 'stature,' i.e. is viewed as meritorious, and that this stature is 'recognized' by art experts, other members of the artistic community, or by some cross-section of society. In making this showing, plaintiffs generally, but not inevitably, will need to call expert witnesses to testify before the trier of fact.[153]

In Martin v. City of Indianapolis,[154] a creator of a large outdoor stainless steel sculpture filed a lawsuit under VARA after the city of Indianapolis demolished the sculpture as part of an urban renewal project. The federal district court granted the plaintiff's motion awarding him statutory damages under VARA. The Seventh Circuit accompanied the finding that the sculpture was of "recognized stature."[155] The

---

[148] 17 U.S.C. § 106A (1999) Section 106A provides:

> Rights of attribution and integrity—Subject to section 107 and independent of the Exclusive rights provided in section 106, the author of a work of visual art—
> (1) shall have the right—
> (A) to claim authorship of that work, and
> (B) to prevent the use of his or her name as the author of any work of visual art which he or she did not create;
> (2) shall have the right to prevent the use of his or her name as the author of the work of visual art in the event of a distortion, mutilation, or other modification of the work which would be prejudicial to his or her honor or reputation; and
> (3) subject to the limitations set forth in section 113(d), shall have the right—
> (A) to prevent any intentional distortion, mutilation, or other modification of that work which would be prejudicial to his or her honor or reputation, and any intentional distortion, mutilation, or modification of that work is a violation of that rights, and
> (B) to prevent any destruction of a work of recognized stature, and any intentional or grossly negligent destruction of that work is a violation of that right.

[149] Carter v. Helmsley-Spear, Inc., 71 F.3d 77 (2d Cir. 1995).

[150] Id. at 83.

[151] Id. at 80.

[152] Id. at 80.

[153] Carter v. Helmsley-Spear, Inc., 861 F. Supp. 303, 325 (S.D.N.Y. 1994), aff'd in part, vacated in part, rev'd in part, 71 F.3d 77 (2d Cir. 1995).

[154] Martin v. City of Indianapolis, 192 F.3d 608 (7th Cir. 1999).

[155] Id. at 609.

court did not find the city's conduct to be willful, effectively precluding the plaintiff from receiving enhanced damages.[156]

Canadian authors have a moral right of integrity in all literary, dramatic, musical, and artistic works as well as sound recordings.[157] Digital modification of a photograph posted at a web site, for example, may constitute an infringement of copyright and a violation of a photographer's moral rights.[158] As a preventive law measure, companies should enter agreements with authors permitting materials to be digitized or modified on its web site.

[2]   Right of Publicity

A web site audit should determine whether all materials posted on its site are owned or licensed by the company. The audit should determine whether any photographs, voices, or images on its web site potentially violates a right to publicity or privacy. The online company needs to obtain rights to use names, faces, images, voices or other likeness in photographs, video clips or other images of living persons. One of the other privacy-based torts may apply to displaying photographs of living persons on its web site. Section 5.06 in Chapter Five covers Internet-related privacy torts including the right of publicity.

[J]   Software Copyrights

Software did not evolve as a separate industry until the early 1980s. By the mid-1980s, it was clear that software could be copyrighted.[159] By then, the trend in the law was for courts "to accord software a relatively thin protection," as one circuit after another followed the abstraction-filtration-comparison test.[160] Courts will examine the program at various levels of abstraction from the most detailed to the most general. The court makes a decision as to which aspects of the software are not susceptible to copyright protection at each level of abstraction from specific to general. After filtering out all of the nonprotectible elements, the court

---

[156] *Id.* at 617.

[157] Brian MacLeond Rogers & Sheldon Burshtein, The Information Highway: The Canadian Perspective on the Bumps in the Road, Software L. Bull., Mar. 1996, at 46.

[158] *Id.*

[159] Raymond T. Nimmer and Patricia Ann Krauthaus, Software Copyright: Sliding Scales and Abstracted Expression, 32 Houston L. Rev. 317, 320 (1995) (nothing that "Early court opinions focused on whether any copyright protection exists for computer programs," but the "question was resolved: software is copyrightable").

[160] Stephen M. McJohn, Software Copyright Developments, presented at the Fourth Annual High Technology Law Conference, Suffolk University Law School, Boston, Massachusetts (Sept. 1998); *See generally,* Stephen M. McJohn, Fair Use of Copyrighted Software, 28 Rutgers L.J. 1 (1997).

compares the original to the copy to determine whether there is a "substantial similarity."

The United States Supreme Court, in Lotus Development v. Borland Int'l,[161] let stand the First Circuit's holding that the "look and feel" of the menu command structure of the 1-2-3 Lotus spreadsheet program are not copyrightable under Section 102 of the Copyright Act.[162] The First Circuit compared the Lotus 1-2-3 menu to the buttons on a VCR: "Just as one could not operate a buttonless VCR, it would be impossible to operate Lotus 1-2-3 without employing its menu command hierarchy. Thus, the Lotus commands are not equivalent to the labels on the VCR's buttons, but are instead the equivalent of the buttons themselves."[163] If a copycat developed a web site with the same feel as a company's site, the company may have a possible action for unfair business competition or trademark dilution. Dilution occurs when a trademark loses its distinctive quality because of unauthorized use by another party.[164]

➤ **[K] Preventive Law Pointers**

It is late Friday afternoon and SPC executives need advisory opinions on a number of copyright issues arising out of the launch of the SPC site: *http://www.spc.com.* SPC recently launched a web site with streaming video, music, software, and an online ordering system.[165] SPC's web site contains a wide range of copyrightable text, artwork, audiovisual material, sounds, and music.

[1] Notice of Copyright

SPC should affix proper copyright notices on its web site even though copyright notice is no longer required after the United States adhered to the Berne Convention on March 1, 1989. Also, because prior law did contain such a requirement, the use of notice is still relevant to the copyright status of older works. Notice was required under the 1976 Copyright Act. This requirement was eliminated when the United States adhered to the Berne Convention, effective March 1, 1989. Although works published without notice before that date could have entered the public domain in the United States, the Uruguay Round Agreements Act (URAA)

---

[161] Lotus Development v. Borland Int'l, 49 F.3d 807 (1st Cir. 1995), *aff'd by,* 116 S. Ct. 817 (1996) (accompanied by a 4-4 vote).

[162] *Id.*

[163] *Id.* at 816.

[164] Trademarks are divided into five general categories of distinctiveness: (1) generic; (2) descriptive; (3) suggestive; (4) arbitrary; and (5) fanciful. Spear, Leeds and Kellogg v. Rosado, 2000 U.S. Dist. LEXIS 3732 (S. D. N.Y. Mar. 24, 2000).

[165] Suffolk Personal Computer (SPC) is a hypothetical company. Our use of the SPC™ is for illustration purposes only and is not affiliated with SPC Software of Walled Lake, Michigan, or Software Professional Consultants or the Software Productivity Center (SPC).

restores copyright in certain foreign works originally published without notice. The Copyright Office does not take a position on whether copies of works first published with notice before March 1, 1989, which are distributed on or after March 1, 1989, must bear the copyright notice.

A copyright notice is notice that the work is protected by copyright; it identifies the copyright owner, and it is evidence of the year of first publication. Furthermore, in the event that a work is infringed, if a proper notice of copyright appears on the published copy or copies to which a defendant in a copyright infringement suit had access, then no weight shall be given a defense based on innocent infringement. Innocent infringement occurs when the infringer does not realize that the work was protected before making a copy.

The notice for visually perceptible copies should contain the following three elements:

1. The symbol © (the letter C in a circle), or the word "Copyright," or the abbreviation "Copr."
2. The year of first publication of the work. In the case of compilations or derivative works, incorporating previously published material, the year date of first publication of the compilation or derivative work is sufficient. The year date may be omitted where a pictorial, graphic, or sculptural work, with accompanying textual matter, if any, is reproduced in or on greeting cards, postcards, stationery, jewelry, dolls, toys, or any useful article.
3. The name of the owner of copyright in the work, or an abbreviation by which the name can be recognized, or a generally known alternative designation of the owner.

An example of a copyright notice is © 2001 SPC or Copyright © 2001 by Michael L. Rustad and Cyrus Daftary.

The "C in a circle" notice is used only on "visually perceptible copies," which is a copyright law concept. The "visually perceptible copy," for example, does not apply to certain kinds of copyrighted works, such as a sound recording. Certain kinds of works—for example, musical, dramatic, and literary works—may be fixed not in "copies" but by means of sound in an audio recording. If SPC employs sound, music, or spoken words on its web site, it will need to comply with the special rules for the form of notice for sound recording. Sound recordings include musical, spoken, or other sounds, but not sounds accompanying a motion picture or other audiovisual work. Common examples include recordings of music, drama, or lectures.

A sound recording, however, is not the same as a phonorecord. A phonorecord is the physical object in which works of authorship are embodied, and includes tapes, CDs, LPs, 45 r.p.m. disks, and other sound formats. The "C in a circle" notice, therefore, is not used to indicate protection of the underlying musical, dramatic, or literary work recorded, and a separate notice is required. The notice for phonorecords embodying a sound recording should contain all the following three elements:

1. The symbol Ⓟ (the letter P in a circle);
2. The year of first publication of the sound recording; and
3. The name of the owner of copyright in the sound recording, or an abbreviation by which the name can be recognized, or a generally known alternative designation of the owner. If the producer of the sound recording is named on the phonorecord label or container, and if no other name appears in conjunction with the notice, the name of the producer shall be considered a part of the notice.

An example of a phonorecord notice is Ⓟ 2001 SPC.

Copyright registration is a predicate to obtaining statutory damages or attorneys' fees.[166] Registration is also a means of proving ownership of a copyright, though it is not a requirement of copyright ownership. The owner of a copyright, or the assignee of the exclusive right of publication, must deposit within three months of the date of publication two complete copies of the best edition.

[2] Benefits of Copyright Registration

SPC should "register with the Copyright Office to obtain statutorily prescribed benefits, including eligibility for statutory damages and legal fees in the event of infringement."[167] For SPC, copyright registration is a simple and inexpensive means of protecting information. When SPC registers its copyright, it is essentially staking a public claim in the Copyright Office. Copyright registration is highly recommended because SPC seeks the certificate of copyright registration, which will be useful in case of a copyright infringement lawsuit. If SPC files a copyright registration at the time of first publication, it may use the registration as *prima facie* evidence of ownership of a copyright. SPC has an exclusive right to obtain a copyright registration during the period of copyright protection.[168]

SPC should register its web site and copyrighted materials posted at its web site. Copyright registration is a legal formality intended to make a public record

---

[166] Copyright Act, 17 U.S.C. § 412 (1999).

[167] Carey R. Ramos and David S. Berlin, Three Ways to Protect Software, 16 The Comp. Law. 16 (Jan. 1999) (noting that copyright law only protects against copying of the work and that if "someone independently creates a similar or even identical work, he or she does not violate the copyright").

[168] Copyright Act, 17 U.S.C. § 408 (1999).

of the basic facts of a particular copyright.[169] Copyright notices prevent "accidental infringement" placing web site visitors on notice that SPC owns rights in information. Copyright registration is not a predicate for SPC obtaining copyright protection but is strongly recommended.[170]

Despite the fact that registration is not required for protection, it provides SPC with several strategic advantages. First, registration serves as a public record for establishing the date of copyright creation. Second, copyright registration is a prerequisite if SPC wishes to file a copyright infringement lawsuit. Third, copyright registration is also evidence to establish the validity of the copyright. If registration is completed before or within five years of publication, registration is treated as *prima facie* evidence of the validity of the copyright and the facts stated in the copyright registration certificate. Fourth, if registration is completed within three months after publication of the work or before an infringement of the work, statutory damages and attorneys' fees will be available to the copyright owner in court actions.

If there is no copyright registration completed three months after publication or before infringement, the copyright owner may not seek statutory penalties. If there is no copyright registration, the total remedy is limited to an award of actual damages and profits. One of the essential issues to understand is whether the registration will extend to the entire scope of SPC's online work. Registration for all online works extends only to the copyrightable content of the work as received in the Copyright Office and identified as the subject of the claim. The Copyright Office has different forms that correspond to the type of work registered. Because a web site contains many different types of work, the form used for a web site containing more than one type of authorship will be the form that corresponds to the predominant material (see Table 4.5).[171]

---

[169] Information on registering copyrights is available through the Copyright Office web site. The Copyright Office provides copies of all circulars, announcements, regulations, other related materials, and all copyright application forms on its web site. The registrant may access all of these forms at the Copyright Office homepage at http://www.loc.gov/copyright. In addition, information (but not application forms) is available by Fax-on-Demand, at (202) 707-2600. For general information about copyright, call the Copyright Public Information Office at (202) 707-3000. The TTY number is (202) 707-6737. Information specialists are on duty from 8:30 A.M. to 5:00 P.M. eastern time, Monday through Friday, except federal holidays. Recorded information is available 24 hours a day. Specific application forms and circulars can be requested from the Forms and Publications Hotline, at (202) 707-9100, 24 hours a day. Information on registration is also available by regular mail: Library of Congress, Copyright Office, Publications Section, LM-455, 101 Independence Avenue, S.E., Washington, D.C. 20559-6000.

[170] Registration may be made at any time within the life of the copyright. Unlike the law before 1978, when a work has been registered in unpublished form, it is not necessary to make another registration when the work becomes published, although the copyright owner may register the published edition, if desired.

[171] U.S. Copyright Office, Copyright Registration for Online Works (Circular 66) (visited Apr. 7, 2000), http://lcweb.loc.gov/copyright/circs/circ66.html.

TABLE 4.5
Copyright Application Forms

For Original Registration

Form PA	For published and unpublished works of the performing arts (musical and dramatic works, pantomimes and choreographic works, motion pictures and other audiovisual works).
Form SE	For serials, works issued or intended to be issued in successive parts bearing numerical or chronological designations and intended to be continued indefinitely (periodicals, newspapers, magazines, newsletters, annuals, journals, etc.).
Form SR	For published and unpublished sound recordings.
Form TX	For published and unpublished nondramatic literary works.
Form VA	For published and unpublished works of the visual arts (pictorial, graphic, and sculptural works, including architectural works).
Form G/DN	A specialized form for registering a complete month's issues of a daily newspaper, when certain conditions are met.
Short Form/SE and Form SE/GROUP	Specialized SE forms for use when certain requirements are met.
Short Forms TX, PA, and VA	Short versions of applications for original registration. For further information about using the short forms, request Circular SL-7.
Form GATT and Form GATT/GRP	Specialized forms to register a claim in a work or group of related works in which U.S. copyright was restored under the 1994 Uruguay Round Agreements Act (URAA). For further information, request Circular 38b.

For Renewal Registration

Form RE	For claims to renew copyright in works copyrighted under the law in effect through December 31, 1977 (1909 Copyright Act) and registered during the initial 28-year copyright term.

For Corrections and Amplifications

Form CA	For supplementary registration to correct or amplify information given in the Copyright Office record of an earlier registration.

For a Group of Contributions to Periodicals

Form GR/CP	An adjunct application to be used for registration of a group of contributions to periodicals in addition to an application Form TX, PA, or VA.

Finally, SPC is a multinational dot-com company, which needs to protect others from importing infringing copies of its software. When SPC registers its copyrights, it should also record the copyright registrations with the United States Customs Services for confiscating infringing copies.[172]

[3] Registration Procedures

Copyright registration transforms a particular copyright into a public record. An original registration of copyright is made in the Copyright Office of the Library of Congress. A work may be registered any time during the life of the work of authorship. It is advisable, however, that copyrighted material be registered early in the life of the copyrighted work. An online work may be registered using any of the Copyright Office forms, with the sole exception that sound should be registered using Form SR. The applicant needs to describe the nature of authorship being registered.

The applicant should use terms that refer to copyrightable authorship, such as text, music, artwork, photographs, audiovisual material, and sound recordings. The Copyright Office advises the applicant not to refer to elements not protected by copyright, such as "user interface," "format," "layout," "design," "lettering," "concept," or "game play."[173] The Copyright Office's definition of "publication" does not "specifically address online transmissions."[174] The paper-based definition of publication refers to the distribution of copies to the public for sale or other transfer of ownership by rental, lease, or lending. A public performance or display of a work does not constitute publication.[175]

The application requires the online publisher to determine whether the work is published with the complete date and nation of first publication.[176] It is unclear when an online publication is published or if it is published. The country where the work was first uploaded defines the nation of publication for an online publication.[177] If the online applicant determines that work is unpublished, the Copyright Office requests that the applicant leave the nation of first publication blank

---

[172] Registration allows the owner of the copyright to record the registration with the U.S. Customs Service for protection against the importation of infringing copies. For additional information, request Publication No. 563 from Commissioner of Customs, ATTN: IPR Branch, U.S. Customs Service, 1300 Pennsylvania Avenue, N.W., Washington, D.C. 20229 (visited Sept. 14, 2000) http://www.customs.gov.

[173] U.S. Copyright Office, Copyright Registration for Online Works (Circular 66) (visited Apr. 7, 2000), http://www.lcweb.loc.gov/copyright/circs/circ66.html.

[174] Id.

[175] 17 U.S.C. § 101 (1999).

[176] For revised works, the publication date is the date the revised version was first published, not the date of the original version. Circular 66, id.

[177] Id.

rather than fill the space with *Internet* or *homepage*.[178] It is unclear how works transmitted online should be deposited with the Copyright Office. The Copyright Office is developing new rules for depositing online materials. The deposit requirement for registered software on a CD-ROM is to deposit the CD-ROM, operating software, and manual.[179]

The three elements of a copyright registration are: (1) a completed application; (2) a filing fee of $30;[180] and (3) a deposit copy of the work being registered. The Copyright Office requires the applicant to place the copyright registration application, filing fee, and deposited work in the same envelope or package and to send them to the following address.

> Library of Congress
> Copyright Office
> Register of Copyrights
> 101 Independence Avenue, S.E.
> Washington, D.C. 20559-6000

SPC's copyright registration is effective on the date the Copyright Office receives all the required materials in acceptable form. The time that it takes to process SPC's application and mail the certificate of registration does not affect the date of copyright registration. The Copyright Office acknowledges that the time that it takes to process an application varies considerably.

In 1999, the Copyright Office reported it was averaging over 600,000 applications each year. The Copyright Office does not acknowledge the receipt of an application. The Copyright Office issues a certificate of registration. The Copyright Office cites statutory reasons if it rejects a copyright application. SPC should send its application, filing fee, and deposited material by registered or certified mail in order to obtain a return receipt.

[4] Who May File an Application Form?

SPC's web site is a collective work protected by copyright. SPC's copyrights in the materials that compose the web site are distinct from copyright in the web site as a collective work. SPC's web site may also be protected by trademark, if the "look and feel" of the web site is distinctive, to obtain trade dress protection under the federal Lanham Act.[181] If SPC's employees develop the web site, it is quite likely that the work qualifies as "work for hire." If SPC employs consultants

---

[178] Space 3b should not be filled in if the work is published. *Id.*

[179] *Id.*

[180] All remittances should be in the form of drafts, that is, checks, money orders, or bank drafts, payable to: Register of Copyrights. The Copyright Office does not accept cash.

[181] The leading case for trade dress is Two Pesos, Inc. v. Taco Cabana, Inc., 505 U.S. 763 (1992).

or outside developers to develop its web sites, however, it is advisable that SPC enter into agreements that would make it the owner of the content copyright.

The Copyright Office considers the following persons to be legally entitled to submit an application form. First, the author who is the creator or, if the work was made for hire, the employer or other person for whom the work was prepared can claim copyright. Second, the copyright claimant, as defined in Copyright Office regulations, may be either the author of the work or a person or organization that has obtained ownership of all the rights under the copyright initially belonging to the author.[182] The owner of a copyright may not necessarily be the original creator. Third, a publisher or an authorized agent of an author or of the owner of exclusive right(s) may register copyrights. Any person authorized to act on behalf of the author, another copyright claimant, or the owner of exclusive rights may apply for registration.

[5] Internet Copyright Searches

SPC may wish to conduct a search before attempting to register its copyrights. The records of the Copyright Office are open for inspection and search by the public. In addition, the Copyright Office will conduct a search of its records at the statutory hourly rate of $65 (effective through June 30, 2002) for each hour or fraction of an hour. The Copyright Office publishes Circular 22, "How to Investigate the Copyright Status of a Work," and Circular 23, "The Copyright Card Catalog and the Online Files of the Copyright Office." Another option is for SPC to conduct an Internet search through the Copyright Office's web site. The Copyright Office has copyrights in a machine-readable form, cataloged from January 1, 1978, to the present, including registration and renewal information and recorded documents.[183]

[6] Content Licenses

If SPC hires consultants or other nonemployees to provide content for its web site, it needs to obtain ownership or assignments to use copyrighted materials, since the "work for hire" doctrine does not automatically confer ownership rights onto SPC. If SPC's web site incorporates text, video, audio, pictures, or other content protected by a third party's copyright, it will need to enter into content license agreements. If SPC employs outside consultants, artists, or other content providers, it will need that party to assign or transfer ownership for all

---

[182] Copyrights are freely transferable, assignable, or conveyed. Anyone who has obtained the right to a copyright may register it with the Copyright Office.

[183] The Copyright Office web site is at http://www.loc.gov/copyright/rb.html. The Telnet site can be found at locis.loc.gov.

copyrighted materials. SPC may decide to enter a content license agreement with the copyright owners. A content license agreement may be as simple as an authorization giving permission to use the materials. The effective date for the license is an important term to include in every agreement. The content license agreement should have the authorized signatures of the licensor and the licensee.

It is essential that SPC's content licenses clearly extend the scope of the agreement to include the Internet as well as print media. What is being transferred or licensed? What is the geographic scope of the license agreement? If SPC is the licensee, it should seek to obtain the right to use the content for all media worldwide.

[a] Granting Clause for Content License Agreements

The granting clause is the heart of the content license agreement. A licensor will typically want to grant limited rights in nonexclusive agreements, while the licensor will frequently want an exclusive license to use the content for all purposes. The content license may be structured as exclusive, semiexclusive, or exclusive. Another issue is whether a content license is extended to the use of copyrighted material by subsidiaries.

A content license agreement may commence at the execution of the agreement. Another possibility is that the terms of the agreement will begin on the date of delivery of the content. A license agreement needs both a termination date and a list of designated events of default that constitute grounds for termination. Each party to SPC's content licenses will have a right to cancel the agreement in the event of a material breach. The failure to pay license royalties is a standard event of termination in license agreements. Insolvency of either party is another standard event of default in a content license agreement. The parties should also decide whether there should be a period in which to cure defaults as well.

[b] Payment/Royalty Reports

A licensee may agree to pay a licensor a set fee for content, even if it is a nominal fee. There are a vast number of payment options available, depending upon the type of content agreements. An important issue to consider is whether the company seeks an exclusive or nonexclusive license. On certain occasions, content may be prepared especially for the web site. The company may require the developer of the content to assign all rights to the company in return for compensation. Another option is to enter a license agreement with the author of the content. This may involve the need for up-front fees, annual fees, royalties, or fees based upon the number of web site visitors viewing or downloading content. A multitude of methods can be used to compute royalties. A licensor, for example, may receive a given percent of the net sales.

Payment streams are generally greater if the license agreement is exclusive. The licensee may want to obtain warranties and an indemnity to protect it from claims for intellectual property infringement. The danger is that a licensee may be subject to a copyright or trademark infringement lawsuit if a third party believes that the licensed material infringes their rights.[184]

[c]   Warranties and Infringement

SPC should complete a due dilegence report of content to reduce the potential for contributory infringement arising out of SPC's participation in infringing activities. A company may otherwise be liable for contributory infringement if copyrighted materials from a third party's sources are posted without an appropriate license or assignment. Even if contributory infringement is not proven, SPC may be liable for vicarious infringement because of its relationship with a primary infringer.[185] A company is liable for vicarious infringement where it (1) has the right and ability to control the infringer's acts, and (2) receives a direct financial benefit from the infringement.

To further reduce the liklihood of infringement, SPC should obtain content licenses from all third-party providers. The content licensee will typically require the licensor to warrant that it owns all rights in the content. The licensee will seek indemnification for infringement of a third party's intellectual property rights in a content license agreement. A licensee will want the licensor to indemnify and "hold harmless" the licensee for liabilities or claims arising from claims of infringement. A common warranty is that the content will conform to the specifications in the license agreement.

A licensor will typically want to limit what it warrants. The licensor will typically limit liability for express or implied warranties such as the warranty of merchantability and fitness for a particular purpose. The licensor will often seek to limit liability for express or implied warranties, or consequential damages, for example. Many licensors substitute an exclusive remedy instead of all express or implied warranties.

[d]   Acceptance Testing

It is customary in the software industry to have a 30-day acceptance period. A licensor will find it advantageous to have a long acceptance period during which to

---

[184] To succeed in a trademark infringement lawsuit, SPC must establish that it has a protectable trademark and that the infringer's use of that trademark is likely to cause confusion in the same channel of trade.

[185] The leading vicarious liability case is Shapiro, Bernstein & Co. v. H.L. Green Co., 316 F.2d 304 (2d Cir. 1963) (articulating the doctrine of vicarious infringement).

cure any defaults. A licensee will want a broad license to use content that allows the transfer of content to backup computers.

[e] Choice of Law and Forum/Dispute Resolution

As with every other web site agreement, it is critical that parties determine the applicable law and/or method for resolving disputes. The case law on Internet jurisdiction is uncertain as to which law is applicable in a situation that involves multiple jurisdictions. The parties should tailor their agreements to include a specific choice of forum and law.

[f] Franchise Rules

If SPC enters a trademark license agreement with other sites, it may be subject to franchise rules. An agreement between a licensor and a licensee to license a trademark, trade name, service mark, or advertising may be deemed as franchises. A franchise is a commercial relationship in which a franchisee sells or distributes products on the Internet using SPC's marks. If a franchisee uses SPC's trademarks, service marks, or trade names, it may create a franchise.

The Federal Trade Commission (FTC) regulates franchise sales, whether on the Internet or in the brick and mortar world. The FTC requires compulsory disclosures in "Franchising and Business Opportunity Ventures," 16 C.F.R. § 436. SPC may also have to comply with state laws governing franchise sales.

[7] Linking Agreements and Disclaimers

SPC may permit free linking to its site, but it will thus risk links with adult entertainment sites or other sites that may tarnish the company's good will. SPC may wish, therefore, to reserve the right to determine the nature of the entity that links to its site. SPC may wish to have a linking clause on its web site terms of service agreement. The following language is an example of a linking clause:

> You are free to establish a hypertext link to this site so long as the link does not state or imply any endorsement or sponsorship of you, your company, or your site by SPC.com. However, without the prior written permission of SPC.com, you may not frame any of the content of SPC.com nor incorporate into another web site or other service any intellectual property of SPC or its licensors. You may not, without prior written permission of SPC, deep link into the interior of SPC's site. You must link directly into the home page of SPC, which is the first page of its web site, unless you have written permission from SPC. Requests for permission to frame alternatively or to deep link our content may be sent to our Customer Service Manager, either by e-mail

or at the SPC address. SPC may decide to enter a promotional linking service agreement to gain more potential customers. SPC may enter into revenue-sharing linking agreements with computer outlets offering discount software.

SPC will need to make a decision on whether other web linking license requirements are necessary. The revenue-sharing agreement will spell out web link specification, commissions, reporting, ownership, termination, representations, and indemnification. Even if SPC does not enter promotional linking agreements, it will need a linking policy for web sites that maintain links to its web site. SPC may require, for example, notification of links to its web site and the linkers' acceptance of SPC's terms and conditions. As an alternative, SPC may use "click through" web site license agreements to reduce transaction costs, rather than nego-tiating each linking agreement.

SPC may also enter web linking agreements to promote its web site or to share resources with another web site through linking. Model provisions for web linking agreements are available through the American Bar Association's Business Law Section.[186] The following terms are common in web linking agreements: (1) granting clauses of the right to link; (2) details about the integrity and operation of the sites; (3) descriptions of ownership rights to information in sites; (4) indemni-fication and disclaimers noting that the parties are agents for named or unnamed principals; and (5) term limits, termination, and limitations on warranties, liability, and remedies.[187] A linking agreement could be modeled on the following language:

> SPC grants to XYZ Company a nonexclusive, nontransferable license to hyperlink ("link") your Internet web site to SPC's link logo and/or SPC's web site, provided XYZ Company accepts all of the following terms and conditions. To indicate XYZ's acceptance of all of the terms and conditions of this web linking agreement, an authorized representative of XYZ Com-pany must click the button marked "XYZ Company Accepts" after its review of the terms and conditions. If XYZ does not agree to all the terms and con-ditions of this agreement, their authorized representative should click the button "XYZ Company does not accept" the terms and conditions. In order to link to the SPC web site and/or use SPC's link logo, XYZ must agree to all of the following terms and conditions:
>
> XYZ company must include the following notice on any World Wide Web page it creates which includes the SPC link or SPC link logo: SPC and

---

[186] Subcommittee on Interactive Services, Committee on the Law of Commerce in Cyberspace, ABA Section of Business Law, Web-Linking Agreements: Contracting Strategies and Model Provi-sions (1997).

[187] Bruce Gaylord, Web Linking Agreements: Understanding Unique Legal Issues: The Judicial System Is Only Starting to Address Related Privacy Matters, 15 Comp. L. Strat. 1 (Mar. 1999).

the SPC link logo are licensed trademarks of SPC Inc. XYZ Company has no rights to the intellectual property of SPC, and in particular, has no rights to distribute SPC hardware or software.

XYZ may not use the name "SPC," the SPC link, and/or the SPC link logo to disparage SPC, its personal computers, software, and/or services.

XYZ company is not permitted to tarnish or diminish SPC's trade name, trademarks, service marks, logos, or good will by linking it to web sites, including but not limited to content such as pornography, obscene materials, political commentary, hate speech, or web sites that incite unlawful activity.

XYZ may not change the appearance of the SPC logo on its web site. The SPC logo must not be attached to any XYZ or third party's logo and must have a minimum amount of 30 pixels of empty space around it. SPC's link logo may not be used as the design element of any XYZ logo or third party's logo or link logo.

XYZ may not use the name SPC, the link, and/or the SPC link logo in any way that implies SPC sponsorship or endorsement of XYZ's product services, and/or SPC's web site.

You may not display the name "SPC," the SPC link, and/or the SPC link logo more prominently than XYZ's product, Internet web site name, or logo. Links from the SPC web site does not constitute an endorsement from SPC.

SPC reserves the right to alter, modify, or discontinue the SPC web site and/or SPC logo at any time, at its sole discretion. SPC makes no warranties, whether express or implied, and specifically disclaims the implied warranty of merchantability and fitness for a particular purpose related to SPC's web site and/or services. SPC is not liable for any damages or losses arising out of this web linking agreement with XYZ.

XYZ agrees to defend, indemnify, and "hold harmless" SPC, its officers, directors, employers, agents, and any of its affiliated companies for any loss or damages caused to SPC arising out of XYZ's use of the name "SPC," the SPC link, and the SPC link logo. XYZ acknowledges that it is responsible for the contents of its web site and acknowledges that SPC is not liable for the defamatory, offensive, or illegal conduct of other users, links, or third parties. SPC is not responsible for hypertext links to web sites that are defamatory, offensive, or illegal.

SPC is not responsible for the contents of XYZ's web site or off-site page references by the XYZ web site.

SPC reserves the right to review XYZ's use of the name "SPC," the SPC link, and the SPC link logo. SPC is hereby granted unrestricted access to XYZ's web site in order to review XYZ's use of the name "SPC," the SPC link, and the SPC link logo.

SPC has the sole discretion to cancel XYZ's use of the trade name SPC, the SPC link, and the link logo for any reason.

XYZ agrees that the laws of the Commonwealth of Massachusetts govern construction of the disclaimers above and resolution of disputes.
Please fill out the following information:
Name of XYZ's authorized representative _____
Title of XYZ's authorized representative _____
Company name and mailing address _____
URL of link to SPC's web site _____
Web site/company _____

Please click "I Accept" if the above information is correct and you agree to the terms of the SPC web link and logo license agreement. If you do not agree to the terms, click "I Do Not Accept" to clear the form and leave the SPC web site.

I Accept	I Decline

[8] Disclaimers

SPC's web site should also contain corporate disclaimers of links made to corporate home pages or subsequent pages. SPC's disclaimer should state that links are made available by the company's home page, which permits the user to go to other Internet sites. The disclaimer should make it clear that the linked sites are not the property of the company or under its control. The company should emphasize that the company makes no express or implied endorsement of linked sites, and it should conspicuously post on its web site a disclaimer similar in language to the following:

CORPORATE DISCLAIMER

NOTE: Some of the links made available to you through Suffolk Personal Computer's (SPC) home page and subsequent pages will allow you to leave the SPC web site. Please be aware that the Internet sites available through these links, and the material that you may find there, are not under the control of SPC. SPC cannot and does not make any representation to you about these sites or the materials available there. The fact that SPC has made these links available to you is not an endorsement or recommendation to you by SPC of any of these sites or any material found there. SPC provides these links only as a convenience to you.[188]

---

[188] The example adapts language from the GTE Internetworking Legal Documentation, *id.*

[9]   Content Posted on SPC's Services

If SPC has a computer bulletin board or other service in which third parties post materials about products or services, it may be advisable to obtain a content license agreement as depicted below:

> YOU AGREE THAT UPON POSTING ANY MATERIAL ON THE SPC "SPC" [SPECIFY SERVICE], YOU GRANT SPC AND ITS SUCCESSORS AND ASSIGNEES A NONEXCLUSIVE WORLDWIDE ROYALTY-FREE, PERPETUAL, NONREVOCABLE LICENSE TO USE, MODIFY, OR RETRANSMIT MATERIAL YOU POSTED. YOU HEREBY GRANT SPC THE RIGHT TO DOWNLOAD, DISTRIBUTE, DISPLAY, REPRODUCE, AND PRINT IN WHOLE OR IN PART ANY MATERIAL YOU HAVE POSTED [TO THE SERVICE]. YOU AGREE TO TAKE ANY NECESSARY STEPS TO PROTECT WHATEVER OTHER INTELLECTUAL PROPERTY RIGHTS YOU HAVE IN SUCH CONTENT, INCLUDING POSTING APPROPRIATE COPYRIGHT NOTICES.

§ 4.03   TRADEMARKS IN CYBERSPACE

[A]   Overview

The Internet raises challenging issues for trademark law. Any company operating a web site needs to understand how trademark law impacts their choice of a domain name, their development of a brand, and their relations with competitors, cybersquatters, or other entities who want to exploit their name. On a practical level, the company must know how to register its trademarks and domain name with the United States Patent and Trademark Office and what remedies are available if someone infringes on their mark (see Table 4.6).

[B]   Types of Marks

A trade name "means any name used by a person to identify his or her business or vocation."[189] A trademark, in contrast, is "any word, name, symbol, or device . . . used by a person in commerce."[190] Trademarks are classified along a spectrum from weakest to strongest: generic, descriptive, suggestive, and arbitrary or fanciful. Four types of trade symbols are (1) trademark; (2) service mark; (3) certification mark; and (4) collective mark. Anyone who claims rights in a mark may use the ™ (trademark) or SM (service mark) designation with the mark to alert the public to the claim. It is not necessary to have a registration, or even a pending application, to use these designations. The claim may or may not be valid. The

---

[189] Trademark Act of 1946, 15 U.S.C. § 1127 (defining "trade name" and "commercial name").
[190] *Id.* (defining trademark).

TABLE 4.6
Protection and Remedies for a Trademark

Method for Obtaining Protection	Trademarks, service marks, certification marks and collective marks, are registered in the USPTO. Registration is also available in states.
Remedies for Infringement	SPC must prove that its mark is entitled to protection and that the defendant's use of SPC's mark will likely cause confusion with its mark. SPC may seek injunctive relief under the Lanham Act, profits, damages, costs, and attorneys' fees; courts balance (1) threat of irreparable harm to the moving party against (2) the state of the balance between this harm and the injury to the other party; (3) the probability of success on the merits; and (4) public interest in determining whether to grant injunction. The Federal Trademark Dilution Act of 1995 provides protection against dilution for "famous" marks. It also protects against dilution for nonfamous marks under state trademark laws, under theories of blurring and dilution by tarnishment.

symbol ® may only be used by SPC if the mark has been registered in the USPTO.[191] The ™ symbol should be displayed even if a company has not yet registered its trademarks.

Trademarks identify goods made by sellers and distinguish them from those of other companies. Ford Motor Company is a trade name used in commerce. CBS is a trade name, whereas CBS marks include CBS™ and the CBS "eye" design. CBS also has an Internet web site, *CBS.com*, as well as television, radio, cable, and other Internet web sites.

If a company's marks are not inherently distinctive, they are not registrable on the USPTO's Principal Register. A mark not qualifying for the Principal Register may be registered on the Supplemental Register if it is capable of acquiring distinctiveness or secondary meaning. The question of whether SPC's marks have acquired distinctiveness is a matter of fact. The Lanham Act's remedies for infringement will apply only to a company's registered marks.

On the web, trademark information on a company's logos, products, service name, and trademarks must be stated on a company's terms of service page. The trademark notice should state that the trademarks are the intellectual property of the company and are not to be used without the company's prior permission. The clickwrap or webwrap "terms of service" agreement should include a clause that

---

[191] *Id.*

the site visitor or user agrees not to display or use a company's trademarks in any manner.

[1] Trademark

Suggestive, arbitrary, and fanciful marks are deemed inherently distinctive; descriptive marks receive protection only upon a showing that they have acquired secondary meaning; and generic marks are not protectable.[192] The "strength" of particular trademark refers to the distinctiveness of the mark or "more precisely, its tendency to identify the goods sold under the mark as emanating from a particular source."[193] Arbitrary or fanciful marks have the highest level of strength, or distinctiveness. Suggestive marks are inherently distinctive, whereas descriptive marks are slightly more distinctive than generic marks. A generic term can never receive trademark protection, although it may acquire a secondary meaning.[194] Terms such as onions.com or toiletpaper.com are generic domain names.

Although a trademark may be found distinctive, it may not be protected by the Lanham Act if it "comprises immoral, deceptive or scandalous matter, or consists of matter which may disparage or falsely suggest a connection with persons, living or dead, institutions, beliefs, or national symbols or bring them into contempt or disrepute."[195] An adult entertainment site, for example, will not be permitted to register obscene trademarks.

Courts impose a variety of tests to distinguish suggestive marks from merely distinctive ones. If a mark is not inherently distinctive, acquiring secondary meaning in the minds of consumers may protect it. A company should choose inherently distinctive marks so that they may be registered on the Principal rather than the Supplemental Register. A descriptive mark that has the potential of acquiring distinctiveness or secondary meaning is registered on the Supplemental Register.

Ford is a surname that has built up secondary meaning. Descriptive marks are not protectible as trademarks unless they acquire secondary meaning. Secondary meaning is acquired in the marketplace, rather than emanating from its natural meaning.[196] The New Ford Explorer is an example of a Ford trademark. The Cadillac car company uses the trademarked slogan "Creating a higher standard." Trademarks prevent consumers from confusing Donald Trump's luxury hotels

---

[192] United States Patent and Trademark Office, Basic Facts About Registering a Trademark (Apr. 9, 2000), http://www.uspto.gov/web/offices/tac/doc/basic/basic_facts.html.

[193] Northern Light Technology, Inc. v. Northern Lights Club, 97 F. Supp. 2d 96 (D. Mass. 2000).

[194] 1 J. Thomas McCarthy, McCarthy on Trademarks and Unfair Competition § 12:47 at 12-92 and 12-93 (1996, 1999).

[195] 15 U.S.C. § 102(b) (1999).

[196] Arthur R. Miller and Michael H. Davis, Intelletual Property: Patents, Trademarks, and Copyrights 165 (2d ed. 1990).

with the Holiday Inn or Motel 6. Pier 1 Imports is a trade name for a chain of stores that sell stylish but inexpensive home furnishings and accessories. The Dollar Stores, on the other hand, are a chain of stores catering to the less affluent. Both use trademarks to identify the types of goods they offer for sale.

Marinated pepper sets are marketed under a trademark owned by Catalago Italiano, whereas French Dijon mustard is trademarked as Dijon Originale by Umberto Sal Maille. Nike's swoosh and the "N'yuk, n'yuk, n'yuk" of the Three Stooges are trademarked. Branding of distinctive goods and services is occurring in cyberspace at a rapid pace. Amazon.com is an example of one of the most famous marks in cyberspace, being used for the sale of books, music, and videos.

[2] Service Mark

A "service mark" is a word, name, symbol, or device used in commerce "to identify and distinguish the services of one person."[197] In the off-line world, Midas is a service mark for automobile mufflers. America Online registered its "Buddy List,"[198] "You Have Mail," and "Instant Message" features as service marks. When AT&T used the phrase "Buddy List"[199] on its competing service, AOL filed a lawsuit for unfair competition. A federal court found AOL's "Buddy List" to be generic and not entitled to protection.[200]

The title of a television program such as "Dawson's Creek," "Friends," or "The Awful Truth," may be registered as service marks. Garrison Keillor's "Prairie Home Companion," a syndicated radio program produced by Minnesota Public Radio, is a syndicated service mark. An Internet company that provides classified advertising for products and services will register its service mark identifying its information services. Call numbers for radio and television stations, such as KNOX or KCND, may be service marks. Like trademarks, service marks are the intellectual property of the owners and may only be used with permission.

[3] Collective Mark

A "collective mark" is a trademark or service mark used by the members of a cooperative, an association, or another collective group or organization. The National Fluid Milk Processor Promotion Board is a collective mark. The slogan,

---

[197] *See supra* note 192.

[198] A Buddy List provides for real-time chat between two or more persons simultaneously using the AOL Service. Its members refer to "instant messages" or "IM" to signify the real-time chat component.

[199] A buddy list permits real time chat between "Buddy List" AOL members.

[200] America Online, Inc. v. AT&T Corp., No. 98-1821-A 1999 U.S. Dist. LEXIS 12615 (E.D. Va., Aug. 13, 1999).

"Got milk?" is a trademarked slogan owned by the board. The Cabot Cooperative of Cabot, Vermont, has a collective market. The Cabot Co-op produces trademarked products under the mark, Cabot of Vermont. The Humboldt Elevator Association of Humboldt, Minnesota, could file for a collective mark for its grain, seed, and fertilizer products. Collective marks differ from trademarks and service marks only in ownership; they may also only be used with the permission of the owners.

[4] Certification Mark

The e-Trust mark is one of the most important certification marks in Internet-related commerce. Web sites that display the e-Trust mark follow certain minimum privacy standards. A "certification mark" is a "word, name, symbol or device used to certify regional or other characteristics of such person's goods or services, or that the work or labor on the goods or services was performed by members of a union or other organization."[201] The French, for example, could apply for a certified mark for Roquefort cheese or Burgundy wines.[202] A labor union such as the AFL/CIO may apply for a certification mark. Consumers rely upon certification marks for information about goods and services. The failure to observe formalities in the use of certification marks may result in cancellation of the registration.

The Lanham Act does not permit self-application for a certification mark because of the potential problem of the lack of objectivity in owners acting as certifiers of their own marks. Owners of certification marks must police their marks or lose them. The Vermont Maple Syrup producers are vigilant in protecting their mark against producers who make syrup with high proportions of cane sugar or other deviations in quality.

[5] Trade Name

A trade name is a name, word, or phrase employed in identifying the source of products or services. Trademarks at common law require that the mark be affixed to the goods. Surnames are not a good choice for trademarks, since there is a "judicial reluctance to enjoin use of a personal name."[203] A court will be reluctant to register surnames, such as Rustad or Daftary, because all persons bearing those surnames should have an equal opportunity to utilize the surnames as distinguishing marks. The Fairbanks Brothers of St. Johnsbury, Vermont, however, obtained trademark protection for their scales because the geographic meaning of

---

[201] *Id.*

[202] *See, e.g.,* Community of Roquefort v. Faehndrich, 303 F.2d 494 (2d Cir. 1962).

[203] Nissan Motor Co., Ltd., v. Nissan Computer Corp., 2000 U.S. Dist. LEXIS 3718 (C.D. Ca., Mar. 23, 2000) (citing Gallo Winery v. Gallo Cattle Co., 967 F.3d 1288 (9th Cir. 1992)).

the marks was deemed to be as great as the surname, Fairbanks. Marks that are primarily a surname may be registered on the USPTO's Supplemental Register.

The Vermont company Ben & Jerry's Ice Cream uses first names as a trade name and a surname in its brand, Cherry Garcia. Ford and Dodge are surnames that have acquired secondary meaning as trade names for automobiles. "Secondary meaning indicates that through 'long and exclusive use and advertising in the sale of the user's goods, [the mark] has become so associated in the public mind with such goods that it serves to identify the source of the goods and to distinguish them from the goods of others.' "[204]

Secondary meaning in this context means that a surname has "developed a quality that distinguishes the goods of the producer."[205] Louis Vuitton and Nissan are surname trademarks that have "secondary meaning." Giorgio Armani, Calvin Klein, Ralph Lauren, and Walt Disney are surnames that have gained secondary meaning. Consumers associate luxury leather goods with Louis Vuitton and well made cars with Nissan, which has been a registered mark since 1959. The Nissan mark benefits from the presumption of incontestability.[206]

Hermès Paris trademarked the term "*Caleche Soie de Parfum*," meaning silk calash perfume or silk bonnet perfume. The Lanham Act permits the registration of foreign words or phrases as trademarks. The Lanham Act defines the "trade name" or "commercial name" to "mean any name [used] by a person to identify his or her business or vocation."[207]

[6] Trade Dress

Section 43(a) of the Lanham Act protects against infringement of unregistered marks and trade dress as well as registered marks.[208] Trade dress is the overall image, design, or appearance of a product and its packaging but does not include functional elements.[209] Functional trade dress that serves to enter Internet commands does not identify the origin of products and services and is therefore not protected by trademark law. Trade dress of a product may serve as a trademark if it identifies the goods or services in its package, distinctive shape, or color.

---

[204] Shade's Landing, Inc. v. Williams, 76 F. Supp. 2d 983 (D. Minn. 1999) (citation omitted).

[205] Arthur R. Miller and Michael H. Davis, Intellectual Property: Patents, Trademarks, and Copyright 164 (1990).

[206] *Id.* at 165 (noting that "[A] user who comes to the Patent and Trademark Office with a mark he has used for five continuous years may benefit from a presumption despite the fact that the mark is facially descriptive or nondescriptive in some other way").

[207] *Id.*

[208] GOTO.COM, Inc. v. The Walt Disney Co., 202 F.3d 1199 (9th Cir. 2000) (prohibiting Disney from using a logo confusingly similar to GOTO's mark.).

[209] Pecos, Inc. v. Taco Cabana, Inc., 505 U.S. 763, 765 (1992).

Examples of trade dress include the shape of the Coca-Cola bottle, Ralph Lauren's tapered square perfume bottle, and McDonald's golden arches. Color may be used as a type of product ornamentation, as with Owens-Corning's use of pink its in fiberglass insulation. A company may obtain trademark registration of the overall color scheme of its web site if it can prove the look and feel of color scheme is an accepted symbol in the trade. Examiners will determine whether the colors used as ornamentation on a company's web site function as trademarks. The color scheme of a company's web site may be protected as a mark depending upon the number of color combinations and how color is used in marketing for hardware and software sales. If a company's web site uses distinctive colors, color combinations, graphics, icons, or other features, for example, and someone else uses the same design and layout for a different site, the company may bring a trade dress action.

[C] Strength of Trademarks

The greater the distinctiveness of a mark, the higher the level of trademark protection. The hierarchy of distinctiveness has five descending levels, ranging from the most distinctive to the least distinctive marks: (1) fanciful or coined; (2) arbitrary; (3) suggestive; (4) descriptive; and (5) generic. Fanciful or coined marks have the highest level of protection, followed by arbitrary, suggestive, and generic marks, which reside at the bottom of the distinctiveness hierarchy. A coined or fanciful trademark consists of a made-up phrase or words that have no purpose other than to identify the goods or services.

[1] Fanciful or Coined Trademarks

A company should choose a fanciful word that identifies the source of its computer products but that is not descriptive.[210] Coined phrases enjoy the highest level of protection. Kodak is an example of a fanciful or coined mark that enjoys the highest level of protection. Polaroid, Exxon, and Vaseline are also fanciful trademarks that enjoy strong trademark protection. The name "Vornado," combining the words "vortex" and "toronado," is an example of fanciful mark. Vornado also has descriptive content when used to market a household fan.[211] Prozac® is a fanciful word that carries no meaning apart from its use to identify a product.

---

[210] The Seventh Circuit in Polaroid Corp. v. Polaroid, Inc., 319 F.2d 830, 837 (7th Cir. 1963) stated that a fanciful word is entitled to the greatest trademark protection.

[211] Vornado Air Circulation Systems, Inc. v. Duracraft Corp., 58 F.3d 1498, 1501 (10th Cir. 1995).

[2] Arbitrary Trademarks

An arbitrary mark is unlike a real word or phrase that can be remembered and associated in the public's mind with the mark's owner. The essence of an arbitrary trademark, however, is that it uses an ordinary word in an extraordinary way. Banana Republic, GAP, Express, and Polo are arbitrary trademarks for clothing. Morningside No-Load Funds is an arbitrary mark used for financial services. Crest is an arbitrary trademark for toothpaste. An arbitrary mark may not be used without permission if the use refers to the product it identifies.

[3] Suggestive Trademarks

A suggestive trademark is a word that describes qualities of a product or service (see Table 4.7). The use of Greyhound for a bus line, for example, suggests speed, since the greyhound is the fastest of all dog breeds. Suggestive trademarks "suggest" but do not directly describe a feature of a product. Coppertone is a suggestive trademark, as is Cap'n Crunch cereal. Coppertone's "Bug-Sun" is a suggestive trademark for sunscreen combined with insect repellent. "Hot Spots for Tots" is a suggestive trademark for a facial sun block marketed for children. Toys 'R' Us is a suggestive trade name for stores carrying children's toys. Playboy, Penthouse, and Hustler Magazine all employ suggestive trade names. Nair is a suggestive trademark for a hair removal product. Champion is a trademark for a company that sells licensed sports jerseys and other sportswear.

[4] Descriptive Trademarks

The fourth level of trademarks is the descriptive trademark, which enjoys the least amount of protection. "A suggestive mark is one that may be partly descriptive but is primarily distinctive. If a mark conveys the nature of the product only through the exercise of imagination, thought and perception, it is suggestive."[212] The boundary between suggestive and descriptive trademarks "is not altogether clear and ultimately . . . is a question of fact."[213] Descriptive terms are not inherently distinctive, and they are entitled to protection only if they acquire secondary meaning.

A descriptive mark directly describes an ingredient, quality, or use of goods or services. New York taxi drivers have the Wooden Bead Seat, which helps them sit for long periods without discomfort. A geographic term like Vermont Maple Syrup is a descriptive mark, as is a trademark using a surname such as Colonel

---

[212] *See supra* note 205.
[213] Shade's Landing, Inc. v. Williams, 76 F. Supp. 2d 983 (D. Minn. 1999).

TABLE 4.7
Examples of Suggestive Trademarks

"LA"	Low alcohol beer[a]
Dietene	Food supplement for people on a diet[b]
"Roach Motel"	Suggestive mark for anti-roach product[c]
"Coppertone"	Suggestive mark for suntan oil
Nair	Suggestive mark for hair removal product

[a] Anheuser-Busch, Inc. v. Stroh Brewery Co., 750 F.2d 631, 635 (8th Cir. 1984).

[b] Dietene Co. v. Dietrim Co., 225 F.2d 239, 243 (8th Cir. 1955) (holding that Dietene is more suggestive than descriptive for diet product).

[c] American Home Prods. Corp. v. Johnson Chemical Co., Inc., 589 F.2d 103, 106 (2d Cir. 1978) (holding that "roach motel" was a suggestive mark for anti-roach product).

Sander's Kentucky Fried Chicken. These marks are not registrable on the Principal Register of USPTO until they have acquired secondary meaning. Kool is a descriptive mark that suggests qualities of that brand of cigarettes. Cabot, Vermont, is a descriptive mark that describes geographic origin. "The Heart of Snow Country" is a descriptive trademarked phrase used by Sugarbush and Mad River Glen ski resorts.

[5] Generic Terms

A generic mark is in general use in a trade or industry. Generic means that a term refers to the genus of which the particular product is a species. The concept of a trademark identifies a unique source for goods or services. The term "shredded wheat" was held to be a generic term generally known to the public in Kellogg Co. v. National Biscuit Co.[214] Generic terms are so common that they do not differentiate goods or services in the minds of Internet users. America Online's "Buddy List," "Instant Message or IM" and "You Have Mail" have been deemed generic.[215]

Internet trade names seek to build up good will, protect business identity, and prevent confusion in the global marketplace. Trademark law can never protect generic marks. A famous or distinctive trademark can descend into the disfavored generic category if it comes to describe a general class of goods rather than an individual product. Companies should prevent competitors or others from using its trademarks in a generic way, to avoid the fate of marks such as aspirin, thermos, or the phrase "March Madess," which have all been ruled generic.[216]

---

[214] Kellogg Co. v. National Biscuit Co., 305 U.S. § 111 (1938).

[215] America Online, Inc. v. AT&T Corp., No. 98-1821-A, 1999 U.S. Dist. LEXIS, 12615 (E.D. Va., Aug. 13, 1999).

[216] Illinois High School Ass'n v. GTE Vantage, Inc., 99 F.3d 244, 247 (7th Cir. 1996) (finding that "March Madness" was generic and citing examples of "aspirin" and "thermos").

[D] Concurrent Use in Cyberspace

Trademark law evolved in a market economy in which goods and services were sold in markets separated by physical distance. Before the rise of a national economy, concurrently used trademarks could be used in geographically dispersed marketplaces. Two trademark owners could sell essentially the same products in different markets using the same marks. The concept of "likelihood of confusion" occurs only when two identical or similar marks are competing in the same market.[217] The Lanham Act permits concurrent registration when more than one party is entitled to use the mark and the likelihood of confusion is low.[218] An owner may establish priority rights with registration on the Principal Register, which places the world on notice that it claims exclusive rights in a mark.[219] The USPTO presumes that the first user is entitled to priority.[220]

The Internet creates the possibility that concurrent use of trademarks will create confusion. Under the common law, the trademark owner's protection extended to any area in which the goods and services became associated with the use of the mark.[221] The rise of the Internet leads to the possibility that previously geographically remote trademark owners using their marks on the Internet will create a likelihood of confusion.[222]

[E] Trademark Infringement

Sections 32(1) and 43(a) of the Lanham Act generally govern trademark infringement.[223] Trademark law prevents competitors from "free-riding on their rivals' marks and capitalizing on their rivals' investment of time, money, and resources."[224] Trademark infringement may be based on the simultaneous use of two trademarks "likely to cause confusion" or dilution. To prove trademark infringement, "a trademark owner must prove that the competing use of the mark is capable of generating a likelihood of confusion concerning the source of its

---

[217] Polaroid Corp. v. Polarad Electronics Corp., 287 F.2d 492, 492 (2d Cir. 1961) (measuring likelihood of confusion by eight factors).

[218] *See supra* note 205.

[219] Paul J. Cronin, Tea Roses, and Donuts in Cyberspace: Is the Concurrent Use of Trademarks Possible on the Internet? High Technology Law Program Thesis, Spring 1997, Suffolk University Law School.

[220] *Id.*

[221] *Id.* at 29.

[222] *Id.* at 3.

[223] *Id.*

[224] New Kids on the Block v. New America Publishing, Inc., 971 F.2d 302, 306 (9th Cir. 1991).

product."[225] The parties' lines of business need not be the same, so long as their products or services are "the kind the public attributes to a single source."[226]

[1] Likelihood of Confusion Test

The use of similar trademarks on different web sites creates a likelihood of confusion for site visitors.[227] The test used to measure a likelihood of confusion is whether "the similarity of the marks is likely to confuse customers about the source of the products."[228] Courts consider the following factors in determining whether a likelihood of confusion or unfair competition exists: (1) strength or weakness of plaintiff's mark; (2) the degree of similarity with defendant's mark; (3) class of goods; (4) marketing channels used; (5) evidence of actual confusion; and (6) intent of the defendant.[229] No one factor is determinative as the likelihood of the confusion test considers the totality of facts under the circumstances.[230] Likelihood of confusion relies heavily on whether web sites offer similar goods or services and use the Internet as a channel for advertising.

Actual confusion between marks is often demonstrated through empirical studies. A company will be more likely to obtain a remedy for infringement if it produces evidence of actual confusion. Empirical evidence such as questionnaires filled out by consumers may establish that trademarks are confusingly similar. If trademarks are being used in the same market, the likelihood is greater that consumers will be confused.

A company's hosting agreement and acceptable use policy needs to address the issue of customers who post materials that infringe on the trademarks of third parties. A host will typically disclaim liability for the infringing activities of customers. The hosting and acceptable use policies need to address the question of indemnification for infringement claims against a company. If a company mounts an online advertising campaign mentioning competitors' trademarks, service marks, or logos, it may be sued by competitors. The use of similar marks selling similar products may trigger an infringement claim based on consumer confusion.

A trademark owner may seek a preliminary injunction to prevent a web site from using its trademarks but first it must show that its mark is entitled to trademark protection. Labrador Software filed a lawsuit against an Internet search service, which used a black Labrador retriever image in its Internet search product.

---

[225] Stratus Computers, Inc. v. NCR Corp., 2 U.S.P.Q. 2d (BNA 1375, 1378 (D. Mass. 1981)), cited in Michael D. Scott, Internet and Technology Law Desk Reference 505 (1999).

[226] Eli Lilly & Co. v. Natural Answers, Inc., 86 F. Supp. 2d 834 (S.D. Ind., 2000).

[227] GOTO.COM v. The Walt Disney Co., 202 F.3d 1199 (9th Cir. 2000).

[228] E. & J. Gallo Winery v. Gallo Cattle Co., 967 F.2d 1280, 1290 (9th Cir. 1992).

[229] See, e.g., Americana Trading Inc. v. Ross Berrie & Co., 966 F.2d 1284, 1287 (9th Cir. 1992).

[230] Hotmail Corp. v. Van$ Money Pie Inc., 47 U.S.P.Q. 2d 1020 (N.D. Cal. 1998).

The court denied the injunction holding That Labrador Software's trademark was only descriptive and not entitled to protection absent a showing of secondary meaning.[231]

[2] Dilution

[a]   *Federal Trademark Dilution Act of 1996*

There are two recognized forms of dilution: blurring and tarnishment. The Federal Trademark Dilution Act (FTDA)[232] provides new remedies for the trademark dilution of famous trademarks. To meet the famousness element of protection under the FDTA, a mark must be prominent and renowned.[233] The owner of a "famous mark" may obtain an injunction against another "person's commercial use in commerce of a mark or trade name, if such use begins after the mark has become famous and causes dilution of the distinctive quality of the mark. . . ."[234] Eight factors determine whether a mark is famous: (1) the degree of inherent or acquired distinctiveness of the mark; (2) the duration and extent of use of the mark in connection with the goods or services with which the mark is used; (3) the duration and extent of advertising and publicity of the mark; (4) the geographical extent of the trading area in which the mark is used; (5) the channels of trade for the goods or services with which the mark is used; (6) the degree of recognition of the mark in the trading areas and channels of trade used by the mark's owner and the person against whom the injunction is sought; (7) the nature and extent of use of the same or similar marks by third parties; and (8) whether the mark was registered on the principal register.[235]

Distinctive trademarks identify origins of goods and services. In Avery Dennison Corp. v. Sumpton,[236] the Ninth Circuit held that the trademarks "Avery" and "Dennison" on the USPTO Register were insufficiently famous for purposes of the Federal Trademark Antidilution Act. The federal district court held that Sumpton's domain name registrations for "avery.net" and "dennison.net" diluted two of Avery Dennison's separate trademarks, "Avery" and "Dennison." The district court ordered the defendant to transfer the domain name registrations to Avery Dennison in exchange for $300.

The Ninth Circuit reversed the district court's summary judgment in favor of Avery Dennison ruling that the domain names did not dilute Avery Dennison's

---

[231] Labrador Software, Inc. v. Lycos, 32 F. Supp. 31 (D. Mass. 1999).

[232] 15 U.S.C. § 1125(c) (2000).

[233] Avery Dennison Corp. v. Sumpton, 189 F.3d 868 (9th Cir. 1999) (holding the Avery and Dennison trademarks were not sufficiently distinctive to warrant a federal cause of action for dilution).

[234] 15 U.S.C. § 1125(c)(1) (1999).

[235] 15 U.S.C. § 1125(c)(1) (1999).

[236] 51 U.S.P.Q. 2d 1801 (9th Cir. 1999).

trademarks within the meaning of the Federal Trademark Dilution Act. The court found the plaintiff's trademarks acquired secondary meaning but were not famous marks entitled to dilution protection. "Dilution is a cause of action invented and reserved for a select class of marks—those marks with such powerful consumer associations that even noncompeting uses can impinge on their value."[237] To meet the "famous" element of the federal statute, the "mark must be truly prominent and renowned."[238]

To qualify as a famous mark requires something greater than mere distinctiveness, whether inherent or acquired. The court found both "Avery" and "Dennison" to be used as trademarks on and off Internet, with no conflict between channels of trade. Sumpton, the defendant, was in the business of selling vanity e-mail addresses, whereas Avery Dennison sold office products and industrial fastenings. The court found no evidence that Sumpton was focusing on Avery Dennison's customer base.

No one factor is determinative in establishing whether a mark is famous, and a court may receive evidence beyond the statutory factors in the federal antidilution statute.[239] Unlike state antidilution acts, the federal antidilution statute does not require a plaintiff to show injury or a likelihood of confusion. A company can establish that its mark is distinctive by pointing to national or international advertising providing strong, unobtrusive evidence of consumer recognition.[240] A defendant, in turn, may assert a defense of a valid registration under the 1881 or 1905 Trademark Act or on the principal registrer. The Trademark Act exempts use of a famous mark in comparative advertisements, promotions, news reports, or in noncommercial uses.[241]

[i] Blurring of Internet trademarks. Before the passage of the FTDA, a trademark owner's only recourse for dilution was to seek relief in the state courts for blurring or tarnishment. The FTDA applies to the Internet, for example, if a web site blurs a famous trademark by using it in a domain name or in metatags.[242] Blurring whittles away the capacity of a distinctive and famous mark to identify and distinguish goods or services, regardless of the presence or absence of competition between the owner of the famous mark and other parties. Aspirin, for example, was once a distinctive mark. Gradually, however, the word lost its distinctive qualities.

---

[237] *Id.*

[238] The court cited I.P. Lund Trading Aps v. Kohler Co., 163 F.3d 27 (9th Cir. 1998) (quoting Thomas McCarthy, McCarthy on Trademarks).

[239] 15 U.S.C. § 1051(c)(1) (1999).

[240] *Id.*

[241] 15 U.S.C. § 1125(c)(3) & 1125(c)(4).

[242] 15 U.S.C. § 1125(c) (1999).

[ii] Tarnishment of Internet trademarks. Tarnishment occurs when a famous mark is linked to products of poor quality or is portrayed in an unwholesome manner."[243] A company must prove four elements to establish a tarnishment or blurring federal trademark dilution claim: (1) the company's mark is famous; (2) a competitor adopted its mark after the original company's mark became famous; (3) the competitor diluted the company's mark; and (4) the competitor used the company's mark in commerce. In Toys 'R' Us Inc. v. Akkaoui,[244] the defendant used the Barbie trademark in its adult entertainment web site. The court held that the use of the Barbie trademark combined with particular fonts and a particular color scheme tarnished the mark.[245] In contrast, blurring may occur when a company's mark is used on a number of different goods and services and, though distinctive, loses its association with the company.[246]

The federal act restrains those who use similar trade names as domain names on the Internet. Antiproduct and antiservices web sites are common on the Internet. A critic of Bally's Total Fitness filed a lawsuit against a former member's web site entitled "Bally sucks." The theme of the anti-Bally web site was criticism of the health chain.[247] Bally's sued for trademark dilution because the defendant was using its trademarks in an unauthorized manner.[248] The federal court in California granted summary judgment in favor of the defendant, holding that "no reasonable person would think Bally's is affiliated with or endorses" the anti-Bally site.[249] The court also found "fair use" in the anti-Bally site's use of the plaintiff's trademarks.[250] Finally, the court found the anti-Bally web site did not tarnish Bally's mark simply because of the name link between the sites. The court also upheld the use of Bally's metatags to promote the anti-Bally site.

In another tarnishment case, an adult web site used the domain names "papalvisit1999.com" and "papalvisit.com" to draw more visitors to its adult entertainment sites. The Archdiocese of St. Louis and Papal Visit 1999 discovered

---

[243] Panavision Int'l, L.P. v. Toeppen, 945 F. Supp. 1296, 1304 (C.D. Cal. 1996), *aff'd*, 141 F.3d 1316 (9th Cir. 1998).

[244] 48 U.S.P.Q. 2d 1467 (S.D.N.Y. 1998). Hasbro Inc. v. Internet Entertainment Group, Ltd., 1996 U.S. Dist. LEXIS 11626 (W.D. Wash. Feb. 9, 1996) (finding that adult entertainment web site tarnished mark of famous board game).

[245] *Id.*

[246] Hormel Foods Corp. v. Jim Henson Prods. Inc., 73 F.3d 497, 506 (2d Cir. 1996).

[247] Bally Total Fitness Holding Corp., 29 F. Supp. 2d 1161 (C.D. Cal., 1998). *See also* Lucent Technologies, Inc. v. Lucentsuck.com, 95 F. Supp. 2d 528 (E.D. Va., 2000) (dismissing claim because plaintiff failed to satisfy due diligence clause of the Anticybersquatting Consumer Protection Act).

[248] *Id.*

[249] *Id.*

[250] Around the Web, 11 The Internet News: Legal & Bus. Aspects 14 (Feb. 1999).

that the adult web sites were using their marks in adult-oriented sites.[251] A federal judge ruled in favor of the plaintiffs and issued an order enjoining the link of the trademarks to the adult entertainment sites. The federal judge found the plaintiffs' marks to be famous, triggering the protection of the Trademark Dilution Act as well as state dilution law.[252]

[b] State Antidilution Remedies

State antidilution statutes provide remedies for the dilution of the distinctive quality of trademarks. The concept of dilution is that a mark's uniqueness or selling power is gradually lost over time. Plaintiffs are required to prove a likelihood of dilution that will diminish the economic value of a mark versus actual dilution under the FDTA.

State antidilution laws protect a senior user's mark even when the junior user is not a competitor and no likelihood of confusion exists between the two users' products or trademarks.[253] To prevail on a state antidilution claim, the senior user must demonstrate that it has a senior mark and that the junior user's conduct damages the senior's interest in the mark "by blurring its product identification or by damaging positive associations that have been attached to it."[254]

If a company's brand names do not qualify as famous marks, they may be protected under state antidilution statutes or state common law. State antidilution claims, whether under statute or the common law, provide a remedy when there is similarity between two marks that either tarnishes or blurs the senior mark, even though the marks are noncompeting and do not create a likelihood of confusion. A state antidilution claim may be filed under the common law or by statute.

State antidilution statutes vary in their provisions. The Illinois Antidilution Act provides a remedy for a prior trademark user who proves that "its mark is distinctive and that the subsequent user's use dilutes that distinctiveness."[255] Illinois does not require the prior user to prove "competition between the users or confusion."[256] Ohio, for example, recognizes state common law antidilution claims.[257]

---

[251] Judge Issues Written Ruling Enjoining Adult Site's Use of Papal Marks, 16 Comp. & Online Indus. Litig. Rep. 12 (Mar. 2, 1999) (reporting on Archdiocese of St. Louis v. Internet Entertainment Group, Inc., No. 4:99CV27SNL (E.D. Mo. Feb. 12, 1999)).

[252] Id.

[253] The FTDA provides that possession of a valid federal trademark registration is a complete bar to a dilution claim "under the common law or a statute of a State." 15 U.S.C. § 1125(c)(3).

[254] Ameritech Inc. v. American Info. Technologies Corp., 811 F.2d 960, 961 (6th Cir. 1987) (applying Ohio Law).

[255] Eli Lilly and Co. v. Natural Answers, Inc., 86 F. Supp. 2d 834 (S.D. Ind. 2000) (citation omitted).

[256] Id.

[257] See, e.g., Guild & Landis, Inc. v. Liles & Landis Liquidators, Inc., 207 N.E.2d 798, 800 (Ohio Com. Pl. 1959) (comparing similar marks). See Ringling Bros.-Barnum & Bailey Combined Shows v.

[F] Trademark Registration

An owner of a mark must apply to the federal Patent and Trademark Office in Washington, D.C., in order to register it nationally for trademark or service mark protection. The USPTO Act specifies that the application must state "the date of applicant's first use of the mark, the date of applicant's first use of the mark in commerce, the goods in connection with which the mark is used, and the mode or manner in which the mark is used in connection with such goods."[258] The trademark applicant must attest that she or he owns the mark, that it is used in commerce, and that there is no similar mark that will create confusion.[259]

The requirements for an application include the name of the applicant; citizenship of the applicant; domicile; and post office address of the applicant. The applicant must also describe the class of goods or services the mark is for, according to the USPTO international classification system. The USPTO recognizes 34 classes for trademarks. An applicant may register for more than a single class in a single application. The date of the applicant's "first use of the mark as a trademark or service mark must be noted on the application."[260] The filing date is the date on which the elements of an application are received in the USPTO.[261]

The federal registration of trademarks is governed by the Trademark Act of 1946, as amended, 15 U.S.C. § 1051 *et seq.*; the Trademark Rules, 37 C.F.R. Part 2; and the Trademark Manual of Examining Procedure (2d ed. 1993). The USPTO uses the terms "trademark" and "mark" to "refer to both trademarks and service marks whether they are word marks or other types of marks. A trademark owner will use trademarks on the product and its packaging, while service marks advertise services."[262] The application and all other correspondence should be addressed to The Assistant Commissioner for Trademarks, 2900 Crystal Drive, Arlington, Virginia 22202-3513. The initial application should be directed to Box NEW APP/FEE." An AMENDMENT TO ALLEGE USE should be directed to "Attn. AAU." A STATEMENT OF USE or REQUEST FOR AN EXTENSION OF TIME TO FILE A STATEMENT OF USE should be directed to Box ITU/FEE. The applicant should indicate her or his telephone number on the application form. Once a serial number is assigned to the application, the applicant should refer to the serial number in all written and telephone communications concerning the application.

Utah Division of Travel Development, 170 F.3d 449 (4th Cir. 1999) (noting that courts applied the [state antidilution] statutes reluctantly and many states found it difficult to apply the dilution concept).

[258] *Id.*

[259] *Id.*

[260] 37 C.F.R. § 2.33(v).

[261] 37 C.F.R. § 2.21(stating requirements for receiving a filing date).

[262] *Id.*

The owner of a trademark may theoretically file and prosecute his or her own application for registration before the Patent and Trademark Office. Corporate counsel will likely hire a trademark company specializing in prosecuting trademark applications. A trademark application is given a filing date once all of the elements of an application have been filed.[263]

In addition to registration, companies must remember to obtain permission to use any trademarks owned by others.[264] An Internet company must use its marks in connection with goods or services on its web site in a manner that is not likely to cause confusion among consumers as a result of a third party's prior registration of identical or similar marks for goods or services that are similar. Internet sales make trademark disputes more likely because sales on the Internet are made on the same channel of trade and are directed to the same class of consumers.[265]

[1] The Benefits of Federal Registration

A trademark registration may be applied for by filing an application with the USPTO. The USPTO sends a filing receipt to the applicant approximately six months after filing. The filing receipt includes a serial number of the trademark application. Registrations issued after November 16, 1989 have a ten-year term and may be renewed every ten years forever. However, an Affidavit of Use must be filed between the fifth and sixth year following registration and within the year before the end of every ten-year period after the initial registration. Information on registering trademarks is available free of charge from the U.S. Patent and Trademark Office at http://www.uspto.gov or 1-800-786-91999. The Official Gazette is the official journal of the USPTO relating to trademarks and contains information about registered trademark.

Federal registration is not required to establish rights in a mark, nor is it required to begin use of a mark. Federal registration, however, can secure benefits beyond the rights acquired by merely using a mark. The owner of a federal registration, for example, is presumed to be the owner of the mark for the goods and services specified in the registration and is entitled to use the mark nationwide.

Each trademark application must be filed in the name of a company as owner of the mark. If a company is listed as the owner of the mark, it is responsible for the nature and quality of the goods or services identified by the mark. A company should remember to register trade name, trademarks, service marks, collective

---

[263] *See*, Rules of Practice in Trademark Cases, 37 C.F.R. §§ 2.1-2.189.

[264] The licensing of trademarks is typically the method of obtaining rights. Trademarks, however, are frequently assigned or purchased.

[265] It is uncertain whether courts will classify the Internet as the same channel of trade involving sales to the same class of consumers.

marks, and certification marks promptly.[266] The first user of a mark to file is conferred "a right of priority, nationwide in effect."[267] The right of priority to federal registration does not necessarily mean the right of priority to use the mark nationwide. The nationwide right to use a mark could, for example, be impeded by the common law right of an earlier use.

Unlike copyrights or patents, trademark rights can last indefinitely if the owner continues to use the mark to identify its goods or services. A trademark receives protection when it is used in commerce in connection with the sale of goods or services. The definition of being "in commerce" may refer to interstate commerce or foreign commerce.

The Lanham Act permits two types of use application: (1) actual use, and (2) intent to use. The Trademark Commissioner may accept evidence that an applicant has used a mark "in commerce" for five years as *prima facie* evidence of distinctiveness.[268] Alternatively, an applicant may attest that the mark will be used in the future. The applicant must state how the mark is (or will be) used in the course of the sale of goods or the rendering of services. The applicant must attest that she or he is the owner of the mark and that the mark is (or will soon be) used in commerce.[269]

[a] Actual Use

If a company has already used its marks in selling, for example, computer software or hardware, it will file an "actual use" application. The elements of an application consist of a page with the mark drawing, an application form, documentation of use, and the application fee of $245 per class.[270] If an examiner determines that the mark is distinctive, and it thus passes the examination stage, a registration issues. If no opposition arises following publication in the registry, the trademark registration is issued.

---

[266] SPC's marks can be in the form of a word, design, symbol, or device that fulfills the purpose of differentiating its goods and services. SPC plans on using its marks on labels on its software, tags on its monitors, screen-savers for its personal computers, brochures, magazine advertisements, and its web site, to name just a few of its uses in commerce.

[267] 15 U.S.C. § 1057(c) (1998).

[268] 15 U.S.C. § 1054(f) (1999) (stating that the Commissioner may accept as *prima facie* evidence that the mark has become distinctive, as used on or in connection with the applicant's goods in commerce . . . for the five years before the date on which the claim of distinctiveness is made").

[269] *Id.*

[270] SPC will file a multiple-class application to cover the wide breadth of goods and services. It may decide to apply for use of a trademark on its personal computers, for example, and another for use with its online services division. The classification of goods and services is in accordance with the World Intellectual Property Organization (WIPO) categories.

[b] Intent to Use

A company may also file an intent-to-use application. This means that if a company files its trademarks before other filers, it has a claim on use of the mark.[271] In an intent-to-use application, the applicant must provide a drawing of the mark and attest to a *bona fide* intention to use the mark on goods that are to be sold.[272] The intent-to-use application states that the applicant has a *bona fide* intention to use the mark in commerce regulated by Congress.[273] The dates of first use of the mark in Internet commerce will be noted on the application to prove use in commerce.[274] After a company files an intent-to-use application, an examination and opposition stage follows. The company's marks are not registered until the mark is used, although the registration date is the filing date of the intent-to-use application.

Federal trademarks may be renewed every ten years so long as the mark is used in commerce. A company's trademark counsel must remember to keep the registration alive by filing an affadavit with the USPTO between the fifth and sixth year after the date of initial registration. The failure of the registrant to provide the affidavit will result in the cancellation of the trademark registration.

[2] International Registration

The owner of a registered trademark has exclusive rights only in the United States. An online business may wish to file trademark registrations in foreign countries. Trademarks may be registered in different countries, especially those where goods and services are sold on the Internet. In the United Kingdom, for example, trademarks are regulated under the Trademark Act of 1938. A subsequent body of laws, the Trade Description Act of 1968, deals with false trade descriptions and imported goods bearing trademarks of U.K. manufacturers. Trademark registration in the United Kingdom is for 7 years initially and may be renewed for periods of 14 years. Germany also permits trademarks to be registered in the German Federal Patent Office. Most U.S. law firms specializing in intellectual property will have affiliations with trademark counsel in essential countries where protection is required.

The House of Representatives has also approved the Madrid Protocol Implementation Act, which would make it easier to file for an international registration

---

[271] The filing date constitutes a constructive date of first use.

[272] 37 C.F.R. § 2.52 (stating requirements of drawings).

[273] 15 U.S.C. § 1051(b) (1998).

[274] SPC must have clear documentation of the date of first use in commerce, although technically the owner does not have to show the exact date to the USPTO. If the filing date of the first use fails, the entire application fails. With an intent-to-use application, SPC may amend its application to include the first use in commerce. SPC's safest course is to file an intent-to-use application if any doubt might arise as to when first use in commerce occurred.

of marks by filing an international application with the USPTO.[275] Madrid Union signatory countries have agreed to a method for the international registration of marks. The Madrid Protocol formed the International Bureau of the World Intellectual Property Organization. The application for international registration of a mark is filed with the International Bureau.[276]

[G] Protecting Trademarks

Trademarks must be used "in commerce," or they will be treated as abandoned. A company can monitor the use, misuse, and abuse of trademarks on the Internet by hiring a search service. Counsel will frequently send "cease and desist" letters and threaten legal action where a company's trademarks are infringed on the Internet. A distinctive trademark may descend into the generic abyss if many others in Internet commerce use it.

Many owners of famous marks assert that similar trademarks are causing consumer confusion in Internet commerce. In one legendary case, the father of a young girl named Veronica registered the domain name of Veronica.com. Archie Comics, whose comic character, Veronica, was a trademarked term, sued Veronica and her father. The owner of the trademarks dropped its lawsuit and settled the case after purchasing the Veronica.com domain name.

Trademark infringement and counterfeiting is increasing at an exponential rate for products and services sold on the Internet. Companies selling trademarked goods need to keep in contact with the U.S. Customs Service (Customs), which polices the importation of counterfeited goods into this country. Customs recently published guidelines on restraining the importation of "gray market" goods bearing genuine trademarks but that are different from goods authorized for importation.[277]

[H] Use and Abandonment of Trademarks

The rule for trademark protection is to "use it or lose it." The concept of use means that the mark is used in the ordinary course of trade. A mark is presumed abandoned if it is discontinued or if a company shows intent not to resume use of

---

[275] Microsoft Law & Corporate Affairs, Summary of Global Internet Legal Developments (for the period Jan.-Mar. 1999) 56 (Apr. 1999) (reporting that H.R. 769 would permit a U.S. trademark owner to seek registration of its mark internationally by filing an international application with the U.S. Patent and Trademark Office, but the U.S. has yet to ratify the Madrid Protocol).

[276] Protocol relating to the Madrid Agreement Concerning the International Registration of Marks, art. 2 (entitled "Securing Protection Through International Registration").

[277] U.S. Customs Service, Gray Market Imports and Other Trademarked Goods, 19 CFR Part 133 (T.D. 99-21) RIN 1515-AB49 (Sept. 29, 1999), http://www.customs.UStreas.gov/fed-reg/notices/914486.htm.

a mark. Intent not to resume use is determined from the circumstances. The trademark owner's failure to use a trademark for three consecutive years is *prima facie* evidence of abandonment. Trademark applications may also be abandoned if "an applicant fails to respond, or to respond completely, within six months after the date an action is mailed; the application shall be deemed to have been abandoned."[278]

[I] Unfair Competition

Section 43(a) of the Lanham Act provides rights and remedies for unfair trade practices such as the "false designation of origin, false or misleading description of fact, or misleading representation of fact."[279] Section 43(a) covers false or misleading misrepresentations of fact "likely to cause confusion, or to cause mistake, or to deceive as to the affiliation, connection or association of such person with another person, or as to the origin, sponsorship, or approval of his or her goods, services, or commercial activities by another person."[280] A web site that falsely alleges endorsement, for example, may be liable for federal unfair competition.

Section 43(a) also covers unfair trade practices in the form of false or misleading advertising. The essence of a false or deceptive advertising claim under the Lanham Act is an advertisement that "misrepresents the nature, characteristics, qualities, or geographic origin of his or her or another person's goods, services, or commercial activities."[281]

[J] Defenses to Trademark Infringement

[1] Noncommercial and First Amendment-Related Defenses

The use of a trademark is not actionable where such use, even if dilutive, is part of a public commentary or journalistic report. An e-commerce publication, for example, may use a company's trademarks in a feature story about how its web site became an e-business success story. Editorial comment is constitutionally protected expression, as is comparative advertising in which another company's marks are mentioned.[282] Anticompany web sites may be protected by the First

---

[278] Rules of Practice in Trademark Cases, 37 C.F.R. § 265 (describing abandonment of trademark applications).

[279] 15 U.S.C. § 1125 (1999) (providing regulations for Section 43, "False Designations of Origin and False Descriptions Forbidden").

[280] 15 U.S.C. § 1125 (a)(1)(A) (1999).

[281] 15 U.S.C.§ 1125(a)(1)(B) (1999).

[282] *See* Seuss Enter, L.P. v. Penguin Books USA, Inc., 924 F. Supp. 1559 (S.D. Cal.), *aff'd,* 109 F.3d 1394 (9th Cir.), *cert. denied,* 118 S. Ct. 27 (1997) (holding uses of a trademark not to be actionable as dilution where the commentary is on an issue of public importance).

Amendment and the news commentary exemption to trademark infringement. The use of trademarks in journalistic reports, comparative advertising and other non-commercial uses developed as a common law "fair comment" or fair use defense.[283] In Patmont Motor Works, Inc. v. Gateway Marine, Inc.,[284] a federal court held that the use of a trademark owner's product name in the text of search engines to constitute fair use.

[2] Statutory Fair Use

The Lanham Act also recognizes a "fair use" defense, "the concept that a trademark registrant or holder cannot 'appropriate a descriptive term for his exclusive use and so prevent others from accurately describing a characteristic of their goods.' "[285] The Lanham Act's fair use defense permits the use of registered marks in a descriptive and fair way to describe the goods and services of the trademark owner. The defendant's use of a trademark owner's trademarks must not be used in conjunction with the sale of goods and services.[286]

Similarly, the FDTA extends the common law fair use doctrine to famous trademarks. Section 1125(c)(4) states that: "All forms of news reporting and news commentary" are classified as fair use.[287] The use of a competitor's advertisement in a comparative advertisement was also validated by Section 1125(c)(4) of the FDTA:

> (A) Fair use of a famous mark by another person in comparative advertising or promotion to identify the competing goods or services of the owner of the famous marks.[288]

A federal court found fair use as a defense to liability under the Lanham Act in Playboy Enterprises v. Welles.[289] Terri Welles, a former Playboy playmate, opened a web site including photographs of herself and a heading entitled Terri Welles: Playmate of the Year 1981. Ms. Welles also used Playboy and Playmate as keywords in the metatags. The court found Ms. Welles' use of the Playboy and Playmate marks in web site advertisements were descriptive and used in good faith. Another court found the descriptive use of a trademark owner's marks in the URL of a web address to be protected by fair use.[290]

---

[283] See supra note 205.

[284] 1997 U.S. Dist. LEXIS 20877 (N.D. Calif. Dec. 17, 1997).

[285] Playboy Enterprises v. Welles, 1999 U.S. Dist. LEXIS 21047 (S.D. Calif., Dec. 1, 1999).

[286] Sealed Indus., Inc. v. Chesebrough-Ponds USA Co., 125 F.3d 28 (2d Cir. 1997).

[287] 15 U.S.C. § 1125(c)(4) (1999).

[288] Id.

[289] 1999 U.S. Dist. LEXIS 21047 (S.D. Calif., Dec. 1, 1999).

[290] Teletech Customer Care Management, Inc. v. Tele-Tech Co., Inc., 977 F. Supp. 1407-1414 (C.D. Calif. 1997) (holding that domain name did not confuse web site visitors when placed in the context of web site content).

[K] Internet Domain Name Issues

[1] Domain Name Registration Procedure

Domain names, like the real estate market, are all about location, location, location. The choice of a domain name is one of great strategic importance. Corporate web sites need to register their domain names with one of the Internet Corporation for Assigned Names and Numbers (ICANN) accredited registrars. There are 61 accredited registrars. When registering, applicants must represent that: (1) the registration is complete and accurate; (2) the domain name does not infringe trademarks of third parties; (3) the domain name is not registered for unlawful purposes; and (4) the domain name owner will not knowingly use the domain name to violate any laws or regulations.

Many companies will want to use their trade name as a domain name, if it is available. The fee for a domain name is $35 a year, and InterNIC requires payment two years in advance.[291] A registrar of Internet domain names is not liable for direct, contributory, or vicarious infringement for accepting registrations of Internet domain names confusingly similar to a plaintiff's service or trademark.[292]

The last several characters of a domain name refer to type of organization that runs the site. The *.gov* in the following URL for the Census Bureau denotes a government site: *http://www.census.gov/*. The URL for ABC television is *http://www.abc.com/*. The *.com* signifies a commercial site. General Motors also is a commercial site, found at *http://www.gm.com*. Suffolk University Law School has an *.edu* at the end of its URL: *http://www.suffolk.acad.edu*, which signifies that this URL is an educational institution. National Public Radio has an organization top-level domain: *http://www.npr.org*. The *.org* signifies a noncommercial organization. An address with a *.mil* at the end signifies a military site. A two-character code at the end of an address signifies a particular country: *AU* (Australia), *BR* (Brazil), *CA* (Canada), *UK* (United Kingdom), and *JP* (Japan), are examples.[293]

Domain names may be cancelled, transferred or changed if: (1) the owner requests it; (2) there is an order from a court or tribunal; or (3) there is a decision from an administrative panel. A domain name may be cancelled or changed if the

---

[291] Absolute Solutions, Starting on the Web, Free Hosting, Domain Names, Email (visited July 13, 1999), http://www.absolute-solutions.com/starting-on-the-web.html.

[292] The leading case is Lockheed Martin Corp. v. Network Solutions, Inc., 985 F. Supp. 949 (C.D. Calif. 1997) (granting summary judgment in favor of registrar of Internet domain names because the registrar's use of Internet domain names was not connected with their trademark functions; acceptance of domain names is not a commercial use and thus does not infringe trademark law).

[293] Bruce J. McLaren, Understanding and Using the Internet 37, 38 (1997).

plaintiff proves the domain name (1) is identical or confusingly similar to trade-marks or service marked owned by another; (2) is owned by a party with no legit-imate interests to the name; and (3) was registered in bad faith.

[2]   Network Solutions and ICANN

Network Solutions was once a quasi-public entity that administered all domain name registrations. ICANN was created as a nonprofit public sector corporation to serve the operational standards of the Internet. Network Solutions is only one of the ICANN Accredited Registrars but is still a dominant player due to its comprehen-sive data base. Prior to the formation of ICANN, Network solution had a dispute res-olution, which placed domain names on hold if challenged by trademark owners.

Corporate defendants who held registered trademarks could restrain a domain name as long as they could produce a trademark registration predating the domain name registration. The Network Solutions dispute resolution policy has been supplanted by the ICANN dispute resolution policy for trademark/domain name disputes. ICANN's Board of Directors adopted a dispute resolution policy applicable for all ICANN accredited registrars in the .com, .net. and .org top-level domains[294] ICANN utilizes a procedure partially online designed "to take less than 45 days and expected to cost about $1,000 in fees."[295]

[3]   ICANN Domain Name Dispute Resolution Policy

The World Intellectual Property Organization (WIPO) devised a new Uni-form Dispute Resolution Policy applicable to generic top-level domains (*.com*, *.net*, and *.org*) adopted by the Internet Corporation for Assigned Names and Num-bers (ICANN). The purpose of the ICANN policy is to "establish a uniform and mandatory administrative dispute-resolution system to address cases of bad faith cybersquatting."[296] Under ICANN's dispute policy, most trademark-based domain name disputes are resolved by agreement, court action, or arbitration before a reg-istrar cancels, suspends, or transfers a domain name.[297]

ICANN adopted the Uniform Domain Name Dispute Resolution Policy on October 24, 1999, and began accepting cases in January 2000. It has so far resolved approximately 500 trademark disputes over primary top-level domain disputes

---

[294] ICANN, The Internet Corporation for Assigned Names and Numbers, Frequently Asked Ques-tions (FAQ), FAQ on Uniform Dispute Resolution Policy (Posted Sept. 13, 1999) (visited Sept. 23, 2000) http://www.icann.org/general/faq1.htm.

[295] *Id.*

[296] WIPO Press Release, First Cybersquatting Case Under WIPO Process Just Concluded, PR/2000/204 (Jan. 14, 2000), http://www.wipo.org/eng/pressrel/2000/p204.htm.

[297] ICANN, Uniform Domain Name Dispute Resolution Policy (visited Feb. 10, 2000), http://www.icann.org/udrp/udrp.htm.

(*.com*, *.net*, *.org*, *.edu*, and so on) by arbitration.[298] The ICANN dispute resolution policy developed by WIPO is available at: *http://www.domainmagistrate.com/disputepolicy*.

Cybersquatting is the abusive practice of registering domain names of famous companies and then seeking to sell their names back for a profit. Cybersquatting cases are resolved through an expedited administrative proceeding in which the holder of the trademark files a complaint with an approved dispute-resolution service provider. The ICANN procedure is triggered by the trademark owner's filing of a complaint, in a court of proper jurisdiction, against the domain-name holder.

ICANN employs an expedited administrative proceeding that the holder of trademark rights initiates by filing a complaint with an approved dispute-resolution service provider.[299] The ICANN procedure also permits *in rem* actions against domain names. The ICANN dispute resolution policy does not, however, allow for suspension of a name during the dispute or for temporary restraining orders.

ICANN's dispute resolution system employs panels of either one or three experts who resolve claims quickly. ICANN, however, defers to the courts to resolve difficult and complex cases.[300] The cost of resolving disputes using the ICANN dispute resolution method is far less than filing a lawsuit in federal court. Costs range "between $750 and $1,000, and you have a decision within 56 days."[301]

The ICANN procedure permits the plaintiff to file complaints electronically, choosing between the WIPO panel and the National Arbitration Forum.[302] WIPO's Uniform Dispute Resolution Policy is administered through its Arbitration and Mediation Center. WIPO recently issued its first domain name dispute ruling in favor of the World Wrestling Foundation (WWF) in a dispute over ownership of the domain name, *worldwrestlingfederation.com*. The WWF filed a lawsuit with WIPO's Arbitration and Mediation Center under the new Uniform Dispute Resolution Policy applicable to generic top-level domains against a California resident who had registered the domain name and then offered to sell it to WWF for a large sum.[303] WWF argued that the defendant registered the domain name in question in bad faith in order to abuse its trademark.[304] ICANN's dispute resolution policy resolves disputes quickly and is far less expensive than filing suit in federal court.

WIPO's first international domain name dispute was initiated when the World Wrestling Federation submitted a dispute over the domain name *www.worldwrestlingfederation.com* to WIPO in Geneva. The WIPO arbitrator ruled that the registrant had acted in bad faith by offering to sell the name for a

---

[298] Joe Borders, New Process Can Dislodge Cybersquatters, Tex. Law., Mar. 14, 2000, at 1.

[299] *Id.*

[300] *Id.*

[301] Joe Borders, New Process Can Dislodge Cybersquatters, *id.*

[302] *Id.*

[303] *See supra* note 296.

[304] *Id.*

significant profit. In addition, the arbitrator found the domain name was confusingly similar to WWF's trademark and service mark and that the defendant had "no rights or legitimate interests in the domain name. The ruling transferred the registration of the domain name *worldwrestlingfederation.com* to WWF.[305]

In another case, Mohamed Al Fayed, whose son Dodi was killed in a 1997 Paris car crash with Britain's Princess Diana, won control of the Internet domain name dodiafayed.com.[306] WIPO's arbitrator "ruled that Robert Boyd of Dayton, Ohio, who registered it first and offered it for sale for $400,000, had 'no legitimate interest' " in the domain name.

[4]   Anticybersquatting Consumer Protection Act of 1999

President Clinton signed the Anticybersquatting Consumer Protection Act of 1999 (ACPA) on November 29, 1999.[307] (See Table 4.8). Part of an omnibus appropriations bill, ACPA was passed to deter the unauthorized registration or use of trademarks of others as Internet domain names. The Senate Committee Report stated that the bill was "to protect consumers and promote electronic commerce by amending certain trademark infringement, dilution and counterfeiting laws."[308] The Act is a response to the trafficking in domain names where there is a bad-faith intent to profit from the goodwill of another's marks.[309] The ACPA amends Section 43 of the Trademark Act of 1946, 15 U.S.C. § 1125, and applies to domain names registered before, on, or after the date of enactment. The ACPA creates *in rem* jurisdiction over domain names that are registered in bad faith.

The *in rem* provisions of the ACPA allow, under limited circumstances, the owner of a federally registered trademark overruled of Porsche Cars, North America, Inc. v. Porsche.com.[310] In that case, Porsche, the owner of the trademarks "Porsche" and "boxster," filed an action against 128 domain name owners claiming that they had diluted Porsche's famous trademarks.[311] The actions were filed *in*

---

[305] *Id.*

[306] Reuters, Dodi's Still His Father's Son, Mar. 17, 2000 (visited Mar. 17, 2000), http://www.wired.com/news/print/0,1294,35031,00.html.

[307] Congress passed S. 1948 (incorporated in H.R. 3194). The Anticybersquatting act will create a new cause of action under Section 43(d) of the Lanham Act, 15 U.S.C. § 1125(d) (2000).

[308] The Anticybersquatting Consumer Protection Act, Hearings on S. 1255 Before the Committee on the Judiciary, 106th Cong., 1st Sess. (1999).

[309] *Id.* at § 2.

[310] Porsche Cars North America, Inc. v. Porsche, 51 F. Supp. 2d 707 (D. Va. 1999) (dismissing federal antidilution action since the FDTA did not provide for *in rem* remedy). *See,* Porsche Cars North America, Inc. v. Porsche, 2000 U.S. App. 12843 (4th Cir. 2000) (applying ACPA's *in rem* remedy retroactively); *see also* Lucent Technologies v. Lucentsucks. Com, 95 F. Supp. 2d 528 (E.D. Va. 2000) (dismissing plaintiff's *in rem* action because personal jurisdiction was possible.).

[311] *Id.*

TABLE 4.8
Anticybersquatting Consumer Protection Act of 1999 (ACPA)

Who is defined as a cybersquatter?	A person who registers a domain name that "consists of the name of another living person, of a name substantially and confusingly similar thereto, without that person's consent, with the specific intent to profit from such name by selling the domain name for financial gain to that person or any third party, shall be liable in a civil action by such person." Section 47 of the ACPA; 15 U.S.C. § 1129(1)(a) (2000).
What is the test for bad-faith intent?	(1) Trademark or intellectual property rights of the person in the domain name; (2) extent to which the domain name consists of a legal name of the person or a name that is commonly used to identify that person; (3) person's prior use of the domain name for offering of goods and services; (4) person's noncommercial or fair use of the mark in a site accessible under domain name; (5) intent to divert consumers from the trademark owner's online location; (6) offer to transfer, sell, or assign domain name to the mark owner; (7) material and misleading false contact information; (8) registration and acquisition of multiple domain names identical or confusingly similar to the marks of others or to famous marks; and (9) extent to which the mark incorporated in the person's domain name registration is not distinctive and famous. 15 U.S.C. § 43(d)(1)(B).
Who is given cyberpiracy protection?	All entities or individual that own trademarks not just individuals with famous trademarks.
What damages and remedies are available?	An *in rem* remedy is available where the owner is not able to find a defendant after due diligence. The *in rem* remedy applies retroactively. *See* 15 U.S.C. § 1125(d)(2)(A) (2000). "A court may order the forfeiture or cancellation of the domain name or the transfer of the domain name to the owner of the mark."[a] The ACPA permits a plaintiff to "elect at any time before final judgment is rendered by the trial court, to recover, instead of actual damages and profits, an award of statutory damages in the amount of not less than $1,000 and not more than $100,000 per domain name, as the courts consider just."[b]
What defenses and limitations on liability are available?	In the event of good-faith registering of a domain name or name of another living person that is substantially or confusingly similar, the domain registry is not liable for monetary relief.

[a] 15 U.S.C. § 1125(d)(1)(C) (1999).

[b] If the plaintiff does not opt for statutory damages, the court may award damages under 15 U.S.C. § 117(a)(b) based on damages, profits, and the cost of the action. 15 U.S.C. § 1125(d)(1)(C) (1999).

rem, rather than as *in personam* actions against the registrants. The court observed that even if the federal antidilution act permitted *in rem* actions against domain name holders, such a procedure might be unconstitutional because there is no requirement of minimum contacts.[312] In addition to the *in rem* and injunctive remedies, the ACPA provides for statutory damages between $1,000 and $100,000 for each domain name that has been encroached by cybersquatters.[313]

Sporty's Farm LLC v. Sportsman's Market Inc.[314] was the first appellate case considering the applicability of the ACPA. In that case, Sportsman's Market, Inc. was the owner of the Sporty's federal trademark. Sportsman's is a mail order catalog company selling products tailored to aviation. Sportsman's used the logo "sporty" to identify its catalogs and products. In 1985, Sportsman's registered the trademark Sporty's with the USPTO. Sporty's was used on the cover of Sportsman's catalogs, and Sportsman's spent $10 million per year advertising its Sporty's logo.

Sporty's Farm sold Christmas trees and advertised its trees on a *sportys.com* web page. Sporty's Farm filed suit seeking a declaratory judgment that it owned the domain name *sportys.com*. The federal district court determined that Sporty's was distinctive as well as a famous trademark and that Sporty's Farm's use of *sportys.com* diluted the famous mark owned by Sportsman's. The lower court found no infringement, however, since Sportsman's and Sporty's Farms were in different lines of business. While the appeal was pending, President Clinton signed the federal ACPA.

The Second Circuit ruled that the ACPA applied not the FTDA and order the transfer of the sports.com domain name to Sportsman's Market finding it to be distinctive, declining to rule on whether it was famous.

In Shields v. Zuccarini,[315] a court found that a wholesaler of Internet domain names was liable under the ACPA. The plaintiff registered *www.joecartoon.com* as his web site and sold Joe Cartoon merchandise. The defendant in *Zuccarini* registered five World Wide Web variations on the plaintiff's site: *joescartoon.com*, *joecarton.com*, *joescartons.com*, *joescartoons.com*, and *cartoonjoe.com*. The defendant "mousetrapped" web visitors seeking the plaintiff's site *http://www.joecartoon.com*. A mousetrap does not permit the visitor to exit without clicking through a succession of ads. The defendant received between ten cents and twenty-five cents from the advertisers for each click. The court issued a preliminary injunction against the defendant's site based on the ACPA. The court found the defendant's domain mark to be confusingly similar to the plaintiff's domain name. The court also found that the defendant intended to profit from the plaintiff's distinctive and famous mark, Joe Cartoon. The court ordered the defendant to deactivate the infringing domain names.

---

[312] *Id.*

[313] 15 U.S.C. § 1125(d)(1)(C) (1999).

[314] 202 F.3d 489 (2d Cir. 2000).

[315] 2000 U.S. Dist. LEXIS 3350 (E.D. Pa., March 22, 2000).

Harvard University brought suit against a domain name entrepreneur who registered 55 domain names relating to the Harvard and Radcliffe trademarks.[316] Harvard received an e-mail from a principal officer of Web-Pro offering to sell the university domain names incorporating the Harvard and Radcliffe trademarks. Harvard charged Web-Pro with federal trademark cyberpiracy, trademark infringement, unfair competition, and trademark dilution under the Lanham Act, as well as trademark dilution, unfair methods of competition, and deceptive practices and unfair competition under Massachusetts state law.[317] Harvard charged the defendant with "willfully adopting, registering, maintaining and offering to sell or license numerous Internet domain names incorporating these marks."[318]

[5] Domain Name Case Law

Domain name disputes are litigated under diverse causes of action including (1) federal trademark infringement; (2) federal trademark dilution; (3) state dilution; and (4) other state common law causes of action.

[a] *Infringement*

A Massachusetts federal district court found the use of the domain name *energyplace.com* to be infringement of the plaintiff's service mark, "Energy Place."[319] A California court found the use of the plaintiff's trademark in the "path" or "second level" of a domain name did not constitute trademark infringement, since the second level does not identify the origin of the web site; it only describes the site's type of organization.[320] The court found the defendant has limited use of the plaintiff's federally registered mark describing a product that was being sold. This use constituted "nominative fair use of the mark" and was not infringing.[321] The court took notice that the plaintiff's product was one not readily identifiable without the use of the mark.[322]

---

[316] Harvard Uses Cybersquatting Law for Infringement Suit, E-Commerce Law Weekly, Dec. 1999 (reporting on President and Fellows of Harvard College v. Michael Rhys, D. Mass., No. 99CV12489RCL, filed Dec. 6, 1999).

[317] *Id.*

[318] Harvard seeks to restrain Web-Pro from using domain names or offering them for sale. The domain names that were the subject of the litigation included: *www.harvard-lawschool.com, www.harvarddivinity.com, www.harvardgraduateschool.com* and *www.radcliffecollege.com.*

[319] Public Serv. Co. of N.M. v. Nexus Energy Software Inc., 36 F. Supp. 2d 436 (D. Mass. 1999).

[320] Patmont Motor Works, Inc. v. Gateway Marine, Inc., 1997 U.S. Dist. LEXIS 20877 (N.D. Ca., Dec. 8, 1997) (ruling that use of mar in path or second level of the domain name was not likely to cause confusion.).

[321] *Id.*

[322] *Id.*

[b] Federal Dilution

Net entrepreneurs register thousands of domain names, including famous trademarks, in the hope of selling them to the trademark owners. The new generation of domain case is based on the tendency of web surfers to make careless typographical errors when typing in URL addresses. Domain name entrepreneurs are registering domain names that are a letter or space different from those of famous trademarks; those who do this are called *typosquatters*. In one recent case, a defendant registered the domain name of WWWPainewebber.com, capitalizing on the mistake made by some users who fail to type the period after WWW when looking for the PaineWebber site."[323] A Virginia federal court enjoined the defendants from operating the confusingly similar web site, stating that it was tarnishing the plaintiff's trademark.[324]

In Panavision v. Toeppen,[325] the Ninth Circuit held that the Federal Trademark Dilution Act was implicated because the defendant was registering domain-name combinations using famous trademarks and seeking to sell the registrations to the trademark owners.[326]

In a notorious cybersquatting case, Dennis Toeppen registered scores of domain names containing the trademarks of famous companies and then sought to sell them to the owners of the marks. Toeppen attempted to show legitimate use of the Panavision domain name by posting aerial photographs of Pana, Illinois, at the web site *Panavision.com*. The Ninth Circuit found Toeppen was misappropriating the trademark of Panavision through his practice of registering trademarks as domain names and then selling them to the trademark owners.[327]

[c] State Dilution

In Planned Parenthood v. Bucci,[328] a federal court ordered an injunction against a pro-life web site that used the domain name *plannedparenthood.com*. The injunction of the court was based on a finding that the domain name would cause confusion and dilute the plaintiff's mark, Planned Parenthood Federation of America, in violation of state law. Planned Parenthood had a diametrically

---

[323] PaineWebber Inc. v. WWWPainewebber.com, 1999 U.S. Dist. LEXIS 6552 (E.D. Va., Apr. 9, 1999), http://www.phillipsnizer.com/int_synopses.htm.

[324] *Id.*

[325] 945 F. Supp. 1296 (D.C. Cal. 1996), aff'd, 141 F.3d 1316, 1324 (9th Cir. 1998).

[326] Panavision, 141 F.3d at 1324.

[327] *Id.* at 1325.

[328] Planned Federation of America, 42 U.S.P.Q. 2d 1430 (S.D.N.Y. 1997) (granting preliminary injunction finding sufficient likelihood of confusion and false designation of origin).

opposed mission to that of the plannedparenthood.com web site, which was put up by an antiabortion activist.

Musician and television personality John Tesh sued Celebsites, a Nevada corporation, and its officers. Celebsites operated a celebrity and entertainment web site, *Celebsites.com*, a site dedicated to celebrities. In addition, the site also offered advertising, contests, reports, and news.[329] *Celebsites.com* registered the domain name, *JohnTesh.com* and offered to sell it back to Tesh for a large sum. Tesh filed an action under the federal trademark act, the Anticybersquatting Act, and California state law. Tesh charged the defendant with marketing the *John-Tesh.com* web site as the official site for Tesh and, as a result, creating a substantial risk of confusion for Internet users.[330]

[6] Metatags*

Increasing the traffic to one's web site has a high priority to site owners, especially for commercial sites. Thus, marketing web sites requires creativity. Some webmasters surpass acceptable levels of creativity when they resort to deception by embedding popular nonrelevant, common words, such as "sex," and the trademarks of others in their web site's metatags. Such webmasters deceive users because they use words that may be of interest to the users to divert them to sites that may be of no interest. A user seeking to purchase a "Healthy Ways" product would not likely be interested in viewing a pornographic site for which "Healthy Ways" is used in the pornographic site's metatags to draw visitors.[331] Such misuse of trademarks, whether by competing or noncompeting businesses (including providers of add-ons and complementary products or services), may be termed "invisible infringement."[332]

These webmasters engage in a pursuit of attention and divert web traffic from the rightful trademark owner's site. They intend to increase their business or the advertising value of their sites, which is similar to the advertising value of television shows: The more "hits" a site has, the greater its sales will be or the more its owners can charge for advertising on it. Often, these webmasters deliberately manipulate search engine results in order to profit commercially from the reputation of another.[333] This tactic may help the unscrupulous webmaster, but it is a detriment to the public because the resulting metatags do not always accurately

---

[329] John Tesh Sues for Trademark Infringement and Cybersquatting, E-Commerce Law Weekly (Jan. 1999).

[330] *Id.*

* The section on Metatags was written by Lucy Elandjian.

[331] Healthy Ways is a hypothetical company used to illustrate the problem with metatags.

[332] Inventor of the term "invisible infringement" is unknown; the term is widely used.

[333] *See* Robert Scheinfeld and Parker Bagley, Emerging Issues on the Internet, N.Y. L.J., Nov. 26, 1997, http://www.ljx.com/Internet/1126netissue.html.

reflect the content of the web page making it more difficult for users to find the information they seek.

Search engines do not have any explicit policies for policing the use of trade-marks to prevent misuse.[334] Some search engines, however, such as Excite, may inadvertently benefit the trademark owners because they do not use keyword metatags, hoping in this way to protect users from unreliable information and to avoid influencing a site's ranking in the search results.[335] Where no metatags are allowed, as in the indexing at Excite, unscrupulous webmasters cannot confuse potential customers by diverting web traffic to their sites by using others' trade-marks. Search engines automate the indexing process by using programs called "spi-ders" that search the Web and pull keywords from the text within a site and/or from the web pages' invisible metatags.[336] These spiders index and rank the relevant web sites using algorithms proprietary to the search engine, with the most relevant site having the highest rank.[337] Because most search engines give most weight to words at the beginning of a web page, metatags that appear in the header of the page heav-ily influence the ranking of a web page.[338] The frequency of words also influences the ranking, such that a word that appears in a web page or its metatag five times will give that web site a higher rank than is achieved by the web page that contains that word only three times.[339] Thus, webmasters use controllability of metatags as a tool to influence the ranking and increase the likelihood of "hits" on their web site.

Not all search engines index the same way. Some will take the contents of a document and index it, but if the search engine limits its examination to the first 250 characters, the site will not be accurately indexed if those characters do not contain anything of relevance to the major part of the site's contents. Metatags serve a useful purpose by allowing such search engines to more accurately list the web site in their indices.

Many companies, such as Lycos, sell advertisements on the web pages of their search engines. Lycos, for example, enters advertising contracts that take one of the following forms:

1. A *run of site* contract, under which a customer is guaranteed a number of impressions;

2. A *keyword* contract, in which a customer purchases the right to advertise in connection with specified word searches; or

---

[334] *See* Elizabeth Gardner, Trademark Battles Simmer Behind Sites, Aug. 8, 1997 (visited Oct. 28, 1998), http://www.web week.com/current/news/19970825-battles.html.

[335] *See* Understanding Metatags—What is a Metatag? (visited Nov. 12, 1998), http://www.excite.com/Info/listing7.html.

[336] *See* Fine, *supra.*

[337] *See* Halpern, *supra.*

[338] *Id.*

[339] *Id.*

3. A *targeted* contract, where the customer purchases a specified number of impressions in one of the targeted categories, or on a specified page or service.[340]

There are growing number of metatag disputes, but most cases are settled or result in an injunction. Metatag litigation is generally predicated upon trademark causes of action seeking remedies for trademark infringement, trademark dilution, and unfair competition. Most of the metatags have little precedential value, rarely resulting in an appellate opinion.

[a]   *Insituform Technologies v. National Envirotech*[341]

National Envirotech, an industrial plumbing supplier, used the registered trademarks—*Insituform®* and *Insitupipe®*—of its competitor, Insituform, as metatags in its web site.[342] The contents of the offensive site did not refer to Insituform or its products, even in a comparative advertising manner.[343] Defendant's act caused search engines to link Insituform's trademarks with National Envirotech's site, and searches for plaintiff's site, via its trademarks, returned a list of matching sites, including defendant's site.[344] Insituform filed suit and brought a motion for a preliminary injunction against National Envirotech.[345]

Insituform argued that defendant's conduct constituted unfair competition. Insituform analogized defendant's conduct to an alteration in Directory Assistance's database such that potential customers requesting Insituform's telephone number would be given National Envirotech's number.[346] These potential customers would then call National Envirotech and purchase its plumbing supplies rather than purchasing Insituform's products. Misdirecting potential customers to its web site appears as the sole plausible reason for National Envirotech's conduct. Insituform suffered damages of lost potential sales and profits because of National Envirotech's action.

The suit was resolved with a settlement, and a court issued permanent injunction.[347] National Envirotech agreed to remove Insituform's trademarks from its

---

[340] Lycos, Inc., Notes to Condensed Consolidated Financial Statements (visited July 2, 1999), http://www.sec.gov/Archives/edgar/data/1007992/0000927016-99-002346.txt.

[341] *See* Insituform Technologies v. National Envirotech, No. 97-2064 (E.D. La. July 1, 1997).

[342] *See id.*, Complaint.

[343] *See id.*

[344] *See id.*

[345] *See id.*

[346] *See* Cowan, Liebowitz and Latman, P.C., CL&L Successfully Stops a Competitor's New Form of Web Site Unfair Competition (visited Nov. 11, 1998), http://www.cll.com/keyword.htm.

[347] *See* Insituform Technologies v. National Envirotech, No. 97-2064 (E.D. La. order Aug. 27, 1997) (visited Oct. 28, 1998), http://www.cll.com/case1.htm.

web site's keyword metatag section, to notify all the search engines of the court's order in order for them to delete from their databases the links that associated plaintiff's trademarks with the defendant, to resubmit their web pages for indexing, and to file a report evidencing their compliance.[348] National Envirotech, however, did not stipulate that it was suggesting an affiliation with Insituform or that it was attempting to deceive anyone.[349] Nevertheless, this case has significance for having the first order on metatag settlement.

[b] *Playboy Enterprises, Inc. v. Calvin Designer Label*[350]

Playboy Enterprises sued an adult web site operator for using its registered trademarks, Playboy® and Playmate®, in the offensive web site's domain name, metatags, and contents.[351] Defendant's unauthorized acts resulted in the retrieval of the offensive web site whenever a search was conducted to locate plaintiff's site using "Playboy" or "Playmate." Plaintiff claimed that defendant acted with knowledge and intent to cause confusion, mistake, or deception, and that defendant's unauthorized use of its famous trademarks would dilute their distinctive quality and destroy the public's association of the marks with Playboy Enterprises.[352]

Plaintiff sought a permanent injunction prohibiting defendant from using Playboy marks, or terms similar to these marks, in any domain name, directory address, metatags, or web page content.[353] Playboy also sought $5,000,000 in damages, any profits defendant made, and punitive damages.[354] The trial court, however, limited the remedy to an immediate preliminary injunction enjoining defendant from using Playboy's trademarks or similar terms in its domain name, directory address, metatags, or web page. The injunction also prohibited the use of Playboy's trademarks in connection with retrieval of data or with advertising the defendant's products in a manner that would create a likelihood of confusion. Metatags should not be used to convey the impression that the defendant's web site was authorized or licensed by Playboy.[355] Although favorable to trademark owners, this ruling does not have a significant effect on wrongful metatag use

---

[348] *See id.*

[349] *See* Danny Sullivan, Metatag Lawsuits (visited Oct. 27, 1998), http://searchenginewatch.com/resources/metasuits.html.

[350] *See* Playboy Enterprises, Inc. v. Calvin Designer Label, 44 U.S.P.Q.2d (BNA) 1156 (N.D. Cal. 1997).

[351] *See id.* at 1157, Complaint, Sept. 8, 1997 (visited Feb. 1, 2000), http://www.patents.com/ac/playcpt.sht.

[352] *See id.*

[353] *See id.*

[354] *See id.*

[355] *See id.* at 1158, Order, Sept. 27, 1997 (visited March 1, 2000), http://www.patents.com/ac/playord.sht.

because it also involved other issues, such as wrongful use of trademarks in domain names.

[c] Playboy Enterprises, Inc. v. AsiaFocus International[356]

Playboy Enterprises sued two Hong-Kong based web site operators for using its federally registered trademarks Playboy® and Playmate® as metatags embedded in their web sites.[357] Defendants' sites existed as click-through sites, where defendants earned money whenever users clicked on banners that routed them to pornographic web sites. As the web pages did not contain any references to the trademarks, it appears that the sole purpose of defendants' act was to capture traffic using Playboy's established reputation in its trademarks for commercial gain.

Playboy claimed trademark infringement, due to customer confusion, and dilution by blurring of its well-known marks.[358] A federal judge in Virginia ruled that Playboy's marks have acquired goodwill through Playboy's national and international advertising, causing the public to associate these marks only with the plaintiff, and awarded Playboy three million dollars in damages, plus costs.[359]

[d] Playboy Enterprises, Inc. v. Terri Welles[360]

Playboy Enterprises sued its former playmate, Terri Welles, for using the terms *Playboy* and *Playmate of the Year* in her commercial web site's metatags and content.[361] Welles uses her web site to sell erotic photographs of herself and her services as a spokesmodel. Plaintiff asserted federal trademark infringement, false description of origin, and dilution causes of action and asked for an injunction plus damages of $5,000,000.[362] Although Welles was not contractually restricted from using these terms, Playboy brought this action to stop her from competing with its CyberClub subscription web site.[363]

Courts look to the factual circumstances relating to the use and intention of the defendant rather than automatically declaring against the unauthorized use of trademarks as metatags. The judge in this case refused to grant an injunction based on fair use because the law allows descriptive use of a trademark.[364] Ms. Welles'

---

[356] *See id.*

[357] *See id.*

[358] *See id.*

[359] *See* Courtney Macavinta, Playboy Wins Piracy Suit, Apr. 4, 1998, http://www.news.com/News/Item/0,4,21370,00.html.

[360] *See* Playboy Enterprises, Inc. v. Terri Welles, 7 F. Supp. 2d 1098 (S.D. Cal. 1998).

[361] *See id.*

[362] *See id.*

[363] *See id.* at 1103.

[364] *See* 15 U.S.C. § 1115(b)(4).

use constituted descriptive use because the plaintiff gave the title to her, and it became a part of her identity to the public.[365] Thus, she had the right to use these marks to describe herself and to catalog her web site appropriately with the search engines. The judge also stressed that by using disclaimers in the web pages, the defendant did not use plaintiff's marks to mislead users to believe that her site belonged to Playboy.[366] Implications of this case are quite limited due to the narrow facts; the Lanham Act can easily be used because the fair use exception applies. The court found the use of Playboy's metatags in Ms. Welles' lawsuit to constitute fair use because the marks were used to describe her status as a former Playmate, not Playboy's goods and services.

[e] *Oppedahl & Larson v. Advanced Concepts*[367]

Oppedahl & Larson, an intellectual property law firm, sued Advanced Concepts, Code Team-LBK, Inc., Professional Web Site Development, MSI Marketing, Inc., and Internet Business Services, based on misuse of trademarks. The law firm conducted an Internet search on their names and respondents' web sites appeared on the search results.[368] No references to the plaintiff were found in the offensive web site. Examination of the site's underlying source document revealed that the names Oppedahl and Larson were each used eight times as metatags.[369] Plaintiff brought its cause of action under federal unfair competition and trademark dilution, as well as state unfair competition and trademark infringement.[370]

The law firm and Carl Oppedahl have an established reputation in the domain name area. Plaintiff stated in the complaint that although Advanced Concepts is not a competitor, it willfully intended to trade on that reputation or to cause dilution of their trademark.[371] Defendants were charged with using the plaintiff's trademarks to draw traffic to their site and commercially advertise their services. Defendants intended to profit from Oppedahl & Larson's established good name. Plaintiff alleged that defendants' practice would confuse and mislead users into believing that plaintiff endorsed or sponsored defendants' site.[372] Oppedahl & Larson claimed that defendants' acts would injure their business reputation and diminish the distinctive quality of their mark.

---

[365] *See* Playboy Enterprises, Inc., *supra* at 1102.

[366] *See id.* at 1104.

[367] *See* Oppedahl & Larson v. Advanced Concepts, No. 97-Z-1592 (D.C. Colo. 1997).

[368] *See id.*, Complaint, July 23, 1997, http://www.patents.com/ac/complaint.sht.

[369] *See id.*

[370] *See* Kuester, *supra* at 276.

[371] *See* Oppedahl & Larson, *supra.*

[372] *See id.*

Plaintiff sought an injunction against the defendants to enjoin them from using its trademarks or any colorable imitation in their web pages or in advertising or promotions. Plaintiff also sought destruction of any materials containing the marks, award of damages greater than three times defendants' profits or plaintiff's damages, reasonable attorneys' fees, and punitive damages.[373] The court-entered judgment in favor of Oppedahl & Larson, however, limited it to the granting of a permanent injunction against the defendants.[374]

[f]   *Nettis Environmental Ltd. v. IWI, Inc.*[375]

In *Nettis*, a competitor used the plaintiff's name Nettis in metatags on its web site. When the defendant registered its web site with hundreds of search engines, it submitted the term *Nettis* and *Nettis Environment* as keywords. The federal district court enjoined the defendant from using the Nettis® trademarks as metatags. The defendant complied with the injunction and removed the metatags from its web site. The defendant, however, was found to be in contempt of court for failing to remove the Nettis keywords in its registrations with the search engines. The court imposed sanctions against the defendant and awarded attorneys' fees to the plaintiff.

[g]   *Brookfield Communications, Inc. v. West Coast Entertainment Corp.*

In Brookfield Communications, Inc. v. West Coast Entertainment Corp.,[376] the Ninth Circuit reversed the district court's denial of an injunction prohibiting a competitor's use of another company's trademarks in the domain name as well as metatags on its web site. Brookfield is an information content provider for the entertainment industry. West Coast is a video rental store chain which used terms similar to Brookfield's trademark, "MovieBuff" in metatags and buried code. The Ninth Circuit was asked to determine whether trademark and unfair competition law prohibited West Coast from using Brookfield's trademark (or similar terms) in the domain name and metatags of the video store's web site.

---

[373] *See id.*

[374] *See* Oppedahl & Larson, *supra*, Order (Dec. 19, 1997), http://www.patents.com/ac/welchord.sht.

[375] No. 1:98 CV 2549, 1999 U.S. Dist. LEXIS 5655 (N.D. Ohio, Apr. 14, 1999).

[376] 174 F.3d 1036 (9th Cir. 1999). SNA, Inc. v. Array, 51 F. Supp. 2d 554 (E.D. Pa. 1999); New York State Society of Certified Public Accountants v. Eric Louis Assocs. Inc., 79 F. Supp. 2d 331 (S.D.N.Y. 1999); N.V.E. Pharm. Inc. v. Hoffman-LaRoche, Inc., 1999 U.S. Dist. LEXIS 20204 (D.N.J., Dec. 27, 1999) (holding that use of competitor's trademarks in metatags unfairly diverted traffic from mark owners' sites).

The case arose out of Brookfield's failed attempt to register the domain name *moviebuff.com* with Network Solutions, a domain name registrar. Network Solutions informed Brookfield that the *moviebuff.com* name was already registered by West Coast. Brookfield then registered the domain names, *brookfieldcomm.com* and *moviebuffonline.com*. Brookfield used its web sites to sell "MovieBuff" software and to market its "MovieBuff" database. In 1998, Brookfield applied to the U.S. Patent and Trademark Office for a federal registration of "MovieBuff" as a mark to designate its goods and services The federal trademark registrations were issued in September 1998.

In October 1998, Brookfield learned of West Coast's plans of launching a web site at *moviebuff.com* also offering a searchable computer database. Brookfield sought an injunction in the federal district court alleging that the West Coast's online services using the term *moviebuff.com* constituted trademark infringement and unfair competition. Brookfield sought a temporary restraining order against any use of the mark "MovieBuff" or similar term likely to cause confusion. Brookfield objected to West Coast use of "MovieBuff" in its metatags as well as the video stores's use of the domain name, *moviebuff.com*.

West Coast opposed the injunction on the grounds that it was the senior user of the "MovieBuff" not Brookfield. West Coast also argued that it was the first user of "MovieBuff" because it has used the term in its federally registered trademark, "The Movie Buff's Movie Store" since 1986. West Coast also claimed common-law rights in the mark in using the domain name, *moviebuff.com* prior to Brookfield's use of the term in marketing its electronic data base. Finally, West Coast argued that its use of *moviebuff.com* would not cause confusion with Brookfield's MovieBuff mark. The district court refused to order an injunction. The Ninth Circuit reversed and remanded the case to the district court with an order to enter the injunction in favor of Brookfield.

The Ninth Circuit began its opinion by establishing that Brookfield, not West Coast, was the senior holder of the "MovieBuff" trademark. The court granted the injunction on the grounds that West Coast's use of MovieBuff and similar terms in its domain name and metatags was likely to cause "initial interest" confusion. Even though consumers would not be confused as to source, they would initially be confused by West Coast's use of "MovieBuff" and related terms in metatags and the domain name. The court found that a web surfer entering "MovieBuff" into a search engine was likely to turn up the West Coast as well as Brookfield's site. The court reasoned that West Coast's use of "moviebuff.com" in metatags would divert traffic from Brookfield. Some web users would use West Coast's site while looking for Brookfield. The court stated that some users would be diverted to the West Coast's site because of "initial interest confusion." The court acknowledged that West Coast's misuse of metatags (and domain name) did not constitute source confusion. However, initial interest confusion could constitute unfair competition and infringement.

The court acknowledged that West Coast could make "fair use" of the "MovieBuff" in describing Brookfield's products. However, West Coast caused initial interest confusion by using the term "movie buff" in metags and this use of Brookfield's mark was not protected by fair use. The Ninth Circuit used a hypothetical to explain how that use by West Coast of Brookfield's mark in a metatag could constitute unfair competition:

> Using another's trademark in one's metatag is much like posting a sign with another's trademark in front of one's store. Suppose West Coast's competitor (let's call it "Blockbuster") puts up a billboard on a highway reading—"West Coast Video: 2 miles ahead at Exit 7"—where West Coast is really located at Exist 8 but Blockbuster is located at Exit 7. Customers looking for West Coast's store will pull off at Exit 7 and drive around looking for it. Unable to locate West Coast, but seeing the Blockbuster store right by the highway entrance, they may rent there. . . . Customers are not confused in the narrow sense; they are fully aware that they are purchasing from Blockbuster and they have no reason to believe that Blockbuster is related to, or in any way sponsored by, West Coast. Nevertheless, the fact that there is only initial consumer confusion does not alter the fact that Blockbuster would be misappropriating acquired goodwill of West Coast.[377]

The court acknowledged that use of competitors' trademarks for nondeceptive comparative advertising would be protected by the doctrine of fair use.[378] An online company may use another's trademark in a web site to describe a competitor's products and services, but may not use marks in metatags or domain names to divert traffic. Online companies risk claims for infringement and unfair competition by using metatags to divert traffic looking for their competitor's site.

[7] Keywords in Banner Advertisements

Keywords sold to advertisers of Internet web sites are an increasing source of revenue for search engines. When a web site visitor types in the keywords, banner advertisements appear along with the search results. If a user types the keyword "beer," the search results include web sites for "Guinness Global," "Pub-Crawler," "Labatts Beer.\\" and an advertisement for Amazon.com with a hyperlink for books on beer. Similarly, a user typing the keyword "automobile" on the Excite search engine receives banner advertisements along with the search results. Autotrader.com is the banner advertisement that comes with the keyword "automobile." The selling of banner advertisements for keywords is a means of generating revenue for search engines.

---

[377] Id. at 1063.
[378] Id. at 1065-66.

Playboy sued the Excite and Netscape search engines for selling a prese-lected package of search queries containing terms such as *playboy* and *playmate* to banner advertisers operating adult entertainment web sites.[379] Playboy Enterprises argued that the keywords *playboy* and *playmate* were confusingly similar to the trademarks, Playboy® and Playmate®.[380] The Ninth Circuit found no trademark infringement or evidence of dilution because of the practice of keying banner ads with words similar to trademarks. The court observed that the firms offering Web portal services were not in competition with Playboy's adult entertainment publications.[381] Moreover, the search engines were not using Playboy's trademarks to identify the source of any goods or services.[382] The court found a user of Excite or Netscape could easily find Playboy Enterprises on the search result pages for "playboy" and "playmate."[383] The court found "no evidence that the banner advertisements on Excite's and Netscape's Search Results pages 'keyed' to the words 'playboy' or 'playmate' are likely to cause confusion as to source, sponsorship, or affiliation."[384] Finally, the court noted that if Playboy was granted an injunction, it would essentially restrain the use of the words "playboy" and "playmate" on the World Wide Web.

➤ **[L] Preventive Law Pointers[385]**

[1] Metatags

It's late Friday afternoon, Maxwell A. Turney, general corporate counsel of SPC, Inc., calls their outside intellectual property counsel, Amanda Adams, for advice. When one of their marketing people conducted an Internet search using their trademarks, SUFFOLK 2000 and MILLENIUM-II, the search retrieved a web site that ranked higher on the list than did SPC's site. That site belonged to Neeto Corporation, a manufacturer of a low-quality line of computer peripherals. Helga Hunter, SPC's chief computing and information systems officer, examined the contents of the site and found no references to SPC or its trademarked products. Neeto's site, however, contained invisible source code that used each of SPC's trademarks, SUFFOLK 2000 and MILLENIUM-II, seven times.

---

[379] Playboy Enterprises, Inc. v. Netscape Comm. Corp., 55 F. Supp. 2d 1070 (9th Cir. 1999).

[380] *Id.* at 1078.

[381] *Id.*

[382] *Id.* at 1083.

[383] *Id.*

[384] *Id.* at 1086.

[385] Copyright © 2000 Lucy Elandjian. All rights reserved. The author is an alumnus of Suffolk University Law School High Technology Law Concentration and a corporate patent attorney, practicing in Cincinnati, Ohio.

Metatags comprise the HTML code and contain information about the contents of a web page.[386] Of the several types of metatags, keyword and description tags provide the most useful information.[387] *Description tags* contain the description of the site, and *keyword tags* specify keywords or synonyms that pertain to site contents, in addition to words that appear in the text of the site.[388] Metatags of SPC's web site are written as follows:

<META NAME="description"=content="world's largest manufacturer of personal computers">

<META NAME="keywords"=content="personal computers, SUFFOLK 2000, MILLENIUM-II">

Moreover, Neeto's keyword metatag was discovered to be the following:

<META NAME="keyword"=content="peripherals, computers, NEETO, SUFFOLK 2000, SUFFOLK 2000, SUFFOLK 2000, SUFFOLK 2000, SUFFOLK 2000, SUFFOLK 2000, SUFFOLK 2000, MILLENIUM-II, MILLENIUM-II, MILLENIUM-II, MILLENIUM-II, MILLENIUM-II, MILLENIUM-II, MILLENIUM-II">

Webmasters use metatags for indexing web pages to enable the retrieval of sites during searches.[389] Terms that appear in metatags are invisible because the page that a web browser opens does not display the metatags.[390] One can, however, view them using the "view page source," or an equivalent command from the browser; the lines that start with "<meta" contain the hidden terms.[391]

[a]   *Potentional Causes of Action*

Mr. Turney believes that SPC's growing reputation for quality computer products, along with their recent successful IPO (initial public offering of stock) are being used by Neeto to bring traffic to their site. He has also heard rumors that

---

[386] *See* David Loundy, Hidden Code Sparks High-Profile Lawsuit, Chicago Daily Law Bulletin, Sept. 11, 1997, http://www.Loundy.com/CDLB/Meta_Tags.html.

[387] *See* Danny Sullivan, How To Use Metatags (visited Nov. 12, 1998), http://searchenginewatch. Internet.com/web masters/meta.html.

[388] *See* Web Developer's Virtual Library, Metatagging for Search Engines (visited Nov. 11, 1998), http://www.stars.com/Search/Meta/Tag.html.

[389] *Id.*

[390] *Id.*

[391] *See* Marcelo Halpern, Meta-tags Effective marketing or Unfair Competition? 7 CYBER. L. 2, 3 (1997).

Neeto is planning to enter the personal computer business. He wants to know what SPC's rights and remedies are with respect to its trademarks, business, and reputation. This scenario focuses on federal and state causes of action that SPC may have against Neeto regarding unauthorized use of its trademarks as metatags.

SPC's complaint will be for: (1) trademark infringement for Neeto's violation of the Lanham Act; (2) unfair competition under the Lanham Act; (3) unfair competition under Massachusetts tort law (tort of misappropriation); and (4) dilution of the distinctiveness of plaintiff's trademarks, trade names and logos in violation of the Federal Antidilution Act. SPC will need to prove that its marks are famous to qualify for protection under the federal antidilution act. SPC may seek an injunction to enjoin Neeto from using its trademarks in metatags.[392]

[i] Trademark infringement. The use of SPC's trademarks in a metatag may divert traffic away from SPC's web site and violate the Lanham Act. If SPC's trademarks, trade names, and logos are used as "metatags" on a competitor's web site, there may be a trademark infringement or dilution action. The more times the trademarked terms appear in the metatags, the greater the liklihood of hits.[393]

SPC can argue that upon Neeto's entry into the personal computer business, Neeto will be infringing SPC's trademarks because Neeto will be confusing potential purchasers by luring them to Neeto's site, using SPC's marks as metatags, to sell them similar products. In such a situation, Neeto will be intentionally riding on SPC's goodwill and the strength of its trademarks to compete in the same markets.

[ii] Unfair competition. In our example, Mr. Turney is particularly concerned that Neeto is unfairly competing against SPC. A federal cause of action for unfair competition provides remedies for common law passing off, unfair competition, and state statutory unfair trade practices.[394] The Lanham Act prohibits anyone from misleading or misrepresenting facts in commerce that are likely to cause confusion, mistake, or deception as to origin, sponsorship, affiliation, or endorsement of the unauthorized user's products by the trademark owner.[395] A finding of passing off requires an association between the mark and its owner in the mind of the consumer and a likelihood of consumer confusion when the mark is used with

---

[392] *See, e.g.*, Niton Corp. v. Radiation Monitoring Devices, Inc., 27 F. Supp. 2d 102 (D. Mass. 1998).

[393] Brookfield Communications, Inc. v. West Coast Entertainment Corp., 174 F.3d 1036, 1045 (9th Cir. 1999).

[394] *See* Federal Unfair Competition Statute derived from Lanham Act § 43(a).

[395] *See* 15 U.S.C. § 1125(a)(1) (1998).

the goods or services of another.[396] *Passing off* rests on the premise of misappropriation of the skill, labor, and investment of another.[397]

Neeto deceives potential customers as to the origin of its site, as well as the origin of the products featured on the site, when it lures these customers to its web pages using SPC's trademarks as its web site's metatags; Neeto leads customers to think that SPC is somewhat associated with Neeto. These customers may then associate Neeto's computer-related products with SPC. Thus, Neeto's act results in the passing off of its low-quality computer peripherals on the tails of SPC's standards of high quality and its goodwill, earned through significant investment of time and money. Unfair competition usually accompanies trademark infringement and dilution causes of action.

[iii] Misappropriation. In our example, SPC may argue that Neeto's action constitutes misappropriation. The tort of misappropriation is governed solely by state law, as there is no federal statute providing remedies for misappropriation. Misappropriation is a tort exclusively governed by state law. A successful misappropriation claim requires the trademark owner to prove that the owner has invested time, money, and effort in the mark, that the unauthorized user appropriated the mark at insignificant cost, and that the unauthorized user's act injured the trademark owner, as by loss of profits or royalties.[398] Misappropriation, a judge-constructed legal hybrid of unfair competition, fills in the gaps where patent, copyright, and traditional trademark laws do not provide an adequate remedy for the protection of intellectual property right.[399]

Assuming SPC invested significant amounts of time, money, and effort in building its goodwill in the marks, Neeto's unauthorized use injured SPC's business because potential customers were diverted to Neeto's site. Although the marks were used invisibly, Neeto accomplished its purpose of using them to help its business at the cost of SPC, thereby misappropriating SPC's trademarks.

[iv] Trademark dilution. SPC can also seek relief under the Federal Trademark Dilution Act of 1995, which added section 43(C) to the Lanham Act, and under the more limited state antidilution statutes. Trademark dilution differs from infringement because it does not require proof of confusion.[400] The Federal

---

[396] *See* Kuester, *supra* at 250.

[397] *See* American Footwear Corp. v. General Footwear Co., 609 F.2d 655, 662 (2d Cir. 1979) (defining passing off).

[398] *See* McCarthy, *supra* at 10-95.

[399] *Id.* at 10-90.

[400] *See* McCarthy, *supra* at 24-117.

Trademark Dilution Act, section 43(C) of the Lanham Act, provides remedies for trademark dilution of well-known marks.[401] The Act defines dilution as "the lessening of the capacity of a famous mark to identify or distinguish goods and services without regard to competition between the owner of the mark and others or to likelihood of confusion, deception or mistake."[402] Dilution is an "erosion of the distinctiveness and prestige of a trademark caused by the sale of other goods or services under the same name . . . although there is no confusion as to source."[403]

Dilution would be a desirable legal cause of action to SPC in this situation, because there is no requirement that the potential customers be confused between marks. SPC may argue that Neeto's use of SUFFOLK 2000 and MILLENIUM-II constitutes dilution by blurring because Neeto uses these trademarks to lure potential customers to its site. The potential customers who are led to Neeto's site may no longer think that SPC's marks are exclusively associated with SPC. SPC may claim that Neeto's conduct is also dilution by tarnishment. Potential customers, who expect to see high-quality computers, enter Neeto's site and find instead low-quality computer peripherals. Neeto's action will reduce SPC's goodwill and high standard of quality in the mind of those potential customers because they may think that SPC is somewhat associated with these low-quality computer peripherals. It is unlikely that SPC's mark is famous or distinctive enough to qualify for protection under the Federal Dilution Act, but it may become famous through online advertising and publicity.

[b] *Limitations of Current Law*

It may be claimed that the confusion of SPC's customer is similar to the point of sale confusion in traditional business practices. Thus, if the initial interest confusion subsides before the consumer makes a purchase at Neeto's site, there is arguably no commercial injury.[404] This is a narrow view, however, because it does not take into consideration the uniqueness of Internet commerce, such as when potential consumers are misled to other sites and never return to the trademark owner's site. Others may claim that it is not the customer, but the search engine

---

[401] Section 43(C)(1) provides:

> The owner of a famous mark shall be entitled, subject to the principles of equity and upon such terms as the court deems reasonable, to an injunction against another person's commercial use in commerce of a mark or trade name, if such use begins after the mark has become famous and causes dilution of the distinctiveness of the mark, and to obtain such other relief as is provided in this subsection.

15 U.S.C. § 1125(c) (1999).

[402] 15 U.S.C. § 1127 (1998).

[403] Elly Lilly & Co. v. Natural Answers, 86 F. Supp. 2d 834 (S.D. Ind. 2000) (citation omitted).

[404] *See* Jeffrey Kuester, Link Law on the Internet: A Panel Discussion, 38 IDEA 197, 218 (1998).

that is being misled, thus there is no consumer confusion violating the Lanham Act.

It may be argued, however, that the original misrepresentation to the search engine caused the customer's confusion, with the misuse of the trademark causing the original confusion.[405] One can argue that in both of these scenarios the damage is done to the potential customers because the manipulative metatagging has increased their search costs (primarily in time), and it is the goal of trademark law to reduce consumer search costs.[406] Current laws do not specifically define such a violation of trademarks. Courts may extend trademark protection to redress the inconvenience of increased search costs. Some courts may consider the policy rationale and some may not. Such interpretive process can result in different outcomes in different jurisdictions; hence, it can lead to forum shopping by the parties. Furthermore, different jurisdictions may interpret differently the degrees of confusion in traditional analysis of infringement, or the degree of fame ("fame" not defined in statute) required for protection, which may also lead to forum shopping.

The Federal Dilution Act limits action to misuse of famous marks. This leaves start-up companies and owners of nonfamous marks without a remedy. Misuse of a nonfamous mark may be just as damaging to its owner as misuse of a famous mark would be to its owner. SPC's marks, SUFFOLK 2000 and MILLENIUM-II, may not be famous, like IBM™ or MOBILE™, but SPC has every right to the protection of these marks, because it has expended great effort and resources to gain recognition for them in conjunction with its products.[407] The use of SPC's marks in connection with poor-quality computer peripherals dilutes the value and whittles away the selling power of those marks as applied to SPC's products. Where the Federal Dilution Act is the primary source of remedy for misuse of trademarks in noncompeting situations (as infringement or unfair competition may not be on point), its limitation to famous marks prevents a fair application of the law to all marks.

Fair remedies for misuses are limited due to the difficulty of applying current statutes and case laws to varying or novel fact patterns. Consequently, a plaintiff has to plead multiple causes of action, such as trademark infringement, trademark dilution, unfair competition, and misappropriation, and hope that at least one cause of action will provide him with a remedy. Thus, if SPC is not able to persuade the court that Neeto's conduct constitutes trademark infringement, dilution, or unfair competition, SPC would not have a remedy nor a means of protecting its business, its trademarks, and its customers. This is typical, as many potentially unfair uses of metatags may go undeterred because no remedy applies.

---

[405] *See* Halpern, *supra.*

[406] *See* McCarthy, *supra* at 2-3.

[407] IBM is a registered trademark of IBM Corp., MOBILE is a registered trademark of Mobil Corp.

[c]   SPC's Best Course of Action

Ms. Adams informs SPC that they can bring action against Neeto under traditional theories of protection, such as federal and state trademark infringement, trademark dilution, and unfair competition. She advises that these theories have limitations when applied to new and nebulous areas, such as metatags, and that SPC may be unable to secure an injunction. Ms. Adams mentions that use of trademarks invisibly in metatags is one of the newer ways of misusing trademarks, and that there is a weak fit between the misuse of metatags and traditional intellectual property remedies. Interpretations of the available laws are similar to a coin toss, differing from court to court. Thus, SPC may be left a victim of the electronic age.

[2]   Trademark Searches

Before a trademark is registered, counsel must conduct a trademark search to determine whether a selected mark is already being used. The trademark search begins with the USPTO's federal register; it is also possible to search some state registers. Other possible ways to search a trademark include the following:

1. The Principal and Supplemental Registers of the USPTO. The Principal Register is for marks that are or will become distinctive, while the Supplemental Register is for descriptive trademarks. Notice of registration is published in the USPTO's Official Gazette. Notice of opposition to a pending mark must be filed within 30 days of the mark's publication in the Official Gazette.

Companies may also use an Internet Jumpstation, which permits searches of scores of trademarks. Keep in mind that trademark law is national or state, and the Internet is transnational. It is too expensive to register trademarks for every country connected to the Internet. A company's trademark should be registered in countries where the company is doing a significant amount of business.

2. Industry trade publications for similar marks. After completing initial searches, it is possible to hire a search company, such as Thomson & Thomson, to do a complete trademark search.

3. Internet domain names. The same domain name may be used with a different high-level domain. *Suffolk.edu* and *Suffolk.org* may coexist under the same domain name registration. Most domain name battles are fought over "the right to use the same domain."[408] Only one owner can possess the domain *Suffolk.edu.*

(a) If a trademark is being used, it may be possible to purchase, license, or assign trademark rights. A growing number of trademark owners

---

[408] Linda A. Heban, Live and Let Live: Tips for Sharing Domain Names, 5 Intell. Prop. Strat. 1 (July 1999).

are filing lawsuits against holders of domain names that contain their registered trademark or similar marks.

(b) Trademarks are registered with the USPTO. The types of registered marks are (1) trademarks; (2) service marks; and (3) collective marks.

[3] Dislodging Cybersquatters

Cybersquatting is the practice of registering domain names for the purpose of reselling them for a profit. The mere fact that another party registered *SPC.com* for use as a domain name does not necessarily support an infringement or dilution claim. In addition, evidence must exist showing that a defendant is acting as a cybersquatter.[409] Assume SPC timely registered the domain name, *www.SPC.com*, but not *www.spc.net* or *www.spcsucks.com*. SPC has several options. First, it can pay the domain name owner to assign or sell the domain names *SPC.net* or *www.SPCsucks.com*.

Second, it may file a trademark or unfair competition lawsuit against the speculator in domain names. A number of courts have ruled that a cybersquatter's registration of a domain name incorporating a well-known tradename or trademark blurs or dilutes the famous mark. Evidence must exist, however, that the SPC mark met the standard for protection as famous and that the defendant's use would cause dilution.[410] SPC will seek the assignment or transfer of the domain name incorporating its trademarks from the defendant to the company. SPC may have an action under ACPA if a cybersquatter registered domain names, such as *www.suffolkpersonalcomputers.com,* and attempted to sell them.

A great deal of uncertainty persists as to whether ACPA would apply to a cybersquatter located in another country. Suppose a cybersquatter located in Russia registered the domain name, *www.spc.ru* to divert business to its site. In a similar case involving Kodak, the Russian Institute of Public Networks ruled that United States' intellectual property rules do not apply in Russia.[411]

§ 4.04   TRADE SECRETS IN CYBERSPACE

[A] Overview

An Internet company can acquire four broad categories of information, which are classified as (1) public domain; (2) proprietary; (3) confidential; and (4)

---

[409] HQM, Ltd. & Hatfield, Inc. v. Hatfield, 1999 U.S. Dist. LEXIS 18598 (D. Md., Dec. 2, 1999).

[410] In Avery Dennison v. Sumpton, 1999 U.S. App. LEXIS 19954 (9th Cir., Aug. 23, 1999) the plaintiff held that the trademarks "avery" and "dennison" were distinctive but not famous for purposes of the federal antidilution act.

[411] John T. Aquino, Why Foreign Internet Laws Are So Important, 4 The Internet Newsltr, Feb. 2000, at 1.

trade secrets.[412] *Public domain* information, as its name suggests, consists of common knowledge or easily available information; it is available for anyone's use without permission. Government documents, such as state and federal statutes, agency hearings, and Congressional Reports, are in the public domain. Copyrighted works go into the public domain after the term of copyright expires. Thus, the works of Louisa May Alcott, Oliver Wendell Holmes, and Robert Louis Stevenson are in the public domain, because the copyright has expired on them. Similarly, inventions go into the pubic domain after the patent term has expired.

A second type of information is *proprietary information*. The predicate of proprietary information is some claim of ownership. Patent and copyright law may protect proprietary information.[413] The third form of information is *confidential information*, "that is restricted from unlimited disclosure by the person or entity who knows it."[414]

The fourth category of information is *trade secrets,* which are protected by state tort law. Trade secrets protect against the misappropriation of proprietary information by third parties, including competitors.[415] In order for a company to recover for misappropriation of a trade secret, it must prove that the defendant put the proprietary information in question to some commercial use. A trade secret is neither known by others nor readily ascertainable by proper means.

The classic example of a trade secret is the formula for Coca-Cola, which has been a closely held secret for more than a century. An Internet company's software, hardware design, computer networking technology, and future design specifications may be protected as trade secrets. Also protectable as trade secrets is proprietary information such as financial data, including pricing, cost information, customer lists, buyer contacts, and vendor information.

Trade secrets may not be patentable or subject to copyright, since these require disclosure in return for a limited monopoly.[416] That said, there is no requirement that trade secrets be trademarked, patented, or copyrighted, and no registration procedure exists for doing so. A trade secret is protected by keeping it secret. For SPC, a trade secret would be any information used in the operation of its online business that is valuable and that gives the company a competitive edge. Judge Richard Posner has stated that trade secrets are "of growing importance to the competitiveness of American industry . . . [and] the future of the nation

---

[412] Fenwick and West, Trade Secrets: A Practical Guide for High Technology Companies 2-3 (1995).

[413] *Id.* at 2.

[414] Fenwick and West, *supra.*

[415] University Computing Co. v. Lykes-Youngstown Corp., 504 F.2d 518 (5th Cir. 1974).

[416] National Conference of Commissioners on Uniform State Laws, The Uniform Trade Secrets Act: A Summary (visited Mar. 19, 2000), http://www.nccU.S.l.org/summary/utsa.html.

Table 4.9
Overview of Trade Secrets

Method for obtaining protection	Use of commercially reasonable means to protect secret; nondisclosure agreements with employees and consultants; information security
Remedies for infringement	Injunctive relief and damages; tort of misappropriation; punitive damages and compensatory damages

depends in no small part on the efficiency of industry, and the efficiency of industry depends in no small part on the protection of intellectual property. Trade secrets have become part of the currency of the services and software-based economy built upon an infrastructure of information assets."[417]

The trade secret owner must use reasonable means to protect its trade secrets (see Table 4.9). The principal dangers to trade secrets are from insiders who have access to a company's confidential information. To qualify as a trade secret, confidential information must be not readily ascertainable by proper means and not generally known. Typically, companies require employees to sign agreements to transfer creative works on the web site to the company, and these "work for hire" agreements generally contain a duty of confidentiality that continues after the termination of the employment relationship.

[1] Uniform Trade Secrets Act

[a] *Misappropriation of Trade Secrets*

The Uniform Trade Secrets Act (UTSA) defines misappropriation as the use of improper means, such as misrepresentation or breach of a duty, to maintain secrecy.[418] UTSA is a model statute that provides a statutory state law remedy in all but a few states.[419] One of the broadly stated policies behind trade secret law is

---

[417] Rockwell Graphics Systems v. DEV Industries, 925 F.2d 174, 180 (7th Cir. 1991).

[418] UTSA, § 1(1)(2).

[419] Uniform Trade Secrets Act ("UTSA") § 1 (2000). The Uniform Trade Secrets Act (UTSA) was approved by the National Conference of Uniform State Laws (NCCUSL) in 1979 and amended in 1985. Forty-four states have adopted UTSA: Alaska, Arkansas, Alabama, Arizona, California, Colorado, Connecticut, Delaware, District of Columbia, Florida, Georgia, Hawaii, Idaho, Illinois, Indiana, Iowa, Kansas, Kentucky, Louisiana, Maine, Maryland, Michigan, Minnesota, Mississippi, Missouri, Montana, Nebraska, Nevada, New Hampshire, New Mexico, North Dakota, Ohio, Oklahoma, Oregon, Rhode Island, South Carolina, South Dakota, Tennessee, Utah, Vermont, Virginia, Washington, West Virginia, and Wisconsin.

"the maintenance of standards of commercial ethics."[420] A trade secret owner has the right to control use and access and to take measures to prevent disclosure. If reasonable measures are in place to prevent disclosure and a wrongdoer uses improper means to access or use information, the owner will have a remedy for the tort of misappropriation; there may also be a crime of computer fraud if the information was gained by means of unauthorized access.

[b]   Definition of Trade Secret

Internet trade secrets are often more vulnerable because the interconnected system of computers makes it possible for hackers, competitors, and experts in corporate espionage to steal information without leaving physical evidence. The Internet economy is known for a rapid turnover in employees, and online companies face the constant danger that an ex-employee will appropriate trade secrets for use in a competitor's business.

The first requirement for a plaintiff suing under the UTSA is that their claim involve an actual trade secret. The UTSA defines trade secrets to include "information, including a formula, pattern, compilation, program, device, method, technique, or process, that:

> (i) derives independent economic value, actual or potential, from not being generally known to, and not being readily ascertainable by proper means by, other persons who can obtain economic value from its disclosure or use, and (ii) is the subject of efforts that are reasonable under the circumstances to maintain its secrecy.[421]

[c]   "Improper Means" Test

The second requirement is that the information derives actual or potential economic value from not being disclosed or readily ascertainable by improper means[422] by other persons.[423] Since a trade secret is lost through public knowledge,

---

[420] Kewanee Oil Co. v. Bicron Corp., 416 U.S. 470 (1974).

[421] UTSA, § 1(4).

[422] Comment 1 to UTSA sets forth five legitimate means of obtaining knowledge of trade secrets: "1. Discovery by independent invention; 2. Discovery by 'reverse engineering,' that is, by starting with the known product and working backward to find the method by which it was developed. The acquisition of the known product must, of course, also be by a fair and honest means (i.e., purchase of the item on the open market for reverse engineering to be lawful); 3. Discovery under a license from the owner of the trade secret; 4. Observation of the item in public use or on public display; and 5. Obtaining the trade secret from published literature." UTSA, § 1, comment.

[423] The comment to UTSA, § 1 states:

> The definition of "trade secret" contains a reasonable departure from the Restatement of Torts (First) definition which required that a trade secret be "continuously used in

the unauthorized disclosure of a trade secret also constitutes the tort of misappropriation.[424] Unlike patents, there is no requirement that trade secrets be novel. Mathematical algorithms, not protectable by patents, may be protected as trade secrets if not readily ascertainable or known.

An ex-employee who bypasses a company's information security procedures to appropriate trade secrets is using improper means. An ex-employee who sells confidential information to a foreign competitor is using an improper means to appropriate trade secrets. Another example of an improper means would be intercepting an e-mail message containing trade secrets.[425] The concept of acquiring trade secrets by "improper means" is key to obtaining relief under UTSA. Section 1(1) of UTSA defines misappropriation as acquisition of trade secrets by improper means, including "theft, bribery, misrepresentation, breach or inducement of a breach of a duty to maintain secrecy, or espionage through electronic or other means."[426]

The UTSA requires that information that is the subject of a trade secret be protected by means that are "reasonable under the circumstances to maintain its secrecy."[427] Theft, bribery, fraud, or other improper means may accomplish misappropriation.

Trade secret law does not restrain an employee, competitor, or third party from acquiring confidential information through proper means. If so-called confidential information is freely available on the Internet or otherwise readily ascertainable, it is not classified as a trade secret. If a company's employees publish confidential information on the Internet, the information is available through proper means. If information was previously disclosed in court proceedings, it is no longer secret and may be freely used.

Reverse engineering is a *proper* method of learning about trade secrets. Competitors are free to "reverse engineer" a company's software, hardware, and web site

---

one's business." The broader definition in the proposed Act extends protection to a plaintiff who has not yet had an opportunity or acquired the means to put a trade secret to use. The definition includes information that has commercial value from a negative viewpoint, for example the results of lengthy and expensive research which proves that a certain process will not work could be of great value to a competitor.

UTSA, § 1, comment.

[424] For liability to exist under UTSA, a Section 1(4) trade secret must exist and either a person's acquisition of the trade secret, disclosure of the trade secret to others, or use of the trade secret must be improper under Section 1(2). The mere copying of an unpatented item is not actionable.

[425] Improper means could include otherwise lawful conduct which is improper under the circumstances; e.g., an airplane overflight used as aerial reconnaissance to determine the competitor's plant layout during construction of the plant. E.I. du Pont de Nemours & Co., Inc. v. Christopher, 431 F.2d 1012 (CA5, 1970), *cert. denied,* 400 U.S. 1024 (1970).

[426] UTSA, § 1(1).

[427] UTSA, § 1.4 (ii).

to learn about its methods of doing business. Trade secret law only restrains insiders and outsiders from using *improper* means of appropriating SPC's trade secrets.

[d] Reasonable Efforts to Maintain Trade Secrets

A company must use reasonable efforts to protect its trade secrets, not every possible or conceivable step.[428] The UTSA requires that a trade secret owner use reasonable efforts to maintain the secrecy of its information. The efforts required to maintain secrecy are those "reasonable under the circumstances." The courts apply a negligence-based formula, in which the burden of precaution need not be greater than the radius of the risk in protecting trade secrets. If trade secrets are transmitted on the Internet, it may be reasonable to encrypt the message. Competitors or unknown hackers may also intercept trade secrets if transmitted in an unencrypted form. Digital signatures with encrypted messages may be the only reasonable means of protecting trade secrets. It may be reasonable to transmit confidential information in an encrypted envelope with a digital signature providing proof of authorship and privacy.[429] A court might find, however, that it is unreasonable to transmit trade secrets on the Internet since hackers may launch cryptographic attacks against the algorithms used to encrypt trade secrets.

[e] UTSA Remedies for Misappropriation

The UTSA provides a wide array of remedies for trade secret misappropriation including preliminary injunctive relief, monetary damages, lost profits, consequential damages, lost royalties, attorneys' fees and punitive damages. Section 3 of UTSA, entitled "damages," provides:

> a) Except to the extent that a material and prejudicial change of position prior to acquiring knowledge or reason to know of misappropriation renders a monetary recovery inequitable, a complainant is entitled to recover damages for misappropriation. Damages can include both the actual loss caused by misappropriation and the unjust enrichment caused by misappropriation that is not taken into account in computing actual loss. In lieu of damages measured by any other methods, the damages caused by misappropriation may be measured by imposition of liability for a reasonable royalty for a misappropriator's unauthorized disclosure or use of a trade secret.

---

[428] Rockwell Graphic Systems, Inc. v. DEV. Indus., Ind., 925 F.2d 174, 180 (7th Cir. 1991).

[429] Bruce Schneier, Applied Cryptography: Protocols, Algorithms, and Source Code in C 227 (2d ed. 1996).

(b) If willful and malicious misappropriation exists, the court may award exemplary damages in an amount not exceeding twice any award made under subsection (a).[430]

UTSA adopts a three-year statute of limitations, and it is uncertain whether courts will apply the "continuing wrong" theory to extend it. A court may toll the trade secret cause of action at the "initial misappropriation."[431] The UTSA statute of limitations is three years after the misappropriation is discovered or after it should have been discovered, had reasonable diligence been exercised.[432]

The remedies for the misappropriation of trade secrets include damages,[433] injunctive relief,[434] and attorneys' fees if bad faith is proven.[435] A reasonable royalty may be obtained for the loss of revenue attributable to the misappropriation of a trade secret. Punitive or exemplary damages are capped at twice compensatory damages.

Preliminary injunctive relief is also available under UTSA, which permits the owner of a trade secret to seek an injunction for actual or threatened misappropriation.[436] The purpose of injunctive relief is to preserve the status quo and to

---

[430] UTSA, § 3.

[431] Section 6 of UTSA states that: "An action for misappropriation must be brought within 3 years after the misappropriation is discovered or by the exercise of reasonable diligence should have been discovered. For the purposes of this section, a continuing misappropriation constitutes a single claim." The Comment to UTSA § 6 states: "There presently is a conflict of authority as to whether trade secret misappropriation is a continuing wrong. Compare Monolith Portland Midwest Co. v. Kaiser Aluminum & Chemical Corp., 407 F.2d 288 (CA9, 1969) (9th Cir. 1969) (no not a continuing wrong under California law—limitation period upon all recovery begins upon initial misappropriation) with Underwater Storage, Inc. v. U. S. Rubber Co., 371 F.2d 950 (C.D. Ca. 1966), cert. denied, 386 U.S. 911 (1967) ("continuing wrong under general principles—limitation period with respect to a specific act of misappropriation begins at the time that the act of misappropriation occurs").

[432] Id. at § 6 (noting that the statute of limitations is within three years after the discovery of misappropriation).

[433] UTSA, § 3 (explaining that damages may be recoverable for misappropriation of trade secrets).

[434] Uniform Trade Secrets Act § 2 (noting that actual or threatened misappropriations may be enjoined).

[435] Id. at § 4 (noting that attorneys' fees may be recoverable where a claim of misappropriation is made in bad faith, a motion to terminate an injunction is made or resisted in bad faith, or willful and malicious misappropriation exists).

[436] The Comment to Section 3 notes that damages are set for the period in which information is entitled to protection, "plus the additional period, if any, in which a misappropriator retains an advantage over good faith competitors because of misappropriation." UTSA, § 3, Comment. The measure of damages then includes actual damages plus the unjust benefit to a misappropriator caused by misappropriation during this time alone. Id.

The comment further notes that: "A claim for actual damages and net profits can be combined with a claim for injunctive relief, but, if both claims are granted, the injunctive relief ordinarily will preclude a monetary award for a period in which the injunction is effective." Id.

prevent defendants from destroying "smoking gun" evidence.[437] A temporary restraining order or other injunctive relief is ordered if a disclosure threatens harm to the trade secret owners.[438]

UTSA permits the owner of a trade secret to recover exemplary damages up to two times the actual amount of damages if the misappropriation is willful and malicious.[439] Exemplary damages may also be recoverable, though the amount is capped at twice the actual damages. Exemplary (or punitive damages, as they are called in most states) are designed to punish and deter the defendant. If an ex-employee has sold trade secrets to a competitor, punitive damages may be sought against both parties. The legal standard of willfulness and malice must be met before statutory punitive damages are recoverable. Attorneys' fees are also recoverable if the misappropriation is willful and malicious.[440]

---

[437] Scott D. Marrs, Trade Secrets: Preliminary Relief in Trade Secret Cases, Texas Bar J., Oct. 1998, at 880.
Section 2, titled injunctive relief, provides:

> (a) Actual or threatened misappropriation may be enjoined. Upon application to the court, an injunction shall be terminated when the trade secret has ceased to exist, but the injunction may be continued for an additional reasonable period of time in order to eliminate commercial advantage that otherwise would be derived from the misappropriation.
>   (b) If the court determines that it would be unreasonable to prohibit future use. In exceptional circumstances, an injunction may condition future use upon payment of a reasonable royalty for no longer than the period of time for which use could have been prohibited. Exceptional circumstances include, but are not limited to, a material and prejudicial change of position prior to acquiring knowledge or reason to know of misappropriation that renders a prohibitive injunction inequitable.
>   In appropriate circumstances, affirmative acts to protect a trade secret may be compelled by court order.

UTSA, § 2.

[438] Section 2(a) permits threatened misappropriations to be enjoined and it is common to seek injunctions restraining future harm from use and disclosure of misappropriated trade secrets, UTSA, § 2(a), comment.

[439] The comment to Section 3 states:

> If willful and malicious misappropriation is found to exist, Section 3(b) authorizes the court to award a complainant exemplary damages in addition to the actual recovery under Section 3(a) an amount not exceeding twice that recovery. This provision follows federal patent law in leaving discretionary trebling to the judge even though there may be a jury; compare 35 U.S.C. Section 284 (1976).

UTSA, § 3, comment.

[440] UTSA § 4 permits a court to award attorney's fees: "If (i) a claim of misappropriation is made in bad faith, (ii) a motion to terminate an injunction is made or resisted in bad faith, or (iii) willful and malicious misappropriation exists, the court may award reasonable attorney's fees to the prevailing party." UTSA, § 4.

[f] Potential UTSA Defendants

Employees have a duty not to disclose trade secrets acquired in the employment relationship independent of any express nondisclosure agreement.[441] Information may be disclosed to employees, business partners, or others in the normal course of doing business without loss of trade secret protection. Companies frequently require that their employees sign nondisclosure agreements to maintain secrecy. If a current employee or ex-employee discloses a trade secret to a competitor without permission, civil and criminal liability attaches for the theft of trade secrets. Even if there is employment without a nondisclosure clause, the employee may nevertheless be bound by a duty not to disclose confidential information.

[2] Alternative Claims

[a] Restatement of Torts

Under the tort of misappropriation, the Restatement of Torts is an influential source of law in the states that have yet to adopt the Uniform Trade Secrets Act. The Restatement defines a trade secret as information used in the operation of a business or other enterprise, "that is sufficiently valuable and secret to afford an actual or potential economic advantage over others."[442]

[b] Breach of Confidence

In addition to the tort of misappropriation for trade secrets, a company may also have a breach of confidence claim. To prevail in a breach of confidence claim, the plaintiff must show that: (1) it conveyed confidential and novel information; (2) defendants had knowledge that the information was being disclosed in confidence; (3) there was an understanding between plaintiff and defendants that the confidence be maintained; and (4) there was disclosure or use in violation of the understanding.[443]

[3] Criminal Prosecution for Trade Secret Theft

The Economic Espionage Act of 1996 (Economic Espionage Act) criminalizes the theft of trade secrets,[444] by making the theft of trade secrets a federal

---

[441] Scott D. Marrs, *supra* note 437.

[442] The Restatement (First) of Torts § 757 and § 758 (1939) provided tort remedies for the misappropriation of trade secrets. In 1995, the National Conference of Commissioners on Uniform State Laws approved the Restatement (Third) of Unfair Competition § 39 (1995) (providing tort remedies for misappropriation of trade secrets).

[443] Cinebase Software v. Media Guaranty Trust, Inc., 1998 U.S. Dist. LEXIS 15007 (D. N.D. Calif. Sept. 21, 1998).

[444] Economic Espionage Act of 1996, 18 U.S.C. §§ 1831-1839 (1999).

crime. An individual whose misappropriation of a trade secret benefits a foreign government, instrumentality, or agent may be sentenced to a federal prison for up to 15 years and fined up to $500,000.[445] An entity that steals a trade secret benefiting a foreign government can be fined up to $10,000,000.[446] The theft of trade secrets for the benefit of "anyone other than the owner" is also punishable by criminal and civil penalties.[447]

The defendant must knowingly have stolen, duplicated, downloaded, or received trade secrets belonging to an owner.[448] Individuals found guilty of trade secret theft benefiting parties other than foreign governments may be fined or imprisoned for not more than 10 years, or both.[449] Any organization that knowingly transmits, receives, or possesses misappropriated trade secrets not benefiting foreign governments may be fined "not more than $5,000,000."[450]

Like UTSA, The Economic Espionage Act defines trade secrets broadly to include the following:

> All forms and types of financial, business, scientific, technical economic or engineering information, including patterns, plans, compilations, program devices, formulas, designs, prototypes, methods, techniques, processes, procedures, programs or codes, whether tangible or intangible, and whether or not stored, compiled, or memorialized physically, electronically, graphically, photographically, or in writing if: (A) the owner thereof has taken reasonable measures to keep such information secret; and (B) the information derives independent economic value, actual or potential, from not being generally known to, and not being readily ascertainable through proper means by the public.[451]

The Economic Espionage Act applies to any individual who transmits, receives or possesses stolen trade secrets.[452] Individuals convicted of violating the Economic Espionage Act may be punished by fines of $500,000 and up to ten years in prison.[453] Corporate defendants may be fined up to $5,000,000.[454] The standard of proof for criminal prosecution is "beyond a reasonable doubt that an individual or corporation knowingly received, bought, or possessed misappropriated or stolen trade secrets."

---

[445] 18 U.S.C. § 1831(a)(5) (1999).

[446] 18 U.S.C. § 1831(b) (1999).

[447] 18 U.S.C. § 1832 (1999).

[448] 18 U.S.C. § 1832(1)(5) (1999).

[449] 18 U.S.C. § 1832(5) (1999).

[450] 18 U.S.C. § 1832(b) (1999).

[451] 18 U.S.C. § 1839(3) (1999).

[452] 18 U.S.C. § 1832(a)(3) (1999).

[453] 18 U.S.C. § 1838 (1999).

[454] 18 U.S.C. § 1832(a) (1999).

In addition, every state has a computer crime statute. A wrongdoer who steals trade secrets may be liable for criminal fraud, for theft, or for computer crimes. In a recent case a high technology company sued a rival accusing it of stealing software, copyright infringement, and conspiracy.[455] Trade secret theft is increasingly prosecuted as a criminal offense. A former vice president of Borland and a chief executive officer of Symantec Corporation, a competitor of Borland, were indicted by a California court for criminal theft of trade secrets.[456]

[4] Preventing Losses: Nondisclosure Agreements

High technology employers should require their employees to sign standard nondisclosure agreements, which are evidence that a company is taking reasonable steps to protect its trade secrets.[457]

The Comment to Section 2 of UTSA states:

> Finally, reasonable efforts to maintain secrecy have been held to include advising employees of the existence of a trade secret, limiting access to a trade secret on "need to know basis," and controlling plant access. On the other hand, public disclosure of information through display, trade journal publications, advertising, or other carelessness can preclude protection.[458]

A written agreement is proof that a company's employees had notice of their duty to maintain confidentiality. A defendant may argue that a company's failure

---

[455] Lawrence M. Fisher, Avant Wins Ruling in Cadence Copyright Suit, N.Y. Times, Sept. 10, 1999, at C2.

[456] People v. Eubanks, 38 Cal. App. 4th 114, 44 Cal. Rptr. 2d 846 (1995).

[457] Companies may also want to consider entering *noncompete* agreements to establish that they are taking reasonable efforts to protect its trade secrets. Courts will enforce reasonable *noncompete* agreements so long as the agreement does not restrain commerce or does not impede an ex-employee's ability to earn a livelihood. Whether a noncompetition agreement is reasonable depends upon

> (1) the agreement's geographic and temporal limits; (2) whether the employee represents the sole customer contact; (3) whether the employee possesses confidential information or trade secrets; (4) whether the agreement seeks to restrain ordinary, rather than unfair, competition; (5) whether the agreement stifles inherent skills of the employee or whether employee's talents were developed during the employment; (6) the balance of the agreement's detriment to employer and employee; (7) whether the agreement restricts employee's sole means of support; and (8) whether the restricted employment is merely incidental to the main employment.

LEXIS-NEXIS v. Beer, 41 F. Supp. 2d 950 (D. Minn. 1999).

[458] UTSA, § 2, comment.

to secure a nondisclosure agreement reflects a too casual attitude toward secrecy, potentially destroying the trade secret status of software or other information.[459]

Nondisclosure agreements may be customized to cover employees, contractors, trade partners, licensees, consultants, grantees, bidders, or government entities who have access to a company's trade secrets. Trade secrets should be marked with a notice that they are confidential. As with military intelligence, however, there is a danger when either too much or too little information is classified as confidential. Most importantly, a company's security policy must be enforced.

A nondisclosure or confidentiality agreement, frequently used by trading partners, can take diverse forms. A nondisclosure agreement must address the question of who owns confidential or copyrighted information. Nondisclosure agreements must be customized to the type of business activity and the form of corporate organization they address. A Fortune 500 company with subsidiaries in many countries should tailor its nondisclosure agreements to take into account cultural and regulatory differences.

[5] Trade Secrets and the Internet

Web sites may contain secrets in the form of data on log files and information obtained from an audit of what visitors do at a corporate web site. If a web site developer is building a specialized company web site, corporate counsel may wish to draft noncompetition and nondisclosure agreements. The purpose of a *noncompetition* agreement is to prevent a web site developer from disclosing information on the web development project to competitors and third parties.[460]

Companies must make reasonable efforts to maintain the secrecy of information. The use of encryption and the other information security tools described in Chapter Three are essential in protecting trade secrets on the Internet. The Internet and e-mail usage policies described in Chapter Nine also contain useful information on protecting trade secrets on the Internet. It may not be enough to have a formal policy regarding confidentiality of documents if there is no mechanism of enforcement. At minimum, documents should be labeled with a confidential and proprietary mark as evidence that they are confidential.

Amazon.com and Wal-Mart Stores settled a trade secrets case in which the online bookseller was charged with hiring Wal-Mart's essential computer systems

---

[459] Weseley Software Development Corp. v. Burdette, 977 F. Supp. 137 (D. Conn. 1996) (noting defense argument that failure of plaintiff to demand nondisclosure agreement as evidence of lax attitudes about confidential information).

[460] Geoffrey G. Surgis, Web Site Development Agreements: A Guide to Planning and Drafting (visited May 20, 1999), http://www.digidem.com/legal/wda/wda.html.

managers in order to steal trade secrets.[461] In Religious Technology Center v. F.A.C.T. Net, Inc.,[462] the Church of Scientology sued former members for copyright infringement and trade secret misappropriation for posting Church trade secrets and copyrighted material on the Internet. The federal district court denied injunctive relief, finding that the defendant's actions were primarily covered by the fair use doctrine and that the disputed documents lost their status as trade secrets.[463] The court held that despite the best efforts of the Church to maintain the secrecy of the works, Internet publication destroyed the trade secret.

> ### [B]   Preventive Law Pointers: Trade Secrets on the Internet

[1]   Drafting Nondisclosure Agreements

The purpose of a nondisclosure agreement is to emphasize to the employee or other party that SPC is providing them with access to confidential company documents, which must be kept in confidence. The nondisclosure agreement should set forth the responsibilities that employees and others have in protecting trade secrets. The nondisclosure agreement should include a general obligation to protect information, as well as set forth any specific responsibilities. The nondisclosure agreement should state the possible sanctions for breaching a nondisclosure agreement, and there should also be a termination clause, which requires the return of all copies of confidential documents held by the signer. Each nondisclosure agreement should have a choice of law and forum clause and should include an integration clause stating that this agreement supersedes all prior or contemporaneous agreements.

SPC needs nondisclosure agreements for all nonemployees working on its web site. Nondisclosure agreements should be included for web site development contracts, web site service and maintenance agreements, web site consulting agreements, sales agreements, and for all other joint venturers granted access to SPC trade secrets. In the event of litigation, SPC should seek a court order early in the litigation to protect its trade secrets. A court, for example, can use *in camera* inspections of SPC's trade secrets. A nondisclosure agreement must be included in the employee handbook as well as posted on the company's web site. Confidential documents should be stamped with a notice that the employee has a

---

[461] Associated Press, Amazon and Wal-Mart Settle Accusations Online Bookseller Stole Trade Secrets, Boston Globe, April 5, 1999.

[462] Religious Technology Ctr. v. F.A.C.T. Net, Inc., 901 F. Supp. 1519 (D. Colo. 1995) (denying preliminary injunction where balance of harms weighed against plaintiff in case involving trade secrets of church).

[463] *Id. See also* Religious Tech. Ctr. v. Lerma, 908 F. Supp. 1362 (D. Va. 1995) (holding that newspaper's publication of church's confidential documents protected by "fair use" defense).

duty to guard the secrecy of the document. It is critical that the nondisclosure agreement have a continuing obligation not to disclose information after termination of employment. The nondisclosure agreement should set forth what constitutes a breach or violation of the agreement by a terminated employee. It is also advisable to include a provision in the employee's agreement stating that the company may file for injunctive relief in case of default. This may be an important clause, since many nondisclosure agreements require the plaintiffs to resolve disputes by arbitration.

Employees violating nondisclosure agreements should be warned that violating a confidentiality agreement may subject them to criminal as well as civil liability. Employees that breach nondisclosure agreements also may be punished with a punitive damages award for misappropriating trade secrets. Moreover, a breach of fiduciary duty may result in lawsuits for trade secrets theft, conversion, tortious interference, unfair competition, and other business torts. The Economic Espionage Act of 1996, for example, applies to anyone who receives, buys, or possesses trade secrets knowing that they have been stolen or misappropriated.

SPC will need to enter into confidential and nondisclosure agreements to provide a contractual remedy against the misappropriation of trade secrets and unauthorized disclosure of confidential information. Nondisclosure agreements will also be appropriate when making confidential information available to customers, potential customers, consultants, independent contractors. A nondisclosure agreement is a safeguard that can help satisfy the secrecy element key to the existence of a trade secret. The essential clauses of the agreement are:

1. Who gets to review, examine, inspect, or use confidential information for what purposes?
2. What are the conditions for various levels of access?
3. Who should sign the nondisclosure agreement?
4. Which employees, co-venturers, or third parties are classifiable as trustworthy insiders?
5. Who has a "need to know"? Closely held subsidiaries of parent corporations may be classifiable as trusted insiders with access to confidential information.
6. Which employees need access to trade secrets in order to perform their job?
7. Has the agreement been properly executed and signed?
8. Who has unlimited access to confidential information?
9. What are the potential consequences if the nondisclosure agreement is violated?
10. Who has the authority to substitute other agreements for the nondisclosure agreement?

[a]   Checklist for Nondisclosure Agreement for Web Sites

I.   What is the subject matter that is not to be disclosed?

- ☐   Technical specifications for software
- ☐   Source code
- ☐   Customer lists
- ☐   Business plans
- ☐   Online business methods
- ☐   Technical data for software and hardware
- ☐   HTML code and method of monitoring web site traffic
- ☐   Information security controls
- ☐   Other web business information (please list)
- ☐   Other technical information (please list)

II.   What is the nature of the obligation to keep information secret?

- ☐   Clear definition exists of what information is encompassed within the agreement
- ☐   Access limited to "need to know" basis in recipient company
- ☐   Recipient indemnifies SPC and holds SPC harmless for harming interests of third parties if proprietary information disclosed
- ☐   Proprietary information furnished by either party has been marked with "Confidential," "Trade Secret," or "Proprietary Information—Not to Be Disclosed"
- ☐   Recipient of proprietary information has agreed not to make copies except as needed to perform web site tasks

III.   Who should be subject to a nondisclosure agreement?

- ☐   Employees and ex-employees
- ☐   Web site designers
- ☐   Web site maintenance contractors
- ☐   Web site service personnel classified as independent contractors
- ☐   Co-venturers or partners

293

❐   Web site contractors

❐   Web site sales agents at co-branded sites

❐   Parties to litigation

IV. What clauses are essential for the nondisclosure agreement?

❐   **Recitals:** In order to protect SPC's confidential information, Suffolk Personal Computers and its [subsidiaries, co-venturers, etc.] disclose to _____.

❐   **Effective date:** Effective Date _____ 2000.

❐   **Disclosure period:** The agreement pertains to SPC's confidential information in Attachment A that is disclosed between Effective Date _____ and _____.

❐   **Granting clause:** In consideration of the promises and the mutual promises made in this agreement, _____ and _____ agree to be mutually bound. The parties agree to protect SPC's proprietary information in Attachment A. All proprietary information supplied to _____ [recipient] must be marked with the legend "Confidential."

❐   **Mutual promises or consideration clause.**

❐   **Warranty:** Each discloser warrants that it has the right to make the disclosures under this agreement. No other warranty is given including the warranty of merchantability, fitness for a particular purpose, or warranty of title or infringement. Neither SPC nor _____ makes any other warranty.

❐   **Standard of performance:** "SPC expects _____ [recipient of disclosed information] to protect the disclosed proprietary information by using the same degree of care, but no less than a reasonable standard of care, to prevent the unauthorized use or disclosure of the confidential information as _____ [recipient] will use in protecting its own confidential information of similar importance."

❐   **Ownership rights:** Neither party to this agreement acquires any intellectual property rights under this agreement except the limited rights necessary to carry out this agreement.

❐   **Notification by receiving party:** Neither party shall be restricted from disclosing proprietary information of the other party pursuant to a judicial or governmental order.

❏ **Antiassignment and delegation clause:** The agreement does not permit the obligations or duties under this agreement to be assigned or delegated.

❏ **No partnership clause:** This agreement does not create an agency, partnership, or joint venture.

❏ **Modifications in writing:** This agreement does not permit additions or agreements except in writing signed by both parties.

❏ **Choice of law:** This nondisclosure agreement is governed by the Commonwealth of Massachusetts.

❏ **Choice of forum:** Disputes concerning this nondisclosure agreement are adjudicated in the state and federal courts of Suffolk County, Massachusetts.

❏ **Events of termination:** Either party may terminate the use of its proprietary information by the receiving party at any time without liability upon written notice to the other party. The recipient of proprietary information must return all copies of information.

❏ **Integration clause:** This nondisclosure agreement supersedes all prior or contemporaneous agreements, whether oral or written, between the parties.

❏ **Discloser's authorized representative:** [Name; title; date; contact information, including e-mail address], signature.

❏ **Disclosing party's authorized representative:** [Name; title; date; contact information, including e-mail address] signature.

❏ **Appendix A:** Proprietary information included in nondisclosure agreement between SPC and _____ [recipient], Effective Date: _____.

[b] Sample Clauses

[i] **RFPs.** The following is a nondisclosure agreement to bind bidders on contracts for requests for proposal (RFPs):

IMPORTANT: This agreement including Attachment A hereof, is entered into and made effective as of _____ [date] is between Suffolk Personal Computers (SPC) and _____ [prospective bidder]. The prospective Bidder [name], by receipt of specifications and information provided by SPC, acknowledges that such specifications and information which may subsequently be supplied by SPC have been, or will be disclosed to it in strictest confidence. The Bidder acknowledges that SPC has a continuing proprietary interest in all such specifications and information. The Bidder [name] acknowledges that SPC has the sole right and privilege to use, patent, manufacture, or otherwise exploit the processes, ideas, and concepts described or revealed as belonging to SPC. In consideration of SPC's disclosure of specifications and information disclosed to Bidder [name], Bidder agrees that all precautions will be taken to ensure that such specifications and information will not be revealed or divulged to any third party at any time, through the use of copies, summaries, or like material, made without the knowledge or consent of SPC. All such specifications, information, and materials, including any copies, summaries, or the like, will be promptly returned to Suffolk Personal Computer without demand.

[ii] SPC's Nondisclosure Agreement.

This agreement is entered into and made effective on the date of the last signature affixed by SPC, a Massachusetts corporation having a place of business at: 120 Tremont Street, Boston Massachusetts 02108-4977 and [employee]. In consideration of being employed by SPC, the undersigned [employee] acknowledges that: During the course of my employment at SPC, there may be disclosed to me certain Confidential Information, which may consist of, but is not necessarily limited to, how SPC: (1) designs its distinctive software, computer systems, business plans, and online marketing models; (2) manufactures, assembles, designs, and tests its software; (3) designs, tests, and monitors its web site; (4) solves clients' problems; (5) markets its products online; (6) implements its metering software; (7) answers customer's inquiries online; (8) arrives at strategies for prices, discounts, and rebates; (9) develops customer lists as well as lists of potential customers; (10) develops its source code; (11) analyzes its potential and actual Internet customer list and market; and (12) develops its other business and strategic planning information.

[iii] Duty of Confidentiality Clause.

The employee agrees to maintain the confidentiality of all Confidential Information and to take all reasonable precautions to prevent disclosure, use, duplication, reverse engineering, and/or reverse compilations of any Confidential Information or any part or parts thereof for any purpose whatsoever. Upon termination of employment, and/or any other time that employment ends, the employee agrees to turn over to SPC any confidential information in his or her possession.

[iv] Restrictive Covenants.

As an employee of SPC, I agree not to solicit (or assist any third party in soliciting) on behalf of myself or on behalf of any third party, any "business opportunity" from any customer.* This agreement defines a business opportunity to mean and include any matter, which SPC, in its reasonable judgment, deems competitive or potentially competitive to its business or to the relationship between SPC and the subject customer.[464]

---

*A customer means and includes: (1) any Licensee of a Company product or service; (2) any person or entity for whom the Company provided or was obligated to provide, within six (6) months prior to such Termination Date, maintenance or other services, or a fee, pursuant to a formal agreement or otherwise; (3) any person or entity to whom, within six (6) months prior to such Termination Date, the Company had made a presentation or solicitation wholly or partially in writing, or for whom the Company had performed or provided, a "savings analysis"; and (4) any joint venturer or subcontractor of the Company. *See* Weseley Software Development Corp. v. Burdette, 977 F. Supp. 137 (D. Conn. 1996) (discussing employment agreement with definition of customer).

[2]   Web Site Trade Secrets

Material published on a web site cannot qualify as a trade secret because it is no longer secret. SPC's trade secrets must remain secret during the period of exploitation. If SPC permits third parties to have access to trade secrets, reasonable means must be taken to maintain secrecy. Hidden aspects of web sites or software may be deemed as trade secrets provided reasonable steps are taken to keep information secret. In many trade secrets claims, adequate protection has been questionable. Employees or consultants who have access to computer applications with software should be required to sign nondisclosure agreements. Web site trade secrets "should be marked with legends which alert a reader of the nature of the document as proprietary."[465] Software applications may be protected by license agreements prohibiting reverse engineering. A European Union Directive, however, gives residents in member states a "right to reverse engineer" to encourage the interoperability of computer systems.[466]

[3]   Security Measures to Protect Trade Secrets

SPC must take measures to guard the secrecy of information transmitted on the Internet; business espionage on the Internet has become an illicit means of stealing trade secrets. Foreign governments, foreign corporations, competitors, independent hackers, or disgruntled employees may use the Internet to steal trade secrets.[467] SPC may lose its trade secrets if disgruntled ex-employees post

---

[464] This clause tracks the restrictive covenant in the employment agreement discussed in Weseley. This clause tracks the restrictive covenant discussed in Weseley Software, *id.*

[465] David B. Himelstein, Web Sites and Software as Trade Secrets (visited March 19, 2000), http://www.himels-computer-law.com/trdscrt.htm.

[466] European Union Software Directive 91/250 (1991).

[467] Computer Security Institute, The 1998 Computer Crime and Security Survey (1998) (reporting the most likely sources for Internet attacks).

confidential information to the Internet anonymously, using false return addresses.[468]

Once a trade secret is transmitted on the Internet, potentially viewable by millions of users, it is no longer secret. Trade secrets consist of technical and non-technical information, such as processes, recipes, plans, strategies, data, systems, sketches, technology, customer lists, and client lists. The security measures used to protect SPC's trade secrets should be calibrated to the value of the information and the adverse consequences if the information is disclosed. Risk analysis is a quantitative means of determining whether expenditures for information security are cost-effective. An effective security policy has the best available technologies, coupled with a workplace culture committed to safety.

Trade secret protection lasts as long as the information is kept secret. Information security may consist of relatively simple access devices, such as a lock and master key or a checkpoint guard to protect a trade secret. Chapter Three provides a description of security tools used to protect trade secrets; these include digital signatures; repeat-back passwords; keyboard and screen locks; date/time stamps; trusted third parties; double-key and single-key encryption; digital signatures; mass-marketed security products; audits of computer systems; and a company-wide policy for using security protocol.

[4] Confidentiality of Trade Secret Trial

Section 5 of UTSA places a duty on a court in a trade secret litigation to "pre-serve the secrecy of an alleged trade secret by reasonable means, which may include granting protective orders in connection with discovery proceeding." Section 5 also notes that the court may hold in-camera hearings and seal the records of trade secrets proceedings to protect confidentiality. If SPC is involved in trade secret litigation, it should file pretrial motions for in-camera hearings and sealed records and an order imposing confidentiality on all persons involved in the litigation.

[5] Inevitable Disclosure/Noncompetition Agreements

SPC may be able to prevent a former employee working for an online com-petitor by invoking the "inevitable disclosure" doctrine. Courts, however, have been reluctant to enforce similar clauses in noncompetition agreements because of the public policies of free competition, the mobility of skilled labor, freedom to change jobs, and the freedom to take one's skill and experience to new employers.

In *LEXIS-NEXIS v. Beer*,[469] a court found a noncompetition agreement that prevented a low level employee from engaging in "competitive activity" for one

---

[468] *Id.*
[469] 41 F. Supp. 2d 950 (D. Minn. 1999).

year after leaving the company was overly broad. The clause in question included the following language:

> As used herein, the term "competitive activity" shall include acting directly or indirectly as an agent, employee, officer, director . . . partner or in any other capacity whatsoever, in any business, venture, association, or organization which engages in programming, designing, or marketing computerized information retrieval systems, or system components anywhere in the United States of America, the United Kingdom, Canada, France, or any country in which LEXIS-NEXIS offers services or products to the public.[470]

The *Beer* court found the noncompetition agreement to be over broad in that it prevented a low-level employee from "working any capacity anywhere in the world."[471] The court found the agreement failed "to sensibly identify the kind of competitive businesses that an employee . . . must stay out of in order for LEXIS-NEXIS to protect its legitimate business interest."[472]

Courts are reluctant to permit companies to use trade secret law as a vehicle for unreasonable restraints on competition.[473] In some cases, though, if the employee in question is at a senior level, it is more likely that a court will enforce a noncompetition agreement that has reasonable limits on time and geography. Courts balance the purposes of trade secret law against the strong public policy against inhibiting competition in the marketplace.[474] The common law of trade secrets distinguished between an employee's "head knowledge" and "trade secrets."

Courts consistently refuse to enjoin an employee's use of his or her "head knowledge" in competition with the former employer when there is no evidence that the employee misappropriated any of the former employer's documents containing business information.[475] Courts refuse to restrain "head knowledge" because it is unrealistic to require employees to forget what they learned on the job. A New Jersey court, for example, held that an employee's knowledge of price and cost data could not be enjoined since the employee need not "force himself to

---

[470] *Id.* at 957.

[471] *Id. See also,* Earthweb, Inc. v. Schlack, 71 F. Supp. 2d 299 (S.D.N.Y. 1999) denying injunction against former employee preventing him from pursing employment with competitor).

[472] *Id.*

[473] *See, e.g.,* Cudahy Co. v. American Labs, Inc., 313 F. Supp. 1339, 1343 (D. Neb. 1970) ("The status given trade secrets is not to be used as a sword to prevent employees from rendering their services, based on knowledge and experience, to somebody other than that one employer."). *See also* DoubleClick v. Henderson, 1997 N.Y. Misc. LEXIS 577 (App. Div. 1997) (declining to grant injunction for a full year in forming own Internet company given rapidly evolving Web advertising business).

[474] Fleming Sales Co. v. Bailey, 611 F. Supp. 507, 511-12 (N.D. Ill. 1985).

[475] *See, e.g.,* Metal Lubricants Co. v. Engineered Lubricants Co., 284 F. Supp. 483, 486-88 (E.D. Mo. 1968) (refusing to enjoin competition where former employees took no documents containing confidential data).

forget."[476] In general, a former employee's use of his memory of former employer's data and information may not be restrained.

§ 4.05   E-COMMERCE RELATED PATENTS

Patents provide stronger protection for intellectual property but are "more difficult, time consuming and expensive than other forms of intellectual property protection"[477] (see Table 4.10). A patent is a property right possessed or held by an inventor with constitutional roots in Article I, Section 8, Clause 8 of the United States Constitution, which states:

> Whoever invents or discovers any new and useful process, machine, manufacture, or composition of matter, or any new and useful improvement thereof may obtain a patent therefor, subject to the conditions and requirements of this title.[478]

[A]   The Concepts and Methods of Patent Law

An online company may seek protection under the federal Patent Act for Internet-related inventions. If a company holds the patent on an e-commerce business process, it can file an infringement lawsuit against competitors who copy the process. The patent owner can raise revenues through its licensing of patents. If a company, for example, invents a method of Internet payment, it may receive patent protection provided the business process is novel, useful, and nonobvious. Alternatively, a company may make a business decision to license the e-commerce business patents of others.

To obtain patent protection, a company must file an application with the Patent and Trademark Office (USPTO), an office of the Department of Commerce. The USPTO is the repository for "records, books, drawings, specifications, and other papers and things pertaining to patents and to trademark registration."[479] The USPTO is headed by the Commissioner of Patents and Trademarks who is appointed by the President and approved by the United States Senate. Other essential officers of the USPTO are the Deputy Commissioner, Assistant Commissioners, and Examiners-In-Chief.[480]

---

[476] Midland Ross Corp. v. Yokana, 185 F. Supp. 594, 604 (D.N.J. 1960).

[477] Carey R. Ramos and David S. Berlin, Three Ways to Protect Computer Software, 16 The Comp. L. 16 (Jan. 1999).

[478] 35 U.S.C. § 101.

[479] 35 U.S.C. § 1 (1999).

[480] 35 U.S.C. § 3 (1999).

TABLE 4.10
Patent Overview

Method for obtaining protection	File application and prosecute application with the USPTO.
Remedies for infringement	Injunctive relief, damages, treble damages in the appropriate cases, attorneys' fees, costs

The Patent Act of 1952, 35 U.S.C. §§ 1-376, is the federal statute governing patents.[481] A patent gives the patent holder the right to exclude others from making, using, or selling an invention in the United States.[482] The subject matter for a patentable invention may consist of useful processes, machines, articles of manufacture, and the composition of matter and material.[483]

A patent requires three conditions: (1) novelty; (2) utility; and (3) nonobviousness.[484] The statutory test for nonobviousness is whether "the subject matter as a whole would have been obvious at the time the invention was made to a person having ordinary skill in the art to which said subject matter pertains."[485]

Patents are classified by the Patent Act into three ideal types: (1) utility patents; (2) design patents; and (3) plant patents.[486] Each patent examination includes an abstract, the field of invention, summary of the invention, drawings, and a detailed description of the patent claim. The patent claim is what defines an invention. The specifications contain a written description of the invention and the exact terms to make and use the invention.

[B]   The Patent and Trademark Office Procedure

[1]   Patentability and Patent Examiners

A USPTO examiner determines whether a patent meets the conditions for patentability. The examiner compares the subject matter sought to be patented with the prior art. If prior art references anticipated the claim of a patent, the claim is found invalid. The differences between the prior art references and the patent claim must be significant.

---

[481] "Whoever invents or discovers any new and useful process, machine, manufacture, or composition of matter, or any new and useful improvement thereof, may obtain a patent therefor, subject to the conditions and requirements of this title." 35 U.S.C. § 101 (1999).

[482] *Id.*

[483] 17 U.S.C. § 101(b) (1999).

[484] 35 U.S.C. § 101-103 (1999).

[485] 35 U.S.C. § 103 (1999).

[486] 35 U.S.C. §§ 101, 102 (1999).

Patent examiners are "persons of legal knowledge and scientific ability" who determine the patentability of inventions.[487] A patent examiner may reject a claim because it is nonstatutory subject matter. "Every case involving a § 101 issue must begin with this question: What, if anything, is it that the applicant 'invented or discovered?' "[488] A patent claim consists of the elements that comprise the invention. An examiner's job is to determine whether the combination of claimed elements exists in prior art, and if so, reject the claim.

An examiner may also reject a patent claim on the grounds of nonobviousness. Certain categories of subject matter are not entitled to patent protection such as "laws of nature, natural phenomena and abstract ideas."[489]

[2] Patent Prosecution

The Board of Patent Appeals and Interference is the first level of appeal for adverse decisions of examiners or other issues of priority and patentability.[490] Every appeal and interference is required to be "heard by at least three members of the Board of Patent Appeals and Interference."[491] An applicant for a patent who has twice been rejected may appeal from the decision of the primary examiner to the Board of Patent Appeals.[492] An applicant dissatisfied with the Board's decision can appeal an adverse decision to the United States Court of Appeals for the Federal Circuit.[493]

The USPTO Commissioner prescribes rules for the "conduct of agents, attorneys, or other persons representing applicants, or other parties before the Patent and Trademark Office."[494] Members of the patent bar prosecute patents. A practitioner must have a background in a designated scientific discipline and pass a two-part patent examination as part of the necessary background to practice before the USPTO. The patent bar examination is described by the USPTO's Manual of Patent Examining Procedure. The rules for practice for members of the patent bar are set forth in the Patent Rules of Practice.

Patent counsel will work with the company in filing patent applications with the USPTO. Challenging the validity of patents is a strategic defense for claims of infringement. In the 1970, two-thirds of the patents reviewed by courts were found invalid.[495]

---

[487] 35 U.S.C. § 7 (1999).

[488] In Re Alappat, 33 F.3d 1526 (Fed. Cir. 1994) (dissenting opinion by C.J. Archer, citations omitted).

[489] Diamond v. Diehr, 450 U.S. 175, 185 (1981).

[490] 35 U.S.C. § 7 (1999).

[491] *Id.*

[492] 35 U.S.C. § 134 (1999).

[493] 35 U.S.C. § 141 (1999).

[494] 35 U.S.C. § 31 (1999).

[495] Ramos and Berlin, *supra* note 477.

[C]   Anatomy of a Patent

Patent protection is available for the invention of "any new and useful process, machine, manufacture, or composition of matter, or any new and useful improvement thereof. . . ."[496] Patents are not granted where "the differences between the subject matter sought to be patented and the prior art are such that the subject matter as a whole would have been obvious at the time the invention was made to a person having ordinary skill in the art to which the said subject matter pertains."[497]

[1]   Specifications

A patent application will typically include: (1) a specification; (2) a drawing; and (3) an oath by the applicant.[498] The specification concludes with "one or more claims particularly pointing out and distinctly claiming the subject matter which the applicant regards as his invention."[499] The two principal ways of describing claims are on dependent forms or on multiple dependent forms. With a dependent form, reference is made to a claim previously described. "A claim in dependent form shall be construed to incorporate by reference all the limitations of the claim to which it refers."[500] Multiple dependent claims "shall be construed to incorporate by reference all the limitations of the particular claim in relation to which it is being considered."[501]

[2]   Drawings of Inventions

An applicant for a patent will frequently include a drawing "where necessary for the understanding of the subject matter sought to be patented."[502] A patent examiner may require a drawing where the "subject matter admits of illustration by a drawing and the applicant has not furnished such a drawing."[503]

A patent gives the owner the right to exclude others from making or using a patented invention. A patent claim describing the invention is filed with the USPTO. Inventions that may be patented include "any new and useful process, machine, manufacture or composition of matter, or any new and useful improvement."[504] Every patent begins with a short title of the invention. The specifications

---

[496] 35 U.S.C. § 101 (1999).

[497] 35 U.S.C. § 103 (1999).

[498] 35 U.S.C. § 111 (1999).

[499] *Id.*

[500] *Id.*

[501] *Id.*

[502] 35 U.S.C. § 113 (1999).

[503] *Id.*

[504] *Id.*

are a "written description of the invention, and of the manner and process of making and using it, in such full, clear, concise, and exact terms . . . to make and use the same."[505]

[3]   Oath

A patent applicant makes an oath attesting that he or she is the original and first inventor of the process; machine; manufacture; composition of matter; or improvement of matter.[506] Joint inventors must each make the required oath.[507]

[4]   Examination of Application

Patent examiners study the application and determine whether the applicant is entitled to protection under the law. The patent claim describes the features of the invention that make it patentable. "The specification shall conclude with one or more claims particularly pointing out and distinctly claiming the subject matter which the applicant regards as his invention."[508] Drawings are submitted to aid in the understanding of the claim.[509] The USPTO Commissioner may require a patent applicant to "furnish a model of convenient size to exhibit advantageously the several parts of his invention."[510]

The Commissioner's patent examiners will study the application and compare it to prior art. If a claim for a patent is rejected or some other objection made, the Commissioner notifies the applicant with the reasons for the rejection or objection.[511] An applicant's failure to prosecute the application within six months after any action by the USPTO is regarded as "abandonment."[512]

Two dates are critically important for a patent: (1) the date of the filing of the patent application; and (2) the date of the granting of a patent. The term for a utility or plant patent filed on or after June 8, 1995, is 20 years from the date the application is filed with the USPTO. Patent prosecution begins with the filing of an application. The patent term for utility or plant applications filed before 1995 is 17 years from the issuance of the patent or 20 years from the filing, whichever is greater. The term for design patents is 14 years from the date the patent issues.

---

[505] *Id.*

[506] 35 U.S.C. § 115 (1999) (covering Oath of Applicant).

[507] 35 U.S.C. § 116 (1999).

[508] *Id.*

[509] 35 U.S.C. § 113 (1999).

[510] 35 U.S.C. § 114 (1999).

[511] 35 U.S.C. §§ 131, 132 (1999).

[512] 35 U.S.C. § 135 (1999).

[D]   Software Patents

Software is frequently classified as a utility patent and may encompass long distance communications networks, voice, video and data communication as well as Internet-related business methods. Software and hardware patents are also essential to broadband distribution technologies, telephone-based access services, and other advanced digital services. The term of a utility patent "filed prior to June 8, 1995 is the later of (1) 17 years from the date of issuance of the patent, or (2) 20 years from the first United States filing date for the patent."[513]

IBM, Oracle, Novell, and Microsoft are owners of many of the patents important to e-commerce. IBM is the world's leader in owning software patents and earned $650 million in royalties from its patent portfolio in 1996.[514] Software patents are growing exponentially because of the greater competence of the United States Patent and Trademark Office and the formulation of Examination Guidelines for Computer-Related Inventions.[515] In addition the USPTO has made a concerted effort to recruit and train examiners trained to use the guidelines. Software patents have been awarded that administer programs, sharpen images, store data, build status indicator, edit graphical resources, facilitate database access, allocate data, organize user interface objects, customize programs, control access point tracking, optimize multidatabase systems, and manage distributed database.[516]

[E]   Patent Infringement

Patent infringement, which occurs when a person or entity without authority "offers to sell or sells any patented invention, within the United States or imports into the United States any patented invention during the term of the invention,"[517] is a widespread problem in the information economy and a source of revenue for companies with large patent portfolios. Polaroid filed a patent infringement lawsuit against Kodak seeking hundreds of millions of dollars. IBM holds thousands of software patents subject to infringement. One of the problems with software patents is that they provide an exclusive monopoly that may make it difficult for

---

[513] Oppedahl and Larson LLP, General Information About Patents (visited May 27, 1999), http://www.patents.com/patents.sht.

[514] Big Blue is Out to Collar Software Scofflaws, Bus. Week, March 17, 1997, at 29.

[515] United States Patent & Trademark Office, Examination Guidelines for Computer-Related Invention, 1184 U.S. Pat. & Trademark Off. Official Gazette 87 (1996).

[516] Robert Greene Sterne, et al., Software Patent Law 1997—Strong Rights Coming of Age (listing software patents granted in 1996 and 1997).

[517] 35 U.S.C. § 271 (1999).

hardware and software producers to avoid infringement.[518] IBM, for example, patented "the software to automatically return the cursor to the start of the next line on a computer screen."[519]

A direct infringer is a person or entity who does not have a license or other authority to use an invention but who nevertheless, "uses, offers to sell or sells any patented invention within the United States" during the patent term.[520] An indirect infringer is a person or entity who actively encourages another person or entity to infringe a patented invention. Contributory infringement is knowingly selling or supplying a part of a patented invention unless there is a substantial noninfringing use.[521]

The remedies for infringement include (1) injunctive relief against the infringer; (2) damages or monetary relief against an infringer;[522] (3) treble damages awarded by the fact finder in appropriate circumstances;[523] and (4) reasonable attorneys' fees to the prevailing party in "exceptional cases."[524] Defenses in infringement suits include "(1) Noninfringement, absence of liability for infringement or unenforceability; (2) Invalidity of the patent or any claim in suit; and (3) Any other fact or act made a defense" by the Patent Act."[525]

➤ [F] Preventive Law Pointers: Patents in Cyberspace

[1] Patents for Push Technologies

One of the strategic decisions that SPC will need to make is how it can quickly gain a positive online identity. Many web sites are content with a "pull method" of attracting visitors and potential customers to the web site. With a pull method, visitors type in the URL or use a standard search engine such as Lycos, Alta Vista, or Excite to find SPC's web site. The user employs search engines to "pull" information or content about SPC's products and services from the web site. With "pull technologies" the user requests information, in contrast to "push technologies," which target potential customers and web site users.

---

[518] Legal Analysis and Commentary, Big Blue Is Out to Collar Software Scofflaws, Bus. Wk. 29 (Mar. 17, 1997) (quoting Greg Aharonian as stating: "It's hard to be in the computing business—hardware or software—and not infringe on a couple of dozen IBM patents").

[519] *Id.*

[520] *Id.*

[521] 35 U.S.C. § 271[c] (1999).

[522] 35 U.S.C. § 284 (1999) (noting that damages award must be "adequate to compensate for the infringement, but in no event less than a reasonable royalty for the use made of the invention by the infringer, together with interest and costs as fixed by the court").

[523] The ordinary measure of damages is reasonable royalties, 35 U.S.C. § 285 (1999).

[524] "The court in exceptional cases may award reasonable attorney fees to the prevailing party." 35 U.S.C. § 285 (1999).

[525] 35 U.S.C. § 282 (1999).

SPC may soon join the growing number of companies using "push tech-nologies" to transmit knowledge to customers—that is, SPC may decide to "push" content to customers and potential customers. If SPC makes a business decision to use "push" techniques to reach out to potential customers, it will likely need to enter license agreements with the vendors owning the patents or having rights in "push technologies."

[2]   Internet-Related Patents[526]

[a]   Roundup of Internet-Related Patents

The USPTO has recently issued many Internet-related patents, which affect a wide range of Internet sales and services. ChequeMARK Patent Inc. received an allowance for a "new patent [that] covers Internet purchases where payments from checking accounts are authorized electronically."[527] ChequeMARK's patent, U.S. Patent Number 5,484,988, is titled: a "Checkwriting Point of Sale Systems." Day traders on the Internet will be able to use a patented business method to analyze risk online in real time. The newly allowed patent is entitled: "System and Method for Determination of Incremental Value at Risk for Securities Trading."[528] The Securities Trading patent allows "value-at-risk" analysis for "real-time" securities transactions.[529] Online brokerage houses will likely need to obtain a license to compete in electronic data trading after the issuance of the "value at risk" patent.

A new patent permitting online loan applications and approvals will likely affect the financial services and home mortgage insurers. The real time loan approval method is titled "System and method for real time loan approval."[530] This "online loan approval" patent constitutes a method and apparatus for closed loop, automatic processing of a loan. The real time loan patent consists of a cradle-to-grave loan application: (1) application, (2) underwriting, and (3) the transfer of funds to the successful applicant. The real time loan patent permits intelligent electronic agents to interact with and obtain necessary information from the loan applicant. This computer application collects all of the information needed to process a loan and contains computer-based decision rules for determining

---

[526] This section was written by Peter Stecher, who holds a Bachelor of Science in Electrical Engineering from Massachusetts Institute of Technology and who entered Suffolk University Law School in September 2000. He has also earned approval as a patent agent.

[527] News.excite.com, LML Enters e-Commerce Arena with New Patent Protecting Authorization of Payments from Checking Accounts Made Over the Internet (visited April 2, 2000), http://news.excite.com/news/pr/000327/bc-lml-enters-e-comm.

[528] The patent that calculates risks in real time is U.S. Patent 5819237 (1998).

[529] Robert Sachs, Method Madness, Patenting Financial Inventions After State Street Bank, Daily Journal, 1999 (visited Feb. 25, 2000), http://www.fenwick.com/pub/ip_pubs/Bob/bob.html.

[530] U.S. Patent 5870721 (1999) is entitled "System and method for real time loan approval."

approval of the loan. The application can even trigger electronic fund transfers to the applicant's deposit account and arrange for automatic withdrawals to repay the loan.[531]

Online auctions are growing at an exponential rate. The operators of virtual online auctions will be interested in the "reverse auction" patent, U.S. Patent 5794207 (1990).[532] The reverse auction permits prospective buyers of goods and services to communicate a binding purchase offer globally to potential sellers. The "reverse auction" patent permits sellers to locate relevant buyers in an efficient manner. This business application software permits the purchasing of offers and a method for binding the buyer to a contract based on the buyer's purchase offer.[533]

Amazon.com is the owner of the famous "single-click method of shopping" entitled "Method and system for placing a purchase order via a communications network."[534] U.S. Patent 5960411 (1999) ("the 411 Patent") permits web sites to solve the problem of web site customers abandoning virtual shopping centers because of the difficulties of placing an order. The 411 Patent is a business method in which a consumer can complete a purchase order for goods or services with a single click of the mouse.[535] The 411 method works because the retailer has saved information about the web site visitor's address and credit card information.[536] The patent facilitates the placing of an order to purchase an item via the Internet, resulting in more online sales and services.[537]

Web site scheduling will likely be improved by "Scheduling system for use between users on the web," a patent issued to eCal, which allows scheduling of events between end users of a system.[538] Double Click is the owner of U.S. Patent 5948061 (1999), which is entitled: "Method of delivery, targeting, and measuring advertising over networks." Double Click's patent permits the management of advertising over the web.[539] The issuance of these patents permits the owner to enter preventive law license agreements to minimize infringement actions.

---

[531] *Id.*

[532] The "Method and apparatus for a cryptographically assisted commercial network system designed to facilitate buyer-driven conditional purchase offers" patents the business model of the "reverse-auction."

[533] Brian Logest, Brian Logest's Software Patent News: Patent Software Inventions, Oct./Nov. 1999 (visited Feb. 25, 2000), http://www.softwarepatentnews.com.

[534] U.S. Patent 5960411 (1999) is the patent for the business method of "one-click shopping."

[535] "Industry studies show that between sixty and sixty-five percent of shopping baskets are abandoned before they are checked out." Ralph Libshon, Madness in the Method: Will 'Method of Doing Business' Patents Undermine the Web ? Netcommerce Mag., Mar. 2000, at 7.

[536] Amazon.com v. Barnesandnoble.com, Inc., 1999 U.S. Dist. LEXIS 18660 (W.D. Wash., Dec. 1, 1999).

[537] *Id.*

[538] *Id.*

[539] *Id.*

In August 1998, Netdelivery was issued a patent "covering the method of receiving information over the Internet via an URL."[540] Netdelivery is licensing its new technologies to Microsoft, Netscape, and other "push" vendors.[541] The U.S. Patent and Trademark Office has recently issued Internet patents that facilitate electronic online commerce. Amazon.com received a software patent to "secure credit card processing of book orders."[542]

[b] *The Impact of* State Street

Prior to 1998, methods for doing business were thought to be unpatentable. This argument was predicated upon the well-established principle that mathematical algorithms were not patentable.[543] The USPTO, however, has been increasingly more receptive to the idea, to the point of patenting several software business methods. In 1989, the USPTO issued patents for cash management accounts and refund anticipation loans.[544] For many decades, the courts and legal scholars were skeptical of the claim that software business methods were patentable.[545]

No single development has spurred the growth of software patents more than State Street Bank & Trust Co. v. Signature Financial Group, Inc.[546] In *State Street*, Signature appealed from the decision of a federal court in Massachusetts granting summary judgment in favor of State Street, holding that the "hub and spoke" financial method was a business method not patentable.[547] Signature owned U.S. Patent No. 5,193,056 (the 056 patent), which manages and coordiantes mutual funds. The hub facilitates a structure, whereas the spokes pool their investment portfolio in a hub organized as a partnership. State Street negotiated with Signature for a license to use the multitiered partnership financial service business method. When negotiations broke down, State Street sought a declaratory judgment that the patent was invalid and unenforceable.

The federal district court for Massachusetts granted State Street's motion for partial summary judgment of finding the 056 patent invalid because it was based

---

[540] Albert Panq, E-Commerce Breakthrough? Netdelivery Gains Patent for Invited Pull, ZDTV (visited Feb. 16, 1999), http://www.zdnet.com/zdnn/st..nn_smgraph_display/0,341,2129869,00.html.

[541] *Id.* (describing how U.S. patent 5,790,793 will be useful to diverse electronic-commerce applications).

[542] *Id.*

[543] *Id.*

[544] The Cash Management Account patent is U.S. Patent 4346442. The Refund Anticipation Loan is U.S. Patent 4890228.

[545] Seth Shulman, "Patents Tangle the Web," Technology Review, March/April 2000 at 71.

[546] State Street Bank & Trust Co. v. Signature Financial Group, Inc., 149 F.3d 1368, *cert. denied,* 199 S. Ct. 851 (Fed. Cir. July 23, 1998).

[547] The hub and spoke business method was encompassed by U.S. Patent No. 5,193,056 (the "056 patent").

on mathematical alogrithms and was therefore an unpatentable business method. The federal district court found the 056 patent merely input numbers and made calculations and, therefore, did not constitute a patentable invention.[548] The trial court found the patent invalid because the subject matter was not encompassed by 35 U.S.C. § 101.

The Federal Circuit reversed and remanded concluding that the patent for computing interest on mutual funds, the so-called "hub and spoke" method, was directed to statutory subject matter.[549] The Federal Circuit eliminated the business method exception. The Court of Appeals for the Federal Circuit's holding unequivocally stated that "the transformation of data, representing discrete dollar amounts, by a machine through a series of mathematical calculations into a final share price, constitutes a practical application of a mathematical algorithm, formula, or calculation, because it produces 'useful, concrete, and tangible results' — a final share price momentarily fixed for recording and reporting purposes."[550]

The *State Street* court narrowed the court-made doctrine that mathematical formulas were unpatentable subject matter.[551] The court limited the prohibition against the patenting of mathematical algorithms in the abstract. The *State Street Bank* case validated computer-related patents for doing business that will continue to have a profound impact on the Internet economy.

The immediate impact of the *State Street* case has been to stimulate software patents. Since the June 1998 decision by the federal circuit court, there "was a 45 percent increase in the number of data processing and computer-related patents issued during its 1998 fiscal year."[552] The development cycle for software for Internet applications is rarely greater than six months. Patents for electronic commerce have been awarded in increasing numbers, but the application period continues to have a longer tail than the product cycle of many software products.

There is strong empirical evidence that the *State Street* case represents a paradigm shift for the new information economy. Since *State Street*, the filing of so-called "business method patents" has skyrocketed.[553] In 1997, the United States Patent and Trademark Office assigned 12 examiners to work on 920 business method patents. In 1999, the number of business method patents was up to 2,600.[554] The Commissioner reports that the USPTO is receiving more than 2,500 applications per year.[555]

---

[548] State Street Bank v. Signature Financial Group, 927 F. Supp. 502, 515 (D. Mass 1996).

[549] *Id.*

[550] State Street Bank v. Signature Financial Group, 149 F.3d at 1373.

[551] Diamond v. Diehr, 450 U.S. 175 (1981).

[552] John T. Aquino, Patently Permissive: USPTO Filings Up After Ruling Expands Protection for Business and Net Software, ABA J., May 1999 at 30.

[553] Seth Shulman, *id.* at 69.

[554] Sabra Charytrand, Patents: What's in a Name? A Sign of Other Changes at the United States Patent and Trademark Office, N.Y. Times, Apr. 3, 2000, at C6.

[555] *Id.*

The courts will play a significant role in determining the reach of e-commerce patents. Priceline.com owns a patent for its "name your price" method of sales and services on the Internet. Priceline recently sued Microsoft for infringing its business method. The infringement action arises out of Microsoft's fall of 1999 plan to let web users name their price for hotel and travel accommodations on Microsoft's Expedia web site. Priceline.com had previously been issued a patent on a "reverse-auction" system that is substantially similar to what Expedia offers to web users.[556] Priceline.com is suing Microsoft for infringement based on their patent.[557] This case may determine the contours of patent infringement damages in business patent cases.

Amazon.com filed a complaint against Barnesandnoble.com alleging that its "Express Lane" method infringed Amazon.com's 411 Patent for "1-Click" ordering of goods.[558] Amazon.com filed suit only 23 days after the "One-Click" patent was issued, alleging that the defendant's "Express Lane" ordering scheme infringed on their "single-click method" patent.[559] Barnesandnoble.com's chief defense was that Amazon.com's patent was obvious and therefore invalid. The Express Lane stored information on prior customers, permitting "registered customers to bypass the Shopping Cart and purchase a book with a single mouse click."[560] A Washington court granted a preliminary injunction enjoining Barnesandnoble.com from using the patent and ordering it to remove the Express Lane feature from its web site.[561] The injunction restrained and enjoined Barnesandnoble.com from continuing to infringe the 0411 patent.

Internet-related patents will shape the future of e-commerce because the patent gives the holder control of the use of their technology. The level and extent of the control varies depending on the business model of the inventor. A patent holder may obtain a patent for a defensive purpose to discourage competitors. An inventor may realize value from its invention by selling the patent, assigning it, licensing it, or doing nothing with it. The USPTO issues the patent but does not dictate the business model. Patent portfolios are key to market differentiation and control.[562]

Our hypothetical Internet company, SPC, needs to conduct a thorough comparative analysis of risks and utilities before seeking patent protection. The cost-benefit equation is the cost of securing the patent balanced against the potential

---

[556] Suzanne Galante, Selling the Priceline Way: Company Patents Its Buyer-Driven Form of E-Commerce, The Street.com (visited Mar. 1, 2000), http://abcnews.go.com/sections/business/TheStreet/priceline991028.html.

[557] Id.

[558] Brian Logest, Brian Logest's Software Patent News: Patent Software Inventions, Oct./Nov. 1999, (visited Feb. 25, 2000), www.softwarepatentnews.com.

[559] 73 F. Supp. 2d 1228 (W.D. Wash. 1999).

[560] Libshon, *supra* note 535.

[561] Id.

[562] Michael B. Einschlag, Simplifying Patent Portfolio Evaluation By Using Product Differentiators, (Spring 1997), pg. 2 (visited Feb. 25, 2000), www.giocities.com/ResearchTriangle/Facility/3078/einsch1.html.

revenue stream. Internet-related e-commerce patents have a high potential for revenue if they cover critical infrastructure, such as one-stop shopping.[563]

E-commerce patent litigation is a war of attrition: an uneven battlefield where a simple patent dispute may result in expenses of $1.2 million.[564] A small or medium competitor may be unable or unwilling to expend resources to challenge the validity of a patent. Assuming SPC determines that an e-commerce "business" product is useful, concrete, and produces tangible results, the company should retain a registered patent counsel to assist in the steps necessary to file a patent application.[565]

The USPTO recently announced that it was instituting new policies for the examination of e-commerce patent applications. The revised policy will result in second reviews of applications and "better searches of previous inventions and industry practices."[566] The USPTO plans to immediately "double the sample size of computer-business method patents that get a final quality check."[567] The revised policy will require examiners to search databases to look for prior art to determine whether business methods are widely used or in the public domain.

[c]　*Licensing E-Commerce Patents*

Patent licenses are a major source of revenue for dot-com companies holding e-commerce patents. An exclusive license, as its name suggests, prevents the licensor from licensing its technology to more than one party[568] and "bars the licensor from practicing the invention unless he has specifically reserved the right to do so."[569]

SPC may wish to reserve the right to use its own e-commerce patents because an exclusive license would allow only the sole exclusive licensee to practice the invention.[570] An alternative is that SPC expressly reserve the right to use its own technology in its patent license agreements. SPC can warrant that it will not issue other licenses to other competitors.[571] In the absence of a specific reservation of the right to use its own invention, SPC may not enter agreements with other licensees to use the patented technology.[572]

---

[563] *Id.*

[564] Seth Shulman, *id.* at 72.

[565] Only counsel who have passed the patent examination of the USPTO and are members of the patent bar can prosecute a patent claim. Specialized knowledge and experience is necessary to draft software patents or Internet-related business model claims.

[566] Reuters, Inc., U.S. to Revise Net Patent Process (visited Apr. 2, 2000), http://www.news.cnet.com/news/0-1007-200-1596357.html?tag+st.

[567] *Id.*

[568] Seth Shulman, *id.* at 71.

[569] *Id.*

[570] Cutter Laboratories, Inc. v. Lyophile-Cryochem Corp., 179 F.2d 80 (9th Cir. 1949).

[571] Harold Einhorn, Patent Licensing Transaction, § 1.01 (1997).

[572] Ackerman v. Hook, 183 F.2d 11 (3d Cir. 1950).

A nonexclusive license allows SPC to practice its inventions and to grant that same right to others.[573] Additionally, SPC "may freely license others, or may tolerate infringers; and, in either case, no right of the license is violated."[574] SPC is in a position to file an action against possible infringers if it has entered a nonexclusive patent license.[575] The nonexclusive licensee, however, has no standing to sue for infringement.[576] Nonexclusive licenses are a "waiver of infringement under the licensed invention."[577] Depending on SPC's business objectives, a nonexclusive license may be an optimum solution in that it permits royalty streams while maintaining control over the invention.

The patent license agreement sets the term of the license and conditions of use for patented technology.[578] The nonexclusive license permits SPC to use its own technology and to license it to any number of other licensees in the global marketplace. It is the exclusive licensee's responsibility to file an infringement claim. The "field of use" exception permits an exclusive licensor to be named as an unwilling party in an infringement action. The disadvantage, however, is that SPC will need to initiate and pay for the considerable costs of an infringement lawsuit. SPC should choose the form of its licensing agreements based upon its business goals. If the goal is to maximize royalties, SPC may wish to enter an exclusive license or to sell its patent.

SPC needs a strategy to manage its patent portfolio for the purposes of commercialization of its invention. Antitrust issues often go hand in hand with licensing. SPC faces the possibility of violating antitrust laws if it is too aggressive in its pursuit of market control. Courts look at the following factors in determining whether a company has too much market power: "(1) when the government has granted the seller a patent or similar monopoly over a product; (2) when the seller's share of the market is high; and (3) when the seller offers a unique product that competitors are not able to offer."[579]

SPC seeks to balance antitrust concerns against market dominance in managing its e-business patents.[580] SPC's legal audit should take into consideration the advantages such as "goodwill, skilled personnel, well established distribution channels, access to raw materials and economies of scale."[581] SPC will use its

---

[573] *See, e.g.,* L.L. Brown Paper Co. v. Hydroloid, Inc., 32 F. Supp. 857, 44 U.S.P.Q. 655 (S.D.N.Y. 1939).

[574] Harold Einhorn, Patent Licensing Transaction, *id.*

[575] Ortho Pharmaceutical v. Genetics Institute, 52 F. 3d. 1026, 34 U.S.P.Q. 2d 1444 (Fed. Cir. 1995).

[576] *Id.*

[577] *See supra* note 573.

[578] Fariba Rad, The New Role of MBA in Licensing, Intellectual Property Today, *id.*

[579] Tominga, 682 F. Supp. at 1493; Mozart Co., 833 F.2d at 1345-46.

[580] Fariba Rad, *supra* note 578.

[581] Thomas G. Field, Jr., Seeking Cost-Effective Patents, Franklin Pierce Law Center (visited Feb. 28, 2000), www.fplc.edu/TFIELD/sEeking.htm.

patent licensing audit as a basis for "developing and prototyping, and securing broad patent coverage, and marketing to qualified licensees."[582]

§ 4.06   GLOBALIZATION OF INTELLECTUAL PROPERTY RIGHTS

E-businesses must be concerned with international protection of intellectual property. Country-specific regimes only have jurisdiction over acts committed in the individual nation-state. French courts, for example, apply French trademark law in resolving domain name disputes.[583] Intellectual property rights are obtained separately in every nation state where protection is desired. In the "brick and mortar" world, corporations must obtain trademarks for overseas operations. McDonald's invests an average of $900 million each year in promoting its 14,000 restaurants in more than 70 countries.[584]

McDonald's trademarks and logos are registered in the individual countries where it desires protection.[585] Internet companies need to protect their marks against local companies in essential countries. Since there is no single international agency, the owner of intellectual property must seek protection in each country.

[A]   World Intellectual Property Organization (WIPO)

The World Intellectual Property Organization (WIPO) is an agency of the United Nations "dedicated to helping to ensure that the rights of creators and owners of intellectual property are protected worldwide."[586] With the rise of the Internet, WIPO is increasingly important in protecting intellectual property rights. The globalization of trade that occurs with the rise of e-commerce has made harmonization of intellectual property rights more critical. There are 171 member-states

---

[582] Frederic P. Zotos, Unlocking the Potential of Innovations, Intel. Prop. Today, July 1997 (visited March 1, 2000), http://www.lawworks-iUSPTOday.com/07-97/zotos.htm.

[583] Andre Bertrand, Recent Developments in French Cyberspace Litigation, 3 Cyber. Law 12 (Jan. 1999 (discussing French cases such as Saint Tropez v. Eurovirtuel, TGI de Draguignan 21 Aout 1997, PIBD, 1997, Ill, 588, Les Petites Affiches 9 mars 1998 n [degrees] 29 anote Drefus-Weill (holding that web page www.saint.tropez infringed the name of the city of Saint-Tropez).

[584] Anthony D'Amato and Doris Estelle Long, International Intellectual Property Law 348 (1999).

[585] McDonald's sought protection for its trademarks in South Africa, for example. In the lower court, McDonald's Corporation lost its claim to its well-known trademarks because McDonald's marks were already registered by lesser known local South African companies. A South African Appellate Court reversed the lower court holding that McDonald's Corporation could introduce survey research to establish that its marks were well known in many sectors of South Africa. *Id.* at 344-348.

[586] World Intellectual Property Organization, An Organization for the Future (visited Jan. 17, 2000), http://www.wipo.org/eng/infbroch/infbro99.htm#P23_2347.

of WIPO, representing 90 percent of the countries of the world.[587] WIPO has succeeded in helping to harmonize diverse intellectual property regimes.

WIPO entered a cooperative agreement with the World Trade Organization (WTO) in 1996[588] and is also the sponsoring agency behind the influential Madrid Agreement.[589] As e-commerce expands, WIPO will play an even more significant role in harmonizing Internet-related intellectual property rules.

WIPO presently has 171 member states and is responsible for administering 21 treaties. WIPO's general polices are to harmonize national intellectual property legislation and procedures, facilitate trade, and the exchange intellectual property information. WIPO seeks to provide legal and technical assistance to developing and other countries in the following ways:[590]

- Harmonize national intellectual property legislation and procedures.

- Provide services for international applications for industrial property rights.

- Exchange intellectual property information.

- Provide legal and technical assistance to developing and other countries.

- Facilitate the resolution of private intellectual property disputes.

- Marshall information technology as a tool for storing, accessing, and using valuable intellectual property information.[591]

[B] Copyright and National Origin of the Work

Copyright protection is available for all unpublished works, regardless of the nationality or domicile of the author. Published works are eligible for copyright protection in the United States if *any* of the following conditions is met:

1) On the date of first publication, one or more of the authors is a national or domiciliary of the United States, or is a national, domiciliary, or

---

[587] *Id.*

[588] The United States is a World Trade Organization (WTO) member and a signatory to the Berne Convention.

[589] The Madrid Agreement concerning the international registration of marks and the protocol relating to that agreement is not in effect in 52 countries. *See* World Intellectual Property Organization, International Protection of Industrial Property Introduction (visited Jan. 17, 2000), http://www.wipo.int/eng/general/ipip/intro.htm.

[590] WIPO critics assert that the agency is superimposing the cultural and legal values of the United States and other countries on less developed countries.

[591] World Intellectual Property Organization, WIPO Today (visited Jan. 17, 2000), http://www.wipo.org/eng/infbroch/infbro99.htm#P52_8261.

sovereign authority of a treaty party, or is a stateless person wherever that person may be.

2) The work is first published in the United States or in a foreign nation, that, on the date of first publication, is a treaty party. For purposes of this condition, a work that is published in the United States or a treaty party within 30 days after publication in a foreign nation that is not a treaty party shall be considered to be first published in the United States or such treaty party, as the case may be; or

3) The work is a sound recording that was first fixed in a treaty party; or

4) The work is a pictorial, graphic, or sculptural work that is incorporated in a building or other structure, or an architectural work that is embodied in a building and the building or structure is located in the United States or a treaty party; or

5) The work is first published by the United Nations or any of its specialized agencies, or by the Organization of American States; or

6) The work is a foreign work that was in the public domain in the United States before 1996 and its copyright was restored under the Uruguay Round Agreements Act (URAA). Request *Circular 38b,* "Highlights of Copyright Amendments Contained in the Uruguay Round Agreements Act (URAA-GATT)," for further information.

Title I of the Digital Millennium Copyright Act of 1998 (DMCA) amends the 1976 Copyright Act so that the United States complies with the World Intellectual Property Organization (WIPO) Copyright Treaty agreed to in December 1996. The DMCA also contains conforming amendments so that United States copyright law is harmonized with the WIPO Performances and Phonograms Treaty enacted on the same day as the copyright treaty.[592]

§ 4.07   WEB SITE INTELLECTUAL PROPERTY AUDIT[593]

Before a company—such as our hypothetical SPC—launches a web site, it needs to complete an audit to protect its intellectual property and to avoid infringing the rights of others. A legal audit for intellectual property in cyberspace begins with SPC's survey of what property it owns. SPC needs to view content on its web site as one of the intangible assets that fuel its dot-com business activities. What

---

[592] The "Geneva Phonograms Convention" is the Convention for the Protection of Producers of Phonograms Against Unauthorized Duplication of Their Phonograms, concluded at Geneva, Switzerland, on October 29, 1971.

[593] Amy P. Wilson, Esquire, who served as Professor Rustad's research assistant in spring 1999, researched the practice pointers in this section.

types of intellectual property are used in SPC's online business? What steps has SPC taken to protect each intellectual property right? SPC's goal is to maximize the value from its intellectual property assets. SPC needs to complete a web site audit of its own intellectual property as well as of its exposure to infringement claims for intellectual property owned by third parties.

Does SPC, for example, own the HTML code that comprises its site? If outside web site consultants and designers have been used, does SPC have assignments or work-for-hire agreements with them? The intellectual property owned by SPC has, potentially, diverse sources. SPC may choose to use software license agreements to protect its software, such as diskettes or CDs. If software is downloaded directly from its web site, SPC will need to enter web wrap or "click through" license agreements. If SPC's site is co-branded with a co-venturer, who owns the content? Does SPC have clearance to use the trademarks and trade name of its co-venturer? Has SPC spelled out the uses that can be made of its own trademarks and trade names? All of these questions must be considered.

Preventive law should be the focus of a intellectual property audit undertaken prior to launching a web site.[594] Preventive law is the fence at the top of the cliff versus the ambulance in the valley below. What are the specific hazards and risks that SPC should consider before engaging in online commercial transactions? SPC could lose millions of dollars from the infringement of a company's literary or artistic works. SPC should also be concerned with the tarnishment, or dilution, of its corporate name and reputation as well as dilution or tarnishment of its trade name, trademarks, or service marks when it becomes a dot-com company.

A legal audit of SPC's intellectual property also "endeavors to identify legal soft spots and [the need for] legal improvements."[595] SPC's legal audit is particularly warranted when trying to avoid legal trouble with intellectual property in cyberspace. The SPC web site may contain pictures of famous movie stores or content belonging to third parties. If this content is in the public domain, however, it may be used without permission.

[A] Risk/Exposure Analysis

SPC's web sit exposes it to the risk of trademark infringement, copyright violations, trade secret misappropriation, and related risks. SPC should also use a search service to determine whether others are infringing on its intellectual property. SPC must monitor the use by others of its trademarks, copyrighted materials, patents, and trade secrets.

---

[594] It is an open question whether a web site needs to exist to be sued for trademark infringement.

[595] Louis Brown, Preventive Law, Glossary, Part II, Prevent. L. Rptr., Sept. 1988, at 19.

[1]   Internet Copyright Issues

1. Are works displayed on SPC's web site protected by copyrights held by third parties? The display of content on a computer screen is in a sufficiently fixed medium of expression to qualify for copyright protection. The existence of any of the following should be noted:

    (a) Music;
    (b) Text;
    (c) Video-clips;
    (d) Software code;
    (e) Graphics;
    (f) Photographs;
    (g) Audio; and
    (h) Streaming video.

2. Does SPC.com have a "terms and conditions of use" agreement? Does the agreement use a clickwrap or webwrap agreement such as the following?

> By using the SPC web site, you signify your agreement to all terms, conditions, and notices contained or referenced herein (SPC's "Terms of Use"). If you do not agree to SPC's terms of use, please do not use this site. SPC reserves the right to update or revise the SPC Terms of Use. Please check the SPC Terms of Use periodically for changes. Your use of the SPC site following posting of the changes at the Terms of Use page constitutes your acceptance of those changes.

3. Does SPC give notice that copyrights, trademarks, service marks, patents, trade secrets, or other proprietary rights protect all content and materials on its sites?

4. Does SPC give a limited license to use content? SPC should require that visitors warrant or represent that they will not "distribute, copy, reproduce, transmit, publicly display, publicly perform, publish, adapt, edit, or create derivative works from materials or content on SPC's web site."[596]

5. If SPC's web site permits visitors to post or submit content to designated pages on its site, does SPC obtain a limited license to use, reproduce, display, perform, adapt, modify, distribute, have distributed and promote the content in any form, anywhere, and for any purpose?[597]

6. Does SPC require its web site visitor who posts materials to warrant that the materials do not infringe the copyright or other rights of any third party?

---

[596] This clause is adapted from AOL.com, AOL.com Terms and Conditions of Use (visited Apr. 21, 2000), http://www.aol.com/copyright.html.

[597] *Id.*

> By posting materials on the [SPC] web site, you warrant and represent that you own or otherwise control all the rights to the content and that public posting and use of your content by America Online will not infringe or violate the rights of any third party.[598]

7. Does SPC disclaim warranties and limit liability for its products, services, and content? Many web sites use UCC Article 2 methods for disclaiming warranties. The "as is" or "without all faults" disclaimer effectively disclaims the implied warranty of merchantability. SPC should, however, specifically exclude warranties of title, merchantability, and fitness for a particular purpose as well as liability for the infringement of third party's intellectual property rights. SPC should give no warranty as to the accuracy of content.

> SPC [and its subsidiaries, joint venturers etc] do not warrant that the content on its web site is accurate, reliable, or correct. SPC makes no warranty that content will be available at a given time or location. SPC also makes no warranty that its content is free of viruses or other harmful components. Your use of SPC content is at your own risk.[599]

8. Does SPC limit its liability for content supplied by others? SPC must also limit the liability of its subsidiaries for incidental, consequential, noneconomic, direct, indirect, special, or other damages resulting from the use of content. It is important for SPC to disclaim consequential damages as well as incidental damages. The limitation should also mention that SPC is not liable for damages under contract (that is, UCC, common law, Convention for the International Sale of Goods) tort, strict liability, or any other cause of action. SPC should also post a notice that some jurisdictions do not allow the exclusion of limitation of incidental or consequential damages.[600]

9. Has SPC sought indemnification from web site visitors that post content to its site? SPC should require web site visitors who post content to indemnify and hold harmless SPC and its subsidiaries (affiliated companies, employees, contractors, officers, directors, and so on) for any liabilities, claims, or expenses that arise from a users' violation of the terms of use or their misuse of the site. SPC should reserve the right to assume the exclusive control of the defense, subject to indemnification. Visitors should guarantee that they will cooperate with SPC in asserting any available defense.[601]

---

[598] *Id.*

[599] This clause is modeled after AOL.com's disclaimer of warranty in AOL.com Terms and Conditions of Use, *Id.*

[600] Massachusetts' UCC 2-316A of chapter 106 does not permit sellers to disclaim implied warranties of merchantability in consumer sales. The Magnuson-Moss federal warranty act permits sellers of consumer to limit the duration, but not to disclaim the implied warranty of merchantability entirely.

[601] AOL.com, Terms of Use, *supra* note 599.

10. Is the content sufficiently original to qualify for copyright protection? Databases may lack the originality necessary to qualify for protection, but they may be protected by license agreements governing access and conditions of use.

11. Who owns the copyrighted material? If SPC employees have produced work, is it within their scope of employment to qualify as a work made for hire? If independent contractors produce web site content, does SPC have permission to use the work?

12. Has work produced by independent contractors been assigned, transferred, or purchased by SPC? SPC needs agreements, assignments, or transfers of the right to use content created by third parties unless covered by the work for hire doctrine.

13. Is SPC a joint author with another entity or person? If SPC produces a web site in partnership with another entity, the site may be classified as a joint work. SPC must enter an agreement setting forth the rights of joint authors.

14. Have all text, images, and other copyrighted materials been cleared for copyright ownership? Does SPC have a license or assignment to use copyrighted materials posted on its web site but belonging to others? If SPC does not own or license content, it must not post content on its web site unless it is in the public domain or protected by fair defense. If content is not owned, licensed, or assigned, it may be displayed if it is in the public domain or covered by the defense of fair use.

15. Is posted content public domain material not protected by the U.S. Copyright Act?[602]

16. Is SPC claiming fair use for materials not covered by its own copyrights? Is SPC's use of the copyrighted materials commercial or noncommercial? What is the nature of the work? What is the amount or substantiality of the portion of the work displayed on SPC's web site? What is the potential effect of SPC's copying on the potential market for the materials?

17. Is there a copyright notice on SPC's web site and on all of its web pages? Notices need to be included for text, graphics, music, video, and all other copyrightable materials. In addition, a notice of copyright should cover the graphics, selection, arrangement, and overall design of the SPC web site.

18. Does SPC have a designated agent and posted contact information, to comply with the ISP safe harbor provisions of the Digital Millennium Copyright Act (DMCA)? Does SPC qualify as a provider for the limitation on liability for caching, storing, or routing copyrighted materials owned by third parties?

---

[602] Government reports, such as White Papers produced by the Department of Commerce or Copyright Office, may be published without permission, as they are in the public domain. The Copyright Office, for example, has a list of photographs in the public domain.

19. Does SPC have a linking, framing, and metatag policy posted on its web site? Does SPC freely permit linking, or does it require linkers to meet certain conditions? Is framing or deep linking prohibited in the absence of agreement?

20. Does SPC monitor the Internet for copyright infringement? Does SPC protect itself against copyright infringement by including digital watermarks in its materials or other technological devices to monitor copyright use?

21. Is SPC using likenesses, voices, or images of famous personalities or celebrities? Have rights of publicity been cleared?

22. Do copyrighted photographs depict nonfamous SPC employees or non-employees? If so, have the right to use these photographs been cleared to avoid invasion of privacy or false light lawsuits?

23. The digitalization of a photograph, for example, arguably modifies an author's moral right against modification. Do agreements to purchase copyright also include waivers of the authors' moral rights? It may be advisable to include an "international use" clause, such as the following, in the terms of use.

> SPC makes no representations that materials in this site are appropriate or available for use in locations outside the United States, and accessing them from territories where contents are illegal is prohibited. Those visitors who choose to access this site from locations outside the United States do so on their own initiative and are responsible for compliance with local laws.[603]

24. Does the copyrighted material comply with language restrictions? Web sites originating in Quebec or France, for example, must include a French language translation. If there is no French translation, the international use notice should state that SPC makes no representation that materials from its site are appropriate for or available in Quebec or France.

25. Are databases protected and licensed by a separate license agreement setting forth terms and conditions of use?

26. Does SPC have a choice of law and forum clause that takes into account intellectual property rights? The choice of law and forum clause makes the user's web site activity conditional on agreeing to an exclusive jurisdiction in the event of a claim or action arising out of use of the web site.

27. Does the Uniform Computer Information Transactions Act (UCITA) apply to a terms of services agreement? UCITA limits the licensor's discretion in choice of law and forum for consumer licensees.

28. Has SPC reserved the right to terminate a user's access to the web site or to remove content posted by visitors? SPC should also reserve the complete discretion to cancel access to the site as a self-help remedy. SPC should also warn

---

[603] AOL.com, Terms of Use, *supra* note 599.

users that it has the discretion to remove posted material that is potentially infringing or illegal.[604] Yahoo! reserves the right to "terminate the accounts of users who infringe the intellectual property rights of others."[605] SPC's "copyrights and copyright agent" clause, below, is based upon the Yahoo! terms of service agreement.

> If you believe that your work has been copied in a way that constitutes copyright infringement, please provide SPC's Copyright Agent the following information:
>
> 1. An electronic or physical signature of the person authorized to act on behalf of the owner of the copyright interest;
> 2. A description of the copyrighted work that you claim or believe has been infringed;
> 3. A description of where the material that you claim is infringing is located on the site;
> 4. Your address, telephone number, and e-mail address;
> 5. A statement by you that you have a good faith belief that the disputed use is not authorized by the copyright owner, its agent, or the law;
> 6. A statement by you, made under penalty of perjury, that the above information in your Copyright Infringement Notice is accurate and that you are the copyright owner or are authorized to act on the copyright owner's behalf. SPC's Copyright Agent for Notice of claims of copyright infringement can be reached as follows:
>
> By mail:
> Michael L. Rustad
> 120 Tremont Street
> Boston, Massachusetts 02108-4977
> By telephone: 617-573-8190
> By fax: 617-305-3079
> By e-mail: profrustad@aol.com

29. Has SPC obtained permission to post electronic postings for print publications? SPC should update each of its grants-of-copyright agreements to include electronic or Internet-related publishing as well as other media, such as CD-ROMS or technologies yet to be developed. The purpose of this clause is to avoid copyright infringement lawsuits by including print publication in electronic databases.

30. Does the Terms of Service Agreement warn users about posting content that is illegal, infringing, harmful, threatening, abusive, defamatory, obscene, hateful, or otherwise objectionable?

---

[604] The Digital Millennium Copyright Act gives the provider a statutory right to remove potentially infringing materials.

[605] Yahoo!, Yahoo! Copyrights and Copyright Agent (visited Apr. 21, 2000), http://docs.yahoo.com/info/copyright/copyright.html.

31. Are there any moral rights in copyrighted works created for SPC's web site? Has SPC entered an agreement with the creator to alter or modify works on its web site?

32. Does an infringing web site violate criminal law for criminal copyright infringement?

[2] Trademark Ownership

1. Has SPC registered all of its online trademarks, service marks, or certification marks? Have any of SPC's trademarks been registered at the state level? Are the marks distinctive, or have they acquired secondary meaning?

2. Are the words descriptive of the trademark's goods or services so that they will not qualify for protection? Descriptive terms are not protectable unless invested with secondary meaning acquired by use in commerce.

3. Are these marks distinctive enough to qualify for trademark protection? The domain name *http://www.computers.com* is inherently generic and therefore can never be registered as a trademark. Can secondary meaning be built up with descriptive marks through online advertising, promotions, or other publicity?

4. Are any of SPC's trademarks confusingly similar to another party's mark? What is the strength of SPC's mark? What is the similarity of the mark to a senior mark used on the Internet? Is there evidence of actual confusion? What is the likelihood of confusion on the Internet?

5. Has SPC conducted a search to determine whether trademarks are available? Has SPC completed an Internet-based search as well as a search of USPTO's database?

6. Has SPC filed trademark applications for each of its marks? SPC may consider applying for trademark protection for its domain name. SPC's applications may be based upon "actual use" or "intent to use."

7. Have SPC's marks been examined by the USPTO? Have SPC's marks been published in the *Trademark Gazette*? Have the trademarks been challenged in the opposition period?

8. Has SPC posted trademark notices for each of its trademarks, service marks, certification marks, or collective marks?

9. Are SPC's trademarks used as keywords for banner advertisements in third party Internet search engines?[606] If so, is this an infringing use of the trademarks?

10. Are third parties using marks identical to or confusingly similar to SPC's trademarks?

---

[606] P.T. Barnum advised "Advertise your business. I owe all my success to printer's ink." Banner advertisements are the online functional equivalent of printer's ink.

11. Are competitors using SPC's marks in a way that blurs the distinctiveness of its marks or tarnishes the mark?

12. Does SPC's mark qualify as a famous mark, so that it may obtain federal antidilution action?

13. If SPC's marks do not qualify for federal antidilution protection, are they protected by state antidilution statutes or the common law?[607]

14. May injunctive relief or damages be recovered under the Federal Trademark Dilution Act of 1995?[608]

15. Is SPC using its trademarks to sell goods or services? Whether an action is for infringement or dilution, a plaintiff must prove that its trademark (1) is used in commerce; (2) is nonfunctional; and (3) is distinctive.[609]

16. Is SPC using the registration symbol, ®, for its online brands? SPC may only use the symbol when its mark has been registered in the USPTO. It is improper to use this symbol at any point before the registration issues.

17. Is the registration symbol, ®, used in SPC's trademark applications? SPC should not use the registration symbol mark in a drawing submitted with an application; the symbol is not considered part of the mark.

18. If the metatags of other parties are critical to SPC's marketing plan, it must enter co-branding or license agreements to use those metatags.

19. Is SPC granting the right to license its trademarks on another party's web site? What conditions are placed on the other party's use of SPC's trademarks? Does the license include notice of trademarks and service marks?

20. Does SPC monitor the Internet to determine whether its trademarks are properly used? One danger is that distinctive trademarks may be become genericized. Aspirin is an example of a once distinctive trademark that has lost its ability to distinguish the source of goods. Are competitors or others using SPC trademarks in a manner that will tarnish or blur its marks? Are competitors copying SPC web site interfaces and the "look and feel" of the site in a way that constitutes trade dress infringement? Is the competitive web site similar to SPC's site in its use of video, graphics, colors, background, and overall web site design?

---

[607] Most states have antidilution statutes, which protect the distinctive quality of trademarks. California, for example, provides protection against injuries to business reputation, or dilution, even "in the absence of competition between the parties or the absence of confusion as to the source of goods or services." Cal. Bus. & Prof. Code § 14330 (1999).

[608] The federal act requires that the plaintiff prove that "(1) its mark is famous; (2) defendant is making commercial use of the mark in commerce; (3) the defendant's use began after the plaintiff's mark became famous; and (4) the defendant's use presents a likelihood of dilution of the distinctive value of the mark." Panavision Int'l, L.P. v. Toeppen, 141 F.3d 1316, 1324 (9th Cir. 1998) (interpreting 15 U.S.C. § 1125(c)(1)).

[609] I.P. Lund Trading v. Kohler Co., 163 F.3d 27, 36 (1st Cir. 1999).

21. Are competitors using SPC marks in a way that constitutes unfair competition by falsely inferring origin?

22. Has a competitor removed SPC's trademarks from copyrighted material, a practice that may constitute unfair competition as "reverse passing off"?

23. Does SPC have state remedies for dilution or unfair competition, in addition to Lanham Act remedies?

24. Are there any other potential defendants who may be charged with either contributory infringement or vicarious infringement?

25. Are competitors using SPC's marks in a manner that may be defended on the grounds of "fair use"? SPC's trademarks, for example, may be referred to in a comparative advertisement on a competitor's web site. Noncommercial use of SPC marks in online publications is protected by fair use.

[3]   Avoiding Trademark Infringement in Cyberspace

1. Is SPC using another entity's trademark, trade name, or trade dress on its web site?

2. Has SPC obtained authorization or licenses to use another's trademark, trade name, or trade dress?

3. Is SPC's use of trademarks, trade names, or trade dress protected by "fair use"?

4. Is SPC's use of trademarks, trade names, or trade dress covered by a license agreement?

[4]   Domain Names in Cyberspace

1. Has SPC registered its domain name with an ICANN accredited registry? All registrars in the .com top-level domains follow the Uniform Domain Name Dispute Resolution Policy?

2. If SPC's domain name is being used by a cybersquatter or other abusive registration, will the company submit a complaint to the approved dispute-resolution service provider?

3. Does SPC have a cause of action under the Anticybersquatting Consumer Protection Act of 1999, the Federal Antidilution Act or under Section 43(a) of the Lanham Act?

[5]   Clearance of Publicity Rights

1. Have releases been obtained for any commercial uses of the right of publicity (name or likeness of individuals) for content on the web site?

2. Have releases been obtained for electronic reproduction rights for any photographs of identifiable persons?

[6]   Trade Secret Preventive Law

1. A trade secret is information has potential or actual value in SPC's business and must be kept secret. Does SPC have a company-wide trade secret protection program? What steps has SPC taken to avoid the disclosure of trade secrets on the Internet?

2. What limitations have been placed on the time of nondisclosure?

3. Have all employees signed nondisclosure agreements reasonable in duration and scope? Have departing employees been briefed on the continuing duty of confidentiality?

4. Have reasonable security precautions been implemented to encrypt confidential information? Have legends of confidentiality been applied to data and other information considered to be trade secrets?

5. Have reasonable steps been taken to prevent the inadvertent disclosure of trade secrets or patentable technologies disclosed on SPC's web site?

6. Does SPC avoid misappropriating the trade secrets of others or acquiring confidential information by improper means?

7. Does SPC's employee handbook, personnel policies, and training all emphasize the continuing obligation of confidentiality and nondisclosure?

8. Does an instance of theft of trade secrets violate criminal law, such as the Economic Espionage Act of 1996? Have public authorities been contacted?

9. What steps have been taken to prevent the publication of trade secrets on the Internet which publication would make these secrets generally known?[610]

[7]   Linking or Framing Agreements

1. Has SPC monitored links to its site to determine whether any of the links tarnish the company's reputation?

2. Does SPC reserve the right to enter licensing agreements to link or frame third party's sites? Simple linking probably does not require a licensing agreement, but deep linking or framing may be an infringement of a third party's intellectual property rights or a business tort. SPC needs to monitor the Internet to detect unauthorized framing or deep linking.

[8]   Indemnification from Content Providers and Third Parties

1. Does SPC enter indemnification and hold harmless agreements with content providers, joint venturers, web designers, and other parties providing content or developing its site?

---

[610] Central Point Software v. Nugent, 903 F. Supp. 1057 (E.D. Tex. 1995) (posting of software to computer bulletin board destroyed trade secret).

2. Is an indemnification clause included on SPC's "terms and services" agreement? If SPC permits outside parties to post information to the web site, is there a notice that the company is not liable for third party infringement?

3. Has SPC sought indemnification for third parties for any infringement actions arising out of content provided by them?

[9]   E-Commerce Patents

1. Does SPC's site publish information about its e-business inventions that would cause it to be bared from obtaining a U.S. patent under 35 U.S.C. sec. 102(b)? Internet publicity about inventions may be construed as prior art triggering the statutory bar under Section 102(b).

2. Has SPC posted materials on its web site that may create a risk of the statutory prepublication bar to obtaining a patent?

3. Has SPC obtained a license to use another's e-commerce business method covered by a patent?

4. Is SPC's use of e-commerce business methods noninfringing?

[B]   Licensing Intellectual Property

SPC will use licensing agreements as the principal tool with which it protects its intellectual property rights and avoids infringing the rights of third parties. "A license is a contract by which the owner of an intellectual property right (such as a patented invention) conveys to another the right to make, use, and/or sell the intellectual property. In return, the owner receives financial or other consideration, typically a share of the revenues or profits."[611] SPC should consider entering agreements with content providers to share revenue generated through a web site linked to a content area.[612]

1. Do SPC's license agreements clearly specify what intellectual property rights are granted, the term of the license agreement, geographic restrictions, reverse engineering restrictions, assignability, warranties, remedies, events of default, and method of termination? With multimedia licenses, it is necessary to obtain permission to use video, sound, text, and images.

2. Has SPC determined which party owns the content on its web site? A web site with hundreds of thousands of pages presents the challenge of determining which rights have to be cleared. SPC will typically license content from third

---

[611] Stites & Harbison, Licensing Your Intellectual Property Rights (June 1999), http://www.iplawky.com/wcsb/licensin.htm.

[612] Adam H. Lehman, Negotiating Content and Interactive Services Agreements, American Bar Association Section of Business Law (Aug. 5, 1996) (providing guidelines for the essential terms of content and distribution license agreements).

parties or enter agreements with parties who will provide content as well as web site design. A traditional print media disseminator may grant the service provider the right to distribute a magazine or newspaper.

[C] Web Site Development

Companies with web sites may decide to outsource the development of the web site, in which case the following questions should be considered.

1. Who owns the trade dress of the web site?
2. Who owns the information posted on the web site?
3. Is the web site a "work for hire?"
4. What will the developer own?
5. Who is responsible for obtaining license agreements for information posted on the web site?
6. If a company has a license agreement to use information, does the scope of the license cover posting information on a web site?
7. Does a company care that its content is copied from the web site?
8. If a developer provides content, will the developer indemnify the company for any third party infringement lawsuits?

[D] Sample Content License Agreement

The following agreement, annotated with comments, is a sample agreement entered into between SPC and a content provider.

SAMPLE AGREEMENT

This agreement ("Agreement") is entered into as of the _____ day of [month, year] ("Effective Date"), by and between SPC, a Massachusetts Corporation, located at 120 Tremont Street, Boston, Massachusetts 02108-4977 ("SPC") and XYZ Content Provider, a _____ [state], located at [address] ("Content Provider").[613]

I. RECITALS[614]

A. SPC maintains a web site on the Internet ("SPC.com"). SPC's site allows its users to search for and access content, an online catalogue, as well as providing other sites on the Internet.

---

[613] It is important to specify the effective date of the agreement. If the beginning and termination dates are available, both dates should be stated. It is also essential to specify who is bound by the agreement.

[614] The recitals are treated as part of the agreement and provide context for interpreting the license. The recitals should state the objectives for the agreement.

    B. Content Provider owns or has the right to distribute certain software content and maintains a related site on the Internet.

    C. SPC and Content Provider wish to distribute content provider's software-related content through the SPC web site.

II. AGREEMENT[615]

Therefore, the parties agree as follows:

A. CONTENT PROVIDED TO SPC

    (1) Content provider will provide to SPC the content described in Exhibit A ("software-related content"). The software-related content will comply with the description in Exhibit A. The Content Provider, however, does not warrant that the content is error free, only that the content complies with the description and technical specifications in Exhibit A.

    (2) SPC may incorporate the software-related content on its web site.

B. CONTENT OWNERSHIP AND LICENSE AGREEMENT

    (1) Content Provider retains all rights, title and interest in and to the software-related content worldwide (including all Intellectual Property rights). Content Provider hereby grants SPC a nonexclusive, worldwide license to use, reproduce, distribute, transmit, and publicly display the Content in accordance with this agreement. Content Provider also grants SPC the nonexclusive right to sub-license Content to its wholly owned subsidiaries and to joint ventures in which SPC participates for the sole purpose of using, reproducing, distributing, transmitting, and publicly displaying the Content in accordance with this Agreement.

    (2) SPC will retain all right, title, and interest in and to the SPC web site and all of its pages worldwide (including, but not limited to, ownership of all copyrights, the look and feel of its web site, trademarks, trade names, logos, patents, the right of publicity, and all other intellectual property rights).[616]

C. TRADEMARK OWNERSHIP AND LICENSE

    (1) Content Provider will retain all right, title, and interest in and to its trademarks, services marks, and trade names worldwide, including any goodwill associated therewith, subject to the limited license

---

[615] The agreement is the heart of the license, which states a present intention to be bound, and the consideration, which may be the form of mutual promises.

[616] It is also advisable to include definitions and rules of construction for the agreement. Definitions of intellectual property rights, enhancements, derivative works, SPC brands, and other properties should be specified.

granted to SPC hereunder. Any use of any such trademarks by SPC shall inure to the benefit of Content Provider.

(2) SPC agrees not to take any action inconsistent with Content Provider's trademark ownership.

(3) SPC retains all rights, title and interest in its trademarks, service marks, and trade names worldwide, and in addition, certification marks worldwide, including any good will associated with its rights. Any use of SPC's trademarks by Content Provider shall inure to the benefit of SPC. Content Provider agrees not to take any action inconsistent with SPC's trademark ownership.

(4) The parties grant to the other, a nonexclusive, limited license to use its trademarks, service marks, or certification marks only as specifically described in this agreement.

(5) Upon termination of this agreement, SPC and Content Provider agree to cease using the other party's trademarks, service marks, certification marks, and trade names, except as the parties agree in writing.[617]

D. TERM AND TERMINATION

Initial Term. The initial term of this Agreement will begin on the Effective Date and will end on _____ [date] _____ unless automatically terminated by an Event of Termination.

(1) **Events of Automatic Termination**

   (a) This Agreement will terminate automatically if SPC no longer sells software at its web site or an equivalent web site.

   (b) This Agreement will terminate automatically if SPC no longer supports its web site or an equivalent web site.

II. EVENTS OF TERMINATION BY MATERIAL BREACH

A. Termination Due to Breach. Either party may terminate this Agreement, effective upon thirty (30) days' written notice, if the other party fails to cure any material breach of its obligations under this Agreement within thirty (30) days following written notice to such party.

B. A material breach occurs if there are two or more material errors, failures, or outages of the Content in any thirty (30) day period. SPC may elect to immediately terminate this agreement upon written notice to Content

---

[617] The grant of rights clause should spell out what is granted and what is not granted in a content license agreement. It is important that the parties acknowledge who has the rights, title, and interest in SPC brand features, trademarks, and trade names.

Provider. In addition, SPC may enter into other arrangements for the acquisition of similar content.

C. A material breach occurs if SPC fails to pay it licensing fees within 30 days after being billed. If the agreement is terminated, SPC is responsible for any unpaid licensing fees.

D. Upon termination of this agreement, SPC agrees to purge Content Provider's software-related content from its web site. SPC must delete or purge all content within 7 days of the termination of this agreement.

E. SPC may retain Content in its off-site storage network archive for regulatory or other purposes related to the archiving of information and not for redistribution or use of the content therein.

III. REPRESENTATIONS AND WARRANTIES

A. Each party to this Agreement represents and warrants to the other party that: (1) such party has the full corporate right, power, and authority to enter into this Agreement and to perform the acts required of it hereunder; (2) the execution of this Agreement by such party, and the performance by such party of its obligations and duties hereunder, do not and will not violate any agreement to which such party is a party or by which it is otherwise bound; and (3) when executed and delivered by such party, this Agreement will constitute the legal, valid, and binding obligation of such party, enforceable against such party in accordance with its terms.

B. Content Provider warrants that it owns, or has obtained the right to distribute and make available as specified in this Agreement, any and all Content provided to SPC as described in Exhibit A.

C. Except for the Content, SPC warrants that it owns, or has obtained the right to distribute the material on its web site.

IV. INDEMNIFICATION

Each party will indemnify the other party and its customers and affiliates for, and hold them harmless from, any loss, expense (including reasonable attorneys' fees and court costs), damage or liability arising out of any claim, demand or suit resulting from (a) a breach of any of its respective covenants or warranties under this Agreement, (b) the failure of such party to have all rights and authority necessary in order to fulfill or perform its obligations pursuant to this Agreement in compliance with applicable laws; and (c) the infringement of intellectual property rights of any third party or the violation of any law by such parties' contributions and/or performance here under (e.g., in the case of SPC.com and the Content Provider's software-related content described in Exhibit A).

SPC will indemnify, defend and hold harmless Content provider, its affiliates, officers, directors, employees, consultants, and agent from any and all third party claims, liability, damages, and/or costs (including but not limited to attorneys' fees) arising from:

(i)   Its breach of any warranty, representation or covenant in this agreement;

(ii)   or any claim arising from content displayed on SPC.com from any modification made to the content by SPC or by content provider at the direction of SPC.

(iii)   Content provider will promptly notify SPC of any and all such claims and will reasonably cooperate with SPC with their defense and/or settlement. The defense and settlement will be controlled by SPC.

        Content provider will indemnify, defend and hold harmless SPC, its affiliates, officers, directors, employees, consultants, and agent from any and all third party claims, liability, damages, and/or costs (including but not limited to attorneys' fees) arising from:

(iv)   Its breach of any warranty, representation, or covenant in this agreement.

(v)   Alternatively, any claim arising from content provided by Content Provider displayed at the SPC web site.

(vi)   Any claim that the content infringes or violates any third party's copyright, patent, trade secret, trademark, right of publicity, or right of privacy, or contains any defamatory content.

(vii)   SPC will promptly notify Content Provider of any and all such claims and will reasonably cooperate with Content Provider with the defense and/or settlement. Content Provider will control its defense and settlement.

(viii) As a condition to indemnification, (a) the indemnified party will promptly inform the indemnifying party in writing of any such claim, demand, or suit, and the indemnifying party will fully cooperate in the defense thereof; and (b) the indemnified party will not agree to the settlement of any such claim, demand, or suit prior to a final judgment thereon without the consent of the indemnifying party.

V. CONFIDENTIAL INFORMATION

A. Definition: "Confidential Information" means all nonpublic confidential and proprietary information which the disclosing party identifies in writing as confidential before or within thirty (30) days after disclosure to the receiving party or which, under the circumstances surrounding disclosure, the receiving party should have understood was delivered in confidence.

B. Nondisclosure. Each party agrees (1) to hold the other party's Confidential Information in strict confidence, (2) not to disclose such Confidential Information to any third party, and (3) not to use the other party's Confidential Information for any purpose other than to further this Agreement. Each party may disclose the other party's Confidential Information to its responsible employees, and, in the case of SPC, the employees of SPC with a bona fide need to know such information and subject to a nondisclosure agreement, but only to the extent necessary to carry out this Agreement.

C. Each party agrees to instruct all such employees not to disclose such Confidential Information to third parties, including consultants, without the prior written permission of the disclosing party.

D. Exceptions.

Confidential Information will not include information which (1) is now, or hereafter becomes, through no act or failure to act on the part of the receiving party, generally known or available to the public; (2) was acquired by the receiving party before receiving such information from the disclosing party and without restriction as to use or disclosure; (3) is hereafter rightfully furnished to the receiving party by a third party, without restriction as to use or disclosure; (4) is information which the receiving party can document was independently developed by the receiving party without use of the disclosing party's Confidential Information; (5) is required to be disclosed by law, provided that the receiving party uses reasonable efforts to give the disclosing party reasonable notice of such required disclosure and to limit the scope of material disclosed; (6) is disclosed with the prior written consent of the disclosing party; or (7) is SPC.com content provided by SPC pursuant to this Agreement.

Upon the disclosing party's request, the receiving party will promptly return to the disclosing party all tangible items containing or consisting of the disclosing party's Confidential Information.

E. Injunctive Relief.

Each party acknowledges that all of the disclosing party's Confidential Information is owned solely by the disclosing party (or its licensors) and that the unauthorized disclosure or use of such Confidential Information would cause irreparable harm and significant injury to the disclosing party, the degree of which may be difficult to ascertain.

F.   General Provisions.

(1) Governing Law and Venue. This Agreement and any disputes arising under, in connection with, or relating to this Agreement will be governed by the laws of the Commonwealth of Massachusetts, excluding its conflicts of law rules. The state and federal courts in Boston, Massachusetts, will have exclusive venue and jurisdiction for such disputes, and the parties hereby submit to personal jurisdiction in such courts. The prevailing party in any such dispute will be entitled to recover costs of suit (including the reasonable fees of attorneys and other professionals).

(b) Notices. All notices or other communications to or upon SPC.com and Content Provider under this Agreement shall be by telecopy or in writing and telecopied, mailed, or delivered to each party at its address set forth in the introductory paragraph of this Agreement or such other address or telecopier number as either party shall notify the other. All such notices and communications, when sent by delivery service, shall be effective on the third business day following the deposit with such service; when mailed, first class postage prepaid and addressed as aforesaid in the mails, shall be effective upon receipt; when delivered by hand, shall be effective upon delivery; and when telecopied, shall be effective upon confirmation of receipt.

Suffolk Personal Computers By /s/ Cyrus Daftary

Title: Chief Operating Officer, SPC

Content Provider By /s/

Title: Chief Operating Officer, Content Provider

CHAPTER FIVE

TORT LIABILITY IN CYBERSPACE

§ 5.01   GENERAL PRINCIPLES OF TORT LAW

[A]   The Three Branches of Tort Law

A tort is "a private or civil wrong or injury, including an action for bad-faith breach of contract, for which the court will provide a remedy in the form of an action for damages."[1] The three branches of tort law include (1) intentional torts; (2) negligence; and (3) strict liability. Table 5.1 lists some illustrative examples of each of the three branches of tort law, which may be adapted to cyberspace. Whether a plaintiffs' complaint seeks monetary damages or injunctive relief, torts contain four elements: duty, breach of duty, damages, and causation.[2]

This chapter examines the online company's potential for tort liability by examining recent case law and developments and applying traditional tort law principles. Tort law is readily adaptable to Internet and web site injury cases. Torts may be committed in chat rooms, videoconferences, news groups,[3] listservs,[4] bulletin boards,[5] or in information or data transfers.[6]

---

[1] Black's Law Dictionary 1489 (St. Paul: West, 6th ed. 1991).

[2] "Proximate cause" means that cause which, in a natural and continuous sequence, produces an event, and without which cause such event would not have occurred. In order to be a proximate cause, the act or omission complained of must be such that a person using ordinary care would have foreseen that the event might occur. Proximate cause "has little to do with physical causation, emphasizing instead the continuity of the sequences that produces an event." Bryan A. Garner, A Dictionary of Modern Legal Usage 211 (2d ed. 1995).

[3] A news group is an "electronic discussion group, serving as a bulletin board for users to post universally accessible messages, and to read and reply to those from others." Michael Scott, Internet and Technology Desk Reference 339 (1999) (quoting Religious Tech. Ctr. v. F.A.C.T.Net, Inc., 901 F. Supp. 1519, 1524 n.4 (D. Colo. 1995)).

[4] A listserv is "an automatic mailing list services . . . that allow communications about particular subjects of interest to a group of people." American Civil Liberties Union v. Reno, 929 F. Supp. 824, 834 (E.D. Pa. 1996), aff'd, 521 U.S. 844 (1997).

[5] A bulletin board system (BBS) is "an electronic forum for exchanging electronic mail, reading notices and features, carrying on unstructured multilogs and copying programs stored on the host computer. Bulletin boards are videotext systems that provide quick access to information held in databanks. They can be used to transmit information back and forth. They can be used to provide information to a closed group or an open group. Bulletin-board services are sometimes provided as a free service, but may be subject to a charge. They function as electronic notice boards and as electronic mail services." Michael Scott, Internet and Technology Law Reference 51 (1999) (quoting In re Application by International Computers Ltd., 5 I.P.R. 263 (Austl. Pat. Off.)).

[6] See, e.g., Martin C. Loesch, Surveying Cyberspace: A Guide to Insurance Defense and Coverage in the Age of Technology, ch. 2, 1998 DRI 1-5, observing that "[d]efamatory statements may be published over private e-mail systems or distributed through the Internet [and] Service provider discussion lists, roundtables, real-time conferences, news groups, listserves and bulletin boards."

TABLE 5.1
Branches of Tort Law

Intentional Torts	*Negligence*	*Strict Liability*
Intentional Interference with the Person: Battery, assault, false imprisonment, intentional infliction of mental distress, invasion of privacy, and defamation	**Direct Negligence:** Violation of duty of care; medical malpractice; failure to provide sufficient security; negligent retention and supervision of employees	**Strict Liability:** Abnormally dangerous activities such as blasting, releasing hazardous wastes, or other unnatural uses of land
Intentional Interference with Business: Trespass to land, trespass to chattels, conversion, and nuisance	**Indirect Negligence:** Vicarious liability for the acts of employees; *respondeat superior*; joint venture; negligent entrustment; duty to control third parties	**Strict Product Liability:** Manufacturers who place a defective product in the stream of commerce that causes injury to a consumer are strictly liable
Intentional Interference with Property: Trade libel, interference with contractual relations, and interference with prospective advantage	**Negligence:** Nuisance or the disturbance in possession or enjoyment of property; activities that interfere with the enjoyment of property	**Trespass to Land:** A person entering the land of another without authorization is strictly liable

[1]   Intentional Torts

Intentional torts are injuries committed with the purpose to bring about a desired result or a substantial certainty to bring about desired consequences.[7] The Restatement of Torts[8] sets the general standard of liability: "One who intentionally causes injury to another is subject to liability to the other for the actual harm incurred, if his conduct is culpable and not justifiable."[9] Battery, assault, false

---

[7] Edward J. Kionka, Torts in a Nutshell 146 (1999).

[8] The Restatements of the Law are projects of the American Law Institute, which seeks to bring uniformity to the common law. The Restatements are codified "to promote the clarification and simplification of the law and its better adaptation to social needs to secure the better administration of justice, and to encourage and carry on scholarly and scientific legal work." The American Law Institute (visited Nov. 14, 1999) http://www.ali.org/index.htm. ALI's Council and its membership approve the Restatements for enactment in the states. The Restatement (Second) of Torts is an influential source of tort law in virtually every state. The Restatements are cited by courts or adopted by state legislatures. Nearly every state, for example, adopted Restatement (Second) of Torts § 402A on strict product liability.

[9] Restatement (Second) of Torts § 870 (1965).

imprisonment, intentional infliction of emotional distress, conversion,[10] trespass to land, and trespass to chattels[11] are examples of intentional torts.

Online companies have utilized some intentional torts. The tort of outrage, for example, may apply where an employee intentionally or recklessly sends harassing e-mail messages to a co-employee. A business competitor that floods a company's computer with spurious messages may interrupt its business and constitute an interference with contract or prospective economic relationships. Similarly, the deliberate introduction of a computer virus into a company's computer system that causes destruction of computer files may be the basis for a conversion lawsuit. A company may be liable for trespass to chattels for sending e-mail spam to subscribers of online services without permission.[12]

EBay, a leading online auction house, recently sued a competitor for trespassing on its web site with robotic agents.[13] The robotic agents allegedly searched and copied files from eBay's web site. This is an example of how creative lawyers use traditional torts to punish unlawful access and copying from web sites.

Online chats may seem relaxed, but a conversation in a chat room, newsgroup, or web site may become the basis of a defamation lawsuit.[14] A company may be liable for defamation for repeating false rumors about individuals or entities. Messages on the Internet may be retransmitted and posted to newsgroups by anonymous individuals leading to costly lawsuits.[15]

Anonymous posters may use the Internet to tarnish the reputation of a company by posting false information to an electronic bulletin board.[16] An anonymous false posting to an Internet web site, for example, led to one individual receiving thousands of angry telephone calls, e-mails, and threatening letters.[17]

---

[10] Conversion is the unlawful exercise of dominion or control over the personal property of another.

[11] Trespass to chattels is an interference with the personal property of another. Conversion differs from trespass to chattels only in the measure of damages. With conversion, the remedy is for a forced sale of the personal property, whereas the damages for trespass to chattels is the diminution in the value due to the defendant's interference.

[12] *See, e.g.,* America Online Inc. v. IMS et al., No. 98-0011-A (E.D. Va. Oct. 29, 1998) (holding defendant liable for trespass to chattels for the unauthorized mailing of unsolicited bulk e-mail to millions of AOL subscribers).

[13] ZDNET.COM, eBay Sues Bidder's Edge, ZDNET NEWS, Dec. 10, 1999 (visited Dec. 13, 1999), http://www.zdnet.com.

[14] Denis Kelleher, Blaming the Messenger, The Irish Times, May 3, 1999, at 18.

[15] *Id.*

[16] A nonresident who posted allegedly defamatory statements about Virginia residents on a Usenet server was held to have sufficient contact with the forum under the state's long-arm statute to support the exercise of personal jurisdiction. Bochan v. LaFontaine, No. 1:98-CV-1749 (E.D. Va., May 26, 1999).

[17] Zeran v. America Online Inc., 129 F.3d 327, 330 (4th Cir. 1997) (false posting stated that the plaintiff was selling offensive t-shirts celebrating the bombing of the federal court house in Oklahoma City).

A disgruntled ex-employee of Smith Barney was charged with sending phony e-mails to the company's top executives charging the company with questionable ethics and morals.[18] The ex-employee was an impostor who pretended to be the chief executive officer of a parent company of Salomon Smith Barney.[19] The ex-employee was charged with eight counts of harassment.[20]

In another recent case, a Washington law firm was accused of launching a "cyber war" against the Internet site, Dig Dirt.[21] The company charges the law firm with posting defamatory messages about company officials on Usenet and covering up its activities with a false e-identity.[22]

A company may also be charged with knowledge of its employee's business torts committed within the scope of their employment. What constitutes guilty knowledge of the principal depends on the circumstances of the case.[23] Business torts may be committed face-to-face or by e-mail messages or postings to electronic bulletin boards[24] or newsgroups.[25] A company may also be a plaintiff in a lawsuit where a competitor is unfairly competing with the company, interfering with prospective advantage, or commiting torts such as disparagement. These intentional business torts will be discussed in detail in § 5.02.

Other intentional torts, such as battery, assault, and false imprisonment cannot be used by online companies, as these torts involve the infliction of bodily harm, the apprehension of harm, or confinement, all situations without obvious parallels in cyberspace.

---

[18] Reuters, Charge Over Smith Barney E-Mail, CNETNEWS.COM (visited Nov. 25, 1999), http://news.cnet.com/news/0-1005-200-332432.html.

[19] The unsavory practice of posting a message on the Internet while pretending to be another person is called *trolling*. Meeka Jun, 'Trolling' on the Internet: Win for On-Line Services, N.Y.L.J., Nov. 21, 1999, at 15.

[20] *Id.*

[21] The law firm of Steptoe and Johnson LLP was accused of cracking into Dig Dirt's web site 750 times and posting defamatory statements using a stolen e-identity. Craig Bicknell, Strange Corporate Hacking Saga, WIRED NEWS Nov. 12, 1999 (visited Nov. 29, 1999), http://www.wired.com/news/politics/0,1283,32488,00.html.

[22] *Id.*

[23] *Id.*

[24] Usenet is a term that refers to the "worldwide community of electronic BBS that is closely associated with the Internet and the Internet community. The messages in Usenet are organized into thousands of topical groups, or 'Newsgroups.'" Michael D. Scott, Internet and Technology Desk Reference 523 (1999) (quoting Religious Tech. Ctr. v. Netcom On-Line Comm. Servs., Inc., 907 F. Supp. 1361, 1365 (N.D. Cal. 1995)).

[25] Usenets are postings on various subjects on servers on the worldwide Internet. A newsgroup is a collection of posted topics on a given subject. A group of law professors, teaching Internet Law, for example, might subscribe to a newsgroup on the topic of cyberspace law. Netscape and Microsoft browsers "provide support and access to any newsgroup on the Internet. What Is.com, Usenet (A Definition) (visited Nov. 22, 1999), http://www.whatis.com/usenet.htm.

[2] Negligence

Negligence is conduct which departs from the reasonable standard of care imposed by law for the protection of others. The elements of a negligence cause of action are (1) duty of care; (2) breach of a duty of care; (3) proximate cause between breach of the duty of care; and (4) damages. "Negligence" is an act or omission where there is a failure to use ordinary care; it is the failure to do that which a person of ordinary prudence would have done under the same or similar circumstances.[26] Ordinary care means that degree of care that would be used by a person of ordinary prudence under the same or similar circumstances.

Courts have had little difficulty in adapting negligence principles to the online world. A company's exposure to negligence stems from its web site, its online communications, inadequate security, or retention of unfit employees. A company may potentially be liable for computer malpractice for its engineer's failure to design hardware or software consistent with high professional standards. A company may also be liable for negligent information security if its firewall or other security technologies fail to protect electronic communications. Courts have been reluctant to recognize the tort of computer malpractice for negligent design of hardware or software. A company has exposure for negligent statements made on its web site as well as for employment-based torts such as the negligent retention of unfit employees. Negligence-based cybertorts are discussed in detail in § 5.07.

[a] *Duty and Breach*

Negligence is conduct that falls below a standard of care for the protection of others in society. A person is not liable for injuries unless there is a duty of care. The general standard of care is based upon the reasonable person-standard. In the case of corporate negligence, the duty of care is that of the reasonable company acting under the circumstances. Violation of a statute, industry standard, or customary usage of trade often establishes corporate negligence.

The definition of a duty of care by one member of society to another is a legal question determined by the court.[27] "In the usual run of cases, a general duty to avoid negligence is assumed, and there is no need for the court to undertake detailed analysis of precedent and policy."[28] The duties owed to a plaintiff by an online company may arise from private duties, such as contract, or public duties, based on a statute or an ordinance. A duty of care may also arise in a company's

---

[26] Restatement (Second) of Torts § 282 (1965).

[27] Hamilton v. ACCU-TEK, 1999 U.S. Dist. LEXIS 8264 (E.D. N.Y., June 3, 1999).

[28] *Id.* (citing Restatement (Third) of Torts: General Principles § 6) (Discussion Draft, Apr. 5, 1999) (finding of no duty rare).

failure to anticipate tortious or criminal acts of others, although "courts are reluctant to impose a duty to anticipate the criminal or tortious conduct of third parties."[29]

The question of whether a defendant owes a duty to a member of society is a question of law often decided on public policy grounds. A company, for example, could be potentially liable for negligently permitting third parties to hack into its web site and steal data or proprietary information owned by others, where that inadequate security results in injuries to third parties.

[b]   Proximate Cause and Damages

The plaintiff must also meet the proximate cause requirement,[30] that is, that the breach of duty had a causal connection to the plaintiff's injury.[31]

[3]   Strict Liability

The third branch of tort law is strict liability, which imposes liability without a showing of fault or negligence. At common law, for example, a landowner that harbored wild animals on his land was strictly liable for the consequences if the animal escaped. Similarly, a nuclear processing plant is strictly liable for the escape of plutonium, even if it complied with federal nuclear regulatory regulations. Strict liability is based on a public policy decision that certain risky activities should bear the cost of wrongdoing, irrespective of the amount of care taken by the defendant. It is no defense to strict liability that the defendant followed statutory or industry standards of care.

[a]   Strict Products Liability

In the early 1960s, courts began to apply strict product liability to defective products. The Supreme Court of California was the first court to apply strict liability to a dangerously defective product in Greenman v. Yuba Power Products, Inc.[32] In *Greenman,* the plaintiff was severely injured when a malfunctioning lathe,[33] called the "Shopsmith," suddenly released a piece of wood, turning the

---

[29] *Id.*

[30] Proximate cause, like torts, is an elusive concept, difficult to define. Justice Benjamin Cardozo noted that "General definitions of a proximate cause give little aid. Our guide is the reasonable expectation and purpose of the ordinary businessman when making an ordinary business contract. It is his intention, expressed or fairly to be inferred, that counts." Bird v. St. Paul F. & M. Ins. Co., 224 N.Y. 47, 51 (1918).

[31] *Id.*

[32] 59 Cal. 2d 57, 377 P.2d 897, 27 Cal. Rptr. 697 (1962).

[33] The woodworking machine was suppose to hold the wooden block in place, while the lathe turned at high speed. When the wood suddenly released, it was propelled at high speed striking the plaintiff.

wood into a missile that injured him.[34] Justice Roger Traynor applied the law of strict product liability rejecting sales law defense:

> Under these circumstances, it should not be controlling whether plaintiff selected the machine because of the statements in the brochure, or because of the machine's own appearance of excellence that belied the defect lurking beneath the surface, or because he merely assumed it would safely do the job it was built to do. . . . To establish the manufacturer's liability it was sufficient that plaintiff proved that he was injured while using the [lathe] in a way it was intended to be used and as a result of a defect in design and manufacture, of which plaintiff was not aware that made the [lathe] unsafe for its intended use.[35]

Strict product liability swept the country after the American Law Institute adopted Section 402A, allowing strict liability for all product liability defendants.[36] The Restatement (Third) of Torts: Product Liability applies to distributors of defective computer hardware and may also apply to software.[37] The Restatement Third supersedes Section 402A of the Restatement Second and provides comprehensive rules dealing with the liability of commercial product sellers and distributors.[38] Section 19 of the Restatement Third defines a "product" as "tangible personal property."[39] If software is classified as a product, a vendor may be liable for product liability.

Strict product liability focuses on whether a dangerous defect in a product causes physical harm to the ultimate consumer. In a products liability action, a plaintiff must prove that (1) a product is defectively designed; (2) the manufacturer failed to warn of a known hazard; or (3) there was a manufacturing defect. A seller is strictly liable for placing a defective product into the stream of commerce that causes physical injuries to the plaintiff.

[b] Economic Loss Doctrine and Computer Law

Computer systems were historically sold as turnkey computer systems. The "hardware and software [was] a complete package such that a purchaser could utilize it for his business as a working system without having to perform any additional programming or system work."[40] Beginning in the 1980s, computer

---

[34] 377 P.2d at 898, 27 Cal. Rptr. at 698 (describing accident).

[35] 377 P.2d at 901, 27 Cal. Rptr. at 701.

[36] Restatement (Second) of Torts § 402A (1965).

[37] Restatement (Third) of Torts: Product Liability (1997).

[38] American Law Institute Press Release, The American Law Institute Publishes Restatement of the Law (Third) Torts: Products Liability May 1997 (visited Nov. 22, 1999), http://www.ali.org/ali/pr-526.htm

[39] Restatement (Third) of Torts, Product Liability, § 19 (1997).

[40] Michael D. Scott, Internet and Technology Law Desk Reference 512 (1999) (citing Management Consultants Ltd. v. Data General Corp., 8 Comp. L. Serv. Rep. 66 (E.D. Va. 1980)).

hardware and software began to be sold separately. A company's computer hardware, if sold separately, is clearly a product, but software is arguably an intangible.

A company can be liable for manufacturing defects in its computers. If a company's computer hardware deviates from its intended design, it would be liable even if it proved that it exercised all possible care. If a plaintiff can establish that the foreseeable risks of harm posed by computer hardware could have been avoided by a reasonable alternative design, the manufacturer may be liable for product liability under a theory of design defect. Finally, if the foreseeable risks of harm posed by a computer could have been reduced or avoided by reasonable instructions or warnings, it would be liable for inadequate instructions or warnings. Section 5.08 examines strict liability causes of action in cyberspace.

Few courts have considered the extension of strict liability to defective computer hardware or software, "but the potential liability is enormous."[41] One of the reasons why there have been so few strict product liability cases in the field of computer law is because of the "economic loss rule." It bears noting that strict product liability does not apply to purely economic losses caused by defective hardware or software. Courts could, however, find a manufacturer liable for defective hardware or software where there is loss of life or serious injury caused by bad software. Software failure, for example, was the probable cause of the crash of a Boeing 757 that killed 70 persons in Peru.[42] Courts may be receptive to permitting plaintiffs to bring strict liability actions where defective software causes physical injury.[43]

The failure of computer systems have been the proximate cause of "chemical leaks or explosions at chemical or nuclear plants, truck, train or plane collisions; physical injury or death where the systems have involved medical applications; and improper architectural/stress analysis."[44] There is some case law on treating defective information as a "product." A California court imposed liability on the seller of an inaccurate instrument approach chart.[45]

[B] Bases for a Company's Liability for an Employee's Wrongdoing

There are two bases of a company's liability for an employee's torts: direct liability and vicarious liability. (See Table 5.2 on page 348). An employer is not

---

[41] Lessons to Learn Regarding Restatement Products Liability, 15 Comp. Law Strat. 5 (Oct. 1998).

[42] Robert Cortijo, Computer Failure & Peru Airplane Crash, Agence-France-Presse, Oct. 4, 1996, at 1.

[43] *See generally* Patrick J. Miyaki, Computer Software Defects: Should Computer Software Manufacturers Be Held Strictly Liable for Computer Software Defects? 8 Santa Clara Comp. & High Tech. L.J. 121 (1992).

[44] Diane Savage, Avoiding Tort Claims for Defective Hardware and Software Strategies for Dealing with Potential Liability Woes, 15 Comp. Law Strat. 1 (Oct. 1998).

[45] Flour Corp. v. Jeppesen & Co., 216 Cal. Rptr. 68, 71 (Ct. App. 1985).

liable for torts of employee where it does not know or have reason to know of an unreasonable risk to others.

[1] Direct Liability

Direct liability is based on agency principles. The agency relationship always involves a principal, an agent, and a third party harmed by the agent's wrongdoing. An agency is a "fiduciary relationship that arises when one person (the 'principal') manifests consent to another person (the 'agent') that the agent shall act on the principal's behalf and subject to the principal's control."[46] The common law of agency follows the principle of vicarious liability or *respondeat superior.* The concept of *respondeat superior* embodies the common law maxim "let the principal answer."[47] Under agency principles, online companies will be liable for contracts made by their employees as well as their employees' tortious activities on company computers.

[a] *Agent's Actual Authority to Act*

Actual authority is when the principal consents to having an agent act on its behalf. A CEO, for example, may consent to have a high-level manager negotiate a contract on the company's behalf. A company may draft a power of attorney authorizing its subsidiary to sell a piece of real estate. The idea of actual authority requires some writing or other record of the principal's agreement to give the agent authority to act on its behalf. The Restatement (Third) of Agency draft defines actual authority as when "the agent reasonably believes, in accordance with the principal's manifestations to the agent, that the principal wishes the agent so to act."[48]

A company may create actual authority in a diverse set of circumstances in its Internet activities. A company, may, for example, give a high-ranking agent written authority to negotiate an online contract on its behalf. A senior officer may negotiate for the design of a web site. The term *implied authority* is "often used to mean actual authority either to do what is necessary, usual or proper to accomplish the agent's express responsibilities."[49]

---

[46] Restatement (Third) of The Law of Agency § 1.01 (American Law Inst. Council Draft No. 1, Nov. 18, 1999).

[47] Bryan Garner, A Dictionary of Modern Legal Usage 766 (2d ed. 1995) (noting that "under the ordinary rules of *respondeat superior*, the shipowner is responsible for his actions").

[48] American Law Institute, Restatement (Third) of the Law of Agency § 2.01 (Council Draft No. 1, Nov. 18, 1999).

[49] *Id.* at § 2.01, cmt.

TABLE 5.2
Liability for Employee's Torts

Direct Liability for Employee's Torts	Vicarious Liability for Employee's Torts	No Liability for Employee's Torts
Standard: Employee's high rank makes him or her a company's alter ego; imputed liability; high-level employee is acting as the company. The company may have intended the consequences of the employee's actions by ordering the high-level employee to commit wrongdoing. **Exceptions:** Does not apply to acts actually nor apparently authorized. A company official is liable for misappropriating a competitor's trade secrets.	**Standard:** Doctrine of *respondeat superior* makes the company liable for the legal consequences of its employee's actions. Company is liable for torts (intentional, negligence, or strict liability) committed within the scope of employment. **Exceptions:** Doctrine does not apply where employee, with apparent authority, defrauded company with third party; does not apply to independent contractors where there is no right to control actions.	**Standard:** Not liable for torts of employee where it does not know or have reason to know of an unreasonable risk to others. **Exceptions:** May be liable in limited circumstance where the duty is nondelegable. May also be liable for "frolic and detour" of errant employee where there is a foreseeable risk of harm.
Typical Example: Inadequate security for computer system leading to loss of confidential information; failure to protect the privacy of customer information.	**Typical Example:** Company is most likely liable for employee's negligence resulting in physical injury to a person or property. Manager sexually harasses co-worker or third party using e-mail system; employee misappropriates trade secrets of a competitor; imputed tort liability.	**Typical Example:** Company is not liable for employee's conduct outside scope of employment and where it does not realize unreasonable danger to others; company is not liable for its employees' hate speech using company computer absent knowledge.

[b]   Apparent Authority

Apparent authority is the situation where a third party has a "reasonable belief that the actor has authority to do actions consistent with the position."[50] An agent has the apparent authority for acts necessary or incidental to achieving the principal's objectives.[51] The underlying idea behind apparent authority is the appearance of authority conferred by a company. An agent who appears to a third

---

[50] *Id.* at § 2.03.
[51] *Id.* at § 2.02(1).

party to be authorized, but who lacks actual authority, may nevertheless bind the company.

[2]   Vicarious or Imputed Liability

Vicarious liability is technically a form of strict liability because the doctrine imposes liability where there is no direct fault on the part of the company. General agency principles make an employer subject to liability for the torts of its employees committed while acting in the scope of employment. An employer, however, can also be vicariously liable for torts committed by an employee.

Vicarious liability evolved out of the medieval law, covering the relationship of master and servant in feudal societies, and the Restatement of Agency (First) continued to use the feudal concepts of master and servant. A "master is a principal who employs an agent to perform service in his affairs and who controls or has the right to control the physical conduct of the other in the performance of the service."[52] A servant is an agent employed by a master to perform services that the master controls or the master has "a right to control."[53] The Restatement further defined the master/servant relationship as follows:

> A master is under a duty to exercise reasonable care so to control his servant while acting outside the scope of his employment so as to prevent him from intentionally harming others or from so conducting himself as to create an unreasonable risk of bodily harm to them, if: (a) the servant is upon premises in possession of the master . . . and (b) the master knows or has reason to know of the necessity and opportunity (i) that he has the ability to control his servant, and (ii) knows or has reason to know of the necessity and opportunity for exercising such control.[54]

The black letter law was that a "master is subject to liability for the torts of his servants committed while acting in the scope of their employment."[55] In contrast, "a master is not subject to liability for the torts of his servants acting outside of the scope of their employment."[56] A master will only be liable for the torts of his servant "outside the scope of employment if the master intended the conduct or the consequences, was negligent or reckless or violated a non-delegable duty."[57]

---

[52] Restatement (Second) Agency § 2(1) (1958).

[53] *Id.* at § 2(2).

[54] Restatement (Second) of Torts § 317.

[55] Restatement (Second) Agency § 219(1) (1958).

[56] *Id.* at § 219(2).

[57] *Id.* at § 219(2)(a)-(c).

[a] Internet Service Provider's Imputed Liability

Prior to 1996, courts were sharply divided on whether Internet Service Providers could be held liable for torts committed by its subscribers. The Communications Decency Act of 1996 (CDA) immunizes providers for torts of third parties. Section 230 of the Communications Decency Act states that: "[n]o provider . . . of any interactive computer service shall be treated as the publisher or speaker of any information provided by another information content provider."[58] A company's computer system would likely qualify as an "interactive computer service" under the Communications Decency Act of 1996. A company's web site, for example, qualifies as "any information service, system or access software provider that provides or enables computer access by multiple users to a computer server."[59] An "information content provider" is another term of art under the Act. An "information content provider" is defined as "any person or entity that is responsible, in whole or in part, for the creation or development of information provided through the Internet or any other interactive computer service."[60] Section 230 would treat third parties who posted defamatory or other tortious materials on a company's web site as an interactive content provider. As an interactive computer service provider, a company is immunized for content supplied by unknown information content providers. The courts have expanded Section 230 to include cases where an interactive computer service is being charged with liability as in a defamation lawsuit.[61]

Countries vary in their approaches to Internet-related defamation actions. In the United States, an Internet Service Provider (ISP) is provided broad immunity for torts committed by third-party subscribers. In other countries, an ISP may be liable for defamatory statements and infringing third-party rights.[62] A company's online activities expose it to different legal regimes covering online conduct, electronic commerce, and online communications. In the United Kingdom, for example, an ISP may be liable for defamatory material where the provider has notice of content.[63] A company's chief exposure, however, is to tort liability in a United States jurisdiction because of the relative numbers of Internet users.

---

[58] 47 U.S.C. § 230(c)(1)(3) (1996).

[59] 47 U.S.C. § 230(e)(2) (1996).

[60] *Id.* at § 230(e)(3).

[61] *See, e.g.,* Blumenthal v. Drudge, 992 F. Supp. 44, 49 (D.D.C. 1998) (dismissing America Online from lawsuit on the grounds of the § 230 Good Samaritan immunity of the Communications Decency Act of 1996).

[62] *Id.* at 34-39.

[63] *See, e.g.,* Godfrey v. Demon Internet (London High Court, United Kingdom, March 26, 1999) (holding that service provider was immune from Section 230 of the CDA for statements in a gossip column made available to its subscribers), reported in Perkins Coie Internet Case Digest (visited Nov. 26, 1999), http://www.perkinscoie.com/resource/ecomm/netcase?Cases-06.htm.

[b]   Imputed Liability and Independent Contractors

A company is generally not liable for the torts of independent contractors under traditional principles of the law of agency. An "independent contractor is a person who contracts with another to do something for him but who is not controlled by the other nor is subject to the other's right to control with respect to his physical conduct in the performance of the undertaking."[64] A company, however, may be liable for an independent contractor's conduct if the duty is nondelegable.

A company may have a nondelegable duty to protect the personal information of customers that is not disclaimable. The company's counsel should seek indemnity from third parties for torts that may arise out of nondelegable duties. Suppose a company hires an independent contractor to design its web site. A company, for example, may be vicariously liable for the designer's copyright or trademark infringement for incorporating text, music, video, or logos without the owner's permission as well as an employee may be held liable for improper use of e-mail or the Internet.

➤   [c]   Preventive Law Pointer: Adopt a Communications Policy

An online company needs to adopt an electronic mail and Internet usage policy to minimize tort liability. Chapter Nine provides detailed policy guidelines on how to develop an e-mail or Internet usage policy. Employers need to train employees on the potential tort liability in postings to discussion groups or e-mail messages. The case law discussed in Chapter Nine illustrates the diverse circumstances in which an online employer as well as an employee may be held liable for improper use of electronic communications.

[3]   Joint Tortfeasors

A company may seek damages from more than one defendant. Assume that networks of hackers are seeking to deny service to a company's web site. The hackers, who are acting in concert, may be sued separately or together for economic injuries caused by the attack.

Joint and several liability makes each co-defendant liable for the entire harm. The plaintiff may sue each defendant separately or together. If a co-defendant is insolvent or unavailable, the plaintiff may seek the entire judgment from the solvent and available defendant. If a co-defendant pays the entire judgment, it may seek contribution from its joint tortfeasor. The right of contribution is a co-defendant's right to seek reimbursement where it has paid more than its share of harm. Indemnity is a

---

[64] *Id.* at § 3.

closely related tort doctrine, which means roughly that a person promises to make good for incurred losses.

§ 5.02   INTENTIONAL TORTS IN CYBERSPACE

Intentional torts are divided into torts that interfere with the person and those that interfere with property. Intentional torts against the person include assault, battery, false imprisonment, and the intentional infliction of emotional distress.[65]

Torts such as trespass to land, trespass to chattels, and conversion arise out of the intentional interference with property interests. A trespass to chattel is committed when the defendant intermeddles with the personal property of another.[66] Conversion is the intentional exercise of dominion or control over the personal property of another, which seriously interferes with the plaintiff's right to control it.[67] In order to state a claim for conversion, the plaintiff must allege that the defendant is responsible for "the deprivation of another's right of property, or use or possession of a chattel . . . without the owner's consent and without legal justification."[68] The defendant must cause the consequences of its act of depriving the owner of property or believe that the consequences are substantially certain to follow from its actions.

The legal definition of intent does not mean that the defendant must act maliciously or with an evil motive. Intent requires that the actor desire to cause the consequences of his act or that he believes that the consequences are "substantially certain." *Specific intent* exists if the defendant desires that its conduct will cause the resulting consequences. The defendant has the requisite *general intent* if it acts, knowing with substantial certainty, that its conduct will cause the resulting

---

[65] The elements of intentional infliction of emotional distress are set forth in Section 46 of the Restatement (Second) of Torts (1965). Section 46 requires that the plaintiff prove that the defendant by extreme and outrageous conducts intentionally or recklessly caused severe emotional distress. The Restatement requires that the plaintiff prove actual damages, which may be in the form of physical injury, costs for medical care, or other damages. Sams v. Doug Hannon Internet Waterworld, Inc., The Blue Sheet of Northeast Texas (No. 58, 995, Hunt County (Tex.), Apr. 19, 1999). A computer consultant and minority shareholder filed a lawsuit against a nationally known bass fishing expert and his company claiming that they stalked and defamed him and his family over the Internet. The plaintiff received a $510,000 damage, which consisted of compensation for his share in the company.

[66] Chattels are defined as personal property as opposed to real property. The trespass to chattels is an interference with property other than land.

[67] The difference between trespass to chattels and conversion is in the seriousness of the interference. Where the extent and duration of exercise of dominion or control is great, the defendant is liable for the full value of the chattel. In contrast, the trespass to chattels defendant is only responsible for the harm done to the personal property of another.

[68] Universal Premium Acceptance Corp. v. York Bank & Trust Co., 69 F.3d 695, 704 (3d Cir. 1995).

consequences. Torts in cyberspace are often untraceable, being committed with the help of anonymous remailers, forged e-mail addresses, or computer servers located in distant lands.[69]

[A]   Assault and Battery

Torts in cyberspace are rarely committed face-to-face and are often committed anonymously by the use of devices such as anonymous remailers or servers located in distant forums. An unauthorized or unconsented touching of one person by another is a battery. An assault "is an act which arouses in the plaintiff a reasonable apprehension of an imminent battery."[70] Some physical contact or touching is necessary in order for there to be a battery.[71] Battery cannot be committed over the Internet because there can be no unwarranted physical contact. In order for a defendant to be liable for an assault, however, he must place the other person in apprehension of an "imminent contact."[72] Assault is almost impossible to prove in an Internet transmission or e-mail because the recipient is generally not in apprehension of an imminent contact. It is theoretically possible for the recipient of an e-mail message to believe that contact is imminent if a co-employee whose workstation is nearby sends the message. An e-mail message threatening unwanted contact in the future is not an assault. An e-mail message alone "does not make the actor liable for assault unless together with other acts or circumstances they put the other in reasonable apprehension of an imminent harmful or offensive contact with the person."[73]

Cyberstalking refers to the use of the Internet, e-mail, or other electronic means to repeatedly threaten, follow, or harass another person. A company may be vicariously liable for failing to warn third parties if it has prior knowledge of a stalker using company computer systems. California defines stalking as a pattern of conduct the "intent of which was to follow, alarm or harass the plaintiff."[74] California prosecuted a former security guard that used the Internet to impersonate a

---

[69] An anonymous remailer is an Internet term describing how "identifying information on the original message is removed, and the message is then forwarded anonymously to its intended destination." Michael D. Scott, Internet and Technology Desk Reference 17 (1999).

[70] Edward J. Kionka, Torts in a Nutshell 151 (1999).

[71] Unprivileged and unconsented physical contact as in Garratt v. Dailey, 279 P.2d 1091 (Wash. 1955) where a court found a child liable for battery for deliberately pulling a lawn chair out from under his elderly neighbor, which caused her to break a hip. The court found the intent of the defendant may be based upon conduct that is substantially certain to injure the plaintiff.

[72] Section 29(1) of the Restatement states that: "[t]o make the actor liable for an assault he must put the other in apprehension of an imminent contact." Restatement (Second) of Torts § 29(1) (1965).

[73] Restatement (Second) of Torts § 31 (1965).

[74] Cal. Civ. Code § 1708.7 (Deering 1999).

woman posting Internet messages of her fantasies of being raped.[75] Objectionable messages, however, do not make the sender liable for assault, because the defendant does not typically place his victim in apprehension of an imminent contact.

Electronic stalking that involves harassing e-mail may create a crime or tort of outrage, even if the defendant lacks the present ability to carry out a threat. It is black letter law that mere "words, unaccompanied by some act apparently intended to carry the threat into execution, do not put the other in apprehension of an imminent body contact, and so cannot make the actor liable for an assault. . . ."[76] Flaming is the functional equivalent of a "verbal lashing in public."[77] Flaming is a term that refers to "terse, angry, or insulting thoughts communicated via e-mail between employees in a company or published on computer bulletin boards."[78] Messages printed in all capital letters are considered to be flaming.[79] E-mail or online "flaming" may result in fright or humiliation, but still it lacks the imminence requirement. Abusive or insulting e-mail messages, mail-bombs, or flaming do not constitute assault because they are typically threats to inflict bodily harm in the future and are, therefore, not imminent threats.[80]

Flaming, though it probably does not satisfy the imminence requirement, may constitute defamation. One of the first online defamation cases arose out of a dispute between two Australian anthropologists who waged a "flame" war on the Internet attacking each other's professional reputations.[81] Damages for libel were based upon messages posted to an anthropology computer bulletin board. The objectionable statements accused the plaintiff anthropologist of sexual misconduct, racism against Australian aboriginal peoples, and academic incompetence. The court found that the anthropologist was defamed and awarded $40,000 to

---

[75] "On at least six occasions, sometimes in the middle of the night, men knocked on the woman's door saying they wanted to rape her. The former security guard pleaded guilty in April 1999 to one count of stalking and three counts of solicitation of sexual assault. U.S. Attorney General, 1999 Report on Cyberstalking: A New Challenge for Law Enforcement and Industry 5 (August 1999).

[76] Restatement (Second) of Torts § 31, cmt. (a) (1965) ("For this reason it is commonly said in the decision that mere words do not constitute an assault, or that some overt act is required").

[77] Whatis.com, "What Is . . . Flaming (a Definition) (visited Nov. 14, 1999), http://www.whatis.com/flaming.htm.

[78] Frah Farouque, E-Mail Chatter Could Lead to a Cybersuit, The Age (Melbourne Australia), June 3, 1995 (quoting Robert Todd of the Sydney, Australia law firm of Blake Dawson and Waldron).

[79] Michael D. Scott, Internet and Technology Law Desk Reference 210 (1999).

[80] Self-help may be useful in preventing harassing e-mails. A kill file, for example, may be used to automatically delete files with certain phrases or words. A kill file may block e-mail messages coming from objectionable persons or dealing with objectionable topics.

[81] Rindos v. Hardwick, No. 1994 of 1993 (W. Austl. Sup. Ct., March 31, 1994).

compensate him for harm to his personal and professional reputation. The tort of defamation will be discussed in detail later in this chapter.

[B] Intentional Infliction of Emotional Distress

The Restatement (Second) of Torts sets forth the basic elements of the tort of intentional infliction of emotional distress as one who: "by extreme and outrageous conduct intentionally or recklessly causes severe emotional distress to another" and states further that such person is "subject to liability for such emotional distress."[82] The elements of a prima facie case of intentional infliction of emotional distress are (1) outrageous conduct by the defendant; (2) the defendant's intention of causing, or reckless disregard of the probability of causing, emotional distress; (3) the plaintiff's suffering severe or extreme emotional distress; and (4) actual and proximate causation of the emotional distress by the defendant's outrageous conduct.[83] States vary in requiring physical injury or manifestation as a required element for a claim of intentional infliction of emotional distress.[84] Some jurisdictions permit a plaintiff to recover for the negligent infliction of emotional distress, but in that case the plaintiff must prove evidence of physical injury or emotional distress.[85]

The tort of intentional infliction of emotional distress, often called the tort of outrage, allows recovery if a defendant intentionally subjects the plaintiff to serious mental distress. The key question is whether the defendant acted in a manner that may be characterized as extreme or outrageous. "Mere insults, indignities, inconsiderations or petty oppressions do not rise to the level of the outrageous conduct essential to the plaintiff's right of recovery."[86] Some states require a physical manifestation of mental distress or medical evidence to prove emotional distress.

Cyberstalking or the sending of threatening or harassing electronic communications may constitute a crime as well as a tort if transmitted in interstate commerce by e-mail or the Internet. Employees of a Massachusetts high technology company, for example, filed an action for the intentional infliction of emotional distress after being fired for sending disparaging e-mail messages about their chief

---

[82] Restatement (Second) of Torts § 46 (1965).

[83] *Id.*

[84] Curtis v. Firth, 123 Idaho 598, 850 P.2d 1282, 1288 (Ct. App. 1984) (stating that evidence of physical harm may bear on the severity of emotional harm).

[85] Thomas Moffatt, Tort and Insurance Deskbook: Tort Law, "Recovery of Damages for Emotional Distress," (visited Nov. 13, 1999), http://www.moffatt.com/deskbook/desk1009.html.

[86] Restatement (Second) of Torts § 46, cmt. (1965) (stating that the tort requires outrageous conduct of the magnitude that arouses the resentment of the "average member of the community . . . and lead him to exclaim, 'Outrageous!' ").

executive officer. In that case, the employees were not told that their e-mail messages were stored and monitored.[87] The court did not find the actions of the company's president to "exceed all possible bounds of decency and . . . utterly intolerable in a civilized society."[88]

An ISP will not be held responsible for e-mail messages causing intentional infliction of emotional distress unless it knew of the contents of the message, "a circumstance that will rarely, if ever, be proved."[89]

> **[1]   Preventive Law Pointer: Preventing Misuse of the Internet**

Sexual and racial harassment should also be included in the company's e-mail and Internet policies examined in Chapter Nine.[90] A company may prevent some forms of harassment by restricting or forbidding access to the Internet. Software is available to block access to objectionable sites. The culture of a company is critical to reducing the risk of many online torts. A company should have a contact person so those employees have a method for reporting cyber-harassment or other misuses of e-mail or the Internet. Co-employees should also be encouraged to report misuses and abuses of e-mail and the Internet.[91] A company may consider dismissing employees for distributing pornography on the Internet. The dean of Harvard's Divinity School was recently forced to resign after pornography was discovered on his computer.[92] A company must designate a contact person to whom misuses and abuses of company computer systems can be reported in order to detect and deal with warning signs of legal trouble.

[C]   Title VII Claims

Title VII of the Civil Rights Act of 1964 provides that it is unlawful to discriminate against an individual with respect to the terms of employment because

---

[87] Restuccia v. Burk Technology Inc., No. 95-2125 (Mass. Super. Ct., Middlesex County (Mass.), Dec. 13, 1999).

[88] *Id.* (quoting Restatement (Second) of Torts § 46).

[89] Lunney v. Prodigy Servs. Co., 250 A.D.2d 230, 237 683 N.Y.S.2d 557, 562 (1998) (entering summary judgment in favor of ISP who was held not liable for the transmission of offensive electronic messages sent in the 15-year-old plaintiff's name to his Boy Scout leader).

[90] *See, e.g.,* Rudas v. Nationwide Mut. Ins. Co., 1997 WL 11302 (E.D. Pa., Jan. 10, 1997) (lawsuit based upon sexual harassment by co-worker in the form of graphic e-mail messages).

[91] One company executive suggests encouraging "whistleblowing on employees who download potentially offensive material." *Id.*

[92] Margie Wylie, Fix and Tell? Since There is No Code of Ethics, Computer Technicians Who Find Sensitive Personal Files Usually Wonder What to Do, The Times-Picayune, July 15, 1999, at E1 (reporting that Harvard University's computer support technicians found pornographic images stored on Ronald Theimann's Harvard-owned computer, which was kept at home).

of sex or race.[93] Plaintiffs filing sexual harassment claims may have tort actions for the "intentional infliction of emotional distress."[94] In addition, Title VII provides tort-like remedies for individuals who are discriminated against in the workplace. Sexual or racial harassment claims are generally based upon discrimination in the conditions of employment.[95] In addition, courts impose vicarious liability principles in hostile workplace claims. An employer may be charged with maintaining a "hostile environment" in violation of federal law.[96]

Courts have determined that employees may establish a "hostile workplace" claim if (1) the conduct in question was unwelcome; (2) the harassment was sex or race-linked; (3) the sexual or racial harassment was severe; and (4) there was a causal connection to the employer.[97] E-mail or Internet communications may be the basis of a hostile workplace claim. An employer may minimize its exposure to hostile workplace claims by enforcing its e-mail and Internet usage policy. In addition, the employer must promptly investigate claims of sexual harassment. In one recent case the transmission of racially insensitive jokes led to a hostile workplace claim.[98] In another case, a racial discrimination claim was based upon jokes containing "racial undertones" sent on a company's e-mail system.[99] The employer needs to inform its employees of its e-mail policy and to train employees not to send jokes that may be offensive via e-mail.[100]

Employees may base a hostile workplace claim upon co-employee's abuse of company computer systems. Continental Express Airlines was found responsible

---

[93] Hateful e-mail messages may also be a violation of federal civil rights law. In United States v. Machado, No. SACR 96-142-AHS (S.D. Cal. 1998), a University of California–Irvine student was convicted of a federal civil rights violation for sending e-mail messages on a university computer signed "Asian Hater" and threatening Asian students.

[94] Anne Saker, The Law on Sexual Harassment, The News Observer, Aug. 20, 1996.

[95] A government employer may be subject to restrictions in prohibiting state employees from accessing sexually explicit materials online. In Urofsky v. Allen, 1998 U.S. Dist. LEXIS 2139, 1998 WL 86587 (E.D. Va. 1998), a court held that a Virginia statute forbidding state employees from accessing sexually explicit materials to be violative of the First Amendment. The court observed that there were legitimate purposes of researching sexually explicit topics that potentially could benefit the public.

[96] *See generally* 29 C.F.R. § 1604.11(a)(1999).

[97] *See, e.g.*, Spicer v. Virginia Dep't of Corrections, 66 F.3d 705, 709-10 (4th Cir. 1995) (*en banc*).

[98] Curtis v. DiMaio, QDS:02760859 (E.D.N.Y., Apr. 23, 1999) (rejecting employee's claim that the transmission of two racially sensitive jokes over the company's e-mail system created a hostile work environment).

[99] Daniels v. WorldCom Corp., No. Civ A 3:97-CV-0721-P, 1998 WL 91261 (N.D. Tex. Feb. 23, 1998) (rejecting plaintiffs' Title VII and 1981 and 1983 of the Civil Rights Act of 1964 claims based upon jokes sent on company computer system).

[100] In *Daniels,* the employer was found not liable because of its prompt remedial measures after learning of the offending messages. In that case, the employees sending the jokes were given oral and written reprimands. *Id.*

for sexual harassment in a hostile workplace claim filed by a female pilot.[101] In that case, a male pilot used computer equipment to superimpose his female co-worker's face onto other female bodies, depicted in pornographic poses. The humiliating pictures were shown to other Continental pilots and transmitted over the Internet.[102] In that case, Continental was found liable under the theories of hostile work environment, ratification of sexual harassment, and negligent retention, training, and supervision. The plaintiff was awarded compensatory damages for the intentional infliction of emotional distress, defamation, and invasion of privacy, as well as punitive damages.

In another case, a group of women who worked as models for an online adult entertainment service filed an intentional infliction of emotional distress and gender discrimination claim against their employer in a sexual harassment case.[103] The online models claimed that their employer encouraged a sexually hostile work environment. The online models alleged that the employer allowed "other employees to view the models performances." They objected to the videotaping of their sexual acts and the distribution of the tapes to fellow employees and customers without their consent.[104]

[D] Trespass to Cyber-Chattels

Trespass is a broad "form of action that, at common law, provided for a wide spectrum of injuries, from personal injuries caused by negligence to business torts and nuisances."[105] A trespass to enter upon another's land without consent is actionable. In contrast, "trespass to chattels . . . occurs when one party intentionally uses or intermeddles with personal property in rightful possession of another without authorization."[106] Trespass to chattels is an interference with personal property that includes "tangible goods or intangible rights, as in patents, stocks or shares."[107] Trespass to chattels is only actionable if the defendant dispossesses chattels belonging to another and the chattel is impaired as to its condition, quality, or value. This tort is triggered when the possessor is deprived of the use of the chattel for a substantial period of time. If harm is caused to some person or thing in which the possessor has a legally protected interest, there may also be a trespass to chattels.

---

[101] Butler v. Krebs & Continental Express, Inc., No. 96-1204096, The Blue Sheet of Southeast Texas (Montgomery Cty. Dist. Ct. (Tex.), June 8, 1998).

[102] Id.

[103] Nude Models Sue Online Service Over Working Conditions, Comp. & Online Indus. Litig. R. Dec. 2, 1997, at 10.

[104] Id.

[105] Bryan A. Garner, A Dictionary of Modern Legal Usage 995 (2d ed. 1995).

[106] Restatement (Second) of Torts § 217(b) (1965).

[107] Id. at 149.

An ex-employee of Intel Corporation was found to have committed trespass to chattels by sending thousands of e-mails to current employees of the company.[108] His purpose was to form an organization of former Intel employees who have filed claims against the company. Intel ordered the ex-employee to stop sending mass e-mails to its employees. When the ex-employee continued sending messages, Intel charged him with trespass to chattels. The company argued that the ex-employee's e-mails constituted an unauthorized use of Intel's computer system.[109] The court agreed, rejecting the former employee's First Amendment defense because there was no state action, as Intel was a private corporation.[110]

[E] Spamming as Cyberspace Trespass

Spamming is the practice of sending unsolicited or unwanted e-mail in an indiscriminate fashion. *Spam* is unsolicited commercial bulk e-mail, akin to the junk mail sent through the postal mail. The number of junk e-mails has been estimated at 25,000,000 messages per day.[111] The sending of spam e-mail, which can take up a substantial amount of a company's computer resources, is arguably a trespass to chattels.

Spammers abuse accounts created at AOL, Hotmail, Prodigy, or other e-mail systems to facilitate their spamming activities. Spammers create particular problems for ISPs by setting up accounts to facilitate the transmittal of bulk e-mails to all ISP subscribers. The e-mail accounts are used to collect responses to the spammer's e-mails and "bounced back" messages.

Hotmail, a Silicon Valley company that provides free electronic mail on the World Wide Web, filed a trespass to chattels action against a spammer who sent thousands of unsolicited e-mails to its subscribers advertising pornographic materials and get-rich financial schemes.[112] In one case, a court found that the spammers trespassed on Hotmail's computer space by causing tens of thousands of misdirected and unauthorized e-mail messages to occupy company computer resources.

In a similar case, AOL filed a lawsuit against a spammer for sending large numbers of unauthorized and unsolicited bulk e-mail advertisements to its members.[113] AOL's complaint alleged false designation of origin and the dilution of

---

[108] Ex-Employee's E-Mails to Intel Workers Are Not Protected Speech, Judge Rules, 16 Comp. & Online Indus. Litig. R. 8 (May 18, 1999).

[109] *Id. See generally*, Dan L. Burk, The Trouble With Trespass 4 J. of Small and Emerg. Bus. Law 27 (2000) (arguing that courts "mangled" the common law in its analysis in Internet trespass to chattels).

[110] *Id.*

[111] James W. Butler, "The Death of Spam and The Rise of DEM: A Bill to Ban It Could Backfire," The Internet Newsl: Legal & Bus. Aspects, Sept. 1998, at 3.

[112] *Id.*

[113] AOL, Inc., v. LCGM, Inc., 1998 WL 940347 (E.D. Va., Nov. 10, 1998).

interest in a service mark under the Lanham Act;[114] exceeding the scope of its subscription agreement, therefore exceeding authorized access in violation of the Computer Fraud and Abuse Act; impairing its computer facilities in violation of same Act; violating Virginia's Computer Crimes Act; and trespass to chattels and violations of both federal and state computer crime statutes.[115] In each case, the court found in favor of AOL.

Spammers have filed antitrust claims against providers as counterclaims to antispam lawsuits. AOL was charged with monopolization[116] by a bulk-e-mailer, a claim rejected by a federal court.[117] In that case, the spammer charged AOL with blocking all of their bulk e-mailings.

The Internet industry is currently developing standards governing spamming, which include the use of false headers and other fraudulent or misleading mailings. AOL has filed scores of lawsuits in many states to deter spammers. In AOL, Inc. v. LCGM, Inc.,[118] AOL sued spammers who sent unsolicited bulk e-mails to AOL subscribers. The spammers used false "aol.com" addresses in their spam headers. AOL's complaint included charges of trespass to chattels, false designation, and dilution by tarnishment. The federal district court ruled in favor of AOL finding that the defendants violated the Lanham Act's false designation of origin and dilution, breached its terms of services, and violated the Computer Fraud and Abuse Act. The Virginia federal court imposed punitive damages, treble damages, and attorneys' fees against the spammer, who had sent more than 60,000,000 pieces of unauthorized bulk e-mail to AOL subscribers.[119]

---

[114] To state a claim of trademark infringement under the federal Lanham Act, the plaintiff must allege that (1) the mark is valid and legally entitled to protection; (2) the plaintiff owns it; and (3) defendant's use of the mark is likely to confuse consumers. Chapter 3 provides a detailed analysis of trademarks arising out of online activities.

[115] *See also* AOL, Inc. v. Prime Data Sys., Inc., 1998 U.S. Dist. LEXIS 20226 (E.D. Va., Nov. 20, 1998) (entering a default judgment against defendant spammers for violating state and federal computer law, the Lanham Act, tort law, and common law conspiracy to commit trespass to chattels).

[116] In order to prevail on a monopolization claim, a party must show "(1) possession of monopoly power in a relevant marked; (2) willful acquisition or maintenance of that power in an exclusionary manner; and (3) causal antitrust injury." AOL Inc. v. GreatDeals.Net, reported in 16 Comp. & Online Litig. R. 3 (June 15, 1998).

[117] America Online Inc. v. GreatDeals, Net, No.99-62-A (E.D. Va., May 4, 1999).

[118] *Supra* note 113.

[119] *Accord* Seidl v. Greentree Mortgage Co., 30 F. Supp. 2d 1292 (D. Colo. 1998) (The owner of an Internet domain name sued a mortgage company, which had conducted a bulk e-mail advertising campaign, claiming that the mortgage company used his domain name as an e-mail identifier. The plaintiff alleged that Greentree violated Colorado's Deceptive Trade Practices Act and the Junk Fax Statute. He also alleged the commission of common law torts, including trespass to chattels, negligence, violation of right of publicity, and false light invasion of privacy.).

§ 5.03   BUSINESS TORTS IN CYBERSPACE

[A]   Fraud and Misrepresentation

Fraud and misrepresentation are torts for willfully deceiving another with intent to cause injury. To prove fraud, the plaintiff must establish that the defendant essentially (1) made a false representation of material fact; (2) knew it was false (or made it with reckless disregard of its truth or falsity); and (3) intended that plaintiff rely upon it; and (4) the plaintiff must be injured by reasonably relying on the false representation. A plaintiff claiming fraud must show injury proximately caused by its reasonable reliance on a misrepresentation. Fraud may be based upon making a statement without reasonable grounds for believing it is true or by suppressing a fact where there is a duty of disclosure.

A *prima facie* case for the tort of misrepresentation occurs when the defendant (1) makes a misrepresentation (2) of material fact (3) for the purpose of inducing the other to act or to refrain from acting in reliance upon it and (4) causes pecuniary loss, (5) even though it is not made fraudulently or negligently.[120] The measure of damages for misrepresentation is the "difference between the value of what the [victim] has parted with and the value of what he has received in the transaction."[121]

Fraud or misrepresentation can also be based on making a promise without any intention of performance, which in turn causes injury or loss to the plaintiff. Misrepresentation, or the common law tort of deceit, occurs when a plaintiff is injured by another's false representations. Liability for fraud or misrepresentation may be actionable under the common law, or state or federal consumer protection statutes.

The reliance element is different for commercial transactions than for consumer transactions. Commercial parties are held to the standard of "justifiable reliance" or "reasonable reliance" standards.[122] The policy justification for the reliance requirement is to encourage recipients of statements to be skeptical about statements that are patently false.[123] The "reasonable reliance" standard determines "the issue of reliance based on all of the circumstances surrounding a transaction, including the mental capacity, educational background, relative sophistication, and bargaining power of the parties."[124] The question of whether the plaintiff's reliance on the representation is justifiable is a factual determination.[125]

---

[120] Restatement (Second) of Torts §§ 525, 552 (1977).

[121] *Id.* at § 552(c).

[122] The standards are objective based on what is reasonable in the industry or in the usage of trade.

[123] Hickox v. Stover, 551 So. 2d 259 (Ala. 1989).

[124] Foremost Ins. Co. v. Parham, 692 So. 2d at 418.

[125] AT &T Information Sys., Inc. v. Cobb Pontiac-Cadillac, Inc., 553 So.2d 529, 532 (Ala. 1989).

A company may be liable for the tort of deceit for products and services it sells online. Fraudulently representing goods or services on the Internet subjects the seller to liability for the pecuniary losses of those who relied on the misrepresentations.[126] A person selling a baseball bat autographed by Ted Williams or golf clubs purportedly used by President Kennedy, for example, is liable for any misrepresentations made about goods sold in an online auction. Misrepresentation in an online transaction may occur with the sale, licensing, lease, exchange of goods, or the rendering of services.

A company may be found liable for the tort of misrepresentation if it suppresses facts or conceals information material to a consumer's decision to purchase its computers or software. The elements of a suppression claim are (1) a duty to disclose the facts; (2) concealment or nondisclosure of material facts by the defendant; (3) inducement of the plaintiff to act; and (4) action by the plaintiff causing injury.[127] Silence is not fraud unless the company has an obligation to communicate material facts about its computer systems.

[B] Misappropriation and Unfair Competition

Unfair competition refers to the torts that punish and deter economic-based deceptive and unfair practices. Unfair competition is subdivided into two parts: (1) consumer confusion as to the source of products, and (2) unfair trade practices (which is a residual category of all other unfair competition laws).[128] The tort of unfair competition arose out of the 1918 case of International News Service v. Associated Press[129] in which the United States Supreme Court recognized misappropriation as a form of unfair competition. In *International News*, the plaintiff, Associated Press (AP), and the defendant, International News Service (INS), each had news wires that sold subscription services to individual newspapers. The defendant would copy AP stories and dispatch them to their subscribers. The Court recognized the defendant's misappropriation of AP's stories as a form of unfair competition.[130]

The Second Circuit in National Basketball Assoc. v. Motorola, Inc.,[131] determined that the following elements were necessary to approve misappropriation of

---

[126] Restatement (Second) of Torts § 531 (1976).

[127] *See, e.g.,* Wilson v. Brown, 496 So. 2d 756 (Ala. 1986).

[128] "Legal Information Institute, Unfair Competition Law Materials" (visited July 1, 1999), http://www.law.cornell.edu/topics/unfair_competition.html.

[129] 248 U.S. 215 (1918).

[130] The court found that the defendant "in appropriating [the news] and selling it as its own is endeavoring to reap where it has not sown, and by disposing of it to newspapers that are competitors of complainant's members is appropriating to itself the harvest of those who have sown." *Id.* at 239-40.

[131] 105 F.3d 841, 845, 847 (2d Cir. 1997). *Cf.* Raymond T. Nimmer, Information Law, ¶3,16 at 3-77 (1996) (arguing "that the general doctrine of misappropriation divorced of any breach of confidence, trademark, goodwill, or similar elements, is not universally accepted").

news or information: "(i) the plaintiff generates or collects information at some cost or expense; (ii) the value of the information is highly time-sensitive; (iii) the defendant's use of the information constitutes free-riding on the plaintiff's costly effort to generate or collect it; (iv) the defendant's use of the information is in direct competition with a product or service offered by the plaintiff; (v) the ability of other parties to free-ride on the efforts of the plaintiff would so reduce the incentive to produce the product or service that its existence or quality would be substantially threatened."[132]

An action for unfair competition encompasses state[133] and federal deceptive trade practices acts as well as the Lanham Act. Unfair competition encompasses state and federal deceptive trade practices acts as well as misappropriations of trade secrets. A California jury awarded $19,000,000 in a case in which a business partner misappropriated valuable proprietary information and trade secrets.[134]

Misappropriation is the use of another's name for one's benefit, as, for example, in advertising services on the Internet. Commercial web sites have found advertising is the chief source of revenue. Advertisers pay to be seen by users of free web sites. News organizations such as the *Washington Post, Life, Fortune,* and *Entertainment Weekly* sell advertising, which is their primary source of revenue from their web sites. TotalNews, Inc. designed a web site featuring the content of major publishers by inserting a "frame on the computer screen that includes the totalnews.com logos and URL as well as the defendants' advertising."[135]

The *Washington Post* and a number of other news organizations sued Total-News for creating a frame around their content.[136] The plaintiffs contended that TotalNews was a "parasitic web site" designed to pocket advertising revenue.[137] The national publications argued that they expended "substantial resources to gather and display the news and information found on their web sites."[138] The defendants caused "each of plaintiffs' web sites to appear within a window on defendants' site . . . misappropriat[ing] valuable commercial property."[139] The plaintiffs further argued that TotalNews promoted their web site to advertisers on

---

[132] *Id.* at 845, 852 (cited in Wehrenberg v. Moviefone, Inc., 1999 U.S. Dist. LEXIS 17574 (E.D. Mo., Nov. 1, 1999)).

[133] The misappropriation is a form of state common law unfair competition. Wehrenberg v. Moviefone, Inc., 1999 U.S. Dist. LEXIS 17574 (E.D. Mo., Nov. 1, 1999).

[134] Zachariades v. Smith, No. 336, 999 (San Mateo Cal., 1993) (reported in Calif. Jury Verdicts & Settl. Rep.) (available on LEXIS, JRVRDCT; ALLVER file).

[135] Complaint of Washington Post Co. v. TotalNews, Inc. (S.D. N.Y. filed Feb. 20, 1997).

[136] *Id.*

[137] *Id.*

[138] *Id.*

[139] *Id.*

the basis of featuring plaintiffs' content. The plaintiffs argued that framing constituted misappropriation and unfair competition because it took "the entire commercial value of the news reported at each of the plaintiffs' respective [news] sites
and literally sells it to others for defendants' own profit."[140] Misappropriation
claims occur in a wide variety of web site activities where the defendant is seeking to divert business to its site.

[C]   Interference with Business Contracts

Intentional interference with contract and economic opportunity may also
occur in a wide variety of Internet activities. This tort involves three parties: "the
plaintiff, a person with whom he has a valuable economic relationship, and the
person who disrupts that relationship."[141] A company could have an action for economic harm if an online competitor interfered with would-be customers or buyers
by planting false rumors about its financial solvency.

The factual circumstances for actionable interference are broad. The *prima
facie* case must, however, show "(1) the existence of a contract (or economic
opportunity) involving the plaintiff and another; (2) the defendant's knowledge of
it; (3) the defendant's malicious, improper, or intentional interference with it; (4)
breach of the contract or other legally cognizable disruption of economic opportunity; and (5) resulting damage to the plaintiff."[142]

Tortious interference with contract may be divided into two separate causes
of action, one for interfering with contract and one for inducing breach of contract. The Restatement (Second) of Torts divides interference torts into first, those
concerning existing contractual rights and, second, those for inducing prospective
contractual relations.[143] The second branch of interference of contract, interference with prospective contractual relations, requires (1) a prospective contractual
relation; (2) the purpose or intent to harm the plaintiff by preventing the relation
from occurring; (3) the absence of privilege or justification on the part of the
defendant; and (4) actual damage resulting from the defendant's interference with
contract.[144]

The Restatement (Second) of Torts § 768 provides the factors to determine
whether a business competitor's interference with a prospective business relationship is proper or improper. The section provides as follows:

---

[140] *Id.*

[141] Dan B. Dobbs, The Law of Torts 1257 (2000).

[142] *Id.* at 1260.

[143] Restatement (Second) of Torts § 766 (1979).

[144] *Id.*

(1) One who intentionally causes a third person not to enter into a prospective contractual relation with another who is his competitor . . . does not interfere improperly with the other's relation if:

      (a) the relation concerns a matter involved in the competition between the actor and the other and

      (b) the actor does not employ wrongful means and

      (c) his action does not create or continue an unlawful restraint of trade and

      (d) his purpose is at least in part to advance his interest in competing with the other.[145]

The Seventh Circuit upheld a ruling of a lower court that a consultant was liable for inducing a breach of contract in JD Edwards & Co. v. Podany.[146] The plaintiff company had hired the defendant consultant to review the computer system. The consultant expressed a derogatory opinion about the software without having a basis of knowledge about its functions.[147] The consultant concluded "that the software system . . . was unsound . . . and he advised the company to stop installing the software and to stop payment" to the licensor.[148] The court found that a reasonable trier of fact could reject the defense of consultant's privilege if asserted by the defendant.[149]

[D]   Breach of Fiduciary Duty

A fiduciary duty arises out of a relationship between two parties "when one of them is under a duty to act for or to give advice for the benefit of another upon matters within the scope of the relation."[150] The breach of fiduciary duty depends first on whether a "fiduciary relationship exist[s] at the time of the alleged misconduct."[151] The concept of a fiduciary relationship arises out of the law of trust, and fiduciary duties may be imputed to a wide variety of corporate actors. A breach of fiduciary duty cause of action may be brought against directors, officers, employers, business partners, or joint venturers. The breach of fiduciary duty may also arise when key employees set up a competing business or work for a competitor.[152]

---

[145] Restatement (Second) of Torts § 768 (1979).

[146] 168 F.3d 1020 (7th Cir. 1999).

[147] *Id.*

[148] *Id.*

[149] *Id.*

[150] Restatement (Second) of Torts § 874, cmt. a (1979).

[151] Robert A. Kutcher and Benjamin W. Bronston, Breach of Fiduciary Duties, Chapter 1 in George F. McGunnigle, Jr., Business Torts Litigation 1 (1992).

[152] Dobbs, *supra* note 141.

Breach of fiduciary duty is a cause of action that may arise in many different situations arising out of online activities. If a company owes a fiduciary duty to a trade partner, it must conduct its online businesses in good faith and in the spirit of fair dealing. An online company that places its own interest ahead of a party to which it owes a fiduciary duty may be assessed punitive damages for ill-gotten gains.[153]

§ 5.04   INTERNET TORTS

[A]   Identity Theft

A company's employees may be victimized by "identity fraud" on the Internet. Any anonymous user can claim to have a given occupation or a given expertise.[154] The Internet makes it easy for impostors to assume false identities, and it is therefore a haven for identity theft. In Andrews v. Trans Union Corp.,[155] for example, an impostor used a plaintiff's Social Security number to apply for credit. The California federal court held that the plaintiff had a valid claim against the credit-reporting agency. The plaintiff had the burden of proving that it used reasonable procedures for assuring maximum accuracy.[156]

A company needs reliable means for identifying and for authorizing potential customers in order to develop reliable e-commerce. Otherwise, it may be subject to tort liability if it permits impostors to gain access to sensitive financial or proprietary information belonging to third persons. New technologies, such as digital certificates, are being developed to combat identity theft.[157]

[B]   Computer Viruses

Electronic viruses are virulent codes that may end up destroying the hard drive of a company computer and altering or destroying data or information. These malicious programs infect "executable files or the system areas of hard and floppy disks and then make copies of [themselves]."[158] A computer virus threat is a serious concern for companies who may lose money, time, and key information assets

---

[153] See, e.g., DeRance, Inc. v. PaineWebber Inc., 872 F.3d 1312 (7th Cir. 1989) (court upholding a $7,000,000 punitive damages award against broker who intentionally misled his client, filing reports under-reporting losses and acting in opposition to express agreement of trading practices between the client and broker).

[154] David L. Wilson, Your Passport Please: Helping to Ferret Out Fakes and Frauds on the Web, Buff. News, Jan. 13, 1998, at 7D.

[155] 7 F. Supp. 2d 1056 (C.D. Cal. 1998).

[156] Id. at 1076.

[157] Wilson, supra note 154.

[158] Computer Virus FAQ for New Users (visited July 19, 1999), http://www.faqs.org/faqs/computer-virus/new-uers.

is a malicious code is unleashed in their systems. In May 1999, computers throughout the world were infected with the CIH virus.[159] In March 1999, the Melissa Virus infected thousands of computers worldwide.[160]

A 1999 e-mail virus called "Bubble Boy"[161] infects computers simply by being viewed in the preview pane of an e-mail program, such as Microsoft's Outlook.[162] Viruses are spread by the execution of a "program code that's infected by a virus."[163] The "Bubble Boy" virus, however, "infects computers without being opened."[164]

Deliberately introducing a virus into a computer system can constitute criminal as well as tortious trespass, and it violates criminal state and federal laws. A company that knowingly distributed computer software with viruses would be theoretically liable for fraud or misrepresentation. The introduction of a computer virus could, theoretically, constitute conversion or trespass to chattels as well.[165]

➤   **[1]   Preventive Law Pointer: Preventing Computer Viruses**

The risk of introducing malicious codes into computer systems needs to be managed by prevention rather than legal remedies.[166] Employees need to be educated on how to avoid catching viruses. Topics should include (1) an overview of the types of virus, including PC viruses,[167] Mac viruses,[168] UNIX viruses,[169] macro

---

[159] *Id.*

[160] John D. Penn, Beyond the Quill: Big Brother Really Is Watching: Following Computers' Trails, 1999 ABI JNL. LEXIS 75 (June 1999).

[161] The virus is named after a famous episode of the "Seinfeld" television show called the Bubble Boy episode.

[162] Robert Schoenberger, Bubble Boy E-Mail Virus Lurks, Gannett News Service, Nov. 11, 1999, at ARC.

[163] "When you execute program code that's infected by a virus, the virus code will also run and try to infect other programs, either on the same computer or on other computers connected to it over a network. And the newly infected programs will try to infect yet more programs." *Id.*

[164] Schoenberger, *supra* note 162.

[165] Robin A. Brooks, Deterring the Spread of Viruses Online: Can Tort Law Tighten the 'Net? 17 Rev. Litig. 343, 365 (1998).

[166] In the summer of 1998, my home and school computers were infected with the Anti-Exec virus, which probably originated in a diskette transmitted from Suffolk's Computer Resource Center. At the time, I thought that all floppy disks had been scanned for viruses. While writing this chapter, I found this was not the case when Anti-Exec again infected my personal computer. The host for the virus was an old diskette that apparently had not been scanned. Without an infected diskette or other host, a virus cannot spread. Viruses cannot be eradicated unless all infected objects are replaced with clean backups.

[167] PC stands for *personal computer*. A *PC virus* is a term referring to viruses that infect personal computers.

[168] A MAC virus attaches itself to Macintosh computer systems.

[169] UNIX is "a software program that controls the operation of computer hardware and the interaction of software applications on that software." Michael D. Scott, Internet and Technology Desk Reference 519 (1999).

viruses,[170] Trojan horses,[171] worms,[172] logic bombs,[173] and other viruses; (2) the harm viruses can do; (3) how viruses spread; (4) technologies and workplace practices that will reduce the radius of the risk of viruses; (5) antivirus software used by the company; and (6) the name of a contact person who checks on virus alerts and is responsible for preventing or mitigating losses due to viruses.

Employees need to be prepared to implement prompt remedial measures once they discover that the company's computer system is infected. A company's systems administrator needs to know how to promptly mitigate the consequences of malicious codes. Companies may need to initiate data recovery and emergency preparedness measures, such as checking off-site storage networks for viruses. Once a virus, such as Anti-Exec, is detected, it is important to take prompt remedial measures. The user will need to run scan programs on all floppy disks, as well as computer systems. Antivirus programs such as Norton Utilities or McAfee should be used to scan all computer drives as well as diskettes.[174]

It is important to remember that a virus cannot be transmitted unless a program is executed. A program is executed by "running an application program (like a text editor or game), booting from a disk with an infected DOS boot sector or master boot record, or launching an infected document in one of the components of MS-Office (i.e., Word, Excel, Access, etc.)."[175] Simply browsing web sites, for example, does not expose the computer system to viruses; the downloading of unknown databases, however, does pose a risk of transmitting viruses. Viruses strike software, not hardware, and experts agree that no known virus has ever damaged computer hardware.[176]

It is arguable that a disabling routine built into the software is also a virus, unless the license agreement gives notice that the licensor reserves the right to use

---

[170] A macro is a "single instruction that initiates a sequence of operations or module interactions within the program." Scott, *supra* note 169, at 305 (quoting Computer Assoc. Int'l. v. Altai, Inc., 982 F.2d 693, 698 (2d Cir. 1992)).

[171] A Trojan horse is a computer program that conceals malicious code. "Typically, a Trojan horse masquerades as a useful program that users would want or need to execute. It performs, or appears to perform, as expected, but also does surreptitious harm." Scott, *supra* note 169, at 510.

[172] *Worm* is an acronym for "write once, read many." A worm is a "self-contained program containing malicious code that copy versions of themselves across electronically connected nodes." Scott, *Id.* at 550.

[173] "A desirable program which performs some useful function such as logic but which contains a parasite or viral infection within its logic which is undetectable upon casual review. [M]ore properly called a 'time bomb' or 'logic bomb.'" Scott, *supra* note 169, at 303 (citation omitted).

[174] There is no "bullet-proof anti-viral program. One expert recommends comparing products at the following web sites: Virus Test Center (UNI-Hamburg), http://agn-www.iformatik.uni-hamburg.de/vtc/naeng.htm, Virus Research Unit (Uni-Tampere), http://www.uta.fi/laitokset/virus; *Virus Bulletin* (Industry Periodical), http://www.virusbtn.com (visited July 19, 1999), http://members.tripod.com/~k_+wismer/common.htm.

[175] *Id.*

[176] *Id.*

disabling software, such as time bombs.[177] An active restraint affects the licensee's ability to access its own information, whereas a passive restraint prevents unauthorized use but does not lock the user out of his own computer. Installing an active disabling routine into software may subject a software vendor to intentional tort liability for spreading a computer virus.

[C] Cyberstalking

A tort action can be brought based on cyberstalking by e-mail or the Internet. In Hitchcock v. Woodside Literary Agency (WLA),[178]Jayne Hitchcock, a University of Maryland teaching assistant and writer, answered a web site advertisement soliciting writing samples from "published and unpublished authors."[179] Mrs. Hitchcock received a letter from WLA that praised her writing and solicited her to forward a full manuscript to the agency, along with a $75 "reading and market evaluation fee."[180] Ms. Hitchcock sent a different sample of her writing to WLA using her maiden name, to which WLA responded to by sending her a letter that was "virtually identical" to the letter sent in response to the first writing sample, save for the soliciting of a $150 "reading and market evaluation fee."[181] Ms. Hitchcock concluded that WLA was nothing more than a scam for soliciting bogus fees from aspiring writers.[182] She then posted various notices on Internet bulletin boards denouncing WLA and noting that "legitimate literary agencies did not charge reading fees."[183]

The company responded to Hitchcock's actions by launching a campaign of harassment against her on the Internet. The harassment took many forms, including the posting of messages that falsely claimed that the plaintiff was the author of hard-core pornography.[184] Hitchcock was also sent crude messages, which threatened her with sexual assault. WLA mail-bombed Hitchcock's e-mail accounts and posted offensive messages to third parties about her.[185] The defendant flooded her e-mail accounts and posted offensive messages to third parties in such a manner as to make it appear she had authored them.[186] Ms. Hitchcock's "name, address, and phone number [was posted] in news groups for sadomasochists."[187] Postings, in her name, were made on electronic bulletin boards for beer lovers which called

---

[177] Id.

[178] 15 F. Supp. 2d 246 (D. Md. 1998).

[179] Id. at 249.

[180] Id. at 249

[181] Id.

[182] Id.

[183] Id.

[184] Id.

[185] Id.

[186] Id.

[187] Michael Dresser, New Maryland. Law Will Ban Harassment by E-Mail, id.

the members "drunks and morons."[188] The online literary agency even went so far as to transmit crank messages, posing as the plaintiff, to insult her co-workers.[189]

The victim filed a lawsuit charging that the agency deliberately placed her in danger of imminent sexual assault by posting Internet messages in her name containing crude sexual propositions.[190] The plaintiff sought to recover damages for personal and professional injury, including the cost of therapy. The federal court dismissed the plaintiff's complaint in its entirety for failure to state a claim.[191] The plaintiff had no alternative for the e-harassment but to close her e-mail account. The online agency was discovered to be the harasser when "it slipped up and left her name and e-mail address in one of the literary agency's Internet ads."[192] Despite this smoking gun, the federal court granted the defendant's motion to dismiss the plaintiffs' RICO claim for failure to state a claim upon which relief could be granted.[193] In the end, there was no remedy available for e-mail harassment and the "e-mail bombs" that shut her e-mail account down.[194]

The Internet makes it easy for harassers to trace the telephone numbers and e-mail addresses of potential victims.[195] The common law agency relationship between an employer and an employee makes an employer liable for torts that the agent commits when acting within the scope of the agency.[196] A company may, therefore, be liable for torts that arise out of an employee's online activities. An employer may be liable for failing to warn others of the dangerous propensities of ex-employees.[197]

---

[188] *Id.*

[189] *Id.*

[190] *Id.*

[191] The plaintiff's dismissal was partially attributable to defective pleading. The plaintiff stated claims under New York law rather than Maryland law, resulting in dismissal of the state claims. The plaintiff, in addition, failed to plead that WLA was a distinct enterprise, which is a requirement of the Racketeer Influenced and Corruption Organizations Act (RICO). All claims were dismissed, and the plaintiff's motion to amend her pleadings was denied. *Id.*

[192] *Id.*

[193] *Id.*

[194] *Id.*

[195] One company has a database that will take a telephone number and "find the owner's name, where they live, and provide a map showing how to get there, a technique known as a reverse look up search." Andrew Brown, "Hidden Dangers of the Internet," It.mail (visited June 18, 1999), http://www.dailymail.co.uk/story1703_2.html.

[196] American Law Institute, Restatement of the Law Third of Agency § 2.04 (Preliminary Draft No. 3, June 11, 1999).

[197] An employer faces a dilemma in providing information on ex-employees for reference checks. On the one hand, employers may be subject to defamatory statements about their employees. On the other hand, employers may be held liable for failing to warn others of known *propensities of ex-employees to commit crimes. See e.g.,* Randi W. v. Morc Joint Unified School Dist., 14 Cal. 4th 1066, 60 Cal. App. 2d 273 (1997) (ex-employer of school molested 13-year-old student; liability for failing to warn new school district that teacher had been dismissed for molesting students).

Vicarious liability would make a company liable for torts that its employees commit while acting within the scope of their employment. The rationale underlying vicarious liability is that the "principal chooses the agent and has the opportunity to train and instruct the agent, as well as the opportunity to install safeguards against predictable forms of misconduct."[198] A company must therefore institute procedures to prevent its employees from using the computer to stalk co-employees or third parties, otherwise it risks being exposed to the possibility of vicarious liability.

§ 5.05   PUBLISHING TORTS IN CYBERSPACE

[A]   Defamation in Cyberspace

The development of new information technologies poses new challenges to the law of defamation. The elements of a defamation action require the plaintiff to prove that the statement (1) is defamatory; (2) is about the plaintiff; (3) was published by the defendant; (4) was made maliciously; and (5) resulted in damages to the plaintiff.[199] The Restatement of Torts defines defamation as:

> a false and defamatory statement concerning another; an unprivileged publication to a third-party; fault amounting to at least negligence on the part of the publisher, and either actionability of the statement irrespective of special harm or the existence of special harm caused by the publication.[200]

Defamation is a communication "which tends to hold the plaintiff up to hatred, contempt, or ridicule, or to cause him to be shunned or avoided."[201] Whether a communication is defamatory is judged from the viewpoint of the reasonable person. The test for defamatory meaning is whether the communication "lowers the person's reputation in the community or deters third persons from associating or dealing with him."[202] A statement may be defamatory on its face or defamatory because of context or by innuendo.[203] "A defamatory communication is made concerning the person to whom its recipient correctly, or mistakenly but reasonably, understands that it was intended to refer."[204] Whether words are reasonably construed as defamatory is a preliminary question of law determined by the court.[205]

---

[198] *Id.*

[199] *Id.* at § 7.02[A].

[200] *Id.* at § 558.

[201] W. Page Keeton, et al., Prosser and Keeton on The Law of Torts 773 (5th ed. 1984).

[202] *Id.* at 774.

[203] *Id.* at 780.

[204] *Id.* at 783.

[205] *Id.* at 781.

The U.S. Supreme Court in New York Times v. Sullivan reshaped the law of defamation, concluding that it must recognize the "profound national commitment to the principle that debate of public issues should be uninhibited, robust, and wide-open."[206] Publisher liability, too, was transformed by the case when, in 1964, the United States Supreme Court applied First Amendment standards to the tort of defamation in New York Times Co. v. Sullivan.[207] In *Sullivan,* a city commissioner of Montgomery, Alabama, sued the *New York Times* for an advertisement published in the newspaper to raise money for a legal defense fund for Dr. Martin Luther King, Jr.[208] The plaintiff contended that the *New York Times* advertisement, placed by four black civil rights leaders defamed him. An Alabama jury agreed, assessing damages of $500,000 against both the civil rights leaders, and the newspaper. The U.S. Supreme Court reversed, holding that in public official cases, the plaintiff must prove with "convincing clarity" that the defamatory statements were made with actual malice.[209]

Defamatory statements may be classified into statements that are defamation "*per se*" or statements that have a defamatory statement due to "extrinsic facts." Slander, on the other hand, is traditionally divided into slander *per se* and slander *per quod.* Slanderous *per se* statements are presumed defamatory, and no special damages must be proven. Showing that the statements refer to a plaintiff and that the plaintiff suffered special damages must be proven for slander *per quod* claims. A growing number of states have codified the law of defamation. The Oklahoma statute, for example, states that: "Slander is a false and unprivileged publication which (1) charges a person with a crime; (2) accuses him of having an infectious, contagious or loathsome disease or being impotent or promiscuous; (3) maligns him with respect to his office, profession, trade or business; or (4) causes actual damages by its natural consequences."[210]

Written defamation is classified as libel, whereas oral defamation is slander. Courts traditionally will not permit an action for slander absent proof of special damages.[211] It is uncertain whether it is slander if the defendant makes an allegedly defamatory statement about the plaintiff in a "chat room." An e-mail message may be printed out and is therefore likely to be libel.

The Internet makes it possible to falsify return e-mail addresses to defame individuals as well as business entities. It is quite common for Internet users to

---

[206] New York Times Co. v. Sullivan, 376 U.S. 254 (1964).

[207] *Id.*

[208] *Id.*

[209] *Id.*

[210] Okla. Stat. tit. 12, 1442 (199(1).

[211] The specific exceptions to the special damage rule for slander are statements that impute a crime, a loathsome disease, or constitute trade libel, which "affect the plaintiff in his business, trade, profession, office, or calling." W. Page Keeton, Prosser and Keeton on The Law of Torts § 111 at 788 (1984).

"flame" fellow users on the Internet. Flaming is not only a breach of netiquette,[212] but it may be the basis for a defamation lawsuit against a company and its employees.[213]

One of the known e-business risks is that anonymous individuals can post false information on online forums that will defame other sellers or interfere with contracts. The eBay system of posting comments on participants appears to function as part of the course of dealing and usage of trade in the electronic auction place.[214] The online auction recently changed the process and form for posting reputation comments. A person's rebuttal now appears immediately after the comments submitted by other users.

Recently, negative feedback by a purchaser on eBay led to a defamation lawsuit in Maryland.[215] The customer purchased a "Color Magic" Barbie doll from a collector using the eBay site. The customer later posted a disparaging comment about purchasing a "Balding Barbie" from the plaintiff.[216] The seller filed a defamation lawsuit, arguing that the disparaging comments thwarted attempts to bid on other items. EBay argued that it builds trust by soliciting positive and negative feedback from customers.[217]

White House aide Sidney Blumenthal and his wife brought a defamation action against the Internet gossip columnist, Matt Drudge, for his false allegation that Mr. Blumenthal was a chronic wife-beater.[218] The plaintiffs also sued AOL, an interactive computer service provider that was the publisher of the electronic version of the Drudge Report. AOL was dismissed from the case, as it was an ISP immunized by § 230(C) of the Communications Decency Act. The District of

---

[212] Netiquette is an "abbreviation for 'Internet etiquette.' Netiquette also refers to the informal norms and rules that develop in the use of the Internet." Michael D. Scott, Internet and Technology Desk Reference 336 (1999).

[213] Flaming may occur in a Usenet newsgroup, Web forum, or e-mail to a distribution list. "Certain issues tend to provoke emphatically stated responses, but flaming is often directed at a self-appointed expert rather than at the issues or information itself and is sometimes directed at unwitting but opinionated newbies (new Internet users) who appear in a newsgroup." Whatis.com, What Is . . . Flaming (A Definition), (visited Nov. 14, 1999), http://www.whatis.com/flaming.htm.

[214] Section 1-205 of the Uniform Commercial Code defines a usage of trade as "any practice or method of dealing having such regularity of observance in a place, vocation or trade as to justify an expectation that it will be observed with respect to the transaction in question. The existence and scope of such a usage are to be proved as facts. If it is established that such a usage is embodied in a written trade code or similar writing the interpretation of the writing, is for the court." U.C.C. § 1-205 (1995).

[215] Zena Olijnyk, Balding Barbie Lawsuit Typifies Peril of E-Commerce, The National Post, Apr. 16, 1999, at CO1.

[216] Id.

[217] "E-Bay feedback is the post-transaction commentary that builds trust for customers in on-line auctions." Troy Wolverton, E-Bay User Subject of Auctioneer's Libel Suit, CNET NEWS.COM (visited June 18, 1999), http://www.news.com/News/Items/0,4,35814,00.html.

[218] Drudge v. Blumenthal, 992 F. Supp. 44 (D.D.C. 1998).

Columbia court found that Drudge's interactive web site specifically focused on D.C. political gossip and that the columnist regularly distributed his writings to D.C. residents. The court, therefore, refused to dismiss the defamation action based upon the defendant's purposeful activity in gathering, soliciting, and receiving D.C. gossip.

Many users of e-mail or those who post to Internet news groups feel free to express opinions they would not make in a business letter or in person.[219] Postings to Internet news groups may result in defamation lawsuits. An AOL subscriber, for example, was sued for libel based on its online criticism of a Caribbean resort and its diving instructor in an anonymous posting.[220]

Libel or slander must be communicated or published to a third person in order to constitute defamation. The concept of publication "does not mean that the defamatory statement was committed to paper; it means that the statement was conveyed to someone besides the person defamed."[221] Publication may be difficult to establish in an online environment.

➤ [1] Preventive Law Pointer: Pleading and Proof of Defamation

Counsel must consider whether a publication is protected by the First Amendment or is constitutionally protected speech. They must also consider state variations in the law of defamation. It is always the trial court's province to determine initially whether statements are capable of having a defamatory meaning.[222] A plaintiff may file for a temporary restraining order or injunction against use of the Internet to transmit untrue factual accusations. The defendant may be enjoined from transmitting defamatory statements via the Internet or discussion groups.[223] Before filing a claim, plaintiffs must determine the elements to be pleaded and proven in the jurisdiction. To plead a cause of action for a defamatory publication in Pennsylvania, for instance, a plaintiff must prove (1) the defamatory character of the communication; (2) its publication by the defendant; (3) its application to the plaintiff; (4) the understanding by the recipient of the defamatory meaning; (5) that the defamatory statement's intent is to be applied to the plaintiff; (6) special harm resulting to the plaintiff from its publication; and (7) abuse of a conditionally privileged occasion.[224]

---

[219] Simon Halberstam, Closing the Portals on Defamation, New Media Age, Oct. 14, 1999, at 25.

[220] Horizon Hotels d/b/a/ Caribbean Inn v. AOL (filed Nov. 1995, Cook County, Ill. (no published opinion), reported in Perkins Coie LLP: Internet Case Digest (visited June 18, 1999), http://www.perkinscoie.com/resource/ecomm/netcase/Cases-06.htm.

[221] George B. Delta and Jeffrey H. Matsurra, Law of the Internet § 7.02[A] at 7-7 (1998).

[222] Resnick v. Angel Manfredy, 1999 U.S. Dist. LEXIS 5877 (E.D. Pa. Apr. 26, 1999).

[223] See, e.g., Internet Am. Inc. v. Massey, No. 96-10955C (Tex. Dallas Cty. Dist. Ct., Oct. 14, 1996).

[224] Furillo v. Dana Corp. Parish Div., 866 F. Supp. 824, 847 (E.D. Pa. 1994) (applying Pennsylvania law).

[2] Parties to a Defamation Action

[a] *Plaintiffs in General*

The plaintiff in a defamation action is a living person or entity, although a few states "have made defamation of the dead a crime."[225] Corporations or other entities can not be defamed in the same personal sense as can a living person.[226] A company in Washington, D.C., filed a lawsuit against Specialty Car Sales of Miami, alleging that the owners and employees of Specialty posted two defamatory messages about a FedTrust employee through the eBay feedback system.[227] The negative comments warned potential buyers about the employee, noting that he was "dishonest about the origin of his cars" and potential buyers should "stay away."[228] The online auction house argued that it was protected from defamation lawsuits by the Good Samaritan provision of the Communications Decency Act.[229]

In a New Hampshire federal case, a defendant posted false information about the plaintiff's company on the Internet to drive down stock prices.[230] Presstek Inc., the plaintiff, was a New Hampshire developer of digital imaging technology. Presstek sued three individuals for posting defamatory comments to an online chat room to drive down the price of the high technology company's stock.[231] The defendants were "short sellers," who sell borrowed stock and profit when a company's stock price declines.[232] In a related case, the First Circuit affirmed the dismissal of a defamation and legal malpractice case filed by the principals of Presstek.[233] The objectionable statements alleged organized crime links between the short sellers and the defendants in a federal securities case accused of stock manipulation.[234]

A Seattle financial education company filed a slander lawsuit against ten users of Yahoo! message boards.[235] The plaintiff named ten "John Doe" defendants and sought to subpoena Yahoo! for their identities. One of the posting defendants

---

[225] Keeton, Prosser and Keeton on Torts § 111, at 778-79.

[226] *Id.* at 806.

[227] *Id.*

[228] *Id.*

[229] *Id.*

[230] Presstek Inc. v. Lustig, No. 97463-M (D. N.H. filed Sept. 17, 1997) (claiming that defendants posted false statements to an Internet chat room, in order to manipulate price of company's stock).

[231] "Once Again an ISP is Open to Liability for Defamation," 14 Computer Law Strategist 6 (Sept. 1997).

[232] *Id.*

[233] Hugel v. Milberg, Weiss, Bershad, Hynes & Lerach, LLP, 175 F.3d 14 (1st Cir. 1999).

[234] *Id.*

[235] Reuters, Slander Suit Served against Yahoo! Users, Special to CNET NEWS.COM, Mar. 9, 1999 (visited June 18, 1999), http://www.news.com/News/Item-0, 4,33503,00.htm/st.ne.fd.mdh.

claimed that one of the financial company's founders "had been arrested for accepting kickbacks."[236]

A plaintiff received a libel award to compensate him for having been called a liar on a posting to an Internet discussion group. The dispute arose out of an exchange of e-mail followed by an argument. The litigants then "posted electronic 'he-said-she-said' accounts about how the phone call ended" on an Internet discussion group.[237] The objectionable message was the defendant's posting a message entitled, "Ken McCarthy is a liar—be warned." The plaintiff filed a defamation lawsuit and received a $5,000 award, which was later overturned on appeal.[238]

A Utah federal court ordered that a web site be removed from the Internet for a short time for allegedly defaming a business.[239] The judge lifted the preliminary injunction in February 1999.[240] In another case, a California court set aside a default motion in a defamation case against a woman who charged a California Highway Patrol officer with sexual harassment on her web site.[241] A British court ordered a Canadian to pay "damages for libeling English physicist Laurence Godfrey during an Internet discussion forum."[242]

[b] Public Officials and Public Figures

The law of defamation merges with the First Amendment when the plaintiffs are public officials and public figures. For public officials and public figures, defamatory statements must be proven, by clear and convincing evidence, to have been made with knowledge of their falsity or with reckless indifference to the truth.[243] There is no defamation for matters in a person's life that relate to the public interest.[244] Public officials are "those who are commonly classified as public officers, but also public employees who exercise any substantial governmental power."[245]

The public figure doctrine was first articulated by the Court in Gertz v. Robert Welch, Inc.[246] There are two kinds of public figures: general and limited.

---

[236] *Id.*

[237] Diana Walsh, Woman Cleared of Net Libel for Calling Man Liar, S.F. Examiner, Apr. 3, 1998, at A-11.

[238] *Id.*

[239] *Id.* at 87.

[240] *Id.*

[241] *Id.* at 88.

[242] *Id.* at 95.

[243] Keeton, Prosser and Keeton on Torts § 113, at 806-07.

[244] *Id.*

[245] W. Page Keeton, Prosser and Keeton on Torts § 113, at 106.

[246] 418 U.S. 323 (1974).

The general public figure is a public figure for all purposes, whereas a limited public figure is a "public figure only because they have voluntarily injected themselves into the resolution of particular controversies or issues of importance to the general public."[247] The following are the three factors determining whether a plaintiff is a limited purpose public figure. (1) Does a public controversy exist? (2) What is the nature and extent of the plaintiff's participation in the controversy? (3) Is the alleged defamation germane to the plaintiff's participation in the controversy?[248]

Commentators argue that individuals who engage in discussions of topics on Internet news groups may be "limited purpose public figures" for purposes of defamation law.[249] Whether a plaintiff is a limited public figure will depend, however, on whether a topic discussed on news groups is deemed to be a public controversy, the extent and nature of the controversy, and the extent and nature of the plaintiff's postings to a newsgroup.

[c]   Online Service Providers

Publishers under traditional defamation law are liable for defamatory statements contained in their works even if they had no knowledge of the statement's objectionable content.[250] In contrast, distributors are not liable for defamatory statements contained in their materials unless it is proven that they have actual knowledge of the defamatory statements.[251] Publishers are liable for any defamatory statements they publish, whereas distributors are liable only if they knew or had reason to know that the statements were defamatory.[252]

Courts were divided on how to apply defamation law to Internet Service Providers (ISPs) for the libelous postings of third parties. The Communications Decency Act of 1996 immunized providers for a wide variety of torts committed by third parties. The role of the ISP resembles a pipe for transmitting data, more like a telephone carrier than a newspaper or distributor.[253]

---

[247] Keeton, Prosser and Keeton on Torts § 113, at 806.

[248] Waldbaum v. Fairchild Publications, Inc., 627 F.2d 1287, 1296-98 (D.C. Cir. 1980).

[249] Martin C. Loesch, et al., Chapter 2, Defamation, in Surveying Cyberspace: A Guide to Insurance Defense and Coverage in the Age of Technology 1998 DRI 1-5.

[250] W. Page Keeton et al., Prosser and Keeton on Torts § 113, at 810 (5th ed. 1984).

[251] Id. at 811.

[252] Jeffrey P. Cunard, Internet Legal Developments, in Communications 1998, G4-64036 (PLI, 1998).

[253] Traditionally, telephone companies, telegraph operators, and other communication carriers were not liable for defamation. The rise of commercial ISPs, such as AOL, CompuServe, Prodigy, and Delphi, raises novel issues as to whether the provider should be held liable for the torts of its subscribers.

Prior to the enactment of the Communications Decency Act (CDA), the Southern District of New York addressed, in Cubby, Inc. v. CompuServe Inc.,[254] whether an Internet Service Provider could be liable for defamatory statements posted on one of its news groups or online forums. CompuServe's bulletin board had an electronic newsletter called Rumorville. The plaintiff began publishing a competing publication he called "Scuttlebutt." A subscriber on CompuServe's bulletin board labeled the Scuttlebutt publication as "a start-up scam." The plaintiff brought a defamation action against Rumorville as well as CompuServe, on the legal theory that it was a republisher.[255] The court found that CompuServe exercised no editorial control over materials made available to its subscribers and was therefore a distributor and not a publisher for purposes of the law of defamation. The legal consequence of being defined as a mere conduit or distributor was that CompuServe was not liable for defamatory statements on Rumorville. The court was persuaded that CompuServe was a distributor because it did not review the content and therefore had the same status under defamation law as a public library, bookstore, or newsstand.[256]

In another case decided prior to the Communications Decency Act of 1996, a New York court found Prodigy to be a publisher rather than a distributor potentially liable for defamatory content made in its newsgroups. The New York court denied Prodigy's motion to dismiss a defamation action made by a subscriber in a Prodigy newsgroup, in Stratton Oakmont Inc. v. Prodigy Services Co.[257] Prodigy was a family-oriented ISP that advertised that it screened its content, unlike many other providers. Prodigy used software that detected objectionable words and automatically notified the user that their message would be censored.[258] After a message accusing Stratton Oakmont, Inc., of fraudulent securities offerings appeared on Prodigy's electronic bulletin board, Stratton Oakmont filed a defamation lawsuit demanding $100 million in punitive damages from Prodigy.[259] Prodigy's defense was that it was a mere conduit of information and not a publisher.[260]

The court in *Stratton Oakmont* held that the provider could be liable for defamatory statements since it was exercising control over the content of materials available on its services. The court was of the opinion that by reviewing and

---

[254] 776 F. Supp. 135 (S.D.N.Y. 1991).

[255] *Id.* at 139.

[256] *Id.*

[257] 23 Media Law Rep. (BNA) 1794 (N.Y. Sup. Ct. 1995).

[258] Rex S. Heinke and Heather D. Rafter, Rough Justice in Cyberspace: Liability on the Electronic Frontier, Comp. Law., July 1994, at 1.

[259] Stratton Oakmont, Inc. v. Prodigy Servs. Co., 1995 WL 323710 (S.D. N.Y., May 26, 1995) (unpublished decision).

[260] *Id.* The Prodigy case was criticized by many legal academics and in electronic discussion groups on the Internet. Professor I. Trotter Hardy found sentiment running "in favor of Prodigy and for unfettered expression on computer bulletin boards." Matthew Goldstein, "Prodigy Case May Solve Troubling Liability Puzzle," Nat'l L. J., Dec. 19, 1994, at B1 (quoting Professor Hardy).

deleting notes from its bulletin boards on the basis of offensiveness, Prodigy was making decisions as to content and exercising editorial control. On October 24, 1995, the case was settled while the appeal was pending.[261] In an unusual procedural move, Stratton Oakmont agreed to drop its demand for $100 million in damages for defamation in an exchange for Prodigy's apology.[262]

Stratton Oakmont also agreed not to contest Prodigy's motion to ask the court to reverse or set aside its prior ruling on Prodigy's status as a publisher.[263] The Stratton Oakmont case was troubling for ISPs because of the vast potential liability for torts such as defamation, misappropriation, or the invasion of privacy.

If ISPs can be held liable for infringing material on their services, there is little reason why the ISP should not be liable for infringing material uploaded by its customers to web sites resident on its server computer. The Clinton Administration's Working Group on Intellectual Property and the National Information Infrastructure favored that tort law for copyright-infringing materials governs ISPs uploaded to their systems.[264] It is hardly surprising that injured plaintiffs will seek to hold the ISP vicariously liable for online injuries. Individual online defendants can avoid repercussions for their actions by simply disguising their messages and postings.[265]

The Communications Decency Act (CDA) expressly overruled the *Stratton Oakmont* case, granting Internet Service Providers a broad immunity for defamatory materials and other tortious activities occurring on their service. Section 509 of the CDA provides that "[n]o provider or user of an interactive computer service shall be treated as the publisher of any information provided by another information content provider."[266] Section 230(c)(1) provides that "no provider or user of an interactive computer service shall be held liable on account of . . . any action voluntarily taken in good faith to restrict access to or availability of material that the provider or user considers to be obscene, lewd, lascivious, filthy, excessively violent, harassing, or otherwise objectionable, whether or not such material is constitutionally protected."[267]

---

[261] Peter H. Lewis, After Apology From Prodigy, Company Drops Suit, N.Y. Times, Oct. 25, 1995, at D1.

[262] *Id.*

[263] Prodigy Plaintiff Reach Agreement in Libel Case, Deal May Let Online Companies Off the Hook, Chi Trib., Oct. 25, 1995, at 3.

[264] U.S. Patent and Trademark Office, Information Infrastructure Task Force, Intellectual Property and the National Information Infrastructure: The Report of the Working Group in Intellectual Property Rights 114 (Sept. 5, 1995).

[265] *See generally* Anne Wells Branscomb, Anonymity, Autonomy, and Accountability: Challenges to the First Amendment in Cyberspace, 104 Yale L. J. 1639, 1641 (1995) (arguing that anonymity and accountability are conflicting values for Internet users).

[266] 47 U.S.C. § 230(c)(1).

[267] *Id.*

The law is evolving quickly on whether online service providers are to be regarded as publishers or distributors. The clear trend in the law is to expand Internet Service Provider immunities to cover a broad range of torts. In America Online v. Zeran,[268] the court found that AOL was a publisher entitled to immunity for defamatory statements posted on its service. The *Zeran* court observed that: "[I]f computer service providers were subject to distributor liability, they would face potential liability each time they receive notice of a potentially defamatory statement—from any party, concerning any message."[269] The plaintiff in *Zeran* argued that the Internet Service Provider was negligent in permitting an anonymous poster (content provider) to defame him by making a false posting on a computer bulletin board that romanticized the Oklahoma City bombing. The false posting stated that Zeran was selling offensive t-shirts celebrating the Oklahoma City bombing. The plaintiff received hundreds of threatening telephone calls and flaming e-mails as the result of the anonymous third party's actions.

The court held that Section 230(c) (1) immunized the AOL from "distributor liability" for postings made by content providers.[270] In another case, a Florida court found that AOL was shielded by the CDA's immunity shield for liability for subscriber's use of a chat room to advertise pornographic images of a child.[271] AOL was also shielded from liability for allegedly defamatory statements made by Matt Drudge on the online version of the Drudge Report published on AOL's service.[272]

In a 1997 case, an anonymous user of an ISP posted false messages that the plaintiffs were performing satanic rituals on children. The plaintiff sued the provider for negligence and the intentional infliction of emotional distress. The court held that the actions were barred by the safe harbor provision of the CDA.[273]

Section 230 of the CDA provides immunity from lawsuits for ISPs who fail to screen messages that allegedly constitute defamation, fraud, or other torts.[274] ISPs have been dismissed from lawsuits based on content supplied by third-party content suppliers. A New York court dismissed another action against Prodigy for failing to screen out defamatory e-mail and bulletin board messages that constituted libel, negligence, harassment, and the intentional infliction of emotional distress. The court held that the provider "was not liable because it had no 'participatory function' in disseminating the messages."[275]

---

[268] 129 F.3d 327 (4th Cir. 1998).

[269] *Id.* at 333.

[270] *Id.*

[271] Doe v. AOL Inc., No. CL 97-631 (Fla. Cir. Ct., Palm Beach Cty, June 26, 1997) (relying upon Zeran v. AOL).

[272] Blumenthal v. Drudge, 992 F. Supp. 44 (D.D.C. 1998).

[273] Aquino v. Electriciti, Inc., 26 Media L. Rep. (BNA) 1032 (Cal. Super. Ct. 1997).

[274] 47 U.S.C. § 230.

[275] Microsoft Law & Corporate Affairs, Summary of Global Internet Legal Developments (for the period Jan.-Mar. 1999) 162 (Apr. 1999).

The global trend in the law is that the ISP is not liable for third-party content. A French appellate court, however, upheld a $70,000 verdict against a French ISP for hosting anonymously posted nude photos of model Estelle Halliday.[276] The court held that the ISP had a duty to protect the rights of third parties.[277] There is cross-national variation in the potential liability of the ISP for torts or crimes committed online.

[3] Retraction Statutes

Most states have "retraction" statutes that require libel plaintiffs to seek a retraction from the defendant before filing a lawsuit. A Wisconsin appellate court held that libel on an online discussion group was not subject to the retraction requirement because the online libel was not classifiable as a "publication" for purposes of that state's retraction statute.[278] Retraction may be easier on the Internet than with print media.

[4] Defenses to Defamation

The two chief common law defenses to defamation are truth and privilege. There is no defamation unless that publication is both defamatory and false.[279] If a "defendant publishes a defamatory statement on a constitutionally privileged occasion, he can either prove truth or require the plaintiff to prove fault."[280] There is absolute immunity from defamation actions for judicial proceedings,[281] legislative proceedings,[282] executive communications,[283] communications between husband and wife,[284] for political broadcasts,[285] and where the plaintiff has given his or her consent.[286] There are a large number of other situations where there is a qualified privilege.[287] Statements that are fair comment on matters of public concern are conditionally privileged,[288] as are communications to one who may act in the public interest.[289]

---

[276] *Id.* at 163.

[277] *Id.*

[278] It's in the Cards, Inc. v. Fuschetto, 535 N.W.2d 11 (Wis. Ct. App. 1995).

[279] W. Page Keeton, Prosser and Keeton on Torts 839 (5th Ed. 1984); Restatement (Second) of Torts § 613, cmt. J.

[280] *Id.* at 840.

[281] *Id.* at 817.

[282] *Id.* at 820.

[283] *Id.* at 821.

[284] *Id.* at 824.

[285] *Id.*

[286] *Id.*

[287] *Id.* at 825.

[288] *Id.* at 831.

[289] *Id.* at 830.

[B] Right of Publicity

The right of publicity is the commercial value that a public person or celebrity has in his or her likeness, name, or voice. The Restatement (Third) of the Law of Unfair Competition states: "One who appropriates the commercial value of a person's identity by using without consent the person's name, likeness or other indicia of identity for purposes of trade is subject to liability for [monetary or injunctive] relief."[290] The private life of another is invaded if the matter "(a) would be highly offensive to a reasonable person; and (b) is not of legitimate concern to the public."[291] A majority of states recognizes the right of publicity giving a person a right to enjoin an unauthorized use of his or her name, likeness, or voice.[292] California's right of publicity statute provides a cause of action for celebrities and personalities that extends 50 years from the death of the deceased personality.[293]

It is arguable that a federal or even international statute can protect rights in cyberspace.[294] An online company needs to do a legal audit to determine whether it is infringing rights of publicity on its web site, news group, and chat rooms. Right of publicity claims may be avoided by licensing the right to use likenesses, voices, and names of celebrities or public figures.[295]

§ 5.06 PRIVACY IN CYBERSPACE

[A] The Internet as a Transparent Society

Under the common law, "[o]ne who intentionally intrudes, physically or otherwise, upon the solitude or seclusion of another or his private affairs or concerns, is subject to liability to the other for invasion of his privacy, if the intrusion would be highly offensive to a reasonable person."[296] The essence of privacy was first

---

[290] Restatement (Third) of the Law of Unfair Competition 46 (1995).

[291] Restatement (Second) Torts § 652(d) (1979).

[292] *See* Karen S. Frank, "Recent Developments in Right of Publicity Law," 533 PLI/Pat 111, 1113 (1998) (listing states that recognize a right of publicity statutorily as California, Florida, Indiana, Kentucky, Massachusetts, Nebraska, New York, Oklahoma, Rhode Island, Tennessee, Texas, Utah, Virginia, Wisconsin as well as states recognizing the right under common law: California, Connecticut, Florida, Georgia, Hawaii, Illinois, Michigan, New Jersey, Ohio, Texas, and Wisconsin).

[293] *Id.* (citing Cal. Civil Code § 990).

[294] Eric J. Goodman, A National Identity Crisis: The Need for A Federal Right of Publicity Statute, 9 DePaul-LCA J. Art & Ent. L. 227 (1999).

[295] Karen Franks, an Internet attorney asks: "What should be the degree of First Amendment protection against right of publicity liability for web sites, news groups, chat-rooms, fan-sites?" Karen S. Frank, "Recent Developments in Right of Publicity Law," 533 PLI/Pat 111, 1113 (1998).

[296] Restatement (Second) of Torts, § 652B. Samuel D. Warren and Louis D. Brandeis first articulated the tort of invasion of privacy in an 1890 Harvard Law Review article. Samuel D. Warren & Louis D. Brandeis, The Right to Privacy, 4 Harv. L. Rev. 193 (1890).

defined as "right to be left alone."[297] Four kinds of interests are protected by a person's right to privacy: (1) unreasonable intrusions upon the seclusion of another; (2) appropriation of the other's name or likeness; (3) unreasonable publicity given to the other's private life; or (4) publicity that unreasonably places the other in a false light before the public.[298]

Tort law is traditionally state law, and therefore online activities may trigger privacy-based torts in any one of fifty plus jurisdictions. Whether an individual state constitutional right to privacy has been violated depends on whether the individual had a reasonable expectation of privacy.[299] The reasonable expectation of privacy varies depending on the setting.[300] In the absence of a reasonable expectation of privacy, there is no cause of action for either the common law invasion of privacy or the constitutional right to privacy.[301]

States vary in their law of privacy. Virginia law, for example, does not recognize the tort of invasion of privacy, in any form, whether intrusion upon seclusion or disclosure of private facts.[302] The majority of the states, however, follow the Restatement (Second) of Torts approach to invasion of privacy.

Selling, transferring, retransmitting, and manipulating data is the life-blood of e-commerce. Cookies, for instance, are text files saved "in Netscape Communicator or Microsoft Internet Explorer (the major browsers) directory or folder and stored in RAM while your browser is running."[303] Cookies permit companies to trace online activity of any online visitor, as well as of its customers. The latest device for tracking computer users without their knowledge is the use of "web

---

[297] Judge Thomas Cooley coined the phrase, "the right to be left alone." W. Page Keeton, et al., Prosser and Keeton on Torts § 117, at 849 (5th ed. 1984).

[298] Restatement (Second) of Torts § 652A (1965) (stating that the right of privacy is invaded by (a) unreasonable intrusion upon the seclusion of another . . . (b) or appropriation of another's name or likeness; or (c) unreasonable publicity given to the other's private life . . . or (d) publicity that unreasonably places the other in a false light before the public").

[299] Alarcon v. Murphy, 201 Cal. App. 3d 1 (1988).

[300] Private employees, for example, have no reasonable expectation of privacy in company owned computer systems. *See, e.g.,* Smyth v. Pillsbury Co., 914 F. Supp. 97 (E.D. Pa. 1996) (holding that an employee has no reasonable expectation of privacy in internal e-mail). A military officer, however, was held to have a reasonable expectation of privacy in his private AOL account. United States v. Maxwell, 45 M.J. 406, 1996 C.A.A.F. 116 (1996).

[301] Bourke v. Nissan Motor Co., No. B068705 (Cal. Ct. App. July 26, 1993) (holding that an employee had no reasonable expectation of privacy because of Nissan's monitoring of their e-mail messages).

[302] Jessup-Morgan v. AOL, Inc., 20 F. Supp. 2d 1 (E.D. Mich. 1998) (citing Brown v. American Broad. Co., Inc., 704 F.2d 1296, 1302-03 (4th Cir. 1983)).

[303] Cookie Central, The Unofficial Cookie FAQ (visited Apr. 27, 1999), http://www.cookiecentral.com.

bugs."[304] Web bugs are able to identify computer users by name, which is an intrusion even greater than that made by cookies. Computer users who are able to block cookies do not have the same ability to disable web bugs.[305] This device was given the name *web bug* because, in its ability to track online computer users, it is the functional equivalent of a hidden microphone.[306]

> ### [1]   Preventive Law Pointer: Cookie Warnings

If an online company uses cookies or text files stored in visitors' computers, it should make a full disclosure as to its use of cookies. Web site visitors may object to the storage of cookies in their computer's RAM.

[B]   Privacy Torts

[1]   Unreasonable Intrusion upon Seclusion

There are two elements to an unreasonable intrusion upon seclusion action: (1) an intentional intrusion, physically or otherwise, on another's solitude, seclusion, or private affairs or concerns, which (2) would be highly offensive to a reasonable person.[307] The rise of the Internet and of e-mail threaten privacy today just as the invention of the telephone and of photography did at the beginning of the twentieth century. A company may be liable for the tort of intrusion on a plaintiff's seclusion or solitude into private affairs if it misuses information collected on corporate web sites. The Ninth Circuit recently commented on the new forms of electronic surveillance that have evolved:

> Something as commonplace as furnishing our credit card number or bank account number puts each of us at risk. Moreover, when we employ electronic methods of communication, we often leave electronic "fingerprints" that can be traced back to us. Whether we are surveilled by our government, by criminals or by our neighbors, it is fair to say never has our ability to shield our affairs from prying eyes been at such low ebb.[308]

---

[304] Michael Geist, Internet Law News, Nov. 15, 1998 (reporting story from Washington Post on the growing use of "web bugs" to track computer users' habits). *See* http://www.washingtonpost. com/wp-srv/business/feed/a60184-1999nov13.htm.

[305] Robert O'Harrow, Jr., Fearing a Plague of "Web Bugs," Wash. Post, Nov. 13, 1999, at E1 (visited Nov. 10, 1999), http://www.washingtonpost.com.

[306] *Id.* (quoting Richard M. Smith, computer security specialist).

[307] Valenzuela v. Aquino, 853 S.W.2d 512, 513 (Tex. 1993).

[308] Bernstein v. Justice Dept., No. 97-16686, LEXIS 4214, 4242 (9th Cir., May 6, 1999).

Corporate employees have no reasonable expectation of privacy against their employers' monitoring of their e-mails.[309] The courts have ruled that e-mail systems are company-owned and that employees will not have a reasonable expectation of privacy as to stored messages.[310] In McClaren v. Microsoft,[311] an employee of Microsoft was suspended pending an investigation of sexual harassment. McClaren was terminated, and he then filed suit against the company, alleging invasion of privacy. The plaintiff argued that Microsoft had invaded his privacy by "breaking into" some of his personal folders maintained on his office computer. The court held that the e-mail messages contained on the company computer were not McClaren's personal property, "but were merely an inherent part of the office environment."[312]

The *McClaren* court held that the plaintiff had no reasonable expectation of privacy in the content of the e-mail messages. Even if he had some reasonable expectation of privacy, Microsoft's accessing of his e-mail messages was relevant to its sexual harassment investigation. The court held that the company's interest in preventing inappropriate and unprofessional comments outweighed the plaintiff's claimed privacy interest in those communications.[313]

➤ **[a]   *Preventive Law Pointer: Employee Handbook and E-Mail Policy***

Corporate counsel should include a conspicuous statement in the employee handbook that employees have no expectation of privacy in e-mail communications. In its e-mail and Internet usage policies, the employer should specifically warn employees that their e-mail messages are considered company records.

[2]   Tort of Misappropriation

The tort of misappropriation is the taking of another's name or likeness; this was the first form of invasion of privacy recognized by courts.[314] There have been

---

[309] Chapter Nine discusses the issue of workplace privacy in detail. Corporate monitoring of e-mail has been upheld by numerous cases. *See, e.g.*, Bourke v. Nissan Motor Co., No. YC003979 (Cal. Sup. Ct., Los Angeles Cty. 1991) (upholding right of company's systems administrator to read employees' e-mail and to terminate employees based on the contents of e-mails that criticized supervisor); Shoars v. Epson Am., Inc., No. YC003979 (Cal. Sup. Ct., Los Angeles Cty., 1989).

[310] *See, e.g.*, "Privacy Claim Rejected in Employer Access to E-Mail Files," 16 Comp.& Online Litig. Rep. 9 (June 15, 1999).

[311] No. 05-97-00824-CV (Ct. App., 5th Dist. Tex., May 28, 1999).

[312] *Id.*

[313] The court cited Smyth v. Pillsbury Co., 914 F. Supp. 97, 101 (E.D. Pa. 1996) in support of its holding that the plaintiff had no reasonable expectation of privacy in e-mail messages stored on a company computer.

[314] W. Page Keeton, Prosser and Keeton on Torts, at 863.

several cases where plaintiffs have sued for misappropriation based on their likenesses appearing on the Internet.

A New York court rejected claims for misappropriation and invasion of privacy[315] where the defendant published a photograph of Howard Stern's bare buttocks on a computer bulletin board. Howard Stern was then running as a candidate for governor of New York. Stern claimed that the use of his name and photograph was a commercial misappropriation. The court rejected this claim finding the online network to be analogous to a bookstore rather than to a publisher. The court found that the defendant's use of Stern's photograph was incident to a publication that concerned the public interest. The court held that the photograph and likeness of Stern was sufficiently newsworthy and refused to enjoin its publication.

In NBA v. Motorola,[316] the National Basketball Association (NBA) sued Motorola, charging the company with misappropriation for offering a pager connected to a web site that would continuously update sports scores as NBA games were being played. Although the court held that copyright law did not preempt the tort of misappropriation claim, it found that reporting scores on Motorola's web site did not constitute the tort of misappropriation.[317]

[3]   Right of Publicity

The private life of another is invaded if the matter "(1) would be highly offensive to a reasonable person and (2) not of legitimate concern to the public."[318] The right of publicity gives a person a right to enjoin an unauthorized use of his or her name or likeness. A federal court reduced a punitive damages award from $850,000 to $350,000 in a right of publicity case against a tabloid for the unauthorized use of a photograph in its print magazine.[319] A celebrity has a property right to "control the exploitation of his or her persona."[320] An online company that uses photographs of any famous entertainment figure needs to obtain rights to use the images or risk exposure to a tort lawsuit. Actress Pamela Anderson Lee and musician Brett Michaels successfully enjoined an adult entertainment web site from displaying images of them engaged in sexual intercourse on the grounds that the publication of the tape invaded their right of publicity under California law.[321]

---

[315] Stern v. Delphi Internet Servs. Corp., 626 N.Y.S.2d 694 (Sup. Ct. 1995).

[316] 105 F.2d 841 (2d Cir. 1997).

[317] Id.

[318] Restatement (Second) of Torts § 652(d) (1979).

[319] Mitchell v. Globe International Publications Co., 817 F. Supp. 72 (E.D. Ark. 1993) (apply Arkansas law).

[320] Michael Scott, Internet and Technology Law Desk Reference 403 (1999).

[321] Michaels v. Internet Entertainment Groups, Inc., 5 F. Supp. 2d 823 (C.D. Cal. 1998).

Summary judgment and an injunction were entered against the operators of a web site containing images of the comedy team, the Three Stooges.[322] The web site violated the right of publicity held by the estate of the actors who had played the Three Stooges.

[4] False Light

The fourth privacy-based tort is "publicity which places the plaintiff in a false light in the public eye." The false light in which the other is placed must be highly offensive to a reasonable person. False light is not a strict liability tort, and the actor must have knowledge of or have acted in reckless disregard as to the falsity of the publicized matter and the false light in which the plaintiff was placed.[323]

[C] Statutory Regulation of Privacy

The U.S. Constitution does not explicitly grant a right to privacy. "What a person knowingly exposes to the public, even in his own home or office, is not a subject of Fourth Amendment protection."[324] The United States Supreme Court has, instead, recognized zones of privacy.[325] Public employees may sometimes enjoy a reasonable expectation of privacy in the workplace from searches by an employer.[326] The constitutional right to privacy protects against intrusions by the government, however, not by private corporations.[327] Corporations that transmit information about a person's identity may face liability for the common law tort of invasion of privacy.

➤ [1] Preventive Law Pointer: Online Privacy Policies

All corporate web sites should conspicuously display their online privacy policy. The policy should describe the type of information collected about users browsing the web site. If a web site sells goods online, an exception in the privacy

---

[322] Comedy III Productions, Inc., v. Class Publications, Inc., 95 Civ. 5552 (SS), 1996 U.S. Dist. LEXIS 5710 (S.D. N.Y. Apr. 30, 1996).

[323] *See, e.g.,* McCormick v. Oklahoma Pub. Co., 613 P.2d 737, 740 (Okla. 1980).

[324] Katz v. United States, 389 U.S. 347, 351 (1967).

[325] *See, e.g.,* Roe v. Wade, 410 U.S. 113, 152-53 (1973) (recognizing privacy right in decision to seek an abortion); Griswold v. Connecticut, 381 U.S. 479, 485-86 (1965) (recognizing privacy right in seeking information on contraception).

[326] O'Connor v. Ortega, 480 U.S. 709 (1987).

[327] Katz v. United States, 389 U.S. 347, 360 (1967) (stating that "[t]he Fourth Amendment can not be translated into a general constitutional right to privacy. That Amendment protects individual privacy concerns against certain kinds of governmental intrusion, but its protections go no further, and often have nothing to do with privacy at all.").

policy should be made for its carriers, such as Federal Express, United Parcel Service, or other companies that deliver the product to the purchaser. The privacy policy should give notice that customer information is given to third parties for the purposes of delivery only.

Commercially reasonable methods, facilities, and systems to protect information from unauthorized access should augment the online privacy policy. Employees and contractors should be required to sign confidentiality agreements not to disclose information without authorization. In the case of children, nonpublic information should not be transmitted without parental consent.[328]

An online company that sells consumers' personal data to another company operating computer databases is subject to FTC enforcement actions, tort law suits, and unwanted publicity. A number of major newspapers, including *USA Today* and *The Washington Post* have given widespread negative publicity to companies that sell consumers' personal data collected on the Internet without the users' permission.[329] Even if the FTC does not file an enforcement action against the nonconsensual sale and usage of consumers' personal data, the negative publicity can tarnish a company's reputation. The integrity of an online company's trade and brand names is a key information asset that must be protected.

The Internet connects hundreds of different countries, many of which have different views of privacy. There is no regulatory framework to guarantee the privacy of personal data transmitted on the Internet.[330] Even though some Internet providers have millions of subscribers, companies such as AOL, EarthLink, or CompuServe are private actors, and their activities will typically not qualify as state action. The Internet has diminished privacy more than any other technological innovation. Specially designed software has been developed to sniff data packets, intercept e-mail, and conduct electronic espionage—all without a trace.

The prohibition in the Fourth Amendment of the United States Constitution against unreasonable searches and seizures by government entities does not apply to the private workplace. If the employer is the government, an employee is protected from unreasonable searches and seizures. Employees in private workplaces, however, do not enjoy similar protection from their employer.[331] Private businesses

---

[328] These principles were adopted as Individual Reference Services Industry Principles following the Federal Trade Commission's workshop on information privacy issues. EPLR: Commercial Database Vendors' Privacy Principles (visited Nov. 25, 1999), http://www.bna.com/e-law/docs/dbguides.html.

[329] October 8, 1996, letter to Hon. Robert Pitofsky, Chairman Federal Trade Commission from Senators Bryan, Hollings, Presser (visited Nov. 25, 1999), http://www.bna.com/e-law/docs/bryan.html.

[330] Neal J. Friedman, The Legal Challenge of the Global Information Infrastructure, Cyberspace Lawyer, (Jan. 1998).

[331] O'Connor v. Ortega, 480 U.S. 709 (1987).

are free to secretly monitor their employees' Internet usage and e-mails, even if they have assured their employees that their use of the computer system is private.[332]

In a Massachusetts case, a CEO spent eight hours reading his employees' e-mail messages and then fired those workers who had made disparaging, but accurate, comments about his sexual liaison with a coworker. The court rejected the employees' claim that the secret monitoring violated the wiretap statute or the common law right of privacy.[333] The courts have uniformly held that computer systems are the property of the employer, and, therefore, the employee has no reasonable expectation of privacy in e-mail communications.

[D]   EU Directive on Protection of Personal Data

The European Union Directive on Protection of Personal Data, adopted on October 24, 1995, imposes restrictions on the transfer of "personal data."[334] A "profile" is "a hierarchical collection of personal profile information . . . describing an end user."[335] The concept of informed consent is drawn from the law of medical malpractice, where a patient must consent to undergoing a procedure after receiving information on risks and alternative procedures. "A party requesting an end user's profile must receive the informed consent of the source(s) before collecting and using their information in any manner."[336] Electronic agents may manage the end user profile as well as manage profiles.[337]

European Union Member States are required to harmonize their domestic laws with the Directive by October 23, 1998. The EU Directive was formally adopted by European Commission's Council of Ministers "to guarantee free movement of personal data."[338] Article 25 prohibits the transfer of "personal data" from EU member states to a country lacking "an adequate level of protection" for such data.[339] Article 26 provides exceptions to Article 25 that would allow the transfer to countries lacking an adequate level of protection in delimited

---

[332] Smyth v. Pillsbury Co., 914 F. Supp. 97 (E.D. Pa. 1996).

[333] Restuccia v. Burk Tcomm, Civil Action No. 95-2125 (Mass. Super. Ct., Middlesex Cty., Dec. 31, 1996).

[334] The European Union Directive of 95/46/EC on the protection of individuals with regard to the processing of personal data and the free movement of such data, 1995 O.J. (L. 28(1))31.

[335] *Id.*

[336] *Id.*

[337] *Id.*

[338] European Commission Press Release: IP/95/822, July 25, 1995, "Council Definitively Adopts Directive on Protection of Personal Data" (visited June 18, 1999), http://www.privacy.org/pli/intl_ors/ec/dp_EC_press_release.txt.

[339] *Id.,* art. 25, 1995 O.J. (L28(1) at 45-46.

circumstances.[340] The free movement of data is important to the banking, insurance, and financial services industries.[341]

The aim of the EU Directive is to afford any person whose personal information is transmitted an equivalent level of protection irrespective of the member state transmitting or processing the data.[342] The EU Directive employs general standards, such as "fundamental fairness," rather than bright-line rules in determining compliance. Companies can sell advertising based on the content of sites without notice or disclosure to consumers.[343] The use of electronic identifiers that enhance the ability of web sites to collect information and track users may violate the European Commission Directive on Protection of Personal Data (EU Directive).[344]

At minimum, web site visitors, must be given the option of providing personal information or not.[345] The EU Directive consists of legal grounds for processing personal data. The Directive seeks a "balance between the legitimate interests of the people controlling the data and the people on whom data is held" or data subjects.[346] Sensitive data "on an individual's ethnic or racial origin, political or religious beliefs, trade union membership or data concerning health or sexual life" may only be processed with the individual's consent.[347]

Member States "endorse appropriate exemptions and derogation . . . which strike a balance between guaranteeing freedom of expression while protecting the individual's right to privacy."[348] New technologies, such as the World Wide Web Consortium's Platform for Privacy Preferences (P3P), may provide technical fixes for the problem of user profiling. In the interim, a company should give complete disclosure as to what information is collected and what is done with that information. Many web site policies give individual users an opportunity to visit a site without collecting personal information. Industry groups are in the process of developing industry standards for the exchange of profile information. One proposal is to develop industry standards for profile exchanges and a mechanism for service provider control of the profiling of web site visitors.[349]

---

[340] The Directive permits data transfers that lack "adequate protection" where the private individual consents to the transfer. *Id.,* art. 26(2), 1995 O.J. (L28(1) at 46.

[341] *Id.*

[342] *Id.*

[343] *Id.*

[344] Most information technology companies are opposed to the European privacy directive. *See, e.g.,* Benjamin Thorner, Privacy on the Internet (visited July 20, 1999), http://www.brobeck.com/docs/98featurs/0498.htm.

[345] *Id.*

[346] *Id.*

[347] *Id.*

[348] *Id.*

[349] Proposal for an Open Profiling Standard Document Version 1.0, June 2, 1997 (visited June 18, 1999), http://developr.netscape.com/ops/proposal.html.

The core guiding principle for open profiling is "control by source, informed consent, and value exchange."[350] The EU Directive applies to the sale or other transfer of data from country to country, whereas the FTC may "prosecute any inquiry necessary to its duties in any part of the United States."[351] The FTC is the agency that scrutinizes the business practices that impact the exchange of personal data. A company will need to comply with FTC regulations and will need to follow the EU Directive if it handles data from member countries.[352]

In July 2000, the European Parliament rejected the "safe harbor" provisions approved by the United States Department of Commerce and the European Commission. The United States and the European Union continue negotiations over what steps the United States must take to protect personal data originating in European Union countries. The proposed safe harbor provision creates a presumption that the online company adequately protects data privacy. In the absence of a safe harbor, there is a possibility that online companies will have disruptions in transborder data flows to and from European Union countries. The key terms in the safe harbor provision are "notice, choice, onward transfer, security, data integrity, access, and enforcement."[353] The proposed safe harbor will be based on industry self-management where companies will "self-certify their adherence to the privacy principles.'[354] The proposed safe harbor will make companies' self-certification practices subject to FTC regulation.[355]

➤   [E]   **Preventive Law Pointer: Principles of Privacy**

Companies may reduce exposure to privacy actions by adopting privacy policies. If a company has a web site, it should keep potential customers or subscribers informed as to what is done with any personal information that is collected. Internally, a company should require every employee to understand and follow its privacy policy. Mindless data mining may lead to needless litigation. A growing number of corporate web sites subscribe to the requirements of TRUSTe. The TRUSTe certification serves as a warranty that the web site adheres to privacy

---

[350] *Id.*

[351] 15 U.S.C. § 43 (1995).

[352] TRUSTe Press Release, Survey Reveals Consumer Fear of Privacy Infringement Inhibits Growth of Electronic Commerce (visited July 17, 1999), http://www.truste.org/press/article003.html.

[353] Department of Commerce, Department of Commerce Requests Comments on Data Privacy Principles, Apr. 27, 1999.

[354] The United States Mission to the European Union, Brussels, Belgium, Joint Report on Data Protection Dialogue to the EU/US Summit, July 21, 1999 (visited Feb. 27, 2000), http://www.useu.be/SUMMIT/dataprotect0699.html. *See also,* Walter F. Kitchenman, European Privacy 'Setback May Be Opportunity, ABA Banking J. Sept. 2000 at 127 (describing European Parliament's rejection of U.S. safe harbor for personal data).

[355] *Id.*

guidelines followed by the industry.[356] Companies are increasingly mining personal data from their web sites without sufficient protection for that personal data.

An employer should require every employee to follow its privacy policy. The privacy policy should be published on the company's web site and incorporated into employee training. All employees may be required to acknowledge that they understand and will comply with the privacy policy. The FTC published the following privacy policy for its web site, which may also be used as a template for private industry:

> This is how we will handle information we learn about you from your visit to our web site. The information we receive depends upon what you do when visiting our site. If you visit our site to read or download information, such as consumer brochures or press releases:
>
> We collect and store only the following information about you: the name of the domain from which you access the Internet (for example, aol.com, if you are connecting from an AOL account, or princeton.edu if you are connecting from Princeton University's domain); the date and time you access our site; and the Internet address of the web site from which you linked directly to our site.
>
> We use the information we collect to measure the number of visitors to the different sections of our site, and to help us make our site more useful to visitors.
>
> If you identify yourself by sending an e-mail: You also may decide to send us personally identifying information, for example, in an electronic mail message containing a complaint. We use personally identifying information from consumers in various ways to further our consumer protection and competition activities. Visit or talk to us to learn what can happen to the information you provide us when you send us e-mail.
>
> We want to be very clear: We will not obtain personally identifying information about you when you visit our site, unless you choose to provide such information to us.[357]

One effective method of transmitting the privacy policy would be through pop-up screens or initial screens that appear when employees log on to their computers or are asked to give their passwords. Employees must be told that they owe a duty to potential customers, co-employees, and other parties to abide by the privacy policy. A company should also require its independent contractors, consultants, and trade partners to abide by the company's privacy policy. Legal counsel should regularly review the company's privacy policy to ensure that it complies with fast-moving national and international developments.

---

[356] *See*, TRUSTe, Building a Web You Can Believe In (visited July 20, 1999), http://www.truste.org.

[357] Federal Trade Commission, Privacy Policy for FTC Web Site (last updated June 16, 1999) (visited July 20, 1999), http://www.ftc.gov/ftc/privacy1.htm.

§ 5.07   NEGLIGENCE IN CYBERSPACE

[A]   Introduction

Negligence is conduct that causes an unreasonable risk of harm. The Restatement (Second) of Torts takes the view that any invasion of a legally protected interest, whether based in negligence, strict liability, or intentional misconduct, can be punished under tort law. Torts arising out of the misuse of computer systems are more likely to be based on intentional torts rather than negligence. *Negligence* is defined as a departure from the conduct expected of a reasonably prudent person under like circumstances. Companies may create an "unreasonable risk of harm" in cyberspace by engaging in conduct that does not meet industry standards or the standard of exercising reasonable care in the circumstances.

A company's duty to consumers and others may stem from its online business activities. An online company may, for example, be found negligent for failing to screen or train key personnel. Third parties may pursue a negligence action against a compny that fails to protect confidential information, such as trade secrets. A company may have a duty of special responsibility to safeguard the confidential or proprietary data on its computer system. A hospital has a duty not to disclose treatment records and will be liable if it does not prevent patient information from being disclosed to third parties. A company has a duty to use reasonable care in protecting the confidential information of trading partners, customers, and web site visitors.[358] A company is negligently engaging in conduct if the company does not exercise reasonable care under all the circumstances.

Industry standards as required by state statutes or federal laws may set the standard of care. It is customary to set the standard of care based on the burden of precaution measured against the radius of the risk. Judge Learned Hand's algebraic formulation of the concept of reasonable care was articulated in United States v. Carroll Towing Co.[359] Judge Hand's risk/utility formula of whether the burden of precaution was less than the probability and extent of damages ($B < P \times L$) was applied to a case regarding a breakaway barge:

> Since there are occasions when every vessel will break from her moorings, and since, if she does, she becomes a menace to those about her, the owner's duty, as in other situations to provide against resulting injuries is a function of three variables: (1) the probability that she will break away; (2) the gravity of the

---

[358] *See* Holtz v. J.J.B. Hilliard W.L. Lyons, Inc., 185 F.3d 732, 744 (7th Cir. 1999) (holding that where there is a special relationship between the parties, each party has a duty to act in reasonable manner).

[359] United States v. Carroll Towing Co., 159 F.2d 169 (2d Cir. 1947).

resulting injury, if she does; and (3) the burden of adequate precautions. Possibly it serves to bring this notion into relief to state it in algebraic terms: if the probability be called P; the injury, L; and the burden, B; liability depends upon whether B is less than L multiplied by P: i.e. whether $B < PL$.[360]

Learned Hand's formula is applicable to negligence in Internet transactions as well. Generally, a corporation will be held negligent in Internet transactions where its failure to use due care results in a foreseeable security breach. A company that has a duty to protect the confidentiality of personal information may be negligent under Judge Hand's risk/utility formula. The key question is whether the cost of precaution is warranted, that is, whether the cost is less than the probability of harm multiplied by the gravity of the resulting injuries.[361]

The Learned Hand test excuses a corporation from taking precautionary measures when the costs of such measures are greater than the potential loss. Accident avoidance on the Internet may also be evaluated by comparing the radius of the risk to the cost of prevention.[362] The Learned Hand formula may be difficult to apply in cyberspace, where there is little empirical data on the potential for injury. No reliable data exists on basic facts such as the number of attacks by hackers or financial losses due to the misappropriation of trade secrets. Similarly, there is little available data on the probability of harm, severity of harm, or the cost of instituting precautions to protect the integrity of online commercial transactions. Efficiency, however, is the starting point for establishing what "ought to be done" by the prudent company in cyberspace. An employer will likely be found negligent where it does not implement reasonable information security devices to protect its information assets.

[B]   Setting the Standard of Care

Customary or industry standards are frequently used to calibrate reasonable care. A threshold question for setting the standard of care for the Internet is to examine customs or industry practices. Judge Hand held that compliance with an industry standard or custom may set the floor but not the ceiling of due care.[363] There may be circumstances, however, where a defendant is negligent despite adhering to weak or undeveloped industry practices.

---

[360] *Id.* at 171.

[361] Car manufacturers, for example, do not have an obligation to place foam rubber throughout the passenger compartment or run automobiles on tracks, even though such precautions may reduce the cost of avoidable injuries.

[362] *See generally* Guido Calabresi, The Cost of Accidents (1961).

[363] The T.J. Hooper, 60 F.2d 737 (1932).

[1] Industry Standard-Setting

A violation of a well-accepted industry or other safety standard may be a sufficient basis for a finding of negligence. The infrastructure for Internet commerce is based on technical standards governing modems or configured telephone connections. Industry groups formulate new specifications for network access. Multimedia groups of the telecommunications industry are developing a "low-cost gateway device that will pass voice, video, fax, and data traffic between conventional telephone networks and packet-based data networks such as the Internet."[364] The United Kingdom's Federation of the Electronics Industry organized the "Cards UK 98" conference to help formulate standards for smart card technology and electronic commerce.[365] In Denmark, for example, a self-regulating governing body was formed to police abuses, such as domain name cybersquatting, spamming, and fraud in electronic commerce.[366]

A difficult issue to determine is which industry's standard is applicable to cyberspace. The leading producers of cable modems in Europe, for example, observe a different standard for dealing with digital video broadcasting and audio broadcasting than do procedures of the recently adopted U.S. cable modem standards.[367] Industry standards are relatively undeveloped for Internet businesses. It may be premature to turn to industry standards in many areas where there is no consensus as to custom or standard.[368]

When the issue is negligence in conducting online transactions, compliance or lack of compliance with industry standards is often considered to be probative evidence. The plaintiff's violation of an Internet industry standard may be evidence of negligence. The tort doctrine of avoidable consequences denies the recovery of damages that could have been avoided by the plaintiff's reasonable care.[369] The rule of avoidable consequences comes into play in assessing implementation of industry standards. The Direct Marketing Association (DMA), for example, adopted a privacy policy to protect consumers. The Electronic Privacy Information Center (EPIC) found that "only a handful" of the DMA members followed their own industry-set standards.[370]

---

[364] Microsoft Law & Corporate Affairs, Summary of Global Internet Legal Developments 136 (Jan. 1999).

[365] Id. at 106.

[366] Id. at 142.

[367] Id. at 138.

[368] "The Internet computer industry is still developing standards for conduct, thus providing the courts little guidance. Software providers, ISPs, and other members of the World Web Consortium and Internet Engineering Task Force have not yet agreed to standards for network security." Robin A. Brooks, Deterring the Spread of Viruses Online: Can Tort Law Tighten the 'Net'? 17 Rev. Litig. 343, 357 (1998).

[369] W. Page Keeton, Prosser and Keaton on Torts § 65, at 458.

[370] Marc Rotenberg, Federal Legislation, Strict Enforcement Will Protect People, USA Today, July 7, 1998, at 12A.

[2]   Statutory Standard of Care

It is quite likely that legislatures will begin to set statutory standards of care for certain Internet activities. A few jurisdictions, for example, require lawyers to encrypt e-mail messages to clients or to obtain the consent of their clients to use unencrypted messages. There are hundreds of examples of legislators setting the standard of care under traditional tort law. When there is a statutory standard of care, plaintiffs may prove negligence by showing (1) that they are members of the class of persons protected by the statute; (2) that the statute protects against the particular interest invaded; and (3) that they suffered the particular harm or hazard envisioned by the statute.[371]

The promulgation of statutory or administrative standards of care might take the form of state standards as to encryption, digital signatures, and other information security devices. In the interests of promoting the development of e-commerce, the federal or state government may adapt commercial-sector standards. The National Computer Security Center of the National Security Agency (NSA) administers the process for the C2 level of computer security certification.[372]

Commercial-sector security standards are modeled after government-published standards. With the rise of statutory standards of care, a wide variance exists on its evidentiary status. Some jurisdictions provide that the violation of a statutory rule is only some evidence of negligence in determining whether a defendant exercised due care in the circumstances. Other jurisdictions provide that an unexcused violation of a statute that results in harm to the class protected by the statute is negligence *per se* as to the consequences that the statue is designed to prevent. The probative value of a statute violation needs to be uniformly treated across states and nations connected to the Internet.

[3]   Professional Standard of Care

Professionals such as lawyers, doctors, architects, engineers, and others may have a higher standard of care when it comes to activities on the Internet.[373] It is

---

[371] Restatement (Second) of Torts § 286 (1965).

[372] *De facto* evaluation of security products vis-à-vis government standards is already occurring. Novell, Inc., formally applied for federal certification for their general-purpose network operating system. According to a research director: "A C2 rating . . . has become a standard for commercial businesses as well as government and military organizations. Customers are using it as a differentiator when making product purchasing decisions." "NetWare 4 Enters Final Phase of C2 Evaluation: On Track to Receive First Client-Server Network Rating," PR Newswire, Aug. 28, 1995 (statement of John Pescatore).

[373] *See* Steiner Corp. v. Johnson & Higgins of California, 135 F.3d 684, 688 (10th Cir. 1998) (holding that where a professional that held himself out as a professional was liable for the negligent performance of duties undertaken); *In re* Daisy Sys. Corp, 97 F.3d 1171, 1175 (9th Cir. 1996) (holding that where a duty of professional care required the plaintiff to show that the defendant should

quite likely that information security professionals will be held to a higher professional standard of care, similar to those currently imposed on doctors, lawyers, accountants, and so on. Courts, however, have been slow to recognize the concept of computer malpractice.[374] Unlike law or medicine, there is no licensing body or minimal educational requirements for computer technicians. There are only optional certification examinations provided by various vendors that may be useful in setting the standard of care.[375]

[C] Premises Liability

A property owner who invites the public onto his property for business purposes is potentially liable if those invitees are harmed by negligent or accidental attacks by third parties. Courts will impose liability if the risk of harm to visitors was reasonably foreseeable.[376] Premise liability lawsuits have traditionally been applied to shopping malls, parking lots, or apartment complexes.

Courts have yet to expand premise liability concepts to cyberspace. It is arguable that the owner of a web site, like any other retail establishment, may be liable for dangers associated with third parties that injure customers.[377] Potential and actual liabilities to web site visitors may include torts such as the conversion of credit card numbers, the invasion of privacy, or defamation. Courts may find that an online business has breached an implied contract to provide a secure web site.[378] A web site owner may avoid premises liability by providing reasonable

---

have used such skill, prudence, and diligence as other members of his or her profession commonly possessed and exercised); *see also* Hospital Computer Sys., Inc. v. The Staten Island Hosp., 788 F. Supp. 1351, 1361 (D. N.J. 1997); Heath v. Swift Wings, Inc., 252 S.E.2d 526, 529 (N.C. App. 1979).

[374] Thomas G. Wolpert, Product Liability and Software Implicated in Personal Injury, 60 Def. Couns. J. 519, 521 (1993).

[375] Certification exams are provided by Cisco Systems Inc.; "Cisco Certified Internetwork Expert" (CCIE) (visited Apr. 18, 1999), (http://www.cisco.com/warp/public/625/ccie; *See also*, Microsoft Corp., "Microsoft Certified Professional" (MCP) (visited Apr. 18, 1999), http://www.microsoft.com/mcp; and Novell, Inc., "Certified Novell Engineer" (CNF) (visited Apr. 18, 1999) http://education.novell.com/cnc/cnebroch.htm.

[376] *See, e.g.,* Isaacs v. Huntington Memorial Hosp., 695 P.2d 653 (Cal. 1985).

[377] Premises liability is based on the notion of prior similar acts that establishes the foreseeability of harm. A hospital, for example, was held not liable for a patient's sexual assault where no such assault had occurred previously. *See, e.g.,* K.L. v. Riverside Medical Ctr., 524 N.W.2d 300 (Minn. Ct. App. 1994).

[378] There is no case law on whether an implied contract to provide a secure environment applies to cyberspace. In K.M.H. v. Lutheran General Hospital, 431 N.W.2d 606 (Neb. 1988), the Nebraska Supreme Court held that the hospital entered into an implied contract to provide patients with a secure environment. In *K.M.H.*, a male employee performing a bed check sexually assaulted a patient. A hospital seemingly would owe a higher duty to vulnerable patients than an online business would owe to its customers.

information security and monitoring the web site to reduce the potential for torts or crimes committed against web site visitors or customers.

[D]   Defenses Against Negligence in Cyberspace

[1]   Contributory Negligence

The defense of contributory negligence bars recovery entirely if the plaintiff's own negligence contributed to the injury. A web site, for example, could defend against a claim for Internet security on the grounds that plaintiffs contributed to their injuries by losing their passwords. In a contributory negligence jurisdiction, plaintiffs are precluded from any recovery for contributing to the injury.

[2]   Comparative Negligence

Most American jurisdictions have adopted some form of comparative negligence. In a comparative negligence jurisdiction, the negligence of the defendant is compared to that of the plaintiff. Plaintiffs' recovery is diminished by the degree of their negligence, as compared to a contributory negligence regime in which plaintiffs' fault relieves the defendant entirely from liability.[379] Comparative negligence jurisdictions may be classified as "modified" or "pure" comparative negligence systems. In a modified system, negligent plaintiffs may recover provided their negligence is neither equal to nor greater than that of the defendant. In a pure comparative negligence regime, plaintiffs' recovery is diminished by the degree of negligence, even if their negligence is greater than or equal to that of the defendant. A plaintiff's failure to use standard antiviral software might constitute comparative negligence in a lawsuit over the transmission of software containing an antiviral.

[3]   Assumption of Risk

If plaintiffs voluntarily assume a known risk, they cannot recover for harm, even if the defendant is at fault. This defense is based on the public policy that one who "knows, appreciates and deliberately exposes himself to a danger assumes the risk."[380] If a web site, for example, warns the user that they do not employ standard security devices, a plaintiff may have voluntarily assumed a known risk.

---

[379] Ballentine's Law Dictionary 252 (3d ed. 1969).
[380] *Id.* at 103.

§ 5.08   STRICT LIABILITY IN CYBERSPACE

[A]   Strict Product Liability

Product liability is the legal liability of manufacturers for injuries caused by the marketing of defective products. Strict product liability evolved out of the societal judgment "that people need more protection from dangerous products than is afforded by the law of warranty."[381]

Injured consumers suing under the theory of strict liability must only prove that they were injured by an unreasonably dangerous product. The tort victim need not prove that the manufacturer knew or should have known about the problem or that the company was negligent. The strict liability rule permits consumers to recover so long as their injuries are causally connected to an unreasonably dangerous product. The policy underlying strict product liability is to place responsibility for dangerously defective products on corporations rather than on the injured claimant.

The ALI superseded Section 402A of the Restatement (Second) of Torts replacing it with the Restatement (Third) of Torts Product Liability. The new Restatement is a significant retreat from strict liability, to a more negligence-based law of product safety. The Restatement Third makes it more difficult for plaintiffs to prove design defects because part of the burden of proof is to demonstrate that the harm would be avoided by an alternative design. Section 17 of the Restatement (Third), for example, reduces a plaintiff's recovery based on the comparative negligence of third parties. It remains to be seen whether courts will adopt the Restatement (Third), which substitutes fault-based principles for strict liability.

[B]   Computer Malpractice

Courts have been reluctant to extend product liability as a remedy for defective computer programs.[382] Defective software has the potential to place life and limb in peril. Consider the following, for example:

[1] An energy management system in a high school that was programmed to be inoperable under 6:30 a.m. and that prevented an exhaust fan in a chemistry lab from working, thus causing a teacher to inhale chlorine gas.

[2] A computer system that generated a warning label for a prescription drug that was inadequate.

---

[381] East River Steamship Corp. v. Transamerica Delval, Inc., 476 U.S. 858 (1986).

[382] *See, e.g.,* Chatlos Sys., Inc. v. National Cash Register Corp., 479 F. Supp. 738 (D.N.J. 1979), *aff'd*, 635 F.2d 1081 (3d Cir. 1980).

[3] A computer system used by a pretrial service agency that failed to warn an arraignment judge that an arrestee was out on bond for two previous armed robberies, a circumstance that resulted in the release of the arrestee and grave injuries to a person wounded in another armed robbery attempt.

[4] A defective computer and software program that was used to assist physicians in calculating doses of radiation received for patients who were being seeded with radioactive implants to treat cancer of the prostate.[383]

§ 5.09   IMMUNITIES AND PRIVILEGES

[A]   Immunities

Immunity is a term that refers to the special protections that the law accords designated categories of defendants, such as public entities, family members, charities, and other protected groups.[384] The law of torts has historically recognized a number of immunities.

Sovereign immunity was the "principle that the sovereign cannot be sued in his own courts or in any other court without its consent and permission."[385] Judges, for example, are not liable for torts committed in the exercise of their judicial functions.

Congress enacted the Good Samaritan provisions of the Communication Decency Act (CDA) to immunize Internet Service Providers for torts committed by subscribers. The Good Samaritan immunity applies to all lawsuits after the enactment of the CDA.[386] The Internet Service Provider immunity has been extended to apply to a wide variety of torts committed by content providers.

[B]   Privileges

A privilege is a rule of law "by which particular circumstances justify conduct which otherwise would be tortious."[387] The two principal intentional tort privileges are (1) consent, and (2) "privileges created by law irrespective of consent."[388] Consent, for example, may be interposed as a defense to most torts. In addition, a defendant may be privileged by self-defense or defense of others.

---

[383] Thomas G. Wolpert, Product Liability and Software Implicated in Personal Injury, 60 Def. Counsel J. 519, 519 (1998).

[384] Dan Dobbs, The Law Of Torts 575 (2000).

[385] Ballentine's Law Dictionary 1195 (3d ed. 1969).

[386] Section 230(d)(3) states that: "[n]o cause of action may be brought and no liability may be imposed under any state or local law that is inconsistent with this section." 47 U.S.C. § 230(d)(3).

[387] Edward J. Kionaka, Torts 178 (1999).

[388] *Id.*

At present, there are few Internet privileges. A law enforcement unit of a cybercrime unit may have a privilege to hack into an online company's web site or to decrypt a message. The evolving cyberlaw will define the circumstances in which defendants have justification for conduct that otherwise would be tortious.

§ 5.10   SPECIAL ISSUES IN CYBERSPACE TORT LAW

[A]   False and Deceptive Advertising in Cyberspace

[1]   Regulation of Internet Advertising

An online company needs to do a complete audit of Internet advertising and promotions. This section provides a brief overview of three matters: (1) public regulation of Internet advertisements; (2) private tort-based regulation of Internet advertisements; and (3) tort liability for Internet advertisements. Internet torts governing Internet advertisements include trade libel or commercial disparagement,[389] personal defamation, interference with prospective or existing contractual relations, and unfair competition. In addition to advertising torts, there is liability for regulatory actions.

[a]   Federal Trade Commission Regulation

[i]   Section 5(a) of the FTC Act. The Federal Trade Commission (FTC) chiefly regulates advertising in the United States, but other federal agencies may regulate the advertising of specific products.[390] The laws of advertising and advertising regulations are general in scope and extend to Internet commercial transactions.[391] False and deceptive advertising will subject the online company to regulatory actions by the Federal Trade Commission.

Online companies that use unfair methods of competition or unfair or deceptive advertising, such as false claims about products or services, may be challenged by FTC enforcement. The FTC's enforcement arm has devoted attention to eliminating advertising practices considered to be "deceptive." Section 5 of the Act

---

[389] Trade libel is defined as "an intentional disparagement of the quality of property, which results in pecuniary damage." Aetna Casualty & Surety Co. v. Centennial Ins. Co., 838 F.2d 346, 351 (9th Cir. 1988).

[390] "Advertising is regulated in the United States at the federal level by the Federal Trade Commission ('FTC'), the Food and Drug Administration ('FDA') and the Bureau of Alcohol, Tobacco and Firearms ('ATF'). Thomas J. Smedinghof, Introduction to Electronic Commerce: A Road Map to the Legal Issues, American Bar Association, Science and Technology Committee Presentation, adapted from Thomas J. Smedinghof, ed., Online Law (1996).

[391] *Id.* at 14.

declared: "[u]nfair methods of competition in commerce, and unfair or deceptive acts or practices in or affecting commerce" unlawful.[392]

In Federal Trade Commission v. Sperry & Hutchinson Co.,[393] the Court held for the first time that consumers as well as competitors were to be protected from unfair or deceptive acts. The *Sperry* case armed the FTC with authority for its so-called unfairness doctrine. The unfairness doctrine was the FTC interpretation that Section 5(a) of the Act allowed it to determine what was "unfair" to consumers, rather than the more limited jurisdiction of determining which trade practices were deceptive. The FTC jurisdiction extends to advertisements that have the capacity to deceive consumers[394] and to materially affect their purchasing decisions.[395] The test for Internet advertisements considers as well whether advertisements will materially affect the purchasing decisions of online customers.

Online advertisements may be outright fraudulent or misleading because of inaccurate claims about products or services. Misleading statements about software or hardware performance that would deceive the consumer acting reasonably under the circumstances would expose an online company to potential enforcement action. A company found to be engaging in unfair or deceptive acts is subject to "cease and desist" orders as well as monetary penalties.

[ii] False Internet advertising claims. Internet advertisements may be found to be "deceptive" by the FTC if the online advertiser makes false claims about goods or services. As with Article 2 of the UCC, courts distinguish between actionable deceptive advertisements and mere puffery. Puffery is unenforceable seller's talk and refers to "opinion claims about goods that do constitute the basis of the bargain.'[396] The adjective "delicious" in an advertisement would be a puff and not an enforceable warranty. In contrast, a warranty of quality is a statement of fact about goods that goes to the "basis of the bargain."

To constitute the "basis of the bargain, the seller's statement must: (1) relate to the goods and (2) become the basis of the bargain."[397] The primary issue for either an express warranty or an FTC enforcement is whether a seller's statement about goods creates an enforceable warranty or constitutes unenforceable puffery or "seller's talk." The FTC has long presumed that a seller's mere expression of

---

[392] 15 U.S.C. § 45(a)(1) (1995).

[393] 405 U.S. 233 (1972).

[394] The "capacity to deceive" is closely related to the "likelihood of confusion" test employed in Section 43(a) unfair competition actions under the federal Lanham Act.

[395] Charles McManus, The Law of Unfair Practices 350 (1983).

[396] Ivan L. Preston, Dimensions at the FTC in Identifying Consumer Response to Advertisements, Washington Regulatory Reporting Association, FTC Watch, June 1996.

[397] U.C.C. § 2-313 (1995).

opinion or seller's talk is not calculated to deceive.[398] The greater the specificity, the more likely a seller's statement will be deemed an express warranty.

The FTC has the authority to police unfair or deceptive advertising in diverse fact-settings, including e-mail, web sites, or other Internet related communications channels.[399] An Internet advertisement may be deceptive not only because of a company's misrepresentations but also by its omissions likely to "mislead consumers . . . and affect consumers' behavior or decisions about the product or service."[400] An act or practice is unfair if the injury caused or likely to be caused, is "substantial . . . not outweighed by other benefits . . . and not reasonably avoidable."[401]

The FTC requires that Internet advertisers, like all advertisers, have a reasonable basis for substantiating advertising claims made about products and services.[402] The FTC first articulated the "reasonable basis for substantiation" test in a case involving advertising claims made for Unburn sunburn lotion. The Commission held that it was an unfair trade practice to make an affirmative comparative product claim that a lotion instantly solved the effects of sunburn without a reasonable basis for making the claim.[403] The FTC has the jurisdiction to file enforcement actions against sellers, advertising agencies, web site designers, and any one who disseminates deceptive representations on a web site, in e-mail communications, or in other Internet transmissions.

[b]   State Enforcement Against Unfair or Deceptive Internet Ads

Advertising is regulated by individual states under little FTC acts. These statutes are called "little FTC acts" because they are modeled on Section 5(a) of the FTC Act. Many states have adopted a version of the Uniform Deceptive Trade Practices Act (UDTPA).[404] Deceptive or misleading advertisements may be deemed to be deceptive trade practices in states adopting the UDTPA.

---

[398] Carlay Co. v. FTC, 153 F.2d 493, 496 (7th Cir. 1946) (holding representation that a car could go an "amazing distance" without oil to be "nothing more than a form of 'puffing' not calculated to deceive").

[399] Federal Trade Commission, "Advertising and Marketing on the Internet: The Rules of the Road"(visited Nov. 27, 1999), http://www.ftc.gov/bcp/conline/pubs/buspubs/ruleroad.htm.

[400] *Id.*

[401] *Id.*

[402] The FTC gives strict scrutiny to claims about health, safety or performance. If an Internet advertisement specifies a given level of support for a claim—"tests show X"—the company must be able to substantiate the claim. *Id.*

[403] *In re* Pfizer, Inc., Trade Reg. Rep. (CCH) ¶ 20,056 (FTC 1972) (articulating the test as two steps: [1] What substantiating evidence constitutes a reasonable basis for making a product claim? and [2] Did the respondent in the case produce such evidence?).

[404] A number of states have adopted statutes modeled on the Uniform Deceptive Trade Practices Act. *See, e.g.,* Fla. Stat. ch. §§ 501.201 to 501.213 (1998); Ga. Code Ann. § 10-1-370 to 375 (Harrison 1995); 390-407 (Harrison 1993); Haw. Rev. Code § 481A (1995); Idaho Stat. § 49-1629

[c]   Regulation of Online Spam

A number of states have enacted antispam statutes punishing companies for sending unsolicited e-mail.[405] Washington passed an antispam law that permits the recipients of unsolicited commercial bulk e-mail to recover damages if the e-mail conceals the true identity or location of the sender or contains a misleading subject line.

The Washington State Attorney General filed a statutory action against an Oregon company that sent spam to millions of state residents advertising its new book on how to profit from the Internet. In a related case, a Washington ISP is suing a mortgage company for sending "4,800 unsolicited commercial messages with phony return addresses."[406] Washington's antispam statutes has been declared unconstitutional as unduly restrictive and burdensome violating the Interstate Commerce Clause of the U.S. Constitution.[407] Virginia makes unsolicited spam e-mail a criminal offense and awards successful litigants with attorneys' fees.[408]

[d]   International Regulation of Internet Advertising

The Internet, by its very nature, is subject to international regulations. The European Commission, for example, adopted a proposal for a Directive to regulate distance selling of financial services in 1998.[409] Many European countries have limitations on comparative advertising that would not be objectionable in the United States.

(1995); Ill. Ann. Code § 815 ILCS 510/1 *et seq.* (Smith-Hurd 1995); Kan. Stat. Ann. §§ 50-623 to 50-643 (1998); La. Stat. 51:1401 to 1418 (West 1995); Maine Stat. tit. 10 §§ 1211 to 1216; tit. 5 §§ 206 to 214 (West 1995); Mass. Gen. Laws Ann. Ch. 93A; Minn. Stat. Ann. § 325D.43-48; Miss. Rev. Stat. § 63-7-203 (1995); Mont. Code Ann. § 61–607 (1995); Nev. Rev. Stat. § 484.6062 (Michie 1995); N.H. Rev. Stat. § 358A (1995); N. M. Rev. Stat. §§ 57-12-1, *et seq.* (Michie 1995); Ohio Rev. Code Ann. §§ 4549.24, 46, 49 (Anderson 1995); Okla. Stat. Ann. tit. 15 §§ 751 to 765 (1995); Ore. Rev. Stat. §§ 646.605 to 656 (1998); Wyo. Stat. §§ 40-12-101 to 112 (1998).

[405] Spammers routinely inundate e-mail systems with hundreds of thousands of misdirected responses. E-mail systems will typically also have transaction costs in answering complaints to subscribers who receive unsolicited e-mail. Unsolicited e-mail will also occupy computer space.

[406] "ISP See No Gift in Spam 'GIFT' Message," 4 The Internet Newsletter: Legal & Business Aspects 14 (May 1999) (noting that the subject line of the message was "A gift for you," a deceptive and illegal message for which a $1,000 penalty may be assessed for each message).

[407] New Anti-Spam Law Unconstitutional, Nat'l L.J., April 17, 2000, at A6.

[408] Va. Code Ann. § 18-2-152.1 et. seq. (Michie 1998).

[409] Microsoft Law & Corporate Affairs, Summary of Global Internet Legal Developments (for the period Oct.-Dec. 1998) 93 (Jan. 1999).

[2]   Private Attorney General Tort-Based Enforcement

One of the distinctive features of advertising law is enforcement by private attorneys general.[410] The Lanham Act gives commercial parties standing to sue defendants for unfair and deceptive acts in federal courts. Section 43(a) provides private litigants with private tort-like consumer remedies against unfair practices. Section 43(a) of the Lanham Act provides:

> Any person who shall . . . use in . . . tending falsely to describe or represent the same, and shall cause such goods or services to enter into commerce . . . shall be liable to a civil action by . . . any person who believes that he is or is likely to be damaged . . .[411]

Courts have long interpreted Section 43(a) to create a federal statutory tort action providing relief for a broad class of injured or likely to be injured plaintiffs.[412] Two types of advertising are actionable under Section 43(a): "false designation or origin" and "false descriptions or representations." Five elements are necessary to state a *prima facie* claim for false advertising in this section: (1) the defendant made false statements about its *own product or services* by the use of misleading statements, partially correct statements, or the failure to disclose material facts; (2) that the advertisements actually deceived or have the tendency to deceive a substantial segment of their audience; (3) that the deception is material; (4) that defendant caused its falsely advertised goods to enter interstate commerce; and (5) that the plaintiff has been or is likely to be injured by false advertising.[413]

A false and misleading advertisement on the Internet must meet the five elements of the *Skil* test to be actionable. An Internet advertisement will be regarded as a "false designation of origin" if it is "likely to cause confusion or to deceive purchasers concerning the source of the goods."[414] The key legal test in a "false designation action" is the creation of "likelihood of confusion by the consuming public as to the source of goods."[415] Section 43(a) prohibits "false descriptions or representations" that apply to Internet advertisements. To prevail on a Section 43(a) claim, the plaintiff must prove by a preponderance of the evidence that the Internet advertisement it challenges is false or deceptive.[416] An

---

[410] Private attorneys general are plaintiffs who bring legal actions on behalf of themselves as well as the larger society.

[411] 15 U.S.C. § 1125(a) (1999).

[412] *See, e.g.*, L'Aiglon Apparel v. Lana Lobell, Inc., 214 F.2d 649 (3d Cir. 1954).

[413] Skil Corp. v. Rockwell Int'l Corp., 375 F. Supp. 777, 783 (N.D. Ill. 1974).

[414] Salomon/North Am. v. AMF Inc., 484 F. Supp. 846 (D. Mass. 1980).

[415] Pignon S.A. DeMecanique v. Polaroid Corp., 657 F.2d 482, 486-87 (1st Cir. 1981).

[416] Courts will likely apply the analysis in American Home Products Corp. v. Johnson and Johnson, 436 F. Supp. 785 (S.D. N.Y. 1977, *aff'd,* 577 F.2d 160 (2d Cir. 1978)) to Internet advertisements.

Internet advertisement must make false statements about its own products or services under Section 43(a). It is not actionable under Section 43(a) to disparage a competitor's product.[417] The standing to sue under Section 43(a) provides remedies to "commercial parties only" who have been sued or are likely to be damaged by falsehoods in advertisements.[418] The standard for preliminary injunctive relief under Section 43(a) is "irreparable harm flowing from the alleged infringement and either (a) a likelihood of success on the merits or (b) sufficiently serious questions going to the merits to make them a fair ground for litigation" and a balance of hardships tipping decidedly in favor of the moving party.[419]

State little FTC acts modeled on UDTPA provide for private tort-like enforcement as well as public enforcement actions. Chapter 93A of the Massachusetts General Law, for example, authorizes lawsuits by the Attorney General,[420] individual consumers,[421] or business competitors.[422] Chapter 93A provides for monetary damages and equitable relief for consumers "injured" as the result of an unfair or deceptive trade practice. While there is no case law on whether false and deceptive Internet advertisements violate Chapter 93A or other UDTPA inspired acts, it is quite likely that courts would extend these state-based causes of action in the proper case. Section 11 of Chapter 93A provides for punitive damages, such as multiple damages for "willful or knowing violations."[423] Attorneys' fees may be recoverable along with injunctive relief, monetary damages, and treble damages. Relief under Chapter 93A supplements and is in addition to traditional tort remedies as well as relief under the Lanham Act.[424]

[3]   Private Common Law Tort Actions

In addition to federal and state statutory causes of action for false advertising, plaintiffs may recover for damages under traditional tort law. False and deceptive advertisements may be the basis for diverse business torts, including unfair competition, disparagement, trade libel, and common law fraud. Comparative

---

[417] *See, e.g.,* Bernard Food Indus., Inc. v. Dietene Co., 415 F.2d 1279 (7th Cir. 1969) (holding that false statements must be made about defendant's own product to be actionable under § 43(a) of the Lanham Act). *See also* Skil Corp. v. Rockwell Int'l Corp., 375 F. Supp. 777 (N.D. Ill. 1974) (holding that the plaintiff's advertisement misrepresented its own product as well as impugning a competitor's product).

[418] *See, e.g.,* Johnson v. Johnson v. Carter-Wallace, Inc., 631 F.2d 186, 189 (2d Cir. 1980) (restricting standing to commercial parties injured by false advertisements).

[419] *See, e.g.,* Frisch's Restaurants, Inc. v. Elby's Big Boy of Steubenville, Inc., 670 F.2d 642, 646 (6th Cir. 1982).

[420] M.G.L.A. ch. 93A, § 4.

[421] *Id.* at § 9.

[422] *Id.* at § 11.

[423] *Id.*

[424] Linthicum v. Archambault, 379 Mass. 381, 383 (1979).

advertisements, which disparage competitor's products and services, may constitute possible trade libel or disparagement.

[a] Unfair Competition

Unfair competition includes: "false advertising, 'bait and switch' selling tactics, use of confidential information by former employee to solicit customers, theft of trade secrets, breach of a restrictive covenant, trade libel, and false representation of products or services."[425] Unfair competition is primarily a matter of state law.[426] Unfair competition is a common law cause of action generally defined "as the passing off by a defendant of his goods or services as those of another, by virtue of substantial similarity between the two, leading to confusion on the part of potential customers, or the misrepresentation by a defendant of the qualities, origin or contents of his products or services."[427]

[b] Trade Libel or Disparagement

Trade libel or commercial disparagement is a common law tort action to redress derogatory statements made about a competitor's products. Modern commercial disparagement cases are relatively rare and often pleaded as pendent claims to Lanham Section 43(a) actions.

➤ [c] Preventive Law Pointer: Insuring Advertising Injuries

An online company needs to have liability insurance policies that cover lawsuits based on advertising on the Internet. Advertising injury must be defined under the policies as injuries occurring in the course of Internet activities. A Nationwide insurance policy defined "advertising injury" as injury arising out of one or more of the following offenses:

1. Oral or written publication of material that slanders or libels a person or organization or disparages a person's or organization's goods, products, or services;
2. Oral or written publication of material that violates a person's right to privacy;
3. Misappropriation of advertising ideas or style of doing business; or
4. Infringement of copyright, title, or slogan.[428]

---

[425] *Id.*

[426] *Id.*

[427] Resnick v. Angel Manfredy, 1999 U.S. Dist. LEXIS 5877 *18 (E.D. Pa., Apr. 26, 1999).

[428] Micotec Research, Inc. v. Nationwide Mut. Ins. Co., 40 F.3d 968 (9th Cir. 1994).

[d]   Conversion of Cyber-Chattels

Conversion is the unlawful exercise of dominion or control over the personal property of another.[429] At common law, only tangible property could be converted, not intangibles such as software or data.[430] Software and other intangible assets cannot be possessed and may not be literally dispossessed or converted. Modern courts have expanded the tort of conversion to include intangible propery.[431] An "employee's destruction of a WordPerfect directory was held to be conversion."[432] In that case, a former secretary deleted the directory on her last day of work, supposedly to free up computer space. The court found that deleting the directory without a review of the contents was not a standard practice and therefore constituted conversion.[433]

The Restatement (Second) of Torts distinguishes conversion from the lesser offense of trespass to chattels based upon the seriousness of the interference. Trespass to chattels is a diminution in value, whereas conversion is a serious interference with property rights. The doctrinal difference between conversion and trespass to chattels is the measure of damages. Less serious incidents of interference are classified as the trespass to chattels. In Prosser's words, "[t]respass to chattels survives today, in other words, largely as a little brother of conversion."[434] Trespass to chattels may result where a licensor exceeds the scope of its license agreement and thereby trespasses on a computer system.[435]

With the evolution of the information-based economy, there is an argument for expanding conversion to intangibles.[436] Conversion is such a pervasive interference with chattels that the tortfeasor "may justly be required to pay the other

---

[429] Conversion is an intentional tort where the "defendant must intend to exercise substantial dominion over the chattel." Dan B. Dobbs and Paul T. Hayden, Torts and Compensation: Personal Accountability and Social Responsibility for Injury 54 (1997). The measure of damages is for the defendant to pay the full value of the chattel, if the interference is serious enough to justify imposing such liability and if a number of factors were important, including: (a) extent and duration of control; (b) the defendant's intent to assert a right to the property; (c) the defendant's good faith; (d) the harm done; and (e) the expense or inconvenience caused. *Id.* (citing Restatement (Second) of Torts § 222A (1965)).

[430] *Id.* (stating that [t]he traditional common law rule was that conversion would lie only for tangible personal property).

[431] *Id.*

[432] Richard A. Raysman and Peter Brown, Conversion, Trespass and Other New Litigation Issues, 221 N.Y. Law J. 1 (May 11, 1999) (discussing Mundy v. Decker, 1999 Neb. App. LEXIS 3 (Neb. Ct. App. Jan. 5, 1999)).

[433] *Id.*

[434] W. Page Keeton, Prosser and Keeton on Torts § 14, at 85-86 (5th ed. 1984).

[435] Hotmail Corp. v. Van Money Pie, Inc., 1998 U.S. Dist. LEXIS 10729 (D. N.D. Cal., Apr. 16, 1998).

[436] *Id.* at 92.

the full value of the chattel." Trespass to chattels originally required asportation[437] and did not include mere unauthorized use or access to documents that were not destroyed or even modified.[438]

[B] State Enforcement of Online Gambling

At least 450 web sites offer Internet gambling: Online casinos and sport-books offer traditional wagering and straight-line betting operations.[439] Internet gambling web sites are available to residents located in states where gambling is illegal.[440] Minnesota's attorney general places a warning to Internet users and providers that they are subject to enforcement for illegal activities on the Internet.[441] In particular, the Minnesota attorney general states: "Persons outside of Minnesota who transmit information via the Internet are subject to jurisdiction in Minnesota courts for violations of state criminal and civil laws."[442]

The Minnesota attorney general has targeted Internet gambling that offers Minnesota residents the opportunity to place bets, purchase lottery tickets, or participate in casino-type games.[443] In 1995, the Minnesota attorney general filed a consumer protection lawsuit against Granite Gate Resorts, doing business as On Ramp Internet Computer Services, and its officers.[444] The Minnesota attorney general alleged deceptive trade practices, false advertising, and consumer fraud, filing for injunctive and declaratory relief. The attorney general argued that the defendants' online casino reached thousands of Minnesota citizens whose computers enter the Internet web site. The Minnesota district court found sufficient jurisdiction, finding that the defendant purposefully availed of itself of jurisdiction by crossing Minnesota borders through Internet advertisements and by soliciting business for their gaming venture.[445]

---

[437] Asportation means the "act of carrying away." Asportation is the taking or absolute control of the property. Ballentine's Dictionary 97 (3d ed. 1969).

[438] CompuServe, Inc. v. Cyber Promotions, Inc., 962 F. Supp. 1015, 1020 (S.D. Ohio 1997).

[439] *See, e.g.,* http://dir.yahoo.com/Business_and_Economy/Shopping_and_Services/Gambling/Web_Site_Gambling (visited Aug. 14, 2000).

[440] *See, e.g.,* SportBet.com, Winners Internet Network, and World Sports Exchange.

[441] A large number of Internet gambling web sites advertise services to residents of jurisdictions where gambling is illegal. Some online casinos employ nude hostesses as part of their online casino and sportsbook. *See* Winners Internet Network (visited Jan. 25, 1999), http://www.winr.net/english/benefits.asp.

[442] Statement of Minnesota AG on Internet Jurisdiction, reprinted at Lewis Rose, Advertising Law, Arent Fox law firm web site (visited Nov. 28, 1999), http://www.webcom.com/lewrose/article/minn.html.

[443] *Id.*

[444] Complaint of State of Minnesota v. Granite Gate Resorts, Inc., No. C6-95-7227 (Minn. Dist. Ct., Ramsey Cty. July 18, 1995).

[445] State of Minnesota v. Granite Gate Resorts, Inc., No. C6-95-7227 (Minn. D. Ct., Ramsey Cty., Dec. 1996) (order finding jurisdiction over online gambling defendants).

In 1997, Missouri's attorney general sued an Idaho Indian tribe, contending that the tribe's online lottery violated Missouri law "offering betting services to state citizens."[446] A number of federal bills have attempted to regulate the advertising of Internet gambling web sites.[447] The United States Department of Justice charged offshore gambling sites with violation of the Interstate Wire Act.[448] Many of the online casinos are located offshore, making enforcement difficult.[449] The Interactive Gaming Council (IGC) is a standards-setting organization developing a Code of Conduct for online casinos.[450] The government of Antigua and Barbuda formed an alliance with the IGC to establish consumer protection for cyber-gaming.[451]

Internet gambling and other activities that may be deemed to be fraudulent or deceptive are subject to consumer protection regulation. Many states have enacted the Uniform Deceptive Trade Practices Act (UDTPA). The UDTPA varies from state to state, but generally it permits actions by the attorney general as well as by private parties. In many states, injunctive relief, double or treble damages, attorneys' fees, and costs are recoverable.[452] Many states that have not adopted the UDTPA have criminal statutes governing false advertising.[453] Internet advertisers may also be subject to enforcement actions brought by the National Advertising Division of the Council of Better Business Bureaus.[454]

[C] Telecommuting and Negligence

Millions of American workers telecommute to work from home with the help of virtual private networks, the Internet, e-mail, and other new technologies.

---

[446] Tim Ito and Sharisa Staples, "The Odds on Prohibiting Web Webs, Washingtonpost.com (visited Jan. 25, 1999), http://www.washingtonpost.com/wp-s.../longterm/intgambling/overview.htm.

[447] Section 1085 of S.474, The Internet Gambling Prohibition Act of 1997, would have made it unlawful for a person "engaged in the business of bettering or wagering to engage in that business through the Internet or through any other interactive computer service in any State." That bill died in committee, as did a 1996 bill filed in the House of Representatives, H.R. 3526, "to amend title 18, United States Code, with Respect to Transmission of Wagering Information."

[448] Tim Ito and Sharisa Staples, *supra* note 446.

[449] The Gaming Commission of Antigua and Barbuda, for example, regulates World Sports Exchange. SportBet.com has an online link to Australia's largest sports and racing bookmaker. Internet Gaming & Communications Corp. is a publicly traded company that accepts wagers phoned to Antigua. See, Cynthia R. Janower, "Gambling on the Internet" (visited Jan. 25, 1999) http://www.ascusc.org/jcmc/vol2/issue2/janower.html.

[450] Interactive Gaming Council, IGC, "Press Release: Antigua Gambling" (visited Jan. 25, 1999), http://www.igcouncil.org.

[451] *Id.*

[452] *See, e.g.*, Mass. Gen. Laws Ann. Ch. 93A.

[453] *See, e.g.*, Alaska Stat. § 45.50.471; 18 (1998); Cal. Civ. Code § 17500 (Deering 1995); Col. Rev. Stat. § 42-6-206 (1998); Fla. Stat. Ann. §§ 501.201 (West 1999); Kan. Stat. Ann. § 50-626 (1999); Ky. Rev. Stat. § 367.170 (Baldwin 1998); N.D. Cent. Code §§ 51-12-01; 15-1208 (1998).

[454] Mark Sableman, Business Liabilities on the Internet, 16 SPG Comm. Law. 3 (1996).

Telecommuting is defined as an employer permitting performance of work to occur on a regular basis in a location, usually the employee's home or a telecenter, other than a principal office. For 2000, the number of telecommuters is expected to grow to 25,000,000, up from the 11,000,000 workers who telecommuted in some fashion in 1997.[455] President Clinton identified telecommuting as a means of fostering a family-friendly work environment.[456]

The National Performance Review recommended that federal agencies promote flexiplace and telecommuting.[457] In Japan, one telecommuting center combines telecommuting with a resort setting.[458] Sweden invented the "office train," where managers work for half-pay during an 80-minute train ride in and out of Stockholm.[459] The first teleservice center in the United States was established by Pacific-Bell in 1985. IBM, AT&T, Ernst & Young, and a number of other companies are furnishing employees with furniture, equipment, workstations, and other accommodations for telecommuting.[460]

Although it may be difficult to show an employer's vicarious liability for injuries on the physical property of the telecommuter, this may not be the case for direct liability for injuries suffered via the telecommuter's cyberspace. While the use of the telecommuter's property is primarily residential, the Internet connection provided by the employer to the telecommuter is predominately commercial. Millions of Internet telecommuters today work from home and connect to their employer's internal network over the Internet.[461] Telecommuting creates a new security risk because of the possibility that careless telecommuting employees may place an employer's otherwise formidable Internet security systems at risk.

If telecommuters do not comply with information security policies, all confidential and trade secret information to which the telecommuter has access is at risk. Employers could also be liable to third parties for the negligent actions of telecommuters. An employer may protect itself from these lawsuits by following the highest standards of information security. A basic tunnel providing encryption that does not prevent a hacker's access may be viewed as a failure of due care. The

---

[455] Beverly W. Garofalo, Telecommuting: Interaction of Employment Law and Tech Change: Employers Are Well Advised to Draw Up Agreements for At-Home Workers, 15 Comp. L. Strat. 1 (Apr. 1999).

[456] Interagency Telecommuting Program, Overview of Telecommuting Today (visited May 29, 1999), http://www.gsa.gov/pbs/owi/overview.htm.

[457] Id.

[458] Id.

[459] Interagency Telecommuting Program, Overview of Telecommuting Today (visited May 29, 1999), http://www.gsa.gov/pbs/owi/overview.htm.

[460] Id.

[461] Mark Maier, The Law and Technology of Internet Telecommuting, SMU Computer L. Rev. & Tech. J. (Fall 1999).

heightened standard of an advanced tunnel providing both encryption and access prevention would likely be an adequate standard of care.[462]

➤ [1] Preventive Law Pointer: Tips for Reducing the Risks of Telecommuting[463]

"Multi-tiered firewalls" . . . "demilitarized zones" . . . "reverse DNS lookup." . . . Internet security products do an acceptable job at protecting an employer's internal networks. But what if an attack circumvents all these precautions by coming from a computer that the security system classifies as a trusted machine? Online companies face new risks from its telecommuting employees remotely accessing the company's system. Today, millions of Internet telecommuters work from home and connect to their employer's internal network over the Internet by tunneling through the security systems. The inherent risk is that a hacker could backdoor the security by first compromising a telecommuter's computer and then using its trusted connection to access the employer's internal network. In this way, a hacker would appear to be the trusted telecommuter and would circumvent even the strongest firewall security. This consequently puts at risk all the trade secret and confidential information to which the telecommuter has access.

Although these are dire results, an employer's use of appropriate security precautions reduces the radius of the risk. First, it is critical that telecommuting employees follow the security guidelines of the company's information technology department. While these precautions may add a slight delay in performance, this is more than compensated for in the level of protection they provide.

A second type of critical security tool, and one that is fairly common, is a product to prevent front-door attack on the network. One such security product is encryption technology known as Pretty Good Privacy (PGP). Encryption products protect information by scrambling it; without the correct deencryption key, the information remains scrambled and of little value. Another precaution is to prevent access to an employer's internal network by the use of firewalls. These products, such as Cisco's PIX Firewall, are placed between the Internet and the employer's internal network and interrogate every piece of data that attempts to access the network. If the particular source address or data type is not approved, the firewall discards the packet.

A third common security measure is antivirus products, such as Norton AntiVirus from Symantec, that protect the system in the event a virus gains access

---

[462] *Id.*

[463] Mark Maier wrote this section. He is a managing consultant for Compaq Computer Corporation. He received his B.S. in Electrical Engineering from the Pennsylvania State University in 1987, and will receive his J.D. in May 2000 from Suffolk University Law School, where he is in the top five percent of his class.

to a computer. Here, the antivirus product scans everything that enters the computer and takes appropriate action if a virus is detected.

In addition to the above security measures, telecommuters should be protected by tunnel products.[464] "Basic tunnels" protect many Internet telecommuters by encrypting the information to which they have access. Basic tunnels, available from Microsoft and AltaVista, for example, create an encrypted path between the telecommuter and the employer's network, which goes over the Internet and through the firewall. "Advanced tunnels," available from Altiga and 3Com, to name but two products, prevent access with firewall-like features, as well as protect information with encryption. While these advanced tunnels are more costly, they also provide the additional feature of access prevention.

A larger question for employers is how much security is appropriate for any given telecommuter. Although a separate risk-utility analysis should be performed for any given situation, some industry standards are emergent. Take, for example, a typical U.S. corporation with 1,000 or more telecommuters. The cost to implement basic tunnel protection is approximately $5,000, while the cost to implement more secured advanced tunnels is $55,000.[465] Each company will weigh the cost of information security technologies against the value of the information at risk. If one of these telecommuters has access to information worth $50,000 or less, it is not cost-efficient to implement tunnel protection.[466] If the information is valued between $50,000 or $1,000,000, there is likely a need for basic tunnel protection. If the information is worth millions of dollars, advanced tunnel protection should be implemented. The cost of security precautions weighed against the value of the information will also be important in determining whether the company is exercising due care.

[D] Successor Liability for Online Companies[467]

In 1998, there was a record $1.7 trillion in domestic mergers and acquisition activities in a single year.[468] The surge of spin-offs, mergers, takeovers, and other

---

[464] Tunnels are known as Virtual Private Networks (VPNs). *See* Microsoft Corp., Virtual Private Networking: An Overview (May 29, 1998) (visited Apr. 14, 1999), http://msd.microsoft.com/workshop/server/feature/vpnovw.asp.

[465] *Supra* note 461.

[466] *See id.* (contending that for risk-utility analyses of when basic tunnels providing encryption but not preventing access are sufficient protection, as well as when a heightened standard of advanced tunnels providing both encryption and access prevention are mandated).

[467] Amy Wilson, Class of 1995, Suffolk University Law School, completed the research for this section.

[468] Thomas J. Dougherty, "Takeovers," Securities Litigation: Planning and Strategies, American Law Institute-American Bar Association Continuing Legal Education, SD79 ALI/ABA 567 (1999).

acquisitions among Internet and media companies is gaining momentum. The American Online/Netscape, TCI/AT&T, Adelphia/Century Communications, MCI/WorldCom, and Intel/Dialog mergers are just a few examples. In addition, parent companies are merging with wholly owned subsidiaries, as with Intel's merger with and into Dialogic Corporation. Dialogic Corporation became a wholly owned subsidiary of Intel in July 1999.[469]

Successor corporations need to do a due diligence to determine whether they have assumed the tort liabilities of predecessor corporations in the online environment. Although there is no case law pertaining to the successor liability of online companies, traditional principles will easily be extended. The traditional rule of successor liability "provides that a corporation that acquires all, or part, of the assets of another corporation does not thereby assume the liabilities and debts of the predecessor."[470] The general rule is that a corporation that purchases the assets of another corporation is not liable for the liabilities and debts of the predecessor corporation.[471] The four exceptions to the "no liability" for successor corporations are (1) when the successor corporation either expressly or impliedly assumes the liabilities; (2) when the sale is essentially a consolidation or merger of the two corporations; (3) when the successor corporation is merely a continuation of the predecessor corporation; or (4) when the transaction is entered into fraudulently for the purpose of escaping predecessor.[472]

The first exception is when the purchaser either expressly or impliedly agrees to assume the seller's liabilities.[473] The second exception occurs when a successor corporation is a continuation of the predecessor corporation and there is a continuity of ownership or corporate structure. Successor liability is transferred from the predecessor to the continuing successor corporation. The "mere continuation" exception is not satisfied unless the predecessor is extinguished.[474] The third exception is where a court finds a *de facto* merger instead of an assets purchase.[475] The continuity doctrine requires a number of other findings including (1) that there be no remedy against the predecessor; and (2) that a transfer of the corporate

---

[469] Intel, Intel Completes Merger With Dialogic, Intel Press Release (visited Nov. 26, 1999), http://intel.com/pressroom/archive/releases/Cn71399.htm.

[470] Annotation, "Successor Products Liability: Form of Business Organization of Successor or Predecessor As Affecting Successor Liability," 32 AL.R.4th 196 (1999).

[471] Araserv, Inc. v. Bay State Harness Horse Racing & Breeding Assoc., Inc., 437 F. Supp. 1083 (D. Mass. 1977).

[472] Dayton v. Peck, Stow & Wilcox Co., 739 F.2d 690 (1st Cir. 1984); Schumacher v. Richard Shear Co., 59 N.Y.2d 239, 464 N.Y.S.2d 437 (1983).

[473] *See, e.g.,* Polius v. Clark Equip. Co., 802 F.2d 75 (3d Cir. 1986).

[474] Liability of Successor Corporation, Generally, 86 N.Y. Jur. Products Liability § 9 (1998).

[475] *See, e.g.,* McCarthy v. Litton Industries, Inc., 410 Mass. 15, 570 N.E.2d 1008 (1991); Cargill Incorporated v. Beaver Coal & Oil Co. 424 Mass. 356 (1997) (holding that a corporation was liable for obligations of predecessor corporation under the *de facto* merger doctrine).

assets must have occurred.[476] The fourth exception is that tort liabilities will be assumed by the successor in the event that the merger or acquisition was a fraudulent transaction, intended to evade liability on debts.[477]

In the field of product liability, a product line exception also holds a successor corporation liable if it continues to market and produce the same product line as the predecessor corporation. A successor product liability manufacturer "steps into the shoes" of its predecessor if the successor produces the same product. In Sheppard v. A.C. & S. Co.,[478] an asbestos company argued that it was only a successor corporation. The court disagreed, holding that uncertainty existed as to whether the successor continued producing the same harm-causing product line, subjecting it to possible punitive damages.[479]

Assuming one of the four exceptions to the "no liability" rule applies, punitive damages are recoverable against the successor corporation for the torts of its predecessor corporation.[480] Successor liability for the torts of a predecessor is a significant risk for the online company for claims arising out of product liability,[481] environmental issues,[482] and labor and employment relations. An online successor may also be liable for the predecessor corporation's employment law obligations, including collective bargaining agreements and responsibility for unfair labor practices.[483]

---

[476] Diaz v. South Bend Lathe, Inc., 707 F. Supp. 97 (E.D. N.Y. 1989) (noting that a *de facto* merger had occurred based on evidence of assumption of liabilities, continuity of management and personnel, and the dissolution of the predecessor corporation).

[477] Raytech Corp. v. White, 54 F.3d 187 (3d Cir. 1995).

[478] 484 A.2d 521 (Del. Super. Ct. 1984).

[479] An online company that merges with another company needs also to consider the risk of assuming environmental cleanup costs. Successor liability is especially important in situations where environmental problems can arise, as the cost for cleanups can be substantial. Under CERCLA (the Federal Comprehensive Environmental Response, Compensation and Liability Act), individuals or corporations who own or operate contaminated sites are liable for any cleanup costs. Environmental cases have found that where a successor acts as "a mere continuation" of a predecessor, it will inherit environmental liabilities despite explicit contractual provisions to the contrary. Blackstone Valley Electric Co. v. Stone & Webster, Inc., 867 F. Supp. 73 (D. Mass. 1994).

[480] Annotation, Liability of Successor Corporation for Punitive Damages for Injury Caused by Predecessor's Product, 55 AL.R.4th 166 (1999).

[481] *See, e.g.,* Holzman v. Proctor, Cook & Co., 528 F. Supp. 9 (D. Mass 1981); Billy v. Consolidated Machine Tool Corp., 51 N.Y.2d 152, 412 N.E.2d 934 (1989).

[482] *In re* Acushnet River & New Bedford Harbor Proceedings re: Alleged PCB Pollution, 712 F. Supp. 1010 (D. Mass. 1989).

[483] *See, e.g.,* Dealing with Labor and Employment Law Issues in Mergers & Acquisitions, ALI/ABA (July 1998 Course of Study). See generally Mark J. Roe, Mergers, Acquisitions and Tort: A Comment on the Problem of Successor Corporation Liability, 70 Va. L. Rev. 1559 (1984).

§ 5.11   AVOIDING CYBERSPACE LIABILITY

An online company needs to complete a self-audit of its web site to minimize tort liability. The legal audit should include the company's web site, e-mail communications, and other Internet channels. The activities of predecessor corporations, trading partners, consultants, telecommuters, and employees using Internet channels should also be included. The legal audit should address the following questions. See also the more extensive checklists in Chapter Eight.

I. JURISDICTIONAL RISKS IN CYBERSPACE

- **Is the web site a passive web site or an active web site subject to personal jurisdiction in many states under applicable long-arm statutes?**[484]

- **Does the company have a "choice of law" notice?**

- **Does the web site disclaim all consequential damages from the company?** From its suppliers or any third parties? In particular, does the web site specifically disclaim incidental and consequential damages, lost profits, and damages from lost data or business interruption? Does the web site specifically mention that the company and its affiliates are not liable, whether based on contract, tort, or any other legal theory? Does the disclaimer make it clear that the web site owes no duty to the web site visitor? Web site visitors should be advised that they use the company's web site at their own risk. The company should make it clear that in delivering the service it is not liable to the web site visitor or to anyone else for losses or injuries. In addition, the company should retain the sole discretion to add, modify, or delete materials on the web site.

- **Has the company considered the impact of global Internet access and the possibility that a web site may subject the company to liability in foreign jurisdictions?**

- **If the company does not desire to accede to laws or regulations of given foreign jurisdictions, does it have limited exposure to liability in these nation states?**[485]

---

[484] A web site that is purely informational is likely to be deemed a "passive" web site, in contrast to an "active" web site where goods and services are sold. The greater the commercial activity, the more likely a web site activity will subject a company to jurisdiction in the United States and in foreign countries.

[485] A gambling web site, for example, should post a notice that it is not intended for use in the specifically named states where online casinos are illegal.

II. INTERNET ADVERTISEMENTS

- **Does the web site comply with federal, state, international and industry regulations governing (1) prior substantiation; (2) objective claims for products or services; and (3) comparative advertisements?**

- **Does the web site meet the Guidelines on Marketing and Advertising on the Internet formulated by the International Chamber of Commerce?** Does the company provide adequate self-identification? Fair information practices? Special rules for online advertising to children? Opt-out options to avoid unsolicited advertisements? Does it respect cultural and national norms and sensitivities?

- **Does the web site comply with the regulations of government agencies, including the Federal Trade Commission, Food and Drug Administration, and state attorneys general?**

- **Does the web site contain representations, omissions, or practices that may be deemed to mislead consumers, exposing the company to regulatory action or tort liability?**

- **If the web site collects information from children, does the web site comply with FTC regulations regulating contact with children?**[486] (The FTC charged a web site covering money and investing issues and directed to children and teens with misrepresenting that personal information collected from the young visitors would be maintained anonymously.[487]) Does the web site comply with the Children's Online Privacy Protection Act of 1998?[488]

- **Does the web site adhere to industry guidelines, such as the Children's Advertising Review Unit (CARU) of the Council of Better Business Bureaus, Inc.?**[489] CARU guidelines require advertisers to children who collect identifiable information to secure parental permission. Children are also to be told "when they are being targeted for the sale of a product or service."[490]

---

[486] The FTC has proposed implementing regulations for the Children's Online Privacy Protection Act of 1998.

[487] Federal Trade Commission, Young Investor Website Settles FTC Charges, May 6, 1999, Press Release (visited June 18, 1999), http://www.ftc.gov/opa/1999/9905/younginvestor.htm.

[488] Parental consent is required to collect personal information on children under the age of 13.

[489] The Better Business Bureau, CARU Gains Support From AOL and Microsoft for Child Privacy Standards (visited Nov. 29, 1999), http://www.bbb.org/advertising/carujoi.html.

[490] *Id.* (The web site should offer a "click here to order" button or instructions that clearly and prominently state that a child must get a parent's permission to order.)

III. MINIMIZING EXPOSURE FOR INTENTIONAL TORTS

- Train employees to avoid defamatory statements in e-mail messages, messages posted to listservs, Usenet groups, and online discussion groups.

- Obtain licenses or authorization for photographs and other images for which an individual may have a right to publicity.

- Avoid disparaging comments about competitors in online advertisements, e-mail messages, and other Internet channels of communications.

- Provide adequate information or computer security to protect electronic information.

- Train employees to avoid "flaming" and other misuses of e-mail that may be construed as online harassment.

- Incorporate e-mail and Internet modules in sexual and racial harassment training materials.

- Train employees in the legal consequences of harassment in the form of e-mail messages or Internet transmitted messages.

- If the company monitors e-mail messages, give notice of monitoring.

- Perform a due diligence to determine whether information posted on web sites violates the right of privacy.

IV. PUBLICATION-BASED TORT LIABILITY

- Is the company's e-mail system used in connection with surveys, contests, Pyramid schemes, chain letters, junk e-mail, spamming, or other unsolicited messages that may make the company vicariously liable?

- **Are employees educated in the proper use of the company's e-mail system?** Does this training include modules on defamation, stalking, harassing, right of privacy, and intentional infliction of emotional distress, as well as other torts that may occur if the computer system is misused or abused?

- Are employees advised that they must not distribute or disseminate profane or obscene material that may subject the company to vicarious liability for sexual or racial harassment?

- Are information security measures in place to protect the privacy of web site visitors and of third parties, such as employees, customers, patients, and others, to whom the online company may owe a legal duty?

- Are employees instructed on how to avoid transmitting viruses, Trojan horses, worms, time bombs, and other destructive code?

- **Are sufficient information security technologies in place to prevent unauthorized access?**

- **Are employees advised of the dangers of Internet identity theft and on how to avoid losses due to password mining and other harmful practices?**

V. EMPLOYMENT-RELATED TORTS

- **Are measures in place to prevent liabilities due to telecommuting employees?**

- **Are proper information security devices, such as tunnels, in place to prevent data loss from negligent telecommuters?**

- **Is an Internet usage and e-mail policy formulated and enforced?** Is the policy updated to meet changing technologies and emerging problems? Are employees warned about possible sanctions for sending inappropriate e-mail messages? Are employees informed that e-mail should be used only for business purposes?

- **Are e-mail messages monitored?** Are employees warned that e-mail messages and Internet usage are subject to monitoring by the company? Are employees trained that e-mail messages are business documents discoverable and admissible in lawsuits?

- **Are employees warned about sending racially or sexually charged jokes or other objectionable e-mail messages?**[491]

- **Has the company obtained indemnification agreements to hold the company (parent corporation, subsidiaries, affiliates, officers, and employees) harmless for the torts of consultants,[492] web site designers, and online partners?**

- **If an employee has committed an online tort or crime, has the employer taken appropriate disciplinary action?** Is the method of discipline progressive? Is the e-mail and Internet usage policy part of continual training?

VI. TORTS AND CUSTOMERS

- **Is the company's current privacy policy available on its web site?** What is the company's policy about selling the web site user's name, address, e-mail address, or personal information to third parties? Does the web site obtain information before transmitting information about customers? If an Internet

---

[491] *See e.g.,* Owens v. Morgan Stanley & Co., 1997 WL 403454, at *1 (S.D. N.Y., July 17, 1997) (lawsuit filed because of "smoking gun" racist e-mail messages).

[492] Internet consulting service is projected to grow to "$78.5 billion by 2003, 10 times the $7.89 billion for 1998." Diane Anderson, "The Young and the Restless, The Industry Standard, Nov. 8, 1999, at 95.

Service Provider hosts the company's web site, does the web site comply with the provider's privacy policy?[493]

- **Does the company require web site visitors to enter into webwrap agreements regarding the use of software, documents, and services available on the web site?**[494]

- **Does the webwrap agreement disclaim all warranties of any kind, including all implied warranties of merchantability, fitness for a particular purpose, title, and noninfringement?**

- **Does the webwrap agreement warn users that the company is not responsible for special, indirect, or consequential damages from losses due to relying upon web site information?** Is the web site offered on an "as is" basis, without warranties of any kind?

- **Does the company's web site have a legal page and disclaimers?** Does the web site disclaim liability for actions whether based upon contract, intentional tort, strict liability, or negligence arising out of use of the web site?[495]

- **What other types of contracts are required to shift or allocate the risk of liability?** Does the company have sufficient contract protection for indemnification, warranties, or insurance coverage for cybertorts?

- **Does the web site use the latest technology to protect credit card information?** Does the web site use SSL encryption for telephoning, faxing, or e-mailing credit card information?

---

[493] America Online requires its AOL Certified Merchants to comply with AOL's privacy policies. In general, an ISP will provide that a web site will not share personal information without the user's consent.

[494] Yahoo! for example, structures its webwrap agreements as Terms of Service (TOS). Yahoo! offers its service subject to the visitor agreeing to the TOS. A company's TOS agreement should note that the terms might be updated from time to time without notice. *See, e.g.,* Yahoo! Terms of Service (visited Sept. 7, 1999), http://docs.yahoo.com/info/terms. The terms of service for Yahoo! is divided into clauses covering the following points: (1) acceptance of terms; (2) description of service; (3) registration obligations; (4) Yahoo! privacy policy; (5) member account, password, and security; (6) member conduct; (7) special admonitions for international use; (8) public content posted to Yahoo! (9) indemnity; (10) no resale of service; (11) general practices regarding use and storage; (12) modifications to service; (13) termination; (14) dealings with advertisers; (15) links; (16) Yahoo!'s proprietary rights; (17) disclaimer of warranties; (18) limitation of liability; (19) exclusions and limitations; (20) special admonition for services relating to financial matters; (21) notice; (22) trademark information; (23) copyrights and copyright agents; (24) general information; and (25) violations.

[495] Courts will not enforce disclaimers of tort liability where there is personal injury, but they may enforce such agreements where losses are purely economic.

- **Does the web site have all proper legal notices as to copyright, trade-marks, patents as well as disclaimers for any errors or omissions relating to information on the web site?**

VII. AVOIDING LIABILITY FOR PRIVACY-BASED TORTS

- **Does the web site disclose what personally identifiable data, such as names, addresses, or e-mail addresses, will be collected and for what purposes?** If the company plans only to use this data for internal purposes, it should say so. Such a statement, however, is a warranty that personally identifiable data will not be sold or transferred to third parties.

- **Does the company's web site comply generally with the European Union Data Protection Directive, which came into effect in October 1998?** Does the web site disclose what types of personal information are collected and for what purpose? Do web site visitors have an opportunity to opt out of giving personal information that will be shared or collected?

VIII. PRIVACY CONCERNS

- **Does the web site meet the privacy principles of the Direct Marketing Association (DMA)?**[496]

- **Does the web site have the certification of TRUSTe?**[497] Is the TRUSTe "trustmark" prominently displayed? The TRUSTe is a "licensing program [that requires] participating Web sites to disclose their online information gathering and dissemination practices."[498] The TRUSTe "trustmark" gives visitors assurance that the web site complies with privacy principles, oversight, and resolution processes.[499] Each TRUSTe certified web site must post a privacy statement disclosing the following: (1) What is being gathered? (2) Who is the gatherer? (3) Uses of the information? (4) How will the information be shared? (5) Choices for collection, use, and distribution. (6) Security procedures to protect personal information. (7) Mechanism for updating and reporting inaccuracies.[500]

- **Does the web site comply with international comparative advertising laws?**

---

[496] The DMA, for example, requires its members to post their online privacy policies.

[497] Thomas Dabney, Mastering Consumer Contracting on the Internet, Third Annual High Technology Law Conference, Suffolk University Law School, Boston, Massachusetts, March 1999.

[498] *Id.*

[499] *Id.*

[500] *Id.*

- Does the web site comply with the requirement that advertisements be in a specific language?[501]

- Does the web site employ online promotions, sweepstakes, or contests that may subject the company to enforcement by state, federal, or international law enforcement?

- Does the web site comply with any industry regulations governing online promotions?[502]

- Do products or services sold on the web site comply with "Made in USA" claims in product advertising, labeling, and packaging?[503]

- Does the web site harvest or otherwise collect information about others, including e-mail addresses, without the user's consent?

- Does the web site have reasonable security to protect the integrity of personally identifiable information?

IX. OTHER TERMS, CONDITIONS, AND CONCERNS

- Does the web sites disclaim endorsements for specific products, processes, or services by trade name or trademark?

- If the company is defined as a service provider, it must designate an agent to receive complaints regarding copyright violations under § 512(c)(2) of the Digital Millennium Copyright Act. Has the company designated an agent or contact person to receive complaints for copyright infringement in connection with the web site?

---

[501] The province of Quebec, for example, requires advertisements to be in French as well as English. There are similar language requirements for advertisements directed to French citizens in France. As an alternative, the web site may have a notice that the advertisements are not directed to citizens of Quebec, France, etc.

[502] Promotions, sweepstakes, and contests "should expressly state which countries entrants must be residents. Such a disclosure should be clearly and prominently placed in all advertising for the promotion." Lewis Rose and John P. Feldman, Internet Marketing: Practical Suggestions for International Advertising and Promotions, Arent Fox (visited Sept. 7, 1999), http://www.webcom.com/lewrose/article/intl.html.

[503] Arent Fox Alert, FTC Enforces Made in USA Standard Against Six Major Corporations (visited August 31, 1999), http://www.arentfox.com/alerts/ftc_made_in_usa_2-4-1999.html.

[A]   **Payment Instruments**
　　　[1]　**Credit Cards**
➤　　　　　[a]　**Preventive Law Pointer: Web Sites and Credit Cards**
　　　[2]　**Debit Cards**
　　　[3]　**Electronic Negotiable Instruments**
　　　　　[a]　**UCC Articles 3 and 4**
　　　　　[b]　**Article 4A Wire Transfers**
[B]   **Internet Banking**
[C]   **E-Cash Payment Systems**
[D]   **European Union Euro**

§ 6.09　**International E-Commerce Developments**
[A]   **Convention on Contracts for the International Sale of Goods**
[B]   **Distance Selling Directive**
[C]   **Electronic Commerce Directive**
[D]   **Product Liability**
[E]   **Data Protection Directive**
[F]   **International Use of Web Site Materials**
[G]   **International Usage of Trade**
[H]   **International Enforceability Issues**
[I]   **Checklist of International Issues for Online Contracts**
　　　[1]　**Computer Hardware Web Site Sales**
　　　[2]　**Export and Reexport Licenses**
　　　[3]　**Licensing of Software at Web Sites**
　　　[4]　**Electronic Data Interchange (EDI)**

§ 6.01   OVERVIEW

The digital economy is based upon "assuring shoppers their communications are secure, their personal data is protected, and they will get what they paid for, and the underlying infrastructure is stable no matter where they shop on the Internet."[1] This chapter describes how online contracting rules are evolving to adapt to the business realities of e-commerce in a digital economy,[2] and it examines the contract law issues confronting an enterprise seeking to conduct e-commerce.

E-commerce regulation at the state level is evolving rapidly, with many states having enacted or considering legislation governing digital signatures, the e-filing of documents, and online licensing. The majority of states have enacted or are considering e-commerce-related legislation.[3] New model laws relating to e-commerce are an important part of this movement. This chapter provides extensive coverage of the Uniform Computer Information Transactions Act (UCITA), approved by the National Conference of Commissioners on Uniform State Laws (NCCUSL) in July 1999.[4] UCITA "represents the first comprehensive uniform computer information licensing law" and adapts traditional contract law to the Internet.[5] UCITA applies to a wide range of Internet-related contracts and is the single most comprehensive body of contract law dealing with cyberspace. UCITA has recently been adopted in Maryland and Virginia and has been introduced in legislatures in Delaware, the District of Columbia, Hawaii, Illinois, Louisiana, New Jersey, and Oklahoma.

In July 1999, NCCUSL also approved the Uniform Electronic Transaction Act (UETA) for enactment in the states. UETA treats electronic records and signatures as the functional and legal equivalent of paper and pencil writings and of

---

[1] Vice President Albert Gore, Towards Digital Equality: The U.S. Government Working Group on Electronic Commerce 1 (2d ed., 1999).

[2] E-commerce is defined as "the buying and selling of goods and services on the Internet, especially the World Wide Web" (http://whatis.techtarget.com/WhatIs_Definition_Page/0,4152,212029,00.html).

[3] See, e.g., CONN. GEN. STAT. § 19a-25a (1997) (adopting electronic signatures for medical records).

[4] UCITA is a statute sponsored by the National Conference of Commissioners on Uniform State Laws (NCCUSL). NCCUSL proposes model statutes "on subjects where uniformity is desirable and practicable, and work toward their enactment in legislatures. See National Conference of Commissioners on Uniform State Laws (NCCUSL) (visited Oct. 12, 2000) http://www.nccussl.org. UCITA is a successor to Article 2B, which was a proposal of NCCUSL and The American Law Institute (ALI) to make computer information a separate article of the Uniform Commercial Code. ALI withdrew from the Article 2B draft proposal which led NCCUSL to propose UCITA (Article 2B's successor) as a stand-alone statute. As of October 15, 2000, UCITA has been enacted in Maryland and Virginia and proposed in a number of other states.

[5] NCCUSL, A Few Facts About . . . Uniform Computer Information Transactions Act (May 9, 2000), http://www.nccusl.org/uniformact_factsheets/uniformacts-fs-ucita.htm.

manually signed signatures.[6] UETA supports the use of electronic contracts, digital evidence, electronic filing, electronic records, and computer-generated signatures. UETA has already been adopted in 17 states.[7]

The Electronic Signatures in Global and National Commerce Act, which validates electronic signatures and records, went into effect October 1, 2000.[8] The Uniform Commercial Code is being entirely revamped to take into account Internet-related transactions. Revised Article 2 of the UCC provides for new electronic contracting rules but does not address whether computer information qualifies as goods.[9] Revised Article 9 of the UCC updates the law of secured transactions for the online economy; for example, a security agreement or financing statement may now be authenticated through electronic means.[10] Revised Article 9 also contains special rules for perfecting security interests in software- or Internet-related assets,[11] and the 2000 revisions provide rules for perfecting security interests in "electronic chattel paper."[12]

To help put the issue in perspective, this chapter applies case law and statutory developments to the activities of our hypothetical company, Suffolk Personal Computers (SPC). Before SPC launches its web site, it must consider a wide range of contracting issues to protect its rights. SPC strives to become a dot-com with access to customers in a global Internet marketplace through a virtual online kiosk that will be open for business 24 hours a day, 7 days a week.

SPC permits its customers to download software from its web site. For tangible products, however, SPC must also have contractual arrangements with Federal Express or other shipping services.[13] SPC's virtual store, for example, permits it to merge its software and hardware offerings with those of other individual retailers in electronic catalogs. These transactions may be governed by a patchwork of laws. Revised Article 2 of the UCC applies to goods with embedded com-

---

[6] *Id.*

[7] The states are Arizona, California, Florida, Idaho, Indiana, Iowa, Kansas, Kentucky, Maryland, Minnesota, Missouri, Nebraska, Oklahoma, Pennsylvania, South Dakota, Utah, and Virginia. *Id.*

[8] The Electronic Signatures in Global and National Commerce Act, S.761, 15 U.S.C. § 7001 (2000).

[9] National Conference of Commissioners on Uniform State Laws, Revision of Uniform Commercial Code, Article 2-Sales (2000 Annual Meeting Draft, July 28, Aug. 4, 2000) (hereinafter Revised Article 2).

[10] UCC § 9-102 (7) (2000 Revisions).

[11] UCC § 9-102 (75) (2000 Revisions) defines software for the first time in Article 9. Electronic records are defined in § 9-102(69) (2000 Revisions), including amendments dating from May 20, 1999, to Mar. 3, 2000.

[12] UCC § 9-105 (Revised Final Draft, 2000); *see also,* The American Law Institute, Uniform Commercial Code [New] Revised Article 2A Leases (Council Draft No. 1, Oct. 5, 2000) (updating Article 2A to include electronic agents, records, and signatures).

[13] Michele Midgette, Two Shipping Giants Boost Productivity and Lower Costs Online, Net Com.Mag. Mar. 1999, at 8.

puter software or chips, whereas UCITA applies to the transfer of intangibles such as software or data.

In mid-2000, a flurry of activity surrounded e-commerce at the state, federal, and international levels. Early in the year, for example, the European Union enacted a Directive on Electronic Commerce, applicable to the 15 member states. The Directive governs unsolicited e-mail or "spam,"[14] defined as "[t]he sending of unsolicited commercial communications by electronic mail."[15] Article 9 of the Directive on Electronic Commerce provides that "Member States shall ensure that their legal system allows contracts to be concluded by electronic means."[16] The European Commission has adopted an EU-wide proposal validating electronic signatures and the receipt of data on electronic networks.[17] The Commission also proposes directives on e-mail, electronic money, and digital-copyright protection.[18]

Section 6.02 provides a brief introduction to the most common e-business models. Section 6.03 describes the sources of e-commerce contract law. Section 6.04 examines the evolving legal framework for electronic contracting. Section 6.05 follows with an analysis of the Uniform Computer Information Transactions Act (UCITA), while Section 6.06 covers the specifics of licensing agreements. UCITA governs software, web site, and Internet-related contract issues. Section 6.07 provides a multijurisdictional survey of Internet taxation. A brief discussion of Internet payment systems appears in Section 6.08. The chapter concludes with Section 6.09, a discussion (including an annotated checklist) of international issues in e-commerce.

§ 6.02 E-BUSINESS MODELS

IBM describes e-business as a process by which companies meld "the standards, simplicity and connectivity of the Internet with the core processes that are the foundation of business."[19] SPC's e-business will evolve through stages of development, beginning with its web site, established as an interface through which to improve customer service. SPC's e-business plan is to redesign its business process to cut costs, increase revenues, create new channels of distribution,

---

[14] The term "spam" comes from a Monty Python skit in which the word Spam™ is used repeatedly. Matisse's Glossary of Internet Terms (Mar. 11, 2000), http://www.matisse.net/files/glossary.html.

[15] Directive on Electronic Commerce, 2000/C I28/02 (adopted by the Council on Feb. 28, 2000); *see also,* Directive on Community Framework for Electronic Signatures, Directive 1999/93/EC (adopted by the Council on Dec. 13, 2000).

[16] *Id.*

[17] The European Commission, Electronic Commerce: Commission Proposes Electronic Signature Directive (visited May 5, 2000), http://europa.eu.int/comm/internal_market/en/media/infso/sign.htm.

[18] *Id.*

[19] IBM.com, What Is E-business? (visited Feb. 5, 2000), http://www.ibm.com/e-business/info.

improve customer service, and offer global support for its medley of hardware and software products.

E-commerce may be broadly divided into four types: business-to-business (B2B); business-to-consumer (B2C); business-to-government (B2G); and consumer-to-consumer (C2C). E-commerce also encompasses diverse commercial practices in which the parties interact over electronic networks rather than by traditional human-to-human exchanges.[20] Additionally, a growing number of federal and state agencies permit government-to-consumer transactions (G2C). SPC is likely to conduct extensive B2B commercial transactions as well as B2C sales from its web site. In addition, SPC will electronically transact B2G business with state and federal agencies.

[A]   Business-to-Business

The B2B marketplace brings businesses together with other businesses to exchange goods, materials, supplies, and services. B2B involves electronic contracts that permit companies to lower costs "via point-and-click comparison shopping or electronically auctioning contracts."[21] B2B supply networks, which are evolving rapidly as a way for entire industries to buy and sell goods online, have recently been established in the steel, aeronautics, automobile, retail, farming, consumer products, paper, and medical products industries.[22]

A B2B model may take the form of a "virtual mall" or electronic catalogs "for purchases between companies [that] allow corporate buyers to search for products based on features and price."[23] B2B is also used in "just in time" strategies for ordering inventory, streamlining administrative tasks, and connecting suppliers.

B2B transactions account for far more dollars than do B2C retail transactions. Businesses spent $92 billion on B2B transactions in 1999, compared to only $15.3 billion in online consumer sales in 1998. By 2003, 25 percent of all B2B sales will be conducted on the Internet or computer-to-computer,[24] and Forrester Research projects that B2B Internet commerce will skyrocket to $1.3 trillion.[25]

---

[20] ISPO, Electronic Commerce and the European Union (visited Jan. 7, 2000), http://www.ispo .cec.be/Ecommerce/answers/introduction.html (defining electronic commerce).

[21] John Witty, Tech's Best Stock Play, Bloomberg B2B Business to Business 53, 55 (June 2000).

[22] Clare Ansberry, Let's Build an Online Supply Network! Wall St. J., Apr. 17, 2000, at B1.

[23] Steffano Korper and Juanita Ellis, The E-Commerce Book: Building the E-Empire 8 (2000).

[24] Boston Consulting Group, New BCG Study Re-Evaluates Size, Growth and Importance of Business-to-Business E-Commerce (visited Dec. 12, 1999), http://www.bcg.com/practice/ ecommerce/press_coverage_supage4.asp.

[25] AllEC.com, Ecommerce Reports, Surveys & Trends (visited Apr. 1, 1999), http://www.allEC .com/allec/News/rs.htm.

[1]   Electronic Data Interchange

Electronic data interchange (EDI) refers to the process by which goods are ordered, shipped, and tracked computer-to-computer using standardized proto-col.[26] EDI permits the "electronic settlement and reconciliation of the flow of goods and services between companies and consumers"[27]; financial EDI permits electronic payment and remittance over an automated clearinghouse (ACH).[28] EDI saves money because the computer, and not an office staff, submits and processes orders, claims, and other routine tasks. It represents a significant advance over snail mail in transmitting business information. In one version, business forms may be e-mailed to a trading partner who then "re-keys the data into another busi-ness application."[29] Under a more efficient approach, computer-to-computer trans-actions solve the problem of "poor response time" in the supply chain and reduce the rate of errors in filling orders because of the greater reliability of computer-to-computer messaging.[30]

EDI is made possible because trading partners enter into master agreements to employ electronic messaging permitting computer-to-computer transfers of information and validates computer-to-computer contracts.[31] In the early days of EDI, the lack of universal standards made it difficult for companies to communi-cate with many of their trading partners.[32] Since the development of the ANSI X12 protocol, described below in § 6.02[A][2], master trading agreements generally specify the use of the ANSI X12 protocol.

In the early days of EDI, companies developed their own proprietary format for interchanging data messages. Internet-based B2B commerce evolved out of the EDI that took hold in the 1960s and allowed corporations to transfer purchase orders, invoices, and other business documents electronically.[33]

---

[26] *See* George B. Delta and Jeffrey H. Matsuura, Law of the Internet § 9.02[A] (1998) (stating EDI is the transmission, in standard syntax, of unambiguous information between computers of two or more independent organizations).

[27] Robert Teitelman and Stephen Davis, How the Cash Flows, Institutional Investor 22, 26 (Aug. 1996).

[28] Federal Reserve Bank of Boston, Fed Flash (June 2, 1998) (visited May 1, 1999), http://www .bos.frb.org.

[29] National Institute of Standards, EDI Tutorial: The Problem Addressed by EDI (May 7, 2000), http://www.nist.gov/itl/div896/ipsg/eval_guide/subsection3_5_1.html.

[30] *Id.*

[31] Electronic Messaging Services Task Force, The Commercial Use of Electronic Data Inter-change: A Report and Model Trading Partner Agreement, 45 Bus. Law. 1645 (1990).

[32] National Institute of Standards, EDI Tutorial: History of EDI (visited May 7, 2000), http:// www.nist.gov/itl/div896/ipsg/eval_guide/subsection3_5_2.html.

[33] *See generally* Benjamin Wright and Jane K. Winn, The Law of Electronic Commerce (3rd ed., 1998) (describing a wide variety of e-commerce and e-commerce issues).

Today EDI is a well-established B2B means of transmitting information from one computer to another. In 1998, total B2B e-commerce was $671 billion, comprising $92 billion in Internet-based transactions and $579 billion in transactions using EDI over private networks.[34]

Interconnected B2B computer systems, for example, link providers, insurers, and suppliers in the health care industry.[35] Physicians employ EDI to make electronic insurance claims, saving $.50 per claim over paper filings.[36] EDI is used to access commercial, dental, Medicare, Medicaid, and Blue Cross/Blue Shield payers.[37] Electronic trading communities connect health care providers, insurers, and other players in the health care industry.

[2] Industry Standards for EDI

To resolve the difficulties resulting from the lack of universal EDI standards, the American National Standards Institute (ANSI) developed X12 for the electronic exchange of information. ANSI is the clearinghouse for all industry standards in the United States; once ANSI standards are approved, they are widely adopted by the respective industry. The ANSI X12 standard encompasses nearly 200 transaction sets for diverse activities including "communications and controls, product data, finance, government, materials management, transportation, purchasing, industry standards transaction, distribution, warehousing, and insurance."[38] ANSI transaction sets are divided into data segments representing elements of business forms. Each segment within a set is in turn divided into data elements.

Trading partners thus have a standard protocol for specifying price, product code, or other attributes in B2B or B2G transactions. The federal government's adoption of ANSI X12 is covered in Federal Information Processing Standards Publication 161 (FIPS 161-1), available at the U.S. Government Printing Office.[39] The National Institute of Standards and Technology (NIST) administers the federal government's EDI activities.[40] The Department of Defense's Electronic Commerce Acquisition-Program Management Office (ECA-PMO) has published the

---

[34] Boston Consulting Group, New BCG Study, *id.*

[35] Envoy.com, Providing Electronic Data Interchange to the Healthcare Industry (visited Sept. 24, 1999), http://www.envoy.com/about/edi.cfm.

[36] *Id.*

[37] *Id.*

[38] U.S. Small Business Administration, Standards Governing EC/EDI (visited June 4, 2000), http://www.onlinewbc.org/Docs/procure/standard/html.

[39] *Id.*

[40] National Institute of Standards and Technology, EDI Implementation Conventions (May 7, 2000), http://www.nist.gov/itl/div896/ipsg/eval_guide/subsection3_5_5.html.

transaction sets and documents for doing business with the military.[41] The goal is to develop a single set of EDI standards with universally understood protocol.[42]

Other entities promote different standards. The European Community has implemented the Guidelines on Trade Data Interchange (GTD) as its standard syntax.[43] The United Nations is the sponsor of a standard titled EDI for Administration, Commerce, and Transport (EDIFACT).[44] EDIFACT represents a "syntax adopted by the International Organization for Standards (ISO) in 1987." EDIFACT is primarily used in Europe and Asia, not in North America. The EDIFACT standard draws upon both the GTD and the ANSI X12 standards. To attain a worldwide standard for the Internet, ANSI X12 and EDIFACT must be harmonized into a single standard.[45]

[B] Business-to-Consumer

Business-to-consumer (B2C) commerce is perhaps the most familiar Internet business model, exemplified by "e-tailers" such as Amazon.com™ and eToys.com™. In the basic B2C model, consumers purchase goods by ordering from a company's web site, much as they might from a catalog. B2C or e-tailing purchases are projected to grow exponentially from $15.3 billion in 1998 to $100.5 billion by 2002.[46]

In addition to sales of tangible goods, B2C activities include online investing, enrollment in distance learning courses, and downloading of music or software from B2C sites. Hundreds of thousands of eMarketplaces target consumers, ranging from Motley Fool™ for financial information to Quake™ for sports. Online casino games, adventure games, and gaming sites are also popular with consumers, as are sites providing cash incentives or sweepstakes. Adult entertainment, including streaming video, is a highly profitable business that attracts hundreds of millions of consumer dollars.

A Harris poll found that 44 percent of those with Internet access had made at least one online purchase in the previous year.[47] Customers located around the world may pursue online shopping through web shopping malls, purchasing things

---

[41] *Supra* note 38.

[42] *Id.*

[43] *Id.*

[44] *Id.*

[45] ANSI has agreed to align the X12 standard with EDIFACT, but this alignment is still in its early stages. *Id.*

[46] Bob Woods, Consumer E-Commerce to Grow by 67% Yearly-Report, CNN Fin. Network, Sept. 24, 1998 (visited Feb. 13, 1999), http://www.cnnfn.com/digitaljam/newsbytes/118544.html.

[47] Comment on Behalf of National Consumers League, Electronic Commerce Policy: Public Comment on Barriers to Electronic Commerce (visited May 5, 2000), http://osecnt13.osec.doc.gov/ecommerce/barriers.ns.../76A4A98D573CC8D5852568CF0067121.

as varied as wine, glass and crystal, pet products, and countless other goods. Online shoppers have an unparalleled opportunity to do comparison shopping. Auto-by-Tel™, for example, specializes in the sale or lease of new and used cars, car loans, and car insurance.[48]

People around the world vary in their acceptance of online shopping. In Germany, for example, online shoppers remain concerned about Internet security, uncertain legal rights, high telephone costs for Internet use, poor web site design, long downloading times, and "the lack of a shopping atmosphere."[49] German respondents complained that online stores were often late in delivering goods. Respondents also report frequent lapses of security due to the failure of online sellers or suppliers to encrypt orders.[50] Until recently, the retail online market was predominately a U.S. market. Online sellers will need to adapt their virtual stores to local languages, cultural sensitivities, and legal systems as they expand into European and Asian eMarketplaces.

[C] Business-to-Government

Particularly in the areas of procurement and contracts, various levels of government have begun to use EDI and other electronic commerce methods for business-to-government (B2G) transactions. Governmental agencies cut costs and bring more efficient methods to the procurement process by using e-commerce to transact business. State governments are combining resources in order to improve their negotiating position with vendors through B2G online malls. A growing number of federal and state agencies use electronic requests for proposals (RFPs) and catalogs. Federal agencies use B2G online transactions to improve supply chain management. State governments, too, are using B2G for procurement and the solicitation of government bids.

A number of dot-com companies are partnering with cities or government agencies in "electronic payments for taxes, permits, utility bills and other transactions."[51] Vendors contracting with state government agencies in Massachusetts, for example, are encouraged to use B2G ordering, billing, and accounting systems.

Government agencies vary in their web site designs and user friendliness in bidding or procurement. SPC will have transaction costs associated with learning how to use government web sites, which may be poorly or inefficiently designed.

---

[48] *See* http://www.autobytel.com.

[49] Alex McCallum, German Consumers Remain Cautious about E-Commerce, 2 Global E-Commerce: Law and Business Report 1 (Jan. 2000).

[50] *Id.; see also,* Forrester Research, Europe: The Sleeping Giant Awakens (visited Oct. 10, 2000) http://www.forrester.com (reporting Europe has the potential to reach $1.6 trillion in online trade by 2004).

[51] Glenn R. Simpson, Putting Government on the Web, Wall St. J., May 17, 2000, at B1.

[D]   Consumer-to-Consumer

A consumer-to-consumer (C2C) model facilitates both transactions between consumers who might otherwise face high transaction costs in finding buyers or sellers and transactions in goods not commonly available through retailers. Online auctions such as eBay™ are a popular C2C model, linking up consumer sellers with consumer buyers interested in auction jewelry, pens, collectibles, electronic equipment, artwork, books, and hundreds of thousands of other consumer goods.[52]

Online trading posts may also be specialized to niche products such as Pokemon™ cards, kitchen products, jewelry, sporting goods, or Hollywood memorabilia. GoAuction.com specializes in art, antiques, collectibles, and sports memorabilia, whereas SkyAuction.com™ is an Internet travel auction site. Stampfair Online Auctions specializes in packets of collectible postage stamps. The BidMore™ online auction permits bidders to purchase foreign stamps in a global auction marketplace.

Auctions may take the form of a traditional auction in which purchasers bid against each one another or of a reverse auction in which purchasers name their price. A growing number of web sites use "reverse auctions"; Priceline.com™ permits a consumer to place a bid for a flight to Copenhagen, for example, at a price no greater than $500 one-way. The reverse bidder specifies departure and return dates, departure and arrival airports, flight times, number of tickets, passenger names, maximum number of connections, airlines, offer price, and the manner of delivery. If the airline accepts the offer price, the purchase is automatically charged to the visitor's credit card.[53] Users must have typed their initials in an icon box "to indicate that they have reviewed the terms and agree to abide by priceline.com's terms and conditions."[54] Bid 4 Vacations uses a similar methodology for vacation and travel packages. Other sites, such as Bid.com™, Bidder's Edge™, BidFind™, BidNow™, and Bidstream™, use auction search engines to conduct meta-searches of popular auction web sites. A consumer can locate the lowest price on the Internet for any consumer product and use that price as a basis for bargaining at a brick and mortar business, such as a car dealership.[55]

Another variation of the online auction has customers band together in groups to increase their purchasing power. The greater the number of interested

---

[52] The auction model developed by eBay and other online auctions for a C2C market extends to B2B markets as well. *See, e.g.*, Harbinger.com, Harbinger Named to Information Week's E-Business 100 List (visited Feb. 5, 2000), http://www.harbinger.com/news/1999/121319999a.html.

[53] Priceline.com, Airline Tickets (visited May 9, 2000), http://www.tickets.priceline.com; *see also* Ronna Abrahamson, Airlines Get Cheap, The Industry Standard, Oct. 2, 2000 at 96 (reporting Priceline has two new online airline ticket competitors, savvio.com and Hotwire).

[54] *Id.*

[55] Some auction brokers offer business applications for online auction sources. Auctionshare.com, for example, sells custom auction sites for various products and services.

buyers seeking a particular item, the lower the price per purchaser.[56] Consumer sites providing information have also evolved. Sites like ancestry.com permit visitors to perform genealogical searches, using the site's message boards, classified by family surname. This site also has a location at which consumers can post their family data along with that of other users, thus creating an evolving family tree for that surname.

Online auctions evolved four decades after the rules for sale by auction were drafted in Article 2 of the Uniform Commercial Code (UCC).[57] The Article 2 rules for auctions were drafted to apply to human auctioneers selling goods in lots. The auctioneer's "falling of the hammer" constituted acceptance of the bidder's offer. This symbolic act has no close parallel in Internet auctions, although judges may extend Article 2 rules by analogy to the online auction house.

Under the UCC rules, a court will look to the "usage of trade"[58] to clarify the contracting parties' intent in light of the industry's established practices. The "usage of trade" for auctions generally take the form of an auction "with reserve" or "without reserve." The traditional auction is "with reserve," meaning that the auctioneer has the discretion to reject the highest bid if it is too low; a sale is "with reserve" unless the goods are explicitly sold "without reserve."[59]

In an online auction, no "fall of the hammer" can signify acceptance, so the operators of virtual or online auctions are developing their own customary practices for listing goods, documenting bid histories, communicating bidding guidelines, and dealing with liability. Online auction sellers frequently set minimum prices and sell their goods explicitly "with reserve" or "without reserve." As in the real world, a virtual auction "with reserve" permits the seller to withdraw the goods at any time. Unlike the real world, however, no auctioneer announces the completion of the sale.[60] An auction "without reserve" means that the auctioneer cannot withdraw the goods unless no bid is made within a reasonable time. In either case, a bidder may retract his bid until the auctioneer announces the end of the bidding period. The existing rules for virtual auctions must be accommodated to evolving online auction practices.

Online auctions use consumer measures of a seller's reputation to build trust in C2C transactions. Consumers give online ratings of their satisfaction with their course of dealing with a given vendor. In a face-to-face auction, the buyer can inspect the lots of goods being auctioned. Many online auction sellers provide

---

[56] *See, e.g.,* http://www.mercata.com.

[57] UCC § 2-328 (2000).

[58] UCC § 1-205(2) provides that a "usage of trade is any practice or method of dealing having such regularity of observance in a place, vocation or trade as to justify an expectation that it will be observed with respect to the transaction in question." UCC § 1-205 (2000).

[59] UCC § 2-328 (2000); *see also,* The American Law Institute, Uniform Commercial Code [New] Revised Article 2, Sales § 238 (Council Draft No. 1, Oct. 5, 2000) (updating the concept of "hammer falling" with the "process of completing the auction sale.").

[60] UCC § 2-328 (3) (2000).

photographs of objects being sold, but a photo of an item for sale is hardly the same thing as a hands-on inspection. State and federal regulators are increasingly scrutinizing online fraud at Internet auction sites. It is unclear whether courts will enforce disclaimers of liability by the virtual auction host.

[E]   Government-to-Consumer

Finally, the Internet allows government-to-consumer (G2C) business transactions. Soon drivers will be able to pay parking tickets online. Most federal agencies already have web sites that provide citizens with government services. The Small Business Administration, for example, offers online courses on implementing business plans.[61] State auditors and attorneys general have sites at which whistleblowers can report unethical or illegal transactions. Federal agencies, such as the Department of Defense, Justice Department, and the USPTO, provide consumers with extensive resources relevant to their services. Citizens can now apply for passports online or, in many jurisdictions, file their tax returns. Millions of American consumers accessed the online version of the Starr Report on President Clinton. Courts, too, increasingly release opinions in well-publicized cases on the Internet.[62]

§ 6.03   SOURCES OF E-COMMERCE LAW

The substantive law of e-commerce law consists largely of commercial and contract law. Article 2 of the Uniform Commercial Code (UCC), the chief source of law for the sale of online goods, governs online offers, acceptance, consideration, warranties, risk of loss, performance and remedies for tangible goods. The Convention for the International Sale of Goods (CISG) applies to online sales of goods between merchants in different signatory countries. It is unclear how traditional substantive contract law applies to software downloadable from a web site. In the absence of new substantive rules, courts will stretch traditional principles to apply to web site contracts. The parties may develop their own rules governing web site contracts. Courts will generally enforce contracts entered into by commercial parties in the absence of fraud or a violation of public policy. Increasingly, regulatory agencies are policing unfair or oppressive contract provisions such as choice of law, choice of forum, or limitations of liability. Unfair or deceptive trade practices may be policed by courts, or by state or federal regulatory agencies.

---

[61] Small Business Administration, Business Plan (visited June 7, 2000), http://www.sba.gov.

[62] *See, e.g.,* Mary Beth Regan, Surfers Face a Flood of Facts, Atlanta J. & Const., Sept. 1998 (noting that Judge Zobel released his opinion online in the highly publicized murder trial of a Massachusetts nanny.) The state attorneys general have millions of documents online in the continuing tobacco litigation. Most of the documents in the Microsoft antitrust litigation are also available online.

[A]   Federal Trade Commission

The Federal Trade Commission (FTC) is the chief federal agency governing online sales and services. The FTC has promulgated rules to implement the Magnuson-Moss Act, which applies to the sale of consumer goods on the Internet, and it has recently issued the Children's Online Privacy Protection Rule, which governs commercial practices of sites directed to children under the age of 13. The FTC is considering amending its Telemarketing Sales Rule to govern abusive or deceptive web site sales acts or practices. The FTC is considering regulations to ensure that consumers receive adequate information when purchasing computer information products and services.

[1]   Magnuson-Moss Act

The Magnuson-Moss Warranty Federal Trade Commission Improvement Act (Magnuson-Moss Act) applies to consumer products on the Internet with the same force it does to products in the offline world. The Magnuson-Moss Act applies to written warranties "made in connection with the sale of a consumer product by a supplier to a buyer that relates to the material or workmanship."[63] This broad language applies to written warranties for consumer products sold over the Internet. The term "consumer products" means "any tangible personal property which is distributed in commerce and which is normally used for personal, family or household purposes."[64]

The threshold for applying the Magnuson-Moss Act is whether a transaction involves consumer products "distributed in commerce" costing more than $15.[65] Courts will have little difficulty holding that Internet sales constitute "use in commerce." It is unclear whether the Magnuson-Moss Act applies to computer software transactions or information products, since software is an intangible rather than a movable good. Courts will apply the Magnuson-Moss Act to hybrid transactions in which computer hardware is the substantial part or predominant purpose.

The Magnuson-Moss Act requires all written warranties to be conspicuously designated as either "full" or "limited." The label "full warranty" signifies that the seller provides all federal warranties, such as a right to a refund if a seller is unable to correct defects. In contrast, the concept of "limited warranty" means that the seller is offering a limited remedy. Few sellers have offered a "full warranty" in the history of the Magnuson-Moss Act. The Magnuson-Moss Act does not apply

---

[63] 16 C.F.R. § 701(b) (2000).

[64] Disclosure of Written Consumer Product Warranty Terms and Conditions, 16 C.F.R. § 701(b) (2000).

[65] 15 U.S.C. § 2301(13) (2000).

to merchant-to-merchant sales (B2B) and is chiefly a consumer protection statute governing B2C transactions.[66]

Under the Magnuson-Moss Act, the implied warranty of merchantability is not completely disclaimable.[67] The Magnuson-Moss Act provides that a supplier may not disclaim or modify any implied warranty to a consumer if (1) the supplier makes any written warranty to the consumer or, (2) at the time of the sale, or within 90 days thereafter, the supplier enters into a service contract with the consumer relative to the consumer product.[68] If a seller gives only a limited warranty, the implied warranty of merchantability may be limited for the duration of a limited written warranty. The limited duration period must, however, be conscionable and explained in clear and unmistakable language.[69]

If a manufacturer of computer hardware has not corrected or cured problems in its computer system after a reasonable number of attempts, the consumer must receive a refund or replacement without charge, plus reasonable expenses. The Magnuson-Moss Act would provide a remedy to consumers in cases where there are repeated failures to pass acceptance tests as well as failure to provide deliverables, such as source codes, which caused the licensee to withhold payment. If the Magnuson-Moss Act were extended to Internet-related licenses, the implied warranty of merchantability would be nondisclaimable in consumer transactions.

➤ **[a]   *Preventive Law Pointer: Complying with the Magnuson-Moss Act***

SPC must comply with the Magnuson-Moss Act warranty provisions for any online sales to consumers. It is unclear whether the Magnuson-Moss Act would apply to licenses related solely to software. The Magnuson-Moss Act creates a federal private cause of action for consumers damaged by the failure of a warrantor "to comply with any obligation under . . . a written warranty."[70] Although the Magnuson-Moss Act does not require SPC to extend a warranty with its computer product, any written warranty offered with a computer product sold to consumers

---

[66] The Magnuson-Moss Act applies "to written warranties on tangible personal property which is normally used for personal, family, or household purposes." 16 U.S.C. § 700.1 (2000): "Nothing in the Act provides that a consumer product be warranted or that a product be warranted for any specific length of time. If however, a written warranty is offered, full disclosure is required, and the warranty information must be made available to consumers before the product is sold." *Id.*

[67] The implied warranty of merchantability is not disclaimable if goods are used for personal, household, or family purposes. For further discussion of warranties, *see* § 6.05[G].

[68] 15 U.S.C. § 2308(a)(1) (2) (2000).

[69] *Id.* § 2308.

[70] *Id.* § 2310(d)(1).

is subject to the requirements of the Act. A Magnuson-Moss written warranty is defined as any affirmation of fact that becomes part of the "basis of the bargain."[71]

Section 103 of the Act provides that warrantors must either conspicuously designate written warranties as "full" or "limited."[72] The term "full" warranty means that the warrantor is promising all of the federal remedies in the Magnuson-Moss Act. In contrast, the term "limited" means that the written warranty does not meet the Federal minimum standards. SPC may limit the duration of an implied warranty "to the duration of a written warranty of reasonable duration."[73] To comply with the Magnuson-Moss Act, SPC should prominently label its written warranties as "limited." SPC must clearly and conspicuously limit the duration of implied warranties. SPC can accomplish this by using "clear and unmistakable language and prominently displaying the limitations on its web site."[74]

The Federal Trade Commission also monitors disclaimers and disclosures to ensure that they are clear and conspicuous. An FTC guideline states that a "consumer must be able to notice, read, or hear and understand the information."[75] Offers and claims for all online products and services must not be unfair or deceptive. Section 5 of the Federal Trade Commission Act gives the Commission the power to prevent deceptive and unfair acts or practices.[76]

[2]   Children's Online Privacy Protection Rule

The FTC regulates unfair or deceptive acts or practices in connection with the collection, use, or disclosure of personal information harvested from children at web sites in B2C transactions.[77] Commercial web sites will need to comply with the FTC's Children's Online Privacy Protection Rule, which implements the Children's Online Privacy Protection Act (COPPA). COPPA's regulations must be complied with by operators of web sites that target online advertisements, promotions, and games to children under the age of 13.[78] COPPA applies to any site that (1) requests that children submit personal information online; (2) enables children to make personal information publicly available through a chat room, message board, or other means; or (3) uses cookies or other identifying codes to track children's activity on the Internet.[79]

---

[71] *Id.* § 2301(6).

[72] *Id.* § 2303.

[73] *Id.* § 2308.

[74] *See id.* § 2308(b).

[75] Federal Trade Commission, Advertising and Marketing on the Internet: The Rules of the Road, Apr. 1998 (visited June 8, 2000), http://www.ftc.gov/bcp/conline/pubs/buspubs/ruleroad.htm.

[76] *Id.*

[77] Children's Online Privacy Protection Rule, 16 C.F.R. § 312 (2000).

[78] *Id.* § 312.2.

[79] *Id.* § 312.2(a)(b)(c).

The web site operator must make a threshold determination of whether the web site or online service is directed to children under 13. A web site that sells children's products such as games, books, or other entertainment products needs to comply with COPPA's safe harbor provisions. Web sites directed to children or that collect information from children must post a notice before collecting, using, or disclosing information about a child. However, consent is not required when a site is collecting an e-mail address of a child for the sole purpose of responding to a one-time request from the child.[80]

The FTC considers a number of factors in determining whether a given web site targets children. The most important factors include the subject matter (visual or audio content), the age of models on the site, the age of the actual or intended audience, and "whether a site uses animated characters or other child-oriented features."[81] The FTC considers an entity an "operator" depending on who owns, controls, and pays for the collection of information.[82] COPPA applies to "individually identifiable information about a child that is collected online, such as full name, home address, email address, telephone number" or other means of identifying or contacting a child.[83] If COPPA applies, the operator must "link to a notice of its information practices on the home page of the web site or online service and at each area where it collects personal information from children."[84] The FTC requires the link to be "clear and prominent."[85]

Personal information is defined to include (a) an individuals' first and last name; (b) home or other physical address; (c) an e-mail address or other online contact information; (d) a telephone number; (e) a Social Security number; (f) a persistent identifier, such as a code; and (g) any other information concerning the child or the parents of that child that the operator collects online from the child.[86] Personal information may be collected directly from a child or passively through devices such as cookies.[87]

The FTC requires the site to obtain parental consent and to give conspicuous notice of their information practices.[88] A site must obtain verifiable parental consent *before* collecting a child's personal data. Parents have a right to review personal information provided by a child and to delete the information or to have it

---

[80] *Id.* Federal Trade Commission, How to Protect Kids' Privacy, Feb. 2000 (visited Oct. 13, 2000), http://www.ftc.gov/bcp/conline/pubs/online/kidsprivacy.htm.

[81] *Id.*

[82] *Id.*

[83] *Id.*

[84] *Id.*

[85] *Id.*

[86] *Id.* § 312.2((2)(a)(g).

[87] Federal Trade Commission, How to Comply with the Children's Online Privacy Protection Rule (visited June 8, 2000), http://www.ftc.gov/bcp/conline/pubs/buspubs/coppa.htm.

[88] 16 C.F.R. §§ 312.4, 312.5 (2000).

deleted.[89] A web site may not condition a child's participation in the web site on the collection of personal information.[90] A child's parents must be given the opportunity to restrain further use or collection of information.[91]

A web site must have reasonable security to protect the confidentiality, security, and integrity of personal information collected from children.[92] The FTC COPPA rule provides a safe harbor for sites as long as they comply with approved self-regulatory guidelines formulated by marketing or online industries.[93] At a minimum, the self-regulatory guidelines must subject operators to the same or greater protections for children as those contained in Section 312.2 through 312.9 of the FTC's COPPA Rule.[94]

A web site is not entitled to the safe harbor unless it requires operators to comply with the guidelines. The site is required to conduct "periodic reviews of subject operators' information practices."[95] The FTC may be requested to approve self-regulatory guidelines.[96] Industry groups who seek safe harbor must maintain records on compliance for a period of not less than three years.[97] The FTC plans to implement a sliding scale approach to parental consent by April 2002.[98] The method of consent will vary depending on how the web site operator intends to use information. If the use of the information is purely internal, a less stringent method of consent will apply. If the operator is harvesting data for others, however, a more rigorous consent will be required.

[3]   Telemarketing Sales Rule

The FTC's Telemarketing Sales Rule, which prohibits "deceptive telemarketing acts or practices,"[99] has yet to be expanded to telemarketing over the Internet. On February 23, 2000, however, the FTC announced a five-year review of the rule. Under the rule, telemarketers are required to make material disclosures *prior* to a customer's payment for goods or services. The customer must be provided with the total costs to purchase, receive, or use any goods or services.[100] Further,

---

[89] *Id.* § 312.6.

[90] *Id.* § 312.7.

[91] *Id.* § 312.5.

[92] *Id.* § 312.8.

[93] *Id.* § 312.10(a).

[94] *Id.* § 312.10(b).

[95] *Id.* § 312.10(b)(1).

[96] *Id.* § 312.10(3)(4).

[97] *Id.* § 312.10(3)(d).

[98] Federal Trade Commission, How to Comply with the Children's Online Privacy Protection Rule, Nov. 1999 (visited June 8, 2000), http://www.ftc.gov/bcp/conline/pubs/buspubs/coppa.htm.

[99] Telemarketing Sales Rule, 16 C.F.R. § 310.3 (2000).

[100] *Id.* § 310.3(a)(1).

telemarketers must make specific disclosure about any material limitations or condition to the purchase of goods or services.[101] A telemarketer must disclose its policy for "refunds, cancellations, exchanges or repurchases."[102]

In any prize promotion, the telemarketer must give the odds of winning a prize and the factors used in calculating the odds, as well as any costs of or conditions for receiving or redeeming a prize.[103] A telemarketer is liable for deceptive telemarketing acts for misrepresenting information on costs, limitations, or conditions to purchase or use goods or services.[104] The FTC's telemarketing regulations prescribe rules for a merchant's payment system. A customer's express verifiable authorization is required for payment by check or other negotiable instruments.[105] False or misleading statements or assisting others in deceptive telemarketing schemes is strictly prohibited by the FTC.[106]

The Federal Trade Commission also governs abusive telemarketing acts or practices. The FTC considers it an "abusive telemarketing act or practice" for the telemarketer to use threats, intimidation, or obscene language in requesting or receiving payment.[107] A telemarketer may not request or receive payment for removing derogatory information from a person's credit history, record, or rating.[108] Telemarketers may not repeatedly cause any telephone to ring continuously "with intent to annoy, abuse or harass any person at the called number."[109] Every online company needs to institute written procedures and to train their personnel to comply with telephone calling restrictions, which may extend to its online sales and collection practices.[110] A web site should also voluntarily comply with best practices of industry standards in its online sales practices.

[B]   The Role of Industry Standards

The usage of trade and evolving business practices are explicitly incorporated into the Uniform Commercial Code (UCC).[111] The UCC's underlying public policy is to "simplify, clarify and modernize the law governing commercial transactions."[112] Karl Llewellyn, Reporter of the UCC, conceptualized the UCC as a

---

[101] *Id.* § 310.3(a)(2)(ii).

[102] *Id.* § 310.3(a)(2)(iii).

[103] *Id.* § 310.3(a)(2)(IV).

[104] *Id.* § 310.3(a)(2)(2).

[105] *Id.* § 310.3(a)(3).

[106] *Id.* § 310.3(4)(b) (2000).

[107] *Id.* § 310.4(a)(1).

[108] *Id.* § 310.4(2).

[109] *Id.* § 310.4(b)(I).

[110] *Id.* § 310.4(b)(1)(ii)(iii).

[111] *See* UCC § 1-205(5) (noting that the concept "applicable usage of trade" is used to interpret all UCC agreements).

[112] *Id.* § 1-102(2)(a).

semipermanent statute that would continually be updated to "permit the continued expansion of commercial practices through custom, usage and agreement of the parties."[113] The goal of the comprehensive commercial statute was a permanent modernity project that would continually be updated to reflect technological and social change.

The UCC was designed to be updated periodically to accommodate new technologies and business practices. The Uniform Computer Information Transactions Act (UCITA), which expands the concepts of the UCC to cyberspace commercial transactions, follows the example of the UCC by anticipating that its rules will evolve as the Internet unfolds.[114] As a result, UCITA, like the UCC, will continually expand through customs, usage of trade, and industry standard.[115] Increasingly, the law of e-commerce is found in industry standards such as those formulated by the International Standards Organization (ISO) and other entities.

[1] OECD Guidelines

The 28 countries of the Organization for Economic Cooperation and Development (OECD) have agreed to new consumer protection guidelines for the electronic marketplace. The guidelines emphasize the importance of providing "truthful, accurate and complete information to consumers" and of avoiding deceptive, misleading, or unfair claims in order to "build consumer confidence in the global electronic marketplace."[116] Under the OECD guidelines, an e-business should do the following:

a. use fair business, advertising, and marketing practices;
b. provide accurate, clear, and easily accessible information about the company and the goods or services it offers;
c. disclose full information about the terms, conditions, and costs of the transaction;
d. ensure that consumers know they are making a commitment to buy before closing the deal;
e. provide an easy-to-use and secure method for online payment;
f. protect consumers during electronic commerce transactions;
g. address consumer complaints and difficulties;

---

[113] UCC § 1-102(2)(b).

[114] UCITA § 113 (2000).

[115] *Id.*

[116] Federal Trade Commission, Electronic Commerce: Selling Internationally, A Guide for Business (Mar. 2000), http://www.ftc.gov/bcp/conline/pubs/alerts/ecombalrt.htm.

h.   adopt fair, effective, and easy to understand self-regulatory policies and procedures; and

i.   help educate consumers about electronic commerce.[117]

[2]   International Chamber of Commerce

The International Chamber of Commerce (ICC) formulates guidelines, codes, and rules for advertising and marketing on the Internet.[118] The ICC also proposes ethics for online advertising which take the form of voluntary guidelines.[119] The ICC's voluntary guidelines on interactive marketing advertising cover issues such as online privacy, the protection of personal data, advertising directed at children, and "the varied sensitivities of global audiences."[120] The ICC guidelines require marketers to clearly disclose their identities when posting messages and to not use false headers.[121] The ICC has formed guidelines giving online users the right to control personal information.

An online advertiser is required to state its reasons for collecting information and must safeguard the security of data.[122] The ICC ethical guidelines update the ICC's International Code of Advertising Practices to apply to Internet-related advertising, marketing, and distribution.[123] The ICC also requires online advertisers and marketers to comply with advertising law in the country where the advertising message originates.[124]

[C]   Revised UCC Article 2

Article 2 of the UCC applies to online sales of goods just as it would apply in the "brick and mortar world." Written long before the rise of e-commerce, Article 2 is being revised to update sales law for Internet commercial transactions such as online sales contracts or Internet sales transactions.[125] Revised Article 2 has electronic contracting provisions which are consistent with the Computer

---

[117] *Id.*

[118] International Chamber of Commerce, ICC Guidelines on Advertising and Marketing on the Internet, 2 Apr. 1998 (visited May 17, 2000), http://www.iccwbo.org/home/menu_advert_marketing.asp.

[119] International Chamber of Commerce, New International Code Covers Ethics of On-Line Advertising (visited May 17, 2000), http://www.iccwbo.org/home/news_archives/1998/new_international_code_covers.asp.

[120] *Id.*

[121] *Id.*

[122] *Id.*

[123] *Id.*

[124] *Id.*

[125] The American Law Institute, Uniform Commercial Code: [New] Revised Article 2—Sales (Council Draft No. 1, Oct. 5, 2000) (hereinafter cited as UCC § R2).

Information Transactions Act and the Electronic Signatures in Global and National Commerce Act of 2000.[126] Presently, for example, Article 2 requires a signed writing for sales of goods valued at $500 or greater. Revised Article 2 raises the statutory minimum to $5,000 and permits the parties to substitute an electronic record for a paper-based writing.[127] Currently the UCC defines a signature or the term "signed" as "any symbol executed or adopted with the present intent to authenticate a writing."[128] Revised Article 2 defines "authenticate" broadly to encompass any encrypted signature or other electronic records.[129]

Increasingly, trading partners employ software or electronic agents for procurement, orders, and other commercial transactions.[130] Trading partner agreements form rules in advance for protocols for the ordering of goods and for payment through electronic messages. The revised draft of Article 2 provides rules that will bring greater determinacy and certainty to cyberspace sales of goods. It promulgates a number of legal concepts useful to electronic transactions and e-commerce, including "electronic agent," "electronic messages," and information.[131] Revised Article 2 defines the record as information "inscribed on a tangible medium or that is stored in an electronic or other medium and is retrievable in perceivable form,"[132] whether sold in a "bricks and mortar" store or in a virtual mall.

Electronic events, such as the transmittal of data messages, for example, may be attributed to a person if it was "the act of the person or the person's electronic agent."[133] Contracts by electronic agents or "bots" may be formed with or without human review.[134] Electronic agents may be used to purchase tangible goods or computer information.

---

[126] UCC § R2-102 (19) (defining "electronic messages" as "an electronic record or display stored, generated, or transmitted by electronic means for purposes of communication to another").

[127] UCC § R2-201 (Proposed Final Draft, May 1, 1999).

[128] UCC § 1-201 (39) (2000).

[129] UCC § R2-102(a)(1) (defining "authenticate" as to sign or "to execute or otherwise adopt a symbol, or encrypt or similarly process a record in whole or in part, with present intent of the authenticating person to identify the person or to adopt or accept a record or term").

[130] *See generally* Wright and Winn, *supra* note 33 (describing a wide variety of e-commerce and e-commerce issues).

[131] UCC § R2-102(17) and (18) defines electronic agents and electronic records while § 2R-102(27) defines the information processing systems as an "electronic system for creating, generating, sending, receiving, storing, delaying, or processing information."

[132] UCC § R2-102(34) (2000).

[133] UCC § R2-212 (2000).

[134] According to the Whatis.com glossary (visited June 14, 2000 at http://www.whatis.com), a "bot" is short for robot and refers to a program, such as a "spider" or web crawler, that simulates human actions.

[D] Digital Signatures

Thirty-six states have either already enacted or are proposing electronic signature acts, according to a survey by the Internet Law and Policy Forum (ILPF).[135] Forty-seven states have considered or enacted electronic authentication legislation, and thirteen states have formed task forces to examine the need for digital signatures and other legal infrastructure for electronic contracting.[136] The ILPF survey distinguished between electronic and digital signatures. An electronic signature means

> any identifiers such as letters, characters, or symbols manifested by electronic or similar means, executed or adopted by a party to a transaction with intent to authenticate writing. A writing, therefore, is deemed to be electronically signed if an electronic signature is logically associated with such writing.[137]

Digital signatures use a branch of mathematics called cryptography to transform writings into unintelligible code that is subsequently translated back into its original form.[138] The attributes of a digital signature are that (1) it is unique to the user; (2) it is capable of verification; and (3) it is under the control of the user. Digital signatures use algorithms that are "encrypted and decrypted using public and private keys."[139]

The trend in the law is to accord legal validity to digital signatures and electronic records. Revised Article 2 shares common ground with UCITA in its validation of electronic contracting as a business model.[140] Revised Article 2 gives legal recognition to the concept of the electronic record, which is the functional equivalent of a signed writing.[141] The American Bar Association's Science and Technology Committee has proposed Digital Signature Guidelines, which have been models for statutes adopted by a number of states.

---

[135] Internet Law and Policy Forum, Update: Survey of State Electronic and Digital Signature Legislative Initiatives (survey completed by the Seattle law firm of Perkins Coie) (visited Aug. 16, 2000), http://www.ilpf.org/digsig/update.htm.

[136] *Id.*

[137] *Supra* note 135.

[138] *Id.*

[139] Technology and the Internet, Digital Signatures, Security Tutorial (visited July 2, 1999), http://www.privacyexchange.org/tsi/digitalsig.htm.

[140] *See* UCC § R2-201(a), § R2-203(e) (Proposed Final Draft, May 1, 1999).

[141] UCC § R2-102(18) (Council Draft No. 1, Oct. 5, 2000).

[1] Purpose and Meaning

[a] Authentication

A digital signature is an electronic identifier, created by encryption technology, intended by the party to have the same effect as a paper-based signature. Traditionally, paper-and-pen signatures are critical to a large number of statutes. In the field of wills and trusts, for example, the signature is evidence that the document is authentic. Under current UCC Article 2, contracts for sales of goods over $500 must be evidenced by a signed writing against which enforcement is sought.[142] Negotiable instruments in order form are indorsed by the signature of the payee on the back of the instrument. An "indorsement" means a signature, other than that of a signer as maker, drawer, or acceptor . . . made on the instrument."[143]

In our information age, "a signature authenticates a writing by identifying the signer with the signed document."[144] As electronic mail becomes more established, the need has grown for legislation to establish the validity of e-mail signatures. Courts will increasingly consider the extent to which an e-mail message is a "writing" or statements that an electronic message has been "signed" by the maker in various contexts.[145]

[b] Ceremony

Signatures play a symbolic role in memorializing legal agreements. "The act of signing a document calls to the signer's attention the legal significance of the signer's act, and thereby helps prevent inconsiderate engagements."[146] The ceremonial role may be found in the last testament and will of a testator. A signed writing plays a ceremonial role in the enactment of legislation. A signature must accompany contracts for the sale of land interests. Relatively little case law exists on how the ceremonial role of signatures might be adapted to the Internet.

---

[142] UCC § 2-201(2000).

[143] UCC § 3-204(2000).

[144] Information Security Committee, Section of Science and Technology, American Bar Association, Digital Signature Guidelines 5 (Aug. 1, 1996) (Digital Signatures Tutorial).

[145] *See, e.g.,* Doherty v. Registry of Motor Vehicles, No. 97CV0050 (Suffolk Dist. Ct. 1997) (visited Apr. 14, 2000), http://www.loundy.com/CASES/Doherty_v_RMV.html (upholding an administrative license suspension initiated by the Massachusetts State Police where the police officer's report of the arrest for driving under the influence was transmitted by e-mail to the Registry of Motor Vehicles without his handwritten signature).

[146] Digital Signature Guidelines, *supra* note 144.

[c]   Approval

The ABA's Digital Signature Guidelines state that signatures are used for approval in a wide variety of laws and customs.[147] "Paper-and-pen" signatures have played multiple roles in Anglo-American contracts for many centuries. A person is not liable on a negotiable instrument, such as a check or promissory note, unless "the person signed the instrument."[148] The signature of the party against whom enforcement is sought frequently proves the acceptance of a contract. A payor bank, for example, certifies a check by placing its signature on the back of the check. A signature also indicates certification of a check, which indicates that the bank intends to honor the check. A payee indorses a check or promissory note by her or his signature. The ABA Information Security Committee observes, "In certain contexts defined by law or custom, a signature expresses the signer's approval or authorization of the writing or the signer's intention that it have legal effect."[149] In the law of agencies, writings are used to prove that the agent is authorized to act on behalf of the principal.

[d]   Efficiency and Logistics

Signatures on writings "often impart a sense of clarity and finality to the transaction and may lessen the subsequent need to inquire beyond the face of a document."[150] The ABA Information Security Committee cites the example of a negotiable instrument in which the holder may rely upon the four corners of the instrument to determine the terms of the agreement. A negotiable instrument is a signed writing, which takes a prescribed form.[151] The signature of a drawer of a negotiable draft is evidence of a contract on a negotiable instrument.[152] Electronic commerce requires technologies to allow negotiable instruments to be electronically "signed" by digital signatures.

[2]   Digital Signature Statutes

Within the past three years, two dozen states have enacted "digital signature laws," with Utah the first to do so.[153] Utah's statute designates a government agency as the certification authority (CA). The role of the CA is to confirm that

---

[147] *Id.*

[148] UCC § 3-401 (2000).

[149] Digital Signature Guidelines, *supra* note 144.

[150] *Id.*

[151] *See* UCC § 3-104 (2000).

[152] *Id.* § 3-401.

[153] Department of Commerce, Public Forum on Certificate Authorities and Digital Signatures: Enhancing Global Electronic Commerce, EPLR: Department of Commerce Notice on Digital Signature Forums (visited July 2, 1999), http://www.bna.com/e-law/docs/digisigcom.html.

the subscriber is the person listed in the digital signature, that the information in the certificate is accurate, and that the subscriber is a rightful holder of the private key which corresponds to the public key designated in the certificate.[154] The trend in the law is to treat the digital signature as the functional equivalent of a manual signature. The concept of a digital signature is the electronic equivalent of a signed writing.

Electronic signature and digital signature laws are classified by the Internet Law and Policy Forum (ILPF) survey as falling "into three categories: prescriptive, criteria-based, and signature enabling."[155] The ILPF concluded, "[t]here is no uniformity in state approaches to electronic authentication."[156] One of the difficult issues is whether states should enter into a "cross-border recognition of electronic or digital signatures."[157] The Internet not only crosses state law boundaries but foreign boundaries. To date, none of the state digital signature laws address the international validity of electronic signatures and writings. Electronic commerce is conducted in an evolving legal framework with problems of "regulatory fragmentation and the lack of national and international harmonization of policies."[158] The uncertainty as to the validity of electronic signatures and writings is a trade barrier that can be dismantled only with an international initiative.[159]

[a] *Prescriptive Model*

The prescriptive approach is a comprehensive and specific regulatory framework such as the Utah Digital Signature Act[160] that generally "prescribes" particular detailed technologies rather than standards. The Utah Digital Signature Act provides for a statewide licensing of certification authorities (CAs). A CA has been compared to an Internet passport office, because it is a trusted third party that establishes the identity of transacting parties.[161] The CA establishes the identity of an organization and issues "a certificate that contains the organization's public key and signs it with the CA's private key."[162] A certificate authority issues security certificates used in Secure Socket Layer (SSL) connections.[163] Utah is the only state to have adopted a digital signature law that is classified as purely prescriptive.

---

[154] Utah Digital Signature Act, Utah Code Ann. §§ 43-3-105 to 504 (1997).

[155] *Supra* note 135.

[156] *Id.*

[157] *Id.*

[158] *Id.*

[159] *Id.*

[160] Utah Code § 46-3-101 et seq. (2000).

[161] Verisign, About Secure Server Ids: Frequently Asked Questions (visited May 13, 2000), http:// digitalid.verisign.com/server/about/aboutFAQ.htm.

[162] *Id.*

[163] Matisse's Glossary of Internet Terms (Mar. 11, 2000), http://www.matisse.net/files/glossary.html.

Minnesota and Washington have enacted statutes that borrow some of the features of Utah's digital signature statute.[164]

[b] Criteria-Based Model

The Internet Law and Policy Forum Survey classifies California's act as the exemplar statute for criteria-based authentication statutes characterized by flexibility and broad standards. The California "criteria-based" model has been enacted in ten states.[165] California does not prescribe any particular technology but incorporates an evidentiary standard into its definition. California treats electronic signatures as legally effective if the signature is:

1. Unique to the person using it.
2. Capable of verification.
3. Under the sole control of the person using it.
4. Linked to the data in such a manner that if the data is changed the signature is invalidated.
5. In conformity with regulations adopted by the appropriate state agency, usually the Secretary of State.[166]

The digital signature statutes that follow the criteria-based approach, in turn, can be divided into "limited" and "general" statutes. A limited statute applies to a given substantive field, such as online contracts, whereas a general statute legitimates electronic records in all substantive fields of law. Georgia, Kansas, New Hampshire, and Virginia have enacted general statutes based on California's model.[167]

[c] Signature-Enabling Approach

"Signature-enabling" statutes are defined as minimalist because they are standards-based and do not prescribe specific technologies, such as biometrics, for authentication or criteria for validating signatures. The ILPF cites Florida's Electronic Signature Act of 1996 as an example of a statute that accords the digital and electronic signature the same status as a physical writing.[168] Therefore, the Florida statute gives legal recognition to electronic writings and signatures. The statute defines a "writing" to include information "stored in any electronic medium and retrievable in a perceivable form."[169] An electronic signature "means any letters,

---

[164] *Supra* note 135 (site visited May 13, 2000).

[165] *Id.* at 6.

[166] *Id.* at 6 (citing CAL. GOV'T CODE § 16.5 (a) (1995).

[167] *Id.*

[168] *Id.* at 7.

[169] *Id.* (citing Florida Electronic Signature Act of 1996, Fla. Stat. § 1.01 (1996 Fla. H.B. 942).

characters, or symbols, manifested by electronic or similar means, executed or adopted by a party with an intent to authenticate a writing. . . . An electronic signature may be used to sign a writing and shall have the same force and effect as a written signature."[170]

The Division of Information Technology of the Commonwealth of Massachusetts, for example, proposed a minimalist statute for writing and signature requirements.[171] The concept of a record for electronic writings and signatures was drawn from the Model Law on Electronic Commerce put out by the United Nations Commission on International Trade Law (UNCITRAL). The Massachusetts minimalist model has been proven to be influential in the recent model statutes of the National Conference of Commissioners on Uniform State Laws. NCCUSL, in turn, has incorporated the concept of the "record" in its Uniform Computer Information Transaction Act and the Uniform Electronic Transactions Acts.

[3]   Electronic Notaries

"CyberNotaries" have been proposed to deal with the problem of authenticating and certifying electronic documents in international Internet commercial transactions. The Science and Technology Committee of the American Bar Association has a CyberNotary Committee to study the role of trusted third parties in electronic commerce.[172]

The CyberNotary Committee is exploring the possibility of setting global certification standards for electronic notaries that would be modeled after international notarial practice.[173] The CyberNotary concept has yet to be adopted in any state or federal law for authenticating electronic documents on the Internet.

[4]   Technology

Digital signatures are based upon cryptographic algorithms, also called ciphers, that permit encryption and decryption.[174] The recipient of the message will turn the ciphertext back into "plaintext," a process called decryption.[175]

---

[170] *Id.*

[171] *Id.*

[172] American Bar Association, Science and Technology Committee, CyberNotary Committee, CyberNotary Committee Home Page (Apr. 10, 2000), http://www.abanet.org/scitech/ec/cn/home.html.

[173] *Id.* In the United States, the qualifications of a notary are rather minimal, compared to those in other countries.

[174] Bruce Schneier, Applied Cryptography: Protocols, Algorithms, and Source Code in C (2d ed., 1996), at 2.

[175] *Id.* at 1.

Public key cryptography "is a method for securely exchanging messages, based on assigning two complementary keys (one public, one private) to the individuals involved in a transaction."[176] The public key is publicly available, but only the "signer" knows the private key. Digital signatures "have private hashing and public verification but only one person can produce the hash for a message."[177]

Single key cryptography is used to help the parties keep a restrictive algorithm secret.[178] The single private key is never published, unlike the public key, which is widely available in books similar to telephone directories. It is not practical for parties in distant locations on the Internet to share a restricted key. Public key cryptography or asymmetric cryptosystems use a public key to encrypt a message and a private key to decrypt it.

[5] Attribution Procedures

The International Chamber of Commerce proposed a broad self-regulatory program governing online contracts, including guidelines for secure and trustworthy digital transactions over the Internet.[179] Trustworthy e-commerce depends on attribution procedures that verify the integrity of transactions and the authenticity of electronic messages. An attribution procedure may be used to detect changes or errors in information. UCITA notes that attribution procedures may use "algorithms or other codes, identifying words or numbers, encryption, callback or other acknowledgments, or other procedures reasonable under the circumstances."[180]

[6] Other Initiatives

A number of electronic authentication initiatives have been proposed by private standards-setting organizations:[181]

*   In May 2000, the European Commission released a Model Directive on Electronic Commerce.

*   The Organization for Economic Cooperation and Development (OECD) has proposed Cryptography Guidelines.

---

[176] Verisign, Inc., About Secure Server Ids (visited May 13, 2000), http://digitalid.verisign.com/server/about/aboutFAQ.htm.

[177] Cryptography FAQ (07/10 Digital Signatures (visited Apr. 10, 2000), http://www.uni-konstanz.de/misc/faqs/Computer/msg00012.html.

[178] *Id.*

[179] *Id.* at 85.

[180] UCITA § 102(5) (2000).

[181] *See* United States Council for International Business (USCIB), Electronic Commerce (May 13, 2000), http://www.uscib.org/trade/eleccomm.htm.

- The International Chamber of Commerce (ICC) has proposed General Usage for Digitally Ensured Commerce (GUIDEC).

- The World Trade Organization (WTO) has formulated comprehensive rules for online contracting, in addition to digital signature rules.

- The United Nations Commission on International Trade Law (UNCITRAL) has promulgated a Model Law on Electronic Commerce.

Article 7 of UNCITRAL's Model Law defines a legal requirement for the signature of a person if (a) a method is used to identify that person and to indicate that person's approval of the information contained in the data message, and (b) that method is as reliable as was appropriate for the purpose for which the data message was generated or communicated, in the light of all the circumstances, including any relevant agreement.[182] UNCITRAL is preparing uniform rules for electronic signatures and certificate authorities.[183] The American Bar Association's Science and Technology Committee has developed Digital Signature Guidelines which are also in line with UCITA's e-commerce concepts of attribution and authentication.

[E] Privacy in Information Contracts

Online contracts are increasingly subject to regulation by the Federal Trade Commission (FTC), the chief federal agency formulating principles of fair information practices, which include "consumer awareness, choice, appropriate levels of security, data integrity and consumer access to their personally identifiable data."[184]

The FTC is increasingly policing how web sites collect, compile, sell, and use consumers' personal information.[185] If a corporate web site compiles or collects data about users who are children, for example, the company needs to comply with industry guidelines.[186] Web sites should also allow visitors to opt out of allowing the company to share their personal information with other companies.[187]

---

[182] UNCITRAL Model Law on Electronic Commerce, Article 7 (1999).

[183] Microsoft Law and Corporate Affairs, Summary of Global Internet Legal Developments, Jan. 1999 at 88.

[184] Department of Commerce, Elements of Effective Self-Regulation for the Protection of Privacy and Questions Related to Online Privacy, 63 FR 30729 (June 5, 1998).

[185] Notice Requesting Industry Guidelines and Principles Regarding Online Information Practices, 63 FR 10916 (Mar. 5, 1998).

[186] *Id.*

[187] The FTC is studying the tactical decision of companies in making "opt out" an arduous process. Companies have a perverse incentive to discourage opt-outs because revenue is dependent on harvesting personal data. Companies, therefore, because their web sites earn revenues from data collection, have an incentive to make it difficult to "opt out" by convincing the consumer not to stop the information flow.

[F]   Procedural Law of E-Commerce; Choice of Law

Subject to certain qualifications, parties to a contract may choose which state's law will govern interpretation of the contract. The parties' choice of law is subject to the statutory directives of each state.[188] It is advisable to include a choice of law clause in license agreements because states vary significantly in their law of contracts, tort remedies, and commercial law. The UCC is supplemented by common law and equity principles, as well as by state consumer protection acts, which vary from state to state. In addition, states have adopted many nonuniform amendments to the UCC. Colorado, for example, requires punitive damages to be proven beyond a reasonable doubt, while its neighbor, Nebraska, does not recognize punitive damages at all. Many companies choose the law and forum in the state where it has its chief place of business. "The use of contractual choice of forum clauses has expanded as judicial hostility to them has failed."[189] Most countries will enforce a parties' choice of law clauses, but they may not enforce provisions inimical to consumer welfare.

[1]   Uniform Commercial Code

The current version of Article 1 of the Uniform Commercial Code (UCC) permits parties to choose the law provided it bears a "reasonable relation" to the commercial contract.[190] The UCC contains relatively few statutorily mandated provisions.[191] An online company would easily satisfy the "reasonable relation" test if it chose to interpret its license agreements under the law of its state of incorporation. A web site may find it advantageous to choose the law where rights and remedies are favorable. The reasonable relation test would not permit a site to apply the law of Bermuda, for example, unless a reasonable relation existed between Bermuda and the parties to the license agreement.

[2]   Revised Article 1

Article 1 of the UCC is being updated "for electronic commerce and communications."[192] The Drafting Committee for Uniform Commerce Code is

---

[188] Restatement (Second) of Conflicts § 6(1) (1971).

[189] UCC § R1-301, cmt. (Revised Article 1 Members Consultative Group Draft, Feb. 28, 2000).

[190] UCC § 1-105.

[191] The UCC carves out exceptions to the parties' choice of law. The parties, for example, are not permitted to bypass the place of filing for financing statements under § 9-402. Third parties would not be able to determine whether a security interest has been perfected unless filing conforms to the proper place of filing. Multistate transactions under § 9-103 also constrain freedom of choice of law.

[192] Neil B. Cohen, Reporter, and H. Kathleen Patchell, Associate Reporter, Memorandum to Members Consultative Group for Uniform Commercial Code Article 1: Key Issues to Consider, Feb. 28, 2000.

recommending changes to choice of law to update the rules for electronic commerce and communications. Revised UCC § 1-301 changes the substantive rules currently found in § 1-105. Section 1-105 permits the parties to choose the jurisdiction whose law applies, providing the transaction bears a "reasonable relation" to the jurisdiction. Section 1-301 provides that if one of the parties to a UCC transaction is a consumer, an agreement to choose the applicable law is not effective unless certain conditions are satisfied.[193]

Revised 1-301(b) would enforce choice of law clauses for consumers only if the jurisdiction designated is the "[s]tate or country in which the consumer resides at the time the transaction becomes enforceable or within 30 days thereafter."[194] An agreement may also be effective if the chosen state or country is the place where "the goods, services or other consideration flowing to the consumer are to be used or used by the consumer" or her or his designee.[195] A consumer is "an individual who enters into a transaction primarily for personal family, or household purposes" as opposed to professional or commercial purposes.[196]

In nonconsumer transactions, the parties have even greater discretion to choose the applicable law in Revised § 1-301, which does not require that the chosen jurisdiction bear a "reasonable relation" to the transaction.[197] Section 1-301 will not, however, enforce agreements to choose the applicable law if they contravene "a fundamental policy of the State or country whose law would otherwise govern."[198]

[3] Uniform Computer Information Transactions Act

The Uniform Computer Information Transactions Act (UCITA) permits the parties to choose the applicable law for computer information transactions.[199] The parties to a computer information transaction may not, however, use the choice of law to bypass a consumer protection rule.[200] The jurisdiction where the licensor is located when an access contract is entered into applies in the absence of an agreement.[201] In the absence of an agreement, for example, UCITA will apply to millions of AOL access contracts because UCITA has recently been enacted in Virginia.

In a consumer contract that includes delivery of a diskette, CD-ROM, or other tangible medium, the law of the jurisdiction applies where "the copy is or

---

[193] Uniform Commercial Code: Revised Article 1: General Provisions, § 1-301 (Members Consultative Group Draft, Feb. 28, 2000).

[194] *Id.* § 1-301(b)(1).

[195] *Id.* § 1-301(b)(2).

[196] *Id.* § 1-301(f).

[197] *Id.* § 1-301(a).

[198] *Id.* § 1-301(c).

[199] UCITA § 109(a) (2000).

[200] *Id.*

[201] *Id.*

should have been delivered to the consumer."[202] In all other computer information transactions, "the law of the jurisdiction having the most significant relationship to the transaction" applies.[203] SPC will use choice of law clauses so that it may apply a familiar body of law to disputes.

[G]   Choice of Forum Clauses

The parties to online contracts will be free to choose an exclusive judicial forum and it is likely that forum selection clause will be enforced. The Supreme Court in Carnival Cruise Lines, Inc. v. Shute,[204] enforced a forum selection clause on a cruise contract even though it specified that all disputes be litigated in Florida, a forum distant from the consumer's residence. Choice of forum clauses are generally enforceable unless "unreasonable and unjust."[205] Choice of forum clauses are also subject to unconscionability and public policy.

➤   [1]   Preventive Law Pointer: Mandatory Arbitration Clauses

In Brower v. Gateway 2000,[206] a New York court upheld a click-through agreement that required any dispute arising out of the plaintiff's purchase of a computer and software to be resolved by arbitration. Gateway shipped its personal computers in a box containing a printed warning stating that, "This document contains Gateway 2000's Standard Terms and Conditions."[207] The license agreement also stated, "By keeping your Gateway 2000 computer system beyond thirty (30) days after the date of delivery, you accept these Terms and Conditions."[208] One of the clauses of the contract mandated that all controversies arising out of the computer contract were to be arbitrated in Chicago, Illinois, applying the "Rule of Conciliation and Arbitration of the International Chamber of Commerce."[209]

The court upheld the arbitration clause, holding it did not render the contract an unenforceable adhesion contract. The court stated that because "the consumer has affirmatively retained the merchandise for more than 30 days—within which the consumer has presumably examined and even used the product(s) and read the

---

[202] Id. § 2.

[203] Id. § 3.

[204] 499 U.S. 585 (1991).

[205] Bremen v. Zapata Offshore Co., 407 U.S. 1 (1972); UCITA § 110 (stating that parties may choose an exclusive judicial forum unless the choice is unreasonable and unjust).

[206] 676 N.Y.S.2d 569 (N.Y. App. Div. 1998); see also Westendorf v. Gateway 2000 Inc., No. 17913 (Del. Ch., Mar. 16, 2000), reported in 13 Software L. Bull. 95 (May/June 2000) (upholding mandatory arbitration clause in computer contract even though service contract made no reference to arbitration).

[207] Id. at 570.

[208] Id.

[209] Id.

agreement . . . the contract has been effectuated."[210] The court, however, did find that the $4,000 fee to arbitrate a dispute was unconscionable and excessive "and surely serves to deter the individual consumer from invoking the process," leaving consumers "with no forum at all in which to resolve a dispute."[211] The fee to arbitrate the dispute far exceeded the price of the software, depriving the consumer of any effective remedy. The court remanded the case to the trial court with instructions to appoint an arbitrator who would not charge excessive fees.[212]

It may be advisable to choose a nonlitigation forum, such as arbitration, in standard online contracts. An example of such a clause follows:

> Any Unresolved Dispute shall be settled at the election of either party, by final and binding independent arbitration conducted before the American Arbitration Association (AAA) in New York, New York, U.S.A., and shall be conducted under the rules of the Commercial Arbitration Rules of the AAA then in effect.

> Any party intending to initiate an arbitration of an Unresolved Dispute shall give fifteen (15) days' prior written notice to the other party of its intention to commence an arbitration proceeding. The arbitrator shall interpret the Agreement and any dispute arising from performance or breach governed by the laws of the state of New York. New York's conflicts of law principles are not applicable.

The benefits of arbitration are cost, speed, and the greater probability that the case will be tried before a tribunal with some understanding of the business context.

The Drafting Committee of the Proposed Revision of the Uniform Arbitration Act (RUAA) found that unconscionability and adhesion issues arise frequently with arbitration clauses.[213] The plaintiffs in the class action against Gateway 2000 argued that the mandatory arbitration clause was unconscionable as well as invalid under the "battle of the forms' provision in § 2-207" of Article 2.[214] The battle of the forms will rarely occur in mass-market license agreements, since only the vendor supplies a form. Arbitration clauses may be challenged, however, if a court finds procedural and substantive unconscionability. The RUAA Reporter noted that unequal bargaining claims arise frequently in "arbitration provisions involving employers and employees, sellers and consumers, health maintenance organizations, and patients, franchisors and franchisees, and others."[215] Web sites

---

[210] *Id.* at 573.

[211] *Id.* at 574.

[212] *Id.* at 574-575.

[213] Tim Heinsz, Reporter, Proposed Revision of the Uniform Arbitration Act (RUAA), Memorandum to RUAA Drafting Committee Members, Liaisons, and Academic Advisors, Contracts of Adhesion and Unconscionability, Sept. 28, 1998 (visited Dec. 6, 1999), http://www.law.upenn.edu/bll/ulc/uarba/arb1098m.txt.

[214] Brower v. Gateway 2000, 676 N.Y.S.2d at 573-75.

[215] Heinsz, *supra* note 213.

that require consumer visitors to submit to arbitration will be embroiled in similar litigation.

Courts consider the following factors in deciding whether to enforce arbitration clauses: (1) unequal bargaining power; (2) whether the weaker party may opt out of arbitration; (3) the clarity with which the arbitration clause is drafted; (4) whether the stronger party enjoys an unfair home-court advantage; (5) whether the weaker party had a meaningful opportunity to accept the arbitration agreement; and (6) whether the stronger party used deceptive tactics.[216] Courts have generally "been reluctant to find arbitration agreements to be unconscionable."[217]

At minimum, an arbitration clause must be prominently displayed and clearly written so those visitors understand that they are waiving their jury right and the right to a full trial on the merits. One-sided webwrap agreements that take away many substantive rights without giving consumers meaningful remedies are legally risky. If an exclusive arbitration clause is struck by a court, a web site visitor will have the full array of rights and remedies available under the UCC or common law.

The trend in the law is for courts to enforce post-sale license agreements incorporating arbitration clauses provided an opportunity is offered to manifest assent.[218] UCITA defines the manifestation of assent as when "a person, acting with knowledge of, or after having an opportunity to review the record or term or a copy of it: (1) authenticates the record or term with intent to adopt or accept it; or (2) intentionally engages in conduct or makes statements with reason to know that the other party or its electronic agent may infer from the conduct or statement that the person assents to the record or term."[219]

§ 6.04 ELECTRONIC CONTRACTING RULES

Every e-business, large or small, must enter into a large number of contracts in the online world. A contract is simply defined as "an agreement upon consideration to do or refrain from doing, a particular lawful thing."[220] The UCC defines the contract as "the total legal obligation which results from the party's agreement."[221] In Revised Article 1 of the UCC, the obligation of good faith is imposed in the performance and enforcement of every commercial transaction.[222]

---

[216] *Id.*

[217] *Id.* (citing authorities).

[218] Baker and McKenzie, IT/Communications Law Alert, Arbitration Clauses and Shrinkwrap Licenses (visited Dec. 6, 1999), http://www.bakerinfo.com/publciations/documents/720_al.htm.

[219] UCITA § 112(a)(1)(2) (1999).

[220] Ballentine's Law Dictionary 263 (3rd ed., 1969).

[221] UCC § 1-201 (11) (2000); *see also* UCITA, § 102(17) (2000) (defining contract as "the total legal obligation resulting from the party's agreement).

[222] American Law Institute, Uniform Commercial Code: Revised Article 1: General Provisions, § 1-304 (Members Consultative Group Draft, Feb. 28, 2000).

[A]   Electronic Contract Formation

Modern contract law makes it possible to make agreements by any reasonable method, including the exchange of electronic records. Article 2 of the UCC notes that "[a] contract for sale of goods may be made in any manner sufficient to show agreement, including conduct by both parties which recognizes the existence of such a contract."[223] At common law, an offer is a manifestation of the offeror's intent to enter into an agreement.[224] The offer may be communicated by the offeror to the offeree orally or in writing. At common law, the offeror was master of the offer and could specify the manner of acceptance. The mirror image rule required that an offeree accept the offer in the precise manner called for in the offer.

An advertisement placed in a newspaper or magazine is generally regarded as an invitation to entertain offers rather than an enforceable offer.[225] SPC needs to decide whether it is inviting offers or making definite offers in its web site promotional materials. If SPC only wishes to entertain invitations of offers and not to make definite offers, it needs to make adequate disclosures "to ensure that any promotional material placed on the Web is not capable of being construed as an offer."[226] On the other hand, SPC may have a business goal of securing online orders and will therefore need to structure its electronic catalog to constitute definite offers rather than mere advertisements to make offers.

[1]   Electronic Data Interchange

One theoretical difficulty of online contracting is that computers do not "manifest assent" or make offers.[227] E-commerce requires a legal framework that permits computers to make and accept offers. Electronic data interchange (EDI) is one well-established contracting practice for building an electronic trading community; brick-and-mortar companies use electronic networks to communicate

---

[223] UCC § 2-204 (2000).

[224] Contracts are generally governed by state law, either the common law for service contracts or the UCC for sales of goods. In contrast, e-commerce typically involves online contracts that "span multiple jurisdictions and may be regulated by the laws of more than one country." J. Fraser Mann and Alan M. Gahtan, Overview of the Legal Framework for Electronic Commerce, in Law of International Online Business: A Global Perspective (Dennis Campbell, ed., 1998).

[225] *Id.* at 40.

[226] *Id.*

[227] Contract law focuses on whether a manifestation of assent exists between humans. One advantage of computer-to-computer contract will be a decrease in cases asserting that offers were made insincerely or in jest. *See* Lucy v. Zehmer, 196 Conn. 194, 175 A. 574 (1934) (annulling marriage because it was entered into in jest). Electronic agents will not lack capacity to contract due to drunkenness, mental illness, infancy, or other human infirmities. However, computer software may malfunction due to viruses, defects, or programmer error.

with warehouses, distributors, and suppliers all over the world.[228] One United Kingdom supermarket uses EDI trading links to communicate with "customers as far apart as Thailand, Zimbabwe and Guatemala."[229]

The difficulty of the EDI model, however, is that it requires trading partners to agree in advance to accept the validity of electronic contracts. Trading partner agreements set the ground rules for permitting the ordering of goods or services through computer-to-computer communications, such as given transaction sets that provide for electronic offers and acceptance. Parties to an e-commerce transaction are unlikely to have a contractual relationship predating the transaction.

[2] Mass-Market Licenses

[a] Shrinkwrap Agreements

A shrinkwrap or mass-market license is an "unsigned software license agreement used in consumer and commercial transactions."[230] Mass-market licenses accompany software modules and may even be printed on the outside of the box. The first paragraph of a typical shrinkwrap license usually provides that the opening of the package indicates acceptance of the license terms.[231] Servicewrap licenses may be used to distribute software support services just as shrinkwrap is used to transfer software licenses.

The shrinkwrap license conditions access to and use of a company's software on acceptance of its terms and conditions.[232] The licensor's purpose is to create a "reverse unilateral contract,"[233] which is structured so that the customer who opens the plastic wrap and uses the software is bound to the one-sided terms of the shrinkwrap license.[234] Clickwrap and web site terms of service agreements take a similar form. Adobe Systems, for example, provides that the customer's downloading of software from its site signifies agreement to its terms and conditions.[235]

---

[228] Kewill-Xetal EDI Services, Case Study: Saphir Produce Ltd., Communicating with Supermarkets (visited Sept. 24, 1999), http://www.kewillxetal.co.uk/case2.htm.

[229] *Id.*

[230] Celeste L. Tito, The Servicewrap: "Shrinkwrap" for Mass-Marketed Software Services, 13 Computer Lawyer 19 (May 1996).

[231] This example is drawn from Morgan Laboratories, Inc. v. Micro Data Base Systems, Inc., 41 U.S.P.Q.2d 1850 (N.D. Cal. 1997); *see* Celeste L. Tito, The Servicewrap Shrinkwrap, *id.*

[232] Real Networks (visited Feb. 9, 1999), http//www.real.com/company/legal.html.

[233] Mark A. Lemley, Intellectual Property and Shrinkwrap Licenses, 68 S.CAL. L. REV. 1239, 1241 (2000).

[234] *Id.* at 1241.

[235] Adobe, CustomerFirst Support (visited Feb. 1, 1999), http://www.adobe.com/supportservice/custsupport.

Shrinkwrap license agreements were developed "to avoid the federal copyright law first sale doctrine."[236] The first sale doctrine of copyright law gives the owner of the lawfully made copy the power to "sell or otherwise dispose of the possession of that copy without the copyright holder's consent."[237] Without this doctrine, the purchaser of the first sale of a copy of the software could copy the software and distribute it for himself with impunity. Software is licensed to avoid the first sale doctrine.

Suppose the shrinkwrap license states, "Opening the envelope containing the diskette will constitute your agreement to the license which is contained on the outside of the envelope." The theory is that the license becomes effective when the licensee breaks the shrinkwrap. Courts have refused to enforce shrinkwrap licenses on various grounds. In Step-Saver Data Systems v. Wise Technology,[238] the Third Circuit held that the terms of a shrinkwrap license agreement were not enforceable against a reseller. In that case, Step-Saver was a value-added retailer for IBM products. Step-Saver's business was to combine hardware and software to meet the data needs for professionals such as lawyers and doctors.[239] Step-Saver provided a box-top license with all software which disclaimed all warranties. Almost immediately after installing the software on its systems, Step-Saver began receiving complaints from its customers.[240] Step-Saver referred the complaints to the licensor, who was unable to solve the problems. The court refused enforcement of the box-top license finding that it was a proposed addition to an already existing contract never accepted by the licensee. The court found that the trial court erred and dismissed the licensee's warranty claims since the disclaimers found in the box-top license were not enforceable.

The Fifth Circuit in Vault Corp. v. Quaid Software, Ltd.,[241] affirmed a district court's finding that a shrinkwrap license was an unenforceable contract of adhesion. A contract of adhesion derives its name from the fact that the weaker party must adhere to the terms of the stronger party. The court refused to enforce a contractual term that prohibited reverse engineering.[242] The court also concluded that federal copyright law preempted Louisiana's Software License Enforcement Act.

---

[236] Step-Saver Data Systems v. Wise Technology, 939 F.2d 91 (3d Cir. 1991).

[237] *Id.* at 96 n.7 (quoting Bobbs-Merrill Co. v. Strauss, 210 U.S. 339 (1908)).

[238] 939 F.2d 91 (3d Cir. 1991).

[239] *Id.* at 93.

[240] *Id.*

[241] 847 F.2d 255 (5th Cir. 1991).

[242] Reverse engineering is a process by which a computer or software engineer works backward to determine how the software works. The Supreme Court defined reverse engineering broadly as "starting with the known product and working backwards to divine the process which aided in its development or manufacture." Kewanee Oil Co. v. Bicron Corp., 470 U.S. 470, 476 (1974). Software reverse engineering is a social good because it enables programmers to develop software that is interoperable with established platforms, such as the Microsoft Office products.

Prior to the mid-1990s, U.S. courts were reluctant to enforce shrinkwrap agreements. The recent trend in the law, however, is to enforce shrinkwrap, click-through, webwrap, and other mass-market license agreements. In ProCD v. Zeidenberg,[243] the Seventh Circuit upheld the enforceability of a shrinkwrap license located inside the packaging of the computer program.[244] The *ProCD* case involved shrinkwrap agreement that could only be characterized as "pay now" and "you'll see the terms later after you pay." The plaintiff compiled a computer database called SelectPhone consisting of more than 3,000 telephone directories.[245] ProCD however, sought to limit the use of the database through a software licensing agreement. The defendant, Matthew Zeidenberg, purchased a copy of Select-Phone in Madison, Wisconsin, but chose to ignore the terms of the agreement.[246] Zeidenberg formed a company to resell the information in ProCD's database.[247]

Zeidenberg charged its customers for access to the information in Select-Phone and made the information available over the World Wide Web.[248] ProCD filed a lawsuit seeking an injunction "against further dissemination that exceeds the rights specified in the license."[249] The federal district court held that ProCD's license agreements were ineffective, since the terms did not appear on the outside of the package and that a customer could not be "bound by terms that were secret at the time of purchase."[250]

The Seventh Circuit reversed, upholding the shrinkwrap agreement. The court applied Article 2 to the license agreement, noting that the UCC permits contracts to be formed in "any manner sufficient to show agreement."[251] The *ProCD* court found that the licensor invited acceptance by silence. The court found that the licensee accepted the software "after having an opportunity to read the license at leisure."[252] In this case, ProCD "extended an opportunity to reject if a buyer should find the license terms unsatisfactory."[253] The court rejected the defendant's

---

[243] 86 F.3d 1447 (7th Cir. 1996).

[244] *Id.*

[245] *Id.* The U.S. Supreme Court in Feist Publications, Inc. v. Rural Telephone Service Co., Inc., 499 U.S. 340 (1991) held that a database of telephone numbers lacked the "originality" necessary for protection under the Copyright Act. The United States does not otherwise provide copyright protection for mere compilations. In contrast, European Union countries provide *sui generis* protection as well as copyright protection for data bases. That would not qualify for copyright protection in the U.S.

[246] 86 F.3d at 1449.

[247] *Id.*

[248] *Id.*

[249] *Id.*

[250] *Id.* at 1450 (citing 908 F. Supp. at 654).

[251] *Id.* at 1451 (citing UCC § 2-204(1)).

[252] *Id.*

[253] *Id.* at 1452.

argument that he had no choice but to adhere to ProCD's terms once he opened the package.[254]

The court also rejected the defendant's argument that shrinkwrap license agreements must be conspicuous to be enforced.[255] The Seventh Circuit in *ProCD* also rejected the argument that the Copyright Act preempts software licenses.[256] The court did not find the rights created by the license agreement to be within any of the exclusive rights of the Copyright Act.[257] The court noted that strong policy arguments favored the validation of shrinkwrap, "Licenses may have other benefits for consumers: many licenses permit users to make extra copies, to use the software on multiple computers, even to incorporate the software into the user's products."[258]

In Hill v. Gateway 2000,[259] the Seventh Circuit relied on *ProCD* in upholding an arbitration clause in Gateway's software license agreement. Gateway's practice was to mail its computer system with a software license agreement inside the box mailed to the customer. The Seventh Circuit observed that the "terms inside Gateway's box stand or fall together."[260] The court found that the license agreement was enforceable because of the consumer's decision to retain the Gateway system beyond the 30-day period specified in the agreement. The court reasoned that there was acceptance by silence and that the entire mass-market agreement was binding, including the arbitration clause.

The Court of Appeals of Washington recently upheld a standard software license agreement in M.A. Mortenson Co. v. Timberline Software Corp.[261] Mortenson, the plaintiff, used a software program to prepare a construction bid and discovered that the bid was $1.95 million less than it should have been because of the malfunctioning of the software. Timberline moved for summary judgment, arguing that the limitation on consequential damages in the licensing agreement barred the plaintiff's recovery. The lower court ruled that the license terms were part of the contract and entered summary judgment in favor of the defendant. The Washington Supreme Court upheld the judgment, ruling that the terms of Timberline's licensing agreement were enforceable and adopting the approach of the *ProCD*, *Hill* and *Brower* courts.

---

[254] *Id.*

[255] *Id.*

[256] *Id.*

[257] *Id.* at 1453.

[258] *Id.* at 1455.

[259] 105 F.3d 1147 (7th Cir. 1998).

[260] *Id.* at 1148.

[261] 2000 Wash. LEXIS 287 (May 4, 2000); *see also* Groff v. America Online, 1998 Westlaw 307001 (R.I. Super. Ct., May 27, 1998), Kaczmorek v. Microsoft Corp., 39 F. Supp. 2d 974 (N.D. Ill., 1999) (upholding mass market licenses).

Despite this recent trend in favor of enforceability, a climate of uncertainty persists. Consumer groups and legal academics are critical of the *ProCD* court's validation of "silence by acceptance" for adhesive contracts. The next generation of software litigation will center on Internet mass-market licenses. The trend in the law is to permit the enforcement of layered, standard-form license agreements so long as the terms are conspicuously displayed. A licensor needs to explicitly reference the fact that the software is licensed and to explain the legal consequences of licensing. In the *Mortenson* case, the licensor included the terms of the license agreement in every copy of the software and manuals and noted that the software was licensed on the introductory screen display each time the software was used.

[b] Content and Interactive Service Agreements

Internet Service Providers (ISPs) such as CompuServe, America Online, and Prodigy enter into two main types of contracts. First, they contract with subscribers to provide Internet access and, often, proprietary content. Second, they enter into license agreements to obtain content from magazines, reports, newsletters, television, radio, and other media so that they can offer subscribers additional value.

When licensing content, an ISP ideally will obtain an international license for all media, including an explicit license to cache a linked web site.[262] If a provider distributes content on ancillary platforms, such as CD-ROM, the license agreement should address this right.[263]

ISPs should give their subscribers notice that the ISPs may be forced to reveal the identities of subscribers in John Doe lawsuits.[264] A number of companies have filed lawsuits to uncover the identities of users who posted "anonymous defamatory opinions . . . on the Internet."[265] Subpoenas resulting from the suits have forced ISPs to reveal the names of individuals who posted the messages using screen names. Providers typically "clickstream" contracts to bind customers.

[c] Clickwrap Agreements

A "clickwrap" or webwrap agreement permits a consumer to assent to the terms of an online agreement by his or her conduct. With a clickwrap license, the

---

[262] *See* Adam H. Lehman, Negotiating Content and Interactive Services Agreements, American Bar Association: Section of Business Law, Committee on Law of Commerce in Cyberspace, Aug. 5, 1996, 1996 ABA Annual Meeting, Orlando, Florida.

[263] *Id.*

[264] John Doe subpoenas are generally addressed to Providers to uncover the identity of customers committing torts or crimes. Mark Gibbs, Responsible Anonymity and John Doe, Network World, July 28, 1999, at 82.

[265] *Id.*

subscriber signifies acceptance or rejection by clicking the mouse on the high-lighted "I accept" or "I decline" text. Netscape Navigator, for example, is distrib-uted with the following end-user clickwrap license:

> BY CLICKING ON THE "ACCEPT" BUTTON, YOU ARE CONSENTING TO BE BOUND BY
> AND ARE BECOMING A PARTY TO THIS AGREEMENT. IF YOU DO NOT AGREE TO ALL
> OF THE TERMS OF THIS AGREEMENT, CLICK THE "DO NOT ACCEPT" BUTTON AND
> THE INSTALLATION PROCESS WILL NOT CONTINUE.

Clickwrap agreements are either express contracts or implied-in-fact con-tracts. Certain elements of the contract are implied from the act of clicking the "I accept" highlighted area. If consumers do not accept the terms of the agreement, they may not use the web site or complete the transactions.

Microsoft Network requires prospective subscribers to enter into clickwrap agreements with exclusive forum clauses. In Caspi v. the Microsoft Network,[266] a New Jersey court upheld Microsoft's clickwrap agreement enforcing a forum selection clause.

In Hotmail v. Van Money Pie Inc.,[267] the court upheld an injunction against a Hotmail subscriber who violated the terms of the Hotmail's Terms of Service agreement by sending unsolicited e-mail messages, or spam. The clickwrap agree-ment at the top of the Hotmail Terms of Service (HTS) had a single button read-ing "I accept" but no button reading "I decline." The subscriber was advised that "BY COMPLETING THE REGISTRATION PROCESS AND BY CLICKING THE 'I ACCEPT' BUT-TON, YOU ARE INDICATING YOUR AGREEMENT TO BE BOUND BY ALL OF THE TERMS AND CONDITIONS OF THE HTS." The consideration for the Hotmail agreement is the mem-ber's providing current, complete, and accurate information in the registration. Hotmail, which requires its subscribers to give their name, mailing address, e-mail address, and account and phone number, agrees not to disclose this information unless required to do so by law or legal process. The *Hotmail* court found that the HTS agreement was enforceable, even though there was no "I decline" button.

➤ [3] Preventive Law Pointers

[a] *Webwrap or Clickwrap License Agreements*

The clickwrap license agreement, sometimes called a webwrap, is a limited license structured as Terms and Conditions of Use (TOC). Web site user agree-ments are generally structured as licenses to use information. E*Trade, an online

---

[266] 732 A.2d 528 (N.J. Sup. Ct., App. Div., 1999).

[267] No. C98-20064 (N.D. Cal., Apr. 10, 1998) (upholding clickstream contract and restraining defendant from spam-related activities).

brokerage house, requires users to agree to a "user agreement" governing online tax filing and active trader services.[268] E*Trade's user agreement states that by accessing other web sites through links provided by E*Trade, the user agrees to the terms and conditions dictated by the online broker.[269] Most web site user agreements parallel software license agreements in that they give no express or implied warranties with respect to information. Amazon.com gives notices that content "such as text, graphics, logos, button icons, images, audio clips and software is the property of Amazon.com."[270] Web sites that offer services to users should require users to agree to Terms of Service (TOS) as a condition of use.

The webwrap agreement requires users to agree to the terms of use or to leave the site. The "webwrap" agreement for Ben and Jerry's Homemade, Inc., provides that the use of the site or downloading of material signifies the user's agreement with the company's "terms of use." It gives users notice of restrictions on the use of materials: "No information, software or other material (collectively referred to as 'Materials') from this Site may be copied, modified, reproduced, republished, uploaded, posted, transmitted or distributed in any way."[271] Another term of use is that the user is given no rights under the law of trademarks or copyrights.[272]

The web site use agreement should have a prominent notice that use is subject to compliance with the TOC agreement. Visitors should be required to click assent to the TOC or be transported automatically off the site. Visitors should be given an opportunity to review the terms and, if a subscriber is required to pay for using the site, to manifest assent.

The online company should reserve the right to change TOC rules and regulations from time to time at its sole discretion. The TOC agreement should be structured as a clickwrap or webwrap agreement, even if no payment is required to access the site or use its services. Many webwrap agreements take the form of a license agreement. Lycos licenses its services for the limited use of online viewing permitting "no further reproduction or distribution of the Services."[273] The webwrap agreement will generally have a term such as: "By using this site, you agree to these terms of use. If you do not agree to these terms, you may not use this site."[274] The web site "terms of use" agreement will set forth the terms and

---

[268] E*Trade, Securities, Inc., User Agreement (visited Feb. 8, 1999), http://www.etrade.com/cgi-bin/gx.cgi/AppLogic%2bHome.

[269] *Id.*

[270] Amazon.com, Inc., Copyright and Disclaimer Page (visited Feb. 8, 1999), http:www.amazon.com/exec/obidos/subst/misc/copyright.html/.

[271] *Id.*

[272] *Id.*

[273] Lycos, Inc., Legal Services, http://www.lycos.com/.

[274] eToys, Terms of Use (visited Dec. 19, 1998), http://www.etoys.com/html/e_etoysterms.html.

conditions for use of the site. The site should note that the user is expected to comply with all applicable federal, state, and local laws governing access. The company's site should state that the company owns its trademarks, logos, and service marks, as displayed on the web site. The site should post a general disclaimer that it is not warranting the accuracy of information on its web site or rendering personal services. The site should assume no responsibility for the accuracy of the information. The online company must reserve the right to change programs or products mentioned at any time without notice. The following is a general disclaimer that may be adapted to a particular company's webwrap or clickwrap agreement.

> ALL INFORMATION PROVIDED ON SPC'S WEB SITE IS PROVIDED "AS IS," WITH ALL FAULTS OR WITHOUT WARRANTIES OF ANY KIND EITHER EXPRESS OR IMPLIED. SPC AND ITS SUPPLIERS DISCLAIM ALL WARRANTIES, EXPRESS AND IMPLIED, INCLUDING, WITHOUT LIMITATION, THOSE OF MERCHANTABILITY, FITNESS FOR A PARTICULAR PURPOSE, AND NONINFRINGEMENT OR THOSE WARRANTIES ARISING FROM COURSE OF PERFORMANCE, COURSE OF DEALING, OR USAGE OF TRADE. SPC AND ITS SUPPLIERS SHALL NOT BE LIABLE FOR ANY INDIRECT, SPECIAL, CONSEQUENTIAL, INCIDENTAL, OR PUNITIVE DAMAGES, INCLUDING, WITHOUT LIMITATION, LOST PROFITS OR REVENUES, COSTS OF REPLACEMENT OF GOODS, LOSS OR DAMAGE TO DATA ARISING OUT OF THE USE OR INABILITY TO USE THE SPC WEB SITE OR ANY SPC PRODUCT OR DAMAGE RESULTING FROM USE OF OR RELIANCE ON THE INFORMATION PRESENT, EVEN IF SPC OR ITS SUPPLIERS HAVE BEEN ADVISED OF THE POSSIBILITY OF SUCH DAMAGES.[275]

The TOC agreement should specify that it limits remedies as well as warranties. If goods are sold or software licensed for a price, the site should provide a minimum adequate remedy, or the company risks having its limitation of remedy clause struck under the doctrine of "failure of essential purpose."

[b]   Terms and Conditions of Use Checklist

1. **Does the Terms and Conditions of Use (TOC) agreement provide for acceptance of terms through use?** Does the TOC agreement provide that the visitor cannot use the site without agreeing to the terms? Does the TOC agreement reserve the company's right to update or revise the terms and conditions of use?

2. **Does the TOC agreement give the web site visitor notice that any right not expressly granted is reserved by the owner of the site?**

---

[275] This disclaimer is based on Cisco Systems, Important Notices (visited May 9, 2000), http://www.cisco.com/public/copyright.html.

3. **Is the web site visitor asked to check the TOC agreement periodically for any changes?**

4. **Is there a provision for displaying any changes in the terms of use or for e-mailing registered visitors concerning any changes?**

5. **Is there a disclaimer of any responsibility for links to third-party sites?** Does the TOC give notice that the company is not responsible for the content of any linked sites? The TOC should also note that the company is not responsible for accuracy, copyright compliance, legality, decency, or compliance with local cultural and legal norms.

6. **Does the TOC state that the company does not endorse any sites to which it is linked and takes no responsibility for content on linked sites?** The linking notice should warn users that the linked sites are not under the control of the company.

7. **The TOC agreement should state that content and materials available on the web site are protected by trademarks, copyrights, patents, trade secrets, license agreements, or other proprietary rights.** Visitors should be required to agree not to sell, license, distribute, or create derivative works from the web site content.[276]

8. **Is there a term or condition by which the visitor agrees not to "sell, license, rent, modify, distribute, copy, reproduce, transmit, publicly display, publish, adapt, edit or create derivative works from such materials or content?"**[277]

9. **What rights of reproduction, copying, or redistribution does the company give users?** AOL.com, for example, grants the user the right to make one copy of materials on the web site for personal, noncommercial use.[278]

---

[276] AOL.Com has a broad proprietary rights clause:

> You acknowledge and agree that all content and materials available on this site are protected by copyrights, trademarks, service marks, patents, trade secrets, or other proprietary rights and laws. Except as expressly authorized by America Online, you agree not to sell, license, rent, modify, distribute, copy, reproduce, transmit, publicly display, publicly perform, publish, adapt, edit, or create derivative works from such materials or content. Notwithstanding the above, you may print or download one copy of the materials or content on this site on any single computer for your personal, non-commercial use, provided you keep intact all copyright and other proprietary notices. Systematic retrieval of data or other content from this site to create or compile, directly or indirectly, a collection, compilation, database or directory without written permission from America Online is prohibited. In addition, use of the content or materials for any purpose not expressly permitted in these Terms of Use is prohibited.

AOL.com, Terms and Conditions of Use (visited May 15, 2000), http://www.aol.com.

[277] *Id.*

[278] *Id.*

10. **Does the TOC Agreement warn users against removing or altering copyright or trademark notices from any copied material?**[279] If copying is permitted, the visitor should be warned to keep intact all copyright notices.

11. **Does the TOC require express written permission to create a compilation or database from content on its site?**[280]

12. **Is written permission from the company required for commercial use of data or intellectual property from its site?** Is the name and contact information for seeking permissions posted on the site?

13. **Does the TOC agreement grant a limited license agreement for a visitor who submits or posts content to the site?** Does the TOC require visitors who submit or post content to warrant that they own or otherwise control all of the rights to the content? AOL, for example, obtains its limited license from visitors with the following terms:

> By posting or submitting content to this site, you:
>
> 1. grant America Online and its affiliates and licensees the right to use, reproduce, display, perform, adapt, modify, distribute, have distributed and promote the content in any form, anywhere and for any purpose; and
> 2. warrant and represent that you own or otherwise control all of the rights to the content and that public posting and use of your content by America Online will not infringe or violate the rights of any third party.[281]

14. **Does the TOC set forth a procedure for making claims of copyright infringement?** A TOC agreement might model its procedure for responding to copyright infringement on that of America Online. The TOC might be structured with a hyperlink to click for obtaining further instructions on making a copyright claim. The Digital Millennium Copyright Act requires that SPC appoint an agent designate to handle copyright claims. SPC's TOC must identify an agent to receive notices of copyright infringement that may occur on its web site. Secondly, SPC must register the agent with U.S. Copyright Office. Finally, SPC's TOC must note the company's policy for dealing with subscribers or users who are repeat infringers. If these safe harbor rules are followed, a site or provider exercising no editorial control will not be liable for infringement by third parties that post content on the site.

---

[279] *Id.*

[280] *Id.*

[281] *Id.*

15. Does the TOC disclaim all warranties for information accuracy on its web site? Does the TOC also disclaim warranties of merchantability, fitness for a particular purpose, and other express or implied warranties, including title or infringement? The TOC should also disclaim any accuracy of information posted on its site, claiming only accuracy to the extent of its best efforts.

[B] Offer and Acceptance

An offer is a definite statement or conduct manifesting a willingness to enter into a contract. The person making an offer is the offeror. The person to whom an offer is made is the offeree. It is the offeree who accepts an offer by manifesting assent to the terms of the offer. An exchange of consideration must occur in order to have an enforceable contract.[282] Consideration generally takes the form either of a promise or of some performance by the offeree in response to an offer. A bilateral contract is a promise for a promise; a unilateral contract is a promise in exchange for a requested act. Online contracts, like traditional contracts, require an offer, acceptance, and consideration, whether under the common law or under Article 2.

Traditional contract law does not permit silence or inaction to constitute acceptance. Acceptance requires that an offeree communicate her or his assent to the terms of the offer. Acceptance may be manifested by acts such as "speaking or sending a letter, a telegram, or other explicit or implicit communication to the offeror."[283] The mere receipt of an e-mail message may constitute acceptance.

[1] E-Mailbox Rule

Under the traditional mailbox rule, an offeree's acceptance was effective when the offeree dispatched a letter out of his or her control. Delivery of an offer occurs when it is placed in the mail. It is questionable whether the traditional mailbox rule should apply to electronic or Internet-related offers. The ABA Model Trading Partner Agreement declined to follow the mailbox rule.[284] The e-mailbox rule has been updated so that an offer is only effective upon actual receipt. The

---

[282] The UCC does not define offer, acceptance, and consideration, incorporating concepts of the common law.

[283] Len Young Smith, Essentials of Business Law and the Legal Environment 171 (4th ed., 1989).

[284] Jeffrey B. Ritter and Judith Y. Gliniecki, Symposium: Electronic Communications and Legal Change: International Electronic Commerce and Administrative Law: The Need for Harmonized National Reforms, 6 Harv. J. Law & Tech. 263 (1993).

e-mailbox rule is possible because technology exists for determining when an offeree has received an e-mail.

[2] Electronic Contract Formation Rules

The UCC presents liberal contracting rules that may be accommodated to electronic contracting. The common law required a "meeting of the minds" of the offeror and offeree for the result to be a contract. In contrast, sales contracts may be formed in any manner sufficient to indicate agreement, including conduct.[285] Article 2 sales contracts do not fail for indefiniteness so long as (1) the parties intend to form a sales contract, and (2) a reasonably certain basis exists for giving an appropriate remedy.[286]

The UCC assimilates common law concepts of offer, acceptance, and consideration. The UCC permits the offeror to demand a particular mode of acceptance. If an offer does not invite a specific means of acceptance, however, the offeree may accept by any reasonable manner or medium.[287]

Great uncertainty persists as to whether mass-market license agreements are enforceable. At common law, an offer could be revoked until acceptance since the promise was not yet supported by consideration. Option contracts were an exception to the general rule because an option supported by consideration was irrevocable for the period stated. Section 2-205, Article 2's "firm offer" rule, is also an exception to the common law rule of revocability of offers. Unlike common law option contracts, company offers by merchants need not be supported by consideration. If a merchant makes a signed written company offer, it is irrevocable for a reasonable period not to exceed three months.

The Uniform Computer Information Transactions Act (UCITA) validates shrinkwrap, clickwrap, webwrap, and other mass-market license agreements as long as the licensor gives the prospective licensee an opportunity to review the terms and to manifest assent. In general, UCITA creates, defines, and governs computer information transactions. UCITA provides the ground rules not only for electronic contracts but also for Internet-related licenses. For a complete discussion of UCITA, see § 6.05.

The model statute provides elaborate rules for online contracting, software licensing, electronic warranties, and remedies. UCITA's scope is wide ranging and applies to webwrap agreements, software licenses, access contracts, and a host of Internet-related contracts.

---

[285] UCC § 2-204 (2000).

[286] *Id.* § 2-204(3).

[287] *Id.* § 2-206(1)(a).

[C] Legal Proof Issues

[1] Electronic Authentication

The question of whether data messages are admissible on the same terms as are handwritten signatures is an important issue encompassing many substantive fields of law. The common law of contract evolved in an age of "pen-and-pencil." Parties in EDI transactions exchange information in an agreed-upon electronic format from computer to computer. Parties to other online transactions may have no prior agreement, and, in the event of a dispute, authentication may become contentious.

The procedural rules for online contracting concern legal proof issues and the rules for enforcing substantive rules.[288] One procedural issue is whether an electronic record or a display generated by electronic means by an electronic agent is admissible in court. Many of the states have extended traditional writing and signature requirements to include electronic writings and signatures; in fact, 40 states have enacted or are considering electronic authentication laws.[289]

[2] Digital Signatures

In order for e-commerce to flourish, electronic records must be validated under rules of evidence and procedure. The procedural question of whether documents may be filed electronically has not been settled in many jurisdictions. The issue of whether an encrypted message is admissible is another unsettled question. The majority of states have enacted digital signature statutes, which are chiefly procedural statutes that validate the admissibility of attribution procedures and digital signatures. Digital signature statutes are chiefly procedural statutes that treat an electronic signature as equivalent to a handwritten signature. For a full discussion, see § 6.03[D].

[D] Uniform Electronic Transactions Act

The Uniform Electronic Transactions Act (UETA) is the most comprehensive statute yet enacted governing procedural rules for contracting. UETA validates electronic records or electronic signatures, in any transaction, except transactions governed by the UCC.[290] UETA "applies to any electronic record or electronic signature created, generated, sent, communicated, received, or stored on or after the effective date" of the Act.[291] UETA does not apply to any articles of the

---

[288] Smith, *supra* note 283, at 5 (defining the distinction between procedural and substantive law).

[289] *Supra* note 135 (April 10, 2000).

[290] UETA § 3 (1999).

[291] *Id.* § 4; *see* NCCUSL, Why States Should Adopt the Uniform Electronic Transactions Act (visited Oct. 13, 2000), http://www.nccusl.org/uniformact_why/uniformacts_why_UETA.htm.

Uniform Commercial Code, to wills or trusts, to UCITA, or to other state laws.[292] In a conflict between Article 2 and UETA, Article 2 governs.[293] The Electronic Signatures in Global and National Commerce Act of 2000 permits UETA to preempt the federal act.

[1] Purpose

The purpose of UETA is to facilitate e-commerce, "to be consistent with reasonable practices concerning electronic transactions," and to make uniform law.[294] UETA treats electronic signatures as the functional equivalent of "paper-and-pen" writings and manually signed signatures. UETA defines the "electronic signature" as "an electronic sound, symbol, or process attached to or logically associated with a record, and executed or adopted by a person with the intent to sign the record."[295] UETA eliminates barriers to electronic commerce and governmental transactions that use electronic records and signatures. The model statute, if widely enacted by the states, will promote the development of a legal infrastructure for electronic commerce and governmental transactions.

The case for adopting UETA is that it will advance the following commercially reasonable policy goals:

a. To facilitate and promote commerce and governmental transactions by validating and authorizing the use of electronic records and electronic signatures;

b. To eliminate barriers in electronic commerce and governmental transactions resulting from uncertainties relating to writing and signature requirements;

c. To simply, clarify, and modernize the law governing commerce and governmental transactions through the use of electronic means;

d. To permit the continued expansion of commercial and governmental electronic practices through custom, usage, and agreement of the parties;

e. To promote uniformity of the law among the states (and worldwide) relating to the use of electronic and similar technological means of affecting and performing commercial and governmental transactions;

f. To promote public confidence in the validity, integrity, and reliability of electronic commerce and governmental transactions; and

---

[292] *Id.* § 3(b)(c)(d).

[293] American Law Institute, Uniform Commercial Code [New], Revised Article 2 (Members Consultative Group Draft, March 1, 2000).

[294] UETA § 6.

[295] *Id.* § 2(8).

g. To promote the development of the legal and business infrastructure necessary to implement electronic commerce and governmental transactions.[296]

[2] Scope

UETA applies to transactions related to business, commercial, and governmental matters.[297] Wills, codicils, and testamentary trusts are removed from UETA as are the Articles of the UCC. For states enacting it, UETA "applies to any electronic record or electronic signature created, generated, sent, communicated, received, or stored on or after the effective date."[298]

[3] Validation of Electronic Signatures

UETA does not *require* any party to use electronic signatures or records and was intended to remove barriers to e-commerce.[299] UETA applies "only to transactions between parties, each of which has agreed to conduct transactions by electronic means."[300] The single most important impact of UETA is to validate electronic records, electronic signatures, and electronic contracts. Section 7 of UETA provides that "[a] record or signature may not be denied legal effect or enforceability solely because it is in electronic form."[301] UETA legitimizes the concept of electronic contract, providing that "[a] contract may not be denied legal effect or enforceability solely because an electronic record was used in its formation."[302] Electronic records and digital signatures satisfy the legal requirements for writings and signatures.

[4] Electronic Records

UETA provides the minimum requirements for what constitutes an electronic record. Electronic records must minimally be "capable of retention at the time of receipt."[303] An online communication that "inhibits the ability of the recipient to print or store the electronic record"[304] does not have the status of a retained record.

---

[296] C. Robert Beattie, Draft Uniform Electronic Transactions Act, Presentation at 1998 Annual Meeting of the American Bar Association, July 31-Aug. 4, 1998.

[297] UETA § 3, cmt. 1.

[298] *Id.* § 4

[299] *Id.* § 5(a).

[300] *Id.* § 5(b).

[301] *Id.* § 7.

[302] *Id.* § 7(b).

[303] *Id.* § 8(a).

[304] *Id.*

UETA does not supplant other law that may require that a record be posted or displayed in a certain manner.[305] For electronic contracts to be viable, some mechanism of attribution must exist. An "electronic record or electronic signature is attributable to a person if it was the act of the person."[306] Security procedures are frequently employed to establish attribution.

UETA is technology-neutral and section 9(a) permits electronic records to be "shown in any manner, including a showing of the efficacy of any security procedure applied to determine the person to which the electronic record or electronic signature was attributable." In many states, the parties are free to agree upon a commercially reasonable security procedure used in their business dealings.

Security procedures are useful in protecting the authenticity and integrity of online contracts, verifying that a signature or record is that of the contracting party. A security procedure may also include encryption technology to detect changes or errors in the content of a record or contract. An electronic record or signature is also determined "from the context and surrounding circumstances at the time of its creation, execution or adoption, including the parties' agreement, if any, and otherwise as provided by law."[307]

[5] Effect of Change or Error

UETA has a methodology for allocating the risk of errors in electronic records that occur during a transmission between parties. The model statute places the risk of loss due to a transmission error on the party that failed to use an agreed-upon security procedure like Article 4A of the UCC.[308] If both parties fail to use an agreed-upon security procedure, the rule does not apply. The party that follows reasonable security procedures "may avoid the effect of the changed or erroneous electronic record only if the other party deviates upon the agreed-upon procedure."[309] It is reasonable that the party that cuts corners on reasonable security is allocated the risk of a security transmission error.

In an automated transaction, an individual must be given the opportunity for the prevention or correction of errors.[310] An individual seeking to avoid the effect of an electronic record must promptly notify the other person of the error.[311] The person erroneously receiving an electronic record must "return it to the other per-

---

[305] *Id.* § 8(b).
[306] *Id.* § 9.
[307] *Id.* § 9(b).
[308] *Id.* § 10.
[309] *Id.* § 10(1).
[310] *Id.* § 10(2).
[311] *Id.* § 10(2)(A).

son" or "destroy the consideration received."[312] The person "must not have used or received any benefit or value from the consideration" received from an erroneous message.[313]

[6] Retention of Records

"If a law requires a signature or record to be notarized, acknowledged, verified, or made under oath," an electronic signature of the person authorized to perform those acts of verification satisfies the requirement.[314] If the law requires a record to be retained, the retention of electronic records satisfies this requirement.[315] To satisfy the retention requirement, the electronic record must fulfill two separate requirements: (1) It must accurately reflect the information in the record after it is in final form; and (2) it must remain accessible for later reference.[316]

[7] Admissibility in Evidence

The digitization of electronic records is becoming increasingly important in litigation. Courts increasingly require parties in litigation to produce electronic records. Computerized files are discoverable, and courts will order discovery of computerized files.[317] The Illinois Supreme Court Rule 201 defines documents to include "all retrievable information in computer storage."[318] Section 13 of UETA states that "in a proceeding, evidence of a record or signature may not be excluded solely because it is in electronic form."[319] Computer records have frequently been "smoking guns" in corporate litigation.[320] For a full discussion of smoking guns and e-mail retention, see § 9.03[C] in Chapter Nine. UETA validates the discoverability and admissibility of electronic data and records.

---

[312] *Id.* § 10(2)(B).

[313] *Id.* § 10(2)(C).

[314] *Id.* § 11.

[315] *Id.* § 12.

[316] *Id.*

[317] *See, e.g.,* Gates Rubber Co. v. Bando Chemical Indus., Ltd., 167 F.R.D. 90, 112 (D. Colo. 1996).

[318] Illinois Supreme Court Rule 20.

[319] UETA § 13.

[320] *See, e.g.,* Knox v. State of Indiana, 93 F.3d 1327 (7th Cir. 1996) (finding e-mail messages in which a supervisor asked employee for sex as evidence in sexual harassment lawsuit); Wesley College v. Pitts, 874 F. Supp. 375 (D. Del. 1997) (admitting e-mail messages in employment case for termination of professor).

[8]   Automated Transactions

UETA provides a legal infrastructure for automated transactions using intelligent electronic agents. Section 14(1) validates contracts formed by electronic agents, even without human review of the terms and agreements.[321] Contracts "may be formed by the interaction of an electronic agent and an individual." UETA is a procedural statute and thus "the terms of the contract are determined by the substantive law applicable to it."[322]

[9]   Receipt of Electronic Records

UETA provides that the parties may determine when an electronic record is sent or received. Unless the parties otherwise provide,

> [a]n electronic record is received when it enters an information processing system that the recipient has designated or uses for the purpose of receiving electronic records or information of the type sent and from which the recipient is able to retrieve the electronic record which is under the control of the recipient.[323]

§ 6.05   SOFTWARE AND INTERNET-RELATED LICENSES UNDER THE UNIFORM COMPUTER INFORMATION TRANSACTIONS ACT

[A]   Overview

The Uniform Computer Information Transactions Act (UCITA) is the world's first comprehensive code for computer information including Internet licenses.[324] By the mid-1980s, the American Bar Association's Business Law Section had begun investigating the possibility that Article 2 of the Uniform Commercial Code (UCC) could be expanded to cover computer contracts.[325]

In the early 1990s, the National Conference of Commissioners on Uniform State Laws (NCCUSL) and the American Law Institute (ALI) agreed to update the UCC to include software-licensing agreements. Although initially proposed as Article 2B, a new article of the UCC, the model statute proved too controversial

---

[321] UETA § 14.

[322] *Id.* § 14(3).

[323] *Id.* § 15(b)(1)(2).

[324] The UCITA text and official comments are available at http://www.ucitaonline.com.

[325] Business Law Section, American Bar Association, Ad Hoc Committee on Computer Contracts (1987).

to secure the required support of the ALI.[326] Thus, as finally approved by NCCUSL, UCITA is a stand-alone statute that will not be part of the UCC.[327]

UCITA is broadly applicable to a wide variety of software-related contracts. UCITA applies to "computer transactions,"[328] a term that covers "contracts to create, modify, transfer or license computer information or informational rights in computer information."[329] It proposes a set of uniform rules and a more certain legal environment for a wide variety of Internet-related mass-market licenses,[330] including software contracts,[331] contracts to download software,[332]

---

[326] The scores of drafts of Article 2B, which preceded UCITA, were hotly debated by industry, consumer, and bar association groups. In March 1995, NCCUSL approved a "hub-and-spoke" model that treated Article 2B as a separate spoke sharing hub provisions with Articles 2 and 2A. The "hub-and-spoke" model sought to harmonize Articles 2, 2A, and 2B by forging general principles common to each article. The "hub-and-spoke" model envisioned a common hub and separate spokes for Articles 2, 2A, and 2B corresponding to sales, leases and licenses respectively.

The "hub-and-spoke" model was opposed by a wide variety of stakeholders, such as the Software Publishers Association. NCCUSL eliminated the "hub-and-spoke" concept but retained Raymond Nimmer as the Article 2B reporter. In addition to Professor Nimmer (Article 2B's technology reporter), the key players for the Article 2B project were the American Bar Association, NCCUSL, and the ALI. Approval by both the ALI and the NCCUSL was necessary before a completed draft could be introduced in the state legislatures.

[327] Thom Weidlich, Commission Plans New UCC Article, Nat'l L. J., Aug. 28, 1995, at B1 (noting that NCCUSL appointed Houston law professor Raymond T. Nimmer as technology reporter for the new UCC Article 2B); See also Raymond T. Nimmer, Intangibles Contracts: Thoughts of Hubs, Spokes and Reinvigorating Article 2, 35 Wm. & Mary L. Rev. 1337 (1994).

[328] UCITA § 103(a) (2000).

[329] Id. § 102(12)

[330] UCITA defines the mass-market license as "a standard form that is prepared and used in a mass-market transaction." Id. § 102(45). A mass-market transaction, in turn, means "(A) A consumer contract; or (B) any other transaction with an end-user licensee if: (i) the transaction is for information or informational rights directed to the general public as a whole, including consumers, under substantially the same terms for the same information; (ii) the licensee acquires the information or rights in a retail transaction under terms and in quantity consistent with an ordinary transaction in a retail market." Id. § 102(46).

[331] Software transactions may take diverse forms, including signed development agreements, purchase orders, electronic or online licenses, web site licenses, or "shrinkwrap" license agreements. A license is a contract that specifies what the licensee may or may not do with the software, information, or data.

[332] Adobe Systems Inc., for example, conditions the downloading of software from its web site on agreement with specified terms and conditions. Adobe's license agreement advises web site visitors that they must agree to the terms and conditions of Adobe's end user license agreement as a condition for downloading software. The Adobe license agreement states: "By downloading software of Adobe Systems Incorporated or its subsidiaries ('Adobe') from the site, you agree to the following terms and conditions. If you do not agree with such terms and conditions do not download the software. The terms of an end user license agreement accompanying a particular software file upon installation or download of the software shall supersede the terms presented below." Adobe Systems International, Customer First Support License Agreement (visited Feb. 1, 1999), http://www.adobe.com/supportservice/custsupport/Library.

access contracts,[333] clickwrap agreements,[334] webwrap agreements,[335] electronic data interchange (EDI),[336] and a host of other Information Age contracts. UCITA also validates shrinkwrap agreements that accompany boxed software.[337]

The statutory purposes of UCITA are (1) to facilitate computer or information transactions in cyberspace; (2) to clarify the law governing computer information transactions; (3) to enable expanding commercial practice in computer information transactions by commercial usage and agreement of the parties; and (4) to make the law uniform among the various jurisdictions.[338]

UCITA provides substantive rules for e-commerce not found in any other state or federal statute. UCITA, for example, defines and validates the use of electronic agents[339] to form online contracts. UCITA provides legal rules for electronic

---

[333] An access contract "means a contract to obtain electronic access to, or information from, an information processing system of another person, or the equivalent of such access." UCITA § 102(a)(1) (2000). UCITA will cover access contracts such as Westlaw, LEXIS, Microsoft Network, America Online, and the online version of the Wall Street Journal, which is subscription-based.

[334] Many companies use "clickwrap agreements" where a subscriber signifies acceptance or rejection by clicking the mouse on a highlighted "I accept" or "I decline" icon. Netscape's Navigator is distributed with an end user "clickwrap or "click-stream" license. The typical clickwrap agreement will state: "By clicking the 'accept' button, you are consenting to be bound by and are becoming a party to this agreement. If you do not agree to all of the terms of this agreement, click the 'do not accept' button and the installation process will not continue."

[335] A webwrap or click-stream contract is typically structured as a license agreement. Web site visitors are given a license to use material on a given web site. The license, for example, may restrict the visitor from distributing, copying, or preparing derivative works from a company's web site materials. The license spells out permitted and restricted uses by visitors. Access to and use of the web site is provided subject to the license agreement's terms and conditions. Real Networks for example, conditions use of "information, artwork, text, video, audio or pictures on the visitor's acceptance of its terms of service." Real Networks, Legal Notice, Disclaimer, and Terms of Use (visited Feb. 9, 1999), http://www.real.com/company/legal.html.

[336] EDI is a contracting practice by which the parties set guidelines for what qualifies as an offer or an acceptance. EDI is a means for businesses to communicate electronically computer to computer. EDI eliminates the need for maintaining paper record systems and multiple data entries. In a typical EDI agreement, the parties enter into a trader party agreement with subsequent transactions handled automatically by electronic agents. *See* Robert W. McKeon, Jr., Electronic Data Interchange: Uses and Legal Aspects in the Commercial Arena, 12 J. Marshall J. Computer and Info. L. 511, 512-514 (1994). The major legal questions to EDI contracts are the validity and enforceability of computer contracts. Jeffrey B. Ritter, Scope of the Uniform Commercial Code: Computer Contracting Cases and Electronic Commercial Practices, 45 Bus. Law. 2533, 2555 (1990).

[337] Software is packaged with shrinkwrap plastic surrounding the package. The shrinkwrap license receives its name from the software vendors' practice of printing shrinkwrap licenses beneath the shrinkwrap or in the box containing the software. Some shrinkwrap license agreements are printed on the outside of the box, but others cannot be seen until the software is paid for and the box opened. Other software vendors display the shrinkwrap license agreement only after the software is booted up and the terms are displayed on the user's screen.

[338] UCITA prefatory note (1999).

[339] *Id.* § 102(27).

events, such as the "electronic authentication, display, message, record or performance" of transactions, a role critical to Internet transactions.[340] UCITA follows the
methodology of Article 2 in drawing distinctions between substantive rules for
"merchants" and "non-merchants."[341]

In the absence of a comprehensive statute for computer transactions in cyberspace, judges and practitioners employ legal fictions cornering and cribbing Article 2 to fit software licensing transactions. The UCITA Reporter argues that a
specialized statute is needed for the licensing of information:

> Contracts for computer information are not equivalent to transactions in
> goods, whether the issues focus on development, commercial exchange, or
> mass marketing. Computer information contracts emphasize different issues
> and bring into play a different policy structure on issues ranging from alloca-
> tion of liability risk to questions about how the right to use the informational
> subject matter is determined. One (goods) focuses on rights to a tangible item,
> while the other (computer information) focuses on intangibles and rights in
> intangibles. The contexts entail different contractual, transaction, property,
> and underlying social policies issues.[342]

---

[340] *Id.* § 102 (29).

[341] Special merchant rules for the UCC include the following: § 2-201(2), the Statute of Frauds;
§ 2-205, the merchants' only "company offer" rule; § 2-207, the merchants' confirmatory memo-
randa rule for "battle of the forms"; § 2-209, the merchants' sales contract modification rule; § 2-
312, the merchant rule for warranty against infringement; § 2-314, implied warranty of
merchantability; § 2-316(2), special merchant rule for disclaiming warranties; § 2-103(1)(b), special
merchant rule for good faith; § 2-327(1)(c), the merchants' rule for following reasonable instructions
in "Sale on Approval" or "Sale or Return" contracts; § 2-603, special duties for merchant buyers in
dealing with rejected goods; § 2-605, the merchants' special rule for waiver of buyer's objection by
failure to particularize defects; § 2-509(3), special merchants' rule for risk of loss in the absence of
breach; § 2-402(2), the merchants' rule for rights of sellers' creditors; § 2-403(2) the merchants'
entrusting rule and power to transfer goods to buyers in the ordinary course of business; and § 2-609,
the merchants' right to adequate assurance of performance. UCITA essentially adapts the methodology of Article 2 in having separate rules for merchants and nonmerchants in computer transactions.
UCITA defines the "merchant" as a person that "deals in information or informational rights of the
kind involved in the transaction" or that otherwise "by the person's occupation holds itself out as
having knowledge or skill peculiar to . . . the practices or information involved in the transaction"
or a person to which such knowledge or skill "may be attributed by the person's employment of an
agent or broker or other intermediary that by its occupation holds itself out as having the knowledge
or skill." UCITA § 102(45) (2000). As with Article 2, UCITA has a special Statute of Frauds rule
for merchants. *Id.* § 201(d) (stating that where both parties are merchants there is an exception to the
writing requirement where notice of objection "is not given within 10 days after the confirming
record is received"). *See id.* § 204(d)(2) ("Between merchants, the proposed additional term becomes
part of the contract unless the offeror gives notice of objection before, or within a reasonable time
after, it receives the proposed terms"). As with Article 2, UCITA has a large number of special merchant rules.

[342] UCITA Prefatory Note (NCCUSL Annual Draft, July 2000).

[B]   Structure and Function

The UCC's purpose is "to clarify the law about business transactions rather than to change the habits of the business community."[343] UCITA, like the UCC, permits the parties to vary statutory provisions. As with the UCC, UCITA incorporates default terms as gap-fillers for missing terms "unless the parties otherwise agree." UCITA's underlying jurisprudence is freedom of contract. As with the UCC, the parties may not disclaim the obligations of good faith, diligence, reasonableness, and due care nor certain consumer protections.

UCITA closely parallels Article 2 of the UCC in structure and function. The proposed stand-alone statute is divided into nine parts: (1) Definitions, General Scope and Terms; (2) Formation and Terms; (3) Warranties; (4) Construction; (5) Transfer of Rights and Interests; (6) Performance; (7) Breach of Contract; (8) Remedies; and (9) Miscellaneous Provisions. UCITA is shaped by the software licensing paradigm as well as by the trade practices of the information-based industries. UCITA § 103 sets the scope of the proposed statute as "computer information transactions" with a series of "carve-outs" or exclusions. Section 104 follows the UCC in permitting supplemental principles of law and equity to apply to contracts governed by UCITA.[344] Like Article 2 agreements, a UCITA contract consists of the parties' agreement, course of dealing, course of performance, and usage of trade. UCITA does not supplant fundamental public policies or consumer protections at either the state or federal level.

[C]   Scope

[1]   Computer Information Transactions

The scope of UCITA is to provide the ground rules for "computer information transactions."[345] UCITA excludes newspapers, motion pictures, and printed

---

[343] Grant Gilmore, On the Difficulties of Codifying Commercial Law, 57 Yale L.J. 1341 (1948).

[344] Section 114 of UCITA contemplates that the statute will be supplemented by common law and equity:

> (a) Unless displaced by this [Act], principles of law and equity, including the law merchant and the common law of this State relative to capacity to contract, principal and agent, estoppel, fraud, misrepresentation, duress, coercion, mistake, other validating or invalidating cause, supplement this [Act]. Among the laws supplementing and not displaced by this [Act] are trade secret laws and unfair competition laws.

UCITA also contemplates that the statute will be supplemented by the usage of trade. *See e.g.,* UCITA §§ 210(a), 302(b).

[345] UCITA § 103(a).

information that is in a nondigital format. The UCITA methodology consists of a broad definition of computer transactions with numerous exceptions. Core banking and payment and financial services are outside the scope of the proposed statute.[346] The entertainment industry is largely outside the scope of UCITA, although movies, television, radio, and mass media may be classifiable as computer information, as would MP3. UCITA, however, specifically excludes the distribution of music and entertainment, which already have well-established rules for contract formation and the distribution of visual programming or similar products.

UCITA does not govern broadcast, satellite, or cable programming governed by the Federal Communications Act.[347] The licensing of motion pictures, sound recordings, musical works, and phonograph records are also carved out of the proposed UCITA.[348] UCITA excludes "traditional core businesses" such as information in print form,"[349] such as a newspaper or magazine. The exclusion of the mass media and of the entertainment industry has narrowed the scope of UCITA.[350] UCITA's ill-fated predecessor, Article 2B, was originally drafted to include all information transfers.

In addition, compulsory licenses are excluded from the scope of UCITA.[351] A compulsory license is a license granted by the government to use patents, copyrighted materials, or other types of intellectual property.[352] The U.S. government's authority to issue compulsory licenses stems from antitrust and eminent domain laws.[353] A number of federal statutes provide for compulsory licenses; the Clean Air Act, for example, "provides for compulsory licensing of patents related to air pollution."[354] The policy underlying compulsory licenses is "to broaden access to technologies and information in order to achieve a number of public purposes."[355] The compulsory licenses recognized by legal treaties, such as GATT, NAFTA, and TRIPS, are outside the scope of UCITA.[356]

---

[346] *Id.* § 103(d)(1).

[347] *Id.* § 103(d)(3).

[348] *Id.* § 103(d)(3)(A)(B).

[349] *Id.* § 103, O.C. #3.

[350] UCITA does not apply to "audio or visual programming . . . provided by broadcast, satellite, or cable, as defined or used in the Communications Act of 1935." *Id.* § 103(f)(1); *see also* § 103(d)(3)(A)(B) (excluding core entertainment, cable, and broadcast from UCITA).

[351] *Id.* § 103(d)(4).

[352] Frequently Asked Questions About Compulsory Licenses (visited Jan. 9, 2000), http://www.cptech.org/ip/health/cl/faq.html.

[353] *Id.*

[354] *Id.*

[355] *Id.*

[356] *Id.*

UCITA does not cover "[c]ontracts of employment of an individual other than as an independent contractor,"[357] nor does it apply to service contracts. Law other than UCITA would govern any contract for personal services.

UCITA does not cover the licensing of intellectual property, such as patents, copyrights, trade dress, or other intellectual property rights. Revised Article 2 provides, if UCITA is adopted in a state, that Article 2 should defer to UCITA's scope section.[358] Revised Article 2 adapts to sales law many of the provisions of the Uniform Electronic Transaction Act.[359]

➤ *[a]* ***Preventive Law Pointer: Determining UCITA's Reach***

A large number of information age contracts will be covered by UCITA. Software licenses, unlike the sale of goods, place restrictions on use. Licenses are limiting and may preclude the commercial use of a database, as in a web site. Many web site license agreements limit the downloading of documents for non-commercial use. Licenses may limit the right to access information. LEXIS-NEXIS and Westlaw, for example, place limits on access to their databases. A faculty member of a law school has a limited right to access these materials for academic purposes but may not use the services for a private law practice. License agreements may restrict the use of software to a single computer versus a network computer or outsourcer.

What Is Included under UCITA?

* Licensing of computer information including software, online licenses.

* Internet-related licenses and web site contracts.

* Contracts to develop, modify or create software.

* Data transfers, access contracts, and data processing contracts.

* Commercial transactions where primary or predominant part is computer information.

What Is Outside UCITA?

* Financial service transactions, insurance services transactions.

* Audio or visual programming defined by The Communication Act of 1934.

* Broadcast, satellite, or cable programming.

---

[357] UCITA § 103(d)(4) (1999).
[358] UCC § R2-103(f).
[359] *Id.*

- Motion pictures, musical works, sound recordings, or phonograph records.

- Compulsory licenses.

- Contracts of employment of individuals (other than independent contractor creating or modifying computer information).

- Entertainment services, musical works, or phonorecords.

- Professional services involving performance.

- Licensing of patents, trademarks, copyrights, trade dress, or other intellectual property governed by state or federal law.

- Subject matter covered by Articles 3, 4, 4A, 5, 6, 7, 8, or 9 of the Uniform Commercial Code.

- Sales or leases of a computer program not developed particularly for the transaction, sales on leases of goods.

- Computer programs embedded in goods, i.e., a Mr. Coffee machine or an airplane navigation system.

- Payment, banking, or financial services.

- Print Media, including books, magazines, or newspapers.

- Telecommunication products or services.

[2] Hybrid or Mixed Transactions

Computer transactions may be broadly classified into "four primary categories: sales of goods, licenses of technology, lease agreements and service."[360] Typically sold in a bundled transaction, a computer system consists of hardware[361] and software. Hardware may itself include software components.[362] Purchasing a

---

[360] Raymond T. Nimmer, The Law of Computer Technology: Rights, Licenses and Liabilities (2d ed., 1992) ¶ 6.01, at 6-3.

[361] Computer hardware generally includes the central processing unit (CPU); printed circuit boards, chips, and electronic circuitry; color monitor; keyboard; disk drives, including an internal hard disk, floppy disk, and CD-ROM drives; network card or modem; power source; and ports to connect the computer to outside devices. Hardware also includes peripheral devices, such as a printer, faxphone, scanner, and external disk drives. The CPU is the "brain" of the computer, the logic and control section that executes the binary instructions encoded in software that controls the other parts of the computer. The term "CPU" is often used more generally to refer to the box that contains the CPU, circuit boards, internal drives, and ports.

[362] "Much 'hardware' today is often made up of both hardware and software components. A hard drive most likely contains a microprocessor with some 'firmware' code in it." Robert F. Bodi, Patent

computer system may also involve services such as initial installation or continuing technical support.

The sale of a computer system may potentially be governed by Articles 2, 2A, and UCITA. Article 2 applies to the sale of hardware, Article 2A to the leasing of computer equipment, and UCITA to software loaded into the computer system. UCITA applies to the entire transaction so long as the "computer information . . . is the primary subject matter."[363] The primary subject matter test closely parallels the predominant purpose test developed in Article 2 cases by the courts.

The predominant factor test will examine whether an underlying transaction is primarily a computer information transaction or a common law service. If the underlying transaction is predominately the sale of goods, Article 2 applies. If the service aspect predominates, the common law applies. The question of whether UCITA applies focuses on whether computer information (that is, software) or goods (that is, hardware) predominate in a mixed or hybrid contract.[364]

In a mixed transaction, in which both goods and computer information are transferred, UCITA applies to computer information. If you purchase a computer with a Pentium III processor from Gateway, Dell, or Compaq, it will be loaded with software such as Windows 2000. A computer system may consist of hundreds of operating systems on the hard drive; the same operating system may run different languages on one personal computer. The software application programs will be covered by UCITA. While computer hardware purchases are covered by Article 2, leased hardware is covered by Article 2A. In addition, state and federal consumer protection laws as well as common law and equitable principles supplement a computer information contract. The gravamen test in mixed or hybrid transactions focuses on the source of a complaint. In a computer contract, it is the source of the problem hardware or software. If the hardware is defective, Article 2 or Article 2A applies depending on whether it is sold or leased. In contrast, if the software is defective or fails to perform to specifications, UCITA applies.

[3] Key Definitions

Part I of UCITA deals with definitions and preliminary concerns. Section 102 defines key terms such as access contracts, attribution procedures, authentication, computer information, electronic agents, electronic events, electronic messages, mass-market licenses, receipt, and record. An electronic agent includes a computer program but is not limited to that technology. In order to qualify as an

---

Nonsense—Firmware, Software, Hardware, Nowhere, posting to CYBERIA-1@LISTSERV .AOL.COM (Law and Policy of Computer Communication), June 13, 2000.

[363] UCITA § 103(b)(2) (1999).

[364] *Id.* § 103(b)(2); *cf.* UCITA § 103, cmt. 3(b)(1) (describing UCITA's approach to mixed transactions as a "gravamen test").

electronic agent, the automated system must have been selected, programmed, or otherwise used in a way that binds the parties. In automated transactions, an individual does not deal with another individual but with one or more electronic agents that represent both parties. The legal relationship between the person and the automated agent is not fully equivalent to common law agency, but takes into account that the "agent" is not a human actor.[365] Parties who employ electronic agents are ordinarily bound by the results of their operations.[366]

[4] Choice of Law and Forum

[a] *Choice of Law*

UCITA adopts a choice of law rule similar to the "most significant relationship" test of the Restatement (Second) of Conflicts of Law.[367] Courts will apply the law of the jurisdiction that has the most points of contact with the contractual relationship. The parties may choose the applicable law rather than leave the matter to the courts.[368] For license agreements with consumers, UCITA limits choice of law to avoid an inconvenient forum. A choice of law is unenforceable "to the extent it would vary a rule that may not be varied by agreement under the law of the jurisdiction whose law would apply."[369] UCITA places limits on choice of law for consumer contracts in Section 109, unlike the UCC, which has no special consumer limitations.

[b] *Choice of Forum*

Choice of forum agreements may be found in a variety of online contracts, including license agreements, trading partner agreements, or web site development agreements. The UCITA Reporter notes that by 1999 more than 100 decisions dealt with Internet personal jurisdiction:

> The decisions reveal an uncertainty about when doing business on the Internet exposes a party to jurisdiction in all States and all countries. The uncertainty affects both large and small enterprises, but [it] has greater impact on small enterprises that are and will continue to be the lifeblood of electronic commerce. Choice of forum terms allow parties to control this issue and the risk

---

[365] *Id.* §§ 206, 215; *see also* § 102(27).

[366] "Electronic agent means a computer program or electronic or other automated means, used independently to initiate an action or to respond to electronic messages or performances, on the person's behalf without review or action by an individual at the time of the action or response to the message or performance." *Id.* § 102(27).

[367] *Id.* § 109 cmt. 4.

[368] *Id.* § 109(a) (noting that UCITA enforces agreed choice of law).

[369] *Id.*

or costs it creates. This section allows the agreement to govern, but adds restrictions based on fundamental public policy considerations.[370]

UCITA provides default rules if the parties do not specify choice-of-law governing their license agreements. Similarly, the parties have the discretion to specify an exclusive judicial forum under Section 110 of UCITA. Choice of forum clauses are generally enforceable.[371] In addition, an agreement must specify that the forum is "exclusive" to be enforceable.[372]

➤   **[i]   Preventive Law Pointer: Choice of Law and Forum**

Choice of law is a contractual provision that predetermines the law that applies for any dispute involving the contract. SPC should draft a clause that states that the web site is created and controlled by Suffolk Personal Computers (SPC), in the Commonwealth of Massachusetts, USA. As such, the laws of Massachusetts will govern this agreement, including disclaimers, terms, and conditions, without giving effect to any principles of conflict of law.

SPC should include a choice of law clause in every agreement because it may have customers in any state and hundreds of foreign countries. SPC needs a choice of law clause to be assured that Massachusetts' law applies, versus that of another state or foreign jurisdiction. SPC may find Massachusetts law to be favorable because that state does not recognize the common law remedy of punitive damages. Massachusetts' Article 2 is far more consumer-oriented than are the sales laws of all other jurisdictions. SPC's counsel may nevertheless choose Massachusetts because of the company's greater familiarity with the state's consumer protection statutes.

Suppose there is an online transaction between a Massachusetts business and a New York bank. If New York law applies, punitive damages may be recoverable, but not if Massachusetts law applies. SPC may wish to restrict offers in countries that have radically different contracting practices or where the governments might object to the subject matter of the contract. The following "choice of law" clause

---

[370] *Id.*

[371] Section 110(a) of UCITA enforces choice of forum clauses unless "unreasonable and unjust." *See* UCITA § 110(a). Section 110(a) refers to judicial forums rather than arbitration. Arbitration clauses in mass market licenses are generally enforced. *See, e.g.,* Lieschke v. RealNetworks, Inc., 2000 U.S. Dist. LEXIS 1683 (N.D. Ill. 2000) (finding that clause in a licensing agreement bound the parties to settle their disputes through arbitration); Westendorf v. Gateway 2000, Inc., 2000 Del. Ch. LEXIS 54 (Del. Ch. Ct., March 16, 2000); Levy v. Gateway 2000, Inc., 1997 WL 823611 (N.Y. Sup. Ct., Aug. 12, 1997). *Cf.* Klocek v. Gateway, Inc., 104 F. Supp. 2d 1332 (D. Kan. 2000) (holding that computer manufacturer did not provide sufficient evidence to support finding that plaintiff agreed to arbitration clause contained in its standard terms mailed inside the computer box).

[372] *Id.*

may be included in paper-based license agreements, nondisclosure agreements, and other Internet-related contracts: "This Agreement shall be governed by the laws of the Commonwealth of Massachusetts."

As with any other Internet-related contract, an integration or merger clause should be included:

> This Agreement states the entire agreement and supersedes all prior agreements, written or verbal, between the parties with respect to the subject matter of this agreement. Writing signed by a duly authorized representative of both parties may not amend except this agreement.

Choice of forum "is a contractual provision that predetermines the judicial or arbitral forum in the event of a dispute arising out of the web site agreement. If the parties do not otherwise agree to choice of law, the court will make the decision as to the applicable law based upon the following factors:

a. The needs of the interstate and international systems;
b. The relevant policies of the forum;
c. The relevant policies of other interested states and the relative interests of those states in the determination of the particular issue;
d. The protection of justified expectations;
e. The basic policies underlying the particular field of law;
f. The certainty, predictability, and uniformity of result; and
g. The ease in the determination and application of the law to be applied.[373]

If a court does reach the question of a state's interest, "it should concern itself with the question whether the courts of that state would have applied the rule in the decision of the case."[374]

Courts may also consider the following factors in determining the choice of law:

a. The place of contracting;
b. The place of negotiation of the contract;
c. The place of performance;
d. The location of the subject matter of the contract; and
e. The domicile, residence, nationality, place of incorporation, and place of business of the parties.[375]

To avoid uncertainty as to choice of law, SPC should include a choice of law clause in its terms of service, end-user license agreements, and other contracts.

---

[373] Restatement (Second) of Conflicts § 6.
[374] *Id.* § 186 cmt.
[375] *Id.* § 188.

SPC should require shoppers to adhere to the following choice of law clause: "This site is created and controlled by Suffolk Personal Computers (SPC) in the state of Massachusetts. As such, the laws of the Commonwealth of Massachusetts governs these disclaimers, terms, and conditions, without giving effect to any principles of conflicts of laws. We reserve the right to make changes to our site and to these disclaimers, terms, and conditions at any time."[376]

Courts are predisposed to uphold choice of law clauses given a reasonable relation to the transaction. Occasionally, a court will find that the question of choice of law is covered neither by statute nor by a parties' "choice of law" clause. SPC may also specify arbitration as an exclusive forum for resolving disputes arising under license agreements.

[D]   UCITA's Licensing Rules

Software licensing evolved in the 1980s with the rise of the software industry. By 1992, sales of software were expanding at a rate of two to three times that of sales of hardware.[377] Licensing is a contract to use computer software or other copyrighted information. Software is licensed, not sold, to circumvent the Copyright Act's "first sale" doctrine which permits the owner of a particular copy to sell or otherwise dispose of that copy.

If a software developer sold the first copy of its software, it would, in many cases, be unable to realize its investment. The price of a single copy of mass-market software will not begin to reflect the thousands of hours of programming or software engineering and the other expenses of producing the first copy. When software is copied, it is not used up in the same sense as are tangible goods, such as tons of iron ore, bushels of grain, or yards of lumber. Copies of software may be made for negligible or no cost, as is the case for information products downloaded from a web site. The ease of copying or downloading software is the principal difference between transfers of information and sales of goods.

Software contracts, access contacts, multimedia contracts, and a multitude of other online contracts are structured as license agreements rather than as sales to avoid the first sale doctrine. A license is permission to use information under restricted conditions, such as the software, in only one single-user computer. A sale, in contrast, involves the passage of title to goods for a price. A license may be based on the number of copies licensed, the method of distribution, the type of end user, or the form of a license agreement. Mass-market license agreements, for

---

[376] This form is adapted from Amazon.com, Inc. Copyright and Disclaimer Page (visited Feb. 8, 1999), http:www.amazon.com/exec/obidos/subst/misc/copyright.html/.

[377] Carolyn Van Brussel, Mobile PCs "'90s Their Decade," Speaker Claims, Computing Canada 14 (June 22, 1992).

example, will state: "opening this package indicates your acceptance of these terms and conditions."

Customized software, in contrast, is tailored to the user and is generally negotiated. A software developer will typically restrict use through site or time limitations. License agreements place restrictions on use not typically found in the sale or lease of goods. A license, in contrast, is frequently personal, nontransferable, and nonassignable; such restrictions are generally not made on sold or leased goods. A LEXIS-NEXIS license, for example, is a license to electronically display, print, and download copyrighted materials from its databases. Many license agreements, including those used by Westlaw and LEXIS-NEXIS, provide that the agreement may not be transferred or used by more than one person and that it is subject to a number of terms.

Licensing is the primary legal tool for transferring value and information in a dot-com business. SPC's expansion of licensing from its web site has the potential of driving its Internet-based business. Gateway, for example, in selling systems, states in its license: "By keeping your Gateway 2000 computer system beyond five (5) days after the date of delivery, you accept these Terms and Conditions."[378] With Article 2, title to goods passes when the buyer accepts and pays in accordance with the contract. No title passes with the licensing of software. Location and use restrictions are necessary if software developers are to realize their investment in developing intangible information assets.[379]

Choice of law is a critically important factor in structuring mass market license agreements in the Internet economy. A number of state courts have refused to enforce one-sided software licenses.[380] In the early 1990s, a number of state courts ruled that mass market licenses shipped with computer software was not enforceable because it was not part of the parties' agreement.[381] The Seventh Circuit has broadly enforced mass market licenses even when the terms were presented after the licensee paid for the software.[382] The Seventh Circuit has also

---

[378] Software contracts, access contacts, multimedia contracts, and a host of online contracts are structured as licenses rather than as sales to avoid the "first sale" doctrine of Copyright Law. A license is permission to use software, databases, intellectual property, or other information. A license may be based on the number of copies licensed, the method of distribution, the type of end user, or the form of a license agreement. Klocek v. Gateway, Inc., 104 F. Supp. 2d 1332, 1335 (D. Kan. 2000). Gateway appears to have shortened the period for acceptance. See § 6.03[G][1].

[379] A contract for the sale of goods is one in which a seller agrees to transfer goods that conform to the contract in exchange for valuable consideration. UCC § 2-301 (1999).

[380] See, e.g., Klocek v. Gateway, Inc., 104 F. Supp. 2d 1332 (D. Kan. 2000) (finding issue of fact as to whether mass market licensee agreed to arbitration clause in adhesive agreement).

[381] See, e.g., Arizona Retail Systems, Inc., v. Software Link, Inc., 831 F. Supp. 759 (D. Ariz. 1993) (ruling that shrinkwrap license agreement shipped with computer software was not part of the agreement).

[382] ProCD v. Zeidenberg, 86 F.3d 1447 (7th Cir., 1996).

enforced arbitration clauses in mass market licenses.[383] Maryland and Virginia have enacted UCITA, which broadly legitimates mass market licenses. Licensors will find it desirable to apply the law of a jurisdiction that has enacted UCITA.

➤ **[1] Preventive Law Pointer: Negotiating Points**

Extensive license negotiations are common in customized or other non–mass-market license agreements. Corporate or outside counsel needs to know about the technical needs of their clients in order to serve their clients' business objectives. Lawyers with a strong technical background will be in a strong negotiating position. First and foremost, the negotiating lawyer must understand what rights are to be protected: copyright, patents, trade secrets, databases, or proprietary information.

Software or web site development agreements are relational contracts in which it is common to change specifications or to make adjustments to adapt to a rapidly changing online environment. The negotiating terms will vary depending on whether counsel is representing a licensor or licensee. The need may also arise for negotiating with third parties over intellectual property rights. The negotiation of a development contract should not be an exercise of mechanical jurisprudence. Counsel should be cautious about blindly using templates without tailoring these standard forms to the company's unique problems. Software licensing agreements should not be spun out of formbooks used like legal vending machines. Licensing agreements need to be customized if they are to meet the company's business objectives.

[E] Policing Mass-Market Licenses

UCITA provides a legal infrastructure for mass-market licenses, including access contracts, terms of service agreements, clickwrap agreements, shrinkwrap agreements, and web site user agreements. UCITA's contracting rules apply to the entire transaction if information is the predominant purpose of the transaction. UCITA favors a general freedom of contract, which is moderated by doctrines such as unconscionability, failure of essential purpose, and supplemental consumer protection. UCITA makes it clear that adopting states are free to impose mandatory terms protecting consumers.[384] Adopting states may extend consumer protections applicable to the sale of goods to retail software licenses.

[1] Procedural Protection for Licensees

UCITA broadly validates mass-market licenses so long as "the party agrees to the license, such as by manifesting assent, before or during the party's initial

---

[383] Hill v. Gateway, Inc., 105 F.3d 1147 (7th Cir., 1997).
[384] UCITA § 104(1).

performance or use of or access to the information."[385] The concept of manifesting assent is based on an objective standard rather than a subjective "meeting of the minds." A minimally adequate objective manifestation of assent is an opportunity to review the record, coupled with an affirmative act that indicates assent. Nevertheless, mass-market licenses are a useful legal invention. The alternative to mass-market licensing would be to retain an attorney to negotiate the terms. Negotiated mass-market license agreements are not cost-efficient. One of the difficult policy issues a company must decide is what affirmative conduct constitutes assent. In a paper-based contract, a signature establishes the manifestation of assent.

UCITA permits the manifestation of assent to be fulfilled by an affirmative act such as clicking a display button labeled "I accept the terms of this agreement" or something similar. A licensor must give the licensee a right to a refund if the licensee has not had an opportunity to review the terms and to manifest assent prior to a requirement to pay.[386]

UCITA rejects the doctrine of acceptance by silence for standard-form licenses. Section 112, for example, binds a licensee to the terms of a shrinkwrap or clickwrap agreement as long as the party manifests assent to the terms. Mass-market contracts are enforced if two conditions are met: (1) The user has an opportunity to review the terms of the license; and (2) the user manifests assent after having an opportunity to review the terms. UCITA also validates clickwrap agreements requiring that the party had an opportunity to review terms before assenting. The licensor can create a "safe harbor" proving manifestation of assent with a built-in double click requiring the user to reaffirm assent.

Simply clicking an "I accept" text or icon may accomplish the manifestation of assent. A growing number of web site vendors use a "double click" method, which asks customers whether they are certain that they accept the terms of the license. It is quite likely that the reasonable visitor will click through these icons without reading the license agreement prior to payment. UCITA provides mass-market licensees with a right to a refund if they have "no opportunity to review a mass-market license or a copy of it before becoming obligated to pay."[387] A party adopts the terms of a shrinkwrap or clickwrap license if the customer has an opportunity to review the terms and to manifest assent by some affirmative act. Software licenses typically limit all damages and provide an exclusive remedy. Some software licenses prohibit reverse engineering or limit permissible uses.

---

[385] *Id.* § 210(a).

[386] *Id.* § 210(b).

[387] *Id.* § 210(a)(2)(b).

[2]   Policing Unconscionable License Agreements

UCITA adopts the concept of unconscionability from Article 2 that gives courts the power to strike down unconscionable contracts or terms. A software license with inconspicuous terms or a hidden webwrap agreement may be found unconscionable if coupled with unfair or onerous terms.[388] The basic test is whether the license agreement or term should be invalidated because it is "so one-sided as to be unconscionable under the circumstances existing at the time of the making of the contract."[389] A court will also consider whether the licensee is a consumer and whether deception occurred through surprising terms.

A court has a wide arsenal of remedies when finding evidence of an unfair bargaining process and unfair terms. "A court, in its discretion, may refuse to enforce the contract as a whole if it is permeated by the unconscionability, or it may strike any single term or group of terms" in an online contract or license agreement.[390] A court has the power to police "to enforce the contract, or it may enforce the remainder of the contract without the unconscionable term, or it may so limit the application of any unconscionable term as to avoid any unconscionable result."[391]

[3]   Failure of Essential Purpose

An online store is entitled to limit warranties as well as remedies. Licensors should have a minimum adequate remedy if the exclusive remedy fails of its essential purpose resulting in a right without a remedy. "Section 2-719(2) raises two essential questions: (1) When does an exclusive or limited remedy fail of its essential purpose? and (2) When a remedy fails, what remedies are available to the buyer?"[392] Courts will not enforce a remedy for an adhesive software license that "fails of its essential purpose." If a court finds a remedy has failed of its essential purpose, aggrieved consumers should have the full panoply of UCITA remedies at their disposal.

---

[388] The issue of unconscionability is a question of law and must be decided by the trial judge rather than by the jury.

[389] Maxwell v. Fidelity Financial Services, Inc., 184 Ariz. 82, 88, 907 P.2d 51, 57 (2000).

[390] Defendants are given an opportunity to present evidence of the circumstances existing at the time of the making of the license agreement or other online contract:

> If it is claimed or appears to the court that a contract or any term thereof may be unconscionable, the parties must be afforded a reasonable opportunity to present evidence as to its commercial setting, purpose, and effect to assist the court in making the determination.

UCITA § 111(a) (2000).

[391] UCITA § 111 (2000).

[392] UCC § 2-719 (2000).

White and Summers observe that "it is hard to find any provision in Article 2 that has been more successfully used by aggrieved buyers in the last 25 years than Section 2-719(2)."[393] Official Comment 1 to 2-719 states that the statutory purpose of the failure of essential purpose doctrine:

> [I]t is of the very essence of a sales contract that at least minimum adequate remedies be available. If the parties intend to conclude a contract for sale within this Article they must accept the legal consequence that that there be at least a fair quantum of remedy for breach of the obligations or duties outlined in the contract.[394]

Revised Article 2 retains the doctrine of "failure of essential purpose."[395] Section 803 provides that if an exclusive or limited remedy "fails of its essential purpose, the aggrieved party may pursue other remedies under [UCITA]."[396] The commercial reality is that mass-market license agreements are adhesive contracts offered on a "take it or leave it" basis.

UCITA's adoption of the failure of essential purpose doctrine moderates the harsh effects of the licensor who attempts to offer only a sole and exclusive remedy disclaiming all remedies. Article 2 divides remedies into buyer's and seller's remedies, whereas UCITA does not differentiate remedies for licensors and licensees. Section 804 of UCITA adopts the doctrine of UCC Article 2 covering the "failure of essential purpose"[397] for remedies. If circumstances cause an exclusive or limited remedy to fail of its essential purpose, a licensee has access to all UCITA warranties and remedies.[398]

When electronic agents do unexpected things, a possibility arises that "common law concepts of mistake may supplement UCITA § 206 and § 217. In addition, the unconscionability doctrine may invalidate a term caused by breakdowns in the automated contracting processes."[399] The Official Comment to § 2-719

---

[393] James J. White and Robert S. Summers, Uniform Commercial Code § 12-10, at 449 (5th ed., 1999).

[394] UCC § 2-719, cmt. 1 (2000).

[395] Early drafts of UCITA did not incorporate Article 2's doctrine of "failure of essential purpose." Revised Article 2 adopts the rule that the buyer has a minimum adequate remedy if the sole or exclusive remedy fails. *See* UCC Revised Article 2: Sales § 2-719, at 107 (Reporter's Interim Draft, Nov. 1999). Section 2-719(b) of Revised Article 2 provides:

> (b) Where circumstances cause an exclusive or limited remedy to fail of its essential purpose in a contract other than a consumer contract, remedy may be had as provided in this Act. However, an agreement expressly providing that consequential damages are excluded is enforceable to the extent permitted under subsection d.

[396] UCITA § 803 (2000).

[397] UCC § 2-719(2).

[398] UCITA § 804 (2000).

[399] *Id.*

explains that the purpose of the failure of the essential purpose rule is to guarantee buyers a minimum adequate remedy if the sole or exclusive remedy fails.

➤ *[a] Preventive Law Pointer: Draft Your Own Excuse Sections*

Under Article 2, a disclaimer occurs when a seller of goods uses language or conduct to negate or limit implied warranties.[400] UCITA's methodology for disclaiming warranties parallels those of the provisions in Article 2. UCITA allows vendors to disclaim implied warranties, to limit their liability, and to restrict a licensee's remedies within the broad parameters of good faith, commercial reasonableness, and conscionability. A web site needs to limit liability for late delivery due to sales that tax the capacity of the delivery system. SPC should limit its liability in the event of the failure of a third party or of commercial impracticability. Courts will not excuse late delivery even if the demand was unprecedented or shortfalls occurred in the supply chain. Toysrus.com, for example, was the target of several class action lawsuits for the late delivery of 1999 Christmas gifts.[401]

Our analysis of the decided cases under § 2-613 through § 2-615 reveals that courts are unsympathetic to seller's excuses.[402] The doctrine of commercial impracticality in Section 2-615 is almost never successfully invoked in the event of shortfalls in the supply chain or unprecedented price hikes. Similarly, UCITA excuse sections are unlikely to provide licensors with relief in similar circumstances.

Courts take the position that the parties could have protected themselves by contract terms with floors and ceilings on the price. A clause that conditions availability on supply is also likely to be enforceable in a commercial setting. Do not rely on the UCC defaults to "excuse" performance. Draft your own *force majeure* clauses. The courts expect that commercial sellers are in the best position to devise their own excuse section.

[F] Electronic Contracting Rules

UCITA provides contracting rules that will permit the further expansion of electronic commerce. UCITA's approach is to favor open standards for e-commerce that are technologically neutral:

---

[400] UCC § 2-316 provides the methodology for disclaiming and limiting warranties.

[401] Class actions were filed against toysrus.com in Alabama, Washington, and other states for late delivery of 1999 Christmas gifts. *See* Theresa Forsman, Toysrus.com Sued Again Over Deliveries (visited Feb. 1, 2000), http://www.beren.com/biz/toys19200001193.htm.

[402] The UCC Reporting Service published by Callaghan reprints all decided cases under a given section of the Code.

The advent of the Internet as a commercial information resource has high-lighted the importance of "electronic commerce," including electronic con-tracting issues. UCITA has been one source of principles for development of state law rules on contract aspects of electronic commerce. These rules are coordinated with the Uniform Electronic Transactions Act (UETA). However, they go beyond the purely procedural rules in that Act and provide a general contract law framework for electronic transactions involving computer infor-mation, where a contract can be formed and performed electronically.[403]

UCITA, like Article 2, does not specifically define offer, acceptance, or con-sideration, but instead incorporates common law definitions. It provides legal rules for the use of electronic agents in making and performing contracts and also vali-dates "automated transactions," which are contracts formed or performed by elec-tronic messaging.[404]

Almost one-half of all U.S. states have already adopted legislation authoriz-ing electronic equivalents to writing requirements. UCITA, along with UETA and proposed revisions of Article 2 and Article 2A, establishes a uniform state law principle that allows electronic "authentication" as a form of signature and recog-nizes the equivalence of electronic "records" and paper writings. The second issue deals with how one establishes the terms of an electronic contract. UETA does not generally deal with this issue; UCITA builds on two concepts to set out a frame-work for contracting and establishing contract terms.

Electronic contracts, by their very nature, are dynamic and often multilayered transactions. With a layered contract, agreement to a contract may not occur at a single point in time. Under webwrap contracts, a party will manifest assent to dif-ferent terms at different points in time. Section 112 provides that a manifestation of assent creates a binding contract if the party had reason to know that its acts con-stituted assent.[405] An opportunity to review is a predicate for manifesting assent.

UCITA § 202 follows Article 2 of the UCC in providing liberal contract for-mation rules for cyberspace transactions and other computer information contracts. "Signed" is defined to mean a mark made with the intent to authenticate, which may be broad enough to include clickwrap agreements. The general rules for "offer and acceptance" are covered by § 203 of UCITA. Section 204 governs the problem of acceptance with varying terms. Conditional offer or acceptance is covered by § 205. The use of electronic agents for offer and acceptance is governed by § 206.

UCITA adapts the concept of manifestation of assent to contract terms to apply to Internet or online contracts.[406] UCITA provides the legal infrastructure for

---

[403] UCITA Prefatory Note (NCCUSL Annual Meeting Draft, July 2000).

[404] UCITA § 102(7) (2000).

[405] *Id.* § 112.

[406] UCITA's Reporter adapted the concept of manifestation of assent from the Restatement (Sec-ond) of Contracts.

a wide range of electronic contracts. As with Articles 2 and 2A, an Internet or online contract may be enforced, despite having open terms.

[1] Statute of Frauds in Cyberspace

The Statute of Frauds is a statutory requirement that certain classes of contracts be evidenced by a writing in order to be enforceable. Originally enacted in England in 1677, the statute was intended to reduce the risks of fraud and false testimony.[407] In this country, "virtually all states have enacted their own version of the statute,"[408] and a less restrictive version of the statute has been incorporated in the Uniform Commercial Code.[409] The United States stands alone in adopting the Statute of Frauds for sales, leasing, and licensing transactions of a threshold amount.[410]

UCITA updates the Statute of Frauds for online contracts by treating a "record" as a functional equivalent of "pen-and-paper" signatures. A record "means information that is inscribed on a tangible medium or that is stored in an electronic or other medium and is retrievable in perceivable form."[411]

UCITA is consistent with the Federal E-Signature Act in its treatment of the electronic record as the functional equivalent of writing.[412] UCITA provides essential legal infrastructure for many different forms of electronic contracts. Section 201 of UCITA requires an authenticated record for enforcing license agreements that are $5,000 or greater and the license is for more than a year.[413] As with Articles 2 and 2A, several exceptions apply to the writing requirement: for example, a license agreement is enforceable after completed or partial performance, an admission in court that a contract exists, or a merchant licensor's failure to answer a confirming record from another merchant.[414]

---

[407] E. Allan Farnsworth, Contracts § 6.1 (2d ed., 1990).

[408] *Id.*

[409] *See, e.g.,* UCC § 2-201 ("a contract for the sale of goods for the price of $500 or more is not enforceable by way of action or defense unless there is some writing sufficient to indicate that a contract for sale has been made between the parties and signed by the party against whom enforcement is sought").

[410] *See* UCC §§ 2-201, 2A-201; UCITA § 201.

[411] UCITA § 102(55) (1999).

[412] Section 107(d) binds a person who uses electronic agents, "even if no individual was aware of or reviewed the agent's operations or the results of the operation." *Id.* § 107(d); *see* Electronic Signatures in Global and National Commerce Act (effective Oct. 1, 2000).

[413] *Id.* § 201(a).

[414] *Id.* §§ 201(c)(1), 201(c)(2), 201(c)(2)(d).

[G] Warranties

UCITA adopts the concepts and methods of warranties of authority and quality from Articles 2 and 2A of the UCC. UCITA warranties are updated to adapt to the online contracting world. Warranties of quality consist of express and implied warranties. UCITA divides warranties into two broad categories: warranties of noninfringement or warranties of performance, which parallels the approach to warranties in Article 2 and 2A.

[1] Express and Implied

UCITA permits licensors to contractually exclude all implied warranties provided that the language is clear, unambiguous, and conspicuous; the limitations are not unconscionable; and the license agreement does not violate fundamental public policies. UCITA divides warranties into two types: warranties of authority (or noninfringement) and performance-based warranties of quality.

Section 401 is the chief warranty that the licensor delivered free of infringing computer information. Merchant licensors warrant that information is delivered free of claims of intellectual property infringement but does not apply to patent licenses. The warranty of noninfringement is functionally equivalent to the warranty of title in Article 2.[415] As with Article 2, there are special merchant rules imposing a higher duty on professional licensors.[416] A merchant licensor warrants that information is delivered free of claims of infringement or misappropriation.[417] Section 401(b)(2) notes that exclusive license agreements are limited by fair use, compulsory licenses, and other recognized limits to exclusivity.[418]

UCITA adapts to information transfers the warranty of quiet possession, which originated in transactions in real property followed in Article 2A, but not Article 2 of the UCC. The essence of the quiet enjoyment warranty is the right of a licensee to exercise contractual rights for the duration of the license without interference by a licensor or a third party. The quiet enjoyment warranty applies only to interference caused by acts or omissions of the licensors. The quiet enjoyment warranty that the licensor will not interfere with licensee's enjoyment of its interest lasts for the duration of the license agreement.[419] Licensees receive "peace of mind" that they are not purchasing an intellectual property lawsuit along with

---

[415] UCC § 2-312's warranty of title is adapted to licensing where title does not pass to the licensee. Special rules are devised for exclusive licenses and the interference warranty not found in Article 2.

[416] Merchant/licensors are those who "regularly deal in information of the kind." UCITA § 401(a) (1999).

[417] UCITA § 401(a) (2000).

[418] *Id.* § 401(b)(2)(B).

[419] *Id.* § 401(b)(1).

software. UCITA's noninfringement authority imposes a strict liability standard if the software infringes title or intellectual property rights of others.

[2]   Warranties of Quality

[a]   *Express Warranties*

UCITA's express warranty provisions for computer information transactions are substantially similar to those of UCC § 2-313. Affirmations of fact made by the licensor about computer software or information are express warranties to the extent that they form the "basis of the bargain." Express warranties under UCITA are created by licensors in banner advertisements, sales literature, and advertisements.[420] Web site promotional materials, product descriptions, samples, or advertisements may create e-commerce warranties.

How are express warranties created?	"Affirmations of Fact" made by the licensor to its licensee in any manner including online brochures, advertising, and sales literature posted on a web site.[421]
What is test for an express warranty?	Does the affirmation of fact relate to information and become "basis of the bargain" or is it merely seller's talk?[422]
What words are critical to creating express warranties?	"It is not necessary to use formal words such as 'warrant' or 'guarantee' or state a specific intention to make a warranty."[423]
What web site activity creates express warranties?	(1) Description of information in virtual catalogs; (2) samples, models, or demonstration of software or other products; (3) any banner advertisement, description, sample, or demonstration if it goes to the basis of the bargain. Technical specifications of computer systems.
What is the difference between express warranties and puffery?	Puffery is a mere statement of opinion that does not form an express warranty. Express warranties are actionable representations.[424]

[b]   *Implied Warranties of Merchantability*

Implied warranties of quality for computer information extend the concept of the implied warranty of merchantability of UCC Article 2 to computer information

---

[420] *Id.* § 402.
[421] *Id.* § 402(a)(1).
[422] *Id.* § 402(a)(2).
[423] *Id.* § 402(b).
[424] *Id.* § 402, Reporter's cmt. 2.

transactions. UCITA § 403 extends Article 2's merchantability warranty to cyber-space. Computer programs must be fit for their ordinary purpose. UCITA's implied warranty is that "the computer program is fit for the ordinary purposes for which such computer programs are used."[425] A computer program need not be the most efficient, but it must meet general industry standards for performance. A distributor also receives the warranty that information is adequately packaged and labeled and that the copies are "of even kind, quality, and quantity with each unit."[426]

Performance standards for implied warranty of merchantability	Description
1. Is the computer software fit for its ordinary purpose?	A computer program is fit for the ordinary purpose for which such computer programs are used.[427]
2. Is the program adequately packaged and labeled?	The redistribution warranty is that "the program is adequately packaged and labeled as the agreement requires."[428]
3. Are the copies of computer software within the variations permitted in the agreement?	"[I]n the case of multiple copies, the copies are within the variations permitted by the agreement, of even kind, quality, and quantity, within each unit and among all units involved."[429]
4. Do computer programs conform to labels or descriptions?	"[T]he program conforms to the promises or affirmations of fact made on the container or label."[430]
5. Are there any implied warranties from the parties' course of dealing or from the software industry?	"Unless disclaimed or modified, other implied warranties may arise from course of dealing or usage of trade."[431]
6. Are there any informational content warranties?	Section 403 does not create informational content warranties as to information content such as aesthetics, market appeal, accuracy, or subjective quality.[432]

[c] Implied Warranty of System Integration

UCITA's implied warranty of system integration is the functional equivalent of the warranty in UCC § 2-312 of "fitness for a particular purpose." The systems integration warranty applies where the customer relies on the software licensor's

---

[425] *Id.* § 403(a)(1).
[426] *Id.* § 403(a)(2)(A)(B).
[427] *Id.* § 403(a)(1).
[428] *Id.* § 403(a)(2)(A).
[429] *Id.* § 403(a)(2)(B).
[430] *Id.* § 403(a)(3).
[431] *Id.* § 403(b).
[432] *Id.* § 403(c).

expertise to make computer information suitable for a particular computer system.[433] SPC, for example could be making a systems integration warranty if a sales representative told a customer that its software would perform with a Windows 2000 platform. The licensor must know of "any particular purpose for which the computer information is required and that the licensee is relying on the licensor's skill or judgment to select, develop, or furnish suitable information."[434] If the transaction resembles a services contract, the warranty does not guarantee results.[435] The systems integration warranty is that the computer components will function as a system, but not necessarily as an optimal system.

[d]   Warranties for Information Content

UCITA, unlike Article 2, devises an implied warranty for informational inaccuracies caused by a merchant's negligence.[436] This special warranty applies to merchant licensors or to transfers of information not performed with reasonable care. The warranty for informational content does not arise for published content or when the licensor is merely acting as an information transfer conduit without providing editorial services.[437] Section 404 is based on reasonable care, and this warranty may be disclaimed despite UCITA's general prohibition against disclaiming reasonableness and care.[438]

[e]   Disclaiming and Limiting Liability

Just as does Article 2, UCITA permits the parties to disclaim or modify all implied warranties by words or conduct.[439] UCITA validates the universal practice of the software industry in offering software or other computer information on an "as-is" basis, without warranties. The software industry universally disclaims all implied warranties. Microsoft, for example, disclaims all express or implied warranties for its software products. Microsoft expressly disclaims any warranty using the following clause:

> THE SOFTWARE PRODUCT AND ANY RELATED DOCUMENTATION IS PROVIDED "AS IS" WITHOUT WARRANTY OF ANY KIND, EITHER EXPRESS OR IMPLIED, INCLUDING, WITHOUT LIMITATION, THE IMPLIED WARRANTIES OF MERCHANTABILITY, FITNESS

---

[433] *Id.* § 405.
[434] *Id.* § 405(a).
[435] *Id.* § 405(a)(2).
[436] *Id.* § 404.
[437] *Id.* § 404(b)(1)(2).
[438] *Id.* § 404(c).
[439] *Id.* § 406.

FOR A PARTICULAR PURPOSE, OR NON-INFRINGEMENT. THE ENTIRE RISK ARISING
OUT OF USE OR PERFORMANCE OF THE SOFTWARE PRODUCT REMAINS WITH YOU.[440]

Content providers typically do not make warranties as to the adequacy or
accuracy of information. NEXIS-LEXIS a leading legal information company, and
McGraw-Hill (M-H) make the following limited warranty:

NEITHER M-H [NOR NEXIS/LEXIS OR ITS SOURCES] MAKE ANY WARRANTY, EXPRESS
OR IMPLIED, AS TO ACCURACY, ADEQUACY, OR COMPLETENESS OF INFORMATION
CONTAINED IN THE MATERIALS, WHICH ARE PROVIDED "AS-IS," WITHOUT WAR-
RANTY AS TO MERCHANTABILITY, FITNESS FOR A PARTICULAR PURPOSE OR USE, OR
RESULTS. NEITHER M-H NOR ANY SOURCES SHALL BE LIABLE FOR ANY ERRORS OR
OMISSIONS NOR SHALL THEY BE LIABLE FOR ANY DAMAGES, WHETHER DIRECT OR
INDIRECT, SPECIAL OR CONSEQUENTIAL, INCLUDING LOSS OF PROFITS, EVEN IF
ADVISED OF THE POSSIBILITY. IN NO EVENT SHALL THE CUMULATIVE LIABILITY OF
M-H FOR ALL ACTIONS EXCEED THE AVERAGE MONTHLY FEE PAID BY SUBSCRIBER
FOR ACCESS TO THE MATERIALS.[441]

The disclaimers in the above online contracts follow a methodology that
closely parallels those of Article 2 and Article 2A of the UCC. As with Article 2,
a written disclaimer of the implied warranty of merchantability must mention
"merchantability" or "quality or use words of similar import."[442] To disclaim the
warranty of fitness, the exclusion must be by a written and conspicuous statement.[443] Disclaimers or limitations of liability under UCITA must be conspicuously displayed in a record. Although no particular form of language is necessary
to disclaim UCITA warranties,[444] to disclaim or modify the warranty of accuracy
the record "must mention accuracy or use words of similar import."[445]

UCITA disclaimers and liability limitations are subject to state and federal
consumer law and common law and equitable doctrines such as the covenant of
good faith and fair dealing and unconscionability. Many web sites will place a
notice that they seek disclaimers "to the full extent permissible by applicable

---

[440] Microsoft, Inc., End-User License Agreement for Microsoft Software, clause 8 (stating "limitation of liability").

[441] LEXIS-NEXIS, Services Supplemental Terms for Specific Materials, July 1, 1998 (visited
Feb. 9, 1999), http://www.lexis-nexis.com/incc/about/terms.htm.

[442] UCITA § 406(b)(1)(A) (2000).

[443] *Id.* § 406(b)(1)(2).

[444] Language in the record should disclaim each warranty or use a phrase such as: "this program
is provided with all faults and the entire risk as to satisfactory quality, performance, accuracy, and
effort is with the user." *Id.,* § 406(b)(1)(3). *See also* UCC § 2-316(2) (noting that "language must
mention merchantability and in case of a writing must be conspicuous, and to exclude or modify an
implied warranty of a warranty of fitness the exclusion must be by a writing and conspicuous").

[445] UCITA § 406(b)(1)(B) (2000).

law."[446] Web site disclaimers may not alter consumer protection statutes, which may preclude the disclaiming of implied warranties in consumer transactions.[447]

A UCITA contract may disclaim all liabilities with language such as that the information "is provided with all faults, and the entire risk as to satisfactory quality, performance, accuracy, and effort is with the user" or similar words.[448] Amazon.com, for example, follows UCITA's methodology in disclaiming damages of all kinds:

> THIS SITE IS PROVIDED BY AMAZON.COM ON AN "AS IS" BASIS. AMAZON.COM MAKES NO REPRESENTATIONS OR WARRANTIES OF ANY KIND, EXPRESS OR IMPLIED, AS TO THE OPERATION OF THE SITE OR THE INFORMATION, CONTENT, MATERIALS, OR PRODUCTS INCLUDED ON THIS SITE. TO THE FULL EXTENT PERMISSIBLE BY APPLICABLE LAW, AMAZON.COM DISCLAIMS ALL WARRANTIES, EXPRESS OR IMPLIED, INCLUDING, BUT NOT LIMITED TO, IMPLIED WARRANTIES OF MERCHANTABILITY AND FITNESS FOR A PARTICULAR PURPOSE. AMAZON.COM WILL NOT BE LIABLE FOR ANY DAMAGES OF ANY KIND ARISING FROM THE USE OF THIS SITE, INCLUDING, BUT NOT LIMITED TO DIRECT, INDIRECT, INCIDENTAL, PUNITIVE, AND CONSEQUENTIAL DAMAGES.[449]

[f] Specialized Computer Warranty Rules

UCITA forges special rules for computer information warranties where the licensee reprograms or modifies computer software. Essentially, no warranties cover programs that the licensee modifies or alters.[450] Warranties "must be construed as consistent with each other."[451] Exact or technical specifications for computer information displace or supplant "general language of description."[452]

Samples displace general language of description and express warranties trump inconsistent implied warranties other than system integration warranties.[453] UCITA sets the rules for third-party beneficiaries of information-based warranties.[454] Warranties, in general, extend to end-users or those who will exercise information or informational rights. UCITA extends third-party beneficiary concepts to extend warranties to the licensee's immediate family or household.

---

[446] *Id.*

[447] *See, e.g.*, Mass. Gen. Laws Ann. ch. 106, § 2-316A (2000) (prohibiting sellers from disclaiming the implied warranty of merchantability in consumer transactions including sales and services).

[448] UCITA § 406(b)(1)(3) (2000).

[449] *See* http://www.amazon.com/exec/obidos/subst/misc/copyright.html/.

[450] *Id.* § 407.

[451] *Id.* § 408.

[452] *Id.* § 408(1).

[453] *Id.* § 408(2)-(3).

[454] *Id.* § 409.

TABLE 6.1
Methods for Disclaiming Online Warranties

Type of Warranty	Method of Disclaiming Warranty
Implied Warranty of Quiet Enjoyment and Noninfringement, Section 401. The "quiet enjoyment" warranty is that the licensor will not interfere with the licensee's exercise of rights. Information must also be free of infringement claims by third parties.	"Except as otherwise provided in subsection (e), a warranty under this section may be disclaimed or modified only by specific language or by circumstances that give the licensee reason to know that the licensor does not warrant that competing claims do not exist or that the licensor purports to grant only the rights it may have. In an automated transaction, the language is sufficient if it is conspicuous."[a]
Express Warranty, Section 402.	Express warranties may not be disclaimed by general language of disclaimers. Courts will construe contract terms of disclaimer and language of express warranties as consistent with each other. If there is an inconsistency, the express warranty controls. Express warranties may be excluded by the parol evidence rule.[b]
Implied Warranty: Merchantability of Computer Program, Section 403.	The implied warranty of merchantability may be modified or disclaimed. "To disclaim or modify an implied warranty arising under Section 403 language must mention 'merchantability' or 'quality' or use words of similar import"[c] and if a record must be conspicuous."[d]
Implied Warranty: Informational Content, Section 404.	This warranty may be disclaimed but the "language in a record must mention 'accuracy' or use words of similar import."[e] All implied warranties, but not express warranties "are disclaimed by expressions like 'as is' or 'with all faults' or other language that in common understanding call the licensee's attention to the disclaimer of warranties and makes plain that there are no implied warranties."[f] In addition, implied warranties are disclaimable by inspection of a sample or model and by course of performance, course of dealing, or usage of trade.[g]
Implied Warranty: Licensee's Purpose; System Integration, Section 405.	Specific language or circumstances indicating that the warranty is not given can disclaim warranty. "There is no warranty that this information or efforts will fulfill any of your particular purposes or needs, or words of similar import."[h] A licensor may also track the language of disclaimer in Articles 2 and 2A of the UCC to disclaim or modify "an implied warranty of fitness for a particular purpose."[i]

[a] UCITA § 401(3)(d) (2000).
[b] *Id.* § 406, Reporter's note 2.
[c] *Id.* § 406(b)(1)(A).
[d] *Id.* § 406(b)(5).
[e] *Id.* § 406(b)(1)(B).
[f] *Id.* § 406(c).
[g] *Id.*, § 406(d), (e).
[h] *Id.* § 406(b)(2).
[i] *Id.* § 406(b)(4).

[H]   UCITA's Canons of Contract Construction

UCITA considers a license agreement to consist of the writing plus supplemental terms. Every UCITA contract consists of (1) express terms of the license agreement; (2) course of performance; (3) course of dealing; and (4) custom or usage of trade.[455] If the parties to a license agreement reduce the final expression of their agreement to a computer record, the parol evidence rule will exclude prior or contemporaneous agreements. UCITA's parol evidence rule substitutes the term "record" for a writing but is otherwise parallel to UCC § 2-202. Like Article 2, UCITA permits integrated writings to be supplemented by course of performance, course of dealing, and usage of trade.

Courts may also receive evidence of consistent additional terms, unless the record states that it is "a complete and exclusive statement of the terms of the agreement."[456] UCITA permits background terms—course of performance, course of dealing, and usage of trade—to supplement a final and exclusive record. The policy underlying UCITA's parol evidence rule the preservation of the integrity of a computer record that is a final expression of agreement between the parties.[457] Section 302 establishes a hierarchy of contract terms.[458]

As with § 2-209, UCITA contracts may be modified without "consideration." UCITA also provides a methodology for precluding modification or rescission except by an authenticated record.[459] Many license agreements are structured as rolling contracts. Section 304 provides that terms of a contract with successive performances apply to the whole.[460] Access contracts, for example, may change terms of performance by giving notice to the other party. UCITA follows the liberal philosophy of the UCC in permitting contracts to be formed even through the particulars of performance are open.[461]

Standardized gap-fillers play a key role in commercial law because Article 2 permits parties to form an enforceable sales contract even where open terms are present. The UCC provides a number of gap-filler provisions for sales contracts. UCITA follows the UCC in permitting performance with open terms. The default terms in UCITA are those that "are reasonable in light of the commercial circumstances existing at the time of agreement."[462] Article 2 forges specific gap-fillers

---

[455] *Id.* § 301(1).

[456] *Id.* § 301.

[457] *Id.*

[458] Express terms supplant course of performance, course of dealing, and usage of trade. Course of performance supplants course of dealing and usage of trade. Course of dealing prevails over usage of trade, which is at the bottom of the hierarchy of terms. *Id.* § 302(a)(1)(2)(3).

[459] *Id.* § 303(b).

[460] *Id.* § 304(a).

[461] *Id.* § 305.

[462] *Id.* § 306.

for price, delivery in single or multiple lots, place of delivery, time provisions, and other terms not settled by the parties.[463] UCITA provides gap fillers for what rights are transferred by a license granting clause,[464] duration of a contract,[465] and what it means to perform to another party's satisfaction.[466]

[I]   Transfer of Interests and Rights

Part V of UCITA deemphasizes the role of title, because title does not pass in the typical license agreement.[467] Software is licensed, not sold: Transfer of a copy of software does not transfer informational rights because the licensor retains title and grants only a right to use information.[468]

UCITA supports the free assignability of licenses of information. A purchaser of software may sell or otherwise assign or transfer the rights to use the software unless the agreement otherwise provides. Software or other computer information may be freely assigned unless it "materially increases the burden or risk imposed on the other party" or otherwise materially affects performance.[469] UCITA permits licensors to inject anti-assignment clauses where a licensee cannot voluntarily or involuntarily assign its rights absent the licensor's consent. Part V of UCITA also sets forth the complex rules for financing arrangements for software.[470] UCITA validates contractual restrictions on transfer.

[J]   Performance Standards

The performance of a sale contract usually begins with the seller's tender of conforming goods. Part VI of UCITA deals with the performance of computer information contracts and adopts the Article 2 concept of tender for cyberspace contracts. In Article 2, tender refers to the duty of the seller to make goods available to the buyer that conform to the contract specifications. In a sale agreement, the buyer has the right to reject goods "if the goods or the tender of delivery fail

---

[463] Many of the UCC gap-fillers in § 2-305 to § 2-311 boil down to reasonable business practices, which is the same underlying philosophy as that of UCITA. UCITA, like Article 2, uses gap-fillers to fill in open terms. UCITA's gap-fillers provide general terms based upon reasonable business practices. UCITA §§ 306 to 308 apply unless the parties otherwise agree. Section 306, for example, provides a general interpretation rule for issues not covered by the license agreement. The general default rule is that the term be "reasonable in light of the commercial circumstances existing at the time of the agreement." *See* UCITA, § 306 (2000).

[464] *Id.* § 307.

[465] *Id.* § 308.

[466] *Id.* § 309.

[467] *Id.* § 502.

[468] *Id.* § 501.

[469] *Id.* § 503(1)(B).

[470] *Id.* §§ 507-511.

in any respect to conform to the contract."[471] Article 2 follows "a perfect tender rule that permits a buyer to reject goods if they fail to conform in any respect to the contract."[472] UCITA's concept of tender is that of a licensor transmitting a copy of software or otherwise enabling use or access to software, databases, or other information.[473] An online store may give a licensee access to downloadable software, which will constitute "tender." Westlaw or another online access provider will tender delivery by giving the subscriber an ID to enable use of databases. The seller that tenders goods that conform to the agreement is entitled to payment; the buyer must accept and pay the contract price if the goods conform to the contract.[474]

UCITA adopts a "material breach" standard rather than the perfect tender rule of Article 2. An information contract may be cancelled if the licensor is unable to cure a material breach.[475] UCITA performance standards are concurrent: Substantial performance of one party is conditional on the substantial performance by the other party. As with Article 2, acceptance occurs through three methods: (1) express acceptance; (2) failure to make an effective rejection; or (3) doing anything with the software or information inconsistent with the licensor's ownership.[476]

A buyer of goods has the right to inspect goods before payment or acceptance. A party receiving a copy of computer information has a similar right to inspect copies to ensure that they conform to the license agreement.[477] Under UCITA, a licensee must accept goods provided they conform to the agreement. Once a licensee accepts a tender, the licensor has a right to the contract price.[478] UCITA has special performance standards for access contracts, support agreements, and contracts involving publishers, dealers, and end users.[479]

The risk of loss provision of Article 2 covers situations where neither party is responsible for the loss, destruction, or theft of goods.[480] UCITA adopts rules for risk of loss and excuses for nonperformance from Article 2. The risk of loss to a copy of information passes to the licensee upon receipt.[481] UCITA's risk of loss

---

[471] UCC § 2-601 (2000).

[472] *Id.*

[473] UCITA §§ 2-601 to 602 (2000).

[474] UCC §§ 2-507, 2-511 (2000). *See also id.* § 2-301.

[475] UCITA's concept of "material breach" parallels the "fundamental breach" standard of Article 25 of the Convention on the International Sale of Goods and Restatement (Second) of Contracts § 241.

[476] UCITA § 2-609(a)(5) (2000).

[477] *Compare* UCC § 2-513 *with* UCITA § 2-608.

[478] UCITA § 610 (2000).

[479] *See id.* §§ 611-613.

[480] UCC §§ 2-509, 2-510 (2000).

[481] UCITA § 614(a) (2000).

rules address the problem of copies lost or destroyed. UCITA shares the heritage of the UCC in rules for shipment and destination contracts. For shipment contracts, "the risk of loss passes to the licensee when the copy is delivered to the carrier."[482]

Destination contracts for information require a copy to be tendered at that destination.[483] UCITA adopts the excuse concepts of Article 2 to cyberspace including impracticability.[484] UCITA adopts the common law doctrine of "frustration of purpose" to cyberspace and other online contracts. A license agreement is excused if there is an "occurrence of a contingency whose nonoccurrence was a basic assumption on which the contract was made."[485] UCITA has ground rules for the termination of a contract that pertain to use restrictions in license agreements.[486] Termination has the legal effect of ending the contract and discharging executory obligations.

[K] Tender, Acceptance, Rejection, and Revocation

Part VII of UCITA set forth the basic rules for tender, acceptance, rejection, revocation, and repudiation of computer information transactions. Even if a licensor tenders software with a substantial defect, it will have an opportunity to cure, which is borrowed from UCC § 2-508.[487] A licensee that accepts software or other computer information must notify the licensor of any breach. The failure to notify the other party of a breach has the legal consequence of waiver of all remedies for the breach.[488] The purpose of the notice requirement (as in § 2-607(3)) is to give the licensor an opportunity to cure any defective performance.[489]

A licensee may refuse a defective tender of software, but the seller must have an opportunity to cure any problems. UCITA assumes that if the computer software or other information does not measure up to contract specifications, a right exists to refuse performance.[490] Even if a licensee rightfully rejects performance, it is still bound by contractual restrictions on the use of software.[491] A licensee may revoke acceptance if the nonconformity in software or other computer information constitutes a material breach.[492] UCITA's methodology requires revocation to occur within a reasonable time after discovering the material nonconformities.

---

[482] *Id.* § 614(b)(1).

[483] *Id.* § 614(b)(2).

[484] UCC § 2-615 to § 2-616 has its parallel in UCITA § 615 (1999).

[485] UCITA § 615 (1999).

[486] *Id.* §§ 616-617 (stating rules for termination and notice of termination).

[487] *Compare* UCC § 2-508 *with* UCITA § 701 (2000).

[488] UCITA § 702(b) (2000).

[489] *Id.* § 703.

[490] *Id.* § 704.

[491] *Id.* § 706.

[492] *Id.* § 707.

The licensee must notify the licensor promptly of the breach in revocation just as with rejection. The consequence of failure of notice is that all remedies are waived. Revocation, as with Article 2, places the party in the same position they would have been for rejection or refusal. UCITA § 708 also adopts the doctrine of adequate assurance of performance from § 2-609. The concept of an adequate assurance of performance protects the parties "peace of mind" that a license agreement will be performed.[493] An anticipatory repudiation is intent to breach a contract whose performance is not yet due. A party may seek adequate assurance of performance and suspend performance.

Anticipatory repudiation occurs where a party to a license agreement advises the other that performance will not be forthcoming. Section 709 permits the aggrieved party to await performance or to treat the license agreement as preemptively breached, immediately giving the nonbreaching party the full array of UCITA remedies.[494] UCITA's retraction of anticipatory repudiation provision is identical to § 2-611. A repudiation may be retracted unless the aggrieved party has changed its position.[495] UCITA follows the "avoidable consequences" rule of the common law and expects parties to take steps to mitigate loss.

[L]   Remedies

[1]   UCITA's Validation of Freedom of Contract

UCITA does not permit an aggrieved party to recover more than once for the same loss.[496] UCITA gives the parties freedom to devise their own remedies. Remedies for breach of a license agreement "are determined by the [license] agreement."[497] UCITA remedies are default gap-fillers that apply in the absence of a specific agreement between the parties. The other party must be placed in breach before UCITA's remedies apply. UCITA rejects the doctrine of election of remedies and grants the power to modify default terms, including all remedies. The parties in an online agreement may bypass or contract around UCITA's rights and remedies. UCITA remedies are recoverable if the breach is material or non-material.[498]

[2]   Duties upon Cancellation

A licensee who violates a use restriction in a license agreement or repudiates a contract is in breach. A license agreement may not be cancelled unless a breach

---

[493] *Id.* § 708.
[494] *Id.* § 709.
[495] *Id.* § 710.
[496] *Id.* § 801.
[497] *Id.* § 701(a).
[498] *Id.*

of contract is material. A licensee will have the duty to return software to the licensor at the end of the term. In addition, a licensee may have a continuing duty of confidentiality.

[3] Material Breach

UCITA § 701(b) defines the uncured "material breach" as a substantial failure to perform as essential element of the agreement, a standard paralleling CISG's fundamental breach standard in Article 25.[499] The parties may define what constitutes a material breach in the license agreement. An events of default clause may define specifically what a "substantial failure to perform" or fundamental breach means.[500] Once a license agreement is cancelled, permission to use software or computer information is also cancelled.

UCITA adopts a substantial performance, or material breach, standard that differs from the perfect tender rule for performance in Article 2, which is not the standard in any country outside the United States. A material breach is "a substantial failure to perform an agreed term that is an essential element of the agreement."[501] A substantial breach is one "that deprives the aggrieved party of a significant benefit it reasonably expected under the contract."[502] In contrast, Article 2 of the UCC permits a buyer to obtain substitute goods if the goods fail "in any respect to conform to the contract."[503]

The perfect tender rule is an unrealistic standard for the software industry: Software may be composed of millions of lines of code. A licensee should not be able to cancel a software contract because of a minor bug or errant line of code.

Under a fundamental breach standard, a question exits as to what level of performance deficit in the software would warrant rejection. The vast majority of fundamental breaches occur when software has bugs that prevent it from performing important contract criteria.

A study of software vendors concluded that the principal types of performance problems with software were (a) form of reports; (b) processing speeds; (c) amount of data that could be handled; and (d) number of multiple users or peripherals that could be used with a computer system.[504] The case law reflects that

---

[499] Convention on Contracts for the International Sale of Goods (CISG), art. 25.

[500] UCITA § 701(b) (1999).

[501] *Id.* § 701(b)(2).

[502] *Id.* § 701(b).

[503] UCC §§ 2-601, 2-712.

[504] Cynthia Anthony and Michael Rustad, Breach and Adaptation of Computer Software Contracts: A Report to the ABA Software Licensing Subcommittee (June 15, 1993) (surveying industries which produced software for mass-market design applications; student loans; accounting activities; health care insurance claims; and telecommunications services).

fundamental breach in bad software cases centers on the failure of acceptance testing,[505] deviation from functional specifications,[506] late delivery of computer software and products,[507] the failure of compatibility,[508] and failure to process data at
a specified processing speed.[509]

UCITA requires the nonbreaching party to comply with contractual restrictions on the use of computer software or other information, despite the other
party's breach.[510] Cancellation is a remedy available to the nonbreaching party
only if the breach is material and uncured by the other party.[511] The rightfully
rejecting seller has duties as to rejected goods. Merchant-buyers may also have a
duty to resell rejected goods.[512] Under UCITA, a licensee in possession of licensed
information must follow the instructions of the licensor after cancellation.[513]

[4]   Exclusive and Limited Remedy

UCITA permits the parties to substitute an exclusive and limited remedy for
the default remedies of the statute.[514] Section 803 permits the aggrieved party to
have access to all UCITA remedies if the exclusive or limited remedy "fails of its
essential purpose."[515] Similarly, if an exclusive remedy is found to be unconscionable, the aggrieved party may seek any of the statutory remedies of UCITA.[516]

---

[505] *See, e.g.*, Whittaker Corp. v. Calspan Corp., 810 F. Supp. 457 (W.D. N.Y. 1992) (finding that
"the actual variances from the contract specifications raise a material question of fact as to the value
of the delivered system").

[506] *See, e.g.*, Photo Copy, Inc. v. Software, Inc., 510 So.2d 1337 (La. Ct. App. 1987) (holding that
rejection of a computer system was warranted because the software program could not perform a key
cross-reference function and observing that the disappointed buyer's "principal motive or cause" in
busying the system was to obtain a cross-referencing function).

[507] *See, e.g.*, Cash Management Services, Inc. v. Banctec, Inc., U.S. Dist. LEXIS 10768 (D. Mass.,
Sept. 21, 1988) (finding that the late delivery of equipment prevented the vendee from making
proper acceptance testing; failure to make prompt delivery within a reasonable time or the time specified in the contract may be deemed a fundamental breach).

[508] *See, e.g.*, Foundation Software v. Digital Equipment Corp., 807 F. Supp. 1195 (D. Md. 1992)
(upholding breach of warranty action in case where vendor promised that software would run on the
customer's system).

[509] *See, e.g.*, Midland Management Corp. v. Computer Consoles Inc., U.S. Dist. LEXIS 537 (No.
87 C 971, N.D. Ill., E.D., Jan. 21, 1992) (finding that the computer system could not support more
than 16 concurrent users and that the 32-user capability warranty did not exist).

[510] UCITA § 801(b) (1999).

[511] *Id.* § 802(a).

[512] UCC § 2-603 (2000).

[513] UCITA § 802(c) (1999).

[514] *Id.* § 803(b).

[515] UCC § 2-719(2) (2000).

[516] UCITA § 803(d) (1999).

UCITA permits the licensor to limit consequential and incidental damages "unless the disclaimer or limitation is unconscionable."[517]

[5] Fundamental Public Policies

A court may refuse to enforce an online contract that violates fundamental public policies.[518] Little case law exists on what contract terms a court may find to be contrary to a fundamental public policy. A court would likely find it a violation of public policy to sell hard core pornography or human embryos on a web site. A few software licensors prohibit licensees from publicly criticizing software. Such a draconian term has a chilling effect on free expression and may be invalidated as a violation of public policy. It is unclear whether courts will use the "fundamental public policy" doctrine to invalidate unfair, oppressive, or surprising terms in mass-market agreements. European courts would find that a licensor's strict prohibition against reverse engineering likely to violate a public policy in favor of interoperability of computer systems.[519] UCITA seems to give the courts wide discretion to "avoid any result contrary to public policy," although the case law has yet to evolve.[520]

[6] Liquidated Damages

Section 804 parallels UCC § 2-718 validating the use of liquidated damages for online contracts. UCITA provides that damages "may be liquidated by agreement in any amount that is reasonable in light of the loss anticipated at the time of contracting, the actual loss or the actual or anticipated difficulties of proving loss in the event of breach."[521] UCITA, like § 2-718, will enforce liquidated damages clauses so long as the amount is not "unreasonably large."

[7] Disabling Device

Technologies have long been available for licensors to disable computer software or restrict access to databases. Electronic self-help is a UCITA remedy available to licensors as long as they follow the procedural protections UCITA gives licensees. A licensor must follow the procedural rules in Section 815(b), however,

---

[517] Id.

[518] Id. § 105.

[519] Reverse engineering is necessary to attain interoperability of computer systems. The European Community recognizes a right to reverse engineering to prevent unfair competition or what we refer to as antitrust.

[520] UCITA § 105(b) (1999).

[521] Id. § 804(a).

or be accountable to the licensee for damages. This means that if the conditions of 815(b) are not followed, no electronic self-help is available. The electronic self-help rule follows Part 5 of UCC Article 9, which governs secured transactions. Just as with Article 9, no repossession can take place where a breach of the peace would result. UCITA does not want to give licensors the unbridled right to use electronic self-help or disabling devices that will cause harm to computer systems or other foreseeable damage to persons or property other than the licensed information.

The Reporter's Notes to UCITA § 816 state that there "can be no electronic self-help where a breach of peace would result or where there is a threat of foreseeable damage of personal injury or significant physical damange to property other than the licensed information."[522] The Notes cite an example in which licensed software is integral to the funds transfer or payment systems of a banking institution or where it pertains to national security systems,"[523] and observe that "[i]n such cases, the peremptory remedy of electronic self-help threatens disruption that far exceeds the benefits of allowing its use."[524]

If self-help is unavailable, the licensor may seek injunctive or monetary relief to enforce its rights.[525] UCITA envisions an expedited review of whether a license agreement is justifiably cancelled and electronic disablement permitted. A wrongful repossession of software or information entitles the injured parties to damages. A licensee who suffers a wrongful electronic repossession may seek consequential, incidental, and direct damages. The procedural rights and obligations for electronic repossession are not disclaimable and may not be "waived by agreement."[526]

The use of disabling devices is a very controversial practice in the software industry. Even though UCITA is not yet law in most jurisdictions, it is risky to include disabling devices for self-help repossession without notice to the licensee. An online company, such as SPC, should not use disabling devices unless notice is given to the licensee prior to entering into the license agreement. The disabling device must not be triggered without notice to the licensee.

[8]   Statute of Limitations and Repose

UCITA adopts a complicated statute of limitations that combines a discovery rule with a rule of repose. Section 805 imposes a four-year statute of limitations accruing one year after the breach was or should have been discovered. The absolute limit to file an action, however, is "five years after the right of action

---

[522] *Id.* § 816 cmt. 3.
[523] *Id.*
[524] *Id.*
[525] *Id.*
[526] *Id.*

accrues."[527] The parties may agree to reduce the period of limitations to not less than one year after the cause of action accrues.[528] Different statutes of limitation and repose exist for third-party warranty claims.

[M] UCITA Checklist

Maryland and Virginia have recently adopted UCITA. In those jurisdictions, UCITA applies unless the parties have opted out by choosing another body of law. Licensors may choose to apply Virginia or Maryland law to their transaction. The parties to a UCITA agreement have freedom of contract to opt in or out of various provisions. The parties to a UCITA transaction may agree to incorporate some UCITA provisions but may not contract around duties of good faith, commercial reasonableness, or due care. The parties are not free to opt out of mandatory consumer protection, such as the Magnuson-Moss Act. UCITA cannot be used to cover transactions not otherwise within the scope of the proposed statute. The following is a checklist of issues to consider for all UCITA-related contracts.

1. **Who are the parties?** Who is the licensor or licensee? Does the license agreement use the vocabulary of license versus a sale transferring title? The purpose of licensing is to avoid the "first sale" doctrine of the Copyright Act. A licensor does not "sell" software, but licenses it. A license involves more limited rights than does a sale. If no specific term describes the parties, questions arise as to whether software is licensed on a single- or multiple-user basis.

2. **How exclusive is the license agreement?** Is it exclusive or nonexclusive? The typical mass-market license is non-exclusive, which means that the software is licensed to the general consuming public. A software license agreement tailored to a single organization may be non-exclusive or semi-exclusive.

3. **What is the term of the license agreement?** A mass-market license may be perpetual, whereas a tailored agreement may be for a designated term. When does the term of the license agreement begin? One possibility is that the term of a mass-market software license begins at the time of the downloading of the software from the licensor's site. In a development software contract, the term might begin after a period of acceptance testing or with the initial installation of the software.

4. **What law is applicable to the license agreement?** Have the parties considered the complex factors for opting in or out of UCITA? One reason to opt in is that a company, such as SPC, is engaged in electronic

---

[527] *Id.* § 805(a).
[528] *Id.* § 805(b).

commerce. UCITA validates electronic contracting practices, electronic records, and authentication. UCITA validates contract formation by electronic means, such as "click-through" agreements, as long as minimal procedural standards are met. Are SPC's B2B data messages sent without review by humans? Does SPC have a trading partner agreement supplementing UCITA? Does SPC use electronic agents to initiate or respond to electronic messages without human review?

5. **Have the parties chosen a given law and forum?** UCITA will enforce choice of law clauses to the extent that it does not diminish consumer protection. Is the contractual choice of forum reasonable and just?

6. **Has the licensor implemented an attribution procedure verifying that the digital signature, record, or message is that of the company?** Are attribution procedures commercially reasonable, and do they comply with best practices in the industry?

7. **If contracts are made by electronic agents, have the parties allocated the risk of a transmission error or error in content?** Who is liable if an electronic transmission or information-processing system creates an error? In the case of SPC's transactions, have the parties determined the conditions for attributing electronic messages to SPC? Does the procedure for attribution comply with best practices or computer industry standards?

8. **Do mass-market licenses such as clickwrap or webwrap agreements comply with UCITA's rules for validating mass-market licenses?** Mass-market licenses are not enforceable unless the licensee manifests assent after an opportunity to review the terms. Does SPC, for example, conspicuously provide users with an opportunity to review the terms prior to requiring the user to "manifest assent" by clicking an icon or button? Does SPC give users an opportunity to review a contract record or terms? Does the "opportunity to review" also give reasonably configured electronic agents an opportunity to react? What mass-market warranties are given?—

   a. Quiet Enjoyment and noninfringement?

   b. Implied warranty for merchantability of computer program?

   c. Warranties for system integration or fitness for a particular purpose?

   d. Warranty for informational content?

   e. Express warranties such as sales literature, specifications, television advertisements, or banner advertisements?

   f. Disclaimers and limitations on warranties? Does SPC follow UCITA's prescribed methodology in disclaiming or limiting warranties?

g. Has SPC modified the default remedies of UCITA? What are the events of breach? When do the parties have a right to cancel the contract?

h. Have the parties agreed to a liquidated damage clause? Are the liquidated damages unreasonably small or large?

i. Have the parties elected different remedies from UCITA or Article 2?

j. Have the parties substituted a sole and exclusive remedy for UCITA remedies?

9. **Has SPC substituted a repair or replacement remedy for UCITA's remedies?** If the parties have a sole and exclusive remedy, what is the backup remedy if the exclusive remedy fails of its essential purpose? Have caps been placed on direct damages? Have consequential damages been disclaimed? Does the backup remedy include a refund? Does the right to refund disclaim consequential, incidental, special, and penal damages?

10. **Have the parties reserved the right to disable software or to undertake self-help repossession in the event of default?**

11. **Has the company correctly configured its agreement?**

a. Is the clickwrap structured so that the web site visitor clicks either "I accept" or "I decline"? The form of the clickwrap agreement is acceptance of terms and conditions by use. Is it clear that the visitor signifies agreement to all terms, conditions, and notices? The following is an example of an acceptance of terms through use clause: "By using the SPC site, you signify your agreement to all terms, conditions, and notices contained or referenced by [the Terms of Use]."

b. Does the statement of terms and conditions of use include all applicable terms such as those included in AOL.com's Terms and Conditions of Use clause? These terms are: (1) Acceptance of Terms Through Use; (2) Agreement to Rules of User Conduct; (3) Third Party Sites; (4) Proprietary Rights; (5) User's Grant of Limited License; (6) Procedure for Making Claims of Copyright Infringement; (7) Disclaimer of Warranties; (8) Limitation of Liability; (9) Indemnification; (10) International Use; (11) Choice of Law and Forum; (12) Severability and Integration; (13) AOL Mail on the Web Registration Agreement; (14) AOL Mail on the Web Billing Notice; and (15) Termination.[529]

---

[529] AOL.com, Terms and Conditions of Use (visited June 9, 2000), http://www.aol.com.

§ 6.06   LICENSE AGREEMENTS

License agreements come in an almost infinite variety of flavors. They may be exclusive or nonexclusive, mass-market or tailored, developmental or customized; they may apply for a single use or for perpetuity. An exclusive licensee, as the name connotes, is the only party who may use licensed software, data, or intellectual property. Territory, time period, or other factors may restrict license agreements.

All forms of intellectual property are licensed. Copyrights, for example, are frequently licensed. A record company may license a copyrighted song for the soundtrack of a film. A photographer may license a copyrighted photograph for use in a web advertisement. It is possible, for example, to enter into a license agreement to use midi-music on a corporate web site. An artist may offer the use of one song for $50 for a 12-month period. A corporate multimedia web site may need to obtain licensed text, music, photographs, software, and streaming video and audio. The scope of the license agreement will describe the material licensed and any restrictions imposed on its use.

Rights in patents, trademarks, trade secrets, and software are also licensed. A license may be structured as exclusive, semi-exclusive, or nonexclusive. Mass-market license agreements, such as the use of Microsoft's Windows 2000, are nonexclusive because the value is realized by marketing end-user agreements to millions of users. A software program custom designed to control missile warheads is certain to be exclusive, because the customized program is tailored for a single user, the Department of Defense. Software license agreements may provide for code that disables an application if timely royalties are not paid.

Another common form of web site licensing is the site license agreement. A web site agreement is a limited license to use materials on a corporate or other web site. A growing number of web sites condition access on payments. A web site term of use agreement will give the user notice that the documents, data, software, or other information on the web site are copyrighted. There should typically be notices of trademarks as well. A typical agreement will state that software is made available for specific purposes. The last clause in a web site agreement generally will state, "All rights not specifically granted are reserved."

SPC structures its mass-market computer software contracts as shrinkwrap or click-through agreements. SPC's mass-market license agreements will likely not be enforced unless consumers are given an opportunity to review and read the terms prior to paying for or receiving software. SPC's licenses should be structured so that the user is required to take some affirmative act to manifest assent after having the opportunity to review the license terms. The web site customer will be asked to click "I accept" or "I reject" after being given the opportunity to read the terms of SPC's license agreements.

TABLE 6.2
Types of Internet-Related Contracts

Type of Contract	*Chief Contracting Form*
Access Contract (i.e., America Online, LEXIS, and Westlaw)	Limited license agreement authorizing access to a computer or Internet database. Limited license to copy or use information.
Internet Service Provider (ISP) Agreement. An ISP is traditionally defined as a commercial entity, such as CompuServe or AOL, that charges a monthly access fee to networks connected to the Internet. Section 512(k) of The Digital Millennium Copyright Act defines a service provider as "an entity offering the transmission, routing, or providing of connections for digital online communications." SPC needs to designate an agent with the Copyright Office to receive notices of copyright infringement. In addition, § 512(I) requires SPC to adopt a policy terminating repeat infringers.	Terms and Conditions of Use Agreement: By accessing the site, the user agrees to all terms, conditions, and notices; limited license to use, reproduce, display, perform, adapt, modify, distribute, and promote content. AOL, for example, creates "acceptance of terms through a "use" license: "By using this site, you signify your agreement to all terms, conditions, and notices contained or referenced herein (the 'Terms of Use'). If you do not agree to these Terms of Use, please do not use this site. We reserve the right, at our discretion, to update these Terms of Use. Please check the Terms periodically for changes. Your continued use of this site following the posting of any changes to the Terms of Use constitutes acceptance of those changes."*
Mass-market License Agreements (i.e., shrinkwrap, clickwrap, and webwrap agreements).	Standard form contracts offered to the general public in a retail market.
Content License (license to use various content on an online service; Matt Drudge, for example, was a licensor who granted a content license to AOL to transmit the Drudge Report on its service).	Online services will enter into license agreements with creators of content.
Web Site User License (i.e., Terms of Service, Limited License to Copy Material, and Legal Notices).	Sample statement: "By accessing this web site, the user acknowledges acceptance of SPC's terms and conditions. SPC reserves the right to change these rules and regulations from time to time."
Sales of Computer Hardware (i.e., Article 2 or CISG Sales).	Article 2 of the UCC applies to the sale of computer goods from SPC's web site. The Convention for the International Sale of Goods applies to nonconsumer transactions between parties located in signatory states, unless the parties have opted out.
Licensing of Software (i.e., UCITA or common law contracts).	Any software downloaded from SPC's web site is accompanied by license terms, which accompany the file.

*AOL.com, Terms and Conditions of Use (visited June 9, 2000), http://www.aol.com.

521

[A]   Granting Clause

The granting clause is the most legally significant clause in a license agreement because it specifies what rights are being transferred. The granting clause will specify whether a license is exclusive or nonexclusive. A broad granting clause in a license agreement is "of all possible rights and media including all rights then existing or created by the law in the future."[530] A licensee receives all rights described in the licensing agreement. The granting clause will typically reference the terms and conditions of the license agreement. License agreements may be country-by-country or worldwide, exclusive or nonexclusive, or restricted by territory, site, or time period. The granting clause must also address the question of whether the licensee has a right to sublicense software or other information.

A sale of goods is forever, whereas a license agreement may be nonperpetual or perpetual. A nonperpetual license agreement may be structured as a single use agreement or for a fixed period, such as 30 days or a year. The license agreement should spell out whether the licensed technology is worldwide or restricted to a given country or continent. If a licensee is a multinational corporation, it is possible to negotiate a license agreement that will permit worldwide use of the license.

[B]   Term for Payment

License agreements may structure payment in many different forms. A software developer may demand a large upfront fee. The licensee may structure upfront fees to correspond to milestones. Royalties in web site agreements may be structured on net sales from a web site or the number of web site visitors. Subscribers to Books24X7, for example, an online business that places information technology books on the web, pay $399 for an annual subscription and lower costs for multiple-user agreements.[531] The site has a search engine so a user can search through hundreds of books for desired content.[532]

[C]   Scope of Licensing Agreement; Number of Users

The license agreement should clearly spell out who is the authorized user. A license agreement should specify that use is for one-user only or for multiple users. A license agreement with a multinational corporation should specify whether a foreign subsidiary may use the licensed information. If independent

---

[530] UCC § 2B-307(1) (Tentative Draft, April 15, 1998).

[531] Gavin McCormick, *Books24x7 Puts IT Books on the Web*, Mass High Tech, Aug. 16-22, 1999, at 18.

[532] *Id.* at 1.

contractors are routinely used, the agreement should specify under what conditions they may use the licensed information. A licensor needs to calibrate the royalties or payments based on the number of users. If the license agreement does not specify the number of users allowed at a given time, the industry standard limits use of software or other information products to a single-user. A clause might limit use of software to a single central processing unit. A detailed shrinkwrap license may state that the "software may not be rented, sold, or transferred." The agreement must be clear as to what access is given in the case of an access contract and whether simultaneous use is permitted.

[D] Different Media

A copyright, trademark, trade secret, or patent holder will have the exclusive rights to reproduce and distribute works. The license agreement, for example, will typically specify the type of media for which rights are granted. A license agreement to distribute content on the *New York Times* web site may not cover CD-ROMs. A license to distribute a motion picture may not extend to broadcasting on the Internet. The licensee of software or other information products may negotiate for the rights to obtain updates.

A licensee will need to negotiate specifically for electronic distribution rights. In the software industry, a licensee does not automatically receive updates of a program. In Playboy Enterprises v. Chuckleberry Publishing,[533] the defendant used the trade name in a 1979 magazine it called *Playmen,* a name substantially similar to that of *Playboy.* Fifteen years later the defendant established a web site for Playmen. The court held that the injunction also applied to the Internet, even though the medium was different.[534]

The licensee needs to be certain that the license agreement applies to Internet publishing as well as to other media. A number of writers sued the *New York Times* and the Time-Warner magazine group claiming that the publishers were infringing their rights by distributing articles they wrote on the Internet without permission, even though they had paid for the print versions of these newspaper and magazine articles.[535]

[E] Licensee's Right to Updates

A licensor may take the position that a licensee is not entitled to updates or new versions of software. A licensee may also wish to be informed of improvements or new releases of software. In the case of access contracts, the licensee will

---

[533] 1996 WL396128 (S.D.N.Y. 1996).

[534] *Id.*

[535] Nicolas Baran, Inside the Information Superhighway Revolution 143 (2000).

want to have the latest updates to a database. In the absence of an agreement, a licensee will not automatically receive new releases or updates. A licensee of mass-market software, such as Windows 2000, will generally pay an additional fee for improved versions of the software.

[F]   Termination Clause

A license will generally define the terms of the license agreement. The term of an agreement will begin as of the "Effective Date." A term may begin when software is installed and continue for the life of the license. Licenses may be for perpetuity or for a fixed period, such as a month, year, or other term. The *sine qua non* of a license agreement is that the title to the program and copies remain the property of the licensor. License agreements will have a termination clause for breach or default. The license agreement should specify the events of default. Events of default will include nonpayment of licensing fees, repudiation, or rejection of conforming software.

➤   ### [1]   Preventive Law Pointer: Term and Termination

TERM OF THE AGREEMENT: The term of this Agreement shall begin as of the Effective Date, and shall continue in full force and effect for _____ years until terminated by either party upon at least ninety days' prior written notice to the other or upon the breach of this Agreement by either party.

TERMINATION FOR BREACH OR DEFAULT: Either party to this Agreement may terminate this agreement in the event the other party shall have materially breached or defaulted in the performance of any of its material obligations, and such default shall have continued for ____ (days) after written notice was provided to the breaching party by the non-breaching party.

Termination Checklist

• **How is the license agreement terminated?**

• **What are the events of default giving the parties the right to cancel the agreement?**

• **Are there any obligations, such as confidentiality, which survive termination?**

[G]   Disabling Devices

A licensee may purchase software that contains a variety of disabling routines designed to permit use of the software only until a given date. A company may agree to a perpetual license of the same product at a higher cost. A computer lawyer who frequently drafts and reviews license agreements "agreed with the proposition that the vendor should be free to limit the term of a license agreement through time-bombs and other disabling routines."[536] Computer law would not require a conspicuous warning or label, leaving it to the licensor to communicate the limitation in the product license.

[H]   Warranties, Disclaimers, and Limitations

Warranty exclusion and remedy limitation provisions are a usage of trade in mass-market software licensing agreements. The Uniform Commercial Code permits parties to exclude implied warranties as long as the language is clear, unambiguous, and conspicuous and not unconscionable.[537] Courts apply Article 2 of the Uniform Commercial Code to software licensing agreements in the absence of a specialized body of law governing computer transactions.[538] For a discussion of warranties under UCITA, see § 6.05[G].

[I]   Indemnification

License agreements will frequently contain indemnification or "hold harmless" clauses. A "hold harmless" clause is an essential term in contracts with third parties who supply content to the web site. Development software contracts should contain cross-indemnities in which each party agrees to indemnify the other for third-party claims.

[J]   Assignment and Anti-Assignment

A licensee may want to sublicense content to a third party. A licensor may require the licensee to sign an anti-assignment agreement. The following is an example of an anti-assignment clause: "SPC grants the licensee a nonexclusive, nontransferable, personal license to use the object code version of SPC's XYZ Software on a single central processing unit at the original site where initially installed."

---

[536] This judgment emerged during an interview with a computer lawyer with 15 years' involvement with software and extensive experience advising licensors or licensees of customized software.

[537] *See, e.g.*, NMP Corp. v. Parametric Technology Corp., 958 F. Supp. 1536 (N.D. Okla. 1997) (enforcing warranty exclusion and remedy limitation provisions contained in software licensing agreement).

[538] *See, e.g.*, Vmark Software v. EMC Corp., 37 Mass. App. Ct. 610, 642 N.E.2d 587 (1994) (applying Article 2 of the UCC to a software licensing agreement and holding that the licensee met its burden of proof regarding allegations of misrepresentation by the licensor of a software program). *See generally* Andrew Beckerman-Rodau, Computer Software: Does Article 2 of the Uniform Commercial Code Apply? 35 Emory L.J. 853 (1986) (arguing that software licensing agreements should be treated as Article 2 transactions).

The software license agreement will govern the user's right to assign or resell software. The agreement will govern whether a user moves the physical location of software. A licensor may have objections, for example, if software is assigned to an outsourcing vendor.

[K] Licensee's Rights

An end user should minimally have the right to load and execute software on a single computer. A licensee probably has an implied right to reverse engineer the software to determine and exploit the underlying noncopyrightable ideas. A multinational company will need to negotiate the right to load software on a network file server or to make it available in other ways to multiple users.

[L] Confidentiality and Nondisclosure

A licensor or licensee may be concerned with confidentiality of licensed data or information. Some intellectual property lawyers argue that confidentiality agreements are unnecessary in license agreements. Trade secret or confidentiality agreements impose conditions on the disclosure of confidential or proprietary information.

[M] Export Restrictions

Software agreements may contain a provision by which the licensee agrees not to export or reexport the software product to any country, person, entity, or end user subject to U.S. export restrictions.[539] Microsoft also asks its licensees to warrant that they have not had their export privileges suspended, revoked, or denied.[540] Software licensors are liable if they permit technology to be exported, downloaded, or even reexported to restricted countries. Software, for example, must not be exported to Cuba, Iran, Iraq, North Korea, Sudan, or Syria.[541] Netscape Navigator distributes end-user licenses with the following export control term:

---

[539] The Clinton Administration's encryption policy has been changed, permitting U.S. companies to sell strong encryption around the world. The United States Department of Commerce's Bureau of Export Administration (BXA) administers the export license program for encryption products subject to the Export Administration Regulations (EAR). A company must determine its licensing requirements under EAR by comparing its products against the Commerce Control List, which is available online. *See generally* U.S. Department of Commerce, Bureau of Export Administration, Fact Sheet: How Do I Know If I Need to Get a License from the Department of Commerce? (visited May 15, 2000), http://www.bxa.doc.gov/factsheets/facts1.htm.

[540] Microsoft, Inc., End-User License Agreement for Microsoft Software, clause 6 (stating export restrictions).

[541] *Id.*

NONE OF THE SOFTWARE OR UNDERLYING INFORMATION OR TECHNOLOGY MAY BE
DOWNLOADED OR OTHERWISE EXPORTED OR RE-EXPORTED (I) INTO (OR TO A
NATIONAL OR RESIDENT OF) CUBA, IRAQ, LIBYA, YUGOSLAVIA, NORTH KOREA,
IRAN, SYRIA OR ANY OTHER COUNTRY TO WHICH THE U.S. HAS EMBARGOED
GOODS; OR (II) TO ANYONE ON THE U.S. TREASURY DEPARTMENT'S LIST OF SPE-
CIALLY DESIGNATED NATIONALS OR THE U.S. COMMERCE DEPARTMENT'S TABLE OF
DENY ORDERS. BY DOWNLOADING OR USING THE SOFTWARE, YOU ARE AGREEING
TO THE FOREGOING AND YOU ARE REPRESENTING AND WARRANTING THAT YOU
ARE NOT LOCATED IN, UNDER THE CONTROL OF OR A NATIONAL OR RESIDENT OF,
ANY SUCH COUNTRY OR ON ANY SUCH LIST.[542]

[N] Integration or Merger Clause

An integration clause states that the contract represents the parties' complete
and final agreement. The purpose of the clause is to merge all prior oral and written agreements into the final agreement. An example of a merger clause is, "This
Agreement constitutes the entire understanding of the parties with respect to the
subject matter." It is critical that merger clauses be included in all license agreements, including the web site agreement.

[O] Access Contracts: Terms and Conditions of Access

The typical access contract is formed by acceptance of terms through use.
America Online, for example, provides: "By using this site, you signify your
agreement to all terms, conditions, and notices contained or referenced herein (the
'Terms of Use'). If you do not agree to these Terms of Use please do not use this
site."[543] AOL reserves the right to update or revise the Terms of Use and places the
burden of checking for modified terms on the user. AOL states: "Your continued
use of this site following the posting of any changes to the Terms of Use constitutes acceptance of those changes."[544]

Section 102(1) of UCITA defines an "access contract" as a contract to obtain
electronic access to the information-processing system of another person or the
equivalent of such access. An access to services contract includes online services
for remote data processing, e-mail, or databases. An access contract is an agreement that a subscriber may have electronic access to a company's databases.
America Online, for example, is an access provider because it gives its 38,000,000
subscribers electronic access to or information from its databases. Westlaw or
LEXIS-NEXIS afford their subscribers remote access to hundreds of thousands of

---

[542] Netscape Communications Corporation, Netscape Navigator End User License Agreement
(1996).
[543] AOL.com, Terms and Conditions of Use (visited May 8, 2000), http://www.aol.com.
[544] *Id.*

specialized legal or law-related databases. The LEXIS-NEXIS or Westlaw subscriber is presented with a "take it or leave it" access contract.

Access providers develop standard-form contracts which they offer to their customers on a "take it or leave it" basis. The subscriber agrees to the terms and conditions of use and to the price schedule; these represent the entire agreement, and without the subscriber's acceptance, no contract exists. Access providers signify acceptance of the access agreement by issuing an identification number that permits access to the services. Access agreements typically impose restrictions on the licenses. An access agreement will typically be nontransferable and limited to use by one person at a time.

Access contracts may include "contracts for remote data processing, third party e-mail systems, and contracts allowing automatic updating from a remote facility to a database held by the licensee."[545] The *New York Times*, for example, enters into access contracts with subscribers for its online publication. The term "access contract" does not include contracts that grant a right to enter a building or other physical locale.

§ 6.07   INTERNET TAXATION

[A]   Introduction

The Internet is the ultimate worldwide market, with hundreds of thousands of possible taxing jurisdictions.[546] State and local governments seek to expand their tax base, whereas the business community is concerned about the uncertainty of filing returns in thousands of taxing jurisdictions.[547] A great deal of legal uncertainty exists about the Internet tax environment, despite the Internet Tax Freedom Act, which has imposed a moratorium on sales and use taxes on Internet sales transactions.

One clouded issue is whether a downloadable software program is classifiable as a good, a service, or neither because it is to be classified as an intangible

---

[545] UCITA § 102(a)(1) (1999) (Reporter's Note).

[546] The Framework Communication, A European Initiative in Electronic Commerce, noted that "by its very nature, electronic commerce is transnational and encourages cross border ordering and delivery of goods and services in the Single Market, that it directly stimulates European growth and competitiveness, and that it represents 'a potentially vital factor for cohesion and integration in Europe.'" Communication by the Commission to the Council of Ministers, the European Parliament, and the Economic and Social Committee, COM (96) 328 Final.

[547] David Hardesty, Part I: NTA Issues Report on E-Commerce Tax Policy, Aug. 30, 1999 (visited May 8, 2000), http://www.ecommercetax.com/doc/083099a.htm.

information asset.[548] The European Union takes the position that web site services should be classified as services.[549] The Commission notes that "VAT legislation makes a basic distinction between the supply of goods and the supply of services. All types of electronic transmissions and all intangible products delivered by such means are deemed, for the purposes of EU VAT, to be services."[550]

[B] Internet Taxation: The U.S. Perspective

As we previously discussed, the Internet and the advent of e-business have empowered companies to change the way they do business—buy and sell products and services, interact with suppliers and customers, and hire and interact with employees—in a global economy. Although e-business is, in many cases, clearly a more appealing way of doing business, its means of silently crossing the borders of states and countries complicates the issues of assessing and collecting taxes.

A hypothetical company such as SPC can now sell computer antivirus software programs either by mailing the software on a disk to a customer or by allowing the customer to download the software directly from the SPC web site. Mailing the antivirus software to a customer could take several days, costs more money to distribute, and increases SPC's operating costs, whereas the download procedure is instantaneous, accurate, and reduces distribution and operating costs. The downloading option is clearly more appealing. This convenience, however, complicates the process of assessing and collecting taxes. It is unclear whether a downloadable software program delivered from SPC's web site is a good, a service, or, being an information asset, neither. These characterizations have different tax implications, based in part on how value is created. "E-business has the potential to transform dramatically tax effects by enabling us to control where value is created."[551]

Decades ago, tax laws and regulations were established all over the world and have since served as a means for local governments to generate income. None of these tax laws and regulations contemplated the possibility that new technologies would so thoroughly complicate how a given transaction was taxed. Today

---

[548] The Council of Ministers of the European Parliament argues that the "consequences of taxation should be the same for transactions in goods and services, regardless of the mode of commerce used or whether delivery is effected Online or off-line." Communication by the Commission to the Council of Ministers, the European Parliament, and the Economic and Social Committee, COM (96)328 Final. Ideally, the consequences of taxation should be neutral and nondiscriminatory, whether purchased "from within or from outside the EU." *Id.*

[549] *Id.*

[550] *Id.* The Commission notes that the application of VAT to e-commerce is consistent with the position taken by the EU and its members states at the World Trade Organization (WTO).

[551] E-Business Tax: A Strategic Weapon in the Digital Age 5 (PricewaterhouseCoopers LLP, 2000).

great uncertainty exists in the global marketplace over taxation and tax processes and the extent to which "sales, value added or similar taxes apply to transactions in the International online services industry."[552]

One of the many problems presented by e-business is the possibility that numerous jurisdictions may claim authority over the same transactions, subjecting a given e-commerce transaction to state, federal, and international taxation. In order to prevent double taxation and to facilitate continued growth in e-commerce, the United States enacted the Internet Tax Freedom Act.[553]

[1]   The Internet Tax Freedom Act

The Internet Tax Freedom Act (ITFA) was introduced in March 1997 by Representative Christopher Cox and Senator Ron Wyden and was enacted into law October 21, 1998.[554] Two of the fundamental purposes of ITFA were to ensure the continued growth of the Internet as well as to prevent multiple or discriminatory taxes which could potentially stifle the growth of e-commerce. Companies will enjoy a respite from federal taxes until October 21, 2001.

The highlights of ITFA include the following:

- *No federal taxes.* Congress believed it was imperative that no federal taxes be imposed on Internet access or e-commerce for several years.

- *Declaration that the Internet should be a tariff-free zone.* Congress did not want foreign tariffs to hinder the ability of U.S. businesses to compete in e-commerce activities abroad.[555]

- *Establishment of an advisory commission.* Congress set up a high profile commission to make recommendations for the future taxation of e-commerce. The Advisory Commission on Electronic Commerce consists of eight business executives, three federal government leaders, and eight state and local government officials.[556] The commission presented formal recommendations to Congress in April 2000.

- *Three-year moratorium on multiple or discriminatory taxes on e-commerce.* ITFA prohibits multiple and discriminatory taxes on e-commerce.

---

[552] J. Fraser Mann and Alan M. Gahtar, Overview of the Legal Framework for Electronic Commerce, in Dennis Campbell, Law of International On-Line Business: A Global Perspective 15 (1998).

[553] Internet Tax Freedom Act, Pub. L. 105-277, § 1101(a) (Oct. 21, 1998).

[554] *Id.*

[555] *See* Robert Guy Matthews, Tariffs Impede Trade via Web on Global Scale, Wall St. J., Apr. 17, 2000, at B1.

[556] http://www.ecommercecommission.org/0621tr.htm.

• *Three-year moratorium on new taxes on Internet access fees.* ITFA prohibits state and local governments from imposing taxes on Internet access fees if such a tax was not in place as of October 21, 1998.[557]

The enactment of ITFA was a preventative measure to ensure the continued growth of the Internet over the next several years. Arguably, the most significant part of ITFA was the establishment of the Advisory Commission. The Advisory Commission studied, among other things, state and local taxation of Internet access; e-commerce with other countries; sales and use taxes within the United States; and consumption taxes, such as value-added taxes (VAT). Many scholars believed the Advisory Commission's recommendations would bring about dramatic changes in existing tax laws that could result in uniform statewide tax rates, consolidated state tax returns, limitations on tax rate changes, and uniform definitions of which products and services may be subject to tax.[558]

[2] Federal Taxation

On July 1, 1997, the White House issued a "White Paper"[559] that declared, "the United States believes that no new taxes should be imposed on Internet commerce."[560] The White House took the position in the White Paper that "the same broad principles applicable to international taxation . . . should be applied to subfederal taxation. No new taxes should be applied to electronic commerce, and states should coordinate their allocation of income derived from electronic commerce."[561] The enactment of ITFA ensured that no federal taxes would be placed on Internet access or e-commerce for three years, and, further, restricted individual states from enacting new taxes on e-commerce.

[C] State Taxation of Electronic Commerce

Our hypothetical company, SPC, can potentially be subject to state taxation anywhere within the United States. SPC, a Massachusetts company, could sell a downloadable computer antivirus software program on the Internet to a resident of Batesville, Indiana, without ever knowing the name and address of the end customer. Numerous tax issues can stem from this type of Internet transaction:

---

[557] *See* § 6.07[c][3], note 594 and accompanying text.

[558] Richard Prem, The Battle of Internet Tax, EComm World, Aug. 2, 1999, http://www .ecomworld.com/html/aug99.htm.

[559] White House, A Framework for Global Electronic Commerce (1997), *reprinted in* Daily Tax Rep. (BNA), July 2, 1997, at L-13.

[560] *Id.* at L-15.

[561] *Id.* at L-16.

- Who is the customer?[562]

- Where does the customer live?[563]

- Did the transaction constitute a sale of tangible property, the performance of a service, or the transfer of intangible property?

- Which jurisdiction has the authority to tax the sale?

- What online activities constitute sales for sales tax purposes?

- When may a state impose a sales or use tax on online activities?

- What constitutes a sufficient nexus[564] within a taxing jurisdiction?

- What kind of record retention requirements are necessary for tax purposes?[565]

Congress and the Advisory Commission on Electronic Commerce may resolve many of the Internet tax issues. Until then, traditional tax rules must be utilized to address these complex issues.

[1] Sales and Use Tax

The concept of the sales and use tax was introduced and enacted in the 1930s.[566] State governments use sales and use taxes to generate revenue within their states.[567] Sales and use taxes constitute an estimated 35 percent of states' total

---

[562] When a customer orders a computer from SPC's catalog, the name of the customer placing the order is recorded, which in turn reveals the identity of the customer. The true identity of a customer is not necessarily known when the product is delivered electronically to an Internet address. The customer could be ordering the product from someone else's computer or under an alias name (the assumption of which is often called spoofing).

[563] When a customer orders a computer from SPC's catalog, the product is physically delivered to the customer, which in turn reveals the taxing jurisdiction. The physical location is not necessarily known when the product is delivered electronically to an Internet address.

[564] In the United States, if a taxpayer has sufficient nexus with a state under the Commerce Clause and the Due Process Clause, a state may impose a tax on the interstate transaction. The Supreme Court in Complete Auto Transit v. Brady articulated a four-prong test that enables a state to tax interstate transactions under the Commerce Clause. A state tax is legal if (1) it applies to an activity with a substantial nexus with the taxing state; (2) it is fairly apportioned; (3) it does not discriminate against interstate commerce; and (4) it is fairly related to the services provided by the state. Complete Auto Transit v. Brady, 430 U.S. 724 (1976). Whereas, under the Due Process Clause, nexus is satisfied when a minimum connection exists between the state and the person, property, or transaction subject to tax.

[565] *See generally* Wright and Winn, *supra* note 33, 10-1 to 10-17.

[566] *See* Adam L. Schwartz, Note, Nexus or Not, Orvis v. New York, SFA Folio v. Tracy and the Persistent Confusion Over Quill, 29 Conn. L . Rev. 485, 520 n.28 (citing Richard Pomp & Oliver Oldman, State & Local Tax'n 775 (1996)).

[567] Stewart A. Baker, Beware, the Taxman Cometh to Cyberspace, L.A. Times, Oct. 5, 1995, at 9.

revenue collection opportunities.[568] Sales and use taxes were aimed at generating revenues for states from an industrial economy where the manufacturing and sales of goods were the mainstays of the economy.[569] Now that the world economy has shifted away from an industrial to an information base, the erosion of territorial boundaries threatens to disrupt what has been a significant source of taxation income for many states.

Forty-six states and the District of Columbia impose sales and use taxes on various business transactions.[570] These states impose a sales tax on the purchase or lease of tangible personal property, certain services, and intangible properties[571] used within their state boundaries. Most states, excluding Alaska, Delaware, Montana, New Hampshire, and Oregon, tax the sale of products, while several states, such as Hawaii,[572] New Jersey, New Mexico,[573] South Dakota,[574] Texas, and Washington, tax services. Ignoring the distinction between products and services, consumers are required to pay the sales tax, while the seller, as an agent for the state government, collects and remits the tax.[575] Table 6.3 outlines the taxation policies of those states imposing a tax on the sale of goods over the Internet.

A use tax is a corollary tax aimed at taxing the use, consumption, or storage of tangible property at a rate similar to that of a sales tax.[576] The use tax is collected from the seller when the consumer is domiciled in another state.[577] Assessing the use tax was meant to put local retailers at a competitive parity with out-of-state retailers exempt from sales tax.[578]

[2] Nexus–Taxable Level of Business Activity

One threshold question that must be answered when determining whether sales or use tax is imposed is whether or not nexus[579] actually exists. Nexus has

---

[568] R. Scott Grierson, Legal Potholes Along the Information Superhighway, 16 Loy. L.A. Ent. L.J. 541, 573 (1996).

[569] *See generally* Delta and Matsuura, *supra* note 26.

[570] Four states (Delaware, Montana, New Hampshire, and Oregon) do not assess sales tax. By comparison, nine states (Alaska, Florida, Nevada, New Hampshire, South Dakota, Tennessee, Texas, Washington, and Wyoming) have little or no income tax. These states must rely on sales or property tax for their revenues.

[571] Intangible properties can include intellectual property rights.

[572] Hawaii taxes 155 different services.

[573] New Mexico taxes 155 different services.

[574] South Dakota taxes 130 different services.

[575] Robert J. Fields, Understanding and Managing Sales and Use Tax 205 (3d. ed., 1994).

[576] *Id.*

[577] *See* White Oak Corp. v. Department of Revenue Servs. 503 A.2d 582, 585 (Conn. 1986).

[578] National Geographic Society v. California Board of Education, 430 U.S. 551, 555 (1977).

[579] For a comprehensive discussion of nexus, *see* Julie M. Buechler, Note Virtual Reality: Quill's "Physical Presence" Requirements Obsolete When Cogitating Use Tax Collection in Cyberspace, 74 N. Dak. L. Rev. 479 (1998).

TABLE 6.3
Taxation of Internet Transactions*

State	Sales of Goods over the Internet	Access to the Internet	Download Information/Software
Alabama	Taxable	Exempt	Taxable
Alaska	No sales tax	No sales tax	No sales tax
Arizona	Taxable	Exempt	Taxable
Arkansas	Taxable	Exempt	Exempt
California	Taxable	Exempt	Exempt
Colorado	Taxable	Exempt	Taxable
Connecticut	Taxable	Taxable	Taxable
Delaware	No sales tax	No sales tax	No sales tax
District of Columbia	Taxable	Taxable	Taxable
Florida	Taxable	Exempt	Exempt
Georgia	Taxable	Exempt	Exempt
Hawaii	Taxable	Taxable	Taxable
Idaho	Taxable	Exempt	Taxable
Illinois	Taxable	Exempt	Exempt/Taxable
Indiana	Taxable	Exempt	Exempt/Taxable
Iowa	Taxable	Exempt	Taxable
Kansas	Taxable	Exempt	Exempt/Taxable
Kentucky	Taxable	Exempt	Unknown
Louisiana	Taxable	Exempt	Taxable
Maine	Taxable	Exempt	Taxable
Maryland	Taxable	Exempt	Exempt
Massachusetts	Taxable	Exempt	Exempt
Michigan	Taxable: Use	Exempt	Exempt/Taxable
Minnesota	Taxable	Exempt	Exempt/Taxable
Mississippi	Taxable	Exempt	Taxable
Missouri	Taxable	Exempt	Exempt

*See generally http://www.vertex.com.

TABLE 6.3 Taxation of Internet Transactions (Continued)

State	Sales of Goods over the Internet	Access to the Internet	Download Information/Software
Montana	No sales tax	No sales tax	No sales tax
Nebraska	Taxable	Exempt and/or taxable	Exempt/Taxable
Nevada	Taxable	Exempt	Exempt
New Hampshire	No sales tax	No sales tax	No sales tax
New Jersey	Taxable	Exempt	Exempt
New Mexico	Taxable	Taxable	Taxable
New York	Taxable	Exempt	Taxable
North Carolina	Taxable	Exempt	Taxable
North Dakota	Taxable	Taxable	Exempt/Taxable
Ohio	Taxable	Taxable: Commercial use only	Taxable: Commercial use only
Oklahoma	Taxable	Exempt	Exempt and/or taxable
Oregon	No sales tax	No sales tax	No sales tax
Pennsylvania	Taxable	Exempt	Exempt/Taxable
Rhode Island	Taxable	Exempt	Exempt
South Carolina	Taxable	Exempt	Exempt
South Dakota	Taxable	Taxable	Taxable
Tennessee	Taxable	Taxable	Exempt/Taxable
Texas	Taxable	Exempt	Taxable
Utah	Taxable	Exempt	Taxable
Vermont	Taxable	Exempt	Exempt
Virginia	Taxable	Exempt	Exempt
Washington	Taxable	Exempt	Taxable
West Virginia	Taxable	Exempt	Taxable
Wisconsin	Taxable	Taxable	Exempt/Taxable
Wyoming	Taxable	Exempt	Exempt

been described as the "degree of business activity that must be present before a taxing jurisdiction has the right to impose a tax, or an obligation to collect a tax, on an entity."[580]

The Due Process Clause and the Commerce Clause of the U.S. Constitution address the concept of nexus in relation to states imposing a tax on interstate transactions. The Due Process Clause provides that: "No person shall . . . be deprived of life, liberty, or property, without the due process of law,"[581] "nor shall any State deprive any person of life, liberty, or property without due process of law."[582] The doctrine of Due Process addresses the "traditional notions of fair play and substantive justice"[583] and "requires some definitive link, some minimum connection between a state and the person, property, or transaction it seeks to tax."[584]

The Commerce Clause provides, that "The Congress shall have the power . . . to regulate commerce with foreign Nations, and among several States, and with the Indian Tribes."[585] Although this phrase does not literally address state taxation, under the guise of Congress's dormant commerce clause power it has been interpreted as prohibiting state taxes that would impede interstate commerce.[586] The Supreme Court in Complete Auto Transit v. Brady[587] developed a four-prong test that permits states to tax interstate transactions under the Commerce Clause. The high court held a state tax is constitutional if (1) it applies to an activity with a substantial nexus with the taxing state; (2) it is fairly apportioned; (3) it does not discriminate against interstate commerce; and (4) it is fairly related to the services provided by the state.[588]

E-commerce companies have been compared to mail-order companies because they do not always have a physical presence in the states in which they do business. This is relevant because the U.S. Supreme Court recently addressed the nexus issue when it ruled in Quill Corp. v. North Dakota[589] that Quill's mail-order business did not constitute a physical presence in the state. Consequently, Quill was not required to collect sales and use taxes from customers located within the

---

[580] Karl A. Frieden and Michael E. Porter, State Taxation of Cyberspace, The Tax Adviser, Nov. 1, 1996.

[581] U.S. Const. amend. V.

[582] Id. amend. XIV.

[583] Miliken v. Meyer, 311 U.S. 457, 463 (1940).

[584] Quill Corp. v. North Dakota, 504 U.S. 298, 306 (1992) (quoting Miller Bros. Co. v. Maryland, 347 U.S. 340, 344-45 (1954)).

[585] U.S. Const. art I, 8.

[586] See Jerome R. Hellerstein and Walter Hellerstein, State and Local Taxation 188-305 (2d ed., 1997).

[587] Complete Auto Transit v. Brady, 430 U.S. 724 (1976).

[588] Id.

[589] Quill, 504 U.S. at 312. The Supreme Court ruled that Quill's mail-order business did not constitute a physical presence within the state. Therefore, Quill did not have substantial nexus with the taxing state. Id.

state. The Court did not suggest that *Quill* would have been decided differently if the sales had been made over the Internet. Arguably, sales over the Internet involve even less physical contact with a state than do catalogs sent through the U.S. mail.

In some cases, companies with a brick-and-mortar presence in a state have not been collecting sales taxes for orders processed online. The California Senate recently passed a bill that would require companies with a presence in the state to collect taxes in online transactions.[590]

An e-business strategy allows organizations a wide variety of choices as to where to locate, what employees to hire, and how to buy and sell goods and services. E-businesses should understand that opening new facilities or entering a partnering relationship can trigger significant tax issues, and they should go into those arrangements with full information, including knowledge of the tax implications. Having a single telecommuting employee in a foreign jurisdiction can greatly increase an organization's tax exposure. Strategic planning on these issues, including where to locate brick-and-mortar facilities and employees can help limit an organization's tax exposure. Companies should consult with professional tax advisors or with the members of their corporate tax departments.

[3] Sales and Use Tax on Internet Access

Free Internet access is now available from companies such as Alta Vista, but most users gain access to the Internet through an Internet service provider (ISP) or online service provider (OSP). Accessing an ISP or OSP occurs by dialing a local access number through a local or national telecommunications company. An ISP, such as AOL, charges users a monthly fee (currently around $21.95 per month) for unlimited Internet access.[591] This monthly fee bundles access to the Internet with AOL's own online content. Bundling these services makes it difficult to determine how much of the fee goes toward access versus content. Estimates made even as early as 1995 placed ISP and OSP revenues between $1.6 billion to $2.2 billion.[592] This revenue stream was a result of fees charged for Internet access, online services, and advertising.[593]

Needless to say, states view Internet access fees as a lucrative source of state revenue. How states will ultimately tax Internet access is yet to be determined. The enactment of the ITFA prohibits state and local governments from imposing taxes

---

[590] *See* Megan Holohan, California Ponders Internet Tax (visited Sept. 6, 2000), http://www.infoworld.com/articles/hn/xml/00/08/31/000831hncaltax.xml?0901frap (discussing A.B. 2412).

[591] AOL's monthly access fee charge is published on its web site, at http://www.aol.com.

[592] Charles E. McLure, Jr., Taxation of Electronic Commerce: Economic Objectives, Technological Constraints, and Tax Laws, 52 Tax L. Rev. 269, 311 (1997).

[593] *Id.*

on Internet access fees if such a tax was not in place as of October 21, 1998.[594] This restriction will be effective until October 21, 2001.[595] Table 6.3 on pages 534-535 shows which states currently impose a tax on Internet access.

For those states that tax Internet access, some tax it as if Internet access were a telecommunication service.[596] The Telecommunications Act defines telecommunication as "the transmission between or among points specified by the user, of information of the user's choosing, without change in the content of the information as sent and received."[597] What constitutes transmission is subject to debate.[598] Internet access, e-mail, and bulletin board services are arguably analogous to cellular or regular telephone calls, which are subject to sales tax.[599] Internet access and e-mail involve additional enhanced services, however, such as the ability to store messages on computer servers, that raise questions as to whether they should, in fact, be subject to sales tax.

[4] Sales Tax Treatment of Online Content

E-commerce offers many new products and services for global customers. One of the most lucrative e-commerce opportunities is online content,[600] including computer software programs, digitized books, digitized magazines, digitized newspapers, digitized pictures, movies, music, video games, and much more.[601] In the United States, online content delivered via e-commerce threatens to compete with the likes of the video (annual revenues in excess of $12 billion), music ($12 billion), movie ($6.5 billion), and print publishing industries ($44 billion).[602]

Given the revenue potential of online content, it is not surprising to find that more than a third of the states currently impose sales and use taxes on online content activities. These states include Connecticut, the District of Columbia, Hawaii, New Mexico, New York, Ohio, Pennsylvania, South Dakota, and Texas.[603] These states tax a variety of electronic services including some of the following: e-mail,

---

[594] A grandfather clause enables certain states to tax access fees. The states include Connecticut, Iowa, New Mexico, North Dakota, Ohio, South Carolina, South Dakota, Tennessee, Texas, and Wisconsin.

[595] *Id.*

[596] Karl Frieden and Michael Porter, The Taxation of Cyberspace: State Tax Issues Related to the Internet and Electronic Commerce, 1996 St. Tax Notes 221-257 (Nov. 14, 1996).

[597] Telecommunications Act of 1996, Pub. L. No. 104-104, 110 Stat. 56, codified as 47 U.S.C. § 153(43).

[598] Delta and Matsuura, *supra* naote 26.

[599] *Id.*

[600] McLure, *supra* note 592.

[601] *Id.*

[602] *Id.* at 304.

[603] Delta and Matsuura, *supra* note 26.

data processing, computer bulletin boards, news and weather reports, credit reports, airline reservations, cable television, software downloads, and fax services, "900" telephone number services, and the like.[604] Although a tax may be levied, each state varies as to whether it taxes online sales transactions as an extension of the sales tax imposed on tangible personal property or as a separate category of taxable services.[605]

These jurisdictions also differ as to whether they tax all or just certain aspects of online content. A particular state's approach may be crucial for interpreting ambiguities or challenging possible overreaching of state tax rules. Moreover, the majority of states, including California, Georgia, Maryland, Massachusetts, Michigan, and Missouri, do not tax the electronic transmission of information or other online content-related transactions. Generally, the states that currently do not impose sales taxes on electronic services are those with a narrower sales tax base that encompasses tangible personal property and only a few enumerated services.

For instance, New Jersey has determined that information transferred electronically is not subject to sales tax because no tangible property is involved in the transaction. Other states, such as California, that have issued regulations or rulings on this issue have also generally relied on the fact that the content transferred electronically is nontaxable intangible property, not taxable tangible property.

[5]   Sales Tax Treatment of Computer Software

One common online transaction is the sale of computer software. Neither the Internal Revenue Code (IRC) nor state regulations have provided much guidance as to whether computer software is considered to be tangible or intangible property for sales and use tax purposes. Some states impose a sales tax on software as if it were a tangible personal property while other states tax computer software as if it were the sale of a computer or electronic service.[606] Some states also will not assess a sales tax on computer software sold over the Internet, even if they would tax the same software sold in retail stores.[607]

Court cases that address this issue have also been split. In South Central Bell Telephone Co. v. Barthelemy,[608] the court found that computer program master source codes were tangible property. In Ronnen v. Commissioner,[609] however, the

---

[604] *Id.*

[605] *Id.*

[606] *Id.* at 10-27.

[607] *Id.* These states include California, Maryland, Massachusetts, Missouri, South Carolina, and Utah.

[608] 643 So. 2d 1240 (La. 1994).

[609] 90 T.C. 74 (1998).

court came to an opposite conclusion and ruled that software codes were intangible property. Some cases have determined that computer services can be treated as taxable and nontaxable services.[610]

Whether software is considered tangible or intangible appears to be determined on a case by case basis and varies from state to state. Table 6.3 lists the tax treatment in each state for computer software and downloads from the Internet.

Ideally, the Advisory Commission on Electronic Commerce will grapple with this issue and bring some uniformity to this question. Until then, e-businesses distributing software over the Internet should be aware of the surrounding tax issues, especially as the digital downloading of software from the Internet increases.

[D]   Products vs. Services: The Characterization of Revenue

How a company characterizes its revenue is critical in terms of the ultimate tax treatment. Traditionally, revenue streams for companies are derived from the sale of a product, use of property (rents and royalties), or the provision of a service. With the entrance of the Internet, and particularly of e-commerce, the line between a service and a product often becomes blurred. Many e-commerce companies have multiple revenue streams, which may include a combination of product sales, uses of property, and sales of services. For tax purposes, identifying whether an e-business is a provider of products or a provider of services may be difficult, but is an important decision to make, as products and services are taxed differently in different jurisdictions. Services are not subject to sales and use taxes in the United States, for example, whereas in Europe they are subject to VAT.

A restaurant bill serves to illustrate the confusion between a product and a service. Most people characterize restaurants as service-oriented businesses. But the bill that customers pay encompasses the cost of the meal as well as the cost of the planning, purchasing, cooking, serving, and other services provided. Since the meal is the significant income-producing factor, however, under tax law restaurants are considered providers of products rather than of services.

As the restaurant example illustrates, distinguishing products from services can be surprisingly difficult, especially when the service provided includes a tangible good. Many Internet companies can be viewed as selling both products and services. Take, for example, Amazon.com, which offers books, CD-ROMS, videos, and other products. Once a customer places an order, Amazon.com typically notifies a distributor of the order, who in turn ships the products to Amazon.com. Amazon.com then delivers the product to its customer. Clearly this chain of events indicates that Amazon.com is engaged in the sale of products. Amazon.com also engages in service activities, however, such as banner advertising

---

[610] *See, e.g.*, Creasy Systems Consultant v. Olsen, 716 S.W.2d 35 (Tenn. 1986).

and holding auctions. This analogy can be applied to a multitude of e-commerce companies, such as Barnes & Noble, Beyond.com, and eBay.

Many services that e-businesses provide to customers revolve around either the sale or the use of products. Consequently, it is becoming more difficult for e-businesses to be treated solely as service providers for tax purposes. One possible method of achieving a more favorable tax status would be to separately invoice the sale of products and the provision of services. Pursuant to Section § 446(d) of the IRC, a taxpayer may gain the tax advantages associated with using a different accounting method for each line of business.

[E]   Cash vs. Accrual

Another major issue regarding the distinction between a provider of products and a provider of services is the accounting method used for tax purposes. IRC § 471 states that, in order to reflect income correctly, inventories must be taken at the beginning and end of each taxable year in every case in which the production, purchase, or sale of merchandise is an income-producing factor.[611] Businesses operating with inventory must use the accrual method of accounting. Therefore, providers of products typically use the accrual method of accounting, while service providers utilize the cash method.

In reality, however, it is difficult to identify a business as being clearly either a service provider or a product provider. Two cases illustrate this point: Knight-Ridder Newspapers, Inc. v. United States[612] and Galedrige Construction v. Commissioner of the Internal Revenue.[613] Although both cases have similar fact patterns, the courts reached different results. Knight-Ridder Newspapers claimed that newspapers were a service and that the newspapers themselves were insubstantial inventory, since a day old newspaper was useless; the court, however, required Knight-Ridder to use the accrual method. Similarly, Galedrige's molten asphalt merchandise became useless five hours after it was picked up from the supplier, but the court permitted Galeridge to use the cash method. In both cases, the inventory in question was a significant income-producing factor and a significant cost of total receipts. Neither service could be rendered without the requisite inventory. The conflicting decisions in these two court cases blurs the distinction between a product provider and a service provider.

SPC is an example of an e-business whose tax classification could vary. One of SPC's corporate missions is to sell software online. SPC delivers the software

---

[611] IRC § 471 (1999).

[612] 743 F.2d 781 (1984).

[613] 1996 U.S. App. LEXIS 1792 (1997) (unpublished opinion). The court overruled the Commissioner and ruled that asphalt was not considered merchandise held for sale due to its short five-hour life cycle. Galedrige Construction, therefore, could continue to use the cash method for its paving business. *Id.*

through a distributor to its customer or allows customers to download the software digitally. Consequently, SPC holds little physical inventory and conducts all transactions on a per order basis. Generally speaking, SPC could be characterized as a company that sells products and should use the accrual method. Without taking title of the software it sells, however, SPC could also be considered a service that delivers software. Consequently, it is unclear whether SPC should utilize the cash or the accrual method.

The main difference between utilizing the cash or the accrual method lies in the timing of tax payments. Under Rev. Proc. 71-21, accrual basis taxpayers may defer to include in their income payments received in one taxable year for services to be performed in the next succeeding taxable year.[614] If SPC is classified as a service company, it cannot defer the advance payment of services, since only accrual basis taxpayers can defer such advance payment. According to this Rev. Proc., it would be more advantageous for SPC to use the accrual method of accounting, since SPC could prepay for products and thus lower its taxable income.

Under the accrual method, companies with inventory need to record their expected revenue for taxable income. When using the cash method, companies do not have to account for expected revenue, thereby delaying the time when they will have to pay taxes on the anticipated income. Companies using the cash method have the benefit of not having to pay taxes for income that has not actually been received. Another benefit to the cash method is in regard to inventory. Under the accrual method, companies must capitalize related costs to inventory. These expenses will not be deductible until the inventory is sold, thus increasing company's taxable income and taxes.

Generally speaking, it is more advantageous for companies to be classified as service providers in terms of the cash and accrual methods of accounting, but it has become more difficult for companies to do so. Prior to 1986, the cash versus accrual distinction was important. Service businesses could stay on the cash method if they chose, while businesses that sold property were forced to use the accrual method. After 1996, IRC § 448, which basically forces large corporations (both service and product) to use the overall accrual method of accounting for tax purposes, has applied.[615] The only professions excluded from IRC § 448 are lawyers, accountants, and other large professional service corporations, as defined in IRC 448(d)(2)(A).[616] The choice of whether to use the cash or the accrual method requires some strategic tax planning. Companies should consult with professional tax advisors or with the members of their corporate tax departments.

---

[614] Rev. Proc. 71-21 (1999).

[615] IRC § 448 (1999).

[616] IRC § 448(d)(2)(A) (1999).

[F] International Withholding Tax

The number of Internet users is predicted to exceed 1,000,000,000 by the year 2010.[617] The ability to reach so many potential customers has encouraged businesses around the world to go online. By connecting the entire world to the Internet, traditional territorial boundaries become invisible and "blur . . . the source and character of income."[618] This, in turn, threatens the stability and viability of source-based taxation,[619] the permanent establishment concept,[620] and the meaning of U.S. trade or business as set forth in the Internal Revenue Code.[621]

In order to deal with impending international tax issues, several countries around the world have set up special commissions to study tax issues resulting from e-commerce.[622] Without changes to existing tax laws, the possibility exists that numerous countries may claim taxing jurisdiction over the same transaction, which could result in double taxation.[623] To avoid this problem and provide consistent treatment on various e-commerce transactions, worldwide rules and policies must be adopted.[624]

Taking a lead in this effort, the U.S. Treasury Department in 1996 published a Discussion Paper entitled *Selected Tax Policy Implications of Global Electronic Commerce*.[625] One of the messages in the Discussion Paper was that the Treasury was prepared to work with taxpayers, tax advisors, technology specialists, academics, foreign tax policy makers, and administrators to better understand the emerging technologies and to formulate rational and enforceable global tax rules.[626]

Coming up with a uniform approach to earnings from online transactions and international taxation issues will be critical to the continued growth and success of e-commerce. As it stands now, each country connected to the Internet has different tax rules on service, product, and royalty income, all of which may have to be

---

[617] *See* For the Record, Wash. Post, July 31, 1998, at A24 (reprinting testimony of William Daley, Secretary of Commerce, before the House Commerce Committee).

[618] *See* David R. Tillinghast, Tax Treaty Issues, 50 U. Miami L. Rev. 455, 456 (1996).

[619] The concept of source-based taxation (sometimes referred to as a territorial approach) entitles the "source" country to tax the income of nonresidents earned within its borders. Restatement (Third) of the Foreign Relations Law of the United States § 412(1)(b)-(c) (1986).

[620] *Id.*

[621] Office of Tax Policy, U.S. Dep't of the Treasury, Selected Tax Policy Implications of Global Electronic Commerce 2.4 (1996), *reprinted in* 1996 Daily Tax Rep. (BNA) 226 (Nov. 22, 1996).

[622] Elusive Nature of Commerce on Internet Requires Uniform Rules, Tax Experts Agree, 1998 Daily Tax Rep. (BNA) 36 (Feb. 24).

[623] James D. Ciglar and Susan E. Stinnett, Treasury Seeks Cybertax Answers with Electronic Commerce, Discussion Paper, 8 J. Int'l Tax'n 56, 58 (Feb. 1997).

[624] *Id.*

[625] Office of Tax Policy, *supra* note 621.

[626] *Id.*

modified to bring uniformity to international tax issues. Companies should consult with professional tax advisors or with the members of their corporate tax departments when addressing international tax planning issues.[627]

[G]   Other Sources of Taxes and Duties

Tax treaties seek to alleviate double taxation and to provide certainty in the marketplace.[628] The United States has a large number of bilateral tax treaties with its trading partners. Customs and duties can be a significant expense and may be overlooked when making sourcing decisions. NAFTA and WTO rules will affect these tax rates and should be considered. Companies should also consider how easily customers in Brazil, for example, can purchase items: Shipping, customs, and duty fees must be calculated and charged correctly to ensure that items move smoothly to customers.

[H]   International Taxation of E-Commerce

International tax considerations include sales, use, franchise, income, customs, corporation, and value-added taxes. In addition, currency limitations and export issues may apply to Internet transactions that cross international borders. The management of tax returns is also an issue in the online environment. Online companies may be subject to filing tax returns in multiple jurisdictions. One concern is the possible tax implications of using electronic agents or servers in another country. Internet-initiated value transfers raise thorny regulatory and tax issues. Coverage of the nuances of international tax issues is beyond the scope of this chapter. The International Chamber of Commerce, however, has identified the following broad categories of significant Internet tax issues:

1.   Reliance on existing principles: utilization of internationally accepted tax rules;

---

[627] *See generally,* Reuven S. Avi-Yonah, International Taxation of Electronic Commerce, 52 N.Y. L. Rev. (1999); John Sweet, Comment: Formulating International Tax Laws in the Age of Electronic Commerce: The Possible Ascendancy of Residence-Based Taxation in an Era of Eroding Traditional Income Tax Principles, 146 U. Pa. L. Rev. 1949 (1998); James D. Ciglar and Susan E. Stinnett, Treasury Seeks Cybertax Answers with Electronic Commerce Discussion Paper, 8 J. Int'l Tax'n 56, 58 (Feb. 1997); Peter A. Glicklich, Stanford H. Goldberg, and Howard J. Levine, Internet Sales Pose International Tax Challenges, 84 J. Tax'n 325 (1996); James D. Cigler, Douglas E. Morgan, and James R. Shanahan, Taxation of Electronic Commerce Puts International Issues in New Light, 1 High Technology Industry 37 (1997); James D. Cigler, Harry C. Burritt, and Susan E. Stinnett, Cyberspace: The Final Frontier for International Tax Concepts? 7 J. Int'l Tax'n 340 (1996); Reuven S. Avi-Yonah, The Structure of International Taxation: A Proposal for Simplification, 74 Tex. L. Rev. 1301 (1996).

[628] Sanjeev Doss, Tax Presence Implications for Doing Ebusiness with the U.S. 17 (May 2000) (on file with author Cyrus Daftary).

2. Bases for taxation: global taxation for residents versus source taxation for nonresidents;

3. Role of tax treaties: unlimited taxation for residence countries versus limited taxation for nonresidents;

4. Permanent establishment: establishing a taxable nexus for foreign taxpayers in a treaty country;

5. Characterization of income: tax treatment of digital information;

6. Services income: source rule for services income;

7. Residence: test for corporation residence;

8. Transfer pricing: allocation of income for electronic transactions;

9. Administration and compliance: providing for nonburdensome audits of tax returns for e-commerce related income;

10. Indirect Taxation: VAT taxation in the country of consumption.[629]

The ICC favors an Internet tax policy based on the assumption that income earned through e-commerce should be treated neutrally by applying traditional tax principles to the Internet to the greatest extent possible rather than formulating a completely new tax regime.[630] The ICC takes the position that the Internet should be "source based."[631] Taking a source-based approach means that "service income is only subject to host country income tax if the services are physically performed in the country."[632] The ICC does not recommend replacing a "place of use" test with the source income test.[633] The ICC report argues that the "mind and management" test for corporate residence should apply to the Internet.[634] This corporate residency test focuses on where the management functions of corporations are performed.[635] The ICC favors a tax regime that guards against double taxation for consumption taxes. The ICC opposes the imposition of Value-Added Taxes (VAT) on electronic commerce.[636] The ICC report concludes that no new taxes should be assessed on e-commerce transactions.[637]

---

[629] International Chamber of Commerce, Policy Statement: Tax Issues and Ramifications of Electronic Commerce (Prepared by the ICC Commission on Taxation Jointly with the Business and Industry Advisory Committee to the OECD (BIAC) Dec. 15, 1999) (visited May 17, 2000), http://www.iccwbo.org/home/state.../tax_issues_and_ramifications_of_electronic_commerce.as.

[630] *Id.*

[631] *Id.*

[632] *Id.*

[633] *Id.*

[634] *Id.*

[635] *Id.*

[636] *Id.*

[637] *Id.*

[1]   Value-Added Taxes

The European Commission's report entitled *A European Initiative in Electronic Commerce* contended that "in order to allow electronic commerce to develop, certainty (so that tax obligations are clear, transparent and predictable) and tax neutrality" are necessary.[638] The European Commission, like the U.S. government, supports the principle of "no new taxes" on electronic commerce.[639] Unlike the United States, however, the Commission favors an international taxation of e-commerce based on the value-added tax.[640] The Commission notes that e-commerce is "developing, in the area both of 'indirect' electronic commerce (electronic ordering of tangible goods), and 'direct' electronic commerce (electronic ordering and delivery of products and services Online over the networks)."[641]

The European Community supports a tax initiative that would make all goods and services sold on the Internet subject to the existing VAT, irrespective of country of origin.[642] The Commission acknowledges that it is difficult to administer a VAT tax system where individuals and businesses purchase services outside the European Union.[643] The Commission favors a "common VAT system based on taxation at origin and providing for a single country of registration where an operator would both account for and deduct tax in respect of all his EU VAT transactions."[644] Under the Commission's plan, online services delivered in the EU will be subject to VAT whether supplied by EU or non-EU suppliers.[645] The Commission notes: "Similarly, because many on-line services are currently subject to tax under EU rules at the place of origin, VAT is payable by EU suppliers on all the services they supply to non-EU countries. Such discrepancies in the application of

---

[638] COM (97) 157.

[639] E-Commerce and Indirect Taxation, Communication by the Commission to the Council of Ministers, the European Parliament, and the Economic and Social Committee, COM (96)328 Final.

[640] VAT is designed as a general consumption tax that, in principle, applies to all supplies of goods and services. In all cases transactions taking place within the EU, using the medium of electronic commerce and resulting in consumption within the EU, are subject to EU VAT under existing provisions. However, that is not always the case where supplies from non-EU countries are concerned. In the case of goods supplied from a non-EU country to an EU recipient, normal import procedures ensure that VAT is applied regardless of the means used to conduct the transaction. Similarly, certain descriptions of services received by EU businesses from non-EU countries are subject to VAT. However, it should be noted that with few exceptions, services received by EU private persons are not, under existing provisions, subject to VAT (the volumes of such supplies is at present very small). *Id.*

[641] *Id.*

[642] *Id.*

[643] *Id.*

[644] *Id.*

[645] *Id.*

tax clearly offend against the principle of neutrality."[646] The European Union's VAT Service would implement the following guideline to ensure that services, whether supplied via e-commerce or otherwise, which are supplied for consumption within the EU are taxed within the EU, whatever their origin. Such services, supplied by EU operators for consumption outside the EU are not subject to VAT in the EU but VAT on related inputs is eligible for deduction.[647]

[2] Web Servers and Tax Issues

Another area of uncertainty is whether companies such as SPC are liable for income tax if their web servers are located in another country. The trend in international law is not to base taxes, jurisdiction, or other status on the location of the web server. The Organization of Economic Cooperation and Development (OECD) proposes a tax treaty under which a company is not liable for income tax on business profits merely because it has a web server in another country.[648] The OECD is exploring four international income tax issues: "(1) the effect of a Web server in a country, (2) the effect of in-country Web site hosting services, (3) the character of transactions involving digital products, and (4) transfer pricing in global e-commerce."[649]

[I] Limiting Tax Liability

Tax consequences are key to deciding what entity to form for an online business. Choosing the right entity to do business is one way to limit tax liability. An online company could theoretically be formed as a partnership. Partnerships do not file returns for federal income tax. The partners are liable for federal income tax for partnership income as individuals, however. An online company could be formed as a professional or for-profit corporation to limit personal liability for debts. A growing number of online companies are forming as limited liability companies (LLC) for tax purposes.[650] The LLC gives its members the same limited liability protection accorded to shareholders of corporations.[651] However, "all nonrecourse debt . . . will be allocated to the tax basis of the members' interests

---

[646] *Id.*

[647] *Id.*

[648] Ecommercetax.com, International Taxation of E-Commerce, Oct. 20, 1999 (visited May 8, 2000), http://www.ecommercetax.com/InternationalTax.htm.

[649] Ecommercetax.com, International Income Tax Update, July 9, 1999 (visited May 8, 2000), http://www.ecommercetax.com/International/Tax.htm.

[650] *See generally* Carter G. Bishop and Daniel S. Kleinberger, Chapter 2, Tax Classification of Unincorporated Business Organizations, Limited Liability Companies: Tax and Business Law (2000).

[651] *Id.*

accordingly."[652] A company should consult its state's version of the Uniform Limited Liability Act of 1996 to determine rules applicable to forming an LLC in that state. In general, an LLC applies to the secretary of state for authorization.[653] The phrase "limited liability company" or "limited company" or the abbreviations "L.L.C.," "LLC," "L.C.," or "LC" must be included in the entity.[654] To qualify to do business in a state as an LLC, the name must be distinguishable from names of any corporation, limited partnership or company incorporated."[655] Section 201 of the Uniform Limited Liability Company Act provides the key attribution of the LLC: "A limited liability company is a legal entity distinct from its members."[656] The legal significance of being a distinct legal entity is that "its members are not normally liable for the debts, obligations, and liabilities of the company."[657]

The Uniform Partnership Act, which revised the Uniform Partnership Act of 1914, updates partnership law to provide partners with the possibility of choosing "the registered limited liability partnership form."[658] The objective of the revisions is to give new businesses, including online business, an option to form limited liability partnerships.[659]

[J] Tax Checklists

When preparing to do business on the Internet, companies must ask and answer several questions that can help them better manage their strategic initiatives. These questions might include the following:

1. What are your tax footprints? Can you easily create a taxable nexus? Remember that the lone telecommuting employee can create large tax issues. Employees, agents, or partners can create a tax footprint, so outsourcing some of the company's work may reduce the tax footprint. Strategic planning in advance will help limit your organization's tax liability. Cisco Systems is a good example

---

[652] *Id.*

[653] Uniform Limited Liability Company Act § 105 (1997).

[654] *Id.* § 105(a)

[655] *Id.* § 105(b).

[656] *Id.* § 201.

[657] *Id.* § 201, comment.

[658] *See* Uniform Partnership Act (UPA) art. 10 & cmts. (1997). The following states or territories have adopted the UPA with the 1997 amendments: Alabama, Arizona, Arkansas, California, Colorado, Delaware, the District of Columbia, Hawaii, Idaho, Iowa, Kansas, Maryland, Minnesota, Montana, Nebraska, New Mexico, North Dakota, Oklahoma, Oregon, Puerto Rico, the U.S. Virgin Islands, Vermont, Virginia, and Washington. Connecticut, Florida, West Virginia, and Wyoming have adopted the 1994 version of the Act. National Conf. of Commr's on Unif. State Laws, A Few Facts About the Uniform Partnership Act (1994), http://www.nccusl.org/uniformact_factsheets/uniformacts-fs-upa9497.htm (visited Aug. 18, 2000).

[659] *See* UPA, addendum to prefatory note (1997).

of smart planning by an Internet-enabled company. Cisco claims that it transacts 85 percent of its orders and 82 percent of its customer inquiries over the Internet.[660] Cisco can close its books in one day, and, using the Internet, it can manage 37 manufacturing plants around the world, only two of which it owns.[661]

2. Have you actively decided how to deliver your product or service? Tangible goods sold in stores, such as music CDs, are taxable, while digital delivery (a customer downloads music over the Internet) has a limited tax footprint: In many jurisdictions, such transactions incur no tax at all. Be aware of revenue royalties, however, and consult your tax advisors.

3. Does your organization have inventory? Is that inventory a significant income-producing factor? Remember the restaurant example and check the law. It pays to know the tax law in the jurisdictions in which you conduct business.

4. Do you distinguish the character of your products from that of your services? You could sell your products separately from your services. Sell the computer without the support and charge separately for support services. Selling set-top boxes to allow access to the Internet yields a wholly taxable product sale. Giving away free set-top boxes and accessing a charge for Internet access services is a better tax decision.

§ 6.08   INTERNET PAYMENT SYSTEMS

[A]   Payment Instruments

[1]   Credit Cards

Retail payments are made with diverse instruments, including "cash, checks, credit and debit cards, and the electronic funds transfer system known as the automated clearing house (ACH)".[662] Cash is used for 75 percent of retail transactions in the offline world.[663] Large funds transfers constitute "about 90 percent of the value of noncash transactions made every day."[664]

Credit cards are the dominant means of Internet payment for consumer sales. The law of credit cards is governed by the Truth in Lending Act (TILA) and Regulation Z, enacted by the Federal Reserve Board. TILA, for example, gave consumers the right to dispute billing errors and a methodology for protecting themselves against unauthorized charges.

---

[660] Doss, *supra* note 628.

[661] *Id.*

[662] Alice M. Rivlin, Chair, Committee on the Federal Reserve in the Payments Mechanism 1 (Jan. 1998).

[663] *Id.*

[664] *Id.* at 6.

Cardholders have $50 total cap on liability for the unauthorized use of a credit card. Cardholders are not even liable for $50 unless the credit card is classified as an "accepted credit card." An accepted credit card means simply that it was issued in response to a consumer's request and that the consumer signed it. Cardholders may assert claims or defenses against the issuer of the credit card.[665] Cardholders are entitled to withhold payment from merchants for claims or defenses which cannot be resolved.[666]

Regulation Z requires that a consumer make "a good faith attempt to resolve the dispute with the person honoring the credit card."[667] Another limitation is that the "disputed transaction occur in the same state as the cardholder's current designated address or, if not within the same state, within 100 miles from that address." Most credit card companies, however, are willing to waive the 100-mile rule, permitting consumers to contest credit card transactions.[668] It is quite unclear how the 100-mile or same state rule applies to web site transactions. Does the rule depend on the location of the server, the place of incorporation of the online company, or the location of the consumer?[669]

When many customers have disputes with online merchants, the charge back rate grows unacceptably high. Charge back occurs when a cardholder contests a charge. Cardholders must contest charges within 60 days from the date of the issuance of the credit card statement.[670] Online companies must strive to keep their charge back rate low. Web sites that sell adult entertainment services have a high rate of disputes leading to charge backs.

Visa USA considers computer network and information services as well as computer programming, data processing, and integrated systems design to have a high rate of charge backs.[671] Visa USA and MasterCard have recently developed guidelines targeting online businesses considered high risk.[672] Online companies are required to keep charge back rates to a maximum of "1 percent of transactions or 2.5 percent of monthly revenue."[673] Merchants will generally not have a direct relationship with the bank issuing the credit card.[674] Instead, a written agreement between the merchant and merchant bank will be executed.[675] The merchant bank

---

[665] 12 C.F.R. § 226.12(c).

[666] *Id.* § 226.12(c)(1).

[667] *Id.* § 226.12(c)(3).

[668] Wright and Winn, *supra* note 33, § 20.02[A].

[669] *Id.*

[670] Henry H. Perritt, Jr., Legal and Technological Infrastructures for Electronic Payment Systems, 22 Rutgers Computer & Tech. L. J. 1, 28 (1996).

[671] Randy Barrett, Newsfront: E'Tailers Caught in Card, Interactive Week, Apr. 10, 2000 at 10.

[672] *Id.*

[673] *Id.*

[674] Perritt, *supra* note 670, at 18.

[675] *Id.*

has the job of "collecting receipts from the merchant and transferring them to the issuing bank for credit on its own account at that bank."[676] The merchant bank accepts deposit of credit slips and credits the merchant's account and charges for this service.[677]

➤ [a] Preventive Law Pointer: Web Sites and Credit Cards

The typical payment mechanism for the Internet is authorization through the web site visitor's credit card. Priceline.com, for example, allows consumers to use a variety of credit cards to make payment for airline tickets and other goods or services. The payment system for airline tickets requires the consumer to give a credit card number and authorization to bill the card if an airline is willing to release seats at the visitor's price. Once the web site visitor clicks, "Submit My Request," Priceline will search for a major airline willing to accept the offer. If an airline accepts the visitor's offer price, Priceline immediately locks in the price and charges the visitor's tickets to the credit card number provided.

Visitors give Priceline the authority to charge the price named as well as tax, fees, and shipping charges. The credit card is not charged if the visitor's price is not accepted by an airline. Priceline also permits visitors to store credit card information for future visits. The authorization to charge a credit card is granted by the bank that issued the credit card.

The online merchant designs its web site to prompt customers to enter their credit card numbers and to transmit the information from the Internet to a gateway. The gateway is a server that converts the information entered by consumers into a format that can be read by banks. The gateway transmits the information to the merchant's bank, which uses a "switch" to transmit it to the credit card network, such as American Express, Visa, or Diner's Club. A switch is a server operated by or on behalf of financial institutions. The card network determines the identity of the issuing bank and sends the information to the bank for authorization.

If the credit card transaction is authorized, the authorization is communicated back up the chain to the merchant. The issuing bank reserves the amount of the purchase to the credit card. The entire transaction takes only five to ten seconds.[678] If the credit card authorization is granted, the merchant may ship merchandise or grant the consumer access to services.

The merchant is paid after the goods or services have been shipped. Sending authorizations to the issuing bank pays the online merchant. Specialized methods

---

[676] *Id.*

[677] *Id.* at 22.

[678] This summary of how the credit card payment system works is drawn from First ECOM.COM, Inc., 10A00 Filing, Dec. 10, 1999, Securities and Exchange Commission, Washington, D.C. (visited May 30, 2000), http://www.sec.gov.

to allow secure credit card payment combine encryption with existing banking methods for payment authorization.[679] SPC will need to have online relationships with Visa USA and MasterCard International.

[2] Debit Cards

Debit cards have developed more recently than credit cards. They are virtually indistinguishable in appearance. A debit card, also known as an automated teller machine (ATM) or banking card, is simply a vehicle for drawing upon funds already in a checking account.[680] Barclays Bank in London installed the first ATM in 1967.[681] Debit cards are governed by the federal Electronic Funds Transfer Act (EFTA). EFTA applies to transactions in which an electronic debit is made from the customer's account and a credit for the same amount is made to the merchant's account through a point-of-sale (POS) terminal."[682]

Use of debit cards became widespread in the late 1970s and early 1980s. EFTA and Regulation E issued by the Federal Reserve Board require the issuer of debit cards to make mandatory disclosure requirements about the terms for use of the card. Regulation E, for example, requires that the bank's debit card rules be written in simple English. Regulation E provides rules for resolving disputes over erroneous transactions, unauthorized or false authorizations, and other problems.[683]

[3] Electronic Negotiable Instruments

[a] *UCC Articles 3 and 4*

The Uniform Commercial Code (UCC) was designed to modernize and bring uniformity to the commercial law. Article 3 of the UCC governing negotiable instruments and Article 4 governing bank deposits and collections were last revised in 1990, prior to the widespread use of the Internet for payment. Revised Article 3 provides ground rules for transferring negotiable instruments. Payment by checks, drafts, promissory notes, and other negotiable instruments is covered by Article 3 of the UCC.

The warranties, liabilities, and rules for allocating payment risks are also covered by Article 3. Revised Article 4 authorized the electronic presentment of

---

[679] VISA and MasterCard use a Secure Electronic Transaction (SET) protocol. The SET user encrypts purchase information so that only the bank will be able read it. The merchant encrypts part of the purchase information, ensuring that the buyer cannot repudiate the transaction.

[680] Lynn LoPucki, Commercial Transactions: A Systems Approach (1998), 384.

[681] Teitelman and Davis, *supra* note 27.

[682] Lewis Mandell, The Credit Card Industry: A History (1990), xxiii.

[683] Consumer Credit Protection Act, 15 U.S.C. §§ 1693-1693r (2000).

items as well as validated the practice of truncation. The purpose of the 1990 revisions to Article 4 was to improve the functioning of check collection.[684] Revised Article 4 was designed to permit the presentment of checks to payor banks by electronic transmission of information.[685] An automated clearinghouse (ACH) is designed to facilitate the exchange by banks of checks involving interbank payments.[686]

[b] Article 4A Wire Transfers

Wire transfers governed by Article 4A of the Uniform Commercial Code transfer trillions of dollars.[687] In contrast, point-of-sale and other consumer transactions are covered by the Electronic Fund Transfer Act (EFTA). The two principal systems for wire transfers are the Federal Reserve wire transfer network (FEDWIRE) and the New York ClearingHouse Interbank Payments Systems (CHIPS).

Each payment order contains information, such as the identity of the account from which funds are to be withdrawn, the amount to be transferred, the name and account number of the person to receive payment (the beneficiary), and the name and location of the beneficiary bank. A fund transfer agreement will also contain definitions, funds transfer services, fees, use of communications, customer identity, limitation of liability, choice of law, authority, and other general terms.[688]

International funds transfers are frequently made through the Society for Worldwide Interbank Financial Telecommunications (SWIFT). SWIFT is a "bank-owned utility for exchanging payment and settlement messages."[689] SWIFT is used to send hundreds of millions of messages each year. SWIFT connects 5,300 member financial institutions in 137 countries and is the primary large-value payment system (LVPS).[690]

Assume Big Company wants to pay an obligation owed to SPC. One option is for Big Company to send SPC a check or a promissory note. Another possibility would be for Big Company to use a credit card to purchase software from SPC's site. By giving its credit card number, Big Company enables SPC to obtain payment from the bank backing the credit card. If Big Company is located in the

---

[684] UCC § 401, official comment 2 (2000).

[685] *Id.*

[686] Teitelman and Davis, *supra* note 27, at 26.

[687] LoPucki, *supra* note 680, at 400.

[688] *See* Committee on the Law of Commerce in Cyberspace, American Bar Association Section of Business Law, Model Fund Transfer Services Agreement and Commentary, by the Working Group on Electronic Financial Services of the Subcommittee on Electronic Commercial Practices (1994).

[689] Teitelman and Davis, *supra* note 27, at 26.

[690] *Id.* at 28.

continental United States, it may also use FEDWIRE to transmit funds. An Article 4A funds transfer is another system of payment.

Funds transfers are typically used for large payment transaction. Suppose Big Company purchased one of SPC's subsidiaries for $500 million. The wire transfer will be a quicker payment option than would using the check collection system. A credit card transaction would be impractical for such a large sum. A wire transfer is an efficient payment system that permits the transfer of millions of dollars for a few dollars.[691]

Funds transfers may occur instantaneously and in a single day where a complex network of intermediary banks exists.[692] Article 4A, unlike other UCC articles, is governed by unique rules not found in Articles 3 or 4.[693] Article 4A sought to balance the interests of banks with those of other commercial and financial organizations.[694] Article 4A employs a specialized vocabulary with key definitions being "payment order," "beneficiary's bank," "receiving bank," and "sender."[695]

[B] Internet Banking

Security First Network Bank became the first fully transactional Internet bank federally insured by the FDIC.[696] The Security First Network Bank uses state-of-the-art information security "including a secure operating system, data encryption firewalls and routers."[697] Security First reimburses customers "100% for unauthorized transactions or misdirected payments."[698] A customer accesses account data using mouse clicks.[699] A large number of banks have web sites which permit customers to review balances, transfer funds, and pay bills.[700]

[C] E-Cash Payment Systems

Consumers have been slow to adopt smart cards and e-money methods of payment. CyberCash Inc. was founded in August 1994 to develop a global payments system with secure payment using encryption technology.[701] CyberCash

---

[691] UCC Article 4A: Funds Transfer, prefatory note (1989).

[692] *Id.*

[693] UCC § 4A-102, official comment 1 (2000).

[694] *Id.*

[695] *Id.* § 4A-103 (2000).

[696] Security First Bank, Security First Network Bank, About Security First Network Bank (May 12, 2000), http://www.sfnb.com/infodesk/about.html.

[697] *Id.*

[698] *Id.*

[699] *Id.*

[700] U.S. Department of Commerce, The Emerging Digital Economy, ch. 4 (April 1998).

[701] CyberCash Plans Software Facility in India, Financial Express (Dec. 21, 1995).

sought "to provide secure, convenient systems for secure credit cards, cash, checks, coins or micropayments."[702] CyberCash sought to promote three payments systems: (1) secure card transport; (2) CyberCash or money messaging; and (3) micropayments to replace coins.[703] CyberCash has a platform that permits merchants to accept payments over the Internet with any merchant bank.[704]

CyberCash was the first vendor to develop "electronic purse cards" which is the Internet equivalent of "walk around money."[705] Micropayments are kept in the virtual equivalent of a coin purse and are used to pay for small-scale Internet goods and services (such as an article downloaded from a news service).[706] Cybercash is a smart plastic card with an embedded chip that transmits payment much like a prepaid telephone cards does.[707] A smart card is a "credit card" with a "brain on it, the brain being a small embedded computer chip."[708]

[D]   European Union Euro

The Euro is a possible de facto currency for the Internet. The Euro, as of January 1, 1999, is already the official currency of the member states of the European Union. The European Central Bank (ECB) sets the overall monetary policy for all countries using the Euro as their currency. The Euro has a fixed rate of conversion into national currencies. The ECB is forced to adopt a "one-size-fits-all" monetary policy for the 11 Euro-zone national economies.[709] This poses an array of economic problems for many of the smaller Euro-zone countries. Monetary policy is set with the interests of the entire Euro-zone in mind, which essentially means that the needs of the larger countries will take precedence over those of the smaller countries. Euro notes and coins will be in widespread use beginning in January 1, 2002.[710]

§ 6.09   INTERNATIONAL E-COMMERCE DEVELOPMENTS

International issues occur because a company's web site can sell its goods and services in a global marketplace. A U.S. company must be aware that different rules apply in the global marketplace. The United States, for example, awards

---

[702] CyberCash as a Virtual Smart Card, Electronic Payments Int'l 9 (Aug. 1, 1995).

[703] *Id.*

[704] CyberCash, CyberCash Products (visited June 9, 2000), http://www.cybercash.com/producdts/index.html.

[705] *Id.* (describing smart cards for virtual "'net around" money).

[706] *Id.*

[707] *Id.*

[708] *Id.*

[709] Tony Barber, Spanish Inflation Stretches "One-Size-Fits-All" Policy, Fin. Times (London), May 18,1999, at 3.

[710] European Commission, EURO (visited May 10, 2000), http://europa.eu.int/geninfo/key_en.htm.

patents to the first person to invent something, whereas the rest of the world awards patents to the "first to file" the patent application.[711] The United States Patent and Trademark Office has taken a much broader view of the patentability of e-commerce business methods and software than has been the case elsewhere.[712] To date, the World Intellectual Property Organization (WIPO) has been unable to negotiate a treaty to harmonize patent law.[713]

Likewise, authors, creators, and performing artists have moral rights in the integrity of their works not recognized in the United States.[714] The European Directive on the legal protection of databases protects databases that do not qualify for copyright protection in the European Union.[715] Many databases lack the originality needed to qualify for copyright protection. The information industry is pressing for a federal law to protect databases from misappropriation.[716]

A number of countries have taken steps to regulate the Internet. Private international law also consists of international usages of trade in addition to the work of supranational organizations such as WIPO and the European Union. The World Trade Organization (WTO) is the principal international agency dealing with global rules of trade. The International Standards Organization (ISO) is a partner with the WTO in promoting a free and fair global trading system.[717] The ISO includes national standards bodies such as AFNOR, ANSI, BSI, CSBTS, DIN, and SIS, but it coordinates its activities with some 500 international and regional organizations.[718]

The WTO Code of Good Practice requires its signatories to "accept and comply with a Code of Good Practice for the preparation, adoption and application of standards."[719] Good practices set the basic rules for food safety, plant health, environmental issues, and standards for trade in services.[720] The WTO seeks transparency and nondiscriminatory trade in services and goods through the use of international standards. SPC will need to comply with the technical specifications or other WTO criteria used in its "materials, products, processes, and services." International standardization is rapidly evolving in the field of e-commerce. ISO

---

[711] International Chamber of Commerce, Current and Emerging Issues Relating to Specific Intellectual Property Rights (visited May 17, 2000), http://www.iccwbo.org/home/intellectual_property/current-emerging/roadmap.asp (hereinafter cited as "ICC, Intellectual Property Rights").

[712] *Id.*

[713] *Id.*

[714] *Id.*

[715] *Id.*

[716] Mark A. Lemley, Software and Internet Law (2000), 412.

[717] International Standards Organization (ISO), Standards and World Trade (visited May 13, 2000), http://www.iso.ch/wtotbt/wtotbt.htm.

[718] *Id.*

[719] *Id.*

[720] *Id.*

standards have been widely adopted worldwide for telephone cards, credit cards, and "smart" cards. Without standardization in thickness, for example, these payment devices would not be usable worldwide.[721] Global standards are necessary for online contracting, authentication, digital signatures, and electronic data interchange if the Internet is to fulfill its promise as a worldwide marketplace.

A systematic analysis of international issues is beyond the scope of this section. It is important to note, however, that an online company or Internet portal, such as Yahoo!, that crosses national borders must be prepared to comply with international law, foreign laws, and international usages of trade. The basic principles governing jurisdiction, choice of law, and conflict of law on the Internet are not yet fully developed for the global Internet.

A European Council Working Group was established to revise the Brussels Convention governing the enforcement of judgments and the European Union's Rome Convention on the treatment of contracts.[722] The country of origin principle holds that if a business meets the legal requirements in its country, it may transact business anywhere in Europe.[723] Both conventions adopt the "country of origin" doctrine.[724]

Both conventions, however, also recognize the following exception for consumer transactions: "that under narrow circumstances, a consumer should be allowed to rely upon the courts and the law of the country in which the services are received."[725] The European Commission adopted an Electronic Commerce Directive, which embraces "a country of origin approach to jurisdiction and choice of law."[726] The country of origin approach applies the law of the country where the Internet Service Provider (ISP) is located, with minor exceptions.[727]

Consumer advocates oppose the "country of origin" approach to conflict of law and jurisdiction because "consumers potentially would be subject to the laws of 15 different countries or might have to cross borders to adjudicate disputes."[728]

---

[721] International Standards Organization, Introduction to ISO (visited May 13, 2000), http://www.iso.ch/infoe/intro.htm.

[722] Professor William Woodward notes that the Rome Convention "restricts the effect of a contractual choice of law to non-mandatory law in domestic contracts and . . . affirmatively gives consumers the mandatory protections of their habitual residence notwithstanding a contrary choice of law." William J. Woodward, Letter to Professor Elizabeth Warren, Leo Gottlieb Professor of Law, Harvard Law School, Member, American Law Institute Council, Nov. 23, 1999.

[723] ISPO, Electronic Commerce and the European Union (visited May 3, 2000), http://www.ispo.cec.be/ecommerce/drecommerce/answers/000009.html.

[724] Microsoft Law and Corporate Affairs, Summary of Global Internet Legal Developments 93 (1985).

[725] *Id.*

[726] *Id.* at 92.

[727] *Id.*

[728] *Id.*

The Consumer Affairs Council of Ministers favors a special rule for consumer contracts, which would designate the choice of law and jurisdiction as the consumer's country of residence.[729]

[A] Convention on Contracts for the International Sale of Goods

As a merchant, SPC is selling computer hardware subject to international sales law, the United Nations' Convention on Contracts for the International Sale of Goods (CISG).[730] The United Nations approved CISG in 1980, and the United States became a signatory in 1988. The purpose of CISG was to harmonize international sales law and to promote uniformity in international trade. CISG is a hybrid statute borrowing "concepts and methods from the common law system that the United States inherited from the British system and the civil law system of Europe."[731] CISG applies to "contracts of sale of goods" if two requirements are satisfied: (1) The contracting parties are from countries that have signed the Vienna Convention or CISG, and (2) the sales agreement is between commercial parties and does not cover consumer goods, certain obligations to pay money, ships, vessels, hovercraft, or the sale of electricity.[732]

CISG shares much common ground with Article 2, with important differences. CISG, for example, does not recognize the Statute of Frauds, the parol evidence rule, or the perfect tender rule. CISG remedies are more standards-driven than are those of Article 2, which take a formulaic approach to separating the remedies of buyers and sellers.

Article 6 of the Convention for the International Sale of Goods gives the parties to an international sales contract the right to opt out of the convention.[733] The parties to a CISG transaction have the discretion to choose applicable U.S. or foreign law to govern all or parts of a transaction. SPC's counsel must make a strategic decision on whether it wants its B2B international contracts to be determined by CISG, foreign law, the UCC, or some other body of law. In licensing software, SPC may opt out of CISG in favor of the proposed Uniform Computer Information Transactions Act (UCITA).

---

[729] *Id.*

[730] The United Nations Convention on Contracts for the International Sale of Goods (CISG) was prepared by the United Nations Commission on International Trade Law (UNCITRAL) and issued for signature in Vienna in 1980. Because CISG is classified as a self-executing treaty, no domestic or federal legislation was necessary.

[731] John E. Murray, Jr., Buying Abroad Invokes International Law Challenge: Contracts Governed Under the United Nations, 123 Purchasing 25 (1997).

[732] CISG art. 3(2).

[733] *Id.* art. 6.

[B]   Distance Selling Directive

The European Directive on the Protection of Consumers in Respect of Distance Contracts (Distance Selling Directive) places limitations on online contracts directed to consumers in the 15 member states.[734] Each member state has its own statutory regulation addressing the Distance Selling Directive. The United Kingdom Directive addresses "contracts for the supply of services concluded at a distance" between merchants and consumers.[735]

The Distance Selling Directive applies only to B2C, and not to B2B or B2G, transactions. "The distance contract is one where supplier and consumer do not come face to face up to and including the moment at which the contract is concluded (i.e., mail order, telephone sales, electronic commerce."[736] The Directive applies to the rendering of professional services at a distance as well as to sales.[737] It does not apply to the marketing of financial services.[738] The Directive does not apply to the sale of real property, but it may apply to leases and rental agreements.[739] It does not cover telephone services and other telecommunications operations.[740] It also requires that consumers be provided with information about the seller in "a clear and comprehensible manner and in good time before the conclusion of any distance contract."[741]

The Distance Selling Directive requires that the online seller and other distance suppliers provide the following information prior to conclusion of the contract: (1) name and address of supplier; (2) main characteristics of goods or services; (3) price; (4) arrangements for payment; (5) existence of right of withdrawal where appropriate; and (6) the cost of using the means of distance communication.[742]

Written confirmation in a durable medium must be given to the consumer unless "the information has already been given in writing prior to the conclusion of the contract."[743] The written confirmation must minimally include (1) written information on the conditions for exercising the consumers' right of withdrawal; (2) geographical address of the supplier's place of business; (3) information on any

---

[734] Directive 97/7EC, adopted on May 20, 1997.

[735] Department of Trade and Industry (United Kingdom) Distance Selling Directive—Implementation in the UK (visited June 9, 2000), http://www.dti.gov.uk/cacp/ca/distance/dist.htm (hereinafter cited as "UK Distance Selling Directive").

[736] UK Distance Selling Directive, art. 2.

[737] *Id.*

[738] *Id.*

[739] *Id.*

[740] *Id.* art. 2.3.

[741] *Id.* art. 4.

[742] *Id.* art. 4.

[743] *Id.* art. 5.

after-sales service and guarantees; (4) conditions for canceling the contract where it is of unspecified duration or exceeds one year.[744] Article 6 of the Directive "gives consumers the right to withdraw from contracts within seven working days without penalty and without giving any reason."[745] The period of withdrawal begins from the date of receipt or the date of the conclusion of the contract.

The date of the conclusion of the contract is when the contract is formed, not performed.[746] If the consumer has not received the written confirmation information required by Article 5, the period of withdrawal is extended to three months.[747] A consumer does not have a right to cancel (1) contracts for service already begun; (2) contracts for goods and services where price is calculated by fluctuations in the financial market; (3) contract for goods supplied to the consumer's specifications (for example, a tailored suit); or (4) contracts for supply of video, audio, or computer software where the seal of the shrinkwrap is broken by the consumer.[748]

It is unclear whether a consumer would have a right to cancel a contract for software downloaded from a web site, a process in which no seal is broken.[749] A consumer's assent to a clickwrap agreement may, however, be viewed as the functional equivalent of "breaking the seal" of a shrinkwrapped package.[750] The Directive requires the seller to give the consumer a refund for any money paid. The seller may assess the cost of postage for goods returned. Consumers must be reimbursed within 30 days of giving notice to the seller that they are exercising the right of cancellation.[751]

Sanctions may be imposed against the seller for failing to reimburse the consumer.[752] A seller may be charged with a criminal offense for failing to make repayment within 30 days.[753] Consumers may also request cancellation of payments "where their credit or debit cards have been used fraudulently in a distance contract."[754] It is an offense for a seller to demand payment for "unsolicited goods."[755]

---

[744] *Id.*

[745] *Id.* art. 6.

[746] *Id.*

[747] *Id.*

[748] *Id.* art. 6.3.

[749] The commentary to the Directive states: "In some cases, this wording is not entirely clear (e.g., computer software may be supplied online in which case the term 'unsealed' refers to the user's indicating assent to the terms of the End-User License Agreement)." *Id.*

[750] *Id.*

[751] *Id.* art. 7.

[752] *Id.*

[753] *Id.*

[754] *Id.* art. 8.

[755] *Id.*

[C]   Electronic Commerce Directive

The European Commission's Electronic Commerce Directive proposes rules covering "Information Society services." The Directive seeks to promote the free movement of e-commerce services and to guarantee access for services throughout the member countries. The Directive "will ensure that Information Society services benefit from the Internal Market principles of free movement of services . . . throughout the European Union."[756] The Directive establishes rules for online contracting, marketing and advertising and for provider liability. The Electronic Commerce Directive addresses issues such as rules for the liability of Internet Service Providers, choice of law, electronic contracts, spam e-mail, digital signatures, and e-filing of records. The European Union's Directive on Electronic Commerce seeks to eliminate barriers to an integrated information-based economy.

The European Parliament approved the Electronic Commerce Directive in May 2000. The Directive validates electronic contracts, establishes the liability of Internet intermediaries, provides for online dispute resolution, and institutes other harmonized e-commerce rules.[757] Electronic signatures are not legally discriminated against in European Union member countries. The EU approach does not mandate a particular technology, such as digital signatures, asymmetrical cryptography, or biometrics.[758]

The Electronic Signature Directive was enacted by the European Commission to permit Internet users to send and receive data over electronic networks. The Directive provides legal validity to electronic signatures as long as the signature product meets specific requirements.[759] An electronic signature is considered the equivalent of a handwritten signature and may be introduced into evidence.[760] Electronic signatures are "subject to the legislation [of] and control by the country of origin."[761]

[D]   Product Liability

The European Commission is considering rules for rights and liabilities for the producers of defective products.[762] The European Commission originally

---

[756] European Commission, Electronic Commerce: Commission Welcomes Final Adoptions of Legal Framework Directive (visited June 9, 2000), http://europa.eu.int/comm/intrnal_market/en/media/eleccomm/2k-442.htm.

[757] *Id.*

[758] European Commission, Commission Welcomes a New Legal Framework to Guarantee Security of Electronic Signatures (visited June 9, 2000), http://europa.eu.int/comm/intrnal_market/en/media/sign/99-915.htm.

[759] *Id.* (discussing Directive 1999/93/EC of Dec. 13, 1999, on a Community framework for electronic signatures).

[760] Directive 1999/93/EC of Dec. 13, 1999, on a Community framework for electronic signatures.

[761] *Id.*

[762] Product liability is covered by Directive 85-374/EEC, OJ L 210 (July 25, 1985), as amended by Directive 99/34/EC,OJ L 141, (June 4, 1999).

enacted a directive concerning liability for defective products in 1985, and in 1999 it adopted Directive 99/34/EC, which makes the producers of non-processed agricultural products liable without fault for damages to health caused by defective products. The Commission's Green Paper is considering expanding the principle of strict liability to all products, including computer systems. Product manufacturers already are "obliged to make good any damage to health, safety, and property caused by a defective product" under the 1985 Directive.[763]

[E] Data Protection Directive

The EU's Data Protection Directive went into effect in October 1998. Member states must ensure that personal data transferred to nonmember states is adequately protected.[764] The European Directive requires the protection of personal information transmitted outside the EU. The U.S. Department of Commerce and the European Commission negotiated a "safe harbor" to comply with the Data Protection Directive.[765] The European Commission has adopted a decision recognizing the adequacy of the "safe harbor" principles despite reservations expressed by the European Parliament that remedies for individuals needed to be strengthened.[766] Companies obtain a "safe harbor" by binding themselves to data protection principles.[767]

[F] International Use of Web Site Materials

SPC should conspicuously note "that it makes no representation that materials on this site are appropriate or available in locations outside the United States, and accessing them from territories where their contents are illegal is prohibited. Those who choose to access this site from other locations do so on their own initiative and are responsible for compliance with local laws."[768]

---

[763] The European Commission, The Commission Adopts a Green Paper on Producer Liability (visited May 10, 2000), http://europa.eu.int/comm/internal_market/en/update/consumer/99-580.htm.

[764] The European Commission, Data Protection: Commission Endorses "Safe Harbor" Arrangement with U.S. (visited Apr. 7, 2000), http://europa.eu.int/comm/internal_market/en/media/dataprot/news/harbor4.htm.

[765] *Id.*

[766] *See* European Commission, Data Protection: Commission Adopts Decisions Recognising Adequacy of Regimes in US, Switzerland and Hungary, http://www.europa.eu.int/comm/internal_market/en/media/dataprot/news/safeharbor.htm (visited Sept. 22, 2000).

[767] *Id.*

[768] This International Use clause is based on that used by America Online. AOL.com Terms and Conditions of Use (visited May 12, 2000), http://www.aol.com.

[G] International Usage of Trade

Devising uniform rules for safeguarding commercial transfers of information that would follow a template familiar no matter where the parties reside is a desirable international development. The International Chamber of Commerce proposes a broad self-regulatory program governing electronic commerce, including guidelines for secure and trustworthy digital transactions over the Internet.[769]

The search for uniform contracting rules as a movement in private international law has evolved rapidly over the past century.[770] Past efforts at creating international commercial law have been spearheaded by the United National Commission for International Trade (UNCITRAL), the International Institute for the Unification of Private Law (UNIDROIT), the Council on Europe, and the International Chamber of Commerce (ICC). UNCITRAL's Model Law on Electronic Commerce is consistent with UCITA's e-commerce infrastructure. The Model Law, like UCITA, validates the digital signature as the functional equivalent of the "pen-and-pencil" signature.

[H] International Enforceability Issues

The recent case law validates mass-market license agreements. The proposed UCITA regulations favor the enforceability of shrinkwrap and other mass-market licenses.[771] SPC's mass-market licenses may not be enforceable in the global marketplace. An empirical study of the laws of 24 countries concluded that no clear consensus exists on the enforceability of shrinkwrap licenses in the global marketplace.[772] Professor Lemley's empirical study of cross-cultural licensing practices found no consensus about the enforceability of shrinkwrap. Policies ranged widely, with some countries treating shrinkwrap as presumptively unenforceable while others held the mirror opposite position that shrinkwrap agreements are enforceable. A number of countries either refuse to enforce shrinkwrap licenses at all or place restrictive conditions on the form and content of such licenses.

Relatively few countries freely enforce shrinkwrap licenses.[773] SPC's counsel must consider the diverse contracting laws in its target markets when drafting its license agreements. A number of other contracting rules differ in other important respects. The European Union has a number of directives that must be complied with in the Internet global marketplace.

---

[769] *Id.* at 85.

[770] Anthony D'Amato and Doris Estelle Long, International Intellectual Property Anthology 3 (1996).

[771] UCITA § 103 (1999).

[772] Mark Lemley, Intellectual Property and Shrinkwrap Licenses, 68 S.Cal. L. Rev. 1239 (2000).

[773] *Id.* at 1252-53.

SPC should consider the following checklist of international issues applicable to web site and other mass-market license agreements:

- **Will SPC's choice of law and forum clauses be enforced?**

- **Do SPC's agreements comply with the Unfair Contract Terms Directive of 1993 as it applies to license agreements?** Unfair clauses and contracts are generally unenforceable. Are statements of limitations of liability and disclaimers conspicuous?

- **Does SPC give visitors the opportunity to read the terms prior to indicating assent by clicking "I accept"?**

- **Does SPC comply with the Distance Contract Directive of the European Commission?**

- **Does SPC comply with the EC Directive on comparative advertising?** If SPC directs online sales to Europe, it must comply with Council Directive 84/450/EEC of September 10, 1984, concerning misleading and comparative advertising.[774]

[I]   Checklist of International Issues for Online Contracts

[1]   Computer Hardware Web Site Sales

a. CISG automatically applies to SPC's online sales of computer hardware made to businesses in signatory states. SPC's place of business is in Boston, Massachusetts, which it notes on its web site.[775] If a contract exists with a nonconsumer in a different signatory state, CISG automatically applies unless the parties opt out in favor of another body of law such as the Uniform Commercial Code.

b. What consumer protection statutes apply to a web site sale of goods? Does the EU Distance Selling Directive apply to SPC's web site sales? Has SPC consulted the Distance Selling Directives implemented in member countries? Does it give adequate prior information to consumers concerning web site contracts? Does it give written confirmation via e-mail? SPC should provide consumers with the following information: (1) company's name and address; (2) the

---

[774] OJ L 250, 19.9, 1984, p. 17. Directive as amended by Directive 98/7 EC of the European Parliament and of the Council (OJ L 101, 1.4.1998, p. 17).

[775] Under CISG, if SPC had more than one place of business, the one with the "closest relationship to the contract and its performance" would be the CISG-related place of business. CISG art. 10(a). If SPC or another online company was operating out of an apartment or place of residence, the place of business would be the "habitual residence." *Id.* art. 10(b).

principal characteristics of its goods or services; (3) the price of its goods or services; (4) possible payment arrangements; (5) the existence of and processes for initiating the right of withdrawal; (6) the cost of using distance communications means, such as telephone service. What is SPC's return policy? Does it give consumers a right of withdrawal? Does it permit a cooling off period of at least seven days from the receipt of the customer's order? Does SPC comply with the other provisions of the EU Directive?

c. How do Internet transmitted offers, acceptance, and consideration operate in the global marketplace? Is SPC contracting with a nonconsumer whose place of business is in a different signatory state? If SPC's web site contract is with a nonconsumer from a different signatory state, does CISG apply? CISG applies to contracts for the sale of goods between parties whose places of business are in different states.[776] CISG does not apply to consumer sales, meaning "goods bought for personal, family or household use."[777]

d. Is SPC's contract predominantly a sale of hardware or is it a contract for software services? CISG governs contracts "in which the preponderant part of the obligations of the party who furnishes the goods consists in the supply of labor or other services."[778] Although web site leases of computer equipment are uncommon, these transactions are outside of CISG. SPC may use a choice of law clause to make a lease agreement subject to Article 2A of the UCC, governing the lease of goods.

If the transaction is structured as a lease, different remedies will be available to the lessee than are available to a buyer. In the case of a finance lease, for example, the lessor has no recourse against the lessee for breach of warranty. Consumer leases mandate special protections not found in either CISG or Article 2. SPC's sale of a computer system includes a combination of hardware, software, and documentation. A company such as Cisco custom builds the component parts of its computer systems. The legal issue is whether a computer system tailored to the user is a sale subject to CISG or a service subject to the common law. SPC must include a choice of law clause to eliminate the uncertainty as to choice of law where a computer contract involves a hybrid of sales and services.

e. Has SPC opted out of CISG by excluding application of the convention or varying its provisions?[779] SPC, for example, could have choice of law, opting out of the CISG in favor of Massachusetts' Article 2 of the UCC. In an international commercial transaction, the sales law of another country may apply. The Sale and Supply of Goods Act, for example, applies to sales of goods in the United Kingdom.

---

[776] *Id.* art. 1.

[777] *Id.* art. 2.

[778] *Id.* art. 3(2).

[779] *Id.* art. 6.

f. Does SPC's conduct conform to commercial standards of reasonableness and good faith under the rules of private international law?[780]

g. Do any courses of performance, courses of dealing, or usages of trade apply to SPC's international sales contracts?

h. Is an electronic communication adequate to prove the existence of a contract? May a computer contract be made at a web site? The United States is one of the few countries to have a Statute of Frauds. CISG does not require written evidence of sales contracts. When does an electronic offer become effective? In the case of e-mail offers or other Internet-related acknowledgments, it may be desirable to request a return receipt. Article 15 of CISG provides that "[a]n offer becomes effective when it reaches the offeree."[781] In the bricks-and-mortar world, an advertising brochure or circular in a newspaper is an invitation to make an offer, as opposed to an offer. In the Internet environment, is it reasonable for a web site visitor to rely on SPC's pricing information as an irrevocable offer?

Article 16 of CISG states that an offer cannot be removed "if it was reasonable for the offeree to rely on the offer as being irrevocable and the offeree has acted in reliance on the offer."[782] SPC should consider structuring its online kiosk or electronic catalog as containing mere invitations for offers, as opposed to enforceable offers. CISG provides that an "offer may be revoked if the revocation reaches the offeree before he has dispatched an acceptance."[783] SPC should conspicuously give notice that it may revoke offers or amend its electronic catalog at any time.

i. What performance standards apply to a sale of computer hardware? CISG does not permit the parties the remedy of cancellation of the contract unless a "fundamental breach" has occurred.[784] The standard of performance in a single delivery of goods is the perfect tender rule. If a sales contract fails in any respect, the seller is deemed to be in breach.[785]

j. What warranties apply to personal computers sold from SPC's web site? Although CISG does not use the term "warranty," the EU Convention applies warranty-like provisions to the sale of goods.

k. What supplemental principles, such as consumer protection directives, apply to SPC's sale of hardware? The European Commission adopted a directive regulating distance selling, including sales via the Internet. The European Union's Distance Selling Directive gives consumer's a "right of reflection before

---

[780] *Id.* art. 7(1)(2).

[781] *Id.* art. 15(a).

[782] *Id.* art. 16(2)(b).

[783] *Id.* art. 16(1).

[784] *Id.* art. 25.

[785] UCC § 2-601 (1999).

accepting a contract and establishes a right to withdraw from a contract" under certain circumstances.[786]

[2] Export and Reexport Licenses

a. Do antiboycott regulations apply to any of SPC's software down-loaded from its web site? Does SPC need a license from the Department of Commerce to export software? Exports and reexports are subject to the Export Administration Regulations (EAR) administered by the Bureau of Export Administration of the U.S. Department of Commerce.

b. What item does SPC intend to export or reexport? Is it subject to EAR licensing requirements? Is a license required? The BXA, for example, licenses software with dual use, such as commercial software with a military application.

c. Where is SPC's item going? The BXA maintains a list of individuals to whom and countries to which designated products may not be exported or reexported.

d. Who will receive SPC's item? Is the recipient on the denied person's list?

e. What will the recipient do with SPC's item? The legality of licensing depends on the technical specifications, destination, end-use, and end-user for the exported or reexported item.

f. In what other activities are the recipients of the item involved?[787] This standard requires SPC to determine whether the recipient of the exported (or reexported) software is involved in any questionable activities. In less than clear-cut cases, SPC may wish to consult with the BXA. The BXA web site offers online assistance to help companies determine whether they have obligations under the EAR. Special agents work with the business community to enforce EAR regulations.[788] The BXA operates an advice line and maintains a list of firms and individuals who have been denied export and reexport privileges.[789]

---

[786] Microsoft Law and Corporate Affairs, Summary of Global Internet Legal Developments 93 (1999) (noting that the texts of the Distance Selling Law and the proposed European Commission Directive are available at http://europa.eu.int/comm/dg15/en/index.htm).

[787] U.S. Department of Commerce, Bureau of Export Administration, Fact Sheet: How Do I Know If I Need to Get a License from the Department of Commerce? (visited May 15, 2000), http://www.bxa.doc.gov/factsheets/facts1.htm.

[788] Boston's Export Enforcement Field Office, for example, is located in Room 350 at 10 Causeway Street, Boston, MA 02222 (telephone: 617-565-6030; fax: 617-565-6039). The BXA also has enforcement offices in New York, Washington, Miami, and Chicago. Contact information and web site forms are available at http://www.bxa.doc.gov/factsheets/ExporterAssistance.html. The BXA's Antiboycott Advice Line is 202-482-2381; it operates from 9 A.M. to 4 P.M. EST (fax: 202-482-0913).

[789] The file of denied persons occupies more than 300KB and takes two to three minutes to download. *Id.*

[3]   Licensing of Software at Web Sites

a. Will SPC's shrinkwrap, clickwrap or other mass-market licenses be enforceable according to contract law outside the United States? SPC should note that shrinkwrap and other mass-market licenses are more likely to be enforced in courts in the United States than in those of European countries.

[4]   Electronic Data Interchange (EDI)

a. Does SPC comply with EDI rules of conduct formulated by the Uniform Rules of Conduct for Interchange of Trade Data by Telecommission (UNCID)? Does SPC follow the EDI standard chosen by the contracting parties?

CHAPTER SEVEN

EXPOSURE TO LAWSUITS IN DISTANT FORUMS: JURISDICTION

§ 7.01 INTRODUCTION

Suffolk Personal Computers ("SPC") is about to enter the global electronic marketplace: SPC is developing content on its web site to attract potential customers. It has recently expanded its web site to include a free service offering online help for its personal computer customers. The software division offers online assistance and tips for persons with hardware and software problems. The software services division represents the first time that SPC has marketed a product independently of its personal computers division. SPC also manages its software services through fax, e-mail, and Internet chat sessions. Digital messages at the company are transmitted or received by consultants through cell phones, the telephone, e-mail, and real-time instant messages over the Internet.[1]

Within a few months of offering this service, SPC received a demand letter from an attorney in California. In the letter, the plaintiff's attorney claimed that his client used a technical tip from SPC's web site to repair a computer and suffered a personal injury in the process. The defendant has charged SPC with professional negligence and the tort of computer malpractice, which is not yet a recognized cause of action in Massachusetts.

The letter also contained a summons requesting that SPC make a personal appearance in a California court and noted that the defendant was demanding a jury trial. The issue that concerns SPC's counsel is whether a federal court sitting in California may assert personal jurisdiction over SPC, a nonresident, in an action arising from services from SPC's site. The Internet recognizes no boundaries, and now SPC must defend a computer malpractice case in a distant forum.

This chapter examines jurisdictional issues that arise in the operation of a web site. The Internet is a "global 'super-network' of over 15,000 computer networks used by over 30 million individuals, corporations, organizations, and educational institutions worldwide."[2] No special tribunal decides cases arising out of Internet activities, nor is there a specific jurisdiction known as cyberspace.[3] No international treaty governs Internet jurisdiction. Since no exclusive subject matter jurisdiction exists for cyberspace, courts must apply traditional principles to a new setting.

Defending a suit in a distant state or country is time-consuming, burdensome, and expensive. Doing business over the Internet may expose a company to unfamiliar substantive law and procedural rules in a foreign jurisdiction. Simply

---

[1] This example is loosely based on Cisco's newly formed Internet Communication Software Group. Alex Pham, Cisco Plans to Move into Software: Base for New Efforts to Be in New England, Boston Globe, May 23, 2000.

[2] American Civil Liberties Union v. Reno, 929 F. Supp. 825, 830-31 (E.D. Pa. 1996).

[3] *Id.* at 830-832.

posting information on an electronic bulletin board accessible in a foreign jurisdiction may subject the online company to liability. States generally extend jurisdiction beyond their borders by a long-arm statute, which provides for service of process on nonresidents. At one time, a defendant could flee the jurisdiction, leaving the plaintiff without a remedy. A more mobile, modern society led the legislatures to enact long-arm statutes. The first long-arm statutes were enacted to provide "constructive or substituted service of process on a nonresident motorist" involved in an accident within the jurisdiction.[4]

Today's more modern long-arm statutes permit process to be served on nonresidents for a wide variety of torts and other causes of action. In considering the issue of personal jurisdiction over a nonresident, a court must first apply the forum state's long-arm statute and then determine if the requirements of the long-arm statute are met.[5]

Foreign jurisdictions have functionally similar devices, and the number of cases of online companies litigating in foreign jurisdictions is growing. The key question addressed here is what Internet-related activity subjects SPC to jurisdiction in another state or country. As with other chapters, the focus is on steps SPC may take to minimize the risk of lawsuits in distant forums.

[A]   Subject Matter Jurisdiction

Jurisdiction is defined as the scope of the court's power to adjudicate a controversy.[6] Subject matter jurisdiction is a legal concept that refers broadly to the power of a court to hear a case. Congress limits the actions that U.S. federal courts can decide.

Federal district courts have limited subject matter jurisdiction and may only hear cases involving federal questions or diversity cases involving state claims of a value greater than $75,000. Diversity of citizenship means that the parties are from different states. Diversity jurisdiction was originally conferred on the federal courts to prevent a "home court" advantage. The theory was that a federal court would be a more neutral forum than would the plaintiff's state court. In addition, federal courts have exclusive jurisdiction over patent, trademark, and copyright cases and other statutorily designated categories of disputes.

A federal district court applies the substantive law that would be applied by the state court in the district where the federal court sits. If SPC filed a lawsuit in the federal district court of Massachusetts, the court would apply Massachusetts law. In addition, the Massachusetts federal court would apply Massachusetts's

---

[4] James A. Ballentine, Ballentine's Law Dictionary 754 (3rd ed. 1969).

[5] Cello Holdings LLC v. Lawrence-Dahl Co., 89 F. Supp. 2d 464, 469 (S.D. N.Y. 2000).

[6] *See* Mary Kay Kane, Civil Procedure in a Nutshell, 6 (1985) (discussing subject matter jurisdiction).

conflict of law rules. SPC will include a choice of law and forum clause in its web site, shrinkwrap, mass market, and negotiated contracts. The freedom to choose the law and forum is the greatest for commercial transactions. Courts are unlikely to enforce one-sided choice of law or forum clauses for consumer transactions. A web site order form may be devised to screen out consumer sales, if the risk of jurisdiction seems to be too great. Contractual choice of law, forum, and venue will be enforced in the commercial context, as long as no fundamental public polices are violated.[7]

If parties to an online or other mass-market license agreement choose a particular state law to apply to their contract, the courts will uphold this choice of law absent a fundamental public policy that mitigates against enforcement. The Uniform Commercial Code, for example, states affirmatively the "right of the parties to a multi-state transaction or a transaction involving foreign trade to choose their own law."[8] Section 1-105 grants the parties power to choose applicable law so long as the "transaction bears a reasonable relation to this state."[9]

Most tort or contract disputes are typically adjudicated in the state courts, the law of torts being largely a matter of state law, as are the fields of contract law, property law, and family or probate law. The state courts also have the residual powers to decide cases not allocated to the federal courts under the U.S. Constitution. An Internet-related action originally brought in state court may be removed to federal court provided a court agrees that 28 U.S.C. § 1441(a) is satisfied. A federal court exercising jurisdiction in a lawsuit may resolve state causes of action that are also part of the suit under the doctrine of pendent jurisdiction.

SPC should routinely include a choice of forum as well as choice of law and venue clause in each of its online agreements. Courts will generally enforce a parties' agreement to adjudicate a dispute in a particular forum, applying an agreed upon body of law. The parties to international sales contracts also have the discretion to choose the applicable law.[10] The Convention on Contracts for the International Sale of Goods (CISG) applies to sale of goods between parties whose places of business are in different signatory states.[11] Many private international agreements agree to adjudicate disputes in an exclusive forum, such as arbitration.

There are limits to the parties' ability to choose the applicable law or forum. In many European countries, mass-market or shrinkwrap license agreements are

---

[7] The choice of law, forum, and venue, for example, must bear a "reasonable relationship" to the commercial contract. *See* UCC § 1-105 (2000).

[8] UCC § 1-105, O.C.#1 (2000).

[9] UCC § 1-105 (2000).

[10] Article 6 of the Convention on Contracts for the International Sale of Goods states that "[t]he parties may exclude the application of this Convention or, subject to Article 12, derogate from or vary the effect of any of its provisions." *See* CISG art. 6 (2000).

[11] CISG art. 1 (2000).

not enforceable. Many countries have mandatory consumer protection for distance contracts, which include Internet sales. In the United States, a plaintiff is not entitled to bring an action in federal court in the absence of federal subject matter jurisdiction. The parties cannot agree to submit their dispute to the federal courts, as Congress confers jurisdiction to the federal courts.[12] State courts have been the traditional province of the law of corporations, commercial law, trusts and estates, and countless other substantive fields.

The typical procedural devices for challenging jurisdictions are (1) a motion challenging the sufficiency of jurisdiction; (2) a summary judgment motion; or (3) a request for a hearing on jurisdiction.

[B] Challenging Personal Jurisdiction

For a court to resolve a dispute, it must be able to exercise personal jurisdiction over a defendant, which requires first that the defendant have minimum contacts with the forum state. Businesses with an online presence may not be summoned to a distant forum unless personal jurisdiction is satisfied. If SPC has minimum contacts with a forum state, a court will move to the next step of the due process analysis and determine whether the exercise of personal jurisdiction over SPC offends "traditional notions of fair play and substantial justice."[13]

A defendant challenging personal jurisdiction in federal court will file a motion to dismiss.[14] A defendant may challenge personal jurisdiction with an interlocutory appeal.[15] A court may permit the defendant to conduct discovery for the purpose of challenging a defendant's motion to dismiss. Courts may also allow the filing of briefs on a motion to dismiss.[16] A United States Court of Appeals applies a *de novo* standard of review to a lower court's decision on whether the exercise of personal jurisdiction complies with due process.[17] The lack of personal jurisdiction is a waivable defense in federal courts, whereas subject matter may not be waived.[18]

---

[12] ErieNet, Inc. v. VelocityNet, Inc., 156 F.2d 513 (3rd Cir. 1998).

[13] Soma Medical International v. Standard Chartered Bank, 196 F.3d 1292, 1299 (10th Cir. 1999) (quoting Ashai Metal Industry Co., 480 U.S. at 113).

[14] Most state courts have enacted state rules of civil procedure that parallel the Federal Rules of Civil Procedure.

[15] GTE New Media Services Inc. v. Bellsouth Corp., 199 F.3d 1343 (D.C. Cir. 2000) (noting that an interlocutory appeal may be brought pursuant to 28 U.S.C. § 1292(b) to determine whether the quality and nature of the web site meets the due process standard of minimum contacts).

[16] The court in American Eyewear, Inc. v. Peeper's Sunglasses, 2000 U.S. Dist. LEXIS 6875 (N.D. Tex. May 16, 2000) allowed discovery and briefing on the issue of personal jurisdiction.

[17] Mink v. AAAA Development LLC, 190 F.3d 333 (5th Cir. 1999).

[18] Fed. R. Civ. P. 12 (h)(1).

If a defendant challenges jurisdiction, the burden shifts to the plaintiff to come forward with sufficient facts to establish personal jurisdiction.[19] The plaintiffs meet this burden by making a *prima facie* showing of "sufficient contacts between the defendant and the forum state."[20] The plaintiff can typically meet this burden by establishing jurisdictional facts through affidavits or other sworn evidence demonstrating the interconnections between the defendant, the forum, and the litigation. The "minimum contacts" aspect of the due process analysis for exercising jurisdiction can be established through contacts that give rise to specific personal jurisdiction or those that give rise to general personal jurisdiction.[21]

In an online dispute, the jurisdictional dispute focuses on the connection between the web site and the state where jurisdiction is asserted. Commercial transactions in the form of online sales are often sufficient to satisfy personal jurisdiction. A plaintiff may not rely solely on bare pleadings to withstand a defendant's motion to dismiss for lack of *in personam* jurisdiction. Personal jurisdiction is acquired by satisfying the requirements of the forum state's long-arm statute.

[C]   The Minimum Contacts Test

Contemporary jurisdictional analysis in the United States emerged in 1945, long before the Internet was conceived. The Supreme Court in International Shoe Co. v. Washington[22] held that a court could maintain jurisdiction over an out of state defendant only if the defendant had sufficient "minimum contacts" with the forum state. The public policy underlying the "minimum contacts" test is fairness and justice.[23] Thus, a court may assert jurisdiction over an out of state defendant who is doing business in the forum state. Foreign courts also recognize the doctrine of personal jurisdiction, though they may use different terminology. Canada, for example requires a "real and substantial" connection between the dispute and the forum province.[24] The United States Supreme Court noted, in Hanson v. Denckla,[25] how "[t]echnological progress has increased the flow of commerce between States" resulting in an increase in jurisdiction.[26]

The key question is whether the defendant purposefully availed himself of the benefits of doing business in the forum state. The Supreme Court in Worldwide

---

[19] Zippo Manufacturing Co. v. Zippo Dot Com, Inc., 952 F. Supp. 1119, 1121 (W.D. Pa. 1997).

[20] Mellon Bank (East) PSFAS, N.A. v. Farino, 960 F.2d 1217, 1223 (3rd Cir. 1992).

[21] Mink v. AAAA Development LLC, 190 F.3d 333, 335 (5th Cir. 1999) (quoting Latshaw v. Johnston, 167 F.3d 208, 211 (5th Cir. 1999)).

[22] 326 U.S. 310, 319-20 (1945).

[23] *Id.* at 316.

[24] David Woolford, Electronic Commerce: It's All A Matter of Trust: Industry Trend or Event, Comput. Canada, May 7, 1999, at 13.

[25] 357 U.S. 235 (1958).

[26] *Id.* at 250-251.

Volkswagen Corp. v. Woodson[27] ruled that a car dealer selling a car in one state is not subjected to jurisdiction in a distant court merely because the buyer has a car accident in the forum state. In product liability cases, a defendant's conduct must be purposefully directed to the forum state. A basis for personal jurisdiction may not be based entirely on the manufacturer's act of placing a defective product in the stream of commerce.[28] In the Internet context, the important question is whether the defendant reached out and originated contacts with residents in the forum state.[29] The amount of revenue from interstate or international commerce is a key factor in determining personal jurisdiction.[30]

The flow of e-commerce between countries on the Internet creates the need for a similar increase in jurisdiction between litigants across the globe. The law of the Internet is rapidly evolving without international treaties addressing cyberspace jurisdiction. Courts seek the closest parallel from the offline world adapted to the commercial realities of cyberspace. Courts struggle in deciding whether a web site is closest to a publisher, television station, bookstore, or baby Bell telecom. This chapter explains some of the basic issues of civil procedure that arise in the online world.

§ 7.02   TWO PARADIGMS OF PERSONAL JURISDICTION

Cyberspace places a new twist on the concept of jurisdiction. Is creating a web site purposefully directed to all potential Internet users or is it similar to placing a product in the stream of commerce? Courts have taken different approaches when faced with relatively identical facts.[31] Since it is unlikely that courts will reach a consensus soon, anyone with a web presence faces the remote possibility that they might have to defend themselves in a distant legal forum.[32]

As the World Wide Web evolved, most web sites were strictly informational and not interactive. An Internet presence was the equivalent of an electronic brochure, available for anyone who stumbled across the links. Consequently, early jurisdiction cases usually involved a controversy independent of the Internet. The web presence was used to try to prove that the defendant had contacts with the forum state.

---

[27] 444 U.S. 286 (1980).

[28] Asahi Metal Industry Co. v. Superior Court, 480 U.S. 102 (1987).

[29] Cello Holdings, LLC v. Lawrence-Dahl Co., 89 F. Supp. 464, 470 (S.D. N.Y. 2000).

[30] *Id.*

[31] *See* Todd D. Leitstein, A Solution for Personal Jurisdiction on the Internet, 59 LA. L. Rev. 565, 566 n.2 (1999) (contrasting court opinions in Internet jurisdiction cases).

[32] *See* Martin H. Redish, Of New Wine and Old Bottles: Personal Jurisdiction, The Internet, and the Nature of Constitutional Evolution, 38 Jurimetrics J. 575, 578 (1998) (analyzing Internet jurisdiction issues and potential roadblocks to commerce). The Minnesota attorney general posted a warning to all Internet users and providers that they are subject to Minnesota jurisdiction for any information that will be disseminated in the state via the Internet. T.J. Thurston, Tackling Conflicts of Law Issues on the Internet, Internet Newsletter: Bus. & Law Aspects, Mar. 1997, at 8.

Many courts found that an informational site was insufficient for jurisdiction without some additional contact with the forum state.[33] Courts have generally inquired as to whether the Internet content provider could have reasonably anticipated defending him or herself in the distant jurisdiction.[34]

The courts have carved out two generic types of personal jurisdiction: specific jurisdiction and general jurisdiction.[35] The "minimum contacts" test of *International Shoe* may be satisfied by the exercise of general and specific jurisdiction. General jurisdiction exists when the plaintiff's cause of action arises from the defendant's nonforum-related activities. The quantity and quality of an online company's contacts with a forum determine general jurisdiction.

General jurisdiction is properly exercised even if causes of action do not originate in the forum, provided the defendant has "continuous and systematic contacts with the forum."[36] Specific jurisdiction is found when the plaintiff's cause of action arises out of a defendant's forum-related activities. The defendant may be subject to the state's exercise of specific jurisdiction if the forum activities are sufficiently persuasive.[37] Specific jurisdiction in the online world as well as the offline world depends on whether the defendant could have "reasonably anticipate[d] being haled into court there."[38]

[A]   General Jurisdiction

General jurisdiction exists over a nonresident defendant only if contacts with the forum are so extensive that "it is possible to overlook the fact the cause of action arose elsewhere."[39] The test for general jurisdiction is whether the defendant has engaged in "systematic and continuous" activities in the forum state.[40]

---

[33] Compare Hearst Corp. v. Goldberger, No. 96 Civ. 3620 (PKL) (AJP), 1997 U.S. Dist. LEXIS 2065, at *2 (S.D.N.Y. Feb. 26, 1997) (observing nationwide jurisdiction on basis of Internet presence violates traditional case law and policy) and Pres-Kap v. System One, 636 So. 2d 1351, 1353 (Fla. App. 1994) (noting jurisdiction based on online contacts alone would dangerously broaden state courts' reach) with Telco Communications v. An Apple A Day, 977 F. Supp. 404, 407 (E.D. Va. 1997) (asserting jurisdiction based on Internet advertising) and Inset Sys., Inc. v. Instruction Set, Inc., 937 F. Supp. 161, 165 (D. Conn. 1996) (holding Internet advertisement and a toll-free number were sufficient to establish jurisdiction).

[34] *See* Matthew Oetker, Personal Jurisdiction and the Internet, 47 Drake L. Rev. 613, 626, 1999 (exploring traditional and Internet-based requirements for jurisdiction).

[35] Helicopteros Nacionales de Colombia, S.A. v. Hall, 466 U.S. 408 (1984).

[36] *See, e.g.,* National Paintball Supply, Inc. v. Cossio, 996 F. Supp. 459, 461 (E.D. Pa. 1998) (applying Pennsylvania law).

[37] World-Wide Volkswagen Corp. v. Woodson, 444 U.S. 286, 297 (1980).

[38] *Id.*

[39] Gene R. Shreve and Peter Raven-Hansen, Understanding Civil Procedure 73 (1989).

[40] *Id. See also* Brand v. Menlove Dodge, 796 F. 2d 1070, 1073 (9th Cir. 1996) (noting that standard for general jurisdiction is "fairly high").

Another court described the test for general jurisdiction as contacts that are "extensive and persuasive."[41] General jurisdiction permits courts to exercise jurisdiction on nonresidents for all purposes because of the defendant's extensive activities directed at the state. The difference between general and specific jurisdiction is a matter of degree.

Suppose a Massachusetts company launched a web site entitled "Vermont.com" directed exclusively to Vermont Internet users. Assume further that the company's online sales are made exclusively to Vermont residents. If the Massachusetts company had an extensive network of representatives in Vermont, a court would likely hold that the contact is so great as to confer general jurisdiction. Courts seldom find that there is a sufficient basis for general jurisdiction because it "requires far more extensive contact between the forum and the defendant than does specific jurisdiction."[42]

The doctrine of general jurisdiction is useful when there is little or no causal connection between the defendant's wrongdoing and the forum. If a plaintiff cannot establish specific jurisdiction, a court may exercise general jurisdiction over the defendant, provided that the defendant's contacts are "continuous and systematic" with the forum state.[43] There are no precedents as to what level of activity constitutes general jurisdiction for the online world.

[B]   Specific Jurisdiction

If contacts are not so substantial or continuous to qualify for general jurisdiction, a court may still exercise specific jurisdiction for forum-related acts.[44] Specific jurisdiction exists if: (1) an online defendant availed himself of the privileges of doing business; (2) the claim arose out of forum-related activities, and (3) the exercise of jurisdiction is reasonable.[45]

Consequently, SPC may be exposed to the product liability jurisdiction of any state where the computers are sold. Internet activities that may give rise to specific jurisdiction include defamation, copyright or trademark infringement, false advertising, or breach of contract.[46] SPC's online product liabilities for placing dangerously defective computers in the stream of commerce may be the basis of

---

[41] Reliance Steel Prods. v. Watson, Ess., Marshall, 675 F.2d 587, 589 (3d Cir. 1982).

[42] Gene R. Shreve and Peter Raven-Hansen, Understanding Civil Procedure 67 (1989).

[43] Helikopteros Nacionales de Colombia, S.A. v. Hall, 466 U.S. 408 (1984).

[44] Burger King v. Rudzewics, 471 U.S. 462, 475 (1985); Bancroft & Masters Inc., 2000 U.S. App. LEXIS 20917 (9th Cir. Aug. 18, 2000).

[45] Cybersell, Inc. v. Cybersell, Inc., 130 F.3d 414, 416 (9th Cir. 1997).

[46] Carl W. Chamberlin, To the Millennium: Emerging Issues for the Year 2000 and Cyberspace, 13 Notre Dame J.L. Ethics & Pub. Pol'y 131, 150 (1999). Additionally, specific jurisdiction was proper in a patent infringement case wherein the defendant infringed the plaintiff's patent online coupon system. Coolsavings.com, Inc. v. I.Q. Commerce Corp., No 98 C. 7750, 1999 U.S. Dist. LEXIS 8852 (N.D. Ill. E.D. June 10, 1999).

specific jurisdiction if the computer was ordered by a state resident who visited SPC's site.

[1] *International Shoe* in Cyberspace

A court must determine whether a nonresident web site is subject to jurisdiction under the law of the state as well as due process. The test the Supreme Court articulated in International Shoe Co. v. Washington[47] focuses upon whether the nonresident has minimum contacts with the forum state so as to satisfy "traditional notions of fair play and substantial justice under the Due Process Clause of the Fourteenth Amendment."[48] A web site that sells goods or licenses software is entitled to due process. An online company should not be forced to defend claims where the exercise of jurisdiction offends "traditional notions of fair play and substantial justice."[49]

The minimum contacts test may be established by contacts to support specific jurisdiction or contacts that support general jurisdiction when a company's activities are "systematic and continuous." For the minimum contacts test for specific jurisdiction to be satisfied, "(1) the contacts must be related to the plaintiff's cause of action; (2) the contacts must involve some act by which the defendant purposefully avails itself of the privilege of conducting activities within the forum; and (3) the forum must be such that the defendant should reasonably anticipate being haled into court there."[50]

SPC's aspirations in becoming an e-business may result in a finding that it "purposefully established contacts with the forum state."[51] If SPC is found to have purposely availed itself of the forum by web site sales or other extensive commercial activity, it is likely that a court will find that the exercise of jurisdiction meets the standard of fair play. It is questionable whether a single sale of a computer from SPC's web site would constitute an act of purposeful availment.[52]

In the typical e-commerce case, the online company will not be targeting consumers in any one jurisdiction. The closest parallel is a national television or print advertisement not directed at any one state.[53] Courts frequently focus on

---

[47] 326 U.S. 310 (1945).

[48] People Solutions, Inc. v. People Solutions, Inc., 2000 U.S. Dist. LEXIS 10444 (N.D. Tex., July 25, 2000) (discussing Constitutional limits of minimum contacts).

[49] Burger King Corp. v. Rudzewicz, 471 U.S. 462, 476 (1985) (quoting International Shoe Co. v. Washington, 326 U.S. 310, 320 (1945)).

[50] Kim v. Keenan, 71 F. Supp. 2d 1228, 1235 (M.D. Fla. 1999) (quotation omitted).

[51] *Id.*

[52] *Id.*

[53] A federal court found that a defendant's web site was not directed at Connecticut any more than any other state declining jurisdiction. The courts observed that the defendant's web site was functionally equivalent to an advertisement in a national magazine or web site. Edberg v. Neogen Corp., 17 F. Supp. 2d 104 (D. Conn. 1998).

whether a web site is being used for e-commerce activities rather than merely posting information about the company. Similarly, a Pennsylvania court granted a defendant's motion to dismiss for lack of personal jurisdiction in an antitrust action.[54] The court found that the defendant's passive web page was a mere conduit for corporate information where no business was transacted and therefore no basis existed for exercising general jurisdiction.

A court may find general jurisdiction even if the controversy does not arise out of the defendant's activities in the state. Jurisdiction over a London hotel by a New York resident who was injured in London was proper in New York, for example, because the hotel maintained a reservation agent in New York.[55]

In a more contemporary example, an Internet presence alone was insufficient to support jurisdiction over an out of state defendant in a wrongful death action.[56] Systematic advertising and business contacts, however, in addition to an interactive web presence making online sales, may be sufficient to support general jurisdiction if the server or computer system is also located within state borders.[57]

[2]   Preventive Law Pointer: Personal Jurisdiction

SPC may file a motion to dismiss for lack of personal jurisdiction if it is summoned into a California or other state court. Courts typically apply a three-pronged test to determine whether sufficient basis exists for specific personal jurisdiction: (1) the defendant must have sufficient "minimum contacts" with the forum state; (2) the claim asserted against the defendant must arise out of those contacts; and (3) the exercise of jurisdiction must be reasonable.[58] These principles apply equally well to cyberspace, although they were formulated in the offline world.

SPC will file a motion to dismiss for lack of personal jurisdiction under Rule 12(b)(2) of the Federal Rules of Civil Procedure if there are insufficient minimum contacts. If SPC challenges personal jurisdiction, the plaintiff will bear the burden of making a *prima facie* case by alleging facts sufficient to establish jurisdiction over a nonresident defendant. SPC must allege facts contesting jurisdiction as

---

[54] Santana Products, Inc. v. Bobrick Washroom Equipment, 14 F. Supp. 2d 710 (M.D. Pa. July 24, 1998).

[55] Frummer v. Hilton Hotels Int'l, Inc., 19 N.Y. 2d 533 (1967). *But see* Romero v. Holiday Inn, Utrecht, 1998 U.S. Dist. LEXIS 19997 (E.D. Pa. Dec. 15, 1998) (denying jurisdiction on the basis of defendant's Internet reservation service).

[56] Grutowski v. Steamboat Lake Guides and Outfitters, Inc., 1998 U.S. Dist. LEXIS 20255 (E.D. Pa. Dec. 21, 1998).

[57] Mieczkowski v. Masco Corp., 997 F. Supp. 782 (E.D. Tex. 1998).

[58] Zippo Mfr. Co. v. Zippo Dot Com, Inc., 952 F. Supp. 1119, 1122 (W. D. Pa. 1997) (quoting World Wide Volkswagen Corp. v. Woodson, 444 U.S. 287 (1980)).

"[u]ncontroverted allegations by the plaintiff must be taken as true."[59] If there is a conflict in facts concerning personal jurisdiction, the federal district court must resolve doubts in favor of the plaintiff.[60]

[C]   Conflict of Laws

Three concepts are critical to understanding the question of which law applies to an Internet dispute where the parties are in different states or countries: conflict of laws, choice of law, and contracts where there is a choice of law clause. Conflict of laws is a branch of law that evolved out of private international law, the body of law that applies in international trade. Questions of conflict of laws arise in cases "in which some relevant fact has a connection with another system of law on either territorial or personal grounds, and may, on that account, raise a question as to the application of one's own or the appropriate alternative (usually foreign) law to the determination of the issue."[61]

In an e-commerce patent case, personal jurisdiction will be governed by federal circuit court decisions, not the law of a local U.S. court of appeals.[62] The federal district court will consider both statutory and constitutional issues in deciding challenges to personal jurisdiction. "Determining whether jurisdiction exists over an out-of-state defendant involves two inquiries: whether a forum state's long-arm statute permits service of process and whether assertion of personal jurisdiction violates due process."[63] The due process analysis is the same whether a case arises under federal question jurisdiction or diversity.[64] "A federal diversity court's jurisdictional power over a nonresident defendant may not exceed the limits allowed under state law."[65]

The choice of law occurs in an online setting when a court must choose whether to apply the differing substantive laws of the parties. Choice of law is "a subset of conflict of laws, concerns the necessity the courts choose between differing substantive laws of interested states."[66] Conflict of law is when the court determines the applicable law. Where the parties do not make a choice of law, it is

---

[59] Nutrition Physiology Corp. v. Enviros Ltd., 87 F. Supp. 2d 648 (N.D. Texas, 2000) (citing Mink v. AAAA Development LLC, 190 F.3d 335, 335 (5th Cir. 1999)).

[60] Id.

[61] Bryan A. Garner, A Dictionary of Modern Legal Usage 200 (4th ed. 1995) (quoting R.H. Graveson Conflict of Law 3 (7th ed. 1974)).

[62] See, e.g., Viam Corp. v. Iowa Export-Import Trading Co., 84 F.3d 424, 427 (Fed. Cir. 1996).

[63] Nutrition Physiology Corp. v. Enviros Ltd., 87 F. Supp. 2d 648, 650 (N.D. Tex. 2000).

[64] Id. at 651, n.1.

[65] Butler v. Beer Across America, 83 F. Supp. 2d 1261 (N.D. Ala. 2000) (holding that personal jurisdiction could not be asserted by a federal court sitting in diversity in Alabama over a nonresident Illinois defendant in an action arising from a single online sale of beer from the defendant's web site).

[66] Id. (quoting Robert A. Leflar, The Nature of Conflicts Law, 81 Colum L. Rev. 1080 (1981)).

the court's duty to determine the applicable law. In limited circumstances, the courts where the parties' choice is contrary to a public policy will not enforce the parties' choice of law.

[D] *In rem* Jurisdiction

The application of the concept of *in rem* jurisdiction, jurisdiction over property rather than persons, to cyberspace activities seems anomalous. Yet *in rem* actions exist for Internet domain names, which are a form of intellectual property. Under United States law, *in rem* jurisdiction affects the rights of all persons in a designated property, whereas "*quasi-in-rem* affects the interests of particular persons in designated property."[67] Internet transactions occur in an international legal environment where the concept of *in rem* jurisdiction may be different. *In rem* jurisdiction in the United Kingdom, for example, refers only to admiralty cases.[68] The law for *in rem* jurisdiction for web servers is relatively undeveloped. The only significant *in rem* action is in domain name litigation. The Anticybersquatting Consumer Protection Act (ACPA) allows an "owner of a mark" to bring an *in rem* action where a domain name allegedly violates the owner's right in a trademark.[69] The Act allows for *in rem* proceedings by the owner of a mark against a domain name in the judicial district in which the domain name registry is located.[70]

The plaintiff in an *in rem* action under the ACPA is the owner of a trademark. Potential defendants include the owner of the infringing domain name or its assignee. The *in rem* action may be filed if the domain name violates the rights of an owner of a registered mark or protected mark and the court finds that the owner either could not obtain personal jurisdiction over the defendant or through due diligence was unable to locate the defendant.[71]

Remedies for the *in rem* action include forfeiture or cancellation of the domain name or transfer of the domain name to the trademark owner.[72] The federal district court held that the *in rem* provisions of the federal act did not violate the defendant's due process rights.[73] In Caesars World, Inc. v. Caesars-Palace.com,[74] a defendant challenged the constitutionality of the *in rem* jurisdiction procedures of the federal anticybersquatting act. The defendant also argued that the court lacked

---

[67] Hanson v. Denckla, 357 U.S. 235, 246 n.12 (1958).

[68] Kazunori Ihiguro, Traditional Legal Concepts: Basics from Three Experts, Remarks, ILPF 1999 Annual Conference, Jurisdiction: Building Confidence in a Borderless Medium, Montreal, Canada, July 26, 1999.

[69] 15 U.S.C. § 1125(d) (2000).

[70] Caesars World, Inc. v. Caesars-Palace.com, 2000 U.S. Dist. LEXIS 2671 (E.D. Va. 2000).

[71] 15 U.S.C. § 1125(d)(2)(A) (2000).

[72] 15 U.S.C. § 1125(6)(2)(D) (2000).

[73] *Id.*

[74] 2000 U.S. Dist. LEXIS 2671 (E.D. Va., 2000).

personal jurisdiction over the defendants. The court found that registration with Network Solutions, Inc., of Virginia satisfied *in rem* jurisdiction.[75]

Harrods Department Store of London filed an *in rem* action under the ACPA to obtain 60 Internet domain names containing its trademarks. The ACPA *in rem* action was dismissed because the plaintiff failed to plead bad faith, an essential element.[76] Process may be served to a party in the state where the court is located. Absent a specific statutory remedy, such as the federal anticybersquatting act, it is likely that a court will not permit service of process on a *res* without a showing of minimum contacts.

> ### [1]   Preventive Law Pointer: Obtaining *in rem* Jurisdiction

SPC must follow the prescribed procedures for filing an *in rem* action under the ACPA. First, SPC must have filed an action against a company or person. Second, SPC must have attempted personal service or have served by publication if personal service was not practical. Third, the ACPA requires SPC to obtain court permission before filing an *in rem* action. SPC has the burden of proving that the domain name violates its trademark rights prior to filing an *in rem* action. The court must grant SPC formal permission prior to filing its lawsuit against the infringing domain name(s). While the ACPA does require the filing of an *in personam* suit first, the court may waive that requirement if the circumstances are such that it "would be fruitless and a waste of resources."[77]

[E]   Long-Arm Statutes

A long-arm statute is a means of effecting service of process on a nonresident defendant. Every state has enacted long-arm statutes as the tool for exercising jurisdiction over a defendant located outside of the forum. One of the difficulties of extending the long arm of state law to the Internet is that every state then becomes the regulator of the Internet.[78] State regulation of the Internet may also violate the

---

[75] The court cited Shaffer v. Heitner, 433 U.S. 186 (1977) which held that *in rem* jurisdiction is constitutional providing that the *res* or property in dispute has minimum contacts with the forum state. In the online world, minimum contacts were satisfied when a domain name is registered in the forum state.

[76] Harrods v. Limited v. Sixty Internet Domain Names, 2000 U.S. Dist. LEXIS 11911 (E.D. Va., Aug. 15, 2000); *See also* Porsche Cars N. Am., v. Allporsche.com, 2000 U.S. App. LEXIS 12843 (4th Cir. June 9, 2000) (reinstating trademark dilution claim because of the possible applicability of the *in rem* remedy of the ACPA); Lucent Techs., Inc. v. Lucentsucks.com, 95 F. Supp. 2d 528 (E.D. Va. 2000) (dismissing *in rem* action against defendant domain name because the identity of the registrants was possible).

[77] Caesars World, Inc. v. Caesars-Palace.com, 2000 U.S. Dist. LEXIS 2671 (E.D. Va. 2000).

[78] This point was made by Thomas P. Vartanian, Whose Internet Is it Anyway? George Mason University, 2000 Global Internet Summit, Vienna, Virginia, Mar. 13-14, 2000.

Commerce Clause of the U.S. Constitution and invade the sovereignty of hundreds of other countries.[79]

There are due process limits to the exercise of personal jurisdiction under the U.S. Constitution. Hundreds of decided U.S. cases exist covering Internet jurisdiction, but few foreign ones. To establish personal jurisdiction, the plaintiffs must satisfy a two-step test. First, the plaintiff must establish personal jurisdiction pursuant to the long-arm statute. Second, they must establish that jurisdiction comports with due process.[80] A federal court sitting in diversity must first determine whether the relevant state long-arm statute permits the exercise of personal jurisdiction. Every state has enacted a long-arm statute permitting constructive service of process on a nonresident.

The long arm of the law permits state courts, for example, to acquire jurisdiction over a nonresident motorist who flees the jurisdiction before any action may be commenced against him. Physical presence within the forum is not required to obtain personal jurisdiction over a nonresident defendant. Long-arm statutes are divided into two broad types: (1) statutes that assert jurisdiction over the person to the limits allowed by the Fourteenth Amendment to the U.S. Constitution, and (2) statutes that limit the assertion of jurisdiction. A federal court sitting in diversity undertakes a two-step test: "First the court applies the relevant state long-arm statute to see if it permits the exercise of personal jurisdiction, then the court must apply the precepts of the Due Process Clause of the Constitution."[81] Long-arm statutes vary in what activities may trigger the exercise of jurisdiction.

Pennsylvania's long-arm statute, for example, extends jurisdiction to the "fullest extent allowed under the Constitution of the United States and may be based on the most minimum contacts with this Commonwealth allowed under the Constitution of the United States."[82] Similarly, New Jersey's long-arm statute provides for personal jurisdiction as far as it is permitted by the Due Process Clause.[83]

Massachusetts is another example of a jurisdiction with an expansive long-arm statute.[84] A Massachusetts court may employ the long-arm statute to obtain jurisdiction on any defendant who commits a tort in the Commonwealth, provided the defendant does business in the state or derives substantial revenues from goods or services. These statutory grounds are spelled out in the long-arm

---

[79] *Id.*

[80] Noonan v. Winston Co., 135 F.3d 85, 89 (1st Cir. 1998).

[81] IMO Industries, Inc. v. Kiekert AG, 155 F.2d 254 (3rd Cir. 1998).

[82] Santana Products, Inc. v. Bobrick Washroom Equipment, 14 F. Supp. 2d 710, 713 (M.D. Pa. 1998) (noting that Pennsylvania's long-arm statute is coextensive with the Due Process Clause of the U.S. Constitution).

[83] *See* N.J. Ct. R. 4:4-4 (1999).

[84] Mass. Gen. Law Ann. ch. 223A, § 3 (1999).

statute. A firm entering into a license agreement with a Massachusetts corporation to offer web site services would be transacting business and thus would be subject to jurisdiction.

A tort such as misrepresentation or fraud communicated on a web site may also be a basis for jurisdiction. Delaware's long-arm statute was not broad enough to encompass the activities of a defendant who posted allegedly defamatory statements on his Internet site.[85] The Delaware long-arm statute provided coverage only if the defendant committed a tort and was regularly conducting business in the state. A state's long-arm statute may limit jurisdiction where there is only a passive web site.

Courts addressing the issue of personal jurisdiction focus on "the nature and quality of commercial activity that an entity conducts over the Internet."[86] The courts have identified three types of commercial activity to help determine the existence of personal jurisdiction: (1) the web site is clearly doing business over the Internet and personal jurisdiction is proper;[87] (2) visitors to a web site can interact with the host computer and exchange information;[88] and (3) the web site is a passive repository of information or advertisements.[89] The greater the interactivity and commercial activity, the more likely it is that a state can use its long arm to exercise personal jurisdiction. Web sites that are passive and noninteractive are not likely to have the continuous and substantial contacts that satisfy the due process requirements for personal jurisdiction.

➤ **[1] Preventive Law Pointer: *Forun Non Conveniens* in Cyberspace**

Venue refers to the locality where a lawsuit may be brought and an action may be dismissed because it is an inconvenient forum.[90] The public policy for having a venue requirement "is to protect defendants from being forced to defend lawsuits in a court remote from their residence or from where the acts underlying the controversy occurred."[91] It is the court's duty to determine whether venue was proper at the time the plaintiff's complaint was filed.[92] SPC may seek transfer of

---

[85] Clayton v. Farb, 1998 Del. Super. LEXIS 175 (Del., April 23, 1998), reported in Perkins Coie Internet Law Digest (visited Aug. 25, 1999), http://www.perkinscoie.com/resource/ecomm/netcase/Cases-15.htm.

[86] Zippo Mfg. Co. v. Zippo Dot Com, Inc. 952 F. Supp. 1119, 1124 (W.D. Pa. 1997).

[87] *Id.* at 1124.

[88] Maritz, Inc. v. Cybergold, Inc., 947 F. Supp. 1328 (E.D. Mo. 1996).

[89] An example is Bensuasan Restaurant Corp. v. King, 937 F. Supp. 295 (S.D. N.Y. 1996) (finding no jurisdiction over Columbia Missouri's Blue Note Cafe jazz club allegedly violating the trademark of the famous New York Blue Note Cafe).

[90] Nutrition Physiology Corp. v. Enviros Ltd., 87 F. Supp. 2d 648, 652 (N.D. Texas, 2000).

[91] *Id.* (citation omitted).

[92] Hoffman v. Blaski, 368 U.S. 335, 342-344 (1960).

venue if it can demonstrate that the convenience of the parties and interests of justice dictate a transfer under 28 U.S.C. § 1404(a).[93]

SPC may bring a patent infringement lawsuit where the defendant resides or where the defendant has committed acts of infringement and has a regular and established place of business. SPC has a brick-and-mortar place of business in Massachusetts and may be sued in the federal district court of Massachusetts. It may be difficult, however, to determine where acts of infringement occurred when the infringing activity occurs at a defendant's web site. The definition of "where the defendant resides" may be determined by guidelines set out in 28 U.S.C. § 1391 (c). In e-commerce patent cases, the special venue statute applies as in any patent infringement lawsuits.

§ 7.03   CYBER-JURISDICTION CASES

A number of United States courts have predicated personal jurisdiction based upon minimum contacts in cyberspace.[94] As of August 2000, 228 state and federal cases had dealt with the question of personal jurisdiction on the Internet.[95] In Europe, there is relatively 'little case law concerning jurisdiction on the Internet.' Courts agree that a web site presence alone is not an adequate basis for specific jurisdiction. In order for there to be personal jurisdiction, SPC's e-business activity must be pervasive, interactive, and permit online sales and service. Plaintiffs will typically use several tests to argue that Internet contacts satisfy due process. Modern courts update the "minimum contacts" test with the purposeful availment test. Purposeful availment correlates positively with the nature and quality of commercial activity on a site. The "purposeful availment" test focuses on whether the Internet or dot-com company sought out business from web site visitors.

[A]   Purposeful Availment

The United States Supreme Court first articulated the purposeful availment test in Burger King Corp. v. Rudzewicz;[96] the test focuses on whether the defendant sought contacts in or should have reasonably anticipated "being haled into court" in the forum state.[97] Courts have updated the purposeful availment test in

---

[93] 28 U.S.C. § 1400(b) (2000).

[94] *See, e.g.,* Digital Equipment Corp. v. Alta Vista Technology, Inc., 960 F. Supp. 456 (D. Mass 1997) (upheld jurisdiction on theory that trademark infringed purposefully availed itself of the forum state by soliciting Massachusetts residents to visit the Alta Vista web site); Zippo Manufacturing Co. v. Zippo Dot Com, Inc., 952 F. Supp. 1119 (W.D. Pa. 1997) (dividing Internet jurisdiction cases into interactive web sites doing substantial business versus being passive web sites).

[95] LEXIS search, conducted August 8, 2000.

[96] 471 U.S. 462 (1985).

[97] World-Wide Volkswagen Corp. v. Woodson, 444 U.S. 286 (1980).

torts and contracts arising out of cyberspace activities. Courts focus on whether Internet advertisements are directed to residents. A court found that a web site that permitted Arizona residents to make hotel reservations at the web site did provide a sufficient basis for personal jurisdiction.[98] In contrast, a California court found that Internet advertising, like print advertising in a national magazine, did not constitute purposeful availment of a forum.[99] State courts do not agree on the question of whether Internet advertisements confer jurisdiction.

In State of Minnesota v. Granite Gate Resorts, Inc.,[100] the court found sufficient contacts to constitute jurisdiction over a nonresident defendant who operated a gambling site on the Internet through a server located in Belize. The court found that the web site actively solicited Minnesota subscribers and violated state advertising and gambling laws. In Thompson v. Handa-Lopez, Inc.,[101] jurisdiction was predicated upon the defendant's operation of a casino-type arcade game through its web site in which players entered into contracts to play a game of chance.[102] The application of the purposeful availment test differs depending on whether the underlying claim is a tort or contract claim.

[B]   Contracts and Purposeful Availment

Purposeful availment for Internet contracts is based on the level of business activity in the forum state. Companies that sell goods or render services over the Internet will likely be considered to have purposefully availed themselves of the forum by ongoing business transactions and online contracts with the plaintiff.[103]

Personal jurisdiction was properly exercised in the Internet-based case of CompuServe, Inc. v. Patterson.[104] In *Patterson*, a Texas resident advertised his product on an Internet computer system maintained by CompuServe, which is based in Ohio. The Sixth Circuit found that Patterson took direct actions that created a connection with Ohio.[105] Personal jurisdiction was based on the defendant's license agreement with CompuServe and his loading software onto the CompuServe system for others to use, as well as on his web site advertisements.[106]

An Oregon federal court dismissed a trademark infringement and unfair competition action against a retail music seller in Millennium Enterprises, Inc. v.

---

[98] Park Inns Int'l, Inc. v. Pacific Plaza Hotels, Inc., et al., 5 F. Supp. 2d 762 (D. Ariz. 1998).

[99] Osteotech, Inc. v. GenSci Regeneration Sciences, Inc., 6 F. Supp. 2d 349 (D.N.J. 1998).

[100] 568 N.W.2d 715 (Minn. App. 1997).

[101] 998 F. Supp. 738 (W.D. Tex. 1998).

[102] *Id.*

[103] *See, e.g.,* CompuServe v. Patterson, 89 F.3d 1257 (6th Cir.1996).

[104] 89 F.3d 1257 (6th Cir.1996).

[105] *Id.* at 1264.

[106] *Id.*

Millennium Music, LP.[107] In *Millennium Music,* a retail music seller located in Oregon brought an action against a retail music seller located in South Carolina for trademark infringement and unfair competition. The defendant operated a retail music store in South Carolina under the name "Millennium Music." The defendants sold products through the Internet site as well as in retail outlets. Internet sales totaled only $225 as compared to over $2,000,000 in retail sales from their music stores.

The plaintiff was an Oregon resident who had operated a retail outlet under "Music Millennium" since 1969. The plaintiff purchased a compact disc (CD) from Millennium Music through their web site. The plaintiff objected to the defendants' use of the name, "Millennium Music," arguing that consumers would be confused as to the source or origin of the defendants' CDs. The plaintiff sought damages and injunctive relief under the Lanham Act and common law claims for unlawful trade practices. The defendant moved to dismiss for lack of personal jurisdiction. The court found that the sale of a single CD and sporadic purchases lacked the "continuous and systematic" contacts to satisfy general jurisdiction.

The *Millennium* court also found that a single sale did not constitute purposeful availment.[108] Likewise, the defendants' occasional purchases from an Oregon firm did not satisfy the minimum contacts test.[109] The court also found that the effect of the defendant's infringing activities were not sufficient to satisfy the "effects test."[110] Finally, the court found that the defendants' Internet web site did not constitute a sufficient fair warning so that they would reasonably anticipate being "haled" into court in Oregon.[111] The court held that (1) defendant was not subject to general or personal jurisdiction based on sales of one compact disc to an Oregon resident and purchases from a supplier in Oregon, and (2) maintenance of an Internet web site did not subject the defendant to personal jurisdiction in Oregon.[112]

[C] Tortious Activities and Purposeful Availment

Courts are predisposed to finding that due process is satisfied by Internet-related activities. The New Jersey Superior Court, however, uncovered "only two cases in which a court has declined jurisdiction of a non-resident individual or corporate defendant who has used the Internet, e-mail, and computer bulletin boards or forums to make defamatory statements."[113]

---

[107] 33 F. Supp. 2d 907 (D. Oregon 1999).

[108] *Id.* at 910.

[109] *Id.* at 911.

[110] *Id.*

[111] *Id.* at 920.

[112] *Id.*

[113] *Id.* at *10.

It is reasonable to presume that our common law will adapt to the challenges posed by the Internet. With a click of the mouse, reputations may be ruined. "The commission of crimes or civil wrongs via the Internet can be subtler and more damaging that the same acts committed in traditional fashion."[114] Courts have found purposeful availment when the claim involves an intentional tort allegedly committed over the Internet along with evidence that the defendant intentionally directed its tortious activities at the forum state.

In Jewish Defense Organization v. Superior Court,[115] a plaintiff filed a defamation action against the Jewish Defense Organization and its leader Mordechai Levi based upon allegedly defamatory statements posted on a World Wide Web page. The allegedly defamatory statement characterized the plaintiff as a "snitch, a dangerous psychopath, anti-Semite and other derogatory statements."[116] The defendants filed motions to quash service of summons. The plaintiff argued that the defendants had continuous and systematic contacts with California through the Jewish Defense Organization web site.

The *Jewish Defense* court, reversing the lower court, found no general jurisdiction as a matter of law.[117] The court also found insufficient evidence to support specific jurisdiction.[118] The court found that the fact that although the defendants "may have foreseen the allegedly defamatory statements might be published in California, that alone is not enough to subject them to personal jurisdiction in this state."[119] The court concluded that there was insufficient evidence "to establish that it was foreseeable that a risk of injury by defamation would arise in California."[120] The court compared the defendant's activities to that of the defendant in Panavision v. Toeppen.[121]

In *Toeppen*, the court found the tort-like activity of cyberpirating domain names to be a sufficient basis for jurisdiction because the defendant knew his actions would cause plaintiff harm in the forum state. Unlike Dennis Toeppen, the individual defendant in *Jewish Defense Organization* was not a full-time resident of California, nor did he have clients in California. The defendant had no knowledge that the defamatory statements posted on its web site would "impact a business interest or reputation in California."[122] The court also found the defendant's web site to be passive and not purposefully directed toward the forum state.[123]

---

[114] James Garrity and Eoghan Casey, Internet Misuse in the Workplace: A Lawyer's Primer, 72 Fla. Bar J. 22 (Nov. 1998).

[115] 72 App. 4th 1045, 85 Cal. Rptr. 2d 611 (Ct. of App. June 8, 1999).

[116] *Id.* at 614.

[117] *Id.* at 617.

[118] *Id.* at 618.

[119] *Id.* (citation omitted).

[120] *Id.* at 619.

[121] 141 F.3d 1316 (9th Cir. 1998).

[122] *Jewish Defense Organization, id.* at 619.

[123] *Id.* at 620 (citations omitted).

In Drudge v. Blumenthal,[124] White House employee Sidney Blumenthal and his spouse filed a defamation action against the electronically published gossip columnist Matt Drudge for reporting that Mr. Blumenthal was a spouse abuser. The plaintiffs also sued America Online, an interactive computer service provider that published an electronic version of the Drudge Report. AOL moved for summary judgment, and the columnist moved to dismiss or transfer for lack of personal jurisdiction.

The *Blumenthal* court held that AOL was not liable, as an Internet service provider, for making the gossip column available to its subscribers, but that Drudge had engaged in a persistent course of conduct in the District of Columbia (D.C.), which warranted the exercise of personal jurisdiction. The court found that the columnist's interactive web site specifically focused on D.C. political gossip and that the columnist regularly distributed his electronic column to D.C. residents, solicited and received contributions from D.C. residents, and contacted D.C. residents to gather information for the column. Jurisdiction may be based on tortious activity even if made on a passive web site.[125]

A New Jersey court summarized the case law and found no prior decision where a court had found "personal jurisdiction over a non-resident defendant for allegedly defamatory remarks communicated electronically when the plaintiff did not reside in the forum state, the plaintiff's employment was not based in the forum state, and the defendant's electronically transmitted remarks were not specifically targeted at the forum state."[126]

[1] Relatedness Test

The relatedness test for specific jurisdiction examines the causal connection between the defendant's contacts and the plaintiff's cause of action;[127] it examines the relationship between forum-state activities and the underlying litigation. In an Internet case, the question posed is whether the litigation arose directly from a defendant's online activities or web site. In Panavision v. Toeppen,[128] a California based corporation that specialized in providing film equipment to the movie industry filed suit against Dennis Toeppen, an Illinois resident. The lawsuit grew out of Toeppen's hoarding of Internet domain names identical to Panavision's trademarked names and his attempt to extract a princely sum to pay him to release those names. Toeppen expended $10,000 in his domain name business.

---

[124] 992 F. Supp. 44 (D.D.C. 1998).

[125] Telco Communications v. An Apple A Day, 977 F. Supp. 404 (E.D. Va. 1997) (basing jurisdiction upon defamatory press releases made on a passive web site).

[126] Blakey v. Continental Airlines, Inc., 1999 WL 402897 *8 (N.J. Super. A.D. June 9, 1999).

[127] Ticketmaster-New York, Inc. v. Alioto, 26 F.3d 201, 206 (1st Cir. 1994).

[128] 141 F.3d 1316 (9th Cir. 1997).

Toeppen's domain name business activities are alternatively described as "domain name hijacking" or cyberpiracy.[129] The *Panavision* court found domain name hijacking to constitute "something more" and sufficiently related to Toeppen's web site to warrant the exercise of jurisdiction. The Ninth Circuit held that: (1) Toeppen was subject to specific jurisdiction in California; (2) his registration of plaintiff's marks in his Internet domain names was a "commercial use" under dilution statutes; and (3) his registration of Panavision's mark diluted it. A New York federal district court recently declined to follow *Panavision*'s expansive view of personal jurisdiction on web sites.[130] The *Panavision* court is the high-water mark for the kind of minimum contacts that satisfies due process.[131]

[D]   Effects Test

The effects test focuses on the nonresident's committing a tort knowing it will cause harm to the plaintiff in the forum state. The Indiana Court of Appeals held that the use of a company's trademark on a web site, without more, was an insufficient basis for personal jurisdiction.[132] The court rejected the "effects test" of Calder v. Jones[133] as inapplicable to a commercial web site. The court found the "effects test" to be inappropriate for cyberspace because the web site activities of corporations were not typically localized in the forum state. The effects test says that a defendant purposely avails itself of the jurisdiction of the forum when its intentional conduct causes harm and the defendant knows that harm will occur in the forum or targeted state. Courts will frequently apply an "effects" test in intentional tort cases to determine whether the defendant's conduct was aimed at the forum state.[134]

Personal jurisdiction can be based upon "(1) intentional actions (2) expressly aimed at the forum state (3) causing harm, the brunt of which is suffered and which the defendant knows is likely to be suffered in the forum state."[135] A Massachusetts federal district found that a California defendant's marketing of cigar humidors on its web site was one of the key factors in establishing jurisdiction

---

[129] Domain hijacking or cyberpiracy occurs when an individual registers the domain names of famous trademarks and then demands those corporations pay a ransom to release the registered domain names.

[130] K.C.P.L., Inc. v. Nash, 1998 WL 823657 (S.D. N.Y. Nov. 23, 1998).

[131] See also, Indianapolis Colts, Inc. v. Metropolitan Baltimore Football Club, 34 F.3d 410 (7th Cir. 1994) (holding that the Baltimore Colts team was subject to personal jurisdiction in Indiana even though its only activity was broadcasts of its games on nationwide cable television).

[132] Conseco Inc. v. Hickerson, 698 N.E.2d 816 (Ind. Ct. App. 1998). Panavision International v. Toeppen, 141 F.3d 1316 (9th Cir. 1998) (applying effects test to trademark infringment claim).

[133] 465 U.S. 783 (1984).

[134] Ziegler v. Indian River County, 64 F.3d 470, 473 (9th Cir.1995) (applying effects test).

[135] Core-Vent Corp. v. Nobel Industries AB, 11 F.3d 1482, 1486 (9th Cir.1993).

over the defendant.[136] The court noted that jurisdiction was proper because the defendant actively chose to market his goods in Massachusetts, and the claim arose out of sales in the forum state. The minimum contacts analysis "has no place in determining whether a state may assert criminal personal jurisdiction over a foreign defendant."[137] However, courts consider detrimental effects within the forum in exercising criminal jurisdiciton.

[E]   The Sliding Scale of Jurisdiction

As e-commerce has expanded, so has the long arm of jurisdiction. Courts have carved out different categories of web sites: those with substantial business or e-commerce sites and those that are passive conduits.[138] The degree of interactivity is an important factor in dictating the willingness of a court to exercise jurisdiction over a web site.[139] Passive informational web sites are the least likely to subject a defendant to out of state jurisdictions.[140] In one case, an Arizona corporation brought suit against a Florida corporation of the same name.[141] The court affirmed the dismissal of the lawsuit on personal jurisdiction, discussing the distinction between "passive" and "interactive" web sites.[142] The amount of online commercial activity directed to the forum state was a factor. The Florida corporation's web site invited companies interested in Internet advertising to e-mail them.[143]

Web sites that operate as passive advertisements, with company, product, and contact information (telephone and fax number) are usually insufficient for general jurisdiction.[144] While most courts have followed this standard, some jurisdictions disagree and have found that a passive commercial web site must have resulted in some business transactions, exposing the defendant to jurisdiction.[145]

---

[136] Gary Scott International v. Baroudi, 981 F. Supp. 714 (D. Mass. 1997).

[137] State v. Amorosa, 975 F.2d 505, 508 (Ct. App. Utah 1999).

[138] Zippo Mfg. Co. v. Zippo Dot Com, Inc., 952 F. Supp. 1119, 1123-1125 (W.D. Pa. 1997).

[139] *See* Maura I. McInerney and Edward G. Biester III, I.P. Claims Based on Internet Contacts, Legal Intell., June 3, 1999, at 7 (analyzing Internet jurisdiction controversies).

[140] *See* Pheasant Run, Inc. v. Moyse, No. 98 C 4202, 1999 U.S. Dist. LEXIS 1087 (N.D. Il. E.D. Feb. 3, 1999) (finding no jurisdiction arising out of small Internet advertisement); Grutowski v. Steamboat Lake Guides and Outfitters, Inc., 1998 U.S. Dist. LEXIS 20255 (E.D. Pa. Dec., 1998) (denying jurisdiction in a wrongful death action based on passive web advertisement); Cybersell, Inc. v. Cybersell, Inc., 130 F.3d 414, 418 (9th Cir. 1997) (denying jurisdiction because merely creating Internet site did not purposefully direct action towards forum state).

[141] Cybersell, Inc. v. Cybersell, Inc., 130 F.3d 414, 416 (9th Cir. 1997).

[142] *Id.* at 417-418.

[143] *Id.* at 416.

[144] Atlantech Distribution, Inc. v. Credit General Insurance Co., 30 F. Supp. 2d 538, 1998 U.S. Dist. LEXIS 19950 (D. Md. Nov. 11, 1998).

[145] *See* SuperGuide Corp. v. Kegan, Civ. No. 4:97CV181 (W.D.N.C. Oct. 8, 1997) (asserting jurisdiction over a trademark dispute where trademark was used on defendant's web site).

The passive site may still subject a defendant to specific jurisdiction if the web site is the focus of the controversy. A passive web site may contain a defamatory remark, trademark infringement, or disclosure of trade secrets, for example, subjecting the web site operator to potential liability anywhere the plaintiff may be found.[146] In general, a passive web site without "something more" is insufficient for personal jurisdiction.[147]

Courts are likely to find personal jurisdiction where there is an "interactive web site."[148] The greater the interactivity and more commercial the site, the greater the likelihood of jurisdiction. Moving up the scale of potential jurisdiction, a passive site with a customer e-mail response feature may not be sufficient to establish general jurisdiction.[149] The web site with e-mail response approaches the subjective threshold as to what is defined as interactive and sufficient for jurisdiction. A passive site with a customer e-mail contact feature and an event listing, including some events in the forum state, for example, conferred general jurisdiction.[150] Further along the jurisdiction spectrum, a hotel's web site from which residents of the forum state made online reservations was sufficiently interactive for jurisdiction.[151]

Internet sites that permit visitors to download software are considered sufficiently interactive for jurisdiction.[152] An interactive commercial web site featuring a business telephone directory was sufficiently interactive for a court to obtain jurisdiction over a nonresident defendant.[153] Interactivity is not always the death knell to an online exposure to jurisdiction. Some courts have looked beyond interactivity and now assess the degree of commercial activity that the defendant conducts in the forum state.[154] Interactivity, without proof of Internet sales, does not

---

[146] *See, e.g.,* Naxos Resources (U.S.A.) Ltd. v. Southam, Inc. 1996 U.S. Dist. LEXIS 21757, 21759 (S.D. Cal Aug. 16, 1996) (observing defamatory Internet article intended for distribution in forum state may be sufficient for jurisdiction); Edias Software Int'l v. Basis Int'l, 947 F. Supp. 413 (D. Ariz. 1996) (finding combined activities of defamatory e-mails, critical web page and chat room postings conferred jurisdiction).

[147] Cybersell, Inc. v. Cybersell, Inc. 130 F.3d 414, 418 (9th Cir. 1997).

[148] Zippo Mfg. Co. v. Zippo Dot Com, Inc., 952 F. Supp. 1119, 1124 (W.D. Pa. 1997).

[149] Grutowski v. Steamboat Lake Guides and Outfitters, Inc., 1998 U.S. Dist. LEXIS 20255 (E.D. Pa. Dec. 21, 1998). *See also* Origin Instruments Corp. v. Adaptive Computer Systems, Inc., 1999 U.S. Dist. LEXIS 1451 (N.D. Tex. Feb. 3, 1999) (determining web site with e-mail feature was interactive, but insufficient for general jurisdiction).

[150] Vitullo v. Velocity Powerboats, Inc., et al., 1998 U.S. Dist. LEXIS 7120 (N.D. Ill. Apr. 24, 1998).

[151] Park Inns Int'l., Inc. v. Pacific Plaza Hotels, Inc., et al., 5 F. Supp. 2d 762 (D. Ariz. 1998).

[152] *See* 3DO Co. v. Poptop Software, Inc. 49 U.S. P.Q.2d (BNA) 1469 (N.D. Cal. Oct. 27, 1998) (permitting jurisdiction in copyright and trade secret action since defendant's activities were targeted at forum state).

[153] GTE New Media Services, Inc. v. Ameritech Corp., 21 F. Supp. 2d 27 (D.D.C. Sept., 1998).

[154] *See* ESAB Group, Inc. v. Centricut, L.L.C., 34 F. Supp. 2d 323, 330-331 (D. S.C. 1999) (applying commercial activity test to Internet jurisdiction).

satisfy the minimum contacts test, despite the fact that a web site permits interactivity. An Oregon court, for example, found that an interactive web site that sold products and provided franchise and discount club information was not subject to Oregon jurisdiction since it did not have systematic and continuous contacts in the state.[155] California has also reexamined and refined the interactivity scale, ruling that interactivity is irrelevant without proof that anyone from the state actually accessed the web site.[156]

A state may also obtain specific jurisdiction over an out of state defendant who regularly engages in business via the web or derives substantial online revenue from the state.[157] Direct solicitation of residents in a state via the Internet can expose a defendant to another state's jurisdiction.[158] Also, any defamatory remarks on a web site that is directed to a plaintiff in a specific state or country may give rise to jurisdiction.[159]

The court in Zippo Mfg. Co. v. Zippo Dot Com, Inc.[160] developed a continuum for examining the presence of personal jurisdiction based on the activities of the web site. The court found a basis for personal jurisdiction even if the defendant limited its contacts to providing, over the Internet, a news service subscribed

---

[155] *See* Millennium Enterprises, Inc. v. Millennium Music, L.P., 33 F. Supp. 2D 907, 921 (D. Or. 1999) (finding insufficient conduct or connections to establish jurisdiction with the forum state). Defendants explicitly disclaimed sales or information to Oregon on the web site after they learned of the dispute. *Id.* at 909. This may have removed the risk of further jurisdictional exposure while the lawsuit progressed.

[156] Richard A. Raysman and Peter Brown, Conversion, Trespass and Other New Litigation Issues, 221 N.Y.L.J. 1, May 11, 1999, at 3.

[157] *See* Quality Solutions, Inc., v. Zupanc, 993 F. Supp. 621, 623 (N.D. Ohio 1997) (finding compelling evidence of local solicitation from out of state web site, among other channels).

[158] Telco Communications Group, Inc. v. An Apple a Day, Inc., 977 F. Supp. 404 (E.D. Va. Sept. 24, 1997).

[159] Blakey v. Continental Airlines, Inc., 156 N.J.L.J. 1165, June 21, 1999. A contemporary test in the United States for jurisdiction in a defamation action is the Calder effects test. Calder v. Jones, 465 U.S. 783 (1984). In a recent Internet dispute, the court articulated the requirements of the effects test as (1) the defendant intentionally committed at tort which (2) was aimed at the forum state and (3) the plaintiff suffered the majority of the harm in the forum state. Imo Indus., Inc. v. Kiekert AG, 155 F.3d 254, 265-266 (3d Cir. 1998). *See also* Barrett v. Catacombs Press, 44 F. Supp. 2d 717 (E.D. Pa. 1999), No. 99-736 U.S. Dist. LEXIS 5108 *29-*36 (E.D. Pa. Apr. 12, 1999) (applying effects test to Internet defamation and reviewing Internet cases using effects test). Germany takes a more liberal approach to defamation. John R. Schmertz, Jr. and Mike Meier, German District Court Holds that Defamation Action Based on False Information Published on Internet May be Heard by Court in "Any Place" Where Message Can Be Received, Int'l L. Update, July, 1997, available in LEXIS, Intlaw Library, Ilawup File. In a domestic Internet defamation dispute, the court found that jurisdiction is proper anywhere the plaintiff can receive the defamatory message. *Id.* For further exploration of an Internet defamation case in the United States, *see* Michelle J. Kane, Internet Service Provider Liability: Blumenthal v. Drudge, 14 Berkeley Tech. L.J. 483 (1999) (analyzing online defamation and ISP liability).

[160] 952 F. Supp. 1119, 1125-27 W.D.Pa (1997).

to by residents within that state. A growing number of other courts apply the *Zippo* test for interactivity of web sites.[161] The *Zippo* court's continuum test for determining Internet presence has become an influential test for determining whether the defendant's web site activities are sufficient to establish personal jurisdiction.[162]

National advertising without more is not enough to establish minimum contacts with a forum state.[163] In Bensusan Restaurant v. King,[164] the court observed that "Creating a site, like placing a product in the stream of commerce, may be felt nationwide—or even worldwide—but, without more, it is not an act purposefully directed toward the forum state."[165]

The *Zippo* court made the point this way:

> This sliding scale is consistent with well-developed personal jurisdiction principles. At one end of the spectrum are situations where a defendant clearly does business over the Internet. At the opposite end are situations where a defendant has simply posted information on an Internet web site, which is accessible to users in foreign jurisdictions. A passive web site that does little more than make information available to those who are interested in it is not grounds for the exercise of personal jurisdiction. . . . The middle ground is occupied by interactive web sites where a user can exchange information with the host computer. In these cases, the exercise of jurisdiction is determined by examining the level of interactivity and commercial nature of the exchange of information that occurs on the web site.[166]

[1] Reasonableness Test

The "reasonableness" test is a finding that the plaintiff's claim must arise out of the defendant's forum-related activities once a plaintiff has shown minimum contacts. The exercise of jurisdiction is reasonable if it does not offend "traditional notions of fair play and substantial justice."[167] The reasonableness test examines the fairness of a particular forum, balancing the burden on the defendant against factors such as: "the forum state's interest in adjudicating the dispute; the plaintiff's interest in obtaining convenient and effective relief, at least when that interest is not adequately protected by the plaintiff's right to choose the forum; the

---

[161] *See, e.g.,* Park Inns Int'l, Inc. v. Pacific Plaza Hotels, Inc., 5 F. Supp. 2d 762 (D. Ariz. 1998).

[162] Zippo Mfr. Co. v. Zippo Dot Com, Inc., 952 F. Supp. 1119 (W.D. Pa. 1997).

[163] Giangola v. Walt Disney World Co., 753 F. Supp. 148, 156 (D.N.J. 1990) (denying personal jurisdiction even though Disney World placed advertisements in local newspapers read by the plaintiff).

[164] 937 F. Supp. 295 (S.D. N.Y. 1996).

[165] *Id.* at 301.

[166] *Zippo Mfr. Co.,* 952 F. Supp., at 1124.

[167] Theo. H. Davies & Co. v. Republic of the Marshall Islands, 174 F.3d 969 (9th Cir. 1999).

interstate judicial system interest in obtaining the most efficient resolution of controversies, and the shared interest of the several states in furthering fundamental substantive social policies."[168] A defendant must make a compelling case to show why jurisdiction is unreasonable.

[F]   International Jurisdictional Issues

An Internet presence automatically equates to an international presence. The problem facing many companies is that they may be subject to personal or prescriptive jurisdiction in many distant forums. A company's web site may be accessed from New Delhi to São Paulo.[169] E-commerce sales that are legal in one country may run afoul of local laws in another country.[170] In one instance, a British judge has asserted jurisdiction over the content of American web sites.[171] Despite some inconsistent rulings, when compared with other countries, the United States has the most developed and predictable approach to Internet jurisdiction.[172]

[1]   European Union

The European Union has recognized that the current legal landscape is one of the biggest challenges to international electronic commerce.[173] Indeed, European Internet content providers are concerned with potential liability in every

---

[168] Zippo Mfr. Co. v. Zippo Dot Com, Inc., 952 F. Supp. 1119, 1122 (W.D. Pa. 1997) (quoting World Wide Volkswagen Corp. v. Woodson, 444 U.S. 287 (1980)). *See also* Teracom v. Valley Nat'l Bank, 49 F.3d 555 (4th Cir. 1995) (stating that no single factor is dispositive in determining whether jurisdiction is unreasonable).

[169] *See* Vanessa Marsland and Francois Bloch, Book Review: Drawing Lines in Cyberspace, I.P. Worldwide, Mar.-April. 1999, available in LEXIS, News Library, Curnws File (warning little control over who can access a web site or from where).

[170] Wendy R. Leibowitz, E-Litigation: Borders in Net Space, Nat'l L. J., June 14, 1999, at B21. A United States court would enforce an incorrectly posted price and an acknowledgment of sale in the buyer's favor, whereas the United Kingdom allows a price to be corrected even after a contract was formed. *Id. See* German Court Overturns Pornography Ruling Against CompuServe, N.Y. Times, Nov. 18, 1999, at C4 (overturning conviction of ISP manager in Bavarian court for failing to block child pornography sites).

[171] UK Shows Door for Pornography Made in the USA, Computers Today, July 31, 1999, at 78.

[172] *See* Robert L. Hoegle and Christopher P. Boam, Nations Uneasily Carve Out Internet Jurisdiction, I.P. Worldwide, July/Aug. 1999, available in LEXIS, News Library, Curnws File (listing worldwide Internet jurisdictional challenges).

[173] Commission Resolution on the Communication from the Commission on Globalization and the Information Society: The Need for Strengthened International Coordination, 1999 O.J. (C 104) 128. An ISP from the United Kingdom removed its server from Germany to avoid liability under Germany's strict antipornography laws. Hoegle and Boam, *supra* note 172.

member state of the European Union.[174] Unlike the United States, however, the European Union hopes to harmonize e-commerce regulations across member states rather than allowing each state the sovereignty to develop conflicting laws.[175] The European Commission has been pushing a controversial regulation that gives jurisdiction to the destination country in an Internet transaction.[176]

[2] ABA Project on Cyberspace Jurisdictional Issues

In July 2000, the ABA Committee on Cyberspace Law's Jurisdictional Project released a report detailing default rules for transnational cyberspace transactions. The subcommittee on international transactions has made the jurisdictional initiative prospectus and several research reports on jurisdiction in cyberspace from the U.S. and European perspective available on the ABA web site.[177]

The purpose of the ABA project was to provide default rules for international jurisdiction. The July 2000 Report will address jurisdictional and enforcement issues raised by e-commerce. The model rules will likely be influential as international bodies develop directives or treaties addressing international Internet jurisdiction.

While most Internet conflict of law disputes occur in the United States, it is expected that many more disputes will cross borders as international sales expand.[178] Amazon.com, for example, now has more foreign than U.S. sales. It is

---

[174] *See* Commission Adopts Draft Regulation on Jurisdiction, Recognition, and Enforcement of Judgments in Civil and Commercial Matters, Comm'n of the Eur. Communities, Press Release: IP 991510, RAPID, July 14, 1999, available in LEXIS, News Library, Curnws File (citing challenges in European electronic commerce).

[175] *See* Electronic Commerce: Commission Proposes Legal Framework, RAPID, Nov. 18, 1998, available in LEXIS, News Library, Curnws File (examining proposed ecommerce harmonization directive); Proposal for a European Parliament and Council Directive on Certain Legal Aspects of Electronic Commerce in the Internal Market, 1999 O.J. (C 30) 4 (proposing framework for assessing jurisdiction within the European Union); cf. Cyberspace Regulation and the Discourse of State Sovereignty, 112 Harv. L. Rev. 1680 (discussing the challenges of international Internet jurisdiction and state sovereignty).

[176] Lucy Dixon, EC Ruling on E-Trade Favors Destination, Precision Marketing, July 26, 1999, at 44. European courts have taken the opposite approach in international libel cases by granting jurisdiction where the harm originated. Jan J. Brinkhof, Cross-Border Injunctions: Dead in the EU? I.P. Worldwide, Mar./Apr. 1999, available in LEXIS, News Library, Curnws File.

[177] ABA Business Law, Committee on Cyberspace, ABA Jurisdiction Project (May 31, 2000), http://www.abanet.org/BUSLAW/CYBER/initiatives/jurisdiction.html.

[178] Samuel Goldstein, Courts Can Track a Case Back to You; Your Web Site May Contain Waivers to Protect You, Computer Dealer News, Apr. 2, 1999, at 19. Other countries find the United States' assertion of international jurisdiction unsettling, and this may backfire when other countries expand their jurisdictional reach. *See, e.g.,* Simon Pollard, et al., Domain Names, A View from the Antipodes, Mondaq Business Briefing, May 25, 1999, available in LEXIS, News Library, Curnws File (expressing concern over U.S. assertion of trademark laws in domain name disputes).

quite likely that U.S. companies will be litigating more disputes in foreign countries. A U.S. firm may be exposed to lawsuits that would not state causes of action under U.S. law.[179] Plaintiffs already have some capacity to forum shop.[180] The United Kingdom, for example, affords plaintiffs greater rights and remedies in libel cases. In contrast, the United States is one of a few countries to permit a plaintiff to recover punitive damages in a product liability case. Forum shopping is inimical to traditional principles of international law, which recognize jurisdiction in the country of either the plaintiff or the defendant.[181]

Individuals may strategically forum shop in order to avoid enforcement action in online businesses that offer offshore gambling, pornography, or other sales or services that violate local laws. Belize and Antigua are popular offshore gambling sites, judging by the hundreds of online web sites.[182] In Canada, for example, some wrongdoers used the Internet to intentionally place their illegal activities outside of the reach of local authorities.[183] In a more dangerous example, a disgruntled intelligence agent from the United Kingdom published a list of names of intelligence agents online, and the United Kingdom could do little to control the information outside of the country.[184] Thus, the inconsistency in regulations further underscores the need for a prudent legal screening of any corporate web site. Some companies choose additional safety measures, as well, such as maintaining one web site for each country in which they plan to do business.[185]

---

[179] *See* Jean Eaglesham, Laying Down Cyberlaw, Financial Times (London), June 23, 1999, at 22 (discussing absence of uniform Internet rules).

[180] Compare John R. Schmertz, Jr., and Mike Meier, Applying French Data Protection Laws, Int'l L. Update, Dec. 1998, available in LEXIS, News Library, Curnws File (citing French company's pursuit of antitrust dispute in U.S. on Internet basis against French defendant) with Global Roundtable: Taking On The World: If the Future of Business Is Global, So, Too, Is the Business of Law, American Lawyer, Nov. 1998, at 97 (noting foreign companies desire to avoid American jurisdiction). For an example of international forum shopping, *see* Filetech S.A. v. France Telecom S.A., 157 F.3d 922, 925 (U.S. App. 2d Cir. 1998) (describing French telecommunication antitrust dispute in U.S. court on basis of Internet presence).

[181] *See* I.P. Worldwide, Mar.-April. 1999, available in LEXIS, News Library, Curnws File (suggesting international law may require modification to accommodate Internet issues). Local and international laws have not progressed at the same speed as communications technology. Lesley Stones, Web Site Content Stays Beyond Official Control, Business Day (South Africa), May 20, 1999, at 30.

[182] The Minnesota attorney general filed an action against an online gambling operation with a server in Belize in Minnesota v. Granite Gate Resorts, Inc., 567 N.W.2d 747 (Minn. 1998).

[183] Pierre Trudel, Jurisdiction Over the Internet: A Canadian Perspective, Int'l Lawyer, Winter, 1998, 1027, 1061. *But see* Minnesota v. Granite Gate Resorts, 568 N.W. 2d 715 (Minn. Ct. App. 1997), *aff'd,* 576 N.W. 2d 747 (Minn. 1998) (finding Minnesota jurisdiction proper in Internet gambling case over Nevada corporation with server in Belize).

[184] Stones, *supra* note 181.

[185] Psinet.com, home page (visited May 1, 2000), http://www.psinet.com.

> ### [3] Preventive Law Pointer: Determining the Identity of Visitors

An online company may limit its jurisdiction by not accepting orders from countries where the risk of litigation is too great. In the online order form, it is important to have visitors designate their country of residence. The web site may use blocking software to automatically reject or disable orders from countries presenting unacceptable risks of jurisdiction. Blocking software may also be used to disable orders from countries having an unacceptably high rate of credit card fraud. Software programs exist that permit the site to choose parameters for targeted sales or services. A company offering online sales of wine or spirits, for example, may not want to take the risk of filling orders in countries prohibiting the sale of liquor. In addition, the web site may post a prominent disclaimer that sales or services are not meant to be targeted for a designated list of countries. It is a cost-benefit analysis for the web site operator to determine which countries or jurisdictions they wish to block.

[G] Obtaining Redress in International Internet Disputes

A company that has not been able to satisfactorily resolve an Internet-related dispute stemming from a foreign jurisdiction may find sending a letter from an attorney addressing its complaint to be an effective first step.[186] If the letter is unsuccessful, it could try contacting the local equivalent of the Better Business Bureau in the jurisdiction, if it is appropriate. These options are preferable to filing suit either in United States or overseas, since this can be an expensive prospect. Companies unable to resolve the dispute without litigation, however, may find some U.S. courts sympathetic to their cases and willing to assert jurisdiction. Playboy Enterprises, for example, successfully obtained a judgment in a Virginia court against a Hong Kong company for trademark infringement.[187] Specific jurisdiction was based entirely on the defendant's web site, which contained the infringing marks and regularly solicited business in Virginia.[188] Alternatively, a well-funded plaintiff may opt to hire local counsel in the country where the harm occurred.

Keep in mind, however, that traditional strategies for resolving disputes in the United States, such as sending a cease and desist letter, may violate local laws in other countries.[189] Prince Sports, for example, had sent a letter to Prince claiming prior trademark rights to the Internet domain name "prince.com" and threatened to sue for trademark infringement unless the domain name was transferred to

---

[186] Goldstein, *supra* note 178.

[187] Playboy Enterprises v. Asiafocus International, C.A., No. 97-734-A, 1998 U.S. Dist. LEXIS 10359 (E.D. Va. Feb. 2, 1998).

[188] *Id.*

[189] *See* Internet Cease and Desist Letter Backfires, Intell. Prop. Strat., Nov. 1997, at 1 (recognizing defendant followed what would be standard procedures in United States).

Prince Sports.[190] In response, Prince initiated an action in the United Kingdom against Prince Sports for making "groundless threats of infringement proceedings under section 21 of the British Trademarks Act of 1994."[191] Thus, Prince Sports was exposed to a cause of action in the United Kingdom and was prevented from having the domain name suspended during the dispute.[192]

International forum shopping may be to a plaintiff's benefit. An American company, for example, used its English subsidiary to obtain jurisdiction over a German corporation for online trademark infringement.[193] Although companies may be able to assert jurisdiction over a defendant and win a lawsuit in this manner, the additional challenge arises of enforcing the judgment over the defendant.[194]

[H] International Conventions Governing Jurisdiction

The Internet, by its very definition, involves transborder communications across hundreds of countries at the click of a mouse. The Internet can be characterized as an international network of interconnected computers. Most e-commerce sites are subject to jurisdiction everywhere. International treaties, however, govern Internet jurisdiction. The traditional principles underlying jurisdiction have been based upon the "exercise of physical coercive control over that territory by the sovereign."[195] Modern jurisdictional analysis is a "mixture of territorial concepts and interest analysis."[196]

A growing number of U.S. courts are exercising jurisdiction over web site activity occurring outside the country's territorial boundaries. Conversely, U.S. companies are increasingly being sued in foreign venues for activities occurring on web servers located in the United States. Presently, little European case law covers Internet jurisdiction, and no statutory solutions exist to answer the question

---

[190] *Id.* The British Trademarks Act of 1994 allows relief from a party threatening proceedings for infringement of a registered trademark unless the defendant can show that the acts constituted infringement. *Id.*

[191] Emmanuel Gouge, Legal Update, Brand Strategy, Sept. 19, 1997, at 21.

[192] *See* Dawn Osborne, The Latest Developments in U.K. Trade Marks Law, Mondaq Bus. Briefing, June 16, 1998, available in LEXIS, News Library, Curnws File (suggesting trademark holders with any ownership doubts avoid U.K. jurisdiction in domain name disputes).

[193] Mecklermedia v. D.C. Congress, Ch 40, 1 All E.R, 148 (1997).

[194] John DeAngelis & Melissa Dewey, *Internet Jurisdiction: Policy Issues* (visited July 1, 1999), http://www.unc.edu/~deweyma/policy.html#intjur.

[195] Henry Perritt, Traditional Legal Concepts: Basics from Three Experts, ILPF, 1999 Annual Conference, Jurisdiction: Building Confidence in a Borderless Medium, Montreal, Canada, July 26, 1999 (visited May 23, 2000), http://www.ilpf.org/confer/trans99/conf99d1.htm.

[196] *Id.*

of Internet jurisdiction.[197] Jurisdiction is frequently based on the company's place of business rather than the location of the server.

Courts will presently decide cross-border jurisdictional issues by applying national law principles.[198] Cornell University and a former graduate student were sued in the United Kingdom for defamatory statements posted by the former graduate student on Cornell's computer.[199] In another case, a district court in Virginia ruled it had personal jurisdiction over Hong Kong defendants in a copyright infringement action filed by Playboy Enterprises.[200] The court expressed doubt that the fact that the Hong Kong defendant registered its domain name in Virginia was a sufficient basis for personal jurisdiction. The Virginia long-arm statute, however, contemplated jurisdiction over a nonresident causing tortious injury in that state provided that they do or solicit business in the forum.[201]

A British Columbia court refused to enforce a judgment of a Texas court holding that it had no jurisdiction in a lawsuit brought by a British Columbia company against a Vancouver resident for allegedly defamatory comments made in an Internet chat forum. The plaintiff had an office in Texas, but the court held that the defendant would need to establish some link to the forum state, such as residency or doing business, to be subject to jurisdiction.[202]

The magician David Copperfield sued the *Paris Match* magazine for an allegedly defamatory story about his relationship with model Claudia Shiffer.[203] The federal court found no jurisdiction in California over the French publisher, since the *Paris Match* did not direct the defamation to California.[204] The magazine has only a limited distribution in California, and the publisher's Internet web site was a passive site used primarily for advertising.[205] The court held that the *Paris Match* web site had a presence only where the web site was created or maintained or placed on a host computer.[206]

---

[197] Agne Lindberg, Jurisdiction on the Internet—The European Perspective: An Analysis of Conventions, Statutes, and Case Law, ABA Committee on Cyberspace Law (May 24, 2000), http://www.abanet.org/buslaw/cyber/initiatives/eujuris.html.

[198] *Id.*

[199] Raysman and Brown, *supra* note 156 (reporting that the court entered a default judgment against the former Cornell graduate student and the university settled out of court).

[200] Playboy Enterprises, Inc. v. Asiafocus International Inc., 1998 U.S. Dist. LEXIS 10459 (E.D. Va., Apr. 10, 1998).

[201] *Id.*

[202] Braintech v. Kostiuk, No. CA024459 (B.C. Ct. of App., Mar. 18, 1999), reported in the Perkins Coie Internet Case Digest (visited Aug. 25, 1999), http://www.perskinscoie.com/resource/ecomm/netcase/Cases-15.htm.

[203] Copperfield v. Cogedipresse, 26 Med. L. Rptr. 1185 (C.D. Cal., Nov. 3, 1997).

[204] *Id.*

[205] *Id.*

[206] *Id.*

American courts applying foreign law to Internet disputes apply a two-step analysis: First, does the plaintiff satisfy the jurisdiction's long-arm statute? Second, does the contact with the forum state satisfy due process?[207] For foreign courts applying U.S. laws, personal jurisdiction will frequently take the form of whether the country has an interest in resolving a dispute in addition to the question of fairness to the defendant. In the absence of an international treaty, SPC faces an uncertain risk of being sued in a foreign country.[208]

A British court recently shut down the web site of a former spy maintained by an ISP in Lausanne, Switzerland.[209] A New York court granted an injunction barring an online gambling site with a server in Antigua from doing business with New York residents.[210] In 1997, a German court asserted jurisdiction to resolve a domain name dispute case where the owner had registered the name in the United States.[211] The Internet's interconnected system of jurisdiction raises the possibility that SPC may be served process in hundreds of foreign jurisdictions as well as in American courts in any of the fifty plus jurisdictions. Another issue is whether SPC can enforce its rights against defendants in foreign jurisdictions.

The online company will need to take seriously the possibility that it will be held subject to jurisdiction in a foreign country. Little authority exists on what contacts are sufficient to subject a party to jurisdiction in another country.[212] Many nations are taking action to restrict the flow of information on the Internet. Individual nation states have jurisdiction over their own territory, and international jurisdiction will generally be based upon treaty-making agreements.[213]

[1] Brussels Convention on Jurisdiction and Judgments

The European Union (EU) has enacted a number of directives related to Internet commerce but not Internet jurisdiction. The Brussels and Lugano Con-

---

[207] 15 Comp. L. Strat. 1 (Sept. 1998).

[208] *See generally* Dan Burk, "Jurisdiction in a World Without Borders," 1 Va. J. Tech. 3 (1997).

[209] Polly Sprenger, Britain Shuts Down Spy Sites, Wired News, May 12, 1999 (visited May 17, 2000), http://www.wired.com/news/politics/0,1283,19620,00.html (reporting Swiss injunction against publishing international intelligence information on web site).

[210] State of New York v. World Interactive Gaming Corp., No. 404428/98 (Sup. Ct. N.Y. Cty., July 22, 1999).

[211] Domain Name Challenge, No. 5 U 659/97, 97 0 193/96 (Langericht Berlin, May 26, 1997) Perkins Coie Internet Case Digest (visited June 18, 1999), http://www.perkinscoie.com/resource/ecomm/netcase/Cases-15.htm.

[212] *See generally* Richard A. Crisone and Richard A. Schwartz, Can You Be Sued in Every State in Which Your Site Can Be Viewed? 3 Internet Newsletter: Law & Bus. Aspects (Feb. 1999).

[213] *See generally* Norman J. Vig and Regina S. Axelrod, (eds.), The Global Environment: Institutions, Law and Policy (1999) (exploring the difficulties of developing an international order regulating environmental pollution in a global environment).

ventions apply to the online as well as the offline world.[214] The European Economic Community (EEC) entered into the Brussels Convention on Jurisdiction and the Enforcement of Judgments in Civil and Commercial Matters (the Brussels Convention) on September 27, 1968.[215] The Brussels Convention provided "reciprocal recognition and enforcement of judgments of courts or tribunals" in the EEC.[216] The United States is not a contracting party to the Brussels Convention, which applies only to EEC countries.

If SPC has a subsidiary located in an EEC country, the Convention would "apply in civil and commercial matters whatever the nature of the court or tribunal."[217] It would take "specific unusual circumstances," however, to make SPC liable for its subsidiary's conduct.[218] Article 2 of the Brussels Convention states that "persons domiciled in a contracting court may be sued in the courts of that state."[219] Article 5 provides that "in matters resulting in a contract," the court is the "place of performance of the obligation in question."[220]

Article 6 provides rules by which a person domiciled in a "Contracting State may be sued in the courts of another Contracting State."[221] Tort or tort-like actions are tried "in the courts for the place where the harmful event occurred."[222] In the case of a consumer transaction, the plaintiff may bring an action in the courts of the contracting state in which he or she is located or the courts where the defendant is located.[223] The parties may opt out of the Brussels Convention by agreement or a choice of law clause.[224] The Brussels Convention also provides for recognition and enforcement of judgments.[225] Judgments in a Brussels Convention signatory country are recognized by the other contracting states.[226] A judgment is not recognized, however, if it is "contrary to public policy in the State in which recognition is sought."[227]

---

[214] Agne Lindberg, Traditional Legal Concepts: Basics from Three Experts, ILPF 1999 Annual Conference, Jurisdiction: Building Confidence in a Borderless Medium, Montreal, Canada, July 26, 1999.

[215] European Economic Community, Convention on Jurisdiction and the Enforcement of Judgments in Civil and Commercial Matters (Brussels, Belgium, Sept. 27, 1968).

[216] *Id.* at Preamble.

[217] *Id.* at Art. 1.

[218] Nutrition Physiology Corp. v. Enviros Ltd., 87 F. Supp. 2d 648, 655 (N.D. Tex. 2000).

[219] *Id.*

[220] *Id.* at Art. 5.

[221] *Id.* at Art. 6(1).

[222] *Id.* at Art. 6(3).

[223] *Id.* at Art. 14.

[224] *Id.* at Art. 15.

[225] *Id.* at Art. 25-49.

[226] *Id.* at Art. 26.

[227] *Id.* at Art. 27(1).

Article 29 provides that "[u]nder no circumstances may a foreign judgment be reviewed as to its substance."[228] A judgment may be enforced in a contracting state by application of an "interested party."[229] Article 32 specifies which national court in EEC countries has jurisdiction to decide applications of enforcement.[230] Article 33 states that "the application shall be governed by the law of the State in which enforcement is sought."[231]

The law is yet to develop as to the transnational principles for adjudicating Internet disputes in foreign countries. A Pennsylvania federal judge, for example, dismissed a trademark infringement lawsuit against a Canadian firm regarding the defendant's infringing use of a domain name.[232] The federal district judge in that case granted the defendant's motion to dismiss for lack of personal jurisdiction, finding that the defendant's online customers did not even have the capability to place orders on the site.[233] The greater the level of interactivity and the more commercial the exchange of information on a web site, the more likely it is that there will be a basis for personal jurisdiction.

[2] Lugano Convention on Jurisdiction and Judgments

The European Economic Community's Convention on Jurisdiction and the Enforcement of Judgments in Civil and Commercial Matters, agreed to at Lugano, Italy (the Lugano Convention), on September 16, 1988, also applies to online transactions between member states.[234] The Lugano Convention extends the same principles of jurisdiction and enforcement of judgments to a larger group of countries, including Austria, Belgium, Denmark, France, Finland, the Federal Republic of Germany, Greece, Iceland, Ireland, Italy, Luxembourg, the Netherlands, Norway, Portugal, Sweden, Switzerland, and the United Kingdom.[235]

The Lugano Convention of 1988 simply extends the number of contracting states to the Brussels Convention, adopting identical rules for jurisdiction and the enforcement of judgments. The Convention applies to "judgments given after the date of entry into force of this Convention."[236] The Brussels and Lugano Conven-

---

[228] *Id.* at Art. 29.

[229] *Id.* at Art. 31.

[230] *Id.* at Art. 32.

[231] *Id.* at Art. 33.

[232] Desktop Technologies, Inc. v. ColorWorks Reproduction & Design, Inc., No. 98-CV-5029 (E.D. Pa. Feb. 24, 1999).

[233] Maritz Inc. v. Cybergold, Inc., 947 F. Supp. 1328 (E.D. Mo. 1996).

[234] European Economic Community, European Free Trade Association, Convention on Jurisdiction and the Enforcement of Judgments in Civil and Commercial Matters (Lugano, Italy, Sept. 16, 1988).

[235] *Id.* at Art. 3.

[236] *Id.* at Art. 54.

tions provide a possible model for Internet-wide adoption. The Conventions are territorially based, but could be extended to legal proceedings arising out of Internet-related commerce. At present, the Burssels and Lugano Conventions only apply to judgments between domiciliaries in EU contracting states.

[3]   European Union Commissions on Jurisdiction

The May 1, 1999, Amsterdam Treaty made "jurisdictional cooperation" a "part of the powers of the EU."[237] The country of the residence of the consumer applies to e-commerce consumer transactions.[238] Neither the Brussels nor the Lugano Convention apply to Internet advertising.[239] A leading authority on EU regulation notes that if "an Irish company is advertising towards Swedish customers in Sweden via the Web page (e-mail etc.) you will have great difficulties suing that company in Ireland, because the courts will not deal with public law issues [which involves another country]."[240] As a result, there is a "legal vacuum" when it comes to cross-border regulation of Internet activities.[241]

[4]   Service of Process on Foreign Defendants

Federal Rule of Civil Procedure 4(f) allows service to be made on defendants in foreign countries by three methods: "(1) by any internationally agreed means such as the Hague Convention on the Service Abroad of Judicial and Extrajudicial Documents; (2) if there is not an internationally agreed means, or if the applicable international agreement allows other means of service by a number of ways reasonably calculated to provide notice; or (3) by any other means not prohibited by international agreement, if directed by the court."[242]

If SPC or any online company is filing suit against a foreign defendant, it may seek prior approval from the court of its proposed method of effecting service of process. Online companies frequently have complex corporate structures, and it is critical to determine whether there is sufficiency of service. If SPC is a defendant, it may file a motion to dismiss for service of process. Service to one of SPC's subsidiaries, partners, or overseas subsidiaries may be grounds for dismissal.

---

[237] Agne Lindberg, ILPF 1999 Annual Conference, *supra* note 214.

[238] *Id.*

[239] *Id.*

[240] *Id.*

[241] *Id.*

[242] Nutrition Physiology Corp. v. Enviros Ltd., 87 F. Supp. 2d 648, 652 (N.D. Tex. 2000). *See also* 1958 New York Convention on International Arbitration, United Nations Convention on the Recognition and Enforcement of Foreign Arbitral Awards, June 10, 1958, 21 U.S. 7 2517, 330 U.N. 7.S.3 (enforcing arbitration awards).

[I]   Minimizing Jurisdictional Exposure

Most case analysis suggests that the primary way to reduce jurisdictional exposure is to limit the amount of commerce and interactivity within a web site.[243] Unfortunately, reducing a web site to a passive advertisement may be contrary to the business objectives of companies looking to do business online. Consumers want more than an online yellow pages advertisement. "[T]he likelihood that personal jurisdiction can be constitutionally exercised is directly proportionate to the nature and quality of commercial activity that an entity conducts over the Internet," however.[244]

An alternative to reducing a web presence to passive advertising is posting a forum selection clause within the web pages. A Nevada hotel avoided New Jersey jurisdiction in a personal injury action by posting a Nevada forum selection clause.[245] The court enforced the clause, even though jurisdiction would have been proper because of the commercial, interactive web site and other advertising.[246]

Web sites may also limit jurisdictional exposure by limiting transactions or access by state. A company looking to keep its business and legal exposure to its resident state may require web site visitors to identify their state before proceeding with a transaction.[247] Alternatively, a disclaimer stating that the site is only intended for access from a specific state or disclaiming access from certain states may be a helpful precaution.[248] Sun Microsystems limited its potential international exposure from an online contest by specifically listing which countries were eligible.[249] Irrespective of whether geography is limited, web site operators should monitor where visitors and purchasers come from.[250] Companies should be will-

---

[243] Todd D. Leitstein, A Solution for Personal Jurisdiction on the Internet, 59 La. L. Rev. 565 (1999).

[244] Soma Medical International v. Standard Chartered Bank, 196 F.3d 1292, 1296 (10th Cir. 1999) (citing Zippo Mfg. Co. v. Zippo Dot Com Inc., 952 F. Supp. 1119, 1123-24 (W.D. Pa. 1997)).

[245] Decker v. Circus Circus Hotel U.S. Dist. Ct. (D. NJ) 156 N.J.L.J. 813, May 13, 1999. *See also* Caspi v. Microsoft Network, L.L.C., A-2182-97T5, 1999 N.J. Super. LEXIS 254 (Sup. Ct. App. Div. NJ July 2, 1999) (upholding Washington State forum selection clause in online subscription agreement).

[246] *Id.*

[247] Carl W. Chamberlin, To the Millennium: Emerging Issues for the Year 2000 and Cyberspace, 13 N.D. J.L. Ethics & Pub. Pol'y 131, 155 (1999).

[248] *See, e.g.,* Kathleen Parrish, Old Laws Shelter Student; D.A. Says Boy's Web Posting About Teacher Can't be Deemed Threat, Morn. Call, July 28, 1998, at A1. A youth avoided criminal charges stemming from a threatening web site by using a disclaimer excluding the threatened individuals from the site. *Id.*

[249] Jonathan I. Ezor, Representing the New Media Company: Advertising on the Web, Comp. Law. May, 1998, at 6.

[250] Warren E. Agin, Banks Warned Against Potential Problems Via Internet, Commercial Lending, Litig. News, May 14, 1999, available in LEXIS, News Library, Curnws File.

ing to decline sales to any distant forum where they cannot defend themselves, unless the other party adheres to a choice of law clause.[251]

Maintaining interactivity while limiting online business activity can minimize exposure. A Canadian company, for example, maintained a web site that allowed e-mail and file exchanges, yet specifically stated that online visitors could not place orders through the site.[252] Since web site visitors could only place orders by printing an order form and faxing it to the company, the court found that the company was not transacting business online.[253] For companies who depend on an interactive, commercial online presence, insurance can cushion the threat of international litigation.[254]

[J] Obtaining Redress in Domestic Internet Disputes

An easy first step in an Internet-related dispute is a letter to the other party stating how a company was harmed and recommending how it would like to resolve the matter. If the initial letter is not well received, a follow up letter from an attorney may help the other party to understand the other's perspective. Additionally, firms can seek the assistance of the local Better Business Bureau or even of an attorney general to help resolve the dispute. As with international dispute resolution, filing a lawsuit can be expensive and time consuming.

Although some companies may have the resources and time to litigate the matter, more than likely the defendant will try to have the matter dismissed for lack of jurisdiction. Consequently, much energy and expense will go into establishing jurisdiction. Another potential obstacle is naming the defendant. Porsche Cars, for example, sued several Internet domain names directly because the domains were registered either anonymously or by an entity beyond possible jurisdictional limits.[255] The court found that the domain names themselves were beyond the jurisdiction of the court.[256] In most situations, however, companies will more often than not have direct commercial contact with the other party. Consequently, naming the defendant should not be an issue.

Companies that are injured via the Internet and thus require the assistance of local law enforcement agencies need to supplement the investigation independently. Local authorities may lack the resources and expertise to pursue Internet

---

[251] Robert A. Bourque and Kerry L. Conrad, Avoiding Remote Jurisdiction Based on Internet Web Site, N.Y.L.J. (Dec. 10, 1996), http://ljx.com/internet/1210jurs.html.

[252] Desktop Technologies, Inc. v. Colorworks Reproduction & Design, Inc., No 98-5029, 1999 U.S. Dist. LEXIS 1934, at *8, *9 (E.D. Pa. Feb. 25, 1999).

[253] *Id.* at 9.

[254] *See, e.g.,* A Major Insurance Innovation for Information Technology Firms (visited July 15, 1999), http://www.chubb.com/news/pr19970815.html (listing insurance services for technology businesses).

[255] Porsche Cars v. Porsch.com, 1999 U.S. Dist. LEXIS 8750 (E.D. Va. Alex. Div. June 8, 1999).

[256] *See id.* at 10-15 (discussing *in rem* jurisdiction with regards to trademark infringement).

crime.[257] Consequently, some companies hire their own investigators and obtain sufficient evidence for the police to issue a warrant and pursue the case.[258]

[K] Choice of Law

The traditional choice of law endorsed by the Restatement (First) of the Conflict of Laws is *lex loci delictis,* the law of the place where the wrong occurred. The *lex loci delictis* rule is on the decline, with less than 20 percent of the states following the doctrine. The majority of American jurisdictions follow the "most significant" relationship test.[259] Canada, in contrast, follows a strict *lex loci delictis* rule.[260] Internet torts are frequently committed in multiple jurisdictions, though they may originate on a server in a single jurisdiction. *Lex fori,* or the law of the jurisdiction in which the litigation occurs, has not been adopted widely.[261]

The majority of jurisdictions follow the "most significant relationship" test.[262] The Restatement (Second) of Conflicts presumes that the law of the state where the injury occurs applies unless another state has a more significant relationship.[263] The factors of a "significant relationship" analysis include:

1. The needs of the interstate and international systems;
2. Relevant policies of the forum;
3. Relevant policies of other interested states and the relative interests of those states in the determination of the particular issue;
4. Protection of justified expectations;
5. Basic policies underlying the particular field of law;
6. Certainty, predictability and uniformity of result; and
7. Ease in the determination and application of the law to be applied.[264]

There are few courts that have applied conflict of law principles to cyberspace. Many firms incorporate choice of law clauses into their standard agreements. Since the rules of Internet jurisdiction are still evolving both domestically and

---

[257] *See* Regina Hong, The Safety Zone, Spotlight: Gray Areas Hinder Web Fraud Probes; Limits on Resources, Time, Jurisdiction Often Leave Investigations in Limbo, L.A. Times, May 10, 1999, at B2.

[258] P.J. Huffstutter, Tech Firms Pay Police Agencies to Fight Cyber Crime, L.A. Times, July 26, 1999, at A1.

[259] Richard H. Acker, Comment, Choice-of-Law Questions in Cyberfraud, 1996 U. Chi. Legal F. 437, 440.

[260] Chris Gosnell, Jurisdiction on the Net: Defining Place in Cyberspace, 29 Canadian Bus. J. 344, 344 (1998).

[261] *Id.* at 447.

[262] *Id.* at 452.

[263] *Id.*

[264] Restatement (Second) of Conflicts, § 6 (1971).

abroad, Internet content providers should endeavor to limit their exposure or to reconcile themselves to the potential risks of doing business on the web. Individuals conducting business online should specify their choice of law in the event of a dispute. Those who are injured in an Internet transaction and require legal intervention may face a winding path before finding a forum willing to hear the case.

➤ [L] Preventive Law Pointer

[1] Minimum Contacts in Cyberspace

The "minimum contacts" standard for exercise of personal jurisdiction over a nonresident company may be met in two ways: First, a court may assert specific jurisdiction over a nonresident defendant if the defendant has purposefully directed his activities at residents of the forum and the litigation results from alleged injuries that arise out these activities. Second, general jurisdiction may be based on the defendant's overall business contacts. If the contacts are substantial, the court may nonetheless maintain general personal jurisdiction over the defendant based on business contacts with the forum.[265] To obtain jurisdiction over a nonresident company in a federal diversity case, a plaintiff must show both that jurisdiction is proper under the laws of the forum state and that the exercise of jurisdiction does not offend due process.[266] The minimum contacts test has been expanded to cyberspace.

The Due Process Clause of the Fourteenth Amendment permits the exercise of personal jurisdiction over a nonresident defendant "so long as there exists minimum contacts between the defendant and the forum State."[267] To meet the minimum contacts test, an online company must have reasonably anticipated being subject to a court. In addition, a court's exercise of jurisdiction must meet the standards of "fair play and substantial justice." More than 200 cases have been decided on issues of Internet jurisdiction. Section 7.03[L][2] presents a summary of the factual circumstances where courts found jurisdiction or declined jurisdiction. An increasing number of Internet cases involve multiple factual circumstances. In the first wave of Internet jurisdiction cases, a "sliding scale" applies, in which the greater the commercial activity and interactivity, the more likely that the company is subject to personal jurisdiction.

Courts will seldom find Internet general jurisdiction unless the Internet site specifically directs substantial contacts with the forum. An Internet site directed to contractors in Massachusetts, for example, would warrant a finding of general jurisdiction. General jurisdiction occurs when the contacts are so substantial and of such a nature as to justify a lawsuit for actions arising from dealing, distinct

---

[265] Intercon, Inc. v. Bell Atlantic Internet Solutions, Inc. 205 F.3d 1244 (10th Cir. 2000).
[266] *Id.*
[267] World-Wide Volkswagen Corp. v. Woodson, 444 U.S. 286, 291 (1980).

from those activities. In contrast, specific jurisdiction arises when there is a sufficient relationship among the defendant, the cause of action, and the forum.

[2]   Factual Circumstances Affecting Internet Jurisdiction

[a]   *Web Page Advertisement*

FINDING JURISDICTION

1. A web page advertisement in a local paper soliciting contributions was sufficient to trigger jurisdiction.[268]

2. A web page advertisement and service agreement as well as delivery of software to six New York subscribers was found sufficient for jurisdiction.[269]

3. A mere Internet advertisement and toll-free telephone number for inquiries satisfied jurisdiction.[270]

4. Jurisdiction was found for an out of state corporation operating a web site that sold 3,000 passwords to forum state residents, giving them access to newsgroup postings.[271]

DECLINING JURISDICTION

1. A passive Internet advertisement alone is an insufficient basis for the exercise of personal jurisdiction.[272]

2. A web site presence alone is insufficient to meet the minimum contacts test.[273]

---

[268] Heroes v. Heroes Foundation, 958 F. Supp. 1,4-5 (D.D.C. 1996) (holding that web page and web site advertisement in a local paper soliciting contributions was a sufficient basis for exercise of jurisdiction); Park Inns Intern., Inc. v. Pacific Plaza Hotels, Inc., 5 F. Supp. 2d 762 (D. Ariz. 1998) (advertising hotel on web site); Shoppers Food Warehouse v. Moreno, 746 A.2d 230 (D.C. Ct. App. 2000) (basing jurisdiction upon extensive advertising).

[269] American Network, Inc. v. Access America/Connect Atlanta, 975 F. Supp. 494, 498-499 (S.D. N.Y. 1997). *See also* Standard Knitting Ltd. v. Outside Design, Inc., No. 00-288 (E.D. Pa., June 2000) (predicating jurisdiction on interactivity of size and sales in forum of $50,000).

[270] Inset Systems, Inc. v. Instruction Set, Inc., 937 F. Supp. 161, 165 (D. Conn. 1996); Telco Communications v. An Apple A Day, 977 F. Supp. 404, 407 (E.D. Va. 1997) (holding advertisement and solicitation over the Internet via a web site confers jurisdiction).

[271] Zippo Manufacturing Co. v. Zippo Dot Com, Inc., 952 F. Supp. 1119 (E.D. Pa. 1997).

[272] Cybersell, Inc. v. Cybersell, Inc., 130 F.2d 414, 418-19 (9th Cir. 1997) (holding that an Internet advertisement alone is an insufficient basis for jurisdiction); Ty, Inc. v. Clark, 2000 U.S. Dist. LEXIS 383 (N.D. Ill. Jan. 14, 2000) (declining jurisdiction over Cheshire, England passive site).

[273] E-Data Corp. v. Micropatent Corp., 1997 WL 805282 (D. Conn. 1997) (finding no jurisdiction based on Internet site alone).

3. A passive web site that solicited participation in an essay writing contest for children and that posted a toll-free telephone number for contacting the defendant was an insufficient basis for personal jurisdiction.[274]

4. Passive web site advertisement for Missouri jazz club with the same name as a well-known New York City jazz club was an insufficient basis for jurisdiction.[275]

[b]   Torts or Tort-like Misconduct in Cyberspace

FINDING JURISDICTION

1. Jurisdiction was satisfied in a case involving columnist Matt Drudge, who made an allegedly defamatory statement on his web site about White House aide Sidney Blumenthal.[276]

2. A court found that a web site that permitted Missouri citizens to input their personal information was sufficient to subject a defendant to jurisdiction in a Missouri court.[277]

3. Minimum contacts satisfied due process in an online fraud case where statements about stocks were transmitted via e-mail as well as by telephone.[278]

4. The defendant's posting of a defamatory statement on a web site accessible in Arizona was a sufficient basis for exercising personal jurisdiction.[279]

DECLINING JURISDICTION

1. The operation of a web site available to Indiana residents that allegedly defamed a national corporation and infringed its trademarks was an insufficient basis for personal jurisdiction.[280]

2. A New Jersey court dismissed a female airline pilot's lawsuit for sex discrimination and defamation for statements made on Continental Airline's internal electronic bulletin board. No evidence existed that the pilots targeted

---

[274] American Homecare Federation, Inc. v. Paragon Scientific Corp., No. CV-893 (1998 U.S. Dist Lexis 17962) (D. Conn., Oct 26, 1998) (holding out of state defendant that sponsored passive web site had insufficient contacts with Connecticut to permit personal jurisdiction).

[275] Bensusan Restaurant Corp. v. King, 126 F.3d 25 (2d Cir. 1997).

[276] Blumenthal v. Drudge, 992 F. Supp. 44, 54 (D.D.C. 1998). *See also* Blakey v. Continental Airlines, 751 A.2d 538 (N.J. 2000) (holding that employer's knowledge of sexual harassment subjects it to jurisdiction).

[277] Maritz, Inc. v. Cybergold, Inc., 947 F. Supp. 1328 (E.D. Mo. 1996).

[278] Cody v. Ward, 954 F. Supp. 43, 47 (D. Conn. 1997) (holding that fraudulent misrepresentations made via e-mail and telephone messages satisfied minimum contacts test).

[279] Edias Software International, LLC. v. Basis International Ltd., 946 F. Supp. 413 (D. Ariz. 1996).

[280] Conseco, Inc. v. Hickerson, No. 29A04-9802-CV-85, 1998 Ind. App. LEXIS 1328 (Indiana Ct. of App., Aug. 14, 1998); *see also* Jewish Organization v. Superior Ct. of L.A. Cty., 72 Cal. App. 4th 104 (1999).

their electronic postings for New Jersey, nor was another basis found for personal jurisdiction over the defendant pilots.[281]

[c] Online Contracts

FINDING JURISDICTION

1. Jurisdiction was found where Texas citizens entered into contract to gamble on the Internet.[282]

2. A party that made a software contract with an Internet Service Provider in Ohio was subject to jurisdiction to litigate that contract.[283]

DECLINING JURISDICTION

1. A British bank's passive, informational Internet web site, the filing of Uniform Commercial Code (UCC) financing statements, and filing of five civil cases in Utah to recover monies or foreclose on trust deeds did not constitute substantial and continuous local activity sufficient to subject the bank to general personal jurisdiction under Utah law.[284]

[d] Crimes in Cyberspace

FINDING JURISDICTION

1. A California couple was convicted of Tennessee obscenity laws based on a Tennessee postal employee's downloading of obscene materials from the defendants' web site.[285]

DECLINING JURISDICTION

1. Court upheld dismissal of criminal charges for Internet sales of beer to out of state minors.[286]

---

[281] Blakey v. Continental Airlines, 730 A.2d 854 (N.J. Super. Ct., 1999) (holding that no personal jurisdiction existed for statements made on airline's electronic bulletin board).

[282] Thompson v. Handa-Lopez, Inc., 1998 WL 142300 (W.D. 1998).

[283] Compuserve, Inc. v. Patterson, 89 F.3d 1257 (6th Cir. 1996).

[284] Soma Medical International v. Standard Chartered Bank, 196 F.3d 1292 (10th Cir. 1999) (dismissing action by Utah account-holder against British bank for breach of contract and negligence for disbursing funds upon unauthorized signature). *See also* Bedrejo v. Triple E Canada, Ltd., 948 P.2d 739 (Mont. 1999) (declining jurisdiction over passive web site).

[285] United States v. Thomas, 74 F.3d 701 (6th Cir. 1996) (upholding Tennessee criminal convictions against California couple for transmission of obscene materials over Internet). *See also* State v. Cain, 360 Md. 205, 757 A.2d 142 (Md. Ct. App. 2000) (finding jurisdiction in theft by deception case).

[286] State v. Amorosa, 975 P.2d 505 (Ct. App. Utah 1999).

[e] Regulatory Activity in Cyberspace

FINDING JURISDICTION

1. The Minnesota attorney general filed suit against an online gambling site for violating Minnesota's gambling laws.[287] The court found a sufficient basis for jurisdiction, because the site actively solicited subscribers and was accessed by Minnesota residents.

2. A New York court found sufficient personal jurisdiction against a New York defendant's e-mail sales activities on the Internet.[288]

DECLINING JURISDICTION

1. An Alabama federal court sitting in diversity found no personal jurisdiction where a nonresident defendant made a single sale of beer from its web site.[289] The plaintiff filed a lawsuit against the Illinois corporation for selling beer to her son, asserting a claim under Alabama's Civil Damages Act.[290] The court found an insufficient basis for either general or specific jurisdiction, noting that this was an isolated sale.[291] The court observed that the defendant did not engage in national advertising or otherwise have continuous and systematic contacts with Alabama.[292]

2. A Massachusetts federal court ruled that Massachusetts regulators could not apply Massachusetts cigarette advertising regulations to the Internet.[293]

[f] Intellectual Property in Cyberspace

FINDING JURISDICTION

1. A domain name cyberpirate was found liable to a lawsuit in California because his attempt to sell a domain name containing a corporation's famous trademark was deemed to be sufficient for jurisdiction.[294]

---

[287] State of Minnesota v. Granite Gate Resorts, Inc., 568 N.W.2d 715 (Minn. App. 1997).

[288] Vacco v. Lipsitz, 174 Misc. 2d 571, 663 N.Y.S.2d 468 (Sup. Ct. 1997). *See also* GTE New Media Services Inc. v. Ameritech Corp., 199 F.3d 1343 (D.C. Cir. 200) (finding jurisdiction in antitrust action); State v. Beer Nuts, Ltd., 2000 Mo. App. LEXIS 357 (June 27, 2000) (finding jurisdiction for soliciting and selling beer in forum).

[289] Butler v. Beer Across America, 83 F. Supp. 2d 1261 (N.D. Ala. 2000).

[290] The act provides for a civil action by the parent or guardian of a minor against anyone who knowingly and illegally sells or furnishes liquor to the minor. *Id.* at 1262.

[291] *Id.* at 1266.

[292] *Id.* at 1266, n.7.

[293] Lorillard Tobacco Co. v. Reilly, 2000 U.S. Dist. LEXIS 862 (D. Mass., 2000).

[294] Panavision International v. Toeppen, 938 F. Supp. 616 (C.D. Cal. 1996) (finding that the defendant purposefully availed himself by harmful acts directed to the California plaintiff);

2. A Colorado company was subject to jurisdiction in Massachusetts because it purposefully directed advertising, an interactive web site, and targeted advertising to Massachusetts customers.[295]

3. A Pennsylvania court found that it had no personal jurisdiction over a nonresident corporation in a trademark infringement lawsuit, given that the company had not transacted business or rendered services in that jurisdiction.[296] A passive site that advertises services is not enough contact with the forum.[297]

4. The act of linking a famous trademark to an adult entertainment site in a trademark infringement case satisfied due process.[298]

5. Federal district court in New York had personal jurisdiction over a California domiciliary in a trademark dilution act under the Federal Trademark Dilution Act and the Anticybersquatting Consumer Protection Act.[299]

DECLINING JURISDICTION

1. A passive web site that infringes intellectual property rights on the plaintiff's web site alone is an insufficient basis for jurisdiction.[300]

2. A defendant's passive web site was an insufficient basis for a Texas court asserting personal jurisdiction over a Norwegian defendant in a patent infringement lawsuit.[301]

3. Personal jurisdiction may not be predicated upon mere availability of an interactive web site to forum residents. The court held that there were insufficient contacts even though the trademark infringement lawsuit arose out of material on the web site.[302]

American Eyewear Inc. v. Peeper's Sunglasses and Accessories, 106 F. Supp. 2d 895 (N.D. Tex. 2000).

[295] Hasbro, Inc. v. Clue Computing, Inc., 994 F. Supp. 34 (D. Mass. 1997).

[296] Desktop Technologies, Inc. v. Coloworks Reproduction & Design, Inc., 1999 U.S. Dist LEXIS 1934 (E.D. Pa., Feb. 24, 1999).

[297] Id. at 1267.

[298] Archdiocese of St. Louis v. Internet Entertainment Group, Inc., No. 4:99CV27SNL (1999 U.S. Dist. LEXIS 1508) (E.D. Mo., Feb. 12, 1999).

[299] Cello Holdings, LLC v. Dahl, 89 F. Supp. 2d 464 (S.D. N.Y. 2000) (holding that due process was not violated by the exercise of personal jurisdiction in a trademark dilution case brought by the New York holder of the trademark "cello" for use with expensive audio equipment against a California registrant who owned the Internet domain name "cello.com.").

[300] Hearst Corp. v. Goldberger, 1997 WL 97097 (S.D. N.Y. 1997) (holding that an infringing site alone did not subject a defendant to New York jurisdiction where there were no sales to New York or any other contact; Mink v. AAAA Development, L.L.C., 190 F.3d 333 (5th Cir. 1999) (declining jurisdiction in infringement lawsuit because site lacked interactivity).

[301] Agar Corp. v. Multi-Fluid, Inc., 45 U.S.P.Q.2d (BNA 1444) (S.D. Tex. 1997).

[302] Millennium Enterprises, Inc. v. Millennium Music, No. Civ. 98-1058-AA (D. Ore., Jan. 1999) (holding there were insufficient contacts with the forum for the exercise of personal juris-

[3]   Choice of Law and Forum Clauses

Courts will generally uphold choice of law and forum selection clauses.[303] Many licensors will want to include a choice of law clause, such as the following.

> _____ grants its customers a nonexclusive, nontransferable license to use the _____ software package. This agreement specifically excludes the United States Convention of Contracts for the International Sale of Goods. All users agree that the laws of the State of _____ govern the agreement, excluding the State of _____ conflict of law rules.

It is also advisable to include a choice of forum clause, because a plaintiff's choice of forum is entitled to substantial deference from the courts.[304] A firm's Internet site should contain a forum selection clause requiring buyers of goods or services from the web site to agree to a forum selection as well as a choice of law clause.

The U.S. Supreme Court validated forum selection clauses in international transactions in Carnival Cruise Lines v. Shute.[305] Choices of forum clauses are _"prima facie_ valid."[306] Another court held that there was a rebuttable presumption in favor of the enforcement of forum selection clauses.[307] A New York trial court

---

diction without actual sales or other contacts); Neogen Corp. v. Neo Gen Screening, Inc., 2000 U.S. Dist. LEXIS 12032 (W.D. Mich., Aug. 21, 2000) (dismissing trademark infringement action for lack of personal jurisdiction); Berthold Types Inc. v. European Mikrograf Corp., 102 F. Supp. 2d 928 (N.D. Ill. 2000) (noting no jurisdiction because of passive site in trademark infringement case).

[303] _See, e.g.,_ Caspi v. The Microsoft Network, 732 A.2d 528 (N.J. Super. Ct. App. Div. 1999) (upholding forum selection clause in Internet service provider agreement).

[304] _See, e.g.,_ Apache Prods. Co. v. Employers Ins. of Wausau, 154 F.R.D. 650, 653 (S.D. Miss. 1994) (listing factors relevant to a change of venue).

[305] 499 U.S. 485, 493-494 (1991) (stating that: "A clause establishing ex ante the forum for dispute resolution has the salutary effect of dispelling any confusion about where suits arising from the contract must be brought and defended, sparing litigants the time and expense of pretrial motions to determine the correct forum and conserving judicial resources that otherwise would be devoted to deciding those motions.").

[306] Hirschman v. National Textbook Co., 184 A.D.2d 494, 495 (2d Dept. 1992) (stating that in order to set aside a forum selection clause a party must show either that enforcement would be unreasonable and unjust or that the clause is invalid because of fraud or overreaching, such that a trial in the forum set in the contract would be so gravely difficult and inconvenient that the challenging party would, for all practical purposes, be deprived of his or her day in court); _see also_ Evolution Online Systems, Inc. v. Koninklijke P77 Nederland, N.V., 145 F.3d 505 (2d Civ. 1998) (noting that forum selection clauses are generally enforced).

[307] TAAC Linhas Aereas de Angela v. TransAmerica, 915 F.2d 1351 (9th Cir. 1990) (validating a forum selection clause that mandated arbitration for disputes arising out of air transportation agreement).

approved the following Internet Service Providers forum selection clause in a
1997 case:[308]

> The _____ and your membership shall be governed by the laws of the Com-
> monwealth of Virginia, excluding its conflicts of law rules. Member ex-
> pressly agrees that exclusive jurisdiction for any claim or dispute resides in
> the courts of the Commonwealth of Virginia. Member further agrees and
> expressly consents to the exercise of personal jurisdiction in the Common-
> wealth of Virginia in connection with any dispute or claim involving
> _____.[309]

The court found that under the terms of the above forum selection clause, the
plaintiff agreed to litigate all claims or disputes between the parties in Virginia.
The court rejected a claim that the forum selection clause was an adhesion contract or unconscionable.[310] Litigators will frequently file a motion to dismiss
actions in foreign countries on grounds of *forum non conveniens.*

---

[308] Spera v. AOL, No. 06716/97 (Sup. Ct. N.Y., Dec. 23, 1997) (visited June 30, 1999), http://
legal.web.aol.com/decisions/dlother/spera.html.

[309] *Id.*

[310] *Id.*

CHAPTER EIGHT

CONDUCTING A LEGAL
AUDIT AND MANAGING RISK

§ 8.01   INTRODUCTION: RISK MANAGEMENT

Despite the potential economic benefits, the Internet can be a new source of liability for many companies, ranging from the possibility that a dot-com company will be sued in a distant forum for copyright or trademark infringement to defamation in online forums, from breaches of information security and invasion of privacy to online fraud claims or tax liabilities. Risks experienced by a bricks-and-mortar company may multiply as a company goes online and confronts new dangers such as vicarious liability for telecommuting employees, negligent information security, or Internet-related business torts.

Online companies have also been targeted in class actions filed by investors. Intel was the target of a class action by consumers arising out of a minor defect in its Pentium chip that caused computational errors in rare circumstances. Intel was involved in another firestorm of activity in its launch of the Pentium III chip, incorporating a digital identification of users.[1] A large number of tort lawsuits have arisen over spam e-mail, fraud in e-commerce transactions, identity theft, and business torts. America Online was the target of a class action filed by subscribers for interruption of service. Intel was the primary defendant in a class action lawsuit for marketing defective chips. Microsoft has been embroiled in a high stakes civil antitrust lawsuit with the states and the Justice Department over its Internet browser.

Companies should engage attorneys with e-business backgrounds to analyze the company's web site sales and services. The attorney will identify legal vulnerabilities and offer advice for the drafting of remedial plans, compliance guidelines, legal forms, and employee training. If the company retains outside counsel, the results of the audit may be protected by attorney-client privilege. With the results of the audit in hand, and in consultation with outside counsel, the potential hazards or violations should be ranked, from those posing great danger to those with negligible risk. Not all legal uncertainty should be viewed negatively; some developing legal risks may also prove to be valuable opportunities for improving an organization.

It is crucial that companies balance the costs and benefits of risky Internet business policies and practices. Some developing profiles of legal risk may not be corrected immediately. Lay out the strategic objectives and be flexible when implementing the corrective or remedial measures. No matter how many precautions are taken, potential legal liability may still exist. Nevertheless, conducting periodic self-audits will protect your corporate name and assets while avoiding costly litigation or possible fines and reducing legal bills.

---

[1] Daniel Armor, The E-Business Revolution: Living and Working in an Interconnected World 128 (2000).

The next section of this chapter provides a series of checklists to assist companies in conducting a legal self-audit. Certain activities may raise a red flag, alerting companies that some online practices may expose themselves to serious legal liability. Preventive measures before entering cyberspace will result in enhancing the long-term health of your online company.

In addition to the Internet legal audit, the company should seek out other ways to protect its interests, such as indemnification or insurance. The chapter concludes with a review of e-commerce insurance coverage and providers as well as alternative dispute resolution options.

§ 8.02   LEGAL AUDIT CHECKLISTS

The following checklists ask probing questions and offer guidance on issues confronting e-businesses, as well as suggest legal issues for further research. First are listed the key questions for assembling a comprehensive e-business plan. The activities identified in the e-business plan will largely determine what preventive law steps need to be instituted. Next comes intellectual property concerns, which include copyright, trademark, domain name issues, linking, framing, e-commerce patents, and trade secrets. Also covered are issues that many online businesses may not have considered, such as jurisdiction, privacy issues, tort liability, advertising, and taxation.

[A]   E-Business Plans

SPC needs a comprehensive e-business plan that will attract venture capital.[2] The business plan is critical not only in defining its e-business strategy but also in identifying its legal vulnerabilities. Online legal liabilities are generally predictable, and, thus, avoidable. Companies aspiring to be e-businesses must develop an acceptable antirisk framework. The team conducting a preventive law audit should consult with those persons most familiar with company processes and operations. Self-audits must be continually updated and upgraded to take into account new profiles of risk or danger. E-commerce legal audits should focus on implementing strategic objectives that will be acceptable for the online business community.

Some e-business activities require more frequent quality control review than do others. Access controls, screening software, and programs that examine patterns of e-mail traffic or Internet usage are tools that help auditors identify developing or emergent risks. The audit process must be an integral part of the cor-

---

[2] IBM was the first to use the term *e-business* to mean a "secure, flexible and integrated approach to delivering differentiated business value by combining the systems and processes that run core business operations with the simplicity and reach made possible by Internet technology." *Id.* (quoting IBM definition of e-business).

poration's strategic and tactical goals. The e-business plan for SPC is reprinted in Appendix A of this book. SPC's e-business plan will require tailoring, depending upon the company's business mission. If SPC's principal mission is to sell and deliver computers via its web site, it will have a different set of vulnerabilities than will an online bookstore, auction house, or car dealer.

SPC's mission of online computer sales will present challenging Internet-related contracting, advertising law, international jurisdictional, intellectual property, tax, and regulatory issues. The e-business plan is a roadmap to the legal risks that must be considered prior to the launch of the web site. The e-business plan requires first and foremost a detailed description of the company's business. SPC needs to be clear as to what business it is in as well as why investors should be interested that business. What products or services are offered? Why is SPC in the best position to carry out the business plan?

E-BUSINESS PLAN CHECKLIST

1. Does your company have a comprehensive e-business plan? Will the e-business plan attract sufficient additional venture capital? Why is the Internet the ideal location for your business? What special features make an e-business plan attractive to investors and customers? What distinguishes it from its competitors? Does the e-business plan appoint the right people to staff operations? Will the team present a credible case for funding? Does your company have a specific product to sell? Have appropriate license agreements been obtained? The more comprehensive the e-business plan, the more likely it will be to obtain adequate funding. How much money does your company have? What funding is minimally needed to serve your customers and operate your web site for a year or more without appreciable revenues? What is your projected cash flow? What is your strategy for achieving income projections? Relatively few businesses have a strong e-commerce strategy covering business as well as legal concerns.[3]

2. Are all of the elements of a business plan completed? Is there a cover sheet? Executive summary? Statement of purpose? Table of contents? Supporting materials? Does the cover sheet include the online company's name, mailing address, e-mail address, and identifying information about the principals of the company? Are up-to-date biographies of the principals included? Does the executive summary provide clear statements of investment objectives, business strategies, operations and management, schedules, financial projections, and investor returns? Have you made a convincing case as to why your Internet site will be

---

[3] TechWeb, Study: Companies Lack Comprehensive E-Business Plan, Information Week, Nov. 29, 1999 (visited June 1, 2000), http://www.informationweek.com/story/IWK19991129S0007 (citing KPMG Benchmarking Partner Study of 48 companies, most with $1 billion or more in revenue).

more profitable than those of your competitors? Who are your competitors? Have you researched your competitors' business strategy? Have you conducted online searches of how your competitors do business online? If your competitors are publicly traded companies, have you visited the Securities and Exchange site and searched for 10-Ks, 10-Qs, and other publicly available documents? How is your business different from that of dot-com businesses that already have web site presences?

3. Does your business plan describe the opportunities for launching a web site? To what extent will the web site focus on a global network?[4] Is your company an e-business leader or follower? Does your business plan emphasize quality, pricing, or other variables that will ensure success? Will your goods and services become known for their quality, reliability, or price, or a combination of these factors? What kind of image do you want to project in the online world? Is your customer base high brow, middlebrow, or low brow? What magazines do your potential customers read? How do you intend to personalize advertising and promotions to reach your customers? Will your web site use real-time customer service to ensure customer loyalty? What features have you incorporated in your site to ensure that your customers will not be one-time customers or "one-shotters"? Do you have a strategy for developing "relational contracts" with your customers? Have you given customers the option of being informed about new products and services? An opt-out feature should be included in all e-mail updates on products and services.

4. Is the description of the online business adequate? Is there a description of marketing, competition, operating procedures, personnel, business insurance, and financial data? Are you an established legacy business seeking out a new business channel? Or a new venture? How will your site attract new customers? What are your online business objectives? If you are a legacy business, you will need to explain how your operations will be retooled to become an e-business.

5. Is there a sufficient description of how services are to be rendered? Is there an overview of online sales and services? What is SPC's principal vision for its Internet business? Does the overview describe the company's customer experience, proposed customer base, projected customer growth, and price? Do you own or have the rights to use your proposed e-business methods?

6. Is the business development and marketing section of the business plan sufficiently developed? What are you selling? Why should web site visitors buy your products or services? Why will customers benefit from your product or service? In the early days of the dot-com economy, it was sufficient to state the purpose of the web site as entering the global Internet marketplace. Because the Internet economy has developed, investors today want more detailed business

---

[4] The number of non-U.S. Internet users is steadily increasing and will grow to 65% by 2003. IWord, World Wide Web: The Global Internet Opportunity Unfolds (visited May 26, 2000), http://www.iword.com/iword51/iword51.html.

development and marketing information. Does your marketing plan define your targeted Internet markets? What are your anticipated product offerings? Are you planning to target foreign sales? How do you intend to increase your market share? What will attract customers to your site?

7. Does the financial data reflect loan applications, capital equipment, a balance sheet, a breakeven analysis, and income projections? What supporting documents are needed to support a detailed three-year analysis of income? The e-business plan needs quarter-by-quarter projections for the first year's revenue stream. Does the business plan include the tax returns of the principals?

8. Determine your virtual store's principal customer base. Is it the B2B market or the consumer market?[5] Have you identified your customer base by nationality, age, sex, income, educational level, and other demographic variables? Are you personalizing sales and services tailored to demographic variables? What mechanisms do you have for personalizing your advertising for your customer base? Do you provide real-time customer service? What is SPC's plan to attract customers to its site? Do you have a call center that can handle customer service?

9. What is your online marketing plan to promote goods and services? What is the "look and feel" of your web site? Check out its components. Do you have a customer loyalty program? How will your advertising reach your target market? Will your advertising be directed to other countries? If so, will foreign language advertising text be tested for nuance, meaning, and legal or regulatory effects? What surveys or other empirical research have you completed to better understand your proposed customer base? Is your web site directed to business-to-business, business-to-government, or business-to-consumer market segments? What is your company's online niche?

10. Do you address how you are different from your competition? Did you do an analysis of your competitor's web site? Will your web site create channel conflict? An online bookstore will need to explain why their product or services are superior to those of Amazon.com. Who are your competitors: direct and indirect? What promotions, advertising, and sales strategies will help your company gain an edge on your competitors? What is your projected customer growth? What pricing is necessary to increase customer growth? Is your pricing strategy based on markup or cost? Is your pricing below that of the competition? Will your pricing cover costs as well as projected profit margins?

11. How does your e-business plan describe business development and marketing? What co-branding or partnership development is necessary to achieve

---

[5] The B2B market is expected to increase to $7.3 trillion by 2005. Brokat NetNews Archive: E-Commerce (visited May 30, 2000), http://www.brokat.com/int/netnews/archive-ecommerce.html.

business development? Will your online company partner with: (a) virtual shopping centers; (b) Internet publishing companies; (c) traditional application service providers; (d) Internet infrastructure companies; (e) software companies; (f) Internet Service Providers; (g) Web development companies; or (h) financial institutions? What is your company's online branding strategy?

12. When is the launch site for your web site? Will password-protected demonstrations be given prior to launch? Do you have an adequate startup and operational budget? Does the operating budget cover the possibility of increased personnel for customer service, web site developers, consulting services, and new capital equipment? How will content be refreshed?

13. Will your company demonstrate its products and services at Internet trade shows? Do sales personnel understand the legal issues in promoting products and advertising? Has counsel reviewed the copy used in advertising and promotional materials? Is the copy in advertising and promotional material accurate as well as attractively packaged? Do press releases about the potential success of product offerings and potential market opportunities comply with SEC requirements in not assuring results?

14. What public relations tools will be used to create a buzz about your company's web site? What is your Internet strategy for promoting your site? Are you offering sweepstakes or games of chance that may be illegal in some jurisdictions?

15. Who will perform the e-business legal audit? Has an outside audit system been established to review and document risks? A company may decide to retain a Big Five accounting firm or a law firm experienced in legal and e-business issues. Outside firms need to work closely with corporate counsel and with key personnel who understand your company's e-business plan.

16. What staffing is necessary for operations to create a profitable online business? Who is the president or chief executive officer? Vice president of services? Vice president of technology? Vice president of finance and administration? Vice president of marketing?

17. Are the technology positions staffed with the right people?
> Director of Applications Development
> Director of Web Technologies
> Systems Architect
> Senior Server Engineer
> Director of Operational Development/Risk Management
> Director of Operations
> Manager of Networking Security
> Quality Assurance Manager
> Documentation Manager

18. Who will staff marketing/business development?
> Senior Sales Representatives

Partner Development Representatives
Marketing Manager

19. Who will staff management and production?

Director of Account Management
Accounts Manager
Manager of Training
User Interface Designer

20. Who will staff finance and administration?

Controller
Human Resources Manager
Accounts Receivable
Accounts Payable

21. Has the company sought out experienced persons who understand the commercial realities of online marketing?

Online Marketing and Public Relations Manager

22. Have you considered giving your employees a stake in the company? Self-management and employee ownership plans create incentives for employees who thereby gain a stake in the company. Is your company structured as a Limited Liability Partnership (LLP), Limited Liability Corporation (LLC), or other entity such as a C or S corporation?

23. Who are your online company's management and advisors? Does your plan e-business include a Board of Directors? A management team? Do you have the right people in place to operate your online business? Are they organized into an enterprise-wide team?

24. What types of partnerships, joint venturers, or co-branding strategies should be considered to help scale and leverage your business opportunities on the Internet?

25. Have you completed an e-business legal audit?

The next section describes the principal legal issues relevant to e-business plans.

[B]   Intellectual Property Concerns[6]

Intellectual property is the chief asset of most online companies. Intellectual property must be protected on the Internet just as in the offline world. An audit of intellectual property rights focuses on copyrights, trademarks, patents, and trade secrets. The first step for an intellectual property audit is to inventory the intellectual property owned by the company. A company may not have rights to intellectual property for web site content even if they paid for it. If web site designers are

---

[6] For a complete discussion of intellectual property issues, see Chapter Four.

independent contractors, the "work for hire" doctrine does not apply. Licenses or assignments may convey intellectual property rights.[7] Software and other intellectual property is licensed rather than sold. A license gives permission to use software, data, or other intellectual property for the term of the license agreement.[8]

A licensee must not exceed the terms granted in the license agreement or the result will be breach of contract or infringement, if the information is copyrighted. What content do you own? What content must you acquire? You will need to obtain necessary clearances and assignments to use the content of others on your site.

The second step is to determine how to protect each type of intellectual property on the web site. Copyrights protect the online company's software, manuals, artistic works, and content on its web site. Use copyright notice on web site agreements and on the web site home page itself. Trademarks will protect the online company's trade names, slogans, corporate name, and trade dress on its web site and even its domain name. The USPTO permits domain names to be registered as trademarks if distinctive and used in commerce. Your company's business model may also be patentable. An online computer store's special expertise in online selling may constitute a patentable business process.

Additionally, some organizations list their trademarks and service marks in their web site agreements so that all users are placed on notice regarding the organization's intellectual property.[9] License agreements, confidentiality agreements, and assignments of rights may be used to protect intellectual property on the Internet. The primary goal is to obtain ownership, assignments, or licenses for all content on your web site to avoid infringing the intellectual property rights of others.

A third step is determining whether other companies are infringing your company's intellectual property rights. The Internet can help the user determine whether another company is misusing your trademarks, copyrighted materials, patents, or other intellectual property.

[1]   Copyrights[10]

Copyright issues are a significant part of Internet law, since technology makes duplicating images or sounds relatively easy. The reproduction of images, sound, or text without permission may constitute infringement, exposing the

---

[7] H. Ward Classen, Fundamentals of Software Licensing, Fourth Annual High Technology Law Conference, Licensing in a Network Environment, Suffolk University Law School (Cosponsored with the Boston Patent Law Association), Mar. 10, 2000.

[8] General Talking Pictures, Inc. v. Western Electric Co., 304 U.S. 175, 181 (1938) (defining a patent license as a "mere waiver of the right to sue").

[9] *See* GTE Internetworking (visited Aug. 11, 1999), http://www.bbn.com/legal.htm.

[10] For a full discussion of copyright issues, see § 4.02.

defendant company to civil and criminal liability.[11] All facets of a web site are potentially protected by copyright law: materials, documents, computer programs, pictures, artwork, photographs, images, sounds, video text, articles, designs, HTML code, and JavaScript code, as well as the entire web site itself.[12] The purpose of the audit is to determine what copyright materials are created or developed by the company and what rights need to be acquired. The exclusive rights of a copyright owner to distribute, display, and transmit works of authorship apply to works on the Internet.[13]

A web site operator must protect the company's copyrighted materials and avoid infringing the copyrights owned by others. A company is directly liable for copyright infringement for posting unauthorized copyrighted materials on its web site.[14] Clip art or even HTML code may appear to be free for the taking from other web sites. Do not let your corporation discover the hard way that your web site designer made a costly mistake. Your company must obtain indemnification and hold harmless for infringement claims for content supplied by third parties. The Berne Convention of Literary and Artistic Works grants worldwide copyright protection in member states, which includes the United States.[15]

COPYRIGHT CHECKLIST

1. Has your company evaluated the business issues regarding copyrighted materials used on your web site? Does your web site designer seek to use images that require licensing, or does he or she use original images created just for your web site? What will it take to enhance the "look and feel" of your site? Who will create or supply the written content? What will it take to entice and engage customers at your web site? What copyright issues need to be resolved?

2. Does your company either own, license, or have assigned rights to use all images, including artwork and photographs, on the site?[16] Remember just

---

[11] *See* Juliette M. Passer, It's All in the Details: Tips for Drafting Online Licensing Agreements, Texas Lawyer, Aug. 2, 1999, at 25 (warning of liabilities from doing business online).

[12] *See generally* the U.S. Copyright Office, Basics of Copyright (visited May 15, 2000), http://lcweb.loc.gov/copyright/.

[13] *See generally,* David L. Hayes, Advanced Copyright Issues on the Internet, 7 Tex. Intell. Prop. L.J. 1,3 (1998) (arguing that "[t]he ubiquitous nature of copying in the course of physical transmission gives the copyright owner potentially very strong rights with respect to the movement of copyrighted material through the Internet, and has moved copyright to the center of attention as a form of intellectual property on the Internet").

[14] *See, e.g.,* Playboy Enterprises, Inc. v. Webbworld, Inc., 968 F. Supp. 1171 (N.D. Tex. 1997) (holding an operator of a web site directly liable and the principals vicariously liable for infringement for permitting Playboy's copyrighted materials to be uploaded on its site).

[15] Rodney D. Ryder, Intellectual Propery Rights: The Grey Matters, Computers Today, April 15, 2000.

[16] Neil Harrison, Ten Points to Remember When Using E-Commerce, The Journal, Mar. 18, 1999, at 47.

because a company has the right to publish copyrighted materials in a print publication does not mean it can automatically extend that right to web site publications.[17] If a company has obtained clearance for publishing images, this permission must explicitly include Internet publication. If a third party supplies images, permissions must be obtained in writing. Make sure that contractors use only cleared images or at least provide you with the sources of the images. Some web sites have specific procedures for copyright infringement claims because of the frequency of claims of infringement.[18] If third parties supply content, do they own or have a license to use all content?

3. Has your company registered its web site with the U.S. copyright office? Have copyright notices been posted in the form "© 2001, Suffolk Personal Computers, All Rights Reserved"? Your company may register printed pages or a disk of your web site with the U.S. Copyright Office.[19] Is there a notice on your web site that its pages are copyrighted? The notice should specify authorized uses and whether copying, transmission, or modification of copyrighted materials is allowed. A web site owner should not grant users the right to make derivative works from copyrighted materials. While it is not necessary to register to protect your copyright, registration provides proof of copyright data and makes it possible to receive statutory damages in the event of infringement.[20]

4. Do all posted images appear with independent copyright notices? To protect your artwork and photographs from reuse, affix copyright notices to each image.[21] The notice should state "Copyright [your company] 2001, all rights reserved."[22] The notice should be imbedded in the image file and not in text independently placed below the image. Persons seeking to use the images without permission cannot remove the notice without affirmatively modifying the image.

5. Are copyrighted images posted on the web site protected with digital watermarks to facilitate tracing unauthorized copying? Digital watermarks are hidden code that can help identify the source of an image.[23] The data is only visible through special software and can contain information about the copyright

---

[17] *Id.*

[18] *See* Notice and Procedure for Making Claims of Copyright Infringement (visited May 15, 2000), http://www.msnbc.com/procedurenotice.asp (displaying copyright infringement claim procedure).

[19] *See* Chu Moy, Avoid Copyright Infringement in E-commerce, E-Business Advisor, Dec. 1998, at 12 (explaining copyrightability of web pages).

[20] *See generally,* The U.S. Copyright Office (visited May 15, 2000), http://lcweb.loc.gov/copyright.

[21] *Id.*

[22] *Id.*

[23] *See* Richard Raysman and Peter Brown, The Digital Millennium Copyright Act, N.Y.L.J., Dec. 8, 1998, at 3 (describing technologies to protect copyrighted materials).

holder and provide proof of authenticity.[24] Digital signatures may be used to determine the authenticity of electronic documents, and digital watermarks may be used to determine the authenticity of audio files.[25] A web site designer should require customers to warrant that they have the right to use trademarks, copyrights, patents, and other intellectual property posted on the site. Content providers should be required to give a warranty that materials do not infringe any copyrights, trademarks, trade secrets, e-commerce patents, or other intellectual property of third parties. Content providers should agree to indemnify and hold the company harmless for any claim, demand, and causes of action, debt, or liability arising out of deliverables.

6. Does the web site post general copyright notices encompassing all images, text, sound, code, and content? The entire "look and feel" of the web site should be protected with a general copyright notice on each page. SPC's web site, for example, may be copyrighted and labeled "Copyright © 2001, Suffolk Personal Computers, Inc. All rights reserved." A web site owner may wish to reserve rights to reproduce materials or, alternatively, to encourage copying of posted materials. No warranties should be given for the accuracy of copyrighted materials. Forrester Research, which produces proprietary information on Internet trends, permits "members of the press to cite a copy of each graph, slide, or a portion of text less than a paragraph long contained in the Information, provided that all portions of text are identified as: 'Source: Forrester Research, Inc.' "[26]

7. Does the web site use any clip art or other graphics that may require copyright clearance? Have copyright clearances been verified? If third parties supply clip art or other graphics, have they provided verification of copyright clearances? Clip art may contain use restrictions for electronic media. Check the terms and get clearance in writing.[27] Many web sites borrow clip art from other sites. This approach is inadvisable without prior permission from the web site operator. Some web sites contain copyright waivers. An individual who can enforce the copyright, however, may have originally posted the clipped image.

8. Have copyright notices been embedded within the HTML or other code? Protect your code by placing a copyright notice at the top of the code and within the body of the code. Clearly state your policy in phrasing such as "No part of this document may be reproduced without express written permission of [your company]."

---

[24] *See* Strategies for Protecting Your Web Site Content: Digital Watermarks (last modified May 5, 2000), http://www.zdnet.com/devhead/stories/articles/0,4413,2168620,00.html (suggesting digital watermark sources).

[25] State of Washington Office of the Secretary of State, Frequently Asked Questions About Digital Signatures (visited May 10, 2000), http://www.secstate.wa.gov/ea/ovfaq.htrm.

[26] Forrester Research, Inc., Citation Policy (visited Aug. 30, 2000), www.forrester.com/ER/Press/Citation/0,1774,0,FF.html.

[27] *See generally* U.S. Copyright Office (visited May 15, 2000), http://lcweb.loc.gov/copyright.

9. Does the company own the rights to use the HTML or other code? Make sure that your programmer did not "borrow" any proprietary content from another site. Obtain written permission if any third-party sources were used. Some sites employ code from many different sources. If you notice anything out of the ordinary within your site, check with your programmer about the source.

10. Has the company retained the rights to the computer code or does the programmer retain these rights? Unless there are written terms to the contrary, the copyright in a work for hire goes to the employer. Make sure any third-party agreements with contractors convey the copyright to the employer. Some programmers may offer favorable prices for creating a web site because they recycle their code. If you have any customized features built into your site that you want to protect, have the programmer agree in writing to convey the copyright to you and not to reuse the code. Let all of your employees know that you retain the rights to all materials produced on behalf of the company and that nothing should be reused externally without the company's express permission. It is much easier early in the process to let employees know that you retain the rights to the code rather than to pursue them after they use the code elsewhere.

11. If the programmer retained the rights, does the company have permission to modify or change the web site? The right to make derivative works is one of the exclusive rights of copyright owners. A web site may change daily or even more frequently, and it is therefore important to obtain the right to make derivative works as well as the original web site. Copyright extends to derivative works. If you did convey the copyright to the programmer, check on the limits to modifications. Successful web sites are constantly changing; do not let your firm be exposed to unnecessary liability because of a poorly worded contract. You may find that you are locked into using the contractor for any further changes. This can create a potentially difficult and expensive situation.

12. Is the web site using music, video, or audio that requires copyright clearance or license agreements? The audio industry has taken a firm stance against online infringement.[28] Do not use any popular music without obtaining written permission. If you do not have the resources to license music, consider using original or classic MIDI[29] files that are in the public domain. A web site's copyright issues will turn on the type of activity occurring on a site. A web site inviting visitors to upload and download pirated software would clearly be infringing. Many web site activities are not as clear. The Recording Industry Association of America filed a lawsuit against Napster for providing visitors with access to

---

[28] *See* William Sloan Coats and Vickie L. Freeman, Digital Copyright Act Seen as Win for Industry, Entertainment Law & Finance, Nov. 1998, at 1 (listing audio provisions in Digital Millennium Copyright Act).

[29] The term *MIDI* refers to a computer music format.

MP3 files, which contain copyrighted songs. Dr. Dre, Metallica, and other musicians have filed suits against Napster.[30]

13. Is all the text on the web site original content or, if not, is it attributed to the appropriate third parties? Make sure that any articles from other sources are attributed to the proper author and source. Do not unnecessarily expose your company to a contributory or vicarious infringement lawsuit over copyrighted materials because a content provider you hired used materials owned by a third party. Have a clear attribution and antiplagiarism policy as well as a copyright policy to avoid problems.

14. Have you posted a clearly written "terms and conditions" policy advising visitors of permitted and prohibited uses of materials on the site? Is there a terms of service agreement? Devise clickwrap or webwrap agreements requiring visitors to either agree to the terms of service or be automatically transported from the site. Does the terms of service address the visitor's responsibilities? What are the restrictions in the terms of service? Is there a limitation of warranty and liability? Is there a merger clause stating that prior or contemporaneous agreements are merged into the final agreement? A copyright policy may permit visitors to view, download, scan, and copy articles, software, images, or any other items for redistribution. Some sites encourage such borrowing.[31] Make your policy obvious if you want to discourage reuse.[32] Web site development can be expensive, and you should endeavor to protect your intellectual property. Also, the images, text, and sounds in your site may help make it unique. Any reproduction of your original work can diminish the site's value and appeal.

15. Does the online company qualify for a "safe harbor" from copyright infringement? Section 512 of the Digital Millennium Copyright Act (DMCA) limits a service provider's liability for transmitting, routing, providing connections for, or providing intermediate storage of material that infringes a copyright provided certain conditions are met. To qualify for a "safe harbor" from copyright infringement claims, the provider must implement a procedure for terminating repeat violators. The provider also must have no knowledge of or financial benefit from the infringement. The DMCA requires service providers to post information on how to report copyright infringement. The provider must also remove infringing materials once given notice of the infringing activity on its site. The company must register an agent with the U.S. Copyright Office to receive complaints about infringement. The company must prominently post information how to contact the copyright agent on its web site. Finally, the DMCA requires the

---

[30] Jenny Eliscu, Napster Fights Back: MP3 Site Contests Lawsuit While Users Remain Defiant, Rolling Stone, June 22, 2000, at 29.

[31] *See,* Snap-Shot Wallpaper (visited May 15, 2000), http://www.snap-shot.com/.

[32] *See,* the Anne Geddes Official Web Site (visited May 15, 2000), http://www.annegeddes.com/indexpages.asp?P=Z.

provider to inform account holders and subscribers of its policy of terminating repeat infringers. Infringing copies of JPEG images and MP3 music files are pirated far more often than text.[33]

[2]   Trademarks[34]

"A trademark is often a valuable property of a seller or manufacturer, because it is the symbol of the company's goodwill and of its products and services."[35] Trademarks can represent a significant portion of a corporation's assets. The Internet, however, has opened a new forum for widespread trademark misuse, potentially diminishing the value of that asset. Domain names can be registered as trademarks, assuming that they are sufficiently distinctive. Amazon.com was one of the first Internet companies to register a ".com" trademark.[36]

Trademarks are registered in the U.S. Patent and Trademark Office of the U.S. Department of Commerce. In addition, "[m]any states register trademarks to maintain a public record and allow others to search the record before choosing and using a new trademark."[37] The number of trademarks with ".com" as a suffix increased from only 4 in 1994 to 12,000 in 1999.[38] Trademark rights are acquired by actual use in commerce. The term "use in commerce" means the use of a mark in the ordinary course of trade and not merely a reservation of a right to use marks in conjunction with the sale of goods. goods.[39] Trademarks may be infringed in domain names and metatags and within the web pages themselves.[40]

Corporations must protect their valuable brand names worldwide and also avoid accidental trademark infringement. The U.S. is a signatory to the Trade-Related Aspects of Intellectual Property Rights (TRIPS), administered by WIPO. Each of the 150 signatory countries provides basic trademark protections that member countries must implement.[41] Courts recognize the value of trademarks to

---

[33] Armor, *supra* note 1. *See also* A&M Records, Inc. v. Napster, Inc., 2000 U.S. Dist. LEXIS (N.D. Cal. Aug. 10, 2000) (enjoining Napster from enabling users to copy digital files of copyrighted music without payment or permission).

[34] For a full discussion of trademark issues, *see* § 4.03.

[35] Small Business Administration, Starting Your Business: Patents, Trademarks and Copyrights (visited June 10, 2000), http://www.sba.gov/starting/indextrademarks.html (contributed by J. Thomas McCarthy).

[36] Dechert, Price, and Rhoads, Annual Report on Trends in Trademarks 2000 (visited May 29, 2000), http://www.dechert.com/news/_byline/may_00.html (citing USPTO trademark applications data).

[37] Small Business Administration, Starting Your Business, *supra* note 35.

[38] Dechert, Price, and Rhoads, *supra* note 36.

[39] Maritz v. Cybergold, Inc., 947 F. Supp. 1328, 1335 (E.D. Mo. 1996).

[40] Linda A. Goldstein, Emerging Issues in Online Advertising and Promotion Law, 570 PLI/Pat 821, 860 (1999); *see also* Playboy Enterprise v. Calvin Designer Label, 985 F. Supp. 1220 (N.D. Cal. 1997).

[41] Chu Moy, Protection Your Company's Trademarks for Global E-Commerce, e-Business Advisor, Oct. 1998 at 16.

both consumers and companies and may offer redress to a company claiming infringement from a "cybersquatter."[42] Online trademark disputes can be time-consuming and expensive; use this checklist to reduce any accidental infringement.

TRADEMARK CHECKLIST

1. Has intellectual property counsel audited the key business issues surrounding trademarks? What trademarks can be protected? How important is your brand name? Do you have a good domain name for differentiating online goods and services? Is your domain name distinctive enough to qualify for trademark protection? Can the trade dress of your web site be registered as a trademark? Do you expect your brand name to be significant in the future? Are trademarks being used in commerce? If a trademark is registered, the owner must file an affidavit between the fifth and sixth year of registration certifying that the trademarks are being used in commerce.[43] Use must be proven at the time of every ten-year renewal as well, and even an "'incontestable" registration might be attacked on the basis of fraud in the allegations of use or of abandonment if use has been too scant.[44] The online company must use its marks in Internet sales or services or risk a finding of abandonment due to nonuse. The online company's business plan must incorporate marks used "in commerce."

2. Does the company have the rights to use all trademarks or logos within the site? Is the ™ trademark symbol used with trademarks not yet registered with the U.S. Patent and Trademark Office? Is the registered ® symbol used for trademarks or trade names already registered? If you have created a new brand name or product for sale online, check to see that it does not infringe on someone else's name or product.[45] Second, be very cautious if you are using another company's trademarks in comparisons.[46] Make sure that the comparison is valid and supported by testing. Comparative advertising is illegal in a number of European countries.

---

[42] Avery Dennison Corporation v. Sumpton 1999 WL 635767 (9th Cir. 1999), citing Intermatic Inc. v. Toeppen, 947 F. Supp. 1227, 1239 (N.D. Ill., 1996); *see also* Andrew Baum and Mark Epstein, New Dilution Act Used to Evict "Cybersquatter"; courts have ruled that owners of famous marks are entitled to those marks in domain names. National.Law.Journal Jan. 27, 1997.

[43] Fish & Richardson, P.C., Don't Be Confused About Whether Your Trademark Is Used (visited Jan. 27, 2000), http://www.fr.com/publis/tmthou3.html.

[44] *Id.*

[45] *See generally,* the United States Patent and Trademark Office web site, specifically Basic Facts About Registering a Trademark (last visited Oct. 6, 1999), http://www.uspto.gov/web/offices/tac/doc/basic/basic_facts.html; *see also* Bitlaw, Trademarks on the Internet (last visited Oct. 4, 1999), http://www.btilaw.com/trademark/internet.html1#discovery.

[46] *See* Lanham Act, 15 U.S.C. §§ 1114, 1125(a) (1998).

3. Has your company chosen distinctive trademarks? Fanciful or coined marks are the strongest marks, followed by arbitrary, suggestive, and descriptive marks. Trademarks do not protect generic marks. A descriptive mark, which is quite weak, may gain secondary meaning through online advertising or publishing.

4. Has your company obtained federal registration for its trade name, logos, slogans, and other trademarks? Registration lasts 20 years and may be renewed for subsequent 20-year terms as long as the trademark continues to be "used in commerce." The symbol ® may be used for federally registered trademarks. An online company needs to apply for trademark registration. The USPTO trademark examiners determine whether the mark meets the conditions for trademark protection.[47] The USPTO also permits "intent to use" applications as well as applications where the mark has already been "used in commerce." Trademarks must not be "confusingly similar" to other trademarks. With an intent to use application, there is no need to prove "use in commerce" prior to registration. Federal registration provides protection for trademarks in the continental United States.

5. If any other trademarks are mentioned on your web site, are comparisons protected by the trademark doctrine of "fair use"? Could consumers be confused about the ownership of trademarks mentioned on your site? Do you make any comparisons that may constitute deceptive or unfair advertising? Trademark infringement, like copyright infringement, is a strict liability offense. If your company sells brand name products from other manufacturers, it must spell out the relationship between your company and the original manufacturers to avoid any confusion. Get written permission from the manufacturer to mention their products by name and include pictures (if appropriate) to use in electronic commerce. If you were an independent distributor of Coca-Cola, for example, the site should state that you are only a distributor, not Coca-Cola. Comparative advertising that mentions the trademarks of others must be supported with substantiation by tests, surveys or other evidence.[48]

6. Has your company obtained necessary clearances to use trademarks owned by others? If SPC sold Macintosh computers, for example, SPC must place a notice on the web site indicating that Macintosh is a registered trademark of Apple Computer, Inc.

7. Does your web site employee characters or other content that parody trademarked characters? Parodies are entitled to a degree of First Amendment protection for free speech.[49] L.L. Bean, for example, was unable to enjoin the L.L.

---

[47] Small Business Administration, *supra* note 35 (contributed by Thomas McCarthy).

[48] *See* Ameritech Agrees to Halt Comparative Advertising Against Cellular One, 14 Communic. Daily 4 (Dec. 28, 1994) (reporting Ameritech's agreement to stop comparative advertisement with claims not supported by tests or surveys).

[49] Andrew R. Basile, Chapter 13, Trademark Rights, in Thomas J. Smedinghoff, ed. Online Law; The SPA's Legal Guide to Doing Business on the Internet 221 (1996).

Beam sex catalogue parody under a trademark dilution theory because of First Amendment rights.[50] Parody has also been conceptualized by courts as a form of trademark "fair use." Parodies are protected speech if three conditions are met: (1) Is the object of reference "not readily identifiable without use of the trademark"? (2) Is no more of a mark taken than is reasonably necessary to refer to the object? (3) Does the use of the trademark in no way imply sponsorship or endorsement?[51]

8. Be sure your metatags do not infringe the trademarks of others, which may lead to a trademark infringement or unfair competition lawsuits. Advise your web site designers to avoid using the trademarks of others as metatags. Does your company use metatags derived from the trademarks of others in registering its site with search engines? Do keyword monitoring to determine whether your competitors or others are using your trademarks in metatags in ways that might confuse visitors or tarnish your marks. Use trademarks in metatags in a way that you would want others to use them. Metatags may not be used to unfairly divert traffic from your competitor's site. Competitors may not use your trademarks in metatags to divert traffic to their site. Does your competitor's use of metatags tarnish or dilute your trademarks?[52] Begin with a "cease and desist" notice. Have you conducted online searches to determine how your trademarks are being used, misused, or abused on the Internet? Do not try to generate traffic by exploiting other brands. If you sell other brands on your web site, get written permission to use the names within your metatags. Never use a competitor's name or product names in the metatag.[53]

9. Your company may have an action against a cybersquatter for registering your company's famous mark under the Federal Antidilution Act. Your company may also have remedies under the Anticybersquatting Consumer Protection Act of 1999 if a domain name owner incorporates your company's trademarks. A likely cause of action exists under the federal antidilution act if a cybersquatter registers a famous mark. In addition, the Anticybersquatting Consumer Protection Act of 1999 (ACPA) provides remedies against those attempting to sell domain names for a profit with "bad faith" intent. An *in rem* remedy may

---

[50] L.L. Bean, Inc. v. Drake Publishers, Inc., 811 F.2d 26 (1st Cir. 1987).

[51] Fish and Richardson, Trademark Parody: The Joke's on Who? (Sept. 30, 2000), http://www.fr.com/publis/ththou5.html. (summarizing standards for "fair denominative trademark use").

[52] An adult entertainment or hate speech site using an online company's trademarks in metatags would also tarnish or dilute those marks.

[53] Goldstein, *supra* note 40; *see also* Playboy Enterprises v. Calvin Designer Label, 985 F. Supp. 1220 (N.D. Cal. 1997). *See* Brookfield Communic. v. West Coast Entertainment Corp., 174 F.3d 1036 (9th Cir. 1999) (holding that use of third party's trademark in metatag caused "initial interest confusion"); N.V.E. Pharm., Inc. v. Hoffman-LaRoche, Inc., 1999 U.S. Dist. LEXIS 20204 (D.N.J. Dec. 27, 1999); SNA, Inc. v. Array, 51 F. Supp. 2d 554 (E.D. Pa. 1999).

be sought if a trademark owner cannot locate registrants of allegedly infringing domain names.[54]

10. Is the online company's domain name registrable as a trademark? Advertising sales or service on a web site is probably sufficient to meet the Lanham Act's "use in commerce" requirement. It is also possible to file an "intent to use application" for a domain name used as trademark.

11. Has your company filed trademark registrations in foreign countries? Can your company apply for the European Community Trademark registration? Trademark registrations in the United States Patent and Trademark Office provide trademark protection only within the boundaries of the United States. SPC, for example, may register its marks in other countries where it sells goods or renders services. If SPC has a subsidiary with a principal place of business in a country that is a party to the Madrid Agreement, it may file a registration for a single European Community Trademark registration at the International Bureau in Alicante, Spain. Only residents of countries that have signed the Madrid Agreement may register their trademarks at the International Bureau. The United States has not yet approved the Madrid Protocol permitting U.S. businesses to use the international registration system.[55] SPC should register its marks in essential countries, not all countries, connected to the Internet.

[3]   Domain Names[56]

A domain name represents a company's gateway on the Internet. Memorable domain names can be valuable assets as well as the subject of heated litigation. Multiple companies and speculators are increasingly competing to register the same domain name. Other companies register as many of the most desirable domain names as they can. SPC must also police competitors who register domain names that infringe or dilute its trademarks or trade name. SPC must restrain defendants who intentionally adopt the SPC trademarks as domain names in order to capitalize on its marks.

---

[54] 15 U.S.C. § 1125(d)(2)(A). *See* Broadbridge Media v. Hypercd.com, 2000 U.S. Dist. LEXIS 9516 (S.D.N.Y. 2000) (holding that bad-faith intent is a predicate of an *in rem* action under the ACPA); Harrods Ltd. v. Sixty Internet Domain Names, 2000 U.S. Dist. LEXIS 11911 (E.D. Va. Aug. 15, 2000).

[55] *See* Testimony of Janice F. Bay, Deputy Assistant Secretary, Dept. of State, Investment Treaties and Nominations, Hearing of the Senate Foreign Relations Committee, Sept. 13, 2000. The European Union countries include the United Kingdom, Austria, France, Germany, Benelux, Spain, Portugal, Italy, Greece, Denmark, Finland, Sweden, and Ireland. *See generally* Timothy A. French and Donna M. Weinstein, Fish & Richardson, P.C., European Community Trademark (visited May 23, 2000), http://www.fr.com/publis/f_europe.htm (noting that the cost of a European Community Trademark is approximately $2,500 including fees for filing up to three classes and $400 for each class in excess of three").

[56] *See also* §§ 4.03[L].

Registration in the ".com" domain can be obtained online at http://www.net-worksolutions.com. Network Solutions' web site also contains a search engine to check on the availability of a domain name, at *http://rs.internic.net/cgi-bin/whois.*[57] The Internet Corporation for Assigned Names and Numbers (ICANN) manages the Internet domain name system. ICANN has certified hundreds of registries and administers the dispute resolution system formulated by the World Intellectual Property Organization (WIPO).

DOMAIN NAMES CHECKLIST

1. Has your company registered its domain name? Can your domain name be protected as a trademark? Does your domain name infringe another's trademark? Has your company taken steps to prevent others from using your trademarks as domain names? After spending thousands of dollars and hundreds of hours attracting traffic to your web site, it would be unfortunate if a dispute resolution tribunal or court ordered your company to "cease and desist" using the name and conveying it to another party. Do a trademark search before you decide on your domain name. Consider registering your domain as a trademark.[58] If you have already created the site, and it is potentially infringing on someone else's brand name, consult a trademark attorney to assess the relative strength of the other trademark. You may be able to continue to use the domain name if the trademark is abandoned or in another product class.[59] Otherwise, the trademark holder may grant a license for a reasonable fee.

2. Should you register other domain names to protect your trademark and increase traffic? Since domain name registration is relatively inexpensive, consider registering other names to prevent someone else from registering the name in the future.[60] Make it easy for consumers looking for your web site to locate your online address. Register your name in all top-level domains (TLDs). The online company should register the domain name in the ".com," ".org," and ".net" TLDs. Also, in the event your domain name is prone to being misspelled, register the most common or frequent misspellings. Fidelity Investments, for example, has registered "www.fidelitu.com."[61] It may also be advisable to register domain names in foreign countries. Many countries, such as France or Sweden, require a presence in the country in order to file for domain name protection.

---

[57] Todd Krieger, Internet Domain Names and Trademarks: Strategies for Protecting Brand Names in Cyberspace, 32 Suffolk U. L. Rev. 47 (1998) (hereinafter Krieger).

[58] *Id.*

[59] *Id.*

[60] *Id.*

[61] *Id.*

3. Have you conducted a trademark search to determine whether your domain name may be registered? Have you registered common misspellings of your domain name? Have you registered the .com, .net, and .org versions of your domain name? If a domain name infringes on the trademarks of others, the domain name registration may be cancelled. In addition, the online company is exposed to an unfair competition and trademark infringement lawsuit. Hundreds of lawsuits have been filed against domain name registrants where the domain name incorporates a trademark of another. The Internet Corporation for Assigned Names and Numbers (ICANN) replaced Network Solutions Inc. in administering the management of the domain name system. ICANN has accredited a large number of domain name registrars around the globe to provide competitive registration services for the .com, .net, and .org domains. ICANN adopted a uniform dispute resolution policy to deal with domain name disputes, based on recommendations of the World Intellectual Property Organization (WIPO). Do periodic keyword monitoring to determine whether your trademarks or domain names are being misused or abused. Your company may register its domain name with a national extension, such as .uk for the United Kingdom or .fr from France. Some countries, such as Sweden (.se) and France (.fr), require a local presence (prior assessment) in order to register a domain number, whereas other countries, such as Fiji (.fi) and Tonga (.to), are unrestricted.

4. Does your firm have a cause of action against a domain name under the Anticybersquatting Consumer Protection Act (ACPA)?[62] The ACPA was enacted as an amendment to the Trademark Act to provide remedies for cyberpiracy or cybersquatting. The ACPA provides remedies against parties who are "registering, trafficking in, or using domain names (Internet addresses) that are identical or confusingly similarly to trademarks with the bad-faith intent to profit from the goodwill of trademarks."[63] A domain name may blur the distinctive quality of a mark or tarnish the mark.[64] A plaintiff may proceed with an *in rem* action against a user of a domain name if the plaintiff is unable to obtain *in personam* jurisdiction.[65] It may be difficult to obtain personal jurisdiction where the domain name owner uses false addresses or other misleading personal information. An *in rem* action is against the domain itself, whereas *in personam* or personal jurisdiction is against the owner of the domain name.

5. Does your company have a cause of action under the Lanham Act? To have standing for trademark infringement lawsuits, a company must prove that the

---

[62] 15 U.S.C. § 1125 (2000).

[63] Lucent Technologies v. Lucentsucks.com, 2000 U.S. Dist. LEXIS 6159 (E.D. Va., 2000) (quoting H.R. Rep. No. 106-412, at 7 (1999)).

[64] *Id.*

[65] 15 U.S.C. § 1125(d)(2)(A).

other party was using a mark in commerce in a way that is likely to cause consumer confusion. Another theory is that the unauthorized user is diluting or tarnishing a company's marks.

[4]   E-Commerce Patents[66]

E-commerce patents have skyrocketed after the federal circuit court's decision in State Street Bank and Trust Co. v. Signature Financial Group, Inc.[67] Since 1998, hundreds of patents covering Internet-related business methods have been issued. Amazon.com's "one click" technology for online shopping, for example, was issued a patent.[68] Soon after, Amazon.com sued Barnesandnoble.com for infringing its "single-click" patent.[69] Recently, Priceline.com sued Microsoft over a "name your own price" patent.[70] The large number of new e-commerce patents creates a greater risk of exposure to an expensive patent infringement lawsuit.

An online business may consider obtaining patent protection for its own business methods that satisfy the novelty, utility, and nonobvious standards. Patents are the most expensive and time-consuming methods of obtaining intellectual property rights, however. The software patent examiners of the USPTO do not have good databases for establishing "prior art."[71] A finding of prior art is necessary in making a finding that a proposed patent is unique. This task may be next to impossible "in the digital world [where] software or [information technology] does not necessarily have a prior art."[72] Another complaint about the e-commerce patents is that they are overly broad, having a chilling impact on the development of the Internet.[73]

E-commerce patents for business methods such as online ordering systems may be obtained through a process called patent prosecution. To prosecute its e-commerce patents, your company will need to retain a patent lawyer who is entitled to practice between the USPTO. Next, a company will need to decide whether to license its e-commerce technology, which may be a source of significant revenue.

---

[66] *See* § 4.05.

[67] 149 F.3d 1368 (Fed. Cir. 1998).

[68] L. Scott Tillett, Patent Office Takes a Fresh Look at The Net, Internet Week 1 (May 15, 2000). *See* Kelly Jackson Higgins, The Other IP—It Exploits Patents to Protect E-Assets, Internet Week, July 17, 2000 (reporting 2,600 e-business patents filed in 1999).

[69] Steve Alexander, Patents in E-Commerce, Computerworld, Apr. 24, 2000, at 58.

[70] *Id.*

[71] *Id.*

[72] *Id.* (quoting Marc Perl, general counsel for Information Technology Association of America).

[73] Steve Alexander, *supra* note 69.

E-BUSINESS PATENTS CHECKLIST

1. Does your company have any business methods that are covered by patents held by others? The United States Patent and Trademark Office has recently expanded its patent search information site to include 30,000,000 documents.[74] E-commerce business methods grant the patent owner a 20-year period to prevent others from using the business process.

2. Do any of the web site technologies or business methods infringe on e-commerce patents owned by third parties? Some e-commerce technologies have been patented for routine activities including online coupons and hyperlinks.[75] If your programmer develops anything out of the ordinary, have an attorney verify that it is not infringing on someone else's patent and, if it is unique, consider having the technology patented.

3. Has an audit been conducted of e-commerce business methods used in the online company's virtual store or web site? Priceline.com, for example, is the patent owner of the reverse auction system.[76] Amazon.com owns a patent for the security of credit card transactions, whereas Cybergold holds a patent for paying web site visitors who view advertising on its site.[77] Netincentives holds a patent for an online frequent buyer program, whereas Open Market owns the electronic shopping cart and real-time payments patent.[78] Patents may be invalidated by demonstrating prior use or that the patent was too broad or lacks novelty, or nonobviousness.

4. Are any of your trade secrets patentable? Patents provide broader protection than trade secrets. Assess the value of your trade secrets and consider whether a patent might be more appropriate to protect your competitive advantage.[79] Keep in mind the expense and length of time required to obtain a patent and also a patent's duration. Trade secrets may last until the secret is disclosed, while patents are limited to 20 years. On the other hand, trade secrets offer no protection against reverse engineering, while patents do.[80] The speed of the Internet revolu-

---

[74] United States Patent and Trademark Office (visited May 20, 2000), http://www.uspto.gov.

[75] CoolSavings.com Inc. v. IQ Commerce Corp., 53 F. Supp. 2d 1000, 1001 (N.D. Ill., June, 1999). Laura Rohde, British Telecom Claims to Have Patent for Hyperlinks, Infoworld, June 26, 2000 (claiming patent for linking).

[76] Priceline.com has filed several patent infringement lawsuits against other online firms using the reverse auction method. *See* Juno Charges Qualcomm, Netzero Violated Patent, Electronic Commerce News, June 19, 2000 (reporting case).

[77] *See* Thomas E. Anderson, Aces: Emerging Intellectual Property Issues in Cyberspace, 78 MI Bar Jnl 1260 (Nov. 1999).

[78] *Id.*

[79] Peter Toren, Protecting Prevailing Intellectual Property, New York L.J., Mar. 21, 2000, at S8.

[80] *See* Michael Bettinger and Peter Berger, Can Intellectual Property Be Protected on the Internet? Legal Backgrounder, Apr. 14, 2000, available in LEXIS, News Library, Curnws File (listing online intellectual property threats).

tion, however, no longer rewards those who can warehouse trade secrets; it rewards companies that bring new products quickly to market.[81]

5. Is international protection of patents necessary? European patents are coordinated through the European Patent Convention (EPC) but Europe has yet to achieve a unified patent system.[82] The EPC "specifically excludes patent protection for software in the form of computer programs."[83] The European Directive on the Legal Protection of Computer Software, however, "allows a freedom: opening the door for logic algorithms and programming language—excluded from copyright protection" in Europe.[84] If software patents are in doubt, it is unlikely that most European countries would issue business method patents.

[5] Trade Secrets[85]

While trade secrets may impart a competitive edge to company's intellectual property arsenal, they are vulnerable to mass dissemination over the Internet. Certain business methods that may not qualify for patent protection may nonetheless be trade secrets and intellectual property assets critical to the company's online strategy. Unlike patents, trademarks, or copyrights, however, a trade secret instantly loses its value when it is revealed to the public. Companies must take steps to keep their trade secrets intact and away from broad online publication. E-mail and Internet usage policies should give employees notice of their duty to protect trade secrets or other confidential information. Nondisclosure and confidentiality agreements are critically important to protecting a company's trade secrets.

TRADE SECRETS CHECKLIST

1. Has your company inventoried its trade secrets? By identifying and cataloguing trade secrets, a company can better assess the risks of having its secrets disclosed. A company that relies heavily on trade secrets should implement a comprehensive policy of trade secret protection. Something as simple as a recipe can be a significant competitive advantage to a food processor. Unlike patents, a

---

[81] Edward Iwata, IBM Revs Up to Internet Speed. Tech Alliances Begin Adjustment to New Economy, USA Today, Mar. 14, 2000, at 3B.

[82] Hans Henrik Lidgard, European Perspective on Licensing in a Network Environment, Keynote Address, European Perspective on Licensing in a Network Environment, Fourth Annual High Technology Law Conference, Licensing in a Network Environment, Suffolk University Law School (co-sponsored with the Boston Patent Law Association), Mar. 10, 2000.

[83] *Id.*

[84] *Id.*

[85] *See* § 4.04.

trade secret does not need to be novel and nonobvious—it could be as simple as a minor improvement over existing technology. Step back and examine your products, plans, or processes for any information that has actual or potential value if it is kept secret.

2. Does your company have a systematic policy for protecting trade secrets? What are the requirements for protecting trade secrets in your company's jurisdiction? All relevant documents should be labeled "confidential." Most companies now require all employees and contractors to sign trade secret nondisclosure agreements, giving the companies recourse if the agreements are breached. Educate employees regarding the value and vulnerability of trade secrets.

3. Are your software engineers, web content managers, programmers, or other critical employees familiar with your trade secret policy and the risks of disseminating trade secrets online? Control potential trade secret leaks at the spigot of online publication. A marketing manager wishing to publish a new product announcement online may not realize that the product specifications have economic value if kept secret.

4. Has your company implemented a formal e-mail and Internet usage policy that covers trade secrets? Does your company monitor employee e-mail and Internet usage? Are employees given prior notice that messages are monitored? Employees can easily forward documents within a company and beyond. Confidential data should be labeled and encrypted. Labeling an e-mail "confidential" will put the employee on notice to limit distribution. Any e-mail monitoring policy should also include searching for key words relating to trade secrets. This may provide an early warning system if a secret is forwarded beyond the company's firewall.[86] The Internet usage policy should address the question of downloading files containing viruses. The policy should require that material not be downloaded without first scanning for viruses.[87] No user should download material from the Internet without knowing the source. The policy should state the procedure for reporting virus outbreaks.

5. Does your company encrypt and otherwise protect trade secrets that are transmitted electronically? Sophisticated encryption technology can help protect software or other data distributed over networks. Programmers have also devised methods of creating programs that protect themselves from unauthorized access by self-destructing.[88]

6. Do you require your key employees to sign agreements containing covenants not to compete? Do you require your employees to sign confidentiality agreements agreeing to hold trade secrets and other proprietary information

---

[86] For a more detailed examination of e-mail and Internet usage policies, *see* Chapter Nine.

[87] City of Seattle, Internet Use Policy and Virus Protection Policy, September 1995 (visited Feb. 14, 2000), http://www.mrsc.org/infoserv/seattle.htm

[88] Bettinger and Berger, *supra* note 80.

secret? Does your confidentiality agreement require employees to return all company documents that have been classified as trade secrets?

7. Do you require your key employees to sign agreements assigning to the company inventions completed with company resources and on company time? Are all assignment of inventions clauses reasonable in terms of breadth and period of time?

8. Are confidentiality clauses included in every license agreement, whether standard form or negotiated? A licensor will require a licensee to take all reasonable measures to maintain the confidentiality of all proprietary information in its possession or control. In fulfilling any developmental software contract, the customer may give a developer confidential information relevant to the project. At minimum, the developer should agree to treat all confidential material with the same measures it uses to protect its own confidential information. Source code, for example, is generally regarded as confidential.

9. Is there a confidential information clause in all of your agreements? Are the agreements reasonable in time, scope, and purpose? Does it cover all formulas, patterns, compilations, programs, devices, methods or processes with actual or potential economic value?

10. In the event of litigation, the attorney for the company must have a protective order to protect trade secrets and other confidential information.

[6] Linking[89]

Linking is one of the main vehicles of navigation through the World Wide Web. Simple linking will rarely present legal problems, since it is widely used and an accepted part of the Internet.[90] Without links, online visitors would have to learn about your web site and get its address from potentially expensive traditional media. Yet the free spirit of Internet linking is diminished when companies are the target of unwanted links or of links that bypass a main web page. Would you want your web page to be linked to an unsavory site? Several trademark infringement lawsuits have been filed based on unwanted links with adult entertainment sites.[91]

Alternatively, a visitor to your web page may develop a dispute with a linked destination and sue you for sponsoring the site. Another objectionable practice is

---

[89] *See* §§ 2.05[C], 4.02[G].

[90] Nicos L. Tisilas, Minimizing Potential Liability Associated with Linking and Framing on the World Wide Web, 8 Comnlaw Conspectus 85, 88 (1988).

[91] *See generally,* Walter A. Effross, Withdrawal of the Reference: Rights, Rules and Remedies for Unwelcome Web-Linking, 49 S.C. L. Rev. 651 (1998).

deep linking, that is, bypassing the home page and advertising of the linked site and thus "cherry-picking the best of a linked site."[92] Linking cases have been litigated under theories of copyright, trademark, and unfair competition law.[93] Ticketmaster, for example, sued Microsoft for unfair competition after Microsoft deep linked to its site.[94] Establishing, posting, and enforcing a linking policy are helpful tools for avoiding linking disputes. Linking agreements are the best preventive law device for avoiding trademark and false endorsement claims. The FTC has guidelines for making hyperlink disclosures clear and conspicuous. The courts have provided little guidance on the limits of linking, so a cautious approach is well warranted. Merchant linking agreements should be used where there is any question that the linked suit might object to a link.

LINKING CHECKLIST

1. Have you evaluated the business benefits and risks associated with external links? Can your company be held liable for dilution of a competitor's trademark or copyright infringement because of linking? A useful page of current, relevant links may bring visitors back to your site and generate traffic. On the other hand, does your organization want to provide a vehicle that leads visitors to other web sites? Additionally, does your company want to dedicate resources to ensuring that the relevant links are updated and/or working properly?

2. Do you have permission to link to all destination sites? Some companies do not want other links to their web pages. If you do not have the resources to obtain written permission from all of your linked sites, check to see if the sites have posted a linking policy. Comply with any requests to remove links; better yet, seek permission first.

3. Does your web page have a linking policy posted on its site? Do your web site designers have clear guidance on the company's rules for linking? Do other web site visitors have guidance on what linking practices are permitted? Your web site designers need to understand you linking policy. Let visitors know your linking policy. You may want to require written permission from anyone who wants to link to your site and maintain the right to revoke the link. Some sites may want to eliminate linking completely. Will you permit linking to your main web page but not deep links directly to other pages? Many web sites do not have a link-

---

[92] *Id.* at 87.

[93] Thomas E. Anderson, Aces—Emerging Intellectual Property Issues in Cyberspace, 78 MI Bar J. 1260 (Nov. 1999).

[94] Ticketmaster v. Microsoft settled their lawsuit after Microsoft agreed to cease the deep linking practice. *See* Ticketmaster Corp. v. Microsoft Corp., No. 97-3055 DDP (C.D. Cal. filed Apr. 28, 1997) (Complaint).

ing policy; examine your business needs before you decide which approach is appropriate for your company.

4. Do any of your links use logos or stylized text? While text links usually do not raise an eyebrow from the destination site, logos or stylized text may draw accusations of trademark infringement.[95] Unless you have express written permission, use only text links.[96] Do not use a corporate logo, image, or trademark text.[97] Any confusion regarding unauthorized endorsement from another company can expose your to trademark infringement lawsuit.[98] Use the same text for all external links.

5. Have you disclaimed liability from any external links? Let visitors know that the links are placed for their convenience and should not be interpreted as an endorsement. Note that you accept no liability from use of the linked sites.[99] You do not want to be sued because of a dispute between one of your visitors and a linked web site.

6. Are visitors clearly notified that they are leaving the site? Does the link imply an endorsement or affiliation with the linked site? Let visitors know that the links will take them to another company's web site. Minimize the possibility that a consumer might confuse the linked site with your's and sue your company for something that occurred on the other site.

7. If your linking does not violate trademark or copyright law, will other parties nonetheless find it objectionable?[100] The safest policy complies with the law and links only in ways the linked site finds unobjectionable.[101] If a linked site has objections to a link, it could lead to costly litigation, unfavorable publicity, and ultimately undermine your best interest.[102] Making a linking agreements or getting permission to link is advisable even though a simple link would likely constitute fair use under trademark or copyright law.[103]

---

[95] BitLaw, Linking and Liability (last visited Oct. 6, 1999), http://www.bitlaw.com/internet/linking.html#Trademark Infringement.

[96] *Id.*

[97] *Id.*

[98] Trademark infringement occurs when a seller uses a mark confusingly similar to registered trademark. "Any seller who uses a mark so similar to a registered trademark that it is likely to cause customer confusion is an infringer and can be sued in a state or federal court. The court compares the conflicting trademarks as to similarity in sound, sight and meaning." Small Business Administration, Starting Your Business—Patents, Trademarks and Copyrights (visited June 10, 2000) http://www.sba.gov/starting/indextrademarks.html.

[99] *Id.*

[100] David Mirchin, Can You Be Legally Liable for Hypertext Linking? (visited May 1, 2000), http://www.silverplatter.com/hypertext.html.

[101] *Id.*

[102] *Id.*

[103] *Id.*

8. Does your company have linking agreements with parties who might object to a link between their site and yours? What is the effective date? What is the policy about attribution? The reciprocal linking agreement should begin by naming the parties, providing their addresses, and stating the purpose of the agreement: "This linking agreement is entered into as of January 1, 2002 between Suffolk Personal Computers, a Massachusetts corporation, and The University of Lund, located in Lund, Sweden."

9. Does your web designer follow the FTC staff's guidelines for the labeling, description, and placement of hyperlinks? The FTC offers specific guidelines for hyperlinking to disclosures, including placement on web pages.[104] If your web site complies with the FTC guidelines for hyperlinking to a disclosure, it is likely that your web site disclosures will be found to be sufficiently conspicuous. The FTC states that "[D]isclosures that are an integral part of a claim or inseparable from it . . . should be placed on the same page and immediately next to the claim."[105] The FTC notes that the key factors for hyperlinks are "the labeling or description of the hyperlink, the consistency in the use of hyperlink styles, its placement and prominence on the Web page, and the handling of the disclosure on the click-through page."[106] In addition, the FTC offers the following advice: (a) choose the right label for the hyperlink; (b) make it obvious; (c) label the link to convey the importance, nature, and relevance of the information it leads to; (d) don't be coy; (e) don't be subtle; (f) use hyperlink styles consistently; (g) place links near relevant information and make them noticeable; (h) make it easy to get to the disclosure on the click-through page; (i) get consumers to the message quickly; (j) assess the effectiveness of a hyperlink disclosure; (k) don't ignore data that your hyperlinks are not followed by visitors; (l) don't ignore technological limitations on scrolling; (m) recognize and respond to the characteristics of each technique (that is, pop-up windows or interstitial pages); (n) research consumer behavior to determine the effectiveness of your communication of disclosure information; (o) don't focus only on disclosures for the order page; (p) disclose information required in the banner clearly and conspicuously; (q) incorporate or flag required information creatively; (r) evaluate the size, color, and graphics of the disclosure in relation to other parts of the web site; (s) don't let other parts of an ad get in the way; (t) repeat disclosures on lengthy web sites, as needed; (u) "Repeat disclosures with repeated claims, as needed"; (v) "For audio claims, use audio disclosures;" and (w) "Display visual disclosures for sufficient duration."[107]

---

[104] Federal Trade Commission, Dot Com Disclosures (visted June 8, 2000), http://www.ftc.gov/bcp/conline/pubs/buspubs/dotcom/index.html.

[105] *Id.*

[106] *Id.*

[107] These suggestions paraphrase the applicability of FTC law to the use of links in Internet advertising. *See* Federal Trade Commission, Dot.Com Disclosures (visited June 8, 2000), http://

[7] Framing[108]

Framing is an easy way to bring external content to your site without recreating other web pages.[109] Framing is also a controversial web practice, because the frame retains the look, feel, and content of one web site while visitors are actually viewing another.[110] Frames may block advertising or confuse consumers as to the site's origin.[111] If you employ frames beyond your own site, the following checklist should help you to reduce your risk. If you want to avoid unwanted framing, this checklist will provide some assistance.

FRAMING CHECKLIST

1. Have you examined the benefits and risks of framing? Do you want to provide external content within your own web site?

2. Is your framing policy posted on your site? Many companies oppose framing because frames may obscure banner advertising and make your web site appear within someone else's. On the other hand, you may find that any traffic is helpful, even if visitors view your site through a frame. Post a clear policy. If your company does not want your site framed, programming tricks exist for preventing unauthorized framing.[112] Also, if you find that your site is the target of frequent, unwanted framing, consider changing the addresses of your internal links so any frames are forced to start at your front page.

3. Have you obtained written permission for any external framing? Get written permission for any external framing. Frames can be very useful because they elimate the need to recreate content that exists on another site. Framing can, for example, help you make use of the up-to-date technical specifications posted by the manufacturer of goods you resell. If the manufacturer approves your framing, you can reduce some of the time and expenses associated with web site development.

---

www.ftc.gov/bcp/conline/pubs/buspubs/dotcom/index.html. *See also*, David Connor and Sadie Curlett, Creating a Website and Doing Business on the Internet? A Checklist for Risk Management (visited Oct. 2, 2000) http://www.interactivelaw.co.nz/infocentre/articles/createwebsite.np (noting that content could also violate New Zealand's Fair Trading Act or overseas legislation, i.e., Australia's Trade Practice Act).

[108] *See* §§ 2.05[D], 4.02[G][4].

[109] Digital Equipment Corporation v. Altavista Technology, Inc., 960 F. Supp. 456, 461 (D. Mass. 1997) (citing Maura Welch, Framing the News, Boston Globe, Feb. 27, 1997 at D4).

[110] *Id.*

[111] *Id.*

[112] *Id.*

4. Make the frame obvious. Design the frame so that all external frames are clearly distinct from the web site's content. Avoid the possibility that visitors will become confused about whether they are at your site or at the framed destination.[113] Avoid covering up any critical information on the destination site.

5. Have you disclaimed liability from any framed sites? Do not expose yourself to liability if a visitor to your site is injured by a site that you have framed. Let visitors know that the frame is for their convenience and that you do not endorse the destination site.

6. Have you entered into agreements to permit framing of your site or for your company to frame the content of others? Does the agreement specify how the frame appears on the page? Have the parties agreed as to how the framed site will appear to the visitor? What are events of termination for the framing agreement?

[8] Moral Rights of Authors[114]

The moral rights of authors originate in the copyright laws of civil law countries, but they have not been recognized under U.S. copyright law.[115] Article 6 of the Berne Convention, however, validates the right of integrity and attribution of works of authorship.[116] The right of integrity maintains, essentially, that a work cannot be distorted in a way that will ruin the reputation of the creator.[117] The right of attribution is the right of the true creator to have his or her name on a work and "non-authors are prevented from having their names attached to the author's work."[118] In addition to the moral rights recognized by the Berne Convention, different moral rights are available under national law.[119]

No court decisions have extended the concept of moral rights to web sites. To be on the safe side, however, web site creators should be required to assign any moral rights to the company. It is possible that a European court could find that a company's redesign of a web site violated a web site designer's moral right of integrity. There is little reason to believe, however, that a U.S. court would recognize such a moral right.

---

[113] *Id.*

[114] *See* § 4.02[I][1]. *See* I.S. Sees Administrative Nightmare in Copyright of Web Site Proposals, Comm. Daily, Sept. 25, 2000 (commenting on WIPO's copyright proposal governing moral rights for performers).

[115] *See, e.g.,* Vargas v. Esquire, 164 F.2d 522, 527 (7th Cir. 1947) (stating that the concept of moral rights of the author is not a doctrine recognized under U.S. copyright law).

[116] Ronald B. Standler, Moral Rights of Authors in the USA (visited June 6, 2000), http://www.rbs2.com/moral.htm.

[117] *Id.*

[118] *Id.*

[119] The French, for example, recognize the right of disclosure, the right to withdraw or retract, and the right to reply to criticism. *Id.*

MORAL RIGHTS CHECKLIST

1. Have you obtained assignments for moral rights, such as the right of integrity, attribution, and distortion, from web site designers?

2. Have you obtained assignments for moral rights for all content providers? This includes audiovisual performers, scriptwriters, and other authors.

3. Have you obtained indemnification that content supplied by third parties does not violate the moral rights of authors?

[C] Exposure to Lawsuits in Distant Forums: Jurisdiction[120]

The moment a web site is launched, the online company is not only subject to local or state law, but also potentially to the laws of distant states or countries. Few activities are more time-consuming or expensive than appearing in a distant court to defend your online activities. Many companies enter cyberspace without considering the possibility of becoming subject to lawsuits in distant forums.[121] A company cannot generally be sued merely for having a server in a jurisdiction or a web site offering no commercial sales or services. The rules for jurisdiction are rapidly evolving to accommodate online disputes, however.[122] Still, a strong element of unpredictability remains, especially where the web site is in the gray zone between passivity and interactivity. Courts may set standards based on their current needs, even if these conflict with precedents in cases with similar facts from other jurisdictions; the federal district court's decision in Zippo Mfr. Co. v. Zippo Dot Com, Inc.,[123] however, has been an influential precedent in many jurisdictions.

Few in the online business community understand the legal risks of jurisdiction. Personal jurisdiction cannot be established by using a server in the forum or entering into a contract.[124] Personal jurisdiction "is directly proportionate to the nature and quality of commercial activity that an entity conducts over the Internet."[125] The definition of "minimum contacts" is still unclear with regard to Internet business.

---

[120] For a complete discussion of jurisdiction, *see* Chapter Seven.

[121] *See* Sylvia Hsieh, Small Companies' Web Sites Get Them Out-of-State, Lawyers Weekly, July 26, 1999 (visited May 15, 2000), http://www.lawyersweekly.com/feature.htm (explaining risks of doing business online).

[122] Jill Westmoreland, Multimedia Docket Sheet Recent and Pending Cases, Multimedia & Web Strategist, Jan. 1999, at 8.

[123] 952 F. Supp. 1119 (W.D. Pa. 1997); *see also* Citigroup v. City Holdings Co., 97 F. Supp. 2d 549 (S.D.N.Y. 2000) (holding that a web site alone, even if it offers goods for sale, cannot alone confer jurisdiction); Telebyte v. Kendaco, Inc., 105 F. Supp. 2d 131 (E.D.N.Y. 2000) (same).

[124] Anderson Holdings LLC v. Westside Story Newspaper, 2000 U.S. Dist. LEXIS 12102 (D.N.J. Aug. 22, 2000).

[125] Zippo Manufacturing Company v. Zippo Dot Com, Inc., 952 F. Supp. 1119, 1124 (W.D. Pa. 1997).

Personal jurisdiction is positively correlated with commercial activity; the greater the interactivity and commercial activity, the greater the likelihood a court will find that an online company is subject to personal jurisdiction in a distant forum. Passive web sites that permit neither interactivity nor online sales or services pose a low risk of personal jurisdiction in an out of state forum. Few companies are willing to restrict their web site to a mere conduit of information, however. The majority of web sites permit electronic purchasing and sales activity, according to a 1999 study by the American Bar Association.[126] Less than a third of the companies surveyed had web pages that provided only general information.[127]

EXPOSURE TO DISTANT FORUMS CHECKLIST

1. Does your web site clearly state the limits of its geographic scope? Inform visitors of the geographic limits within which you want to do business. The threat of being sued in a distant court grows in relation to the geographic scope of your business.[128] Some states and countries may have specific regulations about products or services. You may want to let visitors know that you will not make sales to any states or countries whose restrictions you don't plan to observe.[129]

2. Have you posted a choice of law/forum selection clause? Do your agreements also include choice of venue clauses? Are nonmandatory dispute resolution mechanisms offered to consumers? No matter what the scope of your business, you should limit your exposure to your state's courts and laws.[130] Inform visitors that use of your web site is conditioned upon their assent to your forum selection clause.[131] If you are selling products from your web site, reiterate your forum selection clause in the sales transaction page.

3. Does your company comply with the trade regulations of all of the states and countries in which you intend to do business? Do your e-mail advertisements comply with foreign or state antispamming laws?[132] Use ethical direct e-mail marketing. Opt-in e-mail marketing is less risky than indiscriminate spam-

---

[126] American Bar Association, ABA/ACCA Survey of Electronic Commerce Practices, Jan. 17, 1999 (visited June 15, 1999), http//www.abanet.org/scitech/abaacca.html.

[127] Thirty-one percent of respondents did not sell or purchase products or services on web sites. *Id.*

[128] *Id.*

[129] Decker v. Circus Hotel, 49 F. Supp. 2d 743, 748 (D.N.J., 1999).

[130] *Id.*

[131] *Id.*

[132] A Washington state judge recently declared that the Washington antispam law was unconstitutional, being "'unduly restrictive,' 'burdensome,' and placing a burden on business that outweighs any benefit to consumers." Peter Lewis, Anti-Spam E-Mail Suit Tossed Out, Seattle Times, Mar. 14, 2000 (visited June 10, 2000), http://seattletimes.nwsource.com/news/local/html/98/spam_20000314.html.

ming.[133] The FTC considers rules that apply to writing to be adaptable to e-mail. The FTC considers rules that apply to ads or printed material to apply to e-mail advertisements as well.[134]

4. Can you track the extent of your jurisdictional exposure based on sales and visits? Do you require users to identify the forum of residence? Do you require those who access your site to agree to resolve disputes in your jurisdiction? Are choice of forum, law, and venue class prominently posted on the company's web site? Are visitors to your site required to acknowledge acceptance of these terms? The forum selection clause or choice of law is more likely to be enforced in business-to-business than in business-to-consumer transactions. The sales volume and number of visitors per region may help you to evaluate your jurisdictional exposure.[135] If you can provide adequate data, courts may be reluctant to assert jurisdiction in a state where you have done a minimal percentage of your business.[136] Additionally, some states require registration with the secretary of state if you are conducting sufficient business in the state.[137]

5. Is your company considering entering into agreements with arbitration clauses? A decision should be made as to whether arbitration will be mandatory or not. A sample clause could simply state: "Any controversy or claim rising out of or relating to this web site agreement shall be settled by arbitration in Boston, Massachusetts, in accordance with the American Arbitration Association's Commercial Arbitration Rules."

6. Does your company track the states and countries to which its products are shipped or services rendered? You may want screening software that rejects orders or at least red flags orders from jurisdictions likely to cause legal trouble. Your local customers may request shipments to distant addresses. Such transactions may expose you to the laws and courts of the recipient's address. Make sure that any geographic limitations for sales are enforced for shipments as well.

7. Do you have a specific territorial or noncompete agreement for any products, and are those agreements updated to apply to electronic commerce? Do not forget about any territorial restrictions that you might have agreed to long before the Internet became a viable sales channel. If you set North America as your only targeted market, what do you do if you receive an order from Europe? You may be able to amend the agreement to define electronic commerce

---

[133] *See*, Whitehat.com, Inc., Best Practices (visited June 8, 2000), http://www.wh5.com/bestpractices .cfm (describing ethical direct e-mail marketing as opt-in marketing).

[134] Federal Trade Commission, Dot.Com Disclosures (visited June 8, 2000), http://www.ftc.gov/ bcp/conline/pubs/buspubs/dotcom/index.html.

[135] Zippo Manufacturing Company v. Zippo Dot Com. Inc., 952 F. Supp. 1119, 1124 (W.D. Pa. 1997).

[136] *Id.*

[137] Jonathan Bick, Due Diligence for 'Dot-Com' Deals, N.Y.L.J., May 18, 1999, at 5.

restrictions or to modify your web site to forward extraterritorial sales to another site. Consider using an attorney to ensure favorable terms in the contract modification.

8. Is a defendant in an online lawsuit amenable to service of process? Service of process must be provided under a United States statute or under a state's long-arm statute. A defendant is subject to a long-arm statute if it commits a tortious act within the state and the cause of action arises from the act.[138]

9. Is your company's web site interactive, passive, or in the borderland? Having a web site on the Internet is not enough in itself to create jurisdiction, without "something more." Web sites that are highly interactive and permit online orders will likely be found to be subject to specific jurisdiction. Web sites that provide only corporate information will not be found to be engaging in business with the forum.

10. Will the exercise of personal jurisdiction interfere with the sovereignty of another country? The exercise of jurisdiction that does implicate sovereignty concerns is a key factor in declining jurisdiction.

11. Will the exercise of jurisdiction by a court over an online dispute interfere with principles of comity? Comity is a concept referring to the deference that a domestic court must pay to the act of a foreign government not otherwise binding on the forum.

12. Does your company wish to have an offshore secure facility for an e-mail server containing sensitive data? Online gambling web sites have chosen havens such as Antigua for their places of business. HavenCo has created a satellite-linked sovereign nation called Sealand.[139] The goal of the Principality of Sealand is to host B2B financial transactions and "e-mail servers as well as sensitive data backups."[140] HavenCo.com's press release notes that it is "offering the world's most secure managed collocation facility based in the world's smallest sovereign territory."[141] Sealand permits companies to "operate any type of business within the limits of our Acceptable Use Policy without officially registering for that type of business."[142] It is unclear whether data sanctuaries will ultimately succeed as safe havens from regulators. Representatives of the Group of Eight (G8) nations are seeking ways to prevent the formation of "digital havens."[143] Governments and business partners will likely have concerns about the anonymous and pseudonymous nature of "data havens."

---

[138] Lucent Technologies, Inc. v. Lucentsucks.com, 2000 U.S. Dist. LEXIS 6159 (E.D. Va., May 3, 2000).

[139] Declan McCullagh, A Data Sanctuary Is Born, Wired News, June 8, 2000.

[140] *Id.*

[141] HavenCo., Welcome to HavenCo.com (visited June 8, 2000), http://www.havenco.com.

[142] *Id.*

[143] *Id.*

[D] Internet Privacy[144]

If a company invades the privacy of a web site visitor or employee, it is subject to liability for the resulting harm.[145] The courts recognize four privacy-based torts: intrusion upon seclusion or solitude; appropriation of name or likeness; publicity given to private life; and publicity placing a person in false light.[146] It took several years for consumers to be comfortable enough to do business online. The European Union has already adopted comprehensive privacy regulations, and the United States is examining legal measures as well.[147] The United States, unlike EU, lacks a comprehensive privacy policy[148] targeting legislation to specific industries, such as the banking industry, medical institutions, or educational institutions.

The European Union member countries approved a safe harbor, permitting the transfer of data between Europe and the United States.[149] The Directive, which went into effect in October 1998, only permits transfers of personally identifiable data to countries with an adequate standard of privacy protection. Privacy is also a key issue for U.S. regulators, who are concerned with the proliferation of deceptive online privacy practices.[150] As recently as 1998, relatively few web sites had implemented privacy policies. The Federal Trade Commission (FTC) regularly monitors web sites and privacy policies.[151] The European Commission approved a safe harbor that permits personal data from member states to be transmitted to the United States.[152]

The business community is developing new industry standards for online privacy as an alternative to government regulation.[153] The Children's Online Privacy Protection Act (COPPA) requires web site operators to provide safeguards for collecting personally identifiable information from children under the age of 13. The following checklist can help you draft a policy that matches your business needs and your data practices.

---

[144] *See* § 5.07.

[145] Restatement of Torts (2d) § 652A (2000).

[146] The categories of the privacy tort were first articulated in William L. Prosser, Privacy, 48 Cal. L. Rev. 149 (1960).

[147] Rebecca Christie, Delay in Internet Privacy Law Urged, The Financial Times Limited (London), July 28, 1999, at 6.

[148] *See generally,* Robert M. Gellman, Can Privacy Be Regulated Effectively on a National Level? Thoughts on the Possible Need for International Privacy Rules, 41 Vill. L. Rev. 129 (1996).

[149] FTC Recommends Privacy Legislation, 17 E-Commerce 8 (June 2000).

[150] Children's Online Privacy Protection Act, 15 U.S.C. §§ 6501-06, 16 C.F.R. § 312.1-312.2 (2000).

[151] *See* Kathleen Murphy, The Hard Work of Privacy Policies, Internet World, Nov. 1, 1999, at 40 (citing examples of FTC privacy policy enforcement).

[152] EU Member States Approve Safe Harbor Pact With U.S., DM News Daily, June 1, 2000.

[153] The Clinton Administration's July 1997 White Paper, A Framework for Global Electronic Commerce, favored a private sector code of conduct to protect privacy.

INTERNET PRIVACY CHECKLIST

1. Does your company collect personal, individually identifiable data? Does it require and perform data collection and maintenance? Does it have a privacy policy? Internet advertisers tout their ability to track visitors as they navigate through the web. Data harvesters make it possible to tailor web site advertisements to the visitor's interests. A growing number of Internet users, however, will not purchase goods or services from sites that do not have privacy policies. Web sites may also collect personal information through cookie files, usage data, and the harvesting of other personally identifiable information. A web site collecting personal information may be subject to regulatory action by the Federal Trade Commission.

2. Does your web site have a privacy policy statement that describes your company's personal information gathering and dissemination practices? To gain trust of visitors, your company must post its privacy policy on its web site. Internet privacy is a critically important step in gaining the trust necessary for sales or services.[154] New self-regulatory initiatives have been devised to build networks of trust.[155] Many companies subscribe to Internet seal programs to help build consumer trust. PrivaTrust is an Internet privacy assurance service associated with the Toronto accounting firm of Bennett Gold, Chartered Accountants. WebTrust is another certification program that provides a seal of approval assuring visitors that their personal information will not be misused.[156] A company that does not follow WebTrust's privacy policy may be terminated from its seal programs. In addition, a company misleading the public about its privacy policy may be subject to law enforcement or regulatory action.[157] TRUSTe, PrivaTrust, BBB Online, Web Watchdog, BizRate, or WebTrust.net offer web site certification programs. BBB Online, for example, is a self-regulation tool for fostering consumer trust and confidence on the web.[158] BBB OnLine's "Reliability Seal" is the most widely used reliability program used on the Internet.[159] An online seal or certification program should include a method of enforcement. If subscribers are not held accountable to high standards, the value of the seal or certification will erode. The best certification programs have third-party audits by accounting firms or

---

[154] Privatrust.com, PrivaTrust Is the Highest Standard for Internet Privacy Assurance (visited May 28, 2000), http://Privatrust.com.

[155] The Network Advertising Initiative (NAI) is an example of a self-regulatory group (visited May 5, 2000), http://www.network.advertising.org.

[156] Id.

[157] The audience determines whether an advertisement is misleading. Bates v. Arizona, 433 U.S. 350, 383 n.37 (1977).

[158] BBBOnLine, Code of Online Business Practices (June 8, 2000), http://www.bbbonline.org/businesses/code/index.html.

[159] Id.

other third parties. PrivaTrust is working with the Law Research Center of the University of Montreal to develop an electronic mediation and arbitration program for resolving privacy disputes.[160] Each of these self-regulation tools is designed to address Internet consumer protection issues.

3. Has your company adopted and implemented a Personal Data Protection Program?[161] Has the company prominently posted its web site privacy policy? Has the personal data protection policy been made part of a compliance program? Have employees been educated about the data protection program? Use of a third-party enforcement system or "seal system" will make it more likely that visitors will provide personally identifiable information. A growing number of companies refuse to purchase advertisements from web sites that do not have robust privacy policies. The online company may want to build trust by representing the five principles for adequate personal data protection formulated by the Global Business Dialogue (GBDe). The online company needs to first adopt and implement a Personal Data Protection Policy. The policy must be enforced company-wide in the form of a training and compliance program involving key company executives and employees. Second, a company needs an "opt-out" mechanism if it is collecting personal data from site visitors. Third, the company must only use and distribute personal data in accordance with the purpose for which it was collected. Fourth, the company must give visitors assurance of reliability in the protection of their personal information. Finally, the web site must give visitors a right of access, disclosure, and an opportunity to correct or delete personal information.[162]

4. Does your company's web site subscribe to an online privacy seal program? The TRUSTe "trustmark" or seal is awarded to web sites that follow prescribed privacy principles and comply with verification and consumer resolution processes.[163] The verification feature of the TRUSTe seal permits visitors to click on a "click-to-verify" seal. The visitor is then taken to the TRUSTe site, where they can check a list of all licensees who participate in the program.[164] Visitors can locate privacy policies by clicking on the TRUSTe trustmark. TRUSTe charges its 1,300 licensees a fee between $299 and $4,999 for its seal program.[165] Critics of TRUSTe contend that sites offer inadequate checks for determining whether "data siphoning" is occurring.[166]

---

[160] *Id.*

[161] Global Business Dialogue on Electronic Commerce, Protection of Personal Data, Sept. 1999 (recommending adoption of a data protection program); web site: http://www.gbd.org/.

[162] *Id.*

[163] TRUSTe, TRUSTe for Web Users, Frequently Asked Questions (May 28, 2000), http://www.truste.org/users/users_faqs.html.

[164] *Id.*

[165] Privacy Special Report: Should You Trust TRUSTe? PC World 116 (June 2000).

[166] *Id.*

5. Does your web site collect personal data of visitors? Is there an opt-out mechanism and a specified purpose? A growing number of industry groups endorse an opt-out provision for the collection of personal data.[167]

6. Is your company's use of personal data consistent with its policy to protect the privacy of personally identifiable information in company databases? A web site's privacy policy is an enforceable online contract and must be followed.[168] RealNetworks and Alexsa have recently been sued for violating their own privacy policies.[169] The FTC sued Internet Portal GeoCities for failing to abide by its own posted privacy policy.[170] Make sure that your company's data gathering practices matches your policy. The FTC is concerned with four primary areas of privacy: notice, choice, access, and security.[171]

7. Is there a privacy policy posted on the order or sales page? Shoppers are more comfortable ordering from a company with a posted policy. If you do make your mailing list available to other companies, disclose that fact, and give buyers an opportunity to opt-out of that mailing list.

8. Does your commercial web site target children under age 13? Does the web site comply with the Federal Trade Commission implementing the Children's Online Privacy Protection Act (COPPA)? If your site targets advertising, promotions, and other information to children under 13, it is subject to 16 C.F.R. § 312.1-312.2 (2000). COPPA requires verifiable parental consent before your site can collect personally identifiable information from children. Your site needs to limit data harvesting to what is necessary for a child's participation in an activity. The web site's privacy policy must be posted prominently and in clear language. Verifiable parental consent must be obtained prior to collecting, using, or disclosing personally identifiable information from a child. Online sellers should also consult the Children's Advertising Review Unit (CARU) of the Council of Better Business Bureau, which has published guidelines for children's advertising.

9. If your site transmits or receives sensitive information in regulated industries, is it subject to heightened duties of care? A web site dedicated to health care issues may, for example, deal with sensitive medical records. The American Medical Association requires physicians to take the "utmost care and

---

[167] *Id.*

[168] Daniel Tynan, Privacy 2000: In Web We Trust? PC World 103, 112 (June 2000).

[169] *Id.*

[170] Kenneth L. Carson, Internet Privacy: Oxymoron Or Rallying Cry? 27 Mass Law Wkly. 2277, June 14, 1999, at B5 (analyzing recent Internet privacy cases).

[171] *See* Ron N. Dreben and Johanna L. Werbach, Top 10 Things to Consider in Developing an Electronic Commerce Web Site, Computer Lawyer, May 1999, at 17 (highlighting potential online privacy issues). The Online Privacy Alliance sets out three requirements for a privacy policy: what information do you collect, how do you use it, and does the visitor have the option to keep their data from being used? Grant Lukenbill, IBM Sends Out a Shout on Privacy, DM News, April 5, 1999, at 1.

effort in protecting the confidentiality of medical records, including computer records."[172] The unauthorized disclosure of personal medical records may expose your company to federal or state statutory damages as well as common law tort actions.

10. The Fourth Amendment of the U.S. Constitution does not apply to claims of privacy in e-mail or Internet usage for private employees. State statutes may provide more protection for employees. The State of Washington's Privacy Act makes it "unlawful for any individual, partnership, corporation, association of the State of Washington, its agencies and political subdivisions to intercept or record any private communications transmitted by telephone, telegraph, radio or other device between two or more individuals between points within or without the state by any device electronic or otherwise designed to record and/or transmit said communication regardless of how such device is powered or actuated, without first obtaining the consent of all participants in the communication."[173]

[E] Third-Party Content[174]

A message board or program exchange can be helpful for customers and provide a forum for customer support and feedback. But if your web site allows posting of messages or programs, do not let yourself get involved in a lawsuit because a visitor posts objectionable material on your web site. With a carefully crafted policy and good monitoring, you can make postings an asset and not a liability. Web site posters should be warned of the dangers of defamatory, harassing, offensive, or illegal materials. Posters should be required to indemnify and hold the company harmless for causes of action arising out of chat room postings.[175]

THIRD-PARTY CONTENT CHECKLIST

1. Are third parties permitted to post any materials on your site? While it may be impossible for you to monitor content, check to make sure that items posted to the site match your business objectives. If you find that your server is being abused, assess the business risk of censoring or removing the message board.

---

[172] AMA Reg. 5.07.

[173] Revised Code Wash. 9.73.030 (2000) cited in Isabel R. Safora, Municipal Policies on Internet Usage and E-Mail Document Retention (April 1997) (visited Feb. 14, 2000).

[174] See §§ 2.05[C][2], 4.02[F].

[175] The liability for chat room conversations varies from country to country. German courts, for example, have held that there is "criminal responsibility for defamatory statements made during online conversations." Heinder Buenting, The New German Multimedia Law—A Model for the United States? 14 The Computer Lawyer 17 (Sept. 1997).

2. Do you have a policy limiting the scope of posted material? Warn visitors not to post anything defamatory, infringing, or illegal, and let them know that inappropriate material may be deleted. Regularly audit your site for inappropriate postings. Postings by employees on company stocks, for example, may subject the company to a lawsuit for insider trading. The Securities and Exchange Commission recently charged 19 defendants with the first Internet-based insider trading case for passing tips online.[176]

3. Have you clearly disclaimed any liability for defamation, copyright, trademark, or other infringement? Limit your company's liability for lawsuits from a third party's postings on your web site.

4. Have you reserved any rights to reuse the posted materials? You may want to reprint, for example, reviews, laudatory recommendations, or examples of how a product is being used.

5. Have you reserved the right to transmit or retransmit posted materials?

6. Have you reserved the right to remove posted materials or to terminate the visitor's access for any reason or for no reason?

[F]   Torts and Information Security[177]

In the past five years, more than 150 legal decisions have addressed the question of whether personal jurisdiction is proper in Internet tort cases. A climate of uncertainty persists as to whether tort theories apply to defective software or computer malpractice on the Internet.[178] Online companies are concerned about the possibility of class action lawsuits for defective software, computer viruses, inaccurate information on products, and other problems with Internet contracts.

A tort is a civil injury for which the court will provide a remedy for damages. Torts not only protect against intentional invasion but also against negligent invasions of rights.[179] Torts are not only concerned with personal injury but also with economic injuries. Torts may be committed in chat rooms, message boards, forged web sites, by e-mail, or in conjunction with an online sales or service. Prevention and cost avoidance are the primary aims of tort law.

Dot-com companies need to institute preventive law directed to changing policies and practices that are legally risky. The goal of a self-audit is to seek out

---

[176] Michael Geist, Net Insider Trading Action Launched, Internet Law News (March 15, 2000), citing http://news.cnet.com/news/0-1005-200-1572664.html.

[177] *See* Chapter Five.

[178] *See generally,* John M. Conley, Tort Theories of Recovery against Vendors of Defective Software, Practicing Law Institute: Patents, Copyrights, Trademarks and Literary Property Course Book, PLI Order No. G4-3855 (Oct. 25-27 1990).

[179] Restatement (Second) of Torts § 1 (2000).

any operational problems that need to be corrected before they bankrupt the company or result in a public relations disaster. The next step is to correct those issues and reduce the company's exposure to cyberspace-related lawsuits. Although a self-audit is nothing new for most corporations, a cyber legal audit will apply traditional legal principles to the new venue in which the e-businesses operates. A regular self-audit process that reviews e-business processes and procedures is critical to limiting tort liability. Neglecting legal issues that arise from the self-audit might preclude a company from venturing into a particular market, curb the development of a promising new product or service, and/or even potentially bankrupt the developing dot-com business altogether.

In addition to tort liability, other negative legal consequences can follow from failing to anticipate profiles of danger. The negative legal consequences include (1) a particular activity found to be unlawful; (2) a controversial lawful activity that could result in high compliance costs; (3) a particular activity with an unexpected effect resulting in lost revenues and/or a tarnished reputation; (4) loss of ownership, control, or inability to protect certain assets; and (5) a particular activity exposing the company to new sources of liability.[180]

Extending preventive law to cyberspace can serve as an early warning system against even greater corporate troubles. The remedy of punitive damages may result in even larger damage awards. Punitive damages are awarded where there is some "smoking gun" evidence that an online company concealed, suppressed, or knowingly failed to correct a dangerous computer software defect or fraudulent online practice. While employers do not have a duty to monitor the e-mail and Internet communications of their employees, they have a duty to take "effective measures to stop co-employee harassment when the employer knows or has reason to know of such harassment."[181] An employer may also have an interest in monitoring e-mail or Internet usage for the detection of other illegal conduct.[182] An online employer who knows of online torts by employees but fails to take prompt remedial action may be liable for punitive damages. Punitive damages are awarded to punish and deter the defendant and others from repeating wrongdoing. Aggravating circumstances, such as the destruction of evidence, concealment of fraudulent practices, or many prior similar injuries, are key to the awarding of punitive damages.[183]

---

[180] *See generally,* Secure, Defend, and Transform: The Complete E-Business Legal Strategy, PricewaterhouseCoopers, Spring 1999, at 7 (explaining online risks).

[181] Blakey v. Continental Airlines, Inc., No. A-5-99 (New Jersey Supreme Court, June 1, 2000) (visited June 8, 2000), http://lawlibrary.rutgers.edu/courts/supreme/a-5.99.opn.html.

[182] Isabel R. Safora, Municipal Policies on Internet Usage and E-Mail Document Retention (April 1997) (visited Feb. 14, 2000), http://www.mrsc.org/infoserv/safora.htm.

[183] *See generally,* Michael L. Rustad, Unraveling Punitive Damages: Current Data and Further Inquiry, Wisc. L. Rev 14 (1998); Michael L. Rustad, How the Common Good Is Served by the Remedy of Punitive Damages, 64 Tenn. L. Rev. 793 (1997).

An online company that distributes software from its site may be liable for product liability if a defect in the software causes personal injury. Product liability is a field that evolved largely since the 1960s to make sellers or distributors liable for harm to persons or property caused by defective products.[184] Sellers have long been liable for manufacturing defects. It has only been since the 1960s, however, that courts began basing product liability on a strict liability basis in addition to the traditional negligence or warranty actions.[185] Preventive law can result in the design of safer products and services in the online world as well. A host of relevant legal issues should be reviewed. A company with a web site is liable not just for injuries in their store, but also for any injuries incurred online. Online injuries go beyond the traditional "slip and fall" and encompass harms ranging from web site defamation and online harassment to liability for defective software. Additionally, a company can be held responsible not only for its own torts, but also for those of employees or independent contractors.

TORTS AND INFORMATION SECURITY CHECKLIST

1. Does your company have a policy minimizing the risk of online fraud? The tort of deceit or fraud may arise from false statements made on the online company's web site. A company needs a fraud-screening program to avoid being victimized by online fraud. Internet merchants can tailor fraud screens to their business. Screens may be based on risk factors such as expected time of purchase, expected purchase frequency, match between ship-to and bill-to addresses, e-mail/IP host, and orders originating in international locations.[186] It is critical that a fraud screen be able to validate credit cards.[187] Fraudulent credit card activity may account for as much as "39% of total attempted order revenue."[188] Sophisticated fraud detection methods are critical for reducing fraudulent credit card transactions and identity theft. Vendors are using artificial intelligence to screen for fraudulent and nonapproved credit card transactions.[189] State attorneys general have consumer protection divisions that may file criminal or civil actions against companies engaging in consumer fraud.[190]

---

[184] Restatement of the Law Third (Torts) Product Liability § 1 (1997).

[185] *Id.* at § 1, Comment a.

[186] CyberSource FraudScan™, Internet Fraud Screen with Artificial Intelligence (visited Sept. 19, 1999), http://www.cybersource.com/html/solutions/fraud_main.html. *See also* Brian Fonseca, Keeping Internet-Business Fraud in Check, InfoWorld, March 23, 2000 at 28 (noting high risk of Internet-business fraud).

[187] *Id.*

[188] *Id.*

[189] *Id.*

[190] The Massachusetts' attorney general formed a cybercrime unit that has charged online busi-

2. Has the company minimized its exposure to lawsuits for fraudulent sales or services? An online company must avoid being a defendant in a fraud lawsuit. United States investors sued Corel for misrepresenting its financial results.[191] A fraudulent statement made in an e-mail message or on a listserv may expose the company to a fraud action. An online company may also have tort causes of action for computer fraud. Hackers may use false credit card numbers to order software or hardware from the company. Fraud in cyberspace would cover any fraudulent behavior through which another party made misrepresentations to gain a financial advantage.[192] A web site that fraudulently makes a representation of fact about goods or services sold on its site will be liable for fraudulent misrepresentation.[193] A software vendor who licenses software knowing that the performance standards are not as represented in the promotional literature will be liable for misrepresentation.[194] A software licensor may be liable for misrepresentation fraud if he or she "does not have the confidence in the accuracy of his representations that he states or implies."[195] Fraud in online sales may also be found if the seller "knows that he does not have the basis for his representation that he states or implies."[196] An online company may also be liable for negligent misrepresentation if it provides false information in a business deal.[197]

3. If you distribute software, does your company adequately test it? Is there a standards policy? A company may be exposed to the possibility of strict product liability if defective software causes personal injury or death of a user. Inadequate testing or the defective design of software may expose a company to class action suits as well. An online company may also be exposed to product liability under a theory of negligence if it fails to follow accepted industry standards

---

nesses with online fraud. New Jersey's attorney general recently filed civil fraud lawsuits against eight online pharmacies for selling regulated drugs without a license in the state. BNA, New Jersey: State Files Consumer Fraud Charges Against Eight Online Pharmacies, 9 BNA's Health Law Reporter (News: Drugs & Devices) (Apr. 6, 2000).

[191] Michael Geist, Corel Sued Over Financial Misrepresentations, Internet Law News (Mar. 15, 2000).

[192] Restatement (Second) of Torts § 525 (2000) (summarizing the common law of all U.S. jurisdictions).

[193] The plaintiff must prove that she justifiably relied upon the misrepresentation, to her detriment. The representation may concern either an existing or a past fact. Restatement (Second) of Torts § 525, comments d, e (2000).

[194] Restatement (Second) of Torts, § 526 (2000) (explaining state of mind for fraud or misrepresentation).

[195] Id. at § 526(b).

[196] Id. at § 526(c).

[197] Id. at § 552, comment a (stating that liability for negligent misrepresentation is based upon the "failure to exercise reasonable care of competence in supplying correct information").

for assuring software liability.[198] A software company can be found negligent for the failure to test adequately or for defective design. What degree of care would a reasonable software vendor take in testing its software?[199] A software vendor may also be liable for product liability under a theory of breach of implied warranty of merchantability under Article 2 of the UCC. Negligence is a malleable cause of action that may apply to a wide variety of activities. An online software engineer may be liable for negligence for not conforming to professional standards of care in programming software. The standard of negligence may apply to an online company's failure to use due care in preventing computer viruses from infecting the computers of others. Courts have been slow to extend strict liability to computer software because of the economic loss rule.[200] Most courts limit strict product liability to cases where a defective product causes physical injury to the plaintiff. A producer of software has the potential of designing a software product that causes personal injury to the user or third parties. A producer of a coffee machine with a defective computer chip would face the same product liability as a manufacturer of an automobile with a defective fuel system. Software failure has led to airplane crashes, automobile accidents, chemical leaks, and medical product failure. A company can be exposed to breach of warranty lawsuits as well as strict product liability lawsuits for bad software that causes death or physical injury. Product liability lawsuits may be minimized by greater quality control. The correction of errors or bugs prior to release is key to product liability prevention. Once you learn of problems with hardware or software, take prompt measures to correct bugs or errors. Software license agreements will exclude all warranties and consequential damages.

4. Does your company's web site incorporate a terms and conditions agreement disclaiming warranties and limiting consequential damages? Does it offer an online chat service? Are visitors advised not to use the chat room in a manner inconsistent with netiquette as well as applicable laws and regulations? Are visitors advised about the dangers of defamatory remarks, obscene materials,

---

[198] The standard by which negligence is determined is based upon reasonableness. Negligence is a departure from a standard of conduct demanded by the community for the protection of others against unreasonable risk. Restatement (Second) of Torts § 283, comment c (2000). A company, for example, must conform its practices to those of a reasonable company under like circumstances. Industry standards or best practices are often the best proof for what a reasonable company would do under like circumstances. In general, "an act is negligent if the risk is of such magnitude as to outweigh what the law regards as the utility of the act or of the particular manner in which it is done." Restatement (Second) of Torts § 291 (2000).

[199] Restatement (Second) of Torts § 282 (2000).

[200] The "economic loss" rule is a court-constructed doctrine restricting recovery in strict product liability cases to the consequences of defective products that cause personal injury. Strict product liability lawsuits may not be filed where the injury is only to the product itself or consists only of economic losses, such as lost profits.

or misappropriating the rights of others? Are visitors required to specifically agree not to publish, post, or display defamatory, profane, sexually explicit, racially offensive, or illegal materials? The terms and service agreement may also seek indemnity for any losses, costs, or damages arising out of the misuse or abuse of the chat room. Does the company reserve the right to terminate access to the chat room at any time, for any or for no reason? Even though torts may not be limited or disclaimed, you may obtain indemnification for users who cause torts to third parties. A company may limit or disclaim liability for economic losses due to negligent design or operation of the web site. Any web site operator should meet or exceed industry standards for information security for and the design and operation of its web site.

5. Does your company have exposure to business torts? Are your competitors intentionally and improperly competing with your online business? The most common online business torts are fraud or misrepresentation, unfair competition, breach of fiduciary duty, interference with contract, and interference with prospective contractual relation.

6. Does your company have a regularly updated, comprehensive e-mail and Internet usage policy? Are these policies part of an enterprise-wide training program? Employees must be trained in the proper use of e-mail and the Internet. An e-mail and Internet usage policy should be instituted and continually updated.

7. Has your company installed the latest antiviral software and a training program to minimize viruses? Does your company disclaim the warranty for viruses in all software downloadable from your site? The latest antiviral software programs must be updated regularly. Employees must be instructed on the perils of downloading files from unknown or questionable sources. Do you disclaim or limit consequential damages or warranties for the introduction of viruses that destroy data or information? Train employees to avoid viruses caused by opening unknown e-mail messages. Educate employees on how to remove viruses promptly. Create a data recovery plan to minimize losses due to viruses.

8. Is your company liable to third parties or independent contractors? A company should obtain indemnification and hold harmless agreements from web site developers, consultants, partners, employees, and third parties. The goal is to use contractual means to reduce vicarious liability for torts committed by others. An online company is liable for the torts of its employees but not, in most cases, of independent contractors. You may wish to structure contracts as independent contractor relationships versus employment relationships.

9. Monitor incoming spam or unsolicited e-mail. Incorporate screening software if necessary. You may have a cause of action when third parties send unsolicited e-mail to employees. Create a policy against unauthorized and unsolicited bulk e-mail advertisements sent to employees. You may charge the spammer with false designation of origin when false headers are used to reach employees. Also, a company may charge spammers with a variety of other torts stemming from the spammer's impairment of its computer facilities. On the other side, your company may be liable for trespass to chattels for sending unsolicited e-mail advertisements to subscribers of online services.

10. Does your company have and enforce a computer security policy? Web site operators should monitor their web sites to promptly detect and respond to intrusions or attacks on the computer system. Companies need a strong record-keeping system to detect and avoid information security breaches that may trigger a negligence action from third parties. Additionally, a close relationship with law enforcement can minimize the consequences of intrusions to a computer system or web site. Prompt investigations and responses will make it more likely that the company can find third parties using anonymous remailers or servers to commit torts against the company. Also, institute password or other information security controls for access. Keep in mind that a company may be liable to third parties for unwittingly disclosing confidential information, such as trade secrets. Have precautions in place to protect the personal data of customers, employees, and third parties. Companies must use reasonable procedures to protect personal data or be subject to economic losses caused by impostors and other wrongdoers.

11. Has your company completed a preventive law audit to minimize and assess tort liability? If your company has been sued, has it taken corrective action to promptly mitigate the cost of injury? If the company has prior knowledge of the tortious activities of its employees but takes no action, it may be exposed to tort damages, including punitive damages. A preventive law audit provides some evidence that the company is not recklessly indifferent to the public, thus precluding or mitigating punitive damages exposure. Companies that promptly undertake corrective action have, in effect, an early warning system against tort liability. Delay, neglect, and cover-ups are highly correlated with the imposition of punitive damages.

12. Do your company's business contracts take into account online issues? As in the brick-and-mortar world, most of a company's tort liability will stem from business contracts and torts. Review your business contracts to be sure that you are treating competitors, partners, and others fairly. Do not interfere with the contractual relationships of other parties. If you have an online partnership, you may be held to a higher duty of loyalty. The breach of fiduciary duty is commonly asserted in a wide variety of online activities. Companies must monitor their business contracts to be certain that deceptive or opportunistic conduct does not subject the company to punitive damages in class action law suits.

13. Does your Internet usage policy advise employees about the dangers of defamatory messages posted to electronic bulletin boards or transmitted by e-mail? E-mail messages or Internet postings about another company's stock prices or lawsuits or any other derogatory information may expose your company to defamation lawsuits.[201] An online company should regularly monitor anticompany sites, that may be transmitting defamatory, false, or misleading messages. Procter & Gamble, for example, has long been hounded by false rumors about some of its products. A company that is too aggressive in silencing Internet critics, however, may suffer adverse publicity.[202]

Your company should include a prohibition against online harassment in its e-mail or Internet usage policies. Pornographic images left on computer screens may, for example, be evidence of a hostile workplace. Title VII of the Civil Rights Act of 1964 makes it unlawful to discriminate against an individual in an employment setting because of sex or race. The use of e-mail to sexually harass co-employees is common in today's online environment. In addition to Title VII, companies may be liable directly for the tort of outrage because of objectionable online conduct. Vicarious liability for the tort of outrage may be imposed if an employee uses the company's computer to send emotionally distressing messages to customers, co-workers, competitors, or third parties. The use of the Internet or e-mail to sexually harass co-employees may be minimized by prompt progressive discipline against offenders. A company may make a decision to monitor e-mail or Internet usage, but this step should not be taken unless employees receive notice.

14. Does your company have a system for the retention and destruction of electronic documents? A company may be exposed to liability for the deliberate destruction or failure to preserve essential evidence in the event of a lawsuit. Do you have a shadow or dark site off-line that contains key business information in the event your web site is destroyed or altered by hackers?[203]

15. Has your company received clearance from all living persons depicted in web site images who have a right to publicity or to privacy? Have all depicted persons sign a release form allowing the site to transmit online pictures, photographs, or other images? Obtain a release even if the photograph shows just a portion of a person's face or body.[204] If you are using photographs from a third party, have them provide copies of the release and indemnification.

---

[201] CNET.COM, Telco Files Net Defamation Suit, CNET.COM NEWS, May 29, 1999 (visited Feb. 24, 2000), http://news.cnet.com/news/0-1005-200-343372.htm?tag=.

[202] The Internet, by its very nature, makes it relatively easy to mount a protest campaign against a company for overreaching in its pursuit of legal rights. Archie Comics sent a cease and desist letter to the domain name owner of Veronica.com because the domain allegedly infringed the comic book character, Veronica. It turned out that the owner of the Veronica.com domain name had registered it for his infant daughter named Veronica. Archie Comics dropped the infringement claim in the wake of a wave of criticism on Internet listservs.

[203] Armor, *supra* note 1 (recommending a dark site containing important business information as a disaster recovery method).

[204] *See* Cohen v. Herbal Concepts, Inc., 63 N.Y.2d 379, 472 N.E. 2d 307, 482 N.Y.S. 2d 457 (1984) (holding image of woman and child's bare backs constituted unauthorized use).

16. Does the web site potentially infringe celebrities' right to publicity?
Do not use celebrity look-alikes without permission.[205] Several celebrities have successfully sued companies for right to publicity for using their depicted characters without permission.[206] Images that bear a remote resemblance to a famous personality may trigger a right to publicity action. In past cases, even vague similarities gave rise to legal disputes.[207] Consult an intellectual property specialist if the web site designer wants to use a celebrity look-alike or parody.

[G] Internet Advertising[208]

Online advertising is an inexpensive method of reaching a vast audience of potential customers. The web is a worldwide venue, however, and advertising on it may subject a company to consumer or other substantive laws in hundreds of countries.[209] Cultural sensitivities may create new risks for the online advertiser. Regulators in France, for example, fined the Italian firm Bennetton for an advertisement "exploiting the suffering of AIDS victims."[210] The same rules that apply to other forms of advertising apply to electronic marketing.[211] The following checklist can help you identify any issues that could contravene some fundamental areas of advertising law.

INTERNET ADVERTISEMENT CHECKLIST

1. Has an audit of legal risks been completed before launching an online advertisement?

2. Disclosures must be made to prevent online advertisements from being misleading, unfair, or deceptive. Disclaimers must be clear and conspicuous. The disclosures should be prominently displayed on the web site.[212]

---

[205] *See generally,* Onassis v. Christian Dior-New York, Inc., 1984, 122 Misc. 2d 603, 472 N.Y.S.2d 254, affirmed 110 A.D.2d 1095, 488 N.Y.S.2d 943 (observing model in perfume advertisement had close resemblance to Jackie Onassis); *see also* Hoffman v. Capital Cities ABC, Inc., 33 F. Supp. 2d 867 (C.D. Cal. 1999) (affirming judgment in favor of actor Dustin Hoffman, whose face was used in a computer animation).

[206] *See* Allen v. Men's World Outlet, Inc., 679 F. Supp. 360 (S.D. N.Y. 1988) (finding likelihood of confusion in advertisement using Woody Allen look-alike despite disclaimer).

[207] *See* White v. Samsung Electronics America, Inc. 971 F.2d 1395 (9th Cir. 1992) (finding advertisement using robot with wig and gown violated Vanna White's right of publicity).

[208] *See also* § 2.05.

[209] *Id.*

[210] *Id.*

[211] Federal Trade Commission, Advertising and Marketing on the Internet: The Rules of the Road, Apr. 1998 (visited June 8, 2000), http://www.ftc.gov/bcp/conline/pubs/buspubs/ruleroad.htm.

[212] Federal Trade Commission, Dot.Com Disclosures (visited June 8, 2000), http://www.ftc.gov/bcp/conline/pubs/buspubs/dotcom/index.html.

3. Are your online advertisements clear and conspicuous? The FTC recommends placing disclosures near or on the "same screen as the triggering claim."[213] Use text or cues to encourage consumers to scroll down, when necessary, to view a disclosure.[214] Make links obvious and label them appropriately.[215] Use consistent hyperlink styles.[216] Place hyperlinks near relevant information. Make links noticeable.[217] Monitor click through rates.[218] Make appropriate changes to make disclosures clear and conspicuous. Take into account framing and other limitations when making online disclosures.[219] Display disclosures prior to purchase.[220] Make disclosures clear when working in conjunction with banner advertisements.[221]

4. Have you minimized the possibility that your advertising will be regarded as spamming? Are e-mail advertisements or postings to listservs violating antispam laws or netiquette?[222] Does the online advertiser have the copyright, trademark, right of publicity, and right of privacy clearances on any content incorporated in an online advertisement? If an online advertisement contains photographs, music, stills, video, or other copyrighted material, does the advertiser have the proper intellectual property rights? Will any third party providing content indemnify and hold harmless the web site owner for any third party infringement claims?

5. If you list prices, do they match your current price list? Keep all of your information up to date. You do not want to accidentally sell your products at last year's prices or at prices that conflict with your traditional retail strategy. Your pricing must take into account profit margins. Do not charge the customer a higher price than that appearing on your web site. Post your pricing policy, letting consumers know that prices are subject to change without notice and disclaiming liability for typographical errors. If your programmer drops a zero from the price of your product, it could be a costly problem if you did not disclaim liability for

---

[213] *Id.*

[214] *Id.*

[215] *Id.*

[216] *Id.*

[217] *Id.*

[218] *Id.*

[219] *Id.*

[220] *Id.*

[221] *Id.*

[222] The term *netiquette* refers to the informal norms governing appropriate conduct on a listserv, chat room, or other online forum. Sending unsolicited e-mail advertisements or disseminating advertisements to unrelated listservs will provoke a backlash among Internet users, if not a lawsuit for spamming. Internet Service Providers such as America Online or CompuServe will frequently enjoin online advertisers for sending unsolicited e-mail to subscribers. The courts reject advertiser's claims that they have a First Amendment right to send unsolicited e-mail. *See, e.g.,* CyberPromotions, Inc. v. America Online, 24 Med. L. Rptr. 2505 (E.D. Pa. 1996).

the error. Make disclosures noticeable in terms of size, color, and graphics in context with overall web page.[223] Repeat disclosures in lengthy sites.[224] Use audio or video disclosures so the consumer can easily understand them. Use clear language and syntax.[225]

6. Review entire web sites. Are all Internet advertisements nondeceptive and claims backed up by firm substantiation? Internet advertisements must be truthful, not misleading, and not unfair. The Federal Trade Commission (FTC) requires advertising claims be substantiated, especially those concerning health, safety, or performance.[226] The FTC found that Listerine's statements about promising fewer colds was not substantiated.[227] The FTC and other domestic and foreign agencies comb the web for deceptive advertising.[228] Section 5 of the Federal Trade Commission Act gives the FTC the power "to prevent deceptive and unfair acts or practices."[229] The FTC considers a representation, omission, or practice to be deceptive if it is likely to "(1) mislead consumers; and (2) affect consumers' behavior or decisions about the product or service."[230] The FTC considers an act or practice unfair if the injury it causes or is likely to cause is "(1) substantial, (2) not outweighed by other benefits, and (3) not reasonably avoidable."[231] Avoid any deceptive advertising, including unfair comparisons, exaggerations, or other claims that cannot be substantiated by scientific fact.[232] The FTC does regulate advertisements that go to the "basis of the bargain," not seller's talk or "puffery."[233] *Puffery* means an expression of opinion rather than a statement of fact.[234] A company claiming that their computers are compatible with all personal computer peripherals should clarify the limits of compatibility, noting, for example, that the products may not work with older computers or with new, unanticipated technologies. Clearly list all

---

[223] *Id.*

[224] *Id.*

[225] *Id.*

[226] Federal Trade Commission, Advertising and Marketing on the Internet: The Rules of the Road (visited June 8, 2000), http://www.ftc.gov/bcp/conline/pubs/buspubs/ruleroad.htm.

[227] Warner Lambert, 86 F.T.C. 1398, (1975), aff'd, 562 F.2d 749 (D.C. Cir. 1977).

[228] *See* the Federal Trade Commission's web site policy on advertising and marketing at http://www.ft.gov/bcp/conline/pubs/buspubs/ruleroad.htm (visited May 15, 1998); *See also* In the Matter of DoubleClick, Inc., FTC Complaint (filed Feb. 10, 2000) (reporting FTC action for company's misuse of cookies in creating profiles of users), reported in Perkins Coie L.L.P. Internet Case Digest (visited Sept. 30, 2000) http:www.perkinscoie.com/casedigest.

[229] *Id.*

[230] *Id.*

[231] *Id.*

[232] *Id.*

[233] Section 2-313 of Article 2 of the UCC governs affirmative statements of fact that go to the "basis of the bargain," but not seller's talk known as puffery.

[234] Wilmington Chemical, 69 F.T.C. 828, 865 (1966).

potential costs and do not leave out any hidden charges, including shipping, handling, or taxes.[235]

7. Does your company make product comparisons that mention other brands? Are comparisons fair and backed up by substantial evidence? Comparative advertising is a well-established practice in the United States, but it is prohibited in a number of European countries. Avoid listing your competitors' names or brands on your web site.[236] It may be an invitation to a legal dispute. Some countries do not look favorably on product comparisons. A trademark holder may not prevent the use of words necessary to communicate ideas, however.[237] Product comparisons are generally considered fair use under the trademark law.[238]

8. Does scientific testing support all product and service comparisons? If you post product comparisons or claims, make sure that you have the data to back up the claims.[239] It may be helpful to put a link leading to specifics about the tests (for example, date of testing, agency conducting the tests, numeric results, and so on).

9. Demonstrations must depict product performance under conditions of normal use.[240] Do not make questionable claims about performance of software or other products sold online. Stick to performance claims, which are supported by empirical studies or other scientific data.

10. The web site must comply with local, state, federal, and international regulations governing sweepstakes or games of chance. Are online advertising campaigns regarded as lotteries subject to state, federal, or international law?[241] Is the web site designed to screen out visitors from jurisdictions where sweepstakes or games of chance are illegal? Does the web site post notices

---

[235] *Id.*

[236] *See* Lanham Act, 15 U.S.C. §§ 1114, 1125(a) (1998); Abbott Laboratories v. Mead Johnson & Co. 971 F.2d 6, 16 (7th Cir. Ind.); *see also* Bitlaw, Trademarks on the Internet (last visited Oct. 6, 1999), http://www.bitlaw.com/trademark/internet.html#discovery.

[237] *See* New Kids on the Block v. News America Publishing, Inc., 971 F.2d 302, 308 (9th Cir. 1992) (holding that newspaper could print trademarked name of musical band to identify band).

[238] The fair use test consists of three factors: (a) the product must be one not readily identifiable without the use of the trademark; (b) only so much of the mark may be used as is reasonably necessary; and (c) the user must not suggest sponsorship or endorsement. Playboy Enterprises International v. Netscape, 55 F. Supp. 2d 1070, 1084 (C.D. Cal. 1999).

[239] Abbott Laboratories v. Mead Johnson & Co. 971 F.2d 6, 16 (7th Cir. Ind.) (holding that statements technically true may nevertheless be misleading).

[240] Federal Trade Commission, Advertising and Marketing on the Internet: The Rules of the Road (Apr. 1998) (visited June 8, 2000), http://www.ftc.gov/bcp/conline/pubs/pubs/buspubs/ruleroad.htm.

[241] "At least six states (Arizona, Florida, Indiana, Kansas, Maryland and Vermont) prohibit the payment of entry fees in games of skill." Lawrence M. Hertz, Advertising on the Web: Understanding and Managing the Risks, PLI Patents, Copyrights, Trademarks and Literary Property Course Handbook Series, PLI Order No. G0-0044 (Jan. 1999).

that sweepstakes or games of chance are not directed to jurisdictions where these activities are illegal?

11. Does your company sell advertising space on your web site to other companies? Have you obtained warranties, indemnification, and hold harmless clauses that advertising content will not lead to third-party claims? A company may be liable for reviewing the claims in the advertisements of other parties. The FTC maintains that advertisers or web site designers "are responsible for reviewing the information used to substantiate ad claims [and] may not simply rely on an advertiser's assurance that the claims are substantiated."[242]

12. Has your company purchased advertising space from another web site? Have you obtained indemnification or hold harmless clauses for third party-actions? Is the pricing based on impression rates or sales? How will your advertising message be displayed?

13. Does your company comply with state antispam statutes? The typical antispam statute forbids the online advertiser from masquerading as a third party by using false headers. e-mail addresses, or the domain name of a third party without permission.[243]

14. If you have a refund policy, refunds must be made available to dissatisfied online consumers.[244]

15. Your company must have a reasonable basis for stating or implying that your products can be shipped within a certain time. The FTC's Mail or Telephone Order Merchandise Rule states that if you can't ship when promised, you must send customers a notice advising them of the delay and of their right to cancel.[245] It is likely that the FTC Mail or Telephone Order Merchandise Rule applies to Internet sales.

[H] Internet Taxation[246]

President Clinton signed the Internet Tax Freedom Act into law on October 21, 1998. The Internet Tax Freedom Act imposes a moratorium on certain state and local taxes associated with Internet or e-commerce sales or services. The Act established an Advisory Commission on Electronic Commerce, which

---

[242] Federal Trade Commission, Advertising and Marketing on the Internet: The Rules of the Road (visited June 8, 2000), http://www.ftc.gov/bcp/conline/pubs/buspubs/ruleroad.htm.

[243] E. Gabriel Perle, et al., Electronic Publishing & Software: Part III, 17 The Computer Lawyer 27 (Mar. 2000).

[244] Federal Trade Commission, Advertising and Marketing on the Internet: The Rules of the Road (visited June 8, 2000), http://www.ftc.gov/bcp/conline/pubs/buspubs/ruleroad.htm.

[245] Federal Trade Commission, Mail or Telephone Order Merchandise Rule (visited June 8, 2000), http://www.ftc.gov/bcp/conline/pubs/buspubs/ruleroad.htm.

[246] *See* § 6.07.

will make recommendations on issues such as sales and use taxes on Internet sales. The commission also will make recommendations on international tariffs on electronic transmissions. States are considering new proposals to collect sales taxes.

Contrary to popular opinion, the Internet is not tax-free. "Sales tax for items purchased online works exactly like it does for other mail order purchases."[247] On May 30, 2000, California proposed a statute that clarifies its existing rules governing Internet taxation. The proposed statute "would not tax sales from companies that have no brick and mortar stores or warehouses in the state."[248] California would require book retailers and others with stores or warehouses in the state to collect sales taxes on the Internet.[249]

The rules governing taxation are complex: taxes are generally based, however, on value. A good e-business tax advisor will enable you to control where value is created. Careful consideration of tax issues in the planning stages of your enterprise can yield significant benefits to your company in the form of its e-business structure, distribution plan, and sales model. Careful consideration of tax issues from the beginning will help you avoid problems later.

INTERNET TAXATION CHECKLIST

1. Where do online sales occur? Many transactions involve service providers in one jurisdiction, consumers in another, billing in a third , and distribution of products in yet a fourth jurisdiction. Could each one of these jurisdictions impose a tax on the transaction for sales and use tax purposes?

2. Who is the customer? Where does the customer live? If a customer's e-mail address is *cdaftary@aol.com,* can AOL's proprietary database be accessed in order to obtain the location of the consumer?

3. Which jurisdiction has the authority to tax an online commercial or consumer sales or service? Is the authority based on the location of the customer, the jurisdiction that distributes the product or service, the jurisdiction of the server that hosts the web site, or within the jurisdiction that issued the bill?

4. What types of online transactions are acceptable to be subject to sales and use taxes? Is the transaction a sale of tangible property, of services, or of intangible property? Can the sale of tangible property, services, or intangible property be subject to or exempt from tax? Does nexus have to be established before imposing such a tax? Does the presence of a web page located on a server

---

[247] Ann Kandra, Tax-Free Internet? Don't Count on It? PC World 39 (June 2000).

[248] Reuters News Service, California Assembly Approves Internet Tax Measure, May 30, 2000 (visited June 1, 2000), http://legalnews.findlaw.com/legalnews/s/20000530/economycaliforniainternet.html.

[249] *Id.*

create nexus, or is nexus possibly established in the state in which the vendor has access to the Internet via an ISP or OSP?

5. Is there sufficient documentation detailing the taxable transaction? What records do taxing authorities require? Is there an audit trail? How long should electronic records be retained? Is an off-site storage facility such as a SAN, necessary for storing duplicate records?

6. Where are your employees, center of manufacturing, and distribution centers? Where is your company's taxable nexus? Can outsourcing be used to limit your company's tax liability?

7. Does your company have inventory? Many dot-com companies have no inventory, which may be a significant income-producing factor.

8. Are you clearly distinguishing sales from services? If you sell a computer without support or charge separately for support services, the transaction is completely taxable. A few companies give away free set-top boxes with a charge for Internet access services, which reduces tax liabilities.

9. Has your company made a decision on how to deliver products or services? Tax liabilities frequently turn on whether a transaction is structured as a sale or a service. Many states also base tax liabilities on whether computer software is classifiable as tangible goods or as an intangible information product. Software downloadable on a web site does not involve the transfer of tangible goods. The value of software sold in a store lies not in the diskette or CD-ROM but in the information embedded on the media. Software downloadable at a web site may have a limited tax footprint. In many jurisdictions, no tax will apply to downloads.

10. No uniform structure or simplified method of complying with sales taxes exists. The National Governors' Association is calling for the development of a system through which goods or services may be taxed in a uniform and consistent way across state lines.[250] At present, the state tax system is unable to prevent discriminatory or multiple taxation. Another problem for state governments is that no mechanism compels remote Internet sellers to collect state taxes.[251] The Governors have recently proposed exempting small companies (with annual gross sales between $100,000 and $200,000) from collecting state sales taxes on out of state sales.[252] Online companies will need to closely follow state tax liabilities especially where remote sellers are required to collect sales taxes for any state.[253] The Internet Tax Freedom Act established a moratorium on special, mul-

---

[250] National Governors' Association, NGA Policy: Streamlining State Sales Tax Systems (visited Jan. 15, 2000), http://www.nga.org/Pubs/Policies/EC/ec12.asp.

[251] *Id.*

[252] *Id.*

[253] *Id.*

tiple, and discriminatory taxes on e-commerce at the federal, state, and local levels.[254] The World Trade Organization recently declared that its 132 member countries would continue a policy of not imposing customs duties on electronic transmissions.[255] The European Commission (EC) recently presented a proposal urging that the United States adopt a value-added tax (VAT) on online products.[256]

11. Your web site needs a software program that computes and displays sales taxes online. Many web sites do not display the sales tax, but, rather, compute the sales tax in back-room processing.[257]

12. Are there any ways to sidestep taxes? The use tax can be avoided by downloading software, for example.[258] A growing number of e-commerce companies with "facilities in many states sidestep sales taxes by setting up separate companies to handle e-commerce."[259] An online company may need to be formed as a separate corporation for tax planning purposes.

[I]   Online Contract Formation[260]

UCC Article 2 governs the commercial sale of goods, whereas the Uniform Computer Information Transactions Act (UCITA) applies to information licenses, including Internet-related software contracts. UCITA's rules closely parallel those of Article 2 because the drafters originally sought to make software licensing part of the Uniform Commercial Code.[261] In July 1999, the National Conference of Uniform State Law Commissioners approved UCITA for introduction into the states as a stand-alone statute. UCITA tailors Article 2 to fit software, multimedia contracts, access contracts, and other online transactions. As of May 2000, Maryland and Virginia were the only states to have enacted UCITA. In states that have

---

[254] United States House of Representatives, Global Internet Tax Freedom Act (visited Dec. 15, 1999), http://www.house.gov/chriscox/press/releases/1999.

[255] *Id.*

[256] Reuters, EU: VAT is Doing Now? Wired News (visited June 8, 2000), http://www.wired.com/news/politics/0,1283,36701,00.html.

[257] Kandra, *supra* note 247.

[258] *Id.*

[259] *Id.* (noting that Barnes & Noble's bn.com web site is structured as a separate corporation so that only the residents of the four states in which Barnes & Noble has warehouses or offices will be assessed sales tax for Internet sales).

[260] For a complete discussion of electronic contract issues, *see* Chapter Six.

[261] UCITA is a stand-alone statute that evolved from a project to make Article 2B, dealing with information transactions, part of the Uniform Commercial Code. The proposed Article 2B would have expanded the scope of the code to include software contracts, online contracts, webwrap contracts, access contracts, and other information contracts. UCITA, like its predecessor, applies to computer information transactions.

yet to enact UCITA, courts will apply Article 2 by analogy to software licenses, access contracts, and other Internet-related agreements.

SCOPE OF ONLINE CONTRACTS CHECKLIST

1. What law applies to online contracts? Article 2 of the Uniform Commercial Code provides a set of default rules for the sale of goods. Article 2 applies to "transactions in goods," which makes it clear that Article 2 may be extended to transactions in which there is no technical transfer of title.[262] The Uniform Computer Information Transactions Act (UCITA) applies to the licensing of computer information. UCITA deals with computer information transactions dealing with the creation, modification, licensing, and distribution of computer information.[263] An online contract involving both goods and services is a hybrid transaction that may be subject to more than one branch of law. Article 2 applies if goods are movable at the time of identification.[264]

2. Does UCITA apply to software licenses, clickwrap agreements, or other Internet-related transactions? Counsel representing licensors may want citations to UCITA as a way for courts to adapt Article 2 to cyberspace. Section 1-105 permits the parties to a UCC transaction to choose the applicable law, providing it has a reasonable relationship to the contract. The parties are generally free to choose to apply UCITA, the Convention for the International Sale of Goods (CISG), or some hybrid body of law in place of Article 2. CISG excludes any "contract in which the preponderant part of the obligation . . . consists in the supply of labor or other services."[265] Supplementary principles of law and equity may apply to a commercial transaction.[266] UCITA is a set of default rules for Internet licenses which may be varied by agreement.

UCITA Contract Formation Checklist

(a) UCITA applies to computer information transactions.[267] Determine whether your transaction is governed by UCITA. UCITA does not apply to financial services, audio, cable, satellite, and entertainment services.[268] To date, only Virginia and Maryland have enacted UCITA, but courts may apply

---

[262] 1 Ronald A. Anderson, Uniform Commercial Code § 2-102.4 (3d ed. 1981).

[263] UCITA § 103 Official Comment 1 (NCCUSL Draft for Approval, July 1999). *See,* What is UCITA (visited Oct. 2, 2000) http:www.UCITAonline.com.

[264] UCC § 2-105 (2000).

[265] CISG art. 3(2) (2000).

[266] UCC § 103 (2000).

[267] UCITA § 103(a).

[268] The term "computer information transactions" is broad enough to encompass many Internet-related contracts. Section 103(d) provides exclusions or carve-outs for UCITA. See UCITA, § 103(d).

UCITA by analogy. UCITA does not apply to software embedded in goods such as automobile brakes.

(b) A term of license agreements may not create a result contrary to public policy.[269] Little case law covers what terms might be deemed to violate a fundamental public policy.

(c) Online license agreements may not be enforced if they conflict with a consumer protection statute or administrative rule.[270] Online sales of computer hardware that incorporates software must comply with federal warranty laws, such as the Magnuson-Moss Act. It is unclear whether the Magnuson-Moss Act applies to purely software licenses since the federal warranty act applies to consumer goods, not intangibles.

(d) Incorporate a choice of law and forum selection clause in every computer information license agreement. In the absence of an agreement, access contracts such as LEXIS or the law where the licensor is located will govern Westlaw. Minnesota law for example, would govern Westlaw, whereas Ohio law would construe LEXIS access contracts.[271]

(e) If a commercial transaction involves both software and goods, UCITA will apply only to the part of the transaction dealing with software.[272] However, if the primary subject is computer information, UCITA applies to the whole transaction.

(f) Choice of law may not be enforceable for consumer contracts. A choice of law is not enforceable in a consumer contract to the extent that "it would vary a rule that may not be varied by an agreement."[273] An online "consumer contract that requires delivery of a copy on a tangible medium is governed by the law of the jurisdiction in which the copy is or should have been delivered to the consumer."[274] The parties may opt in or opt out of UCITA except in mass market transactions, where "opt-outs" must be "conspicuous."

(g) Parties may generally "choose an exclusive judicial forum unless the choice is unreasonable and unjust."[275] The choice of forum clause, to be enforceable, must state explicitly that the judicial forum is exclusive.[276]

---

[269] UCITA, § 105(b).

[270] Id. § 105(c).

[271] See id. § 109(b)(1).

[272] Id. § 103(b)(1).

[273] Id. § 109(a).

[274] Id. § 109(b)(2).

[275] Id. § 110(a). See Henry K. Lee, "Judge Calls AOL Litigation Terms Unfair," 5 F. Chronicle, Sept. 28, 2000 (reporting California court's refusal to order transfer of lawsuit filed by AOL users to Virginia because it would be unfair and unreasonable).

[276] Id. § 110(b).

(h) Courts will refuse to enforce unconscionable terms in online license agreements.[277] The court must afford parties an opportunity to present evidence of commercial setting, purpose, and effect of allegedly unconscionable clauses.[278] UCITA preserves state and federal consumer protection statutes.

(i) Online contracts should be structured so that a person has an opportunity to review contractual terms before payment.[279] If there is no opportunity to review the terms before a person has an obligation to pay, the person must have the right to a refund.[280] The manifestation of assent may be achieved through the use of electronic agents. There is no manifestation of assent in the absence of an opportunity to review the record.[281] An electronic record is given the same validity as a writing.

(j) Freedom of contract permits any provision of UCITA to be varied by agreement except the obligations of good faith, diligence, reasonableness, and due care or negligence.[282] In addition, the limits on enforceability imposed by unconscionability or fundamental public policy may not be waived or varied by agreement.[283] UCITA also places limits on agreed choice of law, choice of forum, the requirements for manifesting assent, and the opportunity for review.[284] UCITA's mandatory consumer protection rules may not be disclaimed, including limitations on self-help measures such as disabling the software.[285]

(k) A good faith as well as supplemental principle of law and equity applies to UCITA transactions. In addition, commercial reasonableness and usages of trade permeate every provision of UCITA.[286]

(l) Online contracts with a contract fee of $5,000 or more must be authenticated by a record indicating that the contract has been formed.[287]

(m) Online "contracts may be formed in any manner sufficient to show agreement, including offer and acceptance or conduct of both parties or operations of electronic agents which recognize the existence of a con-

---

[277] Id. § 111.
[278] Id. § 111(b).
[279] Id. § 112.
[280] Id. § 112(e).
[281] Id. § 112(a).
[282] Id. § 113(a)(1).
[283] Id. § 113(a)(2).
[284] Id. § 113(3).
[285] Id. § 113(3)(A)-(J).
[286] Id. § 114.
[287] Id. § 201.

tract."[288] Electronic agents may form contracts, but the court may grant relief from "fraud, electronic mistake or the like."[289] UCITA validates messages coming from electronic agents.

(n) The online site needs to establish the type of authentication or record acceptable to it.[290] A party adopts the terms of a record by manifesting assent to a record.[291] UCITA legally validates electronic records, electronic agents, and electronic authentication.[292]

(o) An online company should adopt a commercially reasonable attribution procedure or one approved by both parties.[293]

(p) In Internet-type transactions, a licensor must "afford an opportunity to review the terms of a standard form contract . . . before becoming obligated to pay."[294] Standard terms "must be displayed prominently and in close proximity to a description of computer information."[295]

(q) Attribution procedures for commercial transactions must be commercially reasonable.[296]

(r) The mail box rule of the common law does not apply to online transactions: "Receipt of an electronic message is effective when received even if no individual is aware of its receipt."[297]

3. Consumer goods costing greater than $10 sold at the web site are subject to the federal Magnuson-Moss Act. The Magnuson-Moss Warranty Act applies to written warranties for goods used for personal, family, or household purposes. The FTC is considering expansion of the Magnuson-Moss Act to apply to mass market software. The Magnuson-Moss Act applies "to written warranties on tangible personal property which is normally used for personal, family, or household purposes."[298] The Magnuson-Moss Act does not apply to business-to-business transactions. Web site warranties must be clearly and conspicuously differentiated or labeled as either "full warranty" or "limited warranty." Full warranty means that the seller is meeting the federal minimum standards.[299] If a full warranty is given, a warrantor must provide a minimum remedy without charge if the

---

[288] *Id.* § 202.

[289] *Id.* § 206.

[290] *Id.* § 107.

[291] *Id.* § 208.

[292] *Id.* § 107.

[293] *Id.* § 108.

[294] *Id.* § 211.

[295] *Id.* § 211(1)(A).

[296] *Id.* § 212.

[297] *Id.* § 215.

[298] 16 U.S.C., § 700.1 (2000).

[299] 15 U.S.C., § 2303 (2000).

product does not conform to the written warranty.[300] Few, if any, online sellers will be willing to offer a full federal warranty. The full warranty obligates the supplier to correct defects, malfunctions, or nonconforming quality defects without charge. Full warrantors may not exclude or limit consequential damages for breach of warranty nor limit the duration of implied warranties.[301] If a full warranty is not given, the seller must "conspicuously designate it a 'limited warranty.' "[302] Warning information must be given prior to the online sale of goods.

Implied warranties of quality cannot be entirely disclaimed under the Act, but they may be limited in duration so long as the limitation is in "clear and unmistakable language and prominently displayed on the face of the warranty."[303] A seller may limit the duration of an implied warranty covered by the act. The Magnuson-Moss Act requires sellers to make other mandatory disclosures to consumer-buyers.[304] Warranties that violate the Magnuson-Moss act are ineffective.[305]

4. Does a state's version of the Uniform Deceptive Trade Practices Act (UDTPA) apply to online agreements, clickwrap agreements, and other Internet-related web site practices? The UDTPA, unlike the UCC, provides remedies for attorneys' fees, costs, and double or treble damages in selected cases. The UDTPA may apply in cases of fraudulent or deceptive online business practices.

5. Does the United Nations Convention on Contracts for the International Sale of Goods (CISG) apply to nonconsumer sales of goods between parties in different signatory states? The United States signed CISG in 1988, and most industrialized countries are also signatories. CISG applies "to contracts of sale of goods between parties whose places of business are in different [signatory] states."[306] CISG does not apply to product liability actions for personal injury caused by goods.[307] In contrast, UCC Article 2 permits plaintiffs to recover damages for personal injury as a form of consequential damages.[308] The parties can opt-out of CISG or exclude the application of any of its applications.[309]

6. Does any of the Federal Trade Commission (FTC) regulations apply to online sales? Do your online sales and services comply with FTC regulations? The FTC is considering expanding its telemarketing rules to apply to Internet web

---

[300] *Id.* § 2304.
[301] *Id.*
[302] *Id.* § 2308.
[303] *Id.*
[304] *Id.*
[305] *Id.* § 2308.
[306] CISG, art. 1.
[307] CISG, art. 5.
[308] UCC, § 2-715(2)(b) (2000)
[309] CISG, art. 6.

sites. To be on the safe side, web sites should avoid Internet acts or practices that would be deceptive or unfair if done by a telemarketer. A web site must prominently disclose any material disclosures prior to a customer's payment for goods or services. In an online sale of goods, the customer must be given the total costs to purchase, receive, or use any goods or services.[310] The web site merchant must obtain express verifiable authorization for payment by check or negotiable instruments. FTC rules apply equally to e-commerce, as do state deceptive and unfair trade practices acts.

7. Does the web site comply with the Directive on Distance Selling and the Directive for Contracts for Financial Services? The European Union directives apply to contracts with consumers in European Community countries.[311] Are web site visitors given the right to reflect before concluding a contract with a supplier? The directives give consumers a right of withdrawal after reflection. Are consumers given the right to cancel financial services contracts within 14 days, or 30 days in the case of mortgage loans, life assurance, and operations pertaining to personal pensions?[312] The directives require a consumer's prior consent "for the use of automated distance communications systems without human intervention, such as faxes."[313] Member states "must ensure that adequate and effective complaints and redress procedures to [exist] settle disputes between suppliers and consumers."[314]

8. Are choice of forum clauses included in online contracts to reduce uncertainty about e-commerce jurisdiction? The parties are free to opt in or out of UCITA, subject to protections for mass market transactions. Choice of law, forum, and venue clauses are used to reduce the uncertainty of doing business on the Internet. Choice of forum permits parties to reduce the probability of litigating in a distant forum. UCITA allows parties to a license agreement to choose an exclusive judicial forum unless it is "unjust." It is critical to state that the forum is exclusive. or courts may not enforce a choice of forum.

9. What contracts are required to launch the company's web site?

    (a) Web Design and Hosting Agreement. Web design and hosting agreements are frequently entered into by small and medium companies.[315]

---

[310] Telemarketing Sales Rule, 16 C.F.R. § 310.3 (2000).

[311] *See, e.g.* Directive 97/7/EC (prohibiting the supply of services without the consumer's specific and valid consent) (visited Dec. 19, 1999), http://europa.eu.int/scadplus/leg/en/lvb/l32035.htm.

[312] Financial Services: Distance Contracts for Financial Services, Council Directives 90/619/EEC, 97/7/EC, and 98/27/EC (visited Dec. 19, 1999), http://europa.eu.int/scadplus/leg/en/lvb/l32035.htm.

[313] *Id.*

[314] *Id.*

[315] *See, e.g.,* Aramedia.net, Virtual Web Hosting Agreement (visited Jan. 21, 2000), http://www.aramedia.net/agree.htm.

Web Design and Hosting Checklist

☐ Do you have a web design and hosting agreement? Who is bound by the agreement?

☐ Is there a clause creating a binding contract between the web designer and the customer?

☐ Is the description of services adequate? Does the host acquire the domain name on behalf of the customer?

☐ Is disk storage adequate for the web traffic and quantity of graphics, sound, and video files?Are e-mail autoresponders and forwarding included?

☐ Is the web traffic allowance adequate?

☐ Does pricing reflect expected traffic? Penalties may be assessed by your host if you exceed your traffic allowance, unless the parties otherwise agree. Length of service? Service start date? Renewal by client? Refund policy?

☐ Does the web site provide traffic reports?

☐ Is the setup fee reasonable? The monthly service fee? Does the cost reflect allowances for extra traffic? Is a shopping cart feature available? Real Audio support? CGI programming? Database services? What conditions govern web design and hosting?

☐ What warranties are given in the hosting agreement? Is there a waiver of damages as well as warranties? Is the host liable for the loss of data as the result of delays, non-deliveries or service interruptions?

☐ Does the web host offer a domain name service?

☐ What is the payment term? Is there a set-up fee?

☐ Are cross-indemnities and hold harmless clauses included in the agreement?

☐ Has the online company reserved the right to approve changes in the terms of the agreement? Many web host agreements reserve the right to make changes to the terms and conditions of hosting agreements without notice to the company.

☐ Is there a merger clause?

☐ What are the events of termination? What law applies in the event of a dispute? Have both parties provided contact information?[316]

---

[316] *See, e.g.,* Online Solutions Web Hosting Reseller Agreement, Online Solutions Web Hosting Reseller Agreement (Jan. 21, 2000), http://www.onsol.com/reseller_agree.html.

❑ Your web design and hosting agreement needs a contracting clause such as: "This agreement for web design and hosting is made and entered between Web Hosting Inc., located at 41 Temple Street, Boston, Massachusetts 02108-4977 and Suffolk Personal Computers, located at 120 Tremont Street, Boston, Massachusetts 02108-4977.

(b) Clickwrap License Agreements. Have clickwrap license agreements been developed for downloading software from the company's web site? A license agreement is a contract to use or access software. A licensor is the person who grants a right to use software, and the licensee is the party acquiring the right to use software for the terms of the license.[317] A clickwrap license is a standard form mass-market license entered into by web site visitors when they download software from a web site. A web site visitor may be asked to accept or decline terms with one click and then be asked to confirm with a second click that they are certain they accept. The "double click" method is designed to prevent a user from disaffirming the act of clicking through screens. Do clickwrap agreements comply with the prescriptions of UCITA in providing an opportunity to review terms as well as manifesting assent? A clickwrap agreement should be structured so that the visitor has an opportunity to review the terms prior to clicking the "I accept" icon or text. A single click on an icon or underlined text would satisfy UCITA's requirement of manifestation of assent. Terms of the license agreement should be available to the licensee prior to purchase. UCITA binds a party to the terms of a shrinkwrap or clickwrap agreement if the party had reason to know that his or her acts would be treated as assent to the terms.[318] Mass-market licenses are adopted "only if the party agrees to the license, such as by manifesting assent, before or during the party's initial performance or use . . . or access to the information."[319] A company must afford a web site visitor "an opportunity to review the terms of a standard form license before the information is delivered or the licensee becomes obligated to pay, whichever comes first."[320]

(c) Webwrap Agreements. If a company does not give a web site visitor opportunity to review a mass-market license before becoming obligated to pay, is there a return policy giving the visitor the right to a refund, along with reasonable expenses? UCITA requires licensors to give licensees a refund along with reasonable expenses if software or information is delivered without giving a licensee an opportunity to review terms of a standard form agreement.[321]

---

[317] UCITA, § 102 (40-42) (NCCUSL Draft for Approval, July 1999).

[318] UCITA, § 112 (NCCUSL Draft for Approval, July 1999).

[319] UCITA, § 210(a) (NCCUSL Draft for Approval, July 1999).

[320] UCITA, § 212(1) (NCCUSL Draft for Approval, July 1999).

[321] *Id.*

(d) **Internet-Related Licenses.** Are the terms of Internet license agreements displayed prominently and in close proximity to the description of computer information? A company may also disclose "the availability of the standard terms in a prominent place on the site for which the computer information is offered."[322]

(e) **Cross-Border Internet Sales Contracts.** The Council of the European Union adopted a Directive on the Protection of Consumers in Respect of Distance Contracts.[323] Member states may determine the language used. If you are doing business with European Union states, consider web sites with different languages. Be sure that disclaimers and limitations of liability are accurately translated. The Distance Contract Directive was originally conceived for communications by telephone, where the consumer could not see the product. Where consumers cannot see the products, a right of withdrawal from the contract should be available.[324] An online business in the United States is subject to the Distance Selling Directive if it has a subsidiary in the consumer's country of residence.[325] The web site, as with any distance seller, "must provide consumers with notice of the provisions of the Directive and of codes of practice that may exist in this field."[326] An online contract qualifies as a "distance contract," which "means any contract concerning goods or services concluded between a supplier and a consumer under an organized sales or service-provision scheme run by the supplier."[327] A supplier "means any natural or legal person . . . conducting distance contracts in their professional or commercial capacities."[328] Written confirmation must be given to a consumer prior to conclusion of the contract.[329] At minimum, information must be included on the right of withdrawal, the geographical address of the supplier, information on services and guarantees, and the means for canceling a contract.[330] The right of withdrawal must exist for a period of at least 7 working days.[331] A supplier must execute an order within a period of 30 days

---

[322] UCITA, § 212(1)(b) (NCCUSL Draft for Approval, July 1999).

[323] European Parliament and the Council of the European Parliament, Directive 97/7/EC of the European Parliament and of the Council of 20 May, 1997, on the Protection of Consumers in Respect of Distance Contracts (visited June 9, 2000), http://europa.eu.int/comm/dg24/policy/developments/dist_sell/dist01_en.html.

[324] *Id.*

[325] *Id.*

[326] *Id.*

[327] *Id.* at art. 1.

[328] *Id.* at art. 3

[329] *Id.* at art. 5(1)

[330] *Id.*

[331] *Id.* at art. 6.

from the time the consumer sends his or her order.[332] Member states shall provide means for charge backs and cancellations in the event of fraudulent use of credit cards.[333] Clickwrap or webwrap agreements may not be used to waive consumer rights.[334] UCITA preserves state and federal consumer protection.

10. What forms of ongoing online contracts are necessary?

Online Contract Checklist

(a) Conduct an audit of all online or Internet-related contracts. Update standard form contracts to fit the realities of online contracting. The first step in an online contracting audit is to do an inventory of all Internet-related agreements. Existing contracts may need tailoring to fit e-commerce transactions. Online companies typically have diverse means of contracting, including Private Virtual Area Networks, Internet e-mail, Internet web sites, direct dial, EDI, video auctions, and FPT through the Internet or by fax. Of online companies selling goods, 28 percent sold them at Internet web sites; 17 percent of online consumers purchased goods from sites.[335] Online contracts were entered into through e-mail, mass-market, or standard form contracts; Electronic Data Interchange; customer data formats; web catalogs; or secure sockets via web site processing.[336] Most online contracts are not ever completed on paper forms or reduced to hard copies.

(b) Online offers and acceptance may be formed in any reasonable manner including by e-mail, computer-to-computer, or through webwrap agreements. Offers can invite acceptance by any reasonable manner. Revised Article 2 of the UCC has updated rules validating online contracting, as does UCITA.

(c) Enter into enforceable online contracts. Online contracts may be signed with digital signatures in many jurisdictions. Structure online catalogues as "invitations to offer" rather than as offers. A company may use international certification networks when inviting offers in foreign countries. Vendors such as GlobalSign offer personal digital certificates for assuring the authenticity of electronic signatures.[337]

---

[332] *Id.* at art. 7.

[333] *Id.* at art. 8.

[334] *Id.* at art. 12.

[335] American Bar Association, ABA/ACCA Survey of Electronic Commerce Practices, Jan. 17, 1999, http://abanet.org/scitech/abaacca.html.

[336] *Id.*

[337] GlobalSign, GlobalSign Certificate Center (visited May 28, 2000), http://www.globalsign.net.

(d) Form computer-to-computer contracts without human review. Prior to the development of the Internet, Electronic Data Interchange (EDI) permitted orders to be filled computer-to-computer. Revised Article 2 of the UCC and the Uniform Computer Information Transaction Act permit the formation of online contracts. Electronic agents are computer programs that can be used to initiate an action or to respond to electronic records or performances. Electronic agents "with or without review or action may form contracts by an individual."[338] Revised Article 2, the Uniform Computer Transactions Act and the Uniform Electronic Transactions Act validate the concept of online computer-to-computer contracts. To be on the safe side, however, the parties should enter into trading partner agreements validating computer-to-computer contracts. UCITA treats the "record" as the functional equivalent of a signed writing that has the effect of permitting the electronic signatures to satisfy the Statute of Frauds.[339] A "record" updates a writing to include information inscribed or stored in an electronic medium, provided it is retrievable.[340] The concept of the e-signature has been updated to include signing by digital signatures or other encryption processes.[341]

(e) Digital signatures and electronic records in most jurisdictions may satisfy the Statute of Frauds. The validation of electronic signatures and records is evolving rapidly. Use digital signatures to ensure the integrity of data messages. Article 2 of the UCC requires a writing signed by the party against whom enforcement is sought for goods worth $500 or greater.[342] The proposed revisions to Article 2 require a record for the sale of goods for $5,000 or greater.[343] The United States is one of the few countries to require a Statute of Frauds. The Convention for the International Sale of Goods does not have a Statute of Frauds or parol evidence rule, unlike Article 2 of the UCC.

(f) An electronic record is treated with the same legal effect as paper-based writings. A record is the e-commerce equivalent of a writing.

(g) Structure your terms of service, clickwrap, and other standard form contracts as license agreements. What specifically is being licensed? Who are the parties to the license agreements? There must be a granting clause, which gives the licensee the right to use software or other licensed intellectual property for the term of the license agreement. Also necessary is a choice of law, forum, and venue clause for each license agreement to avoid litigating in distant forums with unfamiliar law. The license agreement must

---

[338] [New] Revised Article 2. Sales, § 2-103(17) (American Law Institute Discussion Draft, Apr. 14, 2000).

[339] UCITA, § 201 (NCCUSL Draft for Approval, July 1999).

[340] UCITA, § 201(a) (NCCUSL Draft for Approval, July 1999).

[341] UCITA, § 102(a)(6)(A) (NCCUSL Draft for Approval, July 1999).

[342] UCC, § 2-201 (2000).

[343] Revised Article 2, § 2-201(a) (American Law Institute Discussion Draft, Apr. 14, 2000).

clearly specify who is covered by the agreement. Is this a license for a single site? Are subsidiaries covered? What other key terms should be defined? Does the licensee have the right to updates? Is there an effective date for each license agreement? What is the grant of rights? Is the license agreement exclusive, semiexclusive, or nonexclusive? May rights under a license agreement be assigned? What is the payment term? What are the specific deliverables? Is there a period of acceptance testing during which a licensor can work out bugs in software? What is the term of the license? Is the license exclusive, semiexclusive, or nonexclusive? Is there any confidentiality provision? Who owns the intellectual property? If the licensor supplies intellectual property, what warranties are given? Are there cross-indemnities given by the parties? May the license agreement be assigned or delegated? What warranties are given? What are the limitations of warranties and damages? Is there an integration or merger clause? What are the events of termination? What are the remedies and method of dispute resolution? What is the venue and jurisdiction for legal actions?

(h) Do liberal contract formation rules apply to Internet-related contracts? UCITA, for example, validates automated transactions in which contracts are formed by bots or electronic agents.[344] In fact, a party is bound by operation of its bot or electronic agent even if no individual reviewed its actions. UCITA validates computer-to-computer contracts and grants records the same legal effect as a paper and pen writing.

(i) The modification of online contracts requires no consideration.[345] An online company may consider drafting a clause specifying that no modifications are valid unless made in writing.

11. What other online contract terms need to be tailored for the specific commercial transaction in cyberspace?

Online Contract Terms Checklist

(a) Offers and acceptance depend upon the "intent of the parties." Contracts may generally be formed in any manner sufficient to show agreement, including conduct. What is the prescribed method of forming contracts at the company's web site? Contracts in the online environment may be formed on web sites, e-mail, or computer-to-computer. A clickwrap agreement may be structured so that a web site visitor signifies acceptance by the action of clicking an "I accept" button or icon. Does your web site offer online con-

---

[344] Knowbots or intelligent agents, e-mail agents, and shopping agents are increasingly used in Internet transactions. The trend in the law is to permit contracts to be formed by electronic agents.

[345] See UCC § 2-209 (2000).

tracts with an opportunity to review the terms prior to the manifestation of assent?

(b) Is there a merger clause, which is evidence of the parties' final expression of its online contracts? Course of dealing, course of performance, and usage of trade may also supplement a final agreement. Supplemental terms such as industry standards are considered part of the contract unless specifically disclaimed or modified by agreement. Article 2, UCITA, and UNIDROIT's "Principles of International Commercial Contract Law" permit evidence of course of performance, course of dealing, and usage of trade to supplement contracts.[346]

(c) Online contracts must not be blatantly unfair or oppressive. A court may void such contracts as unconscionable. The test of unconscionability is whether the weaker party has a realistic choice in acceding to the terms.[347] The basic test for whether an online contract is unconscionable is whether it is one-sided, oppressive, or has unfair or surprising terms.

(d) Is there a legal framework for conducting electronic commerce in your jurisdiction? The European Parliament approved the Directive on Certain Legal Aspects of Electronic Commerce in the Internal Market in May 2000.[348] The Directive validates online contracts and other e-commerce legal infrastructure for the 15 European Union countries.

12. What web site and online warranties are required? See Tables 8.1, 8.2.

TABLE 8.1
UCC Warranties for Online Sales of Goods

Types of Article 2 Warranties	Description
§ 2-312	Warranty of title and noninfringement
§ 2-313	Express warranty
§ 2-314	Implied warranty of merchantability
§ 2-314	Fitness for a particular purpose

---

[346] UNIDROIT'S Article 2.17 states that a "contract in writing which contains a clause indicating that the writing completely embodies the terms on which the parties have agreed cannot be contradicted or supplemented by evidence of prior statements or agreements. However, such statements or agreements may be used to interpret the writing."

[347] Courts require that the weaker party prove both procedural unconscionability (unfair bargaining) and substantive unconscionability (unfair, oppressive, or surprising term) in order to obtain relief. The fact that a shrinkwrap or clickwrap agreement is adhesive does not mean that it is unconscionable and unenforceable.

[348] Proposal for a European Parliament and Council Directive on Certain Legal Aspects of Electronic Commerce in the Internal Market: Com (98) 586 Final; Official Journal 30, 05/02/99.

TABLE 8.2
UCITA Warranties for Online Licensing of Software

§ 401	Warranty and obligations concerning noninterference and noninfringement
§ 402	Express warranties
§ 403	Implied warranty: Merchantability of computer program
§ 404	Implied warranty: Information content
§ 405	Implied warranty: Licensee's purpose—System integration
§ 406	Disclaimer or modification of warranty

Internet Warranty Checklist

(a) Are your products and services displayed in an online store at your web site? Any description of the specification of goods in an online catalog creates express warranties under the Uniform Commercial Code. A Gateway™ computer described as having a 15.1 XGA TFT Color Display, for example, is given an express warranty by description. Inclusion of the words "56K modem" creates a warranty about the qualities of the modem as does the expression "3.5" diskette drive." An advertisement noting that a computer features the Intel Pentium III processor creates a warranty. It would be a breach of warranty if the processor was, in fact, a Pentium II. An express warranty is any "affirmation of fact or promise made by the seller to the buyer which relates to the goods and becomes part of the basis of the bargain."[349] Express warranties cannot be disclaimed once created.

(b) Does the company demonstrate goods or services through virtual tours on the web site? Express warranties are created by descriptions of goods, which go to the basis of the bargain. Online advertisements, catalogs, and advertisements may give rise to express warranties. Any sample or model, which involves a demonstration of goods, creates express warranties. The words of creation and negation of warranties must be reconcilable. The best way to disclaim express warranties is not to make affirmative statements or to act in any way that goes to the "basis of the bargain."[350] Online advertisements and demonstrations should be reviewed

---

[349] UCC, § 2-313(1)(a) (2000).
[350] UCC, § 2-313 (2000).

to determine whether they accurately depict the performance of software or other products.

(c) Has your company completed an audit of what warranties it gives in connection with the sale of goods or services from its web site? Article 2 of the UCC is the applicable law for warranties for the sale of goods, unless the parties otherwise agree. The common law will apply to rendering professional services, such as computing consulting services or web site design. UCC Article 2 recognizes the following warranties: (1) implied warranty of title and noninfringement; and (2) warranties of performance: express warranties, implied warranty of merchantability, and implied warranty of fitness for a particular purpose. Do your goods conform to the six minimal standards of merchantability: (i) Do your goods pass without objection in the trade (§ 2-314(2)(a))? (ii) Are your goods of fair, average quality (§ 2-314(2)(b))? (iii) Are the goods fit for their ordinary purpose (§ 2-314(2)(c))? (iv) Are the goods even in quality (§ 2-314(2)(d))? (v) Are the goods adequately contained (§ 2-314(2)(e))? (vi) Do the goods conform to representations on the label (§ 2-314(2)(f))?

(d) Has your company followed the prescribed methodology for disclaiming warranties for the sale of goods? The Uniform Commercial Code prescribes precise rules for disclaiming warranties and limiting liability. General disclaimers are ineffective to disclaim UCC warranties. Specific language must, for example, be used to disclaim the warranty of title or noninfringement. ("Seller makes no warranty of title or noninfringement.") Section 2-316 of the UCC provides the prescribed method for disclaiming warranties of performance. To exclude or modify the implied warranty of merchantability, the disclaimer must mention merchantability. If the disclaimer is in the form of writing, it must be "conspicuous."[351] General disclaimers such as "there are no express or implied warranties" are unenforceable. To disclaim the warranty of merchantability, the seller must mention the word "merchantability" or use phrases such as "with all faults" or "as is."[352] The fitness for a particular purpose is an implied warranty, which operates as a matter of law. To qualify for a fitness warranty, the buyer must prove: (i) the seller has reason to know of any particular purpose for which the goods are required; (ii) the seller has reason to know that the buyer is relying upon the seller's knowledge; and (iii) the buyer must actually be relying on the seller's skill or judgment in selecting goods.[353] When disclaimers are posted on a web site, the writing must

---

[351] UCC, § 2-316 (2000).
[352] *Id.*
[353] UCC, § 2-315 (2000).

be conspicuous. Implied warranties, unlike express warranties, are generally disclaimable.[354] Express warranties are affirmations of fact, which go to the basis of the bargain of the sale of goods.[355] Express warranties are made in sales literature, banner advertisements, and demonstrations of products. The best way "to avoid liability for an express warranty is to not make it in the first place."[356]

(e) The Federal Trade Commission's Rule on Pre-Sale Availability of Written Warranty Terms applies to consumer products costing $15 or more.[357] The seller must make written warranties available at the point of sale. An online seller must also make warranties from manufacturers available as well as the warranties provided by the retailer.

(f) UCITA Warranties of noninfringement and performance warranties apply unless disclaimed or limited.

UCITA Warranties Checklist

(a) Merchant licensors warrant that information is delivered free of any claims for intellectual property infringement.[358] The noninfringement warranty continues for the entire term of a license agreement.[359] Software delivered to customers must be free of any claims of infringement. The warranty of noninfringement applies only to rights arising in the United States.[360] A licensee may wish to negotiate for a noninfringement warranty covering the world or specified countries.[361] Merchants may give another merchant the equivalent of a quitclaim warranty with respect to infringement or misappropriation.[362]

(b) Express warranties for license agreements closely parallel those for the sale of goods. An express warranty is created for an "affirmation of fact or promise made by the licensor to its licensee, including by advertising, which relates to the information and becomes part of the basis of the

---

[354] The Magnuson-Moss Act does not generally permit sellers to disclaim implied warranties. 15 U.S.C. § 2308 (2000). Even the Magnuson-Moss Act, however, permits sellers to limit the duration of implied warranties.

[355] UCC, § 2-313 (2000).

[356] Douglas J. Whaley, Problems and Materials on Commercial Law 103 (5th ed. 1997).

[357] Federal Trade Commission, Advertising and Marketing on the Internet: The Rules of the Road (visited June 8, 2000), http://www.ftc.gov/bcp/conline/pubs/buspubs/ruleroad.htm.

[358] UCITA § 401 (NCCUSL Draft for Approval, July 1999).

[359] *Id.* § 401(b)(1).

[360] *Id.* § 401(c)(2).

[361] *Id.*

[362] *Id.* § 401(e).

bargain."[363] This means that banner advertisements, online catalog descriptions, demonstrations, or samples may constitute express warranties. An express warranty is created even if there are no words of "warranty" or "guaranty."[364] Seller's talk or puffery, which express merely opinions or commendations, do not qualify as enforceable express warranties.[365]

(c) UCITA updates the implied warranty of merchantability to apply to Internet-related transactions.[366] Merchant licensors warrant that a "computer program is fit for the ordinary purposes for which such computer programs are used."[367] Software must "be adequately packaged and labeled."[368] If there are multiple copies of software or other information, the copies must be of "even kind, quality and quantity."[369] The computer program must conform to any "affirmations of fact made on the container or label."[370] Implied warranties may also arise from the course of dealing between the parties and from usages of trade that arise in the computer industry.[371] There is no implied warranty for the accuracy of information.[372]

(d) No implied warranty for informational content is created under UCITA's Implied Warranty for Informational Content.[373] A merchant that "compiles, processes, provides or transmits informational content warrants to [the] licensee that there is no inaccuracy in the informational content caused by the merchant's failure to perform with reasonable care."[374] The license agreement should contain a similar clause.

(e) If a licensor in an Internet-related transaction has reason to know of a particular purpose for software or other information, it may be making a system integration warranty.[375] The system's integration warranty parallels the warranty of fitness for a particular purpose. For there to be an integration warranty, the licensee must prove that the licensor had reason to know of a

---

[363] *Id.* § 402(a)(1).
[364] *Id.* § 402(b)(1)(2).
[365] *Id.* § 402(3).
[366] *Id.* § 403.
[367] *Id.*
[368] *Id.* § 403(2)(A).
[369] *Id.* § 403(2)(B).
[370] *Id.* § 403(3).
[371] *Id.* § 403(b).
[372] *Id.* § 403(c).
[373] *Id.* § 404.
[374] *Id.*
[375] *Id.* § 405.

particular purpose for software or other computer information. The licensee must be relying upon the licensor's skill or judgment in selecting software or other information.[376]

(f) Licensors need to follow UCITA's methodology in disclaiming or modifying warranties.[377] To disclaim the implied warranty of merchantability for a computer program, the language must mention "merchantability," "quality," or similar words.[378] To disclaim an informational accuracy warranty, "the language in a record must mention 'accuracy' or use words of similar import."[379] The language to disclaim the systems integration warranty "must be in a record and be conspicuous."[380] The integration warranty may be disclaimed with a conspicuous disclaimer that states "There is no warranty that this information, our efforts, or the system will fulfill any of your particular purposes or needs" or similar words.[381]

(g) UCITA permits the licensor to disclaim all implied warranties other than the noninfringement warranty with an expression such as "as is" or "with all faults."[382] It is necessary to disclaim the noninfringement warranty with specific language.

(h) If software or other information can be examined fully, there "is no implied warranty with respect to defects that an examination ought in the circumstances to have revealed to the licensee."[383]

(i) Implied warranties "may also be disclaimed or modified by course of performance, course of dealing, or usage of trade."[384] It is not recommended to rely upon these implied disclaimers. Use clear language specifically disclaiming implied warranties.

(j) Warranties "must be construed as consistent with each other and as cumulative, [unless] that construction is unreasonable."[385]

13. What performance and remedy clauses are necessary?

---

[376] *Id.*

[377] *Id.* § 406.

[378] *Id.* § 406(1)(A).

[379] *Id.* § 406(1)(B).

[380] *Id.* § 406(B)(2).

[381] *Id.*

[382] *Id.* § 406(4)(c).

[383] *Id.* § 406(4)(d).

[384] *Id.* § 406(4)(e).

[385] *Id.* § 408.

Performance and Remedies Checklists

(a) The standard of performance for online contracts is that perform-ance should "perform in a manner that conforms to the contract."[386] A licensor will have a right to a cure if the software does not conform to the contract. An uncured material breach of contract entitles the other party to cancel the contract.[387] UCITA permits cancellation only for material breaches of performance, in contrast to the "perfect tender" rule of UCC Article 2.[388]

(b) Electronic restraints such as software programs or devices may be used to regulate performance. Restraints, for example, may prevent uses inconsistent with a license agreement.[389] It is a good idea to give the licensee notice of electronic restraints on duration or number of uses.

(c) *Force majeure* or excuse clauses should be tailored for the agree-ment rather than rely upon the default provisions of UCITA.[390]

(d) A party in breach of contract may cure the breach at his own expense.[391]

(e) The seller is entitled to notice of breach or the buyer is precluded from recovery.[392] In non-mass market license agreements, the licensor must give "seasonable notice of a specific nonconformity and make a demand for cure."[393]

(f) UCITA adopts the tender, acceptance, rejection, and revocation concepts from UCC Article 2.[394] The refusal of tender parallels the concept of rejection in Article 2. The tender of a copy of software or other informa-tion that "is a material breach of contract" permits the nonbreaching party to "(1) refuse the tender; (2) accept the tender; or (3) accept any commercially reasonable units and refuse the rest."[395] A party accepting a nonconforming tender may revoke acceptance if they had a reasonable assumption that the licensor would seasonably cure the nonconformity.[396] UCITA follows UCC

---

[386] *Id.* § 601(a).
[387] *Id.* § 601((b)(2).
[388] *See* UCC, § 2-601 (2000).
[389] UCITA § 605.
[390] *See id.* §§ 614, 615.
[391] *Id.* § 703.
[392] UCC § 2-607(3) (2000).
[393] UCITA § 703(b).
[394] *See id.* Part 6.
[395] *Id.* § 704(a)(1)-(3).
[396] *Id.* § 707, § (a)(1).

Article 2 in recognizing an adequate assurance of performance, anticipatory repudiation, and the retraction of anticipatory repudiation.[397]

(g) UCITA follows UCC Article 2 in not permitting a party to recover more than once for the same loss.[398]

(h) The nonbreaching party may cancel if there is a material breach that has not yet been cured.[399]

(i) Upon cancellation, executory obligations are discharged. The licensee has no further right to use licensed information after cancellation.[400]

(j) If the online advertisement uses phrases such as "satisfaction guaranteed" or "money-back guarantee," the refund policy must be to give a full refund with no questions asked.

(k) Limit remedies as well as warranties. Many online sellers offer a sole and exclusive remedy in lieu of Article remedies. UCITA provides that "a party is in breach of contract" as "determined by the agreement."[401]

(l) Agreements may modify or substitute for the default remedies of UCITA.[402] The remedy offered buyers must be meaningful. "Failure or unconscionability of an agreed exclusive or limited remedy makes a term disclaiming or limiting consequential or incidental damages unenforceable unless the agreement expressly makes the disclaimer or limitation independent of the agreed remedy."[403] Article 2 buyers may challenge an exclusive remedy with § 2-719(2), which states: "Where circumstances cause an exclusive or limited remedy to fail of its essential purpose, remedy may be had as provided in this Act."[404] UCITA adopts the doctrine of failure of essential purpose from UCC Article 2. If an exclusive or limited remedy "causes the remedy to fail of its essential purpose," the parties may pursue any of the UCITA remedies.[405]

(m) The measurement of damages may not include avoidable consequences. The nonbreaching party has a duty to mitigate damages.[406]

(n) Consequential damages are not recoverable for "the content of published informational content unless the agreement" expressly provides for such damages.[407]

---

[397] Id. § 708-§ 710.

[398] Id. § 801.

[399] Id. § 802(a).

[400] Id. § 802(c).

[401] Id. § 701.

[402] Id. § 803.

[403] Id. § 803(c).

[404] UCC § 2-719(2) (2000).

[405] UCITA § 803(2)(b).

[406] Id. § 807(a).

[407] Id. § 807(b)(1).

(o) Damages must not be speculative and must be reduced to the present value as of the date of breach.[408]

(p) A licensor's damages will generally consist of accrued and unpaid contract fees or the market value of other consideration not received.[409] Licensors may obtain consequential and incidental damages, but all damages must be calculated in a reasonable manner.[410]

(q) The licensee's damages are measured by the "market value of the performance that was the subject of the breach plus restitution of any amounts paid for performances not received."[411]

(r) Specific performance may be ordered provided adequate safeguards are maintained to ensure confidentiality of information.[412]

(s) Electronic repossession or self-help is a controversial means of exercising a licensor's rights. Electronic self-help is not permitted unless a licensee separately authorizes electronic self-help.[413]

(t) A licensor must give notice before exercising electronic self-help, even if the licensee has authorized this remedy.[414]

[J]   Internet Payment Systems

Credit cards are the principal means for payment for B2C sales. A web site will need a merchant account before it can accept credit card orders. Credit card fraud and charge backs are major problems for web sites. Digital money has not yet gained widespread acceptance as a means of payment.

ONLINE PAYMENTS CHECKLIST

1. What payment systems are required for web site sales and services? What credit card agreements? What new bank/customer relationship is needed? What mechanism does the company use to allocate the risk of lost, stolen, altered, or counterfeit credit cards? A cardholder is not liable for the unauthorized use of her or his credit cards unless it is an "accepted" card. An accepted card is defined as a credit card that the cardholder requested and signed. A cardholder is not liable for unauthorized use in excess of $50.[415] The online seller is liable for fraudulent credit card payments, not the merchant bank.

---

[408] *Id.* § 807(2)(e).
[409] *Id.* § 808.
[410] *Id.* § 808(C)(D)(2).
[411] *Id.* § 809(a).
[412] *Id.* § 811.
[413] *Id.* § 816(a)(c).
[414] *Id.* § 816(c)(1).
[415] 12 C.F.R., § 226.12(b)(2).

2. What types of payment methods are used for electronic sales and purchase transactions? Credit card payments are the best-established payment systems for business-to-consumer sales and services. Recently, however, merchants have been exploring alternative payment systems, such as prepaid cash cards. Online companies targeting a broader consumer market are adopting products such as InternetCash.[416] Online music stores, such as Coconuts, Planet Music, and the Wall, use software that permits the use of prepaid cash cards.[417] Online companies use a variety of payment systems, including the use of negotiable instruments, electronic funds transfer,[418] credit card payment at the time of sale, e-checks at the time of sale, electronic fund transfer at the time of sale, subscription accounts, purchase orders, and electronic bill presentment and payment.[419]

3. Does your web site take steps to keep your _charge back_ rate low? The online seller is liable for resolving charge back problems, not the merchant bank. What steps does the company take in resolving disputes with customers? What is your return or refund policy? Cardholders may assert claims or defenses against the card issuer[420] or withhold payment from merchants for claims or defenses that cannot be resolved.[421] The cardholder "may withhold payment up to the amount of credit outstanding for the property or services that give rise to the dispute and any finance or other charges imposed on that amount."[422] If a "cardholder withholds payment of the amount of credit outstanding for the disputed transaction, the card issuer shall not report that amount as delinquent until the dispute is settled or judgment is rendered."[423] Regulation Z requires the "cardholder to make a good-faith attempt to resolve the dispute with the person honoring the credit card."[424] Another limitation is that the "disputed transaction occur in the same state as the cardholder's current designated address or, if not within the same state, within 100 miles from that address." Most credit card companies waive the 100-mile rule to contest a credit card transaction.[425] It is

---

[416] L. Scott Tillett, Merchants Grapple With Payment Options—Integration Still a Hurdle as Credit-Card Alternatives Emerge, Internet Week, May 22, 2000.

[417] _Id._

[418] The Electronic Fund Transfer Act ("EFTA") establishes the rights, liabilities, and responsibilities of participants in electronic fund transfer systems. EFTA requires participants to adopt certain practices for dealing with preauthorized transfers, error resolution, and liability limits for unauthorized transfers. _See_ Federal Trade Commission, Advertising and Marketing on the Internet: The Rules of the Road (visited June 8, 2000), http://www.ftc.gov/bcp/conline/pubs/buspubs/ruleroad.htm.

[419] _Id._

[420] 12 C.F.R., § 226.12(c).

[421] 12 C.F.R., § 226.12(c)(1).

[422] _Id._

[423] 12 C.F.R., § 226.12(c)(2).

[424] § 226.12(c)(3).

[425] Benjamin Wright and Jane K. Winn, The Law of Electronic Commerce § 20.02[A] at 20-4 (3rd ed. 1998).

unclear how the 100-mile or same state rule applies to web site transactions.[426] "It is uncertain whether an Internet transaction will be deemed to have taken place at a consumer's residence, at the site of the e-commerce server, or at the primary place of business of the merchant."[427]

4. Does the online company considers co-branded credit cards as part of a direct mail marketing effort? Sears, Roebuck and Company has a co-branded credit card with MasterCard and Sears logos.[428] Credit card issuers must be careful not to issue credit cards except by special request from consumers.

5. Does your company's virtual store need a Merchant Credit Card Processing Account? A company that sells goods or renders services from a web site needs a credit card processing account. First of Omaha permits web sites to accept Visa, MasterCard, Discover, American Express, Diners Club, and JCB.[429] A web site must be able to accept a wide variety of credit cards. In addition, the web site may have a toll-free telephone number so customers reluctant to transmit credit card numbers on the Internet can supply credit card information personally. A few online web sites accept checks or permit cash on delivery (COD).

6. The company requires secure sessions with processing or merchant banks for its web site. Does the payment system incorporate a Secure Electronic Transaction (SET) Protocol? Secure online payments may also be achieved by the use of Secure Socket Layers (SSL). Secure protocol is not a payment system but a means for assuring party authentication and the secure transmission of data.[430] The American Bankers Association is the parent company of ABAecom, a subsidiary dedicated to facilitating electronic banking and e-commerce.[431] ABAecom has partnered with Digital Signature Trust Co. to provide a public key infrastructure to ensure privacy, authentication, data integrity, and nonrepudiation for Internet-related financial transactions.[432] ABAecom helps banks build trust through its SiteCertain certification program.[433] The SiteCertain seal gives customers verification that they have reached an authentic Internet bank web site. SiteCertain provides a web site authentication seal and is in the process of developing digital certificates to enable banks and customers to engage in secure communications.

---

[426] *Id.*

[427] *Id.* § 20.02[A], at 20-4, 20-5.

[428] Sears Debuts Mailing for Co-Branded MasterCard, DM News Daily, June 1, 2000.

[429] eCommerce, Twelve Steps (visited May 14, 2000), http://www.foomp.com/e_commerce/twelve_9.htm.

[430] Veronique Wattiez Larose, Electronic Payments: Perspective from Quebec, ABA ECP Home Page (visited May 10, 2000), http://www.abanet.org/scitech/ec/ecp/veronique.html.

[431] ABAecom, About ABAecom FAQs (visited May 28, 2000), http://www.abaecom.com/abt_faq.htm.

[432] *Id.*

[433] *Id.*

7. The online payment system needs protection against forgery and the alteration of messages. One of the difficulties of online contracting is to determine the authenticity of messages. An online company needs a means for verifying the source of electronic messages received. Web site visitors also seek assurances of a web site's authenticity. Verisign's "click to verify" seal assures web visitors that they are at the correct site. The ABA Survey found that the use of e-mail return addresses was the most common means of authenticating data messages.[434] Relying on e-mail addresses as the sole method of authentication is hazardous, however, since e-mail addresses and headers may be falsified or altered. Of the respondents, 22 percent used PINs or passwords to verify the source of electronic messages, whereas only 12 percent with digital signatures with public key encryption.[435] A digital signature uses private keys to "sign" a message, and the recipient uses the signer's public key to determine whether or not the digital signature is valid. The online merchant will want to install configurable antifraud detection software.

8. Does the company use signature certificates based on public keys to conduct electronic contracts to ensure an environment of authenticity, message integrity, and nonrepudiation? Public key-based digital signatures, digital images of signatures, SSL certificates,[436] fax confirmations, and verification through trusted third parties such as banks are commonly used as certification mechanisms for companies engaging in e-commerce.[437] Digital signatures were used by 14 percent of survey respondents in the 1998 ABA Science and Technology survey.[438] Digital signatures, encryption, and SSL certificates use encryption to prevent forgery. The American Banker's Association's ABAecom uses digital certificates, issued and signed by a Certificate Authority (CA), that vouch for the identity of the certificate holder.[439] The CA issues a certificate binding the certificate holder's public key to his or her identity.[440] The use of trusted third parties allows for individuals to securely engage in e-commerce "with assurance of sender and recipient authenticity, privacy, message integrity, and non-repudiation."[441]

9. How does your company determine that a data message it receives has not been altered? An online company needs a systematic procedure for verifying document integrity in order to transmit and receive electronic offers and

---

[434] *Id.*

[435] *Id.*

[436] SSL is short for Secure Socket Layer, which is a technology for verifying the identity of visitors. GlobalSign, GlobalSign Digital Certificate Services, and PKI Solutions (visited May 28, 2000), http://www.globalsign.net.

[437] *Id.*

[438] *Id.*

[439] *Id.*

[440] *Id.*

[441] *Id.*

acceptance. If a funds transfer is altered, the addition of an extra digit may result in a multimillion dollar loss. Repeat back acknowledgments were used by 29 percent of the ABA respondents to verify that the messages they received had not been altered, whereas only 11 percent used digital signatures.[442]

10. Implement electronic bill presentment and payment for B2B transactions. A B2B system may be designed to couple billing data with information delivery.[443]

11. Implement payment fraud software. Companies can install software that "flag[s] suspected transactions with higher-than-normal dollar values or exotic mailing address[es] that don't match with other payment information submitted by the consumer."[444]

12. If you are a creditor who bills online customers for goods or services, you must comply with the Fair Credit Billing Act. The act requires you to acknowledge consumer billing complaints promptly and to investigate reported errors. A creditor must post payments to a consumer's account promptly and refund overpayments.[445]

[K] Employment Issues

INTERNET EMPLOYMENT CHECKLIST

1. E-Mail and Internet Usage Policies

(a) Has the online company implemented an e-mail and Internet usage policy? Are the policies included in your training programs? Are the policies updated regularly? Companies should appoint a contact person who can provide advice on compliance. The contact person should be available by e-mail, if not in real time.

(b) Do the policies provide employees with notice that e-mail and Internet access are for business purposes? The policy needs to be realistic and enforceable. A policy strictly prohibiting personal use of e-mail is not enforceable in many work settings. The policy should notify employees that they have no legitimate expectation of privacy in their Internet use.

(c) Does the policy include notice that e-mail or Internet usage is subject to monitoring and that employees have no reasonable expectation of privacy in using these tools? Does the company advise employees

---

[442] *Id.*

[443] Tim Wilson, E-Bills Fire Up Exchanges, Internet Week, May 15, 2000, http://www.internetwk.com/story/INW20000511S0002.

[444] Tillett, *supra* note 416.

[445] Federal Trade Commission, Advertising and Marketing on the Internet: The Rules of the Road (visited June 8, 2000), http://www.ftc.gov/bcp/conline/pubs/buspubs/ruleroad.htm.

that it intends to cooperate with law enforcement in the event that an employee is charged with violating local, state, or federal law in abusing e-mail or the Internet? Increasingly, American online companies partner with the Federal Bureau of Investigation, Interpol, and other law enforcement agencies to curb software piracy and other crimes.

(d) Are employees given specific training on how to avoid misusing or abusing the Internet? Do employees know the boundaries of acceptable use? Are prohibitions in place against downloading intellectual property without authorization? Are employees given notice of the actions the company intends to take to curb abuses? E-mail training should explain the negative consequences of threatening, obscene, harassing, political, or objectionable online communications. In a June 2000 case, the New Jersey Supreme Court considered whether Continental Airlines had a duty to prevent defamatory statements made by its employees on an online computer "bulletin board."[446] A unanimous court held that an employer who has notice that its employees are using the Internet to defame and harass a co-employee has a duty to remedy that harassment.[447] An employer who did not promptly correct offensive online work-related behavior may be liable to a lawsuit for discrimination. The New Jersey Supreme Court found that Continental Airlines might be directly liable for the online harassment of its employees[448] and might also be liable for a co-employee's harassment under an agency theory and remanded the case for further fact-finding.[449]

2. What preventive law precautions need to be taken in other areas related to employment and the Internet?

(a) A company must promptly take measures to stop work-related online harassment. An employer has a duty to take effective measures to stop e-mail or other online harassment when the employer knows or has reason to know that such harassment is taking place.[450] The employer should: institute a mechanism through which employees can promptly report online harassment, and the employer take effective measures to stop online misuse and abuse. Electronic audios of inbound and outbound files transmission to and from the company may be instituted.

(b) Draft nondisclosure and noncompetition agreements to protect trade secrets. Does your company have nondisclosure and noncompetition agreements? Do the confidentiality agreements extend beyond the period of

---

[446] Blakey v. Continental Airlines, Inc., 164 N.J. 38, 751 A.2d 538 (2000).
[447] *Id.*
[448] *Id.*
[449] *Id.*
[450] *Id.*

employment? Are the agreements enforceable by time and geographic limitations? Nondisclosure and noncompetition agreements must be reasonable in scope, territory, activity, and duration.

(c) Employees must be advised of the consequences of misappropriating trade secrets or confidentiality.[451] Do your company's e-mail and Internet policies describe in sufficient detail the specific confidential material that is to be safeguarded?

(d) Nondisclosure and confidentiality agreements are useful in protecting against the disclosure of subject matter that may be patented. Exit interviews should be conducted to remind employees of their continuing duty to maintain the confidentiality of information covered by a nondisclosure agreement.

(e) Determine the legal status of employees, independent contractors, consultants, and partners. A company that takes no effective action to prevent online torts by its employees may be liable directly or under an agency theory such as vicarious liability. Vicarious liability, for example, will frequently turn on whether a person is classified as an employee or an independent contractor. An employer may be liable for its employees' torts committed within the scope of employment, but will generally have no liability for the torts of independent contractors. In the dot-com world, a number of nontraditional employment relationships may exist that present the possibility that an "employee" may be classified by a court as an independent contractor. Conversely, a court may decide that an "independent contractor" should be treated as an employee for tax and social security purposes. Courts will compare form to substance when examining a company's employment classifications.

(f) Employment issues may arise with the development of a web site. A web site development and service agreement should classify the designers and other consultants as nonemployees. If web site designers and providers are not employees, the work for hire doctrine does not apply. It will, therefore, be incumbent on a company to obtain assignments of intellectual property rights. Nondisclosure and confidentiality agreements are critical to a wide variety of web services agreements. Web site provider agreements, Internet service provider agreements, web site advertiser agreements, end-user license agreements, and multimedia development agreements should all have specific clauses addressing confidentiality and nondisclosure. A simple nondisclosure agreement binding co-venturers would state: "Neither party shall disclose the existence of or the terms and conditions of this agreement without prior writ-

---

[451] *See, e.g.,* DoubleClick Inc. v. Henderson 1997 WL 731413 (N.Y. Misc. 1997) (finding that ex-employee of an online advertising agency violated confidentiality agreement in forming a competing online company).

ten consent of the other party." In the case of co-venturers, cross indemnity clauses may be appropriate. Each party should defend, indemnify, and hold the other harmless and pay damages and costs arising out of any claims or actions brought by third parties for infringement of intellectual property rights.

(g) If your company recruits employees online, all recruiting materials must comply with federal and state antidiscrimination laws, just as in the offline world. It is common in cyberspace to have online employment applicants as well as telecommuting employees. Online applications must comply with state and federal employment law. Many online businesses hire a variety of temporary employees. You may minimize negligent screening, hiring, and retention claims by checking the credentials of employment applicants.

3. What steps has your company taken to protect confidential information? The directors, officers, and other key employees owe the online company a fiduciary duty.

4. What steps has your company taken to prevent insider trading under federal securities law? What measures has the company taken to prevent insider trading? SEC Rule 10b-5 prevents company directors, officers, and other insiders from using "inside information" in the sale or trading of securities. Insiders not only have a duty not to trade upon insider information but also not to pass tips on to friends, family members, or associates. An online company may also wish to establish its own policies against securities transactions involving company securities.

[L] Regulatory Issues

State and federal regulatory agencies police unfair and deceptive trade practices. The Federal Trade Commission regulates privacy issues as well as unfair and deceptive trade practices on web sites. Web sites that sell goods or services in regulated industries are subject to regulatory actions. The New Jersey Attorney General's office, for example, targeted web sites selling Viagra and other prescription drugs without a license in the state.[452] State attorneys general in Illinois, Kansas, and Missouri each targeted online pharmacies, alleging violation of state consumer protection statutes.[453] Missouri also prohibits the online "beer of the month" clubs from selling to customers located in the state.[454]

---

[452] BNA, New Jersey: State Files Consumer Fraud Charges Against Eight Online Pharmacies, 9 BNA's Health Law Reporter (News: Drugs & Devices), Apr. 6, 2000.

[453] *Id.*

[454] Michael Geist, Internet Beer Distribution Shut Down, Internet Law News (Mar. 15, 2000), (citing http://www.ago.state.mo.us/031400b.htm).

INTERNET REGULATION CHECKLIST

1. Does your company store records in electronic form that may be required by federal, state, or local regulators? Are there corresponding backup storage facilities for records?

2. What steps does your company take to verify that data messages you receive have not been altered? Do you use electronic authentication tools, such as digital signatures? Are digital signatures treated with the same legal effect as "paper and pen" signatures? Do electronic records have the equivalent legal effect as paper-based records?

3. Does your company do periodic backup of records? Are your confidential records protected by passwords, biometrics, voice verification, or other security tools?

4. Does your company have a systematic document retention policy that includes electronic records? Does your record retention policy follow local, state, and federal rules for record retention?

5. Does your e-mail system have a mechanism for deleting messages after a defined period of time?

6. Does your company provide training in record keeping to employees and other authorized users?

7. Does your e-mail or Internet policy treat e-mail as records? Is there a document destruction policy that applies to e-mail?

8. The Division of Enforcement of the U.S. Securities and Exchange Commission (SEC) investigates possible violations of federal securities laws on the Internet.[455] The SEC has jurisdiction for the sale of securities subject to the registration requirements of the Securities Act of 1933. Sale of securities on eBay or other auction sites would be a violation of the Securities Act of 1933. The SEC polices web sites offering securities, soliciting securities transactions, or advertising investment services offshore.[456]

9. The Federal Trade Commission polices web sites offering online investment opportunities.[457] Offshore investment opportunities are particularly suspect. The FTC Commission publishes a list of the top ten online scams.[458]

---

[455] Securities and Exchange Commission, SEC Division of Enforcement Complaint Center (visited June 8, 2000), http://www.sec.gov/enforce/comctr.htm.

[456] Securities and Exchange Commission Interpretive Release, Interpretation, Statements of the Commission Regarding Use of Internet Web Sites to Offer Securities, Solicit Securities Transactions, or Advertise Investment Services Offshore (visited June 8, 2000), http://www.sec.gov/enforce/intrelrl.htm.

[457] Federal Trade Commission, FTC Consumer Alert! Online Investment Opportunities "Net Profit" or "Net Gloss"? (visited June 8, 2000), http://www.ftc.gov/bcp/conline/pubs/alerts/oinvalrt.htm. *See also* Arent.Fox.com, FTC Seeks to Expand Scope of Telemarketing Sales Rule (visited Sept. 30, 2000) http://www.ARENTFOX.com/publications/Alerts.

[458] *Id.*

10. The United States, as well as other countries, controls the use of cryptography products. Companies must comply with government regulations of cryptographic security products. The Export Administration Regulations (EAR) of the Bureau of Export Administration of the Department of Commerce requires export licenses for shipment to its list of countries subject to embargoes or other special controls.[459] The Bureau of Export Administration (BXA) has several offices with which to consult when determining licensing requirements.[460] To comply with export controls, commodity classifications must be obtained. For encryption products a license from the Department of State may be needed. Forms for license applications and commodity classification requests are available online.[461] The Bureau of Export Administration posts a list of firms and individuals denied export and reexport privileges.[462] To avoid a visit from agents or the EAR Office of Enforcement, do not distribute software with these firms or individuals.

11. Online companies need to be sure that they are not subject to export controls. The BXA maintains on its web site a number of forms and services for requesting assistance.[463] This helps the BXA ensure a level playing field. Special agents work with the business community to discover export violations. The BXA Enforcement Hotline is 1-800-424-2980.

12. Export controls do not apply to U.S. citizens with greater than 56-bit encryption installed on a personal laptop. This exception pertains when traveling to countries under embargo or to countries deemed terrorist by the government.[464] In addition, an encrypted product may be exported to a foreign subsidiary of a U.S. company "to protect company proprietary data" under a license exception.[465]In general, mass-market products using 56-bit DES or RC4 are exportable.[466] The BXA web site should be consulted to determine whether a given country is eligible to receive general-purpose encryption software. The Wassenaar Arrangement was created in July 1996 to restrict control exports.[467] The Wassenaar Secretariat formulated a Dual Control List extending to "c encryption hardware and software cryptography products above 56-bits," including Web browsers,

---

[459] The Bureau of Export Administration, U.S. Department of Commerce, BXA's Assistance to Exporters (visited June 11, 2000), http://www.bxa.doc.gov/factsheets/ExporterAssistance.html.

[460] *Id.*

[461] *Id.*

[462] *Id.*

[463] *Id.*

[464] Georgetown computer scientist Dorothy E. Denning and her colleague William E. Baugh have written an *Easy Guide to Encryption Export Controls,* Sept. 25, 1999 (visited June 11, 2000), htttp://www.cs.georgetown.edu/~denning/crypto/Export/regs.html.

[465] *Id.*

[466] *Id.*

[467] Electronic Privacy Information Center, Cryptography and Liberty 1999: An International Survey of Encryption Policy 13 (1999).

e-mail applications, electronic commerce servers, and telephone scrambling devices.[468] In addition, mass-market products "over 64-bits are subject to controls for two years."[469] The member states of the European Union recognize "the same list of dual-use goods (generally based on the COCOM and Wassenaar lists), destinations and guidelines."[470] If your online company is shipping encryption commodities outside the United States, it has the burden of determining whether such a practice is allowed under the Commerce Department's export licensing jurisdiction.[471]

§ 8.03   INSURANCE POLICIES

[A]   E-Commerce-Related Insurance

E-commerce is growing rapidly as corporations throughout the world leverage information technology and venture into the new frontier of cyberspace.[472] E-commerce offers to save companies a tremendous amount of money by reducing costs and adducing timesaving benefits, all while potentially increasing revenues.[473] Yet, the Internet can involve significant risks, as well. Internet insurance policies covering e-commerce activities are necessary because traditional coverage is uncertain.[474]

In a joint survey by the FBI and the Computer Security Institute, 64 respondents revealed that in the preceding 12 months they had experienced computer related security breaches.[475] Other computer related computer risks include copyright or trademark infringement, domain name disputes, slander or defamation, libel claims, e-mail abuse violations, plagiarism, tort liability, and claims of false advertising.[476] When considering the revenue potentials of e-commerce, of course, these potential risks are easily overlooked.

[B]   Acquiring Internet-Related Insurance

To complicate matters further, it is very easy to be exposed to such risks. Risks come from both inside and outside the company. A disgruntled employee, an outside computer hacker, or a virus program can cause problems. Depending

---

[468] *Id.* at 13.

[469] *Id.*

[470] *Id.* at 18.

[471] The Bureau of Export Administration, U.S. Department of Commerce, Frequently Asked Questions (visited June 11, 2000), http://www.bxa.doc.gov/factsheets/ExpFAQ1.html.

[472] Reliance National, The Choice (1st Quarter, 1999) (visited May 15, 2000), http:/www.reliancenational.com/choice/9901/cyberrsk.htm

[473] *Id.*

[474] *Id.*

[475] *Id.*

[476] *Id.*

on the scale and scope of the violation, a company could have serious financial exposures. As a practical matter, it is impossible for companies to prevent every possible infraction, especially since some exposures are outside their control. Companies should consider, therefore, supplementing their existing insurance policies with policies such as computer network liability, breach of security coverage, crime and intranet insurance,[477] online internet insurance,[478] and errors and omissions policies.[479]

Regardless of what type of coverage is sought, companies should, at a minimum, protect themselves against defamation,[480] viruses,[481] unauthorized access,[482] intellectual property infringement,[483] and failures of their web sites.[484] When purchasing Internet liability insurance for e-mail, Internet, intranet, or e-commerce violations, companies should look for policies that include protection from negligent acts, errors and omissions, breach of duty, infringement of intellectual property rights, breach of confidentiality, unauthorized access, libel and slander.[485] The policy should also protect the company from any of the aforementioned violations not only within the United States but also worldwide.[486]

[C] Internet Insurance Companies

To date, the insurance industry has not devised boilerplate or standard Internet-related policies; therefore, companies need to do some due diligence before purchasing such a policy. The first Internet-specific insurance policy is

---

[477] CNNFN, WISP Insurance Protects Firms from E-Commerce Problems, May 3, 1999 (visited May 15, 2000), http://www.cnnfn.com/digitaljam/newsbytes/130035.html.

[478] *See* Internet Insurance (visited May 15, 2000), http://www.internetinsure.com.

[479] Melvin Simensky and Eric C. Osterberg, The Insurance and Management of Intellectual Property Risks, 17 Cardozo Arts & Ent L.J. 321 (1999). E&O policies should be broad enough to cover Internet transactions; for example, the matter covered should be expanded to include numerical, audio, visual, and any other form of expression. *Id.*

[480] A company may be exposed to defamation lawsuits for the actions of their employees in e-mails, listservs, electronic bulletin boards, and other Internet-related channels of communication.

[481] Virus protection should not only protect the company, but should also ward off third-party claims of damage to hardware or software resulting from a virus received via e-mail or off the corporate web site. A company should disclaim all warranties and limit liability for viruses. Visitors should also receive notice that the company gives no warranty regarding viruses, and they should be advised to use up-to-date antivirus software to prevent damage due to viruses.

[482] Unauthorized access should protect against failure of computer security systems, web site vandalism and theft, destruction of electronic data, and other related occurrences.

[483] Intellectual property issues include disputes over domain names, copyrights, trademarks, trade dress, framing, linking, and the like.

[484] Companies need to protect themselves and third parties from financial losses that may result from any online violations.

[485] Chad E. Milton, Insurance for Internet Content and Services, 520 PLI/Pat 437, 440 (1998).

[486] Simensky and Osterberg, *supra* note 479.

InsureTrust, a policy offered by Reliance Insurance Company of Illinois.[487] The InsureTrust policy offers "claims-made and reported coverage for third-party losses with liability limits of up to $10 million."[488]

The online company should tailor its insurance policies according to its risks. A company that transmits sensitive financial or medical data on the Internet needs a different policy than does a computer company that sells routers worldwide. The consequences of a security breach for a securities firm are different from those of a hospital. A company offering Internet payment services to online stores will need insurance protecting against the theft of credit card numbers. When shopping for Internet insurance, businesses should first evaluate their needs, based on the type of business in which they are engaged.[489] Companies that are primarily content providers should have protection against intellectual property risks, including licensing issues and defamation.[490] Service providers should guard against defamation, invasion of privacy, intellectual property, and failure of the software or online service.[491] Those companies that use the Internet for advertising or e-commerce need to be wary about errors and omissions, intellectual property concerns, and computer security breaches.[492]

When considering insurance, first determine your potential risks and the type of assets you have and then determine the type of insurance you need.[493] Currently, several insurance companies offer specialized insurance policies specifically addressing liability arising from Internet and computer usage; these include American International Group, Chubb Technology Insurance Group, East West Insurance, INSUREtrust.com, Internet Insure, and Techinsurance.com.

[1] American International Group

American International Group launched an insurance policy covering liability for loss of money or electronic funds for insured Internet transactions.[494] The policy, called InsureSite^SM, also provides coverage for personal injury claims, computer equipment, and business interruption caused by vandalism, viruses, and other perils.[495]

---

[487] Robert D. Chesler and Robyn Ann Valle, Internet Insurance: Old and New Policies Protect E-Commerce, Corp. Couns. (Nov. 1999).

[488] *Id.*

[489] Milton, *supra* note 485.

[490] *Id.*

[491] *Id.*

[492] *Id.* at 441.

[493] *Id.*

[494] American International Group (visited Sept. 16, 1999), http://www.aig.com/corpsite/pr2/pro4_17_97.html).

[495] *Id.*

[2] Chubb Technology Insurance Group

Chubb Insurance established the Technology Insurance Group (TIG).[496] TIG takes a global view of insurance needs, tailoring its policies to the electronic industry.[497] TIG offers several policies addressing the insurance needs of technology companies, including Multimedia Liability Insurance.[498] This policy features insurance for copyrighted and trademarked materials; coverage for plagiarism and unauthorized use of titles, slogans, and so on; expanded advertising and personal injury coverage; global coverage; and flexibility.[499] In addition, Chubb offers coverage for errors and omissions, electronic data processing, and machinery breakdowns—all specifically targeted at high technology companies.[500]

[3] East West Insurance

East West Insurance Agency,[501] an agent for Lumley General Insurance, suggests that liability caused by computer or ISP failure may not be covered under umbrella-type business insurance policies.[502] East West, representing itself as an international insurer, outlines policies protecting against losses resulting from computer network breaches or ISP failures.[503] These policies protect companies from lost revenues resulting from computer network or ISP damage that causes a total business interruption and loss of data.[504] Limitations may apply on the costs associated with the reinstatement of the lost data and the consequential losses or liabilities.[505]

[4] INSUREtrust.com

INSUREtrust.com[506] strives to "instill enterprise-wide accountability, responsibility and financial recourse in networked environments."[507] INSUREtrust.com

---

[496] Chubb Technology Insurance Group (visited Sept. 16, 1999) http://www.chubb.com/business/tig/.

[497] *Id.*

[498] *Id.*

[499] *Id.*

[500] *Id.*

[501] East West Insurance Agency Pty Ltd (visited Sept. 16, 1999), http://www.healey.com.au/ewinsurance/.

[502] *Id.*

[503] *Id.*

[504] *Id.*

[505] *Id.*

[506] INSUREtrust.com (visited May 15, 2000), http://www.INSUREtrust.com.

[507] *Id.*

focuses its business not only on providing insurance coverage but also on providing integrated insurance and risk management solutions for e-commerce.[508] INSUREtrust.com offers a variety of insurance policies, including Internet/network computer liability coverage, covering claims from intrusion into a trusted network; digital asset protection, which covers network computer theft, computer viruses, corruption, and business disruption due to network inaccessibility; and network extortion and ransom, which protects against wrongful system takeovers, alteration of passwords, and loss of system control.[509] Additionally, INSUREtrust.com offers public key infrastructure policies for digital certification.[510]

[5] Techinsurance.com

Techinsurance.com offers technology specific insurance plans,[511] including errors and omissions insurance as well as professional and general liability insurance for computer professionals.[512] Some of the key features of these policies include optional coverage for copyright and intellectual property infringement and worldwide coverage.[513] The professional liability policy protects against errors and omissions, intellectual property claims, libel and slander claims, invasion of privacy, and misappropriation.[514] The general liability insurance program allows computer professionals to supplement their policies with electronic equipment and media protection, which protects computer hardware, software, and data, including business interruption expenses.[515]

[D] Commercial General Liability Coverage

Commercial general liability (CGL) policies may cover intellectual property, defamation, or data corruption claims to the extent that they are covered in the advertising or property damage provisions.[516] Courts have construed such language in CGL insurance to provide at least defensive coverage for intellectual property claims arising from the Internet.[517] In Minnesota, the court of appeals has held twice that CGL carriers "were obligated to defend suits involving loss or erasure of data."[518]

---

[508] *Id.*

[509] *Id.*

[510] *Id.*

[511] Techinsurance.com (visited May 15, 2000), http://www.techinsurance.com.

[512] *Id.*

[513] *Id.*

[514] *Id.*

[515] *Id.*

[516] *Id.*

[517] *Id.* at 442.

[518] *Id.* at 443.

Within CGL insurance policies, certain provisions allow for recovery for transactions on the Internet. One such provision is for advertising injury.[519] This type of provision provides coverage for intellectual property claims and is included in most CGL policies.[520] Advertising injury provisions often cover patent infringement and trademark infringement arising in the course of advertising and should be applicable to Internet advertising.[521] It is unclear, however, if online transactions, such as e-mail or chat room conversations, would be covered under advertising provisions.[522] Also at issue are web sites that promote a service or product even though they are set up as question and answer boards that provide information rather than make solicitations.[523]

A personal injury coverage provision may also be afforded under the CGL.[524] Personal injury coverage is relatively uncontroversial; it includes coverage for slander, libel, and invasion of privacy.[525] A conflict may occur, however, if a policy excludes advertising, publishing, or broadcasting.[526] Personal injury provisions will likely cover noncommercial online transactions, such as e-mail, while commercial web sites would be covered under an advertising provision.[527]

[E] Internet Insurance Audit

INTERNET INSURANCE CHECKLIST

1. Does your commercial general liability (CGL) policy cover computer or ISP failure, including loss of valuable data? A CGL policy generally insures against claims for damages from bodily injury, property damage, personal injury, and advertising injury.[528] Whether electronic data constitutes "tangible" property under standard-form CGL insurance policies is a vital point.[529] Many standard-form CGL policies use the term property damage in a narrow sense, meaning only physical injury to tangible property.[530] Thus, you must either prepare for disputes with your insurance company or consider adding statements to the CGL policy to

---

[519] Bruce Telles, Insurance Coverage for Online Torts, 584 PLI/Lit 239, 258 (1999).

[520] *Id.*

[521] *Id.* at 261-265.

[522] *Id.* at 266.

[523] *Id.* at 267.

[524] *Id.* at 273.

[525] *Id.*

[526] *Id.* at 274.

[527] *Id.*

[528] David B. Goodwin and Steven O. Weise, Risk Management in Cyberspace, The Risk Report, Nov. 1998, at 8. See the Heller Ehrman White and McAuliffe web site (visited May 15, 2000), http://www.hewm.com/search/art.shtml?id=295&parea=BA.

[529] Lorelie S. Masters, Professionals Online: Advice for Travels on the Information Superhighway, 16 Computer Lawyer 1 (Mar. 1999).

[530] *Id.*

clarify that property damage coverage includes loss from or of computer software, hardware, or services.[531] Courts have upheld coverage for loss or damage to computer data or databases.[532] Consider adding statements to protect against interruption if your server goes down or from viruses or other particular software losses.

2. Does your CGL policy's "advertising injury" clause adequately cover intellectual property claims? This clause is the one most likely to cover intellectual property claims; to obtain coverage under it, one must demonstrate a causal connection between the injury and the policyholder's advertising activities.[533] Copyright and trademark infringement can fall under the "advertising injury" clause, but you will only receive coverage if you demonstrate that causal connection. The damage from infringing on a trademark most often occurs in the context of advertising, so the causal connection may be easy to demonstrate.[534]

3. Does your CGL policy's personal injury or advertising injury clause adequately protect against defamation claims? Whether web sites constitute "advertising" or "publishing" could affect insurance coverage for defamation claims. Whether Internet-related activities constitute "advertising" is an issue yet to be fully developed, although courts have rejected narrowing the definition of "advertising."[535] You may wish to purchase media or Internet liability policies to ensure that you have coverage for these risks.[536] A 1998 change to the standard-form CGL policies requires that, to be covered, an "offense must occur in the advertisement itself, rather than (as in previous forms) in the insured's advertising activities."[537] Thus, it is important to review a policy's endorsements to ascertain whether the insurer has excluded coverage for a potential claim.[538] Insurance coverage for emerging technologies is tricky business. Yahoo! purchased a CGL policy and, in a fairly straightforward case of trademark infringement, had to settle the claim and then sue its insurer for coverage.[539]

4. Is your errors and omissions coverage sufficient? This is particularly important if your business sells products created by your business. There may be liability for failure of software or a computer system to meet a customer's expectations, and traditional errors and omissions ought to apply.[540]

---

[531] *Id.*

[532] *Id.*

[533] Goodwin and Weise, *supra* note 528.

[534] *Id.*

[535] Masters, *supra* note 529.

[536] *Id.*

[537] *Id.*

[538] *Id.*

[539] *See* Yahoo! Seeks $2 Million in Suit Against Its Insurer, Computer & Online Industry Litigation Reporter, 5 Aug. 1997, at 24448, discussing Yahoo! Inc. v. Federal Insurance Co. No. CV767426 (Cal. Super. Ct. Santa Clara Cty, complaint filed July 9, 1997), which settled out of court.

[540] Masters, *supra* note 529.

5. Are the special insurance policies available for web sites? As discussed above, many special insurance policies cover Internet activities. Such policies include media and Internet liability insurance; crime and fidelity insurance; and tort liability insurance. Media and Internet liability insurance usually covers only broadcasting, publishing, and advertising against defamation liability, but it may include defamation or torts to businesses that have web sites. Crime and fidelity insurance covers employee and third-party theft claims. Most policies do not cover Internet problems, but some are beginning to cover these claims, such as tort liability for harm from products sold online. Bottom line: To minimize risks, e-commerce will require more than CGL insurance. Seek out insurers who will work with you to cover your business risks properly.

§ 8.04 ONLINE DISPUTE RESOLUTION

[A] Introduction

Civil litigation is not an ideal option for Internet-related conflicts. Some online disputes can lead to years of paralysis as companies become mired in the overburdened, technologically challenged legal system.[541] Plaintiffs could drown in legal fees before they have their day in court.[542] Those with the fortitude and resources to make it to trial may be subjected to an unfair ruling by a judge who does not comprehend the technology. Consumers may be reluctant to shop online because an affordable method of recourse against Internet vendors is lacking. International parties may face a choice-of-law nightmare, with courts reluctant to assert jurisdiction.

While insurance policies may be one way to protect Internet transactions, alternative dispute resolution may be ideal for the unique dynamics of conflicts in cyberspace by offering the parties a rapid, cost-effective, predictable, and reasonable solution. Ombuds,[543] the Virtual Magistrate,[544] and the Maryland School of Law mediation site[545] offer online dispute resolution.

---

[541] *See, e.g.,* Interstellar Starship Services, Ltd. v. Epix, Inc., 983 F. Supp. 1331, 1336 (D. Or. 1997) (ruling on a two year domain name dispute).

[542] *See* Mary Allen, Mediators Help Lighten Courts' Load, Capital, Apr. 13, 1998, at A1 (cautioning that parties to litigation will spend thousands of dollars in legal fees).

[543] Ombuds is a dispute resolution site run by Professor Ethan Katsh. Professor Katsh is the co-director of the Center for Information Technology and Dispute Resolution at the University of Massachusetts. *See* http://www.umass.edu/dispute and http://aaron.sbs.umass.edu/center/default.htm (visited May 15, 2000).

[544] The Virtual Magistrate debuted in 1996 to mediate domain name disputes and ISP subscriber problems.

[545] Maryland School of Law Mediation Site (visited May 15, 2000), http://www.mediate-net.org/frequent1.htm.

[B]   The Case for Online Dispute Resolution

[1]   Time Is Money

Online activities are measured in Internet years.[546] A typical calendar year can represent seven Internet years.[547] While Internet time flies by, a company whose name is exploited online may lose thousands of potential customers and countless revenue opportunities to a trademark pirate.[548] The Internet product life-cycle is rapidly diminishing compared with traditional outlets.[549] Consequently, competitive threats, coupled with the distraction and costs of a lawsuit, can quickly relegate a company to the boneyard of online failures. A legal system that has evolved over 200 years lags behind the demands of a technology limited only by the speed of the fastest modem.[550]

In some jurisdictions, the average civil litigation conflict may last for three years.[551] After the trial, one or both parties might appeal seeking a retrial, further extending the length of the conflict. One district court has become popular because it only takes seven months from the time of the complaint to get to trial.[552] Such a time consuming system is completely contrary to the rapidly evolving world of e-commerce.[553] The court system lacks a mechanism for quickly obtaining redress. In some cases, filing a a request for a preliminary injunction with its expedited hearing might suspend the status quo until a full trial on the merits can be held.[554] A preliminary injunction may be ordered when there is irreparable harm and a

---

[546] Internet years may be no longer than 47 days. Lisa Greim Everitt, Tech Worker Shortage Tackled, Denver Rocky Mountain News, Sept. 13, 1999, at 1B.

[547] Thomas Vartanian, If You Build It, They Will Come, Am. Banker, Sept. 10, 1999, at 8.

[548] See Mark Williamson, Business Warned of More to Come From Cyber Squatters, Scotland on Sunday, Sept. 19, 1999, at 4 (examining the cost of recovering a pirated domain name).

[549] See Christine Lepera and Jeannie Costello, The Use of Mediation in the New Millennium, N.Y.L.J., May 6, 1999, at 3 (listing advantages of mediation for intellectual property disputes).

[550] As early as 1994, Internet legal analysts recognized the unique dynamics of computer network disputes and the inappropriateness of traditional legal systems for coping with those dynamics. See David R. Johnson, Dispute Resolution in Cyberspace (visited May 15, 2000), http://www.eff.org/pub/Legal/Arbitration/online_dispute_resolution_johnson.article (proposing a "law of cyberspace" to contend with online disputes).

[551] Jon Schmitz, Where Have All the Judges Gone? Pittsburgh Post-Gazette, Feb. 15, 1998, at A1. This exceeds the American Bar Association's recommendation that 90 percent of civil cases be resolved within one year. Id.

[552] See Scott A. Zebrak, A Step-by-Step Guide to Handling Domain Name Disputes, Computer Lawyer, Apr. 1999, at 21 (suggesting legal strategies for domain name and trademark conflicts).

[553] According to one online dispute resolution service, the average time required by the court system to resolve a civil claim is 30 months. See Phil Borchmann, Web Sites Help End Bad Posturing by Lawyers, Insurance Companies, Chicago Trib., July 19, 1999, at 2 (describing benefits of new online alternative dispute resolution services).

[554] F.R.C.P. § 65(a) (1995).

probability of legal success on the merits of the case. A court will also consider whether sufficient question exists regarding the merits of the case and whether delay will cause additional hardships to the moving party.[555] Meeting the court's requirements to show hardship to obtain a preliminary injunction may still require more time than a plaintiff can afford. A district court judge, for example, denied Playboy's motion for a preliminary injunction in an online trademark case because Playboy could not show sufficient harm.[556] Playboy had already waited two months from the time of filing the complaint until the case came before the court.[557] While the parties were waging their legal battle, thousands of customers may have been diverted to third-party web sites that took advantage of Playboy's name.

Additionally, the fast-moving nature of online communication can create unique conflicts.[558] Internet cases are still novel to many judges and attorneys. Several plaintiffs, for example, have sued the wrong party in domain name disputes.[559] Since no codified rules cover for online activities, parties to an Internet-related lawsuit might be surprised by the results.[560] Unlike arbitration or mediation, litigation can be uncertain in time and cost.[561]

Internet disputes must be settled quickly. Online dispute resolution promises to radically reduce the time required to settle disputes. Commercial dispute resolution sites like clickNsettle.com[562] and Cyber$ettle.com[563] claim that they can settle disputes within hours rather than the traditional 12 to 30 months.[564] Other online dispute resolution benefits include the convenience of each party being able to choose the time for meeting and eliminating the expense and inconvenience of travel.[565] Arbitration and the use of private judges may be more appropriate for resolving high stakes online disputes. Web site development and hosting agreements should have arbitration clauses or agreements for resolving disputes in hearings before private judges.

---

[555] Coca-Cola v. Tropicana Products, Inc., 690 F.2d 312, 315-316 (2d Cir. 1982).

[556] Playboy Enterprises v. Netscape Communications, No SA CV 99-320 AHs, 1999 U.S. Dist. LEXIS 9638 at *13-14 (C.D. Cal. S.D. June 24, 1999).

[557] *Id.* at *1-2.

[558] Robert C. Bordone, Electronic Online Dispute Resolution: A Systems Approach—Potential Problems, and a Proposal, 3 Harv. Negot. L. Rev. 175, 180 (Spring, 1998).

[559] Courts have consistently held that the domain name registrar, NSI, was not liable for third-party registration or domain names that infringed trademarks. *See* Zebrak, *supra* note 552.

[560] Henry H. Perritt, Jr. Electronic Dispute Resolution (visited Sept. 16, 1999), http://www.law.vill.edu/ncair/disres/PERRITT.HTM.

[561] E. Casey Lide, ADR and Cyberspace: The Role of Alternative Dispute Resolution in Online Commerce, Intellectual Property, and Defamation, 12 Ohio St. J. on Disp. Resol. 193, 199 (1996).

[562] *See* http://www.clicknsettle.com (visited May 15, 2000).

[563] *See* http://www.cybersettle.com (visited May 15, 2000).

[564] *See* http://www.thestandard.net/articles/display/0,1449,4609,00.html?home.tf (visited May 15, 2000).

[565] William J. Snyder, Online Settlement: The Future is Now, Metropolitan Corporate Counsel, Aug. 1999, at 26.

Mediation is also a viable option to reduce the cost of litigation, and is likely to become an even more popular option over the next few years. Currently, traditional mediation fees in some areas can total $1,200, whereas online mediators charge approximately $500.[566] Costs are a major factor in driving consumers and businesses toward commercial online dispute resolution web sites. Commercial sites[567] like Cyber$ettle.com and Clicknsettle.com offer their customers low fee structures. Cyber$ettle.com requires insurance companies to pay a $25 registration fee and a $75 engagement fee, and each side pays a $200 settlement fee, regardless of the settlement amount.[568] Clicknsettle.com requires that a claimant pay a $25 registration fee (a $100 registration fee for a high priority case) a $50 engagement fee, and a settlement fee of $100 for cases that settle for less than $10,000 or of $200 for cases that settle for more than $10,000.[569]

Without the opportunity to engage in low-cost online dispute resolution, many companies might be forced to accept a position or to give up rights. Total-News Corp., for example, settled a framing, linking, and trademark dispute with several well-funded plaintiffs because it could not afford a lengthy appeal.[570] Other defendants may quickly give up a rightfully owned domain name rather than face the expense of defending themselves in court. In short, as online alternative dispute resolution sites become more popular, they will prove to be a cost-effective, efficient alternative to the courts.[571]

Relationships are key in the Internet business. Internet commerce has spawned a new type of business environment wherein competitors work together on some projects and compete on others. The adversarial nature of litigation is inappropriate in this business dynamic. Arbitration and mediation can provide a nonadversarial approach and preserve critical business relationships.[572]

[2]   Solutions for Consumers

Online pyramid salesmen and other electronic con artists quickly recognized the Internet as a medium for consumer fraud. Unfortunately, cybermedi-

---

[566] Robert L. Sharpe, Jr., Internet Negations Eliminate Egos and Accusations, Legal Intelligencer, Aug. 31, 1999, at 1.

[567] Another commercial site is settleonline.com.

[568] *See* http://www.insurance.com/gen/cybersettle699.html (visited Sept. 16, 1999).

[569] Mathew Goldstein, Mediator Morphs Into Web Service, and Finally Gets Wall Street's Notice: New Feature Enables Online Settlement, Crain's New York Business, Aug. 9, 1999, at 12.

[570] 97 Civ. 1190 (PKL) (S.D.N.Y., Feb. 20, 1997).

[571] Department of Energy ADR Policy (visited Sept. 16, 1999), http//www.gc.doe.gov/adr/adr-policy.html.

[572] *See* Raymond L. Ocampo Jr., Mediation: The Preferred Route to Resolving High-Tech Disputes, ABA Bulletin of Law/Science & Technology, July, 1999, at 5 (observing software developers competing with operating system licensors).

ation did not provide viable remedies for fraud.[573] Fraud is an impediment to the growth of consumer e-commerce.[574] Online shoppers who fall victim to an unscrupulous cybermerchant may have a difficult time finding help. The United States government has encouraged business to create an internal dispute resolution mechanism to address consumer complaints about online transactions.[575] This would add an additional level of consumer confidence in online transactions.

The Better Business Bureau (BBB) views itself as a provider of consumer information and as a referee. This organization has traditionally been a great resource for consumer tips. With the increased popularity of the Internet, however, the BBB has expanded its service offerings. The BBB provides web site certification to give consumers a degree of comfort when shopping on a certified commercial web site.[576] Businesses certified by the BBB are required to commit to the BBB's dispute resolution process.[577] Consumers and businesses can turn to BBB to resolve traditional and online disputes,[578] or the BBB may be used to assist in resolving conflicts over online privacy policy violations.[579]

[a] Online Product Sales/Auctions

The Internet has triggered an explosion in auction opportunities for a myriad of products, ranging from toys to antiques to vacations. Unfortunately, parties are not always happy with the results of their online transactions. A buyer may receive damaged merchandise, for example, or the parties may disagree about the quality of the goods.[580]

---

[573] The often touted Virtual Magistrate project handled only one case during a three-year experiment. Wendy R. Leibowitz, Let's Settle This, Online, Nat'l L.J., July 5, 1999, at 20. The service may gain more popularity as online arbitration goes mainstream. Information about Villanova's Virtual Magistrate project is available at http://vmag.vcilp.org (visited May 15, 2000).

[574] See, e.g., Matt Roush, Web-Certified: CPAs, Better Business Bureau Approve Sites for Consumers, Crain's Detroit Business, July 19, 1999, at 33 (citing consumer hesitation to provide credit card numbers and personal information online).

[575] OECD Looks to Consumer Internet Regulations, Communications Daily, Sept. 9, 1999, available in LEXIS, News Library, Curnws File.

[576] Supra note 574.

[577] Id.

[578] Bill Lubinger, Better Business Bureau is a Referee, Not Regulator, Plain Dealer, Aug. 23, 1999, at 4C.

[579] BBBOnline Privacy Program (visited Sept. 16, 1999), http://www.bbbonline.org/businesses/privacy/index.html.

[580] See, e.g., Dispute Resolution Resource (visited Sept. 16, 1999), http://www.up4sale.com/dispute.htm (recommending dispute resolution resources for parties using the up4sale.com auction service).

Some auction sites offer mediation services to increase customer comfort.[581] Several online auctions have tested online dispute resolution through the Online Ombuds Office, a service of the University of Massachusetts.[582] The Online Ombuds Office was able to resolve more than 50 percent of the disputes that it mediated stemming from transactions at the eBay and Up4sale auction sites.[583] This matches the success rate for online resolution of non-Internet-related disputes.[584] Cases involving fraud or abuse of the auction system are not suited to alternative dispute resolution.[585]

Online mediation for auction sites adds an additional guarantee of quality service by providing a convenient method for resolving disputes.[586] Other commercial sites selling third-party goods should consider adding an online mediation service. Some web sites include a mandatory mediation clause for any Internet contract to guarantee efficient dispute resolution.[587]

[3]   International Disputes

Potential conflict of law issues abound in Internet disputes, making alternative dispute resolution ideal for some parties.[588] The International Chamber of Commerce, which handles cases from more than 100 different countries, is developing an online arbitration service.[589]

§ 8.05   PREVENTIVE LAW POINTERS

> ### [A]   Suggestions for Handling Copyright and Trademark Infringement

While this book is not intended as a substitute for legal advice, the suggestions in this section may help parties resolve some disputes quickly. Sending -

---

[581] *See* Stephen Labaton, Can Defendants Cry 'E-Sanctuary' and Escape the Courts? NY Times, Sept. 22, 1999, at G39 (explaining challenges of selling goods online).

[582] Online Ombuds Office (visited Sept. 16, 1999), http://aaron.sbs.umass.edu/center/ombuds/default.htm.

[583] Wendy R. Leibowitz, Cybermediation: ADR in the Electronic Age, N.J.L.J. July 5, 1999, at 26.

[584] Cyber$ettle claims a 50 percent success rate in 3,000 cases. Phil Borchmann, Web Sites Help End Bad Posturing by Lawyers, Insurance Companies, Chicago Trib., July 19, 1999, at 2.

[585] Dispute Resolution Resource (visited Sept. 16, 1999), http://www.up4sale.com/dispute.htm.

[586] Leibowitz, *supra* note 573.

[587] *See* Mediation in a Nutshell (visited Sept. 16, 1999), http://www.internetneutral.com/nutshell.htm (explaining online mediation process).

[588] *See* Alejandro E. Almaguer and Roland W. Baggott III, Shaping New Legal Frontiers: Dispute Resolution for the Internet, 13 Ohio St. J. on Disp. Resol. 711 (1998) (listing challenges of resolving online conflicts in traditional legal fora).

[589] International Trade Court Plans Internet Arbitration, Lawyer, Aug. 2, 1999, at 7.

letters incorporating these guidelines may correct the innocent infringer who has "borrowed" some element of your site. If you are infringed by a competitor or experience some economic damage from the other party, seek legal counsel before taking any action.

Taking a nonadversarial stance in letting the other party know of their innocent mistake may lead that party to move quickly to correct the infringement. Before sending the notice of infringement, however, take time to check that you have the rights to the material and that the other web site is using the material without your permission. If you have any doubt, seek the assistance of counsel before sending a request to remove the material. A letter would be appropriate, for example, if a web site made copies of original images appearing on your site. On the other hand, seek counsel if you want to pursue a site using pictures similar but not identical to yours. In the worst-case scenario, your infringement letter could backfire, if your web designer actually borrowed the material from the other site.

Several web sites have posted examples of their infringement notices online. The University of Virginia takes a gentle approach, letting recipients know that they may have violated the Copyright Act and providing information about copyrights.[590] Viacorp's notice of infringement, on the other hand, directly asserts that material on the infringing site was taken from Viacorp's web site without permission.[591]

[1]   Notice of Copyright Infringement

Any notice for copyright infringement should include the following elements:

1.   Specific information on what was taken (which image, text, sound, and so on).
2.   The full Internet address at which the infringement is taking place, including the paths, that is, *www.suffolkpcs.com/computers/info.htm.*
3.   The address of the site (from which the copyrighted material was taken).
4.   The action you want the infringer to take: remove the image, provide attribution, and so on. If you want payment, make sure to check with an attorney before sending the letter.
5.   How the infringer can contact you with questions.
6.   If necessary to clarify the infringing element, a print copy of the web page with the item(s) in question circled.

---

[590] Copyright Policy and Law: Copyright Notice (visited Sept. 21, 1999), http://gopher.lib. virginia.edu/copyright/notice.html.

[591] Infringement Notice From Viacorp (visited Aug. 28, 1999), http://www.viacorp.com/ infringe.html.

[2] Innocent Infringement of Trademarks Accidentally Misused

This section covers trademarks accidentally misused within a web site, not in infringing domain names. Domain name and trademark issues are addressed elsewhere in § 8.02[B][3] and in § 4.03[K]. Refer to legal counsel any infringement by anyone exploiting your trademark for profit. Finally, if you want the trademarked name removed, make sure that the web site infringes your exclusive right to the name.[592]

The letter for trademark infringement should mention the following elements:

1. The identity of your trademark. Specify if it is locally or federally registered.
2. The full Internet address at which the infringement is taking place, including the paths: that is, *www.suffolkpcs.com/computers/info.htm.*
3. Your company's name.
4. The actions you want the infringer to take: remove the trademark, provide attribution, and so on. If you want payment, make sure to check with an attorney before sending the letter.
5. How the infringer can contact you with questions.
6. If necessary to clarify the infringing element, a print copy of the web page with the item(s) in question circled.

➤ [B] SPC'S Proper Use of Its Trademarks[593]

Trademark rights are acquired by the *proper* continuous use of the trademark. Two problems arise when a trademark is used improperly, both of which may result in loss of trademark protection. First, improper use is the same as a finding that a trademark has not been used in commerce. Bear in mind that to support a statement of use you must submit examples of the trademark that show the trademark being used properly. Second, improper use can lead to the trademark becoming generic. A trademark becomes generic when the trademark literally enters the language and becomes the common name for the product. The rationale for creating the category of generic marks is that no manufacturer should be given exclusive right to use words that generically identify a product.

Improper use of trademarks can be costly to a company, if not deadly to a product. Success of an online company, such as SPC, and especially of dot-com

---

[592] *See* Todd W. Krieger, Internet Domain Names and Trademarks: Strategies for Protecting Brand Names in Cyberspace, 32 Suffolk U. L. Rev. 1, 60 (1998) (addressing limits to trademark rights).

[593] Timothy Hadley, Technology Licensing Manager, Abbott Laboratories, Bedford, Massachusetts, is the author of this section.

companies, is mainly attributable to the company's name, its product names, or both. Losing trademark protection because of improper use may result in others using your trademark and profiting off the goodwill associated with your trademark.

The difference between proper and improper use of a trademark is grammatical. Trademarks are adjectives that describe a specific brand of product. Since trademarks are adjectives, they need to be used with a noun that they modify. SPC, in order to remain diligent in protecting its trademarks, should consider implementing guidelines on trademark usage. SPC's Millennium II, for example, is software. The adjective is "Millennium II," and the noun it modifies is "software." It is incorrect to say "when you enter data into the Millennium II, you will see the green light come on." This is incorrect, because in this statement Millennium II is used as a noun. When the term is not used as an adjective—when it does not describe a specific brand of product—it is not being used as a trademark. The correct way to make this statement would be "When you enter data into the Millennium II software, you will see the green light come on."

In addition, it is important to set trademarks apart from the nouns they modify. There are many ways to accomplish this. Capitalizing, italicizing, or boldfacing the trademark will suffice. Alternatively, stylizing the trademark not only sets the trademark apart, but adds strength and character to the trademark.[594] Finally, as previously discussed, adding the appropriate symbol (® or ™) will also set the trademark apart.

Other rules to keep in mind to use a trademark properly include never using the trademark in the possessive or plural form and never shortening, abbreviating, or creating acronyms out of the trademark. Again, using the possessive form or plural form of Millennium II (for example, "Millennium II's new features" or "Buy two Millennium IIs") turns the trademark into a noun. By abbreviating the trademark or creating acronyms you are not using your trademark, regardless of whether it is used as an adjective or not. Internally, for example, especially in R&D, SPC employees refer to Millennium II as "MII." Using it internally in that fashion does not create a problem for the trademark, but if the abbreviation was used in ad campaigns, those ads would not support a statement of use. The best course of action for SPC, given the likelihood that "MII" will become an alternative name for their product, is to seek trademark registration for the acronym. A prime example of the usefulness of registering acronyms and abbreviations is offered by America Online and its abbreviated counterpart, AOL.

---

[594] Stylizing means adding a design, whether a shape, color, or other elements, to the trademark. The application for registration of a trademark makes it possible to use codes to inform the USPTO of your design. Keep in mind that the sine qua non of trademark protection is distinctiveness. The strength of a trademark is determined by how distinctive it is. Accordingly, a mark that is fanciful, such as the unique word Xerox, or stylized, such as the cursive style of type used by Coca-Cola, is afforded the most protection. At the other end of the trademark spectrum, and receiving less protection, are arbitrary trademarks.

The rules for proper use of a trademark can be summarized as follows:

1. Always use trademarks as proper adjectives.
2. Always set trademarks apart from the nouns they modify.
3. Never use trademarks in the possessive or plural form.
4. Never abbreviate or create acronyms out of the trademarks.
5. Always use appropriate trademark symbols (® or ™).

The rules are not meant to be Draconian in their application. If they were, trademarks would lose some of their benefit, because the constant use of symbols and noun descriptors can be costly both financially (especially in software, where each bit is valued) and aesthetically. Accordingly, SPC operates under the following modified guidelines. For each page, noun descriptors are to be used at least 50 percent of the time. In addition, the noun descriptor must be used for the first reference on the page. Trademark symbols must be used at least once per page, either at the first reference or, preferably, where the trademark will be most noticeable.

Administratively, SPC implements its guidelines by having a paralegal review all web pages, advertising material, product packaging, disk labels, and manuals to ensure proper trademark usage. This procedure also facilitates the review of SPC's use of other companies' trademarks in its materials to ensure that they are being used properly and that these companies receive proper attribution. Finally, SPC's paralegal ensures that trademark notice (for example, "Millennium II is a registered trademark in the United States and/or other countries") is given.

It can be said that policing your own use of your trademarks is only half the battle. That is, to be sure that your trademark does not become generic it is also necessary to police the use of your trademarks by others. Third-party use of your trademarks in a noninfringing manner is known as referential use. In the software industry, referential use is critical. In order to sell any software, for example, you must inform the consumer of the disk operating system required to use your software. Combined with plug-ins, drivers, peripherals, and so on, your software package is likely to carry the trademarks of many different companies.

Granting permission for the referential use of your trademarks can be efficiently accomplished by having a dedicated web page that lists all of your trademarks, along with the rules for proper use mentioned above. Examples can be found on the following web sites:

> Sun Microsystems: www.sun.com/policies/trademarks/index.htm
> Corel: www.corel.com/legal/trademarks.htm
> Oracle: www.oracle.com/html/3party.html
> Apple: www.apple.com/legal/guidelinesfor3rdparties.htm
> Microsoft: www.microsoft.com/trademarks
> Netscape: www.netscape.com/legal_notices/trademarks.html

Adobe: www.adobe.com/misc/trademarks.html
IBM: www.ibm.com/legal/copytrade.phtml

➤   **[C]   Copyright Clearance Center**[595]

In 1995, Texaco, Inc., settled a ten-year-old copyright infringement lawsuit stemming from Texaco's practices of photocopying articles from scientific journals and distributing the articles to employees without paying royalties to the publishers.[596] To settle this high profile lawsuit, Texaco paid "slightly more than $1 million, plus a retroactive licensing fee to the Copyright Clearance Center."[597]

Texaco's practice of photocopying articles and distributing them to employees is a widespread practice but one not protected by the copyright law doctrine of fair use.[598] Startup online companies also should be aware of the hazards of distributing copyrighted materials without permission. Furthermore, with the ease and rapidity at which electronic media can be duplicated and shared, companies must protect themselves. If a company distributes software or other copyrighted materials beyond the scope of its license agreement, it can be subject to a copyright infringement lawsuit.

One way companies can protect themselves is by subscribing to the Copyright Clearance Center (CCC). The CCC was formed in 1978 to facilitate compliance with U.S. copyright laws by providing licenses for the reproduction and distribution of copyrighted material.[599] Presently, the CCC manages rights relating to more than 1,750,000 works and represents more than 9,600 publishers and hundreds of thousands of authors.

The CCC offers many forms of licenses, from those designed for academic organizations to others used by for-profit organizations. A license for a for-profit organization, known as an Annual Authorization Service, enables all employees in an organization to lawfully make unlimited photocopies for internal use of excerpts of copyrighted information contained in one of CCC's titles. The single annual fee is determined on the basis of annual photocopying projections by the company using a calculation method based on number of employees and the type of industry in which the company is engaged. By subscribing to CCC, companies do not need to contact individual rightsholders for permission, pay individual royalty fees, or track each photocopy transaction.

---

[595] Timothy Hadley, Technology Licensing Manager, Abbott Laboratories, Bedford, Massachusetts, is the author of this section.

[596] Association of Research Libraries Bimonthly Newsletter, ARL 180, May 1995.

[597] *Id.*

[598] American Geophysical Union v. Texaco, 37 F.3d 882 (2d Cir. 1994).

[599] *See* http://www.copyright.com (last visited Mar. 23, 2000).

CHAPTER NINE

E-MAIL AND INTERNET USAGE POLICIES

§ 9.01   OVERVIEW

This chapter provides a road map of the most common risks and hazards occurring in the online enabled workplace. E-mail and the Internet have profound implications for employment law, as reflected in the following hypothetical example:

> Suffolk Personal Computers (SPC) encourages its employees to develop through continuing education after work. One employee, Peter Atkins, wants to advance in his career and enrolls in an evening law school program. One of his required courses is constitutional law. Peter decides to do some of his homework after working hours on his work computer, after everyone else has gone home. His third assignment requires him to explore the issues surrounding hate speech. Pete decides that the Internet would be a great way to do his research, and he downloads several articles and prints out the contents of a number of controversial web sites. He forgets, however, to pick up his printouts before leaving.
>
> The next day, another employee notices some of the things that Peter had downloaded from the Internet and accidentally left on the printer. The printout she found included offensive racial slurs denigrating her ethnicity. She immediately brought the documents to Peter's boss. Shortly thereafter, his boss received a telephone call from the systems administrator regarding an e-mail with a controversial subject line heading that Peter had sent to his professor. Peter was terminated for abusing the Internet at work by downloading and e-mailing offensive materials.
>
> SPC had no Internet or e-mail use policy, and Peter has retained counsel to bring wrongful discharge and invasion of privacy claims against SPC.

Like many companies, our hypothetical e-business Suffolk Personal Computers considers its e-mail and intranet to be its digital nervous system, and it expects that these tools will be used predominately for business purposes.[1] SPC already uses its e-mail system to foster greater communication among and within departments by distributing corporate documents such as employee-benefit information, employee handbooks, sexual harassment policies, and expense forms.[2]

As the hypothetical illustrates, however, e-mail is fraught with potential pitfalls for unwary companies. On the one hand, the e-mail system can enhance the

---

[1] *See generally* Bill Gates, From Business @ the Speed of Thought: Using a Digital Nervous System (1998) (explaining that a company's digital nervous system begins with the rule that communications flow through e-mail).

[2] Lori Jorgensen, Connection to Risk? Managing the Exposures of Cyberspace, 45 Risk Mgmt. 14 (Feb. 1, 1998) (noting that Microsoft employees use the company's intranet to access a variety of company databases).

risk that an employee will harass or discriminate against co-workers or defame third parties.[3] A minor lapse, such as leaving employees off a distribution list for employment-related information, can provide evidence to support a discrimination claim. On the other hand, a vigilant company that monitors e-mail use to reduce hazards may lay itself open to invasion of privacy claims.[4]

Companies must achieve a balance between protecting business needs and minimizing exposure to potential liability. Monitoring e-mail usage is particularly justified where an employer has reasonable grounds to believe that employees are engaging in illegal conduct or other misconduct that might subject the company to liability.

Similar liability issues exist with the use of the Internet or intranets. Companies that deploy laptop computers to their employees may unwittingly heighten the potential for abuse. Although employees may not violate any policies while at work, after hours they may be more likely to do so. In the privacy and comfort of their homes, they may be tempted to use their company laptops to surf the Internet or e-mail off-color jokes to friends and family or download hardcore pornography.

Section 9.02 begins with an overview of the legal troubles associated with the misuse and abuse of e-mail and the Internet. Section 9.03 focuses on minimizing e-mail and Internet-related hazards. Section 9.04 presents practical tips for instituting effective e-mail and Internet usage policies. Section 9.05 presents important considerations and elements to incororate in policies. Section 9.06 contains checklists covering the full range of issues involved in developing and implementing a policy, and Section 9.07 offers a sample policy.

§ 9.02 RISKS FROM E-MAIL AND INTERNET USAGE

[A] Scope of the Risk

E-mail is becoming the preferred method of business communication. In 1999, almost one in ten of all company documents were transmitted by e-mail. By

---

[3] *See, e.g.*, Lian v. Sedgwick James, Inc., 992 F. Supp. 644, 648 (S.D. N.Y. 1998) (describing defamation action where a supervisor sent an allegedly defamatory e-mail about former employee). As Chapter Five explains, SPC may be liable for wrongdoing committed by its employees within the scope of their duties.

[4] Electronic monitoring involves the collection of information about an employee's use of a company's computer, e-mail, or the Internet. *See, e.g.*, McLaren v. Microsoft Corp., 1999 Tex App. LEXIS 4103 (Ct. of App. Tex. May 28, 1999) (holding that employee's expectation of privacy was outweighed by employer's interest in preventing the inappropriate use of its e-mail system; Bourke v. Nissan Motor Corp., No. B-687-5 (Cal. Ct. of App. July 26, 1993) (holding that employer's review of e-mail did not invade his right of privacy under the California Constitution or common law); United States v. Simons, 206 F.3d 392 (4th Cir. 2000) (holding that FBI's e-mail policy vitiated employer's expectation of privacy).

2002, it is anticipated that the number of documents transmitted via e-mail will increase to 14.6 billion.[5] E-mail makes "it so easy to access, transmit and even alter the most sensitive corporate documents that companies have to worry about their own employees' sharing of confidential information with competitors and unauthorized persons."[6]

Companies need a written e-mail usage policy to avoid or minimize liability caused by employees or independent contractors who have access to the corporate e-mail network, personal digital assistants (PDAs), and pagers.[7] The convenience of these devices must be balanced against the risks of their misuse and abuse. Technical and managerial employees are increasingly using e-mail pagers or PDAs to communicate with vendors, customers, potential customers, and information providers. These communication devices can transmit and receive messages around the globe.

Any e-mail policy must take into account the company's industry and corporate culture and should be tailored to known risks. Although an e-mail policy cannot immunize a business from liability caused by misuse of the company's computer system, the expense of developing a good e-mail policy may be far less than retrofits, lawsuits, and damage to corporate reputations.

It is reasonably foreseeable that SPC's employees will use the company's e-mail system to commit crimes or torts or to infringe intellectual property rights. SPC may be directly liable for negligently hiring or retaining an employee who has engaged in "prior similar" acts. One employee may send sexually charged messages to another, exposing the company to a lawsuit alleging a hostile work environment. An employee may abuse Internet privileges by downloading unlicensed software from the Internet, subjecting the company to either a vicarious or contributory copyright infringement claim or a visit from the Software Publishers Association.[8] Employees may hack into a business competitor's e-mail system, triggering charges of criminal liability.[9] In addition, SPC may be directly liable for regulatory offenses from stock manipulation or false statements made on web sites. Table 9.1 presents an overview of SPC's e-mail and Internet liabilities.

---

[5] Gerard Panaro, Elements of a Successful E-Mail Policy, Part I (visited Mar. 26, 2000), http://www.bankinfo.com/hr/e-mailpol.html.

[6] *Id.*

[7] *See generally* SkyTel5 (visited July 27, 1999), http://www.skytel.com (describing pager device that permits the user to receive and answer e-mail).

[8] The Software Publisher's Association (SPA) uses ex-employees and other informers to root out companies that use unlicensed software. The SPA has a private software police force that seeks to stigmatize the wayward corporation by widely publicizing copyright infringement.

[9] Labwerks, Inc. v. Sladekutter, Ltd., No. 99-160 (W.D. Pa. Feb. 17, 1999), *reported in* Hacking into Competitor's E-mail Violates Wiretap Law, Judge Finds, 16 Comp. & Online Indus. Litig. Rptr. 1 (Mar. 16, 1999); United States v. Simons, 206 F.3d 392 (4th Cir. 2000) (upholding conviction of FBI employee for storing child pornography on company computers ruling that employee had no reasonable expectation of privacy given FBI Internet usage policy.

TABLE 9.1
Examples of E-Mail and Internet-Related Risks

Types of Risk	Direct Liability	Imputed Liability
Intentional Torts: Fraud or misrepresentation; defamation; trade libel, business torts; trespass to chattels; conversion; and invasion of privacy; intentional infliction of emotional distress; spoliation of evidence for destroying e-mails without justification. Torts may also be claimed in a statutory sexual or racial harassment context as in 42 U.S.C. §§ 1981, 1985 or 1986.	Fraudulent misrepresentation of goods or services sold on web site; defamatory statements about individuals or competitors made by corporate officers; spam or junk e-mail sent to subscribers of online services; introduction of computer viruses; public disclosure of private facts about a plaintiff that are offensive to the reasonable person.	Master/servant; *respondeat superior* (liability for torts committed within scope of employment); joint venturer; partners; joint tortfeasors (harm from tortious acts done in concert with others); joint and several liability (suit against SPC separately or together with other defendants); vicarious liability for defamation (if SPC is deemed to be a publisher).
Negligence: An act or omission that falls below the standard of care established by law for the protection of others; computer malpractice; failure to prevent viruses and maintain information security; failure to protect confidential data of third parties due to a security breach; negligent publications.	Violating duties of care imposed by statute, industry standards, or other standards of care, e.g., a negligent misrepresentation of material fact published on SPC's web site.	Negligent acts committed by employees, servants, joint venturers, or partners may cause company to be liable jointly and severally for negligent concerted action.
Strict Liability: Internet sale of defective computer hardware that leads to personal injury or property damage; imputed liability for acts of employees misusing the Internet.	Corporate liability is imposed for defective products that are unreasonably dangerous. Most jurisdictions impose an "economic loss" rule that will not permit tort recoveries where the loss is purely economic.	Corporation is liable for anyone in the distribution chain that sells defective products. SPC may be able to sue its suppliers for strict product liability or to seek indemnification for defective computer components.
Securities Law: SPC is potentially liable for statements made on its web site, e-mail transmissions and other Internet-related communications;	May be imposed for uses and misuses of SPC's web site in conjunction with the Internet or intranet; liability for reaching investing public via web	Statements that employees, partners, or venturers make about SPC's stock. Company may be jointly and severally liable for underwriters' activities;

TABLE 9.1 (Continued)

Types of Risk	Direct Liability	Imputed Liability
SPC's web postings, Internet road shows, or statements made about stocks in chat rooms expose it to federal or state securities enforcement actions. False or misleading web site statements with intent to deceive under SEC Rule 10b-5; online scams; fraudulent sales of stocks; fraudulent sales of securities.	pages. Type of liability: shareholder class action or liability for predictions about stock made on web site; failure to follow SEC guidelines with respect to investor communications via e-mail or the Internet; false statements made in prospectuses; failure to comply with federal securities regulations; failure to post disclosures about stock prices.	failure of web site designer to update or correct information about company's stock offerings or underwriters' IPO; employees' offering to sell securities or stocks prior to registration; failure to screen sales literature of third parties. No vicarious liability for linking to other's security offerings.
E-Mail or Internet-Related Crimes by Employees: Downloading and transmitting obscene and pornographic material on the SPC web sites; hate speech; computer crimes; child pornography; and theft of trade secrets.	A company will not be prosecuted for criminal acts of its essential employees outside the scope of duty. Company must turn over e-mail records or other computer-resources to law enforcement. The company, at minimum, may suffer public relations problems from crimes committed on company computers; transaction costs in investigating pornography on company computers, for example.	SPC may be liable for an employee's accessing a competitor's computer without authorization or for corporate espionage. SPC will not normally be liable for its employee's knowing release of a virus computer code. SPC will not normally be liable for an employee's downloading of pornography on the company computer. SPC is not liable for online stalking or threats via e-mail unless wrongdoing is authorized or ratified by the company.
Privacy Law: Because SPC is a private company, it is not normally liable for constitutionally based privacy actions; SPC is liable under the Electronic Communications Privacy Act for intercepting e-mail without cause or justification; SPC is also liable for privacy-based torts and	Liability under the Electronic Communications Privacy Act (ECPA) for interception of e-mail or other electronic communications; employee's consent is a defense to an employer's monitoring or interception of stored messages; implied right to review messages in	SPC may be liable if one of its employees was authorized to monitor co-employees' e-mail usage; SPC should have a policy limiting employees' reasonable expectation of privacy. Higher risk of a privacy tort in states with a higher level of protection for privacy, such as

(continued)

731

TABLE 9.1 (Continued)

Types of Risk	Direct Liability	Imputed Liability
country-specific data protection, as well as for observing the European Union Data Protection Directive.	administering the computer system. Liability may also include privacy torts (intrusion upon seclusion, false light, or misappropriation or public disclosure of private facts) and state ECPA statutes; European Data Privacy Directive; and privacy statutes of other countries.	California; E-mail and Internet usage policy can limit or eliminate reasonable expectation of privacy.
Regulatory Offenses: Federal Trade Commission (FTC) Regulations of Advertising and Business Practices.	False advertisements on its web site; liabilities for unfair or deceptive trade practices.	SPC may be vicariously liable for the false advertisements of partners and co-venturers.
Infringement of Intellectual Property Rights: Copyright Infringement: Using the Internet to download pirated software, using e-mail to infringe the copyrights of others. **Trade Secrets:** Use of e-mail to steal or transmit trade secrets; criminal liability as well for trade secret theft (Economic Espionage Act of 1996). **Trademarks:** Using company's computer to download material protected by trademarks. **Patents:** Infringing Internet-related patents in web site technologies.	Direct infringement: Ownership of a valid copyright in the infringed work and copying by the defendant with access. Operators of SPC web site may be liable for incorporating copyrighted materials on the web site. Posting of copyrighted materials on company web site, bulletin board, or chat room; using another's trademark or a substantially similar trademark when advertising goods or services in a way "likely to cause confusion," blurring, or tarnishing of marks; using another's mark as a domain name; strict liability for direct infringement; dilution in trademarks; criminal penalties for copyright infringement.	Contributory infringement: (1) SPC had knowledge that others were posting infringing materials on its web site; or otherwise (2) materially contributed to copyright infringement; or (3) culpable conduct for secondary liability. Vicarious Infringement: Employer may be liable for infringement by employees or joint venturers where there is a right to supervise and a financial interest in the copyrighted materials; third-party liability for online conduct.

TABLE 9.1 (Continued)

Types of Risk	Direct Liability	Imputed Liability
Other: Corporate liability for violation of export controls; taxation of e-commerce; failure to provide adequate security on web site; first amendment issues; liability for web site crashes or service outages.	Liability of cross-border data flow of restricted software.	Exporting encryption software to a foreign subsidiary.

[B] Employees and Others Outside Company Offices

[1] Telecommuters

While most companies can enforce and monitor their e-mail policies for employees at their corporate offices, it becomes more difficult for remote offices and telecommuting employees. Home-based telecommuting employees may work anywhere from Burlington, Vermont, to Singapore with remote access to the corporate office. Business travelers often create a temporary "virtual office" in their hotel rooms or in temporary office space, using a direct connection to their companies' computer systems. Most companies provide access to their networks through a virtual private network (VPN) that gives users private, secure access to the company's information assets.

➤ *[a] Preventive Law Pointer: Telecommuting Employees*

If employees are permitted to telecommute, what special safeguards are in place to govern the use of corporate computer systems outside of the office? Telecommuting employees may work from home, remote sites, or satellite offices, using direct access to internal corporate networks. The information accessed by telecommuters can be protected while the employee is in transit by the use of a secure tunnel, that is, over an encrypted path between the telecommuter, via the Internet, to the internal corporate network.[10]

Companies need to address telecommuting issues in their Internet usage policy or in a separate agreement. The telecommuting policy should also address the issue of whether family members may use the employee's computer or access

---

[10] Mark Maier, Corporate Negligence Arising from Internet Telecommuters (1999) (unpublished High Technology Honors Thesis, Suffolk University Law School) (2000).

company computers. The policy should limit the employee's access to confidential company computer files. Companies cannot monitor an employee's Internet use from home—attempting to do so would impose an impossible burden. Suppose, for example, that a family member or another third party sends harassing messages to the president of a competing company. At minimum, a company could be exposed to public scorn, ridicule, and bad publicity, even if they had no knowledge of the telecommuter's wrongdoing. Telecommuting, if unchecked by clear policy directives, can create great potential for liability for companies. At minimum, a telecommuting policy should advise telecommuters that company equipment can be used only for business purposes.

Finally, the policy statement regarding telecommuting should make clear the company's position that such arrangements cannot be made for all employees. Clear guidelines should be made available to all employees regarding how employees are selected for telecommuting arrangements.[11]

[2] Independent Contractors

At times, companies may engage independent contractors for their expertise. Depending on the business's needs, these contractors may have access to the corporate e-mail and other computer or Internet resources. Consequently, at a minimum, access to these electronic resources should be subject to the same terms and conditions that regular employees observe. Agreements with independent contractors should contain indemnification language to ensure that the independent contractors understand that they are responsible for their own actions and any abuses. While the indemnification may be limited to the economic value of the consulting contract, companies should rely primarily upon their own insurance to limit corporate exposure.

➤ *[a] Preventive Law Pointer: Independent Contractor Status*

SPC must have the exclusive right to use, create, or modify materials created by consultants. The consultancy agreement will set forth the specific provisions dealing with time of performance. The consultancy arrangement has some drawbacks as compared with regular employment. Employees, for example, are covered by workers' compensation, whereas consultants are not.[12]

---

[11] Beverly W. Garofalo, Telecommuting: Interaction of Employment Law and Tech Change: Employers Are Well Advised to Draw Up Agreement for At-Home Workers, 15 Comp. L. Strat. 1 (Apr. 1999).

[12] One advantage of the employment relationship for SPC is the exclusivity bar of the workers' compensation act. SPC is immunized from work place related torts if the employee is covered by workers' compensation.

The consultancy agreement should also cover the consultant's use of employer's equipment, e-mail, and the Internet; sexual harassment; and the procedure for protecting a company's trade secrets and other proprietary information. E-mail impersonation, eavesdropping, and threats by employees may result in lawsuits against SPC. The following is a sample clause of a consultancy agreement.

> This independent contract or consultant agreement is between Suffolk Personal Computers ("SPC"), a Massachusetts corporation and _____.
> _____ is an independent contractor and not a partner, joint venturer, or employee of SPC. _____ shall not represent itself as having any other status or relationship than that of independent contractor. SPC, likewise, agrees not to refer to _____ as anything other than an independent contractor or consultant, unless the parties otherwise agree.

[C]   Risks Posed by E-mail

[1]   Abuse of E-Mail

E-mail messages tend to be more informal and emotive than business letters. They can also be forwarded easily throughout the company and beyond with the click of a mouse. Employees should be warned against a "stream of consciousness" approach: Messages that seemed innocuous when dashed off may appear damning during discovery or at trial. Spell-checks, grammar-checks, and other measures should be used: E-mail messages should be written with as much care as any business letter.

If a company establishes and enforces a formal e-mail use policy, employees who claim to be the victims of harassment by co-employees may not prevail in court. While the policy may not forestall a claim, it may provide important evidence of an environment in which objectionable behavior is not sanctioned or tolerated. Employees from a Texas company, for example, filed suit for racial discrimination based on four jokes with racial overtones sent via internal e-mail.[13] The court rejected the plaintiffs' claims, which were based on Title VII and Sections 1981 and 1983 of the Civil Rights Act of 1964. The company prevailed by showing that they pursued the incident with oral and written reprimands to the employee who had sent the offending e-mail. Further evidence in the company's favor was its appointment of a staff member to advise employees of the policy

---

[13] Daniels v. WorldCom Corp., No. Civ. A.3:97-CV-0721-P, 1998 WESTLAW 91261 (N.D. Tex. Feb. 23, 1998); Curtis v. DiMaio, 2000 U.S. App. LEXIS 902 (2d Cir. Jan 25, 2000) (ffirming finding that sending and receiving racially charged e-mail messages did not alone create a hostile workplace).

against using e-mail for nonbusiness purposes. The company still suffered adverse publicity as well as litigation expenses defending the claim.

[2]   Hostile Workplace Claims

The misuse of e-mail by employees can subject a company to claims of a hostile work environment or to a retaliatory discharge claim. Sexually charged e-mails may become the basis of a harassment claim.[14] For example, an employee sued the *Chicago Sun-Times* newspaper for sex discrimination that created a hostile workplace based in part on a veteran employee's repeated offers to another employee of a ride.[15] The smoking gun in that case was an e-mail from the supervisor that stated: "I know I'm getting to be a pain [in] the butt with these ride offers. And I apologize. But I can't help myself."[16] In the even more blatant example in Knox v. Indiana,[17] a sexual harassment claim was based on an e-mail message from one employee to another asking the plaintiff whether she wanted a "horizontal good time." In another case, Litman v. George Mason University,[18] a university student and employee of the university terminated the plaintiff's research position with a professor. The professor sent her an e-mail that stated: "Don't marry someone you live with. Marry someone you can't live without."[19] Although these statements may not be objectionable on their face, they may, nevertheless, serve as evidence of sexual or other harassment.

Sending e-mails with jokes offensive to minorities may create potential liability for a racial discrimination claim against a company.[20] A New York court held that a single e-mail, even though reprehensible, could not constitute a sufficient basis for a hostile workplace claim.[21] On the other hand, in Sattar v. Motorola, Inc.,[22] a supervisor sent an employee hundreds of e-mails that gave the plaintiff dire warnings of the consequences of turning his back on the Islamic religion. The

---

[14] Comiskey v. Automotive Industries Action Group, 40 F. Supp. 2d 877 (E.D. Mich. 1999).

[15] Greenslade v. Chicago Sun-Times, Inc., 112 F.3d 853 (7th Cir. 1997) (affirming dismissal of Newspaper Employee's 7171c VII claim).

[16] *Id.* at 864.

[17] 93 F.3d 1327 (7th Cir. 1996).

[18] 1999 U.S. Dist. LEXIS 261 (Jan. 5, 1999).

[19] *Id.*

[20] Curtis v. DiMaio, 2000 U.S. App. LEXIS 902 (2d Cir. Jan. 25, 2000) (affirming dismissal of hostile work place claim based on sending and receipt of racially charged e-mails).

[21] Owens v. Morgan Stanley Co., Inc., 1997 U.S. Dist. LEXIS 10351, 1997 WL 403454 (S.D. N.Y. 1997).

[22] 138 F.3d 1164 (7th Cir. 1998). *See also* Mieritz v. Hartford Fire Ins. Co., 2000 U.S. Dist. LEXIS 4965 (N.D. Tex. Apr. 15, 2000) (granting summary judgment in favor of employer in dismissal of auditor for attaching scripture verses to his e-mails contrary to company's e-mail policy).

plaintiff in *Sattar* requested 210,000 pages of e-mail messages.[23] Even though the company ultimately won the case, the litigation was expensive, embarrassing, and time-consuming. In another case, a Michigan employee transmitted an e-mail message to female African-American female co-workers about a male African-American client of the company's. The e-mail message was sent to a supervisor who found the e-mail message to be offensive and disrespectful, so the employee was subsequently terminated. The ex-employee filed suit against his former employer for reverse discrimination. Even though the company prevailed on a summary judgment motion, the e-mail misuse resulted in costly and time-consuming litigation as well as negative publicity.[24]

Federal acts other than civil rights statutes may provide a basis for a claim. In United States v. Casciano,[25] for example, a cyberstalker was convicted of violating the Violence Against Women Act. The evidence included numerous unsolicited e-mail messages. The United States Supreme Court recently upheld a section of the Communications Decency Act (CDA) that prohibits indecent e-mail intended to harass or annoy the recipient.[26] Cyberstalking laws may result in liability where the company had knowledge of an employee's wrongdoing and took no remedial steps.

[3] Identity Theft

Identity theft can include obtaining and exploiting an employee's social security number for financial gain or access to corporate security clearance. Identity theft can result in criminals using an employee's security clearance to steal trade secrets, money, or computer data. Adequate security of personal information about employees must be instituted to guard against the possibility that a co-worker may sell personal information to unscrupulous third parties. Some organizations require all personal and confidential information be encrypted. Employees should be instructed that e-mail or the Internet should never be used to transmit personal or sensitive information.

[4] Business Espionage and Trade Secrets

Aside from harassment claims and other torts, some criminal laws can help a company that has been harmed or expose a company to criminal liability for an

---

[23] The supervisor who sent the hundreds of e-mails was transferred to the United Arab Emirate prior to the plaintiff's termination. The court found that the plaintiff was not terminated as the result of not following the Islamic religion and held for the defendant.

[24] Donley v. Ameritech Services, Inc., 1992 U.S. Dist. LEXIS 21281 (E.D. Mich. 1992).

[25] 124 F.3d 106, 109 (2d Cir. 1997).

[26] ApolloMedia Corp. v. Reno, 526 U.S. 1061 (1999) (summarily affirming lower court opinion that Section 223(a) of the CDA may constitutionally prevent the transmission of obscene communications over the Internet).

employee's actions. One of the dangers of the Internet is the possibility that employees or ex-employees will divulge trade secrets online. Malicious employees can make files and records disappear with the push of a button and distribute confidential records worldwide in a matter of minutes.[27] A trade secret includes any information, "including a formula, pattern, compilation, program, device, method, technique or process" that has independent economic value and is subject to reasonable efforts to maintain secrecy.[28] In addition, a trade secret may not be information "that is generally known or ascertainable by proper means."[29] The Restatement of the Law of Unfair Competition defines trade secrets broadly to include "any information that can be used in the operation of a business or other enterprise and that is sufficiently valuable and secret to afford an actual or potential economic advantage over others."[30]

Whether a trade secret has been lost on the Internet depends upon the following factors:

> "(1) The amount of information that was exposed as compared to the 'entire' relevant set of secret data; (2) The amount of time that the information remained exposed; (3) The extent to which the Internet gained actual (as opposed to theoretical) access to the information; (4) Whether the disclosure was referring to a defined group, making notice more practical; (5) The extent to which the information was disclosed to persons who are in a position to understand and use it; (6) Whether the owner took prompt action by giving notice and seeking to correct the situation by self-help and through the courts; and (7) The extent of the *bona fide* reliance by those whom the situation may have be exposed."[31]

Once a trade secret is transmitted on the Internet, the probabilities are that it will no longer be classified as a trade secret. The Uniform Trade Secrets Act requires a company to maintain secrecy and to use reasonable efforts to do so. Access controls must be instituted to prevent employees from posting company secrets to the Internet.

A company's e-mail system or a company computer connected to the Internet may be the instrument used for a trade secrets crime. Software or other proprietary information may be downloaded and transmitted by cybercriminal employees. The threat of misappropriated information being published online is

---

[27] James Garrity and Eoghan Casey, Internet Misuse in the Workplace: A Lawyer's Primer, 72 Fl. Bar J. 22 (Nov. 1998).

[28] Uniform Trade Secrets Act § 1(4) (defining trade secrets).

[29] *Id. See also* Ford Motor Co. v. Lane, 67 F. Supp. 2d 745 (E.D. Mich. 1999) (holding that in absence of confidentiality agreement or fiduciary duty between the parties, injunction could not enjoin publication of trade secrets on the Internet).

[30] Restatement of the Law of Unfair Competition § 39 (1995).

[31] James Pooley, Is Nothing Secret? The Newest Communication Medium Threatens Sensitive Business Information (visited Apr. 6, 1999), http:www.ipmag.com/pooley.html.

not hypothetical. A former member of the Church of Scientology, for example, posted confidential church documents on the Internet. A former Gillette employee was sentenced to 27 months in jail for transmitting "600MB or megs of secret data and drawings from the confidential Gillette project onto his laptop computer and [disclosing] the proprietary information by fax and e-mail to Gillette competitors, including Schick, Wilkinson and BIC."[32]

The Economic Espionage Act of 1996 criminalizes the theft of trade secrets.[33] The criminal statute requires the government to prove beyond a reasonable doubt that an individual acted with specific intent to steal trade secrets with knowledge that the trade secret was proprietary and knowledge that the theft of trade secrets would injure the victim. Prior to the Economic Espionage Act, prosecutors were powerless to pursue criminals who stole sensitive corporate data and crossed state lines.[34]

A growing number of states statutes criminalize the theft of trade secrets and similar intangibles.[35] Criminal liability for trade secret misappropriations may be prosecuted under state criminal or penal codes. In one case, prosecutors filed trade secret charges against two Silicon Valley executives under California's penal law. The smoking gun in the case was deleted e-mail files. Charges were later dropped, though only after a four-year investigation.[36]

The risk of the misappropriation of trade secrets may be correlated with the organizational culture and whether the employment relationship is based solely on a collecting a paycheck, or the "cash nexus."[37] Employers tend to "overestimate employee loyalty, or their own skills in detecting computer-based misconduct."[38]

---

[32] Mark D. Seltzer and Angela A. Burns, The Criminal Consequences of Trade Secret Misappropriation: Does the Economic Espionage Act Insulate Your Company's Trade Secrets from Theft and Render Civil Remedies Obsolete? 16 Comp. & Online Indus Lit Rptr, 13 (Jan. 5, 1999).

[33] 18 U.S.C. § 1832 (1997). The Act defines a trade secret as follows (1) the owner took reasonable measures to keep the information secret commensurate with the value of the trade secret; and (2) the information derives actual or potential independent economic value from not being made known to the public. 18 U.S.C. § 1839(3)(A)(B) (1997).

[34] Dan Goodin, Busting Industrial Spies, The Recorder, Sept. 25, 1996, at 1 (noting how "outsiders had downloaded a sensitive business proposal and run off to New Mexico [and that] the U.S. attorney's office declined to go after the culprits since the theft of intangibles was not yet a federal crime").

[35] Id. (noting that California criminalizes the transmission of stolen trade secrets); see also Ruckelshaus v. Monsanto Co., 467 U.S. 986 (1984) (holding that pesticide manufacturer had protectable trade secrets under the Trade Secrets Act, 18 U.S.C. § 1095 which penalizes any employee of the U.S. Government who discloses trade secret information revealed in the course of his duties).

[36] The case was People v. Eubanks, No. S049490 (Ca. Superior Ct., charges dropped Nov. 19, 1996) reported in DA Drops Prosecution of Executives; Ca Supreme Court Might Rule on Appeal, Software L. Bull. 14 (Jan. 1997).

[37] The concept of the cash nexus was prefigured in Karl Marx and Frederick Engels' Communist Manifesto. Today, the concept of the cash nexus is widely used by industrial sociologists to describe a workplace in which calculation and self-interest predominate versus moral involvement.

[38] Garrity and Casey, supra note 27.

On the other hand, if a spirit of good faith and fair dealing pervades the workplace, a higher standard of behavior will usually result.

Self-control is the best form of control in an organization, and it is attained in an online company by recruiting, training, and retaining quality employees. In the information age, the workplace that treats employees like disposable plug-in, plug-out parts is more likely to have problems with the misappropriation of information.

The risk of trade secret theft is greater where executives as well as employees jump from company to company. In fact, the FBI reports that domestic and foreign espionage resulted in the theft of intellectual property in excess of $300 billion in 1997.[39]

[5] Defamation

The risk of being subject to a defamation lawsuit is a significant exposure. For example, the web content manager at Suffolk PCs maintains a grudge against his former employer. Working late one night, he posts his opinion on the SPC site. The next week, the competitor files a defamation suit against Suffolk. Such online defamation claims may arise out of a wide variety of e-mail or Internet communications: in chat rooms, on web sites, or from forwarded e-mail that defames individuals. In addition, companies may also be subject for trade libel for defamatory statements made about other companies.

Defamation is the communication of an unprivileged false and defamatory statement about a plaintiff, transmitted to a third person, and as we noted in Chapter Five, it is traditionally subdivided into oral slander and written and published libel in physical form.[40] The Internet may provide the means for either: A recorded audio clip or wave file downloaded and replayed may constitute either libel or slander. The traditional rule is that publishers are liable for any defamatory con-

---

[39] Curtis E. A. Karnow, Computer Network Risks: Security Breaches and Liability Issues: The Judicial System Is Only Starting to Address Related Privacy Matters, 15 Comp. L. Strat. 1 (Feb. 1999) (quoting FBI report).

[40] Section 230 of the Communications Decency Act immunizes providers for providing access to defamatory information and other torts. *See, e.g.,* Ben Ezra, Weinstein & Co. v. America Online, Inc., 206 F.3d 980 (10th Cir. 2000) (upholding immunity for defamation cause of action); Zeran v. America Online, 129 F.3d 327 (4th Cir. 1997); John Does v. Franco Productions, 2000 U.S. Dist. LEXIS 8645 (N.D. Ill., June 22, 2000) (dismissing action against provider who transmitted images of college athletes filmed by a secret camera); Jane Doe One v. Oliver, 46 Conn. Supp. 406, 755 A.2d 1000 (2000) (striking claims against provider for improper e-mails on immunity grounds). The Good Samaritan Defense of the Communications Decency Act of 1996 gives interactive computer services immunity for defamation and other torts committed on SPC's web site. SPC may be liable for its own defamatory statements made by company officials acting within their scope of duties, however. *See* 47 U.S.C. § 230 (2000), Ben Ezra Weinstein v. America Online, Inc., 206 F.3d 980 (10th Cir. 2000) (upholding § 230 immunity for provider in defamation action).

tent, but mere distributors are not liable unless they know or have reason to know of the defamatory statement.[41]

Free speech and opinions may take a back seat to the threat of litigation online. A psychiatrist who hosted a web site brought a defamation action against the host of a rival web site for defamation in Barrett v. The Catacombs Press.[42] The statements by the defendant attacked the plaintiff in his capacity as an advocate against health care fraud and in favor of fluoridation of water sources.[43] The plaintiff was a psychiatrist who was involved in investigating and dealing with many aspects of health care. His web site, called Quackwatch, provided information about health fraud and quackery. The Quackwatch web site addressed the fluoridation debate with a web page entitled, "Fluoridation: Don't Let the Poisonmongers Scare You." The plaintiff sent the defendant an e-mail threatening a lawsuit after seeing her web site.[44]

[6] Fraud

SPC may be subject to a number of direct liabilities, such as fraud or products liability for knowingly placing defective software on the market, or it may be indirectly liable for fraud committed by hackers who steal its customer's credit card numbers or personal information. Fraud is frequently invoked in trade libel cases redressing injuries to business reputation.[45] Companies may be held liable for online defamation for the statements of an employee made in advertisements, chatrooms and other Internet-related forums.

In Lunney v. Prodigy Services Co.,[46] the New York Appeals Court extended a common law privilege designed for telegraph services to Internet service providers covering defamatory statements made on their forums. In that case, an unknown third party opened a Prodigy account in the name of a 15-year-old boy scout. The unknown subscriber transmitted an offensive and threatening e-mail to

---

[41] Jeffrey P. Cunard, et al., Communications Law 1998: Internet Law Developments, Practicing Law Institute, Patents, Copyrights, Trademarks, and Literary Property Course Handbook Series, PLI Order No. GA-4039, Nov. 1998.

[42] 44 F. Supp. 2d 717 (E.D. Pa. 1999).

[43] *Id.*

[44] The court declined to exercise jurisdiction over the defendant because he never targeted nor solicited Pennsylvania residents and otherwise did not meet the minimum contact tests.

[45] *See, e.g.,* Barrett v. Cazacombs Press, 44 F. Supp. 2d 717 (E.D. Pa. 1999), Seidl v. Greentree Mortg. Co., 30 F. Supp. 2d 1292 (D. Colo. 1998).

[46] 1998 N.Y. App. Div. LEXIS 14047 (Sup. Ct. N.Y. App. Div. 1998); Lunney v. Prodigy Services Co., 94 N.Y.2d 242, 723 N.E.2d 539 (Ct. of App. of N.Y. 1999), *cert. denied,* 120 S.Ct. 1832 (2000) (upholding finding that provider was entitled to the common-law qualified privilege accorded telephone companies and thus sheltered from liability).

the boy's local Boy Scout leader. The scout leader reported the matter to the boy's scoutmaster, who confronted the boy and demanded an explanation. In response to the report, Prodigy then closed the boy's account because of a breach of the subscriber's agreement, as pointed out by the scout leader's complaint.

The plaintiff brought suit against Prodigy for libel, negligence, and harassment—all the product of a fraudulent e-mail sent using Prodigy's network. The *Lunney* court dismissed the claims against the online service provider, holding that it was not liable for defamatory materials placed on its system without its knowledge.[47] Other companies, however, may not be as lucky as Prodigy and may be held liable for online defamation if their systems carry derogatory statements about competitors' or their products.

[7] Intellectual Property Infringement

E-mail gives the user the capability of sending data files, pictures, and even video, instantaneously.[48] When a user sends material to which someone else holds the copyright, he or she risks infringing the copyright. SPC may reduce its own exposure to infringement actions by owning, licensing, or assigning all copyrightable materials on its web site. At minimum, proper notice of copyright must be given for all content supplied by SPC and third parties. SPC's due diligence should cover all materials provided by third parties, as well as by the company. Copyrights and trademark clearance must be obtained for any pictures, images, cartoons, photographs, illustrations, streaming video, graphics, text, or other content.

To protect its rights, SPC's notices must encompass rights in text, graphics, selection, and arrangement as well as the "look and feel" or overall design of its web site.[49] If the web site developer supplies content, SPC will need a license agreement to use, modify, update, and maintain materials on the web site. The web site agreement should cover all intellectual property rights including copyrights, trademarks, trade secrets, patents, and the right of publicity. SPC should enter into an agreement with the web site developer to obtain the ownership interest in the web site.

If SPC permits web site visitors to post information on chat rooms, listservs, or other pages on its sites, a terms of service agreement should be implemented.

---

[47] *Id.*

[48] America Online and Kodak are developing a technology for sending pictures directly from photo processing shops to e-mail accounts. Polaroid Corporation has licensed technology from NASA that will enable users to send over the Internet images secured from tampering through the use of special digital cameras and digital signatures.

[49] Amazon.com sued a web site in Greece for copyright and trademark infringement. The Greek site registered the domain name "amazon.gr" and replicated "the look and feel" of Amazon.com's web site. Trademarks/RICO, Amazon.com Sues Greek Site for Trademark, Copyright, RICO Violations, Andrews Comp. & Online Indus. Litig. Rep. 3 (Sept. 21, 1999).

SPC needs to make it clear that it is not liable for outside postings by third parties and that it does not endorse individuals or entities posting information.[50]

[8] Ex-Employee Access

The risk posed by disgruntled ex-employees who continue to have access to company computers is far greater than that of industrial espionage. A number of companies have suffered losses because they did not terminate an ex-employee's access to computer systems. Some security breaches are caused by the company's simple failure to prevent ex-employees, consultants, and other insiders from accessing the computer systems. When an employee is terminated, a standard procedure needs to be in place for reviewing the ex-employee's computer files and e-mail messages. Passwords and authentication devices must be changed to prevent the ex-employee from retaining access to company computers. Some companies allow terminated employees, as part of a severance or layoff plan to retain access to the company's e-mail system to assist them in finding new jobs. This benefit presents potential risks if the ex-employee has a grievance against the company or is not acting in good faith.

In one case, a California court held that a former employee of Intel Corporation, who had sent more than 30,000 e-mails critical of the company, committed trespass to chattel, and enjoined him from e-mailing the employees remaining at his former workplace. The California state court enjoined the former Intel employee from sending further e-mails, ruling that his actions were not protected by the First Amendment's Free Speech Clause.[51] Intel successfully argued that the e-mails were clogging their corporate e-mail system, and that the corporate computer system was not a public forum for First Amendment purposes.

The ex-employee argued that the e-mails did not harm Intel. The court, however, stated that "any impairment in the value to Intel of its e-mail system is sufficient to show injury."[52] The court observed that Intel was injured due to the loss in

---

[50] To protect its own intellectual property rights, SPC will need to do the following: (1) Obtain or register its domain name; (2) seek warranties that intellectual property obtained from others does not infringe the intellectual property rights of others; (3) obtain, register, and protect its trademarks and copyrights; (4) obtain patents or licenses to use e-commerce patents; (5) audit all content on its web site; and (6) use license agreements when obtaining content. Section 8.02[B] provides a systematic discussion of the legal audit for intellectual property rights.

[51] Ex-Employee's E-Mails to Intel Workers Are Not Protected Speech, Judge Rules, 16 Comp. & Online Indus. Litig. Rptr. 8 (May 18, 1999) (reporting that California state court granted Intel's motion for summary judgment finding that ex-employees transmission of thousands of e-mails to current Intel employees to constitute trespass to chattels). This case is being appealed with support from the Society of Harvard Law School and the ACLU. *See* Mike Magee, Intel v. Hamidi E-Mail Case Continues, The Register (visited Oct. 2, 2000), http://www.theregister.co.uk/contents/6/12118.html.

[52] *Id.*

productivity from employees wasting time reviewing the thousands of unwanted e-mails they received from the ex-employee. Consequently, Intel also lost time and money in attempting to block the ex-employee's e-mails as well as in responding to employees' concerns about the e-mail messages.[53]

➤   *[a]   Preventive Law Pointer: Terminating Ex-Employees' E-Mail*

Companies need a well-defined procedure for terminating an employee's e-mail and Internet access at the moment of termination of employment. This can usually be done when the employee has an exit interview and/or is required to hand in all keys and security clearances.

[D]   Corporate Liability for Crimes

[1]   Gambling and Games of Chance

Business activities on the Internet permissible in the state where a company is based may nonetheless create a risk of liability in jurisdictions where the activity is prohibited. An offer by SPC of a promotion, sweepstakes, or gambling may be regulated in some states and countries. SPC will need to investigate the laws of multiple jurisdictions before launching an online promotion or sweepstakes. SPC's due diligence will include a notice that the contest or game is void in countries where it is prohibited.

[2]   Pornography and Obscene Materials; Controversial Web Sites

Employees' abuse of corporate e-mail systems and Internet access raises serious productivity concerns. Nearly two-thirds of responding companies reported that employees "accessed sexually explicit web sites at work. Greater than a quarter of companies took disciplinary action against employees for sex site surfing."[54] Another survey found that "employees at three well-known companies spent the equivalent of 350 eight-hour workdays accessing the Penthouse Magazine Web site in a single month."[55] Unlimited access to the Internet may allow wayward employees to locate pornography or other objectionable materials from one of the thousands of web sites that provide it.[56] "Live feed" web sites enable

---

[53] *Id.*

[54] Karnow, *supra* note 39.

[55] Thomas P. Klein, Electronic Communications in the Workplace, Legal Issues and Policies, Third Annual Internet Law Institute 1999 (PLI Patents, Copyrights, Trademarks and Literary Property Course Handbook Series, No. G0-005(1)).

[56] Garrity and Casey, *supra* note 27.

employees to view live performances of sexual acts from their desktop, which may expose their companies to potential liability for a hostile workplace claim.[57]

The e-mail and Internet policy must address company concerns about downloading obscene, indecent, and other questionable content. Even if the material is not illegal or objectionable, downloaded video, music, and other publications may overload the corporate computer system and create a distraction that impedes workplace productivity. Employees have no First Amendment right to misuse proprietary computer systems.

In addition to productivity losses, the company may also be exposed to civil liability, criminal liability, or bad publicity. The e-mail system is an efficient means for forwarding documents, including pornographic or obscene messages, and it is a common practice to forward off-color jokes or other objectionable materials to multiple recipients. The simple act of forwarding these jokes may unwittingly expose a company to a discrimination lawsuit under Title VII of the Civil Rights Act of 1964 and state discrimination laws.[58] A company is also potentially subject to a hostile workplace claim when off-color or racist jokes are e-mailed to company employees.[59]

In some countries, the mere possession of obscene materials not objectionable in the U.S. may be regarded as a serious offense. The federal Child Online Protection Act, for example, that makes it a crime to "knowingly . . . , by means of the World Wide Web, make any communication for commercial purposes that is available to any minor and that includes any material that is harmful to minors."[60] Law enforcement authorities may confiscate company computers involved in distributing child pornography on the Internet.

Many prosecutors take the position that they may prosecute anyone found to have pornographic materials on their computers. A computer specialist working for the U.S. Senate, for example, was arrested for sending pornographic images from his office at the Senate. The Dean of the Harvard Divinity School was recently dismissed for storing large quantities of pornographic images on his university-owned computer.

An employee who downloads pornography may be violating state and federal criminal law. Courts have little difficulty in admitting e-mail messages to

---

[57] General Media, Inc. v. Shooker, 1998 WL 401530 (S.D. N.Y. July 16, 1998) (citing affidavit of A. Guccione, *Penthouse* magazine); *see* Yamagushi v. U.S. Dept. of Air Force, 109 F.3d 1475 (9th Cir. 1997) (basing hostile workplace claim in part upon offensive e-mail messages).

[58] *See, e.g.*, Rudas v. Nationwide Mutual Insurance Co., 1997 WL 11302 (E.D. Pa. Jan. 10, 1997) (dismissing e-harassment case predicated upon sexually charged e-mail messages).

[59] A federal court rejected a claim by African-American employees of Morgan Stanley & Co., alleging that a racist e-mail joke transmitted on the company's computer system created a hostile work environment. Owens v. Morgan Stanley & Co., No. 96 Civ. 9747 DLC (SD NY, July 1997).

[60] United States v. Hall, 2000 WL 32010 (6th Cir. Jan. 4, 2000) (admitting e-mails as evidence of state of mind in child pornography conviction); United States v. Simons, 206 F.3d 392 (4th Cir. 2000) (upholding conviction of employee for storing child pornography on company computer).

show a defendant's state of mind while engaging in illegally sanctioned activity. In United States v. Hall,[61] the Sixth Circuit omitted e-mail messages as evidence of the defendant's online solicitation of child pornography under the other bad act exception to the hearsay rule, which is the exception.

It is unlikely SPC will be prosecuted for the possession of pornography, but it would lose time and money while cooperating with law enforcement if a police unit seized company computers to prosecute an employee.

Even if not liable for downloaded materials, a company will at least suffer adverse publicity, particularly in the case of child pornography. Charges against a high-level employee for possessing pornographic materials would be a public relations disaster. In a worst-case scenario, a company might be found liable for the downloaded materials. SPC should check to be sure that its web site complies with relevant law regarding obscenity and pornographic materials.

An Internet usage policy must take into account the possibility that employees will download offensive material from the Internet. A company must make it clear that employees are not free to download offensive material from the Internet or to forward offensive e-mails.

SPC may also be exposed to adverse publicity if its employees use company computers to post messages to newsgroups or to visit web sites relating to such controversial topics as abortion, white supremacy, or neo-Nazism. Employees should be warned that it is a misuse of company Internet access to visit or contribute to any controversial site. The general standard to be communicated is that the computer system is to be used primarily for business purposes.

In addition to the usage policy, the company may want to institute technological safeguards, such as filters that restrict access to web sites containing hate speech, pornography, or other objectionable materials. SPC will need to decide which sites to restrict in order to avoid legal liability.

Employees should be instructed to use their own e-mail addresses for personal messages. A "business purposes only" policy might be stated as follows:

> If you wish "to send personal e-mail from the office, use your own e-mail software, e-mail account, and ISP, or use one of the free-e-mail services available on the Web."[62] If objectionable materials are transmitted on a company com-

---

[61] United States v. Hall, 2000 WL 32010 (6th Cir. Jan. 4, 2000) (admitting e-mails s evidence of state of mind in child pornography conviction); United States v. Simons, 206 F.3d 392 (4th Cir. 2000) (upholding conviction of employee for storing child pornography on company computer).

[62] Mike Elgan, The Dangers of E-Mail: Follow These 15 Rules for Your E-Mail System and Steer Clear of Legal Woes CMP NET (Apr. 12, 1999). The Internet offers at least 700 free e-mail services.

puter, a search and seizure of a company's computer system may result in adverse publicity to the company.[63]

[3] Unlawful Interception of Electronic Communications

A company that intercepts the e-mail or other electronic communications of a business rival or competitor is subject to criminal and civil liability under the Electronic Communications Privacy Act (ECPA).[64] The ECPA states that any person who "intercepts, endeavors to intercept, or procures any other person to intercept or endeavor to intercept electronic communications" is subject to fines and/or imprisonment.[65] Any person who intercepts electronic communications including e-mail may be subject to civil damages.[66] The ECPA has an exception to liability if the employees or other parties to a communication give prior consent to monitoring and interception. A second exception is that a private communication network may intercept its employees' electronic communications in the course of system maintenance.

The ECPA prohibits employers from intercepting e-mail messages, but the act does not apply if an employee consents to e-mail monitoring.[67] Some companies may decide to monitor e-mail only if a complaint has been filed against an employee. In a Massachusetts case, an employee was fired supposedly for the excessive personal use of e-mail. The president of the company monitored the company's e-mail system and discovered that the employee was e-mailing messages about an affair the employee was having with another employee. The plaintiff filed a lawsuit against the company and its president, alleging unlawful interception of wire communications, invasion of privacy, the negligent and intentional infliction of emotional distress, interference with contractual relations, and loss of consortium.[68]

---

[63] The employee may be subject to criminal liability for transmitting visual images through an online computer system. It is a federal crime to transport obscene materials for the purpose of sale or distribution in interstate or foreign commerce. 18 U.S.C. § 1465 (1997). The Communications Decency Act of 1996 immunizes employers from tort liability "for the obscene or harassing use of electronic telecommunications by their employees 'unless the employee's or agent's conduct is within the scope of his employment or agency and the employer (a) having knowledge of such conduct, authorizes or ratifies such conduct, or (b) recklessly disregards such conduct.'" Peter Brown, Policies for Corporate Internet and E-Mail Use, Third Annual Internet Law Institute, 1999, 564 PLI/Pat 637, 639 (June 14-15, 1999) (quoting Communications Decency Act of 1996).

[64] 18 U.S.C. § 2510 et. seq. (1998). *See* McVeih v. Cohen, 983 F. Supp. 2125 (D.D.C. 1998) (issuing injunction against Navy from discharging plaintiff for homosexual conduct because of possible violation of the Electronic Communications Privacy Act of 1996, 18 U.S.C. § 2703).

[65] 18 U.S.C. § 2510 et seq. (1998).

[66] *Id.* § 2520.

[67] *Id.* § 2511(2)(d).

[68] Restuccia v. Burk Technology, Inc., No. 95-2125 (Middlesex Super. Ct. Aug. 22, 1996) (cited in C. Forbes Sargent III, Electronic Media and the Workplace, 41 Boston Bar J. 6 (May/June 1997)).

Many states have enacted state ECPA wiretap statutes, which parallel the federal statute. Maryland, for example, requires both parties to consent to any taperecording of telephone conversations. Linda Tripp's secret taping of Monica Lewinsky was arguably a violation of Maryland's wiretap statute. "It is a crime in Maryland, for example, for any person to willfully intercept, endeavor to intercept, or procure any other person to intercept or endeavor to intercept, any wire, oral or electronic communication."[69] Maryland's wiretap statute provides heightened fines to punish the unauthorized interception for "commercial advantage, malicious destruction or damage, or private commercial gain."[70]

In another workplace case, a technology coordinator was charged with felony violation of Pennsylvania's ECPA for accessing the e-mail account of his supervisor.[71] The defendant copied e-mail messages from his supervisor's account and distributed them to his supervisor without his authorization. The charges were dismissed because the federal judge found no evidence that the e-mail was accessed simultaneously at the time of transmittal.[72] The judge also found it an issue of material fact as to whether the technology coordinator has the authority to access e-mail messages.[73]

Not only must companies be concerned about liability arising from the actions of their employees, but they must also avoid violating the privacy rights of employees. Obtaining employees' consent to monitoring and reducing employees' reasonable expectation of privacy will reduce the scope of SPC's risks. Therefore, SPC's e-mail and Internet usage policy should condition e-mail usage on consent to monitoring. The policy should state the conditions for monitoring. SPC systems administrators should monitor e-mail only on a "need to know basis."[74]

[4] Computer Fraud and Abuse Act (CFAA)

Gaining unauthorized access to another person or entity's computer system may also constitute a federal or state computer crime. The federal computer crime statute is the Computer Fraud and Abuse Act (CFAA). The federal computer crime statute punishes those who "intentionally access . . . a protected computer without

---

[69] Office of the State Prosecutor v. Judicial Watch, 737 A.2d 592 (Md. Ct. App. 1999) (citing Maryland Wiretap & Electronic Eavesdropping Statute).

[70] *Id.*

[71] Felony Charges Dismissed Against Ex-Employee Who Accessed E-Mail, 16 Comp. & Online Indus. Litig. Rptr. 6 (May 18, 1999).

[72] *Id.*

[73] *Id.*

[74] Elgan, *supra* note 62.

authorization" and cause damage.[75] All actionable under the CFAA are unauthorized access of a computer to obtain information relevant to national security, financial, or credit information; unauthorized interstate or foreign access of a federal government computer; and fraudulent trafficking in stolen passwords. The statutory threshold is that the unauthorized access results in a loss of $1,000 or greater.

In addition, every state except Vermont has enacted "little computer crime statutes."[76] These statutes make it a crime to access computer systems for harmful purposes, but are seldom prosecuted.

§ 9.03   RISK MANAGEMENT

[A]   Reallocating Risks of Loss

Contract is the principal device to allocate or reallocate e-mail and Internet related risks. SPC needs to enter into contracts with employees, such as nondisclosure agreements, to preserve its confidential information. The typical site developer will seek to limit all liability, including consequential and punitive damages.

[1]   Indemnification or "Hold Harmless" Clauses

Indemnification shifts losses from one party to another. Although a company cannot disclaim liability for its own torts, it may seek indemnification for torts committed by third parties.

SPC should seek to be indemnified and held harmless for wrongdoing arising out of misuse and abuse of its e-mail system and the Internet. It should require its outside consultants, web site developers, trading partners, and telecommuting employees who have access to its Internet and e-mail systems to indemnify and hold harmless SPC from any and all losses, liabilities, expenses, and damages from any claims, demands, actions, or proceedings that may be initiated on the grounds of misuse or abuse of SPC's computer system. This indemnification and hold harmless clause applies to claims based on torts, contract, breach of fiduciary duty, and intellectual property infringement actions. Indemnification may also be sought for violations of local, state, federal, and international regulations.

---

[75] 18 U.S.C. § 1030(a) (1999); United States v. Morris, 928 F.2d 504 (2d Cir. 1991) (imposing criminal liability for unleashing "worm" on the Internet causing computer crashes); *see also* North Tex. Preventive Imaging v. Eisenberg, 1996 Dist. LEXIS 19990 (C.D. Cal. Aug. 26, 1996) (holding that CFAA applied to "timebomb" inserted in computer system).

[76] Mark D. Rasch, Criminal Law and the Internet, Chapter 11 in Joseph Ruh, ed. The Internet And Business: A Lawyer's Guide to the Emerging Legal Issues (1995).

SPC may seek indemnification from consultants, developers, and third parties supplying content to its web site. An indemnification agreement should include language requiring the trading partner or consultant to "indemnify, defend, and hold harmless SPC, its directors, officers, employees, and consultants for its own wrongdoing." SPC should require its web site developers to obtain insurance for its web site activities.

Further, the web site developer should be required to make good for any losses caused by torts, crimes, infringement, or other defaults. E-commerce-related patents are on the rise, and one resulting danger is that a developer's web site architecture may violate one or more Internet-related patents. SPC, as the indemnified party, should have peace of mind that the developer is not infringing some third party's copyrights, trademarks, trade secrets, licenses, or other intellectual property rights.

[2] Nondisclosure Agreements

SPC can protect its proprietary information, confidential information, and trade secrets by entering into confidentiality agreements with its trading partners, subsidiaries, and affiliates to protect confidential information. The agreement should cover confidential and proprietary information that has already been disclosed to the other party. SPC's employment agreements should make it clear that confidential and proprietary information and trade secrets are the property of the company.

[B] Employee Training and Supervision

Employee education is the chief risk management device for e-mail and Internet torts committed by employees. SPC needs to develop an e-mail and Internet usage policy that will inform workers about the proper use of its computer system. Despite the dangers, currently only about one in two companies has an e-mail policy in place.[77] E-mail and Internet usage policy needs to be a part of employee training programs if it is to be effective. A written e-mail and Internet usage policy, combined with training, can be used to mitigate or avoid legal liability.

SPC should also provide e-mail and Internet training for both new personnel and existing employees. Internet and e-mail usage is also an issue for departing and ex-employees. An ex-employee should be reminded about the continuing

---

[77] Marcia Stepanek, When the Devil Is in the E-Mails, Bus. Wk., June 8, 1998, at 72 (citing Nov. 1997 study in which only 51% of survey respondents reported training workers in the appropriate use of e-mails).

obligation to keep documents confidential. SPC's training module should emphasize that employees are subject to tort as well as criminal liability for the theft of trade secrets. The training should explain what the company's expectations are for the protection of trade secrets, confidential information, and proprietary information.

Employees must be educated on what is considered a trade secret or confidential information. E-mail may be a means for insiders to accomplish theft, bribery, misrepresentation, or business espionage. In general, the extent of protection of trade secrets depends on what steps the owner takes to protect its confidential information.[78] Including the protection of trade secrets in an Internet or e-mail usage policy is evidence that the trade secret owner is taking reasonable steps to maintain secrecy.

[C] Smoking Guns and Retention of E-Mail Messages

Managing electronic data is very difficult because, unlike paper-based documents, electronic files cannot simply be torn up or incinerated. Oliver North and his secretary, Fawn Hall, thought that he had shredded all paper-copies and deleted all computer files pertaining to the Reagan Administration's involvement in the Iran/Contra affair.[79] North "was confronted with electronic copies of these documents and other information that congressional investigators and forensic experts were able to recover from backup computer tapes."[80] As Iran Contra defendants learned, "the 'delete' key does not obliterate a file . . . files generally remain intact until they are overwritten."[81]

Even if files have been deleted, computer forensics experts are frequently able to undelete computer files and recreate erased materials.[82] Online employers need to view e-mail as evidence and to visualize how a top plaintiff's attorney will use e-mail to show a company's motivation or state of mind.

---

[78] Ruckelshaus v. Monsanto Co., 104 S. Ct. 2862, 2873 (1984).

[79] "One of the most notorious examples [of e-mail smoking guns] was Oliver North's attempt to cover up arm sales to support the Contras in Nicaragua. North believed that he had deleted e-mail messages but the messages were reconstructed with the help of computer forensics experts." Matthew J. Bester, A Wreck on the Info-Bahn: Electronic Mail and the Destruction of Evidence, 6 Commlaw Conspectus 75 (1998).

[80] James K. Lehman, Litigating in Cyberspace: Discovery of Electronic Information, 8 S. Carolina Lawyer 14, 15 (Mar./Apr. 1997).

[81] Laurie Thomas Lee, Watch Your E-Mail! Employee E-Mail Monitoring and Privacy Law in the Age of the "Electronic Sweatshop," 28 J. Marshall L. Rev. 139 (1994).

[82] Linda Himelstein, The Snitch in the System, Bus. Wk., Apr. 17, 1995, at 104 (citing case in which a judge awarded $25.5 million in a trade secrets action against a software developer based on recreated deleted computer files showing incriminating memorandum).

"Investigations of employee e-mail . . . increased an average of thirty percent each year from 1994 to 1996."[83] It is an urban myth that deleted e-mail no longer exists for later discovery.[84] E-mail messages "survive long after the supposed deletion and may only be permanently deleted when the computer needs the then available space." Computer experts can easily recover "deleted" information that the computer has not yet overwritten and can even reconstruct partially overwritten data.[85] Whether for an internal investigation or as part of discovery, companies may employ forensic computer analysts who have the expertise to " 'bag' the employee's computer by copying the entire hard drive onto a high-density disk."[86] E-mail and other data may be deleted by permanently opening up the hard drive and crushing the magnetically coated platters.

One of the difficult decisions employees must make is which e-mail messages constitute business records, the retention policy, and which messages should be archived. Hundreds of millions of messages are transmitted on the Internet. A large multinational corporation may have a million or more messages daily. It may be impossible to track down e-mail messages that have been forwarded or retransmitted. Even if a message is deleted from an employee's computer, a copy of the message may have been printed out or stored on a diskette. The forwarded e-mail may, in turn, have been forwarded to many other locations across the world. Transmitted, forwarded, or stored e-mail messages from SPC employees may prove to be the "star witness" in an antitrust case, business torts, or a sexual harassment, discrimination, or business contracts lawsuit.

E-mails are classified as company documents and must be covered by a document retention and destruction policy. E-mail messages are subject to discovery and are treated as company records.[87] E-mail has no special privilege and is admissible in a court proceeding as evidence.[88] Rule 34 of the Federal Rules of Civil Procedure permits a party to request an inspection and copy of documents, including electronic information.[89] Discovery requests should specifically include all

---

[83] *Id.*

[84] Charles A. Lovell and Roger W. Holmes, The Dangers of E-Mail: The Need for Electronic Data Retention Policies, 44 R.I. Bar J. (Dec. 1995).

[85] *Id.*

[86] Alexander I. Rodriquez, All Bark, No Byte: Employee E-Mail Privacy Rights in the Private Sector Workplace, 47 Emory L.J. 1439, 1439 (1998).

[87] Reuters Ltd. v. Dow Jones Telerate Inc., 1997 WL 545807, at *2 (N.Y. App. Div. Sept. 4, 1997) (noting that subpoena *duces tecum* gave a nonparty "less than two days to go through 30 years of documents, including e-mail, computer data, etc."). *See also* Falise v. American Tobacco Co., 1999 U.S. Dist. LEXIS 20608 (E.D. N.Y. Dec. 28, 1999) (declaring tobacco litigation documents not privileged because of the widespread availability of the documents).

[88] Wesley College v. Pitts, 1997 WL 557554 (D. Del. Aug. 11, 1997).

[89] E-mail messages were admitted, for example, against a defendant charged with fraud and bribery in United States v. Ferber, 966 F. Supp. 92, 99 (D. Mass 1997).

media including backup copies, which have been outsourced to an off-site storage facility.

E-mail messages have proved important in a number of recent cases. In Workers' Compensation Div. v. Pampell,[90] the plaintiff introduced a "a copy of a dated and time stamped e-mail message" as evidence that an appeal was timely. E-mail evidence was also key to establishing a landowner's notice of a security problem in a premises liability case.[91] An e-mail message was key to a false advertising claim brought by a publisher of physics journals against competitors challenging a study ranking journals; the court noted "an e-mail message which criticized [one plaintiff's] prices" and "characterized its journals."[92]

E-mail messages have also been essential for establishing liability in a number of recent employment cases.[93] In Harrow v. Prudential Insur. Co.,[94] e-mail messages were admitted in a wrongful denial of benefits case. A motion to compel production of e-mail uncovered the e-mail messages. In Evans v. Toys R Us-Ohio, Inc.,[95] an e-mail message was used to show a co-employee's predisposition to discriminate against minorities. The smoking-gun message revealed the company's knowledge that the employee in general had a predisposition to be "hard on minorities and men."

Kenneth Starr's investigation of Monica Lewinsky's e-mail messages in the President Clinton investigation were regarded as electronic smoking guns.[96] The House Judiciary Committee, as part of the evidence collected by independent counsel, released e-mail excerpts.[97] It is common for the "electronic smoking

---

[90] 1997 WL 576470, at *2 (Tex. Ct. App. Sept. 18, 1997). *See also* Canizales v. Microsoft Corp, NSWIRComm 118 (Sept. 1, 2000) (noting e-mail exchanges in $9 million judgment in termination of employment action decided by New South Wales (Aust.) Industrial Relations Commission); United States v. Poehlman, 217 F.3d 692 (9th Cir. 2000) (reversing conviction as much of the evidence was in the form of breezy, informal e-mails with numerous grammatical, spelling, and syntax errors).

[91] Holder v. Mellon Mortgage Co., 1997 WL 461982, at *3 (Tex. Ct. App. Aug. 14, 1997) (noting that e-mail from employee "lodge[d] a formal complaint about the virtually non-existent security for our parking garage" showing that employer had notice of security problem).

[92] Amsterdam BV v. American Inst. of Physics, 1997 WL 528086, at *8 (S.D.N.Y. Aug. 26, 1997).

[93] Samuel A. Thumb and Darrel S. Jackson, E-mail Litigation Puts Companies On Alert: Third-Quarter Review, 3 The Internet News. Legal & Bus. Aspects 10 (Dec. 1998) (noting that "e-mail has become a common type of evidence in civil litigation and periodically plays a role in criminal trials.").

[94] 76 F. Supp. 2d 558 (D.N.J. 1999).

[95] 32 F. Supp. 2d 974 (N.D. Ohio 1999).

[96] Roberta Fusarao, Cases Highlight Need for E-Mail Policies, 32 Computerworld 20 (Oct. 5, 1998).

[97] Linda Tripp sent e-mail released by the House Judiciary Committee to Monica Lewinsky on Oct. 27, 1997. Tripp wrote: "From now on, leave me alone. Don't bother me with all your ranting and raving and analyzing of this situation. And don't accuse me of somehow 'skewing' the truth—because the reality is that what I told you is true. I really am finished, Monica. Share this sick situation with one of your other friends, because frankly, I'm past [being] nauseated about the whole thing. LRT" *See,* The Clinton/Starr Texts (visited Aug. 19, 1999), http://www.ardemgaz.com/prev/Clinton/e-mail.html.

guns" to be incriminating e-mails carrying racist jokes or other objectionable messages.[98]

SPC should list specific content "that should never be discussed in e-mail, such as sensitive personnel issues, company secrets, and personal information."[99] If an employee has any doubt about whether e-mail is an appropriate means by which to transmit sensitive information, that employee should not use e-mail in that case. The typical corporate web site denies the general public access to information accessible only to key employees.

SPC needs a retention policy to protect is e-mail messages and systems. E-mail is classifiable as business records critical for "legal, regulatory, tax, contractual and evidentiary purposes."[100] Companies need a full audit to determine where e-mail records and documents will be stored. SPC needs an electronic record-keeping policy to protect itself in litigation as well as in regulatory enforcement actions.

SPC must consider state and federal regulations in determining what e-mail records should be retained or purged. SPC should give notice to all employees that the company will turn over e-mail records in response to a subpoena. The key elements of a record retention policy are: "(1) the types and form of records to retain; (2) retention periods; and (3) record destruction."[101] SPC needs a record destruction policy for e-mail to avoid swamping its computers in a matter of months.

E-mail messages believed to be deleted may be reincarnated with the assistance of data recovery services. The Justice Department initiated a criminal investigation over the disappearance of thousands of White House e-mail messages sought in a campaign finance hearing.[102]

SPC needs a policy delineating what key documents to retain for tax or regulatory purposes and what documents can be purged on a scheduled basis. Federal and state statutes will dictate the minimum periods for which records must be retained. E-mail messages need not be retained or backed up beyond one year unless a specific duty exists to retain messages beyond that period. Retaining outmoded e-mail messages beyond six months exposes the company to unnecessary risks. One danger of retaining e-mail messages beyond a limited period is the expense of complying with discovery orders. Documents deleted in compliance

---

[98] Beverly W. Garofalo, Technology in the Workplace: Can E-Mail Lead to Liability? What Employers Need to Know to Protect Themselves, 13 Comp. L. Strat. 1 (Apr. 1997) (reporting on lawsuit against Morgan Stanley & Company and Citicorp based on racist jokes transmitted on company's e-mail system).

[99] Elgan, *supra* note 62.

[100] Thomas J. Smedinghoff, Online Law: The SPA's Legal Guide to Doing Business on the Internet, ch. 5 (1996).

[101] *Id.* at 66.

[102] Ann Scales, White House Under Probe Over E-Mails, Boston Globe (visited Mar. 24, 2000), http://www.boston.com/dailyglobe2/084nation/White_House_under_probe_over_e_mails+shtml3/24/00.

with the company's retention policy will reduce the risk and cost of litigation substantially.

E-mail may be stored in many locations, and this may make it difficult for SPC to properly purge all records. E-mail may exist on both the sender(s) and the recipient(s)' personal computers, the e-mail servers that provide e-mail services, or on offline backup material. While SPC can do little to prevent the retention of e-mail on foreign servers, they have implemented a Total Security Policy (TSP) to reduce the risk of unwanted e-mail remaining on their own computing equipment. SPC's TSP contains the following provisions:

1. All SPC employees must set their e-mail software to purge or archive e-mail messages after 14 days.
2. All SPC servers will be set to purge e-mail after 14 days.
3. All SPC employees will be informed that any message saved for more than 180 days must have management approval.
4. All SPC employees will use security software, such as PGP, to do a free-space wipe of their hard drive at end of every week.[103]
5. All SPC servers will use security software to do a free-space wipe at the end of every month.[104]
6. At the end of every quarter, the backup library will be reviewed. All archives more than six-months-old will be destroyed, unless a business reason exists for retaining the record.
7. All SPC's backup media in circulation will be replaced with new media every six months.
8. All SPC employees will be instructed to do a secure delete and purge of any document or e-mail according to its security classification.[105]
9. SPC will create an e-mail and document security classification that includes the following designations:

    (a) Top Secret: Message or document may not be sent by e-mail but only by secure courier. The document or message must be destroyed after recipient reads it, and no copies may be made. No additional distribution will be allowed.

---

[103] Deleting a file does not destroy all traces of the document on the storage medium. The document may still exist on the computer's hard drive, and magnetic traces may exist for an extended period of time. Security software will not only delete the file in the operating systems file management table, it will also write over the space the file occupied with a string of 1's followed by a string of 0's. Successive iterations will enhance the chance that the document will be fully purged. By performing the same operation on a hard disk's free space, it will help ensure that deleted documents remain deleted.

[104] *Id.*

[105] *See* discussion of purging software in note 103, *infra.*

(b)   Secret: Message or document may only be sent by e-mail on internal systems and must be encrypted. The document or message should be destroyed as soon as possible by both the sender and the receiver, and in no case should it be retained after 180 days. No additional distribution will be allowed.

(c)   Confidential: Message or document may only be sent on SPC's internal systems. The document or message should be destroyed by both sender and receiver as soon as possible. No additional distribution will be allowed.

(d)   Sensitive: Message or document should only be sent on SPC's internal systems. It should not be shown to anyone outside the company. It should only be retained with express authority of management.

(e)   Proprietary: Message or document should only be sent to employees with a need to know the information. If sent outside SPC, the message must be encrypted. It should only be retained with express authority of management.

SPC's cost of responding to discovery requests may be overwhelming if all e-mail is kept. Keeping everything will also increase the risk that "spontaneous, sound-byte communication . . . common in internal e-mail" will be uncovered.[106] In a Massachusetts case, an "internal corporate e-mail message followed an incriminating conversation between the defendant and a co-worker."[107] The trial court admitted the e-mail under the excited utterance exception to the hearsay rule.[108] Electronic files may contain inflammatory information in prior drafts not accessible in hard-copy form. A retention policy can reduce the cost of burdensome discovery requests. A company may take "steps to protect against abusive discovery and to avoid any inappropriate disclosure."[109] The plaintiff became a defendant and the employee was charged with a felony for falsifying an e-mail message.[110]

An ex-employee of Oracle was charged with perjury for deleting portions of an e-mail message. The e-mail message discovered simply stated that the vice president of the company was terminating an employee. Computer forensic experts located an electronic version of the e-mail message proving that the e-mail was actually created by the former employee, not by the executive. A company

---

[106] *Id.*

[107] Bester, *supra* note 79.

[108] *Id.*

[109] "Rule 34 does not provide for 'roaming' discovery, which may result if a party were granted direct access to a defendant's computer system." *Id.* (citing Belcher v. Bassett Furniture Indus., Inc., 588 F.2d 904, 906-07 (4th Cir. 1978)).

[110] *Id.* at 15.

destroying e-mail messages may be subject to an adverse inference or have a default judgment entered against it.

> ### [1] Preventive Law Pointer: Electronic Discovery

The typical company's organizational attitude toward e-mail is that it is private and informal. E-mail messages are company documents that are discoverable and the companywide attitude should be that e-mail messages are corporate records. Rule 34 of the Federal Rules of Civil Procedure provides that data compilations may be discovered. Companies need a comprehensive policy on how long e-mail messages should be retained in addition to a policy delineating what to save. If e-mail messages are deliberately destroyed, the company may face liability for the tort of spoliation of evidence or discovery sanctions.[111] The destruction of e-mail may result in an adverse inference that the destroyed message contained evidence that was unfavorable to a company's litigation posture.[112] E-mail needs to be purged on a regular basis to prevent the company computer from being swamped with irrelevant and outdated information.

E-mail should be purged at scheduled intervals rather than as a response to discovery. Requests for the discoverability of e-mail make it imperative that a company change its cultural attitude toward e-mail. Off-color jokes, racist comments, flaming, and emotive battles-of-e-mails within the company or with company outsiders are to be assiduously avoided because they increase the risk of litigation. To protect the company from charges of spoliation of evidence or discovery sanctions, it needs a written retention policy that is enforced. If e-mail messages are destroyed because of routine housekeeping or scheduled purging of the system, the probability is much lower that a court will draw an adverse inference against the company.

---

[111] One of the few spoliation cases involving electronic data was in Applied Telematics, Inc. v. Sprint Communications Co., L.P., No 94-4603, 1996 U.S. Dist. LEXIS 14053 (E.D. Pa. Sept. 17, 1996). In *Applied Telematics*, the plaintiff sought "a default judgment where the defendant failed to prevent relevant data from being overwritten on backup tapes once a week in the normal course of business." The court found the defendant at fault and awarded monetary sanctions for the spoliation of evidence. Committee on Federal Courts, Discovery of Electronic Evidence: Considerations for Practitioners and Clients, 53 The Record 656-666 (Sept./Oct. 1998) (reporting *Applied Telematics* case).

[112] *See, e.g.,* Computer Associates Int'l v. American Fundware, Inc., 133 F.R.D. 166, 170 (D. Colo. 1990) (ordering default judgment for destruction of evidence). *Cf.* State ex rel. Wilson-Simmons v. Lake County Sheriff's Dept., 82 Ohio St. 3d 377 (Ohio 1998) (holding that racist e-mail messages exchanged between government employees was not a public record under Ohio's public records act because these messages did not document activities of a public office).

[D] Electronic Monitoring of Employees

A growing number of companies are monitoring e-mail and Internet communications to prevent exposure for the online torts and crimes of their employees. One estimate is that more than "20 million employees have their e-mail, computer files, or voice mail searched by employers."[113] Even if e-mail is not monitored, it is subject to subpoena.

Courts have upheld the employer's right to monitor and police their e-mail system.[114] In the employment context, courts continue to recognize that employers have legitimate interests in policing their e-mail systems. In an early California case, employees filed a class action against Epson America for the company's routine monitoring of e-mail. The Court of Appeals of California dismissed all claims, finding no invasion of privacy and no unlawful wiretap.[115] A company has an obligation to monitor computer systems for improper use.[116] A growing number of companies have been the target of lawsuits for permitting objectionable e-mail messages to be transmitted on their computer systems.[117]

Private employees do not have a general constitutional right to privacy because they do not satisfy the state action requirement. For public employees, the U.S. Supreme Court in O'Connor v. Ortega,[118] held that the test of "reasonableness" applies to searches and seizures conducted by public employers, rather than the usual Fourth Amendment requirement of a warrant supported by "probable cause."[119]

The federal Electronic Communications Privacy Act (ECPA) prohibits the unauthorized interception and disclosure of electronic communications,[120] but employers will generally require that employees provide consent to monitoring.

---

[113] Felhaber, Larson, Fenlon, and Vogt, What's Happening in Employment Law, 9 Minn. Employment L. Letter 4 (1999).

[114] *See generally*, John Arneo, Note, Pandora's (E-Mail) Box: E-Mail Monitoring in the Workplace, 14 Hofstra Lab. L. J. 339 (1996); *compare,* Heather Rowe, UK Developments Monitoring of E-Mails, 4 Cyber. Law. 34 (Nov. 1999) (arguing that monitoring e-mail without guidelines could violate U.K.'s Human Rights Act of 1998).

[115] Flanagan v. Espon America, BC 007036 (1990) (cited in 41 Boston Bar J. 6, 19 (1997)).

[116] C. Forbes Sargent III, Electronic Media and the Workplace: Confidentiality, Privacy and Other Issues, 41 Boston Bar J. 6, 19 (May/June 1997) (arguing that it is an open question whether an employer has a duty to monitor e-mail messages to discover instances of sexual or racial harassment).

[117] *Id.*

[118] 480 U.S. 709 (1987).

[119] *Id.*

[120] 18 U.S.C. §§ 1367, 2232, 2510 et seq., 2701 et seq., 3117, 3121 et seq. (1997).

The monitoring of every e-mail message is not practical or desirable, just as eliminating all personal use of the computer is a policy impossible to enforce. Companies should enact e-mail and Internet policies that are based on common sense, trust, and discretion.[121] The company's ethos should not be that of Big Brother, but companies have a need to know whether its systems are being used in ways that create serious hazards and risks.[122] A company should not monitor its employee's e-mails without notice and a compelling justification. At minimum, the employer that monitors e-mail should give notice to employees that e-mail is subject to review by a systems administrator. Another common problem with Internet access is the tendency of some employees to surf the Internet for online pornography, sports broadcasts, and other sites unrelated to their work; such "goofing" may detract from workplace performance.[123]

Pennsylvania's House of Representatives introduced legislation requiring notice to employees of electronic monitoring by employers.[124] The Pennsylvania bill requires employers who engage in any type of electronic monitoring to give prior written notice of the types of monitoring that may occur.[125] An employer may monitor, without notice, if it has reasonable grounds to believe that a violation of law or other misconduct has occurred or if a message has contributed to a hostile workplace. If an employer fails to provide notice, it is subject to a "maximum civil penalty of five hundred dollars for the first offense, one thousand dollars for the second offense and three thousand dollars for the third and each subsequent offense."[126]

An organization-wide e-mail and Internet usage policy should be designed in part to reduce employees' "reasonable expectation of privacy." Privacy claims arising out of monitoring employees may be defended successfully to "the degree to which the employer has reserved the right to monitor communications, and the reasons it has engaged in monitoring."[127] Invasion of privacy claims based upon

---

[121] "A sensible Internet usage policy allows employees a certain amount of trust and latitude. Most companies don't check the destination of each and every telephone call to ensure that calls are work-related. Most companies don't mind if employees use their PCs for personal reasons during off hours. . . . However there are some very good reasons for tracking employee Web usage." Tim Wilson, Monitoring Employee Web Usage Is Desirable and Necessary, Comm. Wk, Aug. 11, 1997.

[122] *Id.*

[123] *Id.*

[124] Pennsylvania House Bill No. 5398 requires notice to employees of electronic monitoring by employers. *See* Substitute House Bill No. 5398, Public Act No. 98-142, An Act Requiring Notice to Employees of Electronic Monitoring by Employees (visited Mar. 26, 2000), http://www.cga.state.ct.us/ps98/act/pa/pa-01242.htm.

[125] *Id.*

[126] *Id.*

[127] Restatement (Second) of Torts § 652(b) (1979).

employer's monitoring of e-mail or Internet usage have been largely unsuccessful,[128] but these claims have been expensive and time-consuming.[129] SPC needs to give its employees notice that they have no expectation of privacy in their e-mail or Internet usage.

Accordingly, SPC's e-mail and Internet policy should reserve the right to monitor its employees and should give conspicuous notice that e-mail and Internet usage is subject to monitoring.

[E] Information Security

E-mail and Internet usage policies need to be coordinated with the company's information security policy, which must be tailored to its business plan and corporate organization. An Internet usage policy must convey the importance of security. A company must complete an Internet Security Audit prior to going online.

Curtis Karnow has identified six fundamental principles of information security that apply to businesses of all sizes: (1) Authentication: verifying the identity of a participant; (2) Authorization: determining whether personnel have access to a particular operation; (3) Assurance: a basis for users to determine whether a system is secure; (4) Audit: trail or log to detect security breaches and devise responses; (5) Integrity: a basis for determining whether data is uncorrupted; and (6) Confidentiality: privacy of communication and whether system is used by authorized user.[130] Violating any of these principles can result in problems. A company may have liability for lax security if hackers obtain and disclose personal information of employees, customers, trading partners, or other persons.[131] Suppose a hospital permits a hacker with a "previous conviction for child molestation to access computer files to retrieve the phone numbers of young female patients to whom he then made obscene phone calls."[132] The casual use of passwords can result in compromising a company's computer network. In another case, hackers broke into a university computer and retrieved e-mail addresses and encoded passwords and then sent racist messages to 20,000 e-mail users. The falsely identified "originator" of the messages received death threats, and his reputation was severely harmed.[133]

---

[128] *See, e.g.*, Bourke v. Nissan Motor Corp., Case No. B-68705 (Cal. App. July 26, 1993) (rejecting privacy claim where employee signed agreement that e-mail would be used for business purposes and where he had knowledge of the employer's practice of monitoring).

[129] *See* Gregory V. Mersol, Employer/Employee Rights on the Information Highway—Is There a Right of Privacy? 4 Cyber Law 10 (June 1999) (noting that "invasion of privacy claims, are at present, the most significant claims in connection with e-mail communications").

[130] Karnow, *supra* note 39.

[131] John R. Chritiansen, Liability for Information Security, 3 The Internet Newsl: Legal & Bus. Aspects 7 (Jan. 1999).

[132] *Id.*

[133] *Id.*

[1]   Enforcing Information Security

SPC needs to assure third parties of the security of its web site. An information security policy is evidence that SPC took reasonable precautions to protect the trade secrets and confidential information supplied by third parties.

SPC needs the latest anti-hacking technologies to adequately protect confidential information provided by third parties. The company needs filters for smurf or denial of service attacks and other known security intrusions. SPC needs provisions for the back-up of information on its web site and an emergency preparedness system to protect its customers in the event that the web site is crashed by outside hackers or other causes.

[2]   Antivirus Practices

Computer viruses downloaded from the Internet pose a serious risk to corporate computer systems. Viruses have the potential to delete files, corrupt files, alter data, or lock the user out of his or her computer. Some viruses may crash a computer system or destroy the hard drive.[134] Mandatory virus checking software should be installed on all computers. Spot-checks should be made to determine whether users have disabled these features.

The Internet and e-mail policy should warn employees of the risks of viruses. Additionally, employees who bypass virus-scanning programs should incur consequences. The highly destructive Melissa virus of 1999, for instance, was sent as an innocuous-seeming e-mail attachment.

SPC is susceptible to liability if viruses or malicious code are transmitted through its computers and computer software. A virus, for example, may cause the licensee's computer hard drive to crash resulting in significant economic harm. SPC needs to disclaim liability for viruses and to reallocate the risk of viruses to third parties. A standard clause would state that SPC makes "no warranty as to viruses, and it is the responsibility of the assignee to use antivirus software." SPC needs to be certain that antivirus measures are enforced throughout the company. The systems administrator needs to perform regular checks for viruses and other destructive code. Antivirus software, such as the McAfee package, needs to be installed and used on the desktop and at the mail server. Mail servers now have the capacity to detect viruses and "quarantine infected mail." Antiviral programs need to be frequently updated or they fuster a false assurance of protection.

Before a user is allowed to download anything from a web site, a pop-up warning (or window) should note the risks involved. Antivirus software must be activated for anything downloaded from a third party's web site. Employees who

---

[134] Karnow, *supra* note 39.

download material from the Internet may cause the introduction of malicious computer code or viruses that disables or destroys computer files. A company must install the latest antivirus program and instruct employees not to open e-mail attachments without authorization.

[F] Reducing Regulatory Enforcement Actions

SPC needs to comply with the regulations affecting Internet advertisements, sale of securities, taxation, unfair and deceptive trade practices, pricing laws, and consumer protection. SPC, for example, sells computers to consumers as well as to businesses, and it must comply with the mandatory written warranty rules of the Magnuson-Moss Act, including labeling written warranties as either "limited" or "full," or it risks exposure to a consumer protection lawsuit.

[G] Avoiding Privacy Claims

In order to minimize liability for privacy-related lawsuits, SPC needs to fully disclose its own privacy and data protection practices and give web site visitors an opportunity to "opt out" of any data mining of personal information.[135] The Federal Trade Commission (FTC) is studying ways to protect personal information held by Internet e-businesses. SPC will need to disclose its privacy policy to web site visitors. In addition, SPC's terms and services agreements must cover privacy and data protection issues. SPC must take steps to protect the confidentiality of any personal information supplied by its trading partners or customers. Finally, SPC should act to minimize its exposure to common law torts of privacy, including claims arising out of false light, intrusion of seclusion, and public disclosure of private facts.

SPC must also comply with applicable comprehensive privacy and data protection laws that have been enacted in most countries connected to the global Internet.[136] To minimize its liability for violating the privacy of web site visitors, it must comply with the laws of many nations. The European Union Directive on Data Protection requires privacy safeguards where data is transferred to countries that do not provide "adequate protection." The European Directive on Data Privacy became

---

[135] SPC's privacy policy must be balanced against a need to learn about web site business activity. The e-business economy is based on data mining to quantify monthly hits, user sessions, hits per day, and consumer information. *See generally* Matthew M. Neumeier, E-Commerce Storefront Development and Hosting (E-Commerce: Strategies for Success in the Digital Economy, Practicing Law Institute: Patents, Copyrights, Trademarks and Literary Property Course Handbook Series (PLI Order No. Go-0090, Aug./Sept. 1999) (arguing that information about web site visitors and customers is "one of the most valuable assets a business garners from its web site").

[136] Global Internet Liberty Campaign (GILC), An International Survey of Privacy Laws and Practice (visited Dec. 25, 1999), http://www.gilc.org/privacy/survey.

effective on October 25, 1998. The European Commission has negotiated safe harbor with the United States which must be approved by the European Parliament.

The U.S. must also consider privacy regulations of individual nations. The Swedish Data Protection Act, for example, would prohibit SPC from harvesting names, addresses, and other personal information from its web site without prior consent.[137] Ireland published its data protection rules for privacy on the Internet in November 1998.[138] New Zealand has recently brought its privacy policies up to date to "ensure an adequate level of protection."[139] SPC will need to examine the data protection laws and practices of many countries to ensure that it will not be sued in a distant forum. The United States has yet to be classified as a country with an adequate level of protection under Article 25 of the Directive.

§ 9.04   LAUNCHING AN E-MAIL AND INTERNET USAGE POLICY

The launch of a company-wide policy is a complex undertaking, and it may be difficult to institutionalize when the company has subsidiaries in a number of countries and a complex corporate structure. Multinational corporations may need to consult with unions or other local entities. In West Germany, for example, which has a co-determination system of worker control, a company should obtain approval from the worker's council. If a significant number of employees do not speak English, the e-mail or Internet policy will need to be translated into the relevant languages.

An Internet usage policy should be integrated with employee training. It may be made part of the employment handbook or be signed by new employees. The policy should cover whatever computer systems and electronic information are considered company computer systems and data sources. A contact person should be designated to answer questions employees might have about the policy. In a small or medium-sized corporation, it may be possible to obtain signed acknowledgments from the employees that they have read and understand the terms of an Internet access policy.

[A]   Risk Assessment and Internet Access

Before drafting and implementing a policy, SPC's legal team must first perform a legal audit of its computer system to gain a better understanding of the company's specific risks and dangers. The form of the audit will depend on the nature of SPC's operating systems, its applications, its back-up systems, and its

---

[137] Microsoft Law & Corporate Affairs, Summary of Global Internet Legal Developments 65 (Jan. 1999) (summarizing of global Internet legal developments for the period Oct.-Dec. 1998).

[138] *Id.*

[139] *Id.* at 67.

disaster recovery procedures. What are the sources for potentially relevant electronic information that need to be covered by the e-mail and Internet usage policies?[140]

Policies must be customized to fit business models. Boilerplate forms may identify issues, but every policy should be customized to the organization's specialized needs. An Internet and e-mail policy appropriate for the Defense Department, for example, would not be suitable for Amazon.com or eTrade. Each company needs to determine the appropriate purposes to which its e-mail and Internet access can be put, and then devise its policy accordingly.

If e-mail is used solely for internal purposes, one set of consequences follow. In contrast, if e-mail is used for advertising, transmitting data, and the conduct of trade or commerce, other consequences will follow.

[B] Authenticating and Monitoring E-Mail Usage

Routine checks should be conducted on a weekly basis to determine whether subject and personal authorization policies are followed. The greater the need for confidentiality, the higher the security. "Some confidences are so valuable, that the client will want to take extraordinary steps to protect them."[141] Spot-checks should also be conducted periodically to thwart wrongdoing by those familiar with the timing or patterning of scheduled security audits.

A security policy uses techniques of authentication to determine authorization.[142] Authentication means "to sign, or to execute or adopt a symbol or sound, or encrypt a record in whole or in part, with intent to either identify a party or adopt a record."[143] Routine checks should be made as to whether unauthorized modems or other network connection devices, such as routers, bridges or gate-

---

[140] A Federal Courts Committee recommends some of the following questions be asked to determine the radius of the security risk: "Where are all of the potential sources of electronic information? Cover the following possibilities with the client: floppy diskettes kept by the client, or the employees, in their offices or at their homes; files on individual computer hard drives in employees' offices, on portable drives that can be attached to a computer, on laptops used by employees off site, or on personal computers used by employees at their homes; files on a network or central system's hard drive and servers, and on and off site backup files. What is the client's retention policy with respect to electronic evidence?" Committee on Federal Courts, Discovery of Electronic Evidence: Considerations for Practitioners and Clients, 53 The Record 656, 658 (Sept./Oct. 1998).

[141] William Freivogel, Internet Communications—Part II, A Larger Prospective, VIII Alas Loss Prevent. J. 2, 4 (Jan. 1997) (cited in 3 Hawaii B.J. 6).

[142] Karnow, *supra* note 39; *see also* People v. Lee No. C38925 (Cal. Super. Ct., Jan. 30, 1997) (visited Oct. 2, 2000) http://www.perkinscoie.com (reporting first criminal conviction from falsifying e-mail to extort settlement from employer in sexual harassment action).

[143] U.C.C. § 2-102(2) (Dec. 1, 1998).

ways, have been connected to an internal network.[144] The systems administrator or other person should also design a backup system for company computers. Individual desktops should be set to automatically back-up document every 15 or 30 minutes.

[C]   Employee Education

Preventive law for e-mail and Internet-related hazards must focus on employee education. SPC's principal e-mail or Internet-related hazard is imputed liability for the torts, crimes, and other bad acts of its employees. SPC's primary risk management is in its employment, training, and supervision of its employees.

Commentators advising high tech companies recommend the *Providence Journal* Rule: Employees are instructed not to "write anything in e-mail that you do not want to see on the front page of the *Providence Journal*."[145] Another way of stating this is to caution employees "not to say things in an e-mail that they are not willing to have repeated at the water cooler or in court."[146]

Another technique is to ask employees to visualize their e-mail messages in the hands of a plaintiff's attorney or prosecutor attorney. Yet another more realistic visualization is to ask employees to imagine that their e-mail messages are being read to a jury in an employment termination lawsuit. Summaries or synopses of recent e-mail litigation can serve a training purpose by showing how misuse of the computer system can turn into a tort horror story.

[1]   Use of Internet and E-Mail During Off-Hours

If a company provides an employee with a laptop, desktop, or other computer system used at home, a clear statement should be made of what constitutes appropriate use. The Commerce Department, for example, permits employees to use computers for nonofficial uses: The general guideline is that the Department "expects employees to conduct themselves professionally while using Department resources and [to] refrain from using Department resources for activities that are disruptive to the workplace or in violation of public trust."[147] Under this policy, however, employees may not use printers or supplies for personal use. Further, the policy prohibits the use of government computers for political or partisan purposes, including direct or indirect lobbying.

---

[144] *See* Carnegie-Mellon Computer Emergency Response Team, Investigate Unauthorized Hardware Attached to Your Organization's Network (visited Sept. 6, 2000), http://www.cert.org/security-improvement/practices/p006.html.

[145] *See* Peter Lacourtune, Discovery and the Use of Computer Based Information in Litigation, 45 R.I. Bar J. 9 (Dec. 1996).

[146] *Id.*

[147] *See* U.S. Department of Commerce Internet Use Policy, Appendix 9-1 in this chapter.

Corporate users, like government users, should be warned about using computers for engaging in discriminating conduct, obtaining or viewing sexually explicit materials, or violating state, federal, or international law or a professional code of conduct.[148] The online company, like the government, should not permit users access to subscription or paid Internet sites unless such access serves a business purpose.

[2]   Notice of Monitoring

Although some courts have upheld terminating employees on the basis of intercepted messages where no warning of monitoring was given, it is prudent to include a conspicuous notice of monitoring in any e-mail or Internet access policy. The monitoring warning will be useful evidence that the employee did not have a reasonable expectation of privacy. The Commerce Department's monitoring warning states: "Like all other Government computer use, use of Government equipment for personal use of the Internet may be monitored and recorded. Anyone using Government equipment consents to such monitoring."[149]

Many high tech companies are reluctant to prohibit all personal use of e-mail or the Internet. Such a strict policy would be unenforceable for many Silicon Valley companies. If personal use is permitted, a statement in the policy should caution against personal use that interferes with work. The Commerce Department Internet Use Policy provides the following statement on personal use that may be adapted to the private electronic companies. A Fortune 500 company with foreign subsidiaries will need to adapt their policy to accommodate specific organizational realities. The Commerce Department usage policy provides in relevant part:

> Unless prohibited by the specific policies of the employee's bureau/operating unit, limited personal use of e-mail during duty hours is permissible, as such use will help promote proficiency in electronic communications, including use of the Internet, and provides an alternative method for authorized personal communications, which will promote Government efficiency. At no time may Government e-mail addresses be used in a manner which will give the impression that an otherwise personal communication is authorized by the Department. Personal use of e-mail cannot interfere with the official business of the employee or organization, such as spending an inappropriate amount of time during duty hours (e.g. sending more than four brief messages per day), filling up a mailbox with personal messages so as to prevent official messages from being delivered, or disseminating chain letters.[150]

---

[148] *Id.*
[149] *Id.*
[150] *Id.*

Companies need a written corporate Internet usage policy that fits with their corporate cultures and business models. The goal of a usage policy is to minimize liability caused by employees or independent contractors using corporate computer networks.

[3] Cooperation with Law Enforcement Officials

The policy should note that if monitoring reveals telltale evidence of criminal activity or misconduct, the company may provide evidence to local, state, or federal law enforcement officials. A corporation may be the subject of criminal charges for the theft of confidential information from a business rival. An innocent company may face potential liability for the acts of its malicious employees performed within the scope of their duties. Companies also face the risk that employees or unknown third parties will plant false computer evidence.[151] Lost, deleted, or altered e-mail messages may be reconstructed to determine whether a cover-up or attempt to obstruct justice has occurred.

[D] Enforcement of E-Mail and Usage Policies

An Internet policy may become a dead letter without an enforcement mechanism. An employee may argue that an employer's long-standing custom of not enforcing an Internet usage policy creates an *estoppel* argument; that is, because the employer has enforced the policy arbitrarily or not at all, it is precluded from enforcing the policy against the employee.

SPC should designate someone within the organization to be ultimately responsible for overseeing the company's computer system. The SPC systems administrator needs the necessary training and technical background to assure the availability, integrity, and confidentiality of company e-mail and Internet usage. A leading law company warns companies against the danger of adopting draconian policies that will be unenforceable. Many policies state that computer, e-mail, or Internet access is strictly limited to business use and prohibit *any* personal use.[152] An absolutist policy such as this "loses its value for most, if not all, purposes" if not enforced.[153] The company recommends a policy stating that "occasional, careful, nonoffensive personal use is permitted on the employee's own time."[154]

---

[151] Garrity and Casey, *supra* note 27.

[152] Felhaber, Larson, Fenlon and Vogt, *supra* note 113.

[153] *Id.*

[154] *Id.*

[E]   Even-Handed Enforcement of Internet Usage Policy

The reason for an Internet usage policy is to protect the company, which can be accomplished only by enforcement. An employer that selectively enforces the Internet policy may be exposed to lawsuits based on racial or sexual discrimination. An employer that arbitrarily enforces the policy against middle-aged women employees, for example, may be charged with sex and age discrimination. A company that monitors only the e-mail of black women, while not scrutinizing data messages of other groups, may be charged with both sex and race discrimination.

§ 9.05   E-MAIL AND INTERNET USAGE POLICIES

Every company needs an e-mail and Internet usage policy to reduce liability resulting from the misuse and abuse of corporate computers. Although the media may portray litigation as random lightning strikes beyond a company's control, many online hazards are preventable and avoidable. A preventive law program for the e-mail and the Internet is a required component of any risk management program, and corporate auditing of e-mail or Internet usage reduces the radius of the risk. The corporate counsel will play a significant role in preventive counseling, whether by drawing up an Internet or e-mail policy or by reviewing policies drafted by others.

The e-mail and Internet usage policy should be structured as a contract or written agreement. Computer access should be conditioned upon reading and agreeing to the terms of the usage policies. A technology-leading company should not rely upon a template but should undertake a legal audit before devising its policy.

The usage policy should make it clear that the e-mail system and Internet usage is solely for business purposes by stating specifically that: "The company's computer facilities [include all designated computer systems under the policy] are provided to the employee for business uses." The purpose of this disclosure is to eliminate the widely held perception that the company computer belongs to the employee.

The policy should also include a disclosure about the employee's reasonable expectation of privacy. In many organizations in which passwords are issued, employees often believe that their computer use is private; the belief that e-mail is private is even more widespread. The statement may note that "The Company's equipment may be inspected by an authorized employee at any time even though you may have a password, encryption, or other security device in place." If the company monitors employees' e-mail messages, it should describe permitted uses and the consequences of violating the policy.

The e-mail policy should be enforced, and enforcement should be nondiscriminatory and even-handed. Monitoring web sites can lead to abuses. Failure to enforce the policy generally may result in the company being unable to invoke the policy in a specific instance.

The policy should incorporate graduated methods of discipline. Less serious offenses may be dealt with informally. More serious offenses may be punished by verbal warnings, written reprimands or warnings, payroll deductions, suspensions, or terminations.

The basic policy should explain how crimes, torts, and other liabilities accrue from the misuse or abuse of the computer system. The SPC employee should be advised that downloading unlicensed software, installing it from a CD-ROM, or exceeding the permitted number of licensed copies of software may subject the company and the employee to liability.[155] Downloading pornography or transmitting hate speech may likewise result in liability. In addition, employers should warn all employees that their companies will cooperate with local, state, and federal law enforcement authorities investigating any criminal activities by employees, and that in the event of a subpoena, companies may be required to produce e-mail records.

It is important to give employees clear illustrations of what constitutes a misuse or abuse of the Internet or e-mail. Employees should be warned that inappropriate use of the computer may result in sanctions as well as possible criminal or civil liability. Here is an example of such a statement:

> SPC's communication systems are provided for your use in conducting business on behalf of SPC. Prohibited, inappropriate, or unauthorized use of these systems is grounds for disciplinary action. An example of such misuse or abuse includes such acts as sending anonymous messages using company systems to harass or defame an employee, an organization, or other party.

SPC needs in-house training to help its employees understand the proper use of the e-mail system and the Internet and the principles of information security. Computer users should be required to change their passwords or user identifications periodically. Computer systems used to download data or software or to store data for another company will raise more issues than systems for only internal use.[156]

An e-mail policy needs to take into account the industry and corporate culture and must be tailored to known risks. An e-mail fault tree identifies all of the

---

[155] Tom Lowry, Software Pirates Risk Sailing into Stormy Seas, Comm. World, Jan. 29, 1999 (noting also that "the use of illegal software opens up an organization to software viruses and to lost productivity because unlicensed software is not eligible for software technical support or upgrades").

[156] It is a common practice to lease storage space for databases to other companies. EMC Corporation, for example, provides a web site where companies such as Toys R' Us lease storage space for its databases.

paths that are correlated with known hazards. An e-mail policy does not immunize a business from liability caused by misuse of the company's computer, but the expense of developing a good e-mail policy may be far less expensive than retrofits, lawsuits, or damage to corporate reputations.

[A] Key Issues

[1] Legal Audits

Legal audits of Internet usage involve a careful examination of the legally significant facts of employee's use, misuse, and abuse of the company's computer systems. The objectives for a legal audit of computer usage are to promote efficiency, limit liability, and improve productivity. Does the company have a reporting system that allows employees to report violations of the policies? An online company needs to prevent future legal problems through an operations review of e-mail and Internet usage.[157] How can the company improve its use of e-mail and the Internet?

[2] Legal Autopsies and Near Misses

Corporations need to learn from past mistakes in order to avoid repeating their mistakes. The goal of corporate counsel is to help companies become "first trial learners," avoiding repetitions of their mistakes.[158] Some analysts claim that two kinds of companies do business on the Internet: those who have had e-mail litigation disasters and those who will have them in the future. Prior similar mistakes may be the basis for a claim that the company is ratifying or acquiescing in wrongdoing. Disaster recovery is a part of legal prevention for high technology companies. Corporate counsel can play a key role by analyzing the misuse or abuse of the e-mail system or the Internet that resulted in litigation or a "near miss."

Legal counsel will determine whether charges should be filed against wayward employees, ex-employees, or others who had misused the company computer system. Legal counsel determines the civil and criminal causes of action that may be at issue. Legal counsel will also decide whether to contact law enforcement to investigate a computer intrusion. Legal autopsies of e-mail or Internet abuse are completed to prevent future incidents. The purpose of the audit is to uncover the reasons for a company's direct or indirect liability from abuse of the

---

[157] Edward A. Dauer, Preventive Law Dictates Going to Root Causes to Prevent Claims from Arising, 7 Preventive L. Rep. 12, 13 (Sept. 1988).

[158] A one-trial learner changes its practices in the wake of legal disasters, as opposed to becoming a repeat player litigating the same legal problems over and over.

Internet or the computer system.[159] SPC's team will need to carefully document the steps it takes to recover its computer system after any abuse or intrusion.

[3]   Web Site Activities and Jurisdiction

A company may make a strategic decision to limit its web site activities to minimize the possibility of being "haled into a court in a distant forum." A passive web site may be the source of liability in some jurisdictions. The Internet presents a somewhat uncertain legal environment for determining jurisdictional questions. Calls have been made for an international treaty governing Internet jurisdiction. In the absence of a worldwide solution to Internet governance, however, courts have treated jurisdiction as a question of "old wine in new bottles."

The question still lingers of whether a company that establishes an e-mail system and Internet site is exposed to the risks of being sued everywhere. Many companies will use choice of law and forum clauses to reduce the possibility of litigating in a distant or inconvenient forum. The courts, however, continue to apply a minimum contact analysis to determine jurisdiction. It is clear that personal jurisdiction may not be based simply on a web page and an e-mail address.[160] Similarly, the registration of a domain name alone is not enough to establish it, either, because personal jurisdiction is based on commercial activity. A web site and e-mail system may subject a company to personal jurisdiction. The more active the site, the more likely the exercise of personal jurisdiction in a distant forum.

A California court found that a defendant's passive web site, which permitted e-mail and file transfers but not the taking of orders online, did not constitute jurisdiction for a Canadian company in a domain name dispute.[161] The court found that the protocol of the web site, which required customers to print out an order from the site and then to fax the order to company headquarters in Canada, was evidence that it was a passive site.[162] The court concluded that contacts were insufficient to satisfy the due process requirements of personal jurisdiction.[163] The court compared the site's e-mail capability to electronic response cards, and held that

---

[159] *Id.* at 15 ("Legal autopsies and litigation audits are techniques that run a film backwards—analyses of the portfolio of legal claims designed, like an epidemiological study, to locate the underlying factual causes of legal ill health. Every legal claim is just a late chapter in a much longer story.").

[160] Cybersell, Inc. v. Cybersell, Inc., 130 F.3d 414 (9th Cir. 1997) (finding a web page and an e-mail address alone to be insufficient basis for personal jurisdiction).

[161] Jurisdiction: Desktop Technologies, Inc. v. ColorWorks Reproduction & Design, Inc. Judge Finds No Jurisdiction Over Canadian Company In Domain Name Case, 16 Comp. & Online Indus. Litig. Rptr. 9 (Mar. 16, 1999).

[162] *Id.*

[163] *Id.*

this capability did not alter the site's status as a passive advertisement.[164] For a complete discussion of jurisdiction issues, see Chapter Seven.

[B]   Key Components

[1]   Title

The Internet and e-mail use policy may be divided into separate e-mail and Internet use policies or a combined policy may be used. The policy should be titled appropriately: (1) Company Internet Use Policy; (2) Company E-Mail Use Policy; or (3) Company Internet and E-Mail Use Policy. The title of the policy should be conspicuously displayed on a computer screen as well as in printed materials.

[2]   Purpose of Policy

The document should state the company's purpose for enacting a policy. A policy may simply provide guidance for using information technologies, or it may mandate appropriate uses and define misuses and abuses. The policy should state that the employer owns the e-mail and computer system. Some companies state that they own all e-mail messages as well,[165] but this poses the risk that the company adopts all e-mail messages, even those that might subject them to additional liability.[166] The e-mail policy "does not insulate a business from the effects of employee carelessness or stupidity."[167] The company should incorporate e-mail and Internet horror stories into the training employees receive about the policy.

[3]   Table of Contents

Policies should have indexes of topics covered. Online versions could have a search engine to help employees find topics. Topics will vary depending on the company and industry. Every policy should address key definitions, background, scope, policy, sanctions, risks, rights, and responsibilities.

[4]   Contact Person

Every policy should provide a contact person or persons who can provide sure-footed guidance on interpreting the policy. Feedback forms should be

---

[164] *Id.*

[165] One law company recommends ownership of all data on the company's computers as a means of establishing the right to monitor use. *See* Felhaber, Larson, Fenlon, and Vogt, *supra* note 113.

[166] *See, e.g.,* Stauss v. Microsoft Corp., No. 7433 LEXIS (S.D. N.Y. 1995) (describing sexually explicit e-mail messages in sex discrimination case).

[167] Felhaber, Larson, Fenlon, and Vogt, *supra* note 113.

directed to the contact person. Feedback forms should be reviewed regularly, and companies should respond to them, where appropriate. The contact person should provide an e-mail address as well as a telephone number. All inquiries about the policies should be promptly answered.

[5] Definitions

An e-mail and Internet usage policy should have a glossary of definitions written in plain English and other languages where appropriate. Definitions of terms will include basic definitions covering topics such as systems administrator, legal custodian, e-mail messages, flaming, netiquette, firewalls, discovery, electronic smoking guns, listservs, spam, mail headers, Virtual Personal Networks, URLs, domain names, and web sites.

[6] Background

Policies should have information on why computer use is restricted. A public institution, such as the Commerce Department or a state university, may have Internet legal issues not present in the private economy. The University of North Carolina, for example, enacted the Internet and e-mail policies across all branches of the state college system, based on a model developed by the Computer and Internet Legal Issues Committee.[168]

[7] Scope

The e-mail and Internet policy must state clearly the policy's scope. The scope section of the policy sets forth the persons to whom policies and guidelines apply. Do guidelines vary depending on departmental unit, or do they apply across-the-board to all corporate units? Are policies applicable to closely held corporations or foreign subsidiaries? Are consultants and temporary employees bound to follow the policies? Do policies apply only to the use of the Internet at work, or do they also apply to employer-provided computers in employees' private residences? Are telecommuters subject to the Internet or e-mail use policies? The Department of Commerce Internet Use Policy, for example, applies department-wide, including employees using at home computers provided by the government. Policies should state that they supersede all earlier adopted policies. Providing an effective date of enactment for a policy is also appropriate.

---

[168] *See* University E-Mail Retention Policy, The University of North Carolina at Greensboro, Approved by Chancellor Sullivan, May 13, 1998 (visited July 12, 1999), http://www.uncg.edu/apl/POLICIES/iip019.htm.

It is important to have a clause that e-mail or Internet usage is for business purposes.

[8] Mandatory Terms

This chapter provides a number of mandatory and optional terms for policies. The Internet and e-mail policies will typically be cross-referenced with Internet security and other usage policies. Policies will vary in their stance towards personal use. The Commerce Department, for example, permits government computers to be used only for authorized purposes, but distinguishes between the types of use permitted during working and nonworking hours on equipment provided by the Department.[169] It treats the use of Internet services like the use of any other Government equipment and resources. A company's Internet policy will typically have guidelines for responsible use, including, if needed, a specialized protocol for sensitive or confidential information.

[9] Monitoring E-Mail and Internet Usage

Companies that decide to monitor communications should advise their employees that they plan to monitor their e-mail messages. SPC must conspicuously give notice that it has the right to monitor and review all e-mail and Internet messages. SPC can reduce its risk of invasion of privacy lawsuits by obtaining employees' prior consent to monitoring and review of e-mail and Internet usage.

A growing number of developers sell software that electronically examines an employee's Internet usage.[170] A company may install a software package to monitor all e-mail and Internet usage or to monitor intermittently. Kill files may block incoming messages from individuals repeatedly e-mailing employees in the company for unauthorized purposes. Microsoft, for example, used an e-mail filtering device that relegated e-mail greeting cards to the Spam ashbin.[171] Blocking software may be employed to restrict access to objectionable web sites. Employees may also block e-mail from various individuals and entities to screen out objectionable sites.[172]

Whatever technology or policy is adopted, the company must take steps to train employees in the proper use of the corporate computer system.

---

[169] *See* U.S. Department of Commerce Internet Use Policy, Appendix 9-1 in this chapter.

[170] *See, e.g.,* WinWhatWhere Corp. (visited June 20, 1999), http://www.winwhatwhere.com.

[171] TRO Stops Microsoft's Blocking of Blue Mountain's E-Mail Greeting Cards, 16 Litig. Rptr. 1 (Jan. 19, 1999) (reporting that California judge issued a temporary restraining order against Microsoft in Hartford House, Ltd., v. Microsoft Corp.).

[172] *See, e.g.*, MIMEsweeper developed by Content Technologies filters junk e-mail, and blocks URLs and can be useful when developing a content security policy.

[10]   Conscious Delay

Companies should assess the particular risks attendant to e-mail and Internet usage in their company and take steps to minimize risk. A company should not wait until after a major public relations or legal disaster to formulate an e-mail policy.[173] If electronic documents are requested in discovery, counsel should review them. Counsel may need to advise clients of the importance of preserving the integrity of electronic documents.[174] Electronic data is easier to alter or manipulate than are paper-based documents. A litigant may require the producing party to trace the chain of custody and to attest to the integrity of electronic information.[175]

[11]   Mechanics of Implementation

[a]   *Standard Message Signatures*

For official correspondence, create an e-mail signature that is automatically added to the end of the outgoing message stating the sender's name, address, and title or authority. For incidental personal correspondence, the e-mail should have a standard disclaimer that the communication is personal and not to be imputed to the company. Some companies mandate the use of e-mail signatures that make it clear that the employee's message does not speak for the corporation. Companies should minimally post a disclaimer that the company is not responsible for the contents of the message. They may also want to institute digital or automatic signatures in the proper form.

➤   #### [i]   Preventive Law Pointer: E-Mail Notice

Below is an example of the type of e-mail notice that should be placed on all e-mail messages originating from SPC or any other online company:

This is e-mail from Suffolk Personal Computers (SPC), a Massachusetts company. The contents of this e-mail (and any attachment) are confidential to the intended recipient at the e-mail address to which it has been addressed. You are not permitted to disclose the information in this e-mail to anyone other than this addressee, nor may it be copied or otherwise be retransmitted. If received in error, please contact SPC at 617-573-0000 (Massachusetts,

---

[173] *See generally*, Controlling E-mail and Internet Use: Don't Wait Until It's Too Late to Formulate E-mail Policy, 4 Conn. Employ. L. Ltr. 2 (Apr. 1999).

[174] Committee on Federal Courts, Discovery of Electronic Evidence: Considerations for Practitioners and Clients, 53 The Record 656, 663 (Sept./Oct. 1998).

[175] *Id.* at 663.

USA) and delete the message from your e-mail system. Please note that neither SPC nor the sender accepts any responsibility for viruses, and it is your responsibility to scan attachments (if any). No contracts may be concluded on behalf of SPC or any subsidiary of SPC by means of e-mail communications unless expressly stated by a separate signed written agreement.

[b]   Message Filters

A corporate e-mail system may provide filters that specify subjects to be filtered out. If some unknown outside party is harassing a company, the messages out from given addresses can be filtered. Software filters may be used to block pornographic or other objectionable web sites.[176]

[c]   Spelling Checks

To avoid online spelling errors, require spell checkers to be used for all official e-mail communications. Often, persons write e-mails in an informal style that can at times approach stream-of-consciousness, and they may disregard spelling or grammatical errors. The use of spell checks, formal headings, and a formal signature line is critical for e-mail to be treated as company records.

[d]   Corporate Internet Netiquette

Employees should receive training on Internet norms, often referred to as "netiquette." Netiquette boils down to common courtesy and temperate use of e-mail. E-mail messages may descend into personal or emotional attacks that users would rarely allow themselves in a telephone call or formal corporate letter. E-mail training should emphasize the liability associated with inflammatory e-mail statements that use the company's corporate e-mail return address. It should also cover basic style issues such as not typing messages in ALL CAPS, the Internet equivalent of shouting.

§ 9.06   E-MAIL AND INTERNET USAGE CHECKLISTS

[A]   General Concerns

1. Does the company have an acceptable usage policy? Does the chief administrator of the Internet and e-mail system monitor employees' use of the company computer systems?

---

[176] Software may also help block junk e-mail and URLs and permit SPC systems administrators to enforce information security policies.

2. Is the monitoring narrowly tailored so that it does not constitute an invasion of the employee's right of privacy under the U.S. Constitution, state constitutions, or the common law?[177] Massachusetts, for example, has enacted the Massachusetts Privacy Law, which grants persons "a right against unreasonable, substantial or serious interference with his/her privacy."[178] Massachusetts, as with many other states, attempts "to balance the legitimate business interests of the employer with the privacy rights of the employee."[179]

3. Does the usage policy emphasize that online communications are not private and confidential? A common assumption is that "e-mail is as private and confidential as communication via the U.S. Postal Service. However, most e-mail, voice-mail and computer systems are in fact anything but private and confidential."[180] SPC can reduce employees' expectations of privacy by giving them notice that the system is subject to monitoring.

4. SPC needs to monitor the effectiveness of its usage policies by asking a series of questions. Are the e-mail and Internet usage policies enforced? To whom are misuses reported? Is there a standard protocol for investigating security intrusions or other information security disasters?

5. Are employees consulted appropriately in formulating policies? A multinational corporation with subsidiaries in West Germany, France, and other European countries may need to consult with worker's councils or other groups before launching an Internet or e-mail policy.

6. Many e-mail dangers are the direct result of faulty employment practices. As discussed in Chapter 3, it is the "enemy within" the company, not outside hackers, who poses the greatest security threat to an organization. Employees and other knowledgeable insiders who know the computer system's loopholes and know how to avoid getting caught account for most security breaches. In general, it is not the failure of the firewall or other information technology that leads to a security breach, but rather the failure to detect insiders within the system. No firewall, virtual private network, or other technology can thwart computer attacks by disgruntled employees and other insiders.[181]

"Social engineering" is an information security term describing the use of trickery to gain access to a company computer. A wrongdoer, for example, may pose as a telephone or computer technician to gain access to company computers or may call the computer held desk posing as a trusted insider. Firewalls or other technologies will not detect social engineering faults and other "enemies within."

---

[177] Bourke v. Nissan Motor Corp., No. B068705 (Cal. Ct. of App. 2d App. Dist. July 26, 1993).
[178] M.G.L.A. 214, § 1B ("Massachusetts Privacy Law").
[179] Sargent, *supra* note 116.
[180] *Id.* at 6.
[181] Karnow, *supra* note 39.

7. What can users do with SPC's computer systems? Are the foreseeable uses covered by the written policy?

8. What is the scope of the usage policy? It is important to clearly define the scope of the usage policy to determine how it is to be enforced. Below is a checklist of questions to help determine the scope of the usage policy:

(a) Are there separate policies on e-mail and Internet usage?

(b) Are training modules adapted to SPC's e-business activities and plans?

(c) Does the Internet policy cover postings to listservs or USENET discussion groups?[182]

(d) Does SPC's policy address e-mail exchanges both within and beyond the company?

(e) Whom do SPC's e-mail and Internet usage policy cover?

(f) Does the policy cover all employees, including those in foreign subsidiaries?

(g) How should the policy be adapted to meet local conditions? An e-mail policy launched in Switzerland will require translation into German, Italian, and French. A policy launched in Canada will require translation into French to comply with Quebec statutes. A web site launched in France will also need to comply with French language requirements.

(h) Does SPC's policy cover consultants?[183]

(i) May the company monitor the electronic communications of consultants, temporary workers, and other employees?[184]

---

[182] The Internet contains listservs, or mailing list services, that permit communications about particular subjects of interest to groups of people. Subscribers submit messages on the list topic to the listserv; these are then forwarded via e-mail to all subscribers. A corporation may be concerned if employees use the corporate e-mail system to transmit messages on listservs devoted to controversial topics, such as abortion, hate groups, swapping, and many other topics. A policy may prohibit distributing messages on nonwork topics. A listserv can have thousands of participants, and it is possible that a defamatory statement will be attributed to a company not just one or more of its employees.

[183] Consultants may be the source of considerable liability. The Seventh Circuit recently upheld a lower court ruling in which a corporate consultant was held liable for inducing a breach of contract. The Seventh Circuit stated that the consultant's privilege is a qualified privilege limited to advice within the consultant's engagement. *See*, Consultant Liable for Inducing Breach of Contract, 15 Comp. L. Strat. 1 (Mar. 1999) (citing J.D. Edwards & Co. v. Podany, No. 98-2486, 1999 U.S. App. LEXIS 2666 (7th Cir. Feb. 22, 1999)). Uncertainty exists as to what aspects of e-mail policy would apply to a consultant in the absence of a specific agreement with the consultant or a management-consulting company concerning acceptance of the policy.

[184] Anderson Consulting LLP v. UOP and Bicker & Brewer, No. 97 C-5501, 1998 U.S. Dist. LEXIS 1016 (D. Ill. Jan. 23 1998) (visited July 7, 1999), http://www.philipsnizer.com/int_synopses.htm.

(j) What records are kept of e-mail and Internet usage? Are the records monitored or reviewed? Who reviews them? How long are e-mail messages retained?

(k) What type of analysis (if any) is applied to e-mail and Internet usage records? Does the company develop profiles of risk or danger based on empirical studies of its employees' e-mail or Internet usage?

(l) Does the company have an emergency preparedness team to investigate promptly discovered misuses or abuses of e-mail and the Internet? Does the company have a prescribed method for investigating abuses and misuses of its e-mail or Internet systems? Employees should not be disciplined or sanctioned without a proper investigation or due process, as described in employee handbooks or other company policies. The general rule should be that a company should make "no sudden moves" in disciplining employees.

(m) Does the online company have a corporate counsel or consult outside law firms about its e-mail and Internet policies? What role does counsel play in investigating and enforcing these policies? Corporate counsel will often play a critical role as point person in an internal investigation.

(n) What procedures have been instituted for an internal investigation? A thorough internal investigation and appropriate discipline of the transgressing employee may mitigate or obviate vicarious liability of the company.

(o) What "spin control" or disclosures should be made if e-mail abuses are reported outside the company? In some cases, the public relations department may need to make a public statement if e-mail messages with company addresses have exposed the company to bad publicity or worse.

(p) Does the systems administrator monitor the Internet for use of company trade names, trademarks, or return e-mail addresses? The posting of e-mail with a company message to a hate group, for example, may tarnish the company's reputation.

(q) Does a company take prompt steps to punish employees who abuse e-mail or computer systems? A company's prompt disavowal of the employee's action and its disciplining of the employee will, for example, preclude a finding that the company ratified the employee's actions.

(r) Does the online company have a contingency plan for recovering from an intrusion or abuse of its e-mail or Internet systems?

(s) Does SPC have a disaster recovery plan? To reduce the radius of the risk, corporate e-mail systems should not be used by employees to conduct extraneous online businesses, romances, solicitations, or political organizing.

[B] Usage Disclosures

Does the company e-mail or Internet policy incorporate the following provisions?—

- The employer owns the e-mail system.

- Company e-mail is designated for use for business purposes only (no solicitation or distribution).

- The employee acknowledges that e-mail may be monitored and disclosed by the employer.

- Humor and sarcasm, which are often misinterpreted, should not be used in e-mail.

- The e-mail system is not used for personal matters or comments about others.

- E-mail messages should not be sent in anger.

- All messages are to be deleted 30 days after they are sent, unless archived by the recipient.

- Employees should archive only important or critical messages.

- Employees should organize archived messages by subject and should delete groups of messages when they are no longer needed.

- Archived messages will be subject to review and may be required to be produced in the event of litigation.[185]

[C]   Information Security and Usage Policies

All online companies will have usage policies that set forth the conditions for computer usage or access. The following is a checklist of access and usage control issues.

1. Employees must change their passwords regularly and must use difficult-to-guess passwords, that is, not their first names, the names of family members, or other similar, easily "cracked" passwords. The majority of PC purchasers use the default password that comes with the machine. Many other users utilize easily guessed passwords, such as the user's first name. SPC may install a password-cracking program that identifies easily guessed passwords and may require employees to change their passwords regularly.

2. Does the policy limit employees' access to the Internet? Public employers that use blocking software to limit access to sexually explicit content

---

[185] Peter V. Lacoutre, Presentation at the Rhode Island Bar Association Annual Meeting, June 1996, 45 R.I. Bar J. (1998).

may be violating the First Amendment.[186] First Amendment challenges for blocking access to objectionable web sites or for locking employees out of their computer systems may be made for public but not private employers. Unanticipated consequences may occur from well-intentioned efforts to block access to objectionable content. A private university or think-tank, for example, may be researching the topic of silicon breast implants. Software that blocks sites mentioning the word "breast" may inadvertently block web sites critical to the research mission.

3. Does the e-mail system use pop-up disclaimers and warnings before users can access the system that provide conspicuous notice of the prevailing e-mail policies? Disclaimers in the form of conspicuous pop-up windows may also be used in corporate web sites before a user is permitted to view and/or download data, images, or other information. A general disclaimer should, essentially, warn web site users that they access the corporate web site at their own risk. It is theoretically possible that users may be injured by posted information, ranging from bomb making instructions to home remedies. If SPC permits employees and others to post information on a web site listserv, the company should disclaim any responsibility for third party's torts, crimes, or objectionable activities.[187] Pop-up warnings should advise all employees of e-mail policy and should require "click" agreement with the usage policy before they can proceed to log onto company computers.

➤ **[1] Preventive Law Pointer:
Example Of a Log-In Pop-Up Warning**

The log-in process is an occasion to bind the user to terms and conditions of use. By completing the log-in process, you are acknowledging and consenting to the proper use of SPC's e-mail and Internet usage policies. If you are not an authorized user, please discontinue the log-in process now. If you do not agree to the terms of this agreement, please discontinue the log-in process now. If you have any questions about authorized use and related issues, please refer to the following web site: http://inline.SPC.com/legal/e-mail/policy/. All employees are required to sign a consent form that authorizes SPC Corporation to monitor the electronic communications of its employees.

[D] Training and Education

SPC's training and education module on e-mail and Internet usage is critical to its goal of reducing liability. All employees should be required to sign the e-mail and Internet usage policies to indicate that they are aware of the content of the

---

[186] Urofsky v. Gilmore, 216 F.3d 401 (4th Cir. 2000) (holding that the regulation of state employees' access to sexually explicit material did not violate the First Amendment).

[187] *See also* § 5.05.

policies. Even if SPC's employees misuse the system, this evidence of the employee training or education program may mitigate civil penalties or damages. The following is a checklist for employee education and training issues:

1. What methods are used for training the supervisory staff on the proper uses of the corporate e-mail system? What training is given to new employees or has been given to existing employees? Does the training include an explanation of the purposes for which the e-mail and Internet may be used? Employees may be required to agree to the terms and conditions of the e-mail and Internet policies before being given a password. Pop-up screens may be developed to remind the user that the systems are for business use only.

The pop-up message and policy should explain that all messages are stored and are subject to monitoring and review by the systems administrator. The employee may be asked to consent to the terms and conditions of the e-mail system including recording and monitoring of messages.[188] Many companies use a statement specifying that the employees' use of the system constitutes their consent to company usage policies.[189] Are training modules updated in response to changes in the corporate or legal environment?

2. Does the training explain the company's policy on the personal use of e-mail? SPC should consider adding disclaimers to personal messages to the effect that the data message is not an official correspondence from the company. Disclaimers may also state that "the sender does not have authority to enter into contracts on behalf of SPC." SPC's training should explain the special hazards of e-mail, such as its instant transmission.

3. What ongoing activities communicate the corporate e-mail and Internet usage policies? Does the company use warning screens when the user logs onto the computer to advise the user about known security vulnerabilities, restricted activities, and other security-related information?

4. The e-mail training and education program should be part of new employee orientation. The training module should explain and illustrate the legitimate and illegitimate uses of company computers. All employees must be instructed about the consequences of violating the Internet usage or e-mail policies. As e-mail and Internet usage policy evolves, a mechanism should be in place for updating the training of existing employees. Changes to the e-mail or Internet usage policy can be explained in a click wrap agreement.

---

[188] The employee's consent to monitoring is a well-established defense to the Electronic Communication Privacy Act (ECPA). "In order to avoid potentially violating state and federal wire tapping laws, as well as the ECPA, employers may want to include a statement that the employee's use of the e-mail system constitutes their consent to the company's recording and monitoring of the employee's e-mail messages." Sargent, *supra* note 113.

[189] *Id.*

5. Does the e-mail and Internet usage-training module cover the pitfalls of misdirected e-mails? The danger of misdirected e-mail is legendary. Many law companies have notices about the risk of misdirected faxes. A similar warning or disclosure should appear on e-mail messages in the event that they are misdirected. Misdirected faxes and e-mails are a staple of litigation, occurring often when overworked lawyers or paralegals inadvertently include an opponent in an e-mail "cc." A misdirected e-mail became the smoking gun in a Massachusetts trade secrets case.[190] The systems administrator may develop a technical fix to avoid inadvertently sending e-mail messages to competitors or opposing counsel. It is an open question as to whether the inadvertent access of e-mail is an "implied waiver of the attorney-client privilege as it is for misdirected faxes."[191]

6. The e-mail and Internet usage policies should include employee training about the discoverability of electronic information.[192] Is there a training module on electronic smoking guns? What training techniques are used to teach proper e-mail and Internet usage? Does the company use role-playing, video presentations, literature distribution, posters, letters from management, and online information to convey its position on the proper use of the Internet and e-mail? The synopses of cases may be incorporated into training. In a 1994 sex discrimination case, the smoking gun was an e-mail message stating "I want you to get that [redacted] out of here. I don't care what you have to do."[193]

7. Is there a training module on the misuse of e-mail to spread rumors or make derogatory comments about co-employees, supervisors, trade partners, competitors, or other third parties that may result in lawsuits? Does the training program include information on copyright protection accorded web site materials and the legal consequences of unauthorized copying?

8. Is e-mail monitored to determine whether employees are misusing or abusing their computer accounts? A nongovernment employer's search of an employee's computer files will not violate the Fourth Amendment. The court in United States v. Simons[194] held that an employer's search of an employee's computer hard drive did not violate the Fourth Amendment of the United States Constitution. The Fourth Amendment "search and seizure" protection applies against government intrusions and is inapplicable to private employers.

---

[190] Baystate v. Bentley Systems, Inc., 946 F. Supp. 1079 (D. Mass. 1996).

[191] Evan R. Shirley, Dilbert, Supermodels, and Confidentiality of E-Mail Under Hawaii Law, 3 Hawaii B.J. 6 (Mar. 1999).

[192] Discovery of Electronic Evidence: Considerations for Practitioners and Clients, 53 The Record 656 (Sept./Oct. 1998).

[193] Marianne Lavelle, Digital Information Boom Worries Corporate Counsel, Nat'l L.J., May 30, 1994, at B1 (noting that defendant settled the discrimination case for $250,000).

[194] 29 F. Supp. 2d 324 (E.D. Va. 1998).

If a company conducts its search in cooperation with the local, state, or federal government, the right against unreasonable searches and seizures may be triggered. This was not the case in *Simons* where the employer was not acting in concert with the government. As with other constitutional rights, the right against government intrusion is balanced against public or social interests.

9. Does the training explain how cultural attitudes toward e-mail, such as its informality, may result in increased liability? Angry diatribes and "battles of emotional e-mail messages" are a formula for legal liability. The training module should use examples of how informal e-mail messages lead to a lawsuit. The training should emphasize that e-mail is discoverable and will be treated by the courts as e-records.

10. Does the training explain that e-mail messages should have the proper emotional tone? An e-mail message should be composed with care, and employees should avoid overly emotional diatribes or "battles of the e-mails."

11. Is there a feedback form to encourage employees to comment on the e-mail and Internet usage policies? The feedback form should identify a contact person who is available to clarify any aspect of SPC's e-mail or Internet usage policy.

12. Does the training module illustrate the risks of transmitting or forwarding jokes or off-color stories on the company's e-mail system? The training module should cite prior cases in which a company was charged with maintaining a hostile work environment because of the transmission of jokes of a sexual nature. Prior similar acts of e-harassment may make a company directly liable as acquiescing or ratifying a hostile workplace.

13. Are employees advised of the hazard of transmitting or forwarding ethnically, racially, or sexually insensitive jokes over the company e-mail system or the Internet?[195] Courts have held that while one or two racial e-mail messages will not in themselves constitute a hostile work environment, they may represent the beginning of a pattern of harassment.[196] Prior similar harassing messages, however, make it possible for a plaintiff to prevail on a claim of a hostile work environment. If a company had knowledge of prior similar incidents and took no action, an argument may be made that it ratifies the misconduct. A company's reprimand of employees guilty of sending offensive e-mail is key to a

---

[195] A company will likely prevail in a claim in which an insensitive e-mail joke alone constitutes the evidence of a hostile work environment. The cost of defending against these claims, however, is not insignificant.

[196] Owens v. Morgan Stanley & Co., Inc., 1997 Westlaw 403454 (S.D. N.Y. 1997) ("As a matter of law [the sending of a single racist e-mail message], while entirely reprehensible, cannot form the basis for a claim of hostile work environment"). Curtis v. DiMaio, No. QDS 02760859 (E.D. N.Y. Apr. 23, 1999) (holding that the transmission of two racially insensitive jokes did not constitute a hostile work environment) (visited July 7, 1999), http://www.phillipsnizer.com/int_synopses.htm.

defense against claims of Title VII, civil rights claims, or hostile work environment claims.[197] Therefore, an e-mail monitoring policy should also note that formal reprimands will follow when any offensive content is reported or discovered.

[E] Disaster Recovery Checklist

The Computer Emergency Response Team (CERT) at Carnegie-Mellon University was originally started by the Department of Defense following an Internet "worm" attack that crashed computers throughout the country.[198] The CERT Coordination Center provides incident response services to web sites that have been victimized by attacks. CERT also publishes security alerts and research on information security and computer intrusions.

CERT's Coordination Center provides the following tips for disaster recovery, which may be adapted to any misuse or abuse of an e-mail or Internet system.

1. Before you get started.

    (a) If you have a security policy, consult your policy;

    (b) If you do not have a security policy:

        i.   Consult with management;

        ii.   Consult with your legal counsel;

        iii. Contact law enforcement agencies; and

        iv.   Document all of the steps taken to recover from an intrusion.

2. Regain control.

    (a) Disconnect compromised system(s) from the network; and

    (b) Copy an image of the compromised system(s).

3. Analyze the intrusion.

    (a) Look for modifications made to system software and configuration files;

    (b) Look for modifications to data;

---

[197] Daniels v. WorldCom Corp., No. Civ. A.3:97-CV-0721-P, 1998 WESTLAW 91261 (N.D. Tex. Feb. 23, 1998).

[198] *See* www.cert.org/nav/aboutcert.html (visited July 31, 2000).

    (c)   Look for tools and data left behind by the intruder;

    (d)   Review log files;

    (e)   Look for signs of a network sniffer;

    (f)   Check other systems on your network; and

    (g)   Check for systems involved or affected at remote sites.

4.   Contact CERT/CC and other sites involved.[199]

    (a)   Contact company official charged with incident reporting;

    (b)   Contact the CERT Coordination Center; and

    (c)   Obtain contact information for other sites involved.

5.   Recover from the intrusion.

    (a)   Install a clean version of your operating system;

    (b)   Disable unnecessary services;

    (c)   Install all vendor security patches;

    (d)   Consult CERT advisories, summaries, and vendor-initiated bulletins;

    (f)   Cautiously use data from backups; and

    (g)   Change passwords.

6.   Improve the security of your system and network.

    (a)   Review security using the UNIX Configuration Guidelines;

    (b)   Review the security tools document;

    (c)   Install security tools;

    (d)   Enable maximal logging; and

    (e)   Configure firewalls to defend networks.

7.   Reconnect to the Internet and update your security policy.

    (a)   Document lessons learned from being [root] compromised;

    (b)   Calculate the cost of this incident; and

---

[199] Also contact federal, state, and local law enforcement agencies, if appropriate.

(c)   Incorporate necessary changes (if any) in your security policy.[200]

[F]   Checklist for Internal Corporate Investigations

1.   **What circumstances and conditions determine special investigations of employee's e-mail or Internet usage?** What kind of action was taken?

2.   **When is the Internet Service Provider (ISP) contacted?** Is there an ISP contact available 24 hours a day, 7 days a week?

3.   **What records does the ISP keep to document Internet abuses?** Does the company permit its employees to use private chatrooms or send Instant Messages? America Online, for example, keeps no records on private chatrooms or its Instant Message feature.

4.   **What action was taken to punish the employee: verbal warnings, reprimands, suspension, or termination of employment?**

5.   **What type of report is submitted?** Does the Internet usage policy require a report? If so, what is its intended audience? Are incident reports used to develop risk profiles?

6.   **At what point in an investigation is law enforcement contacted?**

7.   **Have SPC's managers been consulted to facilitate internal coordination?**

8.   **Is a legal investigation required?** What is the role of corporate counsel? Is there an emergency preparedness team to deal with severe abuses of the Internet or e-mail usage policy?

9.   **In the case of an attack on SPC's computers or the introduction of malicious code, has law enforcement been consulted?** Has the incident been reported to the CERT Coordination Center at Carnegie-Mellon University? Does SPC receive CERT advisories? Does SPC have telephone numbers and often contact information for CERT Coordination Center advisors?

10.   **What steps have been taken to recover from an intrusion?** Has SPC's security policy been updated to reflect new security vulnerabilities? Is the computer system secure?

11.   **What local, state, or federal laws have been violated?** At what stage should law enforcement agencies be contacted?

12.   **What is SPC's legal responsibility to inform third parties about intrusions?**

13.   **Should the local Federal Bureau of Investigation (FBI) field office be contacted?**[201] Companies should not hesitate to enlist the expertise

---

[200] CERT Coordination Center, *Improving Security* (visited Mar. 17, 2000), http://www.cert.org/tech_tips/root_compromise.html.

[201] The web site for the FBI National Computer Crime Squad (NCCS) is http://www.fbi.gov/nipc/index.htm.

of cybercrime units of the FBI, Department of Justice, or state attorneys general.

14. **Should the U.S. Secret Service be informed?** In general, the U.S. Secret Service should be informed if an intrusion involves the theft or abuse of credit card information, threats to the President of the United States, and impersonation of the President of the United States through forged e-mail.[202] The Secret Service main phone number is (202) 435-7700. The number for the Financial Crimes Division, Electronic Crimes Section, is (202) 435-7607.[203]

15. **What is the nature of Internet-related threats?** If racist or sexist e-mail messages are transmitted to SPC employees or others, has legal counsel been notified? Many companies have human resources departments or equal opportunity units that handle this type of event.

16. **Who else has been notified?** SPC may also need to notify others in the organization responsible for investigating discrimination claims. Doing nothing is not an option, because a company may be deemed to ratify or acquiesce in wrongdoing if it takes no remedial steps. The steps a company has taken to investigate e-mail misuse serve as documents in a defense against charges that the company ratified the wrongdoing of its employees.

17. **Is the internal investigation conducted in a spirit of good faith and fair dealing?** Does it employ procedures specified in the company's usage policies? The investigation of e-mail or Internet misuse must be fair-minded and in accordance with established policy.

18. **Have employees been informed of the negative consequences of violating usage policies?** Employees must have notice of the consequences of misusing e-mail or the Internet. The use of pop-up warnings on computer screens may be used to reinforce training modules.

19. **Is a progressive method used to discipline employees for misuse and abuse of the Internet?** Sanctions for misuse of e-mail or the Internet should consist of graduated steps, ranging from informal reprimands to dismissals. Is a system of progressive discipline in place that includes giving notice of violations and calibrating punishment from reprimands to dismissals?[204]

---

[202] CERT Coordination Center, Improving Security (visited Mar. 9, 2000), http://www.cert.org/tech_tips/root_compromise.html.

[203] *Id.*

[204] English philosopher Jeremy Bentham was the first criminologist to advocate making punishment proportional to the offense.

20. **If a company does not have a prescribed method for conducting internal investigations, it should develop an enforcement mechanism before launching usage policies.**

21. **Who is responsible for internal investigations of the misuse and abuse of computer systems?** Is that committee or person different from the personnel that installed or designed the computer system?

22. **What procedures have been instituted to ensure a fair and orderly investigation?** Is corporate counsel consulted prior to launching an investigation? Does the corporate security committee have good contacts with local, state, and federal law enforcement?

23. **What technologies have been installed for electronic audits of prohibited URLs and other restricted web sites?**

24. **What procedure has been instituted for reporting abuses?** Abuses of e-mail and the Internet may constitute sexual or racial harassment.

25. **Have employees been trained to recognize abusive, unlawful, or inappropriate e-mails?** Has the training explained how e-mail abuse can subject the employee to personal liability? Has the training explained how a company may be found vicariously liable for a hostile work environment claim arising out of e-mail or Internet abuse?

26. **Have employees been warned about accessing objectionable web sites or employing obscene or pornographic screen savers?** Have employees been warned about visiting pornographic commercial or noncommercial web sites? Unlawful pornography is more frequently found on Usenets than on commercial sites. A recent survey of Usenet newsgroups uncovered more than "50 sites whose newsgroup title alone suggests the availability of unlawful content."[205]

27. **Has blocking web sites prevented objectionable materials from being transmitted via computer bulletin boards?**

28. **Has the company given notice that it intends to monitor the e-mail and Internet usage of employees?**

[G] Issues for Systems Administrators

Systems administrators must be trained to police the e-mail and Internet in a manner consistent with the desired business model and corporate culture. The systems administrator's e-mail monitoring must balance the privacy interest of the employees against the employer's legitimate interest in preventing misuse and abuse. The systems administrator will normally have the task of monitoring excessive use or abuse of e-mail or Internet access. The checklist below was designed

---

[205] Garrity and Casey, *supra* note 27.

to help companies to develop an effective systems administrator role; SPC, for example, must designate someone within the organization to take ultimate responsibility for overseeing the e-mail system.

In a large multinational corporation, numerous contact people may be needed to coordinate Internet and e-mail usage so employees can report abuses of the computer systems promptly. A company such as SPC should appoint a central administrator or webmaster to assure that its e-mail and Internet systems are used in compliance with company guidelines. In the absence of such an administrator, a systems administrator should receive the specialized training necessary to assure the integrity, availability, and confidentiality of e-mail and Internet usage. SPC should employ a qualified systems administrator or webmaster to monitor its e-mail policy.

The systems administrator may be appointed to monitor the e-mail system, web site, and Internet usage patterns. The e-mail auditor should *not* be the same person as the e-mail or Internet systems designer, who may have a blind eye to its vulnerabilities. It is critical that e-mail usage be audited by an independent professional that does not have a stake in the design of the computer system and can therefore be open to its vulnerabilities.

1. Does SPC's systems administrator for the e-mail and Internet computer systems understand the hazards, risks, and vulnerabilities associated with the misuse of e-mail?

2. Corporate counsel should meet with the systems administrator to explain legal vulnerabilities and the company's obligation to comply with any electronic discovery ordered by the courts. E-mail messages are considered to be records which may be subject to discovery. A company with millions of e-mail messages originating in a corporate extranet may find it expensive to comply with discovery orders. Courts, for example, may require a company to produce hard copies of e-mail messages.[206] Corporate counsel may want to obtain estimates for the cost of retrieving electronic information, including e-mail, to support motions to share the cost of producing this information.[207]

3. Has the systems administrator been briefed on legal risks and vulnerabilities regarding e-mail and Internet systems? Does the systems administrator have a good understanding of the litigation and other risks attendant on e-mail and Internet access?

4. Does the systems administrator also administer SPC's program of software licensing? Does the software license agreement have established procedures for determining whether software use is in compliance with the company's license agreements?

---

[206] Committee on Federal Courts, Discovery of Electronic Evidence: Consideration for Practitioners and Clients, 53 The Record 656, 663 (Sept./Oct. 1998).

[207] *Id.* at 665.

5. What procedures are in place for training employees in the importance of not downloading unlicensed software? The systems administrator may implement an automatic inventory program to enforce this policy.

6. The systems administrator should give strict scrutiny to questionable hyperlinks to web sites that could expose the company to liability.[208]

7. Does the systems administrator perform regular checks of the e-mail and Internet computer systems? Periodic spot checks must be conducted on a regular basis to investigate known hazards and risks.

8. Does the systems administrator check firewalls and software filters on a regular basis? Does the systems administrator check log files of web site activity at least twice a day?

9. The web site should be periodically checked for applets. "An applet is a program written in the Java™ programming language that can be included in an HTML page, in much the same way an image can be included."[209]

10. Are web site visitors warned about the hazards of applets? Before a visitor is permitted to download an applet, he or she should be warned of their potential dangers. A Java™ technology-enabled browser will cause the applet's code to be transferred to the accessing computer system and executed by its browser.[210] The Java™ Virtual Machine Software may reduce the radius of risk of dangerous applets. The primary risk of applets is that they will infect company computers with malicious codes.

11. Is the systems administrator responsible for updating the e-mail and Internet Usage policies? Are incident reports used to draft modifications to the policies?

[H] Role of Counsel

1. Does corporate counsel review the company e-mail and Internet policy on a regular basis to ensure compliance with new statutes or regulations?

2. Do the usage policies comply with state and federal laws, including the Federal Wiretap Act, the Electronic Communications Privacy Act, the right of privacy, and other applicable laws and regulations?

---

[208] Employees who link the company name to hard core pornography, hate speech sites and other objectionable material will create embarrassment if not liability for the company. Another danger is employee use on company computers of unlicensed versions of popular software. Not only is this against the law, but it subjects the company to potential litigation. *See generally*, Lowry, *supra* note 155.

[209] Java, The Source for Java™ Technology, Java.sun.com, Applets (visited Aug. 18, 1999), http://java.sun.com/applets/index.html.

[210] *Id.*

3. What role does outside counsel play in developing or reviewing the e-mail or Internet usage policies? SPC's corporate counsel may seek the assistance of outside counsel for Internet-related legal issues.

4. Does the corporate counsel play a role in determining the hazards of the e-mail and Internet systems and the probability of their occurrence?

5. Does the due diligence include revising policy in light of legal developments or litigation over e-mail or Internet usage?

6. What steps are taken to avoid known e-mail or Internet legal vulnerabilities? Does the company learn from history, or will it be condemned to repeat its mistakes?[211]

7. How are the e-mail and Internet usage policies revised? By whom? Is an audit conducted on a regular basis? Does this result in revisions to revises and updates in the e-mail and Internet usage policy?

8. Does the audit committee evaluate feedback forms from employees regarding the policy?

9. How are the policies kept up to date? With the Internet, "all things change. . . . There is nothing . . . which is permanent. Everything flows forward; all things are brought into being with a changing nature."[212] Internet and e-mail usage policies need to be continually updated, or they will soon become "too vague, outdated, or not actively enforced."[213]

10. Is information learned about the e-mail and Internet policies incorporated into training modules?

11. What procedures are institutionalized to ensure that employees understand and comply with the e-mail policy?

12. What role does corporate counsel have in developing training modules to prevent legal troubles? Is e-mail and Internet usage part of an ongoing program of corporate education?

13. Are the e-mail and Internet usage policies audited for workability, accessibility, and "plain English"? The usage policy must be tailored for the company's size, economic standing, and scope of business (that is, whether it is a national or multinational online corporation). The type of policy must be customized for the particular needs of the company. If most or many employees do not speak English, is the policy translated into their primary language?

14. Does the policy comply with the laws of other countries? In the case of companies with foreign subsidiaries, policies must be tailored for semantic nuances and cultural differences, as well as for foreign regulations and laws. In many European countries, for example, Internet usage policies may be challenged

---

[211] As George Santayana stated "Those who cannot remember the past are condemned to repeat it."

[212] Shirley, *supra* note 191 (quoting the Roman poet Ovid, 43 B.C.–A.D. 17).

[213] Garrity and Casey, *supra* note 27.

on privacy grounds. If employee consultation is required with worker's councils in a regime of self-management, consultation with employee representatives should take place before, not after, the launch of a policy.

15. Is corporate counsel included in the emergency preparedness team? Does corporate counsel supervise the monitoring of e-mail or Internet usage? Does monitoring balance employees' privacy expectations with the company's "need to know"? The courts have generally upheld the right of employers to monitor and intercept employees' e-mail messages transmitted over the company's computer system.[214]

16. Does the corporate counsel have contacts and readily accessible telephone numbers and e-mail addresses for local, federal, and international law enforcement officials? Does the corporate counsel subscribe to Carnegie-Mellon's CERT Coordination Center advisories?

17. Does the corporate counsel review CERT advisories and receive updates on a regular basis?

18. Does the corporate counsel receive a briefing on computer system vulnerabilities? After security breaches, does the counsel receive a briefing on how the computer system has been reconfigured to prevent similar intrusions in the future? CERT found that hackers were able to victimize nationally known companies with denial of service attacks by exploiting already well-known vulnerabilities. SPC may avoid similar attacks by following CERT advisories and incident notes.

19. What role does counsel play in helping the company to recover from an intrusion or attack by an employee or third party?

20. Has counsel consulted with the usage policy developers and enforcers to be sure that proper steps are followed? The first step in recovery is to consult the company's security policy.

21. Has counsel documented all of the steps taken in recovering from attacks and regaining control of the computer system in the event it is compromised?

22. Is the corporate counsel active in looking for Internet hazards, as opposed to reacting to a litigation disaster?

[I] Workplace Issues

1. Has SPC installed blocking software programs to limit employee access to objectionable sites?

2. Does filtering and logging software monitor e-mail usage?

---

[214] Smyth v. The Pillsbury Co., 914 F. Supp. 97 (E.D. Pa. 1996) (upholding termination of employee based on intercepted e-mail messages, despite giving assurance that there would be no monitoring, because employee has no reasonable expectation of privacy in e-mail messages transmitted on company computers).

3. What methods are used to enforce employee filters? Preventing employees from accessing objectionable sites is less disruptive to company operations than would be the unwanted publicity associated with punishing employees for violating corporate policies.[215]

4. Does SPC prohibit workplace access to sites containing pornographic materials, hate speech, and political content?

5. Does SPC require its employees to obtain specific authorization to visit paid sites or subscriber sites?

6. If SPC has a formal policy of limiting access to objectionable sites, it will reduce the risk of a "hostile workplace" claim based on its acquiescence in the behavior of workers who openly view pornography or racist materials in the workplace.[216] It is quite common for employees to e-mail sexist and racist jokes to fellow employees. All online companies should implement a procedure for reporting misuses of e-mail and the Internet. A contact person should be in place, as well as procedures for reporting violations of company computer or Internet policies.

7. Does SPC have a policy of forbidding the transmission of off-color or objectionable jokes? A female employee of a California software company filed a sexual harassment lawsuit based on messages she received via the company's electronic bulletin board.[217] E-mail transmissions of offensive jokes may be used as evidence that SPC ratifies employee misconduct. A system of graduated discipline with a continuum of sanctions from warnings to suspensions or dismissals must be enforced.

8. Are SPC's employees advised of the legal troubles that may result for them and the company from misuse or abuse of e-mail or the Internet?

9. Employees should be trained in proper use of e-mail and the Internet. Training may use actual case studies of companies found liable for their employee's misuse or abuse of e-mail. Chevron, for example, agreed to settle for $2.2 million a sexual harassment case brought by four female plaintiffs. The plaintiffs in that case claimed they had been sent offensive e-mail messages, including a joke "listing twenty five reasons why beer is better than women are."[218] If employees are not disciplined for abusing the Internet or e-mail system, SPC's policy may be deemed to be abandoned or relegated to the ashcan of dead-letter laws or regulations.[219]

---

[215] *Id.*

[216] *Id.*

[217] Brown, *supra* note 63 (reporting that the software company entered into a confidential settlement with the plaintiff).

[218] Marcia Stepanek, When the Devil Is in the E-Mails, *supra* note 77 at 78.

[219] UCLA law professor Eugene Volokh notes that "Rules mandating punishment are all well and good but they depend on management's willingness to punish. Many employers might be quite reluctant to formally reprimand people who are accessing pornographic sites. . . . If the punishment is based on central monitoring of the sites the employee accesses, this will be just an unpleasant

10. Does SPC provide regular training on the specific issue of harassment in the electronic workplace? E-harassment videos and training sessions should be part of employee education. The e-mail messages that led to litigation in past cases may be used in sociodramas, role-playing, and other training exercises. SPC's training module should describe the problem of misdirected e-mails; e-mails with racist, sexist or offensive jokes; and online stalking.

11. Does SPC have limited access systems in place to protect confidential information?

12. Does the password or other limited access system comply with industry standards?

13. Is there an effective hierarchy of access that limits access to key confidential information?

14. Does the access system apply to paper-based documents as well as to computer systems?

15. Does SPC require encryption of important e-mail messages containing confidential information? The policy may also address the problem of employees misusing encryption by stealing company data, encrypting it, and distributing it to competitors or third parties.[220]

16. What is the employee's reasonable expectation of privacy? Does the employee's expectation of privacy accord with corporate policy on e-mail and Internet access? Most states do not recognize a cause of action for invasion of privacy based on an employer's monitoring of e-mail stored on a company computer.[221] Most courts hold that a company-owned computer system is not the personal property of employees, and therefore employees do not have a reasonable expectation of privacy in e-mail messages.[222] A notice to this effect should be displayed each time employees boot up their computers.

17. Does the computer system contain defensive programs, such as EtherPeeker, which monitor and record the addresses of visitors to its web site? The systems administrator or webmaster should conduct audits of log files to determine who is accessing the web site. In some cases, the log files will show evidence of hacking, business espionage, or other online crimes or torts.

18. Have backup power and storage capabilities been implemented? Off-site storage or a SAN are used in the event that a computer system goes down or is compromised.[223] Some electronic data is transitory and should be erased. Other data, however, needs to be either preserved in the event of dispute or otherwise

---

reminder of the degree to which the employees lack privacy." Eugene Volokh, E-Mail Message to Cyberia-listserv@aol.com (Nov. 11, 1997).

[220] Garrity and Casey, *supra* note 27.

[221] *See, e.g.,* Privacy Claim Rejected in Employer Access to E-Mail Files, 16 Comp. & Online Industry Litig. Rptr. 9 (June 15, 1999) (citing Texas case of McLaren v. Microsoft Corp., No. 05-97-00824-CV (Tx. Ct. App. May 28, 1999)).

[222] *Id.*

[223] An increasing number of companies are backing up backup storage facilities.

erased in compliance with a written document retention policy.[224] E-mail messages deleted pursuant to a retention policy will be defensible in the event of litigation. In contrast, the deletion of e-mail messages in response to a discovery request will result in sanctions or liability for spoliation of evidence.

19. What means of physical security are in place to protect confidential corporate information? Is an effective marking system in place to calibrate documents based on the level of security they require? Are the physical means appropriate to the type of information to be protected? Is access controlled at corporate facilities?

20. What types of access controls are in place? Does the company have locked areas in which authorization for entry is limited? Are monitoring cameras used in high-security areas? Are physical searches conducted in high security facilities? Are biometrics used to control access to computer systems?

21. Do the systems administrator and key company personnel understand the necessity of preserving data in case of a dispute? The federal and state rules of discovery create an obligation to produce relevant electronic data. If litigation is pending, a letter should be sent to opposing counsel informing them of their obligation to preserve all electronic evidence. E-mail discovery requests must be broad enough to taken into account off-site storage facilities, multiple servers, and other computer systems.

§ 9.07   SAMPLE INTERNET USAGE POLICY

I. PURPOSE.

This document is SPC's Internet policy, which provides the ground rules for the use of the Internet by all employees in all SPC divisions. The policy applies to all employees, partners, consultants, and others having access to SPC's computer system. The goal of the policy is to help you use the computer system while minimizing the possibility of creating legal trouble for you and the company. Another goal is to ensure economical, effective, and efficient management of Internet usage and to encourage collaborative efforts within SPC.

II. TABLE OF CONTENTS.

Contact Person for Information and Assistance[225]

Definitions

---

[224] Committee on Federal Courts, Discovery of Electronic Evidence: Considerations for Practitioners and Clients, 53 The Record 656, 657 (Sept./Oct. 1998).

[225] All policies should always provide readers with the name, address, and title or authority of a contact person.

Background

Illustrations of Use, Misuse, and Abuse of the Internet

Scope of Policy

Policy

Restrictions on Business Use

Responsibilities

III. DEFINITIONS.

A. Internet. A global web connecting more than 1,000,000 computers. Currently, the Internet has more than 30,000,000 users worldwide, and that number is growing rapidly. More than 100 countries are linked into exchanges of data, news, and opinions. Unlike online services, which are centrally controlled, the Internet is decentralized by design. Each Internet computer, called a host, is independent. Its operators can choose which Internet services to provide to its local users and which local services to make available to the global Internet community. Remarkably, this anarchy by design works exceedingly well.

B. World Wide Web (WWW or "the Web"). A system of Internet servers that supports specially formatted documents. The documents are formatted in a language called HTML (hypertext markup language) that supports links to other documents, as well as graphics, audio, and video files. This means users can jump from one document to another simply by clicking on hot spots. Not all Internet servers are part of the World Wide Web. Several applications, called web browsers, make it easy to access the World Wide Web; three of the most popular are Mosaic, Netscape Navigator, and Microsoft's Internet Explorer.

C. Suffolk Personal Computers Home Page. The main page of SPC's web site. Typically, the home page serves as an index or table of contents to other documents stored at the site.

D. SPC's Web Site. A web site (location) on the World Wide Web. Each web site contains a home page, which is typically the first document users see when they enter the site. The site may also contain additional documents and files. Each web site is owned and managed by an individual, company or organization. SPC's web site is owned and managed by our company.

E. Firewall. SPC's employees are responsible for maintaining the security of SPC's firewalls. That is, SPC employees are responsible for maintaining the secrecy of their passwords. A firewall can not protect SPC's confidential information unless employees do their part by following the information security policy. SPC has a number of information security devices that enforce a boundary between two or more networks. A network firewall, or packet filter, examines traffic at the network protocol level. Application-level firewalls also re-address outgoing traffic so that it appears to have originated from the firewall rather than from the internal host. A firewall is part of SPC's information security policy.

IV. BACKGROUND.

The Internet, a public telecommunications service, was established as a cooperative effort to provide worldwide networking services among educational institutions, government agencies, and various commercial and nonprofit organizations. High-speed networking technologies and developments have made the Internet a desirable research tool, a good source for an expanding body of research, and a means for information dissemination and general communication. The Internet has expanded to include government information, educational information systems, archives, and business resources. The Internet also includes functions such as those for electronic mail (e-mail), remote computer networks, file transfers, the World Wide Web (WWW), and wide area information servers.

SPC's access and use of the Internet has grown exponentially since the company made the decision to become an e-business. Online services, such as the WWW, have greatly increased user access to a wider, and more diverse, community of information resources. As SPC has a number of employees in divisions throughout the world, a growing number of SPC employees are telecommuting through the use of tunneling technologies that permit remote access to company computers. This increased access has many benefits for the company, but it also poses new dangers and liabilities. This dramatic increase in communication capabilities makes it necessary to establish policies regarding the proper and efficient use of Internet.

V. SCOPE OF POLICY.

SPC considers the Internet a fundamental communications tool for supporting SPC's business model. The policies and guidelines in SPC's Internet policy apply to the management of all Internet services company-wide. The Internet usage policy will be updated from time to time. You will receive e-mail notification of any supplemental policies affecting use of the Internet.

VI. POLICY.

SPC's encourages its employees to use the Internet to advance the business goals of the company. Use of the Internet, however, requires responsible judgment, supervisory discretion, and compliance with SPC's Internet usage policy. In addition, computer users must comply with SPC's information security policy. This requires the user to be aware of information technology security and other privacy concerns. Users must also be aware of and follow SPC's rules for Internet usage. Your use of SPC's computer system is conditional upon your acceptance of the terms and conditions of this policy.

A. Personal Use of E-Mail and the Internet.

Internet services provided by SPC are to be used for business purposes. Internet service represents a corporate resource that must be managed in an efficient and cost effective manner. A user, for example, should not download lengthy video files for personal use. The following list of examples includes some, but not all, improper uses of the Internet.

1. The use of SPC's computer system to pursue private commercial business activities while at work. The use of SPC's computer or web site to conduct a private business venture.

2. The use of SPC's computer system to work for a political party, candidate for partisan political office, or partisan political group.

3. The use of SPC's computer system to participate in nonbusiness chat rooms including religious or political objectives.

4. Accessing web sites for no business purpose that results in additional charges to the company, such as commercial sites.

5. Use of the e-mail system for nonbusiness purposes. You should consider e-mail messages to be the same as any other corporate record, that is, as subject to review by SPC's systems administrator. SPC employees are subject to sanctions, culminating in termination, for unprofessional, threatening, or other abusive behavior on the e-mail or Internet systems. If SPC's systems administrator finds evidence that an employee has used the company's computer system to commit a crime, the company will cooperate with law enforcement in prosecuting the employee. SPC reserves the right to turn over e-mail messages with objectionable content to law enforcement officials.

6. Use of the computer to engage in hate speech or other discriminatory conduct.

7. Downloading, transmitting, or viewing sexually explicit material.

8. Downloading, transmitting, or viewing Internet sites that would embarrass or bring unfavorable publicity to you and the company.

9. Use of the computer system to commit a crime or to violate a statute or regulation.
10. Misuse of the computer system by using it to disrupt the workplace or to violate the trust of the company in any way.
11. Downloading unlicensed software, music, or other material that may infringe the intellectual property rights of others.

B. Duty to Report Offensive, Illegal, or Inappropriate E-Mail.
It is your duty not to transmit offensive, illegal, or inappropriate e-mail. It is also your duty to report the receipt of any such material or any such behavior by others of which you become aware.

C. The Use of SPC'S Computer(s) and Systems Is not Private.
Your use of SPC's computer system, e-mail system, and Internet access may be monitored. E-mail is not private, and anyone using SPC's computers has no reasonable expectation of privacy in their e-mail communications and Internet usage. You waive any right of privacy in e-mail messages and consent to monitoring and disclosure by the company. Anyone using SPC's equipment consents to such monitoring and is advised that if such monitoring reveals possible evidence of criminal activity or employee misconduct, SPC managers may provide the evidence of such monitoring to law enforcement officials. Individuals are not guaranteed privacy while using SPC's computers and should, therefore, not expect it. To the extent that employees wish that their private activities remain private, they should avoid using SPC's Internet or e-mail for illegal or prohibited activities.

D. Limited Personal Use of E-Mail and the Internet.
SPC's general policy is that e-mail and Internet usage is for business purposes and should be used in accordance with company guidelines. In addition, your use of SPC's computer system must be in accordance with other company policies and procedures. Limited personal use of e-mail during working hours is permissible. As a guideline, your personal use of e-mail and the Internet should be similar to your personal use of the telephone. SPC employees should be careful not to create the impression that a personal e-mail has been sent on behalf of the company. At no time may SPC's e-mail addresses be used in a manner that gives the impression that the company authorizes an otherwise personal communication. The privacy of personal e-mail or of Internet communications cannot be guaranteed and is subject to monitoring.

Personal use of e-mail should be occasional and should not be allowed to interfere with your job. You should avoid spending an excessive amount of time on the Internet. Sending more than one or two personal e-mail messages per day should be considered a rough standard of excessive use. You are not authorized to download software, music, or other materials from the Internet without prior authorization. You must avoid filling up the mail boxes of co-employees, as well as your own mail box, with personal messages; this may prevent delivery of business messages.

VII. RESTRICTIONS ON BUSINESS USES.

The e-mail or the Internet should not be used to send confidential information, proprietary informaiton, or trade secrets without prior written authorization from your manager. Authorized confidential information should be conspicuously labeled as confidential and should be sent using encryption software provided by SPC. SPC employees should consult with their managers before transmitting highly sensitive information, even if encryption is used. E-mail messages are easily misdirected, and it is the duty of every SPC employee to take care in determining the correct e-mail address.

VIII. RESPONSIBILITIES.

A. Each manager is responsible for ensuring that the guidelines in this policy are fulfilled.

B. SPC's systems administrator has responsibility for SPC's e-mail system, Internet activities, and overall network data management. The coordinator is expected to have the following skills and background:

- Method and type of communications access.

- Internet host and domain names.

- TCP/IP addresses.

- Domain name services.

- Internet applications, for example, file transfer protocol (ftp), WWW, and others.

- Network security and data integrity.

I, _____, acknowledge that I have read and agree to the conditions and terms of this Internet usage policy. I acknowledge that SPC does not guarantee the privacy of e-mail communications or Internet usage. I understand that SPC has reserved the right to monitor or review all e-mail and Internet communications and use. I consent to the terms and conditions of this e-mail and Internet usage policy. All prior and contemporaneous agreements are merged into this agreement.

Signature   Effective Date

Further information and assistance on this policy may be obtained from

Systems Administrator
Building XYZ
1 SPC Street
SUFFOLK PERSONAL COMPUTERS
Boston, Massachusetts 02108-4977
617-573-0000
sysadmin@spc.com

APPENDIX 9-1
DEPARTMENT OF COMMERCE INTERNET USE POLICY

1. *Purpose*

    This document states the Department's policy and provides guidance for managing the use of the Internet by operating units and other organizational components, and by employees within Commerce.

    The goal is to ensure economical, effective and efficient management of Internet usage and encourage collaborative efforts among the Commerce components to achieve this end.

2. *Contents*

Topic	Paragraph
Information and Assistance	3
Definitions	4
Background	5
Scope	6
Policy	7
Responsibilities	8

3. *Information and Assistance*

    Guidance on this policy may be obtained from:

    Office of Systems & Telecommunications Management (OSTM)
    HCH Building, Room 6086
    202-482-0120

4. *Definitions*

    Internet. A global web connecting more than a million computers. Currently, the Internet has more than 30 million users worldwide, and that number is growing rapidly. More than 100 countries are linked into exchanges of data, news and opinions. Unlike online services, which are centrally controlled, the Internet is decentralized by design. Each Internet computer, called a host, is independent. Its operators can choose which Internet services to provide to its local users and which local services to make available to the global Internet community. Remarkably, this anarchy by design works exceedingly well.

World Wide Web (WWW or "Web"). A system of Internet servers that supports specially formatted documents. The documents are formatted in a language called HTML (HyperText Markup Language) that supports links to other documents, as well as graphics, audio, and video files. This means you can jump from one document to another simply by clicking on hot spots. Not all Internet servers are part of the World Wide Web.

There are several applications called Web browsers that make it easy to access the World Wide Web, three of the most popular being Mosaic, Netscape Navigator and Microsoft's Internet Explorer.

Home Page. The main page of a Web site. Typically, the home page serves as an index or table of contents to other documents stored at the site.

Site. A site (location) on the World Wide Web. Each Web site contains a home page, which is the first document users see when they enter the site. The site might also contain additional documents and files. Each site is owned and managed by an individual, company or organization.

Firewall. A system or combination of systems that enforce a boundary between two or more networks. A network firewall, or packet filter, examines traffic at the network protocol level. An application-level firewall also readdresses outgoing traffic so it appears to have originated from the firewall rather than the internal host.

5. *Background*

The Internet, a public telecommunications service, was established as a cooperative effort providing worldwide networking services among educational institutions, government agencies and various commercial and non-profit organizations. High speed networking technologies and developments have made the Internet a desirable source for expanding research interest and information dissemination and communications. The Internet has expanded to include government information, educational information systems, archives and business resources. The Internet also includes functions such as those for electronic mail (e-mail), remote computer networks, file transfers, World Wide Web (WWW) and wide area information servers.

The Department's access and use of Internet have grown exponentially. On-line services, such as the WWW, have greatly increased user access to a wider and more diverse user community of information resources. This dramatic increase in communication capabilities makes it necessary to establish policies regarding the proper and efficient use of Internet.

6. *Scope*

The Internet is considered to be a fundamental communications tool that may be used to support the Department's missions and information dissemination requirements. These policies and guidelines apply to the management of Internet services within all organizational units of the Department and may be supplemented by additional guidelines developed by departmental operating units, including the use of Government provided telecommunications resources in employees' private residences. To the extent that existing Department-wide policies and directives relating to e-mail and the Internet are inconsistent with this policy, this policy shall supersede the previous policies or directives. The Departmental Public Affairs office and other operating unit offices may also issue policy regarding the content and management of Internet data and information.

7. *Policy*

It is the policy of the Department to allow and encourage the use of Internet services to support the accomplishment of the various missions of the Department. Use of the Internet requires responsible judgment, supervisory discretion and compliance with applicable laws and regulations. Users must be aware of information technology security and other privacy concerns. Users must also be aware of and follow management directives for Internet usage.

Internet services provided by the Department, like other Government equipment and resources, are to be used only for authorized purposes. The Department recognizes that it is in the interest of the Government that Department personnel become proficient and maintain proficiency in using the Internet. To this end, the restrictions outlined below regarding Internet use during official working hours and non-working hours should be followed by Department employees using Internet services provided by the Department.

The following specific statements reflect official guidance on Departmental use of the Internet:

a. Internet services provided by the Department during official working hours are to be used for authorized purposes only. This may include using Internet services to train personnel on using the Internet, provided prior approval is obtained from an employee's supervisor.

b. Internet service represents a corporate resource that must be managed in an efficient and cost effective manner. Departmental operating units should establish guidelines for accountability and responsibility for use of the Internet and e-mail by their respective employees.

c. Internet access should be achieved using standard and commonly available tools, unless a specific requirement calls for a unique approach. The Department's Office of Systems and Telecommunications Management should be informed in advance of requirements for unique solutions or approaches.

d. Operating units should ensure that their presence on the Internet fulfills mission requirements in a professional manner. Operating units should also ensure that information that they make available via the Internet is accurate, relevant, up-to-date, and is professionally presented.

e. Operating units and Departmental offices may use the Internet to exchange information with the public and internally as an information technology tool. It is to be considered as one of a number of tools and an alternative commercial communication network that is available to DOC.

f. Information technology security requirements shall be a primary consideration in the decision process leading to the use of the Internet. Operating Units must take adequate precautions when processing data or storing data on computers connected to the Internet and when transmitting data on or through the Internet. Chapter 10 of the Department's Information Technology Management Handbook defines certification and accreditation requirements for all sensitive and classified general purpose and application systems. These certification and accreditation requirements apply to use of the Internet for processing or transmitting sensitive or classified data. For classified data, the Director of the Office of Security is the Department's Principal Accrediting Authority and the Director for Budget, Management and Information and Deputy Chief Information Officer is the Designated Approving Authority.

Chapter 10 of the IT Management Handbook also addresses malicious software concerns. Given the extreme vulnerability to viruses and other malicious software occasioned by use of the Internet, operating units must ensure that processes and procedures to minimize risk from malicious programs are in place. Operating units may require that virus checking software be used in conjunction with Internet use.

g. Unless prohibited by the specific policies of the employee's bureau/operating unit, the use of Internet services and e-mail provided by the Department during non-working hours is not limited to official purposes only. This policy will assist employees in becoming proficient in using the Internet and will enhance their professional development at de minimis expense to the Government. However, employees may not use government printers or supplies in conjunction with personal Internet and e-mail activities. Activities for which Department Internet and e-mail services may not be used, during working or non-working hours, include the following:

(1) the pursuit of private commercial business activities or profit-making ventures (i.e., employees may not operate a business with the use of the Department's computers and Internet resources);

(2) matters directed toward the success or failure of a political party, candidate for partisan political office, or partisan political group;

(3) prohibited direct or indirect lobbying;

(4)   use of Internet sites that result in an additional charge to the Government;

(5)   engaging in prohibited discriminatory conduct;

(6)   the obtaining or viewing of sexually explicit material;

(7)   any activity that would bring discredit on the Department; or

(8)   any violation of statute or regulation.

Of course, the Department expects employees to conduct themselves professionally while using Department resources, and employees must refrain from using Department resources for activities that are disruptive to the work place or in violation of public trust.

Like all other Government computer use, use of Government equipment for personal use of the Internet may be monitored and recorded. Anyone using Government equipment consents to such monitoring and is advised that if such monitoring reveals possible evidence of criminal activity or employee misconduct, system personnel may provide the evidence of such monitoring to Department and law enforcement officials. Individuals are not guaranteed privacy while using government computers and should, therefore, not expect it. To the extent that employees wish that their private activities remain private, they should avoid using the Department's Internet or e-mail for such activities.

h.   Unless prohibited by the specific policies of the employee's bureau/operating unit, limited personal use of e-mail during duty hours is permissible, as such use will help promote proficiency in electronic communications, including use of the Internet, and provides an alternative method for authorized personal communications, which will promote Government efficiency.

At no time may Government e-mail addresses be used in a manner which will give the impression that an otherwise personal communication is authorized by the Department.

Personal use of e-mail cannot interfere with the official business of the employee or organization, such as spending an inappropriate amount of time during duty hours (e.g., sending more than four brief messages per day), filling up a mailbox with personal messages so as to prevent official messages from being delivered, or disseminating chain letters.

8.   *Responsibilities*

a.   Operating units and Departmental offices must ensure that employees are aware of these policies and guidelines. Ultimately, it is the responsibility of the management official or supervisor who provides the equipment and/or

Internet access to carry out this Internet Use Policy. Accordingly, these organizations should:

(1) Designate a point of contact within each bureau for discussion and coordination of Internet usage and notify OSTM of the representative appointed.

(2) Assure that use of the Internet by the operating unit and its members is consistent with these policies and guidelines and applicable laws, including the Privacy Act and the Paperwork Reduction Act.

(3) Coordinate and oversee their organization's Internet activities and network data management.

(4) Establish their own procedures as necessary to promote Department-wide interoperability and cooperation.

(5) Provide the necessary technical safeguards for appropriate availability, integrity and confidentiality of operating unit systems and procedures.

(6) Adhere to established Departmental electronic mail and network address management policies where applicable.

(7) Participate in the development of Internet information content, usage policy and operating standards with OSTM when requested.

(8) Assess and validate organizational needs for Internet access using their own established business practices and mission program requirements.

(9) Determine appropriate management controls and technical safeguards to be used for Internet usage, establishing supplemental Internet use procedures and user guidelines as necessary. Because the connection of existing user networks to the Internet presents security risks, the use of firewall technology between local networks and the Internet should be considered.

(10) Periodically assess the effectiveness of their established management controls for Internet access within their organization.

(11) Provide access mechanisms in accordance with Department policy for Internet connectivity for employees who have an authorized purpose for Internet access from home or on authorized travel.

b. Operating unit and Departmental office users of Commerce network resources must:

(1) Coordinate Internet access and Internet services with the appropriate telecommunications, network management, and program management officials. Coordination will include, at a minimum:

- Method and type of communications access.
- Internet host and domain names.
- TCP/IP addresses.
- Domain Name Services.
- Internet applications, e.g., file transfer protocol (ftp),WWW, and others.
- Network security and data integrity.

   (2) Ensure that basic principles of accountability and responsibility apply to electronic data dissemination and the use of the World Wide Web.

c. DOC organizational units are encouraged to develop WWW sites that display creativity and mission focus. However, operating units should ensure that all Web sites within their organization:

   (1) Are subject to appropriate management controls.

   (2) Remain official information sources over which the Department retains complete editorial control.

   (3) Are not "personal" home pages or contain personal information unrelated to official business (e.g., in no circumstance should Department-supported Web sites include items such as vacation or family photographs, links to an employee's personal interest information, or links to partisan political organizations).

   (4) Clearly display the DOC seal or text indicating DOC affiliation.

   (5) Clearly display the operating unit's seal, emblem, logo or text indicating the title of the organization.

   (6) Contain a uniform resource locator (URL) reference to the Department of Commerce Home Page. (http:www.doc.gov).

   (7) Contain appropriate contact information (such as name, phone number, and e-mail address) for technical and content questions.

   (8) Include only links to Government sites and to non-government sites that are directly related to the Department's mission or necessary to carry out the Department's business. If links to non-government sites are referenced, operating units should provide a clearly visible statement specifying that the Department of Commerce does not endorse any particular product, company, information provider, or the content of the referenced sites. However, if the link is included as part of legitimate and approved export promotion activities, the statement need not disclaim the companies or products at issue.

(9)   Are not used for direct or indirect lobbying, including links to sites which engage in or advocate indirect lobbying.

(10)   Adhere to any future directives on DOC Web management.

d.   *Use of Trademarks & Service Mark:* When using any trademarks or service marks, it is recommended that the ™ or ® symbols be used, as appropriate. By definition, trademarks are used to identify tangible goods, while service marks are used to identify services (including the provision of online databases).

The ™ symbol is used on marks that are considered to be trademarks by the Department but have not yet been registered. The ® symbol is used only where the mark is actually registered with the U.S. Patent & Trademark Office. Use of these symbols is not mandatory, but suggested. Further, repetitive use of these symbols is not necessary if it becomes cumbersome or awkward.

Where appropriate, it is recommended that the phrase "[name of trademark] is a (registered, if so) trademark of the U.S. Department of Commerce [or name of individual agency]." Example: "NTIS® and FedWorld® are registered trademarks and service marks of the National Technical Information Service."

Please call the Office of the Chief Counsel for Technology for guidance in using Departmental trademarks and service marks.

APPROVED: <u>W. Scott Gould /s/ /</u>   <u>8/28/98</u>
                         Signature   Effective Date

APPENDIXES

APPENDIX A

SPC BUSINESS PLAN

SPC

Business Plan

Edit History
6/1/00 version 0.2

SPC

Business Plan

Mission Statement

SPC's mission is to fundamentally change the way computers are sold and delivered on the Web.

TABLE OF CONTENTS

TABLE OF CONTENTS

1.   EXECUTIVE SUMMARY

1.1   INVESTMENT OBJECTIVE

SPC seeks initial funding of $50 million to build infrastructure and staff for deployment of SPC's systems and services over a twelve month period. SPC seeks three strategic investors who will bring customer relationships and technological solutions to the Company.

1.2   BUSINESS STRATEGY

SPC is a business-to-business Solutions Provider (ASP). SPC allows its customers to simply and effectively purchase hardware via its web site without having to invest large sums in infrastructure and operational support. Each customer can have a machine trailoried to their preferences.

With SPC's unique pricing model, customers can purchase new machines with minimal expense. SPC provides a predictable cost structure that allows customers to expand their business infinitely.

1.3   OPERATIONS AND MANAGEMENT

SPC's patentable technology has already been successfully deployed for major high tech firms. The management and development team is assembled, has a five-year working history, and owns ten patents.

1.4   SCHEDULE

Table 1: Major Milestones for SPC's First Twelve Months of Operations

Date	Milestone
Jan 2001	Identify and contact Strategic Investors
Feb 2001	Finalize terms of first round financing
Mar 2001	Product offering complete and deployed with first customer
	Financing Complete
	Launch of Marketing Web site
Apr 2001	Build-out complete of new offices in Boston & Cambridge
	Customers: 20
	Full-time employees: 15
Oct 2001	Customers: 65
	Full-time employees: 55
Jan 2002	Customers: 100
	Initial Public Offering to enable acquisition strategy
	Full-time employees: 85

1.5   FINANCIAL PROJECTIONS

Table 2: Financial Projections

	2000	2001	2002
Total Revenue (US$ millions)	15.4	61.4	211.7
Net Profit (pre-tax) (US$ millions)	1.5	40.4	184.4
Net Profit Margin (after tax)	-10%	40%	52%

Fiscal Year 2000 begins January 1, 2000

1.6   INVESTOR RETURNS

Based upon projected revenues and profits, and valuations of similar companies, SPC estimates that initial investors will recognize a 1000% return on investment within the first twelve months of operations. This investment will be realized through SPC's initial public offering that will be used to raise additional funds for the company's growth in the business-to-business solutions provider market.

SPC BUSINESS PLAN

2.   THE SPC OPPORTUNITY

The time is right for SPC to fundamentally change the way computers are delivered on the Web.

821

3.   SERVICE DESCRIPTION

3.1   OVERVIEW

SPC has developed several patentable systems, based on prior patents.

3.2 SPC CUSTOMER EXPERIENCE

SPC customers must maintain complete control of their machines. Therefore, there is a need to create a Help Desk service and other customer tools.

Training and Customer Service

New SPC customers receive on-site, hands-on training. Customers work with SPC Account Managers who are available to assist with any technical issues or feature requests. The Company also offers comprehensive 24-hour support, both automated and human.

3.3 SPC CUSTOMERS

SPC's customers of all sizes will include:

- Portal companies
- E-commerce companies
- Educational institutions

3.4 PROJECTED CUSTOMER GROWTH

Table 3: Projected Customers

Year End	Mid-size	Large
2000	50	50
2001	200	150
2002	1000	600

3.5   PRICING

SPC's unique pay-per-use pricing scheme provides a primary benefit to our customers. Customers are only charged when they turn on their machines. Our cost per thousand (CPM) pricing schedule is as follows:

Table 4: Pricing

Page Views per month	Cost per CPM per month FY 1	Cost per CPM per month FY 2	Cost per CPM per month FY 3
0 - 5 million	$25	$22.5	$20
5 - 10 million	$20	$17.5	$15
10 - 15 million	$15	$12.5	$10
> 15 million	$10	$8.5	$7

Our costs per CPM is a maximum of $5 per CPM per month, guaranteeing a gross profit from inception of the service. Each year, prices will be reduced to remain competitive and to maintain 100% customer retention.

4.   BUSINESS DEVELOPMENT AND MARKETING

SPC's business development team will focus initially on establishing customer relationships with 5 mid-size and 5 large Web businesses. SPC has already successfully deployed one large contract with Suffolk University Law School.

4.1   PARTNERSHIP DEVELOPMENT

SPC's key to developing a business customer base will be through strategic partnerships with companies that are already offering segments of the Internet Infrastructure services for a Web site. SPC proposes to partner with the following types of companies in order to gain access to an active customer base:

- Publishing companies
- Internet infrastructure companies
- Traditional application service providers
- Software companies
- Internet service providers
- Web development companies
- Financial institutions

SPC's Business Development Team will use its existing business and personal relationships with these companies to initiate discussions and form strategic partnerships.

4.2   MARKETING

4.2.1 Branding

SPC's cogent message to its business customers is clear: *SPC manages and delivers your hardware needs more effectively, at lower costs, so you can concentrate on your core business.*

We accurately represent the Company as being made up of the most intelligent, most experienced professionals in the world. SPC is committed to delivering reliable, high-performance, innovative solutions with complete customer service.

4.2.2 Web Site

SPC will launch its Web site (www.SPC.com) on March 1, 2000. The site will be simple and straightforward, outlining the benefits of the company's services to the customer and promoting

SPC as "the smartest people on the Web."

4.2.3 Software Demo

SPC will create a password-protected, online demo of its services that it will make available to qualified leads.

4.2.4 Advertising and Trade Shows

SPC will rely primarily on its business development staff and strategic partnerships to identify and win new customers. A modest marketing budget will support them in their effort. Advertising in trade magazines will be used to create awareness of SPC, and the company will establish a presence at two major trade shows a year.

4.3   PUBLIC RELATIONS

Public Relations will be the primary tool used to create the buzz about SPC. The Company will use Chairman and CEO Cyrus Daftary as a primary spokesperson and "character" on the Web. Cyrus, who is the chief architect of SPC's technology and is the former Chief Technology Officer at PricewaterhouseCoopers, is a well-known industry expert and has spoken at numerous conferences, at venues including Suffolk University Law School, the Mass Bar Association and the Rhode Island Bar Association.

SPC will promote its first-mover advantage as an ASP and ride the excitement surrounding this growing market segment.

4.4   COMPETITION

SPC is unique in the marketplace in targeting this service business. However, potential competitors could come from several directions of the vertical integration of the delivery of other solutions.

- **Internet service providers:**
- **Large web development companies:**
- **Application software companies:**

SPC is in position to succeed in this marketplace because we are 100% dedicated to a single aspect of the delivery of hardware from businesses to consumers. In fact the management of the multiple vendor relationships is the foundation of SPC's service offerings.

4.5   RISKS

Given the exponential growth of content and traffic on the Web, the risks faced by SPC are small in relation to the increasing demand for its services.

An external audit firm is reviewing and documenting any potential risks.

827

5.   OPERATIONS

5.1   STAFFING

SPC's staff will be kept to a minimum when operations begin. We are confident that with a staff of fewer than 100 persons we can create a profitable business managing and distributing machines for 50 customers. However, our rapid expansion plans will require additional staffing after the first six months of operation.

5.1.1 Management

- Chief Executive Officer: Responsible for determining the strategic direction of the company, delivering return on investment to investors, identifying new business opportunities, and winning new accounts for SPC.

- Vice President of Services: Responsible for product definition, customer service and training, PR and marketing.

- Vice President of Technology: Responsible for application and operational development and quality assurance.

- Vice President of Finance and Administration: Responsible for managing the relationships with strategic investors. Manages capital structures and financial needs of SPC. Manages legal aspects of the company and human resources.

- Vice President of Marketing: Responsible for marketing, public relations, and business development.

- President/COO: Responsible for overall day-to-day operations of the company, including marketing, services, and technology.

5.1.2 Technology

- Director of Applications Development: Responsible for development of front-end and back-end of new software offerings.

- Director of Web Technologies: Responsible for front-end development of new software offerings.

- Systems Architect: Responsible for design and implementation of systems schema.

- Senior Server Engineer: Responsible for design, development and integration of back-end software.

- Director of Operational Development: Responsible for the development of new systems and architectures for the management and delivery of content for our customers.

- Director of Operations: Responsible for the day-to-day operations of SPC's technical infrastructure.

- Manager of Networking/Security: Responsible for security and operation of the SPC network. Defines standards and best practices while continuously monitoring the health of the network.

- Quality Assurance Manager: Responsible for the quality of software produced by the applications development group and for the quality of services provided by the operational development group. Establishes standards and processes for the delivery of services.

- Documentation Manager: Responsible for documenting all systems and processes used by the company.

5.1.3 Marketing/Business Development

- Senior Sales Representative: Responsible for identifying new sales opportunities and closing contracts with customers.

- Partner Development Representative: Responsible for identifying strategic partners and defining contracts for strategic partnerships.

- Marketing Manager: Oversees public relations, marketing, and advertising efforts.

5.1.4 Account Management and Production

- Director of Account Management: Responsible for overseeing account manager and ensuring satisfaction of all customers.

- Account Manager: Responsible for managing individual customers, ensuring satisfaction of assigned customers.

- Manager of Training: Responsible for training new customers on use of SPC's services.

- User Interface Designer: Responsible for the design and information architecture of the service for ease-of-use and efficient task completion.

5.1.5 Finance and Administration

- Controller: Responsible for managing day-to-day expenditures and cash flows.

- Human Resources Manager: Manages and supports the COO in recruiting and building a strong team of the smartest Web professionals in the world.

- Accounts Receivable.

- Accounts Payable.

5.1.6 Marketing

- Marketing and PR Manager: Responsible for marketing efforts and public relations.

5.2   LOCATION OF BUSINESS

SPC will be located in Boston, with a satellite office in Cambridge, MA.

5.3   EMPLOYEE OWNERSHIP

As an incentive for long-term employees, SPC has reserved 20% of the company's shares for ownership by employees, including executives, issued as stock options over a four year vesting period.

6.   SPC MANAGEMENT AND ADVISORS

6.1   BOARD OF DIRECTORS

- Cyrus Daftary, Chairman and CEO, SPC
- Mike Rustad, CEO Rustad Technologies
- Jonathan Frank, CEO Frank Sawyer Management Consulting Practice.

The remaining two Board positions will be filled by Strategic Investors.

6.2   MANAGEMENT

- SPC's management team is assembled and has already successfully deployed their first solution for an online education portal, funded by a major player in the Internet industry. The team has a five-year history of working together and has built hardware and software infrastructure for dozens of some of the most recognizable names on the Web.

7.   FINANCIAL PROJECTIONS

The financial projections demonstrate that SPC will be operating profitably within its first seven months of operations. The results are summarized below:

Table 5 : Financial Projections

	2000	2001	2002
Total Revenue (US$ millions)	15.4	61.4	211.7
Net Profit (pre-tax) (US$ millions)	1.5	40.4	184.4
Net Profit Margin (after tax)	-10%	40%	52%

Fiscal Year 2000 begins January 1, 2000

By the twelfth month of operations, the Company will realize annualized revenues of $31 million and a net profit of $13 million, a margin of over 40%. This tremendous upside in profitability is possible because once the infrastructure is in place, costs are shared across large numbers of our customers.

For the first year of operations, SPC will realize total revenues of $15.3 million, with a net loss of $1.5 million. In the second year of operation, revenues are projected to quadruple as we leverage the infrastructure against a greater number of large and mid-size customers. The large margins of 40% and 50% projected for the year 2001 and 2002 are feasible because of SPC's revolutionary technology and publishing methods.

7.1   ASSUMPTIONS

- ☐ Financing is received by March 1, 2001.
- ☐ Intellectual property is transferred from VC to SPC on March 31, 2001.
- ☐ First day of operations is April 1, 2001. Company begins receiving revenue on the first day of operations, from our first customer, VC.
- ☐ Fiscal Year begins on January 1.

8.   RETURN ON INVESTMENT

SPC's current valuation of $100 million is justified by its revenue projections and desirable profit margins forecast for the next three years. Based upon analysis of similar companies within the industry (see table 6), SPC can conservatively expect to have a valuation of $1 to $3 billion within twelve months of operation. Investors would realize a tenfold return on their investment within twelve months.

8.1   GROWTH OPPORTUNITIES

SPC's entry into the hardware market is a "foot in the door" to providing any number of services to our customers. SPC anticipates growing revenues through the development and hosting of additional standard and custom solutions for our customers.

In early 2001, SPC will raise additional funds through an initial public offering in order to acquire additional companies. We will focus on acquiring operations that minimize our bottom line and provide more vertical integration with our partners and vendors.

Table 6: Market Capitalization of Comparable Internet Infrastructure Companies

Company	Most Recent Annualized Revenues	Current Market Capitalization
Company 1	N/A	$25 billion
Company 2	$76 million	$11 billion
Company 3	$6.4 million	$1 billion
Company 4	$33.2	$0.9 billion

8.2   CONCLUSION

The way computers are sold on the Web will change significantly in the next three years. SPC has the idea, the technology, and the team to revolutionize the way the Web is used. With unique software and hardware and an existing customer base, SPC is set to become the dominant force in the marketplace. Investment by a complementary set of strategic partners is all that is needed to complete the picture and launch this company to the market leader position.

9. CALENDAR

Date	Milestone
Jan 2001	Identify and contact strategic investors
	Obtain angel investment funds
	Full-time employees: 5
Feb 2001	Determine terms of first round financing
	Obtain letters of intent from strategic investors
	CEO to present at Harvard University Internet Conference
	Management recruiting of VP Finance
	Sign lease on office space
Mar 1, 2001	Product offering complete and deployed with first customer, Suffolk University Law School
	Financing complete
	Hire VP of Business Development
	Launch of marketing web site
	Customers: 1
Mar 15, 2001	Money received from strategic investors
Apr 1, 2001	Build-out complete of new offices
	Customers: 65
	Full-time employees: 26
Oct 2001	Secondary production facility operational at vendor's facilities in Waltham
Jan 2002	Customers: 75
	Initial Public Offering to enable acquisition strategy
	Full-time employees: 100

INTERNET RESOURCES FOR LAWYERS: LEGAL RESEARCH, ISSUES AND PRACTICE

NOTE: The URLs cited in this Appendix were current as of April 2000.

INTERNET RESOURCES FOR LAWYERS

With the tremendous growth of the Internet, the search is on for ways to incorporate the web technology into the legal profession. To date, the Internet has been useful for the legal profession as a research tool, a method of disseminating traditional materials, and communicating with the outside world. The purpose of this Appendix is to provide you with a starting point of where to begin your legal research on the Internet.

Please keep in mind that the following list of World Wide Web locations is only a tiny fraction of the useful legal resources that can be found on the Internet. This document is not meant to be exhaustive, nor is it comprehensive in scope. It is offered as an example of the types of information one can find on the web, as well as an introductory, organizational tool for locating selected law-related resources. The web site addresses listed have recently been verified for accuracy. However, keep in mind that the Internet is a somewhat fluid mass of information, and web site locations are often modified.

OVERVIEW—WHAT IS THE INTERNET?

The Internet is a giant network that interconnects many smaller groups of linked computer networks (a network of networks). The Internet enables users to access files stored on computer servers anywhere in the world as long as they are part of the Net. The Internet has experienced phenomenal growth in recent years as the number of web sites (URLs) has rapidly increased, thereby increasing the amount of information available on the Internet.

This hypergrowth has in turn increased the availability of legal materials on the Internet. Please keep in mind that there are literally thousands upon thousands of documents added to the Net everyday. Consequently, it is impossible for one to have a current list of every URL.

Generally speaking there are three ways to find legal related materials on the Internet. First, you can search legal mailing lists/newsgroups. Second, you can purchase a legal Internet directory. Finally, you can use Internet search engines, which may be described as crawlers, indexes, spiders, or worms.

OVERVIEW—UNDERSTANDING SEARCH ENGINES

If you find yourself at the very beginning of an issue with little or no information, the following search engines available on the Internet will help you retrieve documents relating to your search request.

A. YAHOO!

YAHOO! is one of the best ways to access information. Yahoo! functions like a "yellow pages" of the Internet. It is divided into various categories, including Government:Law and numerous web sites are listed under each category. If you are unsure of the correct category, you can simply input several key terms and search both the categories and all sites. It is important to note that site links are placed on Yahoo! at the discretion of its administrators. Therefore, unlike other search engines that canvass the entire Net, Yahoo! has, by its very nature, "edited" what is made available. Yahoo! can be found at: http://www.yahoo.com.

B. ALTA VISTA

In contrast to Yahoo!, Alta Vista enables you to search millions of web pages by term(s). You can conduct a simple search by inputting a search term or a more advanced search that uses Boolean search logic. The Boolean search logic on the web is similar to that of LEXIS and Westlaw. Alta Vista can be found at: http://altavista.digital.com.

C. FINDLAW—A LEGAL SEARCH ENGINE

Just as Yahoo! is the starting point for many searches on the Internet, Findlaw is probably one of the best starting points for conducting legal Internet research. FindLaw can be found at: http://www.findlaw.com.

D. HIEROS GAMOS—A LEGAL SEARCH ENGINE

Although there are numerous other legal search engines, Hieros Gamos is another legal search engine that deserves special mention. Hieros Gamos, a site maintained by a collection of law firms, contains many of the links referenced in Findlaw and Cornell's LII but adds many other original documents. These documents include more than 200 practice areas, numerous "Doing Business" guides, as well as other types of material not commonly available on the Internet. Hieros Gamos can be found at: http://www.hg.org.

E. LAW CRAWLER—A LEGAL SEARCH ENGINE

The LawCrawler uses intelligent agents combined with the AltaVista search engine and database and other legal code and case law databases to retrieve information geared towards the specific needs of legal professionals. LawCrawler has an official license to use AltaVista Search. The LawCrawler provides legal researchers with precision by enabling them to focus their searches on sites with legal information and within specific domains. Law Crawler can be found at: http://www.lawcrawler.com.

F. OTHER SEARCH ENGINES

TDSNET has assembled a home page that links users to every commercial search engine that exists on the Internet. Keep in mind the various search engines will retrieve different search results, depending on how the algorithm is encoded. Therefore, you should try the same search request using various search engines in order to truly get an accurate feel for what exists on the Internet. TDSNET can be found at: http://www.abanet.com.

GENERAL LAW SITES

The following sites can be used as gateways to law-related resources. Of most importance is the organizational structure these sites impose on the web. They each provide an impressive array of links to legal information and their user friendly subject arrangements provide easy navigation throughout the Internet.

American Law Sources On-Line   **http://www.lawsource.com/also**
Their stated purpose is to "provide a comprehensive, uniform, and useful compilation of links to all on-line sources of American law that are available without charge." Focus is on U.S., Canadian, and Mexican federal and state legal resources.

FindLaw   **http://www.findlaw.com**

Emerging as the favorite gateway to legal resources. Well-organized, comprehensive arrangement of law sites, including primary and secondary sources. This is the site for the LawCrawler search engine.

Hieros Gamos   **http://www.hg.org**

Billed as the largest comprehensive legal site with more than 50,000 links to U.S. federal and state law, legal organizations, and every government in the world. Also includes links in more than 200 practice areas, 300-plus discussion groups, and 50 doing-business guides.

Internet Lawyer   **http://www.internetlawyer.com**

Incorporates various legal research needs including but not limited to: basic legal research needs, fact-finding research, a legal Internet column, and legal technology briefs. Internet Lawyer is published by GoAhead Publications.

LawCrawler   **http://www.lawcrawler.com**

The LawCrawler uses intelligent agents combined with the AltaVista search engine and database and other legal code and case law databases to retrieve information geared toward the specific needs of legal professionals. LawCrawler has an official license to use AltaVista Search. The Law-Crawler provides legal researchers with precision by enabling them to focus their searches on sites with legal information and within specific domains.

LawLinks: the Internet Legal   **http://lawlinks.com**
Resource Center

LawLinks' aim is to provide a place for all people interested in the law to congregate and obtain information. Users can conduct research, generate referrals, purchase legal products, collaborate, and recruit. LawLinks provides separate "Centers" for attorneys or consumers.

Legal Information Institute   **http://www.law.cornell.edu**
at Cornell University

An award winning pioneer in the electronic dissemination of legal materials. Provides useful background commentary and full text of United States Supreme Court and New York court decisions, the UCC, the U.S. Code, and selected state and federal laws. Also noted for its extensive links to law related sources worldwide.

Legal Computer Solutions, Inc.   **http://www.lcsweb.com**

Contains, among other things, a very comprehensive legal virtual library. The various links include those to current, essential legal resources, and secondary sources and professional information.

Rominger Legal Services   http://www.romingerlegal.com/
  On-Line Research Page
   This site acts as a one stop search option for search engines like Findlaw, DivorceNet, Lycos, Alta Vista, and Yahoo!. Additionally, the site provides links to various sources like Federal Links, Professional Directories, and Non-Legal Resources.

Seamless Website   http://www.seamless.com
   This web site is broken down into four parts. The first section, The Chamber, contains news and information about Seamless and its clients. The second section, The Commons, contains original works on a broad range of legal topics. The third section, entitled the Shingle, features homepages of lawyers, legal associations, as well as legal service providers. The final section, entitled the Cross Road, links this site to 1,000 other legal sites.

Virtual Law Library   http://www.law.indiana.edu/law
                                   /v-lib/lawindex.html
   A collection of materials and pointers to law-related Internet sources. Includes U.S. and state government links, law journals, legal organizations, law firms, law schools, and publishers.

WashLaw   http://lawlib.wuacc.edu
   Maintained by the staff of the Washburn Law Library, this is one of the most extensive legal sites currently available on the web. It links to law schools, law firms, international, state, and federal materials, directories, news sources, and much more.

U.S. GOVERNMENT

General Government Sites

GPO Access   http://www.access.gpo.gov
   This web server for the Government Printing Office is the source for most electronic government documents, including the Congressional Record, CFR, Federal Register, Congressional bills, U.S. Code, agency publications, and much more. It is reliable because it is the official publisher.

GPO Access Searching Tips   http://www.II.georgetown.edu
                                         /wtaylor/gposrch.html

Library of Congress   http://www.loc.gov
   Extremely versatile site features the *American Memory* and the *American Treasures* projects which provide documents, photographs, motion pictures

and sound recordings from the Library's collections and exhibits. It also provides search capabilities for the library catalog, direct access to THOMAS (full text of U.S. House and Senate documents), the Global Legal Information Network, the U.S. Copyright Office, as well as links to other internet research sources.

Federal Web Locator   **http://www.law.vill.edu/fed-agency
                                    /fedwebloc.html**

The most impressive collection of links to federal government web sites. Lists more than 550 separate government information sites.

Administrative/Executive Branch

Department of Commerce	http://www.doc.gov
Department of Justice	http://www.usdoj.gov
Department of Labor	http://www.dol.gov
Department of Treasury	http://www.ustreas.gov
Environmental Protection Agency	http://www.epa.gov
Federal Communications Commission	http://www.fcc.gov
Federal Trade Commission	http://www.ftc.gov
FedLaw: General Services Administration	http://www.legal.gsa.gov
FedWorld	http://www.fedworld.gov
Internal Revenue Service	http://www.irs.ustreas.gov
Pension Benefit Guaranty Corp.	http://www.pbgc.gov
Securities and Exchange Commission	http://www.sec.gov
U.S. Government Information	http://www-libraries.colorado.edu/ps/gov/us /federal.htm
U.S. International Trade Commission	http://www.usitc.gov
U.S. Trade Representation	http://www.ustr.gov
White House	http://www.whitehouse.gov

Book Reviews (Legal)

Bi-Monthly Review of Law Books	http://www.law.suffolk.edu/faculty/ebander /ind19.html.

Courts/Judicial Branch

Administrative Office of the Federal Courts	http://supct.uscourts.gov
Court Rules	http://www.law.cornell.edu/rules
District of Columbia Circuit	http://www.ll.georgetown.edu:80/Fed-Ct /cadc.html

Federal Appellate Courts	http://www.ljx.com/cgi-bin/cir
Federal Circuit Court	http://www.law.emory.edu/fedcircuit
First Circuit	http://www.law.emory.edu:80/1circuit
Second Circuit	http://lawtouro.edu:80/abouttlc/2ndcircuit
Third Circuit	http://vls.villanova.edu/library/express
Fourth Circuit	http://law.emory.edu:80/4circuit/
Fifth Circuit	http://www.law.utexas.edu:80/us5th/us5th.html
Sixth Circuit	http://www.law.emory.edu:80/6circuit
Seventh Circuit	http://www.law.emory.edu:80/7circuit
Eighth Circuit	http://www.wulaw.wustl.edu:80/8thcir
Ninth Circuit	http://vls.villanova.edu/library/express
Tenth Circuit	http://www.law.emory.edu:80/10circuit
Eleventh Circuit	http://www.law.emory.edu:/11circuit/index.html
Federal Court Locator	http://vls.villanova.edu/library/express
Federal Court Finder	http://www.law.emory.edu/FEDCTS
Federal Judicial Center	http://fjc.gov
FedLaw	http://fedlaw.gsa.gov
FLITE Supreme Court Database	http://www.fedworld.gov/supcourt/index.htm
Oyez Oyez Supreme Court Resource	http://oyez.at.nwu.edu/oyezhtml
U.S. Circuit Court of Appeals Decisions	http://supct.law.cornell.edu/federal/opinions/html
U.S. Federal Courts Finder	http://www.law.emory.edu/FEDCTS
U.S. Federal Courts Home Page	http://www.uscourts.gov
U.S. Supreme Court	http://www.law.cornell.edu/supct http://www.usscplus.com/
U.S. Supreme Court Oral Arguments	http://oyez.at.nwu.edu/oyez.html
Virtual Court Web Site	http://www.courtbar.org

Legislative Branch/Federal Materials

THOMAS	http://thomas.loc.gov

"In the spirit of Thomas Jefferson, a service of the U.S. Congress through its Library." Provides access to the legislative documents of the both the House and Senate, plus links to many other government sources.

Code of Federal Regulations (CFR)	http://law.house.gov//cfr.htm
Congressional Bill Tracker	http://www.unipress.com/will-t-bill.html
Congressional Law Library	http://law.house.gov
Congressional Record	http://www.access.gpo.gov/su_docs/aces/aces150.html
Electronic Federal Resources	http://www.bna.com

Federal Register	http://gopher.nara.gov:70/1/register
Federal Rules of Civil Procedure	http://www.law.cornell.edu/rules
Federal Rules of Evidence	http://www.law.cornell.edu/rules
Library of Congress	http://lcweb.loc.gov
	http://thomas.loc.gov
UCC Articles 1-9	http://www.law.cornell.edu/rules
U.S. Code	http://law.house.gov/usc.htm
	http://www.law.cornell.edu/uscode
U.S. House of Representatives	http://www.house.gov
U.S. Federal Government Agencies	http://www.lib.lsu.edu/gov/fedgov.html
U.S. Senate	http://www.senate.gov
United States Constitution	http://www.law.cornell.edu/constitution
U.S. Tax Code	http://www.fourmilab.ch/ustax/ustax.html

STATE GOVERNMENT

General Sources

Council of State Governments	http://www.csg.org
Municipal Codes Online	http://www.spl.lib.wa.us/collec/lawcoll
	/municode.html
National Center for State Courts	http://www.ncsc.dni.us
National Conference of Commissioners on Uniform State Laws	http://www.law.upenn.edu/library/ulc/ulc.htm
National Conference of State Legislatures	http://www.ncsl.org
State & Territorial Laws	http://law.house.gov.17.htm
	http://www.legal.gsa.gov.intro5.htm
State caselaw & statutes via Hieros Gamos	http://www.hg.org/usstates.html
	http://www.hg.org/govt.html
State Court Directory	http://www.piperinfo.com/pl03/statedir.html
State Court Locator	http://vls.villanova.edu/library/express
State Documents Checklist	http://www.law.uiuc.edu/library/check.htm
State Law and Legislative Materials	http://lawlib.wuacc.edu/washlaw/uslaw
	/statelaw.html
State Legislator Directory	http://www.piperinfo.com/pl03/staterep.html
State Tax Forms	http://www.sm-b.com
State Web Locator	http://vls.villanova.edu/library/express
State Cases on Line	http://www.wolfenet.com/~dhillis/index/htm
	http://magnet.state.ma.us
Massachusetts Municipal Association	http://www.mma.org
Boston Public Library State & Local Gov	http://www.bpl.org

AREAS OF LAW

Advertising Law

Arent Fox Advertising Law   http://www.arentfox.com/quickGuide/busine...
advert/advertisingLaw/advertisinglaw.html

Antitrust

ABA, Section of Antitrust Law   http://www.abanet.org/antitrust/home.html
Antitrust Policy   http://www.antitrust.org
Dept. of Justice Antitrust Division   http://www.usdoj.gov
University of Chicago   http://www.lib.uchicago.edu/~llou/antitrust.html

Associations and Organizations

American Bar Association   http://www.abanet.org
American Association of Law Libraries   http://www.aallnet.org
Boston Bar Association   http://www.bostonbar.org
Massachusetts Bar Association   http://www.massbar.org

Banking and Bankruptcy

*AAA*dir:Directory of World Banks   http://aaadir.com
ABI World   http://www.abiworld.org
Bankruptcy Creditor's Service   http://bankrupt.com
Cornell's Legal Information Institute   http://www.law.cornell.edu/topics/banking.html
Electronic Banking Resource Center   http://www2.cob.ohio-state.edu/~richards
/banking.htm

Federal Reserve   http://www.bog.frb.fed.us
FDIC   http://www.fdic.gov
Internet Bankruptcy Library   http://bankrupt.com
KnowX   http://knowx.com
Mortgage Calculator   http://ibc.wustl.edu/mort.html
Office of the Comptroller of Currency   http://www.ustreas.gov/treasury/bureaus/occ
Universal Currency Converter   http://www.xe.net/currency
U.S. Bankruptcy Court S.D.N.Y.   http://www.nysb.uscourts.gov
World Bank   http://www.worldbank.org

Criminal Law

Kelley Blue Book   http://kbb.com

Yahoo!   http://www.yahoo.com/Society_and_Culture
                                                /Crime/

Divorce

DivorceNet   http://www.divorcenet.com/
KnowX   http://knowx.com

Electronic Commerce

Suffolk University Law School Law Library   http://www.law.suffolk.edu/library/pubs
                                                /cyber.html

Uniform Computer Information Transaction   http://www.ucitaonline.com
  Act Online

Software Industry Issues   http://www.softwareindustry.org/issues
                                                /index.html

Environmental Law

Alpha Analytical Labs   http://world.std.com/~alphalab
  (A full-service environmental analytical lab home page.)

Australian Environmental Law   http://www.erin.gov.au/human_env/env_leg

CIESIN (Consortium for International   http://www.ciesin.org
  Earth Science Information Network)

EnviroSense–Common Sense Solutions   http://es.inel.gov
  to Environmental Problems

Environmental Data Sources Around the World   http://bordeaux .uwaterloo.ca/enviro.html

Environmental Protection Agency   http://www.epa.gov

Environmental Law Information Center   http://www.webcom.com/~staber/welcome.html

Environmental Law Around the World   http://www.igc.apc.org/envlaw

Greenpeace Multilateral Environmental   http://www.globalaw.com
  Treaties

Indiana University   http://www.law.indiana.edu/law/v-lib
                                                /envlaw.html

NEIRC   http://www.gwu.edu/~greenu
  (National Environmental Information Resources Center is a partnership between George Washington University, the Institute for the Environment, and the EPA.)

Environmental Sciences Division, Oak   http://www.esd.ornl.gov/main.html
  Ridge National Laboratory (ORNL)

Pace Global Environmental Law Network   http://www.law.pace.edu

United Nations   http://www.unep.org
                                                http://www.undp.org/env.html

United Nations Scholar's Workstation   http://www.library.yale.edu/un/index.htm

U.S. Geological Survey Home Page   http://info.er.usgs.gov

European Union

Community Research & Development	http://www.cordis.lu
ECHO (European Commission)	http://www2.echo.lu
Europa	http://www.europa.eu.int
European Parliament	http://www.europarl.eu.int
European Union	http://www.eurunion.org

Human Rights

Amnesty International	http://www.amnesty.org
Australian Human Rights Info Centre	http://www.austlii.edu.au/ahric
DIANA	http://www.law.uc.edu:81/Diana
Human Rights Web	http://www.traveller.com
International Committee of the Red Cross	http://www.icrc.ch
OAS Inter-American Court of Human Rights	http://www.umn.edu/humanrts/iachr
University of Minnesota	http://www.umn.edu/humanrts
U.S. Dept. of State Foreign Affairs	gopher://dosfan.lib.uic.edu

Immigration

American Immigration Center	http://www.us-immigration.com
Immigration Forms	http://www.wave.net/upg/immigration/forms.html
Immigration Law	http://www.visalaw.com/~gsiskind
Immigration Lawyers on the Web	http://www.ilw.com

Intellectual Property

ABA Section–Intellectual Property Law	http://207.49.1.6/intelprop/home.html
American Intellectual Property Law Association	http://www.aipla.org/
BNA's PT & C Journal	http://suhumi.bna.com:80/hub/bna/legal/ptcindex.html
Copyright Act	http://www.law.cornell.edu/usc/17
Copyright Guide	http://www.ilt.columbia.edu/projects/copyright/index/html
Copyright Office	http://lcweb.loc.gov/copyright
Copyright Regulations	http://www.law.cornell.edu/copyright/regulations/regs.overview.html
Copyright Rights	http://www.uark.edu/depts/comminfo/www/copyright.html

Computer Law Internet Resources	http://www.kentlaw.edu/lawlinks/computers.html
Cyberlaw and Cyberlex	http://cyberlaw.com
IBM Patent Server	http://www.patents.ibm.com/ibm.html
International Trademark Association	http://www.inta.org/
Intellectual Property Owners	http://www.ipo.org/
Federal Courts Finder—Emory University	http://www.law.emory.edu/FEDCTS/
Patents.com, Oppedahl & Larson LLP	http://www.patents.com
Franklin Pierce Law Center	http://www.fplc.edu
General Laws (U.S. House)	http://law.house.gov/105.htm
Lanham Act	http://www.law.cornell.edu/lanham /lanham.table.htm
Law Journal	http://www.ljextra.com/practice /intellectualproperty
Official Gazette	http://www.micropat.com
Patent Act	http://www.law.cornell.edu/patent /patent.table.html
Patent Images	http:// patent.womplex.ibm.com/
Patent FAQ	http://www.sccsi.com/DaVinci/patentfaq.html
Patent Portal	http://www.law.vill.edu/~rgruner/patport.htm
Texas Intellectual Property Journal	http://www.utexas.edu/law/journals/tiplj /index.htm
Title 37 of CFR	http://www.law.cornell.edu/copyright/regulations /regs.overview.html
Trademark Act	http://www.law.cornell.edu/lanham/lanham .table.html
Trade Secrets	http://execpc.com
United States Patent Office	http://www.uspto.gov
Universal Copyright Convention	http://wiretap.spies.com/gopher/gov/copyright /us.universal.copyright/conv.txt
USC Title 17—Copyrights	http://www.law.cornell.edu/usc/17/
U.S. Court of Appeals for the Federal Circuit	http://www.fedcir.gov/
Wacky Patents	http://colitz.com/site/wacky.htm
Yahoo!	http://www.yahoo.com/Government/Law /Intellectual_Property/

International and Foreign Law

Australasian Legal Information Institute	http://www.austlii.edu.au
Electronic Embassy	http://www.embassy.org
FindLaw	http://www.findlaw.com
Foreign and International Law, J.W. Long Law Library, Willamette University	http://www.willamette.edu/~slewis/forint.htm

GODORT Foreign Law Links	http://www.library.nwu.edu/govpub/idtf
Guide to Electronic Resources for International Law/American Society of International Law	http://www.asil.org/resource/home.htm
Hieros Gamos	http://www.hg.org
Foreign Government Sites	http://www.hg.org/govt.html
Foreign and International Law	http://lawlib.wuacc.edu/forint/intro.htm
International Court of Justice	http://www.icj.org
International Law Locator	http://www.law.vill.edu/international
International Trade Law	http://ra.irv.uit.no
International Trade Law Monitor	http://anase.irv.uit.no/trade_law/nav/trade.html
Multilaterals Project of Fletcher School of Law & Diplomacy	http://www.tufts.edu/fletcher/multilaterals.html
OAS Inter-American Court of Human rights	http://www.umn.edu/humanrts/iachr
OECD	http://www.oecd.org
Organization of American States	http://www.sice.oas.org
United Nations	http://www.un.org
University of Chicago	http://www.lib.uchicago.edu/~llou
U.S. Department of State	http://www.state.gov
U.S. House of Reps (Foreign laws & treaties)	http://law.house.gov
U.S. International Trade Commission	http://www.usitc.gov
War Crimes Tribunal	http://www.igc.org/tribunal
Washlaw	http://lawlib.wuacc.edu
World List	http://www.law.osaka-u.ac.jp/legal-info/worldlist/wordlst.html

Internet Law

Perkins Coie International Resource Center	http://www.perkinscoie.com

Labor and Employment

AFL-CIO Homepage	http://www.aflcio.org
Bureau of Labor Statistics	gopher://stats.bls.gov
Center for Mobility, CMR Salary Calculator	http://www.homefair.com/homefair/cmr/cmr.html
Department of Labor	http://www.dol.gov
DOL Pension Welfare Benefits Admin.	http://www.dol.gov/dol/pwba
OSHA	http://www.osha.gov
Pension Benefits Guaranty Corporation	http://www.pbgc.gov
Social Security Administration	http://www.ssa.gov

Law Schools and Legal Education

Jurist: Law The Legal Education Network	http://www.jurist.law.pitt.edu
Law Student Web	http://darkwing.uoregon.edu/~ddun/l_schl.htm
Virtual Law Library	http://www.law.indiana.edu/law/v-lib /lawschools.html
Index of Law—Related Journals	http://www.usc.edu/dept/law-lib/legal /journals.html
University of Arkansas School of Law	http://law.uark.edu/
Belfast Law School (UK)	http://143.117.33.25/default.html
Legal Information Institute/Cornell Law School	http://www.law.cornell.edu:80/lii.table.html
Basic Legal Citation	http://www.law.cornell.edu:80/citation/citation .table.html
Case Western Reserve Law School	http://lawwww.cwru.edu
Université de Montréal	http://www.droit.umontreal.ca/
Chicago–Kent College of Law	http://www.kentlaw.edu/
University of Chicago	http://www.lib.uchicago.edu
University of Cincinnati College of Law	http://www.law.uc.edu/
Cleveland State University	http://www.law.csuohio.edu/
University of Colorado	http://stripe.colorado.edu
Cornell	http://www.law.cornell.edu
University of Dayton	http://www.udayton.edu/~law/
Denver University	http://www.law.du.edu/library/index.htm
Emory University School of Law	http://www.law.emory.edu
Fletcher School of Law and Diplomacy	http://www.tufts.edu/fletcher
Florida State University College of Law	http://law.fsu.edu/
Franklin Pierce Law Center	http://fplc.edu/ipmall.htm
Georgetown University Law Library	http://www.ll.georgetown.edu/
Georgia State	http://www.gsu.edu/lawlibrary
Harvard Law School	http://www.law.harvard.edu/
HytelNet	http://www.cc.ukans.edu/hytelnet_html /SITES1.html
Indiana University School of Law	http://www.law.indiana.edu/
KentWeb's Guide to Substantive Legal Resources	http://www.kentlaw.edu/lawnet/lawlinks.html
Legal Domain Network	http:// www.kentlaw.edu/lawnet/lawnet.html
Universität Mainz (Germany)	http://radbrunch.jura.uni-mainz.de/
John Marshall School of Law	http:// www.jmla.edu/
University of Massachusetts at Amherst Department of Legal Studies	http://www.umassp.edu/legal/home.html
University of Michigan	http://www.lib.umich.edu/libhome
NOCALL–Northern Association of Law Libraries	http://law.wuacc.edu/nocall//home.html

Ohio Northern University, Petit College of Law	http:// www.law.onu.edu/
Pace	http://www.pace.edu/lawlib/library
Rutgers University Law School	http:// www.rutgers.edu/lawschool.html/
Universität Saarbrücken Lehrstuhl für Rechtsinformatik (Germany)	http:// www.jura.uni-sb.de/
Seattle University Law School	http://192.124.98.48/
Southern California Assoc. of Law Libraries	http://law.wuacc.edu/scall/home.html
University of Southern California Law Center	http:// www.usc.edu/dept/law-lib/index.html
St. Louis University School of Law	http://lawlib.slu.edu/home.html
Suffolk University Law School	http://www.law.suffolk.edu
University of Texas-Austin	http://tarlton.law.utexas.edu/library/netref /internet_legal_ref.html
University of Trento School of Law (Italy)	http://www.gelso.unitn.it/card-admin /Welcome.html
The Law Faculty of University of Tromsø–IRV (Norway)	http://ananse.irv.uit.no/law/nav/hp.html
Vanderbilt	http://www.library.vanderbilt.edu/law
Villanova University School of Law	http://ming.law.vill.edu/VCILP.html
University of Waikato School of Law (New Zealand)	http:// www.waikato.ac.nz/law/homepage.html
University of Warwick Legal Information Services (UK)	http://ltc.law.warwick.ac.uk
Washburn University	http://law.wuacc.edu/washlaw.html
Washington College of Law/ The American University	http://sray.wcl.american.edu:80/pub/wcl.htm
Washington University School of Law	http://www/wulaw.wustl.edu

Legal Forms, Memos and Briefs

'Lectric Law Library	http://www.lectlaw.com//form.html
Electric Legal Source	http://www.e-legal.com/resources/forms
Law Journal Extra	http://www.ljx.com/memos/page.html
Realty Law Net	http://www.realty-lawnet.com/legal_forms.html
Brief Reporter	http://www.briefreporter.com
LawLinks.com	http://www.lawlinks.com

Legal and Business News Sources

American Journalism Review Newslink	http://www.newslink.com
Audio Net	http://www.audionet.com
BNA	http://www.bna.com
Business Week Online	http://www.businessweek.com/index.html

Chicago Tribune	http://www.chicago.tribune.com
CNN Interactive	http://www.cnn.com
Commercial News Services on the Net	http://ww.jou.ufl.edu/commres/webjou.htm
Court TV	http://www.courttv.com
Edgar	http://www.sec.gov/edgarhpt.html
Encyclopedia of Law & Economics	http://encyclo.findlaw.com
Federal Communications Law Journal	http://www.law.indiana.edu./fclj/pubs/
Federal Legislative Information	http://loc.thomas.gov
Forbes	http://www.forbes.com
Harvard Journal of Law & Technology	http://studorg.law.harvard.edu/jolt
Industry Solutions Home Page	http://www.microsoft.com/industry
Intellectual Property Magazine	http://www.ipmag.com
Journal of On-Line Law	http://www.law.cornell.edu/jol/post.html
Law Journal EXTRA!	http://www.ljx.com
Los Angeles Times	http://www.latimes.com
Microsoft Legal Industry Page	http://www.microsoft.com/industry/legal
MSNBC	http://www.msnbc.com/news/default.asp
NASD	http://www.nasdr.com
News Page	http://newspage.com
Newspapers Online	http://newspapers.com
New York Times	http://www.nytimes.com
NPR	http://www.npr.org
PointCast	http://pointcase.com
PR Newswire	http://www.prnewswire.com
Red Herring Online	http://redherring.com
Reuters	http://www.moneynet.com
Richmond Journal of Law & Technology	http://www.urich.edu/~jolt/
Securities in the Electronic Age	http://www.wallstreetlawyer.com
Small Business Association	http://www.sbaonline.sba.gov
Texas Intellectual Property Journal	http://www.utexas.edu/law/journals/tiplj /index.htm
USA Today	http://www.usatoday.com
United States Law Week	http://www.bna.com/resources/LAW2
Wall Street Journal	http://update.wsj.com
Wall Street Journal Interactive	http://interactive.wsj.com
Washington Post	http://washingtonpost.com

Legal Publishers

Aspen Law & Business	http://www.aspenpublishers.com

Bureau of National Affairs	http://www.bna.com
Lawyers Cooperative Publishing	http://www.lcp.com
LEXIS-NEXIS	http://www.lexis-nexis.com
Martindale Hubble	http://www.martindale.com
Matthew Bender	http://www.bender.com
Prentice Hall	http://prenhall.com
Shepard's	http://www.shepards.com
Westlaw	http://www.westpub.com

Litigation

Association of Trial Lawyers of America	http://www.atla.org
The Expert Pages	http://www.expertpages.com
Expert Witnesses	http://lawlib.wuacc.edu/washlaw/expert/expert.html http://www.nocall.org/experts.html
Reference Manual on Scientific Evidence From the Federal Judiciary Center	http://www.fjc.gov/pibs/html
Sentencing Commission Federal Sentencing Guidelines Update Newsletter	http://www.fjc.gov
Uniform Acts	http://www.kentlaw.edu
Verbatim Reporters Center (court reporters)	http://www.verbatimreporters.com

Medical and Health Sources

American Cancer Society	http://www.cancer.org
American Medical Association	http://www.ama-assn.org/register/register.htm
Center for Disease Control	http://www.cdc.gov
Center for Health Administration Studies	gopher://gopher.chas.uchicago.edu

(The Center, located at the University of Chicago, offers health and demographic statistics as well as an annotated index of local and national health policy related data.)

Department of Health & Human Services	http://www.os.dhhs.gov
Drug Formulary	http://www.intmed.mcw.edu/drug.html
Health Care Financing Administration	http://www.hcfa.gov
Health Info	http://www.pobox.com/~subhas/health.heml
Mediconsult.com, Inc. (Virtual Medical Center)	http://www.mediconsult.com
Medical Education Information Center	http://dpalm2.med.uth.tmc.edu
Medical Matrix Hypermedia Guide to Internet Health and Medicine Related Resources	http://www.medmatrix.org/index.asp
Medical resources by subject	http://www1.huji.ac.il/me/med_link.html
Medscape	http://www.medscape.com
MedWeb	http://emory.edu/WHSCL/medweb.html

National Cancer Institute	http://imsdd.meb.uni-bonn.de/cancernet
National Institute of Health	gopher://gopher.nih.gov/11
National Library of Medicine	http://www.nlm.nih.gov
National Library of Medicine Medline Database	http://www.4.ncbi.nlm.nih.gov/PubMed
New York Academy of Medicine: Medicine and Health Information Server	http://www.nyam.org
Organizing Medical Networked Information	http://omni.ac.uk
Virtual Hospital	http://vh.radiology.uiowa.edu
Web of Addictions	http://www.well.com/www/woa
World Health Organization	http://who.ch

Professional Responsibility

ABA/BNA Lawyers' Manual on Professional Conduct	http://www.bna.com/prodhome/bus/mopc.html
ABA Center for Professional Responsibility	http://www.abanet.org/cpr/home.html
American Legal Ethics Library	http://www.law.cornell.edu/ethics
Law Journal Extra—Professional Responsibility	http://www.ljxextra.com/practice/professionalresponsibility/index.html
Legalethics.com	http://www.legalethics.com
Legal Ethical Opinion Database	http://www.mwbb.com/leo/leo.htm
Massachusetts Ethics Rules	http://www.state.ma.us/obcbbo http://www.massbar.org/rules/contents.html
Massachusetts Ethics Opinions	http://www.state.ma.us/obcbbo
NetEthics	http://www.computerbar.org/netethic/netnav.htm
State Legal Advertising Restrictions	http://www.wld.com/direct/restrict.htm

Research and Writing

Citation Format

| Beyond the MLA Handbook | http://falcon.eku.edu/honors/beyond-mla |

(Features citation format for Internet sources.)

| The Bluebook | http://www.law.cornell.edu/citation/citation.table.html |
| Citing Electronic Information | http://www.wilpaterson.edu/wpcpages/library/citing.htm http://www.mla.org/main_stl.htm#sources |

Periodical Indexes

| CARL Uncover | http://uncweb.carl.org |
| Index to Legal Periodicals | http://tarlton.law.utexas.edu/tallons/content_search.html |

Real Estate

KnowX   http://www.knowx.com

Securities

New York Stock Exchange   http://www.nyse.com
Nasdaq Stock Exchange   http://www.nasdaq.com
American Stock Exchange   http://www.amex.com
EDGAR   http://www.sec.gov/edgarhp.htm
Quicken Financial Network (stock valuation)   http://networth.quicken.com
Securities & Exchange Commission   http://www.sec.gov
Security APL Quote Server   http://www.secapl.com/cgi-bin/qs
StockMaster   http://www.stockmaster.com
Wall Street Research Net   http://www.wsrn.com

Taxation

ABA Tax Section   http://www.abanet.org.tax
AccountingNet   http://accountingnet.com
American Accounting Association   http://www.aaa-edu.org
American Institute of CPAs (AICPA)   http://www.aicpa.org
American Taxation Association   http://www.uni.edu/ata
Association for Computers & Taxation   http://taxact.org
Bureau of National Affairs   http://www.bna.com
CCH Incorporated   http://www.cch.com
Code of Federal Regulations   http://www.access.gpo.gov/nara/cfr
Commerce Clearing House   http://tax.cch.com
Commission of European Union   http://europa.eu.int/index-en.htm
Current Legal Resources   http://www.currentlegal.com
Estate Planning Legal Research Guide   http://www.law.ukans.edu/library/este_res.htm
Ernst & Young   http://www.ey.com/tax/default.htm
Euro   http://europa.eu.int/euro
Forms, Instructions, & Publications Directory   http://www.taxsites.com/forms.html
Federation of Tax Administrators   http://www.taxadmin.org
House Ways & Means Committee   http://www.house.gov/ways_means
Institute of Property Taxation   http://www.ipt.org
Internal Revenue Bulletin   http://www.irs.ustreas.gov/prod/bus_info
                                                    /bullet.html

IRS Forms	http://www.irs.ustreas.gov/prod/forms_pubs /index.html
	http://www.fedworld.gov/taxsear.htm
IRS Home Page	http://www.irs.ustreas.gov
IRS Regulations	http://www.irs.ustreas.gov/prod/tax_regs
IRS Topic Index	http://www.irs.ustreas.gov/prod/search /site_tree.html
Equipment Leasing Association	http://www.elaonline.com
Federation of Tax Administrators	http://www.taxadmin.org
Federal Tax Law	http://www.taxsites.com/federal.html
Joint Committee on Taxation	http://www.house.gov/jct
Law Journal Extra	http://www.ljx.com/practice/taxation/indexhtml
Michigan Probate & Estate Planning Jrnl	http://www.icle.org/sections/probate/journal /about.htm
Multistate Tax Commission	http://www.mtc.gov
National Conference Of State Legislatures	http://www.ncls.org
Policy and Tax Reform Groups Directory	http://www.taxsites.com/policy
Research Institute of America	http://checkpoint.riag.com
Revenue Rulings	http://www.taxlinks.com
RIA	http://www.riatax.com
RIA Estate Planner's Alert	http://www.riatax.com/estate.html
Senate Finance Committee	http://www.senate.gov/~finance
State & Local Taxes Directory	http://www.taxsites.com/state.html
State & Local Tax Professionals	http://www.willyancey.com/tax-salt.htm
State Tax Agencies	http://www.taxsites.com/agencies.html
State Tax Forms	http://www.sm-b.com
State Tax Links	http://www.taxweb.com/state/index.html
Tax & Accounting Academia	http://www.taxsites.com/academia.html
Tax and Accounting Sites Directory	http://www.taxsites.com
Tax Analyst	http://www.tax.orgs/
Tax Analysts' Discussion Groups	http://www.tax.org/Discuss/discussion.htm
Tax Associations Directory	http://www.taxsites.com/associations.html
Tax Help, Tips & Articles Directory	http://www.taxsites.com/help.html
Tax Library (Thompson Publishing Group)	http://taxlibrary.com

Tax Professional's Corner (IRS)
http://www.irs.ustreas.gov/prod/bus_info/tax_pro

Tax Prophet	http://www.taxprophet.com
Tax Publishers & CPE Directory	http://www.taxsites.com/publishers.html
Tax Resources	http://shell5.ba.best.com/~ftmexpat/html /taxsites.html
	http://www.taxresources.com

Tax Software Directory	http://www.taxsites.com/software.html
Tax Treaties—Bradley Smith	http://www.intltaxlaw.com
Tax Treaties—Danziger's FDI	http://www.danzigerfdi.com
TaxWeb	http://www.taxweb.com
Thomas Legislative Information	http://thomas.loc.gov
Trust & Trustees	http://www.trust-and-trustee.com
U.K. Presidency of European Union	http://presid.fco.gov.uk
U.S. Tax Code	http://www.fourmilab.ch/ustax/ustax.html
	http://law.house.gov/usc.htm
Various Tax Links	http://www.sm-b.com
Will Yancey's Home Page	http://www.willyancey.com
Yahoo!	http://yahoo.com/government/taxes

Torts

Internet Grateful Med	http://igm.nlm.nih.gov

Year 2000 Legal Issues

Y2K	http:// www.year2000.com
	http://www.rightime.com
	http://www.tyler.net
	http://www.phoenix.com/techsupp/biosfaq.html
	http://www.itaa.org
	http://www.y2k.com
	http://www.software.ibm.com/year2000 /resource.html
	http://www.microsoft.com/cio/articles /year2000.html
	http://quickforms.com
	http://www.y2ktimebomb.com
	http://www.ljextra.com/practice/computer /ct_y2k.html
	http://www.gahtan.com/year2000
	http://www.comlinks.com
	http://www.year2000.com/y2klawcenter.html
	http://www.abanet.org/tech/ltrc/2000/home.html
	http://www.bna.com/new/y2k.html
	http://www.2000law.com
	http://www.2000legal.com
	http://pcprofile.com

BUSINESS

Barron's Online	http://www.barrons.com
Barron's Online: Market Surveillance	http://www.corpfinet.com
Business Know-How	http://www.businessknowhow.com

Business Information Server (Dun & Bradstreet) http://www.dbisna.com

Business Plans   http://www.bplans.com

Business Resource Center   http://www.morebusiness.com

Census Bureau   http://www.census.gov

CNNfn: the Financial Network   http://www.cnnfn.com

CommerceNet   http://www.commerce.net

Consumer Price Index   http://stats.bls.gov:80/newsrels.htm#OPLC

The Emerging Companies Network   http://www.capital-network.com/entp.htm

Hoover's Online   http://www.hoovers.com

Idea Cafe   http://www.ideacafe.com

International Business Resources Page   http://sunsite.unc.edu/reference/moss/business

International Small Business Consortium   http://www.isbc.com

Internet Business Resources   http://www.oak-ridge.com

Market Research Center   http://www.asiresearch.com

Marketing Resource Center   http://www.marketingsource.com

Maryland Business Information Network   http://www.mdbusiness.state.md.us

National Federation of Independent Business   http://www.nfibonline.com

Small Business Administration Online   http://www.sbaonline.sba.gov

Small Business Advisor   http://www.isquare.com

Small Business Journal   http://www.tsbj.com

STAT-USA   http://www.stat-usa.gov

   (A giant, fee-based subscription service providing economic, business, and social/environmental
   program data produced by more than 50 federal sources.)

Thomas Register   http://www.thomasregister.com/index.html

Young Entrepreneurs' Organization   http://www.yeo.org

People and Company Finders

Many of these sites permit the user to search by name, street address, or phone
number. They supply a variety of data about individuals and businesses, such as
e-mail addresses, financial information, profiles, and maps and directions.

AmericN Business Information   http://www.lookupusa.com

Bigbook   http://bigbook.com

Database America   http://www.databaseamerica.com/html/gpfind.htm

Four11   http://www.Four11.com

Infospace   http://www.infospace.com

   (Includes maps, radius searching, and a phone/ad directory for the U.S. and some foreign countries.)

Internet Address Finder   http://www.iaf.net

Internet Who's Who	http://web.city.ac.uk/citylive/pages.html
Phone White Pages	http://www.switchboard.com
	http://www.angelfire.com/webfind/index.html
	http://www.555-1212.com
Switchboard	http://www.switchboard.com
WhoWhere	http://whowhere.com
Yellow Pages	http://s12.bigyellow.com
	http://www.yellownet.com
	http://www.ypo.com
	http://www.switchboard.com
	http://www.bigfoot.com
	http://www.four11.com
Reverse Directory	http://www/yahoo.com/search/people
Social Security Death Index	http://www.ancestry.com/home/freesearch.htm
Stalker's Home Page	http://www.glr.com/stalk.html

   (Combines several people finder search sites, plus additional privacy information.)

| Webgator: Investigative Resources on the Web | http://www.inil.com/users/dguss/wgator.html |
| WhoWhere | http://www.whowhere.com |

Online Brokers

Accutrade	http://www.accutrade.com
Ameritrade	http://www.ameritrade.com
Bidwell & Co.	http://www.bidwell.com
Brown & Co.	http://www.brownco.com
Datek	http://www.datek.com
Discover Brokerage	http://discoverbrokerage.com
E*Trade	http://www.etrade.com
Jack White & Co.	http://www.jackwhiteco.com
Quick & Reilly	http://www.quick-reilly.com
Charles Schwab	http://www.schwab.com
Scottsdale Securities	http://www.scottrade.com
Suretrade	http://www.suretrade.com
Waterhouse Securities	http://www.waterhouse.com
Web Street	http://www.webstreet.com

INTERNET

Current Awareness

| Law Library Resource Xchange | http://www.llrx.com |

LegalOnline   http://www.legalonline.com

Scout Report   http://wwwscout.cs.wisc.edu/scout/report/

Law-Related Discussion Lists

LawLists by Lyonett Louis-Jacques   http://www.lib.uchicago.edu/~llou/lawlists
                                         /info.html

LISZT: Directory of E-Mail Discussion Lists   http://www.liszt.com

Internet Legal Research Guides

The Internet Lawyer   http://www.internetlawyer.com

Internet Legal Resource Guide   http://www.ilrg.com/lsahq
                                         http://www/studylaw.com

The Legal List   http://www.lcp.com/The-Legal-List
                                         /TLL-home.html

Search Engines

AOL   http://netfind.aol.com

AltaVista   http://altavista.digital.com

Ask Jeeves! Smart Answers Fast   http://askjeeves.com

CNN Webspace Search Engine   http://cnn.com/SEARCH/index.html

Dog Pile   http://www.dogpile.com

Excite   http://www.excite.com

HomeWiz—Home Page Search Engine   http://www.800go.com/homewiz/homewiz.html

HotBot   http://www.hotbot.com

Infoseek   http://www.infoseek.com

Internet Sleuth—Legal Information   http://www.charm.net:80/~ibc/sleuth/lega.html

Jump City   http://www.jumpcity.com/NEWHOME.html

LawCrawler   http://www.lawcrawler.com

LookSmart   http://www.looksmart.com

Lycos   http://www.lycos.com

Magellan   http://www.mckinley.com

MetaCrawler   http://www.metacrawler.com

News Index—Current News Search Engine   http://www.newsindex.com

Northern Light   http://www.northernlight.com

OpenText   http://www.opentext.com

Snap   http://home.snap.com

Starting Point   http://stpt.com

Yahoo!   http://www.yahoo.com

Master Sites for Search Engines

These sites incorporate many search engines into one page of links. Some allow for combined searching with more than one search engine at a time.

All-in-One Internet Search   http://www.albany.net/allinone

800go.com   http://800go.com

   (Links to 12 separate search engines.)

SavySearch   http://savvy.cs.colostate.edu:2000

   (Links to 19 separate search engines. Allows user to search all 19 search engines at once.)

SAMPLE LAW FIRM HOME PAGES

Arent Fox   http://www.arentfox.com

Pepper & Corazzini   http://www.commlaw.com

Day, Berry & Howard   http://www.dbh.com

Clifford Chance   http://www.cliffordchance.com

Family Law Advisor   http://www.divorcenet.com/law/fla.html

Foley, Hoag & Eliot   http://www.fhe.com

Glovsky & Koenig   http://www.fcr.com/lawinc/glokoe.html

Hale & Dorr   http://www.haledorr.com

Lucash, Gesmer & Updegrove   http://www.lgu.com

Peabody & Brown   http://www.peabodybrown.com

Shearman & Sterling   http://www.shearman.com

Tax Prophet   http://www.taxprophet.com

FINDING A LAWYER ON THE WEB

ABA   http://www.abanet.com

Attorneys' Registry   http://www.legal.net/attorney/viewlist.html

Counsel Connect   http://www.counsel.com

Findlaw   http://www.findlaw.com

Law Journal EXTRA!   http://www.ljx.com

Martindale Hubble   http://www.martindale.com

Seamless   http://www.seamless.com

Westlaw Legal Directory   http://wld.com

MISCELLANEOUS

Amazon Bookstore   http://www.amazon.com

      Building/Designing a Law Firm Web Page
      http://www.zoom.com/weblegal

	http://www.1st-tech.com
	http://www.a-d-m.com
	http://www.wolfenet.com/~dhillis
	http://www.brickbuilt.com
	http://ccrich.com/
	http://www.collegehill.com/
	http://www.virtual411.com/cspmedia/
	http://www.demoline.com
	http://www.s6000.com/dci
	http://www.inherent.com
	http://internet-assist.net
	http://www.internetlawyer.com
	http://www.intranetix.com
	http://www.juris-net.com
	http://www.lawgirl.com
	http://seamless.com
	http://www.webcounsel.com
	http://www.romingerlegal.com/WPdesign.htm
CD Now	http://www.cdnow.com
Free E-mail Service	http://bigfoot.com
	http://hotmail.com
	http://juno.com
	http://mailcity.com
	http://rocketmail.com
Internet Index	http://www.openmarket.com/intindex/
Movie Links	http://www.movielink.com
Public Mailing Lists	http://www.neosoft.com/Internet/paml
Microsoft Sidewalk (local events)	http://sidewalk.com
United States Post Office Zipcode Lookup	http://www.usps.gov/ncsc

INDEX

References are to section numbers.